HANDBOOK OF STRUCTURAL EQUATION MODELING

HANDBOOK OF
STRUCTURAL EQUATION MODELING

EDITED BY
RICK H. HOYLE

THE GUILFORD PRESS
New York   London

© 2012 The Guilford Press
A Division of Guilford Publications, Inc.
72 Spring Street, New York, NY 10012
www.guilford.com

Paperback edition 2015

Printed in the United States of America

This book is printed on acid-free paper.

Last digit is print number: 9   8   7   6   5   4   3   2

Library of Congress Cataloging-in-Publication Data

Handbook of structural equation modeling / edited by Rick H. Hoyle.
    p. cm.
  Includes bibliographical references and index.
  ISBN 978-1-60623-077-0 (hardback : acid-free paper)
  ISBN 978-1-4625-1679-7 (paperback : acid-free paper)
  1. Structural equation modeling.   I. Hoyle, Rick H.
  QA278.3.H36 2012
  519.5—dc23
                                     2011039804

Preface

Structural equation modeling (SEM) has come of age. As recently as the 1980s, SEM was perceived by many students and researchers in the social and behavioral sciences as virtually intractable—esoteric notation, difficult-to-use computer programs, and little published guidance targeted to would-be users with basic graduate-level training in statistical methods. The traditional LISREL notation system is now more familiar to many students and researchers, and alternative, more intuitive systems have been developed. Whereas there was once only LISREL for mainframe computers, there now are multiple computer programs for implementing SEM that run on desktop computers using syntax that does not require knowledge of matrix algebra. And one could now fill a shelf with textbooks and edited volumes devoted to SEM and SEM-related topics. A statistical approach that once was accessible only to social and behavioral scientists with advanced coursework in statistical methods and strong computing skills is now part of the methodological mainstream.

Despite the growing literature on SEM targeted to graduate students and researchers, there has, to date, been no single resource that offers broad and deep coverage of both the mechanics of SEM and specific SEM strategies and applications. This handbook is that resource. If offers comprehensive coverage of SEM, beginning with background issues, continuing through statistical underpinnings and steps in implementation, then moving into basic and advanced applications of SEM. In a single volume, it offers virtually complete coverage of SEM and its use.

The book is intended for advanced graduate students and postgraduate researchers with graduate-level training in applied statistical methods that include multiple regression analysis and at least basic coverage of factor analysis. The structure of the book, described below, is designed to lead readers from basic, foundational material through coverage of the increasing number of modeling approaches and model types for which SEM is appropriate. As such, the book could serve as the primary textbook for a graduate-level course on SEM. Alternatively, it could serve as a resource for students and researchers who have completed their statistical training but need to know more about how SEM works and how it could be used in their work. In either case, the goal is to provide coverage at a level suitable for graduate students and postgraduate researchers who have had basic statistical training typical of the social and behavioral sciences.

To that end, the authors, of whom many are at the forefront of developments related to the topic about which they have written, were challenged with producing focused chapters that balance sophistication and accessibility. The level of sophistication necessarily varies but, generally, increases from early to later chapters. Some chapters in the last part of the book cover highly specialized applications at a level that assumes a solid grasp of the statistical underpinnings of SEM. Yet, even in these chapters, the authors have provided conceptually oriented descriptions and revealing examples. Many of the chapters offer fully explicated analyses, including access to data and syntax files for readers interested in trying their hand at reproducing the authors' results. (These can be accessed at the website for the *Handbook*: *www.handbookofsem.com*.) The result is a set of chapters that provide up-to-date, accessible, and practical coverage of the full array of SEM topics.

The 40 chapters are arrayed in five parts designed to move the reader from foundational material through the statistical underpinnings and practicalities of using SEM, to basic and advanced applications. The chapters in Part I provide important background, beginning with a historical account of key advances and including material on path diagrams, latent variables, causality, and simulation methods. Part II is the "nuts-and-bolts" portion of the book, comprising chapters on assumptions, specification, estimation, statistical power, fit, model modification, and equivalent models. Also included is a chapter on the use of categorical data in SEM. Part III, a practically oriented "how-to" portion of the book, covers preparing data, managing missing data, bootstrapping, choosing computer software, and writing the SEM research report. Parts IV and V cover the many types of models and data for which SEM is appropriate. Part V includes chapters on "basic" applications—those that have been in use for the longest period of time and/or serve as building blocks for newer, more complex or specialized applications. These include confirmatory factor analysis; models of mediation and moderation; models of longitudinal data; models focused on means; models for the construction and development of measurement scales; and models for evaluating measurement equivalence for different populations. Part V includes a dozen chapters that showcase the newest and most specialized SEM models and modeling strategies. Some chapters focus on the use of SEM to model data generated by relatively new methods such as brain imaging, genotyping, and geocoding. Others cover strategies for more general types of data that pose particular challenges but offer unique opportunities; these include multilevel data, categorical measurement data, longitudinal growth data, data from intensive longitudinal assessments, dyadic data, and data from heterogeneous samples for which the source of heterogeneity is not observed. Also included in Part V are chapters on emerging strategies—Bayesian methods and automated model specification.

Together, these parts form a coherent whole that provides comprehensive, in-depth, coverage of SEM in a style appropriate for advanced graduate students and researchers in the social and behavioral sciences.

Acknowledgments

My own introduction to SEM was provided by Kenneth A. Bollen, a master teacher whose classic textbook has been *the* source of information about SEM for a generation of graduate students in the social and behavioral sciences. I had the good fortune of taking Ken's graduate seminar on SEM at the University of North Carolina at Chapel Hill in 1987. It was a privilege that continues to pay professional dividends, including the publication of this handbook.

As the structure and likely content of the *Handbook* took shape, it became apparent that, if it were to be of the highest quality, I would need assistance recruiting authors and helping them shape their contributions. This assistance was provided by three leading scholars on SEM, who served on the advisory board. The outstanding slate of contributors and the overall quality of the book owe in no small measure to their contributions. I thank Advisory Board members David Kaplan (University of Wisconsin–Madison), George A. Marcoulides (University of California, Riverside), and Stephen G. West (Arizona State University). They helped finalize the list of topics to be covered, recruit authors, and manage the review of selected chapters. These are critical contributions for which I am most thankful.

The lead authors of most chapters reviewed and provided feedback on another chapter in the book. In addition, several individuals who were not contributors to the *Handbook* reviewed selected chapters. I gratefully acknowledge the efforts of Hei Ning Cham (Arizona State University), Erin K. Davisson (Duke University), Amanda Gottschall (Arizona State University), Wolfgang M. Hartmann (Heidelberg, Germany), Patrick L. Hill (University of Illinois), Karin Schermelleh-Engel (University of Frankfurt), and Jodie Ullman (California State University, San Bernardino). Their incisive reviews and constructive feedback helped selected authors strengthen and polish early drafts.

Working with the staff at The Guilford Press has been a genuine pleasure. C. Deborah Laughton, Publisher of Guilford's Methodology and Statistics program, with whom I've now had the privilege of developing three books, is without peer. Her wisdom, experience, and commitment to the project were key to its development and completion. In addition, members of the production staff at Guilford handled the challenging manuscript with skill, turning a complex set of chapter manuscripts delivered in various states of (in)consistency with guidelines into a polished final product. The contributors and I owe a debt of gratitude to Editorial Assistant Mary Beth Wood, Managing Editor Judith Grauman, Senior Book Compositor Oliver Sharpe, and Senior Production Editor Laura Specht Patchkofsky.

Projects like this always seem to take more time than anticipated, stealing time from other important obligations and pursuits. I am grateful for the unflagging support of my wife, Lydia, who gave more than her share of time to our shared responsibilities when I needed to give more time than expected to finish the book.

RICK H. HOYLE
Duke University
rhoyle@duke.edu

Contents

■ ix

PART V. ADVANCED APPLICATIONS

Computer input, output, and data files for example models and applications described in selected chapters are available online at *www.handbookofsem.com*.

PART I

BACKGROUND

CHAPTER 1

Introduction and Overview

Rick H. Hoyle

Structural equation modeling (SEM) is a growing family of statistical methods for modeling the relations between variables. Although the data from which these relations are modeled and estimated are observed, models may include variables that are unobserved, or latent. For this reason, SEM has been referred to as latent variable modeling. The primary data for most uses of SEM are covariances, which explains why SEM has also been referred to as covariance structure modeling. And the intent of many uses of SEM is to estimate causal effects between variables, explaining why SEM is sometimes referred to as causal modeling. Regardless of the label, the family of methods referred to as SEM in this handbook is a comprehensive, flexible, and increasingly familiar approach to hypothesis testing and modeling in the social and behavioral sciences.

Unlike more widely used statistical methods such as analysis of variance, multiple regression analysis, and factor analysis, SEM is not yet fully developed. Although the core capabilities of SEM have been well established since the early 1970s and generally accessible to researchers since the early 1980s, new capabilities are being developed and incorporated into computer programs for SEM analyses with regularity (see Matsueda, Chapter 2, this volume, for an informative history of SEM). These emerging capabilities, coupled with powerful and intuitive computer programs for implementing them, have spurred phenomenal growth in the amount and diversity of SEM usage. This handbook is a response to that growth. Our goal is to provide detailed coverage of SEM, beginning with foundational concerns and moving through an impressive array of modeling possibilities.

In this opening chapter, I offer an introduction to SEM that also serves as an overview of the remainder of the handbook. I begin by discussing the relation between SEM and statistical methods with which many readers new to SEM will be familiar. I then provide a brief description of the basic logic of SEM as it typically is used in the social and behavioral sciences. The heart of the chapter is the presentation of an implementation framework that serves as both context for the remainder of the chapter and an outline of the first three parts of the handbook. In the final section of the chapter I succinctly describe types of data and models for which SEM can be profitably used, and point the reader to chapters in the fourth and fifth parts of the book that offer detailed descriptions and demonstrations.

■ 3

SEM IN RELATION TO OTHER STATISTICAL MODELS

As a linear model concerned with accounting for the relations between variables, SEM is not unrelated to narrower and more familiar statistical models such as analysis of variance (ANOVA), multiple regression analysis, and principal factor analysis. Indeed, any of these analyses could be accomplished, and would yield identical results, using SEM. As such, SEM can be described as a generalization, integration, and extension of these familiar models.

Consider, for example, tests involving means. In the most limited case, a single mean estimated from a sample is compared against a population value, often zero, and the difference tested for significance. This test can be usefully generalized to the situation in which both means are estimated from samples, which may be independent or dependent; alternatively, the means may come from two observations of the same sample. The same comparison could be made using ANOVA, which offers the additional benefit of allowing for both more than two means and means generated by more than one factor. The number of levels a factor might reasonably take on in ANOVA is relatively small, making it unsuitable for independent variables measured on a continuous or quasi-continuous scale such as survey items. Multiple regression analysis can accommodate both traditional ANOVA factors and quantitative measures that take on many values; thus, it has all the capabilities of ANOVA and more. Although both ANOVA and multiple regression analysis can accommodate multiple dependent variables, they are limited in how the relations between those variables are specified. Furthermore, a variable can be an independent or dependent variable, but not both. SEM can accommodate both analytic situations. For instance, a set of variables might be used to predict a pair of outcomes that are correlated, uncorrelated, or related in such a way that one is regressed on the other. In the latter case, one of the dependent variables is also an independent variable in that it is used to predict the other dependent variable.

An alternative path to SEM that highlights additional capabilities begins with the zero-order correlation coefficient, which indexes the commonality between two variables. The degree to which that commonality can be attributed to a common influence can be evaluated using partial correlation analysis, assuming the putative influence has been measured. In the case of three or more variables, this logic can be extended to consider common influences that are not measured using factor analysis. The traditional factor analysis model is referred to as exploratory factor analysis (EFA) because those influences, even in the presence of well-developed hypotheses, cannot be specified a priori. More an inconvenience than a limitation is the fact that an infinite number of factor scores can be derived from the parameters (factor loadings and uniquenesses) estimated by EFA (Steiger & Schönemann, 1978). Finally, EFA requires that uniquenesses be uncorrelated. Within SEM, factors have traditionally been referred to as latent variables and are modeled in a more flexible, mathematically defensible manner that allows for a wide array of models that could not be evaluated using EFA. Applications of SEM that focus exclusively on the relations between latent variables and their indicators are referred to as restricted factor analysis or, more commonly, confirmatory factor analysis (CFA). Both labels are apt because it is the restrictions that CFA requires that make it confirmatory (i.e., subject to statistical testing). Conditional on appropriate restrictions (illustrated below), CFA permits specification and testing of a wide array of factor models.

Although each of these generalizations of basic statistical models is impressive in its own right, it is the integration of the two that constitutes the core strength of SEM. The traditional approach to integrating multiple regression analysis and factor analysis involves factoring a set of indicators of one or more predictors and outcomes, generating factor scores (which, as noted, are indeterminate) or creating unit-weighted composites of the highest-loading indicators, then using these variables as predictors or outcomes. SEM allows for these two components of the analytic strategy to be done simultaneously; that is, the relations between indicators and latent variables and the relations between latent variables are evaluated in a single model.

This integration of regression analysis and factor analysis is depicted in three ways in Figure 1.1. The model in question is one in which an outcome, Y, is regressed on a predictor, X. Y is operationally defined by three indicators, y_1, y_2, and y_3, and X is operationally defined by four indicators, x_1, x_2, x_3, and x_4. These indicators could be survey items, total scores on different instruments designed to measure X and Y, behavioral observations, physical characteristics, or some combination of these and other fallible indicators of the constructs. Regardless of how the values on these indicators were generated, it is assumed that x_1 to x_4 share in common their reflection of construct X but not

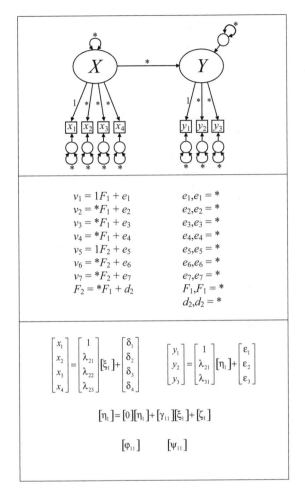

$$v_1 = 1F_1 + e_1 \qquad\qquad e_1, e_1 = *$$
$$v_2 = *F_1 + e_2 \qquad\qquad e_2, e_2 = *$$
$$v_3 = *F_1 + e_3 \qquad\qquad e_3, e_3 = *$$
$$v_4 = *F_1 + e_4 \qquad\qquad e_4, e_4 = *$$
$$v_5 = 1F_2 + e_5 \qquad\qquad e_5, e_5 = *$$
$$v_6 = *F_2 + e_6 \qquad\qquad e_6, e_6 = *$$
$$v_7 = *F_2 + e_7 \qquad\qquad e_7, e_7 = *$$
$$F_2 = *F_1 + d_2 \qquad\qquad F_1, F_1 = *$$
$$d_2, d_2 = *$$

$$\begin{bmatrix} x_1 \\ x_2 \\ x_3 \\ x_4 \end{bmatrix} = \begin{bmatrix} 1 \\ \lambda_{21} \\ \lambda_{22} \\ \lambda_{23} \end{bmatrix}[\xi_1] + \begin{bmatrix} \delta_1 \\ \delta_2 \\ \delta_3 \\ \delta_4 \end{bmatrix} \qquad \begin{bmatrix} y_1 \\ y_2 \\ y_3 \end{bmatrix} = \begin{bmatrix} 1 \\ \lambda_{21} \\ \lambda_{31} \end{bmatrix}[\eta_1] + \begin{bmatrix} \varepsilon_1 \\ \varepsilon_2 \\ \varepsilon_3 \end{bmatrix}$$

$$[\eta_1] = [0][\eta_1] + [\gamma_{11}][\xi_1] + [\zeta_1]$$

$$[\varphi_{11}] \qquad\qquad [\psi_{11}]$$

FIGURE 1.1. Alternative depictions of a model.

Y and, conversely, y_1 to y_3 reflect construct Y but not X. In order to estimate the effect of X on Y using regression analysis, composite scores would need to be produced, perhaps by summing x_1 to x_4 and y_1 to y_3 or, if the indicators were on different scales, standardizing scores and taking a mean. As illustrated in the top panel of Figure 1.1, the regression portion of the model involves only latent variables (i.e., factors), designated by ovals. These are unobserved forms of X and Y that reflect the commonality among observed indicators of them, designated by squares. Variance in each indicator is attributable to two unobserved sources: one of the latent variables of interest, X or Y, and unique-

ness, or specificity, designated by the small circles. The straight lines indicate directional effects, and the sharply curved lines indicate variances. The asterisks designate parameters to be estimated. These include factor loadings, uniquenesses, a regression coefficient, a disturbance (regression error of prediction), and the variance of X. This approach to depicting a model is called a path diagram, about which detailed information is provided by Ho, Stark, and Chernyshenko (Chapter 3, this volume).

Two additional ways of depicting the same model are shown in the remainder of Figure 1.1. In the middle panel, the model is outlined in a series of equations and "double-label" terms (Bentler & Weeks, 1980). In this notational scheme, observed variables are designated as v and latent variables as F, uniquenesses as e, and disturbances as d. As in the path diagram, parameters to be estimated are denoted by asterisks. In the left column are equations; the first seven are measurement equations, which specify the relations between indicators and latent variables, and the last one is a structural equation, which specifies the directional relation between the latent variables. In the right column are variances corresponding to the uniquenesses, the latent predictor, and the disturbance. The scheme draws its name from the approach to designating parameters. The double-label format is evident for the variances. The same format could be used for the equations; for instance, the factor loading for v_2 on F_1 could be written $v_2, F_1 = *$, and the regression coefficient for the structural equation could be written $F_2, F_1 = *$. Note that every asterisk in the path diagram has a counterpart in the double-label depiction.

In the bottom panel of Figure 1.1, the model is depicted using matrix notation, sometimes referred to as LISREL notation in recognition of its use in the original computer program for implementing SEM (Jöreskog & Sörbom, 1999). In this scheme, observed variables are denoted as x (independent) or y (dependent), whereas variables defined in the model and parameters are denoted by Greek letters. ξ_1 corresponds to X and F_1 in the previous panels, and η_1 corresponds to Y and F_2. The parameters are now differentiated, with λ corresponding to factor loadings, and δ and ε variances of uniquenesses. The regression coefficient is denoted by γ. The remaining parameters are the variance of ξ_1 and the disturbance, denoted by ϕ and ψ, respectively. As with the scheme illustrated in the middle panel, equations corresponding to the measurement and structural components of the model are distinguished. Unlike the earlier scheme, a further distinction is made between the measurement equations for the independent (ξ_1) and dependent (η_1) latent variables.

In many applications of SEM, the observed variables are assumed to be measured on a continuous scale, and any latent variables are assumed to be continuous as well. Yet variables often are measured coarsely (e.g., 5- or 7-point response scales) and sometimes categorically (e.g., *true–false*), raising questions as to the appropriateness of standard SEM approaches to estimation and testing (see Edwards, Wirth, Houts, & Xi, Chapter 12, this volume). Fortunately, much of the recent expansion of SEM is attributable to the development of models, estimators, and fit statistics for categorical data. This suggests a third path of generalization from simpler models to the general and integrated models for which SEM is appropriate. At the most elemental level is the simple cross-tabulation of categorical variables. More general models for modeling categorical data include logistic regression analysis and latent class analysis. The integration of latent class analysis and factor analysis yields factor mixture modeling and the possibility of categorical latent variables. These latent variables are unobserved categorical variables that reflect homogeneous groups, or classes, of individuals from a population that is heterogeneous with reference to the parameters in a factor model.

To this point, my description of SEM and comparison with other statistical models has focused on modeling the relations between variables. In some cases, however, the hypothesis of interest requires modeling patterns of means or means of latent variables. SEM is appropriate for testing such hypotheses; however, doing so requires moving beyond covariance structure modeling, which typifies most uses of SEM, to models that include a mean structure. This addition allows for the expansion of models such as the one shown in Figure 1.1 to include intercepts in the measurement, and structural equations and means of the latent variables. It also allows for modeling individual patterns of means over time, capturing variability in latent growth variables. When these variables are examined in relation to latent variables that reflect the commonality among sets of indicators (e.g., *X* and *Y* in Figure 1.1), the model includes three components—measurement and structural equations, which together constitute the covariance structure, and the mean structure. The full generality and flexibility of SEM would be evident in a model that includes all three components, and both continuous and categorical observed and latent variables.

BASIC LOGIC AND APPLICATION

The chapters in the second and third parts of this book provide detailed coverage of the basic logic and general application of SEM. I offer a summary in this introductory chapter both as an overview of the contents of Parts II and III, and as background for the chapters that follow in Part I of this handbook.

A fundamental difference between SEM and more familiar statistical models such as ANOVA and multiple regression analysis is the target of parameter estimation. In typical applications of multiple regression analysis, for example, the regression coefficients are estimated using ordinary least squares (OLS). The coefficients define a regression line that minimizes the average squared distance between the individual data points (the target) and the line. Residuals index the degree to which the estimated line misses each data point, that is, the degree of error in predicting the observed data from those estimated by the model. The goal of estimation in SEM is the same: Find values of the parameters that best account for the observed data given a substantively interesting model. A major difference, however, is what constitutes the observed data, or target. In the prototypic application of SEM—as, for example, the model shown in Figure 1.1—the data are the observed covariances between the variables and their variances. The goal of estimation, typically by the maximum likelihood method, is to find values for the parameters that, given the model, maximize the likelihood of the observed data. Stated differently, as with OLS regression, the goal is to minimize the difference between the observed and estimated data, but the observed and estimated data in SEM are variances and covariances. Thus, the residuals are the differences between the observed variances and covariances, and those estimated by the model given the data.

Returning to the model depicted in Figure 1.1, the data are the seven variances of the observed variables plus the 21 covariances between them (easily calculated as $p(p + 1)/2$, where p is the number of observed variables). As with the casewise observed data in OLS regression, the degrees of freedom available for model testing are derived from the number of data points. Unlike degrees of freedom for casewise data, the number of degrees of freedom available for model testing is equal to the total number of data points—28 in this case. As with tests involving casewise data, the number of degrees of freedom for a given test is the number of available degrees of freedom minus the number of parameters to be estimated. Referring either to the top or middle panel of Figure 1.1 and counting asterisks, there are 15 parameters to be estimated, leaving 13 degrees of freedom for tests of model fit. Working from the matrix notation in the lower panel, the same outcome is reached by counting the λ's, δ's, ε's, γ's, φ's, and ψ's.

Models such as the one shown in Figure 1.1 are specified by researchers; that is, there is no default model provided by SEM software for covariance matrices based on seven observed variables. A given specification offers a putative explanation for the pattern of observed covariances and reflects the researcher's hypotheses about those relations; it also reflects certain technical constraints necessary to ensure the model can be estimated. When the parameters in a model are estimated from data, they can be used in combination with the data to produce an estimated covariance matrix equivalent to estimated scores on the outcome variable in OLS regression. The difference between the estimated and observed matrices is the residual matrix, which is implicated directly or indirectly in various tests and indices of fit. Generally speaking, a model fits the data when the elements of the residual matrix are uniformly near zero. Models initially specified by researchers often result in one or more residual covariances that are nontrivially different from zero, meaning they are not adequately explained by the model given the data. In such cases, models often are respecified, estimated, and tested, the equivalent of post hoc comparisons in ANOVA. When support is obtained for either an a priori or respecified model, it is interpreted and presented. Each of these steps in the use of SEM is discussed and illustrated in chapters in Parts II and

III of this volume. In the next section of this chapter, I present a framework that integrates the steps involved in the implementation of SEM and offer a brief description of each one.

IMPLEMENTATION FRAMEWORK

Despite its flexibility and generality, in practice SEM is nearly always implemented following the same series of discrete steps. In this section, I present an implementation framework that positions these steps in relation to each other, providing context for processing material in the remainder of the book. For each step I provide an overview and refer to the relevant chapters. The framework, shown in diagram form in Figure 1.2, comprises four steps—specification, estimation, evaluation of fit, and interpretation and reporting—that are always followed, and a fifth step—respecification—that is included in most implementations of SEM. Because they are important considerations for how the steps are implemented, I also include the related concerns of data acquisition/preparation and identification; these are shown in Figure 1.2 as boxes connected by dashed lines to one or more of the primary steps in implementation.

SEM can be used with different intents, and it is useful to review them here as context for the presentation of the implementation framework. Specifically, Jöreskog (1993) described three common intents when using SEM. Although somewhat rare in practice, SEM can be used with strictly confirmatory intent. In such cases, a single a priori model is specified and evaluated. Either it provides an acceptable account of the data or it

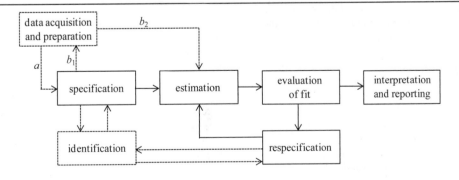

FIGURE 1.2. Steps in the implementation of SEM.

does not. No attempts are made at modifying the model or comparing it with alternative models. Alternatively, the researcher's intent may include both evaluating the fit of a model in an absolute sense and comparing it with alternative models that reflect competing theoretical accounts or offer a more parsimonious account of the data. When SEM is used with the intent of comparing alternative models, these models should be specified a priori and, when possible, specified in such a way that direct statistical comparisons can be made. Finally, the intent of an SEM analysis might be the generation of a model for subsequent evaluation in a strictly confirmatory or alternative models analysis. Although an initial model must be specified, it either follows from results of prior analyses (e.g., multiple regression analysis, factor analyses) of the same data, or offers a sufficiently poor account of the data that it must be modified or abandoned. Many uses of SEM begin with strictly confirmatory or alternative model comparison intent, but they become exercises in model generation when a priori models do not meet fit criteria. At the other extreme, it is possible to begin with a commitment to no particular model and use data mining strategies to generate models (see Marcoulides & Ing, Chapter 40, this volume). With these distinctions in mind, I now turn to an overview of the implementation framework displayed in Figure 1.2.

Specification

The use of SEM always begins with the specification of a model. A *model* is a formal statement of the mechanisms assumed to have given rise to the observed data. Those mechanisms reflect the substantive hypotheses that motivated the analysis, as well as characteristics of the sample and research design. As discussed later in this section, the model also includes features that ensure unique values can be obtained for the parameters to be estimated.

As shown in Figure 1.2, specification can take place either before or after data are acquired and prepared for analysis. The dashed line labeled a corresponds to the situation in which specification follows data collection, whereas the line labeled b_1 corresponds to the situation in which data collection follows specification then, as indicated by line b_2, leads to estimation. Again using the model depicted in Figure 1.1 as an example, a researcher might have access to a set of data that includes x_1 to x_4 and y_1 to y_3. These may be data she collected

herself but did not collect with this specific model in mind, or data she acquired from a secondary source (e.g., U.S. Census data). Note that in this situation the options for specification are constrained by the contents of a set of data that were not collected with the researcher's model in mind. In such cases, multiple indicators might not be available, precluding the specification of latent variables; the spacing of longitudinal data might not be ideal for the mechanisms being modeled; or in any number of other ways the data might limit the researcher's ability to specify the model she ideally would test. For this reason, the preferred approach is the acquisition of data that allow for estimation and testing of a model that comprises all that the researcher believes relevant to the process being studied. Referring again to Figure 1.1, the model depicted there, when specified before the data are acquired, serves as a guide to data collection or the selection of a secondary data source. Only a data set that includes x_1 to x_4 and y_1 to y_3 would be suitable for the analysis.

The specific actions and concerns in specification are the same whether a model is specified before or after the acquisition and preparation of data. In terms of actions, specification involves designating the variables, relations among the variables, and the status of the parameters in a model. With regard to designating variables, the decisions are which observed variables to include and which latent variables, if any, to model (see Bollen & Hoyle, Chapter 4, this volume, for a detailed treatment of latent variables). Having decided which observed and latent variables to include in the model, the researcher must then decide which variables are related and, for those that are related, whether the relation is nondirectional or directional. Finally, the status of parameters in a model must be specified. In general, a parameter can be specified as either fixed or free. Fixed parameters are those whose values are set by the researcher and, therefore, not estimated. For instance, in the model shown in Figure 1.1, the loading of x_1 on X (or F_1 or ξ_1) is fixed to 1. Less apparent is the fact that the loadings of x_1 to x_4 on Y and the loadings of y_1 to y_3 on X are fixed to 0. Otherwise the loadings are free parameters and will be estimated from the data. I provide detailed information about these actions in Chapter 8 (this volume).

As demonstrated earlier, a specified model is expressed formally using a system of notation coupled with either a set of equations or a diagram. Historically, each computer program for conducting SEM analyses accepted only one means of depicting a model. For example, early versions of the LISREL program required specification using matrix notation. Early versions of the EQS program required equations and double-label notation. The first program designed specifically for use on desktop computers, AMOS, accepted either line-by-line code or path diagrams constructed using built-in drawing capability. These and other commercial programs such as Mplus now allow for model specification using multiple means, including one or more of the means illustrated in Figure 1.1 as well as program-specific shorthand coding schemes. These programs are reviewed by Byrne (Chapter 19, this volume). In Chapter 20, Fox, Byrnes, Boker, and Neale review two open-source programs for SEM analyses implemented in the R environment.

A key concern in specification is identification. Each parameter in a specified model must be identified and, if all parameters are identified, the model is an identified model. A parameter is identified when it takes on a single value given the model and observed data. Parameters can be identified in two ways. The most straightforward and direct means of identifying a parameter is to fix its value. Because a fixed parameter can, by definition, assume no other value, it is identified. Free parameters are identified if there is but one estimated value for them that satisfies the estimation criterion and is obtained when the data are used to solve relevant structural and measurement equations. In some models, there is more than one way to obtain the estimate for a free parameter from these equations. As long as all such computations produce the same estimate, the parameter is overidentified. If a single value for a given parameter cannot be obtained through estimation, the parameter is unidentified and, as a result, the model is unidentified. Although a few straightforward rules of thumb offer some assurance that a model is identified, the only way to ensure identification is to show mathematically that a single value can be obtained for each parameter in all ways it might be expressed as a function of other parameters in the model. As illustrated in Figure 1.2, identification is linked to (re)specification. Ideally, prior to estimation, researchers would verify that all parameters are identified. That said, it bears noting that not all identification problems are related to specification. Parameter estimates near zero and highly correlated parameters can result in empirical underidentification, which can only be detected by attempting estimation. Kenny and Milan (Chapter 9, this volume) offer a relatively nontechnical treatment of identification.

An additional concern related to specification is the statistical power of tests of model fit. The model that best reflects the researcher's hypotheses about the mechanisms that gave rise to the data may be perfectly captured in the specification with all parameters identified, but the likelihood of finding support for the model or specific parameters in the model given the specification and data is too low to justify the analysis. The statistical power of SEM analyses is affected by multiple factors (e.g., degrees of freedom, sample size, correlations between parameters) that may vary from one fit index or statistical test to the next. The role of degrees of freedom—which derive, in part, from model specification—in the statistical power of SEM analyses argues for the consideration of statistical power as part of model specification. Detailed treatment of statistical power in the SEM context is provided by Lee, Cai, and MacCallum (Chapter 11, this volume).

Estimation

Once a model has been specified, its parameters identified, and the data prepared for analysis (see Malone & Lubansky, Chapter 16, this volume, for recommendations), the implementation moves to estimation. The goal of estimation is to find values for the free parameters that minimize the discrepancy between the observed covariance matrix and the estimated, or implied, covariance matrix given the model and the data. The means by which parameter estimates are derived depends on which of a number of possible estimation methods are used. Examples are maximum likelihood, unweighted least squares, generalized least squares, weighted least squares, and asymptotically distribution-free estimators (see Lei & Wu, Chapter 10, this volume, for detailed coverage of estimation and estimation methods). By far the most commonly used method of estimation is maximum likelihood, the default in most SEM computer programs. Because the validity of model evaluation rests most fundamentally on the integrity of estimates, a critical concern for researchers is whether maximum likelihood estimation is appropriate given their data and model. If it is not, then a decision must be made as to which alternative estimator overcomes the limitations of maximum likelihood without introducing additional concerns about the integrity of estimates. The key assumptions and how they are evaluated are discussed by Kline (Chapter 7, this volume). The robustness of different estimators to violations of assumptions often is determined by simulation studies, the logic and interpretation of which are covered by Bandalos and Gagné (Chapter 6, this volume). An approach to constructing indices of fit and statistical tests of parameters when assumptions are not met is described and illustrated by Hancock and Liu (Chapter 18, this volume).

Most estimation methods, including maximum likelihood, are iterative. They begin with a set of start values for the free parameters. These values are, in effect, used along with the fixed parameter values to solve the equations that define the model and produce an implied covariance matrix. The degree of discrepancy between the observed and implied covariance matrices is reflected in the value of the fitting function, the computation of which varies from one estimator to the next. The goal of estimation is, through iterative updating of parameter estimates (beginning with the start values), to minimize the value of the fitting function, which takes on a value of zero when the observed and implied covariance matrices are identical. Because the start values are nothing more than guesses at the values of the free parameters, the starting point often is a wide discrepancy between the observed and implied covariance matrices reflected in a relatively large value of the fitting function. The first few iterations typically result in substantial reductions in the discrepancy between the two matrices and relatively large declines in the value of the fitting function. When the value of the fitting function can be minimized no further through updates to the parameter estimates, the process is said to have converged on a solution. Often convergence is achieved in 10 or fewer iterations, though complex models or estimation situations in which start values are highly discrepant from the final estimates may require more. Unidentified models and models estimated from ill-conditioned data typically do not converge, forcing the researcher to revisit the model specification or data evaluation and preparation. Although convergence is necessary for evaluation of model fit, the number of iterations required for convergence has no relevance for that evaluation.

Evaluation of Fit

Although a set of parameter estimates obtained from suitable data for an identified model are those estimates that minimize the discrepancy between the observed

and implied covariance matrices, that discrepancy may be relatively large or small. That is, the fixed and estimated parameters may imply a covariance matrix that is sufficiently similar to the observed covariance matrix to support an inference that the model fits the data; or it may imply a covariance matrix in which one or more values are sufficiently discrepant from the observed data that the model does not fit the data. In an SEM analysis, the evaluation of fit concerns whether the specified model offers an acceptable account of the data or should be rejected (if the intent is strictly confirmatory) or respecified (if the original or reconsidered intent is model generation). How this evaluation is done and a decision reached remains a topic of research and debate among methodologists.

A useful starting point for considering how decisions about fit are made is the so-called χ^2 test. In reality, the value typically labeled χ^2, under conditions rather typical of SEM analyses, is a poor approximation. Moreover, the statistical test, when it is legitimate, is of a hypothesis that few researchers would venture: that the specified model fully accounts for the observed data (i.e., there is no discrepancy between the observed and implied covariance matrices). Nonetheless, it is prototypic of goodness-of-fit tests, the goal of which is to find no difference between the observed data and data implied by a model.

Relatively early in the history of SEM, the χ^2 goodness-of-fit test fell into disfavor as a test of the absolute fit of a specified model. The earliest alternatives were indices that reflected the improvement of a specified model over a model that assumed no relations between the variables (i.e., the independence, or null, model). In some cases these values were standardized so that their values ranged from 0 to 1, with higher values indicating greater improvement of the specified model relative to the model that offered no account of the relations between variables. A drawback to these comparative fit indices is that because they do not follow a known probability distribution, they cannot be used to construct formal statistical tests. As such, their use is governed by rules of thumb, typically involving the designation of a criterion value that must be exceeded for a model to be considered acceptable.

Because of the critical importance of the decision to accept or reject a specified model, the development of new statistics and fit indices has continued. The most promising of these follow a known probability distribution, focus on absolute rather than comparative fit, evaluate the hypothesis of approximate rather than perfect fit, and account for the complexity of the model. West, Taylor, and Wu (Chapter 13, this volume) review a wide range of fit statistics and indices, and offer recommendations for using them to judge the adequacy of a specified model or to choose between alternative models.

Two additional aspects of evaluating fit bear mention. If the intent of an SEM analysis is strictly confirmatory or model generating, then the strategy I have described is appropriate for judging model adequacy. If, however, the analysis involves the comparison of alternative models, this strategy is not appropriate. Ideally the models to be compared are *nested*; that is, one model is produced by changing the status of one or more parameters in the other. In the same way that hierarchical multiple regression models can be formally compared by testing change in F or R^2, nested models in SEM can be compared by testing change in χ^2. The comparison of alternative models that are not nested is more informal and less precise but may be necessary when the alternatives cannot be specified to be nested.

Beyond these tests of overall model adequacy are tests of the estimated parameters. These typically are tested for difference from zero using a test that is comparable to the test of coefficients in multiple regression analysis.

Respecification

Referring back to Figure 1.2, the evaluation of fit can send the researcher in one of two directions—to interpretation and reporting or to respecification (the exception being when SEM is used with strictly confirmatory intent, in which case respecification is not an option). Although interpretation and reporting is the desired direction, often the evaluation of fit does not produce support for the specified model and any alternatives, sending the researcher in the direction of respecification. Note that respecification requires a reconsideration of identification, then a return to estimation and evaluation of fit. Once a researcher engages in respecification, regardless of his original intent, the goal has shifted to model generation.

Decisions about how a model might be modified to improve its fit are based on specification searches, the goal of which is to find sources of misspecification among the fixed and free parameters in the initially specified model. Specification searches can be manual, which involves a visual inspection of the residual matrix in search of subjectively large residuals, or auto-

mated, which involves the use of a statistical algorithm that evaluates the incremental improvement in fit if each fixed parameter is freed or each free parameter is fixed. In Chapter 14, this volume, Chou and Huh offer a detailed treatment of specification searching, including discussion of how modified models should be interpreted given their post hoc nature.

Interpretation and Reporting

When the evaluation of fit yields support for a model— either the originally specified model or a modified version of it—the researcher moves to the final step in the implementation framework. Given the technical challenges associated with specification, estimation, and evaluation of fit, it is perhaps surprising that many of the criticisms leveled at SEM have focused on the interpretation and reporting of results. For that reason the researcher who uses SEM must take special care in interpreting results and reporting information about the analysis and results.

With regard to interpretation, the primary concerns are the basis for the model, the meaning of particular parameters in the model, and the degree to which the model is unique in accounting for the observed data. Generally speaking, the basis for the model can be either a priori, as in models that reflect theoretical models or form a set of interrelated hypotheses that perhaps derive from multiple theories, or post hoc, as in models that include modifications to the initially specified model or have their basis in exploratory analyses of the same data to which they were fit. The former affords stronger conclusions and allows for more straightforward interpretation based primarily on the concepts and their interrelations. The latter requires qualifying with reference to the means by which the model was derived or modified. A second interpretational issue concerns the meaning of certain parameters in the model. Specifically, I refer to parameters associated with directional paths and the degree to which they can be interpreted as reflecting causal effects. In this regard, the prevailing wisdom among methodologists has moved from a willingness to view tests of parameters as tests of causal effects in the 1960s and 1970s, to an increasing reluctance to interpret parameters in this way beginning in the 1980s and continuing into the early 2000s. As detailed by Pearl (Chapter 5, this volume), there is evidence of a move away from such conservative interpretation of directional effects to a view that, when properly justified, parameters can be interpreted as tests of causal effects even when the design is cross-sectional and the data are correlational. Finally, an issue that has received too little attention from researchers who use SEM, despite repeated expressions of concern by methodologists (e.g., Breckler, 1990; MacCallum, Wegener, Uchino, & Fabrigar, 1993), is the degree to which the model accepted by the researcher is the only model that offers an acceptable account of the data. Of particular concern are equivalent models, models that yield fit statistics and indices that are identical to those of the accepted model but include paths that directly contradict those in the accepted model. Means of detecting such models and the interpretational issues they raise are treated by Williams (Chapter 15, this volume). The degree to which the researcher can successfully manage these interpretational concerns often determines whether the findings are taken seriously by other researchers.

Beyond these interpretational concerns is a more mundane set of concerns that focuses on what is to be included in research reports describing SEM analyses and results. Given the flexibility of SEM and the multiple approaches to estimation and evaluation of fit, the research report must include information that generally is not expected in reports of ANOVA, multiple regression, or factor analysis. At the most basic level, the reader needs full information regarding the model specification, including the full array of fixed and free parameters and an accounting for degrees of freedom. Additional information includes the estimation method used and the outcome of evaluating its assumptions, the information to be consulted in order to evaluate fit, and the specific criteria that distinguish a model that offers an acceptable account of the data from one that does not. Information about missing data, if any, and how they are managed in the analysis is important, particularly given the fact that some approaches to managing missing data affect model specification (e.g., inclusion of auxiliary variables; see Graham & Coffman, Chapter 17, this volume, for information about methods for addressing missing data in SEM analyses). Once this background information has been provided, the researcher must decide which parts of the large amount of statistical information generated by an SEM analysis to report and how to report them. General guidelines for reporting statistical results and suggestions related to specific types of models are provided by Boomsma, Hoyle, and Panter (Chapter 21, this volume).

This general framework captures the primary steps in any implementation of SEM, regardless of the type of model or data under study. In the final major section of the chapter, I describe the various types of models and the types of data for which they would be appropriate. Variations on each type are discussed in detail and illustrated in Parts IV and V of this handbook.

TYPES OF MODELS

A covariance matrix to be modeled using SEM, especially a large matrix, affords a wide array of modeling possibilities, constrained only by features of the sampling strategy, the research design, and the hypotheses or patterns the researcher is willing to entertain. In fact, an infinite number of models is possible with even a few observed variables (e.g., Raykov & Marcoulides, 2001). Of course, not all models that might be specified and estimated are plausible or interesting. The point is that SEM allows for the study of a wide array of models using a single comprehensive and integrative statistical approach. In the remainder of this section, I describe a sample of the models for which SEM is well-suited; references are provided to relevant chapters in the latter half of the book. Although these models do not sort cleanly into a small number of categories, for efficiency, I present them in relatively homogeneous groups based on the type of data and hypotheses for which they are appropriate.

Models Focused Primarily on Latent Structure

The variables implicated in many research questions cannot be directly observed in pure form, if at all. Rather, they must be inferred from fallible indicators such as administrative records, observer ratings, self-reports, or the status of some biological characteristic such as heart rate or changes in blood volume in selected regions of the brain. A means of separating variance in these indicators attributable to the variable of interest from variance attributable to other factors is to gather data on multiple indicators that share in common only their reflection of the variable of interest. This commonality—the latent variable—is assumed to be a relatively pure reflection of the variable of interest, free of the error and idiosyncrasies of the individual indicators (see Bollen & Hoyle, Chapter 4, this volume, for further details and discussion of other types of latent variables). This notion of commonality-as-latent-variable is familiar to many researchers as the basic premise of EFA. In the

SEM context, it is the basic logic and building block for a large number of models.

The most straightforward model concerned primarily with the latent structure of a set of indicators is the first-order factor model. The two factors in the model depicted in Figure 1.1 are first-order factors that account for the commonality among the seven indicators. Unlike EFA, indicators are assigned a priori to factors and, ordinarily, each indicator is assumed to reflect only one factor. This prototypic model can be used to test a wide array of hypotheses such as whether the factors are correlated and, if so, whether they are distinguishable; whether each item is, in fact, a reflection of only one factor; whether the loadings are equal; and whether subsets of the uniquenesses are correlated. The basic first-order model and extension of it are discussed by Brown and Moore (Chapter 22, this volume).

If the model includes enough first-order factors, the researcher might choose to explore the latent structure of the first-order factors. In the same way that the commonality among indicators can be attributed to a smaller number of latent variables, it is possible that the commonality among first-order factors can be attributed to a smaller number of second-order factors. The classic example is Thurstone's use of EFA to argue for the presence of seven primary (i.e., first-order) mental abilities but later to concede that a single (i.e., second-order) thread, presumably general intelligence, ran through them (Ruzgis, 1994). With enough first-order factors, it is possible to have multiple second-order factors and the possibility of modeling one or more third-order factors.

Another class of models concerned primarily with the latent structure of a set of indicators includes models with "subfactors," which are additional first-order factors that explain commonality in subsets of indicators that may span the factors of interest (Rindskopf & Rose, 1988). Returning to Figure 1.1 and referencing the second equation in the middle panel, note the model implies that variance in v_2 is attributable only to F_1 (X) and a uniqueness. Imagine that v_2, v_4, and v_6 were negatively worded and for that reason assumed to share a source of commonality not captured by F_1 and F_2. In order to account for this commonality, a subfactor, F_3, could be specified that influences v_2, v_4, and v_6, in which case the equation for v_2 becomes $*F_1 + *F_3 + e_2$. The inclusion of subfactors can be used strategically to tease apart trait and method variance, as in multitrait–multimethod models (Marsh & Grayson, 1995), or trait and state variance, as in trait–state models (see Cole,

Chapter 34, this volume). These models, as well as first- and higher-order models, can be estimated for indicators that are continuous or categorical. The specific concerns of models that include categorical indicators are discussed by Bovaird and Koziol (Chapter 29, this volume).

Regardless of the specific model of latent structure, the question of whether a single model applies to all members of a given population may be of interest. (The same question may be asked of any model, regardless of type.) There are two approaches to studying model equivalence. When the subpopulations for which the model is to be compared can be distinguished by an observed variable (e.g., gender, ethnicity), then multigroup modeling may be used (Sörbom, 1974). In multigroup modeling, a model is estimated separately for different groups subject to constraints placed on individual parameters or groups of parameters. For instance, the loadings in a factor model might be constrained to be equal across groups and compared to a model in which they are free to vary as a means of evaluating the equivalence of the loadings. This approach is described and illustrated by Millsap and Olivera-Aguilar (Chapter 23, this volume). It is also possible that a given model does not describe the data for all members of the population but the variable that defines homogeneous subgroups in terms of parameter values is not observed. In such cases, factor mixture modeling can be used to estimate a categorical latent variable that indexes subgroup membership (Lubke & Muthén, 2005).

Models Focused Primarily on Directional Effects

A second type of model is concerned primarily with the estimation of the directional relations between variables, which may be latent or observed. The most basic model of this type is equivalent to the multiple regression model, in which the relations between a set of potentially correlated predictor variables and a single outcome are estimated. In this simplest structural model, all variables are observed, and there are no directional relations between the predictor variables. SEM allows for the extension of this basic model in three primary ways: (1) Any of the variables may be observed or latent; (2) there may be multiple outcomes among which there are directional relations; and (3) there may be directional relations between predictors. The first extension is illustrated in our example model, in which latent variable X predicts latent variable Y. The second and third extensions are somewhat redundant because they allow for models in which variables are both predictor and outcome. In fact, it is possible to have a model in which only one of many variables is only a predictor, with all other variables serving as predictors with reference to some variables in the model and outcomes with reference to others.

This point is evident in a relatively straightforward but highly useful model: the model that includes an indirect, or mediated, effect. Imagine that we add a variable, Z, to the model depicted in Figure 1.1. This variable is presumed to mediate the effect of X on Y. To evaluate this hypothesis, Z is positioned between X and Y with a directional path running from X to it and from it to Y. Thus, Z is both an outcome and a predictor. This particular model, the topic of Cheong and MacKinnon (Chapter 25, this volume), has received considerable attention from methodologists and is widely used in some research literatures.

Discussions of statistical mediation often compare and contrast it with statistical moderation—the qualification of a direct effect by another variable. Moderation is tested by interaction terms, which are routinely included in ANOVAs, less frequently considered in multiple regression analyses, and rarely included in models analyzed using SEM. In part, the relative neglect of interaction terms in SEM analyses may be attributed to the complexity of specifying interactions involving latent variables. Recent developments regarding strategies for modeling latent interactions have resulted in specification alternatives that significantly reduce the complexity of specification and estimation. These strategies are reviewed and demonstrated by Marsh, Wen, Nagengast, and Hau (Chapter 26, this volume).

A particularly useful class of models focused on directional relations is for data on the same sample at multiple points in time. These models can be distinguished in terms of the intensity of assessment or observation. Traditional longitudinal models involve the collection of data at relatively few points in time (typically two to four) at relatively long time intervals (typically 1–6 months). Intensive longitudinal models involve the collection of data at many time points at short time intervals (occasionally even in a continuous stream). The prototypic model for traditional longitudinal data is the autoregressive model, in which each variable is included in the model at each point in time. This permits estimation of the effect of one variable on another from one wave to the next while controlling for stability of the variables from wave to wave. Autoregressive

models are covered by Biesanz (Chapter 27, this volume). When the data collection is more intensive, as in the case of many observations over a short period of time, SEM can be used to model dynamic change as it is observed taking place. One approach to such data is dynamic factor analysis, by which the latent structure of a set of indicators is simultaneously modeled at each time and across the multiple times for which data are available. Use of the basic dynamic factor model is described and demonstrated by Wood (Chapter 33, this volume). In Chapter 35, Ferrer and Song show how this model is extended to the dyadic case.

These longitudinally intensive data, as well as data used for models described in the next section, are clustered; that is, the individual observations of each individual are almost certainly more related to each other than they are to the individual observations of other individuals in the data set. The same concern applies when each individual observation applies to a different individual, but subsets of individuals share an experience (e.g., treatment by one of several health care professionals) or place in an organization (e.g., one of several classrooms or schools) that is not shared by all individuals in the sample. SEM permits modeling of such clustering while retaining all of the flexibility in modeling described in this section of the chapter. Rabe-Hesketh, Skrondal, and Zheng (Chapter 30, this volume) cover a general method for estimating these multilevel models using SEM methods.

Models That Include Means

The goal of most models estimated using SEM, including all those described to this point, is to account for covariances between variables. An additional model type, which may be integrated with the models reviewed thus far, focuses on estimating the pattern of observed means or estimating latent means. These models require as input an augmented matrix that includes an additional line for the variable means. Models fit to such matrices add intercepts to the measurement and structural equations, which allows for the modeling and comparison of means of latent variables, as well as attempts to account for, and perhaps predict, the pattern of means. The additional considerations raised by the inclusion of means and hypotheses involving means that can be evaluated using SEM are covered by Green and Thompson (Chapter 24, this volume).

Particularly useful is a set of models that are longitudinal, multilevel, and focused on modeling means—

latent growth models. These models express as latent variables the variability between individuals in the pattern of means over time. For instance, bonding to school might be assessed annually on four occasions, beginning with the first year of middle school. These assessments are clustered within individual; thus, the model is multilevel. With four time points, both linear and quadratic patterns could be modeled, yielding three latent growth factors: intercept, linear, and quadratic. In multilevel parlance, these factors are Level 2 variables that can be related to other Level 2 (i.e., individual level) latent and observed variables, as described in the previous section. The basics of this modeling approach and variations on it are described by McArdle (Chapter 32, this volume).

To further extend a model that already comprises many of the capabilities SEM affords, a researcher might ask whether there is evidence in the data of distinct subsets of individuals who show evidence of a similar pattern of bonding to school scores across the four time points. Although it is possible that the researcher has anticipated and measured the characteristic that defines these subsets, more often the heterogeneity in growth either is not expected or, if expected, its source is not known. In such cases, growth mixture modeling can be used to model a categorical latent variable that defines subsets of individuals with similar patterns of bonding to school scores. This latent variable is not unlike the latent variables discussed thus far except that its interpretation is not as simple as inferring the source of commonality among its indicators. Rather, it can be correlated with or predicted by other variables, latent or observed, to examine potential explanations for membership in these emergent groups defined by different patterns of bonding to school. Growth mixture modeling is covered by Shiyko, Ram, and Grimm (Chapter 31, this volume).

These different model types can be adapted to a wide array of data and analytic situations. For instance, SEM is increasingly used to model genetic (Franić, Dolan, Borsboom, & Boomsma, Chapter 36, this volume) and imaging (McIntosh & Protzner, Chapter 37, this volume) data. A relatively new use is for modeling spatial data (Wall, Chapter 39, this volume). And, across an array of data types, SEM has proven useful as an integrative approach to measurement scale development and validation (Raykov, Chapter 28, this volume). Across all these data and model types, parameters can be estimated and models selected using Bayesian methods, which are now available in commercial SEM computer programs. An introduction and demonstration of the Bayesian approach to SEM analyses is provided by Kaplan and Depaoli (Chapter 38, this volume).

CONCLUSION

SEM is a comprehensive and flexible approach to modeling the relations among variables in a set. Historically used primarily to model covariances between variables measured on continuous scales, the capabilities of SEM have expanded dramatically to allow modeling of many data types using an array of estimation methods, and to accommodate means, patterns of means, latent interaction terms, categorical latent variables, clustered data, and models tailored to the needs of researchers working with complex data historically not analyzed using sophisticated multivariate methods. Though SEM is not necessary, or even desirable, for every hypothesis test or modeling need, it is unrivaled in its capacity to fulfill many, varied multivariate hypotheses and modeling needs. How this capacity is harnessed and used to full advantage is the topic of the 39 chapters that follow.

REFERENCES

Bentler, P. M., & Weeks, D. G. (1980). Linear structural equations with latent variables. *Psychometrika, 45,* 289–308.

Breckler, S. J. (1990). Applications of covariance structure modeling in psychology: Cause for concern? *Psychological Bulletin, 107,* 260–273.

Jöreskog, K. G. (1993). Testing structural equation models. In K. A. Bollen & J. S. Long (Eds.), *Testing structural equation models* (pp. 294–316). Thousand Oaks, CA: Sage.

Jöreskog, K. G., & Sörbom, D. (1999). *LISREL 8 user's reference guide.* Lincolnwood, IL: Scientific Software International.

Lubke, G. H., & Muthén, B. (2005). Investigating population heterogeneity with factor mixture models. *Psychological Methods, 10,* 21–39.

MacCallum, R. C., Wegener, D. T., Uchino, B. N., & Fabrigar, L. R. (1993). The problem of equivalent models in applications of covariance structure analysis. *Psychological Methods, 114,* 185–199.

Marsh, H. W., & Grayson, D. (1995). Latent variable models of multitrait–multimethod data. In R. H. Hoyle (Ed.), *Structural equation modeling: Concepts, issues, and applications* (pp. 177–198). Thousand Oaks, CA: Sage.

Raykov, T., & Marcoulides, G. A. (2001). Can there be infinitely many models equivalent to a given covariance structure model? *Structural Equation Modeling, 8,* 142–149.

Rindskopf, D., & Rose, T. (1988). Some theory and applications of confirmatory second-order factor analysis. *Multivariate Behavioral Research, 23*, 51–67.

Ruzgis, P. (1994). Thurstone, L. L. (1887–1955). In R. J. Sternberg (Ed.), *Encyclopedia of human intelligence* (pp. 1081–1084). New York: Macmillan.

Sörbom, D. (1974). A general method for studying differences in factor means and factor structures between groups. *British Journal of Mathematical and Statistical Psychology, 27*, 229–239.

Steiger, J. H., & Schönemann, P. H. (1978). A history of factor indeterminacy. In S. Shye (Ed.), *Theory construction and data analysis* (pp. 136–178). Chicago: University of Chicago Press.

CHAPTER 2

Key Advances in the History
of Structural Equation Modeling

Ross L. Matsueda

Structural equation modeling (SEM) has advanced considerably in the social sciences. The direction of advances has varied by the substantive problems faced by individual disciplines. For example, path analysis developed to model inheritance in population genetics, and later to model status attainment in sociology. Factor analysis developed in psychology to explore the structure of intelligence, and simultaneous equation models developed in economics to examine supply and demand.

These largely discipline-specific advances came together in the early 1970s to create a multidisciplinary approach to SEM. Later, during the 1980s, responding to criticisms of SEM for failing to meet assumptions implied by maximum likelihood estimation and testing, SEM proponents responded with estimators for data that departed from multivariate normality, and for modeling categorical, ordinal, and limited dependent variables. More recently, advances in SEM have incorporated additional statistical models (growth models, latent class growth models, generalized linear models, and multilevel models), drawn upon artificial intelligence research to attempt to "discover" causal structures, and finally, returned to the question of causality with formal methods for specifying assumptions necessary for inferring causality with nonexperimental data.

In this chapter, I trace the key advances in the history of SEM. I focus on the early history and try to convey the excitement of major developments in each discipline, culminating with cross-disciplinary integration in the 1970s. I then discuss advances in estimating models from data that depart from the usual assumptions of linearity, normality, and continuous distributions. I conclude with brief treatments of more recent advances to provide introductions to advanced chapters in this volume.

EARLY HISTORY:
THE DISCIPLINARY ROOTS OF SEM

Sewall Wright's Path Analysis
in Genetics and Biology

In 1918, Sewall Wright, a young geneticist, published the first application of path analysis, which modeled the bone size of rabbits. After computing all possible partial correlations of his measures, he was still dissatisfied with the results, which remained far from a causal explanation. Consequently, Wright developed path analysis to impose a causal structure, with structural coefficients on the observed correlations. His substantive application decomposed the variation in the size of an individual bone to various hereditary causes (Hill, 1995). He subsequently applied path analysis to systems of mating, using data on guinea pigs, which laid the basis for much of subsequent population genetics. For example, in modeling the proportion of white color in spotted guinea pigs, Wright (1920) decomposed the variance into heredity (h), common environment for the litter (e), and other factors, such as developmental noise (d). The path coefficient (h) represents the link between genotype and phenotype, and h^2 is the proportion of variance due to heredity, later termed "heritability" in population genetics. Wright also developed models for systems of mating, showing the consequences of continued inbreeding systems, such as continued brother–sister mating, which results in $m = r'_{00}$, where m is the correlation between mates in one generation, and r'_{00} is the correlation between brother and sister of the previous generation (Li, 1956). He also derived results for intergenerational consequences of assortative mating. Figure 2.1 reproduces a path diagram of environment and heredity, which Hill (1995, p. 1500) calls "surely one of the best known diagrams in biological science."

Wright (1921a, 1934) presented the method of path analysis for estimating causal relations among vari-

ables based on the correlation matrix of observed variables, emphasizing path coefficients (standardized regression coefficients) but also using "path regressions" (unstandardized coefficients). He invented a graphical method of presenting causal relations using path diagrams, consisting of variable labels connected by arrows for direct effects, double-headed arrows for unanalyzed correlations, and the estimated path coefficients listed over single-headed arrows. From path diagrams, Wright could read off total, direct, and indirect effects, and quickly decompose correlations into various causal sources, such as direct effects, indirect effects, common causes, and the like. Among the models Wright estimated by path analysis was a model of multiple causal indicators, or what later became known as the multiple-indicator, multiple-indicator-cause (MIMIC) model. Wright's estimation method was essentially the method of moments, which follows the intuitive principle of estimating a population moment (or function of moments) using the sample analog moment (or function of moments) (Goldberger, 1991). Although he lacked a principle for reconciling multiple ways of expressing a path coefficient in terms of sample moments in overidentified models, he did check to see if they were close, and acknowledged the potential gains in efficiency and reduced standard errors from using full information (Goldberger, 1972b).

While working for the U.S. Department of Agriculture, Wright (1925) worked on corn and hog correlations, developing a complex, highly overidentified, recursive system of equations containing observed, unobserved, lagged, and unlagged variables to describe seasonal data on hog breeding, corn prices, and hog prices. The Department of Agriculture rejected publication of the monograph on the grounds that "an animal husbandman" (Wright's position at the time) "had no business writing about economics" (Crow, 1988). Wright's research was only published after Henry Wallace read the paper and exploited the influence of his father, then Secretary of Agriculture. Although the recursive model had no explicit demand function, Wright (1925, p. 54) noted in a footnote that a direct negative effect of hog quantity on hog price would be desirable but the "treatment of such reciprocal relations between variables requires an extension of the theory of path coefficients" (see Goldberger, 1972b, p. 983).

In 1928, Wright's father, economist Phillip Wright, published a study of the tariff, which included an appendix—the infamous "Appendix B"—that applied instrumental variables and path analysis to reciprocal re-

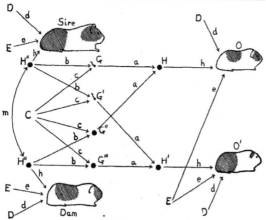

A diagram illustrating the relations between two mated individuals and their progeny. H, H', H'' and H''' are the genetic constitutions of the four individuals. G, G', G'' and G''' are four germ-cells. E and D represent tangible external conditions and chance irregularities as factors in development. C represents chance at segregation as a factor in determining the composition of the germ-cells. Path coefficients are represented by small letters.

FIGURE 2.1. An early path diagram on the importance of heredity and environment in spotted guinea pigs. From Wright (1921b). Copyright granted by the Genetics Society of America. Reprinted by permission.

lations between variables (Wright, 1928). Most scholars presume that the appendix was coauthored with Sewall Wright, although Stock and Trebbi (2003) suggest that Phillip may have been sole author.[1] Phillip Wright, who had mentioned the identification problem as early as 1915 (Wright, 1915), and presented it in graphical form of supply and demand curves, wrote out what later became known as the reduced form equations:

$$P = p_1 \frac{\sigma_P}{\sigma_D} D + p_2 \frac{\sigma_P}{\sigma_S} S \tag{2.1}$$

$$Q = q_1 \frac{\sigma_Q}{\sigma_D} D + q_2 \frac{\sigma_Q}{\sigma_S} S \tag{2.2}$$

where D and S indicate shifts in demand and supply curves after transforming P and Q to trend ratios, and σ's represent standard deviations of variables. Wright (1928) noted that the two equations contain four unknowns. He then suggested that if two external variables, A and B, could be found (based on external knowledge of markets) such that A were correlated with D but not S, and B were correlated with S but not D, the principles of path analysis would yield solutions for the four unknowns. Wright had arrived at a more general treatment than offered by Henry Schultz that year (1928) or "indeed in 1938" (Goldberger, 1972b, p. 984). Sewell Wright (1934) later developed more general solutions, noting that a mere single external variable is sufficient if the supply and demand situations were uncorrelated—that is, the disturbances of the two equations were orthogonal—and also that, in very complex models with many more shifts than external variables, one could solve for parameters by assuming plausible values for some of the unknowns (see Epstein, 1987). This solution to the simultaneous equation problem would be rediscovered by Rejersøl (1945, cited in Morgan, 1990), who used the term "instrumental variable estimates" (which he attributed to Frisch).

At this time, Wright's (1934) path analysis was largely ignored not only in biology but statistics as well, perhaps in part because it contained elements "that were objectionable" to the two dominant schools of statistics (Shipley, 2000, p. 70):

> The Phenomenalist school of Pearson disliked Wright's notion that one *should* distinguish "causes" from correlations. The Realist school of Fisher disliked Wright's notion that one *could* study causes by looking at correlations. Professional statisticians therefore ignored it.

And applied biologists were drawn to Fisher's methods, which included inferential statistics, were rooted in experimental design, and were easier to understand (Shipley, 2000). Later, Wright's path models became foundational for much of population genetics (Li, 1956).

Causal Models and Path Analysis in Sociology

Perhaps the earliest reference to path analysis by a sociologist appeared in an appendix to Blalock's (1961a, pp. 191–193) classic treatment of causal inference in nonexperimental research, where he briefly discussed "some related approaches," and concludes that path analysis "might readily be extended so as to be highly useful in the less precise nonexperimental sciences."[2] Blalock had spearheaded a voluminous literature in sociology on causal models in the 1960s by elaborating on Simon's (1954) method of making causal inferences from correlational data. Building on Yule's (1896) original method of ruling out common causes using partial correlations, Simon (1954) began by noting that a zero partial correlation ($r_{xy.z} = 0$) between independent variable x and dependent variable y holding z constant, implies a *spurious correlation* between x and y when z (a confounder) is causally prior to x and y. However, when z is causally prior to x and causally subsequent to y, z is an *intervening variable* between x and y. Simon (1954, p. 471) correctly asserted that the determination of whether a partial correlation is or is not spurious "can only be reached if a priori assumptions are made that certain other causal relations do not hold among the variables"—namely, exclusionary restrictions on coefficients and uncorrelated errors in equations. He then went on to expound on these conditions in all possible three-variable models. Blalock (1961b, 1962) extended this method to a five-variable model and then to an exhaustive exposition of the four-variable case. Later, Boudon (1965) applied these results to path coefficients, drawing from Wright (1934), but renaming them "dependence coefficients."

But it was Duncan's (1966) classic expository article, "Path Analysis: Sociological Examples," and his monumental monograph with Peter Blau, *The American Occupational Structure* (Blau & Duncan, 1967), that launched the path analysis movement in sociology, and later in political science. Duncan used published correlations to apply path analysis to recursive models of class values, population density, occupational prestige, and synthetic cohorts. Subsequently, Costner (1969) and

Blalock (1969) used path analysis to address multiple-indicator causal models, and in particular, to find that tetrad-difference restrictions on observed correlations provide a way of testing models—a result that emerged from factor analysis in psychology. These papers made important insights into substantive population models, although they tended to gloss over sample–population distinctions, efficient estimation, and formal hypothesis testing.

Substantively, Duncan and Hodge (1963) had earlier published a four-variable status attainment model on data from Chicago, in which son's education intervened between the effects of father's occupation on son's occupation in 1940 and 1950. They estimated the models using equation-by-equation multiple regression. Blau and Duncan's (1967) monograph expanded on this model by using national data, distinguishing hierarchies of occupations and rewards from the process by which individual characteristics sort people into those occupations, and examining whether the American stratification system approximated an open opportunity structure more than a rigid class hierarchy. The study produced an explosion of productive research using path analysis to model status attainment, most notably the Wisconsin status attainment model (e.g., Sewell & Hauser, 1975).

Factor Analysis in Psychology

In psychology, interest in SEM originated in "factor analysis," which is a statistical method for analyzing a correlation or covariance matrix of observed variables to identify a small number of factors, components, or latent variables that contain the essential information in the original variables. Thus, the primary goal is to attain "scientific parsimony or economy of description" (Harman, 1960, p. 4). The method was originally developed to model psychological theories of ability and behavior. Spearman (1904) is often credited as the founding father of factor analysis, although earlier Pearson (1901) published a paper on fitting planes by orthogonal least squares—the foundation for principal component analysis—which was later applied to the analysis of correlation matrices by Hotelling (1933). Spearman's work on factor analysis derived explicitly from his work on intelligence testing. He specified a two-factor theory of intelligence, in which all mental processes involved a general factor g, plus a specific factor s. The general factor enters all activities, some more than others, while the specific factors were unique to the task at hand (the specific mental activity). Spearman claimed

that the disparate items from intelligence tests would reveal two factors: a general factor and an item-specific factor. Moreover, Spearman (1927) showed that four variables cannot be described by a single factor unless their intercorrelations satisfy the conditions of two vanishing tetrad differences[3]:

$$r_{12}r_{34} - r_{12}r_{23} = 0 \qquad (2.3)$$

$$r_{12}r_{24} - r_{14}r_{23} = 0 \qquad (2.4)$$

Criticisms of the two-factor theory of intelligence on theoretical as well as empirical grounds—tetrads often failed to vanish or, equivalently, correlation matrices failed to be of unit-rank, even after considering sampling error—led to interest in multiple factor analysis, in which group factors were identified after extracting a general factor (e.g., Holzinger, 1941). Thurstone (1935), who founded the Psychometric Society, noted that a vanishing tetrad difference implied a vanishing second-order determinant of the matrix of observables, and extended this to the vanishing of higher-order determinants as a condition for more than one factor. He then generalized the result: The number of common factors is determined by the rank of the matrix of observables (see Harman, 1960). In addition, Thurstone (1935) developed the centroid method of factoring a correlation matrix (as a pragmatic compromise to the computationally burdensome principal axis method). Moreover, he developed a definition of simple structure for factor analysis based on five principles (the most important of which are to minimize negative loadings and maximize zero loadings) to facilitate interpretation and ensure that loadings were invariant to the inclusion of other items. This spawned interest in various methods of rotation of the initial solution, such as Kaiser's (1958) Varimax orthogonal rotation. Thurstone's original hand rotation was oblique, allowing factors to be correlated, but it was Jennrich and Sampson (1966) who developed a computational method of achieving an oblique rotation, and Jennrich and Clarkson (1980) who worked out the standard errors of rotated loadings (see Browne, 2000).

The problem of rotating factor solutions is avoided when confirmatory factor analysis is used. Here, the number of factors and the pattern of loadings—including restrictions on loadings—are specified in advance, transforming the problem into one of identification of a model's parameters from observed moments—the same issue that arises in simultaneous equation models.[4] The factor model specifies $y = \Lambda\eta + \varepsilon$, where y is a vector of *p* observables, η is a vector of *m* latent factors, where (*m* < *p*), Λ is a *p* × *m* matrix of loadings, and ε is a vector of *p* error terms representing "unique" variance in *y*. Identification is typically achieved by specifying zero-restrictions on elements of Λ to create, for example, sets of congeneric tests, in which items load solely on single factors (e.g., Jöreskog, 1971b). The zero loadings create tetrad difference overidentifying restrictions on observed covariances, as noted earlier. The covariance structure then becomes

$$\Sigma = \Lambda\Psi\Lambda + \Theta \qquad (2.5)$$

where $\Sigma = E(y\,y')$, $\Psi = E(\eta\,\eta')$, and $\Theta = E(\varepsilon\,\varepsilon')$, and $E(\varepsilon) = 0$. A maximum likelihood approach to factor analysis was developed by Lawley (1940), and fully elaborated by Anderson and Rubin (1956). But, according to Browne (2000, p. 663), computational procedures were not available until "nested algorithms involving eigenvalues and eigenvectors and imposing inequality constraints on unique variance estimates were discovered independently by Jöreskog (1967) and by Jennrich and Robinson (1969)." If *S*, the covariance matrix of observables follows a Wishart distribution, the log-likelihood function of the model is

$$\log L = -\frac{1}{2}n\left[\log|\Sigma| + tr\left(S\,\Sigma^{-1}\right)\right] \qquad (2.6)$$

Jöreskog (1967) and his colleagues developed computer software programs for confirmatory factor analysis estimated by maximum likelihood.

Simultaneous Equation and Errors-in-Variables Models in Economics

The structural equation approach in econometrics is usually attributed to Haavelmo (1943) and the Cowles Commission (1952), most notably Koopmans (1945). But, as Morgan (1990) points out, Frisch and Waugh (1933, pp. 389–390) were first to define "*structural relation*" as a "theoretical relation postulated *a priori*" in a single-equation multivariate linear model in which the partial regression coefficient represented a "structural coefficient": "An empirically determined relation is 'true' if it approximates fairly well a certain well-defined *theoretical* relationship, assumed to represent the nature of the phenomenon studied."

Frisch (1934), however, was critical of the use of probability models for economic data (e.g., variations in the business cycle), which were rarely the result of a sampling process, and of ordinary least squares

(OLS) regression because measurement errors existed on not only dependent variables but also independent variables. This led him to confluence analysis, which treated observed variables as fallible indicators of latent variables, and then examined the interrelationships among all latent and observed variables to distinguish "true relations" from "confluent relations." Frisch developed the method of "bunch maps"—a graphical presentation of regression coefficients—as a tool to discover underlying structure, often obtaining approximate bounds for relationships (for details, see Hendry & Morgan, 1989).

According to Qin (1989), Frisch—who coined the term "econometrics" and helped found the Econometric Society and its journal *Econometrica*—had developed many of the abstract principles of identification of simultaneous equation models, although in a manner confounded with issues of estimation and testing, particularly in his critique of Tinbergen (1939). Tinbergen himself had discussed a formal way of identifying a two-equation model from reduced-form parameters (Tinbergen, 1930, cited in Magnus & Morgan, 1987), although in his monumental models of the Dutch and U.S. economies, he "cleverly constructed his model in the causal chain fashion," using OLS to estimate its parameters, including effects of lagged dependent variables (Anderson, 1991).[5] In his classic works on demand, Schultz (1938) had developed the cobweb model in which lagged price identified the supply–demand model. Remarkably, Schultz was unaware of Sewell Wright's more general instrumental variable solution to the identification problem despite the two participating in intellectual discussions of science, mathematics, and statistics within a hiking group of academics (Goldberger, 1972b, pp. 985–986).

Within this context, Haavelmo (1943, 1944) made two key contributions to structural equation models in economics. First, he built on the work of Wald, Koopmans (1937), and others in specifying a probability model for econometric models, presenting clearly and concisely the Neyman–Pearson (e.g., Neyman & Pearson, 1933) approach to hypothesis testing, and using the probability approach for estimation, testing, and forecasting (see Morgan, 1990). He also distinguished between two models of the source of stochastic components: errors-in-variables models emphasized by Frisch (1934), and random shocks models introduced by Slutsky (1937).[6] This framework is often referred to as the "probabilistic revolution" in econometrics (see Morgan, 1990) and has had a lasting impact on the field, particularly in cementing the Neyman–Pearson approach to inference over others, such as Bayesian approaches (e.g., Jeffreys, 1935; see Heckman, 1992). Second, Haavelmo made major advances in simultaneous equation models, showing that OLS estimates are biased in a two-equation supply–demand model, and distinguishing between structural form equations and what Mann and Wald (1943) termed the "reduced-form equation." He applied maximum likelihood estimation to the system of equations, showing its equivalence to OLS when applied to the reduced form, and specifying necessary and sufficient conditions for identification in terms of partial derivatives of the likelihood function (Haavelmo, 1943, 1944). Haavelmo (1944) also refined the term "autonomy": Parameters representing *relatively* autonomous relations are more likely to be stable, intelligible, and useful for policy analysis (Aldrich, 1989). Parameters, then, are structural when they represent autonomous relations, which are invariant to policy interventions. Haavelmo (1943) also interpreted structural equations in terms of counterfactuals or potential outcomes, presaging the more recent models of Rubin (1974) and Imbens and Angrist (1994).

The advances made by Haavelmo and Mann and Wald led to work on the simultaneous equation model at the Cowles Commission, which moved to Chicago in 1939, led by Marschak and including Koopmans, Haavelmo, Wald, Lurwicz, Klein, and Anderson (Rubin and Leipnik were graduate assistants in Mathematics, and Simon joined later). Work at the Cowles Commission solved the major problems of identification, estimation, and testing of simultaneous equation models. In particular, Koopmans, Rubin, and Leipnik (1950) gave a general treatment of the model's structural and reduced forms:

$$\mathbf{B}y + \mathbf{\Gamma}x = u \qquad (2.7)$$

where y is a vector of p endogenous variables, x is a vector of q predetermined or exogenous variables, u is a vector of p disturbances (assumed normally distributed), and $\mathbf{\Gamma}$ and $\mathbf{B}$ are coefficient matrices in which $\mathbf{B}$ is nonsingular.[7] The reduced form is

$$y = \mathbf{\Pi}x + v \qquad (2.8)$$

where $\mathbf{\Gamma} = -\mathbf{B}\mathbf{\Pi}$, $u = \mathbf{B}v$, $\Sigma = \mathbf{B}\Omega\mathbf{B}'$, and Ω is the covariance matrix of v.

Anderson (1991) summarizes an intuitive way of stating the identification problem. Suppose that in Equation 2.7 some elements of $\mathbf{B}$ and $\mathbf{\Gamma}$ are constrained

to be zero. If we rearrange the matrices so that the first row of $(\mathbf{B}, \mathbf{\Gamma})$ is written as $(\boldsymbol{\beta}, \mathbf{0}, \boldsymbol{\gamma}, \mathbf{0})$, then the first row of $\mathbf{\Gamma} = -\mathbf{B}\mathbf{\Pi}$ becomes $(\boldsymbol{\beta}, \mathbf{0})\mathbf{\Pi} = -(\boldsymbol{\gamma}, \mathbf{0})$. Then partition $(\mathbf{\Pi})$:

$$\mathbf{\Pi} = \begin{pmatrix} \mathbf{\Pi}_{11} & \mathbf{\Pi}_{12} \\ \mathbf{\Pi}_{21} & \mathbf{\Pi}_{22} \end{pmatrix} \qquad (2.9)$$

and we obtain $\boldsymbol{\beta}\mathbf{\Pi}_{11} = -\boldsymbol{\gamma}$, and

$$\boldsymbol{\beta}\mathbf{\Pi}_{12} = \mathbf{0} \qquad (2.10)$$

The vector $\boldsymbol{\beta}$ is identified (except for a multiplicative constant) by Equation 2.10 if and only if the rank of $\mathbf{\Pi}_{12}$ is at least one less than the number of elements in $\boldsymbol{\beta}$ (Anderson, 1991, p. 7). If an equation does not satisfy this condition, it is underidentified and cannot be estimated. If an equation's restrictions on $\boldsymbol{\beta}$ are exactly one fewer than the rank of $\mathbf{\Pi}_{12}$, then the equation is just-identified; if the restrictions are more than one fewer than the rank of $\mathbf{\Pi}_{12}$, the equation is overidentified.[8] Koopmans and colleagues (1950) also specified a maximum-likelihood estimator for the general simultaneous equations model, which made Haavelmo's model accessible for empirical research.[9]

Perhaps the most important empirical applications of simultaneous equation models were Klein's (1950) Keynesian models, culminating with the 15-equation Klein–Goldberger model estimated by limited information methods (Klein & Goldberger, 1955). Others at Cowles had worried about the finite sample properties of estimation and introduced limited information methods as a solution (e.g., Anderson & Rubin, 1949).[10] Later, Theil (1953/1992) developed a two-stage least squares (2SLS) estimator that is consistent but asymptotically efficient only among single-equation estimators. He applied OLS to the reduced form, obtained predicted values for endogenous predictors, and applied OLS to the structural form having replaced endogenous predictors with their predicted counterparts. Zellner (1962) developed a joint generalized least squares (GLS) approach to seemingly unrelated regressions that incorporates information on covariances among errors of equations that are otherwise unrelated. He showed that GLS estimates and standard errors are minimum variance for linear models, and gain efficiency over OLS when the x's differ across equations and covariances among errors of equations are nonzero. Zellner and Theil (1962) developed a three-stage least squares (3SLS) estimator that applies joint GLS to the 2SLS estimates—using information from the disturbance covariances—and showed that, for properly specified models, 3SLS is consistent, asymptotically efficient, and asymptotically equivalent to full-information maximum likelihood (ML).

From its heyday in the 1950s and 1960s, in which Keynesian macroeconomic models proliferated, interest in simultaneous equation models in economics declined (Epstein, 1987). This appears traceable to three events: (1) self-criticism by members of Cowles; (2) Lucas's (1976) rational expectations critique, in which economic agents anticipate policy interventions and then act contrary to linear models—implying that models omitting expectations are misspecified and structural parameters are not policy-invariant; and (3) empirical research suggesting that macro-Keynesian simultaneous equations models were not superior to simple naive models in forecasting the future (e.g., Nelson, 1972), leading to alternative time series models, such as vector autoregressions (Sims, 1980; see Epstein, 1987; Heckman, 2000).

The emphasis of Haavelmo and the Cowles Commission on models of errors in equations led most econometricians to abandon the errors-in-variables model emphasized by Frisch (1934). Two "path-breaking articles"—Zellner (1970) and Goldberger (1972a)—revived empirical interest in errors-in-variables models (Judge, Griffiths, Hill, & Lee, 1980). Zellner (1970) presented GLS (a modification of his joint GLS estimator) and Bayesian approaches to estimating a model with a fallible endogenous predictor with multiple causes. Goldberger showed that GLS is equivalent to ML only when errors are normally distributed with known variances. He also showed that when error variances are unknown, an iterated GLS will converge to ML.[11]

INTERDISCIPLINARY INTEGRATION

The year 1970 was a watershed year for structural equation modeling: Jöreskog (1970) published his general method of analyzing covariance structures; Hauser and Goldberger (1971) presented, at the sociology meetings, their work on unobservables in path analysis; and Zellner (1970) published his GLS results on unobservable independent variables. The year 1970 was also marked by the Conference on Structural Equation Models, an interdisciplinary forum featuring economists, sociologists, psychologists, statisticians, and political scientists, originating from a Social Science Research

Council recommendation and culminating with the published volume *Structural Equation Models in the Social Sciences* (Goldberger & Duncan, 1973). This was presaged by the appearance of Blalock's (1971) edited volume *Causal Models in the Social Sciences*, which featured interdisciplinary contributions.

In this section, I focus on two key papers published in this period by Hauser and Goldberger (1971) and Jöreskog (1973). Hauser and Goldberger's (1971) examination of unobservable variables is an exemplar of cross-disciplinary integration, drawing on path analysis and moment estimators from Wright and sociologists, factor-analytic models from psychometrics, and efficient estimation and Neyman–Pearson hypothesis testing from statistics and econometrics. In a seminal and landmark paper that summarized his approach, Jöreskog (1973) presented his ML framework for estimating SEMs, developed a computer program for empirical applications, and showed how the general model could be applied to myriad important substantive models. Here, I focus on Hauser and Goldberger (1971) because they used limited information estimation to reveal what was going on "behind the scenes" of systems of structural equations estimated by ML.

Hauser and Goldberger (1971) analyze two models: the two-factor multiple indicator "walking dog" model (considered in factor analysis and by Costner and Blalock) and the MIMIC model.[12] Figure 2.2 presents a simple walking-dog model with four observables and two latent factors. We can express the model in matrix form:

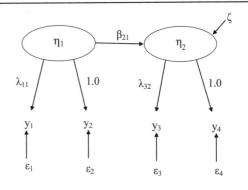

FIGURE 2.2. Path diagram of a walking-dog model in four observables and two latent variables.

$$\begin{pmatrix} y_1 \\ y_2 \\ y_3 \\ y_4 \end{pmatrix} = \begin{pmatrix} \lambda_{11} & 0 \\ 1 & 0 \\ 0 & \lambda_{32} \\ 0 & 1 \end{pmatrix} \begin{pmatrix} \eta_1 \\ \eta_2 \end{pmatrix} + \begin{pmatrix} \varepsilon_1 \\ \varepsilon_2 \\ \varepsilon_3 \\ \varepsilon_4 \end{pmatrix} \qquad \text{(2.11)}$$

$$y \quad = \quad \Lambda \qquad \eta \quad + \quad \varepsilon$$

$$\begin{pmatrix} \eta_1 \\ \eta_2 \end{pmatrix} = \begin{pmatrix} 0 & 0 \\ \beta_{21} & 0 \end{pmatrix} \begin{pmatrix} \eta_1 \\ \eta_2 \end{pmatrix} + \begin{pmatrix} \zeta_1 \\ \zeta_2 \end{pmatrix} \qquad \text{(2.12)}$$

$$\eta \quad = \quad B \qquad \eta \quad + \quad \zeta$$

It then follows that the covariance structure model is

$$\Sigma_{yy} = \Lambda (I - B)^{-1} \Psi (I - B)^{-1\prime} + \theta_{\varepsilon} \qquad \text{(2.13)}$$

where $\Sigma_{yy} = E(y\,y')$ is the (*population*) covariance matrix of observable indicators, Λ is a matrix of loadings, B is a matrix of regression coefficients among latent variables η, $\Psi = E(\zeta\,\zeta')$ is the covariance matrix of structural disturbances, and $\theta_{\varepsilon} = E(\varepsilon\,\varepsilon')$ is a covariance matrix of measurement errors (diagonal in this example). This model is overidentified with one degree of freedom (10 moments and 9 parameters). The overidentifying restriction implies that there is more than one way of computing parameters in terms of moments, and there is a testable overidentifying restriction in the data. This can be seen by computing moments in terms of parameters (normal equations) and then solving for parameters in terms of moments. For example:

$$\lambda_{32} = \sigma_{23}/\sigma_{24} = \sigma_{13}/\sigma_{14} \qquad \text{(2.14)}$$

By cross-multiplying the second two terms and rearranging, we obtain the identical tetrad-difference restriction as found by Spearman (1927) and given in Equation 2.4, but in unstandardized form: $\sigma_{23}\sigma_{14} = \sigma_{24}\sigma_{13}$. Because Equation 2.14 can be satisfied by many different models, a traditional structural equation approach tests a specific nested parameterization of the restriction, rather than testing the tetrad-difference constraint on moments directly.

In estimating overidentified models, the question becomes which moment estimator(s) should be used. We can see this by replacing the population moments in Equation 2.14 with their sample counterparts, and noting we have two moment estimators for λ_{32}. In overidentified fully recursive models, the OLS estimator is unbiased and efficient; therefore, using the moment estimator corresponding to OLS (giving it a weight of one) and ignoring other instrumental variable moment estimators (giving them a weight of zero) is optimal. In the general case, however, one would not want to use only one estimator or a simple unweighted average, but instead weight the moments inversely to their sampling variability. Hauser and Goldberger (1971) show that this is precisely what ML does when minimizing the fit function in Equation 2.6. We can illustrate this point by noting that minimizing Equation 2.6 is asymptotically equivalent to minimizing a quadratic form (Anderson, 1973; Browne, 1974):

$$F_{\text{GLS}} = [s - \sigma(\theta)]'\,W^{-1}[s - \sigma(\theta)] \qquad \text{(2.15)}$$

where s is a vector of nonredundant elements from the sample covariance matrix S, $\sigma(\theta)$ is the corresponding vector of elements of the parametric structure of the covariance matrix Σ—which makes $s - \sigma(\theta)$ a discrepancy vector to be minimized—and W is a weight matrix consisting of the *covariance matrix of the sample moments*. Under normality, the latter consists of products of second-order moments about the mean. Thus, the parameters in $\sigma(\theta)$ are expressed as a function of sample moments s, each of which is weighted inverse to its sampling variability by W. The estimator in Equation 2.15, termed GLS by Browne (1974), has been applied to econometric models by Hansen (1982), who terms it the "generalized method of moments."

The second model analyzed by Hauser and Goldberger (1971), the MIMIC model, is presented in a simple four-variable, three-equation form in Figure 2.3. This model has nine parameters, 10 observable moments and, therefore, one overidentifying restriction. In matrix form, the model is

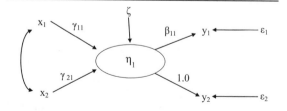

FIGURE 2.3. Path diagram of a multiple-indicator, multiple-indicator cause (MIMIC) model.

$$\begin{pmatrix} y_1 \\ y_2 \end{pmatrix} = \begin{pmatrix} \beta_{11} \\ \beta_{21} \end{pmatrix}(\eta_1) + \begin{pmatrix} \varepsilon_1 \\ \varepsilon_2 \end{pmatrix} \qquad (2.16)$$

$$y \ \ = \ \ B \quad \eta \ + \ \varepsilon$$

$$(\eta_1) = \begin{pmatrix} \gamma_{11} & \gamma_{12} \end{pmatrix}\begin{pmatrix} x_1 \\ x_2 \end{pmatrix} + (\zeta_1) \qquad (2.17)$$

$$\eta \ \ = \ \ \Gamma \quad x \ + \ \zeta$$

and the covariance structure is

$$\Sigma_{yy} = B(\Gamma\Phi\Gamma' + \Psi)B' + \theta_\varepsilon \qquad (2.18)$$
$$\Sigma_{xy} = \Phi\Gamma'B'$$

where $\Sigma_{xy} = E(x\,y')$ contains the covariances between x and y, $\Sigma_{yy} = E(y\,y')$ the covariances among the y's, $\Phi = \Sigma_{xx} = E(x\,x')$ (covariances among x's are unconstrained), $\theta_\varepsilon = E(\varepsilon\,\varepsilon')$ the covariance matrix of measurement errors in y (assumed diagonal here), and $\Psi = E(\zeta\,\zeta')$ the covariance matrix of the structural disturbance(s). Let us fix $\beta_{21} = 1.0$ to normalize the latent variable η and give it a metric; one could also normalize by fixing Ψ to a constant.

Using path analysis, we can compute moments in terms of parameters, solve for the parameters, and obtain two ways of expressing parameters in terms of moments. For example:

$$\beta_{11} = \sigma_{y_1 x_1}/\sigma_{y_2 x_1} = \sigma_{y_1 x_2}/\sigma_{y_2 x_2} \qquad (2.19)$$

Replacing the population moments with their sample counterparts gives us two sample moment estimators of β_{11}. Also, if we cross-multiply the right two terms in Equation 2.19 we get a single tetrad-difference overidentifying restriction, $\sigma_{y_1 x_1}\sigma_{y_2 x_2} = \sigma_{y_2 x_1}\sigma_{y_1 x_2}$. Note that this is the same restriction on observable moments we found for the walking-dog model above (if we denote all variables as y's), which illustrates an important difficulty for structural equation models: Overidentifying restrictions can be satisfied by substantively different models. In general, ML will provide consistent and asymptotically efficient estimates by weighting sample moments inverse to their sampling variability, resulting in optimal weights for multiple moment estimators. Again, minimizing the likelihood function will provide a likelihood ratio χ^2 test of overidentifying restrictions.

Hauser and Goldberger (1971) also use econometric methods to study identification and estimation. By substituting Equation 2.17 into η in Equation 2.16, we obtain the reduced form:

$$\begin{pmatrix} y_1 \\ y_2 \end{pmatrix} = \begin{pmatrix} \pi_{11} & \pi_{12} \\ \pi_{21} & \pi_{22} \end{pmatrix}\begin{pmatrix} x_1 \\ x_2 \end{pmatrix} + \begin{pmatrix} \pi_{\varepsilon 1} \\ \pi_{\varepsilon 2} \end{pmatrix} \qquad (2.20)$$

$$y \ \ = \ \ \Pi \quad x \ + \ \Pi_\varepsilon$$

where $\pi_{11} = \beta_{11}\gamma_{11}$, $\pi_{12} = \beta_{11}\gamma_{12}$, $\pi_{21} = 1.0\gamma_{11}$, $\pi_{22} = 1.0\gamma_{12}$, $\pi_{\varepsilon 1} = \beta_{11}\zeta_1 + \varepsilon_1$, and $\pi_{\varepsilon 2} = 1.0\zeta_1 + \varepsilon_2$. The reduced form can always be efficiently estimated using OLS. The estimation issue arises because there are two ways of expressing structural parameters in terms of reduced-form parameters:

$$\beta_{11} = \pi_{11}/\pi_{21} = \pi_{12}/\pi_{22} \qquad (2.21)$$

This also implies a proportionality constraint on reduced form parameters, providing a test of the MIMIC specification. ML weights the reduced-form parameter estimates $\hat{\pi}_{pq}$ inverse to their sampling variability to obtain asymptotically efficient estimates (Hauser & Goldberger, 1971). In this example, there is one degree of freedom and the single constraint can be expressed in terms of observed moments or reduced-form parameters. Generally, in more complex models, both kinds of restrictions exist, and ML will use both forms of restrictions in estimating parameters.[13] Jöreskog and Goldberger (1975) later expanded on ML estimation of the MIMIC model, and Goldberger (1973) discussed estimation in overidentified models with latent variables and simultaneity. For discussions of indicators as causes of theoretical constructs versus reflections of constructs, see Hauser (1973) and Bollen and Lennox (1991).

In a series of landmark papers, Jöreskog (1970, 1973, 1978) outlined a general approach to covariance analysis and a computer program he called LISREL, which, following econometricians as far back as Frisch and Waugh (1933), stood for "LInear Structural RELations." At about the same time, Keesling (1972) in his PhD dissertation, and Wiley (1973) in the Goldberger–Duncan volume, presented nearly identical models. However, it was Jöreskog's version and software package that came to dominate the field. The LISREL model incorporates factor analysis, simultaneous equation models, and path analysis (as discussed earlier) into a general covariance structure model (e.g., Jöreskog & Sörbom, 2001):

$$\Sigma = \begin{pmatrix} \Sigma_{yy} & \Sigma_{yx} \\ \Sigma_{xy} & \Sigma_{xx} \end{pmatrix}$$

$$= \begin{pmatrix} \Lambda_y (I-B)^{-1}(\Gamma\Phi\Gamma'+\Psi)(I-B)^{-1'}\Lambda_y'+\theta_\varepsilon \\ \Lambda_x\Phi\Gamma'(I-B)^{-1'} \\ \Lambda_y(I-B)^{-1}\Gamma\Phi\Lambda_x' \\ \Lambda_x\Phi\Lambda_x'+\theta_\delta \end{pmatrix} \quad (2.22)$$

Jöreskog showed that ML estimates are obtained by minimizing the following fit function and solving for parameters:

$$F_{ML} = \log|\Sigma| - \log|S| + tr(S\Sigma^{-1}) - p + q \quad (2.23)$$

where S is the sample estimate of the population covariance matrix Σ, and p and q are constants reflecting the number of observed y's and x's, respectively. If we let θ be a vector of t parameters, then the $t \times t$ covariance matrix of parameter estimates, V, is a function of the inverse of Fisher's information matrix:

$$V = \left(\frac{2}{n}\right)\left[E\left(\frac{\partial^2 F}{\partial\theta\partial\theta'}\right)\right]^{-1} \quad (2.24)$$

in which the square roots of the diagonal elements are asymptotic standard errors. Finally, if F_{H_0} is the minimum of Equation 2.23 under the null hypothesis, and F_{H_A} is the minimum under the less restrictive alternative, then –2 times the log likelihood ratio is

$$\nu = N(F_{H_0} - F_{H_A}) \quad (2.25)$$

which is asymptotically distributed χ^2 with $(p+q) - t$ degrees of freedom. Equation 2.25 can be applied to tests of nested models and the model's overall goodness of fit. Jöreskog (1971) also generalized this result to estimate the model in multiple populations, and showed how the model can be applied to simultaneous equations, MIMIC models, confirmatory factor models, panel data, simplex models, growth models, variance and covariance components, and factorial designs (for reviews, see Bentler, 1980, 1986; Bielby & Hauser, 1977).

In 1975, Duncan authored an excellent introductory text for path analysis and structural equation models, in which he echoed Frisch and Haavelmo's concept of autonomy: "The structural form is that parameteriza-tion—among the various possible ones—in which the coefficients are (relatively) unmixed, invariant, and autonomous" (p. 151). He also distinguished forms of social change, from trivial changes in sampling or exogenous variables (that leave structural coefficients intact) to deeper changes in structural coefficients (which provide fodder for explanation by multilevel models), and changes in the model's structure itself (p. 167), and provided sage advice for applying structural models (p. 150): "Do not undertake the study of structural equation models (or, for that matter, any other topic in sociological methods) in the hope of acquiring a technique that can be applied mechanically to a set of numerical data with the expectation that the result will automatically be 'research.'" Furthermore, Duncan noted that if research using structural models "are contributions to science (and not merely exercises in quantitative technique), it is because the models rest on creative, substantial, and sound sociological theory" (p. 151).

The next two decades saw an explosion of the use of structural equation models in many areas of the social sciences, including stratification (e.g., Bielby, Hauser, & Featherman, 1977), social psychology (e.g., Kohn & Schooler, 1982), psychology (e.g., Bentler & Speckart, 1981), marketing (Bagozzi, 1980), mental health (e.g., Wheaton, 1978, 1985), sociology of science (e.g., Hargens, Reskin, & Allison, 1976), criminology (e.g., Matsueda, 1982; Matsueda & Heimer, 1987), adolescence (e.g., Simmons & Blyth, 1987), and population genetics (e.g., Li, 1975). Some extensions of the model were developed during this period. Alwin and Hauser (1975) wrote a systematic treatment of decomposing effects into total, direct, and indirect effects using path analysis. Sobel (1982, 1986) applied the delta method to obtain asymptotic standard errors for total and indirect effects; Bollen (1987) developed a method for determining specific effects and their standard errors (implemented in Mplus); and Bollen and Stein (1990) developed bootstrap confidence intervals for indirect effects. Kenny and Judd (1984) showed how to estimate a LISREL model with product terms among latent exogenous variables, and Jöreskog and Yang (1996) showed that Browne's asymptotically distribution-free (ADF) estimator used on the matrix of augmented moments provides consistent estimates of parameters in the Kenny–Judd model, as well as consistent standard errors and fit statistics.

Matsueda and Bielby (1986) and Satorra and Saris (1985) independently showed how to calculate the power of the likelihood ratio test in covariance structure models—using the noncentral χ^2 distribution—and independently presented a nearly identical way of approximating the noncentrality parameter. They showed that the likelihood ratio test statistic is asymptotically equivalent to a quadratic form:

$$\nu = \left(\hat{\theta}_r - \theta_{r0}\right)' V_r^{-1} \left(\hat{\theta}_r - \theta_{r0}\right) \qquad (2.26)$$

where $\hat{\theta}_r$ is the ML estimator for the rth parameter, θ_{r0} is the corresponding null hypothesis, and V_r is the asymptotic covariance matrix of $\hat{\theta}_r$ or, in other words, r-dimensional submatrix of Equation 2.24. Under the null hypothesis, ν has a central χ^2 distribution with r degrees of freedom. Under the alternative hypothesis, ν has a noncentral χ^2 distribution with r degrees of freedom and noncentrality parameter:

$$\tau = \left(\theta_r - \theta_{r0}\right)' V_r^{-1} \left(\theta_r - \theta_{r0}\right) \qquad (2.27)$$

where θ_r is the population parameter corresponding to the alternative hypothesis and θ_{r0} is the population parameter corresponding to the null hypothesis (see Kendall & Stuart, 1979, pp. 246–247). Matsueda and Bielby (1986) then drew on Hauser and Goldberger (1971) and Goldberger (1973) to show analytically that, in a walking-dog model (Figure 2.2), adding indicators to the endogenous latent variable increases the power of the test of β_{21}, depending on the reliability of the indicators. This is analogous to adding cross sections to a pooled time series cross-section econometric model estimated by GLS. They also gave simulation results for adding indicators to the exogenous latent variable (see Matsueda & Bielby, 1986; Satorra & Saris, 1985).

Applied researchers obsessed over the global goodness-of-fit likelihood ratio χ^2 test because, in large samples, models with many overidentifying restrictions tend to be rejected even when each restriction only departs trivially from the null hypothesis. This gave rise to a cottage industry of fit indices designed to offset the effect of sample size on test statistics. From this literature, it seems that a consensus is emerging that the most useful fit indices are Steiger and Lind's (1980) root mean square error of approximation (RMSEA; see also Browne & Cudeck, 1993; Steiger, 1990) and Raftery's (1993, 1995) application of Schwartz's (1978) Bayesian information criterion (BIC). (For details, see West, Taylor, & Wu, Chapter 13, this volume.) RMSEA is defined as

$$\varepsilon = \sqrt{F_0 / r} \qquad (2.28)$$

where F_0 is the population discrepancy function reflecting the model's lack of fit and r is the degrees of freedom, as earlier. MacCallum, Browne, and Sugawara (1996) have defined the noncentrality parameter for RMSEA index:

$$\lambda = (n - 1) r \varepsilon^2 \qquad (2.29)$$

where n is the sample size. They show that power can be calculated for the null hypothesis of perfect fit (i.e., $\varepsilon = 0$), as well as an approximate or close fit (e.g., $\varepsilon \le .05$). The latter may be useful in very large samples for models with many overidentifying restrictions, whereby reasonably well-specified models are likely to be rejected (see Lee, Cai, & MacCallum, Chapter 11, this volume). To date, RMSEA is the most popular fit index used in empirical applications of SEM, although it recently has been subject to criticism (e.g., Chen et al., 2008, on using a fixed cutoff point).

ADDRESSING VIOLATIONS OF DISTRIBUTIONAL ASSUMPTIONS

At this time, a major criticism of structural equation models is that the assumptions of continuous observed variables, multivariate normal distributions, and large sample sizes—needed to capitalize on the asymptotic properties of maximum likelihood estimation and testing—are rarely met in practice. Some early Monte Carlo studies, such as Boomsma (1983), which created non-normal errors by categorizing continuous variables, found that estimators were robust when samples were greater than 200, but that skewness due to categorization produced spurious measurement error correlations and biased standardized coefficients (see Bollen, 1989, for a review).[14]

ADF Estimator

As noted earlier, Browne (1974) introduced the quadratic form estimator he termed generalized least squares (GLS), which yielded optimal estimates for normally distributed observable variables when W is the covariance matrix of the sample moments (see Equation 2.15). Subsequently, Browne (1984) made a landmark contribution by developing what he termed an "asymptotic distribution-free" (ADF) estimator, by incorporating information about higher-order moments into the weight matrix of Equation 2.15, which can be written in scalar form as

$$F_{GLS} = \sum_{g=1}^{k}\sum_{h=1}^{g}\sum_{i=1}^{k}\sum_{j=1}^{i} w^{gh,ij}$$
$$\left[s_{gh} - \sigma_{gh}(\theta) \right]\left[s_{ij} - \sigma_{ij}(\theta) \right] \qquad (2.30)$$

where s_{gh} is the sample covariance between variables g and h, $\sigma_{gh}(\theta)$ is the corresponding element of $\Sigma(\theta)$ implied by the model, and $w^{gh,ij}$ is a typical element of W^{-1}, which is $u \times u$, where $u = k\ (k + 1)$, and k is the number of observables. Browne showed that if W is a matrix with typical element

$$w_{gh,ij} = m_{ghij} - s_{gh}s_{ij} \qquad (2.31)$$

where m_{ghij} is the fourth-order moment about the mean, then minimizing Equation 2.15 yields the ADF estimator, which is minimum variance consistent within the class of estimators in the form of Equation 2.15 under the mild assumption that eighth-order moments are finite (Browne, 1984, p. 710).[15] Browne presented the asymptotic covariance matrix for $\hat{\theta}_{ADF}$ and an asymptotic χ^2 test statistic, as well as an estimator for elliptical distributions, which have zero skewness but kurtosis that departs from multivariate normality.

Browne's (1984) ADF and elliptical estimators first appeared in Bentler's (1995) EQS program, followed by Jöreskog and Sörbom's (2001) LISREL program. Recent work has examined the finite sample properties of ADF and finds that it works well in very large samples. Other techniques available are using corrections to the covariance matrix of ML estimators to obtain accurate p-values for the χ^2 test under non-normality (e.g., Browne 1984), or a bootstrap method (Bollen & Stein, 1993). Browne's ADF estimator was also crucial for a second important advance: developing models for ordinal, limited, and discrete outcomes.

Models for Ordinal, Limited, and Discrete Outcomes

Structural equation models are often applied to survey data, in which items are measured on dichotomous or ordinal scales, violating the assumption of continuous and normally distributed observed variables. Muthén (1984) has made seminal contributions for analyzing dichotomous, ordinal, and limited dependent variables

within a covariance structure framework. The trick is to estimate scale-appropriate correlation coefficients (e.g., polychoric and polyserial) and then use a variation of Browne's (1984) ADF estimator. The polychoric correlation, which goes back to Pearson (1901), computes a correlation under the assumption that the ordered categories can be represented by contiguous intervals on a continuous scale (correlations between ordinal and continuous variables are termed "polyserial correlations").[16] Thus, the ordinal variable is related to the underlying normally distributed, continuous latent variable through a threshold model. Early work on factor models for dichotomous variables include Bock and Lieberman (1970), who used tetrachoric correlations and an ML estimator for a single factor model, and Christoffersson (1975), who generalized this to multiple factors using a GLS estimator (see also Muthén, 1978). Muthén (1979) developed a multiple-indicator structural probit model, and Winship and Mare (1983, 1984) applied multivariate probit models estimated by ML to multiple-indicator structural equation models and path analysis.

Muthén (1984) provided a general framework for analyzing ordinal variables. Here I focus on the polychoric and ADF approach with a simple example of a pair of three-category ordinal variables. Each ordered variable is related to an underlying continuous variable by two thresholds:

$$y = 1 \quad \text{if } y^* \le \alpha_1$$
$$y = 2 \quad \text{if } \alpha_1 \le y^* < \alpha_2 \qquad (2.32)$$
$$y = 3 \quad \text{if } \alpha_2 \le y^*$$

where the value for y indexes the ordinal category for y, y^* is a latent continuous variable, and α_1 and α_2 are thresholds. If we specify a distribution for y^*—we will assume it is normal—we can then estimate the thresholds by the general formula:

$$\alpha_i = \Phi^{-1}\sum_{k=1}^{i} n_k / N \qquad i = 1,2,3 \quad k = 1,2 \qquad (2.33)$$

where i indexes the category of y, k indexes the number of thresholds, $\Phi^{-1}(\,.\,)$ is the inverse of the standard normal distribution function, n_k is the sample size of the kth category, N is the total sample size, and $N = n_1 + n_2 + \ldots + n_k$. If we apply this to a second three-category ordered variable x, but with thresholds β_1 and β_2, and define π_{ij} as the population parameter denoting that an observation falls into cell (i, j), we can then define the log-likelihood function of the sample (Olsson, 1979):

$$\log L(n_{ij} \mid \pi_{ij}) = c \sum_{i=1}^{3} \sum_{j=1}^{3} n_{ij} \log \pi_{ij} \qquad \textbf{(2.34)}$$

where $\pi_{ij} = \Phi_2(\alpha_i, \beta_j) - \Phi_2(\alpha_{i-1}, \beta_j) - \Phi_2(\alpha_i, \beta_{j-1}) - \Phi_2(\alpha_{i-1}, \beta_{j-1})$, and $\Phi_2(.,.)$ is the bivariate normal distribution function with population correlation ρ. Maximizing Equation 2.34 will yield the ML estimator of the polychoric correlation, $\hat{\rho}_{ML}$. Alternatively, one can use a two-step procedure, estimating the thresholds α_i and β_j from the marginals of the contingency table (e.g., Equation 2.33), and then solving for ρ. See Olsson (1979) for a parallel treatment of the polyserial correlation between continuous and ordered variables, and Poon and Lee (1987) for multivariate ML estimators of both polychoric and polyserial correlations.

Once the polychoric and polyserial correlations $\hat{\rho}$ and their asymptotic covariances have been estimated, Browne's (1984) ADF fitting function can be used to obtain optimal estimates:

$$F_{ADF} = \left[\hat{\rho} - \sigma(\theta) \right]' S_{\rho\rho}^{-1} \left[\hat{\rho} - \sigma(\theta) \right] \qquad \textbf{(2.35)}$$

where $\hat{\rho}$ is a vector of scale-appropriate correlation estimates, $\sigma(\theta)$ is the corresponding vector of the parametric structure generating the correlations, and $S_{\rho\rho}^{-1}$ is the inverse of the asymptotic covariance matrix of the correlation estimates. Standard errors and χ^2 test statistics are obtained as earlier (Muthén, 1984). Muthén (1989) has also developed a tobit factor analysis for censored observed variables. A general method for handling dichotomous and limited dependent variables in SEM was initially programmed in Muthén's LISCOMP program, and then in his recent more comprehensive Mplus program (Muthén & Muthén, 2004), and later in Jöreskog and Sörbom's (2001, 2002) LISREL and PRELIS programs, and Bentler's (1995) EQS. Much of this material is covered in Bollen's (1989) excellent intermediate-level SEM text.

RECENT ADVANCES

Major contemporary advances in SEM make it an exciting and growing field. These include the development of latent growth and latent-class growth models for longitudinal data, the application of Bayesian methods, the integration of generalized linear models and multilevel models within an SEM framework, the adoption of algorithms from artificial intelligence to discover causal structure, and a formal treatment of causality within an SEM framework.

Latent Growth and Latent Class Growth Models

Although the use of factor analysis for modeling panel data on growth was introduced by Tucker (1958) and Rao (1958), it was not until 1990 that Meredith and Tisak (1990) published the treatment within an SEM framework that is still relevant today (see Bollen & Curran, 2006). Meredith and Tisak (1990) showed that individual growth curves, often modeled within a multilevel or mixed model framework (e.g., Raudenbush & Bryk, 2002), can be modeled within a standard SEM framework by treating the shape of growth curves as latent variables with multiple indicators consisting of the variable at multiple time points. This latent growth curve approach models both covariances and means of observed variables. Figure 2.4 presents a path diagram of a four-wave quadratic latent growth curve model. Here, the intercept α gives the value of y implied by the model at the first time point; β_1 is the linear growth component (giving the growth rate at the first time point); and β_2 is the quadratic growth component (giving the change in the growth rate over time). One can then impose a parametric structure on the growth pa-

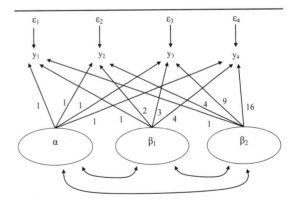

FIGURE 2.4. Path diagram of a four-wave quadratic latent curve model.

rameters α, β_1, and β_2, which would correspond to the second-level equation in a multilevel model.

In criminology, Nagin and Land (1993) developed a finite mixture model for latent classes of individual trajectories. This group-based trajectory model estimates individual trajectories using polynomials and then classifies the trajectories into discrete groups. The latent classes can be viewed as points of support in approximating a continuous distribution of unobserved heterogeneity or as reflections of theoretically important groups (see Nagin, 2005). In criminology, this model has been used to distinguish people with different criminal careers, such as chronic offenders, early starters, and adolescence-limited offenders (see Nagin & Tremblay, 2005). Muthén (2004) shows how to estimate this model within an SEM framework with Mplus. Moreover, Muthén's approach, termed "growth mixture modeling," allows for within-class variation among individual trajectories, a mean curve with variation around it, whereas Nagin's approach does not. The latter is nested within the former and can be subjected to statistical test. These models have become important features of research in child development, adolescent substance abuse, and criminal careers (e.g., Connell & Frye, 2006; Nagin & Tremblay, 2005).

Bayesian Approaches

As noted earlier, work at the Cowles Commission helped cement the Neyman–Pearson frequentist approach to hypothesis testing in econometric simultaneous equation models, which spread to SEM in psychology through Anderson and Jöreskog, and in sociology through Goldberger and Duncan. In recent years, alternatives—particularly Bayesian approaches—have been proposed for SEM (for an early and persistent advocate in economics, see Zellner, 1971). From a Bayesian perspective, estimation is less about deducing the values of population parameters and more about updating, sharpening, and refining our beliefs about the empirical world.

Bayesian estimation begins with a probability model of the data, D, in terms of a vector of parameters, θ (e.g., Raftery, 1995). The analyst's prior beliefs about the uncertainty of θ is denoted by the prior probability density, $p(\theta)$. The probability model for the data, then, is the likelihood function, $p(D|\theta)$, which is the probability of the data given that θ are the true parameters. We then observe the data, D, and update our beliefs about θ using Bayes's theorem:

$$p(\theta \mid D) = [p(D \mid \theta)p(\theta)] / p(D) \qquad (2.36)$$

The data are treated as a fixed set of information to be used in updating our beliefs about the parameters. Therefore, $p(D)$ does not involve θ, and Equation 2.36 reduces to

$$p(\theta \mid D) \propto p(D \mid \theta)p(\theta) \qquad (2.37)$$

where $\propto$ means "proportional to." The marginal density of the data has been dropped; to make this a proper density, a proportionality constant can be added. Thus, the posterior density is proportional to the likelihood times the prior density. Inferences about θ are made from summary statistics about the posterior density, $p(\theta|D)$, such as the posterior mode or Bayesian confidence intervals ("credible intervals"), which have an intuitive interpretation: "The probability that the true value of the parameter lies in the interval is—for example—95%."

Bayesian hypothesis testing entails comparing hypotheses to determine which has the highest probability of being correct. Suppose we have two hypotheses, H_0 and H_1, with *prior* probabilities, $p(H_0)$ and $p(H_1)$ before the data are examined, and define the prior odds ratio as

$$Odds_{\text{prior}} = p(H_0)/p(H_1) \qquad (2.38)$$

After examining the data, the prior probability will be updated, resulting in posterior probabilities for each hypothesis, $p(H_0|D)$ and $p(H_1|D)$, and a posterior odds ratio:

$$\begin{aligned} p(H_0|D)/p(H_1|D) &= Odds_{\text{posterior}} \\ &= B_{01} \times Odds_{\text{prior}} \end{aligned} \qquad (2.39)$$

where B_{01} is the Bayes factor:

$$B_{01} = p(D|H_0)/p(D|H_1) \qquad (2.40)$$

and $p(D|H_0)$ and $p(D|H_1)$ are the marginal probabilities of the data. Equation 2.39, the posterior odds ratio, gives the probability that the data support H_0 over H_1. Note that the posterior odds are equal to the Bayes factor when the prior odds are equal to 1.

Bayesian estimation and testing are currently diffusing into the SEM literature. For example, Raftery (1993, 1995) showed how to approximate the Bayes factor with the BIC, which is computed from the likelihood ratio test statistic. Suppose we wish to compare two models in which M_{k-1} is nested within M_k and has one more parameter than M_k. Then, if v_{k-1} is the likelihood ratio test statistic for model M_{k-1} and v_k is that of model M_k and $v = v_{k-1} - v_k$ is the test statistic for testing the one parameter (see Equation 2.25), then

$$BIC_{k-1} - BIC_k \approx v - \log n \qquad \textbf{(2.41)}$$

where n is the sample size. If this quantity is positive, then the less-restrictive model M_k is preferred (Raftery, 1995). As a fit statistic, BIC has performed exceedingly well in a variety of contexts and is particularly useful for SEM in large samples and with many overidentifying restrictions because trivially small departures from a reasonable model will be rejected using the likelihood ratio test. Although it has become the dominant fit statistic for most models estimated by ML, it has only recently begun to be used in SEM empirical studies.

Bayesian estimation using Markov Chain Monte Carlo (MCMC) algorithms are proving useful for incorporating prior information into confirmatory factor analysis (e.g., Lee, 1981); estimating complex models, such as nonlinear latent variable models (e.g., Arminger & Muthén, 1998); estimating multilevel factor models (Goldstein & Browne, 2002); arriving at a semiparametric estimator (Yang & Dunson, 2010); and drawing inferences about underidentified parameters from the posterior distribution when an informative prior is used (Scheines, Hoijtink, & Boomsma, 1999). For details, see Kaplan and Depaoli, Chapter 38, this volume. The program, TETRAD III, provides an MCMC algorithm using the Gibbs sampler (Scheines, Spirtes, Glymour, Meek, & Richardson, 1997).

Generalized Linear Latent and Mixed Models

When data take on a hierarchical structure—such as individuals nested within families, which in turn are nested within neighborhoods—special methods are needed to obtain consistent estimates of standard errors and test statistics due to dependent observations within clusters. Multilevel regression models allow estimation of models in which random intercepts capture heterogeneity between clusters in the dependent variable, and random coefficients capture heterogeneity in relationships among independent and dependent variables. A multilevel structural equation model would incorporate multiple-indicator measurement models into the

latent variable models. Early attempts to incorporate measurement error into multilevel regression models have assumed that measurement error variances (e.g., Goldstein, 1995) or factor loadings (e.g., Raudenbush & Sampson, 1999) are known and have the advantage that unbalanced designs, in which the number of Level 1 cases varies by Level 2, are easily handled if missing at random (see Rabe-Hesketh, Skrondal, & Pickles, 2004).

Multilevel structural equation models have typically specified separate models for within-cluster and between-cluster covariance matrices. For example, Muthén (1994) has shown how to estimate a two-level SEM using available SEM software. The trick is to specify separate within- and between-cluster models, and then use the multiple-group option to estimate the parameters simultaneously. Muthén argues that an estimator using this method is equivalent to ML in balanced designs, and is consistent (with reasonable standard errors and test statistics) in unbalanced designs (see also Goldstein & McDonald, 1988; Muthén, 1997; for a review of alternate estimators, see Yuan & Bentler, 2007). This approach is easily implemented using existing SEM software but is limited to specific models.

A more general approach is outlined in Rabe-Hesketh and colleagues (2004), and expanded in Skrondal and Rabe-Hesketh's (2004) excellent advanced text. Their generalized linear latent and mixed models (GL-LAMM) framework consists of three components: (1) a response model; (2) a structural equation model for latent variables; and (3) distributional assumptions for latent variables. The response model is simply a generalized linear model conditional on the latent variables and consisting of a linear predictor, a link function, and a distribution from the exponential family (Rabe-Hesketh et al., 2004). The model can handle response variables that are continuous, ordinal, dichotomous, discrete and continuous time durations, counts, polytomous responses and rankings, and mixes of responses. The structural equation for latent variables takes on the usual form, $\eta = \beta\eta + \Gamma\xi + \zeta$, with the exception that latent variables are allowed to vary by different levels. Rabe-Hesketh and colleagues assume the latent variables at level l are distributed multivariate normal with zero mean and covariance matrix Σ_l, although other distributions can be specified. The authors have also written a program, GLLAMM, which maximizes the marginal likelihood using an adaptive quadrature procedure and is available in the software package Stata

(Rabe-Hesketh, Pickles, & Skrondal, 2001). For more details, see Skrondal and Rabe-Hesketh (2004) and Rabe-Hesketh, Skrondal, and Zheng (Chapter 30, this volume). Many of these models can also be estimated using Mplus (Muthén & Muthén, 2004).

Tetrad: The Discovery of Causal Structure

A philosophically distinct approach to SEM developed with the publication of Glymour, Scheines, Spirtes, and Kelly's (1987) *Discovering Causal Structure: Artificial Intelligence, Philosophy of Science, and Statistical Modeling*. Instead of focusing on estimation and testing of structural models specified on a priori grounds, Glymour and colleagues draw on computer algorithms from artificial intelligence to "discover" causal structure with their program TETRAD. Thus, they are returning to the earlier ideas of Spearman, Frisch, Simon, Blalock, and Costner, who tried, in various ways, to induce causal structure from patterns of association among variables.[17] As noted earlier, Spearman's focus on tetrad difference restrictions on observed correlations became superfluous in light of Thurstone's rotated solution to simple structure for factor models; Frisch's confluence analysis and bunch mappings became obsolete with advances in identification and estimation in simultaneous equations; and Simon and Blalock's method of ransacking three- and four-variable models became outdated with the development of estimation and testing using ML and GLS in integrated SEMs. These "outdated" approaches have been resurrected by Glymour et al. (1987).

Beginning with the observation that an infinite number of models is consistent with any covariance matrix of observed variables, Glymour and colleagues (1987) return to Simon and Blalock's method of identifying the vanishing partial correlations that must hold for a given model and to the writings of Wright, Spearman, and others, who identified the tetrad difference equations that must hold for a given model. They provide a fascinating philosophy of science edifice to justify the idea of discovering causal structure. Moreover, they use the terminology of directed graphs—rather than path analysis—in which variables are vertices; causal effects are directed edges that can be into a vertex (the number denoted by indegree) and out of a vertex (the number denoted by outdegree); a recursive model is acyclic; a nonrecursive model (in which a path contains a subpath beginning and ending in the same vertex) is a cyclic model; and a trek is a path or a set of paths that

induce a correlation. Using these notions, they provide basic theorems and definitions about causal relations and a computer program, TETRAD, for discovering causal structure. The program allows users to incorporate a priori information about the data (e.g., a tentative or partial model), identifies the vanishing tetrad differences and vanishing partial correlations of the model, and then provides a test of the constraints. It then modifies the model by identifying the treks needed to satisfy a "false" tetrad equation without altering "true" tetrad equations, and calculates vanishing tetrads and partial correlations implied by the new model. Bollen (1990) develops a simultaneous test statistic to address the multiple testing problem and Bollen and Ting (1993) develop a confirmatory tetrad analysis approach for testing SEMs, including some non-nested and underidentified models.

The TETRAD approach is not without its critics (e.g., Humphreys & Freedman, 1996) and controversies (e.g., Glymour & Cooper, 1999; Spirtes, Glymour, & Scheines, 1993). Robins and Wasserman (1999) have effectively shown that it is not possible, in an observational study, to infer causal relationships between two variables, assuming that the sample is large and the distribution of the random variables is consistent with the causal graph, and assuming no additional substantive background knowledge (as claimed in Spirtes et al., 1993; Pearl & Verma, 1991). Using a Bayesian framework, they demonstrate that the claim assumes that the prior probability of no unmeasured causes is high relative to sample size, and when this probability is low relative to sample size, causal relationships are underidentified from the data. This opens a new puzzle: What kinds of assumptions must be made to discover causal relationships from nonexperimental data (Glymour, Spirtes, & Richardson, 1999)? This puzzle has encouraged cross-fertilization from the causality literature in statistics into the SEM literature.

Nevertheless, TETRAD is certainly a useful empirical tool for exploring causal structures, finding equivalences, and providing an efficient tool for sensitivity analyses. TETRAD has been shown to be more efficient at modifying models than existing procedures available in SEM packages, such as using first-order partial derivatives, residuals, or univariate Lagrange multipliers (termed "modification indexes" in LISREL). Moreover, introducing the language of directed graphs into structural equation models helps bridge the SEM literature with new developments in graphical theory and causal analysis (see Spirtes et al., 1993).

Causality and Structural Equation Models

An exciting recent development, which is slowly filtering into the SEM community, has been an explicit return to causal models using the language and logic of counterfactuals: What would happen if a subject received a different treatment (or value of the independent variable)?[18] As a consequence of Freedman's (e.g., 1987) persistent criticisms of SEM applications for making causal claims when assumptions of linear models are not met, and the more compelling critique of Holland (1988), most members of the SEM community have retreated from making causal claims and using causal language.[19] However, a recent literature, emerging from disparate sources such as statistics, artificial intelligence, philosophy of science, epidemiology, and economics, has developed graphical models for identifying causality under explicit weaker assumptions than are generally made. Such models, which generalize and extend Wright's (1921a) original path analysis, appeared in the social science literature as early as 1982 but did not catch on (see Kiiveri & Speed, 1982). Since then, major advances have been made in artificial intelligence (e.g., Pearl, 1988), statistics (e.g., Spirtes et al., 1993; Wermuth & Lauritsen, 1983), and epidemiology (Greenland, Pearl, & Robins, 1999; Robins, 1986; Robins & Greenland, 1992).

This approach begins with the classical SEM assumption that causality cannot be determined from observational data alone, but requires additional causal assumptions drawn from theoretical or substantive knowledge, which are translated into a structural model represented by a path model. At this point, the approach departs from traditional path analytic and SEM treatments of causality, in which strong and often unrealistic assumptions must be made in empirical applications:

> Structural equation models do little more to justify the causal interpretation of their coefficients than the causal orderings of path analysis. In both approaches, such causal interpretations are established by fiat rather than by deduction from more basic assumptions. (Holland, 1988, p. 460)

The contemporary counterfactual causality literature lays bare the *typically strong assumptions* underlying "causality by fiat," and more importantly, searches for ways of identifying causal effects under *weaker assumptions*.

To get a sense of this literature, consider a fundamental issue of causality in SEM—decomposing total effects into direct and indirect effects (see Figure 2.5). From a causality perspective, by manipulating and randomizing values of the independent variable, causal effects of that variable can be identified because reciprocal causation and omitted variable bias are ruled out. In the case of indirect effects, this requires sequential randomization (Robins & Greenland, 1992). For example, in Model A of Figure 2.5, by randomizing on X we can obtain the causal effect of X on M and the total causal effect of X on Y. However, because M is endogenous—and therefore, neither manipulated nor randomized—we cannot obtain the causal effect of M on Y. Consequently, we cannot obtain the direct causal effect of X on Y, and cannot decompose the total causal effect of X into direct and indirect components. To obtain the causal effect of M on Y we must randomize on M—hence, the need for *sequential* randomization.

In the social sciences, however, such sequential randomization is rarely possible; therefore, the question becomes, "What assumptions are necessary to identify causal direct and indirect effects?" An early paper by Holland (1988) discussed the question within Rubin's (e.g., 1974) model, which carefully separates causal theory from observed data, and which begins with unit causal effects based on counterfactuals and then defines average causal effects. Rubin's model typically assumes independent outcomes, and in particular, that treatment of one individual does not affect the outcome of another.[20] Holland noted that if we can assume that the effect of X on Y operates solely through its effects on M—that is, $c = 0$, which yields Model B of Figure 2.5— then the average causal effect of M on Y is identified and estimable using an instrumental variable estimator. Since X is orthogonal to u (by randomization) and X has no direct effect on Y (because $c = 0$), X can serve as an instrument for M (as long as $a \neq 0$) and a consistent estimator of b, the average causal effect of M

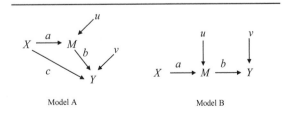

Model A   Model B

FIGURE 2.5. Path diagram of models with direct and indirect effects.

on Y is simply the total average causal effect of X on Y divided by the direct average causal effect of X on M. This estimator is useful for encouragement designs—in which it is reasonable to assume that X, randomized encouragement (e.g., encouraging students to study), affects Y solely through M, the activity encouraged (studying)—but is of limited utility in most observational studies in the social sciences (Sobel, 2008).

A related approach to the separation of causal direct and indirect effects is associated with the work of Robins (e.g., Robins & Greenland, 1992), which builds on Robins's (1986) original graphical approach to causality using tree graphs. Robins and Greenland (1992) show that Robins' g-computation algorithm can be used to separate direct and indirect effects of X if X and M are both randomized, X and M do not interact, and M can be blocked by intervention (i.e., manipulated). When these conditions hold, but M is not manipulated, g-estimation can still estimate the fraction of total effect that could be prevented by blocking M if additional confounding variables are available. Finally, when all conditions hold, except X and M interact in affecting Y, direct and indirect effects cannot be separated, although one can still estimate the fraction of the total effect of X that could be prevented by blocking M.

Recently, Emsley, Dunn, and White (2010) reviewed alternative approaches to estimating mediating effects in controlled trials and showed that under treatment heterogeneity, the interaction terms between randomized treatment and exogenous confounders can be used as instrumental variables to separate direct and indirect effects of treatment when the mediating variable is not randomized. Sobel (2008) shows that instrumental variables can be used to separate direct and indirect effects under weaker assumptions—such as relaxing the assumption of constant treatment effects—than presented by Holland (1988). Jo and Muthén (2002) have used latent growth models to define principal strata of the mediator and estimating, for models with multiple outcomes, complier average causal effects (CACE), which are average effects of treatment in the subpopulation of compliant subjects (e.g., Angrist, Imbens, & Rubin, 1996; Imbens & Rubin, 1997).

In economics, following Imbens and Angrist (1994), CACE, defined as local average treatment effects (LATE), has spawned a spate of randomized experiments using instrumental variables to identify treatment effects (see Imbens & Wooldridge, 2009, for a review). The relative merits of using randomization to identify causal effects versus using structural models, such as

Roy's (1951) counterfactual model, remain controversial among economists (Heckman & Urzúa, 2010). For an excellent discussion of the relative merits of the two approaches in economics, including key trade-offs between internal and external validity, see Deaton (2010), Imbens (2010), and Heckman (2010).

From artificial intelligence and epidemiology, a graphical model approach to causality has emerged. This approach represents the causal assumptions by a graphical model and then logically infers causality from a set of theorems applied to the graph. In addition to Robins's (1986) tree graph approach, Pearl (2000) developed a "nonparametric structural causal model," which holds regardless of distributional and other statistical assumptions about a particular data set. Causal statements can be made that are *conditional on the causal assumptions* encoded into the graphical model.

Pearl's (2000) approach, which is largely consistent with that of Robins (1986), advances SEM by (1) using new mathematical notation to reflect causality, such as replacing the algebraic equals sign with a sign that reflects a causal path; (2) deriving a theorem, the "back door" criterion, to determine which covariates should be controlled to arrive at a causal relationship in an SEM; (3) deriving a theorem, termed "d separation" (directed separation), which gives the necessary and sufficient conditions for independence between two sets of variables conditioned on a third set within an acyclic directed graph; (4) providing some simple mathematical notation for making counterfactual statements, which can be analyzed within the directed graph (for an introduction, see Morgan & Winship, 2007); and (5) providing an algorithm for identifying equivalent models. Taken together, these theorems translate the language of causality into the language of statistics and probability distributions (for distinctions between the approaches of Robins and Pearl, see Robins, 1995, 2003). See Pearl (2000) for an excellent presentation of the graphical approach to SEM and for a lucid introduction to the principles and issues, see Pearl (Chapter 5, this volume).

The importance of a graphical approach can be illustrated with a simple example. Consider Model A in Figure 2.6, a bivariate regression model of Y on X, with two latent variables: ξ affects X and C, and η affects Y and C. Standard SEM texts assume that including an irrelevant variable in a linear regression model leaves estimates unbiased but results in a loss of precision in the estimate (e.g., Greene, 2003, pp. 150–151). However, when Model A is the correct model, regressing Y on X

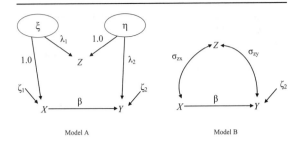

FIGURE 2.6. Path diagram of a model in which controlling for an exogenous variable creates bias.

and Z, which appears irrelevant, results in biased and inconsistent estimates of β. We can see this intuitively from Model A: the covariance between Z and X and Z and Y are spurious due to the latent variables ξ and η. Spirtes, Richardson, Meek, Scheines, and Glymour (1998, pp. 190–191) show that if we simplify Model A to Model B (Figure 2.6), and compute parameters in terms of covariances and partial covariances, we obtain an estimator from regressing Y on X and Z that is biased and inconsistent:

$$E(X,Y \mid Z)/E(X^2 \mid Z) = \beta\sigma_x^2 - \sigma_{zx}\sigma_{yz} / \left(\sigma_y^2\sigma_z^2 - \sigma_{xz}^2\right) \text{ (2.42)}$$

where the term left of the equality sign is the (naive) two-variable regression coefficient, and σ_{xz}^2 is the squared covariance of X and Z. A graphical approach quickly reveals not only that an unbiased and consistent estimate of β is obtained by the bivariate regression of Y on X, but also that a consistent estimator can be obtained by the naive two-variable regression by also controlling for ξ, η, or both (Greenland & Brumback, 2002).

The recent causality literature suggests that the parameters of most applications of SEM in the social sciences cannot be interpreted as causal effects without making strong and often unrealistic assumptions. What, then, are we to make of empirical applications of SEM, such as status attainment models? Perhaps a prudent interpretation, consistent with O. D. Duncan's thinking near the end of his career, is that such models "summarize systematic patterns in population variability" (Xie, 2007, p. 154) or, perhaps more precisely, describe "the probabilistic relationship between successive events in a population of interest" (Sobel, 1992, p. 666). Such a

description—even in the absence of causal language—is a crucial feature of social science research.

CONCLUSION

SEM has progressed through four general stages: (1) early disciplinary-specific developments of path analysis first from genetics and later sociology, factor analysis from psychology, and simultaneous equation models in economics; (2) cross-disciplinary fertilization between economics, sociology, and psychology, leading to an explosion of empirical applications of SEM; (3) a period of developing methods for handling discrete, ordinal, and limited dependent variables; and (4) a recent period of incorporating statistical advances into the SEM framework, including generalized linear models, mixed effects models, mixture regression models, Bayesian methods, graphical models, and methods for identifying causal effects. The recent period is substantially integrating SEM with the broader statistical literature, which—as the chapters of this volume demonstrate—is making SEM an even more exciting and vibrant tool for the social sciences.

ACKNOWLEDGMENTS

During the preparation of this chapter, I received support from the National Institute on Drug Abuse (1 R01 DA018148-01A), the National Science Foundation (SES-0966662), and the Blumstein–Jordan Endowed Professorship in Sociology. I thank Maria Grigoryeva for assistance and comments, Jerry Herting for his lively conversations and SEM books, and Adrian Raftery, Michael Sobel, Lowell Hargens, Ken Bollen, David Gow, and Richard Callahan for comments on an earlier draft. All remaining errors are mine.

NOTES

1. Stock and Trebbi (2003) conduct a stylometric (grammar and writing style) analysis using principal components and discriminant analysis that points to Phillip as the writer. Because one solution used path analysis, it is likely that the two Wrights collaborated—they had done so earlier—although Stock and Trebbi note that Phillip did not mention his son Sewall in his acknowledgments, as he had done in earlier publications.
2. In an essay titled "What If?" Duncan (1992) wondered whether, if he had sooner convinced Blalock that Sewall Wright's path analysis could solve Simon's questions, Blalock's appen-

dix would have been more complete and Duncan would have lost motivation to write his 1966 article.

3. A third tetrad difference, $r_{12}r_{34} - r_{13}r_{24} = 0$, is a function of the first two and will always be true if the first two are true.

4. Anderson (1991) notes that economists like to put restrictions on models, whereas psychologists refused to do so until "Jöreskog (1969) came up with the catchy terms 'exploratory' and 'confirmatory factor analysis'" with zero-restrictions on loading matrices, along with computer programs for maximum likelihood estimation. Jöreskog certainly popularized the terms, but the distinction was originally due to Tucker (1955).

5. This recursive causal chain model was later formalized and extended by Wold (1964), who criticized simultaneous equation models for ignoring the presumption that causality proceeds through time and is best modeled by recursive causal chains.

6. Koopmans (1937) appears to be the first to argue that residual variance in structural models was due not solely to measurement error—which implies deterministic relationships in the absence of such errors—but also to omitting numerous minor variables from the model (see Epstein, 1987, p. 55).

7. For a discussion of the concept of exogeneity, and of super-exogeneity, see Engle, Hendry, and Richard (1983).

8. While at Cowles, Rubin had been attending lectures by Thurstone and raised the identification issue in the context of the factor-analytic model. Anderson and Rubin (1956) concluded that the identification problems of simultaneous equation and factor analysis models were identical, which led to their treatise on maximum likelihood factor analysis (see Anderson, 1991).

9. For excellent discussions of the history of simultaneous equation models in economics, see Epstein (1987) and especially Morgan (1990).

10. For examples of recent returns to limited information methods to obtain estimates more robust to specification errors, see Bollen (1996) and Bollen, Kirby, Curran, Paxton, and Chen (2007).

11. For a lucid discussion of various ways that econometricians have approached measurement error, see Judge et al. (1980, Chap. 13).

12. The term "walking-dog model" originated with Beverly Duncan, who noted that the path diagram (see Figure 2.2) resembled a walking dog, in which η_1 here depicted the dog's face and ζ its tail (Hauser, personal communication).

13. Hauser and Goldberger (1971) also show that in the special case in which all tetrad-difference constraints are satisfied, such as when measurement errors are mutually correlated, modified GLS (GLS with unknown error variances) is equivalent to ML.

14. Wold's (1982) partial least squares "soft modeling" approach to causal chain models provides "instant" estimates under arbitrary distributions but does not necessarily have desirable statistical properties.

15. Note that $m_{ghij} = 1/n\Sigma(x_g - \bar{x}_g)(x_h - \bar{x}_h)(x_i - \bar{x}_i)(x_j - \bar{x}_j)$ is a sample estimator of $\sigma_{ghij} = 1/n\Sigma[x_g - E(x_g)][x_h - E(x_h)][x_i - E(x_i)][x_j - E(x_j)]$.

16. Pearson's tetrachoric correlation, involving pairs of dichotomous variables, led to his famous quarrel with Yule (1912), who argued that many binary outcomes, such as death, cannot be viewed as reflections of a continuous scale, and proposed his Q-coefficient instead (see Pearson & Heron, 1913).

17. A feature of Wold's (1982) soft modeling approach is the further development of a model through a "dialogue between the investigator and the computer."

18. The counterfactual approach to causality is just one of many potential approaches. For a critique of the counterfactual approach in statistics—with a lively discussion from leading statisticians—see Dawid (2000).

19. For a lucid response to Freedman's (1987) critique of Blau-Duncan, see Glymour et al. (1987), and for a lively description of Duncan's personal correspondence with Freedman, see Xie (2007).

20. Rubin (1980) terms this the "stable unit treatment value assumption" (SUTVA); Heckman (2010) has pointed out that Hurwicz (1962) included this assumption under the concept of invariance.

REFERENCES

Aldrich, J. (1989). Autonomy. *Oxford Economic Papers, 41,* 15–34.

Alwin, D. F., & Hauser, R. M. (1975). The decomposition of effects in path analysis. *American Sociological Review, 40,* 37–47.

Anderson, T. W. (1973). Asymptotically efficient estimation of covariance matrices with linear structure. *Annals of Statistics, 1,* 135–141.

Anderson, T. W. (1991). Trygve Haavelmo and simultaneous equation models. *Scandinavian Journal of Statistics, 18,* 1–19.

Anderson, T. W., & Rubin, H. (1949). Estimation of the parameters of a single equation in a complete system of stochastic equations. *Annals of Mathematical Statistics, 20,* 46–63.

Anderson, T. W., & Rubin, H. (1956). Statistical inference in factor analysis. In J. Neyman (Ed.), *Proceedings of the Third Berkeley Symposium on Mathematical Statistics and Probability* (pp. 111–150). Berkeley: University of California Press.

Angrist, J. D., Imbens, G. W., & Rubin, D. B. (1996). Identification of causal effects using instrumental variables (with discussion). *Journal of the American Statistical Association, 91,* 444–472.

Arminger, G., & Muthén, B. O. (1998). A Bayesian approach to nonlinear latent variable models using the Gibbs sampler and the Metropolis–Hastings algorithm. *Psychometrika, 63,* 271–300.

Bagozzi, R. P. (1980). *Causal models in marketing.* New York: Wiley.

Bentler, P. M. (1980). Multivariate analysis with latent variables: Causal modeling. *Annual Review of Psychology, 31,* 419–456.

Bentler, P. M. (1986). Structural modeling and *Psychometrika*: An historical perspective on growth and achievement. *Psychometrika, 51,* 35–51.

Bentler, P. M. (1995). *EQS program manual.* Encino, CA: Multivariate Software.

Bentler, P. M., & Speckart, G. (1981). Attitudes "cause" behaviors: A structural equation perspective. *Journal of Personality and Social Psychology, 40,* 226–238.

Bielby, W. T., & Hauser, R. M. (1977). Structural equation models. *Annual Review of Sociology, 3,* 137–161.

Bielby, W. T., Hauser, R. M., & Featherman, D. L. (1977). Response errors of black and nonblack males in models of the intergenerational transmission of socioeconomic status. *American Journal of Sociology, 82,* 1242–1288.

Blalock, H. M., Jr. (1961a). *Causal inferences in nonexperimental research.* New York: Norton.

Blalock, H. M., Jr. (1961b). Correlation and causality: The multivariate case. *Social Forces, 39,* 246–251.

Blalock, H. M., Jr. (1962). Four-variable causal models and partial correlations. *American Journal of Sociology, 68,* 182–194.

Blalock, H. M., Jr. (1969). Multiple indicators and the causal approach to measurement error. *American Journal of Sociology, 75,* 264–273.

Blalock, H. M., Jr. (Ed.). (1971). *Causal models in the social sciences* Chicago: Aldine-Atherton.

Blau, P. M., & Duncan, O. D. (1967). *The American occupational structure.* New York: Wiley.

Bock, R. D., & Lieberman, M. (1970). Fitting a response model for *n* dichotomously scored items. *Psychometrika, 35,* 179–197.

Bollen, K. A. (1987). Total, direct, and indirect effects in structural equation models. *Sociological Methodology, 17,* 37–69.

Bollen, K. A. (1989). *Introduction to structural equation models with latent variables.* New York: Wiley.

Bollen, K. A. (1990). Outlier screening and a distribution-free test for vanishing tetrads. *Sociological Methods and Research, 19,* 80–92.

Bollen, K. A. (1996). An alternative 2SLS estimator for latent variable models. *Psychometrika, 61,* 109–121.

Bollen, K. A., & Curran, P. J. (2006). *Latent curve models: A structural equation perspective.* New York: Wiley.

Bollen, K. A., Kirby, J. B., Curran, P. J., Paxton, P. M., & Chen, F. (2007). Latent variable models under misspecification: Two stage least squares (2SLS) and maximum likelihood (ML) estimators. *Sociological Methods and Research, 36,* 46–86.

Bollen, K. A., & Lennox, R. (1991). Conventional wisdom on measurement: A structural equation perspective. *Psychological Bulletin, 110,* 305–314.

Bollen, K. A., & Stein, R. A. (1990). Direct and indirect effects: Classical and bootstrap estimates of variability. *Sociological Methodology, 20,* 115–140.

Bollen, K. A., & Stein, R. A. (1993). Bootstrapping goodness-of-fit measures in structural equation models. In K. A. Bollen & J. S. Long (Eds.), *Testing structural equation models* (pp. 111–135). Newbury Park, CA: Sage.

Bollen, K. A., & Ting, K.-F. (1993). Confirmatory tetrad analysis. *Sociological Methodology, 23,* 147–176.

Boomsma, A. (1983). *On the robustness of LISREL (maximum likelihood estimation) against small sample size and non-normality.* Unpublished PhD dissertation, University of Groningen, Groningen.

Boudon, R. (1965). A method of linear causal analysis: Dependence analysis. *American Sociological Review, 30,* 365–374.

Browne, M. W. (1974). Generalized least squares estimators in the analysis of covariance matrices with linear structure. *South African Statistical Journal, 8,* 1–24.

Browne, M. W. (1984). Asymptotically distribution-free methods for the analysis of covariance structures. *British Journal of Mathematical and Statistical Psychology, 37,* 62–83.

Browne, M. W. (2000). Psychometrics. *Journal of the American Statistical Association, 95,* 661–665.

Browne, M. W., & Cudeck, R. (1993). Alternative ways of assessing model fit. In K. A. Bollen & J. S. Long (Eds.), *Testing structural equation models* (pp. 136–162). Newbury Park, CA: Sage.

Chen, F., Curran, P. J., Bollen, K. A., Kirby, J. B., & Paxton, P. M. (2008). An empirical evaluation of the use of fixed cutoff points in RMSEA test statistics in structural equation models. *Sociological Methods and Research, 36,* 462–494.

Christoffersson, A. (1975). Factor analysis of dichotomized variables. *Psychometrika, 40,* 5–32.

Connell, A., & Frye, A. A. (2006). Growth mixture modelling in developmental psychology: Overview and demonstration of heterogeneity in developmental trajectories of adolescent antisocial behaviour. *Infant and Child Development, 15,* 609–621.

Costner, H. L. (1969). Theory, deduction, and rules of correspondence. *American Journal of Sociology, 75,* 245–263.

Cowles Commission. (1952). *Economic theory and measurement: A twenty year research report, 1932–1952.* Chicago: Author.

Crow, J. F. (1988). Sewall Wright: 1889–1988. *Genetics, 119,* 1–4.

Dawid, A. P. (2000). Causal inference without counterfactuals. *Journal of the American Statistical Association, 95,* 407–424.

Deaton, A. (2010). Instruments, randomization, and learning about development. *Journal of Economic Literature, 48,* 424–455.

Duncan, O. D. (1966). Path analysis: Sociological examples. *American Journal of Sociology, 72,* 1–16.

Duncan, O. D. (1975). *Introduction to structural equation models.* New York: Academic Press.

Duncan, O. D. (1992). What if? *Contemporary Sociology, 21,* 667–668.

Duncan, O. D., & Hodge, R. W. (1963). Education and occupational mobility: A regression analysis. *American Journal of Sociology, 68,* 629–644.

Emsley, R., Dunn, G., & White, I. R. (2010). Mediation and moderation of treatment effects in randomised controlled trials of complex interventions. *Statistical Methods in Medical Research, 19,* 237–270.

Engle, R., Hendry, D., & Richard, J. (1983). Exogeneity. *Econometrica, 51,* 277–304.

Epstein, R. J. (1987). *A history of econometrics.* Amsterdam: North Holland.

Freedman, D. A. (1987). As others see us: A case study in path analysis (with discussion). *Journal of Educational Statistics, 12,* 101–223.

Frisch, R. (1934). *Statistical confluence analysis by means of complete regression systems.* Oslo: Universitetets Økonomiske Institutt.

Frisch, R., & Waugh, F. (1933). Partial time regressions as compared with individual trends. *Econometrica, 1,* 387–401.

Glymour, C., & Cooper, G. (Eds.). (1999). *Computation, causation, and discovery.* Menlo Park, CA: AAAI/MIT Press.

Glymour, C., Scheines, R., Spirtes, P., & Kelly, K. (1987). *Discovering causal structure: Artificial intelligence, philosophy of science, and statistical modeling.* Orlando, FL: Academic Press.

Glymour, C., Spirtes, P., & Richardson, T. (1999). Response to rejoinder. In C. Glymour & G. F. Cooper (Eds.), *Computation, causation, and discovery* (pp. 343–345). Menlo Park, CA: AAAI/MIT Press.

Goldberger, A. S. (1972a). Maximum-likelihood estimation of regressions containing unobservable independent variables. *International Economic Review, 13,* 1–15.

Goldberger, A. S. (1972b). Structural equation methods in the social sciences. *Econometrica, 40,* 979–1001.

Goldberger, A. S. (1973). Efficient estimation in overidentified models: An interpretive analysis. In A. Goldberger & O. D. Duncan (Eds.), *Structural equation models in the social sciences* (pp. 131–152). New York: Academic Press.

Goldberger, A. S. (1991). *A course in econometrics.* Cambridge, MA: Harvard University Press.

Goldberger, A. S., & Duncan, O. D. (Eds.). (1973). *Structural equation models in the social sciences.* New York: Academic Press.

Goldstein, H. (1995). *Multilevel statistical models.* London: Arnold.

Goldstein, H., & Browne, W. J. (2002). Multilevel factor analysis modelling using Markov Chain Monte Carlo (MCMC) estimation. In G. Marcoulides & I. Moustaki (Eds.), *Latent variable and latent structure models* (pp. 225–243). Englewood Cliffs, NJ: Erlbaum.

Goldstein, H., & McDonald, R. P. (1988). A general model for the analysis of multi-level data. *Psychometrika, 53,* 455–467.

Greene, W. H. (2003). *Econometric analysis* (5th ed.). Upper Saddle River, NJ: Prentice-Hall.

Greenland, S., & Brumback, B. (2002). An overview of relations among causal modelling methods. *Journal of International Epidemiology, 31,* 1030–1037.

Greenland, S., Pearl, J., & Robins, J. M. (1999). Causal diagrams for epidemiologic research. *Epidemiology, 10,* 37–48.

Haavelmo, T. (1943). The statistical implications of a system of simultaneous equations. *Econometrica, 11,* 1–12.

Haavelmo, T. (1944). The probability approach in econometrics. *Econometrica, 12*(Suppl.), 1–114.

Hansen, L. P. (1982). Large sample properties of generalized method of moments estimators. *Econometrica, 50,* 1029–1054.

Hargens, L. L., Reskin, B. F., & Allison, P. D. (1976). Problems in estimating measurement error from panel data: An example involving the measurement of scientific productivity. *Sociological Methods and Research, 5,* 247–256.

Harman, H. (1960). *Modern factor analysis.* Chicago: University of Chicago Press.

Hauser, R. M. (1973). Disaggregating a social-psychological model of educational attainment. In A. S. Goldberger & O. D. Duncan (Eds.), *Structural equation models in the social sciences* (pp. 255–284). New York: Academic Press.

Hauser, R. M., & Goldberger, A. S. (1971). The treatment of unobservable variables in path analysis. In H. L. Costner (Ed.), *Sociological methodology 1971* (pp. 81–87). San Francisco: Jossey-Bass.

Heckman, J. J. (1992). Haavelmo and the birth of modern econometrics: A review of the history of econometric ideas by Mary Morgan. *Journal of Economic Literature, 30,* 876–886.

Heckman, J. J. (2000). Causal parameters and policy analysis in economics: A twentieth century retrospective. *Quarterly Journal of Economics, 115,* 45–97.

Heckman, J. J. (2010). Building bridges between structural and program evaluation approaches to evaluating policy. *Journal of Economic Literature, 48,* 356–398.

Heckman, J. J., & Urzúa, S. (2010). Comparing IV with structural models: What simple IV can and cannot identify. *Journal of Econometrics, 156,* 27–37.

Hendry, D. F., & Morgan, M. S. (1989). A re-analysis of confluence analysis. *Oxford Economic Papers, 41*, 35–52.

Hill, W. G. (1995). Sewell Wright's system of mating. *Genetics, 143*, 1499–1506.

Holland, P. (1988). Causal inference and path analysis. In C. C. Clogg (Ed.), *Sociological methodology 1988* (pp. 449–484). Washington, DC: American Sociological Association.

Holzinger, K. J. (1941). *Factor analysis.* Chicago: University of Chicago Press.

Hotelling, H. (1933). Analysis of a complex of statistical variables into principal components. *Journal of Educational Psychology, 24*, 417–41, 498–520.

Humphreys, P., & Freedman, D. (1996). The grand leap. *British Journal for the Philosophy of Science, 47*, 113–123.

Hurwicz, L. (1962). On the structural form and interdependent systems. In E. Nagel, P. Suppes, & A. Tarski (Eds.), *Logic, methodology and philosophy of science* (pp. 232–239). Stanford, CA: Stanford University Press.

Imbens, G. W. (2010). Better LATE than nothing: Some comments on Deaton (2009) and Heckman and Urzua (2009). *Journal of Economic Literature, 48*, 399–423.

Imbens, G. W., & Angrist, J. D. (1994). Identification and estimation of local average treatment effects. *Econometrica, 62*, 467–475.

Imbens, G. W., & Rubin, D. B. (1997). Estimating outcome distributions for compliers in instrumental variables models. *Review of Economic Studies, 64*, 555–574.

Imbens, G. W., & Wooldridge, J. M. (2009). Recent developments in the econometrics of program evaluation. *Journal of Economic Literature, 47*, 5–86.

Jeffreys, H. (1935). Some tests of significance, treated by the theory of probability. *Proceedings of the Cambridge Philosophical Society, 31*, 203–222.

Jennrich, R. I., & Clarkson, D. B. (1980). A feasible method for standard errors of estimate in maximum likelihood factor analysis. *Psychometrika, 45*, 237–247.

Jennrich, R. I., & Robinson, S. M. (1969). A Newton–Raphson algorithm for maximum likelihood factor analysis. *Psychometrika, 34*, 111–123.

Jennrich, R. I., & Sampson, P. F. (1966). Rotation for simple loadings. *Psychometrika, 31*, 313–323.

Jo, B., & Muthén, B. O. (2002). Longitudinal studies with intervention and noncompliance: Estimation of causal effects in growth mixture modeling. In S. P. Reise & N. Duan (Eds.), *Multilevel modeling: Methodological advances, issues, and applications* (pp. 71–98). Mahwah, NJ: Erlbaum.

Jöreskog, K. G. (1967). Some contributions to maximum likelihood factor analysis. *Psychometrika, 32*, 443–482.

Jöreskog, K. G. (1969). A general approach to confirmatory maximum likelihood factor analysis. *Psychometrika, 34*, 183–202.

Jöreskog, K. G. (1970). A general method for analysis of covariance structures. *Biometrika, 57*, 239–251.

Jöreskog, K. G. (1971). Statistical analysis of sets of congeneric tests. *Psychometrika, 36*, 109–133.

Jöreskog, K. G. (1973). A general method for estimating a linear structural equation system. In A. Goldberger & O. D. Duncan (Eds.), *Structural equation models in the social sciences* (pp. 85–112). New York: Academic Press.

Jöreskog, K. G. (1978). Structural analysis of covariance and correlation matrices. *Psychometrika, 36*, 109–133.

Jöreskog, K. G., & Goldberger, A. S. (1975). Estimation of a model with multiple indicators and multiple causes of a single latent variable. *Journal of the American Statistical Association, 70*, 631–639.

Jöreskog, K. G., & Sörbom, D. (2001). *LISREL 8 user's reference guide.* Chicago: Scientific Software International.

Jöreskog, K. G., & Sörbom, D. (2002). *PRELIS 2 user's reference guide.* Chicago: Scientific Software International.

Jöreskog, K. G., & Yang, F. (1996). Nonlinear structural equation models: The Kenny–Judd model with interaction effects. In G. A. Marcoulides & R. E. Schumacker (Eds.), *Advanced structural equation modeling: Issues and techniques* (pp. 57–88). Mahwah, NJ: Erlbaum.

Judge, G. G., Griffiths, W. E., Hill, R. C., & Lee, T.-C. (1980). *The theory and practice of econometrics.* New York: Wiley.

Kaiser, H. F. (1958). The Varimax criterion for analytic rotation in factor analysis. *Psychometrika, 23*, 187–200.

Keesling, J. W. (1972). *Maximum likelihood approaches to causal flow analysis.* Unpublished PhD dissertation, Department of Education, University of Chicago, Chicago.

Kendall, M., & Stuart, A. (1979). *The advanced theory of statistics, Vol. 3: Inference and relationship.* London: Griffin.

Kenny, D., & Judd, C. M. (1984). Estimating the nonlinear and interactive effects of latent variables. *Psychological Bulletin, 96*, 201–210.

Kiiveri, H., & Speed, T. P. (1982). Structural analysis of multivariate data: A review. In S. Leinhardt (Ed.), *Sociological methodology 1982* (pp. 209–289). San Francisco: Jossey-Bass.

Klein, L. (1950). *Economic fluctuations in the United States 1921–1941.* New York: Wiley.

Klein, L., & Goldberger, A. S. (1955). *An econometric model of the United States 1929–1952.* Amsterdam: North Holland.

Kohn, M., & Schooler, C. (1982). Job conditions and personality: A longitudinal assessment of their reciprocal effects. *American Journal of Sociology, 87*, 1257–1286.

Koopmans, T. (1937). *Linear regression analysis of economic time series* (Netherlands Economic Institute, Publication No. 20). Haarlem: F. Bohn.

Koopmans, T. (1945). Statistical estimation of simultaneous economic relations. *Journal of the American Statistical Association, 40*, 488–466.

Koopmans, T., Rubin, H., & Leipnik, R. (1950). Measuring the equation systems of dynamic economics (Cowles Commission Monograph 10). In T. Koopmans (Ed.), *Statistical inference in dynamic economic models* (pp. 53–237). New York: Wiley.

Lawley, D. N. (1940). The estimation of factor loadings by the method of maximum likelihood. *Proceedings of the Royal Society of Edinburgh, 60,* 64–82.

Lee, S.-Y. (1981). A Bayesian approach to confirmatory factor analysis. *Psychometrika, 46,* 153–160.

Li, C. C. (1956). The concept of path coefficient and its impact on population genetics. *Biometrics, 12,* 190–210.

Li, C. C. (1975). *Path analysis: A primer.* Pacific Grove, CA: Boxworth Press.

Lucas, R. (1976). Econometric policy analysis: A critique. In K. Brunner & A. Meltzer (Eds.), *The Phillips Curve and labor markets* (pp. 19–46). Amsterdam: North Holland.

MacCallum, R. C., Browne, M. W., & Sugawara, H. M. (1996). Power analysis and determination of sample size for covariance structure modeling. *Psychological Methods, 1,* 130–149.

Magnus, J. R., & Morgan, M. S. (1987). The ET Interview: Professor J. Tinbergen. *Econometric Theory, 3,* 117–142.

Mann, H. B., & Wald, A. (1943). On the statistical treatment of linear stochastic difference equations. *Econometrica, 11,* 173–220.

Matsueda, R. L. (1982). Testing control theory and differential association: A causal modeling approach. *American Sociological Review, 47,* 489–504.

Matsueda, R. L., & Bielby, W. T. (1986). Statistical power in covariance structure models. In N. B. Tuma (Ed.), *Sociological methodology 1986* (pp. 120–158). Washington, DC: American Sociological Association.

Matsueda, R. L., & Heimer, K. (1987). Race, family structure, and delinquency: A test of differential association and social control theories. *American Sociological Review, 52,* 826–840.

Meredith, W., & Tisak, J. (1990). Latent curve analysis. *Psychometrika, 55,* 107–122.

Morgan, M. S. (1990). *The history of econometric ideas.* Cambridge, UK: Cambridge University Press.

Morgan, S. L., & Winship, C. (2007). *Counterfactuals and causal inference: Methods and principles for social research.* Cambridge, UK: Cambridge University Press.

Muthén, B. (1978). Contributions to factor analysis of dichotomous variables. *Psychometrika, 43,* 551–560.

Muthén, B. (1979). A structural probit model with latent variables. *Journal of the American Statistical Association, 74,* 807–811.

Muthén, B. (1984). A general structural equation model with dichotomous, ordered categorical, and continuous latent variable indicators. *Psychometrika, 49,* 115–132.

Muthén, B. (1989). Tobit factor analysis. *British Journal of Mathematical and Statistical Psychology, 42,* 241–250.

Muthén, B. (1994). Multi-level covariance structure analysis. *Sociological Methods and Research, 22,* 376–398.

Muthén, B. (1997). Modeling of longitudinal and multi-level data. In A. E. Raftery (Ed.), *Sociological methodology* (Vol. 27, pp. 453–480). Boston: Blackwell.

Muthén, B. (2004). Latent variable analysis: Growth mixture modeling and related techniques for longitudinal data. In D. Kaplan (Ed.), *Handbook of quantitative methodology for the social sciences* (pp. 345–368). Newbury Park, CA: Sage.

Muthén, B. O., & Muthén, L. K. (2004). *Mplus user's guide.* Los Angeles: Authors.

Nagin, D. S. (2005). *Group-based models of development.* Cambridge: MA: Harvard University Press.

Nagin, D. S., & Land, K. C. (1993). Age, criminal careers, and population heterogeneity: Specification and estimation of a nonparametric mixed Poisson model. *Criminology, 31,* 327–362.

Nagin, D. S., & Tremblay, R. E. (2005). What has been learned from group-based trajectory modeling?: Examples from physical aggression and other problem behaviors. *Annals of the American Academy of Political and Social Science, 602,* 82–117.

Nelson, C. R. (1972). The prediction performance of the FRB-MIT-PENN model of the U.S. economy. *American Economic Review, 62,* 902–917.

Neyman, J., & Pearson, E. (1933). On the problem of the most efficient tests of statistical hypotheses. *Philosophical Transactions of the Royal Society of London: Series A, Containing Papers of a Mathematical or Physical Character, 231,* 289–337.

Olsson, U. (1979). Maximum likelihood estimation of the polychoric correlation coefficient. *Psychometrika, 44,* 443–460.

Pearl, J. (1988). *Probabilistic reasoning in intelligent systems.* San Mateo, CA: Morgan Kaufmann.

Pearl, J. (2000). *Causality: Models, reasoning, and inference.* Cambridge, UK: Cambridge University Press.

Pearl, J., & Verma, T. (1991). A theory of inferred causation. In J. A. Allen, R. Fikes, & E. Sandewall (Eds.), *Principles of knowledge representation and reasoning: Proceedings of the Second International Conference* (pp. 441–452). San Francisco: Morgan Kaufmann.

Pearson, K. (1901). On lines and planes of closest fit to systems of points in space. *Philosophical Magazine, 6,* 559–572.

Pearson, K., & Heron, D. (1913). On theories of association. *Biometrika, 9,* 159–315.

Poon, W.-Y., & Lee, S.-Y. (1987). Maximum likelihood estimation of multivariate polyserial and polychoric correlation coefficients. *Psychometrika, 52,* 429–430.

Qin, D. (1989). Formalization of identification theory. *Oxford Economic Papers, 41,* 73–93.

Rabe-Hesketh, S., Pickles, A., & Skrondal, A. (2001). *GLLAMM manual* (Tech. Rept. 2001/01, Department of Biostatistics and Computing, Institute of Psychiatry, Kings

College, University of London). Downloadable at *www.gllamm.org*.

Rabe-Hesketh, S., Skrondal, A., & Pickles, A. (2004). Generalized multilevel structural equation modeling. *Psychometrika, 69*, 167–190.

Raftery, A. E. (1993). Bayesian model selection in structural equation models. In K. A. Bollen & J. S. Long (Eds.), *Testing structural equation models* (pp. 163–180). Newbury Park, CA: Sage.

Raftery, A. E. (1995). Bayesian model selection in social research. In P. V. Marsden (Ed.), *Sociological methodology 1995* (pp. 111–165). Washington, DC: American Sociological Association.

Rao, C. R. (1958). Some statistical methods for comparison of growth curves. *Biometrika, 51*, 83–90.

Raudenbush, S. W., & Bryk, A. S. (2002). *Hierarchical linear models*. Thousand Oaks, CA: Sage.

Raudenbush, S. W., & Sampson, R. J. (1999). Assessing direct and indirect associations in multi-level designs with latent variables. *Sociological Methods and Research, 28*, 123–153.

Robins, J. M. (1986). A new approach to causal inference in mortality studies with a sustained exposure period: Application to control of healthy worker survivor effect. *Mathematical Modeling, 7*, 1393–1512.

Robins, J. M. (1995). Comment on Judea Pearl's paper, "Causal Diagrams for Empirical Research." *Biometrika, 82*, 695–698.

Robins, J. M. (2003). Semantics of causal DAG models and the identification of direct and indirect effects. In P. J. Green, N. L. Hjort, & S. Richardson (Eds.), *Highly structured stochastic systems* (pp. 70–81). Oxford, UK: Oxford University Press.

Robins, J. M., & Greenland, S. (1992). Identifiability and exchangeability for direct and indirect effects. *Epidemiology, 3*, 143–155.

Robins, J. M., & Wasserman, L. (1999). On the impossibility of inferring causation from association without background knowledge. In C. Glymour & G. F. Cooper (Eds.), *Computation, causation, and discovery* (pp. 305–321). Menlo Park, CA: MIT Press.

Roy, A. D. (1951). Some thoughts on the distribution of earnings. *Oxford Economic Papers, 3*, 135–146.

Rubin, D. B. (1974). Estimating causal effects of treatments in randomized and nonrandomized studies. *Journal of Educational Psychology, 66*, 688–701.

Rubin, D. B. (1980). Comment on "Randomization Analysis of Experimental Data: The Fisher Randomization Test," by D. Basu. *Journal of the American Statistical Association, 75*, 591–593.

Satorra, A., & Saris, W. E. (1985). Power of the likelihood ratio test in covariance structure analysis. *Psychometrika, 50*, 83–90.

Scheines, R., Hoijtink, H., & Boomsma, A. (1999). Bayesian estimation and testing of structural equation models. *Psychometrika, 64*, 37–52.

Scheines, R., Spirtes, P., Glymour, C., Meek, C., & Richardson, T. (1997). *Tetrad 3 user's manual*. Pittsburgh, PA: Department of Philosophy, Carnegie Mellon University.

Schultz, H. (1938). *The theory and measurement of demand*. Chicago: University of Chicago Press.

Schwartz, G. (1978). Estimating the dimension of a model. *Annals of Statistics, 6*, 461–464.

Sewell, W. H., & Hauser, R. M. (1975). *Education, opportunity, and earnings: Achievement in the early career*. New York: Academic Press.

Shipley, B. (2000). *Cause and correlation in biology: A user's guide to path analysis, structural equations and causal inference*. Cambridge, UK: Cambridge University Press.

Simmons, R., & Blyth, D. A. (1987). *Moving into adolescence: The impact of pubertal change and school context*. New York: Aldine de Gruyter.

Simon, H. A. (1954). Spurious correlation: A causal interpretation. *Journal of the American Statistical Association, 49*, 467–479.

Sims, C. (1980). Macroeconomics and reality. *Econometrica, 48*, 1–45.

Skrondal, A., & Rabe-Hesketh, S. (2004). *Generalized latent variable modeling: Multilevel, longitudinal, and structural equation models*. Boca Raton, FL: Chapman & Hall.

Slutsky, E. (1937). The summation of random causes as the source of cyclic processes. *Econometrica, 5*, 105–146.

Sobel, M. E. (1982). Asymptotic confidence intervals for indirect effects in structural equation models. In S. Leinhardt (Ed.), *Sociological methodology 1982* (pp. 290–313). San Francisco: Jossey-Bass.

Sobel, M. E. (1986). Some new results on indirect effects and their standard errors in covariance structure models. In N. B. Tuma (Ed.), *Sociological methodology 1986* (pp. 159–186). Washington, DC: American Sociological Association.

Sobel, M. E. (1992). The American occupational structure and structural equation modeling in sociology. *Contemporary Sociology, 21*, 662–666.

Sobel, M. E. (2008). Identification of causal parameters in randomized studies with mediating variables. *Journal of Educational and Behavioral Statistics, 33*, 230–251.

Spearman, C. (1904). General intelligence, objectively determined and measured. *American Journal of Psychology, 15*, 201–293.

Spearman, C. (1927). *The abilities of man*. New York: Macmillan.

Spirtes, P., Glymour, C., & Scheines, R. (1993). *Causation, prediction, and search*. New York: Springer-Verlag.

Spirtes, P., Richardson, T., Meek, C., Scheines, R., & Glymour, C. (1998). Using path diagrams as a structural equation modeling tool. *Sociological Methods and Research, 27*, 182–225.

Steiger, J. H. (1990). Structural model evaluation and modification: An interval estimation approach. *Multivariate Behavioral Research, 25*, 173–180.

Steiger, J. H., & Lind, J. C. (1980). *Statistically-based tests for the number of common factors.* Handout for a talk at the annual meetings of the Psychometric Society, Iowa City, IA.

Stock, J. H., & Trebbi, F. (2003). Who invented instrumental variable regression? *Journal of Economic Perspectives, 17*, 177–194.

Theil, H. (1992). Estimation and simultaneous correlation in complete equation systems. In R. Baldev & J. Koerts (Eds.), *Henri Theil's contributions to economics and econometrics* (Chapter 6). Dordrecht: Kluwer. (Original work published 1953)

Thurstone, L. L. (1935). *The vectors of mind.* Chicago: University of Chicago Press.

Tinbergen, J. (1939). *Statistical testing of business cycle theories* (2 vols.). Geneva: League of Nations.

Tucker, L. R. (1955). The objective definition of simple structure in linear factor analysis. *Psychometrika, 20*, 209–225.

Tucker, L. R. (1958). Determination of parameters of a functional relation by factor analysis. *Psychometrika, 23*, 19–23.

Wermuth, N., & Lauritsen, S. L. (1983). Graphical and recursive models for contingency tables. *Biometrika, 70*, 537–552.

Wheaton, B. (1978). The sociogenesis of psychological disorder. *American Sociological Review, 43*, 383–403.

Wheaton, B. (1985). Models for the stress-buffering functions of coping resources. *Journal of Health and Social Behavior, 26*, 352–364.

Wiley, D. E. (1973). The identification problem for structural equation models with unmeasured variables. In A. Goldberger & O. D. Duncan (Eds.), *Structural equation models in the social sciences* (pp. 69–84). New York: Academic Press.

Winship, C., & Mare, R. D. (1983). Structural equations and path analysis for discrete data. *American Journal of Sociology, 89*, 54–110.

Winship, C., & Mare, R. D. (1984). Regression models with ordinal variables. *American Sociological Review, 49*, 512–525.

Wold, H. (1964). *Econometric model building: Essays on the causal chain approach.* Amsterdam: North Holland.

Wold, H. (1982). Soft modeling: The basic design and some extensions. In K. G. Jöreskog & H. Wold (Eds.), *Systems under indirect observation* (pp. 1–54). Amsterdam: North Holland.

Wright, P. G. (1915). Moore's economic cycles. *Quarterly Journal of Economics, 29*, 631–641.

Wright, P. G. (1928). *The tariff on animal and vegetable oils.* New York: Macmillan.

Wright, S. (1918). On the nature of size factors. *Genetics, 3*, 367–374.

Wright, S. (1920). The relative importance of heredity and environment in determining the piebald pattern of guinea pigs. *Proceedings of the National Academy of Sciences, 6*, 320–332.

Wright, S. (1921a). Correlation and causation. *Journal of Agricultural Research, 20*, 557–585.

Wright, S. (1921b). Systems of mating: I. The biometric relations between parent and offspring. *Genetics, 6*, 111–123.

Wright, S. (1925). *Corn and hog correlations* (Bulletin 1300). Washington, DC: U.S. Department of Agriculture.

Wright, S. (1934). The method of path coefficients. *Annals of Mathematical Statistics, 5*, 161–215.

Xie, Y. (2007). Otis Dudley Duncan's legacy: The demographic approach to quantitative reasoning in social science. *Research in Social Stratification and Mobility, 25*, 141–156.

Yang, M., & Dunson, D. B. (2010). Bayesian semiparametric structural equation models with latent variables. *Psychometrika, 75*, 675–693.

Yuan, K.-H., & Bentler, P. M. (2007). Structural equation modeling. In C. R. Rao & S. Sinharay (Eds.), *Handbook of statistics: Vol. 26. Psychometrics* (pp. 297–358). Amsterdam: North Holland.

Yule, G. U. (1896). On the correlation of total pauperism with proportion of out-relief: II. Males over 65. *Economic Journal, 6*, 613–623.

Yule, G. U. (1912). On the methods of measuring association between two attributes. *Journal of the Royal Statistical Society, 75*, 579–652.

Zellner, A. (1962). An efficient method of estimating seemingly unrelated regressions and tests of aggregation bias. *Journal of the American Statistical Association, 57*, 348–368.

Zellner, A. (1970). Estimation of regression relationships containing unobservable independent variables. *International Economic Review, 11*, 441–454.

Zellner, A. (1971). *Introduction to Bayesian inference in econometrics.* New York: Wiley.

Zellner, A., & Theil, H. (1962). Three-stage least squares: Simultaneous estimation of simultaneous equations. *Econometrica, 30*, 54–78.

CHAPTER 3

Graphical Representation of Structural Equation Models Using Path Diagrams

Moon-ho Ringo Ho
Stephen Stark
Olexander Chernyshenko

Structural equation modeling (SEM) is one of the most widely used statistical techniques for delineating linear relations in multivariate data among behavioral scientists. Such complex relationships are commonly expressed in either algebraic form[1] or graphical format. The latter representation is usually referred to as a *path diagram*, which is the focus of this chapter.

The path diagram, which originated with Sewell Wright (1921), has become the method of choice for communicating abstract statistical models within the SEM community and is virtually a "must have" in all publications involving SEM procedures. Many researchers find that a path diagram is a clearer and more efficient way of demarcating the relationships among multivariate data than an algebraic system of equations. As a visual presentation tool, a path diagram not only aids the SEM user's thought process for model formulation but also provides an easy communication platform. Some of the current commercial SEM packages, such as AMOS, EQS, and LISREL, even allow users to draw path diagrams and use them as input for data analyses. In our experience, such features are welcomed by SEM users, especially beginners.

Before we discuss how to construct a path diagram, we first introduce the primary symbols that represent the types of variables and relationships. The major sym-

TABLE 3.1. Symbols Used in a Path Diagram

Symbol	Meaning
Y	Square signifies an observed variable.
F	Circle signifies a latent variable.
△1	Triangle signifies a constant / "intercept" term.
→	Directional arrow signifies the direct effect.
⌒	Curved bidirectional arrow signifies nondirectional association between two variables, and also the variance of an exogenous variable.

bols are presented in Table 3.1. Observed variables (i.e., variables that are measured directly) are represented by boxes, and latent (or unobserved) variables are represented by circles. Letters inside boxes or circles serve as variable labels. Latent variables are those variables that are not measured directly. These typically include hypothetical constructs of interest in a study and are often referred to as "common factors" in the factor analysis literature. Another type of latent variables is the error term. Intercepts or constant terms in structural equations are represented by triangles, and a triangle

■ 43

with a "1" on the interior is often used to represent a column of 1's in the "design" matrix of the SEM model that produces the intercept estimate.

In a typical linear structural equation model, there are two types of relationships between two variables; one is simply an association, and the other is a direct effect of an independent variable (i.e., cause, or predictor) on a dependent variable (i.e., effect, or outcome). The former relationship is represented by a curved double-headed (or bidirectional) arrow linking the two variables. The latter relationship is represented by a single-headed (or directional) arrow originating from the independent variable and ending at the dependent variable.[2] A variable in a structural equation model is referred to as "exogenous" if, and only if, it does not serve as an outcome variable in a given model. In a path diagram, this means there are no single-headed arrows pointing to it. Otherwise, the variable is "endogenous." Absence of directional arrow from one variable to another implies the absence of direct effect, whereas the absence of the curved, bidirectional arrow implies that there are no omitted variables explaining their associations.

Taking into account whether a variable is observed or latent, four types of variables can be distinguished in a path diagram—observed exogenous, observed endogenous, latent exogenous, and latent endogenous. A single-headed arrow is used to reflect the direct effect of an exogenous variable on an endogenous variable or the effect of one endogenous variable on another endogenous variable. A double-headed arrow is used to reflect the covariation between two variables. A double-headed arrow can also be used to represent the variance of a variable by letting the two-headed arrow start and end on the same variable. Only means, variances, and covariances for exogenous variables are presented as parameters in a path diagram. Means, variances, and covariances of endogenous variables can be expressed as functions of the means, variances, and/or covariances of exogenous variables, so there is no need to show them explicitly. For example, consider a linear regression model,

$$Y = b_0 + b_1 X_1 + b_2 X_2 + E$$

where Y is an endogenous variable and X_1, X_2 and E are exogenous variables. Assuming error is independent of the predictors in the model, the variance of the endogenous variable, Y, can be expressed as a function of the variances and covariances of the exogenous variables, which is equal to

$$b_1^2 \operatorname{var}(X_1) + b_2^2 \operatorname{var}(X_2) + 2b_1 b_2 \operatorname{cov}(X_1, X_2) + \operatorname{var}(E)$$

where $\operatorname{var}(X_1)$, $\operatorname{var}(X_2)$, and $\operatorname{var}(E)$ are the variances of X_1, X_2, and E, respectively, and $\operatorname{cov}(X_1, X_2)$ is the covariance between X_1 and X_2. Similarly, the mean of Y, $E(Y)$, is given by

$$b_0 + b_1 E(X_1) + b_2 E(X_2)$$

where $E(X_1)$ and $E(X_2)$ are the expectations or means of X_1 and X_2, respectively. Given these algebraic relationships, there is no need to represent the mean and variance of the endogenous variable, Y, in the path diagram, but the variances of the *exogenous* variables, X_1, X_2 and E, and the covariance of X_1 and X_2 must be shown, using the double-headed arrow representations.

CONSTRUCTION OF A PATH DIAGRAM

In constructing the path diagram for a given model of interest, typically three steps are involved:

1. Specification of variables (observed vs. latent).

2. Specification of relationships (directional vs. nondirectional).

3. Specification of parameters (fixed vs. free).

We illustrate these steps with a simple structural equation model. A typical structural equation model has two major parts. One is often referred to as the "measurement model," which shows the relationships between observed variables that are indicators of latent variables, and the latent factors they represent, and the other is known as the "structural model," which shows the relationships among the latent variables in the measurement model, and the observed variables that are not indicators of any of these latent variables.[3]

Consider an example with three latent factors and nine observed variables:

MEASUREMENT MODEL

$$Y_1 = b_1 + \lambda_1 F_1 + E_1$$
$$Y_2 = b_2 + \lambda_2 F_1 + E_2$$

$$Y_3 = b_3 + \lambda_3 F_1 + E_3$$
$$Y_4 = b_4 + \lambda_4 F_2 + E_4$$
$$Y_5 = b_5 + \lambda_5 F_2 + E_5$$
$$Y_6 = b_6 + \lambda_6 F_2 + E_6$$
$$Y_7 = b_7 + \lambda_7 F_3 + E_7$$
$$Y_8 = b_8 + \lambda_8 F_3 + E_8$$
$$Y_9 = b_9 + \lambda_9 F_3 + E_9$$

STRUCTURAL MODEL

$$F_3 = b_{10} + b_{11} F_1 + b_{12} F_2 + D_3$$

where E_1 to E_9 are the error terms in the measurement model (usually known as the "measurement errors") and D_3 is the error term in the structural model (usually known as the "disturbance term"). The parameters λ_1 to λ_9 are the factor loadings, which are the regression weights of the observed variables (Y_1 to Y_9) on the latent factors (F_1 to F_3). The parameters b_1 to b_{10} are the intercept terms.[4] Regardless of the measurement or structural model, the endogenous variables on the left side of any of the preceding equations are expressed as a linear combination of the variables on the right-hand side of the equations. Each of the terms on the right side of an equation is in the form of parameter × random variable. To be precise, subscript i may be added to the random variables in these equations (i.e., Y_{1i} to Y_{9i}, F_{1i} to F_{3i}, and E_{1i} to E_{9i}) to emphasize the fact that these quantities vary from individual to individual. The same can be done in labeling the variables in path diagrams, though such practice is seldom seen in applications. The first nine equations correspond to the measurement model, while the last equation is the structural model. Without loss of generality, we assume all the error terms are uncorrelated and the two exogenous common factors, F_1 and F_2, are correlated.

The first step in drawing the path diagram is to lay out all the observed and latent variables in the model (Figure 3.1a). In this model, there are a total of nine observed variables (Y_1 to Y_9) and 13 latent variables (F_1, F_2, F_3, E_1 to E_9, D_3). Note that the intercept terms can be written as $b_1 * 1$, $b_2 * 1$, . . . , $b_{10} * 1$, where the constant "1" is represented in the diagram as a triangle as discussed before.

The second step involves specifying the relations among these variables (Figure 3.1b). As can be seen, observed variables, Y_1 to Y_3, are the indicators for the

latent factor, F_1, Y_4 to Y_6 are indicators for F_2, and Y_7 to Y_9 are indicators for F_3. Each observed variable is linked to (i.e., loads on) one factor, one measurement error, and an intercept term, as indicated by the single-headed arrows. The structural model specifies the relationships among the three common factors. Latent factors F_1 and F_2 are postulated as the "causes" (explanatory variables) for F_3 but the two factors cannot perfectly account for the variability of F_3. The unexplained component of the endogenous latent factor F_3 is represented by the disturbance term, D_3. Thus, there are three single-headed arrows pointing to F_3, originating from F_1, F_2, and D_3. The double-headed arrow between F_1 and F_2 reflects the fact that these two factors are correlated. There are no double-headed arrows among the error terms, as we assume that they are all uncorrelated. The remaining nondirectional arrows indicate the variances of F_1, F_2, E_1 to E_9, and D_3.

In the last step, parameters are specified in the diagram (Figure 3.1c). There are two major types of parameters: (1) parameters fixed at specific values, and (2) parameters with unknown values that must be estimated from the data (referred to as "free parameters"). In SEM software packages, users can specify that some of the free parameters must be equal to the same value (equality constraints) by assigning to them the same parameter label. More complex constraints (e.g., inequality constraints on factor loadings: $\lambda_1 > \lambda_2$; constraint for expressing one model parameter as a function of the other parameters such as those imposing on the factor loadings for general factor and specific factors in a hierarchical factor analysis model based on a Schmid–Leiman solution; see Yung, Thissen, & McLeod, 1999) can also be imposed in programs, such as LISREL and Mplus, but such constraints are typically not shown explicitly in a path diagram.

Readers should note that each arrow (either single-headed or double-headed) is associated with a parameter. The parameters associated with the single-headed arrows are b_1 to b_{12} and λ_1 to λ_9. For all nine measurement errors and the disturbance term, we can rewrite them as: $1*E_1$, $1*E_2$, . . . , $1*D_3$. Thus, the parameters for the single-headed arrows from these errors are fixed to be 1. There are 12 variances and 1 covariance in the model, which account for the 13 nondirectional arrows, and the associated parameters are denoted as σ^2_{F1}, σ^2_{F2}, σ^2_{D3}, σ^2_{E1} to σ^2_{E9}, and $\sigma_{F1, F2}$ in the path diagram. For model identification reasons, σ^2_{F1} and σ^2_{F2} are fixed to be 1, as shown in the diagram.[5]

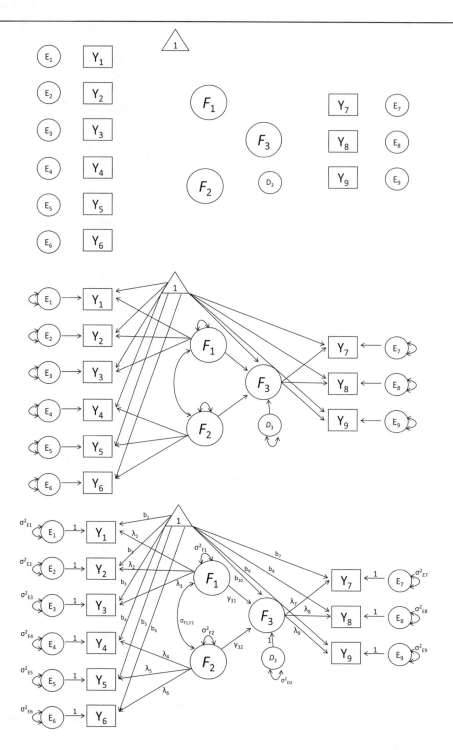

FIGURE 3.1. Steps in constructing a path diagram: (a) listing all the observed and latent variables (top diagram); (b) specifying the relationships (middle diagram); (c) specifying the parameters (bottom diagram).

VARIATIONS IN DRAWING THE PATH DIAGRAM

As remarked in McDonald and Ho (2002), error terms are often not shown in path diagrams for simplicity or ease of presentation (see Figure 3.2a for this variation of the model in Figure 3.1). Alternatively, error terms are shown, but not represented, by circles so as to distinguish them from the latent variables that represent common factors (see Figure 3.2b). We do not argue which is the correct way to draw a path diagram, as both these variations and the traditional representation using circles are common in the SEM literature.

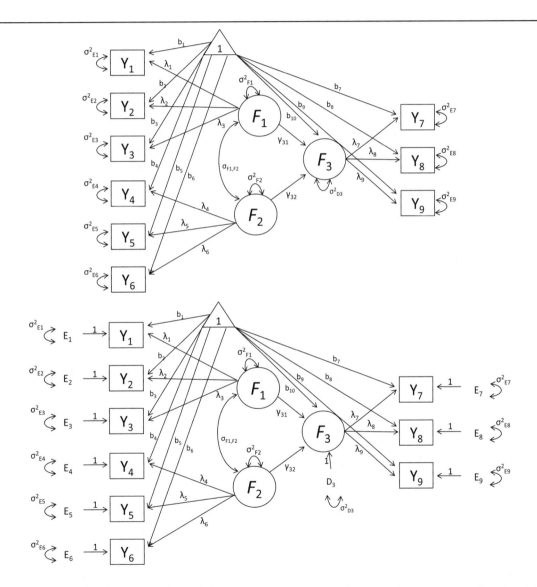

FIGURE 3.2. Error/disturbance variables modeled on curved bidirectional arrows (a, upper diagram) and distinguished from latent factors (b, lower diagram).

EXAMPLES

There have been many new extensions of SEM proposed in recent years, such as growth curve models, multilevel SEM, mixture SEM, and SEM for complex survey data. In this section, we illustrate path diagram representations for some of these advanced models.

Path Diagram for a Growth Curve Model

Growth curve modeling aims to characterize the change of a psychological process of interest by a growth trajectory through a set of repeated measures. The method was proposed independently by Rao (1958), Tucker (1958) and Meredith (Meredith & Tiask, 1990; Scher, Young, & Meredith, 1960). Each individual's growth trajectory is represented by a few basic curves (a.k.a. growth factors), and individual differences on these basis curves are allowed. Typical trajectories that are considered include linear, quadratic, piecewise, and cubic spline. The growth model consists of two parts: One represents within-subject change (growth trajectory), and the other represents individual differences in these changes. Covariates may be included to account for both the intraindividual and interindividual differences in the growth process.

To illustrate, we consider an example of a quadratic growth curve model with four repeated measures (Y_1 to Y_4):

$$Y_{ti} = B_{0i} + t_i B_{1i} + t_i^2 B_{2i} + E_{ti}$$

where Y_{ti} is the repeated measure from subject i at time t. Assuming measurement occasions are the same for all subjects, we can drop the subscript i from t_i and the model is simplified as

$$Y_{ti} = B_{0i} + t B_{1i} + t^2 B_{2i} + E_{ti}$$

The latent variables B_{0i}, B_{1i}, and B_{2i} are the growth factor scores that vary across subjects, which is akin to the common factor in the factor analysis model. B_{0i} defines the intercept factor representing the initial status (when the first time point is coded as 0), B_{1i} is the linear slope, and B_{2i} represents the curvature (or quadratic component) of the growth curve for subject i. In fact, this model can be regarded as a confirmatory factor analysis (CFA) model with factor loadings fixed to a priori values. For illustration, we code the time occasion, t, as 0, 1, 2, and 3 here. Interested readers may refer to

Biesanz, Deeb-Sossa, Papadakis, Bollen, and Curran (2004) for more details on various ways of coding time in growth curve model applications. The growth curve of a measured variable across four measurement occasions can be written as

MEASUREMENT MODEL:
WITHIN-SUBJECT CHANGE

Time occasion 1: $Y_{1i} = B_{0i} + 0\ B_{1i} + 0^2\ B_{2i} + E_{1i}$
$\Leftrightarrow Y_{1i} = 1\ B_{0i} + 0\ B_{1i} + 0\ B_{2i} + 1\ E_{1i}$
Time occasion 2: $Y_{2i} = B_{0i} + 1\ B_{1i} + 1^2\ B_{2i} + E_{2i}$
$\Leftrightarrow Y_{2i} = 1\ B_{0i} + 1\ B_{1i} + 1\ B_{2i} + 1\ E_{2i}$
Time occasion 3: $Y_{3i} = B_{0i} + 2\ B_{1i} + 2^2\ B_{2i} + E_{3i}$
$\Leftrightarrow Y_{3i} = 1\ B_{0i} + 2\ B_{1i} + 4\ B_{2i} + 1\ E_{3i}$
Time occasion 4: $Y_{4i} = B_{0i} + 3\ B_{1i} + 3^2\ B_{2i} + E_{4i}$
$\Leftrightarrow Y_{4i} = 1\ B_{0i} + 3\ B_{1i} + 9\ B_{2i} + 1\ E_{4i}$

STRUCTURAL MODEL:
BETWEEN-SUBJECT DIFFERENCE

$$B_{0i} = \mu_{00} + U_{0i} \Leftrightarrow B_{0i} = \mu_{00}\ 1 + 1\ U_{0i}$$
$$B_{1i} = \mu_{10} + U_{1i} \Leftrightarrow B_{1i} = \mu_{10}\ 1 + 1\ U_{1i}$$
$$B_{2i} = \mu_{20} + U_{2i} \Leftrightarrow B_{2i} = \mu_{20}\ 1 + 1\ U_{2i}$$

For this model, there are four observed variables (Y_{1i} to Y_{4i}), three latent growth factors (B_{0i}, B_{1i}, and B_{2i}) representing the quadratic growth trajectory, and seven error terms (E_{1i} to E_{4i}, U_{0i} to U_{2i}). The μ_{00} is the group average of the individuals' intercepts (B_{0i}), μ_{10} is the group mean of the linear trajectory components (B_{1i}), and μ_{20} is the group mean of the quadratic trajectory components (B_{2i}). The error terms, U_{0i}, U_{1i}, and U_{2i}, represent the individual deviations from the group averages on these growth factors, and their variances reflect the variability of these factors across subjects. Note that it is common to allow these error terms (and thus the growth factors) to covary. The four equations representing "within-subject change" can be regarded as a CFA model with the factor loadings fixed to the values we chose for coding the time occasions. Following the three steps outlined in the previous section, we can therefore construct the path diagram as shown in Figure 3.3.

Path Diagram for a Multilevel CFA Model

Multilevel models have been widely used in social sciences in the last decade. The previous example can also

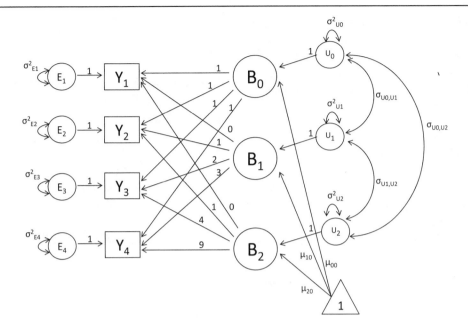

FIGURE 3.3. Path diagram for a quadratic growth curve model.

be regarded as a multilevel model with random intercept and random slope terms, and it can be fitted by any multilevel software package. Interested readers may refer to, for example, Bauer (2003), Curran (2003), and Muthén (1997) for more thorough discussions on the connection between the two statistical techniques. In this chapter, we consider two examples for multilevel analysis. We begin with multilevel CFA, described immediately below, and move to a bivariate two-level linear regression model with random coefficients in the next section.

Consider a two-level CFA model with six observed variables (see Figure 3.4). There are two latent factors in Level 1 (individuals) and one latent factor in Level 2 (groups) underlying these six variables. Each of the observed variables can be expressed in terms of within- and between-group deviations (cf. one-way analysis of variance [ANOVA] decomposition):

$$Y_{pij} = b_p + Y_{pj}^{\,b} + Y_{pij}^{\,w}$$

where Y_{pij} is the score on pth observed variable from subject i in group j, $Y_{pj}^{\,b}$ denotes the corresponding between-group deviations, and $Y_{pij}^{\,w}$ denotes the within-

group deviations, $p = 1, \ldots, 6, i = 1, \ldots, n_j, j = 1, \ldots, J$.

The between- and within-group deviations can be further decomposed following the factor-analytic model. In this example, we assume that the first three observed variables load on the first latent factor in Level 1 ($F_1^{\,w}$), the remaining three load on the second latent factor in Level 1 ($F_2^{\,w}$), and all of them load on a single latent factor in Level 2 ($F_1^{\,b}$). The latent factors in Level 1 account for the structure of observations on individuals within groups, whereas the latent factor in Level 2 accounts for the structure underlying the group means. The between- and within-group deviations can be expressed as follows:

$$Y_{pj}^{\,b} = \lambda_{p1}^{\,b} F_{1j}^{\,b} + u_{pj}^{\,b}$$
$$\text{and } Y_{pij}^{\,w} = \lambda_{p1}^{\,w} F_{1ij}^{\,w} + \lambda_{p2}^{\,w} F_{2ij}^{\,w} + E_{pij}^{\,w}$$

where $\lambda_{p1}^{\,b}$ denotes the factor loading of latent factor in Level 2 (between-level) on variable p, and $\lambda_{p1}^{\,w}$ denotes the factor loading of latent factor in Level 1 (within-level) on variable p. Hence, the two-level CFA model can be written as

$$Y_{pij} = b_p + \lambda_{p1}{}^b F_j{}^{jb} + u_{pj}{}^b + \lambda_{p1}{}^w F_1 ij^w + \lambda_{p2}{}^w F_{2ij}{}^w + E_{pij}{}^w$$
$$\Leftrightarrow Y_{pij} = b_p 1 + \lambda_{p1}{}^b F_{1j}{}^b + \lambda_{p1}{}^w F_{1ij}{}^w + \lambda_{p2}{}^w F_{2ij}{}^w + 1\, u_{pj}{}^b$$
$$\quad + 1\, E_{pij}{}^w$$

To facilitate the construction of the path diagram for this model, it is instructive to write out the equation for each observed variable:

$$Y_{1ij} = b_1\, 1 + \lambda_{11}{}^b F_{1i}{}^b + \lambda_{11}{}^w F_{1ij}{}^w + 1\, u_{1j}{}^b + 1\, E_{1ij}{}^w$$
$$Y_{2ij} = b_2\, 1 + \lambda_{21}{}^b F_{1i}{}^b + \lambda_{21}{}^w F_{1ij}{}^w + 1\, u_{2j}{}^b + 1\, E_{2ij}{}^w$$
$$Y_{3ij} = b_3\, 1 + \lambda_{31}{}^b F_{1i}{}^b + \lambda_{31}{}^w F_{1ij}{}^w + 1\, u_{3j}{}^b + 1\, E_{3ij}{}^w$$
$$Y_{4ij} = b_4\, 1 + \lambda_{41}{}^b F_{1i}{}^b + \lambda_{42}{}^w F_{2ij}{}^w + 1\, u_{4j}{}^b + 1\, E_{4ij}{}^w$$
$$Y_{5ij} = b_5\, 1 + \lambda_{51}{}^b F_{1i}{}^b + \lambda_{52}{}^w F_{2ij}{}^w + 1\, u_{5j}{}^b + 1\, E_{5ij}{}^w$$
$$Y_{6ij} = b_6\, 1 + \lambda_{61}{}^b F_{1i}{}^b + \lambda_{62}{}^w F_{2ij}{}^w + 1\, u_{6j}{}^b + 1\, E_{6ij}{}^w$$

Without loss of generality, the two factors for the within-level are assumed to be correlated, but factors from different levels are usually assumed to be unrelated.

Following the steps described before, we obtain the path diagram for this multilevel CFA model shown in Figure 3.4.

Path Diagram for a Two-Level Model with Random Coefficients

We now consider a bivariate two-level regression model (see Figure 3.5). Both response variables are regressed on predictors from Level 1 (individual level) and Level 2 (group level). We also allow the intercept and the slope terms randomly varying across groups. This model can be expressed as follows:

LEVEL 1 MODEL (CF. MEASUREMENT MODEL)

$$Y_{1ij} = b_{10j} + b_{11j} X_{ij} + E_{1ij} \Leftrightarrow Y_{1ij} = 1\, b_{10j} + X_{ij}\, b_{11j} + 1\, E_{1ij}$$
$$Y_{2ij} = b_{20j} + b_{21j} X_{ij} + E_{2ij} \Leftrightarrow Y_{2ij} = 1\, b_{20j} + X_{ij}\, b_{21j} + 1\, E_{2ij}$$

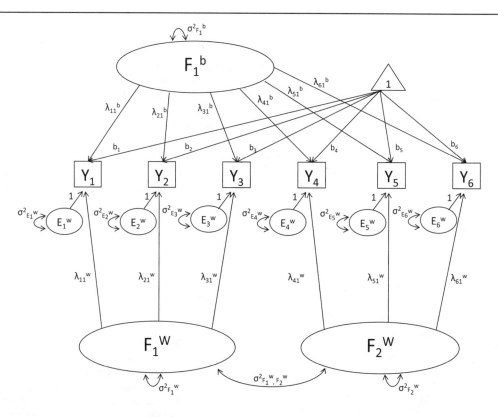

FIGURE 3.4. Path diagram for a two-level CFA model.

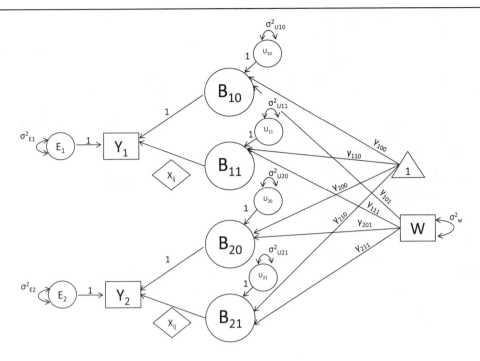

FIGURE 3.5. Path diagram for a two-level regression model using "definition" variable presentation.

LEVEL 2 MODEL (CF. STRUCTURAL MODEL)

$$b_{10j} = \gamma_{100} + \gamma_{101}\ W_j + U_{10j} \Leftrightarrow b_{10j} = \gamma_{100}\ 1 + \gamma_{101}\ W_j$$
$$+ 1\ U_{10j}$$
$$b_{11j} = \gamma_{110} + \gamma_{111}\ W_j + U_{11j} \Leftrightarrow b_{11j} = \gamma_{110}\ 1 + \gamma_{111}\ W_j$$
$$+ 1\ U_{11j}$$
$$b_{20j} = \gamma_{200} + \gamma_{201}\ W_j + U_{20j} \Leftrightarrow b_{20j} = \gamma_{200}\ 1 + \gamma_{201}\ W_j$$
$$+ 1\ U_{20j}$$
$$b_{21j} = \gamma_{210} + \gamma_{211}\ W_j + U_{21j} \Leftrightarrow b_{21j} = \gamma_{210}\ 1 + \gamma_{211}\ W_j$$
$$+ 1\ U_{21j}$$

where Y_{1ij} and Y_{2ij} are responses on two outcome variables, Y_1 and Y_2, from subject i in group j, and X_{ij} and W_j are the Level 1 and Level 2 predictors, respectively.

Following the three steps outlined in a previous section, the path diagram shown in Figure 3.5 results. Note that the Level 1 model is analogous to the growth curve model example except that the "factor loading" is not the same for all subjects but depends instead on individuals' values on the predictors (X_{ij}). Mehta and Neale (2005) refer to such individual-specific values

used for fixing model parameters (i.e., "factor loadings") as a "definition" variable, and they recommend using a diamond symbol for representation, as shown in Figure 3.5.

Overall there is still no general consensus in how to represent a multilevel model using a path diagram. However, Curran and Bauer (2007) recently proposed an alternative systematic scheme that readers may find useful.[6] Their proposal is largely consistent with the conventional way of constructing a path diagram with the following exceptions:

1. A circle is used to represent a random coefficient (or random effect) instead of a latent factor, and each circle is superimposed on the path where the random effect is present.

2. A multilevel model includes intercept terms from multiple levels, and each level's intercept is represented by a triangle, as in a conventional path diagram, with a subscript indicating the corresponding level.

Figure 3.6 presents a path diagram based on Curran and Bauer's (2007) scheme. Note that these authors do not suggest using a circle to denote an error term associated with an observed variable, but we chose to do so in this case for consistency with examples presented earlier in our chapter. When comparing Figures 3.5 and 3.6, it can be seen that the Level 1 predictor, X_{ij}, is represented as a factor loading (diamond symbol) in Figure 3.5, but as an observed variable (square) in Figure 3.6. The Level 1 random coefficients (B_{10j}, B_{11j}, B_{20j}, B_{21j}) are presented as latent factors (circles) in Figure 3.5, but they are represented by circles superimposed on the path where their effects are present in Figure 3.6. Moreover, Level 1 and Level 2 intercepts are represented separately in Figure 3.6, but such a distinction is not made in Figure 3.5. In Curran and Bauer's scheme, subscripts for indexing the levels (i and j) are added in labeling the variables.

Another scheme for representing multilevel models with path diagrams has been used by Muthén and Muthén (1998–2007) in the Mplus software manual. Essentially, the model at each level has its own representation in a path diagram. Level 1 and Level 2 are referred to as within and between parts respectively, as shown in Figure 3.7. In Level 1, which represents the within part, a random intercept is indicated by a filled circle at the arrow head, and a random slope is indicated by a filled circle on the path from the Level 1 predictor to the Level 1 outcome variable. These random intercepts and the random slopes are represented by circles denoting latent factors in the Level 2, or between, part. The random intercept of a variable in Level 2 takes the same label as the original variable in Level 1. Like Curran and Bauer's (2007) scheme, the Muthéns' notation omits error terms, but we have included them in Figure 3.7, as before, for consistency with our previous examples.[7]

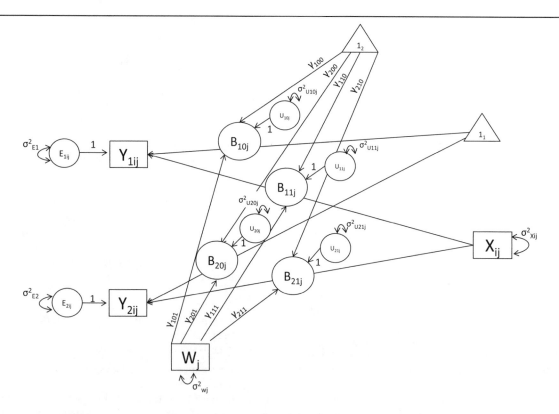

FIGURE 3.6. Path diagram for a two-level regression model following Curran and Bauer's (2007) convention.

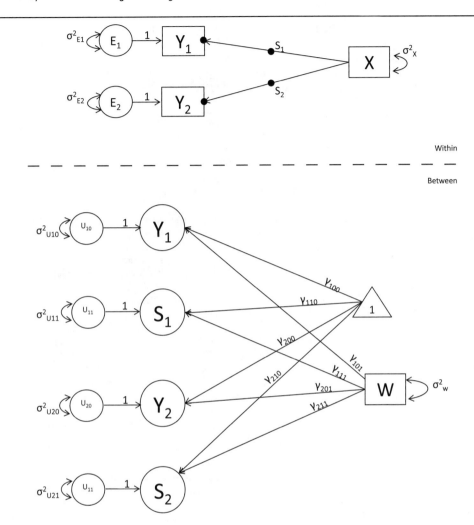

FIGURE 3.7. Path diagram for a two-level regression model following Mplus convention.

CONCLUSIONS

A path diagram provides a systematic visual representation of the linear relationships among a set of variables. SEM beginners typically find path diagrams easier to comprehend and less intimidating than algebraic formulations involving a system of equations or matrices. And advanced modelers generally appreciate being able to present conceptual models in a compact form, while still being able to derive linear equations directly from a diagram when needed, due to the isomorphic

connections between visual and mathematical model representations. Although there is still some variation in the way of notation, particularly in the domain of multilevel models, the process of deriving a system of equations from a path diagram for basic models is relatively straightforward. One must first identify all of the endogenous variables, regardless of whether they are treated as observed or latent. The number of linear equations associated with a model will be equal to the number of endogenous variables. For each endogenous variable, one must trace all of the directional arrows pointing to it. The total number of directional arrows pointing to a particular endogenous variable will be equal to the number of explanatory variables relating to that variable and is equal to the number of terms in the right side of the linear equation. Each term on the right-hand side of a linear equation takes the form parameter × random variable. Readers interested in practicing these steps in conjunction with a relatively simple model are encouraged to refer back to Figure 3.1 and the associated description.[8]

Despite these many attractive features, reliance on path diagrams still presents some challenges and opportunities for further development. For example, although a path diagram can effectively represent linear relationships among a set of variables and there is a one-to-one correspondence between algebraic and path representations, there is not yet consensus on how to represent nonlinear relationships. A nonlinear relationship can be present in a measurement model, such as in the relationship between latent common factors and observed binary responses through logistic or probit functions, or in a structural model involving quadratic or interaction effects between latent common factors. Rapid progress has been made in the last decade in terms of statistical estimation for nonlinear structural equation models, and we believe more attention to this issue in connection with path diagram representations is warranted.

Another area in need of development involves the specification of noncontinuous variables (e.g., binary, categorical observed, or latent). They are typically indicated in path diagrams using a square, just like any other observed variable. However, given the burgeoning literature on the estimation and application of mixture models, involving the use of categorical latent factors, some distinctions in the visual representations seems appropriate. Future work might be of interest in extending current path diagrammatic scheme for handling these new extensions of SEM.[9]

With the recent advances in directed acyclic graph (DAG) theory, conditions for checking parameters' identifiability and various rules for generating equivalent models have been developed and can be easily checked through path diagrams, in particular, on the path model. Due to limited space, we do not elaborate the details of DAG theory here. Interested readers can refer to, for example, McDonald (1997, 2002, 2003), Pearl (1998, 2000, and also Chapter 5, this volume), Shipley (2000), Spirtes, Glymour, and Scheines (2001),

and Spirtes, Richardson, Meek, Scheines, and Glymour (1998) on these conditions and applications in SEM.

ACKNOWLEDGMENT

We thank Pony Chew for her help in preparing the figures in this chapter.

NOTES

1. The algebraic representation is commonly presented in matrix form. In SEM literature, various matrix representation have been proposed including Bentler–Weeks model (Bentler & Weeks, 1979, 1980), COSAN model (McDonald, 1978), Jöreskog–Keesling–Wiley a.k.a. LISREL model (Jöreskog, 1973, 1977; Keesling, 1972; Wiley, 1973), and RAM model (McArdle, 2005; McArdle & McDonald, 1984).

2. Following the directed acyclic graph theory terminology (Pearl, 1998, 2000), the directional relationship is referred to as the *directed arc/edge*, while the nondirectional relationship is referred to as the *nondirected arc/edge*.

3. McDonald and Ho (2002) use path model to refer to the part of the model delineating the relationship between latent common factors. They reserve the term "structural model" for structural equation models without latent common factors but composite scores, which are used as the "proxy" for the latent common factors.

4. In traditional SEM analysis, observed variables are assumed to be mean centered and common factors are assumed to have means equal to zero. Therefore, intercepts are equal to zero and can be ignored. Most of the current SEM software packages no longer require this assumption.

5. An alternative way for model identification is to fix one of the factor loadings for each common factor to be 1 and estimate their variances as free parameters. Rules for identification in SEM are discussed in a separate chapter. Interested readers can refer to Chapters 8 and 9 for more details.

6. Curran and Bauer's (2007) examples focus on multilevel linear models without latent factors.

7. The developers of GLLAMM (generalized linear latent and mixed models; Rabe-Hesketh, Skrondal, & Pickles, 2004), an add-on module to the Stata for a general analysis of multilevel latent variable models, have adopted a convention similar to the one used in a Bayesian analysis package called WINBUGS (*www.mrc-bsu.cam.ac.uk/bugs*). Due to limited space, we do not discuss their path diagram representation here.

8. The conversion from the multilevel model using the Mplus convention to the algebraic representation is possible, though it may not be as straightforward as the other two conventions.

9. In the Mplus manual, Muthén and Muthén (1998–2007) have developed their conventions in representing interaction effects among latent factors and mixture models for ease of presentation of their examples.

REFERENCES

Bauer, D. J. (2003). Estimating multilevel linear models as structural equation models. *Journal of Educational and Behavioral Statistics, 28,* 135–167.

Bentler, P. M., & Weeks, D. G. (1979). Interrelations among models for the analysis of moment structures. *Multivariate Behavioral Research, 14,* 169–186.

Bentler, P. M., & Weeks, D. G. (1980). Linear structural equations with latent variables, *Psychometrika, 45,* 289–308.

Biesanz, J. C., Deeb-Sossa, N., Papadakis, A. A., Bollen, K. A., & Curran, P. J. (2004). The role of coding time in estimating and interpreting growth curve models. *Psychological Methods, 9,* 30–52.

Curran, P. J. (2003). Have multilevel models been structural equation models all along? *Multivariate Behavioral Research, 38,* 529–569.

Curran, P. J., & Bauer, D. J. (2007). A path diagramming framework for multilevel models. *Psychological Methods, 12,* 283–297.

Jöreskog, K. G. (1973). A general method for estimating a linear structural equation system. In A. S. Goldberger & O. D. Duncan (Eds.), *Structural equation models in the social sciences* (pp. 85–112). New York: Seminar Press.

Jöreskog, K. G. (1977). Structural equation models in the social sciences: Specification, estimation and testing. In P. R. Krishnaiah (Ed.), *Applications of statistics* (pp. 265–287). Amsterdam: North Holland.

Keesling, J. W. (1972). *Maximum likelihood approaches to causal analysis.* PhD dissertation, University of Chicago, Chicago, IL.

McArdle, J. J. (2005). Structural equation and related models. In A. Madeau & J. J. McArdle (Eds.), *Contemporary advances in psychometrics* (pp. 225–273). Mahwah, NJ: Erlbaum.

McArdle, J. J., & McDonald, R. P. (1984). Some algebraic properties of the reticular action model for moment structures. *British Journal of Mathematical and Statistical Psychology, 37,* 234–251.

McDonald, R. P. (1978). A simple comprehensive model for the analysis of covariance structures. *British Journal of Mathematical Statistical Psychology, 31,* 59–72.

McDonald, R. P. (1997). Haldane's lungs: A case study in path analysis. *Multivariate Behavioral Research, 32,* 1–38.

McDonald, R. P. (2002). What can we learn from the path equations?: Identifiability, constraints, equivalence. *Psychometrika, 67,* 225–249.

McDonald, R. P. (2003). Specific analysis of structural equation models. *Multivariate Behavioral Research, 39,* 687–713.

McDonald, R. P., & Ho, M. R. (2002). Principles and practice in reporting structural equation analyses. *Psychological Methods, 7,* 64–82.

Mehta, P. D., & Neale, M. C. (2005). People are variables too: Multilevel structural equation modeling. *Psychological Methods, 10,* 259–284.

Meredith, W., & Tiask, J. (1990). Latent curve analysis. *Psychometrika, 55,* 107–122.

Muthén, B. (1997). Latent variable modeling of longitudinal and multilevel data. *Sociological Methodology, 27,* 453–480.

Muthén, L. K., & Muthén, B. O. (1998–2007). *Mplus user's guide* (5th ed.). Los Angeles: Authors.

Pearl, J. (1998). Graphs, causality, and structural equation models. *Sociological Methods and Research, 27,* 226–284.

Pearl, J. (2000). *Causality: Models, reasoning and inference.* Cambridge, UK: Cambridge University Press.

Rabe-Hesketh, S., Skrondal, A., & Pickles, A. (2004). *GLLAMM manual* (U.C. Berkeley Division of Biostatistics Working Paper Series, Working Paper 160). Berkeley: University of California, Berkeley.

Rao, C. R. (1958). Some statistical methods for comparison of growth curves. *Biometrika, 52,* 447–458.

Scher, A. M., Young, A. C., & Meredith, W. M. (1960). Factor analysis of the electrocardiogram. *Circulation Research, 8,* 519–526.

Shipley B. (2000). A new inferential test for path models based on directed acyclic graphs. *Structural Equation Modeling, 7,* 206–218.

Spirtes, P., Glymour, C., & Scheines, R. (2001). *Causation, prediction, and search* (2nd ed.). Cambridge, MA: MIT Press.

Spirtes, P., Richardson, T., Meek, C., Scheines, R., & Glymour, C. (1998). Using path diagrams as a structural equation modeling tool. *Sociological Methods and Research, 27,* 182–225.

Tucker, L. R. (1958). Determination of parameters of a functional relation by factor analysis. *Psychometrika, 23,* 19–23.

Wiley, D. E. (1973). The identification problem for structural equation models with unmeasured variables. In A. S. Goldberger & O. D. Duncan (Eds.), *Structural equation models in the social sciences* (pp. 69–83). New York: Seminar Press.

Wright, S. (1921). Correlation and causation. *Journal of Agricultural Research, 20,* 557–585.

Yung, Y.-F., Thissen, D., & McLeod, L. D. (1999). On the relationship between the higher-order factor model and the hierarchical factor model. *Psychometrika, 64,* 113–128.

CHAPTER 4

Latent Variables in Structural Equation Modeling

Kenneth A. Bollen
Rick H. Hoyle

The use of structural equation modeling (SEM) often is motivated by a desire to model constructs for which there has not been—perhaps could not have been—direct observation or assessment. These constructs often are attributes of people that figure prominently in formal theories about the causal mechanisms that account for behavior. Examples include personality, attitudes, motives, emotions, and abilities. The importance of such constructs in theoretical accounts of behavior coupled with the need to evaluate empirically those accounts necessitates the use of strategies for representing that which is unobserved using variables that can be observed. These strategies allow for the representation of unobserved constructs as latent variables, which, like observed variables, can be used as independent, intervening, or dependent variables in statistical models. SEM is a particularly useful statistical strategy for modeling latent variables and their relations with other latent and observed variables.

A form of latent variable with which readers may be familiar is the common factor, typically referred to simply as a "factor." Factors represent latent sources of commonality among sets of observed variables, or "indicators." As detailed below, variance in each indicator is assumed to be attributable to all latent variables that influence it, a unique factor that is reliable and specific to that indicator, and random error (i.e.,

unreliability). For example, questions about a political candidate might be assumed partly to reflect respondents' attitude toward the candidate, a component unrelated to the attitude but tied to characteristics of the specific question (e.g., wording, response format), and a final part consisting of fleeting influences unlikely to affect responses if the questions were asked again. By separating variance attributable to attitude, assumed to be common to all of the questions, from unreliability and question-specific variance, factor analysis allows for the modeling of the construct of interest—attitude toward the candidate. Factors are one of several types of latent variables that are specified in advance and modeled explicitly in SEM or generated as by-products of analyses using exploratory analysis techniques.

Our goal in this chapter is to elaborate the latent variable concept, with a particular focus on its place in models commonly estimated and tested using SEM. We begin by drawing attention to the different roles of latent variables in basic models. We then review a series of definitions of latent variables, highlighting a recently articulated definition that accommodates the broad range of latent variables in SEM. Next, we return to specific models analyzed using SEM, focusing on those that expand the array of latent variable types encountered in SEM. Building on the presentation of latent variable types and definitions of latent variables, we highlight a number of properties of latent variables that influence how they are specified and interpreted. We close the chapter with a summary of our elaboration of latent variables in SEM and discussion of additional issues related to the interpretation of latent variables.

BASIC ROLES OF LATENT VARIABLES

Displayed in Figure 4.1 is a path diagram showing the relations between seven indicators and two latent variables, and the relation between the two latent variables. As is standard in path diagrams, the observed variables, x_1 to x_3 and y_1 to y_4, are designated by rectangles, and the latent variables, η_1 and η_2, ζ_1 and ζ_2, and ε_1 to ε_4, are designated by ovals. Directional relations are indicated by straight, single-headed arrows. Associated with each directional relation are parameters (e.g., γ_1, λ_1), which are coefficients that give the impact of the variable at the base of the arrow on the variable at the head. Finally, the curved lines that connect two variables (pairs of x's in this case) represent covariances. Implicit in path diagrams like this are parameters for the variances of all exogenous variables and the disturbances or errors, and sometimes the means and intercepts. (See Ho, Stark, & Chernyshenko, Chapter 3, this volume, for a detailed treatment of path diagrams and associated notation.)

This model includes latent variables that play different roles in the model. Most prominent are η_1 and η_2, the variables of primary interest in the model. Notice that the relations between the two latent variables and their indicators differ. The relations between η_2 and its indicators are consistent with the common-factor model described earlier. Variance in the indicators, y_1 to y_4, is assumed to be a function of two variables, one that is common to all the indicators, η_2, and another that is unique to the indicators, ε_1 to ε_4. The fact that ε_1 to ε_4 do not covary is an indication that any covariance between the indicators is attributable to the latent variable. The parameters λ_1 to λ_4 index the relation between each indicator and the latent variable. The equivalent of factor loadings, they are coefficients in a set of measurement equations.[1]

$$y_1 = \alpha_1 + \lambda_1\eta_2 + \varepsilon_1 \qquad (4.1)$$
$$y_2 = \alpha_2 + \lambda_2\eta_2 + \varepsilon_2 \qquad (4.2)$$
$$y_3 = \alpha_3 + \lambda_3\eta_2 + \varepsilon_3 \qquad (4.3)$$
$$y_4 = \alpha_4 + \lambda_4\eta_2 + \varepsilon_4 \qquad (4.4)$$

The α_1 to α_4 are intercepts that give the expected value of each y when the latent variable η_2 is zero. The specification of η_1 differs in three important ways from the specification of η_2. Most fundamentally, the directional arrows run from the indicators to the latent variable. That is, η_1 is a function of its indicators rather than the reverse, which was true for η_2 and is assumed for common factors. Thus, η_1 and η_2 are both latent variables, but they differ in their relationship to their respective indicators. The coefficients on the paths between indicators and latent variable (η_1) are not loadings in the traditional factor-analytic sense but are like regression weights. The equation for η_1 is

$$\eta_1 = \alpha_1 + \gamma_1x_1 + \gamma_2x_2 + \gamma_3x_3 + \zeta_1 \qquad (4.5)$$

A second difference between η_1 and η_2 is that the indicators of η_1 are not influenced by uniquenesses. In fact, neither their variance nor the covariance between them is explained by other variables in the model (i.e., they are exogenous). Finally, whereas the covariance between the indicators of η_2 was effectively zero after accounting for the common influence of η_2, any covariance between indicators of η_1 is explicitly included, because it is not accounted for by η_1. We discuss further this nontraditional form of indicator–latent variable relations later in the chapter.

The model includes two additional types of latent variables, which generally are referred to as "error"

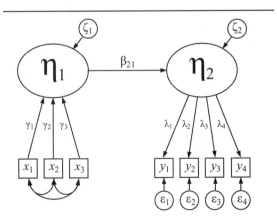

FIGURE 4.1. Model showing latent variables in hypothetical model.

or "disturbance," and are not always discussed as latent variables. Returning to η_2, it is evident that associated with each indicator (y) is a latent variable, ε, which contributes variance to the associated indicator not shared with the remaining indicators. These unobserved sources of variance may include two components. "Random error" is unreliable variance in the indicator; it cannot be attributed to the latent variable of interest or any other latent variable. Moreover, it does not covary with random error in any of the other indicators. "Specificity" is reliable variance in the indicator that is not shared with the remaining indicators of the latent variable of interest. As such, it reflects one or more sources of invalidity. Specific variance may covary with specific variance in one or more (but not all) of the other indicators of the latent variable, or with another variable in the model—a relation referred to as a "specific effect" (Newcomb & Bentler, 1988). The term "uniqueness" often is used to refer to these latent variables, because their influence is unique to a specific indicator, in contrast to the common influence of the substantive latent variable.

The second type of latent variable typically designated as error is the disturbance of the latent variable. Labeled ζ_1 and ζ_2 in the model, these variables correspond to unobserved, or not accounted for, sources of influence on the outcome variables in a model. ζ_1, as shown earlier in Equation 4.5 for η_1, is variance in η_1 not attributable to indicators x_1, x_2, and x_3, but due to all other influences on η_1. Similarly, ζ_2 is a disturbance term that is the collection of all other influences on η_2. It is variance in η_2 not attributable to η_1, as is evident in the structural equation

$$\eta_2 = \beta_{21}\eta_1 + \zeta_2 \qquad (4.6)$$

As with ε_1 to ε_4, ζ_2, is an amalgamation of unobserved contributors to variance in η_2 other than η_1 and may covary with other variables in the model.

These basic types of latent variables are common in models estimated and tested using SEM, as well as other modeling approaches. With rare exceptions, measurement models include the substantive latent variables that are their focus, as well as uniquenesses. Latent variable models may include substantive latent variables but virtually always include disturbances, unless they are exogenous in the model. Later in the chapter, we return to the roles of latent variables in models, expanding our discussion of latent variables such as η_1

in Figure 4.1, and describing less common types of latent variables in specialized models that can be analyzed using SEM.

DEFINITIONS OF LATENT VARIABLES

To this point in the chapter we have described but not defined "latent variable." We now review a number of extant definitions, informal and formal, including our recommended definition. The basis of our recommendation is the need for a definition that applies to the various manifestations of latent variable in SEM, including those pointed out in the previous section and others identified later in the chapter. We begin by reviewing definitions that are primarily conceptual; that is, they do not offer a formal treatment of the relation between observed and latent variables, or latent variables and the unobserved constructs they represent. We then move to a set of formal definitions, beginning with the definition we endorse. We discuss these with reference to the different types of latent variables we have presented thus far.

Conceptual Definitions

In the social and behavioral sciences, latent variables often are referred to as "theoretical" or "hypothetical" variables. For example, Harman (1960) refers to common factors as "hypothetical constructs." Machery (2007) uses the term "theoretical construct" to refer to the abstract and unobservable concepts specified in theories. Sometimes latent variables are referred to simply as "constructs" or "concepts." These labels, though satisfying in their reference to the theoretical context within which latent variables are embedded, offer little in the way of information required to formally specify latent variables in statistical models. Moreover, they imply that the variable may not in reality exist. For instance, Nunnally (1978), in his influential book on psychometric analysis, suggested that such variables exist primarily in the minds of the scientists who posit them. Echoing this sentiment, Skinner (1953) referred to them as "explanatory fiction." Contrasting with this view is the realist position, which suggests that latent variables are real, if unobservable (see, e.g., Borsboom, Mellenbergh, & van Heerden, 2003); that is, they exist apart from the indicators from which they are inferred. This notion of latent variables as theoretical or hypothetical constructs gave rise to a large literature, primarily in psychology, on "construct validation," analytic strategies designed to evaluate the degree to which a set of indicators corresponds to the construct specified by theory (Cronbach & Meehl, 1955).

A second conceptual definition casts latent variables as variables that cannot be observed or measured. Jöreskog and Sörbom (1979), pioneers in the use of SEM to model latent variables, state that latent variables "cannot be directly measured" (p. 105). Writing from an economics perspective, Bannock, Baxter, and Davis (2003) described a latent variable as "a variable in regression analysis that is, in principle, unmeasureable." Definitions of this sort assume that latent variables are impossible to measure. In other words, it is not simply the case that, in a given study, the variable has not been directly observed; it *cannot* be observed. Moreover, presumably it can never be observed, a stipulation that rules out the possibility of new technologies for measurement or observation that might provide a means of direct measurement in the future.

Another conceptual definition views latent variables as ways to reduce the complexity or dimensionality of a set of data. This data reduction method assumes an overabundance of data regarding the variables of primary interest and the need to find a parsimonious means of using the data in tests of the relations between variables. This definition does not necessarily assume that the latent variable exists apart from its indicators. Rather, it views the latent variable as an emergent property of the indicators that, in effect, summarizes them. A related assumption is that the unreliability typical of individual indicators can, to some degree, be overcome by combining them. But rather than doing so using an a priori rule, the variables are discovered through analysis, typically principal components or exploratory factor analysis.

With the exception of the data reduction definition, these conceptual definitions provide an accounting of the relation between latent variables as manifest in statistical models and hypothetical variables specified by theories, but they say little about the relations between indicators and latent variables within models. Also, they generally exclude uniquenesses, errors, and disturbances as latent variables. The data reduction definition is the beginning of a formal definition, but, in conceptual form, does not specify the particular rules by which the observed variables are combined to produce latent variables. It, too, does not encompass the full range of latent variables in SEM.

We now turn to a series of more formal definitions that offer more precise, if not always sufficiently general, accounts of latent variables. We begin with a definition that we feel best captures the broad range of latent variable types in SEM. We follow the presentation of this definition with a discussion of alternative formal definitions, highlighting their limitations as general definitions.

A General Definition

Bollen (2002) provided a *sample realization* definition of latent variables, and it is this definition that best accounts for the full range of latent variables that appear in models estimated and tested using SEM. Unlike the narrower, more restrictive definitions we present later in this section, the sample realization definition is broad and inclusive.

The "sample realization" definition defines a latent variable as a variable "for which there is no sample realization for at least some observations in a given sample" (Bollen, 2002, p. 612). The basis for this definition is the notion of realization in probability and statistics, which differentiates between the values a variable could assume, the "sample space," and the values it does assume when observed or measured, the "state space." Individual elements in the state space are realizations of the variable. Reflecting this relation between what is possible and what is achieved, the sample realizations definition of latent variables refers to latent variables as those for which all or some individuals in the sample do not have a realization in the data set. In SEM the most typical case is that all individuals lack sample realizations for latent variables.

This definition is as general as it is simple. It applies to common factors, as well as uniquenesses, disturbances, and other types of latent variables described in the next section. It does not assume that a variable cannot be measured, either now or in the future. It only assumes that the variable has not been measured for individuals in the sample. It also does not assume that because the variable is latent in one sample, it would necessarily be latent in another sample from the same or a different population. The definition assumes that all variables are latent until there are realizations for the individuals in a sample. And, importantly, the definition can accommodate violations of key assumptions of other formal definitions (e.g., independent uniquenesses for common factors).

Alternative Formal Definitions

A formal definition alluded to earlier in the chapter defines latent variables with reference to the covariances between indicators. Specifically, the *local independence* definition asserts that the covariances between indicators are attributable to one or more latent variables, and when the influence of these latent variables is accounted for, the indicators no longer covary (e.g., Bartholomew, 1987; McDonald, 1981). In the strong form of this definition, any form of relation between the indicators, linear or nonlinear, is attributable to the latent variables. In a weaker form of the definition, only the linear association between the indicators is taken into account (McDonald, 1981). In either case, if, after the specification (or extraction) of a number of latent variables, the covariance between two or more of the indicators is nonzero, then additional latent variables must be added (or extracted; Bartholomew, 1987). Although useful for defining many types of latent variables (e.g., any combination of continuous or categorical latent variables and indicators), the local independence definition does not apply to some variables generally considered latent variables and is therefore inadequate as a general definition. Its limitations primarily stem from its assumptions. These include (1) at least two indicators per latent variable, (2) no covariance between uniquenesses, (3) no effects between indicators, (4) each latent variable must influence at least one indicator, and (5) the indicators do not influence the latent variables. Thus, for instance, only η_2 in Figure 4.1 would be a latent variable given these assumptions, and the definition does not have a label for a variable such as η_1—it is not latent according to this definition and it certainly is not observed, then what is it? In addition, if we consider latent and observed variables as the two possible types of variables, then the definition does not cover variables such as disturbances, unique factors, or higher-order factors.

The definition most familiar to researchers working in the psychometric tradition defines latent variables with reference to individuals' "true score" on the variable. Specifically, and as articulated in classical test theory (Jöreskog, 1971; Lord & Novick, 1968), the expected value of an individual's score on a latent variable is his or her true score. According to this *expected value* definition the mean of independent, repeated assessments of the individual should converge on the true score (i.e., the latent variable). In reality, such repeated assessments are not possible and, as a result, we are forced to rely on estimates of the true score based on a relatively small number of assessments, as in items on a questionnaire. As such, the observed score for an individual reflects both his or her true score and measurement error, as made explicit in the equation

$$y_i = T_i + e_i \qquad (4.7)$$

Though not equivalent, we can find the relation between true scores and factors (see Bollen, 1989, p. 219). Note, however, that the definition does not apply to η_1 in Figure 4.1 or to the disturbances and uniquenesses. As with the local independence definition, it is the assumptions that limit the applicability of the expected value definition to the broad range of latent variables in SEM. These include (1) no covariance between errors, (2) no effects between indicators, and (3) the indicators do not influence the latent variables.

An alternative definition characterizes latent variables in terms of what they are not. Specifically, the *nondeterministic function of observed variables* definition asserts that latent variables are those variables in a model that cannot be expressed as a linear function of the observed variables in the model (Bentler, 1982; Borsboom et al., 2003). This definition elaborates the observed–unobserved distinction, suggesting that variables traditionally considered unobserved (and therefore latent) should be considered observed if their values can be derived through the linear manipulation of model equations given values of observed variables. This definition views η_1 and η_2 in Figure 4.1 as latent variables. However, it would not view the disturbance in a linear regression model as a latent variable, because the disturbance can be expressed as a linear function of the difference between the dependent variable and the predicted dependent variable. What is ambiguous in this regression disturbance example is that virtually always we do not have the population regression coefficients and intercept, but we must estimate them. So in this sense, we can only write the *sample* disturbance as a function of the difference between the dependent variable and the predicted dependent variable using the *sample* regression coefficients. We do not have the population disturbance, since we do not have the population regression coefficients. But the nondeterministic function definition explicitly considers regression disturbances as observed variables. In contrast, the sample realization definition treats the population regression disturbance as a latent variable. The nondeterministic function of observed variables definition also is limited in its assumption of linear equations, which would exclude other variables that we would consider latent (see Bollen, 2002).

These traditional formal definitions account well for an important subset of latent variables—for example, the common factor with uncorrelated uniquenesses. They are found wanting, however, when applied to other unobserved variables frequently encountered in models estimated and tested using SEM. Bollen's (2002) sample realization definition, due in large measure to its lack of assumptions typical of these traditional models, applies to the broad range of unobserved variables, including uniquenesses, disturbances, and additional types of latent variables described in the next section.

ADDITIONAL ROLES OF LATENT VARIABLES

In the early part of the chapter, we pointed out basic roles of latent variables using the model shown in Figure 4.1. These include substantive latent variables of the sort that are the target of factor analysis, as well as random errors of measurement or unique factors, and the disturbances of latent variable equations. In this section, we expand the list of latent variables types in SEM by considering latent variables in models that include features beyond basic models such as the one shown in Figure 4.1. Prior to that consideration, we return to latent variables such as η_1 in Figure 4.1, those in which the latent variable is caused by its indicators rather than being the cause of them.

We begin with a caveat. It is not uncommon for authors to use different labels for latent variables such as η_1 and η_2. We feel this adds to the confusion about how latent variables are defined and the modeling of relations between latent variables and indicators. Latent variables such as η_1 are sometimes referred to as "formative" (e.g., Treiblmaier, Bentler, & Mair, 2011), whereas latent variables such as η_2 are referred to as "reflective" (e.g., Brown, 2006). This distinction confounds the nature of the latent variable and the nature of the indicators and their relation to the latent variable. In the realist view, latent variables exist apart from a specific set of indicators (Borsboom et al., 2003). For that reason, it is not advisable to distinguish substantive latent variables on the basis of the particular set of indicators used to model them in a specific model. In reality, a given latent variable might be modeled using only causal indicators; only reflective, or effect, indicators; or a combination of the two.

Focusing now on the distinction between these two types of indicators, causal and effect, we highlight several salient considerations (see Bollen & Lennox, 1991, for a detailed treatment). Focusing first on η_2, the equivalent of a common factor and consistent with a classical test theory view of measurement, we remind readers that, in this model, the latent variable is responsible for the relations between y_1, y_2, y_3, and y_4. Thus, the indicators are assumed to covary. In fact, the stronger the effects of η_2 on the indicators, the stronger the covariances between them. Moving now to η_1, the inclusion of ζ_1 is an indication that η_1 is more than a simple weighted combination of its indicators (i.e., a composite; Bollen & Bauldry, 2011). Although the model allows x_1, x_2, and x_3 to covary, it makes no assumption about the magnitude of those covariances. Moreover, because η_1 does not determine its indicators, there is no requirement that the indicators covary at all. Thus, although analytic strategies based on classical test theory, such as factor analysis and coefficient alpha, are appropriate for evaluating the adequacy of the indicators of η_2, they are not suitable for evaluating the indicators of η_1. Rather, the concern is one of completeness. Do x_1, x_2, and x_3 capture all essential features of η_1? This judgment is more conceptual than statistical and requires a well-articulated theoretical model of the latent variable apart from a specific set of indicators. Although our example model features latent variables with either causal or effect indicators, it is possible, even advantageous, for a model to include both types of indicators (Edwards & Bagozzi, 2000).

In many, perhaps most, models with latent variables, the indicators and latent variables are assumed to vary on continuous scales. It is possible, however, to model continuous latent variables using categorical indicators, as well as categorical latent variables using either continuous or categorical indicators (Bartholomew, 1987). In practice the most common assumption is that the latent variables are continuous. Indicators can be continuous or categorical. When effect indicators are dichotomous, ordinal, or censored, a common modeling strategy treats the categorical or censored variables as collapsed versions of underlying continuously distributed variables, which are modeled as indicators of latent variables. A model of this sort is shown in Figure 4.2. The model assumes that underlying the categorical observed variables, x_1, x_2, and x_3, are the unobserved continuous variables, x_1^*, x_2^*, and x_3^*, respectively. In this setup the x_1^*, x_2^*, and x_3^* variables are latent variables. These latent variables are nonlinearly related to the

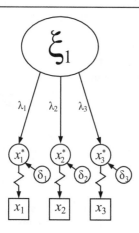

FIGURE 4.2. Latent variable with ordered categorical indicators. Asterisks indicate latent continuous variables assumed to underlie the observed categorical indicators.

observed variables according to a threshold model. Assume, for instance, that the x's are dichotomous variables scored as 0 or 1. The x^*'s are related to their corresponding x in such a way that x is 0 up to a threshold value, after which it is 1. Thus, the observed indicators are categorical, but the indicators influenced directly by the substantive latent variable, ξ_1, are continuous.

When an observed indicator is assessed on multiple occasions, as in longitudinal studies, research questions might concern the pattern of change in scores on the indicator across occasions. In the most straightforward form of this analysis, the focus is the mean pattern of change, such as might be tested using trend analysis in repeated-measures analysis of variance. An alternative form, one that makes strategic use of latent variables, focuses on individual patterns of change (Bollen & Curran, 2006; McArdle, Chapter 32, this volume; Willett & Sayer, 1994). An example is shown in Figure 4.3. This model differs from any described to this point in the chapter. First, the model focuses on a single observed variable, y, though, as indicated by the subscripts, it is observed on four occasions. Second, a focus of the model is to account for means as well as the covariances of the observed variables. Third, all coefficients on the paths from the latent variables to the indicators are fixed. Assuming the spacing between assessments is equal, the coefficients define η_1 as a latent intercept

variable and η_2 as a linear latent slope variable. Finally, this model is multilevel; that is, the latent variables reflect between-subject variability in coefficients associated with the pattern of scores on y across the four assessments. More concretely, imagine that, for each respondent, the four scores are fitted to a straight line, yielding individual intercept and slope values. Collectively, these random coefficients are Level 2 intercepts and slopes, captured in η_1 and η_2, respectively. In other words the random intercepts and random slopes are latent variables. Like any latent variable, η_1 and η_2 can serve as predictors or outcomes in relation to other latent or observed variables.

Some latent curve analyses assume a single characteristic curve that applies to all members of the population. However, for some variables, it is reasonable to assume that different curves characterize different groups within the population. In the most straightforward case, these subpopulations are known and identified by variables in the data set, which are used to predict variability in the latent curve variables. In some instances, there is significant variability in the latent curve parameters but no a priori hypothesis regarding subpopulations or the latent curves that characterize them. In such cases, growth mixture modeling offers a means of detecting heterogeneity and finding latent curves for subpopulations (Shiyko, Ram, & Grimm, Chapter 31, this volume). In growth mixture and other factor mixture models (Lubke & Muthén, 2005), a latent class variable is modeled to account for clustering around specific parameter values (intercept and slope parameters

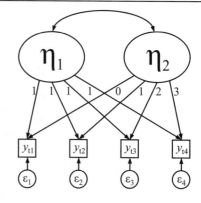

FIGURE 4.3. Latent growth model. η_1 is a latent intercept variable and η_2 is a latent linear slope variable.

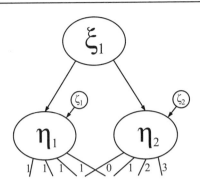

FIGURE 4.4. Growth mixture model. η_1 is a latent intercept variable and η_2 is a latent linear slope variable. ξ_1 is a latent class variable. Indicators are four assessments of an observed variable, as shown in Figure 4.3.

in the growth mixture case) within a population. The relevant portion of a growth mixture model is shown in Figure 4.4. In this model, η_1 and η_2 are as in Figure 4.3, but ξ_1 has been added to account for variability in the intercept and slope values. However, unlike latent variables we have described thus far, ξ_1 is categorical. The number of categories, or classes, represented by ξ_1 is the number required to divide the heterogeneous population into homogeneous subpopulations in terms of the pattern of change in y across the four assessments. For instance, a three-class model might emerge if the pattern for a subgroup of individuals is a low intercept (i.e., Time 1 score) and linear slope near zero; the pattern for a second subgroup is a high intercept and negative slope; and the pattern for a third subgroup is a high intercept and near-zero slope. With regard to the latent class variable, factor mixture (including growth mixture) models are typically exploratory. The number of classes in a population with reference to a particular variable and span of time is not known a priori. Thus, similar to the activity of determining how many factors to extract in exploratory factor analysis, factor mixture modeling requires the use of subjective criteria. Once the appropriate number of classes has been determined and incorporated into a model, information about the classes can be obtained by predicting the latent class variable from other observed or latent variables in the data set.

Returning now to latent variables in factor analysis, we describe two types that appear in models in which

effect indicators reflect two or more latent variables. In Figure 4.5 are path diagrams depicting two models. At the core of each are two latent variables, η_1 and η_2, each influencing three of six indicators, y_1 to y_6. Each model includes a third latent variable, but the models differ in the relation between this latent variable and the indicators. In the model on the left, a second-order factor model, the influence of ξ_1 on the indicators is indirect, transmitted through the first-order latent variables, η_1 and η_2. In this model, the first-order latent variables serve as indicators of the second-order latent variable. Disturbances ζ_1 and ζ_2 are variance in η_1 and η_2 not accounted for by ξ_1. The effect of ξ_1 on y_1 to y_6 requires accounting for the effect of ξ_1 on the relevant η and the effect of that η on the indicator. For example, the influence of ξ_1 on y_1 is the product of λ_{23} and λ_{11}. In the model on the right in Figure 4.5, only two indicators are influenced by the third latent variable, η_3, and the influence is direct. In this bifactor model (Rindskopf & Rose, 1988), the measurement equations for y_2 and y_5 are expanded to include an additional term:

$$y_2 = \alpha_2 + \lambda_{21}\eta_1 + \lambda_{23}\eta_3 + \varepsilon_2 \qquad \textbf{(4.8)}$$
$$y_5 = \alpha_5 + \lambda_{52}\eta_2 + \lambda_{53}\eta_3 + \varepsilon_5 \qquad \textbf{(4.9)}$$

The potential applications of the bifactor model are many. For example, in a set of questionnaire items, of which some are worded positively and others negatively, the model might include a latent variable that influences all of the items to reflect the construct they were intended to measure and two subfactors, one influencing only the positively worded items and the other, only the negatively worded items. A special case of the bifactor model is the multitrait–multimethod model (Kenny & Kashy, 1992), in which variance in each observed variable is attributed to a substantive latent variable, or trait, and a latent variable reflecting the method by which it was assessed (e.g., self-report, observation, collateral report). In such models, "traits" are free of method variance. Moreover, each variance in each trait measure is apportioned according to the influence of latent trait, method, and uniqueness variables, permitting an assessment of the degree to which variance in scores on the measure, as typically used, reflects the measurement method.

Between the basic types of latent variables described early in the chapter and these additional types, the breadth of latent variables that could be modeled in SEM is apparent. These include the standard combina-

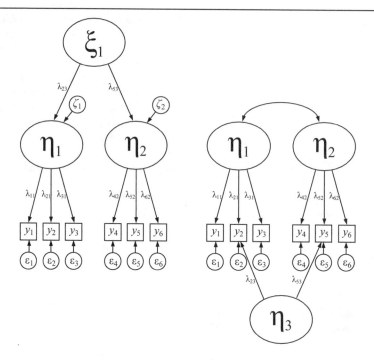

FIGURE 4.5. Second-order and bifactor models.

tion of continuous (or assumed continuous) indicators and latent variables, as well as latent variables estimated from categorical indicators and latent variables that are categorical. We also provided examples of latent variables in multilevel models, in which random coefficients from individual curves estimated at Level 1 are reflected in latent variables at Level 2. In each case, the latent variables reflect quantities for which realizations are not available for members of the sample from which data have been obtained. As such, they are inferred from observed patterns of covariances and/or means.

ADDITIONAL CONSIDERATIONS

The increasing generality of SEM allows for the specification of a growing array of latent variable types. Although the types of latent variables and the forms of models in which they appear are many, several issues arise anytime a latent variable is included in a model to be estimated and tested using SEM. In this section, we touch on several considerations that arise in the specification and interpretation of latent variables in SEM.

A fundamental concern in the specification of models to be analyzed using SEM is identification (Kenny & Milan, Chapter 9, this volume). For current purposes, it suffices to state that a model, or a portion of a model, is identified when a unique value can be obtained for each parameter using the population means and covariance matrix of the observed variables. In models of the sort covered by this chapter, these parameters might include the factor loadings, uniquenesses, variances of the latent variables or disturbances associated with them, covariances between latent variables, and covariances between uniquenesses. A particular concern is the variance of the latent variables, which cannot be estimated without the addition of constraints to specific parameters in the model. The identification of this parameter can be achieved by fixing the loading (i.e., prescribing rather than estimating its value) for one of the variables, the reference variable, typically to a value of 1.[2] This unit loading identification constraint is straightforward for models in which some or all indicators are reflective (Steiger, 2002) but potentially more complicated for models in which all indicators are causal (Bollen & Davis, 2009). Otherwise, assuming a sufficient number of indicators (discussed in the next paragraph), latent variables with reflective indicators are identified. For latent variables with only causal indicators identification is more complex, requiring that the latent variable be embedded in a model in which it serves as a predictor of other variables (Bollen & Davis, 2009). The addition of features such as covariances between uniquenesses, cross-loadings, or subfactors introduces additional identification considerations that must be managed before parameters can be estimated and tested.

Relevant, in part, to the identification concern is the issue of how many indicators should be included for each latent variable. At the most basic level, this concern is one of degrees of freedom. For a single latent variable with reflective indicators, three indicators provides just enough degrees of freedom to permit estimation of parameters (assuming a loading has been fixed as described in the previous paragraph). The addition of a fourth indicator provides degrees of freedom for testing model fit. When a model includes more than one latent variable and the latent variables are related, allowing for latent variables with even fewer indicators is possible. Often in practice, the number of indicators to be included in a model for a given latent variable is dictated by the contents of the available data set. In such cases, the concern shifts from how many indicators to how best to specify the latent variables given the indicators available and identification concerns. In some research contexts, studies routinely produce many potential indicators, as when lengthy psychometric scales are used to measure constructs. Such studies allow for some discretion regarding how many indicators are included for the latent variables reflecting those constructs. Several approaches are available for reducing the number of indicators when the number available is larger than desired (Yang, Nay, & Hoyle, 2010). Countering the appeal of the smallest number of indicators necessary to achieve identification is the observation that when sample size is small, estimation failures are less likely as the number of indicators per latent variable increases (Marsh, Hau, Balla, & Grayson, 1998).

Beyond these considerations related to specification is a concern related to interpretation. It is not uncommon to see or hear latent variables with reflective indicators described as manifestations of the true construct underlying the fallible indicators or as an error-free representation of the construct. Although such claims may be true, there is a decent chance that for a given set of indicators they are not. Referring back to Figure 4.5 and focusing on η_1 and η_2, the latent variables, as common factors, represent variance common to all the indicators

of them. The uniquenesses reflect variance not shared by all of the indicators. This latter point is critical, because although these latent variables are referred to as "measurement errors," they might not capture all of the error variance in the indicators (DeShon, 1998). If, for instance, error is associated with the way in which the indicators were measured (e.g., self-reports), and all of the indicators were measured in the same way, then this source of error will be reflected in the common factor, not the uniquenesses. In practice, indicators of a latent variable typically are measured in the same way and under the same conditions. In such cases, the most appropriate claim is that the latent variable is free of error not common to the indicators. Ideally, the indicators vary independently on potential sources of error, in which case variance attributable to those sources is relegated to the uniquenesses.

SUMMARY AND CONCLUSIONS

We have shown that latent variables are part of virtually all models estimated and tested using SEM. Indeed, it is the capacity for modeling latent variables of various types that initially draws many researchers in the social and behavioral sciences to SEM. Of primary interest are latent variables assumed to represent the constructs articulated in theories. When those constructs are modeled as latent variables using well-selected and soundly measured indicators, estimates of the relations between them provide compelling tests of theoretical propositions. Additional latent variables reflect variance not explained by relations in a model; these include uniquenesses and disturbances. The latent variables share in common with substantive latent variables the fact that observed values are not available for some or all members of the sample to which they apply. SEM provides a flexible and increasingly general means of testing the hypothesized influences of these variables from the observed data.

We summarized several informal and formal definitions of latent variables, concluding that the sample realization definition alone accounts for the full range of latent variables in SEM. The status of variables that are higher-order factors, disturbances, errors, or factors with correlated errors is ambiguous in one or more of the other definitions we reviewed. With its focus on realizations of the variables in a given sample, the sample realization definition does not prescribe the status of variables apart from the information provided by the data for that sample. As such, this definition is consistent with the realist view of variables, which holds that they exist apart from specific models in which they might be included. As such, they could be observed or latent for a given sample; the distinction rests on whether, for that sample, the variable was or was not directly measured for individuals in the sample. If the variable was directly measured for all members of the sample, then, for that sample and measure, it is observed; otherwise it is latent.

We have described a number of roles latent variables assume in models, illustrating the array of hypotheses that can be tested through the strategic specification of latent variables. These range from hypotheses commonly associated with latent variables, such as the relations between indicators and latent variables, to hypotheses not traditionally viewed in latent variable terms, such as the prediction of individual patterns of change over time. Although forms of these hypotheses can be tested in other statistical models, SEM offers a single analytic context within which they can be tested individually or in combinations using continuous or categorical observed variables. For that reason, latent variables, especially as they are modeled in SEM, should become increasingly central to the conceptualization and testing of hypotheses by social and behavioral scientists.

NOTES

1. Given the focus of this chapter, we do not attend to identification concerns in example models. As detailed by Kenny and Milan (Chapter 9, this volume) and discussed later in this chapter, λ_1 typically would be fixed to 1.0 and α_1 set to zero in order to ensure identification of the variance of η_2. We also would need to scale η_1.
2. When intercepts and means are in the model, then the intercept of the scaling indicator can be set to 0 to help identify the parameters (Bollen, 1989).

REFERENCES

Bannock, G., Baxter, R. E., & Davis, E. (2003). *Penguin dictionary of economics*. New York: Penguin. Retrieved from *http://www.credoreference.com/vol/499*.
Bartholomew, D. J. (1987). *Latent variable models and factor analysis*. London: Griffin.
Bentler, P. M. (1982). Linear systems with multiple levels and types of latent variables. In K. G. Jöreskog & H. Wold (Eds.), *Systems under indirect observation* (pp. 101–130). Amsterdam: North Holland.
Bollen, K. A. (1989). *Structural equations with latent variables*. New York: Wiley.
Bollen, K. A. (2002). Latent variables in psychology and the social sciences. *Annual Review of Psychology, 53*, 605–634.
Bollen, K. A., & Bauldry, S. (2011). Three Cs in measurement models: Causal indicators, composite indicators, and covariates. *Psychological Methods, 16*, 265–284.
Bollen, K. A., & Curran, P. J. (2006). *Latent curve models: A structural equation approach*. Hoboken, NJ: Wiley.
Bollen, K. A., & Davis, W. R. (2009). Causal indicator models: Identification, estimation, and testing. *Structural Equation Modeling, 16*, 498–522.
Bollen, K. A., & Lennox, R. (1991). Conventional wisdom on measurement: A structural equation perspective. *Psychological Bulletin, 110*, 305–314.
Borsboom, D., Mellenbergh, G. J., & van Heerden, J. (2003). The theoretical status of latent variables. *Psychological Review, 110*, 203–219.
Brown, T. A. (2006). *Confirmatory factor analysis for applied research*. New York: Guilford Press.
Cronbach, L. J., & Meehl, P. E. (1955). Construct validity in psychological tests. *Psychological Bulletin, 52*, 281–302.
DeShon, R. P. (1998). A cautionary note on measurement error corrections in structural equation models. *Psychological Methods, 4*, 412–423.
Edwards, J. R., & Bagozzi, R. P. (2000). On the nature and direction of relationships between constructs and measures. *Psychological Methods, 5*, 155–174.
Harman, H. H. (1960). *Modern factor analysis*. Chicago: University of Chicago Press.
Jöreskog, K. G. (1971). Statistical analysis of sets of congeneric tests. *Psychometrika, 36*, 109–133.
Jöreskog, K. G., & Sörbom, D. (1979). *Advances in factor analysis and structural equation models*. Cambridge, MA: Abt Books.
Kenny, D. A., & Kashy, D. A. (1992). Analysis of the multitrait–multimethod matrix by confirmatory factor analysis. *Psychological Bulletin, 112*, 165–172.
Lord, F. M., & Novick, M. R. (1968). *Statistical theories of mental test scores*. Reading, MA: Addison-Wesley.
Lubke, G. H., & Muthén, B. (2005). Investigating population heterogeneity with factor mixture models. *Psychological Methods, 10*, 21–39.
Machery, E. (2007). 100 years of psychology of concepts: The theoretical notion of concept and its operationalization. *Studies in History and Philosophy of Biological and Biomedical Sciences, 38*, 63–84.
Marsh, H. W., Hau, K.-T., Balla, J. R., & Grayson, D. (1998). Is more ever too much?: The number of indicators per factor in confirmatory factor analysis. *Multivariate Behavioral Research, 33*, 181–220.
McDonald, R. P. (1981). The dimensionality of tests and items. *British Journal of Mathematical and Statistical Psychology, 34*, 100–117.

Newcomb, M. D., & Bentler, P. M. (1988). *Consequences of adolescent drug use: Impact on the lives of young adults.* Beverly Hills, CA: Sage.

Nunnally J. C. (1978). *Psychometric theory.* New York: McGraw-Hill.

Rindskopf, D., & Rose, T. (1988). Some theory and applications of confirmatory second-order factor analysis. *Multivariate Behavioral Research, 23,* 51–67.

Skinner, B. F. (1953). *Science and human behavior.* New York: Macmillan.

Steiger, J. H. (2002). When constraints interact: A caution about reference variables, identification constraints, and scale dependencies in structural equation modeling. *Psychological Methods, 7,* 210–227.

Treiblmaier, H., Bentler, P. M., & Mair, P. (2011). Formative constructs implemented via common factors. *Structural Equation Modeling, 18,* 1–17.

Willett, J. B., & Sayer, A. G. (1994). Using covariance structure analysis to detect correlates and predictors of individual change over time. *Psychological Bulletin, 116,* 363–381.

Yang, C., Nay, S., & Hoyle, R. H. (2010). Three approaches to using lengthy ordinal scales in structural equation models: Parceling, latent scoring, and shortening scales. *Applied Psychological Measurement, 34,* 122–142.

CHAPTER 5

The Causal Foundations
of Structural Equation Modeling

Judea Pearl

The role of causality in structural equation modeling (SEM) research is widely perceived to be, on the one hand, of pivotal methodological importance and, on the other hand, confusing, enigmatic, and controversial. The confusion is vividly portrayed, for example, in the influential report of Wilkinson and the Task Force (1999), "Statistical Methods in Psychology Journals: Guidelines and Explanations." In discussing SEM, the report starts with the usual warning—"Correlation does not prove causation"—but then it ends with a startling conclusion: "The use of complicated causal-modeling software [read SEM] rarely yields any results that have any interpretation as causal effects." The implication being that the entire enterprise of causal modeling, from Wright (1921) to Blalock (1964) and Duncan (1975), the entire literature in econometric research, including modern advances in graphical and nonparametric structural models, has been misguided, for researchers have been chasing parameters that have no causal interpretation.

The motives for such overstatements notwithstanding, readers may rightly ask: "If SEM methods do not 'prove' causation, how can they yield results that have causal interpretation?" Put another way, if the structural coefficients that SEM researchers labor to estimate can legitimately be interpreted as causal effects, then, unless these parameters are grossly misestimated, why

deny SEM researchers the honor of "establishing causation" or at least of deriving some useful claims about causation?

The answer is that a huge logical gap exists between "establishing causation," which requires careful manipulative experiments, and "interpreting parameters as causal effects," which may be based on firm scientific knowledge or on previously conducted experiments, perhaps by other researchers. One can legitimately be in possession of a parameter that stands for a causal effect and still be unable, using statistical means alone, to determine the magnitude of that parameter given nonexperimental data. As a matter of fact, we know that no such statistical means exist; that is, causal effects in observational studies can only be substantiated from a combination of data and untested theoretical assumptions, not from the data alone. Thus, if reliance on theoretical assumptions disqualifies SEM's parameters from having an interpretation as causal effects, no method whatsoever can endow any parameter with such interpretation, and causal vocabulary should be purged from scientific discourse—an unthinkable restriction.

But then, if the parameters estimated by SEM methods are legitimate carriers of causal claims, and if those claims cannot be proven valid by the data alone, what is the empirical content of those claims? What good are the numerical values of the parameters? Can they inform prediction, decision, or scientific understanding? Are they not merely fiction of one's fancy, comparable, say, to horoscopic speculations?

The aim of this chapter is to lay a coherent logical framework for answering these foundational questions. Following a brief historical account of how the causal interpretation of SEM was obscured (section "SEM and Causality"), the chapter explicates the empirical content of SEM's claims (section "The Logic of SEM") and describes the tools needed for solving most (if not all) problems involving causal relationships (sections "The Causal Reading of Structural Equation Models" and "The Testable Implications of Structural Models"). The tools are based on nonparametric structural equation models—a natural generalization of those used by econometricians and social scientists in the 1950–1960s—that serve as an Archimedean point to liberate SEM from its parametric blinders and elucidate its causal content.

In particular the chapter introduces:

1. Tools of reading and explicating the causal assumptions embodied in SEM models, as well as the set of assumptions that support each individual causal claim.

2. Methods of identifying the testable implications (if any) of the assumptions in (1), and ways of testing not the model in its entirety, but the testable implications of the assumptions behind each individual causal claim.

3. Methods of deciding, prior to taking any data, what measurements ought to be taken, whether one set of measurements is as good as another, and which measurements tend to bias our estimates of the target quantities.

4. Methods for devising critical statistical tests by which two competing theories can be distinguished.

5. Methods of deciding mathematically if the causal relationships are estimable from the data and, if not, what additional assumptions, measurements, or experiments would render them estimable.

6. Methods of recognizing and generating equivalent models that solidify, extend, and amend the heuristic methods of Stelzl (1986) and Lee and Hershberger (1990).

7. Generalization of SEM to categorical data and nonlinear interactions, including a solution to the so-called "mediation problem" (Baron & Kenny, 1986; MacKinnon, 2008).

SEM AND CAUSALITY: A BRIEF HISTORY OF UNHAPPY ENCOUNTERS

The founding fathers of SEM, from Sewall Wright (1921) and the early econometricians (Haavelmo, 1943; Koopmans, 1953) to Blalock (1964) and Duncan (1975), have all considered SEM a mathematical tool for drawing causal conclusions from a combination of observational data and theoretical assumptions. They were explicit about the importance of the latter, but also adamant about the unambiguous causal reading of the model parameters, once the assumptions are substantiated.

In time, however, the causal reading of structural equation models and the theoretical basis on which it rests were suspected of "ad hockery," even to seasoned workers in the field. This occurred partially due to the revolution in computer power, which made workers "lose control of their ability to see the relationship between theory and evidence" (Sørensen, 1998, p. 241), and partly due to a steady erosion of the basic understanding of SEMs, which Pearl (2009, p. 138) attributes to notational shortsightedness (i.e., the failure of the equality sign to distinguish structural from regressional equations).

In his critical paper on SEM, Freedman (1987, p.114) challenged the causal interpretation of SEM as "self-contradictory," and none of the 11 discussants of his paper were able to detect his error and to articulate the correct, noncontradictory interpretation of the example presented by Freedman. Instead, SEM researchers appeared willing to accept contradiction as a fundamental flaw in causal thinking, which must always give way to statistical correctness. In his highly cited commentary on SEM, Chin (1998) surrenders to the critics: "Researchers interested in suggesting causality in their SEM models should consult the critical writing of Cliff (1983), Freedman (1987), and Baumrind (1993)."

This, together with the steady influx of statisticians into the field, has left SEM researchers in a quandary about the meaning of the SEM parameters, and has caused some to avoid causal vocabulary altogether and to regard SEM as an encoding of the parametric family of density functions, void of causal interpretation. Muthén (1987), for example, wrote, "It would be very healthy if more researchers abandoned thinking of and using terms such as cause and effect." Many SEM textbooks have subsequently considered the term "causal modeling" to be an outdated misnomer (e.g., Kelloway, 1998, p. 8), giving clear preference to causality-free nomenclature such as "covariance structure," "regression analysis," or "simultaneous equations." A popular 21st-century textbook reaffirms: "Another term that you may have heard is causal modeling, which is a somewhat dated expression first associated with the SEM techniques of path analysis" (Kline, 2011, p. 8).

Relentless assaults from the potential-outcome paradigm (Rubin, 1974) have further eroded confidence in SEM's adequacy to serve as a language for causation. Sobel (1996), for example, states that the interpretation of the parameters of SEM as effects "do not generally hold, even if the model is correctly specified and a causal theory is given." Comparing structural equation models to the potential-outcome framework, Sobel (2008) asserts that "in general (even in randomized studies), the structural and causal parameters are not equal, implying that the structural parameters should not be interpreted as effect." Remarkably, formal analysis proves the exact opposite: Structural and causal parameters are one and the same thing, and they should *always* be interpreted as effects (Galles & Pearl, 1998; Halpern, 1998; see section "The Causal Reading of Structural Equation Models").

Paul Holland, another advocate of the potential-outcome framework, unravels the root of the confusion: "I am speaking, of course, about the equation: $\{y = a + bx + \varepsilon\}$. What does it mean? The only meaning I have ever determined for such an equation is that it is a shorthand way of describing the conditional distribution of $\{y\}$ given $\{x\}$" (Holland, 1995, p. 54). We will see that the structural interpretation of this equation has in fact nothing to do with the conditional distribution of $\{y\}$ given $\{x\}$; rather, it conveys causal information that is orthogonal to the statistical properties of $\{x\}$ and $\{y\}$ (see section "Counterfactual Analysis in Structural Models").

We will further see (section "Relations to the Potential Outcome Framework") that the SEM language in its nonparametric form offers a mathematically equivalent alternative to the potential-outcome framework that Holland and Sobel advocate for causal inference—a theorem in one is a theorem in another. SEM provides in fact the formal mathematical basis from which the potential-outcome notation draws its legitimacy. This, together with its friendly conceptual appeal and ef-

fective mathematical machinery, explains why SEM retains its status as the prime language for causal and counterfactual analysis.[1] These capabilities are rarely emphasized in standard SEM texts, where they have been kept dormant in the thick labyrinths of software packages, goodness-of-fit measures, linear regression, maximum likelihood (ML) estimates, and other details of parametric modeling. The nonparametric perspective unveils these potentials and avails them for both linear and nonlinear analyses.

THE LOGIC OF SEM

Trimmed and compromised by decades of statistical assaults, textbook descriptions of the aims and claims of SEM grossly understate the power of the methodology. Byrne (2006), for example, describes SEM as "a statistical methodology that takes a confirmatory (i.e., hypothesis-testing) approach to the analysis of a structural theory bearing on some phenomenon. . . . The hypothesized model can then be tested statistically in a simultaneous analysis of the entire system of variables to determine the extent to which it is consistent with the data. If goodness-of-fit is adequate, the model argues for the plausibility of postulated relations among variables; if it is inadequate, the tenability of such relations is rejected."

Taken literally, this confirmatory approach encounters some basic logical difficulties. Consider, for example, the hypothesized model:

$$M = \text{"Cinderella is a terrorist."}$$

Although goodness-of-fit tests with any data would fail to uncover inconsistency in this hypothesized model, we would find it odd to argue for its plausibility. Attempts to repair the argument by insisting that M be falsifiable and invoke only measured variables does not remedy the problem. Choosing

$$M = \text{"Barometer readings cause rain and}$$
the average age in Los Angeles is higher than 3."

will encounter a similar objection; although M is now falsifiable, and all its variables measured, its success in fitting the data tells us nothing about the causal relations between rain and barometers.

The only way to avoid this paradox is to insist that the tested component of M (that the average age is higher than 3) be logically related to its claims (that barometers cause rain), but this stands contrary to the philosophy of confirmatory analysis, according to which the hypothesized model is submitted to a test "of the entire system of variables," irrespective of whether the tested part bears any relationship to the resulting claims.

This simple, albeit contrived, example uncovers a basic logical flaw in the conservative confirmatory approach, and underscores the need to spell out the empirical content of the assumptions behind the hypothesized model, the claims inferred by the model, and the degree to which data corroborate the latter.

The interpretation of SEM methodology that emerges from the nonparametric perspective (Pearl, 2009, pp. 159–163, 368–374) makes these specifications explicit and is, therefore, free of such flaws. According to this interpretation, SEM is an inference method that takes three inputs and produces three outputs. The inputs are:

I-1. A set A of qualitative causal *assumptions*, which the investigator is prepared to defend on scientific grounds, and a model M_A that encodes these assumptions. (Typically, M_A takes the form of a path diagram or a set of structural equations with free parameters. A typical assumption is that certain omitted factors, represented by error terms, are uncorrelated with some variables or among themselves, or that no direct effect exists between a pair of variables.)

I-2. A set Q of *queries* concerning causal and counterfactual relationships among variables of interest. Traditionally, Q concerned the magnitudes of structural coefficients but, in general models, Q will address causal relations more directly, for example,

Q_1: What is the effect of treatment X on outcome Y?

Q_2: Is this employer guilty of gender discrimination?

Theoretically, each query $Q_i \in Q$ should be computable from a fully specified model M in which all functional relationships are given. Noncomputable queries are inadmissible.

I-3. A set D of experimental or nonexperimental *data*, governed by a joint probability distribution presumably generated by a process consistent with A.

The outputs are:

O-1. A set A^* of statements that are the logical implications of A, separate from the data at hand, for example, that X has no effect on Y if we hold Z constant, or that Z is an instrument relative to $\{X, Y\}$.

O-2. A set C of data-based *claims* concerning the magnitudes or likelihoods of the target queries in Q, each conditional on A. C may contain, for example, the estimated mean and variance of a given structural parameter, or the expected effect of a given intervention. Auxiliary to C, SEM also generates an estimand $Q_i(P)$ for each query in Q, or a determination that Q_i is not identifiable from P (Definition 1).

O-3. A list T of testable statistical implications of A, and the degree $g(T_i)$, $T_i \in T$, to which the data agree with each of those implications. A typical implication would be the vanishing of a specific partial correlation; such constraints can be read from the model M_A and confirmed or disconfirmed quantitatively by the data (Definition 3).

The structure of this inferential exercise is shown schematically in Figure 5.1.

Several observations are worth noting before illustrating these inferences by examples. First, SEM is not a traditional statistical methodology, typified by hypothesis testing or estimation, because neither claims nor assumptions are expressed in terms of probability functions of realizable variables (Pearl, 2009).

Second, all claims produced by an SEM study are conditional on the validity of A, and should be reported in conditional format: "If A then C_i" for any claim $C_i \in C$. Such claims, despite their provisional character, are significantly more assertive than their meek, confirmatory predecessors. They assert that anyone willing to accept A must also accept C_i, out of logical necessity. Moreover, no other method can do better; that is, if SEM analysis finds that a set A of assumptions is necessary for inferring a claim C_i, no other methodology can infer C_i with a weaker set of assumptions.[2]

Third, passing a goodness-of-fit test is not a prerequisite for the validity of the conditional claim "If A then C_i" nor for the validity of C_i. While it is important to know if any assumptions in A are inconsistent with the data, M_A may not have any testable implications what-

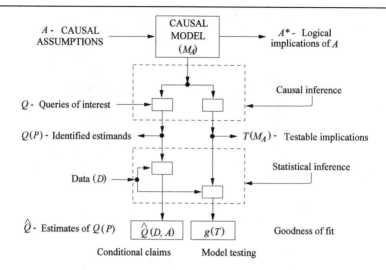

FIGURE 5.1. SEM methodology depicted as an inference engine converting assumptions (A), queries (Q), and data (D) into logical implications (A^*), conditional claims (C), and data-fitness indices ($g(T)$).

soever. In such a case, the assertion "If A then C_i," may still be extremely informative in a decision-making context, since each C_i conveys quantitative information extracted from the data rather than qualitative assumption A with which the study commences. Moreover, even if A turns out inconsistent with D, the inconsistencies may be entirely due to portions of the model that have nothing to do with the derivation of C_i. It is therefore important to identify which statistical implication of (A) is responsible for the inconsistency; global tests for goodness-of-fit hide this information (Pearl, 2004, 2009; pp. 144–145).

Finally, and this was realized by SEM researchers in the late 1980s, there is nothing in SEM's methodology to protect C from the inevitability of contradictory equivalent models, namely, models that satisfy all the testable implications of M_A and still advertise claims that contradict C. Modern developments in graphical modeling have devised visual and algorithmic tools for detecting, displaying, and enumerating equivalent models. Researchers should keep in mind therefore that only a tiny portion of the assumptions behind each SEM study lends itself to scrutiny by the data; the bulk of it must remain untestable, at the mercy of scientific judgment.

THE CAUSAL READING OF STRUCTURAL EQUATION MODELS

The Assumptions and Their Representation

In this section I illustrate the inferences outlined in Figure 5.1 using simple structural models consisting of linear equations and their nonparametric counterparts, encoded via diagrams. Consider the linear structural equations

$$y = \beta x + u_Y, \quad x = u_X \tag{5.1}$$

where x stands for the level (or severity) of a disease, y stands for the level (or severity) of a symptom, and u_Y stands for all factors, other than the disease in question, that could possibly affect Y when X is held constant. In interpreting this equation we should think of a physical process whereby nature *examines* the values of all variables in the domain and, accordingly, *assigns* to variable Y the value $y = \beta x + u_Y$. Similarly, to "explain" the occurrence of disease X, we write $x = u_X$, where U_X stands for all factors affecting X, which may in general include factors in U_Y.

To express the directionality of the underlying process, we should either replace the equality sign with an assignment symbol :=, or augment the equation with a "path diagram," in which arrows are drawn from causes to their effects, as in Figure 5.2. The absence of an arrow makes the empirical claim that Nature assigns values to one variable irrespective of another. In our example, the diagram encodes the possible existence of (direct) causal influence of X on Y, and the absence of causal influence of Y on X, while the equations encode the quantitative relationships among the variables involved, to be determined from the data. The "path coefficient," β, quantifies the (direct) causal effect of X on Y. Once we commit to a particular numerical value of β, the equation claims that a unit increase for X would result in β units increase of Y regardless of the values taken by other variables in the model, regardless of the statistics of U_X and U_Y, and regardless of whether the increase in X originates from external manipulations or variations in U_X.

The variables U_X and U_Y are called "exogenous"; they represent observed or unobserved background factors that the modeler decides to keep unexplained— that is, factors that influence but are not influenced by the other variables (called "endogenous") in the model. Unobserved exogenous variables in structural equations, sometimes called "disturbances" or "errors," differ fundamentally from residual terms in regression equations. The latter, usually denoted by letters ε_X and ε_Y, are artifacts of analysis, which, by definition, are uncorrelated with the regressors. The former are shaped by physical reality (e.g., genetic factors, socioeconomic conditions), not by analysis; they are treated as any other variable, though we often cannot measure their values precisely and must resign ourselves to merely acknowledging their existence and assessing qualitatively how they relate to other variables in the system.

If correlation is presumed possible, it is customary to connect the two variables, U_Y and U_X, by a dashed double arrow, as shown in Figure 5.2(b). By allowing correlations among omitted factors, we encode in effect the presence of *latent* variables affecting both X and Y, as shown explicitly in Figure 5.2(c), which is the standard representation in the SEM literature (e.g., Bollen, 1989). If, however, our attention focuses on causal relations among observed rather than latent variables, there is no reason to distinguish between correlated errors and interrelated latent variables; it is only the distinction between correlated and uncorrelated errors (e.g., between Figure 5.2(a) and (b)) that needs to be made.[3] Moreover, when the error terms are uncorrelated, it is often more convenient to eliminate them altogether from the diagram (as in Figure 5.7, section "Equivalent Models"), with the understanding that every variable, X, is subject to the influence of an independent disturbance U_X.

In reading path diagrams, it is common to use kinship relations such as parent, child, ancestor, and descendent, the interpretation of which is usually self-evident. For example, the arrow in $X \rightarrow Y$ designates X as a parent of Y and Y as a child of X. A "path" is any consecutive sequence of edges, solid or dashed. For example, there are two paths between X and Y in Figure 5.2(b), one consisting of the direct arrow $X \rightarrow Y$, the other tracing the nodes X, U_X, U_Y, and Y.

In path diagrams, causal assumptions are encoded not in the links but, rather, in the missing links. An arrow merely indicates the possibility of causal connection, the strength of which remains to be determined (from data); a missing arrow represents a claim of zero influence, while a missing double arrow represents a claim of zero covariance. Both assumptions are causal,

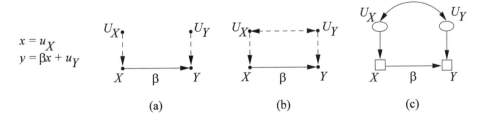

FIGURE 5.2. A simple structural equation model, and its associated diagrams, showing (a) independent unobserved exogenous variables (connected by dashed arrows), (b) dependent exogenous variables, and (c) an equivalent, more traditional notation, in which latent variables are enclosed in ovals.

not statistical, since none can be determined from the joint density of the observed variables, X and Y, though both can be tested in experimental settings (e.g., randomized trials).

Causal Assumptions in Nonparametric Models

To extend the capabilities of SEM methods to models involving discrete variables, nonlinear dependencies, and heterogeneous effect modifications, we need to detach the notion of "effect" from its algebraic representation as a coefficient in an equation, and redefine "effect" as a general capacity to transmit *changes* among variables. The central idea is to exploit the invariant characteristics of structural equations without committing to a specific functional form. For example, the nonparametric interpretation of the diagram in Figure 5.3(a) corresponds to a set of three unknown functions, each corresponding to one of the observed variables:

$$z = f_Z(u_Z)$$
$$x = f_X(z, u_X) \qquad (5.2)$$
$$y = f_Y(x, u_Y)$$

where in this particular example U_Z, U_X, and U_Y are assumed to be jointly independent but otherwise arbitrarily distributed. Each of these functions represents a causal process (or mechanism) that determines the value of the left variable (output) from the values on the right variables (inputs). The absence of a variable from the right-hand side of an equation encodes the assumption that nature ignores that variable in the process of determining the value of the output variable. For example, the absence of variable Z from the arguments of f_Y conveys the empirical claim that variations in Z will leave Y unchanged, as long as variables U_Y and X remain constant.

Representing Interventions and Causal Effects

Remarkably, this feature of invariance permits us to derive powerful claims about causal effects and counterfactuals, despite our ignorance of functional and distributional forms. This is done through a mathematical operator called $do(x)$, which simulates physical interventions by deleting certain functions from the model, replacing them with a constant $X = x$, while keeping the rest of the model unchanged. For example, to emulate an intervention $do(x_0)$ that holds X constant (at $X = x_0$) in model M of Figure 5.3(a), we replace the equation for x in Equation 5.2 with $x = x_0$, and obtain a new model, M_{x_0},

$$z = f_Z(u_Z)$$
$$x = x_0 \qquad (5.3)$$
$$y = f_Y(x, u_Y)$$

the graphical description of which is shown in Figure 5.3(b).

The joint distribution associated with the modified model, denoted $P(z, y \mid do(x_0))$ describes the postintervention distribution of variables Y and Z (also called "controlled" or "experimental" distribution), to be distinguished from the preintervention distribution, $P(x, y, z)$, associated with the original model of Equation 5.2. For example, if X represents a treatment variable, Y a response variable, and Z some covariate that affects the amount of treatment received, then the distribution $P(z, y \mid do(x_0))$ gives the proportion of individuals that would attain response level $Y = y$ and covariate level $Z = z$ under the hypothetical situation in which treatment $X = x_0$ is administered uniformly to the population.

In general, we can formally define the postintervention distribution by the equation

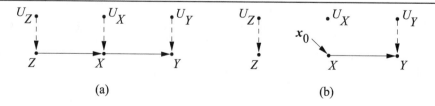

(a)   (b)

FIGURE 5.3. The diagrams associated with (a) the structural model of Equation 5.2 and (b) the modified model of Equation 5.3, representing the intervention $do(X = x_0)$.

$$P_M(y\mid do(x)) = P_{M_x}(y) \qquad (5.4)$$

In words: In the framework of model M, the post-intervention distribution of outcome Y is defined as the probability that model M_x assigns to each outcome level $Y = y$. From this distribution, which is readily computed from any fully specified model M, we are able to assess treatment efficacy by comparing aspects of this distribution at different levels of x_0. However, the central question in the analysis of causal effects is the question of *identification* in partially specified models: Given assumptions set A (as embodied in the model), can the controlled (postintervention) distribution, $P(Y = y\mid do(x))$, be estimated from data governed by the pre-intervention distribution $P(z, x, y)$?

In linear parametric settings, the question of identification reduces to asking whether some model parameter, β, has a unique solution in terms of the parameters of P (say, the population covariance matrix). In the nonparametric formulation, the notion of "has a unique solution" does not directly apply, since quantities such as $Q(M) = P(y\mid do(x))$ have no parametric signature and are defined procedurally by simulating an intervention in a causal model M, as in Equation 5.3. The following definition captures the requirement that Q be estimable from the data:

Definition 1 (identifiability) (Pearl, 2000, p. 77)
A quantity $Q(M)$ is identifiable, given a set of assumptions A, if for any two models M_1 and M_2 that satisfy A, we have

$$P(M_1) = P(M_2) \Rightarrow Q(M_1) = Q(M_2) \qquad (5.5)$$

In words, the functional details of M_1 and M_2 do not matter; what matters is that the assumptions in A (e.g., those encoded in the diagram) would constrain the variability of those details in such a way that equality of P's would entail equality of Q's. When this happens, Q depends on P only and should therefore be expressible in terms of the parameters of P. The section "Identification Using Graphs" will exemplify and operationalize this notion.

Counterfactual Analysis in Structural Models

Not all questions of causal character can be encoded in $P(y\mid do(x))$-type expressions, thus implying that not all

causal questions can be answered from experimental studies. For example, retrospective questions regarding causes of a given effect (e.g., what fraction of death cases are *due to* a specific treatment?) cannot be answered from experimental studies, and naturally this kind of question cannot be expressed in $P(y\mid do(x))$ notation.[4]

To answer such questions, a probabilistic analysis of counterfactuals is required, one dedicated to the relation "Y would be y had X been x in situation $U = u$," denoted $Y_x(u) = y$. Remarkably, unknown to most economists and philosophers, structural equation models provide the formal interpretation and symbolic machinery for analyzing such counterfactual relationships.[5]

The key idea is to interpret the phrase "had X been x" as an instruction to make a minimal modification in the current model, which may have assigned X a different value, say, $X = x'$, so as to ensure the specified condition $X = x$. Such a minimal modification amounts to replacing the equation for X by a constant x, as we have done in Equation 5.3. This replacement permits the constant x to differ from the actual value of X (namely, $f_X(z, u_X)$) without rendering the system of equations inconsistent, thus yielding a formal interpretation of counterfactuals in multistage models, where the dependent variable in one equation may be an independent variable in another.

Definition 2 (unit-level counterfactuals) (Pearl, 2000, p. 98)
Let M be a fully specified structural model and M_x; a modified version of M, with the equation(s) of X replaced by X = x. Denote the solution for Y in the equations of M_x; by the symbol $Y_{M_x}(u)$. The counterfactual $Y_x(u)$ (Read: "The value of Y in unit u, had X been x") is given by

$$Y_x(u) \triangleq Y_{M_x}(u) \qquad (5.6)$$

In words, the counterfactual $Y_x(u)$ in model M is defined as the solution for Y in the "surgically modified" submodel M_x.

We see that every structural equation, say $y = a + bx + u_Y$, carries counterfactual information, $Y_{xz}(u) = a + bx + u_Y$, where Z is any set of variables in the model that do not appear on the right-hand side of the equation. Naturally, when U is a random variable, Y_x will be a random variable as well, the distribution of which is dictated by both $P(u)$ and the model M_x. It can be shown (Pearl,

2009, Ch. 7) that Equation 5.6 permits us to define joint distributions of counterfactual variables and to detect conditional independencies of counterfactuals directly from the path diagram.

Reading Counterfactuals: An Example

This capacity of structural equations to encode and deliver counterfactual information, at both the unit and population levels, is hardly known among SEM researchers, and should receive much greater emphasis in education and the mainstream literature. It is an essential tool to ward off critics who view counterfactuals as an exclusive property of the potential outcome framework (Holland, 1988; Imbens, 2010; Rubin, 2004; Sobel, 2008; Wilkinson et al., 1999). This capacity can be demonstrated by a simple example, using a three-variable linear model; the same one used by Holland (1988) and Sobel (2008) to "prove" that structural models do not have causal or counterfactual content.

Consider the model in Figure 5.4, where X stands for the level of assistance (or "treatment") given to a student, Z stands for the amount of time the student spends studying, and Y, the outcome, stands for the student's performance on an exam. Starting at a unit-level analysis, let us consider a student named Joe, for whom we measure $X = 0.5$, $Z = 1$, $Y = 1.5$, and about whom we ask a counterfactual question:

Q_1: What would Joe's score be had he doubled his study time?

Using our subscript notation, this question amounts to evaluating $Y_{Z=2}(u)$, with u standing for the distinctive characteristics of Joe, namely, $u = (\varepsilon_1, \varepsilon_2, \varepsilon_3)$, as inferred from the observed data $\{X = 0.5, Z = 1, Y = 1.5\}$.

The answer to this question is obtained in three steps.

1. Use the data to compute the exogenous factors $\varepsilon_1, \varepsilon_2, \varepsilon_3$. (These are the invariant characteristics of unit u, and do not change by interventions or counterfactual hypothesizing.) In our model, we get (Figure 5.4(b)):

$$\varepsilon_1 = 0.5$$
$$\varepsilon_2 = 1 - 0.5 \times 0.5 = 0.75$$
$$\varepsilon_3 = 1.5 - 0.5 \times 0.7 - 1 \times 0.4 = 0.75$$

2. Modify the model to form $M_{Z=2}$, in which Z is set to 2 and all arrows to Z are removed (Figure 5.4(c)).

3. Compute the value of Y in the mutilated model formed in step 2, giving:

$$Y_{Z=2} = 0.5 \times 0.7 + 2.0 \times 0.4 + 0.75 = 1.90$$

This example illustrates the need to modify the original model (Figure 5.4(a)), in which the combination $(X = 1, \varepsilon_2 = 0.75, Z = 2.0)$ constitutes a contradiction (see Note 5). This is precisely the contradiction that Freedman (1987) could not reconcile in his criticism of SEM.

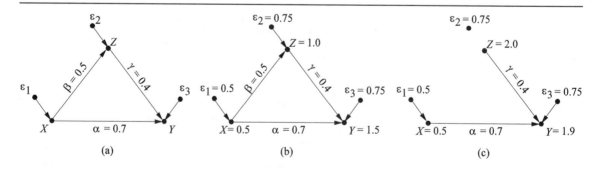

FIGURE 5.4. Structural models used for answering a counterfactual question about an individual $u = (\varepsilon_1, \varepsilon_2, \varepsilon_3)$. (a) The generic model (all intercepts are assumed zero); (b) the u-specific model; and (c) the modified model necessary to accommodate the antecedent $Z = 2$ of the counterfactual question Q_1.

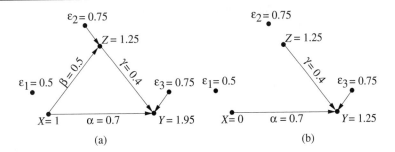

FIGURE 5.5. Unit-specific structural models used for answering a nested counterfactual question concerning the indirect effect of X on Y. (a) Modified model needed for calculating Z_1. (b) Modified model needed for calculating Y_{0,Z_1}.

Let us now ask another hypothetical question about Joe.

Q_2: What would Joe's score be, had the treatment been 0 and had he studied at whatever level he would have studied had the treatment been 1?

This rather intricate question, which involves nested conditionals, is the basis for defining mediation, to be discussed fully in section "Mediation." Using our subscript notation, the quantity sought can be written as Y_{0,Z_1}, where Z_1 is the value that Z would attain had X been one. To compute this quantity we need to form two modified models. The first, shown in Figure 5.5(a), is to compute Z_1, the second antecedent in Y_{0,Z_1}:

$$Z_1 = 1.0 \times 0.5 + 0.75 = 1.25$$

The second, shown in Figure 5.5(b), to compute Y_{0,Z_1}, and thus provide an answer to Q_2:

$$Y_{0,Z1} = Y_{0,1.25} = 1.25 \times 0.4 + 0.75 = 1.25$$

If we compare this value of $Y_{0,Z} = 1.25$ with Joe's outcome had he not received any treatment, $Y_0 = 0.75 \times 0.4 + 0.75 = 1.05$, the difference is, as expected, the indirect effect of X on Y, $Y_{0,Z_1} - Y_0 = 0.20 = \beta \times \gamma$.

This exercise may seem unnecessarily complicated in linear models, where we can compute our desired quantity directly from the product $\beta \times \gamma$. The benefit of using counterfactuals will be revealed in section "Indirect Effects," where indirect effects will be defined

for discrete variables, and estimated from data without assuming any parametric forms of the equations.

Predicting Outcomes and Potential Outcomes in Empirical Studies

Having convinced ourselves that every counterfactual question can be answered (using Equation 5.6) from a fully specified structural model, we next move to population level analysis and ask a policy-related question on a set of 10 individuals, with Joe being participant 1. Each is characterized by a distinct vector $u_i = (\varepsilon_1, \varepsilon_2, \varepsilon_3)$, as shown in the first three columns of Table 5.1.

For each triplet $(\varepsilon_1, \varepsilon_2, \varepsilon_3)$, the model of Figure 5.4(a) enables us to complete a full row of the table, including Y_0 and Y_1, which stand for the potential outcomes under control ($X = 0$) and treatment ($X = 1$) conditions, respectively. We see that a simple structural model like the one in Figure 5.4(a) encodes in effect a synthetic population of individuals together with their predicted behavior under both observational and experimental conditions. The columns labeled X, Y, Z predict the results of observational studies, and those labeled Y_0, Y_1, Z_0, Z_1 predict the hypothetical outcome under two treatment regimens, $X = 0$ and $X = 1$. Many more—in fact, infinite—potential outcomes may be predicted as well, for example, $Y_{X=0.5,Z=2.0}$ computed in Figure 5.4(c), and all combinations of subscripted variables. From this synthetic population one can find the distribution of every counterfactual query on variables X, Y, Z, including, in particular, retrospective counterfactuals, such as the probability that a person chosen at ran-

TABLE 5.1. Potential and Observed Outcomes Predicted by the Structural Model of Figure 5.4(a)

Participant	Participant characteristics			Observed behavior			Predicted potential outcomes				
	ε_1	ε_2	ε_3	X	Y	Z	Y_0	Y_1	Z_0	Z_1	$Y_{00}\cdots$
1	0.5	0.75	0.75	0.5	1.50	1.0	1.05	1.95	0.75	1.25	0.75
2	0.3	0.1	0.4	0.3	0.71	0.25	0.44	1.34	0.1	0.6	0.4
3	0.5	0.9	0.2	0.5	1.01	1.15	0.56	1.46	0.9	1.4	0.2
4	0.6	0.5	0.3	0.6	1.04	0.8	0.50	1.40	0.5	1.0	0.3
5	0.5	0.8	0.9	0.5	1.67	1.05	1.22	2.12	0.8	1.3	0.9
6	0.7	0.9	0.3	0.7	1.29	1.25	0.66	1.56	0.9	1.4	0.3
7	0.2	0.3	0.8	0.2	1.10	0.4	0.92	1.82	0.3	0.8	0.8
8	0.4	0.6	0.2	0.4	0.80	0.8	0.44	1.34	0.6	1.1	0.2
9	0.6	0.4	0.3	0.6	1.00	0.7	0.46	1.36	0.4	0.9	0.3
10	0.3	0.8	0.3	0.3	0.89	0.95	0.62	1.52	0.8	1.3	0.3

Note. Units were selected at random, with each ε_1 uniformly distributed over [0,1].

dom would have passed the exam by getting assistance given that, in reality, he or she failed the example and did not receive any assistance.[6]

This prediction power was facilitated of course with the help of two untestable pieces of information: (1) the structure of the model (which includes the assumption of independent error terms) and (2) the values of the model parameters (which include the distribution of each exogenous variable). Whereas the latter can often be inferred from the data (see section "Identification Using Graphs"), the former depends largely on scientific judgment.

Now assume that we have no information whatsoever about the underlying model and all we have are measurements on Y taken in the experimental study in which X is randomized over two levels, $X = 0$ and $X = 1$.

Table 5.2 describes the responses of the same 10 participants (Joe being participant 1) under such experimental conditions. The first two columns give the true potential outcomes (taken from Table 5.1) while the last two columns describe the information available to the experimenter, where a square indicates that the response was not observed.[7] Randomization assures us that although half of the potential outcomes are not observed, the difference between the observed means in the treatment and control groups will converge to the average of the true difference, $E(Y_1 - Y_0) = 0.9$.

In our model, since all exogenous variables are independent, the slope of the regression of Y on X would

also converge to the average causal effect. Bias will be introduced if ε_1 is correlated with ε_2 or with ε_3. However, such correlation will not bias the average causal effect estimated in the experimental study.

TABLE 5.2. Potential and Observed Outcomes in a Randomized Clinical Trial with X Randomized over $X = 0$ and $X = 1$

Participant	Predicted potential outcomes		Observed outcomes	
	Y_0	Y_1	Y_0	Y_1
1	1.05	1.95	1.05	■
2	0.44	1.34	■	1.34
3	0.56	1.46	■	1.46
4	0.50	1.40	■	1.40
5	1.22	2.12	1.22	■
6	0.66	1.56	0.66	■
7	0.92	1.82	■	1.82
8	0.44	1.34	0.44	■
9	0.46	1.36	■	1.36
10	0.62	1.52	0.62	■

True average treatment effect: 0.90   Study average treatment effect: 0.68

Relations to the Potential Outcome Framework

Definition 2 constitutes the bridge between SEM and a framework called "potential outcome" (Rubin, 1974), which is often presented as a "more principled alternative" to SEM (Holland, 1988; Rubin, 2004; Sobel, 1996, 2008; Wilkinson et al., 1999). Such presentations are misleading and misinformed; the two frameworks have been proven to be logically equivalent, differing only in the language in which researchers are permitted to express assumptions. A theorem in one is a theorem in the other (Pearl, 2009, pp. 228–231), with Definition 2 providing the formal basis for both.

The idea of potential-outcome analysis is simple. Researchers who feel uncomfortable presenting their assumptions in diagrams or structural equations may do so in a roundabout way, using randomized trial as the ruling paradigm, and interpret the counterfactual $Y_x(u)$ as the potential outcome of subject u to hypothetical treatment $X = x$, ignoring the mechanisms that govern that outcome. The causal inference problem is then set up as one of "missing data," where the missing data are the potential outcomes $Y_x(u)$ under the treatment not received, while the observed data are the potential outcomes under the received treatments, as shown in Table 5.2

Thus, Y_x becomes a new latent variable which reveals its value only when $X = x$, through the relation

$$X = x \rightarrow Y_x = Y \qquad (5.7)$$

sometimes written (for binary X)

$$Y = xY_1 + (1 - x)Y_0$$

Beyond this relation (known as "consistency assumption"), the investigator may ignore the fact that Y_x is actually Y itself, only measured under different conditions (as in Figure 5.4(c)), and proceed to estimate the average causal effect, $E(Y_{x'}) - E(Y_x)$, with all the machinery that statistics has developed for missing data. Moreover, since Equation 5.7 is also a theorem in the logic of structural counterfactuals (Pearl, 2009, Chap. 7) and a complete one,[8] researchers in this camp are guaranteed never to obtain results that conflict with those derived in the structural framework.

The weakness of this approach surfaces in the problem formulation phase, where, deprived of diagrams and structural equations, researchers are forced to ex-

press the (inescapable) assumption set A in a language totally removed from scientific knowledge, for example, in the form of conditional independencies among counterfactual variables (see Pearl, 2010a).

For example, to express the fact that, in randomized trial, X is independent on both ε_2 and ε_3 (as in Figure 5.4(a)), the investigator would need to write the cryptic, "strong ignorability" expression $X \perp\!\!\!\perp \{Z_1, Z_0, Y_{00}, Y_{01}, Y_{10}, Y_{11}\}$. To overcome this obstacle, Pearl (2009) has devised a way of combining the best features of the two approaches. It is based on encoding causal assumptions in the language of diagrams or structural equations; translating these assumptions into counterfactual notation; performing derivation in the algebraic language of counterfactuals, using axioms derived from Equation 5.6; and, finally, interpreting the result in plain causal language. The mediation problem discussed in section "Mediation" illustrates how such symbiosis clarifies the conceptualization and estimation of direct and indirect effects, a task that has lingered on for several decades.

THE TESTABLE IMPLICATIONS OF STRUCTURAL MODELS

This section deals with the testable implications of structural models, sometimes called "overidentifying restrictions," and ways of reading them from the graph.

The *d*-Separation Criterion

Although each causal assumption in isolation cannot be tested in nonexperimental studies, the sum total of all causal assumptions in a model often has testable implications. The chain model of Figure 5.3(a), for example, encodes seven causal assumptions, each corresponding to a missing arrow or a missing double-arrow between a pair of variables. None of those assumptions is testable in isolation, yet the totality of all seven assumptions implies that Z is unassociated with Y in every stratum of X. Such testable implications can be read off the diagrams using a graphical criterion known as "*d*-separation" (Pearl, 1988).

Definition 3 (*d*-separation)

A set S of nodes is said to block a path p if either (1) p contains at least one arrow-emitting node that is in S, or (2) p contains at least one collision node that *is outside S and has no descendant in S. If S blocks all paths from set X to set Y, it is said to "d-separate X and Y," and then, it can be shown that variables X and Y are independent given S, written $X \perp\!\!\!\perp Y \mid S$.*[9]

To illustrate, the path $U_Z \to Z \to X \to Y$ in Figure 5.3(a) is blocked by $S = \{Z\}$ and by $S = \{X\}$, since each emits an arrow along that path. Consequently we can infer that the conditional independencies $U_Z \perp\!\!\!\perp Y \mid Z$ and $U_Z \perp\!\!\!\perp Y \mid X$ will be satisfied in any probability function that this model can generate, regardless of how we parametrize the arrows. Likewise, the path $U_Z \to Z \to X \leftarrow U_X$ is blocked by the null set $\{\emptyset\}$, but it is not blocked by $S = \{Y\}$ since Y is a descendant of the collision node X. Consequently, the marginal independence $U_Z \perp\!\!\!\perp U_X$ will hold in the distribution, but $U_Z \perp\!\!\!\perp U_X \mid Y$ may or may not hold. This special handling of collision nodes (or *colliders*, e.g., $Z \to X \leftarrow U_X$) reflects a general phenomenon known as *Berkson's paradox* (Berkson, 1946), whereby observations on a common consequence of two independent causes render those causes dependent. For example, the outcomes of two independent coins are rendered dependent by the testimony that at least one of them is a tail.

The testable implications of any given model are vividly advertised by its associated graph G. Each d-separation condition in G corresponds to a conditional independence test that can be performed on the data to support or refute the validity of M. These can easily be enumerated by attending to each missing edge in the graph and selecting a set of variables that d-separate the pair of variables corresponding to that missing edge. For example, in Figure 5.6, three of the missing edges are $Z_1 - Z_2$, $Z_1 - Y$, and $Z_2 - X$ with separating sets $\{\emptyset\}$, $\{X, Z_2, Z_3\}$, and $\{Z_1, Z_3\}$, respectively. Accordingly, the testable implications of M include $Z_1 \perp\!\!\!\perp Z_2$, $Z_1 \perp\!\!\!\perp Y \mid \{X, Z_2, Z_3\}$, and $Z_2 \perp\!\!\!\perp X \mid \{Z_1, Z_3\}$.

In linear systems, these conditional independence constraints translate into zero partial correlations, or zero coefficients in the corresponding regression equations. For example, the three implications translate into the following constraints: $r_{Z_1 Z_2} = 0$, $r_{YZ_1 \cdot XZ_2 Z_3} = 0$, and $r_{Z_2 X \cdot Z_1 Z_3} = 0$.

Such tests are easily conducted by routine regression techniques, and they provide valuable diagnostic information for model modification, in case any of them fail (see Pearl, 2009, pp. 143–145). Software routines for automatic detection of all such tests, as well as other implications of graphical models, are reported in Kyono (2010).

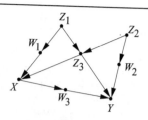

FIGURE 5.6. A Markovian model illustrating d-separation. Error terms are assumed mutually independent and not shown explicitly.

If the model is Markovian (i.e., acyclic with uncorrelated errors), then the d-separation conditions are the *only* testable implications of the model. If the model contains correlated errors, additional constraints are imposed, called "dormant independence" (Shpitser & Pearl, 2008) or Verma's constraints (McDonald, 2002; Verma & Pearl, 1990), generated by missing links that would otherwise be identified (e.g., the missing link from Z to W in Figure 5.7). This means that traditional algebraic methods of recognizing "overidentified models," deriving "overidentifying restrictions" and determining "parameter identification" (Kenny & Milan, Chapter 9, this volume),[10] can be replaced by simple graphical conditions, advertised by nonadjacent variables in the model.

Equivalent Models

d-separation also defines conditions for model equivalence that are easily ascertained in the Markovian models (Verma & Pearl, 1990) as well as semi-Markovian models (Ali, Richardson, & Spirtes, 2009). These

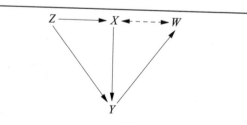

FIGURE 5.7. Showing discrepancy between Lee and Hershberger's replacement rule and d-separation, which forbids the replacement of $X \to Y$ by $X \leftrightarrow Y$.

mathematically proven conditions should amend the restricted (and error-prone) rules currently prevailing in SEM research (Kline, Chapter 7, this volume; Williams, Chapter 15, this volume), based primarily on the replacement rules of Lee and Hershberger (1990). The general necessary rule for any modification of a model to preserve equivalence is that the modification not create or destroy any *d*-separation condition in the modified graph.

For example, consider the model of Figure 5.7. According to the replacement criterion of Lee and Hershberger (1990) we can replace the arrow $X \rightarrow Y$ with a double-arrow edge $X \leftrightarrow Y$ (representing residual correlation) when all predictors (Z) of the effect variable (Y) are the same as those for the source variable (X) (see Hershberger, 2006). Unfortunately, the postreplacement model imposes a constraint, $r_{WZ \bullet Y} = 0$, that is not imposed by the prereplacement model. This can be seen from the fact that, conditioned on Y, the path $Z \rightarrow Y \leftarrow X \leftrightarrow W$ is unblocked and will becomes blocked if replaced by $Z \rightarrow Y \leftrightarrow X \leftrightarrow W$. The same applies to path $Z \rightarrow X \leftrightarrow W$, since Y would cease to be a descendant of X.

Identification Using Graphs: The Back-Door Criterion

Consider an observational study where we wish to find the effect of X on Y—for example, treatment on response—and assume that the factors deemed relevant to the problem are structured as in Figure 5.6; some of these factors may be unmeasurable, such as genetic trait or lifestyle; others are measurable, such as gender, age, and salary level. Using the terminology of section "The Logica of SEM," our problem is to determine whether the query $Q = P(y|do(x))$ is identifiable given the model and, if so, to derive an estimand $Q(P)$ to guide the estimation of Q.

This problem is typically solved by "adjustment," that is, selecting a subset of factors for measurement, so that comparison of treated versus untreated subjects having the same values of the selected factors gives the correct treatment effect in that subpopulation of subjects. Such a set of factors is called a "sufficient set" or "admissible set" for adjustment.

The following criterion, named "back-door" in Pearl (1993), provides a graphical method of selecting admissible sets of factors, and demonstrates that nonparametric queries such as $Q = P(y|do(x))$ can sometimes be identified with no knowledge of the functional form of the equations or the distributions of the latent variables in M.

Definition 4 (admissible sets—the back-door criterion)

A set S is admissible (or "sufficient") if two conditions hold:

1. *No element of S is a descendant of X.*
2. *The elements of S "block" all "back-door" paths from X to Y—namely, all paths that end with an arrow pointing to X.*

In this criterion, "blocking" is interpreted as in Definition 1. Based on this criterion we see, for example, in Figure 5.6 that the sets $\{Z_1, Z_2, Z_3\}$, $\{Z_1, Z_3\}$, $\{W_1, Z_3\}$, and $\{W_2, Z_3\}$ are each sufficient for adjustment because each blocks all back-door paths between X and Y. The set $\{Z_3\}$, however, is not sufficient for adjustment because it does not block the path $X \leftarrow W_1 \leftarrow Z_1 \rightarrow Z_3 \leftarrow Z_2 \rightarrow W_2 \rightarrow Y$.

The intuition behind the back-door criterion is as follows. The back-door paths in the diagram carry spurious associations from X to Y, while the paths directed along the arrows from X to Y carry causative associations. Blocking the former paths (by conditioning on S) ensures that the measured association between X and Y is purely causal, namely, it correctly represents the target quantity: the causal effect of X on Y. The reason for excluding descendants of X (e.g., W_3 or any of its descendants) and conditions for relaxing this restriction are given by Pearl (2009, pp. 338–341).

Identifying Parameters and Causal Effects

The back-door criterion provides a simple solution to many identification problems, in both linear and nonlinear models, and is summarized in the next theorem.

Theorem 1 (causal effects identification)

For any two disjoint sets of variables, X and Y in a causal diagram G, the causal effect of X on Y is given by

$$P(Y = y \mid do(X = x))$$
$$= \sum_s P(Y = y \mid X = x, S = s)P(S = s) \tag{5.8}$$

where S is any set of covariates satisfying the back-door condition of Definition 4.

Since all factors on the right-hand side of the equation are estimable (e.g., by regression) from preinterventional data, the causal effect can likewise be estimated from such data without bias.

In linear systems, identified causal effect expressions such as Equation 5.8 reduce to sums and products of partial regression coefficients. For example, if we wish to estimate the total effect τ_{XY} of X on Y in the linear version of Figure 5.6, we simply take the regression coefficient of Y on X, partialed on any sufficient set S, giving:

$$\tau_{XY} = r_{YX \bullet S} = r_{YX \bullet Z_1, Z_3} = r_{YX \bullet W_1, Z_3} = \cdots$$

Current SEM practices do not take advantage of this capability to decide identification graphically, prior to obtaining data, and to estimate the identified quantities directly, by partialling out sufficient sets (see Kenny & Milan, Chapter 9, this volume). Rather, the prevailing practice is either to engage in lengthy algebraic manipulations, or to identify the model in its entirety by running ML routines on noisy data and hoping for their convergence. This is unfortunate because the target quantity may often be identifiable when the model as a whole is not (see Pearl, 2009, p. 151, for examples). Moreover, estimation accuracy deteriorates when we allow noisy data of irrelevant variables to corrupt the estimation of the target quantity (McDonald, 2004). The back-door criterion enables us to focus the identification of target quantities on the relevant variables and extract an identifying estimand by inspection or through algorithmic routines (Kyono, 2010). We also note that when applied to linear models, all identification conditions are valid for feedback systems as well.

Parametric Identification in Linear SEM

Remarkably, a close cousin of the back-door criterion has resolved an agelong identification problem in linear SEMs: Under what conditions can a path coefficient β_{XY} be estimated by regression, and what variables should serve as the regressors? The answer is given by a criterion called "single-door" (Pearl, 2009, p. 150) which reads:

Corollary 1 (the single-door criterion)
Let β_{XY} be the structural coefficient labeling the arrow $X \rightarrow Y$ and let $r_{YX \bullet S}$ stand for the X coefficient (slope) in the regression of Y on X and S, namely, $r_{YX \bullet S} = \frac{\partial}{\partial x} E(Y|x,s)$. The equality $\beta_{XY} = r_{YX \bullet S}$ holds if

1. *the set S contains no descendant of Y and*
2. *S blocks all paths between X and Y, except the direct path $X \rightarrow Y$.*

In Figure 5.7, for example, β_{XY} equals $r_{YX \bullet Z}$, or the coefficient b_1 in the regression $Y = b_1 X + b_2 Z + \varepsilon$, while β_{YW}, labeling the arrow $Y \rightarrow W$, is equal to $r_{WY \bullet XZ}$. Note that regressing W on Y and X alone is insufficient, for it would leave the path $Y \leftarrow Z \rightarrow X \leftrightarrow W$ unblocked. In a similar fashion we obtain $\beta_{ZY} = r_{YZ \bullet X}$ and $\beta_{ZX} = r_{ZX}$.

If no set S can be found that satisfies the conditions of Corollary 1 then β_{XY} cannot be reduced to a single regression coefficient, and other identification techniques may be invoked, for example, instrumental variables (Brito & Pearl, 2002a).

Recognizing Instrumental Variables

Use of instrumental variables is one of the oldest identification technique devised for linear systems (Wright, 1928). The method relies on finding a variable Z that is correlated with X and is deemed uncorrelated with the error term in an equation (see Pearl, 2009, pp. 242–248, for formal definition). While no statistical test can certify a variable as instrument, the d-separation criterion permits us to identify such variables in the causal graph, and use them to identify parameters that do not satisfy the condition of Corollary 1. Moreover, the graph also shows us how to turn variables into instruments when none exists. In Figure 5.6, for example, Z_1 is not an instrumental variable for the effect of Z_3 on Y because there is a directed path from Z_3 to Y, via W_1 and X. Controlling for X will not remedy the situation because X being a descendant of Z_3 would unblock the path $Z_1 \rightarrow Z_3 \leftarrow Z_2 \rightarrow W_2 \rightarrow Y$. However, controlling for W_1 will render Z_1 a legitimate instrumental variable, since all paths connecting Z_1 to Y would go through Z_3.

The general criterion is given by the following theorem.

Theorem 2 (identification using instrumental variables)
Let β_{XY} stand for the path coefficient assigned to the arrow $X \rightarrow Y$ in a causal graph G. Parameter β_{XY} is identified if there exists a pair (Z, W), where Z is a single node in G (not excluding $Z = X$), and W is a (possibly empty) set of nodes in G, such that:

1. *W consists of nondescendants of Y,*

2. *W d-separates Z from Y in the graph G_{XY} formed by removing $X \rightarrow Y$ from G,*

3. *Z and X are d-connected, given W, in GXY.*

Moreover, the estimand induced by the pair (Z, W) is given by

$$\beta_{XY} = \frac{cov(Y, Z \mid W)}{cov(X, Z \mid W)}$$

Additional identification conditions for linear models are given in Pearl (2009, Chap. 5), McDonald (2002, 2004), and Brito and Pearl (2002a, 2002b) and implemented in Kyono (2010). For example, a sufficient model-identification condition resulting from these techniques is the "non-bow rule" (Brito & Pearl, 2002b), that is, that any pair of variables be connected by at most one type of edge. Accordingly, one can add a bidirected arc between any two nonadjacent variables in Figure 5.6 and still be able to identify all model parameters.[11] In nonparametric models, instrumental variables carry the unique (and rarely utilized) capability of detecting residual (uncontrolled) bias, by comparing $P(y \mid x, z, w)$ and $P(y \mid x, w)$. Complete graphical criteria for a effect identification in nonparametric models is developed in Tian and Pearl (2002) and Shpitser and Pearl (2006a).

Mediation: Direct and Indirect Effects

Decomposing Effects, Aims, and Challenges

The decomposition of effects into their direct and indirect components carries theoretical scientific importance, for it tells us "how nature works" and, therefore, enables us to predict behavior under a rich variety of conditions and interventions. For example, an investigator may be interested in assessing the extent to which the effect of a given variable can be reduced by weakening an intermediate process standing between that variable and the outcome (Pearl, 2013).

Structural equation models provide a natural language for analyzing path-specific effects and, indeed, considerable literature on direct, indirect, and total effects has been authored by SEM researchers (Bollen, 1989), for both recursive and nonrecursive models. This analysis usually involves sums of powers of coefficient matrices, where each matrix represents the path coefficients associated with the structural equations.

Yet despite its ubiquity, the analysis of mediation has long been a thorny issue in the social and behavioral sciences (Baron & Kenny, 1986; MacKinnon, 2008), pri-

marily because the distinction between causal parameters and their regressional interpretations were often conflated, as in Holland (1995) and Sobel (2008). The difficulties were further amplified in nonlinear models, where sums and products are no longer applicable. As demands grew to tackle problems involving categorical variables and nonlinear interactions, researchers could no longer define direct and indirect effects in terms of structural or regressional coefficients, and all attempts to extend the linear paradigms of effect decomposition to nonlinear systems produced distorted results (MacKinnon, Lockwood, Brown, Wang, & Hoffman, 2007). The counterfactual reading of structural equations (Equation 5.6) enables us to redefine and analyze direct and indirect effects from first principles, uncommitted to distributional assumptions or a particular parametric form of the equations.

Direct Effects

Conceptually, we can define the direct effect $DE_{x,x'}(Y)$[12] as the expected change in Y induced by changing X from x to x' while keeping all mediating factors constant at whatever value they *would have obtained* under $do(x)$ (Pearl, 2001; Robins & Greenland, 1992). Accordingly, Pearl defined direct effect using counterfactual notation:

$$DE_{x,x'}(Y) = E(Y_{x',Z_x}) - E(Y_x) \tag{5.9}$$

Here, Y_{x',Z_x} represents the value that Y would attain under the operation of setting X to x' and, simultaneously, setting Z to whatever value it would have obtained under the setting X = x. Given certain assumptions of "no confounding," it is possible to show (Pearl, 2001) that the direct effect can be reduced to a *do*-expression:

$$DE_{x,x'}(Y) = \sum_{zw} [E(Y \mid do(x', z), w) \\ - E(Y \mid do(x, z), w)] P(z \mid do(x), w) P(w) \tag{5.10}$$

where W satisfies the back-door criterion relative to both $X \rightarrow Z$ and $(X, Z) \rightarrow Y$.

In particular, Equation 5.10 is both valid and identifiable in Markovian models (i.e., no unobserved confounders) where each term on the right can be reduced to a "*do*-free" expression using Equation 5.8 and then estimated by regression.

For example, for the model in Figure 5.8(b), Equation 5.10 reads

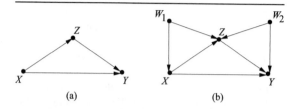

FIGURE 5.8. A generic model depicting mediation through Z (a) with no confounders and (b) with two confounders, W_1 and W_2.

$$DE_{x,x'}(Y) = \sum_z \sum_{w_2} P(w_2)[E(Y \mid x',z,w_2))$$
$$-E(Y \mid x,z,w_2))]\sum_{w_1} P(z \mid x,w_1,w_2)P(w_1) \quad \textbf{(5.11)}$$

while for the confounding-free model of Figure 5.8(a) we have

$$DE_{x,x'}(Y) = \sum_z [E(Y \mid x',z) - E(Y \mid x,z)]P(z \mid x) \quad \textbf{(5.12)}$$

Both Equations 5.11 and 5.12 can be estimated by a two-step regression.

Indirect Effects

Remarkably, the definition of the direct effect (Equation 5.9) can be turned around and provide an operational definition for the *indirect effect* (IE)—a concept shrouded in mystery and controversy because it is impossible, by controlling any of the variables in the model, to disable the direct link from X to Y, so as to let X influence Y solely via indirect paths.

The *IE* of the transition from x to x' is defined as the expected change in Y affected by holding X constant, at $X = x$, and changing Z to whatever value it would have attained had X been set to $X = x'$. Formally, this reads

$$IE_{x,x'}(Y) \triangleq E[(Y_{x,Z_{x'}}) - E(Y_x)] \quad \textbf{(5.13)}$$

which is almost identical to the direct effect (Equation 5.9) save for exchanging x and x' in the first term (Pearl, 2001).

Indeed, it can be shown that, in general, the total effect (*TE*) of a transition is equal to the *difference* between the *DE* of that transition and the *IE* of the reverse transition. Formally,

$$TE_{x,x'}(Y) \triangleq E(Y_{x'} - Y_x) = DE_{x,x'}(Y) - IE_{x',x}(Y) \quad \textbf{(5.14)}$$

In linear systems, where reversal of transitions amounts to negating the signs of their effects, we have the standard additive formula

$$TE_{x,x'}(Y) = DE_{x,x'}(Y) + IE_{x,x'}(Y) \quad \textbf{(5.15)}$$

Since each term above is based on an independent operational definition, this equality constitutes a formal justification for the additive formula used routinely in linear systems.

The Mediation Formula: A Simple Solution to a Thorny Problem

This subsection demonstrates how the solution provided in equations (12) and (15) can be applied in assessing mediation effects in nonlinear models. We will use the simple mediation model of Figure 5.8(a), where all error terms (not shown explicitly) are assumed to be mutually independent, with the understanding that adjustment for appropriate sets of covariates W may be necessary to achieve this independence (as in Equation 5.11) and that integrals should replace summations when dealing with continuous variables (Imai, Keele, & Yamamoto, 2010).

Combining Equations 5.12 and 5.14, the expression for the *IE* becomes

$$IE_{x,x'}(Y) = \sum_z E(Y \mid x,z)[P(z \mid x') - P(z \mid x)] \quad \textbf{(5.16)}$$

which provides a general formula for mediation effects, applicable to any nonlinear system, any distribution (of U), and any type of variables. Moreover, the formula is readily estimable by regression. Owing to its generality and ubiquity, I have referred to this expression as the "mediation formula" (Pearl, 2009, 2012, 2013).

The mediation formula represents the average increase in the outcome Y that the transition from $X = x$ to $X = x'$ is expected to produce absent any direct effect of X on Y. Though based on solid causal principles, it embodies no causal assumption other than the generic mediation structure of Figure 5.8(a). When the outcome Y is binary (e.g., recovery, or hiring) the ratio $(1 - IE/TE)$ represents the fraction of responding individuals that is *owed* to direct paths, while $(1 - DE/TE)$ represents the fraction *owed* to Z-mediated paths.

The mediation formula tells us that *IE* depends only on the expectation of the counterfactual Y_{xz}, not on its functional form $f_Y(x, z, u_Y)$ or its distribution $P(Y_{xz} = y)$. It calls, therefore, for a two-step regression, which, in principle, can be performed nonparametrically. In the first step we regress Y on X and Z, and obtain the estimate

$$g(x, z) = E(Y|x, z) \qquad (5.17)$$

for every (x, z) cell. In the second step we fix x and regard $g(x, z)$ as a function $g_x(z)$ of Z. We now estimate the conditional expectation of $g_x(z)$, conditional on $X = x'$ and $X = x$, respectively, and take the difference

$$IE_{x,x'}(Y) = E_{Z|X}[g_x(z)|x'] - E_{Z|X}[g_x(z)|x] \qquad (5.18)$$

Nonparametric estimation is not always practical. When Z consists of a vector of several mediators, the dimensionality of the problem might prohibit the estimation of $E(Y|x, z)$ for every (x, z) cell, and the need arises to use parametric approximation. We can then choose any convenient parametric form for $E(Y|x, z)$ (e.g., linear, logit, probit), estimate the parameters separately (e.g., by regression or maximum likelihood methods), insert the parametric approximation into Equation 5.16, and estimate its two conditional expectations (over z) to get the mediated effect (Vander-Weele, 2009).

Let us examine what the mediation formula yields when applied to the linear version of Figure 5.8(a), which reads

$$\begin{aligned} x &= u_X \\ z &= b_0 + \beta x + u_Z \qquad (5.19) \\ y &= c_0 + \alpha x + \gamma z + u_Y \end{aligned}$$

with u_X, u_Y, and u_Z uncorrelated, zero-mean error terms. Computing the conditional expectation in Equation 5.16 gives

$$E(Y|x, z) = E(c_0 + \alpha x + \gamma z + u_Y) = c_0 + \alpha x + \gamma z$$

and yields

$$\begin{aligned} IE_{x,x'}(Y) &= \sum_z (\alpha x + \gamma z)[P(z \mid x') - P(z \mid x)] \\ &= \gamma[E(Z \mid x') - E(Z \mid x)] \qquad (5.20) \\ &= (x' - x)(\beta\gamma) \qquad (5.21) \\ &= (x' - x)(\tau - \alpha) \qquad (5.22) \end{aligned}$$

where τ is the slope of the total effect;

$$\tau = (E(Y|x') - E(Y|x))/(x' - x) = \alpha + \beta\gamma$$

We thus obtained the standard expressions for indirect effects in linear systems, which can be estimated either as a difference $\tau - \alpha$ of two regression coefficients (Equation 5.22) or as a product $\beta\gamma$ of two regression coefficients (Equation 5.21) (see MacKinnon et al., 2007). These two strategies do not generalize to nonlinear systems; direct application of Equation 5.16 is necessary Pearl (2010a).

To understand the difficulty, assume that the correct model behind the data contains a product term δxz added to Equation 5.19, giving

$$y = c_0 + \alpha x + \gamma z + \delta xz + u_Y$$

Further assume that we correctly account for this added term and, through sophisticated regression analysis, we obtain accurate estimates of all parameters in the model. It is still not clear what combinations of parameters measure the direct and indirect effects of X on Y, or, more specifically, how to assess the fraction of the total effect that is *explained* by mediation and the fraction that is *owed* to mediation. In linear analysis, the former fraction is captured by the product $\beta\gamma/\tau$ (Equation 5.21), the latter by the difference $(\tau - \alpha)/\tau$ (Equation 5.22), and the two quantities coincide. In the presence of interaction, however, each fraction demands a separate analysis, as dictated by the mediation formula.

To witness, substituting the nonlinear equation in Equations 5.12, 5.15, and 5.16, and assuming $x = 0$ and $x' = 1$, yields the following effect decomposition:

$$\begin{aligned} DE &= \alpha + b_0\delta \\ IE &= \beta\gamma \\ TE &= \alpha + b_0\delta + \beta(\gamma + \delta) \\ &= DE + IE + \beta\gamma. \end{aligned}$$

We therefore conclude that the portion of output change for which mediation would be *sufficient* is

$$IE = \beta\gamma$$

while the portion for which mediation would be *necessary* is

$$TE - DE = \beta\gamma + \beta\delta$$

We note that, due to interaction, a direct effect can be sustained even when the parameter a vanishes and, moreover, a total effect can be sustained even when both the direct and indirect effects vanish. This illustrates that estimating parameters in isolation tells us little about the effect of mediation and, more generally, mediation and moderation are intertwined and must be assessed jointly.

If the policy evaluated aims to prevent the outcome Y by ways of weakening the mediating pathways, the target of analysis should be the difference $TE - DE$, which measures the highest prevention potential of any such policy. If, on the other hand, the policy aims to prevent the outcome by weakening the direct pathway, the target of analysis should shift to IE, for $TE - IE$ measures the highest preventive potential of this type of policies.

The main power of the mediation formula shines in studies involving categorical variables, especially when we have no parametric model of the data generating process. To illustrate, consider the case where all variables are binary, still allowing for arbitrary interactions and arbitrary distributions of all processes. The low dimensionality of the binary case permits both a nonparametric solution and an explicit demonstration of how mediation can be estimated directly from the data. Generalizations to multivalued outcomes are straightforward.

Assume that the model of Figure 5.8(a) is valid and that the observed data are given by Table 5.3. The factors $E(Y|x, z)$ and $P(Z|x)$ can be readily estimated as shown in the two right-most columns of Table 5.3 and, when substituted in Equations 5.12, 5.15, and 5.16, yield

$$DE = (g_{10} - g_{00})(1 - h_0) + (g_{11} - g_{01})h_0 \tag{5.23}$$
$$IE = (h_1 - h_0)(g_{01} - g_{00}) \tag{5.24}$$
$$TE = g_{11}h_1 + g_{10}(1 - h_1) - [g_{01}h_0 + g_{00}(1 - h_0)] \tag{5.25}$$

We see that logistic or probit regression is not necessary; simple arithmetic operations suffice to provide a general solution for any conceivable data set, regardless of the data-generating process.

Numerical Example

To anchor these formulas in a concrete example, let us assume that $X = 1$ stands for a drug treatment, $Y = 1$ for recovery, and $Z = 1$ for the presence of a certain enzyme in a patient's blood that appears to be stimulated by the treatment. Assume further that the data described in Tables 5.4 and 5.5 were obtained in a randomized clinical trial and that our research question is the extent to which Z mediates the action of X on Y or, more concretely, the extent to which the drug's effectiveness depends on its ability to enhance enzyme secretion.

Substituting this data into Equations 5.23–5.25 yields

$$DE = (0.40 - 0.20)(1 - 0.40) + (0.80 - 0.30)0.40 = 0.32$$
$$IE = (0.75 - 0.40)(0.30 - 0.20) = 0.035$$
$$TE = 0.80 \times 0.75 + 0.40 \times 0.25$$
$$\quad - (0.30 \times 0.40 + 0.20 \times 0.60) = 0.46$$

$$IE/TE = 0.07 \qquad DE/TE = 0.696 \qquad 1 - DE/TE = 0.304$$

TABLE 5.3. Computing the Mediation Formula for the Model in Figure 5.8(a), with X, Y, Z Binary

Number of samples	X	Z	Y	$E(Y\|x, z) = g_{xz}$	$E(Z\|x) = h_x$
n_1	0	0	0	$\dfrac{n_2}{n_1 + n_2} = g_{00}$	
n_2	0	0	1		$\dfrac{n_3 + n_4}{n_1 + n_2 + n_3 + n_4} = h_0$
n_3	0	1	0	$\dfrac{n_4}{n_3 + n_4} = g_{01}$	
n_4	0	1	1		
n_5	1	0	0	$\dfrac{n_6}{n_5 + n_6} = g_{10}$	
n_6	1	0	1		$\dfrac{n_7 + n_8}{n_5 + n_6 + n_7 + n_8} = h_1$
n_7	1	1	0	$\dfrac{n_8}{n_7 + n_8} = g_{11}$	
n_8	1	1	1		

TABLE 5.4. The Effect of Drug (X) and Enzyme (Z) on Cure Rate

Treatment X	Enzyme present Z	Percentage cured $g_{xz} = E(Y \mid x, z)$
Yes	Yes	$g_{11} = 80\%$
Yes	No	$g_{10} = 40\%$
No	Yes	$g_{01} = 30\%$
No	No	$g_{00} = 20\%$

TABLE 5.5. The Effect of Drug (X) on Production of Enzyme (Z)

Treatment X	Percentage with Z present
No	$h_0 = 40\%$
Yes	$h_1 = 75\%$

We conclude that 30.4% of all recoveries is owed to the capacity of the treatment to enhance the secretion of the enzyme, while only 7% of recoveries would be sustained by enzyme enhancement alone. The policy implication of such a study would be that efforts to develop a cheaper drug, identical to the one studied but lacking the potential to stimulate enzyme secretion, would face a reduction of 30.4% in recovery cases. More decisively, proposals to substitute the drug with one that merely mimics its stimulant action on Z but has no direct effect on Y are bound for failure; the drug evidently has a beneficial effect on recovery that is independent of, though enhanced by, enzyme stimulation.

In comparing these results to those produced by conventional mediation analyses, note that conventional methods do not define direct and indirect effects in a setting where the underlying process is unknown. MacKinnon (2008, Chap. 11), for example, analyzes categorical data using logistic and probit regressions, and constructs effect measures using products and differences of the parameters in those regressional forms. This strategy is not compatible with the causal interpretation of effect measures, even when the parameters are precisely known; IE and DE may be extremely complicated functions of those regression coefficients (Pearl, 2012). Fortunately, those coefficients need not be estimated at all; effect measures can be estimated directly from the data, circumventing the parametric analysis altogether, as shown in Equations 5.23–5.25.

Attempts to extend the difference and product heuristics to nonparametric analysis have encountered ambiguities that conventional analysis fails to resolve.

The product-of-coefficients heuristic advises us to multiply the unit effect of X on Z

$$C_\beta = E(Z \mid X = 1) - E(Z \mid X = 0) = h_1 - h_0$$

by the unit effect of Z on Y given X,

$$C_\gamma = E(Y \mid X = x, Z = 1) - E(Y \mid X = x, Z = 0) = g_{x1} - g_{x0}$$

but does not specify on what value we should condition X. Equation 5.24 resolves this ambiguity by determining that C_γ should be conditioned on $X = 0$; only then would the product $C_\beta C_\gamma$ yield the correct mediation measure, IE.

The difference-in-coefficients heuristic instructs us to estimate the direct effect coefficient

$$C_\alpha = E(Y \mid X = 1, Z = z) - E(Y \mid X = 0, Z = z) = g_{1z} - g_{0z}$$

and subtract it from the TE, but does not specify on what value we should condition Z. Equation 5.23 determines that the correct way of estimating C_α would be to condition on both $Z = 0$ and $Z = 1$, and take their weighted average, with $h_0 = P(Z = 1 \mid X = 0)$ serving as the weighting function.

To summarize, the mediation formula dictates that, in calculating IE, we should condition on both $Z = 1$ and $Z = 0$ and average while, in calculating DE, we should condition on only one value, $X = 0$, and no average need be taken.

The difference and product heuristics are both legitimate, with each seeking a different effect measure. The difference heuristics, leading to $TE - DE$, seek to measure the percentage of units for which mediation was *necessary*. The product heuristics, on the other hand, leading to IE, seek to estimate the percentage of units for which mediation was *sufficient*. The former informs policies aiming to modify the direct pathway, while the latter informs those aiming to modify mediating pathways.

In addition to providing causally sound estimates for mediation effects, the mediation formula also enables researchers to evaluate analytically the effectiveness of various parametric specifications relative to any assumed model. This type of analytical "sensitivity analysis" has been used extensively in statistics for parameter estimation but could not be applied to mediation analysis, owing to the absence of an objective target quantity that captures the notion of indirect effect in both linear and nonlinear systems, free of parametric assumptions. The mediation formula of Equation 5.16 explicates this target quantity formally, and casts it in terms of estimable quantities. It has also been used by Imai and colleagues (2010) to examine the robustness of empirical findings to the possible existence of unmeasured confounders.

The derivation of the mediation formula was facilitated by taking seriously the graphical–counterfactual–structural symbiosis spawned by the surgical interpretation of counterfactuals (Equation 5.6). In contrast, when the mediation problem is approached from an exclusivist potential-outcome viewpoint, void of the structural guidance of Equation 5.6, counterintuitive definitions ensue, carrying the label "principal stratification" (Rubin, 2004), which are at variance with common understanding of direct and indirect effects (Pearl, 2011c). For example, the direct effect is definable only in units absent of indirect effects. This means that a grandfather would be deemed to have no direct effect on his grandson's behavior in a family where he has had some effect on the father. This precludes from the analysis all typical families, in which a father and a grandfather have simultaneous, complementary influences on children's upbringing. In linear systems, to take an even sharper example, the "principal strata direct effect" would be undefined whenever indirect paths exist from the cause to its effect. The emergence of such paradoxical conclusions underscores the wisdom, if not necessity of a symbiotic analysis, in which the counterfactual notation $Y_x(u)$ is governed by its structural definition, Equation 5.6.[13]

CONCLUSIONS

This chapter casts the methodology of SEM as a causal-inference engine that takes qualitative causal assumptions, data, and queries as inputs and produces quantitative causal claims, conditional on the input assumptions, together with data-fitness ratings to well-defined statistical tests.

Graphical encodings of the input assumption can also be used as efficient mathematical tools for identifying testable implications, deciding query identification, and generating estimable expressions for causal and counterfactual expressions. The logical equivalence of

the structural and potential-outcome frameworks was discussed and the advantages of a symbiotic approach were demonstrated by offering a simple solution to the mediation problem for models with categorical data.

An issue that was not discussed in this chapter is the perennial problem of external validity (Shadish, Cook, & Campbell, 2002), namely, the conditions under which causal conclusions from a study on one population can safely be modified and transported to another. This problem has recently received a formal treatment using nonparametric SEM, and has led to algorithmic criteria for deciding the legitimacy of such transport, as well as the way it ought to be calibrated (Pearl & Bareinboim, 2011).

Some researchers would naturally prefer a methodology in which claims are less sensitive to judgmental assumptions; unfortunately, no such methodology exists. The relationship between assumptions and claims is a universal one—namely, for every set A of assumptions (knowledge) there is a unique set of conclusions C that one can deduce from A given the data, regardless of the method used. The completeness results of Shpitser and Pearl (2006b) imply that SEM operates at the boundary of this universal relationship; no method can do better without strengthening the assumptions.

ACKNOWLEDGMENTS

This chapter has benefited from discussions with Elias Bareinboim, Peter Bentler, Ken Bollen, James Heckman, Jeffrey Hoyle, Marshall Joffe, David Kaplan, David Kenny, David MacKinnon, Rod McDonald, Stanley Mulaik, William Shadish, Leland Wilkinson, and Larry Williams, and was supported in part by grants from the National Institutes of Health (No. IROI LM009961-01), the National Science Foundation (Nos. IIS0914211 and IIS-1018922), and the Office of Naval Research (NO. NOOO-14-09-1-0665).

NOTES

1. A more comprehensive account of the history of SEM and its causal interpretations is given in Pearl (1998). Pearl (2009, pp. 368–374) devotes a section of his book *Causality* to advise SEM students on the causal reading of SEM and how to defend it against the skeptics.

2. This is important to emphasize in view of the often heard criticism that in SEM, one must start with a model in which all causal relations are presumed known, at least qualitatively. Other methods must rest on the same knowledge, though some tend to hide the assumptions under catchall terms such

as "ignorability" or "nonconfoundedness." When a priori knowledge is not available, the uncertainty can be represented in SEM by adding links with unspecified parameters.

3. Causal relationships among latent variables are assessed by treating their indicators as noisy measurement of the former (Bollen, 1989; Cai & Kuroki, 2008; Pearl, 2010b).

4. The reason for this fundamental limitation is that no death case can be tested twice, with and without treatment. For example, if we measure equal proportions of deaths in the treatment and control groups, we cannot tell how many death cases are actually attributable to the treatment itself; it is quite possible that many of those who died under treatment would be alive if untreated and, simultaneously, many of those who survived with treatment would have died if not treated.

5. Connections between structural equations and a restricted class of counterfactuals were first recognized by Simon and Rescher (1966). These were later generalized by Balke and Pearl (1995), using surgeries (Equation 5.6), thus permitting endogenous variables to serve as counterfactual antecedents. The "surgery definition" was used in Pearl (2000, p. 417) and defended in Pearl (2009, pp. 362–382).

6. This probability, written $P(Y_1 = 1 \mid X = 0, Y = 0)$, also known as the "probability of causation" (Pearl, 2009, Chap. 9), quantifies "causes of effect" as opposed to "effect of causes," and was excluded, prematurely I presume, from the province of potential outcome analysis (Holland, 1986).

7. Such tables are normally used to explain the philosophy behind the potential outcome framework (e.g., West & Thoemmes, 2010) in which Y_1 and Y_0 are taken as unexplained random variables. Here they are defined by, and derived from, a simple structural model.

8. In other words, a complete axiomization of structural counterfactuals in recursive systems consists of Equation 5.7 and a few nonessential details (Halpern, 1998).

9. See Hayduk et al. (2003), Mulaik (2009), and Pearl (2009, p. 335) for gentle introduction to d-separation.

10. The nomenclature "overidentifying restriction" is somewhat misleading, because a model may have many testable implications and none of its parameters identified. Likewise, the traditional algebraic distinction between "overidentified" and "just identified" parameters is usually misleading (see Pearl, 2004).

11. This rule subsumes Bollen's (1989, p. 95) "recursive rule," which forbids a bidirected arc between a variable and *any* of its ancestors.

12. Robins and Greenland (1992) called this notion of direct effect "Pure" while Pearl called it "Natural," denoted *NDE*, to be distinguished from the "controlled direct effect," which is specific to one level of the mediator Z. Here I delete the letter N from the acronyms of both the direct and indirect effect, and use *DE* and *IE*, respectively.

13. Such symbiosis is now standard in epidemiology research (Hafeman & Schwartz, 2009; Joffe & Green, 2009; Petersen, Sinisi, & van der Laan, 2006; Robins, 2001; VanderWeele, 2009; VanderWeele & Robins, 2007) and is making its way slowly toward the social and behavioral sciences (Imai et al., 2010; Morgan & Winship, 2007).

REFERENCES

Ali, R., Richardson, T., & Spirtes, P. (2009). Markov equivalence for ancestral graphs. *Annals of Statistics, 37,* 2808–2837.

Balke, A., & Pearl, J. (1995). Counterfactuals and policy analysis in structural models. In P. Besnard & S. Hanks (Eds.), *Uncertainty in artificial intelligence: Proceedings of the Eleventh Conference* (pp. 11–18). San Francisco: Morgan Kaufmann.

Baron, R., & Kenny, D. (1986). The moderator–mediator variable distinction in social psychological research: Conceptual, strategic, and statistical considerations. *Journal of Personality and Social Psychology, 51,* 1173–1182.

Baumrind, D. (1993). Specious causal attributions in social sciences: The reformulated stepping-stone theory of hero in use as exemplar. *Journal of Personality and Social Psychology, 45,* 1289–1298.

Berkson, J. (1946). Limitations of the application of fourfold table analysis to hospital data. *Biometrics Bulletin, 2,* 47–53.

Blalock, H. (1964). *Causal inferences in nonexperimental research.* Chapel Hill: University of North Carolina Press.

Bollen, K. (1989). *Structural equations with latent variables.* New York: Wiley.

Brito, C., & Pearl, J. (2002a). Generalized instrumental variables. In A. Darwiche & N. Friedman (Eds.), *Uncertainty in artificial intelligence, Proceedings of the Eighteenth Conference* (pp. 85–93). San Francisco: Morgan Kaufmann.

Brito, C., & Pearl, J. (2002b). A new identification condition for recursive models with correlated errors. *Journal of Structural Equation Modeling, 9,* 459–474.

Byrne, B. (2006). *Structural equation modeling with EQS: Basic concepts, applications, and programming* (2nd ed.). New York: Routledge.

Cai, Z., & Kuroki, M. (2008). On identifying total effects in the presence of latent variables and selection bias. In D. McAllester & P. Myllymäki (Eds.), *Uncertainty in artificial intelligence, Proceedings of the Twenty-Fourth Conference* (pp. 62–69). Arlington, VA: AUAI.

Chin, W. (1998). Commentary: Issues and opinion on structural equation modeling. *Management Information Systems Quarterly, 22,* 7–16.

Cliff, N. (1983). Some cautions concerning the application of causal modeling methods. *Multivariate Behavioral Research, 18,* 115–126.

Duncan, O. (1975). *Introduction to structural equation models.* New York: Academic Press.

Freedman, D. (1987). As others see us: A case study in path

analysis (with discussion). *Journal of Educational Statistics*, *12*, 101–223.

Galles, D., & Pearl, J. (1998). An axiomatic characterization of causal counterfactuals. *Foundation of Science, 3,* 151–182.

Haavelmo, T. (1943). The statistical implications of a system of simultaneous equations. *Econometrica, 11,* 1–12. Reprinted in 1995 in D. F. Hendry & M. S. Morgan (Eds.), *The foundations of econometric analysis* (pp. 477–490). Cambridge, UK: Cambridge University Press.

Hafeman, D., & Schwartz, S. (2009). Opening the black box: A motivation for the assessment of mediation. *International Journal of Epidemiology, 3,* 838–845.

Halpern, J. (1998). Axiomatizing causal reasoning. In G. Cooper & S. Moral (Eds.), *Uncertainty in artificial intelligence* (pp. 202–210). San Francisco: Morgan Kaufmann.

Hayduk, L., Cummings, G., Stratkotter, R., Nimmo, M., Grygoryev, K., Dosman, D., et al. (2003). Pearl's *d*-separation: One more step into causal thinking. *Structural Equation Modeling, 10,* 289–311.

Hershberger, S. L. (2006). The problem of equivalent structural models. In G. R. Hancock & R. O. Mueller (Eds.), *Structural equation modeling: A second course* (pp. 21–25). Greenwich, CT: Information Age.

Holland, P. (1986). Statistics and causal inference. *Journal of the American Statistical Association, 81,* 945–960.

Holland, P. (1988). Causal inference, path analysis, and recursive structural equations models. In C. Clogg (Ed.), *Sociological methodology* (pp. 449–484). Washington, DC: American Sociological Association.

Holland, P. (1995). Some reflections on Freedman's critiques. *Foundations of Science, 1,* 50–57.

Imai, K., Keele, L., & Yamamoto, T. (2010). Identification, inference, and sensitivity analysis for causal mediation effects. *Statistical Science, 25,* 51–71.

Imbens, G. (2010). An economist's perspective on Shadish (2010) and West and Thoemmes (2010). *Psychological Methods, 15,* 47–55.

Joffe, M., & Green, T. (2009). Related causal frameworks for surrogate outcomes. *Biometrics, 65,* 530–538.

Kelloway, E. (1998). *Using LISREL for structural equation modeling.* Thousand Oaks, CA: Sage.

Kline, R. B. (2011). *Principles and practice of structural equation modeling* (3rd ed.). New York: Guilford Press.

Koopmans, T. (1953). Identification problems in econometric model construction. In W. Hood & T. Koopmans (Eds.), *Studies in econometric method* (pp. 27–48). New York: Wiley.

Kyono, T. (2010). Commentator: A front-end user-interface module for graphical and structural equation modeling (Technical Report R-364). Master's thesis, Department of Computer Science, University of California, Los Angeles. Available at *ftp.cs.ucla.edu/pub/stat_ser/r364.pdf.*

Lee, S., & Hershberger, S. (1990). A simple rule for generat-

ing equivalent models in covariance structure modeling. *Multivariate Behavioral Research, 25,* 313–334 .

MacKinnon, D. (2008). *Introduction to statistical mediation analysis.* New York: Erlbaum.

MacKinnon, D., Lockwood, C., Brown, C., Wang, W., & Hoffman, J. (2007). The intermediate endpoint effect in logistic and probit regression. *Clinical Trials, 4,* 499–513.

McDonald, R. (2002). What can we learn from the path equations?: Identifiability constraints, equivalence. *Psychometrika, 67,* 225–249.

McDonald, R. (2004). The specific analysis of structural equation models. *Multivariate Behavioral Research, 39,* 687–713.

Morgan, S., & Winship, C. (2007). *Counterfactuals and causal inference: Methods and principles for social research.* New York: Cambridge University Press.

Mulaik, S. A. (2009). *Linear causal modeling with structural equations.* New York: CRC Press.

Muthén, B. (1987). Response to Freedman's critique of path analysis: Improve credibility by better methodological training. *Journal of Educational Statistics, 12,* 178–184.

Pearl, J. (1988). *Probabilistic reasoning in intelligent systems.* San Mateo, CA: Morgan Kaufmann.

Pearl, J. (1993). Comment: Graphical models, causality, and intervention. *Statistical Science, 8,* 266–269.

Pearl, J. (1998). Graphs, causality, and structural equation models. *Sociological Methods and Research, 27,* 226–284.

Pearl, J. (2000). *Causality: Models, reasoning, and inference.* New York: Cambridge University Press.

Pearl, J. (2001). Direct and indirect effects. In J. Breese & D. Koller (Eds.), *Uncertainty in artificial intelligence: Proceedings of the Seventeenth Conference* (pp. 411–420). San Francisco: Morgan Kaufmann.

Pearl, J. (2004). Robustness of causal claims. In M. Chickering & J. Halpern (Eds.), *Proceedings of the Twentieth Conference on Uncertainty in Artificial Intelligence* (pp. 446–453). Arlington, VA: AUAI Press. Available at *ftp. cs.ucla.edu/pub/stat_ser/r320-uai04.pdf.*

Pearl, J. (2009). *Causality: Models, reasoning, and inference* (2nd ed.). New York: Cambridge University Press.

Pearl, J. (2010a). An introduction to causal inference. *International Journal of Biostatistics, 6.* Available at *ftp.cs.ucla. edu/pub/stat_ser/r354-corrected-reprint.pdf.*

Pearl, J. (2010b). On measurement bias in causal inference. In P. Grünwald & P. Spirtes (Eds.), *Proceedings of the Twenty-Sixth Conference on Uncertainty in Artificial Intelligence* (pp. 425–432). Corvallis, OR: AUAI Press. Available at *ftp.cs.ucla.edu/pub/stat_ser/r357.pdf.*

Pearl, J. (2011). Principal stratification: A goal or a tool? *International Journal of Biostatistics, 7*(1), 20. Available at *ftp.cs.ucla.edu/pub/stat_ser/r382.pdf.*

Pearl, J. (2012). The mediation formula: A guide to the assessment of causal pathways in non-linear models. In C. Berzuini, P. Dawid, & L. Benardinelli (Eds.), *Causal inference: Statistical perspectives and applications* (pp. 151–179). Hoboken, NJ: Wiley.

Pearl, J. (2013). The causal mediation formula: A guide to the assessment of pathways and mechanisms. *Prevention Science, 13*, 426–436.

Pearl, J., & Bareinboim, E. (2011). Transportability of causal and statistical relations: A formal approach. In W. Burgard & D. Roth (Eds.), *Proceedings of the Twenty-Fifth Conference on Artificial Intelligence (AAAI-*11*)* (pp. 247–254). Menlo Park, CA: AAAI Press.

Petersen, M., Sinisi, S., & van der Laan, M. (2006). Estimation of direct causal effects. *Epidemiology, 17*, 276–284.

Robins, J. (2001). Data, design, and background knowledge in etiologic inference. *Epidemiology, 12*, 313–320.

Robins, J., & Greenland, S. (1992). Identifiability and exchangeability for direct and indirect effects. *Epidemiology, 3*, 143–155.

Rubin, D. (1974). Estimating causal effects of treatments in randomized and nonrandomized studies. *Journal of Educational Psychology, 66*, 688–701.

Rubin, D. (2004). Direct and indirect causal effects via potential outcomes. *Scandinavian Journal of Statistics, 31*, 161–170.

Shadish, W., Cook, T., & Campbell, D. (2002). *Experimental and quasi-experimental design for generalized causal inference*. Boston: Houghton Mifflin.

Shpitser, I., & Pearl, J. (2006a). Identification of joint interventional distributions in recursive semi-Markovian causal models. In Y. Gil & R. J. Mooney (Eds.), *Proceedings of the Twenty-First National Conference on Artificial Intelligence* (pp. 1219–1226). Menlo Park, CA: AAAI Press.

Shpitser, I., & Pearl, J. (2006b). Identification of conditional interventional distributions. In R. Dechter & T. Richardson (Eds.), *Proceedings of the Twenty-Second Conference on Uncertainty in Artificial Intelligence* (pp. 437–444). Corvallis, OR: AUAI Press.

Shpitser, I., & Pearl, J. (2008). Dormant independence. In D. Fox & C. P. Gomes (Eds.), *Proceedings of the Twenty-Third Conference on Artificial Intelligence* (pp. 1081–1087). Menlo Park, CA: AAAI Press.

Simon, H., & Rescher, N. (1966). Cause and counterfactual. *Philosophy and Science, 33*, 323–340.

Sobel, M. (1996). An introduction to causal inference. *Sociological Methods and Research, 24*, 353–379.

Sobel, M. (2008). Identification of causal parameters in randomized studies with mediating variables. *Journal of Educational and Behavioral Statistics, 33*, 230–231.

Sørensen, A. (1998). Theoretical mechanisms and the empirical study of social processes. In P. Hedström & R. Swedberg (Eds.), *Social mechanisms: An analytical approach to social theory* (pp. 238–266). Cambridge, MA: Cambridge University Press.

Stelzl, I. (1986). Changing a causal hypothesis without changing the fit: Some rules for generating equivalent path models. *Multivariate Behavioral Research, 21*, 309–331.

Tian, J., & Pearl, J. (2002). A general identification condition for causal effects. In R. Dechter, M. Kearns, & R. Sutton (Eds.), *Proceedings of the Eighteenth National Conference on Artificial Intelligence* (pp. 567–573). Menlo Park, CA: AAAI Press/MIT Press.

VanderWeele, T. (2009). Marginal structural models for the estimation of direct and indirect effects. *Epidemiology, 20*, 18–26.

VanderWeele, T., & Robins, J. (2007). Four types of effect modification: A classification based on directed acyclic graphs. *Epidemiology, 18*, 561–568.

Verma, T., & Pearl, J. (1990). Equivalence and synthesis of causal models. In P. P. Bonissone, M. Henrion, L. N. Kanal, & J. F. Lemmer (Eds.), *Proceedings of the Sixth Conference on Uncertainty in Artificial Intelligence* (pp. 220–227). Cambridge, UK: Cambridge University Press.

West, S., & Thoemmes, F. (2010). Campbell's and Rubin's perspectives on causal inference. *Psychological Methods, 15*, 18–37.

Wilkinson, L., the Task Force on Statistical Inference, and the APA Board of Scientific Affairs. (1999). Statistical methods in psychology journals: Guidelines and explanations. *American Psychologist, 54*, 594–604.

Wright, P. (1928). *The tariff on animal and vegetable oils.* New York: Macmillan.

Wright, S. (1921). Correlation and causation. *Journal of Agricultural Research, 20*, 557–585.

CHAPTER 6

Simulation Methods in Structural Equation Modeling

Deborah L. Bandalos
Phillip Gagné

Suppose that you are conducting a study in which you plan to use a new technique from within the family of structural equation modeling (SEM). You are aware that the technique is more complicated than those you have used before, and assume that a larger sample size may be needed. You have, however, been unable to find any guidelines regarding how much larger the sample should be. This scenario is indicative of the type of situation in which simulation studies, sometimes referred to as "Monte Carlo studies," might provide guidance to applied researchers. Simulation studies are those in which the researcher generates data using a computer in order to obtain a solution to a problem that is otherwise intractable. In the example scenario, interest is in determining how large a sample will be needed to obtain stable values of parameter estimates, standard errors, and/or fit indexes. To answer this question a simulation researcher might generate many samples at each of several different sample sizes (n), and note the degree to which parameter estimates, standard errors, and fit indexes vary across the set of samples at each value of n.

In this chapter we focus on the purposes of simulation studies, with an emphasis on how these studies can inform the work of applied researchers. We also point out the advantages and disadvantages of simulation studies. A brief overview of the design of simulation studies, including the choice of independent and dependent variables, data generation, and data analysis, is then presented, focusing on how researchers can evaluate the utility of such studies for their own research. Following this we present two examples of simulation studies taken from the literature, with an eye to how these could be used by applied researchers. Finally, we walk the reader through an example simulation study that we have created for the purposes of illustration. This chapter is not intended as a guide for conducting simulation studies. Such resources are already available (see, e.g., Bandalos, 2006; Fan, Felsővályi, Sivo, & Keenan, 2001; Gagné & Furlow, 2009; Muthén & Muthén, 2002), and interested readers are encouraged to consult these references.

PURPOSES OF SIMULATION STUDIES

In SEM, as in inferential statistics in general, inferences are often based on reference to statistical distributions such as the chi-square distribution, which models the behavior of the chi-square likelihood ratio test under the null hypothesis that a model fits perfectly in the population. As is well known, such statistical inferences are premised on a number of assumptions. In the context of the chi-square test of goodness of fit, these include multivariate normality of the observed data, independence of observations, linearity, and sufficient sample size. The latter assumption is necessary because the desirable properties of the chi-square test hold "asymptotically," that is, as the sample size approaches infinity. Although researchers will obviously not have sample sizes approaching infinity, the exact sample size needed to realize the statistic's asymptotic properties is difficult to assess because this depends on other features of the observed data (Chun & Shapiro, 2009; Curran, Bollen, Paxton, Kirby, & Chen, 2002; MacCallum, Widaman, Zhang, & Hong, 1999). If sample size is not sufficiently large, or if assumptions are violated, the tabled chi-square distribution is no longer an appropriate reference distribution for the test and cannot be used to determine p-values. In addition, violation of assumptions can result in bias in parameter estimates and/or standard errors. While the consequences of assumption violations are well known, the *degree* to which p-values, parameter estimates, and standard errors will be affected is difficult to determine for a given study because each study has its own idiosyncratic features.

This is where simulation studies come in. Such studies allow researchers to create data in which various assumptions have been violated in order to determine what effect such violations have on the study results. This is typically done by creating a population model with known parameter values and then generating numerous samples for each combination of violations. SEM solutions are then obtained from each sample; the results are saved into a file and analyzed to determine the effects of the violations. Essentially, simulation researchers create their own empirical sampling distributions that correspond to the conditions in which they are interested. For example, in a later section we use an illustration that investigates the effects of sample size, model size, loading magnitudes, and model misspecification on the values of fit indices for a confirmatory factor model.

In addition to studying the effects of assumption violations and small-sample behavior, simulation studies are commonly used for situations in which no statistical theory is available. For example, many common fit indexes in SEM, such as the root mean square residual, and incremental fit indexes, such as the Tucker–Lewis index (TLI) and comparative fit index (CFI), are not based on known statistical distributions but are ad hoc descriptive indexes. Because of this, values that are indicative of well or poorly fitting models cannot be derived statistically. Instead, guidance regarding acceptable values for these fit indexes has been developed through simulation studies, by creating empirical sampling distributions under different degrees of model misspecification and determining the values of the fit indexes that correspond to each. The well-known studies by Hu and Bentler (1998; 1999) and others (Fan & Sivo, 2007; Herzog, Boomsma, & Reinecke, 2007; Marsh, Hau, & Wen, 2004) exemplify this type of research. Finally, and perhaps most importantly, simulation studies make it possible to study the potential interactions of different assumption violations on the outcomes of interest.

Researchers who use SEM methods in their applied research but who do not conduct methodological research studies may wonder why they need to know about simulation methods. One reason is that the results of simulation studies are often at the core of our knowledge of SEM methods. For example, common guidelines, such as those regarding acceptable values for ad hoc fit indexes and requisite sample sizes, are derived from simulation studies. Researchers who use such findings to guide their own applications should therefore be familiar with the advantages and disadvantages of such studies, and should be able to evaluate their adequacy and rigor.

Researchers also commonly use SEM methods under nonoptimal conditions, such as with small sample sizes, non-normally distributed data, noncontinuous dependent variables, and so forth. Because the statistical properties of most SEM estimators do not necessarily hold under such conditions, researchers must turn to simulation research to support the validity of their inferences. These researchers may need to locate and evaluate simulation research supporting the use of SEM in conditions such as theirs, or even to conduct a small simulation study of their own. Thus, researchers working outside the periphery of conditions that are appropriate for the analysis of interest are more dependent on the results of simulation research than those with access to large sample sizes and normally distributed variables. Having said this, we would argue that virtually all applied researchers are confronted with suboptimal data at some time in their careers.

ADVANTAGES AND DISADVANTAGES OF SIMULATION STUDIES

As we noted in the previous section, the main advantage of simulation studies is that they allow for study of questions that are otherwise difficult, if not impossible, to answer analytically. Although a researcher conducting a study with non-normally distributed data might note that the chi-square value seems unreasonably high, he or she would have no way of determining whether a similar inflation of the chi-square would occur in another, similar study, or whether this was simply due to other idiosyncratic features of his or her data set. Simulation studies allow us to investigate the effects of assumption violations and other factors in a controlled environment because simulation researchers can generate the data to reflect any such factors that are of interest.

On the other hand, some disadvantages of simulation studies should be noted. First, because simulation studies are essentially experimental studies in which the variables of interest are manipulated, they are dependent on the representativeness of the conditions modeled. If these conditions are not similar to those found in real data, the usefulness of the study will be severely limited. This problem is exacerbated by the extreme complexity of most real-world data. In many cases, real data sets include complications such as hierarchically nested structures, data that are missing in a nonrandom fashion, and the existence of heterogeneous subgroups. Given that hundreds or even thousands of samples are typically generated for each combination of design factors, it is easy to see that the inclusion of all factors that might affect the behavior of the statistic under study could render the simulation study impossibly complex. Thus a balance must be found between the generalizability or external validity of the findings; the precision of the findings, represented by the number of samples generated for each combination of conditions; and practicality. Skrondal (2000) expressed the opinion that external validity is generally more important than precision. We agree that if such a choice need be made, as it often is, external validity often trumps precision because precise information about an irrelevant outcome tends to be less useful than somewhat imprecise information about a relevant outcome.

Researchers should also be aware of situations in which simulation studies are not appropriate. One of these situations is that in which an analytical solution is available for the problem. For example, it would be unnecessary to conduct a simulation study to determine the sampling stability of the sample mean because statistical theory (e.g., the Central Limit Theorem) provides the necessary solution analytically. We can therefore derive the appropriate standard error of the mean

for any given sample size by simply applying the appropriate formula. Having said this, there are situations in which simulation studies can be effectively used even when mathematical derivations for the problem being studied are available. One reason for this is the fact that theoretical properties of estimators do not always hold under real data conditions (small sample sizes, etc.). Research questions in simulation studies, however, should be based on statistical theory to the extent possible, indicating the point at which such theory is likely to break down.

Simulation studies are also dependent on proper generation of the data. It is extremely important that simulation researchers check the generated data carefully to verify that they actually reflect the characteristics that were intended. For example, simulation researchers often generate data that are non-normally distributed in order to study the effects of non-normality on fit indexes or standard errors. Moments (e.g., the mean, variance, skewness, and kurtosis) obtained from non-normal distributions, however, have larger standard errors than those obtained from normal distributions, as pointed out by Skrondal (2000). Higher-order moments such as the skewness and especially the kurtosis are particularly variable. This means that it is often difficult, if not impossible, to obtain the desired values at small sample sizes. In such cases, the simulation researcher should report the range of skewness and kurtosis values that were actually obtained.

Another issue related to data generation is the randomness of the data. Most data generation is based on a random seed, which is used as a starting point from which to begin the data generation process. It is important that different seeds be used for different cells of the study design. Failure to do so will result in dependencies among data in different conditions, thus violating the principle of randomness. For example, in our illustrative sample, different seeds were used to generate the data for each of the 63 cells of the design.

EXAMPLES OF SIMULATION STUDIES

We conducted a brief survey of articles using simulation methods in order to investigate methodological issues in SEM in social science journals over the last 10 years. We describe two of the studies here in order to illustrate the nature of simulation studies and the utility of their results. After each study we briefly outline the "take-home message" for applied researchers.

Fan and Fan (2005) conducted a simulation study to investigate the impact of number of measurement occasions and effect size on the power of latent growth models to detect linear growth. They also compared the power of latent growth modeling to that of repeated-measures analysis of variance (ANOVA), repeated-measures analysis via MANOVA (specifically Wilks' lambda), and the dependent-samples *t*-test. In this study the independent variables manipulated were the number of measurement occasions, the magnitude of the growth, and the sample size. The researchers used four different values (i.e., levels) for the number of measurement occasions: 3, 5, 7, and 9. They used six levels for magnitude of growth, defined as "the standardized mean difference between the last and the first measurements" (p. 126) and 10 different values of sample size. Fully crossing the levels of their three independent variables yielded 240 combinations of conditions to be investigated. They ran each combination 1,000 times (i.e., they used 1,000 replications), each time analyzing the data with a dependent-samples *t*-test (using the difference between the first and last measurement occasions), repeated-measures ANOVA, the multivariate version of repeated-measures analysis, and latent growth modeling.

Fan and Fan's (2005) dependent variable was the statistical power of each analysis. To compute statistical power, the number of times the analysis yielded a statistically significant result was divided by 1,000 (the number of replications). Each of the 240 combinations of conditions yielded four power results, one for latent growth modeling, one for the repeated-measures ANOVA, one for repeated-measures analysis via MANOVA, and one for the dependent-samples *t*-test. The researchers also obtained Type I error rates for those four analyses by simulating a seventh "null" effect size condition in which there was no growth.

Fan and Fan (2005) found that larger sample sizes yielded higher values of statistical power for latent growth modeling, but the number of measurement occasions did not seem to affect power. The four methods of analysis did, however, differ in terms of statistical power for sample sizes below 100 with relatively weak linear slopes. Under these conditions, latent growth modeling showed a notable advantage over repeated-measures ANOVA and the dependent-samples *t*-test; it also showed a clear advantage over the multivariate approach. With a medium effect size and a sample size of at least 100, power for all four analyses was comparable and very high.

For applied researchers contemplating a longitudinal study, Fan and Fan's (2005) research study contains a wealth of useful information. For example, if the researcher has to make a choice between including more participants or more measurement occasions, this study suggests that increases in the former would yield greater "bang for the buck" in terms of power, under the conditions investigated. Moreover, if the researchers planned to have a sample size of at least 100 and expected a medium to strong effect size, Fan and Fan's results suggest that any of the four methods could be used. However, researchers should make sure the other conditions included in Fan and Fan's study are similar to those anticipated in their own study. For example, the results of Fan and Fan's study may not hold for nonlinear growth models, so researchers anticipating such growth should be cautious in judging the relevance of that study to their own work.

Grewal, Cote, and Baumgartner (2004) used a simulation to investigate the impact of multicollinearity on Type II error, accuracy of parameter estimation, and accuracy of standard error estimation in latent variable path models. Their study had two parts. In the first part, the independent variables were degree of correlation between the latent exogenous variables (i.e., degree of multicollinearity), which had four levels, composite reliability of the factors (three levels), total explained variance in the endogenous latent variable (three levels), magnitudes of the path coefficients for the effects of the exogenous latent variables on the endogenous latent variable (two levels), and sample size (two levels), yielding 144 cells for the first part of the study ($4 \times 3 \times 3 \times 2 \times 2 = 144$). The second part of the study used a different path model and had three levels of multicollinearity, four levels of composite reliability, three levels of explained variance in the endogenous latent variables, and two levels of sample size, yielding 72 additional conditions, for a total of 216 cells in the study. For each cell, 200 replications were simulated.

Grewal and colleagues (2004) found that as degree of multicollinearity increased, parameter and standard error estimates for the paths leading from the correlated exogenous latent variables to the endogenous latent variables became more inaccurate, and Type II errors for those coefficients increased. The effect was more pronounced in the presence of low composite reliability, with the smaller sample size tested, and with low explained variance in the endogenous variables. Multicollinearity was less influential on the estimates and Type II error rates of the coefficients relating exogenous to other exogenous latent variables; for those coefficients, composite reliability and sometimes variance explained in the endogenous latent variables had a greater effect on estimation and Type II error rates than did multicollinearity.

The ramifications of Grewal and colleagues' (2004) results for applied researchers planning path analytic studies are clear. If the researcher is interested in effects of exogenous on endogenous variables (as is often the case) and anticipates high levels of multicollinearity, he or she should strive to include variables with high levels of reliability and to obtain a large sample, as these conditions will mitigate the deleterious effects of the collinearity. Although high levels of explained variance in the endogenous variables would also serve as a mitigating factor, this is rarely under the researcher's control (unless conducting a simulation study!). Thus, researchers would obtain more accurate results by investing their resources in obtaining better measures and more participants. As always, researchers conducting path analyses under conditions that differ from those studied by Grewal and colleagues., such as models with many more variables, models with interactive or other nonlinear effects, or a large amount of missing data, should apply the results of that study with caution.

EVALUATING SIMULATION STUDIES

Researchers using simulation studies to support their own use of SEM methods under nonoptimal conditions should be able to judge the merit of such studies. Essentially simulation studies are no different from other research studies, in that the research questions should be theoretically based; independent variables, and their levels, should be carefully chosen; the dependent variables should be relevant to the research question of interest; and the data analysis should provide an appropriate summary of the results. These topics will be briefly discussed in the next sections.

Research Questions in Simulation Studies

Determining a research question in Monte Carlo research is no different from doing so in other areas. Good research questions should address gaps in the literature and be designed to advance understanding in a particular area. In simulation studies, research questions are often developed in response to methodologi-

cal problems observed in applied research studies. As in applied studies, the literature review should serve to demonstrate why the study is needed. In simulation research this should include a discussion of why analytical studies would not be appropriate, as well as how the research questions are related to statistical theory and prior research.

Common Independent Variables in Simulation Studies

Although independent variables in simulations are as varied as the studies themselves, certain variables are much more common than others. Most common independent variables can be classified into two areas: characteristics of the data and characteristics of the model. Common data characteristics that are manipulated in simulation studies include sample size, level of measurement, and level of non-normality, while common model characteristics include model type, size, complexity, parameter values, and level of misspecification. Simulation researchers should discuss the reasoning behind their choices of both the independent variables in the study and their levels. The rationales may be based on statistical theory, prior research, or both. The important thing for applied researchers to note is whether a convincing rationale has been presented for the choice of variables and their levels. In addition, researchers should pay attention to the consistency of these variables and levels with the conditions they typically encounter in their own work. Even the most elegantly designed study may not be informative if the conditions included are not relevant to the type of data one typically encounters in practice.

Data Characteristics

Sample Size. Sample size is known to affect many fit statistics in SEM, most notably the values of the chi-square statistic, as well as the magnitude of parameter standard errors. It is therefore commonly varied in simulation studies in SEM. Powell and Schafer (2001) conducted a meta-analysis of simulation studies that investigated the robustness of the chi-square statistic in SEM and found that sample sizes varied from 25 to 9,600 in the studies they reviewed. In some cases interest is in determining the smallest sample size at which reasonably stable estimates or reasonably accurate chi-square values can be obtained. Researchers should keep in mind that fit statistics, parameter values, and standard errors will typically require different samples sizes for stability. Thus, information on the sample size needed to obtain stable parameter estimates cannot typically be generalized to other quantities. Sample size has also been shown to interact with other characteristics of the data, such as non-normality, and with the size and/or complexity of the model in its effects on values of fit statistics and standard errors. These variables should therefore be taken into consideration in evaluating levels of sample size.

Level of Measurement. Because many of the measures used in the social sciences are not at the interval level, applied researchers are often interested in the degree to which the inclusion of categorical or ordinal-level data will affect the results of SEM analyses. In simulation studies, such noncontinuous data are usually obtained through a process of generating data that are normally and continuously distributed, then categorizing these data by "cutting" the distribution into categories. For example, a normally distributed *z*-score could be dichotomized at the mean, resulting in 50% of the observations in each category. Alternatively, scores could be dichotomized at a value of 1.65, resulting in 5% in one category and 95% in the other. Thus, judicious choice of the point(s) at which the continuous distribution is cut can produce greater or lesser degrees of non-normality. Because SEM results are affected most severely by distributions with smaller numbers of categories, simulation research in this area commonly focuses on variables with two, three, or four categories. With five or more categories, the effects of categorization on parameter estimates and standard errors are generally negligible (Dolan, 1994). For more discussion of the analysis of categorical data, see Finney and DiStefano (2006).

Level of Non-Normality. Applied researchers often have data that are non-normally distributed, and for this reason the level of non-normality is commonly varied in simulation studies. Distributional type was included as an independent variable in 76% of the studies in a review conducted by Hoogland and Boomsma (1998) of 62 SEM simulations. There are several ways of generating data that are non-normally distributed. The most commonly used method in Powell and Schafer's (2001) meta-analysis was to generate normally distributed data, then categorize variables in such a way as to induce the desired degrees of skew and kurtosis, as discussed in the previous section. One drawback of this

approach is that the resulting data are necessarily categorized. If continuous data are desired, procedures described by Vale and Maurelli (1983) or Mattson (1997), among others, can be used to induce the required levels of non-normality.

One problem in generating data from populations with prespecified levels of skew and kurtosis is that these characteristics have high levels of sampling variability, as noted previously. Thus, although the desired levels may be obtained for the population, for any given sample they may deviate considerably from these values. This is especially true for kurtosis, and with higher levels of both skew and kurtosis. Finally, researchers who are evaluating the relevance of a simulation study to their own research should consider the degree to which the distributional characteristics of data used in the simulation are consistent with those in their own data.

Model Characteristics

As we stated in an earlier section, model characteristics commonly manipulated in simulation studies include model type, size, complexity, parameter values, and level of misspecification. We briefly discuss each of these in this section.

Model Type. As with data characteristics, applied researchers evaluating the relevance of simulation studies to their own research should carefully consider the degree to which the model characteristics included in the simulation are germane to those they typically encounter. Model characteristics commonly manipulated in simulation studies include the type, size, and level of complexity of the model, as well as the values of the parameters in the model. Before generating data, simulation researchers must decide what type of model to use. In their review of simulation studies in SEM, Hoogland and Boomsma (1998) found that the vast majority (89%) were based on confirmatory factor analysis (CFA) models. Applied researchers using other types of models should carefully consider whether findings based on CFA models would generalize to their own work. This is a particularly important consideration because results obtained from one type of model do not necessarily generalize to another type. For example, in a study by Nylund, Asparouhov, and Muthén (2007), the performance of statistics used to determine the number of latent classes varied considerably across latent class, growth mixture, and factor mixture models.

Once the general type of model(s) to be used (e.g., CFA model, path model, growth model) is determined, the simulation researcher must decide on a specific formulation of that model. There are two basic ways of doing this. One is to review the applied and methodological literature to determine model types and specifications that are commonly encountered in practice. One or more population models can then be constructed based on these. This method allows for model type, as well as model characteristics, to be manipulated experimentally. Because such models are artificial, however, they may not provide ideal representations of real-world conditions. For example, CFA models in simulation studies are often constructed with equal factor loadings or uncorrelated errors, but such conditions do not often occur with real data.

The second and probably less common way of obtaining a population model is to base it on an actual data set. In this method, the researcher would obtain an existing data set, either from his or her own research or from the literature, fit a model to it, and treat this as the population model. The advantage of using this method is that it is more likely to reflect real-world conditions and therefore to produce results that are generalizable to these conditions. The disadvantage is that the researcher may not be able to manipulate all model characteristics that may be of interest. This approach has been endorsed by MacCallum (2003) because it does not make the unrealistic assumption that a model fits exactly in the population.

Model Size. Another important consideration is the size of the model, typically operationalized as either the number of observed variables or the degrees of freedom. In their review of the literature, Hoogland and Boomsma (1998) found that the number of observed variables in SEM Monte Carlo studies ranged from 4 to 33, while Powell and Schafer (2001) found that model degrees of freedom ranged from 3 to 104 in simulations included in their meta-analysis. Model size thus appears to vary more broadly across simulation studies than does model type, and applied researchers should be able to find results that approximate their own situations more readily. Applied researchers may be aware that results obtained from small models do not always hold in larger models. For example, in an early study of asymptotically distribution-free (ADF) estimators in which only four observed variables were used, Muthén and Kaplan (1985) concluded that ADF-based chi-square estimates showed little bias. However, in a later study that included models with up to 15 variables (Muthén & Kaplan, 1992), these authors found that the bias of ADF chi-square tests increased with sample size.

Model Complexity. Closely related to model size is model complexity. The meaning of this term has varied in the literature and is sometimes used synonymously with model size. Here, we define "complex models" as those containing parameters such as cross-loading indicators, reciprocal paths, correlated disturbances or measurement error terms, or nonlinear effects (e.g., interactions or quadratic terms). However, Preacher (2006) suggests a more nuanced conceptualization of model complexity, arguing that, although the number of free parameters represents one aspect of model complexity, other features of a model also contribute to its complexity. Preacher defines model complexity in terms of a model's ability to fit different data patterns. That is, a more complex model can be thought of as one with a greater ability to adapt to differing data patterns. Thus, consideration of model complexity is important because it can play an important role in the fit of a model.

Another consideration regarding model complexity is that the inclusion of nonstandard parameters such as correlated disturbances or quadratic terms can render a model more difficult to estimate. Because of this, results obtained from simulations involving simpler models may not necessarily generalize to models with greater complexity. Applied researchers should be aware of this and, if the models with which they work are more complex than those in a simulation study of interest, results of the simulation should be interpreted with this in mind. Simulation results regarding parameter estimate bias, Type I errors, power, standard errors, and other outcomes might all be affected by the inclusion of complex parameters.

Model Parameter Values. After a simulation researcher has chosen the type and size of the model(s) to be studied, he or she must also decide upon appropriate population values for each parameter in the model(s). The values of parameter estimates can have a considerable influence on simulation outcomes such as power and parameter estimate bias, so applied researchers should determine whether values of parameter estimates chosen for a simulation are similar to those typically encountered in their own research. It may be, however, that applied researchers planning SEM studies are unable to forecast values for each parameter (this is, after all, often the reason for conducting the study). In such cases, researchers might obtain a general sense of possible values by examining other research in their area, or in related areas. Having said this, parameter values in simulation studies are typically varied along a fairly wide range. Given this, applied researchers consulting such studies should be able to obtain at least a rough estimate of the amount of parameter estimate bias or levels of power they might anticipate in their own studies.

Model Misspecification. It is not uncommon in applied studies to find that the model does not fit the observed data. Thus, applied researchers are often interested in the degree to which model misspecification might have affected their results. In simulation research the true generating model is known, for the simple reason that it was generated by the simulation researcher. In simulation research we are therefore in a position to know not only whether or not the model is misspecified, but also the degree to which this is the case. Simulation researchers can misspecify the generating model in various ways in order to determine the effects of the misspecification(s) on parameter estimates, goodness-of-fit measures, and parameter standard errors.

One problem with studies involving misspecification is that the degree of misspecification is often not quantified, making it difficult for applied researchers to gauge the extent to which results of such studies are relevant to their own work. Many simulation researchers simply categorize misspecifications as small, medium, or large, without indicating what this means with regard to the values of omitted parameters and/or fit index values. A more informative method of quantifying misspecification would be to estimate the power associated with the test of the omitted parameter, using methods such as those proposed by MacCallum, Browne, and Sugawara (1996). Alternatively, because the root mean square error of approximation (RMSEA) is a measure of model lack of fit per degree of freedom, this index could be used to quantify the degree of model misspecification. Such quantification not only provides more precise information but also allows simulation researchers to vary the level of misspecification systematically.

For applied researchers, using information regarding the possible effects of model misspecification to inform their own research can be a slippery slope. For one thing, applied researchers rarely have information about the type and level of misspecification in their model(s) until after the analysis has been completed. If such information were available before conducting the analyses, the researcher would presumably develop the model in such a way as to exclude the error(s). Thus, applied researchers can only use information about the possible effects of misspecifications in a post hoc fashion. For example, an applied researcher, upon obtaining unsatisfactory fit index values for a model, might examine residuals or modification indexes (MIs) in an attempt to determine the source(s) of misfit. The researcher could then consult relevant simulation research to determine whether such misspecifications had been studied and, if so, how the misspecifications affected parameter estimates and other outcomes in the simulation. These findings could be used to inform the applied researcher's interpretations of her/his own results.

Although such a procedure is not unreasonable, there are two fairly substantial limitations to such an approach. One is that tracing model misfit back to specific misspecifications through the use of modification indexes is fraught with danger (Kaplan, 1990; Kaplan & Wenger, 1993; MacCallum, 1986; MacCallum, Roznowski, & Necowitz, 1992; see also Chou & Huh, Chapter 14, this volume). The most basic problem with the use of MIs is that they do not necessarily flag the appropriate parameters. A related problem is that large MIs do not always correspond to large misspecifications. This is due to the fact that tests of model parameters have differential levels of power, depending on their correlations with other model parameters (Kaplan & Wenger, 1993). And, of course, changing one's model on the basis of MIs takes advantage of chance and may not provide replicable results. The second and more practical problem is that, even if a researcher were willing to rely on MIs, there are so many ways in which a model might be misspecified that it might prove difficult to find simulation results corresponding to the exact type and level of the misspecifications thought to be present in the applied researcher's study. Given these limitations, the applied researcher should clearly be very cautious in drawing any conclusions about the possible effects of model misspecification on his or her results. Researchers may, however, be able to obtain a rough idea of such effects if the misspecifications thought to be at play correspond closely to those in a relevant simulation study.

Estimation Method

Although maximum likelihood (ML) estimation is used most commonly in SEM studies, many other estimators are available. Perhaps the most popular of these alternative estimation methods are those that have been formulated to be less sensitive to the effects of non-normality or coarse categorization, such as the class of weighted least squares (WLS) estimators. Another approach to analyzing data that violate distributional assumptions has been offered by Satorra and Bentler (1988), and involves scaling the chi-square statistic and standard errors to adjust for the effects of non-normality. Many simulation studies have been conducted to examine the behavior of these and other estimation methods under conditions of non-normality, coarse categorization, and model misspecification (Beauducel & Herzberg, 2006; Finch, West, & MacKinnon, 1997; Fouladi, 2000; Green, Akey, Fleming, Herschberger, & Marquis, 1997; Herzog et al., 2007; Lei, 2009; Nevitt & Hancock, 2004), making estimation method another commonly seen independent variable in simulation research. In such studies, sample data are generated and then analyzed using two or more methods of estimation. Because the same data are analyzed using each of the methods, estimation method is a repeated factor in these studies.

These studies typically include a wide variety of conditions, thus having the potential to provide valuable information for applied researchers. Because methods of estimation differ in terms of their sensitivity to sample size, model size and complexity, level of non-normality, level of categorization, and model misspecification, applied researchers seeking to use simulation results to inform their own work should pay close attention to the match of these simulation conditions to those in their own research.

Common Dependent Variables in Simulation Studies

The primary focus in many simulation studies, and that of interest to most applied researchers, is on the effects of the independent variables on values of parameter estimates, standard errors, and/or fit indexes. These are discussed in turn in this section.

Parameter Estimates

Two aspects of parameter estimate behavior are typically of interest: bias and efficiency. "Bias" is a systematic difference between a sample estimate and the corresponding population value. "Efficiency" has to do with the sampling variability of a statistic, or its standard error. In general, we prefer statistics that vary least across samples.

Bias. Recall that in simulation research the population values are set by the researcher and samples are then generated from models with these population values. By their very nature, sample values exhibit random variation around the population values. In some cases, however, there is also a nonrandom component to such variation, and estimates of the value of a particular parameter are systematically higher or lower than the population value. This is known as "parameter estimate bias" and can occur if, for example, an important path has been omitted from the analysis. In simulation research the population values are known, which allows for relative parameter estimate bias to be quantified as the average deviation of the sample estimate from its population value, relative to the population value, or

$$\text{Bias}\left(\hat{\theta}_i\right) = \sum_{j=1}^{n_r} \left(\frac{\left(\hat{\theta}_{ij} - \theta_i\right)}{\theta_i} \right) / n_r \qquad (6.1)$$

where $\hat{\theta}_{ij}$ is the jth sample estimate of the ith population parameter θ_i, and n_r is the number of replications within the cell. This quantity can be multiplied by 100 to obtain percentage bias values. If certain parameter values, such as factor loadings or error variances, are affected in the same way by the study conditions, relative bias across a set of such parameters is sometimes calculated as a summary measure. If parameter estimates within a set (factor loadings, error variances, etc.) are affected differentially, however, bias should be reported separately for the individual parameters of interest.

There are varying guidelines in the literature for interpreting bias values. For example, Hoogland and Boomsma (1998) suggested that absolute values of Bias($\hat{\theta}_i$) less than .05 could be considered to represent a lack of bias. Muthén, Kaplan, and Hollis (1987) offered the more lenient criterion that bias of less than .10 to .15 might be considered negligible.

Efficiency. The efficiency, or variability, of parameter estimates is often measured by a quantity known as the *mean squared error* (*MSE*), calculated as the average deviation of the sample estimates from their population value, or

$$\frac{\sum_{j=1}^{n_r}\left(\hat{\theta}_{ij} - \theta_i\right)^2}{n_r - 1} \qquad (6.2)$$

In some applications, n_r in the denominator is replaced by $n_r - 1$, but with large samples, the difference will be negligible. When parameter estimates are biased the MSE represents a combination of the squared parameter estimate bias and the variance of the parameter estimate, and can be thought of as the overall accuracy of parameter estimation. If parameter estimates are unbiased, the MSE is a measure of the sampling variance of an estimate and its square root, known as the *root mean square error (RMSE)*, sometimes called the empirical standard error of the parameter. Efficiency or MSE values are sometimes compared across estimators to determine which estimator results in the smallest amount of sampling variability. Estimators that yield the smallest amount of sampling variability are generally preferred because they allow us to pinpoint the values of parameters within a smaller range of error.

Standard Errors

Although the primary focus in most applied and simulation research is on parameter estimates, the importance of accurate parameter standard errors should not be underestimated. Standard errors quantify the amount of sampling error in our parameter estimates and thus provide an estimate of the degree to which these estimates can be expected to vary from sample to sample. Relative standard error bias can be measured in a manner similar to parameter estimate bias as the deviation of each sample standard error from its population value, relative to the population value. Simulation researchers cannot set the population values of standard errors as they can with parameter values. However, recall that in simulation research large numbers of samples are created from which the simulation researcher obtains large numbers of sample parameter estimates. These parameters form an empirical sampling distribution of the parameter estimates, and the standard deviation of this distribution of parameter estimates can be taken as the population standard error. This quantity is also referred to as the "empirical standard error." Formally, standard error bias is calculated as

$$\text{Bias}\left(\widehat{SE}(\hat{\theta}_i)\right) = \sum_{j=1}^{n_r} \left(\frac{\widehat{SE}(\hat{\theta}_i)_j - SE(\hat{\theta}_i)}{SE(\hat{\theta}_i)} \right) / n_r \quad \text{(6.3)}$$

where $SE(\hat{\theta}_i)$ is the empirical standard error of parameter $\hat{\theta}_i$, and $\widehat{SE}(\hat{\theta}_i)_j$ is the estimated standard error of parameter $\hat{\theta}_i$ for the *j*th replication. Hoogland and

Boomsma (1998) have suggested that "acceptable" levels of bias not exceed 5% of the absolute value of Equation 6.3.

Fit Indexes

There are various ways in which the values of fit indexes can be studied in SEM simulations. Perhaps the simplest way is simply to compare average values of the fit indexes across conditions in the simulation. If the model under study is correctly specified, fit index values should approach their optimal values. Thus, use of this method allows researchers to determine the degree to which fit index values are affected by different combinations of study conditions. Because the chi-square statistic has a known sampling distribution in which the expected value is equal to the degrees of freedom, relative bias in that statistic can be expressed as

$$\text{Bias}\left(\hat{\chi}^2\right) = \sum_{j=1}^{n_r} \frac{\hat{\chi}_j^2 - df}{df} / n_r \quad \text{(6.4)}$$

where $\hat{\chi}_j^2$ is the estimated χ^2 value for the *j*th replication, and *df* is the model degrees of freedom.

Another method of assessing the degree to which fit indexes are affected by the study conditions is to calculate the number of samples for which the fit index value fell beyond a particular criterion. For the χ^2 statistic, this criterion is typically the critical value at the .05 or .01 level of significance. For statistics such as χ^2 that have known sampling distributions, this method would allow for calculation of the Type I error rate for correctly specified models, whereas for incorrectly specified models it would yield the level of power. A commonly used guideline for the interpretation of Type I error rates was offered by Bradley (1978), who suggested as a "liberal" criterion that the empirical Type I error rate lie within .5 of the nominal significance level alpha. For example, if alpha were set at .05, the obtained rejection rates should lie between .05 ± .5(.05) or between .025 and .075. Bradley's "stringent" criterion states that the Type I error rate should be within .1 of the nominal alpha value, or between .045 and .055 for an alpha level of .05. In the case of ad hoc fit indexes, it is more difficult to determine what the criterion value should be. In some studies researchers have adopted criteria from the literature, such as the values suggested by Hu and Bentler (1999). Comparison to such criterion values allows researchers to determine the number of samples in which the model would be "rejected" for each combination of study conditions.

Other Dependent Variables

Although parameter estimate bias and efficiency, standard error bias, and fit index values are common dependent variables in simulation studies, these are certainly not exhaustive of the many possibilities. Other choices for dependent variables in SEM simulation studies include power levels and Type II error rates, proportions of convergent and/or admissible solutions, and values or patterns of modification indexes.

DATA ANALYSIS FOR SIMULATION STUDIES

Simulation studies typically include several independent variables with several levels of each, so the amount of information to be conveyed in the results section can quickly become overwhelming. In many cases, simulation researchers rely exclusively on tables of descriptive statistics and graphical techniques to communicate the results of their studies. Although these methods can be very effective in summarizing the voluminous amounts of information that often result from simulation studies, many simulation researchers recommend that inferential statistical models be used to analyze simulation study results (Harwell, 1992, 1997; Hauck & Anderson, 1984; Hoaglin & Andrews, 1975; Skrondal, 2000). Skrondal provides three reasons for this recommendation. First, as he succinctly states, " 'Eyeballing' is an inefficient way of communicating the results" (p. 160). If the study design is complex, as most simulation study designs are, a large number of tables and/or figures is required to convey the results. Such a deluge of information is beyond our usual capacity to comprehend. Second, if there are interactions among the independent variables studied, inferential methods are typically needed to detect these. Few among us would be able to discern complicated interaction patterns from tables of descriptive statistics. Moreover, even if this were possible with the aid of graphical methods, it would be difficult, if not impossible, to gauge the relative magnitudes of the various effects. We would therefore be unable to answer basic questions, such as "Which variable or interaction has the greatest effect on the outcome of interest?" Finally, Skrondal's third reason for using inferential methods is that they result in greater precision in our effect estimates (given that the assumptions of

the inferential method are met). Interestingly, despite this rationale for their use, Harwell, Stone, Hsu, and Kirisci (1996) found that only about 7% of Monte Carlo studies published in the psychometric literature made use of inferential statistics. Unfortunately, this makes it difficult for applied researchers to appreciate the "take home" message in many simulation studies because it is often very difficult to determine the relative effect magnitudes of the variables studied using only graphs or tables.

One common argument against the use of inferential statistics in analyzing simulation study results is that the large number of replications typically used in these studies renders even the smallest of effects statistically significant. Although this is certainly true, the argument does not hold much water because in such situations we can simply rely on measures of effect size to gain perspective on both the practical significance and the relative strength of the various effects. Our recommendation for the analysis and presentation of simulation study results is that appropriate inferential methods be used to analyze the effects, but that interpretation be confined to those reaching a medium effect size. Those effects can then be further illustrated through the use of tables or graphical methods. Of course, researchers might choose different levels of the effect size for interpretational purposes, but the point is that high levels of statistical power due to large numbers of replications need not preclude the use of inferential methods.

Another argument against the use of inferential statistics in analyses of simulation data is that commonly used dependent variables, such as fit index values, may not meet the assumption of normality required for such procedures. For example, if misspecified models are the focus of study, such models will typically have high values of the χ^2 statistic, RMSEA, and standardized root mean square residual (SRMSR), and low values of indexes such as the CFI and TLI, resulting in skewed and leptokurtic values for these indexes. In such cases, researchers could transform index values using a log or other function.

A final point with regard to data analysis for simulation studies has to do with the treatment of nonconverged solutions. As readers may know, most SEM estimation methods are based on iterative techniques in which parameter estimates are successively changed until the fit function or other criterion reaches a minimum value, or converges. In some cases, convergence does not occur; in such cases an error message is typically printed, stating that any resulting output should not be trusted. Lack of convergence can be due to a poorly specified model, poor starting values, a lack of identification, or many other factors. In simulation research such issues are often the focus of study, and this can result in nonconverged solutions in some cells of the design. As noted previously, the degree to which nonconvergence occurs is often one of the dependent variables of interest in such studies. In addition to reporting such percentages, however, researchers must decide if they will generate other samples to replace those that did not converge, or base results only on the samples that do converge. Replacing the nonconverged samples with new ones has the advantage of maintaining a balanced design. However, in studies of extreme conditions, nonconvergence may be so pervasive that replacement of nonconvergent samples would be unrealistic. Most researchers agree, however, that nonconvergent solutions should be screened out before analyzing data from simulation studies.

EXAMPLE SIMULATION STUDY

In this last section we describe a small simulation study to illustrate how a researcher might go about conducting such an enterprise. Our demonstration simulation is a variation of a study by Fan and Sivo (2007) in which the authors investigated the impact on fit indexes of varying sample size, model size, model type, and degree of model misspecification. In that study, the authors used factorial ANOVA to determine the extent to which variation in the fit indexes across cells was attributable to the design facets that they manipulated, as quantified by η^2. They found that a few indexes varied appreciably as a function of sample size (e.g., normed fit index [NFI] and goodness-of-fit index [GFI]), others varied meaningfully as a function of model type (e.g., NFI and SRMSR), and still others varied as a function of model size (e.g., RMSEA and McDonald's centrality index). Of the indexes studied, Gamma Hat was the only one that varied solely as a function of misspecification. From these results, the authors concluded that for most fit indexes, the notion of a global cutoff for declaring a model as fitting the data needs to be revisited in favor of cutoffs that take other factors into consideration.

The demonstration we have prepared is a smaller study of fewer fit indexes than those investigated by Fan and Sivo (2007). Our interest was in extending that study by investigating the impact of loading magnitude and a different type of misspecification on values of the fit indexes. We used a confirmatory factor analysis model with three correlated factors, each of which had the same number of indicators and each of which had a correlation of .4 with the other factors. We manipulated four independent variables, three of which were manipulated by Fan and Sivo: We replaced their use of model type with magnitude of the factor loadings.

We included two different model sizes, 6 indicators per factor (p/f = 6) and 12 indicators per factor (p/f = 12). In the interest of keeping the demonstration small, we used only four sample sizes for p/f = 6 (100, 200, 500, and 1,000) and only three for p/f = 12 (200, 500, and 1,000). The sample size of 100 was not used with a p/f ratio of 12 because we regarded that sample size as insufficient for such a large model. A third independent variable in our study was magnitude of the factor loadings, which had three levels: all $\lambda = .7$; all $\lambda = .4$; for half of the loadings $\lambda = .7$, and for the other half, $\lambda = .4$.

Another independent variable in our study was the type of misspecification. The number of levels for this variable could quickly become unwieldy were we to consider all manner of potential misspecification even for a model as simple as ours. We chose to study two model misspecifications, as well as to include the true model as a baseline condition, for a total of three levels for this design factor. As in Fan and Sivo (2007), one of our misspecifications was to fit a one-factor model to the data, which clearly creates substantial misfit. Our second misspecification was one in which the correct number of factors was modeled, but the indicators were not all specified to load on the correct factors. Specifically, one-third of the indicators that should have been modeled to load only on Factor 1 were modeled as loading only on Factor 2. In this way, a different type of misfit is examined, and the number of affected loadings is held constant proportional to the number of indicators. The correctly specified and misplaced indicators models are shown in Figures 6.1a and 6.1b, respectively. To quantify model misspecification, a single replication was run for each of the 12 misspecified models (2 misspecifications × 2 values of p/f × 3 loading magnitudes), using 1,000,000 cases to obtain the "population" RMSEA; those values ranged from .023 to .144 ($M = .0679$, $SD = .0365$), meaning that the degree of misspecification was generally mild. For the one-factor misspecification, the RMSEA values ranged from .045 to .144 ($M = .0478$, $SD = .0208$), while for the misplaced indicators model, RMSEA ranged from .023 to .079 ($M = .0880$, $SD = .0391$). For both types of mis-

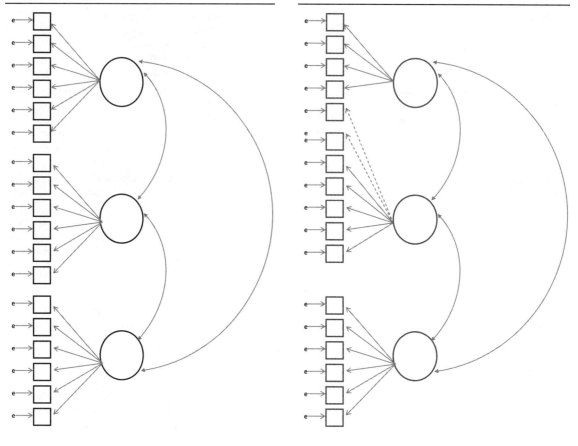

FIGURE 6.1A. True model.   **FIGURE 6.1B.** Model with misspecified factor loadings.

specification, RMSEA values increased as the loading magnitude increased, and they were larger with p/f = 6 than with p/f = 12.

The total number of cells was 63; 36 with p/f = 6 (4 sample sizes × 3 loading combinations × 3 degrees of misspecification) and 27 with p/f = 12 (3 sample sizes × 3 loading combinations × 3 degrees of misspecification). At the lower sample sizes, convergence was a minor issue, so we replaced nonconvergent solutions with new samples until 1,000 properly converged solutions were obtained for each cell. Within each replication, the data were generated using Statistical Analysis Software Interactive Matrix Language (SAS/IML, SAS v9.1; SAS Institute, 2008). Within SAS/IML we included code that caused IML to call the Mplus SEM program, which ran the analysis. We then used IML

commands to read in the Mplus output, strip off the desired output, and analyze the results within SAS. The SAS/IML and Mplus code, as well as a batch file to call Mplus and run the files for selected cells of the design, are included on the website materials for this chapter (*www.handbookofsem.com*). The fit indexes investigated were the model chi-square, TLI, CFI, RMSEA, and its 90% confidence interval, and SRMSR. The purpose of our study was to investigate the utility of commonly recommended guidelines for model fit based on these fit indices. Accordingly, we compared fit index values to the commonly used guidelines suggested by Hu and Bentler (1999). For evaluating model fit, a nonsignificant chi-square indicates good model fit, CFI and TLI indicate good model fit for values greater than .95, and SRMSR indicates good model fit at values below .08.

For the RMSEA, values above .05 indicate lack of a good model fit, values below .05 with a confidence interval including .05 are considered inconclusive, and values below .05 with a confidence interval entirely below .05 indicate good model fit.

Results

True Model

One way of checking to make sure a simulation study has been conducted properly is to evaluate the behavior of the statistic(s) of interest under conditions in which its behavior is known. The chi-square statistic and other fit indices we studied should reach their optimal values for a known true model. This proved to be the case for all indices. The chi-square statistic for correctly specified models was not statistically significant for any condition, with an average *p*-value across all conditions of .37.

The TLI and CFI both had mean values of .98 for correctly specified models across conditions, and the RMSEA averaged .01, with average confidence limits between .002 and .03. Finally, values of the SRMSR averaged .04 across all conditions for the true model. Thus, the data generation and model fitting appears to have functioned as expected for the true model.

Misspecified Models

To quantify the impact of our design factors on the fit indexes, we conducted separate four-way ANOVAs on each of the fit indices and on the boundaries of the RMSEA 90% confidence intervals. Before conducting these analyses, we examined the distributions of the fit indexes and found them to be fairly normal. As we noted in a previous section, statistical tests will almost always yield statistically significant values in simulation studies because sample sizes are typically extremely large. This was the case in our example study, in which only 5 of the 105 effects tested were not statistically significant at the .05 level. As suggested previously, we relied on effect sizes to help us focus on the design factors that had the most impact on fit index values. Specifically, we chose to focus on effects with η^2 values of 0.14 or greater; this value represents a medium effect size. Table 6.1 shows the effect size values corresponding to each main and interaction effect for each of the fit indexes.

For all indexes, η^2 values for interaction effects did not reach our 0.14 criterion. We therefore focus on main effects in most of the ensuing discussion. For χ^2-values, only two of the four main effects had $\eta^2 > .14$: p/f and Misspecification. Values of this index increased with levels of misspecification and of the p/f ratio. Mis-

TABLE 6.1. Values of η^2 for the Effects of the Independent Variables on the Fit Indices

Effect	χ^2	CFI	TLI	RMSEA	RMSEA_LB	RMSEA_UB	SRMSR
Misspecification	.2099	.8570	.8306	.5626	.5777	.4990	.5210
Loadings	.0835	.0006	.0017	.1697	.1849	.1642	.1358
p/f	.1594	.0064	.0024	.0092	.0037	.0250	.0334
n	.0813	.0069	.0050	.0075	.0018	.0472	.0949
Loadings * Misspecification	.0850	.0124	.0099	.1092	.1177	.1105	.1241
p/f * Misspecification	.0580	.0091	.0042	.0058	.0029	.0048	.0309
n * Misspecification	.0840	.0006	.0003	.0046	.0033	.0074	.0093
p/f * Loadings	.0171	.0036	.0042	.0061	.0069	.0057	.0001
n * Loadings	.0348	.0035	.0020	.0001	.0001	.0006	.0066
n * p/f	.0169	.0005	.0006	.0003	.0008	.0000	.0000
p/f * Loadings * Misspecification	.0186	.0029	.0027	.0034	.0038	.0034	.0002
n * Loadings * Misspecification	.0352	.0002	.0001	.0001	.0003	.0004	.0010
n * p/f * Loadings	.0058	.0002	.0003	.0000	.0001	.0000	.0000
n * p/f * Misspecification	.0196	.0000	.0000	.0000	.0001	.0000	.0001
n * p/f * Loadings * Misspecification	.0063	.0000	.0000	.0000	.0000	.0000	.0000

specification explained a substantial proportion of the variance in CFI ($\eta^2 = 0.8570$) and TLI ($\eta^2 = 0.8306$); values of both indexes decreased as misspecification increased. All other effects were negligible for those two indexes. For the RMSEA and its 90% confidence interval boundaries, Misspecification clearly had the largest effect, with loading magnitude coming in a distant second. The impact of changing the loadings was negligible in the true model. However, the loading effect was greater in the more misspecified one-factor model than in the model with misplaced indicators. Finally, for the SRMSR, Misspecification again had the strongest effect ($\eta^2 = 0.5210$), followed by Loadings ($\eta^2 = 0.1358$) and the Loadings × Misspecification interaction ($\eta^2 = 0.1241$). For this index, larger loadings yielded lower SRMSR values when fitting the true model, but in the misspecified models, increasing the loadings increased SRMSR.

In order to investigate our question of whether commonly used guidelines for model fit are reasonable, we examined tables of values of all fit indexes (not shown here) to determine whether there were conditions under which these guidelines might be misleading. We noted several conditions under which the use of such guidelines would result in retention of a model known to be misspecified. For example, the combination of low loading magnitudes and large sample sizes in the misspecified models frequently rendered the entire confidence interval of the RMSEA below .05, meaning that the RMSEA has the potential to be insensitive to mild degrees of misfit when loadings are small and n is large. Similarly, the combination of low loading magnitudes and large sample sizes yielded average SRMSR values below .08 for the misspecified one-factor model. In the misplaced-indicators model, however, SRMSR averaged below .08 in only one cell, revealing greater sensitivity for this misspecification.

Discussion

Our demonstration of a Monte Carlo simulation study illustrated the effects of sample size, model size, loading magnitude, and model misspecification on fit indices commonly used in structural equation modeling. We found that for the conditions tested and the confirmatory factor model we used, many of the variables we studied influence the model chi-square, TLI, CFI, RMSEA, the 90% confidence interval of the RMSEA, and the SRMSR. We found that these fit indexes change in value as a function of more than just degree of model

fit. At lower sample sizes, TLI, CFI, RMSEA, and SRMSR could lead a researcher to reject a well-fitting model, and at higher sample sizes and lower loadings, RMSEA and, to a lesser extent, SRMSR, can result in a failure to reject a model that is nontrivially misspecified. All of these findings are consistent with the results of Fan and Sivo (2007).

In the context of the current chapter, our example simulation was intended to illustrate the process of conducting such a study by briefly discussing how we chose our independent variables and their levels, automated the data generation and analyses, and analyzed the results. Of course, extant simulation studies encompass a wide range of variations on the basic themes we have emphasized. However, we hope that our example will help readers to better understand other simulation studies they may encounter.

As with any other study, our demonstration has limitations. The results of any simulation study should not be generalized beyond the range of values tested. While it is plausible (and often illustrated by results of other studies) that the trends found within the tested range behave in a predictable way outside of the tested range, a given simulation study does not formally have external validity beyond the specific values tested. For instance, in our demonstration, the lowest sample size tested was 100, so any speculation about what would happen at even lower sample sizes would be just that: speculation. Even some of the trends within our tested range are only loosely generalizable. For example, there were several instances of clear differences between results with $n = 100$ and results with $n = 200$, but it is not entirely clear what would happen if n were, say, 150. Other limitations to our study include the narrow range of potential misspecifications tested, the fact that only one type of model was tested, and the fact that interfactor correlations were held constant. It is not unreasonable to assert that our findings would generalize to models in which the interfactor correlations were a little below .4 or a little above .4, but it is quite possible that had we used .3 or .5, the results could differ meaningfully.

CONCLUSION

In this chapter we have discussed what simulation studies are and why it behooves applied researchers to understand them. Because researchers applying SEM methodologies to substantive problems are rarely able to meet all the assumptions necessary for their use, applied researchers are, more often than not, working with data that are suboptimal for the analysis at hand. In situations such as this, researchers must rely for guidance on the results of simulation studies in which the robustness of the parameter estimates, standard errors, and/or fit indexes to similar assumption violations have been studied. Given this reliance on the results of simulation studies, it is important for researchers to understand the basic design and analysis issues associated with these. In essence, these issues are quite similar to those in any study: Research questions should be based on theory; independent variables and their levels should be carefully chosen; dependent variables should relate directly to the research question of interest; and data analyses should be appropriate to the research questions. Of course, the independent and dependent variables included in simulation studies are unique to such studies, and we have discussed some of the more commonly used of these. Throughout the chapter we have emphasized the fact that researchers must be careful in generalizing the results of simulation studies to conditions beyond those actually studied. Although interpolation or extrapolation of results to additional levels of the studied conditions may be reasonable, such generalizations become less defensible as conditions depart further from those studied. Thus, although researchers can often gain beneficial information about the robustness of their own results from simulation studies, researchers should evaluate this information as they would evaluate information from any study: with regard to both the quality of the simulation and its relevance to their own conditions of interest.

REFERENCES

Bandalos, D. L. (2006). The role of simulation in structural equation modeling. In G. R. Hancock & R. Mueller (Eds.), *Structural equation modeling: A second course* (pp. 385–426). Greenwich, CT: Information Age.

Beauducel, A., & Herzberg, P. Y. (2006). On the performance of maximum likelihood versus mean and variance adjusted weighted least squares estimation in CFA. *Structural Equation Modeling, 13*, 186–203.

Bradley. J. V. (1978). Robustness? *British Journal of Mathematical and Statistical Psychology, 31*, 144–152.

Chun, S. Y., & Shapiro, A. (2009). Normal versus noncentral chi-square asymptotics of misspecified models. *Multivariate Behavioral Research, 44*, 803–827.

Curran, P. J., Bollen, K. A., Paxton, P., Kirby, J., & Chen, F. (2002). The noncentral chi-square distribution in misspecified structural equation models: Finite sample results from a Monte Carlo simulation. *Multivariate Behavioral Research, 37*, 1–36.

Dolan, C. V. (1994). Factor analysis of variables with 2, 3, 5, and 7 response categories: A comparison of categorical variable estimators using simulated data. *British Journal of Mathematical and Statistical Psychology, 47*, 309–326.

Fan, X., & Fan, X. (2005). Power of latent growth modeling for detecting linear growth: Number of measurements and comparison with other analytic approaches. *Journal of Experimental Education, 73*, 121–139.

Fan, X., Felsővályi, Á., Sivo, S. A., & Keenan, S. C. (2001). *SAS for Monte Carlo studies: A guide for quantitative researchers.* Cary, NC: SAS Institute, Inc.

Fan, X., & Sivo, S. (2007). Sensitivity of fit indices to model misspecification and model types. *Multivariate Behavioral Research, 42*, 509–529.

Finch, J. F., West, S. G., & MacKinnon, D. P. (1997). Effects of sample size and nonnormality on the estimation of mediated effects in latent variable models. *Structural Equation Modeling, 4*, 87–107.

Finney, S. J., & DiStefano, C. (2006). Dealing with nonnormality and categorical data in structural equation modeling. In G. R. Hancock & R. Mueller (Eds.), *Structural equation modeling: A second course* (pp. 269–314). Greenwich, CT: Information Age.

Fouladi, R. T. (2000). Performance of modified test statistics in covariance and correlation structure analysis under conditions of multivariate nonnormality. *Structural Equation Modeling, 7*, 356–410.

Gagné, P., & Furlow, C. F. (2009). Automating multiple software packages in simulation research for structural equation modeling and hierarchical linear modeling. *Structural Equation Modeling, 16*, 179–185.

Green, S. B., Akey, T. M., Fleming, K. K., Herschberger, S. L., & Marquis, J. G. (1997). Effect of the number of scale points on chi-square fit indices in confirmatory factor analysis. *Structural Equation Modeling, 4*, 108–120.

Grewal, R., Cote, J. A., & Baumgartner, H. (2004). Multicollinearity and measurement error in structural equation models: Implications for theory testing. *Marketing Science, 23*, 519–529.

Harwell, M. R. (1992). Summarizing Monte Carlo results in methodological research. *Journal of Educational Statistics, 17*, 297–313.

Harwell, M. R. (1997). Analyzing the results of Monte Carlo studies in Item Response Theory. *Educational and Psychological Measurement, 57*, 266–279.

Harwell, M. R., Stone, C. A., Hsu, T.-C., & Kirisci, L. (1996). Monte Carlo studies in Item Response Theory. *Applied Psychological Measurement, 20*, 101–125.

Hauck, W. W., & Anderson, S. (1984). A survey regarding the reporting of simulation studies. *American Statistician, 38*, 214–216.

Herzog, W., Boomsma, A., & Reinecke, S. (2007). The model-size effect on traditional and modified tests of covariance structures. *Structural Equation Modeling, 14*, 361–390.

Hoaglin, D. C., & Andrews, D. F. (1975). The reporting of computation-based results in statistics. *The American Statistician, 29*, 122–126.

Hoogland, J. J., & Boomsma, A. (1998). Robustness studies in covariance structure modeling: An overview and meta-analysis. *Sociological Methods and Research, 26*, 329–367.

Hu, L., & Bentler, P. M. (1998). Fit indices in covariance structure modeling: Sensitivity to underparameterized model misspecification. *Psychological Methods, 3*, 424–453.

Hu, L., & Bentler, P. M. (1999). Cutoff criteria for fit indexes in covariance structure analysis: Conventional criteria versus new alternatives. *Structural Equation Modeling, 6*, 1–55.

Kaplan, D. (1990). Evaluating and modifying covariance structure models: A review and recommendation. *Multivariate Behavioral Research, 25*, 137–155.

Kaplan, D., & Wenger, R. N. (1993). Asymptotic independence and separability in covariance structure models: Implications for specification error, power, and model modification. *Multivariate Behavioral Research, 28*, 467–482.

Lei, P.-W. (2009). Evaluating estimation methods for ordinal data in structural equation modeling. *Quality and Quantity, 43*, 495–507.

MacCallum, R. (1986). Specification searches in covariance structure modeling. *Psychological Bulletin, 100*, 107–120.

MacCallum, R. (2003). Working with imperfect models. *Multivariate Behavioral Research, 38*, 113–139.

MacCallum, R., Roznowski, M., & Necowitz, L. B. (1992). Model modifications in covariance structure analysis: The problem of capitalization on chance. *Psychological Bulletin, 111*, 490–504.

MacCallum, R. C., Browne, M. W., & Sugawara, H. M. (1996). Power analysis and determination of sample size for covariance structure modeling. *Psychological Methods, 1*, 130–149.

MacCallum, R. C., Widaman, K. F., Zhang, S., & Hong, S. (1999). Sample size in factor analysis. *Psychological Methods, 4*, 84–99.

Marsh, H. W., Hau, K.-T., & Wen, Z. (2004). In search of golden rules: Comment on hypothesis-testing approaches to setting cutoff values for fit indexes and dangers in overgeneralizing Hu and Bentler's (1999) findings. *Structural Equation Modeling, 11*, 320–341.

Mattson, S. (1997). How to generate non-normal data for simulation of structural equation models. *Multivariate Behavioral Research, 32*, 355–373.

Muthén, B. O., & Kaplan, D. (1985). A comparison of some methodologies for the factor analysis of non-normal Likert variables. *British Journal of Mathematical and Statistical Psychology, 38*, 171–189.

Muthén, B. O., & Kaplan, D. (1992). A comparison of some methodologies for the factor analysis of non-normal Likert variables: A note on the size of the model. *British Journal of Mathematical and Statistical Psychology, 45*, 19–30.

Muthén, B. O., Kaplan, D., & Hollis, M. (1987). On structural equation models that are not missing completely at random. *Psychometrika, 52*, 431–461.

Muthén, L. K., & Muthén, B. O. (2002). How to use a Monte Carlo study to decide on sample size and determine power. *Structural Equation Modeling, 9*, 599–620.

Nevitt, J., & Hancock, G. R. (2004). Evaluating the small sample approaches for model test statistics in structural equation modeling. *Multivariate Behavioral Research, 39*, 439–478.

Nylund, K. L., Asparouhov, T., & Muthén, B. (2007). Deciding on the number of classes in latent class analysis and growth mixture modeling: A Monte Carlo simulation study. *Structural Equation Modeling, 14*, 535–569.

Powell, D. A., & Schafer, W. D. (2001). The robustness of the likelihood ratio chi-square test for structural equation models: A meta-analysis. *Journal of Educational and Behavioral Statistics, 26*, 105–132.

Preacher, K. J. (2006). Quantifying parsimony in structural equation modeling. *Multivariate Behavioral Research, 41*, 227–259.

Reinartz, W., Haenlein, M., & Henseler, J. (2010). An empirical comparison of the efficacy of covariance-based and variance-based SEM. *International Journal of Research in Marketing, 26*, 333–344.

SAS Institute. (2002–2008). SAS IML [Computer software]. Cary, NC: Author.

Satorra, A., & Bentler, P. M. (1988). Scaling corrections for chi-square statistics in covariance structure analysis. *1988 ASA Proceedings of the Business and Economic Section*, 308–313.

Skrondal, A. (2000). Design and analysis of Monte Carlo experiments: Attacking the conventional wisdom. *Multivariate Behavioral Research, 35*, 137–167.

Vale, C. D., & Maurelli, V. A. (1983). Simulating multivariate non-normal distributions. *Psychometrika, 48*, 465–471.

PART II

FUNDAMENTALS

CHAPTER 7

Assumptions in Structural Equation Modeling

Rex B. Kline

Euclid taught me that without assumptions there is no proof. Therefore, in any argument, examine the assumptions.
  —E. T. BELL (1883–1960), Scottish mathematician and author

The least questioned assumptions are often the most questionable.
  —PIERRE PAUL BROCA (1824–1880), French physician and anatomist

The two quotes that open this chapter underscore the importance of assumptions in science. The main purposes of this chapter are to (1) elucidate the assumptions that underlie the application of structural equation modeling (SEM) and (2) emphasize the critical role of assumptions in specification, analysis, and interpretation. The main goal of this presentation is to help readers appreciate just how much the substantive value of basically all phases of SEM depend on the veracity of the underlying assumptions. I also argue that assumptions are given short shrift in perhaps most SEM studies. This inattention implies that the interpretation of results in the typical SEM analysis may be unwarranted, too.

Many researchers in the behavioral sciences use standard statistical techniques that make certain assumptions about the data or model. For example, statistical tests in multiple regression (MR) generally assume that the residuals are normally distributed and have uniform variances across all levels of the predictors (homoscedasticity). Although it is possible to model curvilinear relations or interactive effects in multiple regression by entering the appropriate power or product term into the equation (e.g., X^2 for a quadratic effect when predictor X is also in the equation; Cohen, Cohen, West, & Aiken, 2003), a standard regression analysis assumes linear relations only. The analysis of variance (ANOVA) generally requires normal population distributions, homogeneity of variance, and both equal and uncorrelated error variances when analyzing scores from repeated-measures factors. I would wager that most researchers could name the majority of the MR or ANOVA assumptions just listed. Unfortunately, there is evidence that too many researchers fail to practice what methodologists preach; that is, these assumptions are not taken seriously. For example, few authors of studies in which ANOVA is used provide any evidence about whether distributional or other assumptions were met (Keselman et al., 1998). Without verification of assumptions, the results of statistical tests—and corresponding interpretations based on them—should be viewed with caution. Although the F-test in ANOVA is relatively robust against violation of normality or homogeneity assumptions, this is generally true for large, representative samples with equal group sizes. Otherwise, even relatively minor departures from normality or homogeneity can seriously bias outcomes of the F-test (and the t-test, too) (Wilcox, 1998).

Compared with standard statistical techniques, there are even more assumptions in a typical application of SEM. These assumptions concern the model, inferences about the directionality of effects in structural models or measurement models, and the data. The latter concern distributional and other assumptions required by a particular estimation method, of which the most widely used (and default) method is maximum likelihood (ML) estimation. Each set of assumptions just mentioned is considered next. Major take-home messages of this discussion are that (1) researchers must be even more vigilant about assumptions in SEM compared with using more standard statistical techniques; however, (2) if researchers are just as lackadaisical about verifying assumptions in SEM as they seem to be when using simpler techniques like ANOVA or MR, then results from SEM studies may have little interpretative value.

DIRECTIONALITY ASSUMPTIONS

The specification of directionalities of presumed casual effects, or *effect priority*, is represented in most structural equation models described in the literature. Directionality specifications concern both structural models and measurement models. Briefly, "structural models" in SEM represent hypotheses about presumed direct or indirect causal effects among variables measured either simultaneously (cross-sectional designs) or at different points in time (longitudinal designs). For example, the hypotheses that verbal skills affect delinquency both directly and indirectly through their prior impact on scholastic achievement would be represented in the diagram of a structural model with the paths

Verbal Skills → Delinquency and
Verbal Skills → Achievement → Delinquency

where the presumed direct effects are represented by the line with a single arrowhead. The original SEM technique of path analysis, which dates to the 1920s and the work of geneticist Sewall Wright, concerns the analysis of structural models where each observed variable is the single indicator (measure) of an underlying construct, or latent variable. It is also possible in SEM to specify structural regression models—also known as *latent variable path models*—in which some constructs are measured with multiple indicators (Kline, 2010, Chap. 5). Confirmatory factor analysis (CFA) models

also feature the measurement of latent variables, each with multiple indicators.

A *measurement model* is defined by (1) the distinction between indicators and their corresponding constructs, and (2) specification of directional effects between observed and latent variables. In a standard measurement model, scores on observed variables are presumed to be caused by hypothetical constructs. For example, if a vocabulary test is specified as an indicator of a latent verbal skills factor, then the specification

Verbal Skills → Vocabulary

in the diagram of a measurement model reflects the hypothesis that vocabulary test scores reflect the influence of an underlying verbal skills construct. The presumption that constructs affect observed scores, and not vice versa, corresponds to a traditional view of measurement, also known as *reflective measurement*. Classical measurement theory assumes reflective measurement. For example, the fundamental equation of traditional reliability theory is

$$X = T + E \qquad (7.1)$$

where X represents an observed score, T stands for a true score on the construct, and E signifies a random error component that is normally distributed with a mean of zero. Most measurement models analyzed in SEM studies—and all models tested with CFA—assume reflective measurement.

It is not always appropriate to assume that indicators are caused by underlying factors. Consider this example by Bollen and Lennox (1991): The variables income, education, and occupation are used to measure socioeconomic status (SES). In a standard measurement model, these observed variables would be specified as caused by a single underlying SES factor, or

SES → Income, SES → Education,
and SES → Occupation

But we usually think of SES as the outcome of these variables (and probably others), not vice versa. For example, a change in any one of these indicators, such as a salary increase, may affect SES. From the perspective of *formative measurement*, SES is a composite that is determined by its indicators, not the other way around; that is,

Income → SES,   Education → SES,
and Occupation → SES

The assumption of formative measurement reverses the presumed directionality of effects between indicators and latent variables relative to that presumed in reflective measurement models, and vice versa. Other implications of specifying reflective versus formative measurement are considered later. Discussed next are directionality assumptions of structural models in SEM.

Assumptions of Structural Models

Five general conditions must be met before one can reasonably infer a causal relation between two variables:

1. The presumed cause (e.g., X) must occur before the presumed effect (e.g., Y); that is, there is temporal precedence.

2. There is association, or an observed covariation, between X and Y.

3. There is isolation, which means that there are no other plausible explanations (e.g., extraneous or confounding variables) of the covariation between X and Y; that is, their statistical association holds controlling for other variables that may also effect Y.

4. The form of the distribution of the data is known; that is, the observed distributions match those assumed by the method used to estimate associations.

5. The direction of the causal relation is correctly specified; that is, X indeed causes Y instead of the reverse, or X and Y cause each other in a reciprocal manner.

The requirement for temporal precedence is addressed in experimental studies through random assignment of cases to conditions and in nonexperimental studies through the use of longitudinal designs, also known as *panel designs*, where the putative cause and effect are each measured at different points over time. If all variables are measured simultaneously—which is true in most SEM studies—then it is not possible to demonstrate temporal precedence. In this case, a clear, substantive rationale is needed for specifying that X in fact is a cause of Y. This rationale should have a solid

basis in both theory and results of empirical studies. It should also identify other relevant variables to measure and control for in statistical analysis (second and third requirements). Without such a rationale, any inference about causation in a nonexperimental design has little justification. Data-related assumptions (fourth requirement) are considered later, but a gross mismatch between data characteristics and statistical assumptions of a particular method jeopardize inference accuracy.

The fifth requirement for causal inference may be the toughest, and it highlights an aspect of the logic in causal modeling that is circular: Interpretation of a large coefficient for the path $X \rightarrow Y$ as evidence for causation assumes that the true direction of causality actually "flows" from X to Y. That is, we must assume that the specification $X \rightarrow Y$ is correct in the first place (and also that the other four requirements listed earlier are met). This is a critical characteristic of SEM, one not fully appreciated by all researchers: *Interpretation of statistical estimates of direct effects as indicating causality assumes that the researcher's model is correct.* This is a *huge* assumption, one that should take our collective breath away and give us pause before interpreting results of SEM analyses as evidence for causation.

It is necessary to assume that the model is correct because the statistical association between X and Y could be strong even if (1) the true direct effect is in the opposite direction (i.e., Y causes X), (2) the two variables are causes and effects of each other in a feedback loop, or (3) there is no causal relation, but X and Y have a common cause, which gives rise to a spurious association. That is, the hypotheses of

$$X \rightarrow Y, Y \rightarrow X, X \rightleftarrows Y$$

and that of a spurious (noncausal) association could all be consistent with the same data. Without presuming that X causes Y is the only viable model, there is no basis for interpreting a large coefficient for the path $X \rightarrow Y$ as evidence for this directional effect. This is why Pearl (2000) reminded us that "causal assumptions are prerequisite for validating any causal conclusion" (p. 136). This insight echoes that of Wright (1923) from nearly 80 years earlier, when he noted that "prior knowledge of the causal relations is assumed as prerequisite in the theory of path coefficients" (p. 240).

It is also critical to know that Wright invented path analysis in order to estimate the magnitudes of effects when the basic causal pathways were *already known* (e.g., genetics). That is, given a true causal model, the technique of path analysis could be applied to es-timate it among observed variables. However, this is *not* how we generally use path analysis or related SEM techniques for analyzing latent variables today. In the behavioral sciences, we *rarely* know the true causal model. Instead, we usually *hypothesize* a causal model and then we test that model using sample data. This context of use is very different from that of Wright. Specifically, when the true causal model is unknown but our hypothesized model fits the data, about all we can say is that our model is consistent with the data, but we cannot claim that our model is proven. In this way, SEM can be seen a disconfirmatory technique, one that can help us to reject false models (those with poor fit to the data), but it basically never confirms a particular model when the true model is unknown. In this sense, referring to SEM as "confirmatory" is misleading, es-pecially in the behavioral sciences where true causal pathways are rarely known.

Exogeneity and Endogeneity

Perhaps the most basic specification in structural mod-els is the distinction between exogenous variables and endogenous variables. To summarize, the presumed causes of exogenous variables are not represented in structural models. Instead, (1) the causes of exogenous variables are unmeasured (or unknown as far as the model is concerned), and (2) exogenous variables are considered free both to vary and to covary. The latter (covariance, unanalyzed association) is often repre-sented in model diagrams by the symbol with a curved line with two arrowheads ($\curvearrowright$) that connects every pair of exogenous variables. In contrast, the presumed measured causes of endogenous variables are explicitly represented in the model, which also implies that en-dogenous variables are not free to vary or covary.

Endogenous variables in diagrams have direct ef-fects pointing to them from exogenous variables or other endogenous variables. The specification of at least one endogenous variable as a direct cause of an-other endogenous variable implies an indirect effect. If X is exogenous and Y_1 and Y_2 are endogenous, for in-stance, then the specification $X \rightarrow Y_1 \rightarrow Y_2$ describes an indirect effect, where Y_1 is presumed to mediate at least part of the effect of X on Y_2. The statistical estimate of an indirect effect is the product of the path coefficients for all the direct effects that make up the indirect effect. Kenny (2008) reminded us of the requirements listed

next for interpreting the product of path coefficients as evidence for an indirect causal effect:

1. A mediational model is a causal model. For ex-ample, the specification $X \rightarrow Y_1 \rightarrow Y_2$ assumes that variable Y_1 is actually a cause of Y_2 and not vice versa. It also assumes variable X is causally prior to both Y_1 and Y_2. If either assumption is in-correct, then the results of a mediational analysis are of little value.

2. Mediation is not statistically defined. Instead, statistics such as products of direct effects can be used to evaluate a presumed mediational model.

Kaplan (2004) notes that the distinction between exogenous and endogenous variables is not solely con-ceptual. That is, just because a researcher claims that a variable is exogenous does not make it so. Instead, there are statistical consequences for claiming that the exogenous variables do not depend on (are not caused by) the endogenous variables. These consequences are implied by the assumption of *exogeneity*, a concept that is familiar in the economics literature but is less well known in the behavioral sciences. Briefly, exogeneity means that the parameters of the conditional distribu-tions of the endogenous variables given the exogenous variables are unrelated to those that describe the distri-butions of the exogenous variables by themselves (e.g., their means and variances). That is, knowing a param-eter in the marginal distributions of the exogenous vari-ables gives no information about values of parameters in the structural equation model (Kaplan, 2004). Ways to check whether weaker or stronger forms of exogene-ity may hold in a particular sample are considered later in the section "Data-Related Assumptions."

Exogeneity also implies that the disturbances (error or residual variances) of the endogenous variables in a structural model are unrelated to the exogenous vari-ables. In other words, all omitted (unmeasured) causes of the endogenous variables are uncorrelated with the whole set of exogenous variables. This assumption is referred to as *pseudo-isolation* (Bollen, 1989) or *self-containment* (James, Mulaik, & Brett, 1982), and it permits the estimation of direct effects and disturbance variances holding omitted causes constant. There is a similar requirement in MR: the residuals in ordinary least squares estimation are calculated to be indepen-dent of the predictors, which implies that all omitted predictors are assumed to be independent of predictors in the equation. In SEM, exogeneity thus implies that not only are directionality specifications correct, but also that no unmeasured cause has anything to do with the exogenous variables. These strong requirements emphasize the importance of correct specification of the model in the first place.

Given the specification $X \to Y$, the situation where a putative exogenous variable X actually covaries with the error term for Y is known as *endogeneity*, which indicates that (1) exogeneity does not hold and (2) variable X is not really exogenous. Misspecification of the direction of the causal relation between X and Y can lead to endogeneity. If Y actually causes X ($Y \to X$), then X is clearly not exogenous; a reciprocal relation between X and Y ($X \rightleftarrows Y$) implies the same thing. Here is an example by Antonakis, Bendahan, Jacquart, and Lalive (2010): Suppose that more police are hired in order to reduce the level of crime. However, if an increase in crime leads to the decision to hire more police, then the latter is not exogenous because the two variables reciprocally affect each other. Endogeneity can also arise when there is measurement error in an exogenous variable and that error is not explicitly represented in the model, a point that is elaborated later. See Antonakis and colleagues (2010) for description of other sources of endogeneity.

Disturbances

In most structural models tested in the behavioral sciences, disturbances of the endogenous variables are assumed to be uncorrelated. Independence of error terms is signaled in model diagrams by the *absence* of the symbol for a covariance (↖↗) that connects any pair of disturbances. This specification implies that no two endogenous variables share a common omitted cause; that is, all omitted causes are unrelated to each other. It also implies that the observed correlations among the endogenous variables can be explained by other measured variables in the model, exogenous or endogenous. This presumption is known as the *local independence assumption* that the endogenous variables are independent, given the (correctly specified) structural model. The assumption of no common omitted causes is both restrictive and probably unrealistic, especially for the types of outcome variables studied in the behavioral sciences. For example, it seems unlikely that omitted causes of reading outcomes would be unrelated to omitted causes of arithmetic outcomes among elementary schoolchildren. Also, the error

variances of repeated-measures variables may overlap, which describes autocorrelation among repeated-measures variables.

The specification of a disturbance covariance (for unstandardized variables) or a disturbance correlation (for standardized variables), such as $D_1 \leftrightarrow D_2$, reflects the assumption that the corresponding endogenous variables (Y_1 and Y_2) share at least one omitted cause. Unlike unanalyzed associations between measured exogenous variables (e.g., $X_1 \leftrightarrow X_2$), the inclusion of disturbance covariances in the model is not routine. This is so in part because the addition of each disturbance covariance to the model "costs" one degree of freedom (*df*), and thus makes the model more complicated. If there are substantive reasons for specifying disturbance covariances, however, then it is better to estimate the model with these terms than without them. This is because the constraint that a disturbance covariance is zero when there are common causes tends to redistribute this association toward the exogenous end of the model, which can result in biased estimates of direct effects. In structural models with latent variables, the omission of theoretically justifiable correlated residuals may not in some cases harm model fit, but their omission could change the meaning of latent variables and thus lead to inaccurate results (Cole, Ciesla, & Steiger, 2007).

Recursive and Nonrecursive Models

There are two types of structural models, recursive and nonrecursive. Both assume that the exogenous variables are unrelated to the disturbances of the endogenous variables (no endogeneity). They differ concerning assumptions about direct effects among endogenous variables and whether endogenous variables specified as causes are allowed to covary with the disturbances of other endogenous variables specified as outcomes. In recursive models, all causal effects are unidirectional; that is, there are no feedback loops, so none of the endogenous variables are specified as both causes and effects of each other. Recursive models may also have optional correlated disturbances, but only between pairs of endogenous variables *without* direct effects between them.

Nonrecursive models have feedback loops or they may have optional correlated errors between pairs of endogenous variables *with* direct effects between them. A direct feedback loop involves just two endogenous variables specified as both causes and effects of each other (e.g., $Y_1 \rightleftarrows Y_2$). Indirect feedback loops involve three or more variables, such as

$$Y_1 \rightarrow Y_2 \rightarrow Y_3 \rightarrow Y_1$$

Note that variables involved in feedback loops are each actually each measured only once and also simultaneously. That is, they are estimated with data from cross-sectional designs, not longitudinal (panel) designs. Disturbances of variables involved in feedback loops are often specified as correlated. This specification makes sense because if variables are presumed to mutually cause each other, then it seems plausible to expect that they may have shared omitted causes. In fact, the presence of disturbance correlations in particular patterns in nonrecursive models with feedback loops helps to determine their identification status (Kline, 2010, Chapter 6).

Presented in Figure 7.1 are two structural models.[1] These models are path models because there is a single indicator of every construct, but the same principles apply when some constructs are measured with multiple indicators and the whole model is a structural regression model. Observed variables in Figure 7.1 are represented with squares and the disturbances of endogenous variables are represented with circles. Constants that scale the disturbances are represented in the figure as 1's. The symbol in Figure 7.1 with the two-headed curved arrow that exits and reenters the same variable ($\curvearrowright$) represents the variance of an exogenous variable (i.e., it is free to vary). This symbol also appears next to the disturbances because the computer must estimate the error variance, which is a model parameter. The

model of Figure 7.1(a) is recursive because no endogenous variable is represented as both a cause and effect of another, directly or indirectly. There is a disturbance correlation in Figure 7.1(a), but there is no direct effect between Y_1 and Y_2. The specification $D_1 \curvearrowright D_2$ assumes that there is at least one common unmeasured cause of Y_1 and Y_2.

The model in Figure 7.1(b) has both a feedback loop and a disturbance correlation between a pair of variables with direct effects between them ($Y_1 \rightleftarrows Y_2$). The latter specification ($D_1 \curvearrowright D_2$) implies that a predictor of Y_2, or Y_1, covaries with the disturbance of Y_2. This model-implied association is represented in Figure 7.1(b) by the path

$$D_2 \curvearrowright D_1 \rightarrow Y_1$$

The other predictor of Y_2 is the exogenous variable X_2, but exogenous variables and disturbances are assumed to be orthogonal. The model in Figure 7.1(b) also implies that a predictor of Y_1, or Y_2, covaries with the disturbance of Y_1, or

$$D_1 \curvearrowright D_2 \rightarrow Y_2$$

These model-implied correlations between endogenous predictors and the disturbances of other endogenous outcome variables violate the ordinary least squares assumption that the residuals are independent of all the predictors. This explains why standard MR is generally inappropriate for estimating direct effects in nonrecursive path models, but it is no particular problem for ML estimation or special forms of regression, such as

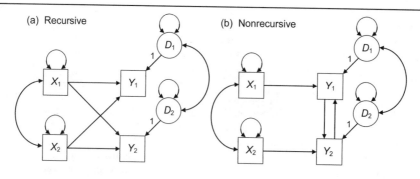

FIGURE 7.1. Examples of recursive and nonrecursive structural models.

two-stage least squares, that correct for model-implied correlations between endogenous predictors and disturbances (Kline, 2010, pp. 156–157).

There are two special assumptions for nonrecursive structural models with feedback loops. Kaplan, Harik, and Hotchkiss (2001) remind us that data from a cross-sectional design give only a snapshot of an ongoing dynamic process. Therefore, the estimation of reciprocal effects in a feedback loop with cross-sectional data requires the assumption of *equilibrium*. This means that any changes in the system underlying a presumed feedback relation have already manifested their effects, and that the system is in a steady state. That is, estimates of the direct effects that make up the feedback loop do not depend on the particular time point of data collection. A second assumption is that of *stationarity*, the requirement that the basic causal structure does not change over time. Both assumptions just described are demanding, and thus probably unrealistic. Also, there is no direct way to verify these assumptions in the data. Instead, these assumptions should be evaluated on rational grounds. However, the assumptions of equilibrium and stationarity are rarely acknowledged in studies where feedback effects are estimated with cross-sectional data. This is unfortunate because results of computer simulation studies by Kaplan and colleagues indicate that violation of the equilibrium assumption can lead to severely biased estimates of the direct effects in feedback loops.

Justifying Specifications in Structural Models

The specification of structural models in SEM relies heavily on the researcher's good judgment to (1) describe and measure variables of interest, while avoiding the omission of causes correlated with those represented in the model; (2) correctly partition the variables into the mutually exclusive subsets of exogenous variables and endogenous variables; (3) accurately lay out patterns of presumed direct and indirect effects; and (4) properly specify the error covariance structure (i.e., independent or correlated disturbances). This process is based on multiple assumptions, the most overarching of which is that the researcher's model is basically correct before any interpretation about causality can be made. It also requires strong knowledge about the phenomena under study. The need for wisdom about the research problem is even greater when there is no temporal precedence (all variables are measured simultaneously). Unfortunately, too many authors of SEM studies in

which structural models are analyzed do not give reasoned accounts of their specifications about exogeneity, directionality, and the structure of the error terms. This is often apparent when the results section of an SEM article is much longer than the introduction, in which the rationale for model specification should be fully explained. That is, too much attention is typically paid to the statistical machinations of SEM and not enough to the assumptions on which it is based. Examples of recent works where the authors presented quite detailed rationales for their directionality specifications (i.e., they are good role models) include Sava (2002), who tested a path model of student educational outcomes, and Houghton and Jinkerson (2007), who tested a structural regression model of job satisfaction.

Another serious shortcoming of SEM studies in which structural models are analyzed is the failure to consider equivalent models. Briefly, an *equivalent model* is based on the same variables as the researcher's original model, has the same number of parameters, and is fitted to same data. Both the original model and the equivalent version have the exact same fit to the same data. Equivalent structural models are generated by applying the *Lee–Hershberger replacing rules* (e.g., Hershberger, 1994; Kline, 2010, pp. 225–228) such that the directionalities of certain paths are changed without affecting model fit. Suppose that a structural model includes the path $Y_1 \rightarrow Y_2$ and that both variables are specified to have common causes. In this case, all of the following paths can be substituted for $Y_1 \rightarrow Y_2$ without changing the overall fit of the model: $Y_2 \rightarrow Y_1$, $D_1 \smile D_2$, and the equality-constrained reciprocal effect $Y_1 \rightleftarrows Y_2$ (i.e., $Y_1 \rightarrow Y_2 = Y_2 \rightarrow Y_1$). The respecified equivalent models say very different things about the directionality of effects between Y_1 and Y_2 (if any), but they all have identical fit to the data. Relatively simple structural models may have few equivalent versions, but more complicated ones may have hundreds or even thousands. However, most researchers fail to even acknowledge equivalent versions of their preferred structural models, which is a form of confirmation bias where alternative explanations of the same data are not recognized (Shah & Goldstein, 2006). This is a serious problem, one that threatens the validity of perhaps most SEM studies. There may also be near-equivalent models that fit the same data just about as well as the researcher's preferred model, but not exactly so. Near-equivalent models may be just as critical a validity threat as equivalent models, but near-equivalent models are rarely acknowledged in SEM studies.

Given these shortcomings, it is no wonder that many behavioral scientists are skeptical of the usefulness of SEM for causal inference in nonexperimental designs (e.g., Freedman, 1991). Pearl (2009) attributes part of this "crisis" in SEM to the absence of a precise, mathematical language for formally evaluating causal hypotheses embedded in (implied by) structural models. Pearl (Chapter 5, this volume) describes this framework in more detail, so it is only briefly summarized here: It features the generation of implications of claims about causation represented in a structural model, and these claims are subjected to logical proofs that are independent of the data. The testable portions of these claims— that is, those derived from the parts of the model for which there is no equivalent version—are represented by graphs with parent and child nodes of the type analyzed in graph theory, such as directed acyclic graphs.

These logical implications are then combined with the data in order to estimate Bayesian-type conditional probabilities of causal claims given the data and the original model. Assessment of global fit of the model to the data—which is tested with the model chi-square statistic—is deemphasized in Pearl's (2009) framework in favor of *local fitness testing* of restrictions implied by testable causal hypotheses. This framework is not easy to learn and still depends on assumptions about causality obtained from theoretical or empirical sources, but it offers greater rigor in the evaluation of testable causal hypotheses, including those about indirect effects (mediational hypotheses). Time will tell whether Pearl (Chapter 5, this volume) is describing a next step in the evolution of SEM practice, but this framework adds needed formalization and rigor to reasoning about causality in SEM.

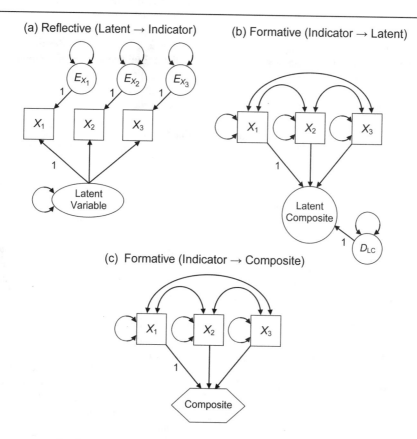

FIGURE 7.2. Examples of reflective and formative measurement models.

Assumptions of Measurement Models

Considered next are directionality and other assumptions of reflective measurement models and of formative measurement models.

Reflective Models

Recall that reflective measurement models are the kind most often analyzed in SEM. Presented in Figure 7.2(a) is a reflective model for a single factor with three indicators, X_1–X_3. The constants in the figure (1's) scale the measurement errors and also the factor. Each observed variable in Figure 7.2(a) is specified as an *effect indicator* caused by an underlying latent variable that corresponds to a hypothetical construct and also by a measurement error term (e.g., E_1 for X_1) that represents unique variance. Thus, in reflective models (1) the indicators are specified as endogenous, and (2) measurement error is represented at the indicator level. Because the indicators are endogenous, their observed variances and covariances can be compared to values predicted by a reflective measurement model. It is generally assumed that the factors and measurement errors in reflective models are uncorrelated; that is, any omitted systematic cause of scores on the indicators has nothing to do with the factors.[2] The factors themselves are assumed to be continuous variables that represent a single domain (i.e., they are unidimensional) and are normally distributed. There are other statistical techniques, such as latent class analysis, that estimate categorical latent variables with levels that refer to membership in different inferred subpopulations, or *classes*, but SEM analyzes continuous latent variables only.

If independent error terms are specified, as in Figure 7.2(a), then it is also assumed that omitted causes of different indicators are all pairwise uncorrelated. This is another variation of the local independence assumption, which for a reflective measurement model is the presumption that effect indicators are independent, given the (correctly specified) latent variable model. The specification of correlated measurement errors relaxes this assumption and, specifically, allows for omitted common causes for the pair of indicators that share an error covariance (e.g., $E_1 \smile E_2$ for indicators X_1 and X_2). An example of a justification for specifying correlated errors is when two indicators share item content or a method of measurement that is unique to those indicators. Another example is for indicators that are repeated-measurement variables, where correlated

errors represent presumed autocorrelation (Cole et al., 2007).

The theoretical model implied by the specifications just described is the *domain sampling model*, and it assumes that a set of effect indicators, such as X_1–X_3 in Figure 7.2(a), are internally consistent. This means that their intercorrelations should be positive and at least moderately high in magnitude (e.g., > .50). It is also assumed that that equally reliable effect indicators of the same construct are interchangeable. That is, effect indicators can be substituted for one another without appreciably affecting construct measurement. This assumption explains why it makes no sense to specify a factor with effect indicators that do not measure something in common. For example, suppose that the variables gender, ethnicity, and education are specified as effect indicators of a factor named "background" or some similar term. There are two problems here: First, gender and ethnicity are unrelated in representative samples, so these variables are not internally consistent; second, none of these indicators, such as a person's gender, is in any way "caused" by the some underlying "background" factor.

Formative Models

The assumptions of reflective measurement are not appropriate for some research problems, especially one where composites, or *index variables*, are analyzed. A *composite* is the total score across a set of variables. In this way, a composite is "caused" by its constituent parts, which are referred to as *cause indicators*. An example of a composite is an estimated monthly rate of inflation that takes account of price changes across different areas, such as energy, housing, food, durable goods, and so on. The meaning of a composite depends on its particular set of cause indictors that contribute to the total score; thus, cause indicators are not generally interchangeable. Also, cause indicators may have *any* pattern of intercorrelations: positive, negative, or even close to zero. This is because composites often reflect the contribution of multiple dimensions, albeit with a single score for each case (i.e., composites are not unidimensional). There are many examples of the analysis of composites in economics and business research (Diamantopoulos, Riefler, & Roth, 2005). Grace (2006) describes the analysis of composites in the environmental sciences.

If one believes that a set of cause indicators does not represent all facets of the phenomenon under study, then it is possible to specify a formative measurement model where a latent composite has a disturbance, which represents unexplained (unmeasured) variance. An example of a formative measurement model for a latent composite with three cause indicators is presented in Figure 7.2(b). In this model, the direct effects point from the indicators, which are specified as exogenous, to the latent composite, which is endogenous and has a disturbance. The constants in the figure (1's) scale the latent composite and its disturbance. The cause indicators in Figure 7.2(b) are allowed to covary in any pattern (i.e., internal consistency is not required). Because cause indicators are usually specified as exogenous, their variances and covariances are not explained by a formative measurement model. This characteristic of formative measurement models makes it more difficult to assess the validity of a set of cause indicators compared with a set of effect indicators (Bollen, 1989). In contrast, effect indicators in reflective measurement models are always endogenous, so the observed variances and covariances of effect indicators can be compared against the values predicted by the model. Also, there is no error term for a cause indicator in a standard specification of a formative model. Thus, the effect of measurement error shows up at the construct level instead of being accounted for at the indicator level, as in a reflective measurement model; compare Figures 7.2(a) and 7.2(b). Note that the model in Figure 7.2(b) is not identified. In order to estimate its parameters, it would be necessary to embed it in a larger model. In contrast, the reflective measurement model in Figure 7.2(a) is identified; specifically, this model has no degrees of freedom ($df = 0$), but it could theoretically be analyzed as a single-factor CFA model.

Formative measurement is also represented in Figure 7.2(c), but the composite in this model has no disturbance. Consequently, this composite is not latent; it is instead just a total score. Grace and Bollen (2008) represent composites in model diagrams with hexagons, which is also used in Figure 7.2(c). This is not a standard symbol, but it does convey the fact that a composite with no disturbance is not latent. These same authors distinguish between a "fixed weights composite," where loadings (weights) are specified a priori (e.g., unit weighting), and an "unknown weights composite," where the weights are estimated with sample data. The model in Figure 7.2(c) assumes an unknown weights composite with a required scaling constant (1) that appears along one of the paths that point from an indicator to the composite.

The main stumbling block to analyzing measurement models where some factors have cause indicators only and the composite is latent (e.g., Figure 7.2(b) but embedded in a larger model) is identification. This is because it can be difficult to specify such a model that both reflects the researcher's hypotheses and is identified. The need to scale to a latent composite was mentioned, but meeting this requirement is not difficult. MacCallum and Browne (1993) noted that in order for the disturbance variance of a latent composite to be identified, the latent composite must have direct effects on at least two other endogenous variables, such as endogenous factors with effect indicators. This requirement is known as the *2+ emitted paths rule*. If a factor measured with cause indicators only emits a single path, its disturbance variance will be not be identified, and the analysis of the whole model will probably fail. Another requirement for models with two or more latent composites is that if factors measured with effect indicators only have indirect effects on other factors that are mediated by different combinations of latent composites, then some of the constituent direct effects may be not be identified.

Jarvis, MacKenzie, and Podsakoff (2003) advise researchers in the consumer research area—and the rest of us, too—not to automatically specify factors with effect indicators only because doing so may result in specification error, perhaps due to lack of familiarity with formative measurement models. On the other hand, the specification of formative measurement is not a panacea for the reasons mentioned earlier (identification, validity testing is more difficult). Howell, Breivik, and Wilcox (2007) were skeptical that these challenges can always be overcome and concluded that (1) formative measurement is not an equally attractive alternative to reflective measurement and (2) researchers should try to include effect indicators whenever other indicators are specified as cause indicators of the same construct, but see Bagozzi (2007) and Bollen (2007) for other views. There is also a special issue in the *Journal of Business Research* about formative measurement (Diamantopoulos, 2008).

MIMIC Factors

There is actually a "compromise" between specifying that the indicators of a factor are either all effect or all causal. It is achieved by specifying a MIMIC (*multiple indicators and multiple causes*) factor with both effect and cause indicators. There are many examples in the literature of the analysis of structural regression models with MIMIC factors. For example, Hershberger (1994) described a MIMIC depression factor with indicators that represented various behaviors. Some of these indicators, such as "crying" and "feeling depressed," were specified as effect indicators because they are symptoms of depression. However, another indicator, "feeling lonely," was specified as a cause indicator. This is because "feeling lonely" may be a cause of depression rather than vice versa. Bruhn, Georgi, and Hadwich (2008) describe the analysis of a MIMIC factor of customer equity management with latent cause indicators and manifest effect indicators.

A way to remedy identification problems of formative measurement models is to add effect indicators for latent composites represented in the original model as measured with cause indicators only; that is, specify a MIMIC factor. For example, adding two effect indicators means that the formerly latent composite will emit at least two direct effects, which satisfies the 2+ emitted paths rule for the identification of the disturbances of latent composites—see Diamantopoulos, Riefler, and Roth (2008) for examples. However, all such respecifications require a theoretical rationale. This means that the specification of measurement as reflective, formative, or MIMIC-type should reflect substantive theory for a particular research problem about the directionality of effects between indicators and latent variables.

DATA-RELATED ASSUMPTIONS

The cardinal assumption of any estimation method in SEM is that the model is correctly specified.[3] Otherwise, model parameters may be estimated with bias. This assumption is especially critical for a *full-information method*, such as the default ML estimation, that simultaneously estimates all model parameters. The reason is the phenomenon of *error propagation*, which can happen in full-information methods when specification error in one part of the model affects estimates for other parameters elsewhere in the model. Suppose that an error covariance for two indicators of the same factor is incorrectly omitted. This specification error may propagate to estimation of the factor loadings for this pair of indicators. It is difficult to predict the direction or magnitude of error propagation, but the more serious the specification error, the more serious may be the resulting bias in other parts of the model. In computer simulation studies with incorrectly specified CFA measurement model, Bollen, Kirby, Curran, Paxton, and Chen (2007) found greater bias when using ML estimation compared with using two-stage least squares estimation. The latter method is a *partial-information method* that analyzes the equation of a single endogenous variable at a time, which may better isolate the effects of error to misspecified parts of the model instead of allowing them to spread to other parts. A drawback of partial-information methods is that there is no statistical test of overall model fit (i.e., there is no model chi-square); see Bollen and colleagues (2007) for more information.

The statistical assumptions of ML estimation concerning the observed variables are listed next and then discussed afterward. See also Chapter 16, this volume, by Malone and Lubansky for discussion of how to prepare the data for analysis in SEM:

1. The observations (scores) are independent and the variables are unstandardized.

2. There are no missing values when a raw data file is analyzed.

3. The joint distribution of the endogenous variables is multivariate normal, which also implies that the endogenous variables are continuous.

4. The exogenous variables are measured without error (i.e., their score reliabilities all equal 1.00).

Nonindependence among scores of repeated-measures variables or among those from variables that share common methods of measurement can be addressed through the specification of correlated error terms. In complex samples (hierarchical data sets) where scores are grouped into higher-order units (e.g., siblings with families), nonindependence among scores at lower levels (e.g., siblings affected by family characteristics such as income) can be addressed through specification of a multilevel structural equation model (Kline, 2010, Chapter 12). If a correlation matrix is analyzed with ML estimation instead of a covariance matrix, then values of model test statistics and standard errors may not be correct. There are special methods for fitting models to correlation matrices (Kline, 2010, p. 175), but default ML estimation requires unstandardized variables. There is a special form of ML estimation for incomplete raw data files, but it is not available in all SEM computer tools. Otherwise, a complete raw data file, or one with no missing values, is required.

Distributional Assumptions

Standard ML estimation makes specific distributional assumptions of the endogenous variables, but not of the exogenous variables. The latter can be either continuous or categorical variables where cases are partitioned into two or more nonoverlapping groups. Group membership is represented in structural models with codes, such as dummy codes or effect codes, that each represent a different contrast ($df = 1$) between two of the groups. The joint distribution of the endogenous variables should be multivariate normal, which implies that (1) all univariate distributions should be normal, (2) all bivariate scatterplots are linear, and (3) the distribution of residuals is homoscedastic. Malone and Lubansky (Chapter 16, this volume) describe how to screen raw data for multivariate normality. The normality assumption in ML estimation is critical. Specifically, if endogenous variables have severely non-normal distributions, then (1) standard errors for parameter estimates tend to be low, which results in rejection of the null hypothesis that the corresponding population parameter is zero more often than is correct (Type I error rate is inflated). Also, (2) the value of the model chi-square tends to be too high, which results in rejection of the null hypothesis that the model has perfect fit in the population more often than is correct (true models tend to be rejected too often). Depending on the particular pattern and severity of non-normality, however, it can also happen that the value of the model chi-square can be too low, which means that model fit is actually worse than it appears. Because it is usually impossible to know the direction of the bias in the model chi-square due to non-normality, it is better to thoroughly screen the data beforehand in order to verify distributional assumptions.

Transformations may be required for continuous endogenous variables with severely non-normal distributions. Another option is to use *robust ML estimation*, where estimates of standard errors and model test statistics are corrected for the degree of non-normality in the data. The corrected model chi-square generated by most robust methods is the Satorra–Bentler statistic, which adjusts downward the value of the standard model chi-square from standard ML estimation by an amount that reflects the degree of kurtosis. Other estimation methods (i.e., not ML) should be selected when some of the endogenous variables are ordinal, such as items with Likert-type scales (e.g., 0 = *disagree*, 1 = *neutral*, 2 = *agree*). When ML estimation is used to analyze endogenous variables that are not continuous,

values of both parameter estimates and their standard errors tend to be too low (DiStefano, 2002). Alternative methods, such as robust forms of weighted least squares (WLS) estimation, are generally better choices than ML estimation for noncontinuous endogenous variables. The issues just discussed imply a general assumption in SEM: *The distributional characteristics of the data must match those assumed by the particular estimation method selected.*

Reliability Assumptions

Basically any estimation method in SEM assumes that observed exogenous variables are measured without error. This includes exogenous variables in path models (e.g., X_1 and X_2 in Figure 7.1), and cause indicators in formative measurement models, for example, X_1–X_3 in Figure 7.2(b) and (c), when such variables are not explicitly specified as indicators of underlying factors. The assumption of no measurement error in exogenous variables is generally unrealistic, especially for measures of psychological traits, such as level of anxiety, instead of for simple demographic variables, such as age. However, it is required for the types of models just described because "stand-alone" exogenous variables have no error terms. In contrast, endogenous variables specified as indicators of latent variables in reflective measurement models have error terms, for example, E_1 for X_1 in Figure 7.2(a), and these error terms represent in part measurement error. This specification permits the estimation of parameters for latent variables, such as their variances and covariances, controlling for measurement error in their indicators.

There is no requirement that endogenous variables in path models are measured without error, but measurement error in endogenous variables is manifested in their disturbances (e.g., D_1 for Y_1 in Figure 7.1). If scores on an endogenous variable are unreliable, then its disturbance variance will be relatively large, which could be confounded with omitted causes (i.e., R^2 is reduced). However, the potential consequences of measurement error in exogenous variables of path models are generally more serious than for endogenous variables. Briefly, bias due to measurement error can affect not only the path coefficient for a particular exogenous variable but also those of other exogenous variables. However, it is difficult to predict the direction and magnitude of this error propagation. Depending on sample intercorrelations, some path coefficients for exogenous variables may be biased upward (too large), but others may be biased in the other direction. If the score reliabilities of exogenous variables are excellent, such as $r_{XX} > .90$, then the magnitude of bias may be slight, but the amount of bias increases as there is more and more measurement error in exogenous variables.

There is a way to respecify models, such as path models, with "stand-alone" exogenous or endogenous variables in a manner that allows direct control for measurement error. An example is presented in Figure 7.3. The path model in Figure 7.3(a) represents the hypothesis of "pure" mediation concerning the effect of exogenous variable X on endogenous variable Y_2; that is, Y_1 is presumed to mediate all of the impact of X on Y_2. Measurement error in X will truncate the estimate of the coefficient for the path $X \rightarrow Y_1$ and thus increase the amount of unexplained variance (that of D_1). Unreliability in the scores of Y_1 is also manifested in its

disturbance D_1. Because Y_1 is specified as a direct cause of Y_2 in Figure 7.3(a), measurement error in Y_1 will attenuate the estimates of the coefficient for the path $Y_1 \rightarrow Y_2$ and will also increase the variance of D_2.

The model in Figure 7.3(b) is a structural regression model, and it features:

1. The specification of X, Y_1, and Y_2 each as the single indicator of a latent variable.

2. The pattern of direct effects in the structural portion of the model in Figure 7.3(b), or

$$A \rightarrow B \rightarrow C$$

also represents the hypothesis of "pure" mediation but now among latent variables instead of observed variables; compare Figure 7.3(a) and (b).

3. Each observed variable in Figure 7.3(b) has a measurement error term.

4. The variance of each measurement error in Figure 7.3(b) is specified to equal the product of the observed variance of the corresponding indicator and the quantity one minus the estimated score reliability for that indicator (i.e., this parameter is fixed, which is required for identification).

Suppose that $r_{XX} = .80$ for variable X in Figure 7.3(b). This result implies that the proportion of variance due to random measurement error in variable X equals (1 − .80), or .20. If the observed variance of X is 15.00, then the product .20 (15.00), or 3.00, estimates the error variance in an unstandardized metric. The error variances for Y_1 and Y_2 in Figure 7.3(b) are interpreted in similar ways. In the structural model of Figure 7.3(b), all path coefficients ($A \rightarrow B$, $B \rightarrow C$) and disturbances (D_B, D_C) are estimated explicitly controlling for measurement error in the indicators (E_X, E_{Y_1}, and E_{Y_2}). See Kline (2010, pp. 276–280) for more information about the specification of single indicators with measurement errors in structural models.

(a) Path model with no measurement errors

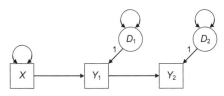

(b) Respecified model with measurement errors

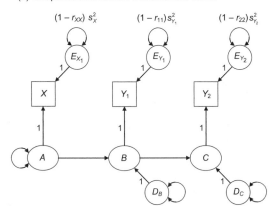

FIGURE 7.3. A path model with no measurement error for any observed variable (a) and a structural regression model with a measurement error for each observed variable (b). *Note.* r_{XX}, r_{11}, and r_{22} designate score reliability coefficients for, respectively, variables X, Y_1, and Y_2.

Exogeneity

Kaplan (2004) described a way to evaluate the assumption of a weak form of exogeneity that is suitable for studies where all variables are measured at once (there is no temporal precedence). Specifically, this assumption is violated if any of the following conditions does not hold: (1) the joint distribution of the endogenous variables and the exogenous variables that are continuous is multivariate normal; (2) all bivariate relations are linear; and (3) the distributions of regression residuals are all homoscedastic. Each condition just stated can be evaluated in data screening. Also, each condition for weak exogeneity is just an extension of a corresponding assumption of ML estimation that applies to the endogenous variables only. That is, conditions for weak exogeneity concern all the continuous variables in the sample, both exogenous and endogenous, but assumptions for ML estimation concern just the endogenous variables. Kaplan described additional tests for stronger forms of exogeneity in panel designs in which presumed exogenous and endogenous variables are each measured at different points in time; that is, the structural model has a temporal structure. These tests involve checking for possible feedback effects that indicate a presumed endogenous variable affects a presumed exogenous variable (i.e., exogeneity is not supported); see Kaplan (2004) for more information.

SUMMARY

Using an SEM computer tool—especially one with a graphical editor that allows the user to specify the model by drawing it on the screen—it is quite easy to add paths (parameters) to a structural equation model. However, one should never forget that each specification about directionality (whether structural or measurement) or about error covariances brings with it an assumption that requires a sound rationale. Without such a rationale, interpretation of estimates for that parameter may be meaningless. Once the whole model is specified, the overarching assumption in the analysis is that (1) the model is reasonably correct and (2) the distributional characteristics of the data respect those assumed by the estimation method. Likewise, any respecification of the original model in the analysis phase requires a rationale and also implies the fundamental assumption about model correctness. Even if the model is ultimately retained because it is consistent with the data, never forget that the model is probably one of perhaps many equivalent versions, each of which would fit the same data equally well. Also, do not falsely assume that closer to fit means closer to truth in SEM. That is, models with poor fit to the data are typically respecified by adding parameters to the model. This makes the model more complex, and more complex models tend to fit the same data better than simpler models, and

this is true even if the more complex model is grossly misspecified. That is, model fit could improve when paths are added not because those respecifications are correct, but simply because new paths capitalize on sample-specific variation.

Given all the assumptions of the typical SEM analysis, the proper view that researchers should take of their retained model is one of skepticism. The latter should also include appreciation of the need to replicate the model across independent samples and also to field test causal assumptions implied by the model that are amenable to the use of quasi-experimental designs among other possibilities discussed by Antonakis and colleagues (2010). This attitude described by the Russian novelist Vladimir Nabokov (1899–1977) is apropos concerning the need for awareness of all assumptions made in the typical application of SEM: "I am sufficiently proud of my knowing something to be modest about my not knowing all."

NOTES

1. Both models in Figure 7.1 assume that all effects are linear, and that there are no interactive effects. It is possible in SEM, just as in MR, to include power or product terms in structural models in order to estimate curvilinear or interaction effects; see Kline (2010, Chapter 12) and Edwards and Lambert (2007) for more information.
2. This assumption is analogous to the one for structural models that exogenous variables and omitted causes of endogenous variables are uncorrelated.
3. This includes the assumption that the exogenous variables and error terms are unrelated.

REFERENCES

Antonakis, J., Bendahan, S., Jacquart, P., & Lalive, R. (2010). On making causal claims: A review and recommendations. *Leadership Quarterly, 21*(6), 1086–1120.

Bagozzi, R. P. (2007). On the meaning of formative measurement and how it differs from reflective measurement: Comment on Howell, Breivik, and Wilcox (2007). *Psychological Methods, 12*, 229–237.

Bollen, K. A. (1989). *Structural equations with latent variables.* New York: Wiley.

Bollen, K. A. (2007). Interpretational confounding is due to misspecification, not to type of indicator: Comment on Howell, Breivik, and Wilcox (2007). *Psychological Methods, 12*, 219–228.

Bollen, K. A., Kirby, J. B., Curran, P. J., Paxton, P. M., & Chen, F. (2007). Latent variable models under misspecification: Two-stage least squares (TSLS) and maximum likelihood (ML) estimators. *Sociological Methods and Research, 36*, 48–86.

Bollen, K. A., & Lennox, R. (1991). Conventional wisdom on measurement: A structural equation perspective. *Psychological Bulletin, 110*, 305–314.

Bruhn, M., Georgi, D., & Hadwich, K. (2008). Customer equity management as formative second-order construct. *Journal of Business Research, 61*, 1292–1301.

Cohen, J., Cohen, P., West, S. G., & Aiken, L. S. (2003). *Applied multiple regression/correlation analysis for the behavioral sciences* (3rd ed.). Mahwah, NJ: Erlbaum.

Cole, D. A., Ciesla, J. A., & Steiger, J. H. (2007). The insidious effects of failing to include design-driven correlated residuals in latent-variable covariance structure analysis. *Psychological Methods, 12*, 381–398.

Diamantopoulos, A. (Ed.). (2008). Formative indicators [Special issue]. *Journal of Business Research, 61*(12).

Diamantopoulos, A., Riefler, P., & Roth, K. P. (2005). The problem of measurement model misspecification in behavioral and organizational research and some recommended solutions. *Journal of Applied Psychology, 90*, 710–730.

Diamantopoulos, A., Riefler, P., & Roth, K. P. (2008). Advancing formative measurement models. *Journal of Business Research, 61*, 1203–1218.

DiStefano, C. (2002). The impact of categorization with confirmatory factor analysis. *Structural Equation Modeling, 9*, 327–346.

Edwards, J. R., & Lambert, L. S. (2007). Methods for integrating moderation and mediation: A general analytical framework using moderated path analysis. *Psychological Methods, 12*, 1–22.

Freedman, D. A. (1991). Statistical models and shoe leather. *Sociological Methodology, 21*, 292–313.

Grace, J. B. (2006). *Structural equation modeling and natural systems*. New York: Cambridge University Press.

Grace, J. B., & Bollen, K. A. (2008). Representing general theoretical concepts in structural equation models: The role of composite variables. *Environmental and Ecological Statistics, 15*, 191–213.

Hershberger, S. L. (1994). The specification of equivalent models before the collection of data. In A. von Eye & C. C. Clogg (Eds.), *Latent variables analysis* (pp. 68–105). Thousand Oaks, CA: Sage.

Houghton, J. D., & Jinkerson, D. L. (2007). Constructive thought strategies and job satisfaction: A preliminary examination. *Journal of Business Psychology, 22*, 45–53.

Howell, R. D., Breivik, E., & Wilcox, J. B. (2007). Reconsidering formative measurement. *Psychological Methods, 12*, 205–218.

James, L. R., Mulaik, S. A., & Brett, J. M. (1982). *Causal analysis: Models, assumptions and data*. Beverly Hills, CA: Sage.

Jarvis, C. B., MacKenzie, S. B., & Podsakoff, P. M. (2003). A critical review of construct indicators and measurement model misspecification in marketing and consumer research. *Journal of Consumer Research, 30*, 199–218.

Kaplan, D. (2004). On exogeneity. In D. W. Kaplan (Ed.), *The Sage handbook of quantitative methodology in the social sciences* (pp. 407–421). Newbury Park, CA: Sage.

Kaplan, D., Harik, P., & Hotchkiss, L. (2001). Cross-sectional estimation of dynamic structural equation models in disequilibrium. In R. Cudeck, S. Du Toit, & D. Sörbom (Eds.), *Structural equation modeling: Present and future: A Festschrift in honor of Karl Jöreskog* (pp. 315–339). Lincolnwood, IL: Scientific Software International.

Kenny, D. A. (2008). Mediation. Retrieved April 20, 2009, from *davidakenny.net/cm/mediate.htm*.

Keselman, H. J., Huberty, C. J., Lix, L. M., Olejnik, S., Cribbie, R. A., Donahue, B., et al. (1998). Statistical practices of education researchers: An analysis of the ANOVA, MANOVA, and ANCOVA analyses. *Review of Educational Research, 68*, 350–368.

Kline, R. B. (2010). *Principles and practice of structural equation modeling* (3rd ed.). New York: Guilford Press.

MacCallum, R. C., & Browne, M. W. (1993). The use of causal indicators in covariance structure models: Some practical issues. *Psychological Bulletin, 114*, 533–541.

Pearl, J. (2000). *Causality: Models, reasoning, and inference*. New York: Cambridge University Press.

Pearl, J. (2009). *Causality: Models, reasoning, and inference* (2nd ed.). New York: Cambridge University Press.

Sava, F. A. (2002). Causes and effects of teacher conflict-inducing attitudes towards pupils: A path analysis model. *Teaching and Teacher Education, 18*, 1007–1021.

Shah, R., & Goldstein, S. M. (2006). Use of structural equation modeling in operations management research: Looking back and forward. *Journal of Operations Management, 24*, 148–169.

Wilcox, R. R. (1998). How many discoveries have been lost by ignoring modern statistical methods? *American Psychologist, 53*, 300–314.

Wright, S. (1923). The theory of path coefficients: A reply to Niles' criticism. *Genetics, 20*, 239–255.

CHAPTER 8

Model Specification in Structural Equation Modeling

Rick H. Hoyle

All applications of structural equation modeling (SEM) begin with the specification of one or more models to be estimated and tested. *Models* are sets of statistical statements about the relations between variables, which may be observed or unobserved (i.e., implied by sets of observed variables). The relations typically are linear, though, as in other linear models such as multiple regression analysis, nonlinear relations can be included. Each specified model offers a parsimonious, plausible, and substantively meaningful account of the processes that gave rise to the observed data.

Whether the focus of a particular analysis is one model or multiple models depends on the researcher's approach to using SEM (Jöreskog, 1993). In the *strictly confirmatory approach*, a single model is proposed and evaluated. Estimation and testing lead to a decision to either accept or reject the model as specified. Importantly, in the event the model is rejected, no attempt is made to modify the initial specification in order to meet some statistical criterion that would lead to its acceptance. Because SEM analyses rarely yield statistical support for initially specified models and, when they do, there is a question as to whether other models might also receive support if tested, use of the strictly confirmatory approach is rare.

When multiple models are specified, typically one, the target model, is of greatest interest or favored by the researcher. Additional models may be specified either before or after the target model is evaluated. In the *alternative models approach*, one or more additional models is specified without knowledge of the adequacy of the target model or, more generally, knowledge of the data. These models are plausible alternatives to the target model and, in the best use of this approach, are directly compared to it. As such, when the alternative models approach is used, the target model is evaluated in two ways. First, and most fundamentally, it is evaluated with reference to the observed data: In an absolute sense, does the model offer an acceptable account of the data? If this evaluation produces support for the target model, then it is evaluated with reference to the alternative model(s): Does it offer the *best* account of the observed data? As illustrated later in this section, not all alternative models can be compared to a target model because they are, in a statistical sense, equivalent to it. For instance, for a data set including two variables, attitude and behavior, a target model specifying attitude as the predictor and behavior as the outcome is equivalent to a model in which behavior is the predictor and attitude the outcome; their fit to the data will be identical and the choice between them will rest on considerations outside the data analysis. Assuming the target and alternative models are not equivalent, two additional outcomes of the analysis are possible when using the alternative models approach. The target model may not offer an acceptable account of the data in an absolute sense, but one or more target models prove acceptable in absolute terms. In such cases, the target model is rejected and, following appropriate comparisons (and assuming nonequivalence), the best fitting alternative model is supported. Alternatively neither the target model nor any of the alternatives provides an acceptable account of the data, in which case either the analysis is abandoned or the approach shifts to model generation.

In the *model-generating approach*, additional models are specified following analyses that do not produce support for a target model and any alternative models. In such cases, the analysis takes a turn, moving away from rigorous testing of a priori hypotheses to exploration aimed at generating models for future testing with new data. Strategies for modifying a priori models for the purpose of generating plausible new models are discussed by Chou and Huh (Chapter 14, this volume). Because these strategies involve examination of the results from estimation of the initially specified model, they run the risk of all such post hoc analyses: They are too likely to yield a model that captures the idiosyncrasies of the current data but is unlikely to prove adequate for another set of data from the same population. This likelihood is particularly high for modifications when sample size is not large (< 1,200) and automated specification searching is used (MacCallum, Roznowski, & Necowitz, 1992). Nonetheless, the model-generating approach is a viable alternative to abandoning a modeling effort altogether and, when used with discipline and interpreted with caution, may lead to a new understanding of a process or phenomenon.

A final, relatively new approach to specification is a generalization and automation of the model-generating approach. In the *model discovery approach*, automated search strategies are used to find all possible models for a given set of variables, sometimes constrained by knowledge or assumptions about the variables and their interrelations. With access to adequate computing power no longer a concern, the generation of all possible models for a modest number of variables is feasible. Yet, because of the wide array of models that can be specified for a given set of variables using SEM, even a relatively small number of variables (e.g., 10–12) yields too many models to be thoughtfully considered. Moreover, some portion of the models will differ in ways that are substantively inconsequential or include relations that are implausible given the variables under consideration. The challenge for automated model discovery strategies is to find those models that are plausible and interesting. Marcoulides and Ing (Chapter 40, this volume) describe and illustrate several heuristic search algorithms for model discovery. A more restricted approach is TETRAD, so named for its reliance on "vanishing tetrads" as a means of identifying models (Scheines, Spirtes, Glymour, Meek, & Richardson, 1998). The no-cost TETRAD computer program can be used to implement this model discovery strategy (Landsheer, 2010). An appealing feature of TETRAD is the ability to constrain the automated model search by specifying model type (e.g., measurement, structural) and background knowledge about the relations between sets of variables. In addition to offering a means of identifying potential models in the absence of sufficient knowledge to specify them a priori, these strategies can be used to identify equivalent models.

Regardless of the approach taken to model specification, the goal is the same: a model that offers a parsimonious and useful account of the data. Importantly, the goal of specification is not to provide a full or complete account of the data. For that reason, all models are, to an extent, incorrect (MacCallum, 2003). They are merely approximations of the real-world forces that produced the data, which are too complex to capture in a specified model. These approximations are nonetheless of value, particularly when they (1) leave relatively little unexplained (i.e., they offer "close fit" to the data), (2) include relatively few unknowns to be estimated from the data (i.e., they are parsimonious), and (3) are high in hypothesis validity (Wampold, Davis, & Good, 1990); that is, they include parameters that correspond to the substantive hypotheses the data were collected to address. Like a street map, which eschews detail in the service of usefulness, such models, though incorrect, are useful.

Equipped now with an understanding of what models are and the various approaches a researcher might take to specifying them, you are ready to consider the mechanics of specification. I begin with an example, followed by a detailed presentation of the steps involved in specifying a model.

A SIMPLE EXAMPLE

Displayed in Figure 8.1 are four models of the relation between two variables, *X* and *Y*. These are examples of specification using the path diagram (detailed information is provided by Ho, Stark, & Chernyshenko,

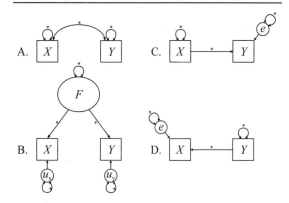

FIGURE 8.1. Different models of the relation between two observed variables, X and Y.

Chapter 3, this volume). In these diagrams, X and Y are observed variables, conveyed by their representation as squares. They are connected, directly or indirectly, by one of two types of paths. The curved line pointing in two directions conveys a nondirectional relation between X and Y. The straight lines pointing in one direction convey a directional relation between the two variables or each variable and F. The sharply curved bidirectional lines denote variances. The ovals denote unobserved variables. These generally are of two types. The larger of the ovals, labeled F, corresponds to a latent variable, or factor, as in factor analysis. The smaller ovals, labeled e and u, correspond to error variances. These represent that portion of variance in one or both of the observed variables not accounted for by the relations in the model. Those labeled e are errors of prediction, as in regression equations. Those labeled u are uniquenesses, or measurement errors, which correspond to variance in the variables, systematic and random, not accounted for by the factor. Finally, the asterisks correspond to parameters to be estimated. Three of the models include three parameters to be estimated, whereas the fourth includes five. In reality, and as discussed below, five parameters are more than a model involving two observed variables could include apart from the imposition of constraints on some of the parameters (e.g., the pair of loadings constrained to be equal and the variance of F fixed to 1.0). This concern is addressed below in the section on identification.

These four models of the same data provide a basis for introducing some basic concepts and concerns related to model specification in SEM. Models A and B are two models of the covariance (unstandardized correlation) between X and Y. Note that, in Model A, the variances of X and Y are included in the model, indicating no attempt to account for variance in X or Y. This model, the equivalent of a zero-order correlation (i.e., the asterisk on the curved line between them, when standardized, would be r_{XY}), ventures nothing more than that the two variables are related. Model B suggests that X and Y are related because their variance can be explained by a single source, F. Notice that, when the effect of F on each variable is included in the model, the variables are assumed to no longer be related. Also notice that, in this model, their variances are not estimated. Rather, their variances are apportioned between the path from F, for which the coefficient is a factor loading, and a uniqueness.

Models C and D posit a directional relation between the two variables. In Model C, variance in X is not accounted for in the model; its estimate can be taken directly from the observed data. The model proposes that the variance in Y is, at least in part, accounted for by X. The degree to which this is the case would be judged by the asterisk on the directional path, equivalent to a regression coefficient. Variance in Y not accounted for by X is reflected in the asterisk associated with e, which reflects the additional, unobserved influences on Y. In Model D, the direction of the path is reversed so that the model now accounts for variance in X. As in Model C, that variance is apportioned between a path coefficient and a latent error variable (i.e., a disturbance).

A key point, to which I alluded earlier and return near the end of the chapter, is that these models are equivalent. That is, in terms of overall fit of the model to the data, each is as good as the other. Thus, a researcher could not compare the fit of these models to determine whether, for instance, X causes Y or Y causes X. Similarly, the comparison between Models A and B could not be used to address the question of whether X and Y are manifestations of the same underlying construct. Thus, apart from additional information, each of these models offers a plausible account of the X–Y relation. Such information might come from three sources. For example, perhaps X is a dummy code for gender or some other biological characteristic unlikely to be attributable to Y. Similarly, perhaps research subjects were randomly assigned to levels of X, which was manipulated. In both of these cases, Models B and D are implausible. Model A is plausible but relatively uninformative. Model C would offer the best account of the data. A third source of information is substantive theory about *X* and *Y*, which might lead to the choice of one model over another. However, for some relations between variables, competing theories might favor more than one model (e.g., the attitude–behavior relation). In such cases, absent additional information such as that provided by randomized experiments, none of the models in Figure 8.1 could be used to support one theoretical account over the other. Model A would provide the most defensible, if least satisfying, account of the data.

These models also provide a glimpse into the modeling possibilities for a given set of variables. As I have shown, with the minimum number of observed variables, at least four different models could be specified. As the number of variables increases, the number of modeling possibilities increases dramatically. Not only are there more possible models of the types shown in Figure 8.1 with more variables; there are more *types* of models, each offering a potentially large number of variations. Some of the variations within and between model types are, as is the case with the models in Figure 8.1, equivalent. Others are not. Among those that are not equivalent, some can be directly compared because they are nested, whereas others cannot. For a modest number of variables, this collection of equivalent, nested, and non-nested models approaches infinity (e.g., Raykov & Marcoulides, 2001). Not all of these models are plausible or interesting, but those that are must be accounted for in the interpretation of the target

model until they can be ruled out on the basis of persuasive theoretical arguments or through the use of rigorous research design (e.g., randomized experiments; Eberhardt, Glymour, & Scheines, 2006).

THE SPECIFICS OF SPECIFICATION

Although the types of models that might be specified and analyzed using SEM are numerous and varied, the specific steps involved in specification are few and common to all model types. Before detailing those steps, I return to the implementation framework I presented in Chapter 1 (this volume) for context. The framework is shown in Figure 8.2, highlighting the portion relevant for model specification. Of particular interest at this point in the chapter are the "specification" and "data acquisition and preparation" boxes and the connections between them, *a* and b_1. Specifically, this portion of the diagram illustrates two possible scenarios in the timing of model specification. Path *a* corresponds to the fairly common scenario in which data have already been acquired, and a model is specified based on the contents of the data set. This scenario is unavoidable in disciplines that rely on archival and other secondary data sources. Although avoidable, this scenario is not unusual in disciplines that typically make use of data from studies designed by researchers with a particular interest or set of hypotheses in mind but no specified model prior to data collection. In both cases, the range of models that can be specified is constrained by the

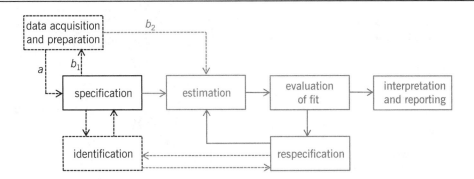

FIGURE 8.2. SEM implementation framework introduced by Hoyle (Chapter 1, this volume) highlighting the position of model specification and related concerns.

variables available in the data set and the conditions under which they were collected.

Path b_1 in Figure 8.2 corresponds to an alternative scenario, one in which the model is specified first, and then the data are acquired and prepared for analysis. Although the range of models that can be specified in this scenario is constrained by what is feasible in terms of data collection given available resources, it at least allows for the possibility of specification and testing of the researcher's ideal model. Such issues as whether to model key variables as latent variables, and if so, how many and what type of indicators to use, shape data collection rather than being shaped by it. In short, model specification can take place before or after data are acquired or collected, but, when possible, specification prior to data collection is to be preferred.

I now turn to the actual mechanics of model specification, which I present as a set of decisions that increasingly shape a set of variables into a model.

Format

The initial decision in specification concerns the format that will be used to convey the specified model. That is, how will the researcher formalize the variables, relations, and parameters in the model; provide this information to the computer program to be used for estimation and testing; and communicate the model in manuscripts and presentations? The format need not be the same for these three functions—the best means of communicating the model to an audience might not be the most efficient means of providing the model to the computer program of choice—but researchers who favor a format for one of these functions tend to favor that format for the others. In any case, for current purposes, the salient consideration is how the variables, relations, and parameters in the model will be formalized.

There are three general formats that may be used to specify a model for estimation and testing in SEM: a diagram, a set of equations, and matrix, or LISREL, notation. I introduced and illustrated the path diagram earlier. The path diagram in Figure 8.3 depicts a model I use to illustrate the different formats for specifying a model. The benefits of a graphical presentation are readily apparent. It is immediately evident which variables are in the model, whether they are observed or latent, and the type of relations between them. Free parameters, those that will be estimated from the data, are clearly indicated. Selected fixed parameters, those set

by the researcher, are evident. Despite these strengths, two potential drawbacks to the path diagram as a format for specification bear mention. Although the diagram shows selected fixed parameters (the 1s for the loadings of v_1 and v_5 on F_1 and F_2, respectively), it does not show them all. Specifically, it does not show those parameters fixed to 0. These include the "off loadings" for the indicators, such as the loading of indicator v_4 on latent variable F_2, and the covariances between error terms, which are assumed to be 0 but often are not. A second drawback is one of aesthetics. Although the path diagram functions well for this rather simple model, for more complex models the number and direction of lines and curves can result in a diagram that is ineffective as a means of capturing and communicating model specification. These caveats notwithstanding, the path diagram is, for many researchers, the format of choice for formalizing and communicating the specifics of a specified model.

Before turning to the other formats, I touch briefly on an alternative diagrammatic format for specifying models—graph theory. Although, on the surface, diagrams based on graph theory appear to be directly comparable to path diagrams (e.g., nodes are variables, edges are paths), such is not the case. Graph theory

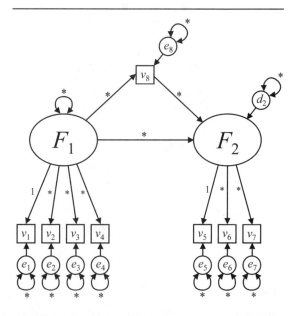

FIGURE 8.3. Path diagram showing model specification.

diagrams communicate substantially more about variables, relations, and parameters than do path diagrams. Moreover, given their basis in mathematical theory, they formalize relations between variables in a way that is neither intended nor accomplished by path diagrams. Pearl (Chapter 5, this volume) makes liberal use of graph theory to discuss issues of causality in SEM. Similarly, the authors of the TETRAD computer program make use of graph theory to develop algorithms and strategies for automated model selection (Scheines et al., 1998). I refer interested readers to the published work of these authors.

An alternative format for model specification makes use of equations to formalize the relations between variables in a model. Although there are a number of approaches to specifying models in this way, the best developed is the Bentler–Weeks (1980) system, which includes two types of equations: measurement equations that specify the relations between indicators and latent variables, and construct, or structural, equations that specify the relations between latent variables. Parameters are identified using a "double-label" system, which I illustrate below. Using the Bentler–Weeks system, the model displayed in Figure 8.3 in path diagram form would be depicted as follows (note that the variable labels in Figure 8.3 correspond to those used in the Bentler–Weeks system):

$$v_1 = 1F_1 + e_1$$
$$v_2 = {*}F_1 + e_2$$
$$v_3 = {*}F_1 + e_3$$
$$v_4 = {*}F_1 + e_4$$
$$v_5 = 1F_2 + e_5$$
$$v_6 = {*}F_2 + e_6$$
$$v_7 = {*}F_2 + e_7$$
$$v_8 = {*}F_1 + e_8$$
$$F_2 = {*}F_1 + v_8 + d_2$$

The equations for v_1 to v_7 are measurement equations. The equations for v_8 and F_2 are structural equations. These equations reflect all of the directional paths in the model, but they do not reflect variances and covariances. The 10 variances are indicated using double-label notation:

$$F_1,F_1 = {*}$$
$$e_1,e_1 = {*}$$
$$e_2,e_2 = {*}$$

$$e_3,e_3 = {*}$$
$$e_4,e_4 = {*}$$
$$e_5,e_5 = {*}$$
$$e_6,e_6 = {*}$$
$$e_7,e_7 = {*}$$
$$e_8,e_8 = {*}$$
$$d_2,d_2 = {*}$$

The model does not include covariances but if, for example, the error terms for v_2 and v_4 were allowed to covary, that parameter would be indicated as $e_2,e_4 = {*}$.

All of the information evident in the path diagram is also evident in this format. Although this format is not subject to the concern about clarity when used for complex models, it shares with path diagrams the concern about making evident all fixed parameters. As in the path diagram, the loadings fixed to 1 are made explicit; however, the loadings fixed to 0 are not. Unlike in path diagrams, those parameters could be included without concern for visual clarity. For instance, the first measurement equation could be expanded to

$$v_1 = 1F_1 + 0F_2 + e_1$$

And the zero covariances between measurement errors could be indicated using double-label notation:

$$e_1,e_2 = 0$$

Compared to the path diagram format for model specification, the equations format offers an advantage and brings a disadvantage. A relative disadvantage is the lack of perspective offered by path diagrams, which provide a global view of models and the variables, and relations between variables they comprise. A relative advantage of equations is the ability to efficiently reference specific parameters in a model using straightforward notation. For example, the loading of v_1 on F_1 is denoted by F_1,v_1. Every parameter has a unique double-label designation by which it can be referred in computer syntax or presentations of results.

The identification of specific parameters in a model is a hallmark of the third format for model specification— matrix notation. Matrix notation is sometimes referred to as LISREL notation because it was the means by which models were specified in early versions of the LISREL computer program. Although LISREL now offers alternative options for specifying models, matrix notation remains the primary means of communicating about SEM in the methodology literature. As such, it is advantageous for researchers to have some familiarity with matrix notation even if they routinely formalize the specification of their models using path diagrams or equations.

Before illustrating the use of matrix notation to convey the details of our example model, I note two distinctions drawn and a convention followed in this framework. As with the equations format, a distinction is made between the measurement and structural components of a model; the former encompasses the relations between indicators and latent variables, and nondirectional relations (i.e., correlations) between latent variables, whereas the later includes directional relations between latent variables. A further distinction is between types of variables. *Exogenous variables* are those for which no explanation is offered by the model;

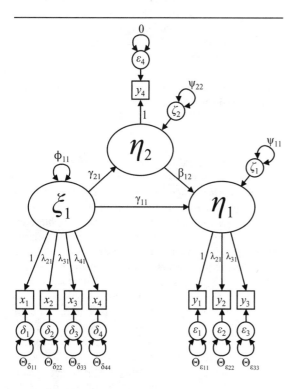

FIGURE 8.4. Path diagram showing a single observed variable specified as a latent variable.

that is, no directional paths point to them (e.g., F_1 in Figure 8.3). *Endogenous variables* are those explained within the model by a combination of other variables in the model and unspecified influences captured by a latent disturbance term (e.g., v_8 and F_2 in Figure 8.3). In matrix notation, the structural model typically includes only directional relations between latent variables. In our example model, v_8, though related to F_1 and F_2 by directional paths, is not a latent variable. The specification for this variable can be adjusted as shown in Figure 8.4, so that all structural relations are between latent variables. In anticipation of the presentation of matrix notation, I also have relabeled the variables using matrix notation conventions. Because the loading of y_4 (formerly v_8) on η_2 is fixed to 1 and the variance of the error term, ε_4, is fixed to 0, η_2 is simply an alternative form of y_4. An advantage of this specification is that it permits fixing of the ε_4 variance to values other than 0 if, for example, the proportion of unreliable variance in y_4 is well established.

Turning now to the formal expression of the model shown in Figure 8.4 using matrix notation, I first specify the exogenous latent variable, ξ_1.

$$\begin{bmatrix} x_1 \\ x_2 \\ x_3 \\ x_4 \end{bmatrix} = \begin{bmatrix} 1 \\ \lambda_{21} \\ \lambda_{31} \\ \lambda_{41} \end{bmatrix} [\xi_1] + \begin{bmatrix} \delta_1 \\ \delta_2 \\ \delta_3 \\ \delta_4 \end{bmatrix}$$

Often, the matrix that comprises the variances of the measurement errors is expressed as a vector, conveying the standard assumption that these terms are uncorrelated. The full variance–covariance matrix of these terms can be expressed in the Θ_δ matrix, which for our example model is populated as follows:

$$\Theta_\delta = \begin{bmatrix} \Theta_{\delta_{11}} & & & \\ 0 & \Theta_{\delta_{22}} & & \\ 0 & 0 & \Theta_{\delta_{33}} & \\ 0 & 0 & 0 & \Theta_{\delta_{44}} \end{bmatrix}$$

The variance–covariance matrix of the exogenous latent variables is Φ. Because there is only one exogenous latent variable, there are no covariances. The lone element in the Φ matrix is ϕ_{11}.

$$\Phi = [\phi_{11}]$$

Next, I specify the two endogenous latent variables, η_1 and η_2.

$$\begin{bmatrix} y_1 \\ y_2 \\ y_3 \\ y_4 \end{bmatrix} = \begin{bmatrix} 1 & 0 \\ \lambda_{21} & 0 \\ \lambda_{31} & 0 \\ 0 & 1 \end{bmatrix} \begin{bmatrix} \eta_1 \\ \eta_2 \end{bmatrix} + \begin{bmatrix} \varepsilon_1 \\ \varepsilon_2 \\ \varepsilon_3 \\ \varepsilon_4 \end{bmatrix}$$

The variance–covariance matrix of the measurement errors, Θ_ε, includes the fixed value of the ε_4 variance $(\Theta_{\varepsilon_{44}})$.

$$\Theta_\varepsilon = \begin{bmatrix} \Theta_{\varepsilon_{11}} & & & \\ 0 & \Theta_{\varepsilon_{22}} & & \\ 0 & 0 & \Theta_{\varepsilon_{33}} & \\ 0 & 0 & 0 & 0 \end{bmatrix}$$

Because the variances of η_1 and η_2 are apportioned to the paths pointing to them and a disturbance term, the variances of these variables and covariances between them are not specified as part of the measurement model.

I now move to the specification of the structural model, which comprises the directional relations between the latent variables. The latent endogenous variables, η_1 and η_2, are a function of the other latent endogenous variable, the exogenous variable, and disturbances:

$$\begin{bmatrix} \eta_1 \\ \eta_2 \end{bmatrix} = \begin{bmatrix} 0 & \beta_{12} \\ 0 & 0 \end{bmatrix} \begin{bmatrix} \eta_1 \\ \eta_2 \end{bmatrix} + \begin{bmatrix} \gamma_{11} \\ \gamma_{21} \end{bmatrix} [\xi_1] + \begin{bmatrix} \zeta_1 \\ \zeta_2 \end{bmatrix}$$

A variance–covariance matrix, Ψ, contains the variances of the disturbances, ζ_1 and ζ_2, and, if specified, the covariance between them.

$$\Psi = \begin{bmatrix} \psi_{11} & \\ 0 & \psi_{22} \end{bmatrix}$$

A significant benefit of matrix notation relative to path diagrams and equations is evident in several of the matrices. Specifically, those matrices reveal that some parameters have been fixed to zero as part of the model specification. The loadings matrix for the endogenous latent variables, Λ_y, shows that the loadings of y_1, y_2, and y_3 on η_2 have been fixed to 0.[1] The variance–covariance matrix for the measurement errors associated with indicators of the endogenous latent variables,

Θ_ε, reveals that the error for y_4 has been fixed to 0. And the variance–covariance matrix for the disturbances, Ψ, makes explicit the fact that the model assumes no covariance between the two disturbances.

These three formats provide viable alternatives for formalizing the specification of a model. The choice of a format may be influenced by the requirements of the computer program to be used for estimation and testing (though, increasingly, programs can accept either format); the norms within the discipline or literature for which the model is relevant; or the personal preference of the researcher. As noted earlier, researchers may use two or more of the formats, for instance, when the model is developed for analysis using equations or matrix notation but described in manuscripts or presentations using a path diagram. In the remainder of the chapter, I illustrate various aspects of the mechanics of model specification primarily through the use of path diagrams. This choice should not be interpreted as an endorsement of the path diagram format for model specification. Rather, it reflects the need for a means of clear and efficient communication of relatively simple models in this didactic forum.

Identification

As shown in Figure 8.2, identification, though a separate consideration in the implementation of SEM, is directly related to model specification. Because identification affects decisions about model specification, I offer a brief summary of it here. Detailed coverage is provided by Kenny and Milan (Chapter 9, this volume).

Each parameter to be estimated in a model must be identified. Parameters are identified if a unique value can be obtained for them from the data given the model. Identification is achieved by incorporating restrictions into the model, for example, when the loadings of v_5, v_6, and v_7 on F_1 were fixed to 0 in the model shown in Figure 8.3. Note also that in that model the loadings of v_1 on F_1 and v_5 on F_2 have been fixed to 1, another restriction that ensures that specific parameters—the variances of F_1 and F_2 in this instance—are identified. When every parameter in a model is identified, the model as a whole is identified. Otherwise, the model is not identified, and parameter estimates and tests, as well as tests of model fit, are not valid (cf. Pearl, 2009).

Because of this need to impose restrictions on models in order to achieve parameter identification, not every model of interest can be estimated and tested.

For example, referring back to Figure 8.1, Model B is not identified. Thus, although the researcher might believe that the correlation between X and Y is attributable to latent variable F, he or she could not evaluate that hypothesis by estimating and testing this model. Identification problems stem from two characteristics of the model. Most fundamentally, it includes more parameters to be estimated than available data points. The "data" in SEM analyses are variances and covariances; in this instance the variances of X and Y, and the covariance between them. With three data points and five parameters to be estimated, the model has –2 degrees of freedom. Although models with negative degrees of freedom are always not identified, models with non-negative degrees of freedom are not necessarily identified. For instance, in this case, an additional problem is that a unique value for the variance of F cannot be estimated from the data given the model. One approach to dealing with this problem is to fix that parameter to a value such as 1.[2] Though this solves the identification problem associated with the variance of F, it still leaves a model with –1 degrees of freedom. This problem might be solved by, for example, constraining the loadings to be equal, thereby, in essence, reducing two parameters to be estimated to one. The result would be a model with 0 degrees of freedom. Such models can be estimated but not tested. That is, their parameters can be estimated and tested, but the model as a whole cannot be tested. A model can only be tested if every parameter is identified and it has positive degrees of freedom.

Identification is substantially more complex than is evident from this brief treatment, but I have provided enough information to make evident three key points relevant to specification:

1. Although SEM is highly flexible for modeling latent variables and the relations between them, that flexibility is tempered by the need to ensure that unique estimates can be obtained for all parameters to be estimated in a model.

2. Data points in SEM are variances and covariances. As such, degrees of freedom are a function of the number of observed variables in the model, not the number of cases for which there are data.

3. As with any statistical method, a model cannot require estimation of more parameters than the number of degrees of freedom. Unlike with other

statistical methods, in the case of SEM these two quantities can be equal. I refer back to these points and illustrate their relevance later in the chapter.

Form

The most basic consideration in model specification is the form the model will take. Specifically, what type of model will it be, and which variables will be included? I defer a lengthy discussion of model type until the last section of the chapter. At this point, I highlight several basic distinctions that set in motion the steps that will result in a fully specified model to be estimated and tested.

A primary consideration is whether the model will include latent variables and, if so, whether the model will venture hypotheses about the directional relations between them. Models in which all observed variables are indicators of latent variables, and the only relations between the latent variables are nondirectional, are measurement models and their analysis using SEM typically is referred to as confirmatory factor analysis (detailed coverage provided by Brown & Moore, Chapter 22, this volume). A basic measurement model is shown on the left in Figure 8.5 (asterisks and values indicating parameters have been omitted because they are not relevant for the discussion of form). The intent of such a model is not to test hypotheses about causal relations between observed or latent variables. Instead, its focus is the modeling of unobserved sources of commonality that account for the pattern of covariances between the observed variables.

The model on the left in Figure 8.5 is typical of measurement models and latent variables in models focused on the directional relations between them. Notice that the directional paths flow from the latent variables to the indicators. This is because the indicators are assumed to reflect the latent variables they represent; hence, their designation as reflective indicators. Indicators in such models also are referred to as *effect indicators* because in the cause-and-effect relations between latent variables and indicators, the latent variables are causes and the indicators are effects. This type of relation between latent variables and indicators is consistent with the common-factor model that underlies exploratory factor analysis (but not principal components analysis). It is the standard characterization of latent variables in SEM and throughout the social and behavioral sciences (see Bollen & Hoyle, Chapter 4, this volume).

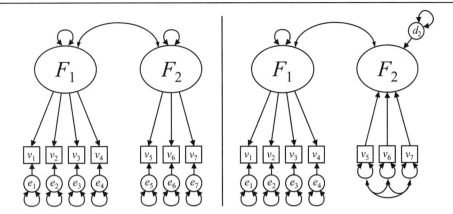

FIGURE 8.5. Measurement models with two correlated latent variables. Indicators v_5, v_6, and v_7 are effect in the model to the left and causal in the model to the right.

On the right in Figure 8.5 is an alternative model, one in which the directional paths between F_2 and its indicators have been reversed. Now the indicators are causes and the latent variable is an effect. In such models, the indicators are referred to as *causal indicators*. This change in the relation between indicators and latent variable produces other important changes in that part of the model. Notice that the errors associated with the indicators have been removed. In fact, the indicators are now exogenous because there is no attempt to account for their variance by relations in the model. Also, the covariances between the indicators have been included. This addition reflects that fact that, unlike for F_1, the latent variable does not offer an account of the relations between the indicators (i.e., it does not reflect commonality). Finally, note the addition of a disturbance term associated with F_2. This term could be fixed to 0, in which case F_2 is simply a weighted composite of v_5, v_6, and v_7, or it could be estimated from the data, which allows for the possibility that F_2 comprises more than v_5, v_6, and v_7 (Bollen, 2011).

The specifications of F_1 and F_2 in the diagram on the right in Figure 8.5 differ in interpretation as well. Each indicator of F_1, that which is common to v_1, v_2, v_3, and v_4, is assumed to be a fallible reflection of it (but see De-Shon, 1998, for a discussion of potential threats to this interpretation). *Fallibility*, that is, variance not shared with the other indicators, is captured by the error terms, e_1 to e_4. The indicators of F_2 are, in this specification, assumed to be infallible; there is no provision for vari-

ance in the indicators not relevant for F_2. Furthermore, although the indicators are allowed to covary, their commonality has no impact on the latent variable. In fact, the best formative indicators covary very little, which means that each indicator brings unique information to the modeling of the latent variable. Critically, F_2 is adequately modeled only if all components of it are captured by the indicators. Unlike with reflective indicators, each of which is assumed to correspond to the latent variable, composite indicators are assumed to correspond to only a portion of the latent variable. Like a puzzle with a missing piece, a latent variable with formative indicators that does not include all such indicators is incomplete.

A final note about reflective and formative indicators of latent variables concerns identification. Assuming the model is constrained in such a way that the variance of F_1 is identified, the portion of the model on the right in Figure 8.5 related to F_1 is identified. The portion of the model related to F_2 is not. Identification is a major concern with formative indicators (MacCallum & Browne, 1993). Only recently have identification rules (Bollen & Davis, 2009) and specification strategies (Treiblmaier, Bentler, & Mair, 2011) been developed to address this concern. These rules and strategies, coupled with broader discussions of types of indicators and latent variables (e.g., Bollen & Bauldry, 2011; Bollen & Hoyle, Chapter 4, this volume; Diamantopoulos, 2011), are paving the way for more frequent use of formative indicators in the specification of latent variables in SEM.

Returning now to general considerations related to models focused primarily on the relations between indicators and latent variables, a key decision is how the indicators are formed. In the simplest case, the data set includes a single measured variable for each indicator. For example, returning to the pure common-factor model on the left in Figure 8.5, perhaps v_1 to v_7 are individual survey items. For identification reasons, three indicators generally are recommended as a minimum and four as a preferred number (see Marsh, Hau, Balla, & Grayson, 1998, regarding additional considerations and alternative recommendations), so there is no decision to be made about how to manage the indicators of F_1 and F_2. Imagine instead that F_1 is "psychological well-being" and a team of researchers has administered a battery of self-report instruments. The data set in its most elemental form includes many potential indicators of the latent variable in the form of individual items on the instruments. The researchers now are faced with a decision: Is each item included as an indicator of the latent variable? Or is the number of potential indicators somehow reduced? Imagine that the researchers administered four 20-item instruments. Clearly 80 indicators is too many. In terms of data reduction, the researchers might score each instrument, producing a single score and four indicators, as in Figure 8.5. In this case, however, v_1 to v_4 are composite scores, each reflecting a measurement instrument. A virtue of this strategy is that each indicator is more reliable than the single items from a survey. A drawback is that within-instrument measurement error is not accounted for. Nonetheless, F_1, a reflection of the commonality across the four instruments, is likely to provide a good account of psychological well-being—almost certainly better than the account provided by four individual items.

Imagine that, instead of four instruments, the researchers administered a single 20-item instrument. Although it now might be feasible to include each item as an indicator of F_1, unless the focus of the model is evaluating the instrument, the researchers would be better served by a smaller number of indicators. To reach a smaller number, the researchers need to answer two questions: How many indicators are preferred? How is that number achieved? Perhaps the researchers decide that four indicators are ideal. That number might be achieved in two ways. In the most straightforward case, the 20 items can be arrayed in four five-item subscales. Subscale scores are produced, and these serve as indicators of F_1. If subscales or other a priori groupings of the items (e.g., previously published fac-

tor analyses of the item set) are not an option, then the researchers could form *parcels*, arbitrary sets of items combined to form a single indicator. For instance, they might assign every fifth item to a parcel or randomly assign one-fourth of the items to each parcel. In either case, a key concern is that properties of the parcels are not known and, as such, their suitability as reflections of F_1 is unclear. This concern is at least partially addressed through the use of nonarbitrary rules for parceling, such as exploratory factor analysis; however, the general practice of parceling remains controversial and should be undertaken with due attention to the relevant methodological literature (e.g., Little, Cunningham, Shahar, & Widaman, 2002).

Although the matters of model form discussed so far in this section apply to models focused on relations between indicators and latent variables, such as those shown in Figure 8.5, they also apply to models focused on the relations between latent variables, such as the one shown in Figure 8.4. For such models, beyond issues concerning the paths between the variables (covered in the next section) are additional considerations about variables to be included in the model and whether they are observed or latent.

A major consideration is whether the model will include interaction effects and, if so, whether the interaction terms involve only observed variables or one or more latent variables.[3] When the variables in the interaction term are observed, the strategy is the same as that for multiple regression models with interaction effects (Aiken & West, 1991): Center the variables, create product terms, and include those terms in a model that also includes the variables involved in the interaction terms. The strategy is even simpler, and easier to implement in SEM, when one of the variables is nominal, with relatively few categories. In that case, the model can be estimated simultaneously for subsamples at each level of the nominal variable and equality constraints used to test whether effects vary across levels of the nominal variable. (This multigroup specification strategy is discussed later in the chapter.)

When one or both variables in the interaction term are latent, the specification of the interaction effect is more challenging. In the most straightforward case, one variable is latent and the other is nominal and observed. In that case, the strategy described in the previous paragraph can be used. For example, referring to the model depicted in Figure 8.4, imagine that data were available for women and men, and a question of interest concerned whether η_2 mediated the ξ_1–η_1 relation to an equivalent degree for these two subgroups. This test of moderated mediation could be accomplished by simultaneously estimating the model for women and men, and using equality constraints on the γ_{21} and β_{12} paths to test their equality. A finding of inequality for these paths is equivalent to finding support for the Gender $\times \xi_1$ and Gender $\times \eta_2$ interactions. Imagine that, rather than gender, the moderator variable of interest was the psychological well-being latent variable from my earlier example, and the data set included four reflective indicators. Referring again to Figure 8.4, this latent variable could be added as a second exogenous latent variable, ξ_2. Now the moderated mediation hypothesis is tested by the $\xi_2 \times \xi_1$ and $\xi_2 \times \eta_2$ interactions. Modeling of the effects requires specification of *latent interaction variables*, the latent equivalent of observed product terms in moderated multiple regression.

Focusing on the $\xi_2 \times \xi_1$ interaction, modeling the effect requires specification of a new latent variable, ξ_3. In a full specification, the reflective indicators are all products of the ξ_2 and ξ_1 indicators. So, for example, if the indicators of the moderator latent variable, ξ_2, were x_5, x_6, and x_7, the indicators of ξ_3 would be 12 new observed variables created by multiplying each indicator of ξ_2 by each indicator of ξ_1 (e.g., x_5x_1, x_6x_2, x_7x_3). For two reasons, this specification, though intuitive, is not practical. First, as in the present case, the number of indicators of the latent interaction variable can be very large even if the number of indicators of the latent variables involved in the interaction is small. Second, the loadings and uniquenesses associated with ξ_3 are nonlinear transformations of their counterparts in ξ_1 and ξ_2 (Kenny & Judd, 1984). Although this nonlinearity can be incorporated into the specification of ξ_3 using constraints, for more than a few indicators of ξ_1 and ξ_2 the specification becomes prohibitively complex (though see Ping, 1995, for a workaround). Fortunately, results of simulation studies comparing the full specification and several more straightforward partial specifications suggest that little is lost by working with less than the full set of product terms and forgoing the nonlinear constraints. Specifically, the unconstrained matched pairs strategy, described by Marsh, Wen, Nagengast, and Hau (Chapter 26, this volume), requires simply specifying a latent interaction variable with only the number of reflective indicators necessary to ensure that every indicator is included in one and only one product term. Because it is important that each indicator be used only once, in situations like the present one, with different numbers of indicators of the two latent variables in the

interaction, the number for the largest set must be reduced. For instance, indicators x_3 and x_4 of ξ_1 might be combined to form a parcel. For our example, in which the indicators of ξ_1 are x_1, x_2, and x_3 (with x_3 now being a parcel combining the original x_3 and x_4) and the indicators of ξ_2 are x_5, x_6, and x_7, the indicators of ξ_3, the latent interaction variable, would be x_1x_5, x_2x_6, and x_3x_7. When the interaction variable is specified in this way, the interaction effect is corrected for attenuation due to unreliability of the indicators of the variables involved in the interaction.

A final consideration regarding the inclusion of variables in a model concerns variables that might be included for the purpose of solving specification or estimation problems. That is, the variables do not have direct relevance for paths of substantive interest in the model, but they need to be included in order to estimate those paths. A little known but highly flexible strategy for imposing certain types of constraints on parameters involves the specification of *phantom variables* (Rindskopf, 1984). These variables have no substantive meaning but allow the imposition of nonlinear constraints when the computer program used for estimation does not allow them to be imposed directly. Such constraints include forcing a parameter to fall within certain bounds (e.g., > 0, < 1) and expressing one parameter as a nonlinear function of another (e.g., one loading equals the square of another). Increasingly, these constraints can be imposed directly using widely available computer software. Another type of variable that fits in this category is the *auxiliary variable*, which has no direct relevance to the substantive hypotheses of interest but contributes to tests of those hypotheses by improving the performance of missing data procedures (Collins, Schafer, & Kam, 2001). Simulation research indicates that the inclusion of auxiliary variables when estimating from incomplete data reduces bias due to systematic reasons for missingness and restores some of the power that would be lost were cases with incomplete data excluded from the analysis (see Graham & Coffman, Chapter 17, this volume). Even the inclusion of auxiliary variables unrelated to the reasons for missingness improves the performance of missing data procedures, suggesting that the liberal use of auxiliary variables when estimating from incomplete data is warranted (Graham, 2003).[4] One additional type of variable that fits into this category is *instrumental variables*, which are included in models for the purpose of estimating causal effects using nonexperimental data (e.g., Heckman, 1997). Well-chosen instrumental variables, when included in a model, have the effect of isolating the putative causes from extraneous influences on the outcomes through those causes. Although not as effective as randomization at isolation, instrumental variable methods strengthen the case for causal inference when randomized experiments are not feasible and confounding variables are known and available in the data set.

Paths and Parameters

When the form of a model has been set and the array of variables to be included selected or created, the focus of model specification moves to paths between variables and parameters associated with those paths and the variables in the model. Models can include two types of paths, and the status of each parameter associated with a path or a variable can be designated in one of three ways. Paths connect variables. Referring to Figure 8.5, the curved line between F_1 and F_2 is a *nondirectional path*. Although its coefficient is estimated as a covariance, in terms of interpretation it corresponds to a zero-order correlation. Such paths account for the relation between two variables, but they offer no claim regarding temporal or causal priority. The paths between the latent variables and their indicators are *directional paths*. The coefficients associated with these paths are regression weights that reflect the amount of change in the outcome (the indicators in this instance) per unit change in the predictor (the latent variables). Such paths might reflect causal claims, but this is not always the case. At the most basic level, they reflect an attempt to account for variance in one variable with another.

Parameters in a model are designated as fixed or free and, if free, constrained or unconstrained. *Fixed parameters* are those that have been assigned values as part of the specification. They are not estimated from the data. Most fixed parameters are set to 0 or 1. Referring to Figure 8.4, one loading on each latent variable (e.g., λ_{11} on ξ_1) has, for identification purposes, been set to 1. Though not apparent in the path diagram, parameters associated with the directional arrows from the uniquenesses and disturbances also have been set to 1. As noted in the section on format, the parameters set to 0 are less apparent in path diagrams. In Figure 8.4, the loadings of x_1 to x_4 on η_1 and η_2 are set to zero, as are all off loadings in the model. Also, the covariances between uniquenesses (the δs and ϵs) have been set to zero. Parameters that are fixed in order to ensure pa-

rameter identification are not open to reconsideration in the event the model is modified. The status of other fixed parameters might be reconsidered when searching for ways to improve the fit of models that do not provide acceptable fit. For instance, perhaps x_1 and x_2 in Figure 8.4 share something in common that they do not share with x_3 and x_4 (e.g., they are negatively worded). This commonality would not be accounted for by ξ_1. Freeing the covariance between δ_1 and δ_2 (i.e., $\Theta_{\delta_{21}}$) would allow this parameter to depart from 0, resulting in an improvement in the fit of the model.

Parameters that are not fixed are free. *Free parameters* are those that have not been assigned values as part of the specification; they are estimated from the data. Associated with each free parameter is a standard error, and the ratio of the parameter estimate to its standard error provides for a test of significance (typically against a null of 0). Because free parameters are estimated from the observed data, each one "costs" a degree of freedom. The total number of degrees of freedom available for a given model specification is the number of variances and covariances associated with the observed variables in the model (calculated as half the product of the number of variables and the number of variables plus 1). The difference between the number of degrees available and the number of free parameters is the number of degrees of freedom available for testing the fit of the model. As noted earlier, it is possible to use all of the degrees of freedom, in which case the model has 0 degrees of freedom and its fit to the data cannot be tested. Such models are referred to as *saturated models* and, despite the fact that their fit cannot be tested, parameter estimates and their standard errors can be generated and used to test individual parameters.

Typically, the value a free parameter might take on is not constrained by the values estimated for other parameters in the model (inherent interdependence between parameters notwithstanding). Sometimes either substantive hypotheses about the relations between parameters or identification concerns necessitate constraining some of the free parameters. *Constrained parameters* are those free parameters for which the range of potential values has been limited in some way. Those limits are of two types. In some instances the limits are absolute. For instance, a parameter might be constrained such that it can only take on values greater than 0 or less than 1. Such constraints sometimes help address estimation problems. More typical are limits tied to the estimation of other parameters in the model. For example, a model might constrain the loadings of all indicators on a latent variable to be equal. Or, in longitudinal models that assume stationarity, corresponding paths at each wave might be constrained to be equal. Such constraints are not limited to equality. For example, a parameter might be constrained to the square or some other nonlinear transformation of another parameter, as in fully specified latent interaction variables. An important distinction between these two types of constraints is their implication for degrees of freedom. When the constraint is absolute (e.g., only values greater than 0 are allowed), no degrees of freedom are saved; the parameter is estimated as it would be were it not constrained, differing only in the values it can assume. When the constraint is with reference to other free parameters, degrees of freedom are saved. For instance, referring back to Figure 8.4, if the three free loadings on ξ_1 were constrained to equality, then 1 rather than 3 degrees of freedom would be used.[5] This example highlights a key point with regard to constraining parameters: Constraints can involve only free parameters. Thus, for example, the first loading on ξ_1, because it is fixed, could not be part of the equality constraint placed on the loadings.

In the remainder of this section, I refer to the model shown in path diagram format in Figure 8.6. The data to which the model applies are for six variables, v_1 to v_6, measured at two occasions, a and b. These variables are indicators of two latent variables, F_1 and F_2. This model includes a number of features that illustrate decisions to be made regarding the inclusion of paths and status of parameters in a model. First, I point out a number of paths and parameters that are not directly relevant to the substantive hypotheses tested by the model but that are necessary in order to account for general features of the data and model. The parameters associated with the exogenous latent variables, F_{1a} and F_{2a}, are common to exogenous variables in structural models. These include the variances of the variables (not shown in Figure 8.6) and if, as in the example, there is more than one exogenous variable, the covariances between them. The fact that these parameters are drawn directly from the observed data (i.e., they are not a function of other parameters in the model) is consistent with their position as exogenous variables. The inclusion of these parameters does not require justification. The nondirectional paths between uniquenesses reflect the panel feature of the design. They account for the fact that any systematic uniqueness associated with an indicator at assessment a is likely to be associated with the indicator at assessment b. As with the variances and covariances of

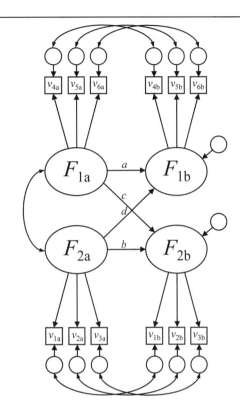

FIGURE 8.6. Cross-lagged panel model with latent variables. (Note: Variances are not shown.)

the exogenous variables, these paths and parameters do not require substantive justification. Finally, the variances elsewhere in the model are free parameters that must be estimated. These include the variances of the uniquenesses and the disturbances.

The remaining paths and parameters in the model are likely to be of substantive interest. These include the loadings of the indicators on the latent variables and the directional paths between the latent variables. Although the test of model fit will consider these paths simultaneously, it is advantageous to think of them as separate sources of potential misspecification. For instance, the paths between latent variables might be correctly specified, but the paths between indicators and latent variables might be inadequate to account for the relations between indicators. For this reason, models such as the one in Figure 8.6 sometimes are assessed in two steps (Anderson & Gerbing, 1988). At Step 1, the evaluation focuses only on the measurement model. For the current example, this would involve replacing the directional paths labeled *a, b, c,* and *d* with nondirectional paths, eliminating the disturbances associated with F_{1b} and F_{2b}, and adding a nondirectional path between F_{1b} and F_{2b}. The fit of that model sets an upper bound on the fit of any model with directional paths. Once support has been obtained for the measurement model, then the nondirectional paths could be replaced by the directional paths between latent variables as shown in the figure and the model reevaluated. Any deterioration in fit would be attributable to those structural paths.

Of primary interest in the model are the directional paths labeled *a, b, c,* and *d.* Paths *a* and *b* are stability paths. Their parameters reveal the degree to which there is change in the latent variables from assessment *a* to assessment *b.* As the magnitude of these paths increases, the likelihood that either latent variable at assessment *b* is predicted by the other latent variable at assessment *a* (paths *c* and *d*) decreases. A model in which paths *c* and *d* are fixed to 0 would be a pure stability model, which assumes that, at least across the time period between assessments *a* and *b*, F_1 and F_2 have not changed. The inclusion of paths *c* and *d* allows for an evaluation of whether any nonstable variance in F_1 and F_2 can be predicted by initial standing on the other variable. Assuming all of the variance in F_1 and F_2 is not stable and standing on each latent variable at assessment *b* is, to some degree, attributable to the other latent variable at assessment *a,* a question often addressed in these cross-lagged panel models is whether the cross-lagged paths are equal. This question would be addressed by constraining parameters *c* and *d* to equality and determining whether there is a significant decline in fit relative to the single degree of freedom saved by imposing the constraint.

The model in Figure 8.6 also provides an opportunity to illustrate the determination of degrees of freedom for a specified model, a value that can be used to estimate the statistical power for tests of model fit given a particular sample size (MacCallum, Browne, & Sugawara, 1996). With 12 observed variables, the data set comprises a total of 78 variances and covariances (computed as 12(12 + 1) / 2). The model includes the following free parameters:

- 2 variances of the exogenous latent variables
- 1 nondirectional path between the exogenous latent variables

- 8 loadings of the indicators on the latent variables (one loading on each latent variable is fixed to 1)
- 12 uniqueness variances
- 6 nondirectional paths between uniquenesses
- 2 disturbance variances
- 4 directional paths between latent variables

With a total of 35 free parameters, 33 degrees of freedom are available for tests of model fit. These degrees of freedom also are available for model modifications that do not introduce identification concerns should the initially specified model not provide an adequate account of the data.

The model in Figure 8.6 shares in common with all models I have presented so far the fact that its intent is to account for the covariances between the variables and for their variances. Yet some research questions concern means, which in the typical specification are effectively eliminated from the model through mean centering of the variables (accomplished by SEM computer programs prior to estimation). For instance, a researcher might be interested in the mean of F_{1a}, either in an absolute sense or in contrast to the mean of F_{1b}. Or, in latent growth models, for example, the means of the latent intercept and slope variables are of primary interest. When means are to be modeled, at least two additional considerations arise. Principally, the data to be modeled must be expanded beyond variances and covariances to include variable means. The model specification must then be expanded to include equation intercepts and latent variable means. How this expansion is represented varies across the three formats for formalizing model specification. In the path diagram format, a constant, typically represented by a triangle, is added to the diagram, with directional arrows running from the constant to the indicators and latent variables. In the equation format, an intercept term is added to the measurement equations and intercept-only equations are added to account for the latent variable means. In matrix notation, new parameter matrices are included for the intercepts and means. A thorough treatment of means modeling strategies is provided by Green and Thompson (Chapter 24, this volume).

Additional Considerations

The basic decisions about model specification—the type of model, the variables to be included, the paths between the variables, and the status of the parameters in the model—once made, result in a model that is fully specified and ready to estimate. Beyond these basic decisions are three additional considerations that affect how the analysis is done and the results interpreted.

All of the examples presented thus far assume that the specified model will be estimated using data from a single sample and the inferences drawn with reference to a homogeneous population. Yet some research questions concern whether the process or structure reflected in a model applies to an equivalent degree for different groups. When the question concerns only a path or two in a model (e.g., the earlier moderated mediation example earlier), the most efficient means of evaluating equivalence between groups is by including relevant interaction terms. When the question concerns multiple paths, particularly when those paths are part of the measurement model, the most efficient approach is to specify a multigroup model. As the name suggests, *multigroup models* concern the equivalence of parameters in a specified model when estimated from data from two or more groups.

The specification strategy for multigroup models is best illustrated using an example. Assume that a researcher had reason to believe that certain paths in the model shown in Figure 8.6 vary as a function of gender. For instance, perhaps there is reason to believe that indicators v_4, v_5, and v_6 are not equivalent in their reflection of F_1. This is a critical concern because, if F_1 is qualitatively different for women and men, the interpretation of the paths between F_1 and F_2 must be different as well. Put differently, if, for instance, the magnitude of path c differs for women and men, it could either be because the influence of F_1 on F_2 varies as a function of gender, or because F_1 is defined differently for women and men. In order to evaluate these possibilities directly, the model is, in effect, duplicated, which allows it to be simultaneously estimated for women and men. This setup allows for the use of equality constraints to test for differences in parameters in the model. As noted, a fundamental concern is that the constructs are equivalent, and this is evaluated through analysis of measurement invariance. Such analyses can focus on any parameters in the measurement portion of the model (see Millsap & Olivera-Aguilar, Chapter 23, this volume, for a full treatment of measurement invariance), but the loadings are of primary interest. Equivalence of loadings would be tested by simultaneously estimating the model for women and men. Using the logic of nested model comparisons outlined below,

the loadings would be constrained to be equal in one version and left free to vary in the other. Any difference in the fit of these two models (accounting for the difference in degrees of freedom) would suggest that one or more of the loadings are not equivalent. This logic can be used to compare any parameter or set of parameters in a model for any number of groups.

In the multigroup model, the groups to be compared are explicitly defined; group membership is reflected in an observed variable. In some cases, a sample is heterogeneous with reference to a specified model, but the source of that heterogeneity is not observed. In such cases, group membership must be inferred from the data with reference to parameters in the model. Using mixture modeling, a latent class variable (i.e., an unobserved categorical variable) can be identified and modeled as the source of nonequivalence in one or more parameters in the model (Lubke & Muthén, 2005; Shiyko, Ram, & Grimm, Chapter 31, this volume). The latent class variable identifies two or more groups that can be identified by differences in model parameters or by differences detected through prediction of the latent class variable from other variables in the data set.

I have alluded to model comparison at several points in the chapter, including the comparison of alternative models as one basic approach to the use of SEM. Model comparison requires the specification of at least two models that differ in their account of the mechanism or process for which they are relevant. In the most effective use of model comparison, these models differ at two levels. At a substantive level, the models offer alternative accounts, perhaps reflecting alternative theories, of the relations between a set of variables. For instance, perhaps one account of a construct as assessed by a particular measure assumes that it is unidimensional, whereas another account suggests that it comprises three related but distinguishable dimensions. At the specification level, model comparison is most effective when the models differ in ways that allow for a statistical comparison of them; that is, they are nested.[6]

Two models are nested if they are of the same form, but the free parameters of one model are a subset of the free parameters of the other model. This basic idea is typified by hierarchical multiple regression analysis, in which the predictors in one multiple regression model—the reduced model—are a subset of the predictors in the other—the full model. In such cases, the difference between the model F statistics and the difference in degrees of freedom can be used to test the hypothesis that the removal of the set of predictors to produce the reduced model results in a significant decline in the predictive power of the model. In SEM terms, the reduced model has been produced by fixing to 0 the coefficients associated with the set of predictors (i.e., their directional paths to the outcome variable) in question. This rather straightforward logic can be generalized to the most complex models to be evaluated using SEM. Referring again to Figure 8.6, a researcher might wish to compare a model that assumes no prospective predictive relation between F_1 and F_2 (accounting for their temporal stability) with the model depicted in the figure, in which prospective prediction is assumed. The first model is produced by constraining paths c and d to 0, producing a model that is nested in the full model. The reduced model, which is the more parsimonious of the two, is to be preferred if the elimination of the two paths in question does not lead to a significant decline in the overall fit of the model. The 2 degrees of freedom and the difference between the model fit statistics can be used to formally address this question. If the fit of the model declines significantly, then one or both of the paths should be retained. Conversely, if the fit does not decline, inclusion of the paths is not justified and the reduced model (as well as the substantive reasoning behind it) is supported. The direct statistical comparison of models that differ in substantively interesting ways yields important information beyond that provided by tests of individual models using absolute criteria.

As noted early in the chapter, alternatives to a model of interest—the target model—are of two types. The most useful and informative alternatives, those described in the preceding paragraph, offer a different account of the data that can be contrasted with the account provided by the target model. Another type of alternative is equivalent models. These are models that differ from the target model, perhaps in substantively interesting and important ways, but cannot be contrasted with it because they produce identical statistical results. A simple set of equivalent models is shown in Figure 8.1. Assuming identifying constraints are added to Model B (e.g., the variance of F fixed to 1 and the loadings constrained to be equal), these four models cannot be distinguished on the basis of their fit to the data. In fact, these are saturated models in which the 3 available degrees of freedom have been exhausted. The concern of equivalent models is perhaps best illustrated in the comparison of Models C and D, which show that the data are equally consistent with a model in which X causes Y, and a model in which Y causes X. There is no statistical basis for choosing one of these models over

the other and, as such, absent certain design features (e.g., randomization to levels of one of the variables) or logical arguments (e.g., one variable is an immutable biological characteristic), the direction of causality between X and Y cannot be addressed.

With larger models, the number of equivalent models increases dramatically. For typical models, most of these can be generated manually using rules proposed by Stelzl (1986) and Lee and Hershberger (1990; reviewed by Williams, Chapter 15, this volume). For larger models, an automated strategy such as the TETRAD computer program is useful for generating equivalent models (Scheines et al., 1998). Once equivalent models have been generated, the researcher faces the challenge of ruling out at least those that most clearly contradict the target model. In some cases, knowledge about how the data were generated and characteristics of the model can be used to eliminate some alternatives. In other cases, compelling equivalent models remain after all such knowledge has been applied. Pearl (Chapter 5, this volume) aptly describes the conundrum facing users of SEM unable to eliminate equivalent models using these relatively unambiguous criteria: "Researchers should keep in mind therefore that only a tiny portion of the assumptions behind each SEM study lends itself to scrutiny by the data; the bulk of it must remain untestable, at the mercy of scientific judgment." Ideally, the same scientific justifications that produced the target model will serve as a basis for selecting it over equivalent models that cannot be ruled out on other grounds. Absent such justifications, a favorable statistical result is necessary but not sufficient support for the target model.

SUMMARY AND CONCLUSIONS

SEM is a remarkably flexible approach to modeling the processes and mechanisms assumed to account for relations and patterns in observed data. That flexibility is most evident at the model-specification stage of implementation. The capacity for modeling latent variables, evaluating direct and indirect relations between latent and observed variables, and flexibly specifying parameters and relations between parameters makes SEM a formidable scientific tool. Yet appropriate and strategic use of SEM requires much of the researcher. From the selection of variables, including those not directly observed, to the designation of the relations between them and the specification of the parameters associated with those relations, the specification of a model for analysis using SEM requires a series of thoughtful decisions. Additional decisions face the researcher who wishes to compare different models of the same data or compare the fit of a single model for different groups. These decisions require balancing the desire to address specific research question with the need to account for the design and methods by which the data were generated and attend to concerns about parameter identification and equivalent models.

In this chapter, I have outlined the decisions involved in specifying a model for analysis using SEM. Along the way, I have provided examples of models and illustrated features of models typical of research in the social and behavioral sciences. Although those examples provided a means of describing the specifics of model specification, they only scratch the surface of modeling possibilities for which SEM is suitable. Many of those possibilities are described and illustrated in Parts IV and V of this handbook. Equipped now with a good understanding the basics of model specification, you are ready for exposure to the full range of possibilities for using SEM to model your own data.

NOTES

1. The loadings of the *x* variables on η_1 and η_2 and the *y* variables on ξ_1 also have been fixed to 0, a feature of the model specification that is lost as a result of the distinction between exogenous and endogenous latent variables.

2. Because variables typically are mean centered in SEM, *F* would have a mean of 0. Assigning it a variance of 1 would result in a standardized variable.

3. I assume only two-way interactions. Although higher-order interactions are possible and feasible when all variables are observed, when all variables involved in the interaction term are latent, only two-way interactions are feasible.

4. When the design is longitudinal and missingness is due primarily to attrition, an alternative strategy is to include *missing data indicators*, which allow for explicit modeling of the systematic missing mechanism (Enders, 2011).

5. Although the focus of this chapter is not estimation and testing, it is worth noting here that the 2 degrees of freedom difference between the models with and without the equality constraints could be used to test the difference in overall model fit, which is a test of whether the equality constraints are supported by the data.

6. It is possible to compare non-nested models using model fit statistics; however, the comparison of those fit statistics does not yield a value suitable for statistical testing. The most promising of these is the Bayesian information criterion (BIC), for which rules of thumb for interpreting the difference have been proposed (Raftery, 1995).

REFERENCES

Aiken, L. S., & West, S. G. (1991). *Multiple regression: Testing and interpreting interactions*. Thousand Oaks, CA: Sage.

Anderson, J. C., & Gerbing, D. W. (1988). Structural equation modeling in practice: A review and recommended two-step approach. *Psychological Bulletin, 103*, 411–423.

Bentler, P. M., & Weeks, D. G. (1980). Linear structural equations with latent variables. *Psychometrika, 45*, 289–308.

Bollen, K. A. (2011). Evaluating effect, composite, and causal indicators in structural equation models. *MIS Quarterly, 35*, 359–372.

Bollen, K. A., & Bauldry, S. (2011). Three Cs in measurement models: Causal indicators, composite indicators, and covariates. *Psychological Methods, 16*, 265–284.

Bollen, K. A., & Davis, W. R. (2009). Causal indicator models: Identification, estimation, and testing. *Structural Equation Modeling, 16*, 498–522

Collins, L. M., Schafer, J. L., & Kam, C.-M. (2001). A comparison of inclusive and restrictive strategies in modern missing data procedures. *Psychological Methods, 6*, 330–351.

DeShon, R. P. (1998). A cautionary note on measurement error corrections in structural equation models. *Psychological Methods, 4*, 412–423.

Diamantopoulos, A. (2011). Incorporating formative measures into covariance-based structural equation models. *MIS Quarterly, 35*, 335–358.

Eberhardt, F., Glymour, C., & Scheines, R. (2006). *N* − 1 experiments suffice to determine the causal relations among *N* variables. In D. E. Holmes & L. C. Jain (Eds.), *Innovations in machine learning: Theory and applications* (*Studies in fuzziness and soft computing*, Vol. 194, pp. 97–112). Berlin: Springer-Verlag.

Enders, C. K. (2011). Missing not at random models for latent growth curve analyses. *Psychological Methods, 16*, 1–16.

Graham, J. W. (2003). Adding missing-data relevant variables to FIML-based structural equation models. *Structural Equation Modeling, 10*, 80–100.

Heckman, J. (1997). Instrumental variables: A study of implicit behavioral assumptions used in making program evaluations. *Journal of Human Resources, 32*, 441–462.

Jöreskog, K. G. (1993). Testing structural equation models. In K. A. Bollen & J. S. Long (Eds.), *Testing structural equation models* (pp. 294–316). Thousand Oaks, CA: Sage.

Kenny, D. A., & Judd, C. M. (1984). Estimating the nonlinear and interactive effects of latent variables. *Psychological Bulletin, 96*, 201–210.

Landsheer, J. A. (2010). The specification of causal models with TETRAD IV: A review. *Structural Equation Modeling, 17*, 630–640.

Lee, S., & Hershberger, S. (1990). A simple rule for generating equivalent models in covariance structure modeling. *Multivariate Behavioral Research, 25*, 313–334.

Little, T. D., Cunningham, W. A., Shahar, G., & Widaman, K. F. (2002). To parcel or not to parcel: Exploring the question, weighing the merits. *Structural Equation Modeling, 9*, 151–173.

Lubke, G. H., & Muthén, B. (2005). Investigating population heterogeneity with factor mixture models. *Psychological Methods, 10*, 21–39.

MacCallum, R. C. (2003). Working with imperfect models. *Multivariate Behavioral Research, 38*, 113–139.

MacCallum, R. C., & Browne, M. W. (1993). The use of causal indicators in covariance structure models: Some practical issues. *Psychological Bulletin, 114*, 533–541.

MacCallum, R. C., Browne, M. W., & Sugawara, H. M. (1996). Power analysis and determining sample size for covariance structure modeling. *Psychological Methods, 1*, 130–149.

MacCallum, R. C., Roznowski, M., & Necowitz, L. B. (1992). Model modifications in covariance structure analysis: The problem of capitalization on chance. *Psychological Bulletin, 111*, 490–504.

Marsh, H. W., Hau, K.-T., Balla, J. R., & Grayson, D. (1998). Is more ever too much?: The number of indicators per factor in confirmatory factor analysis. *Multivariate Behavioral Research, 33*, 181–220.

Pearl, J. (2009). *Causality: Models, reasoning, and inference* (2nd ed.). New York: Cambridge University Press.

Ping, R. A., Jr. (1995). A parsimonious estimating technique for interaction and quadratic latent variables. *Journal of Marketing Research, 32*, 336–347.

Raftery, A. E. (1995). Bayesian model selection in social research. In P. V. Marsden (Ed.), *Sociological methodology* (pp. 111–163). Cambridge, UK: Blackwell.

Raykov, T., & Marcoulides, G. A. (2001). Can there be infinitely many models equivalent to a given covariance structure model? *Structural Equation Modeling, 8*, 142–149.

Rindskopf, D. (1984). Using phantom and imaginary latent variables to parameterize constraints in linear structural models. *Psychometrika, 49*, 37–47.

Scheines, R., Spirtes, P., Glymour, C., Meek, C., & Richardson, T. (1998). The TETRAD project: Constraint based aids to causal model specification. *Multivariate Behavioral Research, 33*, 65–117.

Stelzl, I. (1986). Changing a causal hypothesis without changing the fit: Some rules for generating equivalent path models. *Multivariate Behavioral Research, 21*, 309–331.

Treiblmaier, H., Bentler, P. M., & Mair, P. (2011). Formative constructs implemented via common factors. *Structural Equation Modeling, 18*, 1–17.

Wampold, B. E., Davis, B., & Good, R. H. (1990). Hypothesis validity of clinical research. *Journal of Consulting and Clinical Psychology, 58*, 360–367.

CHAPTER 9

Identification

A Nontechnical Discussion of a Technical Issue

David A. Kenny
Stephanie Milan

Identification is perhaps the most difficult concept for structural equation modeling (SEM) researchers to understand. We have seen SEM experts baffled and bewildered by issues of identification. We too have often encountered very difficult SEM problems that ended up being problems of identification. Identification is not just a technical issue that can be left to experts to ponder; if the model is not identified the research is impossible. If a researcher were to plan a study, collect data, and then find out that the model could not be uniquely estimated, a great deal of time would have been wasted. Thus, researchers need to know well in advance if the model they propose to test is in fact identified. In actuality, any sort of statistical modeling, be it analysis of variance or item response theory, has issues related to identification. Consequently, understanding the issues discussed in this chapter can be beneficial to researchers even if they never use SEM.

We have tried to write a nontechnical account. We apologize to the more sophisticated reader that we omitted discussion of some of the more difficult aspects of identification, but we have provided references to more technical discussions. That said, this chapter is not easy for most readers. We have many equations and often the discussion is very abstract. The reader may need to read, think, and reread various parts of this chapter.

The chapter begins with key definitions and then illustrates two models' identification status. We then have an extended discussion on determining whether a model is identified or not. Finally, we discuss models that are underidentified.

DEFINITIONS

"Identification" is going from the known information to the unknown parameters. In most SEMs, the amount of known information for estimation is the number of elements in the observed variance–covariance matrix. For example, a model with six variables would have 21 pieces of known information, six variances and 15 covariances. In general, with k measured variables, there are $k(k + 1)/2$ knowns. In some types of models (e.g., growth curve modeling), the knowns also include the sample means, making the number of knowns equal to $k(k + 3)/2$.

"Unknown information" in a specified model includes all parameters (i.e., variances, covariances, structural coefficients, factor loadings) to be estimated. A parameter in a hypothesized model is either freely estimated or fixed. Fixed parameters are typically constrained to a specific value, such as 1 (e.g., the unitary value placed on the path from a disturbance term to an endogenous variable or a factor loading for the marker variable) or 0 (e.g., the mean of an error term in a measurement model), or a fixed parameter may be constrained to be equal to some function of the free parameters (e.g., set equal to another parameter). Often, parameters are implicitly rather than explicitly fixed to 0 by exclusion of a path between two variables. When a parameter is fixed, it is no longer an unknown parameter to be estimated in analysis.

The correspondence of known versus unknown information determines whether a model is underidentified, just-identified, or overidentified. A model is said to be "identified" if it is possible to estimate a single, unique estimate for every free parameter. At the heart of identification is the solving of a set of simultaneous equations where each known value, the observed variances, covariances, and means, is assumed to be a given function of the unknown parameters.

An *underidentified* model is one in which it is impossible to obtain a unique estimate of all of the model's parameters. Whenever there is more unknown than known information, the model is underidentified. For instance, in the equation

$$10 = 2x + y$$

there is one piece of known information (the 10 on the left side of the equation), but two pieces of unknown information (the values of x and y). As a result, there are infinite possibilities for estimates of x and y that would make this statement true, such as $\{x = 4, y = 2\}$, $\{x = 3, y = 4\}$. Because there is no unique solution for x and y, this equation is said to be *underidentified*. It is important to note that it is not the case that the equation cannot be solved, but rather that there are multiple, equally valid, solutions for x and y.

The most basic question of identification is whether the amount of unknown information to be estimated in a model (i.e., number of free parameters) is less than or equal to the amount of known information from which the parameters are estimated. The difference between the known versus unknown information typically equals the model's *degrees of freedom*, or *df*. In the earlier example of underidentification, there was more unknown than known information, implying negative *df*. In his seminal description of model identification, Bollen (1989) labeled non-negative *df*, or the *t*-rule, as the first condition for model identification. Although the equations are much more complex for SEM, the logic

of identification for SEM is identical to that for simple systems of linear equations. The *minimum condition of identifiability* is that for a model to be identified there must be at least as many knowns as unknowns. This is a necessary condition: All identified models meet the condition, but some models that meet this condition are not identified, two examples of which we present later.

In a *just-identified* model, there is an equal amount of known and unknown information, and the model is identified. Imagine, for example, two linear equations:

$$10 = 2x + y$$
$$2 = x - y$$

In this case, there are two pieces of unknown information (the values of x and y) and two pieces of known information (10 and 2) to use in solving for x and y. Because the number of knowns and unknowns is equal, it is possible to derive unique values for x and y that exactly solve these equations, specifically, $x = 4$ and $y = 2$. A just-identified model is also referred to as a *saturated model*.

A model is said to be *overidentified* if there is more known information than unknown information. This is the case, for example, if we solve for x and y using the three linear equations:

$$10 = 2x + y$$
$$2 = x - y$$
$$5 = x + 2y$$

In this situation, it is possible to generate solutions for x and y using two equations, such as $\{x = 4, y = 2\}$, $\{x = 3, y = 1\}$, and $\{x = 5, y = 0\}$. Notice, however, that none of these solutions exactly reproduces the known values for all three equations. Instead, the different possible values for x and y all result in some discrepancy between the known values and the solutions using the estimated unknowns.

One might wonder why an overidentified model is preferable to a just-identified model, which possesses the seemingly desirable attributes of balance and correctness. One goal of model testing is falsifiability, and a just-identified model cannot be found to be false. In contrast, an overidentified model is always wrong to some degree, and it is this degree of wrongness that tells us how good (or bad) our hypothesis is given the available data. Only overidentified models provide fit statistics as a means of evaluating the fit of the overall model.

There are two different ways in which a model is not identified. In the first, and most typical, case, the model is too complex with negative model degrees of freedom and, therefore, fails to satisfy the minimum condition of identifiability. Less commonly, a model may meet the minimum condition of identifiability, but the model is not identified because at least one parameter is not identified. Although we normally concentrate on the identification of the overall model, in these types of situations we need to know the identification status of specific *parameters* in the model. Any given parameter in a model can be underidentified, just-identified, or overidentified. Importantly, there may be situations when a model is underidentified, yet some of the model's key parameters may be identified.

Sometimes a model may appear to be identified, but there are estimation difficulties. Imagine, for example, two linear equations:

$$10 = 2x + y$$
$$20 = 4x + 2y$$

In this case, there are two pieces of unknown information (the values of x and y) and two pieces of known information (10 and 20), and the model would appear to be identified. But if we use these equations to solve for x or y, there is no solution. So although we have as many knowns as unknowns, given the numbers in the equation there is no solution. When in SEM a model is theoretically identified, but given the specific values of the knowns there is no solution, we say that the model is *empirically underidentified*. Although there appear to be two different pieces of known information, these equations are actually a linear function of each other and, thus, do not provide two pieces of information. Note that if we multiply the first equation by 2, we obtain the second equation, and so there is just one equation.

GOING FROM KNOWNS TO UNKNOWNS

To illustrate how to determine whether a model is identified, we describe two simple models, one being a path analysis and the other a single latent variable model. Later in the chapter, we do the same for a model with a mean structure. To minimize the complexity of the mathematics in this section, we standardize all variables except disturbance terms. We consider first a simple path analysis model, shown in Figure 9.1:

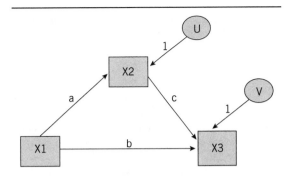

FIGURE 9.1. Simple three-variable path analysis model.

$$X_2 = aX_1 + U$$
$$X_3 = bX_1 + cX_2 + V$$

where U and V are uncorrelated with each other and with X_1. We have six knowns, consisting of three variances, which all equal 1 because the variables are standardized, and three correlations. We can use the algebra of covariances (Kenny, 1979) to express them in terms of the unknowns[1]:

$$r_{12} = a$$
$$r_{13} = b + cr_{12}$$
$$r_{23} = br_{12} + c$$
$$1 = s_1^2$$
$$1 = a^2 s_1^2 + s_U^2$$
$$1 = b^2 s_1^2 + c^2 s_2^2 + bcr_{12} + s_V^2$$

We see right away that we know s_1^2 equals 1 and that path a equals r_{12}. However, the solution for b and c is a little more complicated:

$$b = \frac{r_{13} - r_{12}r_{23}}{1 - r_{12}^2}$$

$$c = \frac{r_{23} - r_{12}r_{13}}{1 - r_{12}^2}$$

Now that we know a, b, and c, we can solve the two remaining unknowns, s_U^2 and s_V^2: $s_U^2 = 1 - a^2$ and $s_V^2 = 1 - b^2 - c^2 - 2r_{12}$. The model is identified because we can solve for the unknown model parameters from the known variances and covariances.

As a second example, let us consider a simple model in which all the variables have 0 means:

$$X_1 = fF + E_1$$
$$X_2 = gF + E_2$$
$$X_3 = hF + E_3$$

where E_1, E_2, E_3, and F are uncorrelated, all variables are mean deviated, and all variables, except the E's, have a variance of 1. We have also drawn the model in Figure 9.2. We have six knowns, consisting of three variances, which all equal 1 because the variables are standardized, and three correlations. We have six unknowns: f, g, h, s_{E1}^2, s_{E2}^2, and s_{E3}^2. We can express the knowns in terms of the unknowns:

$$r_{12} = fg$$
$$r_{13} = fh$$
$$r_{23} = gh$$
$$1 = f^2 + s_{E1}^2$$
$$1 = g^2 + s_{E2}^2$$
$$1 = h^2 + s_{E3}^2$$

We can solve[2] for f, g, and h by

$$f^2 = \frac{r_{12}r_{13}}{r_{23}}, \quad g^2 = \frac{r_{12}r_{23}}{r_{13}}, \quad h^2 = \frac{r_{13}r_{23}}{r_{12}}$$

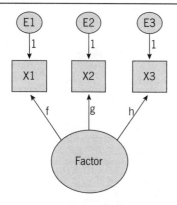

FIGURE 9.2. Simple three-variable latent variable model (latent variable standardized).

The solution for the error variances are as follows: $s_{E1}^2 = 1 - f^2$, $s_{E2}^2 = 1 - g^2$, and $s_{E3}^2 = 1 - h^2$. The model is identified because we can solve for the unknown model parameters from the known variances and covariances.

OVERIDENTIFIED MODELS AND OVERIDENTIFYING RESTRICTIONS

An example of an overidentified model is shown in Figure 9.1, if we assume that path b is equal to 0. Note that there would be one less unknown than knowns. A key feature of an overidentified model is that at least one of the model's parameter has multiple estimates. For instance, there are two estimates[3] of path c, one being r_{23} and the other being r_{13}/r_{12}. If we set these two estimates equal and rearrange terms, we have $r_{13} - r_{23}r_{12} = 0$. This is what is called an *overidentifying restriction*, which represents a constraint on the covariance matrix. Path models with complete mediation ($X \rightarrow Y \rightarrow Z$) or spuriousness ($X \leftarrow Y \rightarrow Z$) are overidentified and have what is called *d-separation* (Pearl, 2009).

All models with positive degrees of freedom (i.e., more knowns than unknowns) have overidentifying restrictions. The standard χ^2 test in SEM evaluates the entire set of overidentifying restrictions.

If we add a fourth indicator, X_4, for the model in Figure 9.2, we have an overidentified model with 2 degrees of freedom (10 knowns and 8 unknowns). There are three overidentifying restrictions:

$$r_{12}r_{34} - r_{13}r_{24} = 0, \; r_{12}r_{34} - r_{14}r_{23} = 0, \; r_{13}r_{24} - r_{14}r_{23} = 0$$

Note that if two of the restrictions hold, however, the third must also hold; consequently, there are only two *independent* overidentifying restrictions. The model's degrees of freedom equal the number of *independent* overidentifying restrictions. Later we shall see that some underidentified models have restrictions on the known information.

If a model is overidentified, researchers can test overidentified restrictions as a group using the χ^2 test or individually by examining modification indices. One of the themes of this chapter is that there should be more focused tests of overidentifying restrictions. When we discuss specific types of models, we return to this issue.

HOW CAN WE DETERMINE IF A MODEL IS IDENTIFIED?

Earlier we showed that one way to determine if the model is identified is to take the knowns and see if we can solve for the unknowns. In practice, this is almost never done. (One source described this practice as "not fun.") Rather, very different strategies are used. The minimum condition of identifiability, or *t*-rule, is a starting point, but because it is just a necessary condition, how can we know for certain if a model is identified? Here we discuss three different strategies to determine whether a model is identified: formal solutions, computational solutions, and rules of thumb.

Formal Solutions

Most of the discussion about identification in the literature focuses on this approach. There are two rules that have been suggested, the rank and order conditions, for path models but not factor analysis models. We refer the reader to Bollen (1989) and Kline (2010) for discussion of these rules. Recent work by Bekker, Merckens, and Wansbeek (1994), Bollen and Bauldry (2010), and Mc-Donald (2002) has provided fairly general solutions. As this is a nontechnical introduction to the topic of identification, we do not provide the details here. However, in our experience, neither of these rules is of much help to practicing SEM researchers, especially those who are studying latent variable models.

Computational Solutions

One strategy is to input one's data into a SEM program and if it runs, then it must be identified. This is the strategy that most people use to determine if their model is identified. The strategy works as follows: The computer program attempts to compute the standard errors of the estimates. If there is a difficulty in the computation of these standard errors (i.e., the information matrix cannot be inverted), the program warns that the model may not be identified.

There are several drawbacks with this approach. First, if poor starting values are chosen, the computer program could mistakenly conclude the model is underidentified when in fact it may be identified. Second, the program does not indicate whether the model is theoretically underidentified or empirically underidentified. Third, the program very often is not very helpful in indicating which parameters are underidentified. Fourth, and most importantly, this method of determining identification gives an answer that comes too late. Who wants to find out that one's model is underidentified after taking the time to collect data?[4]

Rules of Thumb

In this case, we give up on a general strategy of identification and instead determine what needs to be true for a particular model to be identified. In the next two sections of the chapter, we give rules of thumb for several different types of models.

Can There Be a General Solution?

Ideally, we need a general algorithm to determine whether or not a given model is identified. However, it is reasonable to believe that there will never be such an algorithm. The question is termed to be *undecidable*; that is, there can never be an algorithm we can employ to determine if any model is identified or not. The problem is that SEMs are so varied that there may not be a general algorithm that can identify every possible model; at this point, however, we just do not know if a general solution can be found.

RULES FOR IDENTIFICATION FOR PARTICULAR TYPES OF MODELS

We first consider models with measured variables as causes, what we shall call *path analysis models*. We consider three different types of such models: models without feedback, models with feedback, and models with omitted variables. After we consider path analysis models, we consider latent variable models. We then combine the two in what is called a *hybrid model*. In the next section of the chapter, we discuss the identification of over-time models.

Path Analysis Models: Models without Feedback

Path analysis models without feedback are identified if the following sufficient condition is met: Each endogenous variable's disturbance term is uncorrelated with all of the causes of that endogenous variable. We call this the *regression rule* (which is entailed by the *non-*

bow rule by Brito and Pearl [2002]) because the structural coefficients can be estimated by multiple regression. Bollen's (1989) recursive rule and null rule are subsumed under this more general rule. Consider the model in Figure 9.3. The variables X_1 and X_2 are exogenous variables, and X_3, X_4, and X_5 are endogenous. We note that U_1 is uncorrelated with X_1 and X_2, and U_2 and U_3 are uncorrelated with X_3, which makes the model identified by the regression rule. In fact, the model is overidentified in that there are four more knowns than unknowns.

The overidentifying restrictions for models overidentified by the regression rule can often be thought of as *deleted paths*, that is, paths that are assumed to be zero and so are not drawn in the model, but if they were all drawn, the model would still be identified. These deleted paths can be more important theoretically than the specified paths because they can potentially falsify the model. Very often these deleted paths are direct paths in a mediational model. For instance, for the model in Figure 9.3, the deleted paths are from X_1 and X_2 to X_4 and X_5, all of which are direct paths.

We suggest the following procedure in testing overidentified path models. Determine what paths in the model are deleted paths, the total being equal to the number of knowns minus unknowns or model *df*. For many models, it is clear exactly what the deleted paths are. In some cases, it may make more sense not to add a path between variables, but to correlate the disturbance terms. One would also want to make sure that the model is still identified by the regression rule after the deleted paths are added. After the deleted paths are specified, the model should now be just-identified. That model is estimated and the deleted paths are individually tested, perhaps with a lower alpha due to multiple testing. Ideally, none of them should be statistically significant. Once the deleted paths are tested, one estimates the specified model, but includes deleted paths that were found to be nonzero.

Path Analysis Models: Models with Feedback

Most feedback models are direct feedback models: two variables directly cause one another. For instance, Frone, Russell, and Cooper (1994) studied how work satisfaction and home satisfaction mutually influence each other. To identify such models, one needs a special type of variable, called an *instrumental variable*. In Figure 9.4, we have a simplified version of the Frone

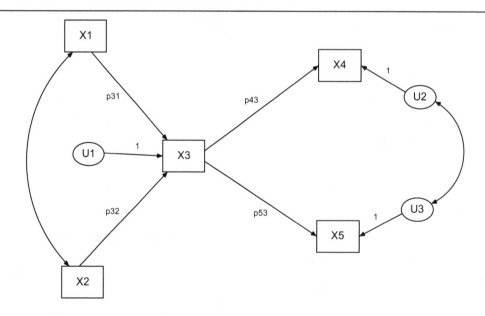

FIGURE 9.3. Identified path model with four omitted paths.

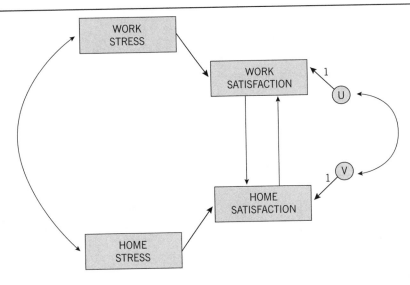

FIGURE 9.4. Feedback model for satisfaction with stress as an instrumental variable.

and colleagues model. We have a direct feedback loop between home and work satisfaction. Note the pattern for the stress variables. Each causes one variable in the loop but not the other: Work stress causes work satisfaction, and home stress causes home satisfaction. Work stress is said to be an instrumental variable for the path from work to home satisfaction, in that it causes work satisfaction but not home satisfaction; home stress is said to be an instrumental variable for the path from home to work satisfaction, in that it causes home satisfaction but not work satisfaction. The key feature of an instrumental variable: It causes one variable in the loop but not the other. For the model in Figure 9.4, we have 10 knowns and 10 unknowns, and the model is just-identified. Note that the assumption of a 0 path is a theoretical assumption and not something that is empirically verified.

These models are overidentified if there is an excess of instruments. In the Frone and colleagues (1994) study, there are actually three instruments for each path, making a total of 4 *df*. If the overidentifying restriction does not hold, it might indicate that we have a "bad" instrument, an instrument whose assumed 0 path is not actually 0. However, if the overidentifying restrictions do not hold, there is no way to know for sure which instrument is the bad one.

As pointed out by Rigdon (1995) and others, only one instrumental variable is needed if the disturbance terms are uncorrelated. So in Figure 9.4, we could add a path from work stress to home satisfaction or from home stress to work satisfaction if the disturbance correlation were fixed to 0.

Models with indirect feedback loops can be identified by using instrumental variables. However, the indirect feedback loop of $X_1 \rightarrow X_2 \rightarrow X_3 \rightarrow X_1$ is identified if the disturbance terms are uncorrelated with each other. Kenny, Kashy, and Bolger (1998) give a rule—we call it the *one-link rule*—that appears to be a sufficient condition for identification: If between each pair of variables there is no more than one link (a causal path or a correlation), then the model is identified. Note that this rule subsumes the regression rule described in the previous section.

Path Analysis Models: Omitted Variables

A particularly troubling problem in the specification of SEMs is the problem of omitted variables: Two variables in a model share variance because some variable not included in the model causes both of them. The problem has also been called "spuriousness," "the third-variable problem," "confounding," and "endogeneity." We can use

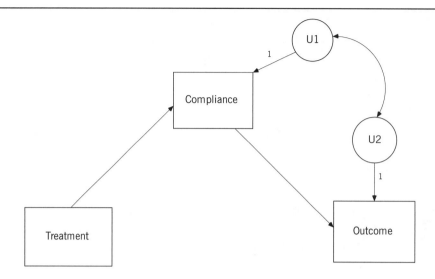

FIGURE 9.5. Example of omitted variable.

an instrumental variable to solve this problem. Consider the example in Figure 9.5. We have a variable, treatment, which is a randomized variable believed to cause the outcome. Yet not everyone complies with the treatment; some assigned to receive the intervention refuse it and some assigned to the control group somehow receive the treatment. Compliance mediates the effect of treatment on outcome, but there is the problem of omitted variables. Likely there are common causes of compliance and the outcome (i.e., omitted variables). In this case, we can use the treatment as an instrumental variable to estimate the model's parameters in Figure 9.5.

Confirmatory Factor Analysis Models

Identification of confirmatory factor analysis (CFA) models or measurement models is complicated. Much of what follows here is from Kenny and colleagues (1998) and O'Brien (1994). Readers who are interested in the identification of exploratory factor analysis models should consult Hayashi and Marcoulides (2006).

To identify variables with latent variables the units of measurement of the latent variable need to be fixed. This is usually done by fixing the loading of one indicator, called the "marker variable," to 1. Alternatively, the variance of a latent exogenous variable can be fixed to some value, usually 1.

We begin with a discussion of a simple structure where each measure loads on only one latent variable and there are no correlated errors. Such models are identified if there are at least two correlated latent variables and two indicators per latent variable. The difference between knowns and unknowns with k measured variables and p latent variables is $k(k + 1)/2 - k + p - p(p + 1)/2$. This number is usually very large and so the minimum condition of identifiability is typically of little value for the identification of CFA models.

For CFA models, there are three types of overidentifying restrictions, and all involve what are called *vanishing tetrads* (Bollen & Ting, 1993), in which the product of two correlations minus the product of two other correlations equals 0. The first set of overidentifying restrictions involves constraints within indicators of the same latent variable. If there are four indicators of the same latent variable, the vanishing tetrad is of the form: $r_{X_1X_2}r_{X_3X_4} - r_{X_1X_3}r_{X_2X_4} = 0$, where the four X variables are indicators of the same latent variables. For each latent variable with four or more indicators, the number of independent overidentifying restrictions is $k(k - 3)/2$, where k is the number of indicators. The test of these constraints *within* a latent variable evaluates the single-factoredness of each latent variable.

The second set of overidentifying restrictions involves constraints across indicators of two different

9. Identification

153

latent variables: $r_{X_1Y_1}r_{X_2Y_2} - r_{X_1Y_2}r_{X_2Y_1} = 0$, where X_1 and X_2 are indicators of one latent variable, and Y_1 and Y_2 indicators of another. For each pair of latent variables with k indicators of one and m of the other, the number of independent overidentifying restrictions is $(k-1)(m-1)$. The test of these constraints *between* indicators of two different variables evaluates potential method effects across latent variables.

The third set of overidentifying restrictions involves constraints within and between indicators of the same latent variable: $r_{X_1X_2}r_{X_3Y_1} - r_{X_2Y_1}r_{X_1X_3} = 0$, where X_1, X_2, and X_3 are indicators of one latent variable and Y_1 is an indicator of another. These constraints have been labeled *consistency constraints* (Costner, 1969) in that they evaluate whether a good indicator within, one that correlates highly with other indicators of the construct, is also a good indicator between, one that correlates highly with indicators of other constructs. For each pair of latent variables with k indicators of one and m of the other (k and m both greater than or equal to 3), the number of independent overidentifying restrictions is $(k-1) + (m-1)$ given the other overidentifying restrictions. These constraints evaluate whether any indicators load on an additional factor.

Ideally, these three different sets of overidentifying constraints could be separately tested, as they suggest very different types of specification error. The first set suggests correlated errors within indicators of the same factor. The second set suggests correlated errors across indicators of different factor or method effects. Finally, the third set suggests an indicator loads on two different factors. For overidentified CFA models, which include almost all CFA models, we can either use the overall χ^2 to evaluate the entire set of constraints simultaneously, or we can examine the modification indices to evaluate individual constraints. Bollen and Ting (1993) show how more focused tests of vanishing tetrads can be used to evaluate different types of specification errors. However, to our knowledge, no SEM program provides focused tests of these different sorts of overidentifying restrictions.

If the model contains correlated errors, then the identification rules need to be modified. For the model to be identified, then, each latent variable needs two indicators that do not have correlated errors, and every pair of latent variables needs at least one indicator of each that does not share correlated errors. We can also allow for measured variables to load on two or more latent variables. Researchers can consult Kenny and colleagues (1998) and Bollen and Davis (2009)

for guidance about the identification status of these models.

Adding means to most models is straightforward. One gains k knowns, the means, and k unknowns, the intercepts for the measured variables, where k is the number of measured variables, with no effect at all on the identification status of the model. Issues arise if we allow a latent variable to have a mean (if it is exogenous) or an intercept (if it is endogenous). One situation where we want to have factor means (or intercepts) is when we wish to test invariance of means (or intercepts) across time or groups. One way to do so, for each indicator, is to fix the intercepts of same indicator to be equal across times or groups, set the intercept for the marker variable to 0, and free the latent means (or intercepts) for each time or group (Bollen, 1989).

Hybrid Models

A hybrid model combines a CFA and path analysis model (Kline, 2010). These two models are typically referred to as the "structural model" and the "measurement model," respectively. Several authors (Bollen, 1989; Kenny et al., 1998; O'Brien, 1994) have suggested a two-step approach to identification of such models. A hybrid model cannot be identified unless the structural model is identified. Assuming that the structural model is identified, we then determine if the measurement model is identified. If both are identified, then the entire model is identified. There is the special case of the measurement model that becomes identified because the structural model is overidentified, an example of which we give later in the chapter when we discuss single-indicator over-time models.

Within hybrid models, there are two types of specialized variables. First are formative latent variables, in which the "indicators" cause the latent variable instead of the more standard reflective latent variable, which causes its indicators (Bollen & Lennox, 1991). For these models to be identified, two things need to hold: One path to the latent factor is fixed to a nonzero value, usually 1, and the latent variable has no disturbance term. Bollen and Davis (2009) describe a special situation where a formative latent variable may have a disturbance.

Additionally, there are second-order factors that are latent variables whose indicators are themselves latent variables. The rules of identification for second-order latent variables are the same as those for regular latent variables, but here the indicators are latent, not measured.

IDENTIFICATION IN OVER-TIME MODELS

Autoregressive Models

In these models, a score at one time causes the score at the next time point. We consider here single-indicator models and multiple-indicator models.

Single-Indicator Models

An example of this model with two variables measured at four times is contained in Figure 9.6. We have the variables X and Y measured at four times and each as-sumed to be caused by a latent variable, LX and LY. The latent variables have an autoregessive structure: Each latent variable is caused by the previous variable. The model is underidentified, but some parameters are identified: They include all of the causal paths between latent variables, except those from Time 1 to Time 2, and the error variances for Times 2 and 3. We might wonder how it is that the paths are identified when we have only a single indicator of X and Y. The variables X_1 and Y_1 serve as instrumental variables for the estimation of the paths from LX_2 and LY_2, and X_2 and Y_2 serve as instrumental variables for the estimation of the paths

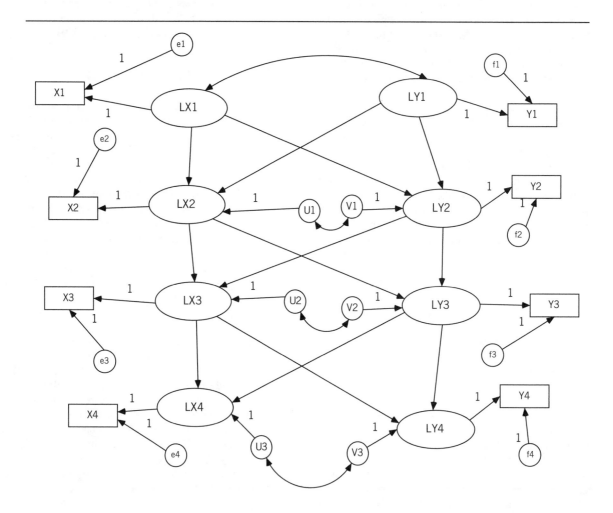

FIGURE 9.6. Two variables measured at four times with autoregressive effects.

from LX_3 and LY_3. Note, in each case, the instrumental variable (e.g., X_1) causes the "causal variable" (e.g., LX_2) but not the outcome variable (e.g., LX_3).

A strategy to identify the entire model is to set the error variances, separately for X and Y, to be equal across time. We can test the plausibility of the assumption of equal error variances for the middle two waves' error variances, separately for X and Y.

Multiple-Indicator Models

For latent variable, multiple-indicator models, just two waves are needed for identification. In these models, errors from the same indicator measured at different times normally need to be correlated. This typically requires a minimum of three indicators per latent variable. If there are three or more waves, one might wish to estimate and test a first-order autoregressive model in which each latent variable is caused only by that variable measured at the previous time point.

Latent Growth Models

In the latent growth model (LGM), the researcher is interested in individual trajectories of change over time in some attribute. In the SEM approach, change over time is modeled as a latent process. Specifically, repeated-measure variables are treated as reflections of at least two latent factors, typically called an *intercept* and *slope* factors. Figure 9.7 illustrates a latent variable model of linear growth with three repeated observations, where X_1 to X_3 are the observed scores at the three time points. Observed X scores are a function of the latent intercept factor, the latent slope factor with factor loadings reflecting the assumed slope, and a time-specific error. Because the intercept is constant over time, the intercept factor loadings are constrained to 1 for all time points. Because linear growth is assumed, the slope factor loadings are constrained from 0 to 1 with an equal increment of 0.5 in between. An observation at any time point could be chosen as the intercept point (i.e., the observation with a 0 factor loading), and slope factor loadings could be modeled in various ways to reflect different patterns of change.

The parameters to be estimated in a LGM with T time points include means and variances for the intercept and slope factors, a correlation between the intercept and the slope factors, and error variances, resulting in a total of $5 + T$ parameters. The known information will include T variances, $T(T-1)/2$ covariances, and T

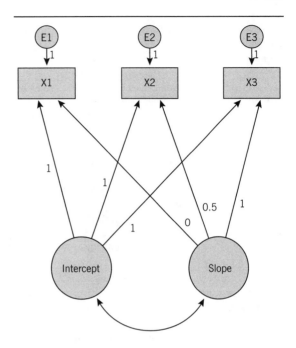

FIGURE 9.7. Latent growth model.

means, for a total of $T(T+3)/2$. The difference between knowns and unknowns is $(T(T+3)/2) - (T+5)$. To illustrate, if $T = 3$, $df = 9 - 8 = 1$. To see that the model is identified for three time points, we first determine what the knowns equal in terms of the unknowns, and then see if we have a solution for unknowns. Denoting I for the intercept latent factor and S for slope, the knowns equal:

$$\bar{X}_1 = \bar{I},\ \bar{X}_2 = \bar{I} + .5\bar{S},\ \bar{X}_3 = \bar{I} + \bar{S}$$
$$s_1^2 = s_I^2 + s_{E1}^2,\ s_2^2 = s_I^2 + .25s_S^2 + s_{IS} + s_{E2}^2$$
$$s_3^2 = s_I^2 + s_S^2 + 2s_{IS} + s_{E3}^2$$
$$s_{12} = s_I^2 + .5s_{IS},\ s_{13} = s_I^2 + s_{IS},\ s_{23} = s_I^2 + 1.5s_{IS} + 0.5s_S^2$$

The solution for the unknown parameters in terms of the knowns is

$$\bar{I} = \bar{X}_1,\ \bar{S} = \bar{X}_3 - \bar{X}_1$$
$$s_I^2 = 2s_{12} - s_{13},\ s_S^2 = 2s_{23+} + 2s_{12} - 4s_{13},\ s_{IS} = 2(s_{13} - s_{12})$$
$$s_{E1}^2 = s_1^2 - 2s_{12} + s_{13},\ s_{E2}^2 = s_2^2 - .5s_{12} - .5s_{13}$$
$$s_{E3}^2 = s_3^2 + s_{13} - 2s_{23}$$

There is an overidentifying restriction of $0 = \bar{X}_1 - \bar{X}_2 + \bar{X}_3$, which implies that the means have a linear relationship with time.

Many longitudinal models include correlations between error terms of adjacent waves of data. A model that includes serially correlated error terms constrained to be equal would have one additional free parameter. A model with serially correlated error terms that are not constrained to be equal—which may be more appropriate when there are substantial time differences between waves—has $T - 1$ additional free parameters. As a general guideline, if a specified model has a fixed growth pattern and includes serially correlated error terms (whether set to be equal or not), there must be at least four waves of data for the model to be identified. Note that even though a model with three waves has one more known than unknown, we cannot "use" that extra known to allow for correlated errors. This would not work because that extra known is lost to the overidentifying restriction on the means.

Specifying a model with nonlinear growth also increases the number of free parameters in the model. There are two major ways that nonlinear growth is typically accounted for in SEM. The first is to include a third factor reflecting quadratic growth in which the loadings to observed variables are constrained to the square of time based on the loadings of the slope factor (Bollen & Curran, 2006). Including a quadratic latent factor increases the number of free parameters by four (a quadratic factor mean and variance and two covariances). The degrees of freedom for the model would be: $T(T + 3)/2 - (T + 9)$. To be identified, a quadratic latent growth model must therefore have at least four waves of data, and five if there were also correlated errors.

Another way to estimate nonlinear growth is to fix one loading from the slope factor (e.g., the first loading) to 0 and one loading (e.g., the last) to 1, and allow intermediate loadings to be freely estimated (Meredith & Tisak, 1990). This approach allows the researcher to determine the average pattern of change based on estimated factor loadings. The number of free parameters in this model increases by $T - 2$. The degrees of freedom for this model, therefore, would be $(T(T + 3)/2) - (2T + 3)$. For this model to be identified, there must be at least three waves of data and four for correlated errors, and to be overidentified, there must be at least four waves of data and five for correlated errors.

The LGM can be extended to a model of latent difference scores, or LDS. The reader should consult McArdle and Hamagami (2001) for information about the identification of these models. Also, Bollen and Curran (2004) discuss the identification of a combined LGM and autoregressive models.

A Longitudinal Test of Spuriousness

Very often with over-time data, researchers estimate a causal model in which one variable causes another with a given time lag, much as in Figure 9.6. Alternatively, we might estimate a model with no causal effects, but rather with the source of the covariation due to unmeasured variables. The explanation of the covariation between variables is entirely due to spuriousness, with the measured variables all caused by common latent variables.

We briefly outline the model, a variant of which was originally proposed by Kenny (1975). The same variables are measured at two times and are caused by multiple latent variables. Though not necessary, we assume that the latent variables are uncorrelated with each other. A variable i's factor loadings are assumed to change by a proportional constant k_i, making $A_2 = A_1 K$, where K is a diagonal matrix with elements k_i. Although the model as a whole is underidentified, the model has restrictions on the covariances, as long as there are three measures. There are constraints on the synchronous covariances, such that for variables i and j, $s_{1i,1j} = k_i k_j s_{2i,2j}$, where the first subscript indicates the time and the second indicates the variable, and constraints on the cross-lagged covariances, $k_i s_{1i,2j} = k_j s_{2i,1j}$. In general, the *df* of this model are $n(n - 2)$, where n is the number of variables measured at each time. To estimate the model, we create $2n$ latent variables, each of whose indicators is a measured variable. The loadings are fixed to 1 for the Time 1 measurements and to k_i for Time 2. We set the Time 1 and Time 2 covariances to be equal, and the corresponding cross-lagged correlations to be equal. (The Mplus setup is available at *www.handbookofsem.com*.) If this model provides a good fit, then we can conclude that data can be explained by spuriousness.

The reason why we would want to estimate the model is to rule out spuriousness as an explanation of the covariance structure. If such a model had a poor fit to the data, we could argue that we need to estimate causal effects. Even though the model is not identified, it has restrictions that allow us to test for spuriousness.

UNDERIDENTIFIED MODELS

SEM computer programs work well for models that are identified but not for models that are underidentified. As we shall see, sometimes these models contain some parameters that are identified, even if the model as a whole is not identified. Moreover, some underidentified models have restrictions that make it possible to test the fit of the overall model.

Models That Meet the Minimum Condition but Are Not Identified

Here we discuss two examples of models that are not identified but meet the minimum condition. The first model, presented in Figure 9.8, has 10 knowns and 10 unknowns, and so the minimum condition is met. However, none of the parameters of this model is identified. The reason is that the model contains two restrictions of $r_{23} - r_{12}r_{13} = 0$ and $r_{24} - r_{12}r_{14} = 0$ (see Kenny, 1979, pp. 106–107). Because of these two restrictions, we lose two knowns, and we no longer have as many knowns as unknowns. We are left with a model for which we can measure fit but we cannot estimate any of the model's paths. We note that if we use the classic equation that

the model's *df* equal the knowns minus the unknowns, we would get the wrong answer of 0. The correct answer for the model in Figure 9.8 is 2.

The second model, presented in Figure 9.9, has 10 parameters and 10 unknowns, and so it meets the minimum condition. For this model, some of the paths are identified and others are underidentified. The feedback paths *a* and *b* are not identified, nor are the variances of U_1 and U_2, or their covariance. However, paths *c, d,* and *e* are identified, and path *e* is overidentified.

Note that for both of these models, although neither is identified, we have learned something important. For the first, the model has an overidentifying restriction, and for the second, several of the parameters are identified. So far as we know, the only program that provides a solution for underidentified models is AMOS,[5] which tests the restrictions in Figure 9.8 and estimates of the identified parameters for the model in Figure 9.9. Bollen's (1996) instrumental variable estimation method would be able to estimate most of these parameters but, unfortunately, that method is not yet implemented in any SEM package. Later in the chapter we discuss how it is possible to estimate models that are underidentified with programs other than AMOS.

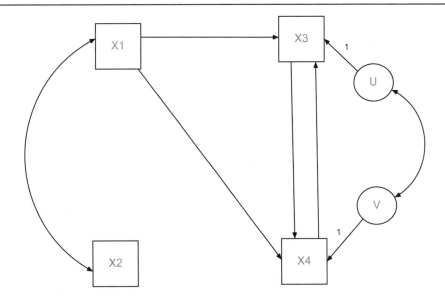

FIGURE 9.8. A model that meets the minimum condition of identifiability, but is not identified because of restrictions.

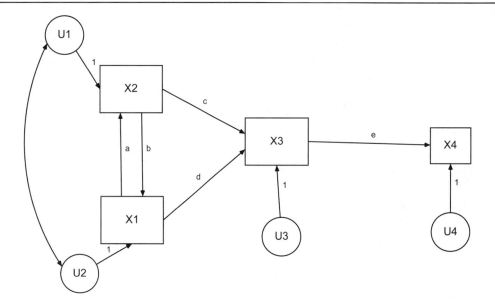

FIGURE 9.9. A model that meets the minimum condition of identifiability, with some parameters identified and others overidentified.

We suggest a possible reformulation of the *t*-rule or the minimum condition of identifiability: For a model to be identified, the number of unknowns *plus the number of independent restrictions* must be less than or equal to the number of knowns. We believe this to be a necessary and sufficient condition for identification.

Underidentified Models for Which One or More Model Parameter Can Be Estimated

In Figure 9.10, we have a model in which we seek to measure the effect of stability, or the path from the Time 1 latent variable to the Time 2 latent variable. If we count the number of parameters, we see that there are 10 knowns and 11 unknowns, two loadings, two latent variances, one latent covariance, four error variances, and two error covariances. The model is underidentified because it fails to meet the minimum condition of identifiability. That said, the model does provide interesting information: the *correlation* (not the covariance) between the latent variables, which equals $\sqrt{[(r_{12,21}r_{11,22})/(r_{11,21}r_{12,22})]}$. Assuming that the signs of $r_{11,21}$ and $r_{12,22}$ are both positive, the sign of

latent variable correlation is determined by the signs of $r_{12,21}$ and $r_{11,22}$, which should both be the same. The standardized stability might well be an important piece of information.

Figure 9.11 presents a second model that is underidentified but from which theoretically relevant parameters can be estimated. This diagram is of a growth curve model in which there are three exogenous variables, Z_1, Z_2, and Z_3. For this model, we have 20 knowns and 22 unknowns (six paths, four covariances, seven variances, three means, and two intercepts) and so the model is not identified. The growth curve part of the model is underidentified, but the effects of the exogenous variables on the slope and the intercept are identified. In some contexts, these may be the most important parameters of the model.

Empirical Underidentification

A model might be theoretically identified in that there are unique solutions for each of the model's parameters, but a solution for one or more of the model's parameters is not defined. Consider the earlier discussed path anal-

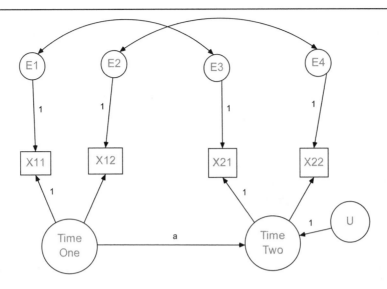

FIGURE 9.10. A model in that does not meet the minimum condition of identifiability, but with a standardized stability path identified.

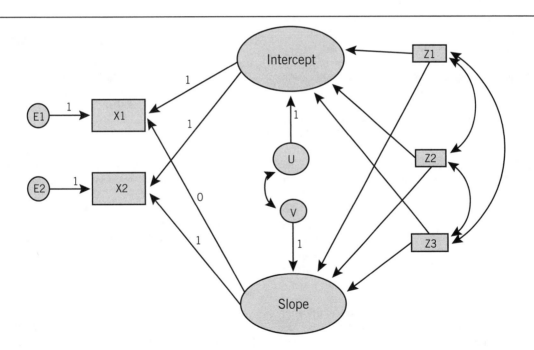

FIGURE 9.11. Latent growth curve model with exogenous variables, with some of the parameters identified and others not identified.

ysis presented Figure 9.1. The standardized estimate c is equal to

$$\frac{r_{12} - r_{12}r_{13}}{1 - r_{12}^2}$$

This model would be empirically underidentified if $r_{12}^2 = 1$, making the denominator 0, commonly called *perfect multicollinearity*.

This example illustrates a defining feature of empirical underidentification: When the knowns are entered into the solution for the unknown, the equation is mathematically undefined. In the example, the denominator of an estimate of an unknown is equal to 0, which is typical of most empirical underidentifications. Another example was presented earlier in Figure 9.2. An estimate of a factor loading would be undefined when one of the correlations between the three indicators was 0 because the denominator of one of the estimates of the loadings equals 0.

The solution can also be mathematically undefined for other reasons. Consider again the model in Figure 9.2 and $r_{12}r_{13}r_{23} < 0$; that is, either one or three of the correlations are negative. When this is the case, the estimate of the loading *squared* equals a negative number, which would mean that the loading was imaginary. (Note that if we estimated a single-factor model by fixing the latent variance to 1, and one or three of the correlations are negative, we would find a nonzero χ^2 with zero *df*.[6])

Empirical underidentification can occur in many situations, some of which are unexpected. One example of an empirically underidentified model is a model with two latent variables, each with two indicators, with the correlation between factors equal to 0 (Kenny et al., 1998). A second example of an empirically underidentified model is the multitrait–multimethod matrix with equal loadings (Kenny & Kashy, 1992). What is perhaps odd about both of these examples is that a simpler model (the model with a 0 correlation or a model with equal loadings) is not identified, whereas the more complicated model (the model with a correlation between factors or model with unequal loadings) is identified.

Another example of empirical underidentification occurs for instrumental variable estimation. Consider the model in Figure 9.4. If the path from work stress to work satisfaction were 0, then the estimate of the path from work to home satisfaction would be empirically underidentified; correspondingly, if the path from

home stress to home satisfaction were 0, then the estimate of the path from home to work satisfaction would be empirically underidentified.

There are several indications that a parameter is empirically underidentified. Sometimes, the computer program indicates that the model is not identified. Other times, the model does not converge. Finally, the program might run but produce wild estimates with huge standard errors.

Just-Identified Models That Do Not Fit Perfectly

A feature of just-identified models is that the model estimates can be used to reproduce the knowns exactly: The χ^2 should equal 0. However, some just-identified models fail to reproduce exactly the knowns. Consider the model in Figure 9.1. If the researcher were to add an inequality constraint that all paths are positive, but one or more of the paths was actually negative, then the model would be unable to reproduce exactly the knowns, and the χ^2 value would be greater than 0, with zero *df*. Thus, not all just-identified models result in perfect fit.

What to Do with Underidentified Models?

There is very little discussion in the literature about underidentified models. The usual strategy is to reduce the number of parameters to make the model identified. Here we discuss some other strategies for dealing with an underidentified model.

In some cases, the model can become identified if the researcher can measure more variables of a particular type. This strategy works well for multiple-indicator models: If one does not have an identified model with two indicators of a latent variable, perhaps because their errors must be correlated, one can achieve identification by obtaining another indicator of the latent construct. Of course, that indicator needs to be a good indicator. Also, for some models, adding an instrumental variable can help. Finally, for some longitudinal models, adding another wave of data helps. Of course, if the data were already collected, it can be difficult to find another variable.

Design features can also be used to identify models. For example, if units are randomly assigned to levels of a causal variable, then it can be assumed that the disturbance of the outcome variable is uncorrelated with that causal variable. Another design feature is the timing of measurement: We do not allow a variable to cause another variable that was measured earlier in time.

Although a model is underidentified, it is still possible to estimate the parameters of the model. Because some of the parameters are underidentified, there is a range of possible solutions and other parameters are identified. Finally, the model may have a restriction, as in Figure 9.8. Let q be the number of unknowns minus the number of knowns and the number of independent restrictions. To be able to estimate an underidentified model, the user must fix q underidentified parameters to a possible value. It may take some trial and error determining which parameters are underidentified and possible values for those parameters. As an example of possible values, assume that a model has two variables correlated .5, and both are indicators of a standardized latent variable. Assuming positive loadings, the range of possible values for the standardized loading is from 0.5 to 1.0. It is important to realize that choosing a different value to fix an underidentified parameter likely affects the estimates of the other underidentified parameters.

A sensitivity analysis involves fixing parameters that would be underidentified to a range of plausible values and seeing what happens to the other parameters in the model. Mauro (1990) described this strategy for omitted variables, but unfortunately his suggestions have gone largely unheeded. For example, sensitivity analysis might be used to determine the effects of measurement error. Consider a simple mediational model in which variable M mediates the X to Y relationship. If we allow for measurement error in M, the model is not identified. However, we could estimate the causal effects assuming that the reliability of M ranges from some plausible interval, from say .6 to .9, and note the size of direct and indirect effects of X on Y for that interval. For an example, see the example in Chapter 5 of Bollen (1989).

Researchers need to be creative in identifying otherwise underidentified models. For instance, one idea is to use multiple group models to identify an otherwise underidentified model. If we have a model that is underidentified, we might try to think of a situation or condition in which the model would be identified. For instance, X_1 and X_2 might ordinarily have a reciprocal relationship. The researcher might be able to think of a situation in which the relationship runs only from X_1 to X_2. So there are two groups, one in a situation in which the causation is unidirectional and another in which the causation is bidirectional. A related strategy

is used in the behavior genetics literature when a model of genetic and environmental influences is underidentified with one group, but is not when there are multiple groups of siblings, monozygotic twins and dizygotic twins (Neale, 2009).

CONCLUSIONS

Although we have covered many topics, there are several key topics we have not covered. We have not covered nonparametric identification (Pearl, 2009) or cases in which a model becomes identified through assumptions about the distribution of variables (e.g., normality). Among those are models with latent products or squared latent variables, and models that are identified by assuming there is an unmeasured, truncated, normally distributed variable (Heckman, 1979). We also did not cover identification of latent class models, for which we refer the reader to Magidson and Vermunt (2004) and Muthén (2002) for a discussion of those issues. Also not discussed is identification in mixture modeling. In these models, the researcher specifies some model with the assumption that different subgroups in the sample will have different parameter values (i.e., the set of relationships between variables in the model differs by subgroup). Conceptualized this way, mixture modeling is similar to multigroup tests of moderation, except that the grouping variable itself is latent. In mixture modeling, in practice, if the specified model is identified when estimated for the whole sample, it should be identified in the mixture model. However, the number of groups that can be extracted may be limited, and researchers may confront convergence problems with more complex models.

We have assumed that sample sizes are reasonably large. With small samples, problems that seem like identification problems can appear. A simple example is that of having a path analysis in which there are more causes than cases, which results in collinearity. Also models that are radically misspecified can appear to be underidentified. For instance, if one has over-time data with several measures and estimates a multitrait–multimethod matrix model when the correct model is a multivariate growth curve model, one might well have considerable difficulty identifying the wrong model.

As stated before, SEM works well with models that are either just- or overidentified and are not empirically underidentified. However, for models that are underidentified, either in principle or empirically, SEM programs are not very helpful. We believe that it would be beneficial for computer programs to be able do the following. First, for models that are underidentified, provide estimates and standard errors of identified parameters, the range of possible values for underidentified parameters, and tests of restrictions, if there are any. Second, for overidentified models, the program would give specific information about tests of restrictions. For instance, for hybrid models, it would separately evaluate the overidentifying restrictions of the measurement model and the structural model. Third, SEM programs should have an option by which the researcher specifies the model and is given advice about the status of the identification of the model. In this way, the researcher can better plan to collect data for which the model is identified.

Researchers need a practical tool to help them determine the identification status of their models. Although there is not currently a method to unambiguously determine the identification status of the model, researchers can be provided with feedback using the rules described and cited in this chapter.

We hope we have shed some light on what for many is a challenging and difficult topic. We also hope that others will continue work on this topic, especially more work on how to handle underidentified models.

ACKNOWLEDGMENTS

Thanks are due to Betsy McCoach, Rick Hoyle, William Cook, Ed Rigdon, Ken Bollen, and Judea Pearl who provided us with very helpful feedback on a prior draft of the chapter. We also acknowledge that we used three websites in the preparation of this chapter: Robert Hanneman (*http://faculty.ucr.edu/~hanneman/soc203b/lectures/identify.html*), Ed Rigdon (*http://www2.gsu.edu/~mkteer/identifi.html*), and the University of Texas (*http://ssc.utexas.edu/software/faqs/lisrel/104-lisrel3*).

NOTES

1. Here and elsewhere, we use the symbol r for correlation and s for variance or covariance, even when we are discussing population values. A population correlation is typically denoted as ρ and population variance or covariance is usually symbolized by σ.
2. The astute reader may have noticed that because the parameter is squared, there is not a unique solution for f, g, and h because we can take either the positive or negative square root.
3. Although there are two estimates, the "best" estimate statistically is the first (Goldberger, 1973).
4. One could create a hypothetical variance–covariance matrix before one gathered the data, analyze it, and then see if the model runs. This strategy, though helpful, is still problematic, as empirical underidentification might occur with the hypothetical data but not with the real data, or vice versa.
5. To accomplish this in AMOS, go to "Analysis Properties, Numerical" and check "Try to fit underidentified models."
6. If we use the conventional marker variable approach, the estimation of this model does not converge on a solution.

REFERENCES

Bekker, P. A., Merckens, A., & Wansbeek, T. (1994). Identification, equivalent models, and computer algebra. *American Educational Research Journal, 15*, 81–97.

Bollen, K. A. (1989). *Structural equation models with latent variables*. Hoboken, NJ: Wiley-Interscience.

Bollen, K. A. (1996). An alternative two stage least squares (2SLS) estimator for latent variable equations. *Psychometrika, 6*, 109–121.

Bollen, K. A., & Bauldry, S. (2010). Model identification and computer algebra. *Sociological Methods and Research, 39*, 127–156.

Bollen, K. A., & Curran, P. (2006). *Latent curve models: A structural equation perspective*. Hoboken, NJ: Wiley-Interscience.

Bollen, K. A., & Curran, P. J. (2004). Autoregressive latent trajectory (ALT) models: A synthesis of two traditions. *Sociological Methods and Research, 32*, 336–383.

Bollen, K. A., & Davis, W. R. (2009). Two rules of identification for structural equation models. *Structural Equation Modeling, 16*, 523–536.

Bollen, K. A., & Lennox, R. (1991). Conventional wisdom on measurement: A structural equation perspective. *Psychological Bulletin, 110*, 305–314.

Bollen, K. A., & Ting, K. (1993). Confirmatory tetrad analysis. In P. M. Marsden (Ed.), *Sociological methodology 1993* (pp. 147–175). Washington, DC: American Sociological Association.

Brito, C., & Pearl, J. (2002). A new identification condition for recursive models with correlated errors. *Structural Equation Modeling, 9*, 459–474.

Costner, H. L. (1969). Theory, deduction, and rules of correspondence. *American Journal of Sociology, 75*, 245–263.

Frone, M. R., Russell, M., & Cooper, M. L. (1994). Relationship between job and family satisfaction: Causal or noncausal covariation? *Journal of Management, 20*, 565–579.

Goldberger, A. S. (1973). Efficient estimation in over-identified models: An interpretive analysis. In A. S. Goldberger & O. D. Duncan (Eds.), *Structural equation models in the social sciences* (pp. 131–152). New York: Academic Press.

Hayashi, K., & Marcoulides, G. A. (2006). Examining identification issues in factor analysis. *Structural Equation Modeling, 10*, 631–645.

Heckman, J. (1979). Sample selection bias as a specification error. *Econometrica, 47*, 153–161.

Kenny, D. A. (1975). Cross-lagged panel correlation: A test for spuriousness. *Psychological Bulletin, 82*, 887–903.

Kenny, D. A. (1979). *Correlation and causality.* New York: Wiley-Interscience.

Kenny, D. A., & Kashy, D. A. (1992). Analysis of multitrait–multimethod matrix by confirmatory factor analysis. *Psychological Bulletin, 112*, 165–172.

Kenny, D. A., Kashy, D. A., & Bolger, N. (1998). Data analysis in social psychology. In D. Gilbert, S. Fiske, & G. Lindsey (Eds.), *Handbook of social psychology* (4th ed., Vol. 1, pp. 233–265). Boston: McGraw-Hill.

Kline, R. B. (2010). *Principles and practice of structural equation modeling* (3rd ed.). New York: Guilford Press.

Magidson, J., & Vermunt, J. (2004). Latent class models. In D. Kaplan (Ed.), *The Sage handbook of quantitative methodology for the social sciences* (pp. 175–198). Thousand Oaks, CA: Sage.

Mauro, R. (1990). Understanding L.O.V.E. (left out variables error): A method for estimating the effects of omitted variables. *Psychological Bulletin, 108*, 314–329.

McArdle, J. J., & Hamagami, F. (2001). Linear dynamic analyses of incomplete longitudinal data. In L. Collins & A. Sayer (Eds.), *New methods for the analysis of change* (pp. 139–175). Washington, DC: American Psychological Association.

McDonald, R. P. (2002). What can we learn from the path equations?: Identifiability, constraints, equivalence. *Psychometrika, 67*, 225–249.

Meredith, W., & Tisak, J. (1990). Latent curve analysis. *Psychometrika, 55*, 107–122.

Muthén, B. (2002). Beyond SEM: General latent variable modeling. *Behaviormetrika, 29*, 81–117.

Neale, M. (2009). Biometrical models in behavioral genetics. In Y. Kim (Ed.), *Handbook of behavior genetics* (pp. 15–33). New York: Springer Science.

O'Brien, R. (1994). Identification of simple measurement models with multiple latent variables and correlated errors. In P. Marsden (Ed.), *Sociological methodology* (pp. 137–170). Cambridge, UK: Blackwell.

Pearl, J. (2009). *Causality: Models, reasoning, and inference* (2nd ed.). New York: Cambridge University Press.

Rigdon, E. E. (1995). A necessary and sufficient identification rule for structural models estimated in practice. *Multivariate Behavioral Research, 30*, 359–383.

CHAPTER 10

Estimation in Structural Equation Modeling

Pui-Wa Lei
Qiong Wu

Model estimation and evaluation are integral parts of any application of structural equation modeling (SEM). Quality of model parameter estimates, their associated standard error estimates, and overall model fit statistics depend on the choice of appropriate estimation methods. Desirable properties of estimators include asymptotic consistency, unbiasedness, and efficiency. An estimator is consistent if it approaches the true parameter as sample size increases toward infinity, unbiased if its expected value equals the parameter that it estimates (i.e., the average of estimates from an infinite number of independent samples from the same population will equal the population parameter), and efficient if its variability is the smallest among consistent estimators. Some estimators are also asymptotically normally distributed, allowing adequate significance testing of individual parameters using the z-test.

SAMPLE DATA AND MODEL PARAMETERS

The basic elements of data for SEM analyses are sample variances and covariances of observed variables. Given a hypothesized SEM model, individual observed variables can be written as a function of unknown parameters (i.e., path coefficients or factor loadings) and other observed or latent variables in the model. These functions describe structural relations (or causal hypotheses) among the variables and are referred to as "structural equations." From the set of structural equations, variances and covariances of observed variables can be expressed in terms of unknown parameters in the model, such as path coefficients, factor loadings, and variances and covariances of latent variables. These variances and covariances are model-specific and are called model-implied variances and covariances.

As an example, suppose that a simple four-variable two-factor confirmatory factor analysis (CFA) model, as depicted in Figure 10.1, is being estimated from a sample variance–covariance matrix (see upper half of Table 10.1). The factors of interest are reading (F_1) and mathematics (F_2). Reading is indicated by basic word reading (X_1) and reading comprehension (X_2) scores. Mathematics is indicated by calculation (X_3) and reasoning (X_4) scores. There are four structural equations (ones that stipulate the causal relationship among variables) for the model in Figure 10.1, one for each observed variable: $X_1 = 1 * F_1 + \delta_1$, $X_2 = \lambda_{21} * F_1 + \delta_2$, $X_3 = 1 * F_2 + \delta_3$, and $X_4 = \lambda_{42} * F_2 + \delta_4$. In the equations, the λ's represent factor loadings, and the δ's represent measurement errors. The equations suggest that each observed variable (outcome) is a function of a common factor (cause) and a unique measurement error (other unspecified causes). Two loadings are fixed to 1 to set

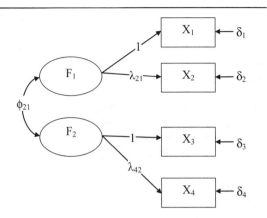

FIGURE 10.1. A CFA model with unknown model parameters.

The complete set of model-implied variances and covariances for this example are arranged in a matrix form, parallel to the sample counterpart, and shown in the lower half of Table 10.1. The model parameters to be estimated for this CFA model include factor loadings, factor variances, covariance between the two factors, and variances of measurement errors. Readers who wish to learn more about covariance algebra can consult Bollen (1989, pp. 21–23). However, standard SEM software programs will calculate the model-implied variance–covariance matrix given a user-supplied path diagram or a set of structural equations.

GENERAL ESTIMATION PROCEDURES

Model parameters (θ, which is a generic notation for all unknown parameters in the model) are estimated by minimizing some form of discrepancy between a sample variance–covariance matrix ($\mathbf{S}$) and model-implied variance–covariance matrix [$\Sigma(\theta)$]. This is similar to the ordinary least squares (OLS) estimation in regression in which the sum of squared differences between observed and predicted values for individual observations is minimized. The difference is that observations in regression are individual scores, while observations in SEM are sample variances and covariances.

Moreover, a closed-form solution (one that can be obtained analytically) is available for regression, but it is often unavailable for SEM. SEM generally relies

the scale for the factors (i.e., F_1 takes the scale of X_1; F_2 takes the scale of X_3).

Assuming independence between latent factors and measurement errors, variances (V) and covariances (C) among the observed variables can be expressed in terms of model parameters based on the structural equations using covariance algebra—for example, $V(X_1) = C(X_1, X_1) = C(1 * F_1 + \delta_1, 1 * F_1 + \delta_1) = V(F_1) + V(\delta_1)$. $C(X_1, X_2) = C(1 * F_1 + \delta_1, \lambda_{21} * F_1 + \delta_2) = \lambda_{21} * V(F_1)$ because the δ's are uncorrelated in the model.

TABLE 10.1. Sample and Model-Implied Variance–Covariance Matrices for the Model in Figure 10.1

	X_1	X_2	X_3	X_4
	Sample variance–covariance matrix (**S**)			
X_1	211.60	—	—	—
X_2	178.78	247.32	—	—
X_3	125.12	158.87	236.12	—
X_4	116.85	163.21	181.20	227.78
	Model-implied variance–covariance matrix [$\Sigma(\theta)$]			
X_1	$V(F_1) + V(\delta_1)$	—	—	—
X_2	$\lambda_{21} * V(F_1)$	$\lambda_{21} * \lambda_{21} * V(F_1) + V(\delta_2)$	—	—
X_3	$C(F_1, F_2) = \phi_{21}$	$\lambda_{21} * \phi_{21}$	$V(F_2) + V(\delta_3)$	—
X_4	$\lambda_{42} * \phi_{21}$	$\lambda_{21} * \lambda_{42} * \phi_{21}$	$\lambda_{42} * V(F_2)$	$\lambda_{42} * \lambda_{42} * V(F_2) + V(\delta_4)$

Note. — indicates redundant symmetric values.

on iterative procedures to solve for unknown parameters in the model. Educated guesses of parameter values, known as starting or initial values ($\hat{\theta}_0$), which are usually supplied by standard SEM programs, are used to start the iterative process. An intermediate model-implied variance–covariance matrix can then be calculated by substituting the unknown parameters with their initial values [$\Sigma(\hat{\theta}_0)$]. Minimizing the discrepancy between the sample and the intermediate model-implied variance–covariance matrices will provide a new set of parameter estimates. This new set of parameter estimates will replace the old set of initial values, and the process repeats until changes in parameter estimates between adjacent iterations become acceptably small. The rules used to stop the iterative process are called "convergence criteria." When convergence criteria are met, the model is said to have converged, and the last set of parameter estimates is taken to be the final solution for the unknown parameters. Parameter estimates for the above example are shown in Table 10.2.

Different estimation methods or estimators minimize different functions of the discrepancy between **S** and $\Sigma(\theta)$, called fit or discrepancy functions (F). A model fit statistic is $T = (N - 1) * F$, where N is sample size, and F is the minimum of the fit function when the model converges. When assumptions of estimators are met, T often approximately follows a χ^2 distribution with degrees of freedom (df) equal to the number of unique variances and covariances minus the number of estimated model parameters. Therefore, overall fit of the model to data can be assessed using a χ^2 test. The asymptotic variance–covariance matrix of an estimator, if it exists, provides standard error estimates of individual parameter estimates for significance tests.

In the following, we introduce some popular estimation methods used in SEM, including the maximum likelihood family, least squares family, and Bayesian method. We also briefly review empirical findings about these methods and illustrate the importance of choosing estimation methods in consideration of commonly encountered conditions in practice. For concern of space, we limit our discussion to basic covariance structure models and estimation methods that are relatively more widely used and studied. Our selection of estimation methods is by no means inclusive or comprehensive.

TABLE 10.2. Parameter Estimates for the Model in Figure 10.1

	Unstandardized parameter estimates	Standard errors	Standardized parameter estimates
Factor loadings			
X_1	1^a		.79
X_2 (λ_{21})	1.34*	.15	.99
X_3	1^a		.87
X_4 (λ_{42})	1.02*	.10	.90
Factor variances and covariance			
$V(F_1)$	133.21*	29.73	1
$V(F_2)$	177.23*	34.78	1
$C(F_1, F_2)$ or ϕ_{21}	118.71*	24.92	.77
Error variances			
$V(\delta_1)$	78.39*	15.09	.37
$V(\delta_2)$	7.39	18.35	.03
$V(\delta_3)$	58.89*	14.95	.25
$V(\delta_4)$	42.52*	14.28	.19

[a]Values are fixed to 1 to set the scale of latent factors.
*Estimates are significantly different from 0 at the .05 level.

MAXIMUM LIKELIHOOD ESTIMATORS

Contemporary SEM appears to originate from econometrics, psychometrics, and mathematical statistics (Bielby & Hauser, 1977). Karl G. Jöreskog is often credited for unifying path analysis from econometrics and factor analysis from psychometrics into a general framework of covariance structure analysis (e.g., Bielby & Hauser, 1977). Lawley (1940) was the first to apply maximum likelihood (ML) estimation in factor analysis, but the iterative numerical procedure used by Lawley and several others (e.g., Bargmann, 1957; Emmett, 1949) was not very successful. A major breakthrough came in the 1970s when Jöreskog and his colleagues (Jöreskog, 1977; Jöreskog & Lawley, 1968) introduced a numerical solution for ML factor analysis and developed the LISREL (LInear Structural RELations) software program (Jöreskog & van Thillo, 1973). The availability of the LISREL program has played a significant role in popularizing SEM. ML remains the most well known and widely used estimator to date. The fit function for ML given by Bollen (1989) is shown in Equation 10.1.

$$F_{ML} = \log |\Sigma(\theta)| + \text{tr}(S\Sigma^{-1}(\theta)) - \log |S| - p \quad \textbf{(10.1)}$$

In Equation 10.1, log(.) is the natural logarithm function, tr(.) is the trace function, and p is the number of observed variables. Under the assumption of multivariate normality of observed variables and a correct model specification, the ML estimator is asymptotically consistent, unbiased, efficient, and normally distributed, and the model fit statistic (T_{ML}) is asymptotically distributed as χ^2 with $df = p(p + 1)/2 - t$, where t is the number of model parameters estimated.

The ML estimator tends to produce relatively unbiased parameter estimates (provided that the proper covariance matrix is analyzed and that the model is correctly specified) but inflate model χ^2 and deflate standard error estimates under non-normality (e.g., Bollen, 1989, pp. 417–418; Chou, Bentler, & Satorra, 1991; Finch, West, & MacKinnon, 1997). Fortunately, a robust asymptotic covariance matrix for the estimated parameters, from which robust standard errors can be obtained, and corrections to the model fit statistic (T_{ML}) to better approximate the reference χ^2 distribution are documented in Satorra and Bentler (1988, 1994). The χ^2 correction entails adjusting the mean of the test statistic alone, resulting in the Satorra–Bentler scaled statistic,

or adjusting both the mean and variance resulting in the Satorra–Bentler adjusted statistic (Fouladi, 2000). The Satorra–Bentler scaled χ^2 statistic is available in most specialized SEM software programs. Both versions of adjustment are available in Mplus (Muthén & Muthén, 1998–2010) with the mean-adjusted version labeled as MLM and mean- and variance-adjusted version as MLMV. Little is known about the performance of MLMV, perhaps because it is not available in most SEM programs other than Mplus.

More recently, Asparouhov and Muthén (2005) developed another more general robust ML estimator (called MLR in Mplus) based on Skinner's (1989) pseudo-ML method and by using adjustments similar to those of Satorra and Bentler (1988) to deal with complex sampling designs. Initial evidence provided by the authors seems to support its use for survey data. Additionally, MLR can be used for non-normal data (Muthén & Muthén, 1998–2010, p. 484).

Another variant of ML developed by Finkbeiner (1979) to handle missing data is referred to as the full-information maximum likelihood (FIML) estimator. Assuming data are missing at random (MAR), FIML maximizes a modified log-likelihood function that makes use of all available individual observations (e.g., Enders, 2006, pp. 322–323). Therefore, raw individual data are required for FIML. This approach to handling missing data is logically appealing because there is no need to make additional assumptions for imputation and no loss of observations. It is regarded as one of the state-of-the-art treatments of missing data (Schafer & Graham, 2002). It has also been found to work better than listwise deletion in simulation studies (Kline, 2010, p. 59).

LEAST SQUARES ESTIMATORS

Before the availability of LISREL, OLS estimation (i.e., multiple regression technique) had been used to derive estimates for recursive path models (e.g., Blalock, 1964; Duncan, 1966). However, the capability of OLS is very limited because it cannot deal with nonrecursive path models or measurement models (Kline, 2005, p. 159). Therefore, the use of OLS in SEM is very rare nowadays.

The two-stage least squares (2SLS) estimation method can be considered an extension of the OLS method for handling nonrecursive models and models with latent variables. The 2SLS method often involves the use of instrumental variables. An instrumental variable has a direct effect on a "problematic" causal variable (i.e., one that is correlated with the equation's disturbance), but no direct effect on the endogenous variable (Kline, 2010, p. 156). See Figure 10.2 for a conceptual illustration of an instrumental variable (I) for a "problematic" causal variable (X) in predicting an endogenous variable (Y). In the enclosed part of Figure 10.2, X is a "problematic" predictor because it is correlated with the disturbance of Y (D). The variable I is an appropriate instrumental variable for X because it has a direct effect on X but not on Y. The 2SLS estimator applies multiple regressions in two stages. In the first stage, the "problematic" causal variable is regressed on the instrumental variable(s) (i.e., $X = \beta_0 + \beta_1 I + e$ for the example, where the β's are regression coefficients, and e is the error term for X). In the second stage, the endogenous variable is regressed on the predicted value of the "problematic" causal variable from the first stage (i.e., $Y = \pi_0 + \pi_1 \hat{X} + u$ for the example, where the π's are regression coefficients, and u is the error term for Y). The purpose of this two-stage process is to replace the "problematic" causal variable with its predicted value (predicted by the instrumental variables) that is uncorrelated with the equation's disturbance. Since not all parameters are estimated simultaneously, 2SLS is a limited-information method. Limited-information methods may be less susceptible to spreading of model misspecification to other equations than full-information estimation methods such as ML (Bollen, Kirby, Curran, Paxton, & Chen, 2007).

Variants of the 2SLS estimator have been developed since the 1950s in econometrics in the context of simultaneous equation models (e.g., Basmann, 1957). Jöreskog (1983) also proposed a 2SLS estimator to estimate starting values for the LISREL program (Jöreskog & Sörbom, 1993). The 2SLS estimator developed by

Bollen (1996a, 1996b, 2001) is probably the most general in that "it permits correlated errors across equations, . . . estimates intercepts, and provides asymptotic covariance matrix of the estimator for significance testing" and that it is equivalent to other versions of 2SLS under certain conditions (Bollen et al., 2007, p. 54). According to Bollen and colleagues (2007), the 2SLS estimator is consistent, asymptotically unbiased, asymptotically normally distributed, and asymptotically efficient among limited information estimators, and the version proposed by Bollen (1996a, 1996b, 2001) provides an accurate asymptotic covariance matrix without assuming normality of observed variables.

One advantage is that the 2SLS estimator does not require a specialized SEM program to implement it. Researchers can use any software programs that have 2SLS procedures or that perform OLS regression; however, researchers may need to make proper adjustments to the estimates of the standard errors manually (Bollen, 1996a). Moreover, Bollen and Bauer (2004) developed an automatic algorithm to help select model-implied instrumental variables and provided a Statistical Analysis Software (SAS)/interactive matrix language (IML) macro to implement it.

Both OLS and 2SLS are noniterative, limited-information estimation methods, and the computation of parameter estimates does not require any starting values. Full-information least squares estimation methods that simultaneously estimate all parameters are generally iterative and require starting values to successively minimize a particular fit function of the difference between the vector of elements in the sample variance and covariance matrix (s) and the vector of elements in the model-implied variance and covariance matrix [$\sigma(\theta)$]. The s and $\sigma(\theta)$ vectors are of order $p(p + 1)/2$ containing unique elements from S and $\Sigma(\theta)$, respectively. The fit function that the least squares family minimizes has the general form of Equation 10.2.

$$F_{\mathrm{LS}}(\theta) = [s - \sigma(\theta)]' W^{-1} [s - \sigma(\theta)] \tag{10.2}$$

Equation 10.2 defines a family of estimation methods sometimes known as generalized least squares (e.g., Anderson & Gerbing, 1988) or weighted least squares (e.g., Bollen, 1989, p. 425; Kline, 2005, p. 159). However, for the purpose of this chapter, we use these terms for specific methods discussed later rather than as a family of methods.

Different least squares estimation methods employ different weight matrices, $\mathbf{W}$'s, which are $p(p + 1)/2$

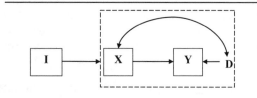

FIGURE 10.2. A conceptual illustration of an instrumental variable (I) for a "problematic" causal variable (X).

by $p(p + 1)/2$ square matrices. If an identity matrix (**I**) is used as **W**, for example, the estimation method is reduced to the unweighted least squares method (ULS). ULS is a consistent estimator, and it makes no distributional assumption about the observed variables (Bollen, 1989, p. 112). However, it requires all observed variables to be measured on the same scale, and it is generally less efficient than the ML estimator (Kline, 2010, p. 176).

Expositions of the normal theory–based generalized least squares (GLS) method appeared in the 1970s (e.g., Anderson, 1973; Browne, 1974; Jöreskog & Goldberger, 1972). One form of the fit function for GLS is $F_{GLS}(\theta) = \frac{1}{2}\text{tr}(\{[S - \Sigma(\theta)]V^{-1}\}^2)$, where $V = S$ is a p by p square matrix. Note that when **V** is chosen to be $\Sigma(\hat{\theta})$, minimizing this form of the fit function leads to the normal theory–based ML (Lee & Jennrich, 1979). According to Bollen (1989, pp. 428–429), F_{GLS} has been shown to be equal to Equation 10.2 by Browne (1974) and can be considered a special case of Equation 10.2. Using the more general form of Equation 10.2, the weight matrix, **W**, for GLS contains elements that are functions of the second-order product moments around the mean, $[W_{GLS}]_{ij,gh} = s_{ig}s_{jh} + s_{ih}s_{jg}$, $i \geq j$, $g \geq h$, where s_{ig} represents the covariance between observed variables i and g. Like ML, GLS assumes multivariate normality or no excessive kurtosis (Browne, 1974) and is consistent, asymptotically unbiased, asymptotically normally distributed, and asymptotically efficient among full-information estimators.

The weighted least squares (WLS) estimator proposed by Browne (1984) relaxes the distributional assumption and is referred to as Browne's asymptotically distribution-free (ADF) method. In spite of this name, it should be noted that Browne's ADF method is not the only one that makes no distributional assumptions. A number of other methods, including the 2SLS and the ULS methods mentioned earlier, also do not make distributional assumptions. The WLS estimator uses the asymptotic covariance matrix of sample variances and covariances as its weight matrix with a typical element consisting of estimates of the second- and fourth-order product moments around the mean, $[W_{WLS}]_{ij,gh} = s_{ijgh} - s_{ij}s_{gh}$, $i \geq j$, $g \geq h$, where

$$s_{ijgh} = \frac{\sum_{n=1}^{N}(X_{ni} - \bar{X}_i)(X_{nj} - \bar{X}_j)(X_{ng} - \bar{X}_g)(X_{nh} - \bar{X}_h)}{N}$$

and N is sample size. Under correct model specification

and multivariate normality, the individual elements of W_{GLS} and W_{WLS} will converge in probability to $\sigma_{ig}\sigma_{jh} + \sigma_{ih}\sigma_{jg}$ (Hu, Bentler, & Kano, 1992). Research has shown that WLS has a strict requirement on sample size and may produce large amounts of bias with small samples (e.g., Hoogland & Boomsma, 1998).

Because inverting the full-weight matrix of WLS is computationally demanding, and it is likely the culprit for the poor performance of WLS with less than large samples, diagonally weighted least squares methods, in which only diagonal elements of the WLS weight matrix are kept in the weight matrix, are often used to lessen the computational burden. A version of the diagonally weighted least squares (DWLS) estimator is available in LISREL, beginning in version 7 (Jöreskog & Sörbom, 1988). Two other versions known as mean-adjusted WLS (WLSM) and mean- and variance-adjusted WLS (WLSMV; Muthén, 1993; Muthén, du Toit, & Spisic, 1997) are available in Mplus (Muthén & Muthén, 1998–2010).

DWLS estimators can be and are often used when some or all observed endogenous variables are nonnormal and categorical. They are commonly used with alternative correlations that estimate association between latent response variables for ordinal data (i.e., polychoric correlation between categorical variables, or polyserial correlation between categorical and continuous variables). WLSM and WLSMV were specifically developed for categorical variable methodology and were referred to as robust WLS estimators by Muthén and colleagues (1997). A robust asymptotic covariance matrix for the estimated parameters and corrected model χ^2 test statistics similar to those of Satorra and Bentler (1994) are available for these estimators. WLSM differs from WLSMV in the adjustment to the model χ^2 test statistic and in their degrees of freedom. Degrees of freedom for WLSMV are estimated from the sample, and they can vary from sample to sample for the same model.

BAYESIAN ESTIMATION

According to Dunson, Palomo, and Bollen (2005), there is a long history of Bayesian methods in factor analysis and general SEM models. The earliest work on factor analysis models (Martin & McDonald, 1975) was cited by the authors in the 1970s, and that on general SEM models (Bauwens, 1984), in the 1980s. Recent developments of Bayesian estimation in SEM have focused on the use of Markov Chain Monte Carlo (MCMC) methods to handle complex cases, including nonlinear structural models and multilevel data (Dunson et al., 2005).

Bayesian methods take a completely different perspective on estimation, in that they assume true model parameters are random and unknown, whereas in ML, true parameters are considered fixed and unknown but their estimates are random (Arbuckle, 1995–2009). In the Bayesian framework, parameters' prior distributions are combined with empirical data likelihood based on Bayes's theorem to form posterior distributions for parameter estimates. Since analytical approaches to obtaining posterior distribution are most often impractical due to the difficulty of estimating high-dimensional integrals, empirical approximations are adopted by simulating values based on Monte Carlo procedures. Regular Monte Carlo procedures that draw independent samples may not be feasible because posterior distributions are often of an unknown form. Under such circumstances, MCMC can be used to draw dependent samples from a series of distributions that is in the limit equal to drawing from the stationary posterior distribution (Gilks, Richardson, & Spiegelhalter, 1996). More details about Bayesian estimation in SEM can be found in Kaplan and Depaoli, Chapter 38, this volume.

Compared to the frequentist approach (i.e., ML and LS), Bayesian estimation has a few advantages. First, ML and LS confidence intervals assume that parameter estimates are asymptotically normal, whereas Bayesian credibility intervals are based on percentiles of the posterior distribution, which is not restricted to any fixed form. Second, when models are computationally intractable for ML, the Bayesian method can come to the rescue. Hence, the Bayesian method can simply be viewed as a computational tool to obtain parameter estimates (Muthén & Muthén, 1998–2010). A disadvantage of the Bayesian method is that it is computationally intensive and may take a long time to obtain a solution with an acceptably low level of Monte Carlo error (Dunson et al., 2005).

SOFTWARE PROGRAMS THAT PERFORM THE DIFFERENT ESTIMATION METHODS

There are a number of software programs that estimate SEM models. We chose the four most frequently used programs (Amos 18: Arbuckle, 2009; EQS 6.1: Bentler, 2005; LISREL 8.8: Jöreskog & Sörbom, 2006; Mplus 6: Muthén & Muthén, 2010) and briefly describe their similarities and differences in terms of their estimation capacities.

Estimators that are available in all four software programs include ML, FIML, GLS, ULS, and WLS or ADF. ML and GLS assume either multivariate normality or no excessive kurtosis of observed variables. ML is the default estimator for all four programs when observed endogenous variables are continuous. When raw data are analyzed, missing code is provided, and when ML is requested, these programs produce FIML solutions. When data distributions deviate from multivariate normality, different estimation options are available in different programs.

The robust ML approach, that is, using regular ML for model estimation, along with robust standard errors and scaled model χ^2 of Satorra and Bentler (1988, 1994) to evaluate model fit, is a popular choice for non-normal continuous data. It is available in LISREL 8.8 (by including an asymptotic covariance matrix of the variances and covariances estimated by PRELIS), EQS 6.1 (with METHOD = ML, ROBUST), and Mplus 6 (with ESTIMATOR = MLM), but not in Amos 18. Bootstrapping is available in Amos 18, so that one can estimate standard errors and model fit statistics empirically by applying this resampling technique on the sample data at hand. Moreover, when the keyword ROBUST is used in EQS 6.1, the program provides three additional residual-based test statistics, including Browne's (1984) original residual-based χ^2, the Yuan–Bentler extension of Browne's residual-based χ^2 test for small samples (Bentler & Yuan, 1999; Yuan & Bentler, 1998), and an even more radical modification of Browne's test called the Yuan–Bentler residual-based F-statistic (Yuan & Bentler, 1998). Another robust ML estimator for non-normal or cluster data, called MLR, is currently available only in the Mplus 6 program.

The ADF estimator can also be considered for model estimation with non-normal continuous data when the sample size is very large (i.e., in the thousands). ADF or WLS is available in all four programs. LISREL 8.8 provides ADF solutions when an asymptotic covariance matrix estimated by PRELIS is submitted as input and the WLS option is requested. Mplus 6 also uses the keyword WLS, while EQS 6.1 uses AGLS and Amos 18 uses ADF for Browne's (1984) ADF estimator. Moreover, EQS 6.1 provides two different adjustments to the model test statistic called the Yuan–Bentler corrected arbitrary distribution generalized least squares (AGLS) test statistic (Yuan & Bentler, 1997b) and the Yuan–Bentler AGLS F-statistic (Yuan & Bentler, 1999). In addition, it provides corrected standard error estimates (Yuan & Bentler, 1997a) for small samples.

When categorical variables are declared in LISREL 8.8 (PRELIS), Mplus 6, or EQS 6.1, all three programs estimate thresholds for categorical variables, polychoric/polyserial correlations among observed variables, and an asymptotic covariance matrix before estimating structural model parameters. The programs differ in the ways these matrices are computed. LISREL 8.8 estimates polychoric/polyserial correlations using Olsson's (1979) procedure. EQS 6.1 uses a partition maximum likelihood approach (PML; Lee, Poon, & Bentler, 1995; Poon & Lee, 1987), while Mplus 6 employs the limited-information likelihood approach of Muthén (1984). The default estimator for categorical variables is WLSMV in Mplus 6; robust ML with robust statistics based on the Lee and colleagues' (1995) optimal weight matrix is the default estimator in EQS 6.1. LISREL 8.8 provides a robust ML solution with Satorra–Bentler scaled statistics by default when a polychoric matrix and asymptotic covariance matrix calculated by PRELIS are submitted as input. Instead of using ML or ADF estimation, Amos 18 only allows Bayesian estimation when non-numeric data (i.e., ordered categorical) are declared.

Bayesian estimation is currently available only in Mplus 6 and Amos 18. Both programs use MCMC as the sampling algorithm. To request Bayesian estimation in Mplus 6, "ESTIMATOR = BAYES" should be specified. Mplus 6 allows different types of Bayes point estimates; users can request mean, median, or mode of the posterior distribution by specifying "POINT = MEAN," "POINT = MEDIAN," or "POINT = MODE," respectively. By default, Amos 18 provides the posterior mean and median for point estimates. The statements used by the four software programs to request the different estimation methods discussed above are summarized in Appendix 10.1.

EMPIRICAL FINDINGS ABOUT DIFFERENT ESTIMATION METHODS

Although Equation 10.2 can be considered the general fit function for normal theory ML, normal theory GLS, and Browne's ADF or WLS, these estimators are not necessarily equivalent. When multivariate normality of observed variables does not hold or sample size is small, F_{WLS} will not be equivalent to F_{GLS} or F_{ML} (Yuan & Chan, 2005). Unfortunately, multivariate normality

of observed variables, assumed by ML and GLS, is rarely satisfied (e.g., Micceri, 1989), and sample sizes required by the theoretically correct ADF estimator under non-normality are often unavailable in practice. It is unlikely that these estimators will be equivalent in realistic conditions. The choice of estimation method becomes essential because it will affect evaluation of model fit and parameter estimates (Bentler & Dudgeon, 1996). Users have to rely on empirical findings about different estimators in various practical conditions to inform their choice in applications of SEM.

Estimators for Continuous Variables

When continuous observed variables are not normally distributed, robust ML estimators (i.e., ML with Satorra–Bentler scaled statistics) appear to work better than Browne's ADF estimator, especially when sample sizes are not large (e.g., Chou et al., 1991; Curran, West, & Finch, 1996; Hu et al., 1992). Sample sizes required for ADF to work satisfactorily increase for larger models, increasingly non-normal distribution of observed variables, or both. The required sample size is often unrealistic for many social and behavioral fields. Hu and colleagues (1992), for example, found that the sample size required for ADF to work well for a 15-variable, three-factor CFA model was 5,000 under a symmetrical but highly kurtotic distribution. The Satorra–Bentler scaled χ^2, however, has been shown repeatedly to work fairly well relative to the ML and ADF χ^2 across various levels of non-normality and sample size (e.g., Chou et al., 1991; Curran et al., 1996; Hu et al., 1992).

Among the modified model fit test statistics for ML, Yuan and Bentler (1998) found that both the Satorra–Bentler scaled χ^2 and the Yuan–Bentler residual-based χ^2 performed well under a variety of conditions at sample sizes of 200 or above. When sample size was 120 or smaller, however, Bentler and Yuan (1999) found the Type I error rate of the Satorra–Bentler scaled χ^2 to be inflated two to four times the nominal level, while that of the Yuan–Bentler residual-based χ^2 was too conservative (underrejected correct models). The Yuan–Bentler residual-based F-test was found to perform better than the Satorra–Bentler scaled χ^2 test, Browne's residual test, and the Yuan–Bentler residual-based χ^2 test under various levels of non-normality and very small sample conditions ($N \leq p(p + 1)/2$ or $N:t \leq 3.64:1$, where t is the number of estimated model parameters; Bentler & Yuan, 1999). Because the theoretical null distribution of the Satorra–Bentler scaled statistic is unknown,

Bentler and Yuan recommend using the Yuan–Bentler residual-based χ^2 or the Yuan–Bentler residual-based F-test for non-normal data when the sample size is medium to large $[N > p(p + 1)/2]$. The Yuan–Bentler residual-based F-test is recommended when the sample size is very small $[df \leq N \leq p(p + 1)/2]$ regardless of sampling distribution (Bentler & Yuan, 1999).

Fouladi (1999) suggested that small-sample performance of Satorra and Bentler's (1988, 1994) test statistics could be improved by incorporating a Bartlett (1950) correction. In a large simulation study, Nevitt and Hancock (2004) examined the performance of a number of modified model fit test statistics for non-normal data under various ratios of sample size to number of estimated model parameters (N:t ranged from 1:1 to 10:1, with N's ranging from 35 to 1,290) and sampling distributions (skewness ≤ 3, kurtosis ≤ 21). The authors found that the Satorra–Bentler scaled statistic exhibited inflated Type I error rate at small sample sizes (N:$t \leq 10$:1) but the Bartlett-corrected version provided good Type I error control and superior power compared to other test statistics in nearly all sample size and distribution conditions they investigated. However, the Satorra–Bentler adjusted statistic and its Bartlett-corrected version tended to provide low rejection rates for both correctly and incorrectly specified models (Nevitt & Hancock, 2004). Regarding the residual-based test statistics, the authors found the performance of the Yuan–Bentler χ^2 and F-test statistics to be "erratic, controlling Type I error rates under some conditions and failing under others" (Nevitt & Hancock, 2004, p. 468). As a result, the authors recommended the Bartlett-corrected Satorra–Bentler scaled statistic for evaluating model fit with small samples.

Besides model fit test statistics (χ^2 or F-test), other fit indices that are functionally related to model χ^2 are often used to evaluate model fit, and standard error estimates are used to test parameter estimates for statistical significance. Yu and Muthén (2002) showed that model fit indices (root mean square error of approximation [RMSEA], Tucker–Lewis index [TLI], and comparative fit index [CFI]) based on Satorra–Bentler scaled χ^2 performed better than those based on regular ML and ADF under moderate to severe non-normality and small sample size conditions. Nevitt and Hancock (2000) also reported improved performance of adjusted RMSEA based on Satorra–Bentler scaled χ^2 when models were properly specified for non-normal data. Similarly, robust standard errors of Satorra and Bentler (1988, 1994) have been found to show less negative bias

than those of regular ML and ADF (Chou & Bentler, 1995; Chou et al., 1991).

Compared to the robust ML approach for continuous non-normal data, Nevitt and Hancock (2001) found that the bootstrapping approach (with Amos) did not work well with small samples ($N = 100$ or N:$t = 5$:1). When sample size was at least 200, bootstrapping provided better Type I error control but lower power than did the Satorra–Bentler scaled statistic under severe non-normality (skewness = 3, kurtosis = 21). Moreover, bootstrapped standard errors were somewhat less biased but more variable than Satorra–Bentler robust standard errors when sample size was not small (Nevitt & Hancock, 2001).

Estimators for Ordered Categorical Variables

When approximately normal ordinal variables with at least five categories are treated as continuous and analyzed with normal theory ML, research has shown that model χ^2 and fit indices are not greatly misleading, but parameter estimates are slightly underestimated, and standard error estimates are negatively biased (e.g., Babakus, Ferguson, & Jöreskog, 1987; Muthén & Kaplan, 1985). When non-normal ordinal variables are treated as continuous and analyzed with normal theory ML, model–data fit is underestimated (e.g., Green, Akey, Fleming, Hershberger, & Marquis, 1997; West, Finch, & Curran, 1995), and negative bias in parameter and standard error estimates is more severe (e.g., Babakus et al., 1987; Muthén & Kaplan, 1985). The performance of the normal theory ML estimator is worse as the number of categories decreases, level of non-normality increases, and sample size decreases (e.g., Babakus et al., 1987; Bollen, 1989; Dolan, 1994).

Because analyzing a polychoric/polyserial matrix leads to consistent estimators of parameters with any fit functions (Bollen, 1989), alternative estimation methods for categorical data in SEM usually begin with estimating polychoric/polyserial correlations, assuming underlying normality of latent response variables. Dolan (1994) found that ML with a polychoric matrix provided better parameter estimates than ML with Pearson matrix for symmetrically distributed variables with up to seven categories. Coenders, Satorra, and Saris (1997) also found that analyzing a polychoric matrix worked better than analyzing a Pearson matrix when normality of latent response variables held, even though intervals between categories of ordinal variables were unequal (the authors called this "high transformation error," p. 273).

However, a polychoric or polyserial correlation may provide a biased estimate of the latent association when normality of latent response variables is violated or when the cell size of the bivariate frequency table is sparse (e.g., Olsson, 1979). Although researchers have found polychoric/polyserial correlations to be fairly robust to moderate non-normality of latent response variables (|skewness| ≤ 1.25 and |kurtosis| ≤ 3.75; e.g., Coenders et al., 1997; Flora & Curran, 2004), they are not robust to severe non-normality (e.g., skewness = 5, kurtosis = 50; Flora & Curran, 2004).

Among estimation methods used on polychoric/polyserial matrices, WLSMV has been found to perform better than the full WLS (e.g., Flora & Curran, 2004, who used Mplus for WLS; Berkovits & Hancock, 2000, who used EQS for WLS). Moreover, Muthén and colleagues (1997) found that WLSMV outperforms WLSM in Type I error control. However, WLSMV appeared to be slightly more sensitive to small samples than robust ML with Satorra–Bentler scaled statistics (Lei, 2009). Lei (2009) found that when sample size was at least 250 ($N{:}t > 10{:}1$), robust ML and WLSMV performed similarly regardless of level of score skewness. When sample size was 100 ($N{:}t < 10{:}1$) and ordinal variables were moderately skewed (skewness = 2.3, kurtosis = 5.3), however, WLSMV provided a slightly higher percentage of invalid rejections, a lower percentage of valid rejections, and more negatively biased standard error estimates than did ML with Satorra–Bentler scaled statistics. Lei also found the Satorra–Bentler scaled χ^2 test to be generally more powerful than the Yuan–Bentler residual-based F-test (at $N > p(p + 1)/2$), although they provided similar Type I error rates.

SUMMARY OF EMPIRICAL FINDINGS

In summary, when simultaneously considering both model test statistics, and parameter and standard error estimates, the literature suggests that normal theory ML with the Satorra and Bentler (1988, 1994) scaled statistics would work better than ML without scaling for continuous variables when normality of variables is violated; it would also work better than the ADF estimator when sample size is not very large. Among methods for improving the model fit test statistic, the Satorra–Bentler scaled χ^2 appears to perform comparably to the Yuan–Bentler residual-based tests and

bootstrapping when sample size is not too small ($N \geq$ 200 or $N{:}t \geq 10{:}1$). When sample size is very small ($N < 200$ or $N{:}t < 10{:}1$), incorporating a Bartlett correction to the Satorra–Bentler scaled χ^2 statistic may improve the accuracy of model evaluation, and it appears to work more consistently than the Yuan–Bentler residual-based F-test.

For categorical observed variables, polychoric/polyserial correlation is recommended for analysis unless normality of the underlying scales is severely violated (e.g., skewness = 5, kurtosis = 50; examined by Flora & Curran, 2004) or the expected bivariate frequencies are small (Olsson, 1979). WLSMV or robust ML with a Satorra–Bentler scaled statistic on polychoric/polyserial correlations would work better than full WLS for ordinal variables at realistic sample sizes. The robust ML approach appears to perform similarly to WLSMV when sample size is not too small (e.g., $N{:}t \geq 10{:}1$) but may perform better than WLSMV when the sample size is small (e.g., $N = 100$ or $N{:}t < 10{:}1$). In general, full WLS estimators are not recommended for either continuous or ordinal variables, unless the sample size is extremely large.

AN ILLUSTRATION

To illustrate the use and performance of various estimators for non-normal variables, we created several simulated data sets with the desired data characteristics (continuous vs. ordinal non-normal data, and small vs. large sample sizes). A simple 18-variable, two-factor CFA model with simple structure is used for illustration purposes. Population parameters, factor loadings, and correlation between the two factors were taken from estimates of a large, actual data set. The two constructs of interest are generalized anxiety (measured with eight items) and depression (measured with 10 items). Original item responses were on a 5-point scale. Respondents were asked to rate brief descriptions of symptoms (e.g., "I have sleep difficulties," "I feel helpless") from 0 (*not at all like me*) to 4 (*extremely like me*).

The number of unique sample variances and covariances for 18 observed variables is 171 [i.e., 18 * (18 + 1)/2]. The 18-variable, two-factor model has 134 *df*, with 18 factor loadings, 18 error variances, and an interfactor correlation (factor variances were fixed to 1 to scale the latent variables), resulting in a total of 37 parameters to be estimated. Two levels of sample size, 200 and 1,000, were included. Both sample sizes were greater than the number of unique sample variances and covariances, but the ratio of sample size to number of estimated parameters was less than 10 to 1 for a sample size of 200 (about 5.4:1) and greater than 10 to 1 for sample size of 1,000 (about 27:1). A sample size of 1,000 is expected to work well for robust ML with Satorra–Bentler corrected statistics or with a Yuan–Bentler residual-based χ^2 or F-test when observed variables are continuous non-normal, and for robust ML and WLSMV analysis with polychoric matrix when observed variables are ordinal non-normal. A sample size of 200 (less than 10 observations per estimated parameter), however, may pose a challenge for these estimators. Nevertheless, a sample size of 1,000 might still be too small for normal theory ML and full WLS χ^2 to behave well when observed variables are non-normal in either continuous or ordinal form.

A large level of non-normality (all indicators had univariate skewness = 3, kurtosis = 21) was simulated for continuous observed variables to challenge the robust ML approach. For ordinal variables, either *non-normality* of latent response variables (univariate skewness = 3, kurtosis = 21) with low transformation error (i.e., equal interval between categories with cut points for categorization at –.75, –.25, .25, and .75) or *multivariate normal* latent response variables with high transformation error (unequal interval and asymmetric categorization at cut points .67, 1.28, 1.645, and 2.05) was simulated. The former resulted in univariate negative skewness (average = –.64) and negative kurtosis (average = –.46) of the observed ordinal variables and the latter univariate positive skewness (average = 2.34) and positive kurtosis (average = 5.16). If normality of latent response variables were important for using a polychoric matrix, then parameter estimates produced by analyzing a polychoric matrix (holding estimators constant) would be expected to be worse in the first case than in the second case despite the more severe level of non-normality of the observed ordinal variables in the second case.

The normal theory ML estimator, the full WLS (or ADF) estimator, and the MLM with Satorra–Bentler scaled χ^2 and fit indices based on scaled statistics were used to estimate the model with Mplus 6 for continuous observed variables. Residual-based model test statistics based on ML were obtained from EQS 6.1 by fitting the same model to the same continuous data sets. For ordinal observed variables, solutions from normal theory ML and MLM were requested from Mplus 6 by treating the 5-point ordinal variables as continuous to see if

ignoring the metric problem was robust to source (from non-normal latent response variables or transformation error) or level (small skewness and kurtosis vs. moderate skewness and kurtosis) of observed non-normality. A polychoric matrix of ordinal variables (PC) was analyzed with ML (referred to as ML + PC in Table 10.3) and robust ML (labeled as MLM + PC in Table 10.3) using EQS 6.1, as well as with full WLS and WLSMV using Mplus 6.

Model fit statistics and bias of parameter estimates (Average % bias and Average % absolute bias of model parameters) based on one replication for the various combinations of non-normality, sample size, and estimation methods are provided in Table 10.3. Bias of standard error estimates could not be evaluated because only one replication for each cell was simulated for illustration purposes.

As can be seen in Table 10.3, all ML χ^2 without adjustment rejected the true model incorrectly, as did some fit indices based on unadjusted ML χ^2 at the small sample size. As expected, Satorra–Bentler scaled χ^2 and fit indices based on the scaled χ^2 performed well for continuous variables despite the large departure from normality. The Yuan–Bentler residual-based χ^2 and F-test also performed well at both sample sizes for continuous non-normal variables, while Browne's residual-based χ^2 did not do well in the small-sample condition. Furthermore, average % bias and average % absolute bias of the ML parameter estimates across model parameters were small for continuous non-normal data. The performance of the robust ML approach with adjusted model test statistics (with Satorra–Bentler scaled χ^2 or Yuan–Bentler χ^2 or F-test) appeared to hold up well under continuous non-normality even in the small-sample condition ($N = 200$), with the ratio of sample size to number of estimated parameters being just over 5 to 1. Consistent with findings from the literature, the theoretically correct estimator under non-normality, full WLS or ADF, performed worse than the robust ML method in estimation of both model fit and model parameters at either sample size.

For ordinal variables, the performance of the estimation methods in parameter estimation appeared to depend on the source or magnitude of non-normality. Treating ordinal variables as continuous and estimating the model with normal theory ML produced a substantial amount of negative bias (about 14% on average) in parameter estimates, regardless of sample size, when transformation error was high (asymmetrical categorization with unequal intervals between adjacent cat-

TABLE 10.3. Fit Statistics for Selected Estimation Methods under Different Non-Normal Variable and Sample Size Conditions

	χ^2 (df = 134)	p	CFI	TLI	RMSEA	Average % bias of parameter estimates	Average % absolute bias of parameter estimates
Severely non-normal continuous variables							
N = 200							
ML	337.52	**.000**	**.911**	**.898**	**.087**	.08	5.88
MLM[a]	149.35	.173	.982	.980	.024	—	—
WLS	398.44	**.000**	**.797**	**.769**	**.099**	5.45	9.65
N = 1,000							
ML	395.39	**.000**	.975	.972	.044	.17	1.69
MLM[b]	150.55	.156	.995	.995	.011	—	—
WLS	149.46	.171	**.949**	**.942**	.011	−7.18	**10.21**
Ordinal variables with moderate observed non-normality (MVN latent response variables + high transformation error)							
N = 200							
ML	197.12	**.000**	**.948**	**.941**	.049	−14.11	**14.11**
MLM	115.99	.867	1	1	.000	—	—
ML+PC	478.67	**.000**	**.854**	**.834**	NA	.06	4.60
MLM+PC[c]	130.74	.564	1	1	NA	—	—
WLSMV	139.53	.354	.997	.997	.014	.70	4.40
WLS	NA	NA	NA	NA	NA	NA	NA
N = 1,000							
ML	238.39	**.000**	.983	.980	.028	−13.74	**13.74**
MLM	122.33	.756	1	1	.000	—	—
ML+PC	497.79	**.000**	.966	.961	NA	.40	2.26
MLM+PC[b]	135.28	.453	1	1	NA	—	—
WLSMV	128.38	.621	1	1	.000	.59	2.36
WLS	149.27	.174	.996	.995	.011	5.09	6.32
Ordinal variables with mild observed non-normality (severely non-normal latent response variables + low transformation error)							
N = 200							
ML	177.34	**.007**	.980	.977	.040	1.67	3.30
MLM	164.97	**.036**	.985	.983	.034	—	—
ML+PC	276.52	**.000**	**.949**	**.942**	NA	7.49	7.90
MLM+PC[a]	158.69	.072	.994	.993	NA	—	—
WLSMV	165.68	**.033**	.994	.993	.034	8.13	8.23
WLS	NA	NA	NA	NA	NA	NA	NA
N = 1,000							
ML	163.22	**.044**	.997	.997	.015	1.84	2.77
MLM	145.59	.233	.999	.999	.009	—	—
ML+PC	273.94	**.000**	.990	.988	NA	7.62	7.62
MLM+PC[b]	136.31	.428	1	1	NA	—	—
WLSMV	154.32	.111	.999	.999	.012	7.67	7.67
WLS	182.35	**.004**	.994	.994	.019	**11.61**	**11.61**

Note. NA, not available; — indicates same as above. **Bolded** fit statistics indicate rejection of the model at their respective recommended criteria (i.e., $p < .05$, CFI < .95, TLI < .95, RMSEA > .06); **bolded** average bias and average absolute bias of parameter estimates are > 10%, a level considered unacceptable by Muthén et al. (1997).

[a]Yuan–Bentler χ^2 and F-test were not significant, but Browne's residual-based χ^2 was at $p < .05$.

[b]All residual-based test statistics were not significant at $p > .05$.

[c] All residual-based test statistics were significant at $p < .05$.

egories) or when observed skewness and kurtosis were large (2.34 and 5.16, respectively). However, the same approach produced fairly unbiased parameter estimates (< 5% on average) when transformation error was low (symmetrical categorization with equal intervals between adjacent categories on severely non-normal latent response variables) or when observed skewness and kurtosis were low (−.64 and −.46, respectively), regardless of sample size. Note that levels of transformation error and of observed non-normality were confounded in this example. That is, high transformation error happened to result in large observed non-normality, and low transformation error happened to result in a low level of observed non-normality. Analyzing PC instead of a Pearson matrix with ML or WLSMV produced acceptable parameter estimates with a small amount of bias (< 10% on average) in both levels of observed non-normality. However, the amount of bias was notably lower when normality of latent response variables held, despite the larger level of observed skewness and kurtosis (average absolute bias < 5%) than when normality of latent response variables was violated (average absolute bias around 8%). Normality of latent response variables appeared to be important when PC was analyzed. More severe departure from normality than the magnitude simulated here may bias parameter estimates to an unacceptable level.

Holding sample size and source of non-normality for observed ordinal variables constant, robust ML analyzing a polychoric matrix with Satorra–Bentler scaled statistics performed similarly to WLSMV in their estimation of model fit and model parameters, both yielding mostly accurate fit statistics about the true model and an acceptable amount of bias in parameter estimates. As expected, full WLS was inferior to WLSMV in all cases. When the sample size was small, full WLS failed to yield a solution; when it did produce a solution at the larger sample size, its parameter estimates were more biased than WLSMV estimates. A sample size of 1,000 did not appear to be large enough for full WLS to outperform WLSMV.

Regardless of the type of matrix analyzed, for ordinal variables or sample size (200 or 1,000), the Satorra–Bentler scaling appeared to successfully reduce the inflation in model χ^2 of the ML estimator and would correctly retain the true model at the .05 significance level in most cases by itself. Moreover, the performance of Satorra–Bentler scaled χ^2 for ML with PC was more consistent than that of the residual-based test statistics.

Although no definitive conclusions can be made from this single-replication simulation, it illustrates the importance of choosing appropriate estimation methods based on considerations of data characteristics, including sample size or sample size per estimated model parameter, metric of measured variables, and distribution of variables. Our simulation results showed that the default normal theory ML estimator in most standard SEM programs did not work well when observed variables were non-normally distributed; it misinformed model–data fit regardless of the metric of the observed variables and underestimated model parameters for ordinal variables with high transformation error or moderate level of observed non-normality. The ML estimator with Satorra–Bentler scaled statistic performed much better in informing model–data fit than the regular ML model fit statistic regardless of the form or magnitude of non-normality and sample size. Bias of parameter estimates provided by the ML estimator was small under continuous non-normality but large when the metric of ordinal variables with high transformation error (or moderate observed non-normality) was disregarded.

The metric of ordinal variables can be taken into account by analyzing a polychoric/polyserial matrix. Robust ML or WLSMV analysis of a polychoric matrix performed well in informing model–data fit and provided parameter estimates with a tolerably small amount of bias, albeit bias of their parameter estimates might be somewhat higher when normality of latent response variables was severely violated (skewness = 3, kurtosis = 21). Moreover, the theoretically correct WLS or ADF estimator for non-normal data did not perform well at realistic sample sizes compared to robust ML or WLSMV, as has been shown in previous studies.

In conclusion, results of this simple simulation appear to be consistent with findings reported in other studies. It demonstrates differential performance of different estimation methods that have been proposed, recommended at some point, or used in applied research under some common practical conditions. It elucidates the importance of choosing estimation methods based on careful considerations of data characteristics such as sample size or sample size per estimated model parameter, metric of measured variables, and distribution of variables. These considerations are imperative because in real-life application in areas of social and behavioral sciences, non-normality of observed variables is common (e.g., Micceri, 1989) and sample size is typically not large.

REFERENCES

Anderson, J. C., & Gerbing, D. W. (1988). Structural equation modeling in practice: A review and recommended two-step approach. *Psychological Bulletin, 103*, 411–423.

Anderson, T. W. (1973). Asymptotically efficient estimation of covariance matrices with linear structure. *Annals of Statistics, 1*, 135–141.

Arbuckle, J. L. (1995–2009). *Amos 18 user's guide*. Crawfordville, FL: Amos Development Corporation.

Arbuckle, J. L. (2009). *Amos 18* [Computer software]. Chicago: SmallWaters.

Asparouhov, T., & Muthén, B. (2005, November). *Multivariate statistical modeling with survey data*. Paper presented at the 2005 Federal Committee on Statistical Methodology (FCSM) Research Conference, Arlington, VA.

Babakus, E., Ferguson, C. E., Jr., & Jöreskog, K. G. (1987). The sensitivity of confirmatory maximum likelihood factor analysis to violations of measurement scale and distributional assumptions. *Journal of Marketing Research, 24*, 222–228.

Bargmann, R. (1957). *A study of independence and dependence in multivariate normal analysis* (Mimeo Series No. 186). Chapel Hill: University of North Carolina, Institute of Statistics.

Bartlett, M. S. (1950). Tests of significance in factor analysis. *British Journal of Psychology, Statistical Section, 3*, 77–85.

Basmann, R. L. (1957). A generalized classical method of linear estimation of coefficients in a structural equation. *Econometrica, 25*, 77–83.

Bauwens, L. (1984). *Bayesian full information analysis of simultaneous equation models using integration by Monte Carlo*. New York: Springer-Verlag.

Bentler, P. M. (2005). *EQS 6.1 for Windows* [Computer software]. Encino, CA: Multivariate Software.

Bentler, P. M., & Dudgeon, P. (1996). Covariance structure analysis: Statistical practice, theory, and directions. *Annual Review of Psychology, 47*, 563–592.

Bentler, P. M., & Yuan, K.-H. (1999). Structural equation modeling with small samples: Test statistics. *Multivariate Behavioral Research, 34*, 181–197.

Berkovits, I., & Hancock, G. R. (2000, April). *A comparison of methods for structural modeling with polytomous and continuous variables*. Paper presented at the annual meeting of the American Educational Research Association, New Orleans, LA.

Bielby, W., & Hauser, R. (1977). Structural equation models. *Annual Review of Sociology, 3*, 137–161.

Blalock, H. M., Jr. (1964). *Causal inferences in nonexperimental research*. Chapel Hill: University Press of North Carolina.

Bollen, K. A. (1989). *Structural equations with latent variables*. New York: Wiley.

Bollen, K. A. (1996a). An alternative two stage least squares (2SLS) estimator for latent variable equations. *Psychometrika, 61*, 109–121.

Bollen, K. A. (1996b). A limited-information estimator for LISREL models with and without heteroscedastic errors. In G. Marcoulides & R. Schumacker (Eds.), *Advanced structural equation modeling: Issues and techniques* (pp. 227–241). Mahwah, NJ: Erlbaum.

Bollen, K. A. (2001). Two-stage least squares and latent variable models: Simultaneous estimation and robustness to misspecifications. In R. Cudeck, S. Du Toit, & D. Sörbom (Eds.), *Structural equation modeling: Present and future* (pp. 119–138). Lincolnwood, IL: Scientific Software.

Bollen, K. A., & Bauer, D. J. (2004). Automating the selection of model-implied instrumental variables. *Sociological Methods and Research, 32*, 425–452.

Bollen, K. A., Kirby, J. B., Curran, P. J., Paxton, P. M., & Chen, F. (2007). Latent variable models under misspecification: Two-stage least squares (2SLS) and maximum likelihood (ML) estimators. *Sociological Methods and Research, 36*, 48–86.

Browne, M. W. (1974). Generalized least squares estimators in the analysis of covariance structures. *South African Statistical Journal, 8*, 1–24. Reprinted in 1977 in D. J. Aigner & A. S. Goldberger (Eds.), *Latent variables in socioeconomic models* (pp. 205–226). Amsterdam: North Holland.

Browne, M. W. (1984). Asymptotically distribution-free methods for analysis of covariance structures. *British Journal of Mathematical and Statistical Psychology, 37*, 62–83.

Chou, C., & Bentler, P. M. (1995). Estimates and tests in structural equation modeling. In R. H. Hoyle (Ed.), *Structural equation modeling: Concepts, issues, and applications* (pp. 37–54). Thousand Oaks, CA: Sage.

Chou, C., Bentler, P. M., & Satorra, A. (1991). Scaled test statistics and robust standard errors for non-normal data in covariance structure analysis: A Monte Carlo study. *British Journal of Mathematical and Statistical Psychology, 44*, 347–357.

Coenders, G., Satorra, A., & Saris, W. E. (1997). Alternative approaches to structural modeling of ordinal data: A Monte Carlo study. *Structural Equation Modeling, 4*, 261–282.

Curran, P. J., West, S. G., & Finch, J. F. (1996). The robustness of test statistics to nonnormality and specification error in confirmatory factor analysis. *Psychological Methods, 1*, 16–29.

Dolan, C. V. (1994). Factor analysis of variables with 2, 3, 5 and 7 response categories: A comparison of categorical variable estimators using simulated data. *British Journal of Mathematical and Statistical Psychology, 47*, 309–326.

Duncan, O. (1966). Path analysis: Sociological examples. *American Journal of Sociology, 72*, 1–16.

Dunson, D. B., Palomo, J., & Bollen, K. A. (2005). *Bayesian structural equation modeling* (Technical Report No.

2005-5). Research Triangle Park, NC: Statistical and Applied Mathematical Sciences Institute.

Emmett, W. G. (1949). Factor analysis by Lawley's method of maximum likelihood. *British Journal of Mathematical and Statistical Psychology, 2*, 90–97.

Enders, C. K. (2006). Analyzing structural equation models with missing data. In G. R. Hancock & R. O. Mueller (Eds.), *Structural equation modeling: A second course* (pp. 313–342). Greenwich, CT: Information Age.

Finch, J. F., West, S. G., & MacKinnon, D. P. (1997). Effects of sample size and non-normality on the estimation of mediated effects in latent variable models. *Structural Equation Modeling, 4*, 87–107.

Finkbeiner, C. (1979). Estimation for the multiple factor model when data are missing. *Psychometrika, 44*, 409–420.

Flora, D. B., & Curran, P. J. (2004). An empirical evaluation of alternative methods of estimation for confirmatory factor analysis with ordinal data. *Psychological Methods, 9*, 466–491.

Fouladi, R. T. (1999, April). *Model fit in covariance structure analysis under small sample conditions—Modified maximum likelihood and asymptotically distribution free generalized least squares procedures.* Paper presented at the annual meeting of the American Educational Research Association, Montreal, Canada.

Fouladi, R. T. (2000). Performance of modified test statistics in covariance and correlation structure analysis under conditions of multivariate nonnormality. *Structural Equation Modeling, 7*, 356–410.

Gilks, W. R., Richardson, S., & Spiegelhalter, D. J. (1996). Introducing Markov Chain Monte Carlo. In *Markov Chain Monte Carlo in practice* (pp. 1–19). London: Chapman & Hall.

Green, S. B., Akey, T. M., Fleming, K. K., Hershberger, S. L., & Marquis, J. G. (1997). Effect of the number of scale points on chi-square fit indices in confirmatory factor analysis. *Structural Equation Modeling, 4*, 108–120.

Hoogland, J. J., & Boomsma, A. (1998). Robustness studies in covariance structure modeling: An overview and a meta-analysis. *Sociological Methods and Research, 26*, 329–367.

Hu, L., Bentler, P. M., & Kano, Y. (1992). Can test statistics in covariance structure analysis be trusted? *Psychological Bulletin, 112*, 351–362.

Jöreskog, K. G. (1977). Factor analysis by least square and maximum likelihood methods. In K. Enslein, A. Ralston, & H. S. Wilf (Eds.), *Statistical methods for digital computers* (Vol. III, pp. 125–165). New York: Wiley.

Jöreskog, K. G. (1983). Factor analysis as an error-in-variables model. In H. Wainer & S. Messick (Eds.), *Principles of modern psychological measurement* (pp. 185–196). Hillsdale, NJ: Erlbaum.

Jöreskog, K. G., & Goldberger, A. S. (1972). Factor analysis by generalized least squares. *Psychometrika, 37*, 243–260.

Jöreskog, K. G., & Lawley, D. N. (1968). New methods in maximum likelihood factor analysis. *British Journal of Mathematical and Statistical Psychology, 21*, 85–96.

Jöreskog, K. G., & Sörbom, D. (1988). *LISREL 7* [Computer software]. Chicago: Scientific Software.

Jöreskog, K. G., & Sörbom, D. (1993). *LISREL 8* [Computer software]. Mooresville, IN: Scientific Software.

Jöreskog, K. G., & Sörbom, D. (2006). *LISREL 8.8 for Windows* [Computer software]. Lincolnwood, IL: Scientific Software.

Jöreskog, K. G., & van Thillo, M. (1973). *LISREL–A general computer program for estimating a linear structural equation system involving unmeasured variables* (Research Report No. 73-5). Uppsala, Sweden: University of Uppsala.

Kline, R. B. (2005). *Principles and practice of structural equation modeling* (2nd ed.). New York: Guilford Press.

Kline, R. B. (2010). *Principles and practice of structural equation modeling* (3rd ed.). New York: Guilford Press.

Lawley, D. N. (1940). The estimation of factor loadings by the method of maximum likelihood. *Proceedings of the Royal Society of Edinburgh* (A), *60*, 64–82.

Lee, S.-Y., & Jennrich, R. I. (1979). A study of algorithms for covariance structure analysis with specific comparisons using factor analysis. *Psychometrika, 44*, 99–113.

Lee, S.-Y., Poon, W.-Y., & Bentler, P. M. (1995). A two-stage estimation of structural equation models with continuous and polytomous variables. *British Journal of Mathematical and Statistical Psychology, 48*, 339–358.

Lei, P.-W. (2009). Evaluating estimation methods for ordinal data in structural equation modeling. *Quality and Quantity, 43*, 495–507.

Martin, J. K., & McDonald, R. P. (1975). Bayesian estimation in unrestricted factor analysis: A treatment for Heywood cases. *Psychometrika, 40*, 505–517.

Micceri, T. (1989). The unicorn, the normal curve, and other improbable creatures. *Psychological Bulletin, 105*, 156–166.

Muthén, B. O. (1984). A general structural equation model with dichotomous, ordered categorical, and continuous latent variable indicators. *Psychometrika, 49*, 115–132.

Muthén, B. O. (1993). Goodness of fit with categorical and other non-normal variables. In K. A. Bollen & J. S. Long (Eds.), *Testing structural equation models* (pp. 205–243). Newbury Park, CA: Sage.

Muthén, B. O., & Kaplan, D. (1985). A comparison of some methodologies for the factor analysis of non-normal Likert variables. *British Journal of Mathematical and Statistical Psychology, 38*, 171–189.

Muthén, B. O., & Muthén, L. K. (2010). *Mplus 6* [Computer software]. Los Angeles: Authors.

Muthén, B. O., du Toit, S. H. C., & Spisic, D. (1997). *Robust inference using weighted least squares and quadratic estimating equations in latent variable modeling with categorical and continuous outcomes.* Unpublished technical report. Retrieved from *http://gseis.ucla.edu/faculty/muthen/articles/Article_075.pdf.*

Muthén, L. K., & Muthén, B. O. (1998–2010). *Mplus user's guide* (6th ed.). Los Angeles: Authors.

Nevitt, J., & Hancock, G. (2000). Improving the root mean square error of approximation for nonnormal conditions in structural equation modeling. *Journal of Experimental Education, 68,* 251–268.

Nevitt, J., & Hancock, G. R. (2001). Performance of bootstrapping approaches to model test statistics and parameter standard error estimation in structural equation modeling. *Structural Equation Modeling, 8,* 353–377.

Nevitt, J., & Hancock, G. R. (2004). Evaluating small sample approaches for model test statistics in structural equation modeling. *Multivariate Behavioral Research, 39,* 439–478.

Olsson, U. (1979). Maximum likelihood estimation of the polychoric correlation coefficient. *Psychometrika, 44,* 443–460.

Poon, W.-Y., & Lee, S.-Y. (1987). Maximum likelihood estimation of multivariate polyserial and polychoric correlation coefficients. *Psychometrika, 52,* 409–430.

Satorra, A., & Bentler, P. M. (1988). Scaling corrections for chi-square statistics in covariance structure analysis. In *Proceedings of the Business and Economic Section of the American Statistical Association* (pp. 308–313). Alexandria, VA: American Statistical Association.

Satorra, A., & Bentler, P. M. (1994). Corrections to test statistics and standard errors in covariance structure analysis. In A. von Eye & C. C. Clogg (Eds.), *Latent variables analysis: Applications for developmental research* (pp. 399–419). Thousand Oaks, CA: Sage.

Schafer, J. L., & Graham, J. W. (2002). Missing data: Our view of the state of the art. *Psychological Methods, 7,* 147–177.

Skinner, C. J. (1989). Domain means, regression and multivariate analysis. In C. J. Skinner, D. Holt, & T. M. F. Smith (Eds.), *Analysis of complex surveys* (pp. 59–87). New York: Wiley.

West, S. G., Finch, J. F., & Curran, P. J. (1995). Structural equation models with non-normal variables: Problems and remedies. In R. Hoyle (Ed.), *Structural equation modeling: Concepts, issues, and applications* (pp. 56–75). Thousand Oaks, CA: Sage.

Yu, C., & Muthén, B. (2002, April). *Evaluation of model fit indices for latent variable models with categorical and continuous outcomes.* Paper presented at the annual meeting of the American Educational Research Association, New Orleans, LA.

Yuan, K.-H., & Bentler, P. M. (1997a). Improving parameter tests in covariance structure analysis. *Computational Statistics and Data Analysis, 26,* 177–198.

Yuan, K.-H., & Bentler, P. M. (1997b). Mean and covariance structure analysis: Theoretical and practical improvements. *Journal of the American Statistical Association, 92,* 767–774.

Yuan, K.-H., & Bentler, P. M. (1998). Normal theory based test statistics in structural equation modeling. *British Journal of Mathematical and Statistical Psychology, 51,* 289–309.

Yuan, K.-H., & Bentler, P. M. (1999). F tests for mean and covariance structure analysis. *Journal of Educational and Behavioral Statistics, 24,* 225–243.

Yuan, K.-H., & Chan, W. (2005). On nonequivalence of several procedures of structural equation modeling. *Psychometrika, 70,* 791–798.

APPENDIX 10.1. Statements Used by Four SEM Software Programs to Request Different Estimation Methods

Estimation methods	Amos 18.0	EQS 6.1	LISREL 8.8 (Simplis)	Mplus 6
FIML	View → analysis properties: Estimation tab → check "estimate means and intercepts" Output tab → check "observed information matrix"	/Specifications matrix=raw; analysis=moment; method=ML; missing=ML; SE=observed	Missing Value Code -999 Raw Data from File 'C:\...' Options: me=ML	Variables: Missing are all (-999); Analysis: Estimator=ML; Information=observed;
ML with Satorra–Bentler scaled χ^2 and robust standard errors	NA	/Specifications matrix=raw; method=ML, robust;	Covariance Matrix from File 'C:\...' Asymptotic Covariance Matrix from File C:\... Options: me=ML	Analysis: Estimator=MLM;
ADF/WLS	View → analysis properties: Estimation tab → check "Asymptotically distribution-free" under "Discrepancy"	/Specifications matrix=raw; method=AGLS;	Covariance Matrix from File 'C:\...' Asymptotic Covariance Matrix from File C:\... Options: me=WLS	Analysis: Estimator=WLS;
Default estimator for categorical data	File → Data files: Check "allow non-numeric data" → OK Analyze → Bayesian Estimation	/Specifications matrix=raw; categorical=V1–Vn; method=ML, robust;	Correlation Matrix from File 'C:\...' Asymptotic Covariance Matrix from File C:\... Options: me=ML	Variable: Categorical are V1–Vn; Analysis: Estimator=WLSMV;
Bayesian	Analyze → Bayesian Estimation	NA	NA	Analysis: Estimator=BAYES;

Note. NA, not available; V1–Vn, user-defined variable names.

CHAPTER 11

Power Analysis for Tests
of Structural Equation Models

Taehun Lee
Li Cai
Robert C. MacCallum

In empirical applications of structural equation modeling (SEM), researchers routinely encounter the need to evaluate the fit of a hypothesized model to sample data for purposes of inferring the correspondence between the model and the true process under investigation. In addition, when researchers fit more than one model to data, the need arises to evaluate differences between models for purposes of selecting one from among competing theoretical models. For such model evaluations, a commonly used statistical method is the likelihood ratio (LR) test. In the case of testing the fit of single models, the null hypothesis (H_0) to be tested by the LR test is that the specified model holds exactly in the population. In the case of comparing nested models, the null hypothesis is that there is no difference in model fit between the two models in the population.[1]

When testing a null hypothesis, it is important to know the probability of drawing the correct conclusion (i.e., the probability of retaining a correct H_0 and the probability of rejecting a false H_0). Because the statistical convention is that the probability of retaining a correct H_0 is fixed at $1 - \alpha$, the probability of rejecting a false H_0 (i.e., the *statistical power* of the test) needs to be determined to fully assess the quality of the test. In the model evaluation context, power analysis informs researchers whether the tests have adequate capability to discern and reject a false hypothesis about model fit.

This chapter presents methods for estimating statistical power of the LR test for model evaluations, along with discussions of relevant methodological issues.

In general, statistical power analysis requires the investigator to define an *effect size* representing the degree to which H_0 is incorrect. In the context of SEM, two approaches to establishing effect size have been proposed. One procedure is based on the work of Satorra and Saris (1985), in which "effect size" is defined in terms of the values of parameters that differentiate the hypothesized model and the alternative model that is assumed to represent the true process of interest. An alternative procedure, proposed by MacCallum, Browne, and Sugawara (1996), defines "effect size" in terms of the lack of fit of the specified models in the population. Once an effect size is specified, computation of power becomes straightforward. In this chapter, these approaches to establishing effect size are described and compared. A closely related problem, determination of minimum sample size necessary to achieve a desired level of power, is also described.

An important issue in the hypothesis testing framework is the specification of the null hypothesis. Classical LR procedures test *exact fit* or *no difference* null hypotheses. Reliance on such null hypotheses is prone to problems. When evaluating a single model, the null hypothesis that the proposed model holds exactly in the population is always false in empirical studies. Similarly, for model comparison, the null hypothesis that there is no difference in fit between two nested models is also always false. Therefore, the best one can hope for realistically is that a model is not grossly wrong, providing a close approximation to real-world relationships and effects (Box, 1979; MacCallum, 2003). When comparing competing models, although exactly equal fit is implausible, small differences in fit would be realistic and interesting. In response to problems associated with the testing of hypotheses that are never true, Browne and Cudeck (1993) proposed procedures for the test of *close fit*, in which the null hypothesis to be tested is that the specified model is a close approximation to the true process of interest. Furthermore, MacCallum, Browne, and Cai (2006) generalized these procedures and provided a mechanism for the testing of the null hypothesis that the true difference between two nested models is small, rather than zero, in the population. MacCallum and colleagues (1996, 2006) provide methods for computing statistical power of the test of such null hypotheses. These procedures are also described in this chapter.

POWER ANALYSIS FOR TESTS OF FIT OF SINGLE MODELS

Here we consider the case where researchers are interested in estimating the power of the test in which the null hypothesis is that the specified model holds exactly in the population, known as the test of "exact fit" in SEM. Following is some basic background material necessary for the statistical power analysis for the test of model fit in SEM.

Statistical Theory

Given p manifest variables, let Σ_0 represent the $p \times p$ population covariance matrix and let γ_0 represent a $q \times 1$ vector of model parameters. Then a structural equation model of interest could be represented as $\Sigma(\gamma_0)$, where $\Sigma(\bullet)$ is a matrix-valued function that specifies the functional relationship between the model-implied covariances and the parameters. We define the exact fit null hypothesis as

$$H_0 : \Sigma_0 = \Sigma(\gamma_0) \qquad (11.1)$$

representing that the specified model holds exactly in the population, or equivalently stated, that there is no

lack of fit of the model-implied covariance matrix $\Sigma(\gamma_0)$ to the population covariance matrix Σ_0.

Suppose, on the other hand, that the null hypothesis does not hold. The alternative hypothesis (H_1) states that one cannot find a vector of parameters γ such that the model-implied covariance matrix $\Sigma(\gamma)$ is equal to the population covariance matrix Σ_0. The degree of lack of fit between the model-implied covariance matrix and the population covariance matrix is captured by a discrepancy function, $F[\Sigma_0, \Sigma(\gamma)]$. A discrepancy function must satisfy a number of mathematical properties (see, e.g., Browne, 1984). Generally, F is non-negative, and it increases as the difference between Σ_0 and $\Sigma(\gamma)$ increases. A most important requirement is that the discrepancy function can take on a value of zero if and only if Σ_0 is equal to $\Sigma(\gamma_0)$ for some γ_0. In other words, $F[\Sigma_0, \Sigma(\gamma_0)] = 0$ when the exact fit hypothesis (Equation 11.1) holds.

In practice, a specified model is fitted to a $p \times p$ sample covariance matrix, $\mathbf{S}$, producing a vector of parameter estimates, $\hat{\gamma}$, and a model-implied covariance matrix in the sample, $\Sigma(\hat{\gamma})$. The objective of parameter estimation is to find a γ among all plausible parameter vectors such that the resulting model-implied covariance matrix $\Sigma(\gamma)$ is as similar to $\mathbf{S}$ as possible. The difference between $\Sigma(\gamma)$ and $\mathbf{S}$ is measured by the same discrepancy function, $F[\mathbf{S}, \Sigma(\gamma)]$, applied to a sample covariance matrix $\mathbf{S}$ instead of a population covariance matrix Σ_0.

A number of different discrepancy functions have been proposed, such as generalized least squares or asymptotically distribution-free (Browne, 1974, 1984), but for the moment, let us assume that we utilize the normal theory maximum likelihood (ML) discrepancy function, defined as

$$F[\mathbf{S}, \Sigma(\gamma)] = \ln |\Sigma(\gamma)| + \text{tr}\,[\mathbf{S}\Sigma(\gamma)^{-1}] - \ln |\mathbf{S}| - p \quad (11.2)$$

And let F_0 represent the discrepancy function value reflecting lack of fit of the model in the population. Then, it is clear that, if the model holds exactly in the population, F_0 will have the value of zero, meaning that there is no lack of fit in the population. Thus, an equivalent way to express the null hypothesis of exact fit could be

$$H_0 : F_0 = 0 \qquad (11.3)$$

In practice, only the sample value of the discrepancy function is known. Let that sample value be designated

$\hat{F}$. Then the null hypothesis that the specified model holds exactly in the population can be tested using the LR test statistic

$$T = (N - 1)\hat{F} \tag{11.4}$$

where N represents sample size. If the distributional assumptions underlying the discrepancy function being used are adequately satisfied, and if N is sufficiently large, then T will be approximately distributed as chi-square with degrees of freedom $d = p(p + 1)/2 - q$, where q is the number of free parameters to be estimated. For a selected α level, one can determine a critical value, χ_C^2, under this chi-square distribution. If the observed value of T exceeds χ_C^2, then H_0 is rejected; if not, H_0 is retained.

To determine the statistical power of the LR test, knowledge of the distribution of the test statistic T under the alternative hypothesis is required. When the specified model does not hold exactly in the population, one must quantify, for the purposes of power analysis, the degree of lack of fit of the specified model in the population. In other words, one must choose an *effect size* in terms of a specific nonzero discrepancy function value. Let that value be designated F^*. The alternative hypothesis, then, could be represented as

$$H_1 : F_0 = F^* \tag{11.5}$$

Under a specific alternative hypothesis, H_1, along with a chosen value of F^*, the LR test statistic, T, is approximately distributed as noncentral chi-square with d degrees of freedom and with the noncentrality parameter[2]

$$\lambda = (N - 1)F^* \tag{11.6}$$

Let us assume for the moment that a value of the noncentrality parameter λ has been specified. Once λ is specified, it follows that statistical power is obtained by computing the area to the right of χ_C^2 under the noncentral chi-square distribution with noncentrality parameter λ. The distributions and relevant areas for a typical case are illustrated in Figure 11.1. The shaded area in the figure shows the probability of rejecting $H_0 : F_0 = 0$ if in fact $H_1 : F_0 = F^*$. This area represents the probability that a value of T drawn from the distribution of T under the (true) alternative distribution exceeds the critical value defined under the (false) null distribution.

Specifying Effect Size

It is clear that the procedure for power calculation requires the investigator to provide the effect size, F^*, or the noncentrality parameter, λ. Of course, this value is not known in practice. Therefore, a procedure is needed for establishing an appropriate value of λ so that statistical power can be computed. In SEM, two approaches have been proposed to this end. In the first approach, establishing λ is based on parametric misspecification of the hypothesized model, whereas in the second approach, establishing λ is based on overall fit of the hypothesized model.

Approaches Based on Parametric Misspecification

One option for specifying effect size can be drawn from the work of Satorra and Saris (1985) on power analysis procedures for tests of model fit of single models. Their procedure for establishing the noncentrality parameter, λ, has the following steps:

1. The parametric structure representing the model of interest to be tested under H_0 is specified. Let the covariance structure implied by this model be $\Sigma_0(\gamma)$, where γ represents a $q \times 1$ vector of model parameters.

2. A new model is specified under the alternative hypothesis (H_1). The new model is the same as the original model under H_0 except that it now includes additional parameters. Let the vector of additional parameters be an $r \times 1$ vector τ. Then a $(q + r) \times 1$ vector $\gamma_1 = (\gamma', \tau')'$ represents the vector of parameters for the alternative model. This alternative model is considered to represent the true model that holds exactly in the population.

3. One must then specify population values for the parameter vector γ_1 in the alternative (true) model. Let that vector of parameter values be designated $\tilde{\gamma}_1$. One can then generate the model-implied covariance matrix, $\tilde{\Sigma}_1 = \Sigma_1(\tilde{\gamma}_1)$.

Finally, the null hypothesized model $\Sigma_0(\gamma)$ is fitted to $\tilde{\Sigma}_1$ to obtain a minimum discrepancy function value, $\hat{F}_1$. Then one can use $(N - 1)\hat{F}_1$ as an approximation to the noncentrality parameter, λ. The degrees of freedom (d) for the noncentral chi-square distribution are taken from the H_0 model.

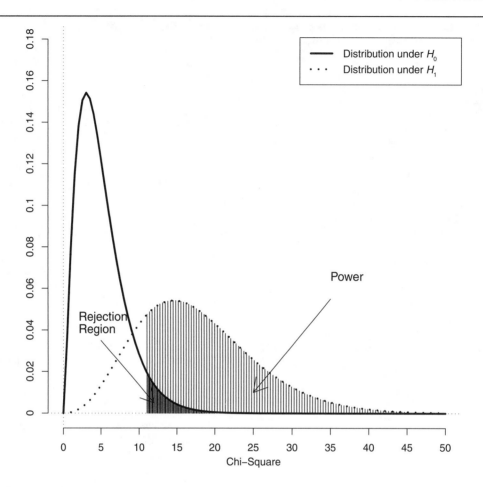

FIGURE 11.1. Null and alternative distributions of the test statistic for determining statistical power.

In sum, the noncentrality parameter, λ, can be approximated by

$$\lambda = (N-1)F[\tilde{\Sigma}_1, \Sigma_0(\gamma^*)] \qquad (11.7)$$

where γ^* represents a vector of parameters for the model under H_0 such that the discrepancy function $F[\tilde{\Sigma}_1, \Sigma(\gamma)]$ is minimized. Satorra and Saris (1985) provide rigorous justifications for the above approximation. See Matsueda and Bielby (1986), Satorra and Saris (1985), and Bollen (1989, p. 338) for examples of this approach.

Notice that in this approach, researchers are required to fully specify values of model parameters under H_1 to establish the value of the noncentrality parameter for power estimation. Once the noncentrality parameter, λ, is established by Equation 11.7, the power of the test is then determined, for a selected α level, as the area to the right of χ_C^2 under the noncentral chi-square distribution with d degrees of freedom and with the noncentrality parameter λ. The resulting power of the test is the probability of detecting when H_0 model is false, under the assumption that the model and specified parameter values under H_1 are correct in the population.

Approaches Based on Overall Model Fit

MacCallum and colleagues (1996) proposed an alternative approach to establishing an appropriate value of the noncentrality parameter. Whereas the procedure based on the Satorra and Saris (1985) framework defines "effect size" in terms of differences in parametric specification between the null hypothesized model and the alternative (true) model, the MacCallum and colleagues approach defines "effect size" in terms of overall model fit.

Because the scale of the discrepancy function, F, is quite difficult to work with directly, specifying the effect size in terms of the discrepancy function value, F_0, is indeed difficult. For this reason, MacCallum and colleagues (1996) employed the root mean square error of approximation (RMSEA) measure (Browne & Cudeck, 1993; Steiger & Lind, 1980), which is directly related to the discrepancy function value, to reframe procedures for testing hypotheses about model fit. In the population, RMSEA(ε, hereafter), is defined as

$$\varepsilon = \sqrt{\frac{F_0}{d}} \qquad (11.8)$$

where F_0 represents the discrepancy function value in the population, and d represents the degrees of freedom of the model. That is, RMSEA is a measure of the discrepancy per degrees of freedom for the model. Like the discrepancy function value, F, RMSEA is bounded below by zero and will be zero only if the model holds exactly ($F_0 = 0$).

Based on practical experience with estimates of the RMSEA, Browne and Cudeck (1993) provide guidelines for evaluation of the RMSEA as follows: $\varepsilon \leq 0.05$ indicates close fit; $0.05 < \varepsilon < 0.08$ indicates fair fit; $0.08 < \varepsilon < 0.10$ indicates mediocre fit; $\varepsilon > .10$ indicates poor fit. Browne and Cudeck recommend against employing a model with a RMSEA greater than 0.1.

Using RMSEA, the conventional LR test of exact fit, $H_0 : F_0 = 0$, can be redefined as a test of

$$H_0 : \varepsilon = 0 \qquad (11.9)$$

Under H_0, the test statistic, T, approximately follows a central χ^2 distribution with d degrees of freedom. Given a chosen significance level, α, if the test statistic exceeds the critical value, χ_C^2, then the hypothesis of exact fit is rejected. If not, the hypothesis of exact fit is not rejected.

For the purposes of power analysis, one must choose an alternative value of ε representing true lack of fit of the model in the population. Let that value be ε_1; then the alternative hypothesis can be written as

$$H_1 : \varepsilon = \varepsilon_1 \qquad (11.10)$$

Under this alternative hypothesis, the test statistic, T, will be distributed as noncentral χ^2 with d degrees of freedom and noncentrality parameter, λ_1. From Equation 11.8, it is easy to see $F_0 = d\varepsilon^2$; therefore, the noncentrality parameter (λ) in Equation 11.6 can be represented alternatively as $\lambda = (N-1)\,d\varepsilon^2$. Thus, under a specific alternative hypothesis with $\varepsilon = \varepsilon_1$, the test statistic, T, will be distributed as noncentral χ^2 with d degrees of freedom and noncentrality parameter

$$\lambda_1 = (N-1)\,d\varepsilon_1^2 \qquad (11.11)$$

In sum, under the overall-model-fit approach, effect size, λ, can be specified by selecting the degree of lack of fit in the population in terms of the RMSEA measure, ε_1. Notice that in this approach neither population parameter values for the true model nor parametric structures of the model of interest is required to be specified for the purposes of establishing the value of the noncentrality parameter.

Given sample size (N), degrees of freedom (d), and a chosen significance level, α, the critical value of the test statistic, χ_C^2, is determined from the central χ^2 distribution. We can then obtain the power of the test by calculating the area under the (true) alternative distribution that lies beyond the established critical value of the test statistic. When ε_1 is specified to be 0.05, for example, then the resulting power of the test indicates the probability of rejecting the false hypothesis of exact fit when true fit of the model is *close*. Graphically this case corresponds to Figure 11.1.

Comparison of Approaches

The two approaches use the same underlying statistical distribution theory for determining power (as illustrated in Figure 11.1), but involve different approaches to defining an alternative hypothesis, thereby employing different methods to establishing a value of the noncentrality parameter, λ. The parametric misspecification approach defines H_1 in terms of an alternative model assumed to be true in the population, where that alternative model defines particular parametric misspecifications of the model being tested. By contrast, the overall-model-fit approach defines H_1 in terms of a specified degree of misfit of the model being tested. In the parametric misspecification approach, λ is a function of the difference in parametric specification between a model under study and a specific alternative model that is considered as the true model in the population and different from the original model, in that it includes additional parameters. In this approach, it is necessary for users to completely specify the alternative model, including parameter values. In contrast, the overall-model-fit approach defines λ in terms of the RMSEA measure (Browne & Cudeck, 1993; Steiger & Lind, 1980), which defines the true lack of fit of the specified model when the specified model does not hold exactly in the population. This value is used to determine a value of the noncentrality parameter for the noncentral χ^2 distribution that is used in turn to determine power. This approach does not require any statement about how the model is misspecified; rather, it requires only the degree of lack of fit in the population.

These differences between the two approaches in establishing the alternative hypothesis and noncentrality parameter lead to the difference in the way of interpreting the results of power analysis. Under the parametric misspecification approach, where the effect size is a direct function of the specified values of the parameters that differentiate the hypothesized model and the true model, the result of power analysis can be readily interpreted in terms of the particular parameters, their assigned values, and their meaningful units. For example, if the hypothesized model does not include a correlation between two latent variables, whereas its value in the alternative (true) model is .40, the power of the test is the probability of detecting the falsity of the hypothesized model if the true factor correlation is .40, assuming other parameters take on the assigned values in the true model. By comparison, under the overall-model-fit approach, effect size is defined in terms of overall fit. Consequently, the result of power analysis is interpreted in terms of overall fit. That is, the power indicates the probability of rejecting the hypothesis of exact fit of the hypothesized model if the true fit corresponds to the specified RMSEA value. For example, when the effect size is defined as RMSEA value 0.08, the power of the test is the probability of rejecting the hypothesis of exact fit when the true fit of the model is mediocre.

Compared to the parametric misspecification approach, the overall-model-fit approach requires considerably less information from the investigator, which can be a clear advantage when the investigator has insufficient information about the correct parametric model structure and its parameter values. However, in those contexts where there is a specific focus on a key parameter or two, the parametric misspecification approach can be more useful because the overall-model-fit approach does not provide a way to interpret the results of a given power analysis in terms of misspecified parameters and their values.

Power of Test of Close Fit

In testing hypotheses about model fit, it is important to test realistic and meaningful hypotheses so as to obtain useful information. Recognizing that all models are wrong to some degree, it is not an overstatement that there is little to nothing to be gained by testing the null hypothesis, that the specified model is exactly correct in the population, and that any lack of fit in the sample arises only from sampling error.

A general lack of fit or degree of imperfection of a model in the population has been known as "model error" (MacCallum & Tucker, 1991) or "approximation discrepancy" (Cudeck & Henly, 1991). The notion of imperfect models reflects a fundamental contradiction between the model and the real world (Meehl, 1990), implying that even if a proposed model, $\Sigma(\gamma)$, is a reasonable structure closely approximating the process of interest, that model will not exactly reproduce the population covariance matrix, Σ_0; hence, $\Sigma_0 \neq \Sigma(\gamma)$ for any γ. This difference in turn yields a nonzero discrepancy function value in the population. All models are wrong to some degree and they cannot exactly capture the complexities of the real world. It is meaningless, therefore, to test the null hypothesis of exact fit because such a null hypothesis is always false. Consequently, the outcome of the test of exact fit is, of course, not really informative or useful.

In addition, a well-known statistical characteristic of the chi-square test of model fit is that even when the true level of misfit in the population is very small, with an adequately large sample this null hypothesis will always be rejected. Essentially the outcome merely tells the investigator whether his or her sample size was large enough to reject the *false* null hypothesis of exact fit.

To address this problem, Browne and Cudeck (1993) proposed the testing of null hypotheses that are of more empirical interest than the traditional null hypothesis of exact fit, redefining the null hypothesis using the RMSEA (Steiger & Lind, 1980) measure. In addition, MacCallum and colleagues (1996) provided procedures for conducting power analysis where the null hypothesis specifies a close fit of the model in the population and the alternative hypothesis specifies a larger misfit in the population.

In their procedures, H_0 specifies a hypothesized non-zero value of RMSEA, the degree of lack of fit to be considered as a close approximation to the real-world relationships; let that value be designated as ε_0. If H_0 is false, then the actual value of ε is some value that is not consistent with H_0; let that value be designated as ε_1. The value of ε_1 represents the degree of true lack of fit of the specified model in the population when ε_0 is false. In power analysis terminology, the difference between ε_0 and ε_1 reflects effect size.

For example, in testing the null hypothesis of close fit ($H_0 : \varepsilon \leq 0.05$), ε_0 takes on a value of 0.05. The value of ε_1 must then be specified as some value greater than 0.05, representing the degree to which the model is considered to be incorrect in the population. For instance, ε_1 could reasonably be specified as 0.08.[3] Then the power of the test can be reframed as the question: If the fit of the model is actually mediocre (i.e., $\varepsilon = 0.08$), and we test the null hypothesis that fit is close (i.e., $\varepsilon \leq 0.05$), what is the probability of rejecting the null hypothesis of close fit?

On the basis of the chosen values of ε_0 and ε_1, we can define two overlapping non-central chi-square distributions. The first, representing the sampling distribution of T under H_0, is a chi-square with the noncentrality parameter, $\lambda_0 = (N-1)d\varepsilon_0^2$. Under H_0, the test statistic, T, follows this distribution. For a given level α, a critical value χ_C^2 is determined that cuts off an area of α in the upper tail of this noncentral chi-square distribution. If H_0 is false in reality, and the true value of ε is ε_1, then the test statistic is distributed as noncentral chi-square with noncentrality parameter $\lambda_1 = (N-1)d\varepsilon_1^2$. Given χ_C^2, the critical value of the test statistic defined under H_0, the power of the test is then defined as the area under this true distribution of the test statistic, to the right of χ_C^2.

Recall that, under the parametric misspecification approach, the population covariance matrix, Σ_0 is constructed by completely specifying a structural equation model, including parameter values, that is assumed to be the true process that generates Σ_0. Notice that within this approach, due to the method for constructing Σ_0, there is no direct way of incorporating model error or approximation discrepancy that represents a fundamental lack of fit of the model to the population covariance matrix. Unless an extra step is taken for adding model errors to Σ_0 (see Cudeck & Browne, 1992, for details of the method), the value of the noncentrality parameter under H_0 is by definition zero in the parametric misspecification approach. This approach, in principle, can apply only to the test of exact fit (cf. Satorra & Saris, 1983).

Therefore, two approaches for power analysis in SEM differ with respect to flexibility in specifying H_0; in the parametric misspecification approach, H_0 can only indicate exact fit of the hypothesized model, whereas in the overall model fit approach, H_0 can indicate exact fit or any degree of misfit.

POWER ANALYSIS FOR TESTS OF DIFFERENCES BETWEEN NESTED MODELS

Statistical Theory and Methods

Model comparisons are routinely conducted in the practice of SEM. Different models represent competing theoretical views on the patterns of relationship among the latent or observed variables. In measurement invariance research, one may compare the fit of various models representing different degrees of invariance across groups or time. In latent curve analysis, one may compare different models for patterns of change over time. In exploratory factor analysis, one may determine the optimal number of factors to retain via comparison of models. These model comparisons are usually performed using the LR test of difference in fit for a pair of nested models.

Test of No Difference

The typical approach involves the specification of two models, a less constrained/baseline model (hereafter Model B) and a more constrained model (hereafter Model A). Model A is nested within Model B in the sense that the set of all possible covariance matrices generated by Model A is a subset of those generated by Model B. Typically this is a result of adding more restrictions to Model B. For example, Model B may reflect configural measurement invariance across two groups of respondents, whereas Model A may reflect metric invariance (Meredith, 1993), with additional equality constraints on the factor loading matrices. The degrees of freedom of Models A and B must therefore satisfy the inequality $d_B < d_A$. Let us refer to the difference in degrees of freedom as $d_{A-B} = d_A - d_B$.

The test of no difference hypothesizes that the added constraints in Model A do not lead to any deterioration in model fit. Assuming the use of the maximum likelihood discrepancy function (Equation 11.2), the null hypothesis of the test of no difference can be written as

$$H_0 : (F_A^* - F_B^*) = 0$$

where F_A^* and F_B^* are, respectively, the population values of the maximum likelihood discrepancy function for Model A and Model B. In other words, the null hypothesis states that the discrepancy (as measured by the maximum likelihood discrepancy function) between the implied covariance matrix of Model A and the true population covariance matrix and that of Model B and the population covariance matrix is equal. Let the sample values of the discrepancy functions be $\hat{F}_A$ and $\hat{F}_B$. The null hypothesis can be tested with the following LR test statistic:

$$T_{\text{DIFF}} = (N-1)(\hat{F}_A - \hat{F}_B)$$

Under the null hypothesis, and when all distributional assumptions are satisfied, T_{DIFF} is distributed as a central chi-square variable with d_{DIFF} degrees of freedom.

To conduct power analysis, we must operate under the alternative hypothesis. For the test of no difference, the alternative hypothesis states that

$$H_1 : (F_A^* - F_B^*) = \delta_1$$

where $\delta_1 > 0$ reflects the population difference in model fit between Models A and B due to the added constraints in Model A. The value of δ_1 is the equivalent of an effect size. Under appropriate distributional assumptions and population drift, the test statistic $T_{\text{A-B}}$ is distributed as a noncentral chi-square random variable with degrees of freedom $d_{\text{A-B}}$ and noncentrality parameter

$$\lambda_1 = (N-1)\delta_1 = (N-1)(F_A^* - F_B^*)$$

Let us assume, for now, that an effect size has been specified and that the noncentrality parameter λ_1 can be computed. From the null distribution of T_{DIFF}, which is a central chi-square with d_{A-B} degrees of freedom, a critical value can be determined. Let us refer to the critical value as χ_C^2. The power of the test of no difference between Models A and B can be found by computing the cumulative probability to the right of χ_C^2 for a non-

central chi-square random variable with d_{A-B} degrees of freedom.

Test of Small Difference

The null hypothesis of no difference in model fit will always be false in empirical studies where the two nested models reflect substantive differences in hypothesized relations among the variables in the structural equation model. While the true difference in fit between the two models may be small, the null hypothesis of no difference will always be rejected given a sufficiently large sample size. This will lead to the conclusion of a statistically significant difference in fit; thus, the researcher must favor the less constrained model. Akin in spirit to MacCallum and colleagues (1996), we resolve this logical inconsistency by proposing the use of a null hypothesis of small difference in fit between Model A and Model B. Based on this null hypothesis, we can also develop power analysis procedures where the alternative hypothesis reflects a larger difference in fit.

More formally, the null hypothesis of small difference states

$$H_0 : (F_A^* - F_B^*) \leq \delta_0^*$$

where δ_0^* reflects the null hypothesized population difference in fit between Model A and Model B. Under the same assumptions as discussed earlier, the LR test statistic T_{DIFF} is distributed as a noncentral chi-square random variable with d_{DIFF} degrees of freedom and noncentrality parameter $\lambda_1^* = (N-1)\delta_0^*$. Using this null distribution one can find the critical value of the LR test χ_C^2. The alternative hypothesis specifies that the difference $(F_A^* - F_B^*)$ is equal to some specific value that is larger than δ_0^*:

$$H_1 : (F_A^* - F_B^*) = \delta_1^*$$

where $\delta_1^* > \delta_0^*$. Under the alternative hypothesis, the LR test statistic is distributed as a noncentral chi-square random variable with d_{DIFF} degrees of freedom and noncentrality parameter

$$\lambda_1 = (N-1)\delta_1^*$$

Power of the test of small difference is then determined by computing the cumulative probability of T_{DIFF} under the alternative distribution to the right of χ_C^2.

Specifying Effect Size

The power analysis procedures just described require the researcher to provide a value of the noncentrality parameter for the test of no difference, and two values for the test of small difference. The noncentrality parameter value is related to the population discrepancy function values F_A^* and F_B^*, and direct specification is difficult.

Approaches Based on Parametric Misspecification

One option for accomplishing this task can be drawn from the work of Satorra and Saris (1985). In their framework, one must specify all parameter values of Model B, generating the implied covariance matrix Σ_B. Model A is then fitted to Σ_B. Because Model A is nested in Model B, it will yield a nonzero discrepancy function value designated F_A^*. Note that Model B will fit Σ_B perfectly, so $F_B^* = 0$. The noncentrality parameter is therefore equal to $(N - 1)(F_A^* - F_B^*) = (N - 1)F_A^*$. Note that in this procedure Model B is considered to be free of misspecification in the population.

In earlier work, Satorra and Saris (1983) proposed a procedure that allows Model B to be considered misspecified in the population. This procedure requires the specification of yet a third model (Model C) that is considered free of misspecification. From Model C, the implied covariance matrix Σ_C is generated and then Models A and B are fitted to Σ_C, yielding nonzero discrepancy function values F_A^* and F_B^*. In this case, the noncentrality parameter is equal to $(N - 1)(F_A^* - F_B^*)$. In either of these two procedures, one must be able to completely specify a model that is assumed to be free of misspecification and the power analysis is conditional on the specification of that model.

Approaches Based on Overall Model Fit

As an alternative, MacCallum and colleagues (2006) proposed an extension of the overall model fit based procedure due to MacCallum and colleagues (1996). In this framework, the noncentrality parameter is specified using a pair of RMSEA values. Let ε_A and ε_B be the RMSEA values associated with Models A and B, respectively. Because the RMSEA is directly tied to the population discrepancy function value, we have

$$\varepsilon_A = \sqrt{\frac{F_A^*}{d_A}}, \; \varepsilon_B = \sqrt{\frac{F_B^*}{d_B}}$$

which implies the following expression for the noncentrality parameter:

$$\lambda = (N - 1)(F_A^* - F_B^*) = (N - 1)(d_A \varepsilon_A^2 - d_B \varepsilon_B^2)$$

Note that the noncentrality parameter is completely determined by the sample size, the pair of RMSEA values, and the degrees of freedom for Models A and B. The relation holds whether we are specifying the noncentrality parameter for the alternative hypothesis for power analysis of test of no difference, or for the null hypothesis of the test of small difference, or for the alternative hypothesis for power analysis of test of small difference.

THE CONDITIONAL NATURE OF POWER ANALYSIS IN SEM

A general framework for power estimation in SEM is as follows. The investigator specifies a null hypothesis to be tested, thereby determining λ_0, then specifies an alternative hypothesis that is assumed to be true in the population, thereby determining λ_1, along with other design and testing features such as N, d, and χ_C^2, then computes statistical power, π, under those specified conditions. As can be seen from Figure 11.1, power is a function of the separation of the two distributions, which is determined by the distance between the two noncentrality parameters for the two distributions, λ_0 and λ_1. Thus, the evaluation of the power of the test is in fact an evaluation of the difference between noncentrality parameters. In addition, one should recognize the fact that a given power analysis in SEM is conditional by nature, in that the result of the power analysis indicates the probability of rejecting H_0 if H_1 is true, assuming all specified conditions yielding a given set of noncentrality parameters hold in the population.

There have been two lines of research attempting to enhance the understanding of the conditional aspects of a given power analysis in SEM. In the first line of research, investigators have examined conditions affecting the location of noncentrality parameters, which in turn affect the power of the test. In the second line of research, investigators have examined (combinations of) conditions that produce the same distance between two noncentrality parameters. In other words, in the first approach, one alters the conditions to be specified in a given power analysis and examines their effects on power, showing how power varies with alterations in various quantities. In the second approach, one investigates alternative sets of conditions producing the same level of power. Both approaches have contributed to illuminating the conditional nature of the result of a given power analysis.

Conditions That Affect Power

Recall that, under the parametric misspecification approach (Satorra & Saris, 1985), the power of the test indicates the probability of detecting when the model being tested is false (for tests of single models) or when the difference in fit between two models is not nil (for tests of differences between models), under the assumption that the alternative (true) model is correct in the population. Moreover, the power of the test is evaluated at a specific parameter vector, $\tilde{\gamma}_1$, assigned to the alternative model and considered to be true in the population.

It should be kept in mind that the result of such power analysis is conditional in that the numerical value of estimated power can change under a set of different conditions (Matsueda & Bielby, 1986; Saris & Satorra, 1993; Saris, Satorra, & Sörbom, 1987). For example, Saris and Satorra (1993), using a two-factor confirmatory factor analysis model, demonstrated that the power of the test for detecting the misspecification of the factor correlation is considerably affected by varying the size of factor loadings (and the sample size), even when the size of factor correlation is held constant. Browne, MacCallum, Kim, Anderson, and Glaser (2002), although the context of the original paper is much broader, showed that the size of unique variances specified in the true model can dramatically affect the power of the test of exact fit. In particular, when unique variances are very small, the test becomes very sensitive to detecting misspecifications of the model being tested and yields higher effect size; hence, the power of the test becomes very high. The effects of measurement properties on the power of the test were also noticed by Matsueda and Bielby (1986). For rigorous explanations of this property, interested readers are referred to Browne and colleagues.

In practice, unless much prior knowledge has been already accumulated so that the investigator can confidently make educated estimates of unknown parameter values, assigning reliable numerical values for model parameters can be a very difficult task. In many cases, the numerical assignment can be made only under a

high level of uncertainty. Therefore, one should keep in mind that the result of a given power analysis should be interpreted in light of a particular set of conditions (i.e., a particular set of parameter values assigned for a particular analysis); under a different set of parameter values, the result of the power analysis can change.

The result of a given power analysis under the overall fit approach is also conditional. In the overall fit approach (both for the test of single models and for the test of the difference between two models), the distance between λ_0 and λ_1 is a function of d, N, ε_0, and ε_1. Thus, any change of these terms that produces a greater difference between λ_0 and λ_1 will increase power. For example, power increases with larger N and with ε_1 more discrepant from a fixed ε_0 for the test of single models. Furthermore, for fixed N, ε_0, and ε_1, power is greater in models with higher d (MacCallum et al., 1996). For the test of the difference between two models, MacCallum and colleagues (2006) show that, holding the difference in RMSEA values fixed, power will change as the location of the RMSEA values on the scale is shifted. Furthermore, the effects of these conditions will change in degree as levels of other conditions change. Again, it should be borne in mind that any change in any specified conditions for a given power analysis will affect the result of a given power analysis. A specified condition in a given power analysis should not be regarded as a rigidly defined true condition. Considering that the specified conditions are all subject to uncertainty and arbitrariness to some degree under a particular investigation, the result of a given power analysis should be interpreted carefully. The interested readers is referred to MacCallum and colleagues (1996, 2006) for details of the conditions that affect power.

Identifying Iso-Power Alternatives

As a second approach to examining the conditional nature of power analysis, instead of varying conditions to examine their effects on power, one can hold power constant and examine alternative sets of conditions that yield the same power, termed "iso-power alternatives." These ideas have been examined first in Saris and Satorra (1993) and generalized in MacCallum, Lee, and Browne (2010). MacCallum and colleagues show that under the parametric misspecification approach, given a particular H_0 model, it is possible to identify an infinitely large class of alternatives to produce the same value of the noncentrality parameter, which in turn yields the same level of power for the test of H_0. Under the overall-model-fit approach, different pairs of ε_0 and ε_1 values produce the same noncentrality parameter, yielding the same level of power. In addition, there will exist various combinations of ε_1 and N that would yield the same power as the original test of H_0 versus the alternative hypothesis $H_1 : \varepsilon = \varepsilon_1$.

The framework presented in investigating iso-power alternatives shows that the result of a power analysis in effect selects a single set of conditions from an infinitely large class of conditions that would produce exactly the same outcome. Members of this class can be defined by different combinations of various conditions, holding other elements fixed. The mere existence of these iso-power alternatives should be taken into account when interpreting and reporting the outcome of any power analysis in SEM. An investigator should state that an obtained result for a power computation is not isomorphic with the particular set of conditions specified in the power analysis, and that different sets of conditions likely exist, probably in infinite number, that would yield the same result. The examination of iso-power alternatives provides the investigator with a tool for explicitly incorporating into a power analysis the uncertainty associated with specifying conditions for that analysis. Such an analysis could more explicitly take into account the conditional and sometimes arbitrary nature of a particular power analysis and provide richer information about the kind and degree of misspecification that can be detected at a given level of power.

DETERMINATION OF NECESSARY SAMPLE SIZE

An important use of power analysis is to determine minimum sample size, $N_{\min}$, required to achieve a desired level of power for a specified test. The determination of $N_{\min}$ in the design stage of a research project could be of value because the knowledge of minimum sample size would provide investigators with a mechanism for avoiding waste and low-power investigations. In SEM, a specific solution to this end is provided in MacCallum and colleagues (1996, 2006). The general idea behind the solution follows.

Under the overall-model-fit approach, power for a test of model fit in SEM could be represented as

$$\pi = f(N, d, \varepsilon_0, \varepsilon_1, \chi_C^2) \qquad \textbf{(11.12)}$$

That is, statistical power of a test of model fit is a function of N (sample size), d (degrees of freedom), ε_0

(RMSEA under H_0), and ε_1 (RMSEA under H_1), and critical value χ_C^2 corresponding to a given α (significance level). Equation 11.12 clearly shows that given a desired level of power, say, π^*, if values of any four arguments are provided, the value of the one remaining argument that produces π^* can be obtained by solving a nonlinear equation with respect to the unknown information. Thus, one can obtain the required sample size by specifying all the necessary information, including a desired level of power, and solving the equation with respect to the unknown quantity, N. Under the overall-model-fit approach for tests of single models, MacCallum and colleagues (1996) provide a method and software program for solving this nonlinear equation, thereby obtaining $N_{\min}$ for achieving a desired level of power for test of single models. By setting a desired level of power to be reasonably high (e.g., 0.80), the obtained $N_{\min}$ can inform the investigator of the sample size needed to have a strong likelihood for detecting when the hypothesis about model fit is false. For tests of differences between models, MacCallum and colleagues provide a method and software program for obtaining $N_{\min}$. The obtained $N_{\min}$ can inform the investigator of the sample size needed for the test to have a desired level of probability for detecting when the hypothesis about the difference in fit of various degrees is false under various conditions.

Table 11.1 is a partial production of original results in MacCallum and colleagues (1996). These results show the minimum sample size to achieve power of 0.80 for selected levels of degrees of freedom, significance level, and RMSEA values under H_0 and H_1. Inspection of the results reveals a strong association between d and $N_{\min}$. When d is small, a very large N is needed to achieve adequate power for such a model test. Studies with small d occur when the number of manifest variables (MVs) is small, when the specified model has a relatively large number of free parameters, or both. Thus, when one wishes to test a relatively complex model on a relatively small number of MVs, one needs a very large sample in order to obtain adequate power for a model test. Based on these results, MacCallum and colleagues (1996) discourage attempts to evaluate models with low d unless N is extremely large. In conjunction with this view, they discourage the introduction of a substantial number of parameters into models so as to improve model fit. Such procedures have been shown to be susceptible to capitalization on chance (MacCallum, 1986; MacCallum, Roznowski, & Necowitz, 1992). Furthermore, it is clear

TABLE 11.1. Minimum Sample Size to Achieve Power of .80 for Selected Levels of Degrees of Freedom

df	Test of close fit	Test of exact fit
2	3,488	1,926
4	1,807	1,194
6	1,238	910
8	954	754
10	782	651
20	435	421
30	314	329
40	252	277
50	214	243
75	161	193
100	132	164

Note. For all analyses, α = .05. For the test of close fit, ε_0 = 0.05 and ε_1 = 0.08. For the test of exact fit, ε_0 = 0.0 and ε_1 = 0.05.

that the resulting reduction in d causes substantial reduction in power of the model tests.

For N_{min} for test of difference in fit and choice of a pair of RMSEAs, see MacCallum and colleagues (2006).

CONCLUSION

In this chapter, we have reviewed two approaches for power analysis in SEM. The first is the parametric misspecification approach, and the second is the overall-model-fit approach. We also pointed out the conditional nature of a given power analysis in SEM. Most conditions necessary for conducting power analysis are unknown, but it is important to establish them as correctly as possible because the result of a given power analysis is considerably affected by the specified numerical values of the conditions. One guiding principle should be that the investigator make use of all available relevant information, thereby making educated estimates of unknown quantities necessary for the power analysis. Parameter estimates and RMSEA estimates reported in prior research could serve as a good source of reference for the educated estimates of the conditions required for the power calculation.

As pointed out earlier, the two approaches require a different amount of information from the investigator for the power calculation. The parametric misspecifi-

cation approach requires complete specification of the true model, including parameter values. The overall fit approach requires only the degree of lack of fit of the model being tested in the population. In practice, information available to the investigator can vary substantially depending on the stage of the research area. For example, when research in a particular domain is sufficiently advanced, the investigator may specify reasonable values for all model parameters using prior information accumulated from previous research. The parametric misspecification approach can then be employed, and the result can be interpreted in light of misspecified parameters and their values. When information about parameter values is insufficient, or the specification of some parameter values is considered too unreliable, such as in earlier stages of research, then the overall-model-fit approach may be preferred, in that it requires considerably less information from the user.

In SEM, the logic of hypothesis testing is different from that of conventional hypothesis testing, in that investigators hope to retain the null hypothesis instead of rejecting it. It should be noted that without knowledge about the power of the test, a nonsignificant result of the LR test cannot be interpreted in a meaningful way because such a result can be a mere consequence of the lack of power for the test to detect when the H_0 is false. In other words, for a nonsignificant result to be interpretable, the power of the test is required to be sufficiently high.

In the context of the test of close fit, knowledge of the power of the test can be more important. In the test of close fit, the H_0 specifies that a model fits reasonably well in the population (e.g., RMSEA of H_0 in the population is less than 0.05). A common result of using the test of close fit is for the model to be retained under the test of close fit, which would be rejected under the test of exact fit. Therefore, the knowledge about the power of the test of close fit becomes even more important because otherwise it is impossible to draw a conclusion whether the failure to reject the H_0 is due to the plausibility of the H_0 or to the lack of the power for the test to detect when the H_0 is false.

It should be kept in mind that the investigator should not use an ad hoc method for calculating the power of the test by taking parameter estimates or RMSEA estimates obtained by fitting the specified model to the sample covariance matrix of the given data set as the assumed population effect size. Power estimates computed from such an approach are sometimes called "observed power." Power computations are most appropriately done in the research design stage before data are collected. Any suspicions that the effect sizes were taken from the data used in the study should be dispelled. It is important to show how effect size estimates have been derived from previous research and theory (Wilkinson & the Task Force on Statistical Inference, 1999). Statistically, it is pointless to calculate the observed power of a test because there is a one-to-one relationship between *p* values and observed power (i.e., nonsignificant *p* values always correspond to low observed powers) (Hoenig & Heisey, 2001).

Procedures of power analysis in SEM require the investigator to be explicit about the kind and (meaningful) degree of misspecification that he or she wishes to be able to detect. That is, in the parametric misspecification approach, the investigator is required to be specific about the misspecification of particular parameters of interest and their magnitudes. In the overall-model-fit approach, the investigator is required to be specific about the degree of misfit of the hypothesized model or difference in fit between two models. It is very clear that a low-power test should be avoided because such a test is unlikely to detect the misspecification of interest. Therefore, power analysis in the design stage is of value in that the result provides a mechanism for adjusting the power of the test. In particular, knowledge about conditions affecting power can be effectively employed for the improvement of the power of the LR test. For example, the investigator may plan on allocating adequate resources to enhance the quality of the measurement model or on securing the necessary sample size, N_{min}, to achieve a desired level of power. In empirical applications of SEM, investigators can have confidence in interpreting the result of a nonsignificant LR test when the power of the LR test is sufficiently high.

ACKNOWLEDGMENTS

Part of this research was made possible by a statistical methodology grant from the Institute of Education Sciences (No. R305D100039). The views expressed in this chapter do not reflect the views and policies of the funding agencies or grantees.

NOTES

1. See Cudeck and Henly (1991), Browne and Cudeck (1993), and Mulaik et al. (1989) for other methods of assessing different aspects of model fit.

2. The use of the noncentrality parameter requires the additional assumption that lack of fit of the model in the population is of approximately the same magnitude as lack of fit arising due to sampling error (see Browne & Arminger, 1995), also known as "population drift."

3. For principles and guidelines for selecting a pair of ε_0 and ε_1, see MacCallum et al. (1996, pp. 138–139).

REFERENCES

Bollen, K. A. (1989). *Structural equations with latent variables.* New York: Wiley.

Box, G. E. P. (1979). Some problems of statistics and everyday life. *Journal of the American Statistical Association, 74,* 1–4.

Browne, M. W. (1974). Generalized least squares estimates in the analysis of covariance structures. *South African Statistical Journal, 8,* 1–24.

Browne, M. W. (1984). Asymptotically distribution-free methods in the analysis of covariance structures. *British Journal of Mathematical and Statistical Psychology, 37,* 62–83.

Browne, M. W., & Arminger, G. (1995). Specification and estimation of mean and covariance structure models. In G. Arminger, C. C. Clogg, & M. E. Sobel (Eds.), *Handbook of statistical modeling for the social and behavioral sciences* (pp. 185–249). New York: Plenum Press.

Browne, M. W., & Cudeck, R. (1993). Alternative ways of assessing model fit. In K. A. Bollen & S. Long (Eds.), *Testing structural equation models* (pp. 131–161). Newbury Park, CA: Sage.

Browne, M. W., MacCallum, R. C., Kim, C., Anderson, B. L., & Glaser, R. (2002). When fit indices and residuals are incompatible. *Psychological Methods, 7*(4), 403–421.

Cudeck, R., & Browne, M. W. (1992). Constructing a covariance matrix that yields a specified minimizer and a specified minimum discrepancy function value. *Psychometrika, 57,* 357–369.

Cudeck, R., & Henly, S. J. (1991). Model selection in covariance structures analysis and the problem of sample size: A clarification. *Psychological Bulletin, 109*(3), 512–519.

Hoenig, J. M., & Heisey, D. H. (2001). The abuse of power: The pervasive fallacy of power calculations for data analysis. *American Statistician, 5*(1), 19–24.

MacCallum, R. C. (1986). Specification searches in covariance structure modeling. *Psychological Bulletin, 100,* 107–120.

MacCallum, R. C. (2003). Working with imperfect models. *Multivariate Behavioral Research, 38*(1), 113–139.

MacCallum, R. C., Browne, M. W., & Cai, L. (2006). Testing differences between nested covariance structure models: Power analysis and null hypotheses. *Psychological Methods, 11*(1), 19–35.

MacCallum, R. C., Browne, M. W., & Sugawara, H. H.

(1996). Power analysis and determination of sample size for covariance structure modeling. *Psychological Methods, 1*(2), 130–149.

MacCallum, R. C., Lee, T., & Browne, M. W. (2010). The issue of power in power analysis for tests of structural equation models. *Structural Equation Modeling, 17*, 23–41.

MacCallum, R. C., Roznowski, M., & Necowitz, L. B. (1992). Model modifications in covariance structure analysis: The problem of capitalization on chance. *Psychological Bulletin, 111*, 490–504.

MacCallum, R. C., & Tucker, L. R. (1991). Representing sources of error in the common factor model: Implications for theory and practice. *Psychological Bulletin, 109*, 502–511.

Matsueda, R. L., & Bielby, W. T. (1986). Statistical power in covariance structure models. *Sociological Methodology, 16*, 120–158.

Meehl, P. E. (1990). Appraising and amending theories: The strategy of lakatosian defense and two principles that warrant it. *Psychological Inquiry, 1*, 108–141.

Meredith, W. (1993). Measurement invariance, factor analysis and factorial invariance. *Psychometrika, 58*, 525–543.

Mulaik, S. A., James, L. R., Van Alstine, J., Bennett, N., Lind, S., & Stillwell, C. D. (1989). An evaluation of goodness of fit indices for structural equation models. *Psychological Bulletin, 105*(3), 430–445.

Saris, W. E., & Satorra, A. (1993). Power evaluations in structural equation models. In K. A. Bollen & J. S. Long (Eds.), *Testing structural equation models* (pp. 181–204). Newbury Park, CA: Sage.

Saris, W. E., Satorra, A., & Sörbom, D. (1987). The detection and correction of specification errors in structural equation models. *Sociological Methodology, 17*, 105–129.

Satorra, A., & Saris, W. E. (1983). The accuracy of a procedure for calculating the power of the likelihood ratio test as used within the LISREL framework. In C. P. Middendorp, B. Niemoller, & W. E. Saris (Eds.), *Sociometric research 1982* (pp. 127–190). Amsterdam: Sociometric Research Foundation.

Satorra, A., & Saris, W. E. (1985). The power of the likelihood ratio test in covariance structure analysis. *Psychometrika, 50*, 83–90.

Steiger, J. H., & Lind, J. (1980, May). *Statistically-based tests for the number of common factors.* Paper presented at the annual meeting of the Psychometric Society, Iowa City, IA.

Wilkinson, L., & the Task Force on Statistical Inference. (1999). Statistical methods in psychology journals: Guidelines and explanations. *American Psychologist, 54*, 594–604.

CHAPTER 12

Categorical Data in the Structural Equation Modeling Framework

Michael C. Edwards
R. J. Wirth
Carrie R. Houts
Nuo Xi

Categorical data are often encountered in the social and behavioral sciences when measuring attitudes, abilities, opinions, and behaviors. They are also commonly found in other areas of science and education that rely, at least in part, on tests, questionnaires, or surveys. Agresti (1996) defines a categorical variable, also commonly called a discrete variable, as one with a measurement scale consisting of a set of categories. Categorical variables often denote some level of group membership such as race, ethnicity, gender, education level, or political party. However, many other categorical variables arise when people answer questions. Often questions are endorsed or scored dichotomously as correct–incorrect, agree–disagree, or using polytomous, "Likert-type" (see Likert, 1932) response sets such as *Strongly Disagree, Disagree, Neither Disagree nor Agree, Agree*, or *Strongly Agree*. Regardless of their makeup, the categorical variables we discuss below must assign one and only one category to each subject.

In this chapter we provide a brief introduction to the use of categorical variables within the structural equation modeling (SEM) framework. We begin with a brief review of levels of measurement. We follow this with an overview of the relationship between structural equation models and linear regression models, intro-

duce the complexities that arise when different types of categorical variables are used in SEM, and discuss some of the estimation options that are available when modeling categorical variables within the SEM framework. We conclude this chapter with a series of examples demonstrating how researchers can use categorical variables within SEM.

LEVELS OF MEASUREMENT

The name "categorical variable" is sometimes used interchangeably with the term "nominal variable," the lowest level of measurement defined by Stevens (1946). According to Stevens's definition, a nominal measure only names or labels distinct classes and is insignificant with regard to the order of these classes. Although it is justifiable to regard the word *category* as a synonym of *class*, we take a more general view of what defines a categorical variable. A category can be derived from observations of qualitative or quantitative data. The rank of a category within a set of possible categories may be meaningful, depending on the data from which the categories are summarized. For example, race/ethnicity is a categorical variable that labels people according to their ethnological trait, and no ranking is assumed. Education level, on the other hand, has an intrinsic order, as people who endorse *High school graduate* have usually spent more years in school than those who endorse *Some school*. It is generally accepted that this same type of ordering is reflected in many of the response scales used in the behavioral sciences. For example, a subject reporting that she "agrees" with the statement "I feel depressed" is likely more depressed (or is higher on depression) than a subject reporting that she "disagrees" with the same statement. Both nominal and ordinal variables are regarded as categorical variables, with the former having no meaningful order[1] and the latter having a meaningful order (Agresti, 1996).

A variable's level of measurement (nominal, ordinal, interval, or ratio) provides a great deal of information about plausible uses for that variable. In general, the higher the level of measurement (with ratio being the highest), the more information contained by the variable. That is, we can say more about its relationship to other variables and more about the relationship between people (or things) measured with that variable. The goal of maximizing information gained from a variable, without assuming the variable contains more information than it does, dictates the appropriateness of a particular mathematical manipulation or operation. Generally speaking, most statistical techniques are developed assuming interval or ratio levels of measurement. Categorical variables, which often have nominal or ordinal levels of measurement, usually require special treatment that takes their level of measurement (i.e., less information available) into consideration. Methods designed for interval or ratio scales might assume the variables involved are continuous, are normally distributed, or represent "real" values. Such methods, as discussed in more detail below, are not appropriate for categorical variables, as they make assumptions that are generally untenable with categorical data. On the other hand, some methods designed specifically for categorical variables can be used on interval or ratio measurements, but these fail to take advantage of the richness of the information available in interval- or ratio-level variables.

The extant literature is full of discussions and rules of thumb about when it is and is not appropriate to use certain analytic methods with certain types of variables. Many of these guidelines can be useful, but they should only be taken as suggestions. For example, while it is generally not advisable to compute a product–moment correlation between two nominal variables (e.g., a per-

son's gender and whether or not he or she owns a dog), there may be circumstances when such a method could provide useful[2] information (e.g., a positive correlation between these variables would indicate that one of the genders is more likely to own a dog). In this chapter we focus on what are generally considered the "proper" models and methods for use with varying types of categorical data. We would be remiss if we did not note the large literature examining when these methods cease to provide meaningful advantages. For example, there are a number of research papers (e.g., Beauducel & Herzberg, 2006; Dolan, 1994; Flora & Curran, 2004) examining the question, "How many categories does a variable have to have before we can treat it as continuous?" It is also important to remember that all models are approximations. To the extent that a researcher can maximize the correspondence between the assumptions of a model and the data, more useful information will be provided. To that end, the remainder of the chapter focuses on understanding how categorical variables can be properly modeled in structural equation models. We leave it to other researchers, and the reader, to decide when these methods should best be employed.

A REVIEW OF SEM

Before addressing the role of categorical variables within the SEM framework, we first provide a brief overview of SEM and how it relates to common linear regression models. At the most basic level, a structural equation model is a regression model in which measurement error can be taken into account. One of the standard assumptions of multiple linear regression (MLR) is that the predictors are measured without error (see, e.g., Cohen, Cohen, West, & Aiken, 2003). In many cases in the social sciences this assumption is untenable. The SEM framework allows one to enjoy the basic features of MLR without requiring the assumption of perfect reliability in the predictors.

Another difference between MLR and SEM is that instead of one regression equation, structural equation models can contain many regression equations. SEM is a method that focuses on the simultaneous analysis of systems of equations (e.g., series of regression equations). Structural equation models can measure the direct influence between variables throughout the system and can thus quantify the degree to which variability at one point in the system is accounted for by variability in another (Wright, 1921). In structural equation models, each regression states a directional influence from a set of independent variables on a single dependent variable. Basically, each equation in a structural equation model is much like the standard linear regression model often taught in introductory statistics courses. At the most fundamental level, SEM and regression share a similar objective—to better understand the relationships among variables. SEM is more powerful and sophisticated than MLR because it takes into consideration the modeling of multiple observed (or manifest) and latent variables. SEM can model the relationship between manifest variables, manifest and latent variables, or multiple latent variables—regardless of whether each of these variables acts as a dependent or independent variable[3] (Kenny & Milan, Chapter 9, this volume). Moreover, SEM can simultaneously examine complex modeling issues such as moderation, mediation, moderated mediation, correlated independent variables, and correlated errors of measurement.

Structural equation models usually have two parts: a *measurement model* and a *structural model*. In its simplest form, a measurement model is a confirmatory factor analysis (CFA) model. Because of the limitations inherent in single-item measures (Churchill, 1979), it is not uncommon to have underlying constructs associated with multiple indicators. Therefore, measurement models typically use multiple manifest variables as indicators of a corresponding latent variable. This helps to provide an empirical representation of the underlying hypothesized construct. More specifically, regressing the manifest variable (e.g., an item response) onto a latent variable (i.e., the hypothesized construct) quantifies the relationship between an item and the latent factor. The regression coefficient, called a "factor loading" or λ (lambda) in structural equation models, provides a measure of the strength of the relationship between an item and a latent variable. When a group of items "load" on a given factor, the estimated coefficients help us to better understand the latent variable being modeled.

Other directional and correlational relationships, usually among independent variables in the measurement model and other exogenous[4] variables, are summarized in the structural model. The structural model is the part of SEM that represents the researcher's explicit theory of the pattern of variation and/or correlation among the variables. Complex relationships, like bidirectional or nonrecursive links, may arise in this part of the model, and the estimated coefficients, often called β (beta) or γ (gamma) coefficients, serve as evidence for or against a researcher's theory.

The measurement and structural models are intuitive in the sense that they directly portray the relationships we observe or expect from a set of variables. The measurement and structural models can be combined to form a "data model," which provides a hypothesized set of relationships in the data. From the data model, a covariance structure involving all the variables (manifest and latent—including error terms) can be derived. By checking the agreement between a sample covariance matrix ($\mathbf{S}$), calculated from data, and a hypothesized covariance matrix ($\mathbf{\Sigma}(\mathbf{\theta})$) derived from the model, structural equation models provide estimates of the model parameters, standard errors, and the degree of correspondence between $\mathbf{S}$ and $\mathbf{\Sigma}(\mathbf{\theta})$ (i.e., the fit of the model to the data).

Conventional SEM is mainly dependent on linear regression to examine the multitude of complex relationships among observed and latent variables. However, linear regression is most appropriate for continuous dependent variables. When the dependent variables are categorical, handling them directly through linear regression is generally inappropriate. Failing to take the categorical nature of a variable into account can lead to assumption violations, model misspecification, poor predictions, and a misunderstanding of the relationships that exist in the data. For example, the predicted value from a linear regression is typically continuous and can take on any value along the real number line. This can often result in predicted values that are outside the range of the possible categorical values. To circumvent this limitation of linear regression, nonlinear regression is employed when the outcome of interest is categorical in nature. For example, logistic regression is commonly used when an individual is interested in predicting a dichotomous outcome such as a pass–fail status on some test. Methods such as logistic regression allow for the nonlinear relationship between predictors and outcomes to be appropriately accounted for in the model and results in the predicted probability of passing a test (in this example) as opposed to the 0–1 outcome of passing. Logistic regression allows us to examine the likelihood, probability, or odds of a particular behavior or choice.

Up to this point, we have reviewed definitions of what categorical data are and provided a brief overview of some of the core ideas underlying SEM. In the next section, we explore the interaction of these two ideas and describe the numerous ways in which categorical variables may be involved in structural equation models.

INCORPORATING CATEGORICAL VARIABLES IN SEM

Categorical Indicators

Though not the only way categorical variables are used in SEM (more on this below), categorical variables frequently emerge as indicators of continuous latent variables. Any time the item-level responses from a scale are either incorporated into a larger structural equation model or the scale is analyzed independently using CFA, categorical data are being used as indicators of a latent, continuous variable.[5] Much like standard regression, when indicators (i.e., outcomes) of a latent variable are categorical, a nonlinear relationship exists between the manifest, categorical variables and the latent variable hypothesized to give rise to the categorical data. This means that the observed product–moment covariance matrix of the categorical variables, S, is not a consistent estimate of the population covariance matrix of the responses that gave rise to the categorical variables, Σ^*. Note the subtle change in language here. We are interested in the responses that *gave rise* to the categorical data and not in the categorical responses themselves. This shift in attention will become very important below.

Much like standard MLR, a structural equation model will assume a linear relationship exists between the predictor (here, a latent variable) and an outcome (here, a categorical response). An alternative method must be used to account for this nonlinearity. While not the only method (as we discuss below), the most common method used in structural equation models to account for the nonlinear relationship between the observed, categorical responses and latent variables is to replace the observed, categorical variables with their underlying latent, continuous responses. For example, we assume that there is a response on the real number line that corresponds to each categorical variable, and that an individual has to take that continuous number (a number that resides only in the respondent's mind) and decide which category best corresponds to that latent value. The goal is to "reverse-engineer" the relationship such that we can take the observed categorical response and translate it back into the latent, continuous value corresponding to that item response. A path diagram expressing this concept is presented in Figure 12.1.

As can be seen in Figure 12.1, the hypothetical model we are interested in suggests that a single latent variable, Reading Ability, underlies the relationship among four reading items (y_1–y_4). However, because these items

are scored dichotomously (*correct, incorrect*) there exists a nonlinear relationship between the hypothesized latent variable of Reading Ability and the observed responses. To circumvent this problem, we assume that there are continuous response distributions (the small circles leading to the observed responses) underlying each item response. The goal of the model presented in Figure 12.1 is to examine the extent to which the hypothesized latent variable of Reading Ability accounts for the correlations among the latent response distributions. Of course, the next logical question is, how do we get to the latent response distributions?

If y is an item that uses a dichotomous response scale, we assume that there is a continuous, latent y^*

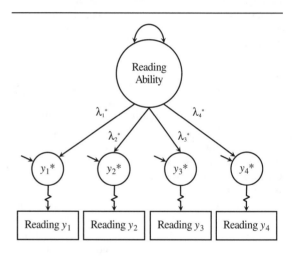

FIGURE 12.1. A path diagram showing the hypothesized relationship between four dichotomously scored (*correct, incorrect*) reading items (y_1–y_4) and the latent variable of Reading Ability. The latent response variables for y_1–y_4 are denoted by y_1^*–y_4^*. Straight, single-headed arrows originating from one latent variable (denoted as circles) and ending at another latent variable denote linear, directional relationships between latent variables. The strength of the relationship is denoted by a factor loading (λ_i^*). Jagged, single-headed arrows between latent variables and manifest variables (denoted as rectangles) denote nonlinear, directional relationships between the variables. Single-headed arrows originating in space and ending at a variable (latent or manifest) denote residual (or unique) variances. Dual-headed arrows beginning and ending at the same variable denote variances.

that dictates which of the two categories a respondent will choose (or whether the respondent gets the item correct). We use cut points (τ) to denote the point on the latent response continuum where a person will no longer respond using category $c - 1$ but will now use category c. This relationship can be formalized for any number of categories such that

$$y = \begin{cases} 1, & \text{if } y^* \leq \tau_1 \\ 2, & \text{if } \tau_1 < y^* \leq \tau_2 \\ \vdots & \quad \vdots \\ C-1, & \text{if } \tau_{C-2} < y^* \leq \tau_{C-1} \\ C, & \text{if } \tau_{C-1} \leq y^* \end{cases} \tag{12.1}$$

where C denotes the number of categories and τ_i ($i = 1$, 2, 3, . . . , $C - 1$) denotes the location of the cut points, also called "thresholds," along the latent response distribution. Tetrachoric correlations, used for estimating correlations between binary manifest variables, or polychoric correlations, used for ordinal manifest variables with more than two categories, can be estimated using these thresholds (see Olsson, 1979). The correlations then become the sample correlations, S^*, used for parameter estimation in SEM.[6] The goal of structural equation model (at least the portion of the model with categorical indicators) becomes maximizing the correspondence between Σ^*, the population covariance matrix of the latent responses (where S^* is a consistent estimate of Σ^*), and $\Sigma(\theta)$, the model-implied covariance matrix (e.g., Bollen, 1989, pp. 433–434; Lei & Wu, Chapter 10, this volume).

A less common method within the SEM framework (but commonplace in the related item response theory framework) is to model the nonlinear relationship between the observed, categorical response and the latent factor directly; see X path in Figure 12.2. In these cases a method much more similar to traditional logistic regression is used. More specifically, as a special case of the generalized linear model (GLM), logistic regression is used for predicting the probability an event (e.g., $y_1 = 1$) occurs by modeling the event with the logistic function, which is commonly expressed as

$$P(y_i = c) = \frac{1}{1 + e^{-z}} \tag{12.2}$$

where z is a linear combination of the independent variables (i.e., the predictor side of a MLR equation). For

example, suppose that z is equal to $a(x - b)$, where x is an independent variable (e.g., Reading Ability), the a parameter is a slope coefficient, and the product of a and b is an intercept. In linear regression, the parameter a (the slope) shows the amount of change in the expected value of the outcome (say, y_1) associated with one unit increase in x, and the intercept indicates at what value of x the expected value of the outcome will be zero. However, just as in traditional logistic regression, logistic regression within the SEM framework results in a logistic function that is an S-shaped curve

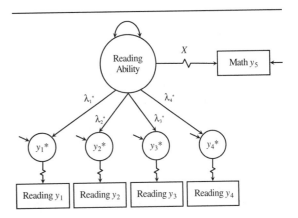

FIGURE 12.2. A path diagram showing the hypothesized relationship between four dichotomously scored (*correct, incorrect*) reading items (y_1–y_4) and the latent variable of Reading Ability, as well as the predictive relationship between the latent variable of Reading Ability and the manifest variable of Math Grade (a standard ABC letter grade denoted by y_5). The latent response variables for y_1–y_4 are denoted by y_1^*–y_4^*. Straight, single-headed arrows originating from one latent variable (denoted as circles) and ending at another latent variable denote linear, directional relationships between latent variables. The strength of the relationship is denoted by a factor loading (λ_i^*). Jagged, single-headed arrows between latent variables and manifest variables (denoted as rectangles) denote nonlinear, directional relationships between the variables. The strength of the nonlinear, predictive relationship between Reading Ability and Math Score is denoted by X. Single-headed arrows originating in space and ending at a variable (latent or manifest) denote residual (or unique) variances. Dual-head arrows beginning and ending at the same variable denote variances.

increasing from 0 to 1 as z goes from $-\infty$ to ∞. This means that the interpretation of the slope and intercept in structural equation models using a logistic function differs slightly from the interpretation of these parameters in standard, linear structural equation models. The parameter a now denotes the slope of the curve at its steepest point, whereas parameter b denotes the location along the curve where the slope is steepest. Just as with standard logistic regression, there are no restrictions on the independent variables, and the predicted value becomes the probability of endorsing an item (or getting the item correct).

Logistic regression is most commonly associated with dichotomous outcomes, but there are extensions of this model that are appropriate for ordered (or unordered) categories. The multinomial logit model can be used to model choices among unordered categories, and a cumulative link model (using the phrasing of Agresti, 1990) can be used to model ordered categories. The cumulative link model is really a general description of a model that can have many possible links. There is a logit version (the cumulative logit model), a probit version, and others (e.g., a log–log link leading to a hazard model). For more information on multiple-category versions of logistic regression, see Chapter 9 in Agresti (1996) or Chapter 5 in Long (1997). The manner in which the nonlinear relationship between the latent variable (e.g., Reading Ability) and the observed, categorical variables is handled (e.g., estimating tetrachoric correlations vs. using a logit link function) will often dictate the method used to estimate the model parameters. We expand on this point in a subsequent section.

Categorical Dependent Variables

Just as with indicators of latent variables, dependent variables or outcomes of latent variables can take on a number of response options. The outcome could be continuous (e.g., the score on a standardized math test),[7] ordered categorical (e.g., a letter grade on a math test), or dichotomous (e.g., pass–fail on a math test). As with categorical indicators of latent factors, categorical outcomes require the nonlinear relationship between the latent factor and the observed, categorical variable to be accounted for appropriately. In many cases, especially when no categorical indicators are in the model, an individual may wish to model the nonlinear relationship between the latent factor and the categorical outcome directly using either a logit or probit link function. In such cases the interpretation of the relationship

between the latent factor and the categorical outcome is the same as with any standard logistic or probit regression model.

More commonly, especially when categorical indicators are also in the model, a categorical dependent variable is treated as if it were another indicator. That is, the outcome is assumed to have an underlying, continuous response distribution that gave rise to the observed, categorical response. All categorical responses are treated the same way; thus, the same assumptions are placed

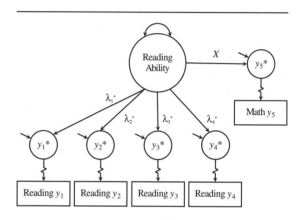

FIGURE 12.3. A path diagram showing the hypothesized relationship between four dichotomously scored (*correct, incorrect*) reading items (y_1–y_4) and the latent variable of Reading Ability, as well as the predictive relationship between the latent variable of Reading Ability and the manifest variable of Math Grade (a standard ABC letter grade denoted by y_5). The latent response variables for y_1–y_5 are denoted by y_1^*–y_5^*. Straight, single-headed arrows originating from one latent variable (denoted as circles) and ending at another latent variable denote linear, directional relationships between latent variables. The strength of the relationship is denoted by a factor loading (λ_i^*). The strength of the linear, predictive relationship between Reading Ability and the latent outcome distribution for Math Score is denoted by X. Jagged, single-headed arrows between latent variables and manifest variables (denoted as rectangles) denote nonlinear, directional relationships between the variables. Single-headed arrows originating in space and ending at a variable (latent or manifest) denote residual (or unique) variances. Dual-headed arrows beginning and ending at the same variable denote variances.

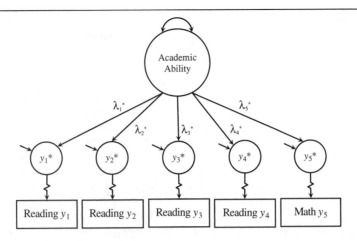

FIGURE 12.4. A path diagram showing the hypothesized relationship between five categorical items and the latent variable of Academic Ability. Four of the items (y_1–y_4) are reading items that were scored dichotomously (*correct, incorrect*). One of the items (y_5) represents math grade scored using a standard ABC letter-grade system. The latent response variables for y_1–y_5 are denoted by y_1*–y_5*. Straight, single-headed arrows originating from one latent variable (denoted as circles) and ending at another latent variable denote linear, directional relationships between latent variables. The strength of the relationship is denoted by a factor loading (λ_i*). Jagged, single-headed arrows between latent variables and manifest variables (denoted as rectangles) denote nonlinear, directional relationships between the variables. Single-headed arrows originating in space and ending at a variable (latent or manifest) denote residual (or unique) variances. Dual-headed arrows beginning and ending at the same variable denote variances.

on all categorical, dependent variables in the model. A path diagram presenting the similarity between the treatment of categorical outcomes and categorical indicators when both are in the model is presented in Figure 12.3. In this hypothetical example we are interested in how well individuals' Reading Ability predicts their math scores, where the math scores are on a standard, ABC letter-grade scale.

It is important to note that in many situations there is no difference between a categorical indicator and a categorical outcome. Indeed, all indicators and outcomes are dependent variables. With regard to the latent variable depicted in Figure 12.3, a 1-unit increase in the latent variable (Reading Ability) results in a unit λ_i^* increase in the ith item's latent response distribution. For example, a 1-unit increase in Reading Ability results in a λ_1^* unit increase in y_1^*. The λ_1^*-unit increase in y_1^* may or may not, depending on the value of y_1^* and the thresholds (see Equation 12.1), result in a higher category being endorsed. The way in which the model is thought about (the outcome being something different from an indicator) and presented graphically often occludes the

equivalence of indicators and outcomes. However, if the model were simply redrawn as in Figure 12.4, one can see that the outcome is no different than another indicator. In many situations the interpretation of the indictor–outcome itself would remain unchanged.

The interpretation of a model that includes a single latent variable with a set of indicators and one or more outcomes can get tricky, regardless of the categorical nature of the dependent variables. When a latent variable is defined, for example, by only reading items, it is easy to justify interpreting the latent variable as Reading Ability (or something similar). However, when an outcome such as math grade is added to the model, the latent variable is now, in part, defined by math. That is, it becomes difficult to label the latent variable as Reading Ability when, in fact, one of the indicators (even if called an "outcome") of the model is a measure of math ability. A more appropriate label for the latent variable may be "Academic Ability." It is wise to keep in mind that the name one provides a latent variable has no impact on what the model defines the latent variable to be.

Categorical Predictors

Up to this point we have discussed only unconditional models. However, categorical predictors of latent variables can also be incorporated into structural equation models. The inclusion of categorical predictors in structural equation models is not much more complicated than including categorical predictors in a standard regression model. When the predictor is dichotomous, the model can be interpreted with regard to the reference group (the group coded 0). The path from the predictor to the latent variable (or any other type of variable) is then the effect of the predictor on the outcome when the predictor equals 1. For example, if we were interested in the effect of school socioeconomic status (SES) on Reading Ability we could include a dichotomously scored predictor variable (0 for low SES and 1 for high SES) into our Reading Ability model. The results may suggest that low-SES schools have an average Reading Ability of zero (zero here is an arbitrary value on a standard normal metric to be used as a reference point for the high-SES group). The effect of being from a high-SES school then would be the value of the regression slope. If this value were 1 (and a standardized estimate) the result would suggest that individuals from high-SES schools are 1 *SD* higher, on average, in Reading Ability than individuals from low-SES schools.

Difficulties arise when the predictor consists of more than two categories. Many standard statistical packages automatically dummy-code predictors with more than two categories (e.g., using the CLASS option in SAS's PROC REG). Unfortunately, standard SEM packages do not currently offer this option. It is up to the researcher to dummy-code the predictors (as well as any interactions). This can become very tedious and lead to mistakes if the number of categorical predictors or categories becomes large.

Depending on the predictor, it may be useful to think of the predictor as a single-indicator latent variable. If parameterized correctly, a single manifest variable can be used to identify a latent variable. In these instances, a 1-unit increase on the latent response scale (now a latent predictor scale) is associated with a *b*-unit increase in the latent variable.

Observed and Latent Groups

In some cases a predictor may denote logical groups (e.g., males and females). In this case the structural equation model may be parameterized such that differ-ent model parameter values can be estimated for each group. The multiple-group model has been used extensively in conjunction with categorical indicators (see, e.g., Curran, Edwards, Wirth, Hussong, & Chassin, 2007; Edwards & Wirth, 2009; Flora, Curran, Hussong, & Edwards, 2008; Muthén, 1984). This method can be extremely useful when one is unsure of whether the same measurement model holds across groups, or whether the same relationship between two latent variables holds across groups. For example, males may interpret one reading item differently than how women interpret the same item. If indicators differ in their relationship to a latent variable across groups (i.e., the factor loadings are not equivalent across groups), the measurement model is generally said to be noninvariant over group or that the item (or items) shows differential item functioning (Millsap & Olivera-Aguilar, Chapter 23, this volume).

In other cases, group membership is not directly observable. In these cases, one may want to implement categorical latent variables. Though these methods originated as a way to model non-normal distributions (see Bauer & Curran, 2003, for a review of this topic), the methods can be useful for defining post hoc groups (Dolan, 2009). These models are generally only categorical in name. The likelihood function for latent-class models generally includes a probability of group membership for each individual. The researcher defines the number of groups to be extracted, and the model assigns (via the fit function) a probability that each individual "belongs" to each group. In most cases, an individual belongs to a single group: The researcher assigns the individual to one and only one group. The models themselves rarely make this level of distinction. For more information on the topic of latent classes in the SEM framework, see Bauer (2007), Bauer and Curran (2004), and Dolan (2009).

THE IMPACT OF CATEGORICAL DATA ON SEM

In this section we review three different aspects of SEM that are impacted by the presence of categorical data. We begin with estimation, which flows naturally into a discussion of model fit. Before leaving the section to review examples of different structural equation models incorporating categorical variables, we touch briefly on ways that categorical data can impact interpretation.

Estimation

Categorical data, by their very nature, pose challenges when it comes to estimating the parameters of a structural equation model. The most common situation in SEM parameter estimation is the pairing of a maximum likelihood (ML) estimator with an observed covariance matrix. The likelihood serves to select parameter values that minimize the deviation between what was observed (the data) and what is expected (the model-implied covariance matrix). For this procedure to work "as advertised," strong assumptions are made about the distribution of the observed variables. Specifically, in the case of ML, it is assumed that the data follow a multivariate normal distribution. In the case of categorical data, this is almost always falsifiable. A number of alternatives exist that are appropriate for use when the data do not satisfy the strong assumption required for ML estimation. These methods can be broadly classified as belonging to one of two categories: limited- and full-information estimators. What follows is a brief overview of each class of estimator, as well as some descriptions of the more popular forms of each. For a more detailed overview of the topic see Wirth and Edwards (2007).

Limited Information

Limited-information estimators use only a summary of the available data. In most cases within the SEM framework, these are variances and covariances (and occasionally means) derived from data. In the case of categorical data, these are most commonly tetrachoric or polychoric correlations. Each correlation is a bivariate measure of association and based on first- and second-order margins (as typically computed). Limited-information estimators sacrifice some of the information available in the data but are often much simpler to implement in practice. The reduction in information comes with a reduction in the size of the data. For example, a 10-item scale with 1 million responses still reduces down to a 10×10 correlation matrix. There are other limited-information methods that do not rely on covariance–correlation matrices (see, e.g., Jöreskog & Moustaki, 2001), but these are generally still rarely used in practice.

In the SEM framework, limited-information estimators still must navigate the fact that the data are not likely to support the assumptions necessary to justify using ML. To correct for the likely non-normal distribution

of the observed data, a weight matrix can be used in conjunction with a least squares estimator. This combination is called, perhaps not surprisingly, *weighted least squares* (WLS). If the weight matrix is an identity matrix, a matrix with ones on the diagonal and zeroes off the diagonal, it is called *unweighted least squares* (ULS) or *ordinary least squares* (OLS). The idea of least squares estimators is, very generally stated, to choose item parameter values to minimize the distance between the way the world is and the way the model says the world should be. It is a very elegant solution, but in the presence of non-normal data ULS cannot provide accurate standard errors or χ^2 values, which play a critical role in assessing model fit. WLS is meant to correct this deficiency. Unfortunately, the required weight matrix is very large, very difficult to work with, and generally not a practical solution. To get around this problem, researchers have discovered that by only using the diagonal of that very large weight matrix it is possible to get answers that can then, after undergoing some subsequent corrective procedures, provide accurate standard errors and χ^2 values. The least squares estimator, combined with the diagonal of the appropriate weight matrix (first suggested by Christoffersson, 1975), is referred to as *diagonally weighted least squares* (DWLS) or *modified weighted least squares* (MWLS) estimator, depending on the source.

If this description sounds somewhat convoluted, there is good reason for this. The approach outlined here reflects researchers' attempts to modify procedures originally developed for continuous data for use with categorical data. Each step closer to an accurate answer seemed to produce an additional hurdle. Despite this, there is much to be said for the analytic simplicity of obtaining estimates through the DWLS/MWLS procedures—especially compared to the full-information methods, to which we turn next.

Full Information

As the name suggests, "full-information estimators" work with the raw data rather than summary statistics. Each datum contributes something to the estimation procedure, and its contribution can usually be tracked fairly directly. Perhaps the most common full-information method is full-information maximum likelihood (FIML). There are a number of variations of the FIML estimator in existence, but a standard feature is the contribution of each data point to the likelihoods being calculated. Although this is more efficient from a statistical standpoint, it is more complex from a computational one. One advantage is that FIML can be applied directly to linear and nonlinear models without any ancillary steps (e.g., the tetrachoric–polychoric correlations described earlier). Thus, it is the standard estimation method used in most software for logistic regression. Logit and probit versions of these regression models are more complex in the SEM framework due to the presence of latent variables, which are unobserved. This necessarily increases the complexity of using FIML with a nonlinear regression in SEM.

Perhaps the biggest difference when using FIML with a nonlinear model in the SEM framework (vs. a nonlinear model where all variables are observed) is the need to perform integration as part of the parameter estimation process. Computer-friendly approximations exist (e.g., numerical integration) for these integrals, but as the number of dimensions being integrated increases, the computational demand increases rapidly. It is only recently, with the advent of Markov Chain Monte Carlo (MCMC) and other computer-intensive estimation routines, that the problem is no longer the major roadblock it once was (see, e.g., Cai, 2010; Edwards, 2010). Increasingly there are FIML options available for nonlinear models in popular SEM software.

Model Fit

Once one has obtained parameter estimates for a model of interest, a next logical question is "How good is this model?" The subject of model fit is a large and active area within the SEM literature (as is true for many areas) and the next chapter in this volume (West, Taylor, & Wu, Chapter 13) focuses exclusively on issues of model fit and model selection. Literally dozens of available fit measures attempt to gauge the quality of structural equation models. The presence of categorical data can complicate the assessment of model fit, but many of these challenges have been overcome. In the limited-information cases, especially those highlighted earlier, which rely on the covariance–correlation matrix as the unit of analysis, there are corrections available that provide an accurate fit function value when using a number of the least squares variants (most notably DWLS/MWLS). An accurate fit function value is extremely important, as it plays a crucial role in almost every widely used measure of fit.

Whether a limited- or full-information estimator is used changes some of the available options. Many of the fit measures for SEM were developed specifically for limited-information estimators. Other measures are available for both limited- and full-information solutions. As currently implemented in most major software packages, though, users will notice a drastic reduction in the available indices of fit when using a full-information estimator combined with a nonlinear model. Also worth noting is that despite a large literature describing the performance of various fit indices (e.g., Hu & Bentler, 1999), little research has been done to assess the extent to which guidelines about model fit developed with continuous data hold when the data are categorical. We feel this is a fruitful avenue for future research and hope to see quantitative methodologists exploring the issue before long.

Interpretation

Before moving to examples of structural equation models involving categorical data, we want to briefly discuss the issue of interpretation. In general, when limited-information approaches are used and the underlying response variable is invoked, the factor loadings are still interpreted as if they were related directly to the measured variable. Things are not quite as simple when a nonlinear model is used (almost always in conjunction with a full-information estimator). One of the most commonly used interpretations of the regression parameters from nonlinear models is called the "odds ratio." In the simplest case, where the outcome is dichotomous, the odds ratio interpretation tells us the impact of a 1-unit change in a particular predictor on the probability of the outcome being 1. To make this interpretation, the researchers must take the additional step of exponentiating the reported regression coefficient. Let's imagine a very simple example where we are using standardized scores from an intelligence test and whether a child has failed a grade to predict graduation from high school. We use logistic regression to better understand the impact of intelligence test scores and failing a grade on graduation from high school. Our analysis produces a slope of –0.355 for failing a grade and a slope of 0.405 for intelligence test scores. These are in logit units, which are not all that interpretable. If we exponentiate them, they become odds ratios. For example, $\exp(-0.355)$ is approximately equal to 0.70. Odds ratios are interpreted relative to 1, which would indicate that an increase in the predictor does not change the likelihood of the outcome. An odds ratio of 0.70 for failing a grade indicates that, holding intelligence test scores constant, failing a grade reduces the odds of graduating by 30%. If we do the same thing for intelligence test scores, we get an odds ratio of approximately 1.5. That means that, holding grade failure constant, every standard deviation increase in intelligence test scores increases the odds of graduating by 50%. Other interpretations are possible, and this is just a brief example of how things can be interpreted in a very simple example. There are excellent resources to aid in the interpretation of regression coefficients from logistic regression (and its various close cousins). Among our favorites are the books by Agresti (1996), Long (1997), and Pampel (2000).

EXAMPLES

In this section, we provide empirical examples that incorporate categorical variables into several different parts of a structural equation model (i.e., as indicators, predictors, or outcomes) and employ both general classes of estimation methods, full- and limited-information, previously discussed. The data are from the National Longitudinal Survey of Youth 1997 (NLSY97), a large-scale survey designed to track the transition from school to work using a nationally representative sample of American youth; the data are collected and maintained by the U.S. Bureau of Labor Statistics.[8] Analyses were performed using LISREL 8.72 and/or Mplus 6.1, as noted.

Categorical Indicator Variable

During data collection in 2006–2007, NLYS97 Wave 10 respondents encountered items soliciting their view on whether the government should be responsible for providing things such as inflation control, environmental protection, and healthcare. Participants responded to these 10 items using a Likert-type scale with four options, ranging from *Definitely should not be* to *Definitely should be*, in which higher values were coded to indicate a greater degree of belief in government responsibility. In total, 1,888 individuals responded to at least 1 of the 10 government responsibility items. With four response options, these data are most appropriately considered categorical as opposed to continuous. As noted, the items had response options with a clear order, suggesting an ordinal level of measurement.

We examined a measurement model as the first step in this example. A unidimensional factor model was specified, in which all 10 items loaded on a single common latent variable, which we term "Government Responsibility"; depicted as a path diagram, this model would closely resemble Figure 12.1. The data were analyzed using two estimation methods described earlier, DWLS (implemented in Mplus as "estimator = WLSM" and in LISREL as "method = DWLS") and FIML, implemented using the MLR estimation method within Mplus.

Item content and factor loadings for all analyses are presented in Table 12.1. There are several points regard-

TABLE 12.1. Standardized Factor Loadings for Government Responsibility Items

	Factor loading		
Indicators	FIML (Mplus) (N = 1,888)	DWLS (Mplus) (N = 1,617)	DWLS (LISREL) (N = 1,617)
Provide a job for everyone who wants one	.58	.60	.60
Keep prices under control	.58	.59	.59
Provide healthcare for the sick	.81	.80	.79
Provide a decent standard of living for the old	.83	.82	.79
Provide industry with the help it needs to grow	.55	.58	.59
Provide a decent standard of living for the unemployed	.60	.64	.60
Reduce income differences between the rich and poor	.58	.62	.61
Give financial assistance to college students from low-income families	.68	.67	.65
Provide decent housing for those who can't afford it	.77	.78	.78
Impose strict laws to make industry do less damage to the environment	.50	.49	.47

Note. FIML, full-information maximum likelihood; DWLS, diagonally weighted least squares.

ing these results that deserve attention. As part of the typical DWLS estimation process, cases with any missing values are excluded from the analysis through listwise deletion, which resulted in a reduced sample size for the DWLS estimations compared to FIML. In the current data, almost 14% of the sample was excluded due to missing values when using DWLS. Examining factor loadings across the three analyses, there is a high level of agreement for the point estimates. However, there are some discrepancies, even across programs using the same sample and comparable estimation methods. In our experience, any such differences tend to be in the third or, less frequently, the second decimal place and typically have little to no impact on the statistical/substantive conclusions drawn. Table 12.2 presents a selection of popular fit indices for the model estimated in three ways. Of particular note, and as discussed earlier, is the lack of typical SEM fit indices for the FIML estimation method. For the models estimated using DWLS, using the suggested cutoff values (e.g., Browne & Cudeck, 1993; Hu & Bentler, 1999) developed for use with continuous data, the model appears to fit adequately, although there is discrepancy between the RMSEA values from Mplus and LISREL, which, if taken alone, could lead to different conclusions regarding the adequacy of the model (see West et al., Chapter 13, this volume, for a more detailed discussion of fit evaluation).

Categorical Predictor Variable

Building upon the measurement model established in the previous section, we investigated whether demographic variables could predict respondents' level of

TABLE 12.2. Fit Indices for Measurement Models.

	FIML (Mplus) ($N = 1,888$)	DWLS (Mplus) ($N = 1,617$)	DWLS (LISREL) ($N = 1,617$)
RMSEA	—	.082	.069
SRMR	—	—	.051
CFI	—	.974	.981
TLI/NNFI	—	.966	.975
AIC	33,831.39	—	—

Note. Cells containing "—" indicate unavailable/unreported indices. RMSEA, root mean square error of approximation; SRMR, standardized root mean square residual; CFI, comparative fit index; TLI/NNFI, Tucker–Lewis index/non-normed fit index.

the latent trait. Gender and race/ethnicity were introduced in the analysis as possible predictors. As discussed earlier, the dichotomous predictor of gender is incorporated as is, with the reference group of males assigned the value of 0 and females assigned 1. For the race/ethnicity predictor, dummy variables were created by hand for the two most commonly reported values, Black and Hispanic; in coding these dummy variables Caucasian served as the reference category. In total, three manifest predictors were used, one for gender and two dummy variables for race.

DWLS in Mplus and LISREL was used to obtain parameter estimates. Some factor loadings within the measurement model changed slightly, due to being estimated from a covariance matrix conditioned on the predictors; however, the rank-ordering of loadings and statistical significance decisions were comparable across the conditional and unconditional models. Across LISREL and Mplus, the coefficient estimates for the predictors differed in only the third decimal place; LISREL estimates are reported. The standardized regressions coefficients for the gender, black, and Hispanic dummy variables are $\hat{\beta} = .14$, .37, and .21, respectively; all predictors were statistically significant ($p < .05$). Because we did not include race by gender interactions, the interpretation applied to the standardized regression paths are straightforward. The standardized regression path from gender to the latent variable suggests that females (regardless of race) are, on average, 0.14 *SD* higher than males in their belief that the government is responsible for providing for its citizens. Similar interpretations would be used for the Black and Hispanic coefficients as well, with the values representing each group's respective average Government Responsibility score compared to that of Caucasians, regardless of gender.

Categorical Outcome Variable

In this example we are interested in whether or not Government Responsibility predicted whether an individual voted in the 2006 election (dichotomously scored: yes–no) and to what extent the individual was interested in politics and public affairs (scored using a 4-point Likert-type response scale). The model is similar to those presented in Figures 12.3 and 12.4. As discussed earlier, adding outcomes to the measurement model is equivalent to including additional indicators of the latent factor. Indeed, we simply added the two new variables to the model as indicators to test the relationship between voting, interest in politics and public affairs, and the latent variable of Government Responsibility. DWLS in both Mplus and LISREL was again used. Due to missing values on the "Vote" variable, the sample size was reduced to 1,206.

Across Mplus and LISREL, the estimates for the two new variables were identical to the third decimal place. The resulting loadings for voting and interest in politics were $\hat{\lambda}^* = -0.05$ and $\hat{\lambda}^* = 0.05$, respectively. Both are statistically nonsignificant, $p > .10$. From this, we conclude that Government Responsibility does not significantly predict 2006 voting behavior or an individual's interest in politics or public affairs. As noted previously, with the inclusion of outcome variables, it is possible that the meaning of the latent factor will become murky, but with statistically nonsignificant loadings it is reasonable to make the simpler conclusion that belief about government responsibility is not associated with respondents' voting behaviors or levels of interest in public affairs/politics.

CONCLUSION

As computing power continues to increase and software continues to expand, it seems likely that the incorporation of categorical data in statistically valid ways will become increasingly common in SEM. Despite the vast literature on categorical data and the equally vast literature on SEM, there is relatively little on the intersection between these two topics. In this chapter, we have reviewed definitions of categorical data, core aspects of SEM, the ways in which categorical data can manifest in structural equation models, the impact of having categorical data in structural equation models, and have provided examples of these methods and issues using real data. Each of these sections is by necessity brief and only covers a small sliver of the possible content that could be covered. However, we hope we have given the reader a useful overview of some of the more critical issues in the use of categorical data in SEM, as well as indicating where readers can turn for more information on the subjects we covered.

NOTES

1. It is also possible for a variable to be nominal because, while it has an order among the response categories, we don't know a priori what that order is.

2. We do not mean to assert that there are not more appropriate ways to examine these relationships. We only wish to note that even suboptimal methods can provide useful information at times.

3. Assuming the model is properly identified. See Bollen (1989) for an extensive discussion of model identification and methods for assessing whether or not a model is identified.

4. As described by Bollen (1989, p. 12), an exogenous variable is "caused" by variables outside the model, whereas an endogenous variable is "caused" by variables within the model.

5. This section provides a brief overview of categorical measurement models. For a more in-depth treatment see Bovaird and Koziol (Chapter 29, this volume).

6. Note that when using tetrachoric or polychoric correlations the **S*** matrix will be a correlation matrix. We use the traditional covariance matrix notation to remain consistent with the standard SEM notation.

7. It is important to note that in many instances even these scores are not continuous, normally distributed variables and alternative modeling methods may be required.

8. Additional information on the NLSY97 is available at *www.nlsinfo.org/nlsy97/nlsdocs/nlsy97/maintoc.html*.

REFERENCES

Agresti, A. (1990). *Categorical data analysis.* New York: Wiley.

Agresti, A. (1996). *An introduction to categorical data analysis.* New York: Wiley.

Bauer, D. J. (2007). Observations on the use of growth mixture models in psychological research. *Multivariate Behavioral Research, 42*, 757–786.

Bauer, D. J., & Curran, P. J. (2003). Distributional assumptions of growth mixture models: Implications for overextraction of latent trajectory classes. *Psychological Methods, 8*, 338–363.

Bauer, D. J., & Curran, P. J. (2004). The integration of continuous and discrete latent variable models: Potential problems and promising opportunities. *Psychological Methods, 9*, 3–29.

Beauducel, A., & Herzberg, P. Y. (2006). On the performance of maximum likelihood versus means and variance adjusted weighted least squares estimation in CFA. *Structural Equation Modeling, 13*, 186–203.

Bollen, K. A. (1989). *Structural equations with latent variables.* New York: Wiley.

Browne, M. W., & Cudeck, R. (1993). Alternative ways of assessing model fit. In K. A. Bollen & J. S. Lang (Eds.), *Testing structural models* (pp. 136–162). Newbury Park, CA: Sage.

Cai, L. (2010). Metropolis–Hastings Robbins–Monro algorithm for confirmatory item factor analysis. *Journal of Educational and Behavioral Statistics, 35*, 307–335.

Christofferson, A. (1975). Factor analysis of dichotomized variables. *Psychometrika, 40*, 5–32.

Churchill, G. A., Jr. (1979). A paradigm for developing better measures of marketing constructs. *Journal of Marketing Research, 16,* 64–73.

Cohen, J., Cohen, P., West, S. G., & Aiken, L. S. (2003). *Applied multiple regression/correlation analysis for the behavioral sciences.* Mahwah, NJ: Erlbaum.

Curran, P. J., Edwards, M. C., Wirth, R. J., Hussong, A. M., & Chassin, L. (2007). The incorporation of categorical measurement models in the analysis of individual growth. In T. D. Little, J. A. Bovaird, & N. A. Card (Eds.), *Modeling contextual effects in longitudinal studies* (pp. 89–120). Mahwah, NJ: Erlbaum.

Dolan, C. V. (1994). Factor analysis of variables with 2, 3, 5, and 7 response categories: A comparison of categorical variable estimators using simulated data. *British Journal of Mathematical and Statistical Psychology, 47,* 309–326.

Dolan, C. V. (2009). Structural equation mixture modeling. In R. E. Millsap & A. Maydeu-Olivares (Eds.), *The Sage handbook of quantitative methods in psychology* (pp. 568–591). Thousand Oaks, CA: Sage.

Edwards, M. C. (2010). A Markov Chain Monte Carlo approach to confirmatory item factor analysis. *Psychometrika, 75,* 474–497.

Edwards, M. C., & Wirth, R. J. (2009). Measurement and the study of change. *Research in Human Development, 6,* 74–96.

Flora, D. B., & Curran, P. J. (2004). An evaluation of alternative methods for confirmatory factor analysis with ordinal data. *Psychological Methods, 9,* 466–491.

Flora, D. B., Curran, P. J., Hussong, A. M., & Edwards, M. C. (2008). Incorporating measurement nonequivalence in a cross-study latent growth curve analysis. *Structural Equation Modeling, 15,* 676–704.

Hu, L., & Bentler, P. M. (1999). Cutoff criteria for fit indexes in covariance structure analysis: Conventional criteria versus new alternatives. *Structural Equation Modeling, 6,* 1–55.

Jöreskog, K. G., & Moustaki, I. (2001). Factor analysis of ordinal variables: A comparison of three approaches. *Multivariate Behavioral Research, 36,* 347–387.

Likert, R. (1932). A technique for the measurement of attitudes. *Archives of Psychology, 140,* 1–55.

Long, J. S. (1997). *Regression models for categorical and limited dependent variables.* Thousand Oaks, CA: Sage.

Muthén, B. (1984). A general structural equation model with dichotomous, ordered categorical, and continuous latent variable indicators. *Psychometrika, 49,* 115–132.

Olsson, U. (1979). Maximum likelihood estimation of the polychoric correlation coefficient. *Psychometrika, 44,* 443–460.

Pampel, F. C. (2000). *Logistic regression: A primer.* Thousand Oaks, CA: Sage.

Stevens, S. S. (1946). On the theory of scales of measurements. *Science, 103,* 677–680.

Wirth, R. J., & Edwards, M. C. (2007). Item factor analysis: Current approaches and future directions. *Psychological Methods, 12,* 58–79.

Wright, S. S. (1921). Correlation and causation. *Journal of Agricultural Research, 20,* 557–585.

CHAPTER 13

Model Fit and Model Selection in Structural Equation Modeling

Stephen G. West
Aaron B. Taylor
Wei Wu

One of the strengths of structural equation modeling (SEM) is the ability to test models that represent a complex set of theoretical hypotheses. The set of hypothesized relationships is specified and commonly represented graphically in the compact form of a path diagram. The model and its associated path diagram contain one or more of three components. It may contain a hypothesized measurement component that relates the observed (measured) variables to underlying constructs (Figure 13.1A). It may contain a structural (path) component that portrays the hypothesized causal relationships between the constructs (Figure 13.1B). It may contain a hypothesized mean component that portrays similarities and differences in the level of the constructs, potentially as a function of other variables (Figure 13.1C). Once a path model is specified, an important question arises: How well does the hypothesized model fit observed data on each of the variables?

The path model diagram implies a set of algebraic equations whose parameters (e.g., factor loadings in Λ_y, factor variances and covariances in Ψ) are estimated, typically through maximum likelihood (ML) or generalized least squares (GLS) estimation procedures. For the confirmatory factor analysis (CFA) model in Figure 13.1A,

$$\Sigma = \Lambda_y \Psi \Lambda_y' + \Theta_\varepsilon \tag{13.1}$$

where Σ is the population covariance matrix of the observed variables, Λ_y is the matrix of factor loadings, Ψ is the matrix of factor covariances, and Θ_ε is the covariance matrix of residuals. The parameters estimated for the specified model, in turn, provide the machinery for calculating what the variances, covariances, and means of the variables would be, *if in fact the model were true* (model-implied estimates). The key question for assessing the overall fit of the model is how well the estimates implied by the model match the variances, covariances, and means of the observed data.

This chapter addresses two related but different questions. First, we may wish to answer the question of model fit: Does the hypothesized model provide an adequate fit to the data? Second, we may wish to answer the question of model selection: If multiple competing models have been proposed, which of these models provides the best account of the data? Or, alternatively, which competing model is most likely to replicate in another sample drawn from the same population? We focus on the model fit question in the initial part of the chapter, returning to brief consideration of the model selection question at the end of the chapter. We also briefly consider other key aspects of model evaluation beyond those of overall model fit.

We begin by reviewing the properties of the chi square (χ^2) test statistic and several "practical" indices

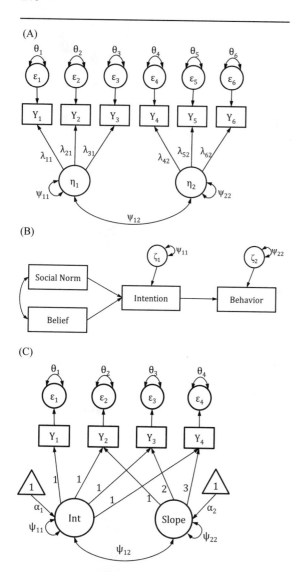

FIGURE 13.1. (A) Two-factor confirmatory factor analysis model. (B) Path model with four measured variables (Fishbein–Azjen model). (C) Linear growth model with four time points.

of overall model fit, focusing on those that are currently being reported in journals by researchers. In the first part of our review we emphasize lack of sensitivity to sample size in estimation, the criterion that dominated the evaluation of fit indices in the last part of the 20th century. We then consider other desiderata for good fit indices, discovering that other model-related factors can make it difficult to establish a threshold for good fit. Most existing work has only studied the performance of fit indices in simple CFA (measurement) models; we initially follow this precedent but later consider the use of fit indices with other, more complex models, such as growth models and multilevel models. We consider evaluating the fit of different model components as well as overall global fit. We also consider other approaches to evaluating the adequacy of a model. Finally, we consider model selection indices useful for selecting the best of a set of competing models.

ASSESSING OVERALL MODEL FIT: THE CHI-SQUARE TEST AND PRACTICAL FIT INDICES

Most of the practical fit indices involve the chi-square (χ^2) test statistic for the hypothesized model, sometimes in conjunction with same test statistic for a baseline model (Yuan, 2005). A summary of some of the equations, original sources, and key properties of several commonly used fit indices is presented in Table 13.1.

For covariance structure models, we use the following notation. The number of observed variables being modeled is denoted p, and their covariance matrix, based on a sample size of N, is $\mathbf{S}$. The corresponding population covariance matrix is Σ. The covariance matrix reproduced by the model using q estimated parameters is $\hat{\Sigma}(\theta)$, where θ represents a vector of free parameters estimated by the model (factor loadings in Λ; factor variances and covariances in Ψ; unique variances and covariances in Θ). Each of the covariance matrices $(\mathbf{S}, \Sigma, \hat{\Sigma}(\theta))$, has p^* nonredundant elements, where $p^* = p(p+1)/2$. The model estimation procedure attempts to minimize a discrepancy function F, which achieves a minimum value f. A general form of the discrepancy function is presented in Equation 13.2 (Browne, 1974):

$$F = (\mathbf{s} - \hat{\sigma}(\theta))' \mathbf{W}^{-1} (\mathbf{s} - \hat{\sigma}(\theta)) \tag{13.2}$$

where $\mathbf{s}$ is a vector containing the p^* nonredundant elements in the sample covariance matrix, $\hat{\sigma}(\theta)$ is a vector containing the $p*$ nonredundant elements in the model implied covariance matrix, and $\mathbf{W}$ is a weight matrix. Equation 13.3 presents the most commonly used discrepancy function for the ML estimation procedure (Jöreskog, 1967):

$$\hat{F} = \log|\hat{\Sigma}(\theta)| + \text{tr}|\mathbf{S}\hat{\Sigma}(\theta)^{-1}| - \log|\mathbf{S}| - p \quad \textbf{(13.3)}$$

where tr is the trace of the matrix.

Chi-Square (Likelihood Ratio) Test

For standard ML estimation (Equation 13.3), under the null hypothesis that the model-implied covariance matrix equals $\Sigma(\theta)$, the population covariance matrix Σ, the test statistic $T = (N - 1)f$ follows a central χ^2 distribution with degrees of freedom (df) equal to $p* - q$. f is the minimum of $\hat{F}$. q is the number of parameters to be estimated. Important assumptions underlying this test statistic are that (1) the observed variables have a multivariate normal distribution, (2) N is sufficiently large, and (3) none of the tested parameters is at a boundary (e.g., variance = 0). We refer to this expression as the χ^2 test (although other such tests are possible; Hu & Bentler, 1995). If the observed χ^2 exceeds the critical value given the df and the nominal Type I error rate (typically $\alpha = .05$), the null hypothesis that $\Sigma(\theta) = \Sigma$ is rejected. This means that the null hypothesis of perfect fit in the population is false, the assumptions are wrong, or both. As we discuss below, this χ^2 test has limitations and is not always the final word in assessing fit.

This χ^2 test can be considered a special case of the likelihood ratio (LR) test for nested models. A model is nested within another if its estimated parameters are a subset of the estimated parameters in the other model (see Bentler & Satorra, 2010). Typically, this occurs when a parameter is set equal to a fixed value (e.g., ψ_{21} = 1) or two or more parameters are set equal (e.g., λ_{11} = λ_{42}, setting the factor loadings of indicators 1 and 4 on their respective factors equal; see Figure 13.1A). The null hypothesis is that the model estimating fewer parameters (Fewer) fits no worse in the population than the model estimating more parameters (More). The LR test statistic is presented in Equation 13.4:

$$\Delta\chi^2 = \chi^2_{\text{Fewer}} - \chi^2_{\text{More}} \quad \Delta df = df_{\text{Fewer}} - df_{\text{More}} \quad \textbf{(13.4)}$$

Given that previous assumptions (1), (2), and (3) are met and that the two tested models are not too discrepant from the true model in the population (Steiger, Sha-

piro, & Browne, 1985), $\Delta\chi^2$, the difference between the two tested models' χ^2 values, follows a χ^2 distribution under the null hypothesis, with df equal to Δdf (Bentler & Bonett, 1980). The χ^2 test of overall model fit tests the null hypothesis that the tested model fits no worse than a saturated model, which estimates $p*$ parameters and fits the data perfectly. The saturated model has a χ^2 value of 0 with $df = 0$. A saturated model exists for all covariance structure models; however, some more complex models do not have a known saturated model or the standard saturated model is incorrect.

Jöreskog (1969), who introduced the χ^2 test of fit in the context of covariance structure models, also noted its limitations (see also Bentler & Bonett, 1980; James, Mulaik, & Brett, 1982; Tucker & Lewis, 1973). A major problem with the χ^2 test is that as N increases, its power to detect even trivial differences between $\Sigma(\theta)$ and $\mathbf{S}$ approaches 1.0. A model that accounts for the major sources of covariance in the data, even if it ignores what Jöreskog termed "minor factors," can still be of practical value—"all models are wrong, some are useful" (Box, 1979, p. 202). Models may be considered to be approximations of reality a priori, so the null hypothesis of exact fit is *not* expected to be retained (Cudeck & Henly, 1991; Jöreskog & Sörbom, 1981; MacCallum, Widaman, Preacher, & Hong, 2001; Steiger & Lind, 1980). In short, the null hypothesis of exact overall fit tested by the χ^2 test is often not of general interest.

Other problems with the χ^2 test have also been raised. Because researchers hope to retain the null hypothesis (thus supporting the theoretically hypothesized model), the use of the χ^2 test statistic encourages the use of small samples (Bentler & Bonett, 1980; Meehl, 1967). Small samples, in turn, potentially obscure poor fit and yield less precise estimates of the free (estimated) parameters in a model. The test statistic T is not likely to follow a χ^2 distribution when the observed variables are not multivariate normal and or when N is small (Bentler, 1990; Jöreskog & Sörbom, 1981). Even when its assumptions are met, the χ^2 test tends to reject true models at higher than the nominal rate in small samples (Boomsma, 1982); conversely, the χ^2 test often has low power to detect meaningful levels of model misspecification in small samples (Gallini & Mandeville, 1984). Researchers have developed practical fit indices in an attempt to overcome some of these problems. Special emphasis has historically been placed on the criterion that the value of fit indices for correctly specified or slightly misspecified models should not be affected by sample size (e.g., Marsh, Balla, & McDonald, 1988).

TABLE 13.1. Fit Indices for Covariance Structure Models

Equation No.	Fit index	Reference	Goodness- or badness-of-fit index	Theoretical range	Cutoff criterion	Sensitive to N	Penalty for model complexity?
T1	$\chi^2 = (N-1)f$	Jöreskog (1969)	Badness	≥ 0	$p < .05$	Yes	No
T2	χ^2 / df (8)	Jöreskog (1969)	Badness	≥ 0	$< 5^d$	Yes	Yes
T3	$GFI = 1 - \dfrac{\mathbf{e'We}}{\mathbf{s'Ws}}$ (10)	Jöreskog & Sörbom (1981)	Goodness	$0\text{–}1^a$	$> .95^d$	Yes	No
T4	$AGFI = 1 - \dfrac{p^*}{df}(1 - GFI)$ (6)	Jöreskog & Sörbom (1981)	Goodness	$0\text{–}1^a$	N/A^{d,e}	Yes	Yes
T5	$GFI^* = \dfrac{p}{p + 2\left(\dfrac{\chi^2 - df}{N-1}\right)}$ (0)	Maiti & Mukherjee (1990); Steiger (1989)	Goodness	$0\text{–}1^a$	$> .95$	No	No
T6	$AGFI^* = 1 - \dfrac{p^*}{df}(1 - GFI^*)$ (0)	Maiti & Mukherjee (1990); Steiger (1989)	Goodness	$0\text{–}1^a$	N/A^e	No	Yes
T7	$RMR = [p^{*-1}(\mathbf{e'1e})]^{1/2}$ (4)	Jöreskog & Sörbom (1981)	Badness	> 0	N/A^{e,f}	Yes	No
T8	$SRMR = [p^{*-1}(\mathbf{e'W_s e})]^{1/2}$ (13)	Bentler (1995)	Badness	> 0	$< .08$	Yes	No
T9	$RMSEA = \sqrt{\dfrac{\hat{\lambda}_N}{df}} = \sqrt{\dfrac{\max(\chi^2 - df,\, 0)}{df(N-1)}}$ (42)	Steiger & Lind (1980)	Badness	> 0	$< .06$	Yes to small N	Yes

	Formula		Citation		Range	Cutoff		
T10	$TLI^c = \dfrac{\chi_0^2/df_0 - \chi_k^2/df_k}{\chi_0^2/df_0 - 1}$	(22)	Tucker & Lewis (1973)	Goodness	0–1 [a, b]	> .95	No	Yes
T11	$NFI = \dfrac{f_0 - f_k}{f_0} = \dfrac{\chi_0^2 - \chi_k^2}{\chi_0^2}$	(7)	Bentler & Bonett (1980)	Goodness	0–1	> .95[d]	Yes	No
T12	$IFI = \dfrac{\chi_0^2 - \chi_k^2}{\chi_0^2 - df_k}$	(3)	Bollen (1989); Marsh et al. (1988)	Goodness	> 0[b]	> .95	Yes to small N	Yes
T13	$RNI = \dfrac{(\chi_0^2 - df_0) - (\chi_k^2 - df_k)}{(\chi_0^2 - df_0)}$	(3)	Bentler (1990); McDonald & Marsh (1990)	Goodness	> 0[b]	>.95	No	Yes
T14	$CFI = \dfrac{\max(\chi_0^2 - df_0, 0) - \max(\chi_k^2 - df_k, 0)}{\max(\chi_0^2 - df_0, 0)}$	(42)	Bentler (1990)	Goodness	0–1	> .95	No	Yes

Note. χ^2, chi-square test statistic; GFI = goodness-of-fit index; AGFI, adjusted goodness-of-fit index. GFI*, revised GFI; AGFI*, revised AGFI; RMR, root mean square residual; SRMR, standardized root mean square residual; RMSEA, root mean square error of approximation; TLI, Tucker–Lewis index; NFI, normed fit index; IFI, incremental fit index; RNI, relative noncentrality index; CFI, comparative fit index; f, minimized discrepancy function; o, baseline model; k, tested or hypothesized model; df, degrees of freedom; N, sample size; p^*, the number of nonduplicated elements in the covariance matrix; $\mathbf{e}$, a vector of residuals from a covariance matrix; $\mathbf{s}$, a vector of the p^* nonredundant elements in the observed covariance matrix; $\mathbf{I}$, an identify matrix; $\mathbf{W}$, a weight matrix; $\mathbf{W_s}$, a diagonal weight matrix used to standardize the elements in a sample covariance matrix; λ_N, noncentrality parameter, normed so that it is not negative. The numbers in parentheses in the "Fit indices" column represent the number out of 55 articles on structural equation models in substantive American Psychological Association journals in 2004 that reported each of the practical fit indices described here (see Taylor, 2008). No other practical fit indices were reported.

[a]Can be negative. Negative value indicates an extremely misspecified model.
[b]When exceeds 1, the fit index indicates extremely well-fitting model.
[c]Also called non-normed fit index (NNFI).
[d]Fit index is affected by sample size.
[e]No cutoff criteria have been proposed for this index.
[f]Not standardized, so will be affected by size of elements in covariance matrix.

Practical Fit Indices

The decade of the 1980s was the heyday of the development of new fit indices, and—with apologies to songwriter Paul Simon—there must be 50 ways to index your model's fit (see Marsh, Hau, & Grayson, 2005, for a list of 40). In this section we focus on several practical fit indices commonly reported in published articles. Table 13.1 reports the fit indices identified based on a computer and manual search of American Psychological Association journals (Taylor, 2008; see also Jackson, Gillapsy, & Purc-Stephenson, 2009). Good (and bad) reasons exist for the use of these particular indices, such as the precedent of use by other researchers, their routine computation by SEM software, and positive evaluations in reviews (e.g., Hu & Bentler, 1998).

Following McDonald and Ho (2002), we distinguish between absolute and comparative fit indices. Absolute fit indices are functions of the test statistic T or of the residuals (Yuan, 2005). In contrast, comparative fit indices assess the improvement in fit of the hypothesized model relative to a baseline model. The most restricted model that is "theoretically defensible" (Bentler & Bonett, 1980) has become the standard baseline model estimated by most SEM software packages (e.g., EQS, LISREL, Mplus). This independence model estimates a variance for each measured variable but permits no covariances between measured variables (see Figure 13.2A). This standard baseline model is not always appropriate for more complex SEM models (McDonald & Marsh, 1990; Widaman & Thompson, 2003; see Figure 13.2B). Other baseline models may be justified in some research contexts, even for CFA models (e.g., Sobel & Bohrnstedt, 1985). Another distinction is between goodness- and badness-of-fit indices. Goodness-of-fit indices increase (often to a maximum value of 1) with improving fit. Badness-of-fit indices decline (often to 0) with improving fit. All comparative fit indices are goodness-of-fit indices; absolute fit indices can be either goodness- or badness-of-fit indices.

Of the fit indices presented in Table 13.1, the root mean square error of approximation, the standardized root mean square residual, the goodness-of-fit index, the χ^2/df ratio, the adjusted goodness-of-fit index, and the root mean square residual are absolute indices; the comparative fit index, the Tucker–Lewis index, the normed fit index, the relative noncentrality index, and the incremental fit index are comparative fit indices. We consider the absolute indices first, followed by the comparative indices, with each group presented in roughly

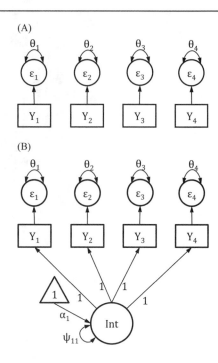

FIGURE 13.2. (A) Baseline model for a confirmatory factor analysis model with four indicators. (B) Baseline (intercept only) model for linear growth model with four time points.

their order of introduction in the literature. Not all of these fit indices are currently recommended; all continue to appear with some frequency in published SEM applications. We note commonly used cutoff values proposed for those indices that are not affected by N.

χ^2/df Ratio

The χ^2/df ratio was never formally introduced as a fit index but appears to have evolved as an easily computed, ad hoc measure of fit. Jöreskog (1969), in his consideration of limitations of the χ^2 test of overall fit, suggested that the χ^2 value be used more descriptively in the evaluation of model fit, with the df acting as a standard of comparison. The rationale for the χ^2/df ratio[1] is that the expected value of the χ^2 for a correct model equals the df. Wheaton, Muthén, Alwin, and Summers (1977) explicitly introduced the χ^2/df ratio with little comment except to indicate that their experience suggested that a value of 5 or less indicated good fit; this proposed reference value is heavily influenced by N (Marsh et al., 1988). Given a fixed N, smaller values of the χ^2/df ratio indicate better fit; it is a badness-of-fit index. The χ^2/df ratio has a minimum of 0, which occurs when a model with positive df has a χ^2 value of 0. Saturated models, which by definition fit perfectly, have 0 df; therefore, they have an undefined χ^2/df. There is no theoretical maximum for the χ^2/df ratio.

Unlike χ^2, which can only remain constant or improve as parameters are added to a model, the χ^2/df ratio can potentially get worse. The χ^2/df ratio penalizes model complexity. If added parameters fail to reduce a model's χ^2 appreciably, the χ^2/df ratio will get worse because adding parameters reduces the model's df. The χ^2/df ratio suffers from the same problem as the χ^2 test—its value is dependent on sample size for misspecified models (Marsh et al., 1988).

Goodness-of-Fit and Adjusted Goodness-of-Fit Indices

Jöreskog and Sörbom (1981) introduced the goodness-of-fit (GFI) and adjusted goodness-of-fit (AGFI) indices. They described these indices as proportions of variance accounted for, but their formulas did not make this interpretation transparent. Bentler (1983, Equation 3.5) later reexpressed the GFI formula, clarifying this interpretation (see Table 13.1, Equation T3). Equation T3 uses a weight matrix $\mathbf{W}$ that is computed from the elements of $\hat{\boldsymbol{\Sigma}}(\boldsymbol{\theta})^{-1}$ for ML and $\mathbf{S}^{-1}$ for GLS. Thus, GFI is calculated using the weighted sum of squared residuals from a covariance matrix and weighted sums of squared variances and covariances. It is similar to the familiar R^2 measure used in ordinary least squares (OLS) regression, which can be expressed as

$$R^2 = 1 - \frac{SS_{\text{residual}}}{SS_{\text{total}}} \quad \textbf{(13.5)}$$

The major difference[2] between Equation T3 and Equation 13.5 is the GFI's use of the weight matrix $\mathbf{W}$. This matrix, which appears in the fit function, relates the GFI directly to the estimation procedure, which is typically a desirable property for a fit measure (Menard, 2000).

Jöreskog and Sörbom (1981) presented the AGFI as an adjustment to the GFI based on a model's df (Table 13.1, Equation T4). The goal of the adjustment was to penalize model overfitting, in which additional parameters are estimated with small resulting improvement in

fit. Equation 13.6 reexpresses Equation T4 to make the relationship between the GFI and AGFI clearer:

$$\frac{(1-\text{GFI})}{(1-\text{AGFI})} = \frac{df}{p*} \quad \textbf{(13.6)}$$

Equation 13.6 shows that the AGFI will be smaller than the GFI for all realistic models in which at least one parameter is estimated ($df < p*$). The AGFI will approach the GFI as fewer parameters are estimated (as df approaches $p*$).

Both the GFI and the AGFI are goodness-of-fit indices, increasing with improving fit. They are proportions that conceptually have a range of 0 to 1, but can potentially be negative (Jöreskog & Sörbom 1981; Maiti & Mukherjee, 1990). The GFI will be negative if $\mathbf{e'We} > \mathbf{s'Ws}$ (see Equation T3 in Table 13.1), meaning that the weighted squared residuals are actually larger than the weighted squared covariances in $\mathbf{S}$! This result is theoretically possible, but only in extremely badly misspecified models that would never be entertained by researchers. In contrast, the AGFI can become negative whenever GFI $< (p* - df)/p* = q/p*$. In other words, the AGFI will be negative whenever the proportion of variance accounted for by a model, as measured by the GFI, is smaller than the proportion of the $p*$ observed covariances used to estimate parameters.

Mulaik and colleagues (1989) noted that the relationship between the AGFI and the GFI is analogous to the relationship between R^2 and adjusted R^2 (Wherry, 1931) in OLS regression. They critiqued the AGFI because, as noted earlier, it can fall below 0 (as can adjusted R^2). Given that the AGFI is in a proportion metric, negative values are mathematically uninterpretable, although such values could only occur with an extremely misspecified model. Mulaik and colleagues also questioned the penalty used by the AGFI to choose more parsimonious models: The GFI is not very sensitive to changes in a model's df when the model has a large df to begin with, particularly as the GFI approaches 1.

Maiti and Mukherjee (1990, Equation 19) and Steiger (1989, Equation 51) suggested a revised index known as GFI* (a.k.a., gamma hat) that improves on the properties of the GFI (Table 13.1, Equation T5). Steiger demonstrated that although the GFI and GFI* asymptotically estimate the same quantity, the GFI is biased and the GFI* is unbiased in smaller samples. An unbiased estimate of the AGFI, the AGFI*, can also be calculated by substituting the GFI* for the GFI in Equation T4, yielding Equation T6 in Table 13.1. In contrast to the GFI and AGFI, which are affected by sample size, the GFI* and AGFI* are expected to have the desirable property of not being affected by N. They are promising global fit indices (see Hu & Bentler, 1998; Taylor, 2008), but to date have been little used in practice.

Root Mean Square Residual and Standardized Root Mean Square Residual

Jöreskog and Sörbom (1981) also introduced the root mean square residual (RMR), which is the square root of the average of the squared residuals (Table 13.1, Equation T7). Recall that residuals are differences between observed covariances and model-implied covariances $(s - \hat{\sigma}(\theta))$ rather than differences between observed scores and predicted scores $(Y - \hat{Y})$. Equation T7 in Table 13.1 clarifies the relationship between the RMR and the GFI. Rather than using a weight matrix W, the RMR uses the identity matrix I. RMR depends on an unweighted rather the weighted function of the residuals.

The RMR's use of unweighted residuals can be a virtue, particularly for observed measures with little measurement error (e.g., some cognitive or biological measures). Browne, MacCallum, Kim, Andersen, and Glaser (2002) demonstrated that the weighting of residuals in the ML and GLS fit functions (see Equation 13.2) can severely overstate a model's badness of fit when the measured variables have small unique variances. The RMR does not weight the residuals in its calculation, so it is unaffected by this problem; all other fit indices discussed in this chapter (except for the standardized root mean square residual, discussed immediately below) are affected. The GFI and the AGFI use the same weighting as the ML or GLS fit functions; other fit indices incorporate the fit function through their use of χ^2, which is equal to $(N-1)f$ in their equations.

The RMR is a badness-of-fit index; it approaches 0 as the fit of a model improves. Unfortunately, its scaling can impede interpretation as it diverges from 0. The RMR will tend to be larger for covariance matrices with larger elements than for matrices with smaller elements, precluding comparisons across data sets. Bentler (1995) introduced the standardized root mean square residual (SRMR) to address this comparison problem. The SRMR converts the residuals into a standardized metric. Each standardized residual that goes into the calculation of the SRMR is the raw residual as a proportion of the element of S being estimated. Because of this standardized metric, SRMR values can

be meaningfully compared across models fit to different data sets. The calculation of the SRMR is similar to the calculation of the RMR (Table 13.1, Equation T8), except that it uses a diagonal weight matrix W_s to standardize the elements in S, whereas the RMR uses an identity matrix, leaving the elements unstandardized. Each diagonal element of W_s is the reciprocal of the square root of the product of the variances on which the corresponding element of S is based. For example, for s_{12} and $\hat{\sigma}_{12}$, the corresponding diagonal element of W_s has a value of $\sqrt{s_{11}s_{22}}$.

The SRMR's weight matrix W_s is diagonal, whereas the weight matrix W in the fit function in Equation 13.2 is, in general, not diagonal. Although the SRMR differs from the RMR in that it is standardized, it is like the RMR in that its weighting of the residuals ignores the possible covariance of the elements in S or $\hat{\Sigma}$, taken into account by the ML or GLS fit function. This outcome implies that it is also like the RMR in being immune to the problem discussed earlier of overstating misfit when several manifest variables in a model have small unique variances (see Browne et al., 2002).

Like the RMR, the SRMR is a badness-of-fit index. It has a minimum of 0 for a perfectly fitting model. In practice, the SRMR will be less than 1, typically far less. An SRMR of 1 would indicate that the residuals were, on average, as large as the elements of S being estimated, an extremely poorly fitting model that no researcher would seriously consider.

Root Mean Square Error of Approximation

The root mean square error of approximation (RMSEA; Steiger, 1989, 1990; Steiger & Lind, 1980) is based on the insight that although $(N-1)f$ asymptotically follows the familiar (central) χ^2 distribution under the null hypothesis, it asymptotically follows a *noncentral* χ^2 distribution under the alternate hypothesis. The noncentrality parameter (λ) of this distribution depends on how badly the model fits, so it can be used to construct a fit index. Since the expected value of a noncentral χ^2 distribution is $df + \lambda$, Steiger (1989) pointed out that the noncentrality parameter could be estimated as

$$\hat{\lambda} = (\chi^2 - df)/(N-1) \qquad \textbf{(13.7)}$$

To keep this estimated noncentrality parameter from taking on an unrealistic negative value, Steiger suggested that λ be given a lower bound of 0.

$$\hat{\lambda}_N = \max(\chi^2 - df, \, 0) / (N - 1) \qquad \textbf{(13.8)}$$

where the N subscript indicates that $\hat{\lambda}_N$ has been normed to keep it non-negative.

Steiger and Lind (1980) suggested two adjustments to $\hat{\lambda}_N$ to improve the RMSEA's interpretation. First, they added a penalty function to discourage researchers from overfitting models, dividing $\hat{\lambda}_N$ by its *df*. Second, they took the square root of this result, so that the RMSEA is in the same metric as the weighted residuals (see Equation T9 in Table 13.1). Steiger (1989; Steiger & Lind, 1980; see also Browne, 1974) showed that the population noncentrality parameter being estimated by $\hat{\lambda}$ could be considered as a weighted sum of squared residuals (see Equation 13.2)

$$\hat{\lambda} = \mathbf{e}'\mathbf{W}\mathbf{e} \qquad \textbf{(13.9)}$$

The residuals are then weighted in the same manner as in the ML or GLS estimation procedure because the weight matrix $\mathbf{W}$ is the same.

The RMSEA is a badness-of-fit index, declining with improving fit. The RMSEA is bounded at a lower value of 0. It has no theoretical maximum. Browne and Cudeck (1993) suggested that a model with an RMSEA of .10 is unworthy of serious consideration.

A confidence interval (CI) for the RMSEA is provided by most computer programs. An iterative procedure is used to find limits of a CI for $\hat{\lambda}_N$, and then these limits are substituted into the left formula of Equation T9 in Table 13.1. Steiger and Lind (1980) advocated using a 90% CI. Browne and Cudeck (1993) extended the use of this CI to a test of close fit. Noting that in their experience, RMSEA values of .05 or less indicated "close fit," they constructed a test of the null hypothesis that the true value of the RMSEA $\leq$ .05, now implemented in many SEM software packages. This null hypothesis that the model closely fits the data is retained if the lower limit of the RMSEA's confidence interval falls at or below .05. Alternatively, an RMSEA whose upper limit exceeded .08 or .10 could be deemed unacceptable. RMSEA underestimates fit at small sample sizes ($N < 200$; see Curran, Bollen, Chen, Paxton, & Kirby, 2003).

Tucker–Lewis Index

Tucker and Lewis (1973) noted that the fit function F (Equation 13.2) is a sum of squares that when divided by *df* yields a mean square M. For exploratory factor analysis they proposed the Tucker–Lewis index (TLI), which compares M_k for the hypothesized model to M_0 for a baseline, independence model. (In this and subsequent equations for comparative fit indices, quantities subscripted with 0 come from the baseline model and quantities subscripted with k come from the hypothesized model.)

Bentler and Bonett (1980) generalized the TLI to the covariance structure analysis context and labeled it the non-normed fit index (NNFI), although the TLI designation remains more common. They formulated the TLI in terms of χ^2/df ratios (see Table 13.1, Equation T10). Their formulation makes clear that the TLI is conceptually in a proportion metric. In terms of χ^2/df ratios, it gives the distance between the baseline and target models as a proportion of the distance between the baseline model and a true model. The 1 in the denominator is the expected value of the χ^2/df ratio for a true model.

Although the TLI is conceptually in a proportion metric, it can potentially fall below 0 or above 1. TLI can occasionally exceed 1 if $\chi_k^2 / df_k < 1$. By contrast, TLI can be negative if the denominator is negative and the numerator is positive. Both conditions under which the TLI becomes mathematically negative, $\chi_k^2 / df_k < \chi_0^2 / df_0 < 1$ and $1 < \chi_0^2 / df < \chi_k^2 / df_k$, require the baseline model to fit the data very well, a condition that is unlikely to occur in practice.

The TLI penalizes models that estimate many parameters. McDonald and Marsh (1990) showed that it could be rewritten in terms of James, Mulaik and Brett's (1982; see also Mulaik et al., 1989) parsimony ratio (PR): PR = df_k/df_0. Thus, PR is the proportion of the number of parameters fixed in the hypothesized model relative to the proportion of the number of parameters fixed in the baseline independence model. McDonald and Marsh's reexpression of the TLI is given in Equation 13.10:

$$\text{TLI} = 1 - \frac{(\chi_k^2 - df_k) / (\chi_0^2 - df_0)}{df_k / df_0} = 1 - \frac{\hat{\lambda}_k / \hat{\lambda}_0}{\text{PR}} \qquad \textbf{(13.10)}$$

Given equal model fit, models with larger PRs yield larger TLI values. Bollen (1986), in an early critique, argued that the TLI would be affected by sample size; however, Monte Carlo studies (e.g., Marsh et al., 1988) have consistently found that the TLI is not affected by sample size (see also Balderjahn, 1988).

Normed Fit Index

Bentler and Bonett (1980) also introduced the normed fit index (NFI), which compares the fit of a target model to the fit of a baseline model. Rather than use χ^2/df ratios as the TLI does, it uses either fit function values or χ^2 values (Table 13.1, Equation T11). The expression shows the NFI indicates the improvement in fit realized by moving from the baseline model to a hypothesized model, as a proportion of the baseline model's fit. The left expression for the NFI (Equation T11 in Table 13.1) can also be used even when the fit function is not related to the χ^2 distribution. The NFI cannot fall below 0 or above 1. The NFI cannot fall below 0 because the baseline model must be nested within the hypothesized model, so the hypothesized model cannot have a worse (larger) χ^2. It cannot exceed 1 because the minimum value of the hypothesized model's χ^2 value is 0, which makes the maximum NFI equal to $\chi_0^2 / \chi_0^2 = 1$. The NFI does not include a penalty function to penalize overfitting and is affected by N, with small sample sizes producing underestimates of the true NFI (Marsh et al., 1988).

Incremental Fit Index

Bollen (1989; see also Marsh et al., 1988) introduced the incremental fit index (IFI) in an attempt to improve on the NFI. The NFI does not approach 1 for correct models in small samples (Bentler, 1990). The key problem is that the expected value of a model's χ^2 for correct models does not equal zero as the NFI assumes, but instead equals the model's df. The IFI subtracts the hypothesized model's df in the denominator, as this is the expected value of a model's χ^2 if the model is correct (Table 13.1, Equation T12). The IFI is theoretically in a proportion metric, but it can potentially exceed 1. It will do so under precisely the same circumstances as the TLI: when the hypothesized model's χ^2 is less than its df. Also like the TLI, the IFI can be negative, but only if $\chi_0^2 < df_k$, again suggesting a remarkably good fit for the baseline model. Like the NFI, the IFI's numerator cannot be negative: The baseline model must be nested in the hypothesized model, so the baseline model's χ^2 cannot be smaller than that of the hypothesized model.

Although proposed as an improvement to the NFI, the IFI introduced new problems. First, McDonald and Marsh (1990) showed that the IFI will tend to overestimate its asymptotic value in small samples; this over-

estimation will be more severe as the misspecification of the hypothesized model increases, as indexed by its noncentrality parameter λ. The IFI's positive bias in small samples is probably a greater concern than the NFI's negative bias, as positive bias leads to conclusions that a model fits better than it actually does. Negative bias can have the virtue of encouraging conservative conclusions about model fit (Marsh, Balla, & Hau, 1996).

Second, the inclusion of the model's df, which should act as a penalty function for overly complex models like that of the TLI, actually works in the wrong direction (Marsh, 1995; Marsh et al., 1996). If a superfluous parameter is added to a model, the model's df will be reduced by 1, but its χ^2 will not decrease, meaning that the IFI's denominator will decrease while its numerator will remain unchanged, resulting in a larger IFI value. Marsh and colleagues (1996) refer to this as a "penalty for parsimony," noting that it runs counter to the more desirable behavior of the TLI, which penalizes for unnecessary complexity.

Comparative Fit Index and Relative Noncentrality Index

Bentler (1990) and McDonald and Marsh (1990) independently introduced two virtually identical fit indices. McDonald and Marsh introduced the relative noncentrality index (RNI), which uses the noncentrality parameter as an index of lack of fit just as the RMSEA does. The noncentrality parameter is estimated using Equation 13.7, just as it is for the RMSEA. The RNI then takes a form similar to that of the other comparative fit indices, giving the reduction in noncentrality realized by moving from the baseline to the hypothesized model, as a proportion of the baseline model's noncentrality (Table 13.1, Equation T13). The RNI converges asymptotically to the same value as do the NFI and the IFI, but has the desirable property of being unaffected by sample size. The RNI can exceed 1 under the same unlikely circumstances that the TLI and the IFI do: when the hypothesized model's χ^2 is smaller than its df.

In defining the CFI, Bentler used the same logic as Steiger and Lind (1980) with the RMSEA and fixed the estimated noncentrality parameter to have a minimum of 0. Doing this replaces $\hat{\lambda}$ from Equation 13.7 with $\hat{\lambda}_N$ from Equation 13.8 and yields the CFI's formula (Table 13.1, Equation T14). In models for which the χ^2 is larger than the df, which likely includes the great majority of models tested in psychological research, the CFI and RNI take on identical values. The RNI and CFI will differ only when a model's χ^2 is smaller than its *df*, characteristic of extremely well fitting models. Under such circumstances, the RNI exceeds 1, whereas the CFI is bounded at the maximum theoretical value of 1. Goffin (1993) pointed out that the RNI and the CFI estimate the same population quantity, but this difference means that they have different strengths. The RNI is a less biased estimator than the CFI because it does not truncate its distribution at 1. The CFI is a more efficient estimator (smaller standard error) because its truncated distribution discards values that the population index cannot possibly take on. Goffin suggested that these qualities make the RNI preferable for comparing competing models, and the CFI preferable for reporting the fit of a single model. Both the CFI and RNI are straightforward to interpret and are not affected by *N*.

Summary

Our review thus far has considered the characteristics of commonly used practical fit indices and their performance in simple CFA models in which each factor has a small number of measured indicators. Researchers have strongly preferred fit indices whose mean values in simulation studies are independent of *N* (e.g., Marsh et al., 1988). This preference parallels psychology's increasing use of effect sizes that are independent of *N* rather than *p*-values, which are strongly related to *N* (Wilkinson and Task Force on Statistical Inference, 1999). Other desirable unique properties of a specific fit index (e.g., the confidence interval of the RMSEA; the proportion of variance interpretation of GFI³) may argue for its use so long as a minimum sample size is exceeded that makes bias in its estimation trivially small. A second important issue is ease of interpretation. Indices in a proportion fit metric or standardized metric that is unaffected by the scaling of the measured variables will be easier to interpret than indices without these qualities. Using these criteria to cull the fit indices reviewed earlier, the fit indices commonly reported in the literature that are worthy of consideration are the SRMR (given its standardized metric), RMSEA (for sample sizes over 200), TLI, and CFI/RNI. The TLI and CFI/RNI are goodness-of-fit indices in a proportion fit metric, whereas the RMSEA and SRMR are badness-of-fit indices that are not in a proportion metric. Other evaluations of more extensive sets of fit indices (Hu & Bentler, 1998; Marsh et al., 2005) also provide favorable evaluations of these fit indices, as well as others with which there is far less practical experience.

Proposed Cutoff Values

Most researchers focus on the first question posed at the beginning of this chapter: Does the hypothesized model provide an adequate fit to the data? Higher values on goodness-of-fit indices and lower values on badness-of-fit indices indicate better overall fit of the model to the data. But, what is an "adequate" fit? Researchers ideally desire a comparison standard that specifies a single criterion value that defines adequate fit.

Bentler and Bonett (1980) originally suggested a standard of .90 for the NFI and TLI (NNFI), fit indices in the proportion metric (also including the CFI/RNI reviewed earlier). Hu and Bentler (1995) proposed a criterion of <.05 for what they termed "good fit" and from .05 to .10 for "acceptable fit" for the SRMR. Browne and Cudeck (1993) suggested for the RMSEA that a value of .05 represented what they termed a "close fitting model" and .08 represented an "adequate" fitting model. These recommendations were based on the researchers' practical experience with the fit indices in the evaluation of many CFA models. Hu and Bentler (1999) later took another approach, conducting a simulation study that addressed the ability of fit indices to distinguish between correctly specified and misspecified models. Based on this study, they proposed a criterion of .95 for the TLI and CFI, a criterion of .06 for the RMSEA, and a criterion of .08 for the SRMR. Thus, Hu and Bentler proposed replacing the initial ad hoc practical guidelines with standards based on the results of a simulation study using a small set of correctly specified and misspecified covariance structure models. The rationale for their proposed standards, which focuses on the acceptance versus rejection of hypothesized models, has been questioned by Marsh, Hau, and Wen (2004) because it implicitly reintroduces sample size as a determinant of the outcome.

We believe that the proposed cutoff values can be guidelines about the overall fit of the model to the data, but we caution readers that the reification of specific cutoff standards for the acceptance versus rejection of a hypothesized model can be fraught with peril. The next section examines three important issues related to the use of cutoff values for fit indices.

ISSUES WITH PRACTICAL FIT INDICES

Model Characteristics and Standards for Fit

We earlier summarized the results of an extensive body of simulation research attempting to identify practical fit indices whose estimates are not affected by sample size. Unfortunately, much less research has investigated the effect of other model characteristics on fit. The available results suggest that other model and data characteristics can substantially affect the performance of fit indices. Within CFA models, Chen, Curran, Bollen, Kirby, and Paxton (2008; see also Savalei, 2011) showed that model specification and *df* can affect the performance of the RMSEA. Marsh, Hau, Balla, and Grayson (1998) have found that as the number of indicators per factor increases, models showed decreased fit to simulated data with properly specified models. Kenny and McCoach (2003) found that all fit indices examined, with the exception of the RMSEA, showed decreased fit as more indicators were added to a single-factor model. Marsh and colleagues note that "this apparent decline in fit associated with larger [number of indicators per factor] must reflect problems in the standards used to evaluate model fit rather than misspecification in the approximating model" (p. 217). Saris, Satorra, and van der Veld (2009) have found that given a constant magnitude of misspecification and sample size, the numerical value of other parameters in a model can affect the value of fit indices, with, for example, higher factor loadings leading to poorer fit index values. Davey, Savla, and Luo (2005) found that the values of fit indices for slightly misspecified CFA models increased as the proportion of missing data increased. Adding random error to a model may improve its apparent fit! This is not a desirable property.

As mean structures are added to models, other issues arise. The SRMR as commonly calculated only addresses the discrepancies between the model's implied and observed covariances; the mean structure is ignored. For practical fit indices based on the χ^2 test statistic, the fit function adds another term to capture the discrepancy between the observed and model implied means. A general discrepancy function extends Equation 13.2 to mean and covariance structures (Browne & Arminger, 1995):

$$F = [\mathbf{s} - \hat{\sigma}(\theta)]\mathbf{W}^{-1}[\mathbf{s} - \hat{\sigma}(\theta)] \\ + [\bar{X} - \hat{\mu}(\theta)]\mathbf{V}^{-1}[\bar{X} - \hat{\mu}(\theta)] \tag{13.11}$$

where $\mathbf{W}$ and $\mathbf{V}$ are weight matrices, and $\bar{X}$ and $\hat{\mu}(\theta)$ are the vectors of observed means and model implied means, respectively. The first term assesses fit in the covariance structure; the second assesses fit in the mean structure. Wu, West, and Taylor (2009) note the complexity of assessing fit for growth models given that misspecification in one structure can affect the other structure. In addition, the metrics of fit in the two structures may be quite different: Taking a traditional standard for the GFI of .90 or .95 for a CFA model in a large sample may be an appropriate proportion of variance for which to account (cf. Tanaka & Huba, 1985), but do we also expect our model to account for 90% or 95% of the variance in the latent means? Experience with other models such as analysis of variance with reliably measured outcomes would not lead us to expect such high values. Based on Wu and West's (2010) study of the effects of different types of model misspecification and different data characteristics (e.g., the ratio of the Level 1 to Level 2 variances) on the fit of growth curve models, Wu attempted to develop standards for fit indices. She abandoned this effort because standards following Hu and Bentler's (1999) accept–reject criterion varied dramatically as a function of the type of misspecification and data characteristics.

Taken together, these results suggest that appropriate cutoff standards may be specific to particular models and data sets. Current standards for interpreting acceptable model fit are only rough guidelines; they become increasingly less reasonable as they are extrapolated to models and data further from the CFA models with complete data studied by Hu and Bentler (1999).

Baseline and Saturated Models

Several smaller but easily overlooked issues relate to baseline and saturated models. For comparative fit indices, most commonly used SEM programs use the baseline model proposed by Bentler and Bonett (1980), which estimates a model in which each variable has a variance, but in which there are no covariances between variables (see Figure 13.2A). Because of the different weight matrices used in estimating the baseline model, comparative fit indices based on different estimation methods (e.g., GLS, ML) will differ (Sugawara & MacCallum, 1993). GLS and ML do produce the same results in large samples if data have the typically assumed multivariate normal distribution and the hypothesized model is close to the true model. The baseline model, though, will never be close to the true model for real applications. Under these conditions, the GLS weight and ML weight matrices computed from the elements $\mathbf{S}^{-1}$ and $\hat{\Sigma}(\theta)^{-1}$, respectively, will typically vary appreciably. Of note, LISREL uses GLS estimation for its baseline model, whereas most other SEM packages use the same procedure (typically ML in practice) as is used to estimate the hypothesized model. Values of comparative fit indices estimated using different estimation procedures will differ, perhaps substantially (Tanaka, 1993).

A second issue identified by Widaman and Thompson (2003) is that the baseline model must be nested within the hypothesized model. When mean structures are included, or certain restrictions are placed on the model, modified baseline models must be used in the calculation of comparative fit indices, or the value of the fit indices will be incorrect, sometimes appreciably so. Wu and colleagues (2009) discuss this and specify an acceptable baseline model (see Figure 13.2B) in the context of growth curve models.

Finally, some models do not have a proper saturated (0 *df*) model in which the number of estimated parameters matches the number of observed means and covariances in the model. Growth curve models in which each individual is measured at a different set of time points (so-called "random time models") and models with certain patterns of missing data do not have a saturated model (Wu et al., 2009). In addition, the standard saturated model used for linear structural equation models is not appropriate for models with interactions or quadratic effects of latent variables. The standard χ^2 test statistic and all practical fit indices based on the χ^2 reported by computer programs will be incorrect. Klein and Schermelleh-Engel (2010) provide a method of estimating χ^2 based on an appropriate saturated model for these cases.

Each of these issues illustrates the need for careful attention to the baseline and saturated models in the calculation of comparative fit indices.

Encouragement of Poor Practices

Reliance on fixed comparison standards for fit indices can also encourage poor practice by researchers. First, researchers, despite hypothesizing a model based on prior theory and research, may add and delete paths and factor loadings based on modification indices until the prescribed threshold standard for adequate fit is met. Traditional post hoc model modification, particularly when undertaken on an atheoretical basis, is unlikely to lead to the development of an improved model (Kaplan,

1990; MacCallum, 1986; MacCallum, Roznowski, & Necowitz, 1992; but see Marcoulides & Ing, Chapter 40, this volume, for newer approaches that are more promising). It is a sobering exercise to modify one's hypothesized model and then to test the hypothesized and post hoc modified model in a new replication sample, only to find that modified model does not lead to any gain in fit over the originally hypothesized model (and perhaps a worse fit, if a fit index with a penalty function is used). Modification of hypothesized models changes the epistemological status of the tested model from confirmatory to exploratory. The LR (χ^2) test no longer has a clear meaning once the model has been modified on the basis of the data. The change requires explicit acknowledgment of the model's new exploratory status; it also requires far more tentative reporting of model fit statistics and hypothesis tests in the absence of replication of the model in a new sample (see Diaconis, 1985). Reporting of fit indices with a parsimony penalty such as the TLI or RMSEA can reduce, but does not eliminate, this problem of capitalization on chance relationships in the data.

Second, fixed standards can lead to poor representation of constructs. From the standpoint of modern test theory, we would like to have a measure with multiple items that covers the full content of the construct and provides a relatively precise estimate of each person's score across the full range of the construct (e.g., Embretson & Reise, 2000). Yet most CFA models utilize only a small number of indicators per construct. As Marsh and colleagues (1998) and Kenny and McCoach (2003) found, fit indices tend to decrease as the number of indicators per construct increases, even when the model is properly specified. Fit indices for hypothesized models will also tend to decrease as the coverage of the hypothesized construct improves because the items will become more dissimilar (cf. Tucker, Koopman, & Linn, 1969). As Marsh and colleagues note, "Because of the importance typically placed . . . on evaluating the fit of one model against a fixed standard . . . , this bias would naturally extinguish the possibly desirable strategy of using larger numbers of indicators. This may explain in part why so many published CFA studies are based on [indicators per factor] = 2 or 3" (p. 217).

In sum, attempting to meet cutoff standards for adequate fit encourages post hoc model modification and the use of a relatively small number of indicators of each latent construct, practices which are often nonoptimal from a scientific viewpoint.

OTHER STRATEGIES FOR EVALUATING FIT

Fit of Model Components

The fit indices considered so far provide information about overall model fit. In models with several components, researchers may place differential importance on the fit of each of the different components. In combining measures of the fit of each component to produce a measure of overall fit, no guarantee exists that the researcher's theoretically desired weights will match those produced by the computer software. Model components with extremely good or extremely poor fit, even if they are of little theoretical interest, may swamp the contribution of other model components in the calculation of global fit indices.

In their consideration of CFA models and structural path models between latent variables, Anderson and Gerbing (1988) originally proposed a two-step approach. The first step involved satisfactory specification of the measurement model by estimating a CFA model (saturating the Ψ matrix of the covariances of latent factors). However, the challenge remained of assessing the fit of the structural model—the weight of the measurement structure in determining the fit of the overall model could potentially make it difficult to detect misspecification in the path model. In the context of multilevel SEM, Ryu and West (2009; see also Yuan & Bentler, 2007) proposed procedures for separately examining the Level 2 (between groups) and Level 1 (participants within groups) components of fit. Ryu and West showed that in the fit function, the between-groups component has far less weight (reflecting the number of groups) than the within-subjects component (reflecting the number of cases), giving the latter component disproportionate importance in determining overall model fit. They showed that improved results could be obtained using procedures that provided separate fit statistics for the Level 1 and Level 2 models. Wu and colleagues (2009) found that misfit in latent growth curve models can result from failure to reproduce the marginal means, the conditional means, the within-persons covariance structure, or the between-persons covariance structure. Wu and West (2010) presented methods for appropriately saturating different components of the model to provide more appropriate examination of the fit of the other components in the model. Such strategies can be useful in isolating the source(s) of model misfit, which is particularly important when some components of the model (e.g., marginal means; between-persons covariance structure) are of particu-

lar theoretical interest and other portions (e.g., within-persons covariance structure) are of far less theoretical interest.

Examination of Individual Standardized Residuals

McDonald (1999, 2010) and McDonald and Ho (2002) have advocated an even more fine-grained analysis of fit—the separate examination of the each standardized residual in the covariance structure and, if applicable, the mean structure in the model. Models in which all residuals are not large are deemed to fit the data adequately. Models in which there are one or more large residuals indicate problems with model fit. By examining the individual standardized discrepancies between the observed and model-implied covariance or mean, "it becomes possible to judge whether a marginal or low index of fit is due to a correctable misspecification of the model, or to a scatter of discrepancies, which suggests that the model is possibly the best available approximation to reality" (McDonald & Ho, 2002, p. 73).

In sum, indices that assess the fit of theoretically important model components and examine individual residuals in the covariance and mean structures can provide a richer, more fine-grained understanding of the strengths and limitations of the hypothesized model in accounting for the data set that complements the use of global fit indices.

WHAT IF THERE ARE ALTERNATIVE MODELS?

So far we have focused solely on cases in which there is assumed to be only one theoretically hypothesized model. However, often one of two other cases will occur. First, there may be alternative a priori theoretical models whose fit the researcher wishes to compare with that of the target model. This case can be particularly informative about the strengths and weaknesses of competing theoretical models in accounting for the data. Second, there may be other exploratory models proposed during the model fitting process that the researcher wishes to compare with the originally hypothesized model. Fit indices and model selection indices can be used to make these comparisons, again with the caveat that the second case requires appropriate acknowledgment of its exploratory status. Many discussions of model comparison emphasize the criterion of parsimony—given similar overall model fit, the model with fewer parameters will be preferred over an alternative model with more parameters (e.g., Mulaik et al., 1989; Preacher, 2006). As considered in a later section, fit indices and model selection indices (see Table 13.2) that penalize model complexity will often, but not always, be preferred.

Comparing Nested Models

As noted earlier, when the researcher wishes to compare two nested models, the likelihood ratio (LR) test discussed earlier can be used to determine whether the imposition of the restrictions on the more restricted model (yielding fewer parameters estimated) makes a statistically significant difference in model fit. Unfortunately, the same issues arise with the LR test for comparison of nested models that arose earlier for the overall χ^2 fit test statistic. Small N's can yield nonsignificant LR tests, masking important differences between the models. Conversely, very large N's can produce statistically significant χ^2 values even when the discrepancies between the two models are trivial.

Recognizing this issue, some researchers have argued that a change in practical fit indices that is less than some cutoff criterion may provide the desired information about differences in the fit between nested models. In the context of measurement invariance, which involves testing a series of nested measurement models (Widaman & Reise, 1997), Cheung and Rensvold (2002) suggested that changes in selected fit indices, including the CFI or GFI* among the fit indices reviewed earlier, appear to provide good performance in the assessment of measurement invariance. They proposed specified cutoff criteria for the change in fit between nested measurement invariance models (e.g., .01 for ΔCFI and .001 for ΔGFI*).

Note that neither of these fit indices includes a penalty for complexity, presumably because it is more difficult to compare corrected fit indices against an absolute standard for change. In addition, many of the same issues noted earlier with respect to the evaluation of fit indices against a cutoff criterion also appear to apply in this context (Fan & Sivo, 2009). Chen (2007) noted that different fit indices tended to be differentially sensitive to different types and amounts of invariance.

The LR test and changes in fit indices provide methods for comparing nested models. Model selection indices, which are the focus of the next section, allow comparison of both nested and non-nested models.

Model Selection Indices

We consider four model selection indices (and some of their variants) whose properties have received analytical and empirical evaluation that have been formally proposed for the comparison of either nested or non-nested models (see Table 13.2 for a summary). The general goal of these indices is to select the model with highest generalizability to samples with the same N drawn from the same population. According to Cudeck and Henly (1991), this model should have the smallest expected discrepancy between the fitted model covariance matrix and the population covariance matrix.

Akaike Information Criterion

The Akaike information criterion (AIC) was proposed by Akaike (1973) to measure the expected discrepancy between the true model and the hypothesized model. The first term of AIC (Table 13.2, Equation T13) is a measure of lack of fit; the second term reflects model complexity, penalizing more complex models. Of importance, the AIC only considers the number of free parameters in determining model complexity. The model with the smallest AIC is selected. Although commonly used, the AIC favors too complex models at small N due to the fact that it fails to take into account the effect of N on model selection. To solve the problem, alternatives to the AIC have been proposed that downweight sample size and therefore may have better performance in these contexts (e.g., bootstrapped information criterion [EIC]; Ishiguro, Sakamoto, & Kitagawa, 1997). For example, Bozdogan (1987) developed a consistent Akaike information criterion (CAIC, Table 13.2, Equation T16). The CAIC performs better than AIC at small N and with a large number of parameters. It does not necessarily favor models with more parameters, unless N is sufficiently large.

Bayesian Information Criterion

The Bayesian information criterion (BIC) aims to select the model that is most likely to have generated the data in the "Bayesian sense" (Myung & Pitt, 2004; Raftery, 1995). The BIC is in fact a large-sample approximation of the Bayesian model selection procedure that we describe below. The first term in the BIC (see Table 13.2, Equation T17) is the same lack of fit measure used by the AIC. The second term is a measure of model complexity, which is the product of the number of free

TABLE 13.2. Model Selection Indices for Non-Nested Models

Equation No.	Index	Rationale	Measure of model complexity	Pros	Cons
T15	$AIC = f + 2k$	Selects the model that had least expected discrepancy from the true model.	Number of parameters.	Easy to calculate. Performs well at large sample sizes.	Tends to select too complex models. Bad in recovering true model at small sample N.
T16	$CAIC = f + [1 + \ln(N)]k$	Selects the model that had least expected discrepancy from the true model.	Number of parameters and sample size.	Easy to calculate. Performs better than AIC at small sample size and large number of parameters.	
T17	$BIC = f + k\ln(N)$	Selects the model that is most likely to have generated the data in the Bayesian sense.	Number of parameters and sample size.	Easy to calculate. Performs well under large sample size.	Tends to select a model with too few parameters. Bad in recovering true model at small N.
T18	$CV = -\ln\int(y_{val} \mid \hat{\theta}_{cal})$	Selects the model that has more generalizability to the sample from the population.	Complexity penalty is implicit.	Easy to calculate. More consistent with the implication of generalizability.	Requires sample split. Estimates are often unreliable, especially for small sample size.
T19	$ECVI = f + \dfrac{2k}{N}$	Expected value of CV.	Number of parameters and sample size.	Can be calculated using one sample. More consistent with the implication of generalizability.	Assumes multivariate normality.
T20	$BMS = \ln\int_{\Theta} f(y \mid \hat{\theta})\pi(\theta)d\theta$	Selects the model with the highest mean likelihood of the data over the parameter space.	Number of parameters, sample size, and functional form of a model.	Includes more accurate measure on model complexity. Leads to more accurate model selection.	Computational burden. Hard to specify and calculate for most SEM models.

Note. AIC, Akaike information criterion; BIC, Bayesian information criterion; CV, cross-validation index; BMS, Bayesian model selection; f, minimized discrepancy function; k, the number of free parameters of the model; N, sample size; ln, natural logarithm; y_{val}, the validation sample; y_{cal}, the calibration sample; $\hat{\theta}_{cal}$, the parameter values estimated by the calibration sample; $\pi(\theta)$, the prior density of the parameters; Θ, the parameter space.

parameters and the natural logarithm of N. Unlike the AIC, the estimation of additional parameters will have a decreasing impact (penalty) in model selection as sample size increases. The model with the smallest BIC is selected. Alternatives to the BIC that may have better performance in some cases have been proposed (e.g., Sclove, 1987).

Cross-Validation Index

Browne and Cudeck (1993) proposed the cross-validation index (CV) as a means of estimating the generalizability of the estimate of model fit in a new sample from the same population. The CV involves two sequential steps: (1) first fitting a model to a calibration sample (y_{cal}) and (2) fitting the same model to a validation sample (y_{val}) with the parameter values fixed at those estimated in the first step. The resulting fit in the validation sample estimates the generalizability of the model to a new sample (see Table 13.2, Equation T18). Cudeck and Henly (1991) also noted that the CV is a measure of overall discrepancy between the fitted model and population covariance matrices.

In practice, the calibration and validation samples are often obtained by randomly splitting the observed data into two subsamples of equal size, which becomes impractical when the available sample is small. Browne and Cudeck (1989, 1993) proposed the expected cross-validation index (ECVI; see Table 13.2, Equation T19) based on a single sample under the assumption of multivariate normality. Conceptually, one can interpret the ECVI as the average discrepancy in the fitted covariance matrices between two samples of equal sample size across all possible combinations of two samples from the same population. Because it considers all possible combinations, it is expected to give more stable estimates than the CV. However, the ECVI can provide misleading information about model selection when the multivariate normality assumption is severely violated.

Bayesian Model Selection

Bayesian model selection (BMS), an approach developed in the Bayesian statistical framework, is theoretically useful but difficult to implement in many contexts (Pitt, Kim, & Myung, 2003; Wu, Myung, & Batchelder, 2010). BMS attempts to select the model with the highest mean likelihood of producing the data. To achieve this goal, BMS takes the logarithm of the mean like-lihood, averaged across the full range of parameter values and weighted by the prior density (Table 13.2, Equation T20). BMS assumes that there exists (1) a true known probability distribution (prior density[4]) from which the data were sampled and (2) a known parameter space that represents the potential values that each of the parameters may take on. BMS represents the Bayesian posterior probability of the model being correct given the data. BMS is potentially of particular value for comparing models that have different functional forms, but which have the same number of freely estimated parameters. In the context of SEM, an example in which this would occur is the comparison of a latent interaction model, $\eta = \gamma_1 \xi_1 + \gamma_2 \xi_2 + \gamma_3 \xi_1 \xi_2$, with a latent quadratic model, $\eta = \gamma_1 \xi_1 + \gamma_2 \xi_2 + \gamma_3 \xi_1^2$. To date, BMS has not been implemented in SEM, except in contexts involving the analysis of correlation rather than covariance structures (see Preacher, 2006, for an example).

Comparison of the Model Selection Indices

Table 13.2 compares six model fit indices for non-nested models. The AIC, CAIC, and BIC all measure model complexity using a number of parameters. The CAIC and BIC also include a weight for sample size, whereas the AIC does not, so that the CAIC and BIC tend to select simpler models than does the AIC at smaller N. BMS considers functional form in addition to the number of free parameters and sample size. Therefore, BMS is expected to perform more accurately in model selection than the AIC, CAIC, and BIC when the competing models have different functional forms. Given the pervasiveness of linear functional forms in SEM, this feature would only rarely be an advantage in practice. The chief disadvantage of BMS is the need to specify a known probability distribution and parameter space for the model, which is very difficult in practice. These can be specified for some well-defined problems, but even then the computational burden can be enormous. The CV implicitly builds model complexity into its calculation procedure. The definition of the CV also seems more consistent with the implication of generalizability. However, it often leads to an unreliable estimate of generalizability in small samples. ECVI provides more stable estimates than the CV but assumes multivariate normality. Wicherts and Dolan (2004) noted that the ECVI has a linear relationship with the AIC. Thus, it leads to the same rank-ordering of competing models as the AIC.

In contrast to fit indices, N plays an important role in choosing among competing models. More complex models are often preferred for large Ns, in the sense that they are more likely to replicate in a new sample, even though a simpler model might provide a better approximation to the population. In contrast, for small Ns, simpler models are typically preferred because there are not enough data to support the estimation of parameters with sufficient precision in a more complex model (MacCallum, 2003). Cudeck and Henly (1991) argued that this effect of sample size should be deemed not as undesirable but as *fundamental* to any statistical decision. It is important to choose the model that performs best in practice given the specified sample size.

SENSITIVITY OF KEY MODEL PARAMETERS

Beyond the consideration of fit, researchers are concerned about producing unbiased and precise estimates of key parameters in their hypothesized models. In some models, such as the Fishbein–Azjen model presented in Figure 13.1B, researchers may consider each of the paths to be equally important. In other models, such as the growth model presented in Figure 13.1C, researchers may believe that some parameters (e.g., the mean intercept and slope) are key parameters, whereas other parameters, such as the values of autocovariances between the Level 1 residuals, are only of importance to the extent they may produce more accurate estimates of the values of the key parameters or their standard errors (Kwok, West, & Green, 2007).

Several approaches have been proposed for probing the sensitivity of the estimates of the model parameters to changes in the model. Saris and colleagues (2009) proposed focusing on key model parameters. They suggest identifying a value that would reflect a meaningful change in that key parameter, and then conducting a series of simulation studies in which the values of other model parameters are varied within plausible ranges. This approach can be used to investigate each key parameter separately in turn, but it has not yet been extended to permit the simultaneous investigation of multiple parameters as a function of changes in other parts of the model. Millsap (in press) has extended this approach to permit the examination of alternative models that fall within a small specified range of the target model on the RMSEA. An alternative approach has been proposed by MacCallum, Lee, and Browne (in press) that more easily allows for the examination

of the joint sensitivity of multiple parameter estimates. They propose allowing a small, nonconsequential increase of F from its minimum f, followed by an examination of the range of values of the key parameters that are permissible given this slight reduction in fit. They find that all potential parameter estimates that satisfy the criterion will fall within an ellipsoid, with one dimension for each key parameter. Analysts can choose to consider dimensions corresponding to two or three of the key parameters simultaneously to permit visualization of the acceptable parameter space. In some cases, the range of parameter estimates will be reasonable and little difference in the conclusions of the model could result. In other cases, the range of potentially acceptable parameter estimates will be large, even permitting analysts to conclude that the direction of the parameter estimates is uncertain, providing the researcher with little confidence in the conclusions based on fitting the model.

DISTINGUISHING BETWEEN EQUIVALENT MODELS

Even when a model fits the data well, other equivalent models that fit the data equally well typically exist. Figure 13.3 presents three path models each having 1 *df* that provide an equally good fit to a 3×3 covariance structure. These models are data equivalent (see Williams, Chapter 15, this volume) but have distinctly different substantive interpretations since the directions of the paths vary. Figure 13.3A presents a model depicting the full mediation of an effect of X through M, which in turn influences Y. Figure 13.3B presents a model of the reverse causal effect, where Y affects M, which in turn affects X. Finally, Figure 13.3C presents a model in which M is a common cause of both X and Y. These models cannot be distinguished with cross-sectional data. Batchelder and Riefer (1999) proposed the use of model validation to distinguish between models. In the present example of a mediational model, developing manipulations that separately target the $X \rightarrow M$ path and the $M \rightarrow Y$ path could provide experimental data that would help the researcher to distinguish between the three models (Spencer, Zanna, & Fong, 2005). Alternatively, a longitudinal panel study (Cole & Maxwell, 2003) in which X, M, and Y were measured at Times 1, 2, and 3 could provide evidence that allows the researcher to establish the temporal precedence of the effects, thereby helping to rule out the alterna-

(A)

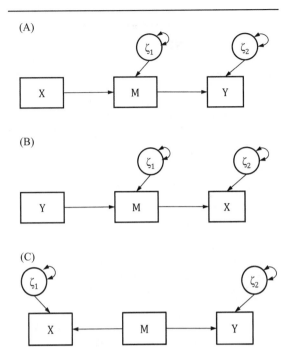

(B)

(C)

FIGURE 13.3. Three data-equivalent path models with cross-sectional data. (A) Mediational model: *X* causes *M*, which in turn causes *Y*. (B) Mediational model: *Y* causes *M*, which in turn causes *X*. (C) Common cause model: *M* causes both *X* and *Y*.

tive models. Conceivably, model validation strategies could even be extended to CFA models, for example, by developing a manipulation expected to affect (1) only the first factor (η_1) but not the second factor (η_2), or (2) only the second factor but not the first factor, as a means of helping to clarify the measurement structure (see Figure 13.1A). Although such strategies have been used widely in other areas (e.g., multinomial tree models), they have not seen much usage with structural equation models.

PARSIMONY REVISITED

The focus on achieving accurate estimates of key parameters raises another issue, the value of parsimony. Other things being equal, science clearly prefers (1) models with fewer parameters and (2) models that

make more precise estimates, so that they place more restrictions on the range of data structures they will fit (Preacher, 2006). The value of parsimony is clearly evident when models involving exploratory components are being compared. On the other hand, other things are not always equal. Cole, Ciesla, and Steiger (2007) have shown that key parameters in structural equation models can be seriously misestimated if theoretically justified residual correlations are not included in the model, even though minimal effects on overall model fit are observed. Marsh and Hau (1996) have shown that the failure to estimate relatively small correlated residuals in longitudinal confirmatory factor analysis models could have effects on estimates of the key stability parameters, even though model fit is little affected. In part for this reason, Bentler (1992) has argued that the assessment of fit and parsimony may often best be kept separate. This strategy lessens the possibility of deleting model parameters that provide important correction for artifacts that may plague the model, a practice that leads to distortion of key model parameters.

SUMMARY AND CONCLUSION

The assessment of fit provides researchers with an overall perspective on how well the theoretical model is able to reproduce the observed data. The χ^2 test statistic provides a statistical test of whether the residuals between the model-implied values and actual data are greater than would be expected on the basis of sampling error, assuming adequate sample size and multivariate normality. However, given that the hypothesized model is an approximation to the unknown true model, and that the χ^2 test statistic is affected by sample size, researchers have sought to develop alternative practical fit indices that provide measures of fit that are not related to sample size. A large number of these fit indices have been proposed, and the properties of several of the more widely used indices are presented in Table 13.1. Several of these (e.g., CFI/RNI, RMSEA, TLI, SRMR, GFI*) have desirable properties, and their estimates are *not* related to sample size. However, the quest for a standard cutoff criterion for each of the fit indices has proven to be elusive. Fit indices are affected by other model properties, such as the number of indicators and magnitudes of factor loadings. As fit indices are applied beyond CFA models to more complex models—multiple group models, multilevel models, growth models, and so forth—this quest for a single, standard cutoff criterion becomes increasingly chimerical and alternative strategies are needed.

One alternative strategy involves separate examination of the fit of each part of the model, for example, in multilevel models and growth curve models. This strategy can be extended even down to examination of the reproduction of the individual means or covariances to identify problem spots in the model. A second strategy involves hypothesizing multiple competing models and then using model selection indices to identify the optimal model. A third strategy involves close examination of key parameter estimates and their sensitivity to other aspects of the model. A fourth strategy involves the use of model validation procedures that can potentially help researchers distinguish between data-equivalent models or even models that produce similar values of practical fit indices. Nearly 20 years ago Bollen and Long (1993) wrote, "The test statistics and fit indices are very beneficial, but they are no replacement for sound judgment and substantive expertise" (p. 8). This advice remains true today, but sound judgment is now aided by several alternative strategies that provide supplemental information on the adequacy of the hypothesized model in accounting for the observed data.

ACKNOWLEDGMENTS

Stephen G. West was supported by a Forschungspreis from the Alexander von Humboldt Foundation during the writing of this chapter. We thank Peter Bentler, Patrick Curran, Edgar Erdfelder, Robert MacCallum, Roger Millsap, Victoria Savalei, editor Rick Hoyle, and an anonymous reviewer for comments on an earlier version of this chapter.

NOTES

1. A value of $\chi^2/df < 1$ can occur due to sampling variation, particularly in small samples.
2. Another difference between the GFI and R^2 is that structural equation models attempt to reproduce observed covariances, so the GFI is based on p^* residual covariances, whereas OLS regression attempts to reproduce observed scores on a dependent variable, so R^2 is based on N residual dependent variable scores.
3. In the case of the GFI, the GFI* appears to have the desired proportion of variance interpretation without the bias of underestimating the true value at small sample sizes.
4. The prior density of the parameter is the probability distribution over the parameter space, prior to seeing the data. The prior density represents the researcher's prior belief or prior

assumptions about the probabilities of different parameter values.

REFERENCES

Akaike, H. (1973). Information theory and an extension of the maximum likelihood principle. In B. N. Petrov & F. Csaki (Eds.), *Second International Symposium on Information Theory* (pp. 267–281). Budapest: Akademiai Kiado.

Anderson, J. C., & Gerbing, D. W. (1988). Structural equation modeling in practice: A review and recommended two-step approach. *Psychological Bulletin, 103*, 411–423.

Balderjahn, I. (1988). A note to Bollen's alternative fit measure. *Psychometrika, 53*, 283–285.

Batchelder, W. H., & Riefer, D. M. (1999). Theoretical and empirical review of multinomial process tree modeling. *Psychonomic Bulletin and Review, 6*, 57–86.

Bentler, P. M. (1983). Some contributions to efficient statistics in structural models: Specification and estimation of moment structures. *Psychometrika, 48*, 493–517.

Bentler, P. M. (1990). Comparative fit indexes in structural models. *Psychological Bulletin, 107*, 238–246.

Bentler, P. M. (1992). On the fit of models to covariances and methodology to the *Bulletin*. *Psychological Bulletin, 112*, 400–404.

Bentler, P. M. (1995). *EQS structural equations program manual*. Encino, CA: Multivariate Software.

Bentler, P. M., & Bonett, D. G. (1980). Significance tests and goodness of fit in the analysis of covariance structures. *Psychological Bulletin, 88*, 588–606.

Bentler, P. M., & Satorra, A. (2010). Testing model nesting and equivalence. *Psychological Methods, 15*, 111–123.

Bollen, K. A. (1986). Sample size and Bentler and Bonett's nonnormed fit index. *Psychometrika, 51*, 375–377.

Bollen, K. A. (1989). A new incremental fit index for general structural equation models. *Sociological Methods and Research, 17*, 303–316.

Bollen, K. A., & Long, J. S. (Eds.). (1993). *Testing structural equation models*. Newbury Park, CA: Sage.

Boomsma, A. (1982). The robustness of LISREL against small sample sizes in factor analysis models. In K.G. Jöreskog & H. Wold (Eds.), *Systems under indirect observation: Causality, structure, prediction* (Part I, pp. 149–173). Amsterdam: North Holland.

Box, G. E. P. (1979). Robustness in the strategy of scientific model building, In R. L. Launer & G. N. Wilkinson (Eds.), *Robustness in statistics* (pp. 201–236). New York: Academic Press.

Bozdogan, H. (1987). Model selection and Akaike's information criterion (AIC): The general theory and its analytical extensions. *Psychometrika, 52*, 345–370.

Browne, M. W. (1974). Generalized least squares estimators in the analysis of covariance structures. *South African Statistical Journal, 8*, 1–24.

Browne, M. W., & Arminger, G. (1995). Specification and estimation of mean and covariance structure models. In G. A. Arminger, C. C. Clogg, & M. E. Sobel (Eds.), *Handbook of statistical modeling for the social and behavioral sciences* (pp. 185–249). New York: Plenum Press.

Browne, M. W., & Cudeck, R. (1989). Single sample cross-validation indices for covariance structures. *Multivariate Behavioral Research, 24,* 445–455.

Browne, M. W., & Cudeck, R. (1993). Alternative ways of assessing model fit. In K. A. Bollen & J. S. Long (Eds.), *Testing structural equation models* (pp. 136–162). Newbury Park, CA: Sage.

Browne, M. W., MacCallum, R. C., Kim, C., Andersen, B. L., & Glaser, R. (2002). When fit indices and residuals are incompatible. *Psychological Methods, 7,* 403–421.

Chen, F., Curran, P. J., Bollen, K. A., Kirby, J., & Paxton, P. (2008). An empirical evaluation of the use of fixed cutoff points in RMSEA test statistic in structural equation models. *Sociological Methods and Research, 36,* 462–494.

Chen, F. F. (2007). Sensitivity of goodness of fit indices to lack of measurement invariance. *Structural Equation Modeling, 14,* 464–504.

Cheung, G. W., & Rensvold, R. B. (2002). Evaluating goodness-of-fit indices for testing measurement invariance. *Structural Equation Modeling, 9,* 233–255.

Cole, D. A., Ciesla, J. A., & Steiger, J. H. (2007). The insidious effects of failing to include design-driven correlated residuals in latent-variable covariance structure analysis. *Psychological Methods, 12,* 381–398.

Cole, D. A., & Maxwell, S. E. (2003). Testing mediational models with longitudinal data: Questions and tips in the use of structural equation modeling. *Journal of Abnormal Psychology, 112,* 558–577.

Cudeck, R., & Henly, S. J. (1991). Model selection in covariance structures analysis and the "problem" of sample size: A clarification. *Psychological Bulletin, 109,* 512–519.

Curran, P. J., Bollen, K. A., Chen, F., Paxton, P., & Kirby, J. B. (2003). Finite sampling properties of the point estimates and confidence intervals of the RMSEA. *Sociological Methods and Research, 32,* 208–252.

Davey, A., Savla, J., & Luo, Z. (2005). Issues in evaluating model fit with missing data. *Structural Equation Modeling, 12,* 578–597.

Diaconis, P. (1985). Theories of data analysis. In D. C. Hoaglin, F. Mosteller, & J. W. Tukey (Ed.), *Exploring data tables, trends, and shapes* (pp. 1–36). New York: Wiley.

Embretson, S. E., & Reise, S. P. (2000). *Item response theory for psychologists.* Mahwah, NJ: Erlbaum.

Fan, X., & Sivo, S. A. (2009). Using Δgoodness-of-fit indices in assessing mean structure invariance. *Structural Equation Modeling, 16,* 54–69.

Gallini, J. K., & Mandeville, G. K. (1984). An investigation of the effects of sample size and specification error on the fit of structural equation models. *Journal of Experimental Education, 53,* 9–19.

Goffin, R. D. (1993). A comparison of two new indices for the assessment of fit of structural equation models. *Multivariate Behavioral Research, 28,* 205–214.

Hu, L., & Bentler, P. M. (1995). Evaluating model fit. In R. H. Hoyle (Ed.), *Structural equation modeling: Concepts, issues, and applications* (pp. 76–99). Thousand Oaks, CA: Sage.

Hu, L., & Bentler, P. M. (1998). Fit indices in covariance structure modeling: Sensitivity to underparameterized model misspecification. *Psychological Methods, 3,* 424–453.

Hu, L., & Bentler, P. M. (1999). Cutoff criteria for fit indexes in covariance structure analysis: Conventional criteria versus new alternatives. *Structural Equation Modeling, 6,* 1–55.

Ishiguro, M., Sakamoto, Y., & Kitagawa, G. (1997). Bootstrapping log likelihood and EIC, an extension of AIC. *Annals of the Institute of Statistical Mathematics, 49,* 411–434.

Jackson, D. L., Gillapsy, J. A., Jr., & Purc-Stephenson, R. (2009). Reporting practices in confirmatory factor analysis: An overview and some recommendations. *Psychological Methods, 14,* 6–23.

James, L. R., Mulaik, S. A., & Brett, J. M. (1982). *Causal analysis: Assumptions, models, and data.* Beverly Hills, CA: Sage.

Jöreskog, K. G. (1967). Some contributions to maximum likelihood factor analysis. *Psychometrika, 32,* 443–482.

Jöreskog, K. G. (1969). A general approach to confirmatory maximum likelihood factor analysis. *Psychometrika, 34,* 183–202.

Jöreskog, K. G., & Sörbom, D. (1981). *LISREL V: Analysis of linear structural relationships by maximum likelihood and least squares methods.* Chicago: International Educational Services.

Kaplan, D. (1990). Evaluating and modifying covariance structure models: A review and recommendation. *Multivariate Behavioral Research, 25,* 237–155.

Kenny, D. A., & McCoach, D. B. (2003). Effect of the number of variables on measures of fit in structural equation modeling. *Structural Equation Modeling, 10,* 333–351.

Klein, A. G., & Schermelleh-Engel, K. (2010). A measure for detecting poor fit due to omitted nonlinear terms in SEM. *Advances in Statistical Analysis, 94,* 157–166.

Kwok, O.-M., West, S. G., & Green, S. B. (2007). The impact of misspecifying the within-subject covariance structure in multiwave longitudinal multilevel models: A Monte Carlo study. *Multivariate Behavioral Research, 42,* 557–592.

MacCallum, R. C. (1986). Specification searches in covariance structure modeling. *Psychological Bulletin, 100,* 107–120.

MacCallum, R. C. (2003). Working with imperfect models. *Multivariate Behavioral Research, 38,* 113–139.

MacCallum, R. C., Lee, T., & Browne, M. W. (in press). Fungible parameter estimates in latent growth curve models.

In M. Edwards & R. C. MacCallum (Eds.), *Current issues in the theory and application of latent variable models.* New York: Routledge.

MacCallum, R. C., Roznowski, M., & Necowitz, L. B. (1992). Model modifications in covariance structure analysis: The problem of capitalization on chance. *Psychological Bulletin, 111,* 490–504.

MacCallum, R. C., Widaman, K. F., Preacher, K. J., & Hong, S. (2001). Sample size in factor analysis: The role of model error. *Multivariate Behavioral Research, 36,* 611–637.

Maiti, S. S., & Mukherjee, B. N. (1990). A note on the distributional properties of the Jöreskog–Sörbom fit indices. *Psychometrika, 55,* 721–726.

Marsh, H. W. (1995). The $\Delta 2$ and χ^2 I2 fit indices for structural equation models: A brief note of clarification. *Structural Equation Modeling, 2,* 246–254.

Marsh, H. W., Balla, J. R., & Hau, K. T. (1996). An evaluation of incremental fit indices: A clarification of mathematical and empirical properties. In G. A. Marcoulides & R. E. Schumacker (Eds.), *Advanced structural equation modeling: Issues and techniques* (pp. 315–353). Mahwah, NJ: Erlbaum.

Marsh, H. W., Balla, J. R., & McDonald, R. P. (1988). Goodness-of-fit indexes in confirmatory factor analysis: The effect of sample size. *Psychological Bulletin, 103,* 391–410.

Marsh, H. W., & Hau, K.-T. (1996). Assessing goodness of fit: Is parsimony always desirable? *Journal of Experimental Education, 64,* 364–390.

Marsh, H. W., Hau, K.-T., Balla, J. R., & Grayson, E. (1998). Is more ever too much?: The number of indicators per factor in confirmatory factor analysis. *Multivariate Behavioral Research, 33,* 181–220.

Marsh, H. W., Hau, K.-T., & Grayson, D. (2005). Goodness of fit in structural equation models. In A. Maydeu-Olivares & J. J. McArdle (Eds.), *Contemporary psychometrics* (pp. 275–340). Mahwah, NJ: Erlbaum.

Marsh, H. W., Hau, K. T., & Wen, Z. (2004). In search of golden rules: Comment on hypothesis-testing approaches to setting cutoff values for fit indexes and dangers in overgeneralizing Hu and Bentler's (1999) findings. *Structural Equation Modeling, 11,* 320–341.

McDonald, R. P. (1999). *Test theory: A unified treatment.* Mahwah, NJ: Erlbaum.

McDonald, R. P. (2010). Structural models and the art of approximation. *Perspectives on Psychological Science, 5,* 675–686.

McDonald, R. P., & Ho, M.-H. R. (2002). Principles and practice in reporting structural equation analyses. *Psychological Methods, 7,* 64–82.

McDonald, R. P., & Marsh, H. W. (1990). Choosing a multivariate model: Noncentrality and goodness of fit. *Psychological Bulletin, 107,* 247–255.

Meehl, P. E. (1967). Theory-testing in psychology and physics: A methodological paradox. *Philosophy of Science, 34,* 103–115.

Menard, S. (2000). Coefficients of determination for multiple logistic regression analysis. *American Statistician, 54,* 17–24.

Millsap, R. E. (in press). A simulation paradigm for evaluating approximate fit. In M. Edwards & R. C. MacCallum (Eds.), *Current issues in the theory and application of latent variable models.* New York: Routledge.

Mulaik, S. A., James, L. R., Van Alstine, J., Bennett, N., Lind, S., & Stilwell, C. D. (1989). Evaluation of goodness-of-fit indices for structural equation models. *Psychological Bulletin, 105,* 430–445.

Myung, J. I., & Pitt, M. A. (2004). Model comparison methods. *Methods in Enzymology, 383,* 351–366.

Pitt, M. A., Kim, W., & Myung, I. J. (2003). Flexibility versus generalizability in model selection. *Psychonomic Bulletin and Review, 10,* 29–44.

Preacher, K. J. (2006). Quantifying parsimony in structural equation modeling. *Multivariate Behavioral Research, 41,* 227–259.

Raftery, A. (1995). Bayesian model selection in social research. *Sociological Methodology, 25,* 111–196.

Ryu, E., & West, S. G. (2009). Level-specific evaluation of model fit in multilevel structural equation modeling. *Structural Equation Modeling, 16,* 583–601.

Saris, W. E., Satorra, A., & van der Veld, W. M. (2009). Testing structural equation models or detection of misspecifications? *Structural Equation Modeling, 16,* 561–582.

Savalei, V. (2011). *The relationship between RMSEA and model misspecification in CFA models.* Unpublished manuscript, Psychology Department, University of British Columbia, Vancouver, BC, Canada.

Sclove, L. S. (1987). Application of model-selection criteria for some problems in multivariate analysis. *Psychometrika, 52,* 333–343.

Sobel, M. E., & Bohrnstedt, G. W. (1985). Use of null models in evaluating the fit of covariance structure models. In N. B. Tuma (Ed.), *Sociological methodology* (pp. 152–178). San Francisco: Jossey-Bass.

Spencer, S. J., Zanna, M. P., & Fong, G. T. (2005). Establishing a causal chain: Why experiments are often more effective than mediational analyses in examining psychological processes. *Journal of Personality and Social Psychology, 89,* 845–851.

Steiger, J. H. (1989). EZPATH: *A supplementary module for SYSTAT and SYGRAPH.* Evanston, IL: SYSTAT.

Steiger, J. H. (1990). Structural model evaluation and modification: An interval estimation approach. *Multivariate Behavioral Research, 25,* 173–180.

Steiger, J. H., & Lind, J. C. (1980, May). *Statistically-based tests for the number of common factors.* Paper presented at the annual meeting of the Psychometric Society, Iowa City, IA.

Steiger, J. H., Shapiro, A., & Browne, M. W. (1985). On the multivariate asymptotic distribution of sequential chi-square statistics. *Psychometrika, 50,* 253–264.

Sugawara, H. M., & MacCallum, R. C. (1993). Effect of estimation method on incremental fit indexes for covariance structure models. *Applied Psychological Measurement, 17,* 365–377.

Tanaka, J. S. (1993). Multifaceted conceptions of fit. In K. A. Bollen & J. S. Long (Eds.), *Testing structural equation models* (pp. 10–39). Newbury Park, CA: Sage.

Tanaka, J. S., & Huba, G. J. (1985). A fit index for covariance structure models under arbitrary GLS estimation. *British Journal of Mathematical and Statistical Psychology, 38,* 197–201.

Taylor, A. B. (2008). *Two new methods of studying the performance of SEM fit indices.* Doctoral dissertation, Arizona State University, Tempe, AZ.

Tucker, L., Koopman, R., & Linn, R. (1969). Evaluation of factor analytic research procedures by means of simulated correlation matrices. *Psychometrika, 34,* 421–459.

Tucker, L. R., & Lewis, C. (1973). A reliability coefficient for maximum likelihood factor analysis. *Psychometrika, 38,* 1–10.

Wheaton, B., Muthén, B., Alwin, D. F., & Summers, G. F. (1977). Assessing reliability and stability in panel models. *Sociological Methodology, 8,* 84–136.

Wherry, R. J., Sr. (1931). A new formula for predicting the shrinkage of the coefficient of multiple correlation. *Annals of Mathematical Statistics, 2,* 440–457.

Wicherts, J. M., & Dolan, C. V. (2004). A cautionary note on the use of information fit indexes in covariance structure modeling with means. *Structural Equation Modeling, 11,* 45–50.

Widaman, K. F., & Reise, S. P. (1997). Exploring the measurement invariance of psychological instruments: Applications in the substance use domain. In K. J. Bryant, M. Windle, & S. G. West (Eds.), *The science of prevention: Methodological advances from alcohol and substance abuse research* (pp. 281–324). Washington, DC: American Psychological Association.

Widaman, K. F., & Thompson, J. S. (2003). On specifying the null model for incremental fit indices in structural equation modeling. *Psychological Methods, 8,* 16–37.

Wilkinson, L., & Task Force on Statistical Inference. (1999). Statistical methods in psychology journals: Guidelines and explanations. *American Psychologist, 54,* 594–604.

Wu, H., Myung, J. I., & Batchelder, W. H. (2010). On the minimum description length complexity of multinomial processing tree models. *Journal of Mathematical Psychology, 54,* 291–303.

Wu, W., & West, S. G. (2010). Sensitivity of SEM fit indices to misspecifications in growth curve models: A simulation study. *Multivariate Behavioral Research, 45,* 420–452.

Wu, W., West, S. G., & Taylor, A. B. (2009). Growth curve modeling: Evaluating model fit and model selection. *Psychological Methods, 14,* 183–201.

Yuan, K.-H. (2005). Fit indices versus test statistics. *Multivariate Behavioral Research, 40,* 115–148.

Yuan, K.-H., & Bentler, P. M. (2007). Multilevel covariance structure analysis by fitting multiple single-level models. *Sociological Methodology, 37,* 53–82.

CHAPTER 14

Model Modification in Structural Equation Modeling

Chih-Ping Chou
Jimi Huh

Structural equation modeling (SEM) has been a popular analytical approach in social science research, especially since the development of computer programs such as LISREL (Jöreskog & Sörbom, 2006), EQS (Bentler, 2006), Amos (Arbuckle, 2006), and Mplus (Muthén & Muthén, 2007). The application of SEM involves an iterative process consisting of five consecutive steps: model specification, model identification, model estimation, model fitting, and model modification (Bollen & Long, 1993; Schumacker & Lomax, 2010). The objective of an application of SEM is to obtain an adequate model that is theoretically meaningful, with acceptable fit to the data. Whereas the meaningfulness of a model depends on the subjective judgment of the researchers, acceptable fit to the data frequently relies on objective statistical criteria for model fitting. The model fitting step is therefore critical in determining when the iterative process of an SEM application should be terminated. Model modification is considered if the model is not adequate and a new model needs to be specified, leading to a new iteration.

In practice, a model is considered adequate if it consists of a compact set of parameters supported by substantive theories and has an acceptable statistical or empirical fit to the data. However, if the fit of the model being evaluated is considered inadequate, model modification, or specification searching, becomes a viable option. An application of SEM is completed once the fit of a model is considered adequate. The model is treated as the final model in a particular application of SEM and results can be reported. It should be noted that the final model is not unique in terms of theoretical meaningfulness and model fitting. There exist a number of alternative and near equivalent models that also yield adequate fit to the data. There are also numerous equivalent models that fit the data equally well (for further discussions on alternative models, see Cliff, 1983; Lee & Hershberger, 1990; MacCallum, Wegener, Uchino, & Fabrigar, 1993; Stelzl, 1986; Tomarken & Waller, 2003; Williams, Chapter 15, this volume). Substantive theories, therefore, should always guide the model specification and model modification steps of an application of SEM.

Two considerations are involved in determining whether a model is adequate. The parsimony of a model is determined by the number of free parameters it includes. Model fit is evaluated primarily by statistical criteria or empirically based fit indices. A model is considered inadequate, requiring modification, if it either (1) has an adequate fit to the data with excessive parameters (i.e., overparameterization) or (2) does not have an adequate fit to the data (i.e., underparameterization;

Hu & Bentler, 1998). In the former case, the initial model needs to be simplified to achieve parsimony by imposing constraints on (or deleting) free parameters to obtain a more compact model. In the latter case, the initial model needs to be modified by releasing constraints on (or freeing) fixed parameters to obtain better fit to the data. The strategies used in these two model modification approaches are termed "backward search" and "forward search," respectively.

Conventionally, the forward or backward specification search approaches are carried out by calculating the difference of χ^2 test statistics for two nested models to evaluate whether the two models are significantly different in model fit. These two approaches can be more efficiently carried out using the Wald (*W*; Wald, 1943) and Lagrange multiplier (*LM*; Aitchison & Silvey, 1958; Lee & Bentler, 1980; Rao, 1948; Silvey, 1959) tests. Because of the a posteriori nature of searches for more adequate models, model modification has been criticized for its data-driven approach (Green, Thompson, & Poirier, 1999; MacCallum, 1986; MacCallum & Austin, 2000; MacCallum, Roznowski, & Necowitz, 1992; McDonald & Ho, 2002). Nevertheless, model modification is difficult to avoid in practice and has become common in the research community. This is especially the case because complex models involving latent variables rarely provide an acceptable fit to the data (Bollen & Long, 1993).

The purpose of this chapter is to describe the model modification step in SEM. In the following section, the concept of nested models in which the likelihood ratio (*LR*, i.e., chi-square difference test), *W*, and *LM* tests can be applied is introduced. Statistical theory of the *LR*, *W*, and *LM* tests is discussed. Two examples from MacCallum (1990) and Chou and Bentler (1990) illustrate the model modification process to highlight information needed to obtain adequate models. Stepwise approaches for the *LM* and *W* tests and the multiple-sample approach for the *LM* test are also discussed. Recommendations based on results of two simulation studies are used to demonstrate how to conduct a successful search.

STATISTICAL BACKGROUND

Some statistical concepts required in the model modification step in SEM are introduced in this section.

Nested Model Comparisons

Specification of a structural equation model is performed by defining fixed and particularly free parameters in a model. If a model is identified, model fit statistics that compare the data structure based on the model and the observed data structure can be generated. Frequently used notation for the number of free parameters and the number of observed data points are q and p^*, respectively, with $p^* = p \times (p + 1)/2$ where p is the number of variables involved in parameter estimation and model evaluation. For model modification, nested models need to be developed to fit the same data set, and comparisons need to be made between their corresponding test statistics. One model, M_1, is considered to be nested within the other model, M_2, if the set of free parameters specified in M_1 is a subset of the free parameters specified in M_2. More specifically, let θ_1 be the set of q_1 free parameters specified in M_1 and θ_2 the set of q_2 parameters in M_2. M_1 is nested within M_2 (expressed as $M_1 < M_2$) if θ_1 is a subset of θ_2 (i.e., $\theta_1 \subset \theta_2$). Fitting the same data set involving p observed variables with p^* data points on variances and covariances, M_1, therefore, yields degrees of freedom $df_1 = p^* - q_1$ and for M_2, $df_2 = p^* - q_2$. These two nested models, M_1 and M_2, are used throughout this chapter to illustrate various statistical concepts involved in model modification.

For two nested models, two approaches to specification searching can be considered for model modification. One is to search from M_1 (the more restricted model) to M_2 (the more general model) if the fit of M_1 is not acceptable and needs to be improved. The other is from M_2 to M_1 if M_2 has acceptable fit and needs to be simplified. These two approaches to specification searching are analogous to the forward and backward stepwise procedures, respectively, in regression analysis. Searching from a more restricted model to a more general model (e.g., from M_1 to M_2) is considered a forward search approach, which requires adding free parameters to the more restricted model. Adding a free parameter to M_1 is the same as releasing the constraint on that parameter fixed at a particular value in M_1. Searching from the more general model to the more restricted model (e.g., from M_2 to M_1), on the other hand, takes a backward search approach by fixing, or constraining, free parameters in M_2 to produce M_1. Conditions relevant to these two approaches to model modification are summarized in Table 14.1.

TABLE 14.1 Conditions Associated with Specification Searching (Model Modification)

Condition	Forward search	Backward search
Purpose	Model improvement	Model simplification
No. of free parameters (q)	Increase	Decrease
Constraints (r)	Reduce	Impose
Degrees of freedom (df)	Decrease	Increase
χ^2 goodness-of-fit test statistic	Decrease	Increase

To summarize, the decision about whether to conduct backward or forward specification searching is straightforward. When the initial model has adequate model fitting statistics and model simplification is needed, backward searching can be performed to drop unnecessary and nonsignificant parameters. Constraining free parameters can primarily be accomplished by imposing constraints on, or dropping, the free parameters (e.g., constraining multiple free parameters to be equal, or fixing free parameters to zero) in the more general model. Forward search is for model fitting improvement and is carried out by releasing constraints, particularly constraints on parameters that were fixed to zero in the more limited model. Generally, procedures involved in forward searching are more complicated and computationally intensive than procedures involved in backward searching. However, both backward and forward searching, as presented in this chapter, are based on the comparison of nested models constructed with consideration of relevant substantive theories.

Test Statistics for Model Modification

Three test statistics that follow a χ^2 distribution are commonly used for model modification purposes. These test statistics are equivalent asymptotically (i.e., when N approaches infinity) when the null hypothesis is correct. The *LR*, or χ^2 difference, test is performed by computing the difference between the χ^2 statistics associated with two nested models. Using the example of M_1 being nested in M_2 discussed earlier, both M_1 and M_2 need to be estimated first to obtain their corresponding χ^2 test statistics, $\chi^2(M_1)$ and $\chi^2(M_2)$, re-

spectively. After estimating the test statistics for both models, the test statistic of the more general M_2 model can be subtracted from that of the more restricted M_1 model $[\chi^2(M_1) - \chi^2(M_2)]$. The difference of the two χ^2 statistics can then be used to evaluate if the two nested models are significantly different.

The other tests used for model modification are the *W* test and *LM* test. Unlike the *LR* test, which requires evaluating both M_1 and M_2, the *W* and *LM* tests only need to estimate one of these models. The *W* test for backward searching estimates a more general model (e.g., M_2) and uses estimation results to search toward more restricted models (e.g., M_1) by dropping nonsignificant parameters without actually estimating the more restricted models. The *LM* test, on the other hand, starts with a restricted model and searches for parameters to be freed in order to obtain the models that can yield better fit to the data.

Statistical Background for the *LR*, *W*, and *LM* Tests

Statistical theory for the *LR*, *W*, and *LM* tests for structural equation models is reviewed in this section. Assume a structural equation model is developed to analyze a data set with N participants and p variables. Let S be the $p \times p$ covariance matrix of this sample randomly selected from a population with mean vector of μ and covariance matrix of Σ_0. The null hypothesis being tested in SEM is that the model-based covariance matrix is the same as the population covariance matrix, H_0: $\Sigma = \Sigma_0$, where $\Sigma = \Sigma(\theta)$ is the model-based covariance matrix that is a function of a vector of free parameters, θ, specified in the model. Various χ^2 distribution-based model fit criteria have been developed to evaluate the appropriateness of the specification of a structural equation model. The maximum likelihood (ML) estimation method is used as an example to illustrate the *LR*, *W*, and *LM* tests used in model modification procedures. The algorithms involved in model modification using the ML estimation method can be similarly generalized to that of other estimation methods. In the ML estimation method, the function to be minimized is:

$$F(\theta) = \log|\Sigma(\theta)| + \text{tr}(S\Sigma(\theta)^{-1}) - \log|S| - p \quad \textbf{(14.1)}$$

The null hypothesis of SEM, H_0: $\Sigma = \Sigma_0$, can be tested with the χ^2 goodness-of-fit test statistic, which equals the sample size N minus 1 multiplied by the ML function, or $nF(\theta)$ with $n = N - 1$.

LR Test

The *LR* test evaluates the difference between the χ^2 test statistics of two nested models. The *LR* test evaluates whether the χ^2 difference, which also has a χ^2 distribution under the null hypothesis, is significant, a test of the null hypothesis that the two model-based covariance matrices are not different, $H_0 : \Sigma(\theta_1) = \Sigma(\theta_2)$. Using the example of M_1 and M_2 and their corresponding parameter vectors θ_1 and θ_2, respectively, θ_1 is a subset of θ_2. Parameter vector θ_2 can be expressed as (θ_1, θ_r), with θ_r being the vector containing the r free parameters that differentiate the M_1 and M_2 models. With q_1 free parameters in the θ_1 vector and r free parameters in the θ_r vector, there are, therefore, q_2 free parameters in the θ_2 vector with $q_2 = q_1 + r$. Fitting the same covariance matrix with p variables, the degrees of freedom associated with M_1 and M_2 are $df_1 = (p^* - q_1)$ and $df_2 = (p^* - q_2) = (p^* - q_1 - r)$, respectively. The *LR* test can be carried out using the χ^2 goodness-of-fit test statistics of the two models obtained from $\hat{\theta}_1$ and $\hat{\theta}_2$, $nF(\hat{\theta}_1)$ and $nF(\hat{\theta}_2)$, or $\chi^2(M_1)$ and $\chi^2(M_2)$, respectively. The degrees of freedom associated with the *LR* test statistic is the difference of the degrees of freedom of the two nested models being compared, or $r = (q_2 - q_1) = (df_1 - df_2)$. For simplicity of illustration, θ_r is fixed at 0 in the M_1 model. Comparing the difference between M_1 and M_2 is the same as testing if θ_r is not different from 0, $H_0 : \theta_r = 0$. Let the estimated θ_1 and θ_2 be $\hat{\theta}_1$ and $\hat{\theta}_2$, respectively; the *LR* test statistic can therefore be expressed as

$$\text{LR} = n[F(\hat{\theta}_1) - F(\hat{\theta}_2)] \sim \chi_r^2 \qquad (14.2)$$

W Test

The *W* test is a test to evaluate whether one or more free parameters in a model is different from zero. The purpose of the *W* test is to simplify an initially well-fitting model by dropping nonsignificant free parameters. The approach is consistent with the common practice in SEM applications of examining the significance of each free parameter specified in the model that is considered statistically acceptable. The parameters are assumed to be normally distributed and the significance test for each parameter is evaluated using the *z*-test, which is referred to as the *t*-value in LISREL. The square of the standard *z*-statistic is the same as the univariate *W* test statistic. Starting with the more general M_2 model, the *W* test focuses on the test of the free parameters in θ_r to evaluate whether these parameters are significantly

different from 0. Let $\mathbf{H}$ be the information matrix associated with the q_2 free parameters in the M_2 model, or θ_2. The diagonal of the $\mathbf{H}^{-1}$ contains the standard errors of the estimates of all the free parameters in θ_2. With an $r \times q_2$ selection matrix $\mathbf{L}$, the corresponding variance and covariance components in $\mathbf{H}^{-1}$ for all the free parameters in θ_r can be properly selected. The multivariate *W* statistic is asymptotically distributed as a χ^2 variate with r degrees of freedom:

$$W = n\,\hat{\theta}_r'(\hat{\mathbf{L}}\,\hat{\mathbf{H}}^{-1}\hat{\mathbf{L}}')\hat{\theta}_r \sim \chi_r^2 \qquad (14.3)$$

The univariate *W* statistic for each of the parameters i in θ_r can be expressed as

$$W_i = n\hat{\theta}_i\hat{\mathbf{H}}_{ii}^{-1}\,\hat{\theta}_i = n\theta_i^2 / \hat{\mathbf{H}}_{ii} \sim \chi_1^2 \qquad (14.4)$$

where $\hat{\theta}_i$ is one of the element in $\hat{\theta}_r$ and $\hat{\mathbf{H}}_{ii}$ is the ith element in the diagonal of the $\mathbf{H}$ matrix.

LM Test

Statistical theory relevant to the *LM* test is more complicated relative to theory for the *LR* and *W* tests. Nevertheless, the basic idea of using the *LM* test for forward specification searching is similar to that of backward searching using the *W* test. To better understand how a forward search is carried out, it is helpful to conceptualize a more limited model (e.g., M_1) as a more general model (e.g., M_2) with some free parameters constrained at 0. For example, with M_1 nested within M_2, M_1 containing q_1 free parameters is the same as M_2 with $q_2 = q_1 + r$ free parameters, while constraining the r additional free parameters in M_2 to 0. From this perspective, a model is defined by not only a set of free parameters but also a set of fixed parameters. Given all the potential parameters that could be used to specify a model, there is generally a greater number of fixed parameters than free parameters. The *LM* test focuses on which of those fixed parameters could be freed in order to improve model fit.

As discussed earlier (see Equation 14.1), minimizing the fit function $F(\theta_1)$ for M_1 is equivalent to minimizing the function of $F(\theta_2)$ for M_2 while assuming $h(\theta_2) = \theta_r = 0$. For the forward search, there exists a *LM* vector (λ) and matrices of derivatives $\Delta(\theta) = (\partial F/\partial\theta)$ and $\mathbf{L} = (\partial h/\partial\theta)$ in minimizing $F(\theta)$ with constraints of $h(\theta) = 0$ such that

$$\Delta(\hat{\theta}) + \hat{\mathbf{L}}\hat{\lambda} = 0 \text{ and } h(\hat{\theta}) = 0 \qquad (14.5)$$

Under the null hypothesis $h(\theta) = 0$, the asymptotic joint distributions of $n^{1/2}(\hat{\theta} - \theta)$ and $n^{1/2}\lambda$ are multivariate normal with zero mean vectors and covariance matrices, $\mathbf{M}$ and $\mathbf{R}$, respectively. The covariance matrices of $\mathbf{M}$ and $\mathbf{R}$ can be derived from the inverse of the information matrix $\mathbf{H}(\theta)$ and $\mathbf{L}$. The multivariate LM statistic is asymptotically distributed as a χ^2 variate:

$$LM = n\hat{\lambda}_r'\mathbf{R}^{-1} \quad \hat{\lambda}_r \sim \chi_r^2 \qquad (14.6)$$

It should be noted that $h(\theta) = 0$ is a very generalized expression of equality constraints. It can be used to constrain combinations of several parameters to be equal to 0 as illustrated in this chapter. In the case of evaluating the more restricted M_1 in a forward specification search, the LM statistic can be used to evaluate the null hypothesis: $h(\theta_2) = \theta_r = 0$. The univariate LM statistic, which is also a χ^2 variate with 1 df, can be used to evaluate whether a specific parameter in θ_r is equal to 0:

$$LM_i = n\hat{\lambda}_i^2 / \mathbf{R}_{ii} \sim \chi_{r1}^2 \qquad (14.7)$$

with $\mathbf{R}_{ii}$ being the ith diagonal of the $\mathbf{R}$ matrix. Modification indices provided in LISREL (Jöreskog & Sörbom, 2006) are the same as the univariate LM statistics presented earlier. Additional technical details of the LM test can be found in papers by Chou and Bentler (1990), Engle (1984), Saris and Satorra (1987), Satorra (1989), and Sörbom (1989).

The LR, W, and LM test statistics have asymptotically a central χ^2 distribution when the null hypothesis is true. However, the three test statistics have noncentral χ^2 distribution when the null hypothesis is not true or does not hold exactly. A noncentral χ^2 distribution can be specified by a noncentrality parameter (ncp) and corresponding degrees of freedom. The ncp reflects the degree of model misspecification of the model being evaluated and it is equal to zero under the central χ^2 distribution. More technical details on the ncp can be found in Saris and Satorra (1993) and Satorra (1989).

In summary, the LR, W, and LM tests discussed in this section can all be used to evaluate whether a specific set of parameters is different from zero by comparing two nested models. With M_1 being nested within M_2 and θ_r the parameter set differentiating the two models, all three tests can be used to evaluate if $\theta_r = 0$. The LR test requires estimating both M_1 and M_2, whereas the W and LM tests only require estimating one model, either M_2 or M_1, respectively. The parameters in θ_r that dis-

tinguish the two models are treated as free parameters in M_2 to be dropped using the W test, whereas they are treated as fixed parameters in M_1 to be freed using the LM test.

Forward specification searching is more commonly utilized in practice, as the need to improve model fit is more frequently encountered than is simplifying a model. However, the success in finding the correct model is usually low in forward searching and depends very highly on the initial model selected in the modification process (Chou & Bentler, 1990; MacCallum, 1986; Saris, Satorra, & ven der Veld, 2009). Although backward searching may be more successful in leading to the correct model (Chou & Bentler, 2002), it has more serious deficiencies when sample size is small (Chou & Bentler, 1990). A more careful examination of the causal sequence and more restricted searching focused on a predetermined set of parameters are critical in finding the correct model (Chou & Bentler, 1990, 2002; MacCallum, 1986).

LM Test in SEM with Multiple Groups

The LM test discussed earlier is primarily for models fit to data from a single group. However, Equation 14.5 with the condition $h(\theta) = 0$ while minimizing the ML function $F(\theta)$ is a very general expression of imposing equality constraints on θ. The simplest form of $h(\theta) = 0$ is to constrain some of the parameters in θ equal to 0. The equality constraints of $h(\theta) = 0$ can be extended to a multiple-group approach while minimizing the multiple-group ML function $F(\Theta)$

$$F(\Theta) = \sum_{1}^{G} n_g F(\theta_g) \qquad (14.8)$$

Similarly, LMs also exist when minimizing the $F(\Theta)$ in Equation 14.8 subject to the conditions of $h(\Theta) = 0$. The Θ vector consists of all the parameters from different groups and therefore permits the constraints of equality of parameters across groups. Univariate LM statistic may be used to evaluate each equality constraint between groups, and multivariate LM statistics can be calculated to evaluate a set of cross-group equality constraints. Tests of equality across groups are frequently conducted to examine moderated effects (e.g., Corning, 2002; Frazier, Tix, & Barron, 2004; Hoyle & Robinson, 2003) or measurement invariance between groups (e.g., Byrne, Shavelson, & Muthén, 1989; Byrne & Stewart, 2006; Pentz & Chou, 1994).

Stepwise *LM* and *W* Tests

The *LM* and *W* tests discussed earlier are multivariate statistical approaches for significance tests of a set of *r* parameters (or $\theta_r = 0$), but these procedures can be decomposed into *r* different steps and implemented in a stepwise fashion. We use the *LM* test to illustrate the stepwise procedure. With a total of *r* parameters to be added, the sequence for selecting each of the parameters step by step into the model is determined based on certain statistical criteria.

The strategy is analogous to the stepwise procedure used in the regression analysis. Let *y* be the dependent variable and x_1 and x_2 be two sets of covariates in a regression model. A multiple regression model without certain covariates, say, x_2, is the same as a regression model with those covariates while constraining their corresponding regression weights at 0, that is,

$$y = \alpha + x_1\beta_1 + e \quad \Rightarrow \quad y = \alpha + x_1\beta_1 + x_2\beta_2 + e,$$
$$\text{subject to } \beta_2 = 0.$$

The forward stepwise procedure for multiple regression analysis includes one predictor in x_2, or releases corresponding constraint in $\beta_2 = 0$, at a time. The predictor added to the model at each step is the one projected to have the strongest impact, or the largest increment in R^2, on the outcome. Similarly, the *LM* test in SEM selects the fixed parameter that, if freed, would yield the largest projected improvement in model fit. Analogously, for the backward stepwise procedure in regression analysis, the predictors with the weakest impact on the outcome measure are dropped from the model one at a time until all the nonsignificant predictors are deleted. Similarly, the *W* test in SEM drops one parameter at a time until there are no more nonsignificant predictors to be dropped. The stepwise procedures for both *LM* and *W* tests have been implemented in the EQS program (Bentler, 2006).

The purpose of the stepwise application of the *LM* and *W* tests is to partition the multivariate χ^2 cumulative statistic into as many steps, or degrees of freedom, as the number of parameters involved. At each step, one parameter is changed from fixed to free, or vice versa. A multivariate χ^2 cumulative statistic and a univariate χ^2 increment statistic associated with the inclusion or exclusion of the current parameter can be calculated. The multivariate statistic is used to test the null hypothesis that the set of all the parameters included up to the current step is equal to 0. The univariate, or χ^2

increment, statistic provides information on the unique contribution of the currently included parameter to the multivariate χ^2 cumulative statistic. The univariate χ^2 increment statistics add up to the multivariate χ^2 cumulative statistic at the completion of each step. Different criteria are used in selecting a parameter at each step between forward and backward searches. The parameter selected at a specific step of the *LM* test is the one that yields the largest *LM* univariate χ^2 increment statistic considering all other parameters that already have been selected in the previous steps. The parameter selected at a specific step of the *W* test is, on the other hand, the one with the smallest *W* univariate χ^2 increment statistic considering all the parameters already selected in previous steps. For both the *LM* and *W* tests, models are not reestimated as new parameters are selected into the test procedure.

To demonstrate how parameters are considered at each step of the *LM* or *W* stepwise procedure, we use the *LM* test searching from M_1 to M_2 as an example. Similarity between the *LM* test and forward searching using *LR* tests is also discussed in this section. Let θ_r be a set of *r* fixed parameters differentiating M_1 and M_2 and targeted by the *LM* test; and let $\kappa_1, \kappa_2, \ldots,$ κ_r be the *r* parameters in θ_r. After obtaining the estimates of the free parameters, θ_1, in M_1, the univariate *LM* statistic (see Equation 14.7) associated with each fixed parameter, κ_i, in θ_r can be computed. Before the stepwise procedure is initiated, *r* univariate *LM* test statistics are computed and then used to decide which of the $(\kappa_1, \kappa_2, \ldots, \kappa_r)$ parameters is to be selected in Step 1. Each univariate *LM* statistic tests a specific κ parameter: $\kappa_i = 0$. Testing each of the κ parameters can also be carried out using the *LR* test. The *LR* tests on the κ_i parameter require developing an $M_{1,i}$ model that contains all the free parameters in M_1 and an additional parameter, κ_i. M_1, therefore, is nested within $M_{1,i}$. With the M_1 model already estimated, estimation results for each $M_{1,i}$ model allow the comparison between these two models: $[\chi^2(M_1) - \chi^2(M_{1,i})]$ to evaluate whether $\kappa_i = 0$. To test the *r* parameters in θ_r, there are *r* different *LR* statistics to be computed after evaluating all *r* $M_{1,i}$ models. It should be noted that though it is necessary to develop and evaluate other *r* $M_{1,i}$ models (*i* = 1, 2, . . . , *r*) in *LR* tests, the *LM* test only needs to evaluate M_1. Under the null hypothesis, $\kappa_i = 0$, the univariate *LM* statistic should asymptotically be equal to the *LR* statistic with 1 *df*.

The *r* univariate *LM* statistics associated with the κ parameters can be rank-ordered to determine which κ_i

has the largest univariate *LM* statistic. The κ_i with the largest *LM* statistic is expected to make the most significant improvement to overall model fit if it is added to the model. At each step of the forward search procedure, two *LM* related statistics—*multivariate LM cumulative statistic* and *univariate LM increment statistic*—can be computed for each of the parameters not yet included in the procedure. The multivariate *LM* cumulative statistic is used for significance testing of the set of all the parameters included in the previous steps plus the specific remaining parameter. The univariate *LM* increment statistic reflects the unique contribution of that specific parameter, if selected, over all the parameters already included in the previous steps. The parameter with the largest univariate *LM* increment statistic is then selected into the current step before proceeding to the next step of the procedure.

At the first step of the *LM* stepwise procedure, the multivariate *LM* cumulative statistic, the univariate *LM* increment statistic, and the univariate *LM* statistic (see Equation 14.7) for each fixed parameter are of the same value. Among the r fixed parameters considered, the parameter with the largest univariate *LM* increment statistic is the one selected into the *LM* procedure. The multivariate *LM* cumulative statistic at Step 1 involves only one parameter.

At the second step, with the parameter selected at Step 1, say κ_1, already in the procedure, univariate *LM* increment statistic controlling for the κ_1 parameter is computed for each of the remaining $(r-1)$ parameters. The multivariate *LM* statistic with 2 *df* is also computed for each of the remaining $(r-1)$ parameters in conjunction with κ_1 already included in the test procedure. The univariate *LM* increment statistic for each parameter in Step 2 is the same as the difference between the multivariate *LM* statistic from Step 2 and that from Step 1. With the *LM* increment statistics calculated for the $(r-1)$ remaining parameters at the beginning of Step 2, the parameter selected in the second step is the one that yields the largest *LM* increment statistic. Similarly, after the parameters selected in Steps 1 and 2 are included in the test procedure, the parameter with the largest univariate *LM* increment statistic in the remaining $(r-2)$ parameters is selected in Step 3. This stepwise procedure can be continued by selecting the parameter with the largest *LM* increment statistic at the next step until all r parameters are included. The multivariate χ^2 cumulative statistic obtained at the completion of each step can be used for the significance test on the parameters selected up to and including that step. The χ^2 increment statistic at the ith step is, in fact, equal to the difference of multivariate χ^2 statistics between the $(i-1)$th and ith steps.

The univariate *LM* increment statistic generally decreases at each step in the stepwise procedure; the statistical significance of this value is usually used as the criterion for deciding when to terminate the forward search. When the largest *LM* increment statistic is not significant, the stepwise procedure can be stopped. More specifically, if the parameter with the largest *LM* increment statistic at the ith step is not significant, then only the parameters selected in Steps 1 through $(i-1)$ should be considered in the new model. The stepwise search procedure can also be executed using the *W* test by dropping the parameter with the smallest *W* increment statistic at each step.

The primary issue with the forward stepwise procedure using the *LM* test is similar to that of forward stepwise regression analyses (Kerlinger & Pedhazur, 1973): Parameters selected in earlier steps are "locked in" and influence the selection of parameters at later steps. In other words, parameters introduced at later steps are dependent on those included in the earlier steps. Furthermore, significant parameters introduced in the earlier steps may become nonsignificant as the stepwise search continues but are forced to remain in the model. In contrast, the backward selection procedure starts with a model containing all the parameters to be examined and drops the ones that are not significant. Consequently, the backward procedure does not "lock in" nonsignificant parameters in the model.

Efficiency of the *LM* and *W* Tests

The *W* and *LM* tests are computationally more efficient than the *LR* test. In the example of M_1 being nested within M_2 with $r \geq 2$ parameters differentiating the two models, there are $(r^2 - 2)$ intermediate models to be searched if model modification is needed. These intermediate models are more general than M_1 but more restricted than M_2. Letting M_k represent one of the intermediate models, the nested relations between M_1, M_k, and M_2 are $M_1 < M_k < M_2$. With the *LR* test, all r^2 models including M_1 and M_2 need to be evaluated and compared. With stepwise searching using the *LM* and *W* tests based on either M_1 or M_2, respectively, the models with adequate fit and parsimonious structure can potentially be detected more efficiently.

The number of free and fixed parameters in a model determines the computational intensity of backward and forward search procedures. The Bentler–Weeks (1980) model is used in this chapter to demonstrate free and fixed parameters that can potentially be defined in a model to be estimated using SEM. In the Bentler–Weeks model, variables are classified in terms of their functions and types. A variable is classified as an independent or a dependent variable. Dependent variables (η) are the ones that are functions of other variables, or those that have lines with an arrow pointing to them in a path diagram. Variables which are not defined as dependent variables are treated as independent variables (ξ). Each variable, whether an independent or a dependent variable, can be classified into one of four types: V (Measured Variable), F (Latent Factor), E (Measurement Error), or D (Disturbance). It should be noted that E and D variables are usually treated as independent variables in the Bentler–Weeks model. With k independent variables in vector ξ, and m dependent variables in vector η, the Bentler–Weeks model with the dimensions of the matrices can be expressed as

$$\eta_{(m \times 1)} = \beta_{(m \times m)}\, \eta_{(m \times 1)} + \gamma_{(m \times k)}\, \xi_{(k \times 1)} \qquad \textbf{(14.9)}$$

with β and γ being matrices of regression weight parameters and $\phi_{(k \times k)} = \xi'\xi$, the covariance matrix of independent variables.

The dimensions of the ϕ, γ, and β matrices reflect the number of parameters that can be defined as either free or fixed parameters in a model. There are a total of k^2 elements in the ϕ matrix, $(m \times k)$ elements in the γ matrix, and $(m \times (m - 1))$ elements in the β matrix that can potentially be defined as free parameters. There are only $(m \times (m - 1))$ elements rather than $(m \times m)$ elements in the β matrix because the diagonal of the β matrix is fixed at 0 (i.e., the dependent variables cannot influence themselves). If only nonrecursive models are to be considered, elements in the β matrix can be further reduced. Elements in the ϕ matrix are associated with variances or covariances, whereas elements in the γ and β matrices are regression weights (including factor loadings). There are q free parameters in a model, and the remaining parameters are fixed.

To simplify the model by dropping excessive parameters without compromising model fit, a backward search in SEM is conducted by removing free parameters that are not significantly different from zero. With the free parameters defined, the number of parameters that can potentially be dropped in a backward search is, in general, relatively smaller compared to the number of fixed parameters embedded in the model. Consequently, backward searching in SEM is more straightforward to carry out, especially because the model typically already has adequate fit to the data.

A forward search using the *LM* test, on the other hand, involves freeing fixed parameters to improve model fit. With the free parameters specified in a model, a forward search focuses on freeing fixed parameters. Consequently, with a significantly larger set of fixed parameters embedded in the model to be freed, forward searching is generally more complicated than backward searching. Among the fixed parameters targeted to be freed in a forward search, most are fixed at zero, although some are fixed at nonzero values primarily for model identification purposes.

EXAMPLES

The purpose of this section is to illustrate how the W and *LM* tests are used. We use models from MacCallum (1986) and Chou and Bentler (1990) to demonstrate decision making in selecting parameters in practice. The former study focuses on forward searching; the latter study demonstrates that backward searching can be more successful than forward searching under certain conditions. Two major sources of error have been identified in specification search procedures such as the W and *LM* tests: sampling fluctuation and model misspecification (Green et al., 1999). To provide a clear presentation of both backward and forward search procedures without the additional complication of addressing both types of error, this section deals only with the model misspecification error.

MacCallum (1986) Model

Model A in MacCallum (1986) is used in this section. The true model (MA_T) presented in Figure 14.1 consists of two dependent factors (F4 and F5) and three independent factors (F1, F2, and F3), with two indicators for each factor. True values assigned to the free parameters for covariances and regression weights among the factors are also presented in Figure 14.1. MA_T consisted of 15 independent variables ($k = 15$) including three factors, 10 measurement errors (not shown in the figure), and two disturbances; and 12 dependent variables

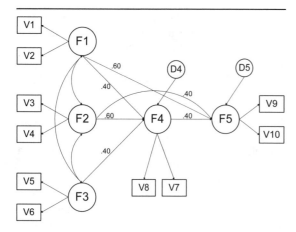

FIGURE 14.1. True model from MacCallum (1986).

($m = 12$), including 10 measured variables and two factors. Based on the Bentler–Weeks model, the ϕ, γ, and β parameter matrices potentially consisted of $15^2 + (12 \times 15) + 12 \times (12 - 1) = 537$ parameters that could be defined as free parameters. We analyzed the population covariance matrix presented in MacCallum (1986) to illustrate search procedures when there is model misspecification error. With 29 free parameters specified and $55 = 10 \times 11/2$ data points, the true model, which is used to generate the population covariance matrix, yielded a perfect fit to the data, as expected, with 26 df.

Backward Searching Using the *W* Test

To illustrate backward searching, a more general model (MA_W) was created by adding the path from F3 to F5, or (F5,F3), to the true model. A successful backward search using the *W* test should lead to the true model (MA_T), which is a more restricted model nested within MA_W. With a total of 30 free parameters in the model (one more than that in MA_T), MA_W also had a perfect fit to the data, as indexed by a value of 0 for the χ^2 test statistic and 25 df. In order to ensure appropriate modifications to the model, restricted searches based on theoretical meaningfulness have been suggested (Chou & Bentler, 1990, 2002; MacCallum, 1986). Such searches focus on parameters that are more essential to the model. Following this guideline, our search was restricted to parameters in the structural model. The model generated to illustrate backward searching, MA_W, contained a saturated structural model. As noted by Chou and Bentler (2002), starting from a saturated structural model helps with identifying the portion of the model—measurement or structural—in which modification is needed. Parameters listed in column 2 of Table 14.2 involved three covariances and seven regression weights between latent factors. The univariate *W* statistic, which is equal to the square of the z-value for a given parameter, was used to examine the significance of each free parameter in the model. The univariate *W* statistics not reported in the table consistently indicated that among the 10 free parameters associated with the structural model only the path from F3 to F5 (F5,F3) was not significant and could be dropped from

TABLE 14.2. Results of Stepwise *W* Test

| Step | Parameter | Cumulative multivariate statistics | | | Univariate increment | |
		Chi-square	df	Probability	Chi-square	Probability
1	F5,F3	.000	1	1.000	.000	1.000
2	F5,F2	11.858	2	.003	11.858	.001
3	F3,F2	26.080	3	.000	14.222	.000
4	F3,F1	37.017	4	.000	10.937	.001
5	F2,F1	47.095	5	.000	10.077	.002
6	F5,F1	71.381	6	.000	24.287	.000
7	F4,F1	92.946	7	.000	21.565	.000
8	F4,F3	140.435	8	.000	47.489	.000
9	F4,F2	257.372	9	.000	116.936	.000
10	F5,F4	544.336	10	.000	286.964	.000

MA_W to obtain a simpler model without loss in fit. By dropping the (F5,F3) parameter, the backward search using the univariate W test statistics correctly reached the true model, MA_T, from MA_W.

In addition to the univariate W statistics for tests of the free parameters, a stepwise W test was conducted on the 10 free parameters associated with the structural model. Results obtained from the EQS program are reported in Table 14.2. To demonstrate the stepwise procedure, specific free parameters in the structural model selected into the test procedure at each step are presented in column 2. Multivariate W cumulative statistics, associated dfs, and probabilities are presented in columns 3, 4, and 5, respectively. Univariate W increment statistics, which have one df (not reported in Table 14.2), and corresponding probabilities are presented in the last two columns. The multivariate W statistic was calculated at each step to test $h(\theta) = 0$, where $h(\theta)$ contains all the parameters up to that specific step. Univariate W increment statistics provide the change of multivariate W statistics between the current step and the previous step as a result of the inclusion of the current parameter. The df for the multivariate W statistic is the same as the number of parameters, or steps, included in the test procedure, whereas the df for the univariate increment is always 1. The parameter entered at each step is labeled using double-label notation. The parameters consisting of two independent variables—for example, (F2,F1), (F3,F1), and (F3,F2)—represent a variance or covariance; parameters with the first variable being the outcome variable and the second variable the predictor variable—for example, (F4,F1), (F4,F2), (F4,F3), (F5,F1), (F5,F2), (F5,F3), and (F5,F4)—represent a regression weight. At each step, probabilities associated with both the multivariate W statistic and univariate W increment statistic are produced.

At the first step of the W search procedure, parameter (F5,F3), the regression weight of F5 on F3, is entered into the test procedure. The multivariate W statistic and the univariate increment of the W statistic are the same with one df at Step 1. The univariate W increment statistic is usually used as the criterion to determine whether the parameter suggested at the current step should be dropped or whether the procedure should be continued to search for additional parameters to drop. With the univariate increment not significantly different from 0, the (F5,F3) parameter did not show a significant contribution in accounting for the variation of F5 and should, therefore, be dropped from the model for the purpose of parsimony. The parameter entered

at Step 2 was (F5,F2), the regression weight of F5 on F2. The multivariate W statistic with 2 df at Step 2 was significant, indicating that the two parameters, (F5,F3) and (F5,F2), were jointly not equal to 0. Furthermore, unlike the previous parameter, (F5,F3), the newly entered (F5,F2) parameter had a significant univariate increment in the W statistic, indicating that this parameter was significantly different from 0 and should, therefore, not be dropped from the model. The significant increment in the W statistic at Step 2 also indicated that no more parameters should be dropped beyond the parameter suggested at Step 1. The stepwise W test procedure for this model should, therefore, be terminated at this point. Dropping the (F5,F3) parameter from MA_W led to MA_T and, in so doing, demonstrated a successful backward search.

Forward Searching Using the *LM* Test

To demonstrate forward searching using the *LM* test, a more restricted model (MA_0) was created by dropping the (F5,F1) and (F5,F2) parameters from the true model (MA_T) and using it as the initial model. MA_0 is nested within the true model, MA_T. With 27 free parameters specified, MA_0 yielded a χ^2 goodness-of-fit test statistic of 33.212 with 28 df and probability of .228. The results in fact indicated that the initial model had an adequate fit to the population covariance matrix. Thus, from a model modification perspective, this model does not require the use of forward specification searching. Nevertheless, for the purpose of demonstrating the use of forward searching from a more restricted model in search of the true and more general model, forward searching using the *LM* test was conducted. A successful forward search using the *LM* test would start from MA_0 and be expected to lead to MA_T.

With 27 out of potential 537 parameters in the ϕ, γ, and β parameter matrices defined as free parameters, there are 510 potential fixed parameters to be examined by the *LM* test based on the initial model, MA_0. Although the *LM* test could be used to examine all of these fixed parameters statistically, many are not theoretically appealing, such as nonsystematic correlated errors, correlated disturbances, and unexpected factor loadings. A systematic pattern of correlated uniqueness may, in fact, imply the existence of other factors not considered in the model. In addition, numerous fixed parameters are dependent on each other and may yield equivalent models. More specifically, freeing just one of these interdependent parameters at a time may create several models with the same overall fit to the data.

Fixed parameters in the MA_0 model with significant univariate *LM* statistics are summarized in Table 14.3. In the large set of fixed parameters embedded in MA_0, only 11 produced significant univariate *LM* statistics. The parameter corresponding to the path from F1 to F5, or (F5,F1) in the EQS output, has the largest χ^2 value of 19.473, followed by three parameters: the path from F5 to F4 (F4,F5), the covariance between D2 and D1 (D2,D1), and the covariance between E7 and E8

TABLE 14.3. Results of Univariate *LM* Test Based on the MA_0 Model

No.	Parameter	Chi-square	Prob.
1	F5,F1	19.473	.000
2	F4,F5	18.727	.000
3	D2,D1	18.727	.000
4	E8,E7	18.727	.000
5	V5,F5	7.718	.005
6	V5,F1	5.633	.018
7	V7,F1	5.626	.018
8	V7,F5	4.771	.029
9	F5,F3	4.728	.030
10	V6,F5	4.653	.031
11	V6,F1	4.103	.043

Note. The MA_0 model is the same as the true model (MA_T) without (F5,F1) and (F5,F2) parameters.

(E8,E7), with the same value of 18.727. These three parameters with the same univariate *LM* statistic indicate that adding only one of them to a previous model may yield three new and equivalent models with the same χ^2 values and *df*. Substantively, however, the (D2,D1) and (E8,E7) parameters represent correlated disturbances and correlated errors, which are substantively not appealing. Adding (F4,F5) to the initial model may generate a recursive model and may not be of interest either. None of these three parameters, therefore, may be considered theoretically appealing. In addition to these four parameters, other parameters with significant univariate *LM* statistics included the fixed path from F3 to F5 (F5,F3) and unexpected factor loadings between measured variables and factors. Freeing these factor loadings would produce a model in which some measured variables have multiple loadings. Notably, the parameter for the path from F2 to F5 (F5,F2) specified in the true model was *not* one of the fixed parameters with significant univariate *LM* statistics. Thus, the results indicate that releasing parameters based on univariate *LM* statistics may not lead to the correct model.

Similarly, results of a stepwise multivariate *LM* test based on MA_0 summarized in Table 14.4 indicate that three fixed parameters should be reconsidered in the following sequence: (F5,F1), (E8,E7), and (F5,F3). Given the second parameter (E8,E7), a correlated error, is not substantively meaningful, we elected not to add this parameter in the new model. *LM* statistics associated with parameters following (E8,E7)—for example, (F5,F3)—were no longer valid due to the "locked-in" problem previously discussed. As a result, the forward

TABLE 14.4. Results of Multivariate *LM* Test Based on the MA_0 and MA_1 Models

		Cumulative multivariate statistics			Univariate increment	
Step	Parameter	Chi-square	df	Prob.	Chi-square	Prob.
			MA_0			
1	F5,F1	19.473	1	.000	19.473	.000
2	E8,E7	30.065	2	.000	10.592	.001
3	F5,F3	35.685	3	.000	5.620	.018
			MA_1			
1	F5,F2	11.610	1	.001	11.610	.0001

Note. The MA_0 model is the same as the true model (MA_T) without the (F5,F1) and (F5,F2) parameters; the MA_1 model is the same as the true model without the (F5,F2) parameter.

search continued by including only (F5,F1) in the new model, MA$_1$.

Compared to the initial model, MA$_0$, MA$_1$ containing the extra parameter of (F5,F1) yielded a significantly smaller χ^2 goodness-of-fit statistic of 11.382 with 27 *df* and a probability of .996. We proceeded with another forward search, beginning now with MA$_1$. Results of the *LM* test summarized in the lower portion of Table 14.4 indicate that only the (F5,F2) parameter should be freed to further improve model fit. Following the stepwise multivariate *LM* test with theoretical guidance, the forward search process in this example led to the true model. This example of using the *LM* test also demonstrates that releasing multiple parameters without theoretical guidance may lead to an incorrect model. The results based on MA$_0$ and MA$_1$ illustrate that the success of finding the correct model with forward specification searching depends heavily on the initial model; MA$_0$ led to the wrong model, but MA$_1$ led to the correct model (Saris et al., 2009). The more the initial model differs from the true model, the less likely forward searching is to suggest the proper modifications.

Chou and Bentler (1990) Model

With significantly more applications of model modification in SEM focusing on forward searching, we use another example to demonstrate the *LM* stepwise test procedure. The true model (MB$_T$) investigated by Chou and Bentler (1990) is presented in Figure 14.2. The model consists of two dependent factors (F3 and F4) and two independent factors (F1 and F2), with three indicators for each factor. The factor loadings assigned were 1, .8, .8 for the three indicators, respectively, assuming reliability of .75 for each indicator. True values assigned to the free parameters in the structural model are also presented in Figure 14.2. For the purpose of forward searching, a more restricted model (MB$_0$) was developed by dropping the covariance between F1 and F2, and two paths: from F1 to F4, and from F2 to F3, or (F4,F1) and (F3,F2), respectively. With sample size of 200, the true model (MB$_T$) contained 29 free parameters and had a perfect fit to the population covariance with 49 *df*. The restricted model (MB$_0$) developed to illustrate forward searching contained 26 free parameters and yielded a χ^2 test statistic of 143.903 with 52 *df* and probability close to 0, indicating very poor overall fit to the data.

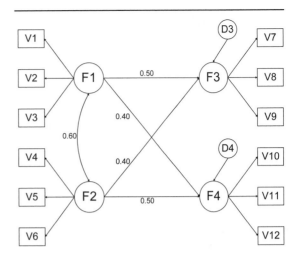

FIGURE 14.2. True model from Chou and Bentler (1990).

Model fitting results for the MB$_0$ model indicate five fixed parameters with significant univariate *LM* statistics. Ordered from high to low, these values are provided in the top portion of Table 14.5. It should be noted that the first three parameters, (F2,F1), (F3,F2), and (F4,F1) are needed for the initial model to reach the true model. Multivariate *LM* test results based on MB$_0$ are presented in the lower portion of Table 14.5. Due to a linear dependency issue, the (F4,F3) parameter was not considered in the multivariate procedure. Univariate *LM* increment statistics suggested that only the first three parameters, (F2,F1), (F3,F2), and (F4,F1), had significant unique contribution to the model and should be freed from the MB$_0$ model. Adding these three parameters led to the true model in this example.

DISCUSSION

The main purpose of model modification, or specification searching, in SEM is to find a parsimonious model that fits the data, while maintaining theoretical meaningfulness through model simplification or improvement (Chou & Bentler, 1990). Statistical information needed to facilitate model modification was discussed in this chapter. Three commonly used tests, the *LR* test, the *W* test, and the *LM* test, were discussed in detail as alternatives for comparing two nested models during

TABLE 14.5. Results of Univariate and Multivariate *LM* Tests Based on the MB$_0$ Model

		Univariate	
No.	Parameter	Chi-square	Prob.
1	F2,F1	71.713	.000
2	F3,F2	23.360	.000
3	F4,F1	23.360	.000
4	F4,F3	10.373	.000
5	F3,F4	10.373	.005

		Multivariate				
		Cumulative multivariate statistics			Univariate increment	
Step	Parameter	Chi-square	df	Prob.	Chi-square	Prob.
1	F2,F1	71.713	1	.000	71.713	.000
2	F3,F2	88.121	2	.000	16.409	.000
3	F4,F1	104.530	3	.000	16.409	.000
4	F3,F4	106.175	4	.000	1.645	.200

Note. MB$_0$ model is the same as the true model (MB$_T$) without the (F2,F1),F3,F2) and (F4,F1) parameters.

specification searching for the purpose of model modification. Backward searching is used to obtain a more parsimonious model from an initially well-fitting, but more general, model. Forward searching, on the other hand, begins with a more restricted, poor-fitting model, and is used to find a "correct" and more general model. Conventionally, the *LR* test has been the primary approach used for model modification through manual specification searching and model comparisons. Model modification based on the *LR* test requires multiple model respecifications and can be both computationally intensive and time-consuming. The *W* and *LM* tests offer more efficient alternatives. The *W* test is used for tests in backward searching resulting from imposing constraints, or dropping free parameters, to simplify a model. The *LM* test is used for tests in forward searching resulting from releasing constraints, or adding free parameters, to obtain better model fit.

We used two examples from simulation studies to illustrate the forward and the backward search procedures. Focusing on model misspecification error, we demonstrated how to utilize both theoretical and statistical decision making in the search to identify critical parameters for model modification purposes. With thorough consideration given to the substantive implication of each parameter suggested by the *W* and *LM*

tests, true models were reached in both examples. The extent to which the degree of misspecification in an initial model affects the success of finding the correct model was also evidenced in the first example. To help avoid failed specification, searching additional strategies, such as expected parameter change and power of parameter tests for forward searching, has been recently suggested (Saris et al., 2009).

SEM is a statistical technique primarily used for confirmatory purposes. However, as often is the case, when the model originally specified is not deemed parsimonious or well-fitting, model modification becomes an option (Chou & Bentler, 1990; Leamer, 1978; MacCallum, 1986; MacCallum et al., 1992; Martens, 2005; Sörbom, 1989). Clearly, the application of statistical approaches to searching for more suitable models makes SEM less confirmatory and more exploratory. Consequently, model modification based on specification searching in SEM has been criticized for its post hoc nature and unacceptable likelihood of capitalization on chance in searching for "better" models. It should also be noted that if a modified model is considered adequate, it simply represents one plausible depiction of the data structure. There are many other models that can yield acceptable fit to the same data set. It is therefore crucial that researchers make theoretical decisions on which specific final models to select that can most adequately address the research questions being pursued given the state of relevant knowledge.

Cautious experts have made several constructive recommendations in conducting model modification. For example, in his seminal paper, MacCallum (1986) suggested four principles to enhance the success of forward specification searches: (1) Carefully specify the initial model; (2) use data from large samples; (3) use a restricted search strategy with rigorous substantive justification; and (4) continue forward searching even with a well-fitted model. These principles also apply when conducting backward searches. Backward searching is also likely to be more successful than forward searching if the measurement model is adequately specified first (Chou & Bentler, 2002). These suggestions and findings underscore the importance of the theoretical justification for specification searches. In addition to theoretical guidance, it is also recommended by researchers that the modified model be re-evaluated using data from an independent sample as a practice of cross-validation (Browne & Cudeck, 1989; Cudeck & Browne, 1983; Kelloway, 1995). Browne and Cudeck (1989) also proposed the single-sample cross-validation index, incorporating both the criteria of model parsimony and model fit to estimate the likely fit of the model being evaluated using a different sample.

In conclusion, model modification is usually an inevitable process in the application of SEM. As models estimated using SEM tend to be complex and are frequently found to provide unacceptable fit to empirical data, model modification through either backward or forward searching is needed. To carry out model modification while reducing the likelihood of capitalization on chance, theoretical guidance is essential in determining how model fit can be improved or simplified. Substantive knowledge about the overall model, specific parameters, and the study population is vital in guiding more restricted and successful searching in model modification. To ensure successful modification and adequate model specification, replication of the model with independent samples should always be done when possible.

ACKNOWLEDGMENTS

Preparation of this chapter was supported in part by National Institute on Drug Abuse Grant No. R01DA027226, USC Clinical and Translational Science Institute Grant No. U54RR026075 from the National Institutes of Health, and Tobacco-Related Disease Research Program Grant No. 19FT-0089. We gratefully acknowledge the invaluable contribution of the editor, Dr. Rick Hoyle, in improving this chapter.

REFERENCES

Aitchison, J., & Silvey, S. D. (1958). Maximum likelihood estimation of parameters subject to restraints. *Annals of Mathematical Statistics, 29*, 813–828.

Arbuckle, J. L. (2006). *Amos (Version 7.0)*. Chicago: SPSS.

Bentler, P. M. (2006). *EQS structural equations: Program manual*. Encino, CA: Multivariate Software.

Bentler, P. M., & Weeks, D. G. (1980). Linear structural equations with latent variables. *Psychometrika, 45*, 289–308.

Bollen, K. A., & Long, J. S. (Eds.). (1993). *Testing structural equation models*. Thousand Oaks, CA: Sage.

Browne, M. W., & Cudeck, R. (1989). Single sample cross-validation indices for covariance structures. *Multivariate Behavioral Research, 24*, 445–455.

Buse, A. (1982). The likelihood ratio, Wald, and Lagrange multiplier tests: An expository note. *American Statistician, 36*, 153–157.

Byrne, B. M., Shavelson, R. J., & Muthén, B. (1989). Testing for the equivalence of factor covariance and mean structures: The issue of partial measurement invariance. *Psychological Bulletin, 105*, 456–466.

Byrne, B. M., & Stewart, S. A. (2006). The MACS approach to testing for multigroup invariance of second-order structure: A walk through the process. *Structural Equation Modeling, 13*, 287–321.

Chou, C. P., & Bentler, P. M. (1990). Model modification in covariance structure modeling: A comparison among likelihood ratio, Lagrange multiplier, and Wald tests. *Multivariate Behavioral Research, 25*, 115–136.

Chou, C. P., & Bentler, P. M. (2002). Model modification in structural equation modeling by imposing constraints. *Computational Statistics and Data Analysis, 41*, 271–287.

Cliff, N. (1983). Some cautions concerning the application of causal modeling methods. *Multivariate Behavioral Research, 18*, 115–126.

Corning, A. F. (2002). Self-esteem as a moderator between perceived discrimination and psychological distress among women. *Journal of Counseling Psychology, 49*, 117–126.

Cudeck, R., & Browne, M. W. (1983). Cross-validation of covariance structures. *Multivariate Behavioral Research, 18*, 147–168.

Engle, R. F. (1984). Wald, likelihood ratio, and Lagrange multiplier tests in economics. In Z. Griliches & M. D. Intriligator (Eds.), *Handbook of econometrics* (pp. 775–826). Amsterdam: North-Holland.

Frazier, P. A., Tix, A. P., & Barron, K. E. (2004). Testing moderator and mediator effects in counseling psychology research. *Journal of Counseling Psychology, 51,* 115–134.

Green, S. B., Thompson, M. S., & Poirier, J. (1999). Exploratory analyses to improve model fit: Errors due to misspecification and strategy to reduce their occurrence. *Structural Equation Modeling, 6,* 113–126.

Hoyle, R. H., & Robinson, J. C. (2003). Mediated and moderated effects in social psychological research: Measurement, design, and analysis issues. In C. Sansone, C. C. Morf, & A. T. Panter (Eds.), *Handbook of methods in social psychology* (pp. 213–234). Thousand Oaks, CA: Sage.

Hu, L. T., & Bentler, P. M. (1998). Fit indices in covariance structure modeling: Sensitivity to underparameterized model misspecification. *Psychological Methods, 3,* 424–453.

Jöreskog, K. G., & Sörbom, D. (2006). *LISREL 8.8 for Windows* [Computer software]. Lincolnwood, IL: Scientific Software International, Inc.

Kelloway, E. K. (1995). Structural equation modelling in perspective. *Journal of Organizational Behavior, 16,* 215–224.

Kerlinger, F. N., & Pedhazur, E. J. (1973). *Multiple regression in behavioral research.* New York: Holt, Rinehart & Winston.

Leamer, E. E. (1978). *Specification searches: Ad hoc inference with non-experimental data.* New York: Wiley.

Lee, S., & Hershberger, S. (1990). A simple rule for generating equivalent models in covariance structure modeling. *Multivariate Behavioral Research, 25,* 313–334.

Lee, S. Y., & Bentler, P. M. (1980). Some asymptotic properties of constrained generalized least squares estimation in covariance structure models. *South African Statistical Journal, 14,* 121–136.

MacCallum, R. C. (1986). Specification searches in covariance structure modeling. *Psychological Bulletin, 100,* 107–120.

MacCallum, R. C. (1990). The need for alternative measures of fit in covariance structure modeling. *Multivariate Behavioral Research, 25,* 157–162.

MacCallum, R. C., & Austin, J. T. (2000). Applications of structural equation modeling in psychological research. *Annual Review of Psychology, 51,* 201–226.

MacCallum, R. C., Roznowski, M., & Necowitz, L. B. (1992). Model modification in covariance structure analysis: The problem of capitalization on chance. *Psychological Bulletin, 111,* 490–504.

MacCallum, R. C., Wegener, D. T., Uchino, B. N., & Fabrigar, L. R. (1993). The problem of equivalent models in applications of covariance structure analysis. *Psychological Bulletin, 114,* 185–199.

Martens, M. P. (2005). The use of structural equation modeling in counseling psychology research. *Counseling Psychologist, 33,* 269–298.

McDonald, R. P., & Ho, M. H. R. (2002). Principles and practice in reporting structural equation analyses. *Psychological Methods, 7,* 64–82.

Muthén, L. K., & Muthén, B. O. (2007). *Mplus user's guide* (5th ed.). Los Angeles: Authors.

Pentz, M. A., & Chou, C. P. (1994). Measurement invariance in longitudinal clinical research assuming change from development and intervention. *Journal of Consulting and Clinical Psychology, 62,* 450–462.

Rao, C. R. (1948). Large sample tests of statistical hypotheses concerning several parameters with application to problems of estimation. *Proceedings of the Cambridge Philosophical Society, 44,* 50–57.

Saris, W. E., & Satorra, A. (1987). Characteristics of structural equation models which affect the power of the likelihood ratio test. In W. E. Saris & I. N. Gallhofer (Eds.), *Sociometric research* (Vol. 2, pp. 220–236). London: Macmillan.

Saris, W. E., & Satorra, A. (1993). Power evaluation in structural equation models. In K. Bollen & J. S. Long (Eds.), *Testing structural equation models* (pp. 181–204). Newbury Park, CA: Sage.

Saris, W. E., Satorra, A., & van der Veld, W. M. (2009). Testing structural equation models or detection of misspecifications? *Structural Equation Modeling, 16,* 561–582.

Satorra, A. (1989). Alternative test criteria in covariance structure analysis: A unified approach. *Psychometrika, 54,* 131–151.

Schumacker, R. E., & Lomax, R. G. (2010). *A beginner's guide to structural equation modeling* (3rd ed.). New York: Taylor & Francis.

Silvey, S. D. (1959). The Lagrangian multiplier test. *Annals of Mathematical Statistics, 30,* 389–407.

Sörbom, D. (1989). Model modification. *Psychometrika, 54,* 371–384.

Stelzl, I. (1986). Changing the causal hypothesis without changing the fit: Some rules for generating equivalent path models. *Multivariate Behavioral Research, 21,* 309–331.

Tomarken, A. J., & Waller, N. G. (2003). Potential problems with "well fitting" models. *Journal of Abnormal Psychology, 112,* 578–598.

Wald, A. (1943). Tests of statistical hypotheses concerning several parameters when the number of observations is large. *Transactions of the American Mathematical Society, 54,* 426–482.

CHAPTER 15

Equivalent Models
Concepts, Problems, Alternatives

Larry J. Williams

Researchers who use structural equation modeling (SEM) techniques across various social science disciplines follow a similar process. They begin by examining the constructs included in their model to determine which constructs will be linked to each other, and the nature of the linkages. Theory and prior empirical results guide this process, and the resulting proposed model is typically represented via a path diagram that shows some constructs to be correlated with each other, others as either independent or dependent variables in some type of causal relationship, and still others as relatively unrelated. Within a structural equation model these constructs are represented by latent variables, and the researcher must next choose the indicators or measures used to operationalize and represent the latent variables. Subsequently, data are collected from a sample using these indicators, and a resulting indicator moment matrix (typically involving only variances and covariances) is used as input to a specialized software package. The resulting software output includes parameter estimates indicating the direction, magnitude, and statistical significance of relationships among the latent variables and between the latent variables, and their indicators.

An important aspect of SEM analysis, as briefly described, is that measures of the adequacy or goodness of fit of the proposed model such as the comparative fit index (CFI; Bentler, 1990) and the root mean square error of approximation (RMSEA; Steiger & Lind, 1980) are also obtained. Although these measures take many forms, they all share a common element. The parameter estimates obtained with a SEM analysis are developed via an iterative process, and once the final estimates are available, based on a converged solution, they are used to generate what is referred to as a predicted covariance matrix for the indicators. This predicted matrix is based on the particular model specification, with different specifications (i.e., different proposed relationships among and between latent and indicator variables) typically resulting in different predicted matrices. More importantly, the differences between a given predicted covariance matrix and the corresponding sample matrix used to obtain the estimates are used in the computation of the values for the various fit indices. These differences are summarized in a residual covariance matrix, and if the model is satisfactory, this residual matrix will have relatively small values, whereas if the model is misspecified (has important relationships omitted or unimportant relationships added), the residual matrix will have relatively larger values. Thus, the residual covariance matrix is the common element linking fit indices, and a good model will have small residuals and values on fit indices that reflect this, whereas a poor model will have larger residuals and unacceptable fit values.

Although the question of what value for a given fit index indicates acceptable fit versus unacceptable fit is hotly debated (e.g., Chen, Curran, Bollen, Kirby, & Paxton, 2008), what is not in doubt is the fact that even when fit is deemed to be adequate, this does not provide proof that the model being examined is the true model underlying the data. It is well understood that alternative models with different proposed patterns of relationships and interpretations might provide different but similar values for the fit indices and could also be viewed as satisfactory. And more importantly for present purposes, in some instances these alternative specifications will result in values for the fit indices that are *identical* (not just similar) to those of the original model. This occurs when the predicted covariance matrices for the original and alternative models are identical, which results in their residual matrices and fit indices also being identical. These types of models, referred to as "equivalent" models, are the focus of this chapter.

Specifically, the types of model specifications that yield equivalent models are first described. Next, the prevalence of equivalent models across some areas of social science research is discussed. Third, emphasis is placed on an important but relatively neglected problem of equivalent models—that conclusions about the relationships in the entire model can be compromised, and not just those associated with the component that changes across the equivalent models. Fourth, strategies that have been proposed for selecting among equivalent models are summarized. Finally, the actions that researchers can take to minimize or avoid problems of equivalent models are discussed, with an emphasis on key decisions related to selection of variables before data collection. The goal of this chapter is to make researchers more sensitive to this major problem that threatens the conclusions they make based on their analyses. The importance of this problem has been emphasized by MacCallum, Wegener, Uchino, and Fabrigar (1993), who stated that "the existence of any, let alone many, equivalent models presents a serious challenge to the inferences typically made by researchers using CSM (another term for SEM)" (p. 196). Or as summarized by Hershberger (2006), model equivalence "exposes the limitations of structural equation modeling to test theories" and requires that "we never test a model, but rather a whole class of models from

which the hypothesized model cannot be distinguished by statistical means" (p. 17).

ALTERNATIVE SPECIFICATIONS YIELDING EQUIVALENT MODELS

Interest in the basic issue of alternative models fitting data equally well can be traced back to classics of SEM, including papers by Duncan (1969), Heise (1975), Kenny (1979), and Bentler (1980). However, additional focus was brought to this area by Jöreskog and Sörbom (1988, 1989), who used the term "equivalent" models in their widely used manual for the LISREL software program to refer to models with alternative specifications (arrangements of paths linking variables) that result in the same predicted covariance matrix and identical overall fit indices. They also contrasted the problem of model equivalence with model identification, stating that the latter involves whether there are two or more sets of parameter values that generate the same covariance matrix, and that by comparison model equivalence involves alternative specifications that might result in the same matrix. It should be noted that Lee and Hershberger (1990) reported the distinction made by Lee (1987) between models with an empirical occurrence of equivalence based on data from a given sample, and equivalence in principle that is not sample-specific and occurs in any data set. This chapter focuses on the latter. Additionally, Hershberger (2006) has distinguished between observationally equivalent models in which one model can generate every probability distribution that another model can generate and requires identity of individual data values, and covariance equivalence in which the covariance matrix generated by one model can be generated by other equivalent models. This chapter focuses on the latter. Finally, equivalent model problems can occur in the measurement portion of a multiple-indicator latent variable model by changing the relationships linking the factors to their indicators and/or the correlations among the factors (for further discussion, see Hershberger, 2006; Mulaik, 2009). In this chapter the discussion focuses on equivalent models in which structural relations linking latent variables to each other, referred to as "path components" by McDonald and Ho (2002), vary across models.

Although, as noted earlier, structural equation experts have long been aware of equivalent model issues, exploration of these issues was limited by a lack of understanding of how to identify possible equivalent models for a given model, other than after the fact through their equivalent implied covariance matrices. In other words, there was not a guide as to which specific paths could be changed in a given model and how they could be changed to result in a new model that was equivalent to the initial model. It should be clarified that in this context, this is viewed as a technical problem, and nothing is implied about the theoretical support needed for such respecifications (which is discussed later). Stelzl (1986) made an important contribution to this area by

developing four rules that could be applied to generate equivalent models for a given theoretical model. These rules focused on cases in which the direction of a causal path could be reversed between two endogenous variables from a model, or a path could be replaced by a correlation among residuals of the equations for the two variables involved in the path. Subsequently, Lee and Hershberger (1990) developed a more general rule that subsumed Stelzl's four rules. To explain this rule I refer to Model A, based on an example provided recently by Mulaik (2009) and presented in Figure 15.1,

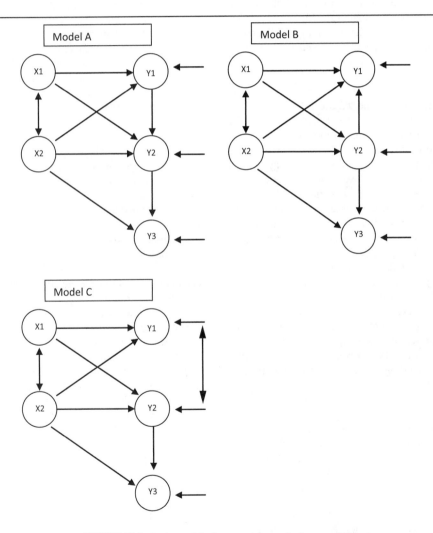

FIGURE 15.1. Path models for example equivalent model.

which includes two correlated exogenous variables ($X1$, $X2$) that each have an impact via structural parameters on two endogenous variables ($Y1$, $Y2$). The model further proposes that $Y1$ has a structural effect on $Y2$, and that $Y2$ and $X2$ have effects on a third endogenous latent variable, $Y3$.

To explain the replacement rule, terminology of Hershberger (2006) is used to refer to three components or blocks in Model A, as shown in Figure 15.1. First, the component consisting of the variables $X1$ and $X2$ is referred to as the "preceding block" because $X1$ and $X2$ causally precede the two variables in the focal block ($Y1$, $Y2$), which contains the path that will be modified using the replacement rule. Mulaik (2009) refers to the preceding block as containing the "parents" of the variables in the focal block and notes that all variables in the focal block must have the same parents or include the parents from the preceding block. In the model shown in Figure 15.1, this requirement is met, in that both $Y1$ and $Y2$ are influenced by $X1$ and $X2$. Hershberger (2006) additionally refers to $Y1$ within the focal block of such a model as the source variable and to $Y2$ as the effect variable, so this requirement can be alternatively stated as saying that the predictors of the effect variable are the same as or include those of the source variable. The special case in which the source and effect variables have the same predictors is referred to by saying the variables in the focal block are symmetrically determined (Hershberger, 2006). Finally, the third block is referred to as the "succeeding block" because it contains a variable ($Y3$) that succeeds the variables in the focal block. Succeeding blocks can also contain multiple variables. As noted by Hershberger, the replacement rule requires limited block recursiveness such that relations between the blocks and within the focal block be recursive or one-way in nature, whereas relations within the preceding and succeeding blocks may be nonrecursive or two-way in nature.

Within such a model, as described earlier, two alternative models that can be easily developed using the replacement rule are equivalent and result in identical predicted and residual covariance matrices. The first alternative model (Model B) replaces the path in the focal block between $Y1$ and $Y2$ with a path in the opposite direction, from $Y2$ to $Y1$. Although this might seem like a small change to a model, as noted by Stelzl (1986), inverting the direction of a path results in a change in the causal hypothesis, which will usually have extreme consequences on the interpretation of results and conclusions about theory. The second alternative model (Model C) replaces the path in the focal block with a correlation between the two disturbance terms for the $Y1$ and $Y2$ equations. This second model thus contains no structural parameter between $Y1$ and $Y2$ in either direction. Following the perspective of Stelzl, the specification of no causal path between $Y1$ and $Y2$ is an extreme position with important ramifications related to theory development for the $Y1$, $Y2$ relation.

Additional equivalent models are possible if the preceding and focal blocks are saturated such that every variable in the block is related to every other variable via a one-way structural path, a covariance/correlation, or a correlated disturbance. In this situation, the preceding and focal blocks can be merged to form a saturated block and, as described by Mulaik (2009), any relation between any two of its variables can be represented by a one-way path in either direction or a correlation between the two disturbances for the equations of the two variables. Our original Model A has preceding and focal blocks that are saturated, so an additional five equivalent models are possible and, as developed by Mulaik, these are presented in Figure 15.2. The saturated block model is referred to as Model D (although Mulaik did not provide a label for this model), and the other four equivalent models, as Models E–H (following Mulaik).

A couple of other comments on equivalent models are in order before proceeding. First, in the special case of a symmetric focal block, yet another equivalent model is obtained using the replacement rule by replacing either recursive path ($Y1$ to $Y2$ or $Y2$ to $Y1$) or the correlation among their disturbance terms with two nonrecursive paths that are constrained to be equal so that the model will be identified (e.g., Hershberger, 2006). In that Model A contains a symmetric focal block, this means another equivalent model with equal nonrecursive paths between $Y1$ and $Y2$ is possible, although this model will not be evaluated further in this chapter. Also, as noted by MacCallum and colleagues (1993) the replacement rule can be applied repeatedly with the same model, which greatly increases the number of possible equivalent models. Finally, models without the characteristics associated with the replacement rule can still be subject to equivalent model problems, and a technique for proving equivalence in this context was recently described by Bentler and Satorra (2010). This approach is described in a later section to verify equivalence of models to be presented.

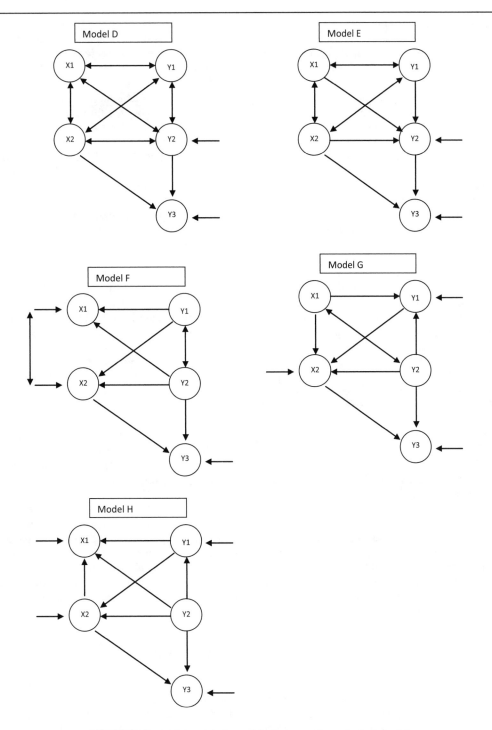

FIGURE 15.2. Additional path models for example equivalent model.

FREQUENCY OF EQUIVALENT MODELS

The preceding section indicates that with one model containing two exogenous and three endogenous latent variables, and with seven out of nine possible structural paths included, at least nine equivalent models are possible. Though useful for demonstration purposes, this example does not address the broader question of how many equivalent models are present in typical areas of social science research. One set of limited answers to this question can be found in the methodological articles and chapters on equivalent models that include demonstration examples. For instance, Stelzl (1986) included three substantive-based examples, and noted that one included four variables and had six possible equivalent models; that a second example included five variables and had two but possibly many other equivalent models; and that yet a third example based on three latent variables had six alternative equivalent specifications. Also, Jöreskog and Sörbom (1988, 1989) presented a hypothetical example with three latent variables, and described and analyzed one equivalent alternative. Bollen (1989) showed how three measured variables could result in 10 equivalent models, including four with latent variables added. Finally, Loehlin (2004) also presented the traditional three latent variable model and described three equivalent versions, whereas Kline (2010) took five measured variables and presented four equivalent models.

Others have described examples of equivalent models occurring in published research across a variety of substantive areas. Breckler (1990) reported a review based on applications of SEM in personality and social psychology. He described several specific examples in detail, and concluded that a first example involving five latent variables (three exogenous, two endogenous) had a number of plausible equivalent alternatives. A second example from Breckler involved three latent variables, and he conducted reanalyses and discussed two alternative equivalent models. In a third example that also included three latent variables, there was one plausible equivalent model consistent with theory. Finally, for a fourth example, Breckler stated that there were at least 26 equivalent models.

MacCallum and colleagues (1993) have perhaps the most comprehensive study of this issue. They examined top journals in three areas of psychology, including educational, industrial organizational, and personality/social psychology for the 3-year period from 1988 to 1991. They found a total of 53 articles relevant to the topic, and across the three areas found that 86%, 74%, and 100%, respectively, of the articles from the three areas had possible equivalent models based on applying the replacement rule. Perhaps more important was their finding that the median number of equivalent models in each article across the three areas ranged from 12 to 21. In a more narrowly focused search, Williams, Bozdogan, and Aiman-Smith (1996) found six articles published between 1986 and 1994 on the specific topic of job satisfaction and organizational commitment relations for which three possible equivalent models were supported by theory and prior research. Finally, most recently Henley, Shook, and Peterson (2006) conducted a review of SEM applications in the area of strategic management research. They found 79 studies from top journals in the time period 1984–2004. Of these, Henley and colleagues concluded that 75% had at least one equivalent model based on applying the replacement rule. Furthermore, in 71% of the studies, the directional causal paths could be replaced by correlated residuals, and the direction of causality could be reversed in 48% of the studies.

Across all of the results presented in this section, it can be clearly seen that researchers cannot ignore the fact that many theoretically plausible equivalent models are likely to exist for the substantive models they consider. Perhaps most importantly, these reviews of published examples indicate that authors typically ignore the problem. There were no cases in the review of MacCallum and colleagues (1993) for which the authors explicitly acknowledged the existence of an equivalent model, and in the Henley and colleagues (2006) review, only one set of authors acknowledged the issue of equivalent models. It may be the case these authors are not aware of the degree to which their conclusions about the relationships proposed by their models are influenced by the chosen specification, and how these conclusions may be changed if, instead, equivalent alternative specifications are responsible for the observed covariances.

PARAMETER ESTIMATES AND CONCLUSIONS FROM EQUIVALENT MODELS

It seems as though much of the scholarship on equivalent models has focused on developing rules to help identify them, and on using these rules to document the degree to which they are a problem as they occur across various social science disciplines. Relatively less attention has been placed on the issue of how parameter estimates vary across different equivalent models assessed using the same data. Of course, one would expect the three parameters being manipulated (paths from $Y1$ to $Y2$, $Y2$ to $Y1$, and the correlation among the two residuals) to have different values. However, what may be more important is the degree to which other parameters in the model are influenced by the alternative model specifications that fit the data equivalently. Conclusions about the direction, statistical significance, and magnitude of these parameters are used to reach conclusions about theory, which may in turn be used to influence practice or policy. That these conclusions may vary considerably across equivalent models cannot be ignored, and researchers need to increase their awareness, reconsider their inferences, and attempt to minimize the problem.

In his seminal paper, Stelzl (1986) noted but did not discuss extensively how parameter estimates varied across one of three empirical examples considered. In one case, a path from a three-variable model became nearly zero as the direction of one of the other two paths was reversed. In another case, less noticeable change occurred when a five-variable model was used. Changes in the statistical significance of paths were not discussed. Similarly, in the previously mentioned review by Breckler (1990), results from alternative versions of a three-variable model were given. These results showed that one of three paths was not statistically different from zero in one model but was significant in the other two. MacCallum and colleagues (1993) also included in their review three empirical examples from diverse areas of psychology. These examples included more variables, so more equivalent models were possible; they examined four for each example. MacCallum and colleagues focused on changes in statistical significance of paths across the models in their examples, and in one example there were no changes. However, in a second example one of seven paths significant in the original model became only marginally significant in an equivalent model that was examined. In a third example, they noted interesting changes in parameter estimates as compared across equivalent models. Although one path that was only marginally significant became significant across the alternative models considered, a different path changed from being positive to negative. Finally, Henley and colleagues (2006) reported reanalysis for three equivalent models from an

example study from the area of strategic management, and found several relationships that changed in significance over the models examined.

The most extensive investigation of changes in sample results associated with equivalent models has been provided by Williams and colleagues (1996). They focused on models with two employee attitudes (job satisfaction, organizational commitment) as endogenous variables, for which theory and empirical results supported paths in both directions between the two variables, as well as support for no significant relation. Results of reanalyses from six previously published studies were reported, and three equivalent models were examined that varied the specification of the relation between the two attitude variables. Across the six examples, the numbers of antecedents of each of the two attitudes were 4, 7, 4, 5, 5, and 4, resulting in a total of 29 antecedent variables across the studies. Although Williams and colleagues reported results separately for each of the six studies they analyzed, they also reported a summary table that will be useful presently.

Williams and colleagues (1996) reported four types of changes in the 29 parameters linking the antecedent variables with the two endogenous satisfaction and commitment variables. First, they summarized the frequency with which there were changes in statistical significance for the 58 paths, and found that such a change occurred 21% of the time for satisfaction and 35% of the time for commitment. Second, they documented changes in the magnitude of the structural parameter estimates that were 20% or more, and found that such change occurred in 59% of the cases for satisfaction and 24% of the cases for commitment. A change in sign of a parameter estimate that remained statistically significant occurred in 6% of the cases across both variables. Finally, in terms of the number of statistically significant predictors, a change occurred in four of the six studies for satisfaction, and in two of these four, more than one change in significance occurred. For commitment, such a change occurred in five of the six studies, and in four of these five, more than two predictors changed in significance. Although these results were obtained for only six studies, there is no reason not to believe a similar pattern of findings would be obtained from equivalent models from other substantive domains.

The strategy of examining changes in parameter estimates across equivalent models using sample data provides one way of demonstrating how conclusions about relations among variables may be different across the equivalent models. It has the advantage of providing information about changes in statistical significance, but has as a limitation the fact that the true parameter values are not known. An alternative approach is a simulation analysis, in which values for the parameters of a model are assumed, and then changes in the parameters across different equivalent versions of the original model are documented. This approach was used by Williams and colleagues (1986) with two examples based on models originally considered by MacCallum (1986) and Mulaik and colleagues (1989). The models from these two examples were mediation models in which a set of exogenous variables influenced mediators, which were then proposed to influence an outcome variable. Williams and colleagues reported important departures from population values of the parameter values across the two sets of equivalent models that were obtained by changing the specification of the relationship between the mediator and outcome variables using the previously discussed replacement rule.

An additional demonstration of this approach uses the previously discussed models based on Mulaik (2009), shown in Figure 15.1. Specifically, a set of values for the parameters shown in Model A were chosen, and these were used to generate the corresponding population covariance matrix for the five variables shown in Table 15.1. Next, the alternative equivalent models (Models B–H) were evaluated with this covariance matrix, and the resulting values for the parameters were examined. It should be noted that for each of the seven models that were proposed as equivalent to Model A, the goodness of fit was found to be equal and perfect, providing confirmation that they were in fact equivalent to Model A based on the approach recently provided by Bentler and Satorra (2010).

The parameter values for all eight models are presented in Table 15.2. In each row are the parameter values for each of 10 bivariate relations between the five variables of the model ($X1$, $X2$; $X1$, $Y1$; $X1$, $Y2$). Each row also contains a symbol for each relation indicating its nature as proposed by that specific model. For these symbols, $\leftrightarrow$ indicates a correlation is specified, $\rightarrow$ indicates a path from the first to the second variable is specified, $\leftarrow$ indicates a path from the second to the first is specified, $\downarrow\leftrightarrow\downarrow$ indicates a correlation between the disturbance terms for the two variables is included, and a 0 shows no relation is proposed. Thus, the first row of Table 15.1 shows the values used to generate the population covariance matrix, which includes a correlation of .25 between $X1$ and $X2$ (column 1) and regression parameters of .3 and .2 linking $X1$ with $Y1$ and $Y2$, respectively (columns 2 and 3). Furthermore, this row indicates that values of .2, .3, and .2 were assumed for regression parameters linking $X2$ with $Y1$, $Y2$, and $Y3$ (columns 5–7), respectively; a value of .2 was assumed for the path linking $Y1$ and $Y2$ (column 8), and a value of .5 was used for the path linking $Y2$ and $Y3$ (column 10). In Table 15.2, the differing values within each column demonstrate how a parameter changes across the alternative equivalent model specifications. It is informative to compare the resulting values to those for Model A (the values used to generate the population covariance matrix).

The values shown in column 1 of Table 15.2 indicate a fairly large change in the parameter linking $X1$ and $X2$, which ranges from .25 as a correlation in Models A–E but drops to .09 as it is represented as a regression parameter in either direction in Models G and H. Columns 2 and 5 show that the parameters linking $X1$ and $X2$ with $Y1$ decrease when specified as structural parameters in Models B, F, G, and H, but increase when specified as a correlation in Models D and E. Alternatively, columns 3 and 6 indicate that relative to the value from Model A, the parameter values increase in Models B, C, F, and H when specified as regression parameters, and a similar increase is demonstrated in Models D and G when the relation between variables is represented as correlations. Finally, columns 7 and 10 indicate no changes in parameter values for $X2$, $Y3$ and $Y2$, $Y3$ relations across different specifications.

Some summary comments related to these results may be helpful. First, across the models, structural parameters that retained their specification as structural parameters (in some instances with a direction change) increased in value as much as 30% (columns 3 and 8), but also decreased as much as 40% (column 2). Second, greater differences were, not surprisingly,

TABLE 15.1. Covariance Matrix for Model A

$X1$	1				
$X2$	.54	1			
$Y1$	.24	.27	1		
$Y2$	.31	.28	.64	1	
$Y3$	.07	.09	.37	.34	1

TABLE 15.2. Parameter Values for Equivalent Models

Model	1 X1 X2	2 X1 Y1	3 X1 Y2	4 X1 Y3	5 X2 Y1	6 X2 Y2	7 X2 Y3	8 Y1 Y2	9 Y1 Y3	10 Y2 Y3
A	↔ 0.25	→ 0.3	→ 0.2	0	→ 0.2	→ 0.3	→ 0.2	→ 0.2	0	→ 0.5
B	↔ 0.25	→ 0.24	→ 0.26	0	→ 0.12	→ 0.34	→ 0.2	← 0.22	0	→ 0.5
C	↔ 0.25	→ 0.3	→ 0.26	0	→ 0.2	→ 0.34	→ 0.2	↔ ↙↘ 0.17	0	→ 0.5
D	↔ 0.25	↔ 0.35	↔ 0.25	0	↔ 0.28	↔ 0.4	→ 0.2	↔ 0.36	0	→ 0.5
E	↔ 0.25	↔ 0.35	→ 0.2	0	↔ 0.28	→ 0.3	→ 0.2	→ 0.2	0	→ 0.5
F	↔ ↙↘ 0.08	← 0.26	← 0.25	0	← 0.15	← 0.35	→ 0.2	↔ 0.36	0	→ 0.5
G	→ 0.09	→ 0.26	↔ 0.34	0	← 0.12	← 0.33	→ 0.2	← 0.27	0	→ 0.5
H	← 0.09	← 0.24	← 0.22	0	← 0.15	← 0.35	→ 0.2	← 0.36	0	→ 0.5

Note. The parameter values are unstandardized. The standardized versions are identical except for a slight difference in the value for Y2–Y3.

obtained when comparing parameters specified as correlations versus structural parameters. For example, a drop of 64% was demonstrated in column 1, and 57% in column 5. Third, it should be emphasized that changes of these magnitudes might likely be associated with changes in statistical significance in research using sample sizes common to social science disciplines. Finally, a focus on changes in magnitudes should not lead one to forget the fundamental differences in specification across the parameters with very different interpretation: Correlation versus paths in opposite directions have fundamentally different implications for theory development. Regarding the latter, in both columns 2 and 3 a comparison of parameter values for Models A, B, and C versus Models E and H indicates how fairly strong parameter values for paths opposite in direction are possible, and fundamentally different conclusions about the relation of X1 with Y1 and Y2 would be obtained depending on which equivalent model was chosen.

SELECTING FROM AMONG EQUIVALENT MODELS

Given the number of equivalent models and the differing results possible for many of the substantive contexts in which social science investigations occur, researchers face the challenge of how to select from among the ones that might be considered given their study. Although Stelzl (1986) did not discuss this issue, after presenting their replacement rule Lee and Hershberger (1990) did discuss two conditions that could be used to identify a better model from among equivalent models. Noting that effects follow causes in time, they suggested that some causal orderings that vary across equivalent models could be ruled out if some of the involved variables were measured at different points in time. Second, they stated that knowledge of mediating mechanisms might help limit the range of equivalent models to be considered in a given situation. They gave an example describing how, if full mediation were assumed in a model in which an exogenous variable influenced a mediator that then influenced an outcome variable (so that a direct effect from an exogenous variable on the outcome variable was assumed to be zero), some equivalent models would be eliminated. This point is elaborated in a later section of this chapter.

Breckler (1990) added to the list of recommendations for selecting among equivalent models by proposing that it might be possible to eliminate some models on theoretical or logical grounds. Though this is similar to the second recommendation of Stelzl (1986), it also appears to have broader applications. With this guideline, a researcher might reject a statistically equivalent model that included paths with little or no theoretical support. Breckler (1990) also added that features of data collection, such as the use of an experimental design or supplemental data, might make some equivalent models implausible.

MacCallum and colleagues (1993) similarly noted that each equivalent model in a given context should be considered for its substantive meaningfulness, with the absence of such meaningfulness then being used to eliminate some models from further consideration. MacCallum and colleagues also emphasized that if a key independent variable is experimentally manipulated, this eliminates alternatives in which the specification is changed, so that this variable becomes an outcome of the nonmanipulated variable that originally served as its dependent variable. MacCallum and colleagues also reinforced the notion of Lee and Hershberger (1990) that when longitudinal data are involved, models in which effects move backward in time may not be meaningful. However, they further cautioned that this would not mean that in another study with a different design that a Time 2 variable might not be proposed as an antecedent of the original Time 1 variable. Perhaps more importantly, MacCallum and colleagues also described how known characteristics of variables might help eliminate as plausible some equivalent models. Specifically, they mentioned demographic variables such as sex or age, and noted that models specifying these often make little sense.

Perhaps the most extensive discussion of how to select from among equivalent models was provided by Hershberger (2006). His discussion was organized by considering strategies before data collection, which are saved for the next section of this chapter, and four strategies for after data collection, which are now summarized. Hershberger's first strategy involved the use of a different type of index for judging a model than the

overall goodness-of-fit measures typically employed, such as the previously mentioned CFI or RMSEA. The use of this new index was originally proposed for dealing with equivalent models by Williams and colleagues (1996) and is referred to as ICOMP (an information complexity criterion). As summarized by Hershberger, ICOMP combines two aspects that should be considered in evaluating a model: model misfit and model complexity. "Model misfit" refers to the traditional discrepancy between the predicted and sample covariance matrices, as summarized in a matrix of residual covariances. Alternatively, "model complexity" summarizes the degree of correlation among the parameter estimates from a given model, with higher correlations representing more complexity.

From this perspective, such high correlations and associated complexity are not desirable because they indicate that information from the data required to estimate each parameter independently from other parameters may be lacking. When the two aspects of model performance are combined in the ICOMP, low values indicate a model that is fitting well (low misfit) with parameter estimates that are relatively independent (low complexity). A model with a relatively low ICOMP value as compared to its equivalent counterparts would be preferred, and Williams and colleagues (1996) demonstrated this type of use in their reanalysis of data from six studies of job satisfaction and organizational commitment described earlier in this chapter.

A second strategy summarized by Hershberger (2006) also focuses on parameter estimates from equivalent models. Instead of their ultimate independence, as captured by the ICOMP, Hershberger focused on how they are obtained during the iterative parameter estimation process mentioned at the beginning of this chapter. He noted specific signs of problems during the estimation process, including a high number of iterations, negative parameter estimates for variances, and parameters that needed to be constrained to avoid improper estimates. The logic behind this recommendation is that such estimation difficulties, which often result from highly misspecified models, would support eliminating them from further consideration.

A practice of comparing R^2 values for endogenous variables from among a set of equivalent models was originally proposed by Jöreskog and Sörbom (e.g., 1988, 1989) and is a third approach discussed by Hershberger (2006). With this tactic, the R^2 values from the endogenous variables are combined into an aggregate measure, and the equivalent model with a higher total value would be preferred. Hershberger did add that this approach has not been systematically investigated, and that use of R^2 values can be compromised by the fact that such values can be greatly influenced by sample size. This characteristic could lead to the selection of different models from among an equivalent set evaluated across different samples, which would not be desirable.

The fourth and final strategy presented by Hershberger (2006) is referred to as extended individual case residuals (EICR), as originally proposed by Raykov and Penev (2001). To understand this strategy, it is important to remember that the residual covariance matrix is identical across equivalent models from a given data set. However, this does not imply that the model applies equally well to all observations in the data set. As summarized by Hershberger, the EICR refers to the difference between data values for observations and their model-based predicted values, with lower values being preferred. And, it is important to understand that the EICR for an individual will differ across equivalent models under some conditions. Thus, Raykov and Penev (2001) suggested that the model with the smallest average standardized EICR value (aggregated across observations in the sample) relative to its equivalent model alternatives be selected.

STRATEGIES FOR AVOIDING EQUIVALENT MODELS

The preceding section offered some approaches to selecting from among a set of equivalent models based on information assessed *after* data collection. However, a much better strategy involves trying to minimize the number of possible equivalent models that may threaten the evaluation of one's original model by decisions made *before* the data are collected. Before proceeding, it should be noted that some of the recommendations already provided may be relevant for decisions made before data collection. For example, including variables that are experimentally manipulated may be appropriate and practical in some contexts, as is using a longitudinal design. Furthermore, adding variables into one's model that are less likely to be endogenous in a given substantive context, such as demographic variables and certain personality variables, may also be helpful. Or, as stated by Mulaik (2009), it can be helpful to embed a path representing a relationship for which an alternative direction of relationship is possible in models for which the directions of other paths are known. This might

help lessen the number of possible equivalent models based on changing the original path of interest. A key point with these recommendations is that they help a researcher eliminate a set of possible equivalent models that might be obtained by reversing the direction of a focal structural path by providing stronger evidence in favor of the original specification.

However, a different type of recommendation is likely to hold more promise, and to explain this, it is important to understand the key characteristic of a model that greatly affects the number of potential equivalent models that threatens the inference process. It appears that MacCallum and colleagues (1993) provided one of the earliest discussions of how the number of proposed *nonzero* relationships in a model influences the number of alternative equivalent models. Specifically, they stated that models with large blocks of variables involved in saturated relationships with other variables (i.e., a given variable is related to all other variables) tend to yield a large number of equivalent models, as in Models D–H shown in Figure 15.2. They further added that in parts of a model where such a pattern of relations exists, described as "saturated blocks," the direction of paths is arbitrary. And, as a result, these paths can be reversed in direction to yield a rather larger number of possible equivalent models. It is important to add that MacCallum and colleagues stated that such saturated blocks cannot be avoided in some situations, and the best researchers can do is to acknowledge that there are many possible alternative equivalent models or simply to treat the involved variables as exogenous and correlated, and be clear that they are not attempting to impose causal order on the variables.

More recently, Mulaik (2009) emphasized this point as he elaborated on the implications associated with saturated focal blocks, as discussed in an earlier section of this chapter. Specifically, Mulaik used an illustration involving a saturated model with three variables, and showed that if one or two of these variables become exogenous (as compared to simply allowing all three to be correlated with each other) there would be 12 distinct recursive equivalent saturated models. Mulaik also extended the illustration to the case involving four variables. Given that one, two, or three of these variables could be treated as exogenous in alternative specifications, Mulaik computed that there would be 130 saturated equivalent recursive models. So, all things being equal, models with lots of paths tend to have more equivalent models because these paths can be reversed or replaced with correlated residuals.

One important implication of this is that it is advantageous to have variables in one's model that are linked to only some of the other variables of the model. It follows from this suggestion that researchers wanting to lessen their equivalent models risk might add variables into their data for which there is strong theoretical and empirical support for them being *unrelated* to some of the other variables in their model. This point appears to have been somewhat neglected by methodologists who have written about equivalent model problems. For example, Breckler (1990) mentioned that, as part of data collection, adding supplemental data might help make some equivalent models implausible, but he did not elaborate on the characteristics of such variables (i.e., being unrelated to other model variables). Similarly, Lee and Hershberger (1990) did claim that being able to rule out as implausible some causal connections could be helpful, but they did not mention doing so by adding variables with no relations to some of the other variables in the model.

More recently, Hershberger (2006) elaborated on the suggestion of adding variables by commenting on the importance of having them be selectively associated with only a few of the original variables in the model. He noted that in doing so, the revised model (with variables added) should retain the most important causal relations specified in the original model, adding that "reducing the number of equivalent models while at the same time retaining the integrity of the original model may be difficult" (p. 206). He also stated that variables added in such a way serve a purpose similar to that of instrumental variables in cases where a model is just identified or underidentified. This important link with the concept of instrumental variables was made, but not described as such, in one of the earliest papers on equivalent models by Stelzl (1986).

Specifically, Stelzl (1986) addressed the issue of what kind of information would help a researcher decide about the direction of a path between two variables. Stelzl discussed this in the context of a simple path model involving three variables in a causal chain A, B, and C. Although there were no paths in the initial figure presented by Stelzl, it can be inferred that this was a partial mediation model with B serving as the mediator, with a direct path from A to C also included. Stelzl initially stated that only adding a variable X_1 that was related to B was not sufficient to eliminate equivalent models, in that the direction of the path from B to C could still be reversed and equivalence maintained. However, by adding a second new variable X_2

that was related to C but whose path to B was fixed to zero, the two models with alternative specifications of the B → C relationship would no longer be equivalent according to Stelz and could be rejected or accepted based on their overall fit. It should be noted that in this instance the added variables of X_1 and X_2 would be serving as instruments of B and C. A revised version of Stelzl's model with these instruments added is shown in Figure 15.3.

Although providing this demonstration, Stelzl (1986) did so within the context of demonstrating the original rules for generating equivalent models and determining the direction of a path between two variables, rather than as a general approach to lessening equivalent model problems. However, it seems like the simple example just presented has much broader implications for researchers as they approach the design of their studies. A key implication is that a simple but effective way of lessening equivalent model problems is to add variables to the research design before data collection. Specifically, with respect to the source and effect variables from a focal block, a researcher could add to the preceding block one or more variables related to the source but not the effect variables, and one or more variables related to the effect but not the source variable. It should be noted that if this occurs, this approach follows the recommendation of Lee and Hershberger

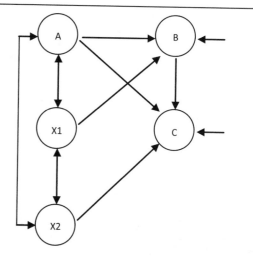

FIGURE 15.3. Additional path models for example equivalent model.

(1990) to assume full mediation. Specifically, adding antecedents of the source variable not related to the effect variable involves assuming that all the influence of the added variables on the effect variable is mediated by the source variable. The same is implied for variables added as antecedents of the effect variable: Their effects on the source variable are fully mediated by the effect variable when the effect variable is modeled as an antecedent of the source variable. The value of this approach has been noted by Mulaik (2009), who stated that "reducing the number of equivalent models with respect to a given model results from fixing more path coefficients to zero" (p. 248).

Referring back to Model A in Figure 15.1, the point is that at least some of the alternative models (B–H) might be eliminated if a researcher investigating the proposed pattern of relationships considered the problem of equivalent models in advance. To address the ambiguity about possible relationships between $Y1$ and $Y2$ (since they are in the focal block), this researcher would be advised to investigate prior theory and empirical findings of antecedents for $Y1$ and $Y2$. In this process, variables found to be related to $Y1$ but not $Y2$ would be worthy of further consideration as antecedents of $Y1$, and it would be appropriate also to specify them as not related to $Y2$. Similarly, variables demonstrated to be antecedents of $Y2$, but with no or very little relation with $Y1$, could play a similar role for $Y2$ (but be modeled as independent of $Y1$). Finally, it should be acknowledged that such a priori analysis by the researcher would require a different perspective than that typically used, in that so much attention is traditionally placed on developing support for paths in the model (as compared to support for leaving them out). However, the importance of placing emphasis on these excluded paths and the recognition that they represent an important aspect of model confirmation and judgment of model fit is increasing within the model evaluation literature (e.g., Mulaik, 2009; Williams & O'Boyle, 2011).

CONCLUSIONS

Since the 1970s the power of SEM has been recognized, and it is seen as the optimal analysis method for many types of research designs and variable types. In the end, SEM's key value is that it can improve theory development by providing effective and efficient theory testing. A key weakness of the method is that even when there is evidence of good model fit, it remains true that

alternative specifications may be plausible, some of which will have the exact same goodness of fit. It is my hope that the material presented in this chapter will help researchers better appreciate the importance of the problem, make better use of developing diagnostics for selecting from among equivalent models, and pay more attention to their research designs and variables before data collection. By doing so these researchers may add key variables that otherwise might not be included, and in the process eliminate from consideration some equivalent models, thereby increasing their confidence in the model of interest.

REFERENCES

Bentler, P. M. (1980). Multivariate analysis with latent variables: Causal modeling. *Annual Review of Psychology, 31*, 419–453.

Bentler, P. M. (1990). Comparative fit indexes in structural models. *Psychological Bulletin, 107*, 238–246.

Bentler, P. M., & Satorra, A. (2010). Testing model nesting and equivalence. *Psychological Methods, 15*, 111–123.

Bollen, K. (1989). *Structural equations with latent variables*. New York: Wiley.

Breckler, S. J. (1990). Applications of covariance structure modeling in psychology: Cause for concern? *Psychological Bulletin, 107*, 260–273.

Chen, F., Curran, P. J., Bollen, K. A., Kirby, J., & Paxton, P. (2008). An empirical evaluation of the use of fixed cutoff points in RMSEA test statistic in structural equation models. *Sociological Methods and Research, 36*, 462–494.

Duncan, O. D. (1969). Some linear models for two-wave, two-variables panel analysis. *Psychological Bulletin, 72*, 177–182.

Heise, D. (1975). *Causal analysis*. New York: Wiley.

Henley, A. B., Shook, C. L., & Peterson, M. (2006). The presence of equivalent models in strategic management research using structural equation modeling: Assessing and addressing the problem. *Organizational Research Methods, 9*, 516–535.

Hershberger, S. (2006). The problem of equivalent structural models. In G. R. Hancock & D. O. Mueller (Eds.), *Structural equation modeling: A second course*. Charlotte, NC: Information Age.

Jöreskog, K. G., & Sörbom, D. (1988, 1989). *LISREL 7: A guide to the program and applications* (2nd ed.). Chicago: SPSS, Inc.

Kenny, D. A. (1979). *Correlation and causality*. New York: Wiley.

Kline, R. B. (2010). *Principles and practice of structural equation modeling* (3rd ed.). New York: Guilford Press.

Lee, S. (1987). *Model equivalence in covariance structure*

modeling. Unpublished doctoral dissertation, Ohio State University, Columbus, OH.

Lee, S., & Hershberger, S. (1990). A simple rule for generating equivalent models in covariance structure modeling. *Multivariate Behavioral Research, 25,* 313–334.

Loehlin, J. C. (2004). *Latent variable models: An introduction to factor, path, and structural equation analysis* (4th ed.). Mahwah, NJ: Erlbaum.

MacCallum, R. C. (1986). Specification searches in covariance structure modeling. *Psychological Bulletin, 101,* 107–120.

MacCallum, R. C., Wegener, D. T., Uchino, B. N., & Fabrigar, L. R. (1993). The problem of equivalent models in applications of covariance structure analysis. *Psychological Bulletin, 114,* 185–199.

McDonald, R. P., & Ho, M. (2002). Principles and practice in reporting structural equation analyses. *Psychological Methods, 7,* 64–82.

Mulaik, S., James, L., Van Alstine, J., Bennett, N., Lind, S., & Stilwell, C. (1989). An evaluation of goodness of fit indices for structural equation models. *Psychological Bulletin, 105,* 435–445.

Mulaik, S. A. (2009). *Linear causal modeling with structural equations.* Boca Raton, FL: Chapman & Hall/CRC.

Raykov, T., & Penev, S. (2001). The problem of equivalent structural equation models: An individual perspective. In G. A. Marcoulides & R. E. Schumacker (Eds.), *New developments and techniques in structural equation modeling* (pp. 297–312). Mahwah, NJ: Erlbaum.

Steiger, J. H., & Lind, J. C. (1980, Spring). *Statistically based tests for the number of common factors.* Paper presented at the annual meeting of the Psychometric Society, Iowa City, IA.

Stelzl, I. (1986). Changing a causal hypothesis without changing the fit: Some rules for generating equivalent path models. *Multivariate Behavioral Research, 21,* 309–331.

Williams, L., & O'Boyle, E. (2011). The myth of global fit indices and alternatives for assessing latent variable relations. *Organizational Research Methods, 14*(2), 350–369.

Williams, L. J., Bozdogan, H., & Aiman-Smith, L. (1996). Inference problem with equivalent models. In G. A. Marcoulides & R. E. Schumacker (Eds.), *Advanced structural equation modeling: Issues and techniques* (pp. 279–314). Mahwah, NJ: Erlbaum.

PART III

IMPLEMENTATION

CHAPTER 16

Preparing Data for Structural Equation Modeling

Doing Your Homework

Patrick S. Malone
Jill B. Lubansky

Most of the previous chapters in this volume have dealt with conceptual issues: the nature of latent variable modeling and thus structural equation modeling (SEM), the fundamentals of specifying and estimating structural equation models, and so on. Most of the subsequent chapters are concerned with practical issues and techniques in SEM, including programming and model development. This chapter, opening Part III, "Implementation," is about something different: the step between deciding one wants to use SEM and beginning the modeling process. That is, the researcher must prepare the data for the specialized software used.

First, we introduce the concept of *homework* in research using SEM, identifying the major components. Most of these are common to other statistical techniques, yet often are given scant attention as the analyst may be eager to move on to modeling and results. Subsequent sections deal with some of the issues that are frequently involved in SEM and less likely to be so in other modeling—especially those that concern preparing the data for translation between general purpose statistical or data management software and the commonly used dedicated SEM programs. Finally, we present a series of examples of increasing complexity (and associated hazard) using a publicly available data set from the National Longitudinal Study of Youth, high-

lighting issues that can arise in working with a data set of some complexity.

THE IMPORTANCE OF HOMEWORK

We, as products of an educational system of a certain time and place, have had ingrained the notion and value of homework. Even beyond the schooling process, the U.S. colloquialism, "She clearly did her homework," means she was fully prepared for the task at hand. In this case, it would be that the researcher began the SEM analysis fully prepared. As to the importance of homework and identifying errors and problems, one need only look at retractions of scientific findings in the popular media, with the attendant embarrassment to the researcher. Even aside from cases of apparently deliberate fraud (e.g., the case of Dr. Hwang Woo-suk, who claimed to have extracted stem cells from cloned human embryos; Sang-Hun, 2009), there have been assorted cases of sometimes terribly costly mistakes, such as the linking of the mumps vaccine to autism (Burns, 2010) or the "discovery" of cold fusion (Browne, 1989).

There are at least two major means by which failing to do the homework can result in flawed conclusions from the data analysis. The first of these we discuss is

■ 263

errors in the data. This may seem simplistic, and it is simple, but a failure to check can cause any number of problems later (especially after publication!). We briefly discuss the problem in general, then turn in somewhat more detail to problems likely to creep into SEM data preparation. The second is data *problems*—not necessarily errors in the sense of the wrong data, but problems in assumptions, in missing data, and so forth. SEM, like any regression technique, not only requires certain assumptions about the nature of the data but also can accommodate certain tools to deal with data problems in a robust way.

DATA ERRORS: SOURCES AND SOLUTIONS

We would first like to emphasize that the only acceptable standard for data errors is *none*—zero errors. The approach described in this section is aimed to that standard, and we return to this point after reviewing error sources and solutions.

Incorrect Responses

The earliest (and perhaps the easiest) occasion for an error to appear in a data set is when the respondent provides a datum. That is, it is almost always possible (except, perhaps, for biological assays) for a respondent to provide incorrect single responses, and it may be possible to provide a contradictory set of responses. There is little recourse for the former case: We must trust our respondents, in the absence of a compelling reason to the contrary. In the latter, early detection is vital for providing an opportunity for correction. For example, in a survey on substance use, a respondent might report never having used marijuana, but then give a nonzero response to a second question asking about frequency of use of marijuana. Depending on the data collection method, it may be impossible to give such a response (e.g., with well-programmed branching in a computer-administered interview), or it might be possible to detect the contradiction early enough to resolicit responses (e.g., in a face-to-face interview), or it might be nearly impossible to resolve the contradiction by the time it is detected (e.g., in an anonymous paper-and-pencil survey). Unfortunately, if the contradiction cannot be resolved by the respondent, there are no good solutions. Setting both contradictory values as "missing" may be the best of a bad lot.

Incorrect Transcription

The next (and perhaps even easier) occasion for an error to enter an electronic data set is when the data point—meaning the value of a given variable for a given observation—first is entered into a computer or other electronic medium. Traditionally, many kinds of data (survey responses, medical data, and many other types) are recorded on paper before being key-entered to an electronic file. The act of transcription from paper is an obvious source of potential errors. In recent years, it has become increasingly feasible to have data directly entered to electronic storage by a respondent or an interviewer, such as in computer-assisted self- or personal interviewing (CASI or CAPI) or in moment-capture studies using a personal digital assistant (PDA), iPod Touch, or equivalent. Some data, especially physiological, can even be directly recorded. However, these electronic means are no panacea for data errors.

Data transcription errors may be common, but they can, with proper precautions, be the most easily detected. The gold standard of "proper precautions" is double entry. It is laborious, but by far the best way to identify transcription errors. Double entry means just what it sounds like—entering all of the data twice, by different operators. Differences between the resulting data sets can be identified by software such as PROC COMPARE in Statistical Analysis Software (SAS), which checks every data point against its mate in a second data set. Discrepancies are resolved by returning to the original data source. This procedure, while time-consuming, nearly eliminates accidents of transcription. A possible compromise sometimes used is "spot-check" double entry. In this situation, a second person inputs a portion (perhaps 10%) of the data to be compared to the original entry. This is intended as a check of the original entry operator's accuracy, *not* of those specific records. If any errors are found in this spot-check, full double entry is warranted.

Problems with Electronic Input

Electronic means of taking the initial record, such as CASI or CAPI, are subject to different sorts of errors. Sometimes there are simple programming errors; other situations include instructions or interfaces that are confusing to the user (also possible with paper records) or possible inputs that are not adequately controlled. Even simple electronic recording can have several benefits over paper data collection, but it is quite easy to inadvertently make things *more* difficult, such as with a confusing data entry screen. The solution to this is extensive procedural pilot testing, to make sure the intended users of the system find it easy and—dare we say—foolproof to operate. A simple step to take on many types of responses is for the system to accept only legitimate response: For example, if the instrument is a questionnaire with 4-point Likert responses, only the responses 1, 2, 3, and 4 should be accepted (though for ethical reasons there needs to be an option for refusal to answer and, depending on the nature of the question, perhaps options for "not applicable" or "do not know"). Of course, such a technique does not apply for open-ended responses, but it can certainly minimize some types of error. A different step to reduce data errors is to allow the user (whether respondent, interviewer, or archivist) to review the entered responses before finalizing them—as the T-shirt has it, "typos happne."

One area in which computer-based input systems shine is in skip and branching patterns of questions. For example, the Educational Testing Service (ETS) changed the Graduate Record Examination (GRE) over to computer-based adaptive testing in the 1990s, rendering it briefer for the respondent, more precise, and far faster to score. As another example, if a respondent indicates that he or she does not drink alcoholic beverages, questions on quantity and frequency of drinking can be omitted, as the answers are effectively known. Skip patterns can also be used in paper forms, but, as noted earlier, contradictions resulting from the respondent not following the directions (e.g., answering both "no drinking" and "3–4 drinks per week") can be difficult or impossible to resolve. Again, procedural pilot testing is crucial. One of us was involved in a project for which the CAPI system had a programming error. In that program, if the "gateway question" was answered in the negative, the skip pattern of missing data codes was applied to the wrong items, *including the gateway question*. The resulting missing data were quite the mystery.

Summary

Detecting errors is absolutely essential. Again, no avoidable errors should be tolerated. However, we must acknowledge that the search can be quite laborious, and therefore costly, especially in the case of full double entry of transcribed data. The process of error searches is costly and time-consuming, but is no less critical for that.

Correcting Errors

Addressing errors in data that one collects is usually relatively straightforward. Errors can be traced back to the original records. When designing a study one tends to be familiar with the coding system and any inconsistencies that occur during the data collection processes. Those who attempt to conduct secondary analysis have fewer options for the detection of errors. However, there are a number of important fundamentals to keep in mind before performing secondary data analysis. First, it is important to familiarize oneself with the codebooks, original measures, and data collection procedures.

Resources

Codebooks offer information about the coding of variables, valid skips (e.g., missed response due to the answer on the previous gateway question), invalid skips (e.g., missing data due to refusal to respond), recoded or reverse-scored variables, and composite score variables. When codebooks are unavailable, incomplete, or unclear, templates of the original measures may prove useful. Information that may be obtained from the original measures includes instructions, information about skip patterns, methods used for tallying scores, and information about reverse scoring. Copies of the original measures may be obtained via websites associated with original studies, by ordering copies of published measures from publishers, or by writing the authors of unpublished measures.

A comprehensive understanding of the data collection procedures will likely yield essential information about dependent observations (e.g., as is the case with clustered sampling strategies), whether weighting is necessary (e.g., as a result of oversampling of a given population group), and planned missingness methods (as is common with longitudinal designs). Many public-use data sets are accompanied by extensive information detailing data collection procedures, codebooks, and measures. This type of information varies in the quality of organization and clarity; often, the process of researching a data set can be cumbersome and frustrating. However, this is one of the most important steps in secondary data analysis.

Understanding the various sources of data errors and problems will help you to understand why a careful examination of your data is an important step to carry out *before* you begin to analyze it. Additionally, you will have an idea of what to look for in your data. It may be tempting to skip the data inspection step and to jump right into data analysis; however, careful inspection of your data prior to analysis may save you a great deal of time and confusion. If you don't take our word for it, you may end up learning this lesson the hard way!

Careful inspection of data for errors should become habit. Each time you begin working with a data set, you should evaluate descriptive statistics, check plots and graphs, examine correlations, and, if your data are ordinal, inspect frequency tabulations. These simple steps will help you to safeguard against unnecessary mistakes and erroneous conclusions about the associations among the variables in your data set.

Descriptive Statistics

Most software programs offer numerous options for easily analyzing descriptive statistics. The first step that we recommend is to check the number of valid cases. Cases may be missing due to a number of reasons, such as mistakes in the syntax you wrote to import your data, your software's default settings for handling missing data (e.g., some programs may use listwise deletion for missing data), or incongruence between missing data codes in your software program and the program initially used to manage your data. Incomplete data do not result in a fatal problem; there are several approaches for handling missing data that minimize bias and maximize power (see Graham & Coffman, Chapter 17, this volume). Before you check any other descriptive statistics, save time by making sure that you are working with the set of data that you think you have.

The next step is to check variability and central tendency. A priori expectations about your data will facilitate this process. Out-of-range data are a common error. Often, such values are simply an indication of inappropriate missing value codes. For example, your original data set may have consisted of values representing missing data, such as −999, that your data management software treats as numeric values rather than symbols for missing data. It is worth noting that, although out-of-range data are typically errors, other extreme values may accurately reflect outliers in the population of interest, requiring decisions about the treatment of these outliers. Standard deviation and measures of central tendency (mean, median, and mode) may offer similar information, though clues from these statistics may not be helpful without a priori expectations. For instance, if you were to evaluate the mean and standard deviation

of IQ scores of a sample of adults, you would expect to find a mean close to 100 and a standard deviation near 15. A mean of 300 and a standard deviation of 100 would be an indication of an error, requiring investigation of the original data set.

The second step is to evaluate distribution graphs (e.g., histograms) of each of your continuous variables. This is another quick way to check for outliers. In addition, you can examine the shape of the distribution. Gaps and bimodal distributions are often indications of errors in your data. Ceiling and floor effects may be indications of a need to recode continuous data, creating new variables that are discrete (e.g., dichotomous or censored binary variables). If working with ordinal data, frequency tabulations or bar graphs are useful tools for examining variables for errors. As with continuous variables, unexpected gaps, impossible or inappropriate values, bimodal distributions, and ceiling and floor effects may indicate errors, but in any case call for investigation and possibly remediation.

The last step is to examine statistics describing relations between variables. An examination of correlations may offer information about multicollinearity. Identify any correlations at or near unity. When your data set includes many variables, correlation matrices offer a more efficient means of quickly investigating a large number of correlations at once. Some software programs offer options to check the variance inflation factors (VIFs) or tolerance values to inspect your data for multicollinearity. These two related statistics may be especially useful for situations in which a correlation between two variables does not approach unity, but nevertheless is large enough to threaten the detection of true effects of individual predictors. An additional potential benefit of inspecting correlations is detecting reverse scoring of items or scales. These are not always clearly documented in codebooks, but a surprising pattern of signs in the correlation matrix tends to be conspicuous on inspection.

If utilizing an SEM software program that is different from your data management program, you will need to inspect your data briefly again. Most SEM programs provide options for evaluating descriptive statistics. Check for consistency between descriptive statistic outputs from your data management program and your SEM program. Oftentimes, discrepancies are due to differences in the defaults for handling missing data. Regardless, the researcher should investigate and identify sources of discrepancies prior to beginning analysis. For example, means may vary due to errors in the data import stage (e.g., mislabeled data), differences in missing data handling techniques (e.g., listwise vs. maximum likelihood), or syntax errors. Investigating and understanding sources of discrepancies may prevent you from having minor bugs in your code that will cause you to have to reanalyze your data when you find them in the end stages of analysis.

DATA PROBLEMS

Assumptions

SEM is a general case of regression analysis and therefore carries similar assumptions. The assumptions vary by both the estimation method (e.g., maximum likelihood or least squares, mean- and variance-adjusted; see Lei & Wu, Chapter 10, this volume, for more detail) and by the type of regression being estimated (e.g., linear or logistic). A comprehensive overview of assumptions is beyond the scope of this chapter. However, we provide a brief discussion of three linear regression assumptions that are most relevant to the data preparation stage of analysis: continuous scale of measurement of the dependent variable, independence of observations, and absence of multicollinearity among independent variables. We also discuss common ways in which these assumptions may be violated. We assert that many assumption violations result from "not doing your homework."

Distributions

The assumption regarding the scale of measurement of the dependent variable is that observations of the dependent variable are measured on an interval or ratio scale. One way in which this assumption may be violated is through the treatment of a dependent variable measured on an ordinal or nominal scale of measurement as though it were measured on a continuous scale. This may be especially problematic if the categories of the dependent variable are not ordered, or if the dependent variable consists of few categories. If one estimates a linear regression equation with a dependent variable that is measured on an ordinal or nominal scale, the results will be difficult to interpret and misleading at best. Many modern SEM programs can accommodate nonlinear link functions (e.g., logit, probit) for discrete data, but only if the researcher is aware of the need.

Another way to violate this assumption is by including a continuous dependent variable (measured on a ratio or an interval scale) that is exceptionally skewed in a linear regression equation. Skewed distributions may be an indication of ceiling or floor effects. With ceiling or floor effects, the variability may be diminished, masking true effects. A second issue is that such limitations of the measurement tend to distort the distribution of residuals, as many predicted values may be out of range. Such distributional problems may indicate a need for partial or complete transformations of the data, as discussed below.

Independence of Observations

Because SEM is frequently utilized to model longitudinal models and multilevel models, the assumption of independence is especially relevant to this chapter. Independence of observations implies that similarities (or dissimilarities) among observations are strictly due to chance. Violations of the assumption of independence may result from temporal or spatial proximity of observations. For example, though it is often assumed that participants are randomly selected from populations of interest, this is rarely the case in social science research. More often, the selection of participants is related to spatial proximity, as is the case with clustered sampling strategies. For instance, a researcher may recruit first graders for a reading intervention study via a fixed number of schools rather than randomly selecting students from the entire population of first graders. Two children from the same school are likely to have more similar reading achievement scores than children from two different schools. Like violations of the assumption of normality, the end result of violations of independence is likely to be underestimated standard errors, resulting in inflated Type I error rates (West, Finch, & Curran, 1995). As with discrete data, such dependencies can be accommodated in select SEM software, but only if the analyst knows to invoke those features.

Multicollinearity

Multicollinearity occurs when there is a linear dependence among the independent variables. Violations of this assumption may occur because two variables measure the same construct. For example, a variable measuring a person's self-reported level of ambition may be nearly perfectly correlated with a variable measuring a person's hoped-for job status. Violations of multicollinearity may also result from analyst error and carelessness in the data preparation stage. For example, a researcher may decide to rescale a variable, so that the variable is on the same metric as other variables in the data set. Poor documentation and unmethodical labeling may result in accidental inclusions of the old and new variables in the same analysis. This may be especially common in situations in which multiple researchers utilize the same data set. The result of this type of violation is inflated Type II error rate, meaning that the true effect of individual predictors (independent variables) may not be detected.

Missing Data

Missing data that are a result of skip patterns are typically easily dealt with in the data management stage, by replacing the "missing" indicator with the known value (often zero, but depending on the nature of the item). Missing data that do not have a known true value present a more complex problem, which is dealt with in detail in Graham and Coffman (Chapter 17, this volume). For our purposes, the key point is that one must understand which situation is at hand.

PREPARING DATA FOR ANALYSIS

After the detail on data cleaning, it may seem that there is little more to do in the stage of data preparation. However, there are, we assert, several key steps remaining in the process before the analysis stage. Depending on one's specific practical details, the first may be unnecessary for a given user, but it still calls for attention for many or most users.

Transferring Data

This section may be skimmed by those using SEM software in the same package as the data management software (e.g., OpenMx for R, Amos for Statistical Package for the Social Sciences (SPSS), TCALIS for SAS). However, several prominent systems at this writing require a transfer of data from the management program to the analysis software (e.g., EQS, LISREL, Mplus). This step involves its own cares and potential hazards.

First, it may be that the entire data set need not, or should not, be transferred between systems. The analysis software may have limitations on the number of variables or the type of variables (e.g., numeric vs. string). Furthermore, some analysis software may be limited in its capacity to exclude observations, as the

analyst might require. So the initial step in the transfer is to identify the cases and variables needed for the SEM step. In addition to the obvious requirement of the analysis variables, this may include nesting/clustering identifiers, sample weights, and, in some cases, identification variables. Some software also can utilize variables in special roles, such as Mplus's facility for using "training data" in mixture models, which one may need to generate in the data management step specifically for use in the SEM package. Records or cases may need to be omitted due to data-screening rules (e.g., based on social desirability scores) or, of course, data errors (e.g., missing sampling weights).

The transfer step may also involve some recoding of data. Examples of this include recoding character variables (potentially, ethnicity, gender, etc.) to numeric codes, as required by the specific SEM software. The software may also have limitations in variable naming not shared by the data management program, such as restrictions on the number of characters or special characters in the variable names. If variable renaming is done in the transfer, the use of systematic naming conventions is at least as important as in the data management processes and can save many a headache in later steps.

A second element that may arise in this stage is the use of missing data codes. The same codes used in the management step may not be appropriate in the analysis step, so wholesale data edits may be required. This is a function of not only software but also analysis strategy. We discuss below certain analyses and data types that could involve potentially elaborate recoding at or before the data transfer step.

In whatever case, there are two essential elements in preparing data for use in a different program. The first is that this should only be done *after* the initial data inspection and cleaning discussed in the first part of this chapter. Otherwise, any subsequently identified data problems will need to be fixed and this step repeated. The second, and this should likely be emblazoned throughout this chapter, is to document everything. Every change made should be transparent to a later user, or a later programmer who may need to replicate the process of preparing the data set.

Preparing Non-Normal Variables

In its early forms, SEM was solely a technique for use with continuous, (multi)normal variables. In the time since, great advances have been made in the accommodation of variables with substantially non-normal distributions and/or discrete scaling. The handling in the data preparation step varies by not only software but also the nature of the variable and its role in the analysis.

The first case we examine is that of exogenous, or source, variables in the model. It is here that scaling and distributional issues typically have the fewest implications, as maximum likelihood estimation does not incorporate distributional assumptions for exogenous variables (Eliason, 1993). An obvious countercase is of nominal variables (i.e., variables in which any numeric coding is simply a set of labels and has no implications for order). Examples might include race/ethnicity, type of community, and so forth. The usual strategy for nominal exogenous variables, as it is in multiple regression, is to recode the variable into a set of predictors— $k - 1$ predictors for k groups. Either "dummy-coding," where a value of zero across codes represents a reference group, or "effect-coding," where a value of zero represents an "average case," is a reasonable solution, with the choice between the two depending on what interpretations are planned for the structural coefficients from these variables and the intercepts of the downstream variables (Aiken & West, 1991).

Endogenous variables that are not normally distributed present a different set of issues. For ordinal endogenous variables, the solution is usually an appropriate estimation method, such as weighted least squares (as opposed to maximum likelihood [ML]), rather than transformation. The options available depend on software, and are dealt with by Lei and Wu (Chapter 10, this volume). Of relevance here is the concern of small cell sizes. Specifically, in a smaller sample, or with a grossly unevenly distributed ordinal variable, some consolidation of response options may be needed to enhance the stability of estimation. Simply put, if a small number of cases exceeds a threshold (in a probit or logit model), the estimation of that threshold will be imprecise. The solution, in most cases, is to combine response options. Nominal endogenous variables are a special case, and not readily accommodated in traditional SEM. Guo, Wall, and Amemiya (2006), for example, have incorporated multinomial logistic regression into mixture and general latent variable models. For our purposes, the issue is the same as for ordinal variables—a large enough portion of the sample in each response category, which may require some recoding. If collapsing of some of the nominal categories is not conceptually appropriate, a last resort of excluding a small subsample from the analysis may be necessary.

Continuous but non-normal endogenous variables present a different issue. If the problem with normality is one of skew or kurtosis, normalizing transformations (e.g., logarithm to reduce positive skew; see Tukey, 1957, for a classic catalog) can be useful but are not without hazards. More precisely, back-transformation holds hazards. By definition, a normalizing transformation, even if monotonic, is nonlinear. It will have different effects at different parts of the distribution of the variable. Any process applied across observations to the transformed data—including calculating a factor loading or structural coefficient, or simply calculating a mean—will be affected by the transformation. If the transformation is conceptually appropriate, such as the logarithmic Richter or decibel scales can be considered, there is little problem. In such cases, the transformed data can often be interpreted directly. However, an ad hoc transformation based solely on the distribution of a variable in a sample might not be. Back-transforming (e.g., exponentiating for a logarithmic transformation) an intercept, for example, can result in a very different sense of the data than was found originally. Which is more "true" or "valid" is often not obvious.

In the last part of this section, we turn to a special case—the semicontinuous variable. Olsen and Schafer (2001) documented this case in the regression model. In their conception, the semicontinuous variable has a different meaning at zero (or some other boundary) than at nonzero values. An obvious example is substance use: Zero cigarettes smoked is qualitatively different from one cigarette, which is, for most purposes, not much different from two. Olsen and Schafer's solution was to recode semicontinuous values to a two-part coding. In the smoking example, one variable would be dichotomous—any smoking versus none. The other variable would be continuous—quantity of smoking. The quantity variable, in this practice, is set to missing if it is not applicable (i.e., for a participant who does not smoke at all). Full-information maximum likelihood (FIML) from raw data, one of the current common practices for missing data, accommodates this transformation nicely, as it readily meets the required condition of missing at random (MAR). The true value of the missing data point is known from the dichotomous indicator.

For purposes of data recoding, a similar situation applies to any continuous variable with a strong floor or ceiling effect. Normalizing transformations cannot rid a variable of a preponderance of values at a boundary. Depending on the research context, a two-part variable may be a conceptually appropriate approach to accommodating a boundary. Regression using the zero-inflated Poisson distribution or, in some cases, negative binomial, might also be appropriate for the specific context. Alternatively, a simple discretizing transformation may be a better match to the nature of the construct. This might be dichotomizing (at the bound vs. otherwise), creating tertiles or quartiles, or any of a number of approaches to setting cut points for a discrete version of the continuous variable. From that point, it is an ordinal endogenous variable and can be handled as discussed earlier.

Structured Missing Data

This chapter is not this volume's primary treatment of missing data (see Graham & Coffman, Chapter 17), but there are certain points we must continue to address. Little in the process of data preparation homework has to do with unplanned missing data (i.e., a lack of valid score in a variable) other than to ensure the proper missing data codes are used for the data management and analysis software. However, two, or three, depending on counting, other cases do have more relevance at this stage of data preparation. One is what we just discussed, semicontinuous or two-part variables. In such cases, known values for variables are actually replaced with missing data codes in order to take advantage of properties of FIML estimation. We now turn to a different situation, that of planned missing data.

Designs with planned missing data again draw on modern missing data techniques, such as FIML estimation or multiple imputation (MI), in this case to address designs where certain blocks of data are simply not collected (and not due to the values being known, as is the case for skip patterns discussed earlier). Graham, Hofer, and MacKinnon (1996) laid out select specific designs and the rationale thereof that make use of planned missingness to reduce respondent burden while retaining maximum power. For our purposes, there is little added preparation work for these designs, but special care must be taken that the variables with and without expected responses are properly aligned and associated with the variable names.

We do address here a more elaborate specific case of planned missing data, that of the cohort-sequential or accelerated longitudinal design. In this widely used design, documented in Schaie (1965), different age cohorts (or cohorts defined by some other timing variable) are assessed in a longitudinal fashion, with the ages overlapping across cohorts. As an example, three birth cohorts—1995, 1998, and 2001—might have been recruited in 2005 and measured annually through 2010. The 2001 birth cohort thus provides data on youth at ages 4, 5, 6, 7, 8, and 9; the 1998 cohort at ages 7, 8, 9, 10, 11, and 12; and the 1995 cohort at ages 10, 11, 12, 13, 14, and 15. The researchers thus have data on their measures reflecting ages 4 through 15, but are able to collect the data in a 6-year rather than 12-year span. (There are, of course, limitations to such a design in terms of cohort effects; a full discussion of the merits is beyond the scope of this chapter.) We consider this an example of planned missing data, as the 1995 cohort's ages 4 through 9 data are never collected, nor is the collection ever attempted, and correspondingly, for the other birth cohorts.

The cohort-sequential design requires extraordinary care in data management and preparation. Most SEM software will not manipulate the timing/age variables directly, and so this must be done in the data preparation stage (Mplus is one exception, but the latest version at this writing, 6.1, applies listwise deletion for any unplanned missingness when utilizing the feature, limiting its application). The key in the preparation process is the development and use of appropriate variable-naming conventions, whether as data are being collected or as they are being prepared for analysis. In our (nonrepresentative) experience with data from such projects, including the National Longitudinal Surveys by the U.S. Bureau of Labor Statistics (BLS), variable names are more likely to be assigned across cohorts based on the time or wave of data collection, rather than assigned differently according to the age of the respondent. Where this is so, a systematic renaming process is required in the data preparation stage. To continue the above example, an aggression variable collected in 2007 might need to be renamed from *AGGR2007* to *AGGR06* for the 2001 birth cohort, *AGGR09* for the 1998 cohort, and *AGGR12* for the 1995 cohort. *AGGR09*, then, contains data collected at age 9 for the 1998 and 2001 cohorts, and is missing data for the 1995 cohort. When preparing for a large analysis, this can be quite an unwieldy, though absolutely vital, programming task.

INSPECTING THE PREPARED DATA

After this lengthy process, the researcher may consider the homework done. But we would require one final step: inspecting the prepared data. The more active the preparation done so far, the more important this is, especially in the case of separate data management and SEM software. Because we have already discussed most of the techniques required here, we content ourselves with mentioning the two issues most likely to have had problems inadvertently introduced in the data preparation process.

The first issue is to check which data are missing. The analyst should be aware of the quantity and location of missingness to be sure it matches the expectations from the limitations or design of the data set. The second is to check the variable distributions. The analyst should repeat the earlier steps, being sure the scale of the (possibly transformed or recoded) variables meet expectations, whether nominal, ordinal, or continuous.

ANALYSIS OF DATA

This step is beyond the scope of this chapter—your homework is complete!

WORKED EXAMPLES

In the final section of the chapter, we present a series of worked examples of increasing complexity, calling on different steps in the homework process. We also highlight some of the problems that can arise from *failing* to do the homework. The examples draw on data from the National Longitudinal Survey of Youth—1997 Cohort (NLSY97), collected by the U.S. Department of Labor's BLS. This large data set includes a nationally representative sample of youth born 1980 through 1984, recruited at the beginning of 1997, with an oversample of African American and Latino adolescents. The initial sample comprised 8,984 respondents, ages 12–16 as of the end of 1996. The cohort has been surveyed annually since. For a comprehensive description of the sample and sampling process, see U.S. Department of Labor (2009). In the interests of simple presentation, our examples do not incorporate measurement models but still highlight the key steps of data preparation.

Example 1: Regression

Our first example is a simple regression. The hypothesis to be tested is that girls' perceptions of their mothers' strictness (vs. permissiveness) negatively predict concurrent reports of having had dates with boyfriends.

Three variables are thus needed: respondent gender and the two study variables.

Because this is secondary data analysis, our ability to detect many types of errors is limited or absent. We can, however, check that the distributions of the variables of interest are as expected. All three variables were measured dichotomously, according to the online codebook. We used the BLS-provided SAS code for collating our working data set, and so use that software (SAS v9.2; SAS Institute, 2009) for the data management steps of our sequence. A frequency tabulation of each of the three variables (with the option for printing missing values as categories) appears in Figure 16.1. The numbers for respondent sex are as expected, and we can refer to the codebook to see that "1" represents males and "2," females. However, the other two "dichotomous" variables include negative numbers! Again, we refer to the codebook and learn that the negative numbers represent different categorizations of missing responses, depending on whether the respondent refused to answer, reported that they did not know the answer, had a "valid" skip of the item (boys were not asked about boyfriends or there was not a mother in the home), or had an "invalid" skip of the item (any other reason for missing). Among the non-negative values for permissiveness, "1" indicated permissive and "2" strict. For dating, "0" indicated no and "1" yes. Thus, the next step was to convert the negative numbers to missing-value codes. We simply changed all negative values for those two items to ".", SAS's default indicator for missing data. Having done so, we ended with three variables, each of which appropriately included only two possible nonmissing values.

The next step was to transfer the data to our analysis software. We use Mplus v6.1 (Muthén & Muthén, 2010) for the examples, both because of its versatility in accommodating different data types, and because the syntax is reasonably transparent. All Mplus syntax and output used in these examples is published on this volume's website (*www.handbookofsem.com*). As part of our homework, we first verified that we had transferred the data correctly. As part of the transfer step, we renamed the variables, giving them labels with more obvious meanings, with the constraints of Mplus's 8-character limit on variable names. This is, of course, an opportunity to introduce error. We utilized the USEOBSERVATIONS option in Mplus to restrict the working sample to girls (per our research question); we could have done so as easily in the transfer step from SAS.

The SAS System

The FREQ Procedure

KEY!SEX (SYMBOL) 1997

R0536300	Frequency	Percent	Cumulative Frequency	Cumulative Percent
1	4599	51.19	4599	51.19
2	4385	48.81	8984	100.00

MOTH PERMISSIVE OR STRICT? 1997

R0325800	Frequency	Percent	Cumulative Frequency	Cumulative Percent
-4	374	4.16	374	4.16
-3	2	0.02	376	4.19
-2	27	0.30	403	4.49
-1	1	0.01	404	4.50
1	3889	43.29	4293	47.78
2	4691	52.22	8984	100.00

R EVER HAD DATE WITH BOYFRIEND? 1997

R0349200	Frequency	Percent	Cumulative Frequency	Cumulative Percent
-4	4600	51.20	4600	51.20
-3	7	0.08	4607	51.28
-2	3	0.03	4610	51.31
-1	11	0.12	4621	51.44
0	2180	24.27	6801	75.70
1	2183	24.30	8984	100.00

FIGURE 16.1. SAS frequency table of raw data with numeric missing codes.

Using the TYPE = BASIC analysis option, and the CATEGORICAL definition for both analysis variables, we obtained sample statistics, including proportions of missing data. The first item we checked was the sample size: 4,379. This does not match the expected 4,385 girls (from Figure 16.1), but Mplus appropriately applied listwise deletion to the six cases missing both the permissiveness and the dating variables, with the warning:

Data set contains cases with missing on all variables.

These cases were not included in the analysis.

Number of cases with missing on all variables: 6.

Thus, the sample size was correct. The raw data proportions for the responses among girls were 53.7% reporting strict mothers and 50.0% having dated. These do not exactly match the numbers from Figure 16.1 due to different exclusion criteria, but they are near enough for reassurance. In a more complex problem, with correspondingly more opportunities for mistakes, we might have rerun the SAS frequencies with the same exclusion criteria as in Mplus to be doubly sure.

Now, for this simple problem (in truth, a logistic regression with robust mean- and variance-adjusted weighted least squares [WLSMV] estimation), we conducted the analysis, resulting in a logistic regression coefficient of −0.226 and standard error of 0.039, a statistically significant negative relation between perceived strictness and dating.

To contrast with those results, we also conducted the analysis in a perfectly blithe and unaware manner, as if we had not inspected missing data codes and frequencies, or checked the distributions of our variables. In other words, we set about as if we knew we wanted a regression coefficient, and leapt straight to that step. This resulted in a *linear* regression coefficient of −0.029 and standard error of 0.007. Coincidentally, we would still have concluded there was a significant negative relation, but it is by sheer chance (and the magnitude is obviously dramatically different).

Example 2:
Regression with Discretized Outcome

Our second example draws on the longitudinal aspect of the NLSY97. Using the same predictor, youth-reported maternal permissiveness, we hypothesized that youth with more permissive mothers would use marijuana more frequently 4 years later. For this analysis, the only new conceptually relevant variable is the marijuana frequency indicator from the 2001 interview. The frequency table from SAS appears in the left panel of Figure 16.2, where (non-negative) numbers indicate the number of days in the past 30 on which the youth used marijuana. Two things are worthy of note. First, there is a new category of missing data codes (negative numbers): −5 indicates the youth was not interviewed in that year. Second, there is quite a large number of observations associated with −4, the "valid skip." Conscientious readers of codebooks that we are, we find that an earlier item asked whether youth had ever smoked marijuana. If youth had, they were not asked the frequency question. In the first example, the valid skips were for cases where the response was truly not applicable (e.g., maternal permissiveness with no mother in the home). Here, the skip has a different meaning. There is a known value of number of days: 0. Thus, we recode −4 to 0, and this yields the frequency table in the right panel of Figure 16.2.

There is a remaining obvious problem with the marijuana frequency variable. It is grossly non-normal in distribution. In addition to a large floor effect at 0 days' use, the distribution is multimodal, with peaks at 10, 15, 20, 25, and 30 days. Substantively, it is likely that many of the respondents are estimating their responses, rather than recalling details of each day of use. How-

ever, in secondary data analysis, we have no access to the youth and cannot obtain revised reports. Thus, we are left with a distribution that does not lend itself to normalizing transformation. This is a case for a blunter tool: a discretizing transformation. There is little in the way of guidance here, except for an attempt to make substantively meaningful and statistically tractable cut points. Zero days' use is an obvious first category. Thirty days' use is the third most frequent response (after 0 and 1) and has unique substantive meaning (daily), so we would choose that as our final category. Arbitrarily, we render our other categories in our new ordinal variable as 1–9 days, 10–19 days, and 20–29 days. This transformation results in the distribution seen in Figure 16.3. The smallest resulting response is category 2, for 10–19 days' use. Even that reflects 180 responses, which is large enough for most logistic regression purposes. Had the original data set been smaller, we would have probably used fewer categories in the transformed variable. This resulting variable is highly skewed, of course. Transformations cannot reduce a floor effect. Thus, we still treat it as categorical in our final analyses, using a cumulative logistic regression.

We do not repeat here the steps taken to verify an accurate transfer of data, but we assert that our tests were passed and proceed to the analysis output. The analysis was, as noted, a cumulative logistic regression. Assuming proportional hazards for the sake of simplicity, the logistic regression coefficient was −0.066, $SE = 0.032$, $p = .040$; a significant negative relation between maternal strictness and subsequent frequency of youth marijuana use.

Our counterexample this time assumes somewhat more sophistication on the part of the researcher who has not done the homework, and we allow for correct handling of missing data, including the skip pattern. We hope that even the most casual investigator would have noticed either a negative mean number of days (retaining the numeric missing codes) or a drop in sample size from nearly 9,000 to approximately 2,000 (neglecting to substitute the known true values for missing). Given those corrections, an analysis that ignores the terrible distributional properties of the number of days variable and treats it as continuous and normal results in a different conclusion: a linear regression coefficient of −0.272, $SE = 0.161$, $p = .092$; no significant relation.

The SAS System

The FREQ Procedure

DAY USE MARIJUANA LAST 30 DAYS 2001

R6535700	Frequency	Percent	Cumulative Frequency	Cumulative Percent
-5	1102	12.27	1102	12.27
-4	5815	64.73	6917	76.99
-2	4	0.04	6921	77.04
-1	2	0.02	6923	77.06
0	531	5.91	7454	82.97
1	300	3.34	7754	86.31
2	194	2.16	7948	88.47
3	101	1.12	8049	89.59
4	64	0.71	8113	90.30
5	96	1.07	8209	91.37
6	26	0.29	8235	91.66
7	26	0.29	9261	91.95
8	16	0.18	8277	92.13
9	9	0.10	8286	92.23
10	84	0.93	8370	93.17
11	3	0.03	8373	93.20
12	8	0.09	8381	93.29
13	3	0.03	8384	93.32
14	3	0.03	8387	93.35
15	65	0.72	8452	94.08
16	2	0.02	8454	94.10
17	5	0.06	8459	84.16
18	4	0.04	8463	94.20
19	3	0.03	8466	94.23
20	93	1.04	8559	95.27
21	4	0.04	8563	95.31
22	6	0.07	8569	95.38
23	4	0.04	8573	95.43
24	1	0.01	8574	95.44
25	71	0.79	8645	96.23
26	2	0.02	8647	96.25
27	17	0.19	8664	96.44
28	30	0.33	8694	96.77
29	18	0.20	8712	96.97
30	272	3.03	8984	100.00

The SAS System

The FREQ Procedure

DAY USE MARIJUANA LAST 30 DAYS 2001

R6535700	Frequency	Percent	Cumulative Frequency	Cumulative Percent
.	1108	12.33	1108	12.33
0	6346	70.64	7454	82.97
1	300	3.34	7754	86.31
2	194	2.16	7948	88.47
3	101	1.12	8049	89.59
4	64	0.71	8113	90.30
5	96	1.07	8209	91.37
6	26	0.29	8235	91.66
7	26	0.29	9261	91.95
8	16	0.18	8277	92.13
9	9	0.10	8286	92.23
10	84	0.93	8370	93.17
11	3	0.03	8373	93.20
12	8	0.09	8381	93.29
13	3	0.03	8384	93.32
14	3	0.03	8387	93.35
15	65	0.72	8452	94.08
16	2	0.02	8454	94.10
17	5	0.06	8459	84.16
18	4	0.04	8463	94.20
19	3	0.03	8466	94.23
20	93	1.04	8559	95.27
21	4	0.04	8563	95.31
22	6	0.07	8569	95.38
23	4	0.04	8573	95.43
24	1	0.01	8574	95.44
25	71	0.79	8645	96.23
26	2	0.02	8647	96.25
27	17	0.19	8664	96.44
28	30	0.33	8694	96.77
29	18	0.20	8712	96.97
30	272	3.03	8984	100.00

FIGURE 16.2. SAS frequency tables of data with raw skip pattern and corrected for skip pattern.

The SAS System

The FREQ Procedure

mrjcat	Frequency	Percent	Cumulative Frequency	Cumulative Percent
.	1108	12.33	1108	12.33
0	6346	70.64	7454	82.97
1	832	9.25	9286	92.23
2	180	2.00	8466	94.23
3	246	2.74	8712	96.97
4	272	3.03	8984	100.00

FIGURE 16.3. SAS frequency table of discretized data.

Example 3:
Regression with Structured Missing Data

Our third and final example takes the question of marijuana use and adds sophistication. While it is certainly true that the responses for the abstinent group (no lifetime use) could legitimately be coded as 0 days in the past 30, it is also true that there is more information to be had. The abstinent group members are qualitatively different in some sense from those who have used marijuana but not in the past month. This is a clear example of a two-part outcome (technically not semicontinuous, as we will leave the quantity "part" of the two-part variable discrete, due to the still multimodal distribution of the raw variable). With slightly different data management coding in SAS, we created two variables. Rather than setting the frequency variable to 0 for the abstainers, we left it coded as missing and created a second, dichotomous variable for lifetime abstention from marijuana.

The remainder of the recoding was identical to that in Example 2. A cross-tabulation of the resulting variables appears in Figure 16.4. As shown, there are no cases in which the ever-use variable is coded as "no" (0) and the recent-use variable is coded as anything other than missing.

In brief, the results indicated a significant negative effect of 1997 maternal strictness on use of marijuana to any degree by 2001, and a logistic regression coefficient of -0.068, $SE = 0.031$, $p = .029$. However, there was no significant relation with quantity of use, among those who had used, with a logistic coefficient of -0.035, $SE = 0.048$.

There is no obvious "bad example" to use here that has not already been illustrated, so we allow this example to highlight the general ease of proper coding of even a relatively complex idea. (We note that recent versions of Mplus, including at least version 6.0, have internal facilities for creating two-part variables. How-

```
The SAS System

The FREQ Procedure

Table of evermj by mrjcat

evermrj     mrjcat
```

Frequency Percent Row Pct Col Pct	.	0	1	2	3	4	Total
.	1102 12.27 100.00 99.46	0 0.00 0.00 0.00	0 0.00 0.00 0.00	0 0.00 0.00 0.00	0 0.00 0.00 0.00	0 0.00 0.00 0.00	1102 12.27
0	0 0.00 0.00 0.00	5815 64.73 100.00 91.63	0 0.00 0.00 0.00	0 0.00 0.00 0.00	0 0.00 0.00 0.00	0 0.00 0.00 0.00	5815 64.73
1	6 0.07 0.29 0.54	531 5.91 25.69 8.37	832 9.26 40.25 100.00	180 2.00 8.71 100.00	246 2.74 11.90 100.00	272 3.03 13.16 100.00	2067 23.01
Total	1108 12.23	6346 70.64	832 9.26	180 2.00	246 2.74	272 3.03	8984 100.00

FIGURE 16.4. SAS two-way frequency table of two-part data.

ever, we opted to present the more general data management solution for users of various analysis software.)

CONCLUSIONS

Our conclusions are simple and, we suspect, hammered home by this point. Nonetheless, we will summarize. Careful data preparation can be time-consuming and even tedious, but it is crucial to obtaining valid research results. Some research and analysis designs (especially involving structured missing data) are more demanding in preparation than others, but it is these designs in which errors are all too easy.

The final point we wish to make is that just like doing homework before the exam, the data preparation must be done *before* the data analysis. It is tempting, as we noted at the outset, to go straight to testing the hypotheses. In such cases, often peculiar results highlight errors and omissions in the data preparation. However, the great hazard is the not-so-peculiar result that does *not* point to the errors. It is far safer to inspect and prepare the data carefully before the analysis stage—and far less embarrassing than having the errors found by others.

REFERENCES

Aiken, L. S., & West, S. G. (1991). *Multiple regression: Testing and interpreting interactions*. Thousand Oaks, CA: Sage.

Browne, M. W. (1989, May 3). Physicists debunk claim of a new kind of fusion. *The New York Times*. Retrieved from *www.nytimes.com*.

Burns, J. F. (2010, May 24). British medical council bars doctor who linked vaccine with autism. *The New York Times*. Retrieved from *www.nytimes.com*.

Eliason, S. R. (1993). *Maximum likelihood estimation: Logic and practice*. Newbury Park, CA: Sage.

Graham, J. W., Hofer, S. M., & MacKinnon, D. P. (1996). Maximizing the usefulness of data obtained with planned missing value patterns: An application of maximum likelihood procedures. *Multivariate Behavioral Research, 31*, 197–218.

Guo, J., Wall, M., & Amemiya, Y. (2006). Latent class regression on latent factors. *Biostatistics, 7*, 145–163.

Muthén, L. K., & Muthén, B. O. (2010). *Mplus user's guide* (6th ed.). Los Angeles: Authors.

Olsen, M. K., & Schafer, J. L. (2001). A two-part random-effects model for semicontinuous longitudinal data. *Journal of the American Statistical Association, 96*, 730–745.

Sang-Hun, C. (2009, October 27). Disgraced cloning expert convicted in South Korea. *The New York Times*. Retrieved from *www.nytimes.com*.

SAS Institute. (2009). *The SAS System* (v9.2). Cary, NC: Author.

Schaie, K. W. (1965). A general model for the study of developmental problems. *Psychological Bulletin, 64*, 92–107.

Tukey, J. W. (1957). On the comparative anatomy of transformations. *Annals of Mathematical Statistics, 28*, 602–632.

U.S. Department of Labor. (2009). *The NLSY97*. Retrieved from *www.bls.gov/nls/nlsy97.htm*.

West, S. G., Finch, J. F., & Curran, P. J. (1995). Structural equation models with nonnormal variables: Problems and remedies. In R. H. Hoyle (Ed.), *Structural equation modeling: Concepts, issues, and applications* (pp. 56–75). Thousand Oaks, CA: Sage.

CHAPTER 17

Structural Equation Modeling with Missing Data

John W. Graham
Donna L. Coffman

The missing data problem has long been an issue for data analysis of all kinds, and structural equation modeling (SEM) was, in the early days, not exempt from such problems. The main problem, as was true of virtually all statistical procedures of the time, was that statistical algorithms were devised for complete data, that is, perfectly rectangular data sets with no missing values. In those early days, new statistical procedures first focused on well-behaved data (e.g., normal distributions, no missing values), and only later began to address problem data (e.g., non-normal data, missing values).

An important year in the history of missing data analysis was 1987. Although important missing data work was done prior to that (e.g., Dempster, Laird, & Rubin, 1977), what happened in 1987 was a kind of a missing data revolution. This year was the beginning of the end of the reign of complete-cases analysis in scientific research. Two highly influential books were written that year: Little and Rubin's (1987) *Statistical Analysis with Missing Data* and Rubin's (1987) *Multiple Imputation for Nonresponse in Surveys*. These two books have been the basis for most of the important missing data developments since that year.

Even more important for SEM was the development in 1987 of the multiple-group SEM (MGSEM)

approach to handling missing data. Allison (1987) and Muthén, Kaplan, and Hollis (1987) each described the procedure, the first truly accessible procedure (accessible to SEM users, at least), for addressing missing data in a principled way. The MGSEM approach is described more fully below.

MISSING DATA THEORY

Defining Key Missing Data Terms

Fundamentally, the concepts and definitions we present here are the same as what are commonly used in the statistical literature. However, following Graham (in press), we take a somewhat different approach to describing these terms than is typically used. Our approach is meant to use simple English, while providing the precision needed to understand these often difficult concepts.

We begin with the idea that we have a variable, Y, that is of substantive interest for the planned analysis. Although we think of Y as being the dependent variable in an analysis (e.g., a multiple regression analysis), it can be any variable of substantive interest in the analysis model. It is key that Y is a variable that is observed for some cases, and missing for other cases.

Missingness

Following the rules of plain English, missingness is the *state* of (*Y*) being missing. So it is important that missingness per se is not a probability. That is, the data point of *Y* is either missing or not. We operationally define missingness as a variable, *R*, which takes on the value 1 if *Y* is observed, and 0 if *Y* is missing.[1] As with its more conceptual counterpart, *R* also is not, in and of itself, a probability. *R* has a (probability) distribution, but *R* is not itself a probability or a probability distribution.

Probability Distributions of *R*

What is the probability that *R* takes on the values 1 and 0? Assuming we are talking about a single variable at this point, the probability of a 0 value is the same as the percent missing on that variable. This distribution is useful, but what is more typically described in this context is the *joint probability distributions* associated with *R*. Here we are not interested in just the probability that *R* takes on the values 1 or 0. Here we are interested in the conditional probability that *R* takes on the value 0, conditional on the value of some other variable. In the sections that follow, we consider four other variables: *Q, Z, X,* and *Y* itself.

Model

Throughout this section, we use the term "model." We use this term in three different ways. First, we refer to the analysis model of substantive interest (referred to hereafter as the *analysis model*). This model includes (but is not limited to) various types of structural equation models. Second, when missing data analyses are performed, we also commonly refer to it as the missing data model. However, in order to distinguish this model from the next, we refer to this model as the *missing data analysis model*. In this case, we are thinking of multiple imputation (MI; most commonly, but not limited to, normal-model MI) or full information maximum likelihood (FIML) analysis. Third, there is the model that describes how the missingness was created. Three examples of such models were described by Collins, Schafer, and Kam (2001) as missing at random (MAR) linear, MAR convex, and MAR sinister. For example, they described MAR linear missingness with these statements:

If $Z = 1$ then prob(Y_{MIS}) = .20
If $Z = 2$ then prob(Y_{MIS}) = .40
If $Z = 3$ then prob(Y_{MIS}) = .60
If $Z = 4$ then prob(Y_{MIS}) = .80

where the values of Z represent the four quartiles of Z. In order to distinguish this model from the missing data analysis model, we refer to this model as the *missing data creation model*.

Causes of Missingness

Although other terms are commonly used to describe the four variables (Q, Z, X, and Y) introduced earlier, we think of them as the *causes of missingness*. Q is a variable that was produced using some completely random process, such as flipping a coin. The key feature of Q is that it is uncorrelated with all other variables, measured or unmeasured. Z is a real variable with substantive meaning. Variables in this category are correlated with Y to varying degrees. A key feature of Z is that it is not part of the analysis model of substantive interest. X is also a real variable with substantive meaning. The difference between X and Z is that X is part of the analysis model of substantive interest. As described earlier, Y is a variable that (1) is part of the analysis model of substantive interest, and (2) has missing data for some cases.

Our intent here is to explain why the Y value is missing. In talking about the causes of missingness, we find it useful to think of these causes as variables (Q, Z, X, and Y); these variables may be measured and available for analysis, or not. This concept is also often referred to as the *mechanisms of missingness*. Whatever the term used, three types of missingness are typically described: missing completely at random (MCAR), missing at random (MAR), and missing not at random (MNAR; Little & Rubin, 2002; Schafer & Graham, 2002).[2]

MCAR Missingness

Missingness is MCAR when Q is the cause of missingness. With this type of missingness, which is a special case of MAR, the word *random* means what most social scientists think of as random. MCAR missingness occurs when the values observed are a random sample of the total sample. That is, the cases that have data for a particular variable are representative of the total sample. Because the cause of missingness in this case (Q) is uncorrelated with all other variables, it need not be included in the missing data analysis model.

MAR Missingness

As it is typically defined, MAR missingness may depend on Y_{OBS}, but not on Y_{MIS}, where Y_{OBS} represents the data that have been observed, and Y_{MIS} represents the data that are missing (Little & Rubin, 2002; Schafer & Graham, 2002). It is commonly said that MCAR is a special case of MAR in which missingness also does not depend on Y_{OBS} (Schafer & Graham, 2002). Unfortunately there is some slippage in these definitions. Thus, following Graham (in press), we prefer definitions that stay close to plain English. We refer to it as "MAR missingness" if Z or X is the cause of missingness, and Z or X is included in the analysis model, or in the missing data analysis model. In particular, statements such as the following do *not* apply:

$$\text{If } Y = 1 \text{ then prob}(Y_{MIS}) = .20$$
$$\text{If } Y = 2 \text{ then prob}(Y_{MIS}) = .40$$
$$\text{If } Y = 3 \text{ then prob}(Y_{MIS}) = .60$$
$$\text{If } Y = 4 \text{ then prob}(Y_{MIS}) = .80$$

Another way of thinking of MAR is that once Y is conditioned on X and Z, any residual missingness can be thought of as being MCAR. In other words, MAR is more reasonably thought of as being *conditionally* MAR. With MAR, the cause of missingness must be included in the analysis model, or in the missing data analysis model, in order to achieve the "conditioning" described earlier. If the variable (X or Z) that is the cause of missingness is included in the missing data analysis model, then there is no estimation bias associated with the missing data. However, if the cause of missingness, even though available, is omitted from the missing data analysis model, then by definition, the missingness is MNAR, and there will be estimation bias.[3]

MNAR Missingness

The common definition of MNAR missingness is that the missingness is due to Y_{MIS} (Schafer & Graham, 2002). We would say that missingness is MNAR when Y itself is the cause of missingness. Missingness is MNAR if, even after conditioning on all X and Z variables, statements such as the following still hold:

$$\text{If } Y = 1 \text{ then prob}(Y_{MIS}) = .20$$
$$\text{If } Y = 2 \text{ then prob}(Y_{MIS}) = .40$$
$$\text{If } Y = 3 \text{ then prob}(Y_{MIS}) = .60$$
$$\text{If } Y = 4 \text{ then prob}(Y_{MIS}) = .80$$

A common example of MNAR missingness is that a question about family income on surveys is generally more likely to be missing among those with high incomes. In adolescent drug prevention research, the concern is that adolescent drug users are more likely than nonusers to drop out of a study. Taken by itself, this would be an example of MNAR missingness. Because with MNAR missingness the cause of missingness cannot be included in the model, this type of missingness produces estimation bias (again, for important exceptions see Collins et al., 2001; Graham, 2009).

Goals of Analysis

The goals of any analysis are (1) to obtain unbiased parameter estimates (i.e., to have estimates that are close to the population parameter values), (2) to obtain a good assessment of the variability around those estimates (i.e., to estimate standard errors or confidence intervals), and (3) to maximize statistical power in the process. The goals of good methods for handling missing data are the same. In the sections that follow, all of the methods we describe for handling missing data are judged using these three criteria.

Old Analysis Approaches
Complete-Cases Analysis

Complete-cases analysis (a.k.a. listwise deletion) involves discarding any case with any missing values on variables to be included in the model. In the early days (i.e., prior to 1987), researchers who made use of SEM (or any statistical) programs had no choice but to be satisfied with complete-cases analysis. Also, because the relatively new SEM analyses were perceived to provide so much, and because handling missing data in any principled way was not the norm, reviewers and editors tended to overlook missing data issues, perhaps requiring only a sentence or two in the discussion section in which the missing data were described as an unavoidable limitation.

In most empirical data sets, the cases that have complete data are very likely to be different from those that have missing data. That is, the sample of complete cases will not be representative of the whole, and the missingness will not be MCAR. Thus, any number of estimated quantities (means, variances, correlations) will not be reflective of the whole sample. On the other hand, it is often the case that variables from the pre-test (for which all cases generally have data), variables that could reasonably be part of the *analysis* model, are causes of missingness, or good proxies for the causes of missingness. When this is the case, and it tends to be the case with a broad array of regression models that are common in SEM analysis, the biases tend to be small, even with complete-cases analysis (e.g., see Graham, Cumsille, & Elek-Fisk, 2003). When it is reasonable to include such variables as covariates, means and correlations will still be biased, but covariate adjusted means and unstandardized regression coefficients are often relatively unbiased. It turns out to be a rather important limitation, however, that with complete-cases models, there is no special way of including the causes of missingness in the model, unless it is reasonable to include those variables as covariates, or as other parts of the analysis model.

An important by-product of using complete cases analysis is that the standard errors associated with the parameter estimates are meaningful. In addition, provided that the number of cases lost to missing data is small (e.g., less than about 5%), the loss of statistical power from throwing away partial cases is relatively small. However, it is often the case that a small amount of missing data on different variables adds up to a meaningful loss of power due to cases lost to missingness. It is especially in these situations that analysis of complete cases is a poor alternative to using one of the recommended analysis procedures.

Pairwise Deletion

Also in those early days researchers flirted with the idea of using as input to the SEM program a covariance matrix generated with pairwise deletion. That is, each variance and covariance element in the matrix was estimated based on cases that had relevant data. This procedure was facilitated by the fact that inputting a covariance matrix was exceptionally easy with SEM programs. Despite problems associated with estimating standard errors with pairwise deletion, this approach had conceptual appeal in that all available information seemed to be used in the analysis. A problem that can occur with this approach is that the pairwise deletion

covariance matrix can be nonpositive definite. Perhaps the strongest reasons for not using the pairwise deletion approach are (1) that parameter estimates may be biased, and, perhaps more importantly, (2) that reasonable standard errors are not estimable directly. Pairwise deletion is not recommended with SEM.

Recommended Missing Data Methods

Model-Based Solutions

As we noted earlier, the problem with missing data for most existing statistical analysis is that the estimation algorithms were originally written with complete data in mind. So with one of the recommended solutions, the model-based solution, one develops new statistical estimation algorithms designed to handle the missing data and perform the usual parameter estimation all in a single step. Also fitting in this category of solutions is the MGSEM procedure, which we describe more fully below. The value of this general approach is that handling the missing data is little more than a by-product of performing the parameter estimation one wanted to do in the first place. The disadvantage of this approach is that a different algorithm must be developed for each new type of analysis. It is important that a primary implementation of model-based solutions for missing data, solutions that have come to be known as FIML solutions, has been in SEM programs.

Data-Based Solutions

The other general class of recommended solutions for missing data are data-based. This is a two-step approach. With this approach, one first deals with the missing data and generates a *product* (e.g., a covariance matrix or complete data). Then, in a separate, second step, one analyzes the product with regular complete cases statistical procedures. The first solution in this general class was the expectation maximization (EM) algorithm (Dempster et al., 1977; Little & Rubin, 1987, 2002). With one common implementation of the EM algorithm, the data (with missing values) are read in, and the product is a maximum-likelihood (ML) variance–covariance matrix and vector of means. This covariance matrix (and means) may then be analyzed as if they were complete data. The biggest advantage of analysis based on EM is that parameter estimates are known to be unbiased and efficient.[4] The biggest drawback to using the EM algorithm in this way, however, is that, as with pairwise deletion, there is no direct way of obtaining reasonable estimates of the standard errors (although two-stage approaches have been studied in this context, e.g., Yuan & Bentler, 2000). In addition, although this is not a huge problem in this context, parameter estimates for latent variable SEM models are not ML when based on the EM covariance matrix (which is ML).

The other major approach that fits within this general class of solutions is MI (Rubin, 1987; Schafer, 1997). MI, which is described a bit more fully below, reads in the data (with missing values), and the products are multiple data sets with the missing values replaced with plausible values. Asymptotically, the parameter estimates based on EM and MI are equivalent. That is, the parameter estimates based on MI are also known to be unbiased and efficient (to the extent that the MAR assumption holds). The key advantage of MI is that it also provides a method for estimating the uncertainty due to the missing data. That is, as a by-product of the analysis, MI provides standard errors for the parameter estimates.

THE MGSEM PROCEDURE

Specific to SEM is the MGSEM procedure (Allison, 1987; Muthén et al., 1987). In this chapter, we lay out the rudiments of the procedure. More detailed descriptions (with LISREL; Jöreskog & Sörbom, 1996) may be found elsewhere (e.g., Allison, 1987; Graham, Hofer, & Piccinin, 1994). In brief, the MGSEM procedure starts by dividing the cases into groups that correspond to different missing data patterns. In the simplest case, suppose we were testing a model with three variables: a program variable, a mediating variable, and an outcome variable. Also suppose that the program variable and outcome variable were always observed, but that the mediating variable was observed for only one-third of the cases. The two patterns of missingness are shown in Table 17.1.

TABLE 17.1. Patterns of Missing and Nonmissing Values

Group	Program	Mediator	Outcome	N
1	1	1	1	667
2	1	0	1	333

Note. 1 = data present; 0 = data missing.

With this procedure, each distinct pattern of missing and nonmissing values is represented in the SEM analysis as a different group. In this simplest case, there would be two groups. Group 1 is the cases with no missing data, and Group 2 is the cases with data missing for the mediator. The input covariance matrices for the two-group analysis are as follows. For Group 1 (complete cases), the covariance matrix is the same as for any one-group SEM analysis. For Group 2 (some missing data), any variance or covariance element for which all relevant variables have data, the element is presented as usual. For any variance or covariance element for which one or both variables are missing, the covariance is fixed at 0, and the variance is fixed at 1.

For analysis, in broad terms, Group 1 parameters are all estimated in the way that is customary for any one-group model. For Group 2, all of the factor-level parameter estimates (factor variances, factor covariances, factor regressions) are constrained to be equal across groups. Then, for item-level parameters (factor loadings, item residual variances and covariances), wherever there are data, the parameter is estimated and constrained to be equal across groups. Where the relevant data are missing, however, the parameter is fixed at 0 (factor loadings and item residual covariances), or 1 (item residual variances). The results of this analysis are ML parameter estimates with reasonable estimates of the standard errors.

Why Even Talk about the MGSEM Procedure?

The MGSEM procedure just described has been supplanted by the FIML models described below. So why even talk about this model, except in a historical sense? One reason for doing so relates to the fact that the MGSEM model allows the researcher to test many kinds of models using the covariance matrix (and means) as input. Because of this, the input matrix can be the population covariance matrix, and parameters and standard errors can be estimated for the population without sampling. This can be an enormous benefit for certain simulations relating to missing data analysis. Because the covariance matrices in the two groups are known, for example, when missingness is MCAR, certain missing data models can be fit easily and quickly using the MGSEM strategy. These models are not possible for every question relating to missing data analysis. But when these models are possible, parameter estimates and standard errors can be estimated for the population in a matter of minutes using the MGSEM procedure that would take many hours or days to estimate using Monte Carlo procedures. Graham and colleagues have used this approach for several years to good effect (see Graham, in press; Graham, Taylor, & Cumsille, 2001; Graham, Taylor, Olchowski, & Cumsille, 2006).

FULL-INFORMATION MAXIMUM LIKELIHOOD

Historically, SEM was estimated via maximum Wishart likelihood (MWL), which required only the sufficient statistics (i.e., means, variances, and covariances). Among SEM researchers, MWL is usually referred to as ML. Historically, this was more efficient computationally, but with the speed of computers today it is easy to maximize the full "raw" data likelihood. Among statisticians, this is usually referred to as ML, but among SEM researchers, this is usually referred to as FIML. For each individual, the log-likelihood is given as

$$l_i(\theta \mid Y) = K - \frac{1}{2}ln \mid \Sigma_i \mid - \frac{1}{2}(y_i - \mu_i)\Sigma_i^{-1}(y_i - \mu_i)$$

where K is a constant. Summing the log-likelihood across the N cases results in the overall sample log-likelihood, that is,

$$l(\theta \mid Y) = \sum_{i=1}^{N} l_i(\theta \mid Y)$$

Because the log-likelihood can be written for each individual, there does not need to be the same number of items, observations, or variables for every individual. Rather, each individual's log-likelihood is written in terms of the individual's observed data. Therefore, we subscript with i to denote that these are subvectors (e.g., μ_i) or submatrices (e.g., Σ_i) of the original mean vector and covariance matrix in which rows and columns for missing variables are removed, and that these subvectors or submatrices may vary across individuals. In the context of factor analysis, this estimation method of maximizing the individual log-likelihood to average across the missing data was first introduced by Finkbeiner (1979). Arbuckle (1996) later introduced FIML in the context of SEM (although FIML had been implemented earlier in software, e.g., Mx and Amos).

FIML yields correct standard errors and a likelihood ratio (chi-square) test statistic when the assumptions are met. Note that Savalei (2010) shows that the observed information matrix rather than the expected information matrix should be used for obtaining standard errors, and that most SEM software packages use expected information by default (the exception is Mplus). For FIML, unlike MI, the analyst specifies a particular density function and, therefore, likelihood function to be maximized. For example, in the previous equation, we specified a multivariate normal distribution. A possible disadvantage of FIML is that it is relatively more difficult to incorporate auxiliary variables, but this has become less relevant with recent advances in statistical software (e.g., Mplus 6 makes it easy for the user to incorporate auxiliary variables).

FIML estimates can also be obtained using the EM algorithm. In the E-step, the missing values are replaced by predicted values assuming known model parameters. In the M-step, the parameters are reestimated by ML assuming complete data. These steps are repeated until convergence occurs. To obtain FIML estimates, other algorithms may be used, such as the pseudo-Newton-type algorithms that are used when there is no missing data, but EM is generally simpler to implement. Whichever algorithm is used, the entire procedure is carried out in one stage. That is, it does not involve obtaining an ML estimate of the means, variances, and covariances via EM and inputting these sufficient statistics into an SEM software program to estimate model parameters via MWL. Nor does it involve performing MI followed by fitting the SEM to each of the complete data sets and combining the results. In other words, when the EM algorithm is used with FIML, the estimates obtained are the factor loadings, error variances, and so forth, but when the two-stage (i.e., data-based) EM procedure is used, estimates of the mean, variances, and covariances are obtained. These estimates are then used to obtain estimates of the factor loadings, error variances, and so forth. For this reason, the two-stage EM procedure may give standard errors that are too small, although point estimates are good.[5]

MULTIPLE IMPUTATION

The most common approach at present for handling missing data in SEM is to make use of the FIML feature within one of the SEM programs. However, there are reasons for employing MI to handle missing data in the SEM context. In this section, we lay out the fundamentals of MI.

Regression-Based Single Imputation

A common form of single imputation is based on multiple regression. With this approach, we start with the idea that one variable (Y) is sometimes missing, and several other variables (say X_1–X_5) are never missing. Based on cases that are not missing for Y, one can perform a multiple regression analysis with X_1–X_5 predicting Y. The regression equation from that analysis may then be employed for cases with Y missing to obtain a predicted score for Y ($\hat{Y}$); that $\hat{Y}$ score may be used in place of each missing Y score.

Problems with Single Imputation

The main problem with the single imputation approach is that the imputed scores have too little variability. There are two sources of this problem. First, the imputed scores (the $\hat{Y}$'s) lie on the regression line. However, for cases with data for Y, it is virtually never the case that the value lies right on the regression line; the score almost always deviates from the regression line by some amount.

The second reason singly imputed scores have too little variability comes from the idea that the regression equation itself was derived from a single sample from the population. Other samples from the same population would be expected to produce a slightly different regression equation.

Restoring Lost Variance in Multiple Imputation

One key to MI, then, is to restore the variance lost from single imputation. Restoring the lost error variance is a simple matter. One could simply sample the error variance from the cases with data for Y. But it turns out that an easier (and usually better) strategy is simply to generate random normal error and add it to each imputed value.

Restoring lost variance from the second source, however, is more of a challenge. Conceptually, one could "simply" generate multiple random draws from the population, and calculate a new regression equation for each random draw. Then if one adds random error to each imputed value from each random draw, one has what Rubin (1987) referred to as *proper* imputations.

Of course, one does not normally have the luxury of being able to make multiple random draws from the population. But one may be able to simulate those random draws. One approach would be to employ bootstrapping (Efron, 1982) to simulate random draws from the population. Another possibility is to use Bayesian sampling methods for this purpose. One could use data augmentation (DA; Tanner & Wong, 1987), or the related Markov Chain Monte Carlo (MCMC) approach for this purpose. DA is a two-step, iterative procedure that bears some similarity to EM. With DA, one first simulates data from current parameter estimates (the imputation, or I-Step), and then one simulates parameter estimates from the current data (the posterior, or P-Step). One continues this process until the distribution of parameter estimates has stabilized.

Some Practical Details in Multiple Imputation

MI is a three-step process. First, impute m data sets. Second, perform the analysis on each of the m data sets using regular, complete-cases statistical analysis (saving the results). Third, combine the results of the m analyses.

A key issue of the first step relates to how many steps of DA (or MCMC) there should be between imputed data sets. As we said earlier, the purpose of DA is to simulate random draws from the population. The idea with any Markov chain analysis is that all of the information for the current iteration is contained in the previous iteration. Because of this, the parameter estimates from adjacent steps of DA are expected to be very similar, much more similar than would be expected from two random draws from the population. However, after many steps of DA, one cannot predict the current parameter values from the original iteration. That is, if the number of DA steps is sufficiently large, the imputed data sets are like two random draws from the population. As it turns out, a good estimate of the number of DA steps required is the same as the number of iterations it takes EM to converge. This is often valuable because implementations of MI often use EM results as starting values for DA (MCMC) iterations.[6]

MI Inference

The key to drawing inferences from MI is to combine the results of the m separate analyses following Rubin's (1987) rules. The parameter estimate itself is simply the average of the parameter estimate over the m imputed data sets. The standard error of the estimate is made up of two sources of variance. The first source is due to regular sampling variability. This is referred to as the "within imputation" variance ($\bar{U}$), and is the squared standard error estimated within each imputation averaged over the m imputed data sets. The second source of variance is due to the missing data. This is referred to as the "between imputation" variance (B), and is the sample variance of the parameter estimate over the m imputed data sets. With Rubin's rules, the two sources of variance are summed to yield the total variance (T), which is given by

$$T = \bar{U} + (1 + 1/m)B$$

The square root of T is the MI estimate of the standard error for that parameter.

The Practical Importance of Automation

In a conceptual sense, the three steps of MI are very simple. The second step, analysis of each of the m imputed data sets, could not be easier. But what is hidden in this step is that there must be some mechanism for saving the results of those m separate analyses. One can imagine simply copying the results (by hand, or by cutting and pasting) to a separate results file. But imagine having 40 parameter estimates and standard errors to deal with, and then imagine multiplying this by the number of imputations; it is easy to see that the process would become highly tedious and error-prone. Thus, automating this process becomes essential.

MI Implementations

Two good, normal-model MI implementations with DA or MCMC for simulating random draws from the population are Norm (2.03; Schafer, 1997; see also Graham, in press; Graham et al., 2003),[7] and SAS PROC MI. A third implementation, SPSS 17-20, does make use of the MCMC approach, but it has other failings that limit its general usefulness for now (see Graham, in press, for a more detailed discussion of the limitations of the multiple imputation feature in SPSS 17-19; Graham also notes, however, that the automation and combining of results with SPSS 17-20 is excellent). Other MI implementations that do not use DA/MCMC but may nonetheless prove to be useful include Amelia II (Honaker, King, & Blackwell, 2007; King, Honaker, Joseph, & Scheve, 2001), and IVEware (Raghunathan, 2004; Raghunathan, Solenberger, & Van Hoewyk, 2002).

Multiple Imputation with SEM

When one's analysis of choice is SEM, it does seem logical to take advantage of the FIML feature of one of the popular programs to deal with missing data. However, there are reasons for using MI with SEM. One reason for using MI rather than FIML relates to addressing the problem that manifest indicators are not normally distributed. For example, when one wishes to estimate robust standard errors (Satorra & Bentler, 1994; e.g., as implemented with LISREL), these standard errors must be estimated with complete raw data. (Note that this limitation does not apply with EQS 6.1 [Bentler, 2006, see *http://www.mvsoft.com/eqs60.htm#new*] or Mplus 6.) Another approach in this context is to make use of the bootstrap option available in several programs (e.g., Amos [Arbuckle, 2006] and LISREL). Again, however, the bootstrap option is available only with complete raw data (this limitation does not apply with Mplus 6).

It may also be the case that the researcher simply prefers analysis with MI. One advantage, for example, is that it is generally much easier to include auxiliary variables with MI than with FIML and SEM (but see "Auxiliary Variables" section below). Finally, not all SEM programs have a FIML feature. One good example of this is PROC CALIS with older versions of SAS. With this program, it is a simple matter to use PROC MI to impute the data, PROC CALIS to perform the analysis, and PROC MIANALYZE to combine the results for final MI inference.[8]

AUXILIARY VARIABLES

In the early days of missing data analysis, researchers often talked about including in the analysis variables that were not part of the analysis model (this applied mainly to the use of MI). It was often said that such variables were included to "help" with the imputation. However, little was written in those early days that would give us details about what was meant by "help" with the imputation. Collins and colleagues (2001) provided us with many of those details. These authors referred to variables included "solely to improve the performance of the missing data procedure as *auxiliary variables.*" The two benefits of including such variables in the missing data model are (1) to reduce estimation bias (due to nonignorable sources of missing data), and (2) to restore some of the power lost due to missing data.

Auxiliary Variable Benefit on Estimation Bias

In one simulation, which is the focus here, Collins and colleagues (2001) studied a system of three variables: X, Y, and Z. The variables of substantive interest were X (always observed) and Y (sometimes missing). The auxiliary variable, Z, was always observed. In their simulation, Collins and colleagues showed that the regression coefficient for X predicting Y (β_{YX}) was biased to an appreciable extent when (1) Z was the (MAR-linear) cause of missingness on Y, (2) Z was omitted from the model (rendering the missingness MNAR), (3) there was 50% missing data on Y, and (4) the correlation between Y and Z (ρ_{YZ}) = .9. However, for all other conditions of their simulation (50% missing on Y, ρ_{YZ} = .4; 25% missing on Y, ρ_{YZ} = .9; 25% missing on Y, ρ_{YZ} = .4), Collins and colleagues judged the bias associated with the MNAR missingness (excluding Z from the model) to be tolerably small.[9]

Collins and colleagues (2001) also studied the effect of adding an auxiliary variable (where Z was correlated with Y, but not with missingness itself, ρ_{ZR} = 0, where R is a dichotomous variable with 0 if the value is missing and 1 if the value is observed) under MNAR missingness. With no auxiliary variable, standardized bias = –138.2, where standardized bias (as used by Collins et al.) represented the percentage of the standard error. Collins and colleagues suggested that standardized bias greater than about 40% (positive or negative) is of practical significance (which implies that values less than 40% represent bias that is tolerably small). When they added an auxiliary variable (Z) to the model, where ρ_{YZ} = .4, the bias improved only slightly, to –131.7. However, when an auxiliary variable with ρ_{YZ} = .9 was added to the model, bias was reduced substantially, to –54.5.

Auxiliary Variable Benefit on Statistical Power

Collins and colleagues (2001) also showed that adding an auxiliary variable (where ρ_{ZR} = 0) reduced the width of the confidence interval for β_{YZ}. Graham and Collins (2011) extended this work, showing details of the statistical power benefits of adding auxiliary variables to the missing data model. They used the concepts of total sample size (N_{TOT}), complete cases sample size (N_{CC}), and effective sample size (N_{EFF}) to capture the benefit from adding auxiliary variables to the model. N_{TOT} was defined as the total sample size, including com-

plete cases and partial cases; N_{CC} was the sample size of complete cases; and N_{EFF} was the sample size (larger than N_{CC}) with no auxiliary variables that yielded the same statistical power as the model that included the auxiliary variables.

Graham and Collins (in press) used a model similar to that used by Collins and colleagues (2001). The model included three variables: X (always observed; the independent variable in a simple regression model), Y (sometimes missing; the dependent variable in the regression model), and Z (an auxiliary variable with ρ_{ZR} = 0). Graham and Collins showed that as the correlation (ρ_{YZ}) increased, the N_{EFF} benefit increased, as shown in Table 17.2, in which the numbers involved N_{TOT} = 1000, N_{CC} = 500, and ρ_{YZ} ranging from ρ_{YZ} = .10 to ρ_{YZ} = .90. As shown in Table 17.2, adding any auxiliary variable will yield some benefits in terms of N_{EFF} increase. For small values of ρ_{YZ}, those benefits are modest. However, with ρ_{YZ} = .50 or greater, those benefits are considerably larger. And with very large ρ_{YZ} (e.g., .90), the benefits are substantial.

The benefits shown in Table 17.2 involve the situation in which all cases missing on Y have data for the auxiliary variable Z. Graham and Collins (in press) also explored the value of having one auxiliary variable where only 25%, 50%, or 75% of the cases missing on Y actually have data for Z. They also explored the value of having a second auxiliary variable, where $\rho_{Y,Z2}$ is less than or equal to the value of $\rho_{Y,Z1}$. Graham and Collins describe a utility for calculating the N_{EFF} benefit of adding one or two auxiliary variables under any circumstances as described earlier.

TABLE 17.2. N_{EFF} Benefits from Adding an Auxiliary Variable

ρ_{YZ}	N_{EFF}	% benefit
.10	502	0.4%
.20	509	1.8%
.30	522	4.4%
.40	542	8.4%
.50	570	14%
.60	608	22%
.70	660	32%
.80	733	47%
.90	839	78%

Note. N_{TOT} = 1,000; N_{CC} = 500; % benefit = $(N_{EFF} - N_{CC})/N_{CC}$.

Incorporating Auxiliary Variables in Structural Equation Models

Graham (2003) described in detail two kinds of models for incorporating auxiliary variables in an SEM. The basics of these two models are described in this section. Some additional details relating to specific SEM programs are given near the end of this chapter.

Extra DV Model

With the extra dependent variable (DV) model (which is best with manifest variable models), one simply specifies the auxiliary variables as extra DVs in the model. Every variable to the left of the auxiliary variable (e.g., independent variables and mediators) is specified to predict the auxiliary variable. For every variable that is also a DV, the residuals are correlated. There is really nothing particularly tricky about this model in any of the SEM programs because models with multiple DVs are common, and this model follows the same form.

Spider Model

The "spider" model, described by Graham (2003) as the "saturated correlates" model, is best for latent variable models. With this model each auxiliary variable is specified to be correlated with every other auxiliary variable, and with any manifest variable that is not predicted by anything (e.g., single items as independent variables). In addition, each auxiliary variable is specified to be correlated with the item residual of any manifest variable that is predicted (e.g., if the variable is an indicator of a latent variable, or if it is a single item that is a mediator or DV). Additional details for some SEM programs are given below.

SEM WITH MISSING DATA AND ORDERED-CATEGORICAL INDICATORS

FIML

When there are no missing data, structural equation models with ordered categorical indicators, such as responses from a rating (e.g., a 5-point Likert) scale, are fit by first estimating a polychoric correlation matrix. To accommodate binary and ordinal categorical indicators, it is assumed that a continuous response variable underlies each observed categorical variable, where the relationship between the observed variable and the underlying response variable is a threshold process. Assuming that the observed categorical variables, y, arise from categorizing the underlying multivariate normal latent response variables, y^*, the polychoric correlation is the estimate of the correlation among the latent response variables. The SEM is then fit to the polychoric correlation matrix using weighted least squares (or robust weighted least squares), which is a limited-information ML procedure. Thus, the input is a correlation matrix and not the raw data. Recall, FIML requires the raw data. However, Amos and Mplus 6 will fit structural equation models with ordinal indicators and missing data using a Bayesian estimation procedure. Using this procedure, each missing value has a posterior distribution, and if a point estimate for the missing value is needed, it is taken as the mean of the posterior predictive distribution.

Multiple Imputation

Norm, SAS PROC MI, and the MI options available in SEM packages (e.g., Amos, Mplus 6) assume that the variables are normally distributed. One possible solution is to impute under the multivariate normal assumption and then round off the values to the nearest integer, thereby creating ordinal data. Although previous simulation studies have shown that this solution is reasonable (Schafer, 1997), other, more recent studies have shown this method can be inadequate and can result in inaccurate results for *binary* (i.e., dichotomous) variables (Allison, 2005; Bernaards, Belin, & Schafer, 2007; Horton, Lipsitz, & Parzen, 2003). Note that these simulation studies were for *binary* data. The approach suggested by Yucel, He, and Zaslavsky (2008) also applied to ordinal data. Also, Finch (2010) showed in a simulation study with ordinal data with five response categories that MI followed by rounding did not result in substantial significant bias.

Existing Options

Five or More Response Categories, Approximately Symmetrical Responses

Simulation studies (see, e.g., Dolan, 1994; Olsson, 1979) have shown that if there are five or more response categories *and* the responses are approximately symmetrical, then the responses may be treated as continuous in the context of no missing data. Thus, one option, if there are more than five response options, is to treat the responses as continuous, and use FIML. In addition, robust standard errors could be obtained. Another fairly simple option would be to multiply impute the missing data using a multivariate normal distribution (i.e., Norm or SAS PROC MI) but retain the imputed values without rounding. MI could then be followed by fitting an SEM for continuous normal data to the imputed data sets and combining results (again, given that there are five or more response categories and the responses are approximately symmetrical). However, given the ease with which more advanced procedures (described next) can now be implemented in SEM software (e.g., Amos, Mplus 6), and given the bias that may result when using ML with ordinal indicators (see, e.g., Babakus, Ferguson, & Jöreskog, 1987; Muthén & Kaplan, 1985), we prefer the more advanced procedures described next.

Less Than Five Response Categories, and/or Responses Not Symmetric

If there are not at least five response categories and/or the responses are not approximately symmetrical, another option would be to consider the FIML methods used in item response theory (IRT) models. Likewise, for linear latent growth curve models in which the factors are slope and intercept, a program, such as SuperMix (Hedeker & Gibbons, 2008), that implements a FIML estimation procedure for ordinal or binary data, could be used. More generally, however, the Bayesian estimation procedures in Amos or Mplus 6 could be used.

Another possible solution would be to impute under a multinomial model using, for example, the "cat" package for R. However, this solution would not take into account the ordinal nature of the responses and instead would treat the responses as strictly multinomial categorical (i.e., nominal). Furthermore, if there are more than a few nominal categorical variables, this approach is impractical (Schafer, 1997). Another R package "mix" is available for handling mixed categorical and continuous data. If the data have a monotone missingness pattern, then either the logistic (or ordinal logistic) regression or discriminate function imputation options in SAS PROC MI could be used. In any case, approaches based on statistical approximations are preferable to complete-cases analysis (i.e., listwise deletion; Bernaards et al., 2007). In previous simulation studies (e.g., Allison, 2005; Bernaards et al., 2007; Horton et al., 2003), most any imputation method resulted in less

biased estimates than listwise deletion (i.e., complete-cases analysis). Furthermore, Bernaards and colleagues (2007) showed that an adaptive rounding procedure performed well. This procedure used a cutoff value for determining whether to round a binary variable to 0 or 1 that was based on a normal approximation to the binomial distribution. More recently, Demirtas (2009) compared six different rounding strategies for binary variables in a simulation study and recommended that researchers avoid uncritical use of rounding and consider the applied context and specific nature of their problem when deciding on a rounding rule.

Finally, perhaps the most practical approach for imputation of mixed categorical and continuous data is a fully conditional specification (as opposed to specifying a joint model for the data as in Norm or "cat"). The fully conditional specification is also referred to as "chained equations" (Raghunathan, 2004; Raghunathan, Lepkowski, Van Hoewyk, & Solenberger, 2001) and is currently implemented in Mplus 6, ICE, IVEware (Raghunathan, Solenberger, & Van Hoewyk, 2002), and the R packages "mice" (van Buuren & Groothuis-Oudshoorn, in press) and "mi" (Gelman, Hill, Yajima, Su, & Grazia Pittau, 2010).[10] The chained equations approach tailors the imputation model to the scale of the incomplete variable, for example, a logistic model for a categorical variable and a linear regression model for a continuous variable, so that a separate conditional model is specified for each variable with missingness. Thus, postprocessing of data, such as rounding, is not needed. The specification of sequential separate conditional models for each variable with missingness as opposed to a joint multivariate model for all variables simultaneously is the reason this approach is so flexible in handling variables with different scale types.

MODEL IDENTIFICATION WITH MISSING DATA

Closely examining the standard errors is a good way of determining the (empirical) identification status of one's model. And this examination can involve comparing standard errors from a part of the model for which identification status is in question with a part of the model that is well identified. It is important that there be a level playing field for these comparisons. With no missing data, the major determinant of differential standard errors is the variance of the indicator variables; a good strategy for estimating identification is to standardize the variables, and to use a parameterization that estimates all factor loadings (these strategies are not necessarily good for actual analysis, but they can be useful to assessing identification status; e.g., Graham, 2005).

In the missing data case, one more factor, sample size, must be taken into account. Parts of the model that are based on smaller N will have larger standard errors, not because of poor identification, but because of the smaller N. Thus, a good strategy for assessing identification is to analyze the EM covariance matrix (with artificially equal N) or to analyze a single data set imputed from EM parameters. Again, although one would never use such data sets for one's main analysis, it is a good strategy for assessing the identification status of one's model.

GOODNESS OF FIT WITH MISSING DATA

We start off with the idea that this situation is complicated. The complications begin with the fact that we talk about "goodness of fit." However, it often helps to think of it as "badness of fit." When a particular parameter is not estimated, the chi-square is incremented to the extent that the parameter value is large.

RMSEA, TLI/NNFI, and CFI

We have observed that when analyzing incomplete data, different programs (LISREL, Amos, Mplus) give different estimates of goodness of fit. Although model chi-square and degrees of freedom (df) are the same across these programs, we have observed differences for independence (baseline) model chi-square and df, and especially for these three indices of practical fit: root mean square error of approximation (RMSEA; Browne & Cudeck, 1993; Steiger & Lind, 1980); Tucker–Lewis index/non-normed fit index (TLI/NNFI; Tucker & Lewis, 1973; see also Bentler & Bonett, 1980); and comparative fit index (CFI; Bentler, 1990). It appears that at least in some cases, the differences are due to small errors in one program or another.

Many questions arise that relate to what should be done with goodness of fit when one has missing data. For at least some of these questions, it is possible to contrive a missing data model and a complete cases model that should have identical (or virtually identical) estimates of fit. Thus, in these cases, it is possible to use logic to help us make the proper decision.

■ *Question 1: What is the proper independence model?*

■ *Answer:* We assume that the appropriate independence model is the model that estimates item variances (and means, if they are estimated in the model of interest) but no covariances (e.g., Bentler & Bonett, 1980; Widaman & Thompson, 2003).

■ *Question 2: Should means be fixed at 0 in the independence model?*

■ *Answer:* No. Consider two data sets. The first has $k = 5$ variables and $N = 1,000$ cases, and no missing data. The second data set is the same, except that one value (out of the 5,000 total values) is missing. Under these two circumstances, we would want to draw the same conclusions about model fit; that is, we would want model fit to be virtually identical in the two data sets, despite the fact that the first data set (complete cases) is estimated one way (and without means), and the second data set (a single missing value) must be estimated with FIML (with means). To achieve this with the FIML analysis, we must estimate means in the independence model (Widaman & Thompson, 2003).

■ *Question 3: How should one estimate TLI/NNFI and CFI with missing data?*

■ *Answer:* First, estimate the model chi-square, χ_h^2, and df, d_h, and independence model chi-square, and df, d_0, χ_0^2, as described under Question 1. Then simply calculate the two indices using the standard formulas for TLI/NNFI,

$$\text{TLI} = \frac{\dfrac{\chi_0^2}{d_0} - \dfrac{\chi_h^2}{d_h}}{\dfrac{\chi_0^2}{d_0} - 1}$$

and for CFI,

$$\text{CFI} = 1 - \frac{\max[(\chi_h^2 - d_h), 0]}{\max[(\chi_0^2 - d_0), (\chi_h^2 - d_h)]}$$

Because sample size is not part of these formulas, there is no need to be concerned with the correct sample size for this analysis.

■ *Question 4: How can one estimate RMSEA with missing data?*

■ *Answer:* This answer is more complicated. In order to answer it, we conceive of two data sets for which we would expect identical estimates of fit. Let's say that we have a simple two-factor model, with one, single-item factor,[11] set to be correlated with a second, 5-item factor. Let's say that all of the (appreciable) badness of fit comes from the need to estimate the residual covariance in the last two items in the 5-item factor. Now suppose that data set 1 has $N = 1,000$ cases with data for the 1-item factor, and $N = 500$ cases with data for the five items making up the second factor. Also suppose that data set 2 has just $N = 500$ complete cases for all variables.

First consider the 500 cases (data set 1) with data for just the 1-item factor. It is clear in this situation that these cases contribute nothing to the badness of fit (because that part of the model is exactly identified). Because of this, in this instance, goodness of fit in the two data sets should be the same. Although rather contrived, this example serves to illustrate the problem many programs have with goodness-of-fit indices, especially the RMSEA, when there are missing data.

Table 17.3 presents goodness-of-fit results for testing this simple, two-factor model with the two data sets just described. Results are shown for LISREL 8.54,[12] Amos 18, and Mplus 6. If the program also presents the independence (baseline) model chi-square and *df* for the FIML model, that is also presented in Table 17.3. Finally, the independence model, as described earlier, was calculated separately (in LISREL); we calculated the three indices (RMSEA, TLI/NNFI, and CFI) using a simple fit calculator, rho.exe (Graham, 2005). We present these fit values for each of three possible sample sizes: (a) the complete cases N (500); (b) the total N (1,000); and (c) N', as suggested by Graham and Hofer (2000), where N' is the total N (1,000 in this case), multiplied by the proportion of nonmissing values throughout the data set. In this instance, $N' = 583$.

As shown in Table 17.3, the correct values for model chi-square and *df*, independence model chi-square and *df*, and TLI/NNFI and CFI were observed for the complete cases and FIML only for Mplus. LISREL presented only the (incorrect) RMSEA value in the FIML model and had the incorrect independence model chi-square in the complete cases model; thus RMSEA, TLI/NNFI, and CFI were all incorrect in the complete cases model. For Amos, all values in the complete cases were correct. However, due to the incorrect independence *df* estimate with the FIML model, the TLI/NNFI and CFI values were incorrect in the FIML model.[13] Note that all of the FIML estimates for RMSEA were too low.

TABLE 17.3. Goodness-of-Fit Tests

	Model		Independence (baseline) model				
	χ^2	*df*	χ^2	*df*	RMSEA	NNFI	CFI
LISREL FIML	26.9	9	—	—	*.0446*	—	—
Amos FIML	26.8	9	487.1	*21*	*.0445*	*.9108*	*.9618*
Mplus FIML	26.9	9	487.6	15	*.045*	.937	.962
LISREL CC	26.8	9	*715.3*	15	*.0644*	*.958*	*.975*
Amos CC	26.8	9	486.7	15	.063	.9371	.9623
Mplus CC	26.9	9	487.6	15	.063	.937	.962
"correct"	26.9	9	487.6	15			
rho.exe ($N' = 1,000$)					.0446	.9369	.9621
rho.exe ($N' = 583$)					**.0584**	.9369	.9621
rho.exe ($N' = 500$)					.0631	.9369	.9621

Note. Values appearing in normal print are correct. Values in *italics* are not correct. The one value in **bold** is meant to be an approximation.

For this particular model, model fit according to chi-square, TLI/NNFI, and CFI is virtually identical for the FIML and complete cases models. We argue that fit in this instance should be the same in these two models. This all illustrates the fact that the FIML estimate for RMSEA is too low. Look now at the three estimates of RMSEA as calculated "by hand" with rho.exe. Note that the value .0446 was obtained when the total N (1,000) was used in the calculations. In this instance, the correct RMSEA value (.063) was obtained when the complete cases N (500) was used in the calculations. In this extreme case, RMSEA based on $N' = 583$ was not a particularly good estimate. However, we argue that in general, the correct value for N in these calculations will be bounded by the total N and the complete cases N, and that N' (Graham & Hofer, 2000) will be approximately correct. Even in this extreme case, RMSEA based on $N' = 583$ was much closer to the correct value than it was to the incorrect value observed in the FIML model.[14]

The strategy we recommend is to estimate one's own independence model in the missing data case and use rho.exe (Graham, 2005) or equivalent calculations to obtain correct values for TLI/NNFI and CFI, and plausible values for RMSEA. With Mplus, one may simply use for these calculations the independence (baseline) model chi-square and df as given by the program. For Amos, one may use the independence model chi-square given by the program, but the df used should be the df given by the program less k, the number of manifest variables in the model. For LISREL, one must calculate the independence model separately to obtain correct estimates of the independence model chi-square for these calculations.

Model Modification

Model modification with missing data is also a challenge. In Amos, modification indices are not provided in the missing data case. In LISREL, they are provided, but they are not trustworthy in the missing data case. So what is the solution? One solution is this: First, generate an EM covariance matrix (e.g., with EMCOV: Graham & Hofer, 1992; with Norm: Schafer, 1997; with SAS PROC MI; or with the SPSS MVA routine), and then analyze that matrix directly using matrix input. Alternatively, impute a single data set from EM parameters (e.g., with Norm or with SAS PROC MI; see Graham, in press; Graham et al., 2003), and analyze that. The

modification indices (at least with LISREL) can be quite helpful in analysis of one of these data sets.

As we have already noted, the chi-square and goodness-of-fit indices are not helpful per se with these data sets. However, the relative improvement for freeing one parameter or another (e.g., as shown by modification indices) will still be helpful in pointing to parameters that could be estimated to improve fit. Of course, once the modification index from analysis of this data set is identified, it would be good to rerun the model with the FIML procedure to verify that chi-square improvement is sufficiently large.

FIML IMPLEMENTATIONS

LISREL

Estimation

Using FIML is straightforward for estimation. One adds a single statement (MI = –9)[15] to the DA (DAta parameters) line in the syntax file.

Goodness of Fit

In order to get plausible indices of practical fit (RMSEA, NNFI, CFI) in LISREL, one must estimate a separate independence model as described earlier, then calculate those indices by hand or using a fit calculator such as rho.exe (Graham, 2005).

Multiple Imputation

LISREL has a feature (the RP option as part of the OU—OUtput—statement) that allows for analysis of stacked (e.g., multiply imputed) data sets. Automation would make use of this feature. An automation utility would (1) stack the input data sets, (2) read the analyst's syntax file and add the necessary syntax for MI (e.g., OU RP = 40), (3) read the single parameter estimate and standard error file output by LISREL (e.g., OU PV = parms.dat, SV = parms.dat), and (4) perform MI inference.

Auxiliary Variables

LISREL statements for including auxiliary variables in the model are given in Graham (2003). The "extra DV" model is set up as described earlier. There is nothing particularly tricky about specifying this model in LISREL.

For the spider (saturated correlates) model (which is best for latent variable models), the setup in LISREL is somewhat complicated. First, each auxiliary variable is set to be a single-indicator factor. In the PSi matrix, all variances and covariances for the auxiliary variables are freely estimated, but correlations between the auxiliary variables and other (substantive) factors are fixed at 0. For example, with two substantive factors and three auxiliary variables, the LY and PSi matrices might look like this (this model assumes a simple correlation between factors, and three items per factor for the two substantive factors; of course, that relationship could be a regression coefficient instead):

PA LY
0 0 0 0 0
1 0 0 0 0
1 0 0 0 0
0 0 0 0 0
0 1 0 0 0
0 1 0 0 0
0 0 0 0 0
0 0 0 0 0
0 0 0 0 0
start 1.0 ly 1 1 ly 4 2 ly 7 3 ly 8 4 ly 9 5

PA PS
1
1 1
0 0 1
0 0 1 1
0 0 1 1 1

The remaining relationships with the auxiliary variables are estimated in the TE matrix, for example, with three indicators for each substantive factor, and three auxiliary variables. The TE matrix would look like this:

PA TE
1
0 1
0 0 1
0 0 0 1

0 0 0 0 1
0 0 0 0 0 1
1 1 1 1 1 1 0
1 1 1 1 1 1 0 0
1 1 1 1 1 1 0 0 0

With these models, the residual variances for the auxiliary variables must be fixed at 0 (assuming the "factor" variances for these single-item factors was estimated). However, the residual correlations may still be estimated as shown.

Amos

Estimation

Using FIML is straightforward for estimation. One simply requests that means and intercepts be estimated, and Amos automatically handles any missing data.

Goodness of Fit

Amos does a good (but not perfect) job with goodness of fit in the missing data case. The chi-square, *df*, and RMSEA estimates are the same as with LISREL (including the RMSEA value that is too optimistic, as described earlier). Amos also presents estimates of other indices of fit, including CFI and TLI/NNFI. However, these latter estimates are not quite correct. The independence model *df* used in the calculations is too large by k, the number of manifest variables in the model. The effect of this is that the TLI/NNFI as calculated automatically by Amos is too small by about .02. The CFI calculation is also incorrect, but by a much smaller amount.

The suggestion about calculating one's own independence model also applies with the Amos program. However, with Amos, the chi-square for the independence model is correct, and only the *df* needs to be adjusted (reduced by k). With this adjustment, along with using N' (Graham & Hofer, 2000) in the calculations, one gets a plausible value for RMSEA, and the correct values for TLI/NNFI and CFI.

Auxiliary Variables

There are two approaches available in Amos for incorporating auxiliary variables: (1) working with Amos Graphics, and (2) text code. We focus on the first approach here (the text approach for Amos 4, provided by Jim Arbuckle, is presented in detail in Graham, 2003).

The "extra DV" model is set up as described earlier. There is nothing particularly tricky about specifying this model in Amos, except that with larger models, the picture does become a bit crowded with boxes and arrows. However, with some prior planning regarding the placement of boxes, and by employing the automation features in Amos ("plug-ins") for drawing covariances and for naming residual variances, the process is manageable, even with larger models.

The spider (saturated correlates) model is also conceptually straightforward in Amos Graphics. Again, the biggest issue is that with larger models, and with larger numbers of auxiliary variables, the picture becomes rather cluttered. However, with the spider model, making use of the automation features (plug-ins) for drawing covariances does help.

Mplus

Estimation

The missing data statement (e.g., "missing are all (–9);" appears in the "Variable:" statement in Mplus.

Goodness of Fit

This version (Mplus 6) does a better job than LISREL or Amos. All model chi-square and *df*, independence model chi-square and *df*, and estimates of TLI/NNFI and CFI are correct in the FIML model. As described earlier, a better estimate of the RMSEA can be obtained by calculating the RMSEA separately from the program, using N' (Graham & Hofer, 2000) as the sample size.

Multiple Imputation

The new MI feature in Mplus is described on the Mplus website (e.g., *www.statmodel.com/verhistory.shtml*).

Auxiliary Variables

A nice feature of Mplus is its capability of including auxiliary variables automatically in the model (see Asparouhov & Muthén, 2008; *www.statmodel.com/download/auxm2.pdf*).

LOOSE ENDS

Missing Data with Growth Modeling/ Longitudinal Models

A question that often comes up is whether longitudinal models (e.g., growth modeling) are appropriately handled with normal-model MI and the equivalent FIML model. Nowhere is this clearer than in the SEM context. For years, SEM researchers have fit growth models in SEM with nothing more than a variance–covariance matrix and vector of means. These parameters (variances, covariances, and means) are all estimated without bias with normal-model MI and the equivalent FIML model. Thus, specialized longitudinal MI programs (e.g., the PAN program for MI; Schafer, 2001; Schafer & Yucel, 2002; Yucel, 2008), although very useful for special-case longitudinal models and for cluster data, are not required for standard growth modeling.

Missing Data with Categorical and Other Complex Models

The main point we would like to make here is that one should take care in employing normal-model MI with categorical (e.g., growth mixture) and other complex (nonlinear) models. Unless one is able to specify the interactions of the continuous variables that are relevant in such complex models, and include them in the normal-model MI, it is likely that the results will be biased. On the other hand, just as Collins and colleagues (2001) demonstrated that not all MNAR circumstances produce appreciable bias, we may find that many complex, nonlinear models can be tested with normal-model MI data with acceptably low bias. Nevertheless, until there is some evidence for this, it would be prudent to proceed with caution.

NOTES

1. Rubin (1974) and Little and Rubin (2002) refer to this as *M* rather than *R*.
2. Little and Rubin (2002) refer to this third type of missingness as NMAR (Collins et al., 2001), and Schafer and Graham (2002) refer to the same concept as MNAR.
3. However, Collins et al. (2001; also see Graham, 2009) have shown that these biases can be tolerably small under a variety of circumstances.
4. Parameter estimates based on the EM covariance matrix (and

based on MI) are unbiased to the extent that the MAR assumption holds.

5. Note that standard errors for two-stage EM could also be too large depending on the choice of N, and that correct standard errors can be obtained using an appropriate procedure (see Savalei & Bentler, 2009; Yuan & Bentler, 2000).

6. Graham (in press) notes that this rule applies to Schafer's (1997) Norm program. However, because other software (e.g., SAS PROC MI) uses different criteria for EM convergence, the number of DA steps between imputations will vary somewhat from program to program.

7. Note that a more recent version, Norm 3, is available for use with R.

8. Automation utilities for use with LISREL, EQS, and Mplus are available on request from John W. Graham (*jgraham@psu.edu*).

9. We focus here on MAR-linear missingness, one of three MAR missingness conditions studied by Collins et al. (2001), who also examined bias for several other parameters (e.g., mean and variance of Y, and correlation between X and Y); we focus here on bias and power benefits relating to the regression coefficient for X predicting Y because this is often the parameter of greatest interest in empirical research.

10. It is likely that many other R packages of which we are unaware perform chained equations, and it is also likely that by the time this chapter is in press, the two R packages mentioned will be updated.

11. For clarification, the single-item factor fixes the loading at 1.0 and the residual variance at 0, and estimates only the "factor" variance.

12. Results for the student version of LISREL 8.80 are identical to those shown for LISREL 8.54.

13. Note that the mistaken independence model *df* causes only a very small error in the CFI.

14. In multiple group models, the correct value for N' is the average N' value for the groups.

15. The "–9" refers to the missing data indicator used throughout one's data set in place of each missing value. The value, –9, is quite commonly used for this, but, of course, any value that is clearly out of the legal range for all variables may be used here.

REFERENCES

Allison, P. D. (1987). Estimation of linear models with incomplete data. In C. Clogg (Ed.), *Sociological methodology 1987* (pp. 71–103). San Francisco: Jossey-Bass.

Allison, P. D. (2005, April). *Imputation of categorical variables with PROC MI*. Paper presented at the annual meeting of the SAS User's Group International, Philadelphia.

Arbuckle, J. L. (1996). Full information estimation in the presence of missing data. In G. A. Marcoulides & R. E.

Schumaker (Eds.) *Advanced structural equation modeling* (pp. 243–277). Mahwah, NJ: Erlbaum.

Arbuckle, J. L. (2006). *Amos (Version 7.0)* [Computer program]. Chicago: SPSS.

Asparouhov, T., & Muthén, B. O. (2008). *Auxiliary variables predicting missing data*. Unpublished manuscript available at *www.statmodel.com/download/auxm2.pdf*.

Babakus, E., Ferguson, C. E., & Jöreskog, K. G. (1987). The sensitivity of confirmatory maximum likelihood factor analysis to violations of measurement scale and distributional assumptions. *Journal of Marketing Research, 24,* 222–228.

Bentler, P. M. (1990). Comparative fit indexes in structural models. *Psychological Bulletin, 107,* 238–246.

Bentler, P. M. (2006). *EQS 6 Structural Equations Program manual*. Encino, CA: Multivariate Software, Inc.

Bentler, P. M., & Bonett, D. G. (1980). Significance tests and goodness of fit in the analysis of covariance structures. *Psychological Bulletin, 88,* 588–606.

Bernaards, C. A., Belin, T. R., & Schafer, J. L. (2007). Robustness of a multivariate normal approximation for imputation of incomplete binary data. *Statistics in Medicine, 26,* 1368–1382.

Browne, M. W., & Cudeck, R. (1993). Alternative ways of assessing model fit. In K. A. Bollen & J. S. Long (Eds.), *Testing structural equation models* (pp. 136–162). Newbury Park, CA: Sage.

Collins, L. M., Schafer, J. L., & Kam, C.-M. (2001). A comparison of inclusive and restrictive strategies in modern missing data procedures. *Psychological Methods, 6,* 330–351.

Demirtas, H. (2009). Rounding strategies for multiply imputed binary data. *Biometrical Journal, 51,* 677–688.

Dempster, A. P., Laird, N. M., & Rubin, D. B. (1977). Maximum likelihood from incomplete data via the EM algorithm. *Journal of the Royal Statistical Society B (Methodological), 39,* 1–38.

Dolan, C. V. (1994). Factor analysis of variables with 2, 3, 5, and 7 response categories: A comparison of categorical variable estimators using simulated data. *British Journal of Mathematical and Statistical Psychology, 47,* 309–326.

Efron, B. (1982). *The jackknife, the bootstrap, and other resampling plans*. Philadelphia: Society for Industrial and Applied Mathematics.

Finch, W. H. (2010). Imputation methods for missing categorical questionnaire data: A comparison of approaches. *Journal of Data Science, 8,* 361–378.

Finkbeiner, C. (1979). Estimation for the multiple factor model when data are missing. *Psychometrika, 44,* 409–420.

Gelman, A., Hill, J., Yajima, M., Su, Y.-S., & Grazia Pittau, M. (2010). mi: Missing Data Imputation and Model Checking. R package version 0.08-06. Available at *cran.r-project.org/package=mi*.

Graham, J. W. (2003). Adding missing-data relevant variables to FIML-based structural equation models. *Structural Equation Modeling, 10*, 80–100.

Graham, J. W. (2005). *Structural equation modeling.* Unpublished manuscript, The Pennsylvania State University, University Park.

Graham, J. W. (2009). Missing data analysis: Making it work in the real world. *Annual Review of Psychology, 60*, 549–576.

Graham, J. W. (in press). *Missing data: Analysis and design.* New York: Springer.

Graham, J. W., & Collins, L. M. (in press). Using modern missing data methods with auxiliary variables to mitigate the effects of attrition on statistical power. In J. W. Graham, *Missing data: Analysis and design.* New York: Springer.

Graham, J. W., Cumsille, P. E., & Elek-Fisk, E. (2003). Methods for handling missing data. In J. A. Schinka & W. F. Velicer (Eds.), *Handbook of psychology: Vol. 2. Research methods in psychology* (pp. 87–114). New York: Wiley.

Graham, J. W., & Hofer, S. M. (1992). *EMCOV user's manual.* Unpublished manuscript, University of Southern California, Los Angeles.

Graham, J. W., & Hofer, S. M. (2000). Multiple imputation in multivariate research. In T. D. Little, K. U. Schnabel, & J. Baumert (Eds.), *Modeling longitudinal and multiple-group data: Practical issues, applied approaches, and specific examples* (pp. 201–218). Hillsdale, NJ: Erlbaum.

Graham, J. W., Hofer, S. M., & Piccinin, A. M. (1994). Analysis with missing data in drug prevention research (National Institute on Drug Abuse Research Monograph Series #142). In L. M. Collins & L. Seitz (Eds.), *Advances in data analysis for prevention intervention research* (pp. 13–63). Washington, DC: National Institute on Drug Abuse.

Graham, J. W., Taylor, B. J., & Cumsille, P. E. (2001). Planned missing data designs in analysis of change. In L. Collins & A. Sayer (Eds.), *New methods for the analysis of change* (pp. 335–353). Washington, DC: American Psychological Association.

Graham, J. W., Taylor, B. J., Olchowski, A. E., & Cumsille, P. E. (2006). Planned missing data designs in psychological research. *Psychological Methods, 11*, 323–343.

Hedeker, D., & Gibbons, R. D. (2008). *SuperMix (Version 1.0)* [Computer software]. Lincolnwood, IL: Scientific Software International.

Honaker, J., King, G., & Blackwell, M. (2007). *Amelia II: A program for missing data.* Unpublished user's guide, Harvard University. Available at *gking.harvard.edu amelia*.

Horton, N. J., Lipsitz, S. R., & Parzen, M. (2003). A potential for bias when rounding in multiple imputation. *American Statistician, 57*, 229–232.

Jöreskog, K. G., & Sörbom, D. (1996). *LISREL 8 user's reference guide.* Chicago: Scientific Software, Inc.

King, G., Honaker, J., Joseph, A., & Scheve, K. (2001). Analyzing incomplete political science data: An alternative algorithm for multiple imputation. *American Political Science Review, 95*, 49–69.

Little, R. J. A., & Rubin, D. B. (1987). *Statistical analysis with missing data.* New York: Wiley.

Little, R. J. A., & Rubin, D. B. (2002). *Statistical analysis with missing data* (2nd ed.). New York: Wiley.

Muthén, B., & Kaplan, D. (1985). A comparison of some methodologies for the factor analysis of non-normal Likert variables. *British Journal of Mathematical and Statistical Psychology, 38*, 171–189.

Muthén, B., Kaplan, D., & Hollis, M. (1987). On structural equation modeling with data that are not missing completely at random. *Psychometrika, 52*, 431–462.

Olsson, U. (1979). On the robustness of factor analysis against crude classification of the observations. *Multivariate Behavioral Research, 14*, 485–500.

Raghunathan, T. E. (2004). What do we do with missing data? Some options for analysis of incomplete data. *Annual Review of Public Health, 25*, 99–117.

Raghunathan, T. E., Lepkowski, J. M., Van Hoewyk, J., & Solenberger, P. (2001). A multivariate technique for multiply imputing missing values using a sequence of regression models. *Survey Methodology, 27*, 85–95.

Raghunathan, T. E., Solenberger, P. W., & Van Hoewyk, J. (2002). *IVEware: Imputation and Variance Estimation software.* Ann Arbor: University of Michigan, Institute for Social Research, Survey Research Center.

Rubin, D. B. (1974). Characterizing the estimation of parameters in incomplete data problems. *Journal of the American Statistical Association, 69*, 467–474.

Rubin, D. B. (1987). *Multiple imputation for nonresponse in surveys.* New York: Wiley.

Satorra, A., & Bentler, P. M. (1994). Corrections to test statistics and standard errors in covariance structure analysis. In A. von Eye & C. C. Clogg (Eds.), *Latent variables analysis: Applications for developmental research* (pp. 399–419). Thousand Oaks, CA: Sage.

Savalei, V. (2010). Expected vs. observed information in SEM with incomplete normal and nonnormal data. *Psychological Methods, 15*, 352–367.

Savalei, V., & Bentler, P. M. (2009). A two-stage approach to missing data: Theory and application to auxiliary variables. *Structural Equation Modeling, 16*, 477–497.

Schafer, J. L. (1997). *Analysis of incomplete multivariate data.* New York: Chapman & Hall.

Schafer, J. L. (2001). Multiple imputation with PAN. In L. M. Collins & A. G. Sayer (Eds.), *New methods for the analysis of change* (pp. 357–377). Washington, DC: American Psychological Association.

Schafer, J. L., & Graham, J. W. (2002). Missing data: Our view of the state of the art. *Psychological Methods, 7*, 147–177.

Schafer, J. L., & Yucel, R. M. (2002). Computational strategies for multivariate linear mixed-effects models with missing values. *Journal of Computational and Graphical Statistics, 11*, 437–457.

Steiger, J. H., & Lind, J. M. (1980, May). *Statistically based tests for the number of common factors.* Paper presented at the annual meeting of the Psychometric Society, Iowa City, IA.

Tanner, M. A., & Wong, W. H. (1987). The calculation of posterior distributions by data augmentation (with discussion). *Journal of the American Statistical Association, 82*, 528–550.

Tucker, L. R., & Lewis, C. (1973). A reliability coefficient for maximum likelihood factor analysis. *Psychometrika, 38*, 1–10.

van Buuren, S., & Groothuis-Oudshoorn, K. (in press). MICE: Multivariate Imputation by Chained Equations in R. *Journal of Statistical Software.*

Widaman, K. F., & Thompson, J. S. (2003). On specifying the null model for incremental fit indices in structural equation modeling. *Psychological Methods, 8*, 16–37.

Yuan, K.-H., & Bentler, P. M. (2000). Three likelihood-based methods for mean and covariance structure analysis with nonnormal missing data. *Sociological Methodology, 30*, 165–200.

Yucel, R. M. (2008). Multiple imputation inference from multivariate multilevel continuous data with ignorable nonresponse. *Philosophical Transactions of the Royal Society A, 366*, 2389–2403.

Yucel, R. M., He, Y., & Zaslavsky, A. M. (2008). Using calibration to improve rounding in multiple imputation. *American Statistician, 62*, 125–129.

CHAPTER 18

Bootstrapping Standard Errors and Data–Model Fit Statistics in Structural Equation Modeling

Gregory R. Hancock
Min Liu

As any student or practitioner of statistics knows, statistical methods rest on many assumptions that were necessary in the formal derivation of those methods and which, technically speaking, should hold in order for the inferences drawn from those statistics to be valid. Under some conditions, violating an assumption may be largely benign, meaning that the method being used will still tend to provide reasonable point and interval estimates of the parameter(s) of interest and sufficiently accurate statistical tests thereof. Under other conditions, however, such violations may compromise one's ability to estimate and test statistically one or more key aspects of the variables under investigation.

Structural equation modeling (SEM) is certainly no different, resting on many assumptions and suffering to varying degrees from violations of those assumptions in terms of assessment of the model as a whole, as well as assessments of parameters within a given model. Consider the familiar maximum likelihood (ML) fit function for covariance structure models:

$$F_{\mathrm{ML}} = \ln|\hat{\Sigma}| + \mathrm{tr}(S\hat{\Sigma}^{-1}) - \ln|S| - p$$

where S is the observed variance–covariance matrix for n observations on the model's p measured variables, $\hat{\Sigma}$ is the corresponding variance-covariance matrix im-

plied by fitting the model to the data, and where $(n-1)$ F_{ML} yields a potentially useful test statistic, T_{ML}, for assessing overall data–model fit. The fit function itself appears to suggest no specific assumptions, but they are indeed embedded in the formula's origins, as well as in the assumed behavior of the resulting F_{ML}, and in turn T_{ML}, statistics. To be more specific, in its derivation the ML function assumes that individuals' scores come from a population whose scores follow a multivariate normal distribution, and that the likelihood of the sample of n observations can be characterized as the product of the likelihoods of the n individual observations' likelihoods (i.e., that the observations are independent). Further, in order for the resulting F_{ML} statistic to facilitate accurate statistical inference through its corresponding test statistic T_{ML}, the latter must follow a known distribution such as $T_{\mathrm{ML}} \sim \chi^2$. In order for this to happen, however, the sample must be sufficiently large and the multivariate normality assumption for the population is again technically required. When such conditions are met, T_{ML} follows a central χ^2 distribution when the model is correctly specified, and a noncentral χ^2 when the model is not correctly specified. Finally, regarding the model's parameter estimates and standard errors, their behavior also assumes a sufficiently large sample size and rests on assumptions of independence of observations and multivariate normality; obviously, as well, one would expect bias in the parameter estimates and standard errors if the model is improperly specified.

For the purposes of the current chapter, the most relevant assumption is that regarding normality. Violations of this assumption typically take two forms in social science data: One is discretization of scores, and the other the presence of skew and/or kurtosis with otherwise continuous data. Concerning the former, as a normal distribution is a continuous distribution, any discretization or categorization of data yields, by definition, non-normality. Thus, for example, Likert scale responses are not normal; in fact, the distribution of adult males' heights in inches, however normal the distribution may appear, is non-normal given the discretization at the metric of inches. Nevertheless, practically speaking, as a variety of studies have shown (see, e.g., Finney & DiStefano, 2006, for a review), the impact of non-normality through discretization is typically minimal when the variables in question have five or more categories (and are otherwise fairly normal in shape). When fewer than five categories are present, and/or the data deviate appreciably from a generally normal shape, problems may arise in the model test statistic T_{ML} as well as in the standard errors associated with parameter estimates. Unfortunately, while the corrective approaches to be discussed in this chapter can be of some value in addressing the non-normality inherent in discrete data, they cannot be completely corrective because of the fundamental attenuation of the relations among the measured variables that occurs due to their discretization. Thus, one should not expect the methods described here to be sufficient to address this form of non-normality.

Instead, the methods to be described in this chapter are primarily for data that are, for all practical purposes, continuous but non-normal; that is, we assume researchers have variables with at least five response categories and whose non-normality stems more from skew and/or kurtosis than any discreteness in the variables' measurement. There has been considerable interest in evaluating robustness of ML (and other) estimation methods to violations of distributional assumptions (for reviews, see Chou & Bentler, 1995; Finney & DiStefano, 2006; West, Finch, & Curran, 1995). As methodological research has shown, non-normality tends to have little impact on the parameter estimates themselves, which remain fairly unbiased (e.g., Finch, West, & MacKinnon, 1997). The value of T_{ML}, however, tends to become upwardly biased under common conditions of non-normality (e.g., heavy-tailed leptokurtic distributions), which in turn can lead to rejections of otherwise satisfactory models when making the normality-dependent assumption that $T_{ML} \sim \chi^2$ (e.g., Browne, 1984; Chou, Bentler, & Satorra, 1991; Curran, West, & Finch, 1996; Hu, Bentler, & Kano, 1992; Yu & Muthén, 2002). Similarly, as T_{ML} is used in the computation of common data–model fit indices (e.g., root mean square error of approximation [RMSEA]), non-normality's inflation of T_{ML} can also lead those derivative indices to suggest poorer and possibly unsatisfactory data–model fit, an effect that can be further exacerbated with smaller sample sizes (e.g., $n \le 250$; see Hu & Bentler, 1999; Yu & Muthén, 2002). Additionally, regarding parameter standard errors, common forms of non-normality tend to make their estimates downwardly biased (i.e., too small), thereby leading to inflated parameter z statistics and hence an increased tendency to deem model relation estimates to be statistically significant (e.g., Chou et al., 1991; Finch et al., 1997; Hoogland & Boomsma, 1998; Olsson, Foss, Troye, & Howell, 2000). Thus, non-normality often alters the behavior of both the model test statistic (T_{ML}) and the parameter test statistics (z), potentially leading to more frequent errors regarding the model as a whole, as well as parameters within the model.

A reasonable and practical question, then, is how much non-normality must be present in one's data to precipitate these problems. This question is actually difficult, if not impossible, to answer, for a number of reasons. To start, simulation studies upon which recommendations are based can only examine a finite number of distribution and model conditions. Regarding distributions, at the univariate level, research has shown that the problems with model and parameter test statistics can arise when univariate distributions have, for example, skew exceeding 2 and kurtosis exceeding 7 relative to a normal distribution, where skew and kurtosis are defined as 0 (e.g., Chou & Bentler, 1995; Curran et al., 1996; Muthén & Kaplan, 1985). However, what if some variables are more non-normal than others, as they most certainly would be in practice? Again, research can only speak to conditions similar to those examined. And at the multivariate level, where the assumption technically resides, Bentler and Wu (2002) have suggested that matters get troublesome when Mardia's normalized multivariate kurtosis (see Bollen, 1989, p. 424, Equation 4) exceeds a value of 3. But, in fact, many different combinations of univariate distributions and correlational structure can lead to precisely the same normalized kurtosis (exceeding 3 or otherwise), and not all would be expected to have the same impact.

To expand upon the earlier point regarding differential impact, the often ignored fact is that the model itself plays a role in determining how distributional shape affects the model T_{ML} and parameter z test statistics. For example, one may have a measured variable path model in which X_1 is connected to relatively few other variables, and X_2 is an integral part of relations among many variables. Non-normality in either X_1 or X_2 can induce a sufficiently large Mardia coefficient, yet non-normality in X_1 would likely be far more benign in its impact on test statistics than would non-normality in X_2. Conversely, one may have data with a Mardia's coefficient that signals no trouble overall, yet in the context of a particular model specific test statistics can indeed be affected (e.g., Hancock & Wasko, 2010). In addition, although seldom discussed, it is also the case that specific combinations of distribution and model can yield test statistics that become smaller rather than larger, thereby leading to a propensity to retain models too frequently and to have less power in the tests of specific model parameters. The implication of all this is that although one can quantify the degree of univariate and multivariate non-normality in one's data, it is much more difficult to foretell the impact of that non-normality in the context of a specific model.

So what, then, are researchers to do in practice? Given the general difficulty of subscribing to the assumption of multivariate normality with any serious conviction, and given the somewhat tenuous relation between distributional shape and test statistics without taking into account the specific model(s) at hand, pursuing strategies that are more tolerant of non-normality may be a reasonable course of action right from the start of a modeling endeavor. Three such strategies are commonly discussed: (1) asymptotically distribution-free estimation (Browne, 1982, 1984), which makes no distributional assumptions in its fit function; (2) rescaled test statistics (Satorra & Bentler, 1988, 1994), which utilize ML estimation but with a subsequent correction to model test statistics and parameter standard errors based on distribution and model conditions; and (3) bootstrapping, which appeals to empirical distributions to facilitate both the assessment of data–model fit and of parameters within the model. The latter strategy is the primary focus of this chapter, and will be illustrated in the context of the example described next.

RUNNING EXAMPLE

For this chapter a classic data set from Holzinger and Swineford (1939) serves as the basis for the bootstrapping examples. These authors collected data from $n = 301$ seventh- and eighth-grade children in the Pasteur and the Grant–White schools in Chicago. These data consisted of 26 psychological aptitude tests, six of which are used in an oblique two-factor model in this chapter. The first factor is Visual Ability, the indicators of which are the tests labeled as *visperc* (visual perception), *cubes*, and *lozenges*. The second factor is Verbal Ability, with the three indicators *paracomp* (paragraph completion), *sentcomp* (sentence completion), and *wordmean* (word meaning).

For our purposes in this current chapter, the original data by Holzinger and Swineford were transformed prior to any analyses. Specifically, scores on each of the six variables were divided by 10 and then raised to the fourth power. The purpose of this transformation was merely didactic, heightening the data's degree of non-normality so as to enhance their illustrative value. Table 18.1 summarizes the relevant characteristics of the data before and after this transformation. From this point on, the transformed data are used in all examples, without reference to the original data. Because the transformation altered not just the distributional characteristics of the data but also their correlational structure, any comparison of modeling results in this chapter using the transformed data with those involving the original data appearing elsewhere would not be useful.

To start, the two-factor model described earlier, with the first indicators' loadings (λ_{11} and λ_{42}) set to 1 (for reasons discussed later), was applied to the transformed data using ML within Amos 17 (Arbuckle, 2008), EQS 6.1 (Bentler, 2008), and Mplus 6 (Muthén & Muthén, 2010). For this model, Amos yielded $T_{ML} = 22.683$ (8 df; $p = .004$), while the parameter estimates (and standard errors) were .218 (.043) for the loading (λ_{21}) of *cubes*, .301 (.055) for the loading (λ_{31}) of *lozenges*, 5.163 (.427) for the loading (λ_{52}) of *sentcomp*, 17.500 (1.387) for the loading (λ_{62}) of *wordmean*, and 69.743 (10.738) for the covariance (ϕ_{21}) of the Visual Ability and Verbal Ability factors. (Note that estimates from EQS and Mplus were quite similar to those from Amos.) These values serve as a basis for comparison with those resulting from the bootstrapping procedures described and illustrated below using these three SEM software packages.

TABLE 18.1. Characteristics of Holzinger and Swineford (1939) Data before and after Transformation

	visperc	cubes	lozenges	paracomp	sentcomp	wordmean
Original data						
Mean	29.61	24.35	18.00	9.18	17.36	15.30
SD	7.00	4.71	9.05	3.49	5.16	7.70
Skew	−0.26	0.48	0.39	0.27	−0.35	0.87
Kurtosis	0.36	0.38	−0.89	0.12	−0.53	0.88
Transformed data						
Mean	102.41	43.68	29.82	1.41	13.72	17.40
SD	87.93	36.68	44.51	2.09	12.47	39.81
Skew	1.97	1.95	1.69	2.81	1.11	4.59
Kurtosis	6.82	3.95	1.70	8.93	0.73	26.01

BOOTSTRAPPING

The area of bootstrapping, pioneered by Efron (1979), has amassed a vast and engaging literature over the last three decades. The scope of this literature far exceeds the goals of this chapter, and the interested reader may consult any of a number of more general resources; the book by Chernick (2008), in particular, has an extensive bibliography on the technique's methodological advances and applications. For our purposes, the general principles of bootstrapping are explained herein to provide orientation.

To start, consider Figure 18.1, which depicts the most basic bootstrapping process. The container on the left represents the population of observations, to which we seldom have direct access but from which our data have been sampled (presumably randomly). That population may be characterized by parameters of interest, which are represented generically in a vector θ. Our sample may be viewed as a microcosm of that population, and for this reason we are accustomed to using its statistics, contained in $\hat{\theta}$, to facilitate inferences about the population parameters in θ. We are able to make such inferences because given specific assumptions about

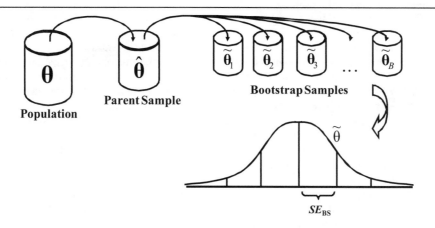

FIGURE 18.1. Naive bootstrapping process.

the population (e.g., normality), we have an analytical understanding of the natural fluctuations in $\hat{\theta}$ would be expected across such random samples. Unfortunately, when those assumptions about the nature of the population do not hold, as portended empirically by a sufficiently deviant sample distribution and/or by strong theoretical rationales that some variables' data should, in fact, be non-normally distributed (e.g., polarizing questionnaire items), our expectations regarding the random behavior of $\hat{\theta}$ may be compromised. A way around this would be to take many samples from the population and examine the empirical behavior of the parameter estimates across those samples' $\hat{\theta}$ vectors, and utilize the parameter estimates' empirical distributions to facilitate inference about the parameters of interest. In practice, however, we typically have only one sample upon which to base our inferences.

Fortunately, a sample is not just a microcosm of the population in terms of the parameters of interest, but also in terms of its distributional shape. That is, observations in a population have a specific distribution, and each random sample one takes from that population would be expected to have a distribution that deviates only randomly from that of the population. Hence, our best window into the distributional characteristics of the population is our sample at hand. So, in an attempt to emulate drawing repeated samples from the population to get an empirical sense of the behavior of the statistics of interest, bootstrapping draws many (B) repeated samples (*bootstrap samples*) from our own single sample (the *parent sample*) of data. For most purposes the size of each bootstrap sample will be the same as that of the parent sample, n, but sampling is with replacement to avoid repeatedly replicating the parent sample precisely. For each bootstrap sample one determines estimates of the parameters of interest, designed here in vector $\tilde{\theta}$, and the empirical distribution of each specific parameter's bootstrap estimates can serve as a foundation for inference regarding the corresponding population parameter. Specifically, as shown at the bottom right of Figure 18.1, the standard deviation of the empirical distribution of bootstrap parameter estimates for a given parameter θ can serve as an adjusted standard error (*bootstrap standard error, SE_{BS}* in Figure 18.1) for conducting inference regarding that parameter (e.g., using $z^* = \hat{\theta}/SE_{BS}$). The adjustment comes because the population's distribution influenced that of the parent sample, which in turn influenced the distributions of the bootstrap samples from which the empirical distri-

bution of parameter estimates was derived. Thus, the parent sample's distributional properties and the random deviations in those properties that propagated to the bootstrap samples set the context for the empirical behavior of the bootstrap parameter estimates and the adjusted nature of SE_{BS}.

Bootstrap Standard Errors in SEM

The generic process just described, sometimes referred to as *simple, naive,* or *nonparametric* bootstrapping, is precisely the strategy employed in SEM to get adjusted standard errors for tests of model parameters. Specifically, from the parent sample of n observations, B bootstrap samples of size n are drawn with replacement; research by Nevitt and Hancock (2001) has suggested that $B = 250$ should be adequate for estimating standard errors in SEM (although many more may be necessary to get precision of bootstrap confidence intervals; see, e.g., DiCiccio & Efron, 1996). For each of the bootstrap samples the structural equation model of interest is fit to the data, yielding B sets of model parameter estimates ($\tilde{\theta}_1, \ldots, \tilde{\theta}_B$). For each individual parameter an empirical distribution is constructed, the mean of which should be near the parameter estimate from the parent sample. From this distribution one could also derive an empirical interval estimate for the population parameter of interest, taking percentile points of the empirical distribution that correspond to the desired confidence level (e.g., fifth percentile, 95th percentile). While this interval (or an adjusted form discussed later) could also be used for testing purposes, more commonly the standard deviation of the empirical distribution is used as the SE_{BS}, leading to the adjusted z statistic mentioned earlier for each parameter.

Regarding the quality of the bootstrap standard errors, while they do not perform as well as ML standard errors under multivariate normality, under a variety of non-normal conditions they can contain less bias than the original ML standard errors and may even tend toward less bias than Satorra–Bentler rescaled standard errors (see, e.g., Nevitt & Hancock, 2001). Such findings, while quite encouraging, must be taken somewhat cautiously. For small samples (e.g., $n < 100$), considerable bias and variability in these standard errors have been observed; one cannot be certain, however, whether such behavior is a general property or specific to the models that have been included in methodological investigations.

Example

Recall the two-factor model described earlier, to be fit to the transformed data of Holzinger and Swineford (1939). Naive bootstrapping for this example, to get empirical standard error estimates for key parameters, was accomplished using $B = 1,000$ bootstrap samples in Amos, EQS, and Mplus; the popular SEM software package LISREL (Jöreskog & Sörbom, 2008) does not currently offer automated nonparametric bootstrapping capabilities (specifically, one must generate bootstrapping samples with PRELIS, analyze all samples using LISREL, and then summarize results with PRELIS). In this example, as with the model analyzed previously using ML, the first indicator of each factor (*visperc* and *paracomp*) served as the scale referent with its loading fixed to 1. Although one might prefer to allow the factors to be standardized, as is a common default in SEM software packages, doing so can artificially inflate the bootstrap standard errors of loadings (for an explana-

tion, see Hancock & Nevitt, 1999). Relevant output from the three packages is summarized in Table 18.2, including bootstrap standard errors and 90% confidence intervals for free factor loadings and the factor covariance. Software code for EQS and Mplus, and screen shots for Amos's graphic user interface, are provided at this handbook's website (*www.handbookofsem.com*).

Looking at Table 18.2, many interesting results are seen. To start, in addition to the slight differences among the ML standard error estimates (SE_{ML}) across packages, both the bootstrap standard errors (SE_{BS}) and the bootstrap 90% confidence intervals (90% CI) also differ. Although no particular pattern is discernible for the relative values of the SE_{BS} estimates, the values for the lower and upper boundaries of the CIs appear systematically lower for Mplus than those of the highly comparable Amos and EQS. Also, while EQS uses the percentile points of the bootstrap distribution for the 90% CI, as described previously, Mplus and Amos employ what is called the *bias-corrected percentile*

TABLE 18.2. Naive Bootstrap Standard Errors and Confidence Intervals

	Amos	EQS	Mplus
λ_{21} ($\hat{\lambda}_{21} = .218$)			
SE_{ML}	.043	.043	.048
SE_{BS}	.107	.109	.108
90% CI	(.103, .441)	(.108, .447)	(.040, .396)
λ_{31} ($\hat{\lambda}_{31} = .301$)			
SE_{ML}	.055	.055	.059
SE_{BS}	.110	.115	.112
90% CI	(.182, .539)	(.186, .538)	(.117, .485)
λ_{52} ($\hat{\lambda}_{52} = 5.163$)			
SE_{ML}	.427	.427	.417
SE_{BS}	.624	.594	.612
90% CI	(4.421, 6.371)	(4.471, 6.364)	(4.157, 6.169)
λ_{62} ($\hat{\lambda}_{62} = 17.500$)			
SE_{ML}	1.387	1.387	1.399
SE_{BS}	2.775	2.654	2.701
90% CI	(13.499, 22.869)	(13.648, 22.322)	(13.056, 21.943)
ϕ_{21} ($\hat{\phi}_{21} = 69.743$)			
SE_{ML}	10.738	10.773	11.242
SE_{BS}	24.624	23.994	23.665
90% CI	(36.308, 120.143)	(33.433, 110.053)	(30.817, 108.676)

method (e.g., DiCiccio & Efron, 1996; MacKinnon, Lockwood, & Williams, 2004); this approach is intended to provide more accurate interval estimates for parameters whose estimates' sampling distributions are asymmetric. Given that the distributions for the factor covariance and factor loadings should be near neither a ceiling nor a floor, one would not expect this correction to have much impact. Indeed, the trivial difference betwen the uncorrected EQS intervals and the corrected Amos intervals would seem to support this.

With regard to the SE_{BS} values themselves, irrespective of the software package, these values are considerably larger than the original SE_{ML} values that depend upon normality. Overall, for the current example, the bootstrap standard errors appear to be approximately twice as large as their ML counterparts, although usually a bit more (e.g., for λ_{21}) and sometimes a bit less (e.g., for λ_{52}). The implication of these larger standard errors is that the corresponding parameter test statistics using the bootstrap standard errors (i.e., $z^* = \hat{\theta}/SE_{BS}$) will be appropriately smaller than those based on ML standard errors (i.e., $z = \hat{\theta}/SE_{ML}$), thereby preventing spurious inferences of nonzero relations regarding specific parameters (i.e., Type I errors). In the current example, although parameter test statistics were approximately halved by employing SE_{BS} values, all did remain statistically significant at a .05 level.

Bootstrap Data–Model Fit Statistics in SEM

While the previous section details the process for using bootstrapping to assess parameters within a given model, in fact one should have determined that the model is satisfactory prior to assessing its parameter estimates. The T_{ML} statistic is one tool for assessing data–model fit, where statistically large values compared to a reference sampling distribution (typically a central χ^2) begin to call into question the model. Unfortunately, as discussed previously, the distribution of the data can affect T_{ML} (and its derivative indices, such as RMSEA and comparative fit index [CFI]), causing its behavior to depart from the reference distribution and thereby rendering it a tenuous foundation upon which to build a case for or against a given model.

As the reader no doubt understands by now, bootstrapping is a process well suited to deriving an empirical sampling distribution when the theoretical one resting on violated assumptions is no longer appropriate. Interestingly, however, the naive bootstrapping process described previously cannot be employed for T_{ML}. If

one applied the same process to generate B naive bootstrap values for T_{ML}, its empirical distribution would likely not represent the null condition necessary for facilitating a test of T_{ML}, but rather would contain noncentrality reflective of the degree to which the model under scrutiny is misspecified (even if only slightly). Thus, the naively bootstrapped empirical sampling distribution for T_{ML} would not be appropriate for gauging the magnitude of T_{ML} for the parent sample, and hence would not facilitate an accurate statistical assessment of data–model fit.

In order to circumvent the problem of the empirical distribution likely reflecting a non-null condition, Bollen and Stine (1992; see also Beran & Srivastava, 1985) suggested that the data from the parent sample with covariance matrix $\mathbf{S}$ be transformed to have covariance matrix equal to $\hat{\Sigma}$ so as to have perfect data–model fit. Specifically, for original data in matrix $\mathbf{Y}$, transformed data in matrix $\mathbf{Z}$ are obtained as $\mathbf{Z} = \mathbf{Y}\mathbf{S}^{-1/2}\hat{\Sigma}^{1/2}$. The idea is that the transformed data retain the distributional characteristics of the parent sample but now represent a null (true model) condition from which to draw bootstrap samples and construct an empirical sampling distribution for bootstrap T_{ML} values. This process, known as *Bollen–Stine* or *model-based* bootstrapping, is summarized in Figure 18.2.

Now the transformed parent sample has distributional characteristics from the original parent sample but represents the null condition of a perfectly fitting model; in fact, if one were to compute T_{ML} for these data, it would be precisely zero. From these transformed data the bootstrapping process continues as in the naive process, drawing (with replacement) B samples of size n and determining the bootstrap model test statistic $\tilde{T}_{ML}$. The empirical distribution of the B values of $\tilde{T}_{ML}$ constitutes the frame of reference for judging the magnitude of the original parent sample's T_{ML} value. Specifically, the bootstrap p-value (p_{BS}) is determined as the proportion of the B bootstrap test statistics exceeding T_{ML}, where smaller values (e.g., $p_{BS} < .05$) can be used as a statistical basis on which to proclaim the original model inadequate.

Regarding the quality of the bootstrap for data–model fit assessment, work by Fouladi (1998) and by Nevitt and Hancock (2001) has supported this approach's improvement over using the normal theory T_{ML} value. Specifically, the Bollen–Stine bootstrapping has been found to control the Type I error (false model rejection) rate considerably better than ML approaches under conditions of extreme to moderate non-normality. In

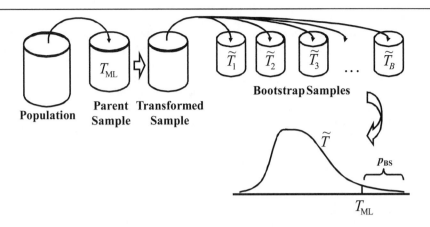

FIGURE 18.2. Bollen–Stine bootstrapping process.

fact, Nevitt and Hancock found that the bootstrap was often conservative in its control over the rejection rate irrespective of whether the model was correct, implying that its control in the null case of a correct model would be adequate, but that it might compromise power to some extent under conditions where the model at hand should indeed be rejected.

Example

For the oblique two-factor model applied to the transformed Holzinger and Swineford (1939) data, Bollen–Stine bootstrapping to assess data–model fit was accomplished using $B = 1,000$ bootstrap samples in Amos and Mplus; the LISREL software package does not currently offer Bollen–Stine bootstrapping capabilities, and EQS does the Bollen–Stine bootstrapping process but does not determine its *p*-value (it merely lists individual results for all B replications). As discussed previously, the first indicator of each factor (*visperc* and *paracomp*) served as the scale referent with its loading fixed to 1. Software code for Mplus and screen shots for Amos's graphical user interface are provided at this handbook's website (*www.handbookofsem.com*).

The key result from each software package is the Bollen–Stine *p*-value (p_{BS}) representing the proportion of bootstrap samples whose model test statistic exceeded the parent sample's ML test statistic value (22.683, as reported by Amos). Results from the two software packages were as follows: for Amos, $p_{BS} = .051$; for

Mplus, $p_{BS} = .075$. Although differing in exact value, both would lead to the same conclusion if held to a traditional $\alpha = .05$ level standard; that is, both would lead to a retention of the current model. Recalling that the *p*-value associated with the parent sample's T_{ML} statistic was .004, we see that a different conclusion would have been reached had we failed to take steps to adjust for the non-normal distributional characteristics of the parent sample.

ISSUES AND EXTENSIONS

As described in this chapter, bootstrapping is a viable option within the SEM framework for addressing non-normality in continuous data. Specifically, the naive process leads to empirical distributions for parameter estimates, which in turn lead to more robust standard errors for testing parameters within a model and constructing empirical confidence boundaries for interval estimates of those parameters. The Bollen–Stine process, in addition, facilitates an assessment of overall data–model fit. With regard to the latter, the traditional ML model test statistic was bootstrapped (i.e., $\tilde{T}_{ML}$), as is common when conducted within current SEM software packages. One could certainly bootstrap other fit indices as well (see Bollen & Stine, 1992), again determining the proportion of bootstrap sample fit index values that exceed the corresponding parent sample fit index value. The principle here is the same as for the ML test statistic, in this case deriving an empirical distribution for a descriptive data–model fit index that does not otherwise have a clearly accessible asymptotic distribution, especially under non-normality. This extension, however, is not really akin to having an alternative method of data–model fit assessment. That is, irrespective of the index bootstrapped, in the end one is conducting a statistical test of a model that is, in all likelihood, incorrect for reasons beyond its distributional violations. Indeed, indices to supplement, if not supplant, the statistical test of a model were derived for reasons related to the belief that slightly incorrect models might still be theoretically useful. Alas, although forays into using Bollen–Stine bootstrapping results to develop adjusted fit indices have been attempted (e.g., Nevitt & Hancock, 2000), their instability has thus far left us with no bootstrap-based assessment of data–model fit that tolerates misspecification.

This limitation notwithstanding, the versatility of bootstrapping within standard SEM practice makes it an attractive option for dealing with non-normality. It has also been extended, for example, to models involving mean structures (e.g., Yung & Bentler, 1996), to scenarios with missing data (e.g., Enders, 2002, 2005; Savalei & Yuan, 2009) and with complex samples (e.g., Asparouhov & Muthén, 2010; Stapleton, 2008), and it has been suggested to assist in power analyses within covariance structure models (Yuan & Hayashi, 2003). It has been used to develop more robust tests of indirect/mediation effects (e.g., Bollen & Stine, 1990; G. W. Cheung & Lau, 2007; M. W. Cheung, 2007; Finch et al., 1997; MacKinnon et al., 2004; Shrout & Bolger, 2002), as well as tests of model comparisons of covariance structure models (e.g., Raykov, 2001), of mixture models differing in numbers of classes (e.g., Lo, Mendell, & Rubin, 2001), and of competing latent variable models more generally (Levy & Hancock, 2011). Bootstrapping methods have even been used to stabilize other robust estimation techniques, such as asymptotically distribution-free estimation (e.g., Yung & Bentler, 1994).

In sum, as this chapter has illustrated, bootstrapping is a viable option for dealing with non-normality in continuous data within SEM, facilitating the derivation of standard errors, confidence intervals, and a statistical data–model fit assessment that are more robust than their default ML alternatives under samples of sufficient size and representativeness. As we mentioned earlier, given the difficulty of subscribing to the assumption of multivariate normality in general, pursuing strategies that are more tolerant of non-normality would seem to be a reasonable course of action right from the start of a modeling endeavor. Bootstrapping appears to be a strong contender for this role, and advances in software capabilities to incorporate existing and new developments in this area will only serve to enhance bootstrapping's attractiveness in this capacity.

REFERENCES

Arbuckle, J. L. (2008). *Amos 17 users' guide.* Chicago: SPSS.

Asparouhov, T., & Muthén, B. (2010). *Resampling methods in Mplus for complex survey data* (Mplus Technical Report). Los Angeles, CA: Muthén & Muthén.

Bentler, P. M. (2008). *EQS for Windows* [Computer software]. Encino, CA: Multivariate Software, Inc.

Bentler, P. M., & Wu, E. J. C. (2002). *EQS for Windows user's guide.* Encino, CA: Multivariate Software, Inc.

Beran, R., & Srivastava, M. S. (1985). Bootstrap tests and confidence regions for functions of a covariance matrix. *Annals of Statistics, 13,* 95–115.

Bollen, K. A. (1989). *Structural equations with latent variables.* New York: Wiley.

Bollen, K. A., & Stine, R. A. (1990). Direct and indirect effects: Classical and bootstrap estimates of variability. In C. C. Clogg (Ed.), *Sociological methodology* (pp. 115–140). Oxford, UK: Blackwell.

Bollen, K. A., & Stine, R. A. (1992). Bootstrapping goodness-of-fit measures in structural equation models. *Sociological Methods and Research, 21,* 205–229.

Browne, M. W. (1982). Covariance structures. In D. M. Hawkins (Ed.), *Topics in applied multivariate analysis* (pp. 72–141). Cambridge, UK: Cambridge University Press.

Browne, M. W. (1984). Asymptotic distribution-free methods in the analysis of covariance structures. *British Journal of Mathematical and Statistical Psychology, 37,* 62–83.

Chernick, M. R. (2008). *Bootstrap methods: A guide for practitioners and researchers* (2nd ed.). Hoboken, NJ: Wiley.

Cheung, G. W., & Lau, R. S. (2007). Testing mediation and suppression effects of latent variables: Bootstrapping with structural equation models. *Organizational Research Methods, 11,* 296–325.

Cheung, M. W. (2007). The comparison of approaches to constructing confidence intervals for mediating effects using structural equation models. *Structural Equation Modeling, 14,* 227–246.

Chou, C., & Bentler, P. M. (1995). Estimates and tests in structural equation modeling. In R. H. Hoyle (Ed.), *Structural equation modeling: Concepts, issues, and applications* (pp. 37–55). Thousand Oaks, CA: Sage.

Chou, C., Bentler, P. M., & Satorra, A. (1991). Scaled test

statistics and robust standard errors for non-normal data in covariance structure analysis: A Monte Carlo study. *British Journal of Mathematical and Statistical Psychology, 44*, 347–357.

Curran, P. J., West, S. G., & Finch, J. F. (1996). The robustness of test statistics to nonnormality and specification error in confirmatory factor analysis. *Psychological Methods, 1*, 16–29.

DiCiccio, T. J., & Efron, B. (1996). Bootstrap confidence intervals. *Statistical Science, 11*, 189–228.

Efron, B. (1979). Bootstrap methods: Another look at the jackknife. *Annals of Statistics, 7*, 1–26.

Enders, C. K. (2002). Applying the Bollen–Stine bootstrap for goodness-of-fit measures to structural equation models with missing data. *Multivariate Behavioral Research, 37*, 359–377.

Enders, C. K. (2005). A SAS macro for implementing the modified Bollen–Stine bootstrap for missing data: Implementing the bootstrap using existing structural equation modeling software. *Structural Equation Modeling, 12*, 620–641.

Finch, J. F., West, S. G., & MacKinnon, D. P. (1997). Effects of sample size and nonnormality on the estimation of mediated effects in latent variable models. *Structural Equation Modeling, 4*, 87–107.

Finney, S. J., & DiStefano, C. (2006). Non-normal and categorical data in structural equation modeling. In G. R. Hancock & R. O. Mueller (Eds.), *Structural equation modeling: A second course* (pp. 269–314). Greenwich, CT: Information Age.

Fouladi, R. T. (1998, April). *Covariance structure analysis techniques under conditions of multivariate normality and nonnormality—Modified and bootstrap based test statistics.* Paper presented at the annual meeting of the American Educational Research Association, San Diego, CA.

Hancock, G. R., & Nevitt, J. (1999). Bootstrapping and the identification of exogenous latent variables within structural equation models. *Structural Equation Modeling, 12*, 394–399.

Hancock, G. R., & Wasko, J. A. (2010, May). *Preliminary assessments of normality are useless in deciding whether or not to use rescaled model test statistics.* Paper presented at the annual meeting of the American Educational Research Association, Denver, CO.

Holzinger, K., & Swineford, F. (1939). *A study in factor analysis: The stability of a bifactor solution* (Supplementary Educational Monograph, No. 48). Chicago: University of Chicago Press.

Hoogland, J. J., & Boomsma, A. (1998). Robustness studies in covariance structure modeling: An overview and a meta-analysis. *Sociological Methods and Research, 26*, 329–367.

Hu, L.-T., & Bentler, P. M. (1999). Cutoff criteria for fit indexes in covariance structure analysis: Conventional criteria versus new alternatives. *Structural Equation Modeling, 6*, 1–55.

Hu, L.-T., Bentler, P. M., & Kano, Y. (1992). Can test statistics in covariance structure analysis be trusted? *Psychological Bulletin, 112*, 351–362.

Jöreskog, K., & Sörbom, D. (2008). *LISREL 8.80 for Windows* [Computer software]. Lincolnwood, IL: Scientific Software International, Inc.

Levy, R., & Hancock, G. R. (2011). An extended model comparison framework for covariance and mean structure models, accommodating multiple groups and latent mixtures. *Sociological Methods and Research, 40*, 256–278.

Lo, Y., Mendell, N. R., & Rubin, D. B. (2001). Testing the number of components in a normal mixture. *Biometrika, 88*, 767–778.

MacKinnon, D. P., Lockwood, C. M., & Williams, J. (2004). Confidence limits for the indirect effect: Distribution of the product and resampling methods. *Multivariate Behavioral Research, 39*, 99–128.

Muthén, B. O., & Kaplan, D. (1985). A comparison of some methodologies for the factor analysis of nonnormal Likert variables. *British Journal of Mathematical and Statistical Psychology, 38*, 171–189.

Muthén, L. K., & Muthén, B. O. (2010). *Mplus 6.0* [Computer software]. Los Angeles: Authors.

Nevitt, J., & Hancock, G. R. (2000). Improving the root mean square error of approximation for nonnormal conditions in structural equation modeling. *Journal of Experimental Education, 68*, 251–268.

Nevitt, J., & Hancock, G. R. (2001). Performance of bootstrapping approaches to model test statistics and parameter standard error estimation in structural equation modeling. *Structural Equation Modeling, 8*, 353–377.

Olsson, U., Foss, T., Troye, S. V., & Howell, R. D. (2000). The performance of ML, GLS, and WLS estimation in structural equation modeling under conditions of misspecification and nonnormality. *Structural Equation Modeling, 7*, 557–595.

Raykov, T. (2001) Approximate confidence interval for difference in fit of structural equation models. *Structural Equation Modeling, 8*, 458–469.

Satorra, A., & Bentler, P. M. (1988). Scaling corrections for chi-square statistics in covariance structure analysis. In *American Statistical Association 1988 Proceedings of the Business and Economics Sections* (pp. 308–313). Alexandria, VA: American Statistical Association.

Satorra, A., & Bentler, P. M. (1994). Corrections to test statistics and standard errors in covariance structure analysis. In A. von Eye & C. C. Clogg (Eds.), *Latent variables analysis: Applications for developmental research* (pp. 399–419). Thousand Oaks, CA: Sage.

Savalei, V., & Yuan, K.-H. (2009). On the model-based bootstrap with missing data: Obtaining a *p*-value for a test of exact fit. *Multivariate Behavioral Research, 44*, 741–763.

Shrout, P. E., & Bolger, N. (2002). Mediation in experimental and nonexperimental studies: New procedures and recommendations. *Psychological Methods, 7*, 422–445.

Stapleton, L. M. (2008). Variance estimation using replication methods in structural equation modeling with complex sample data. *Structural Equation Modeling, 15*, 183–210.

West, S. G., Finch, J. F., & Curran, P. J. (1995). Structural equation models with nonnormal variables: Problems and remedies. In R. H. Hoyle (Ed.), *Structural equation modeling: Concepts, issues, and applications* (pp. 56–75). Thousand Oaks, CA: Sage.

Yu, C., & Muthén, B. (2002, April). *Evaluation of model fit indices for latent variable models with categorical and continuous outcomes.* Paper presented at the annual meeting of the American Educational Research Association, New Orleans, LA.

Yuan, K.-H., & Hayashi, K. (2003). Bootstrap approach to inference and power analysis based on three test statistics for covariance structure models. *British Journal of Mathematical and Statistical Psychology, 56*, 93–110.

Yung, Y.-F., & Bentler, P. M. (1994). Bootstrap-corrected ADF test statistics in covariance structure analysis. *British Journal of Mathematical and Statistical Psychology, 47*, 63–84.

Yung, Y.-F., & Bentler, P. M. (1996). Bootstrapping techniques in analysis of mean and covariance structures. In G. A. Marcoulides & R. E. Schumacker (Eds.), *Advanced structural equation modeling: Issues and techniques* (pp. 195–226). Mahwah, NJ: Erlbaum.

CHAPTER 19

Choosing Structural Equation Modeling Computer Software

Snapshots of LISREL, EQS, Amos, and Mplus

Barbara M. Byrne

The growth of structural equation modeling (SEM) over the past 35 years or so has been nothing short of phenomenal! An interesting offshoot of this escalation has been the equally expanding, albeit somewhat more subtle growth of computer software capable of handling the statistical rigors demanded by the SEM methodology. In combination, each component of this symbiotic pair serves as a stimulant for the other in advancing the practice of SEM methodology. As substantive researchers increasingly seek more comprehensive answers to their research questions, statistical researchers are challenged to further advance the capabilities of SEM methodology, which in turn necessitates further development of existing SEM software programs.

Since development of the first SEM program in 1974 (LISREL), the ensuing years have witnessed a steady increase in the development and revision of alternative SEM computer software, such that there are now several programs from which to choose, including Amos (*Analysis of Moment Structures*; Arbuckle, 2009), CALIS (*Covariance Analysis of Linear Structural Equations*; SAS, 2009), EQS (*Equations*; Bentler, 2005), LISREL (*Linear Structural Relationships*; Jöreskog & Sörbom, 2006), Mplus (Muthén & Muthén, 1998–2010), Mx (*Matrix*; Neale, Boker, Xie, & Maes, 2003), RAMONA (*Reticular Action Model or Near Approximation*; Systat Software Inc., 2009), and SEPATH (*Structural

Equation Modeling and Path Analysis; StatSoft, Inc., 2009). Although these software programs share many of the same core analytic features, they are also necessarily unique in a variety of ways. Given that a review of each is clearly beyond the scope of this chapter, only a limited selection is included here.

The purpose of this chapter is to provide readers with an overview of four commercial programs (two open-source programs are reviewed in the next chapter) considered to be the most widely used and therefore likely of most interest and potential use to the readers of this volume. I refer, of course, to LISREL, EQS, Amos, and Mplus. More specifically, the intent is fourfold: (1) to provide a brief historical review of development related to each of these programs; (2) to describe the major features of each, highlighting both their strengths and limitations; (3) to outline the manner by which each of these programs addresses one critically important issue in SEM application—the presence of data that are non-normally distributed; and (4) to illustrate and compare an example SEM application based on the EQS (Version 6.1) and Mplus (Version 6.12) programs.

The material in this chapter is presented in five sections. I begin with a historical overview of the four selected programs and highlight major modifications of each throughout the span of its existence. In the second section, I present a general description of each program within the context of its most recent version (as this handbook goes to press), followed by notation of its particularly distinctive elements and major strengths, as well as its possible limitations. The third section describes the approach taken by each of the programs in addressing the issue of non-normal data. In the fourth section, I present an illustrative comparison of the EQS and Mplus programs with respect to components of the input file and selected analytic results in the output file. In the final section, I suggest factors most appropriate to professional and personal needs that one may wish to consider in the selection of a SEM computer program.

HISTORICAL PERSPECTIVES

LISREL (Jöreskog & Sörbom, 2006)

LISREL, the legendary initial SEM computer program, evolved from rekindled interest in path analysis during the 1960s that resulted from a call for social scientists to reconsider making causal interpretations of nonexperimental data. Indeed, a 1970 conference on causal modeling, organized by the Social Science Research Council, appears to have been instrumental in the early development of SEM in general, and of the LISREL program in particular. Two critically important milestones resulted from this conference: (1) the publication of two seminal textbooks on SEM (Duncan, 1975; Goldberger & Duncan, 1973), and (2) presentation of a model that combined features of econometrics with those of psychometrics and allowed for multiple indicators of latent variables. This model became commonly known as the "LISREL" model.

During the early 1970s the LISREL model was generalized to accommodate confirmatory factor analysis (Jöreskog, 1969), multiple-group analysis (Jöreskog, 1971), and more general models for the analysis of covariance structures (e.g., Jöreskog, 1970). It was during this period that the initial structure of the LISREL computer program began to take shape. Initial references to this developing program were cited in a research report by Jöreskog and van Thillo (1972). Although Wolfle (2003) notes that for all practical purposes, this 1972 article describes LISREL I, it was actually not until 1974 that the program officially took on a life of its own, at which time it was known as LISREL III (Sörbom, 2001).

Although the basic form of the so-called LISREL model and the program within which it is implemented has remained unchanged across its nearly four-decade

lifespan, the program itself has undergone substantial improvement and modification. A few of the key enhancements during this period are (1) implementation of automatic start values (LISREL V; Jöreskog & Sörbom, 1981); (2) implementation of modification indices (LISREL VI; Jöreskog & Sörbom, 1984); (3) introduction of PRELIS (LISREL 7; Jöreskog & Sörbom, 1988); (4) introduction of SIMPLIS and the Microsoft Windows interface (LISREL 8; Jöreskog & Sörbom, 1993a, 1993b); and (5) implementation of multilevel and latent growth curve modeling (LISREL 8.30; Jöreskog & Sörbom, 1999). For a more comprehensive review of these program advances, readers are referred to Sörbom (2001).

EQS (Bentler, 2005)

In the early 1980s, applications of SEM in the social sciences were uncommon. This phenomenon likely can be linked to the mathematically sophisticated nature of existing computer programs at that time, the primary one of which was LISREL. Successful use of this program required a sound understanding of both matrix algebra and an arcane command language rooted in Greek mathematical symbols. Recognition of this fact, based on his own empirical work and extensive publication in the areas of personality and applied social psychology (particularly drug abuse), prompted Bentler to develop a computer program that could be more readily understood by the practical/empirical researcher who may not have a strong mathematical background. This pioneering work during the 1980s led to the birth of EQS (Bentler, 1985), the first program to provide a user-friendly, but statistically sound, approach to SEM programming long before such modus operandi became fashionable. Based on the Bentler–Weeks (1980) model, EQS provided an easier, alternative way of thinking about structural equation models, such that the matrix language used in the specification of models was replaced by equations.

In addition to his motivation for making SEM modeling more accessible to a broader spectrum of researchers, Bentler (personal communication, April 16, 2010) also saw many other existing program limitations in need of attention; in particular, these included statistics based only on normal theory tests, the lack of practical fit indices, and the difficulty of model modification based on the existing modification indices at that time. Accordingly, development of the EQS program focused on incorporation of a wider range of statistics that addressed issues such as non-normality and missing data, practical indices of fit such as the normed fit index (NFI; Bentler & Bonett, 1980) and subsequently, the comparative fit index (CFI; Bentler, 1990), and a simplified approach to model modification based on Lagrange multiplier theory.

Continuing development of EQS resulted in its breaking the glass ceiling of SEM computing in several ways as the first program to (1) enable its use on the personal computer (PC)[1]; (b) perform normal, elliptical, and distribution-free estimation based on the Bentler–Weeks (1980) model (Bentler, 1986); (3) provide a simulation module, thereby allowing researchers to study test performance under conditions of correct model specification, as well as under various conditions of violation; (4) incorporate the use of robust statistics (Satorra & Bentler, 1988; Yuan & Bentler, 1998), all of which were completely documented and fully described in the EQS manual; (5) facilitate model specification via path diagrams structured within the Windows graphical interface (Bentler & Wu, 2002; Byrne, 1994); and (6) perform many statistical, graphical, and data management procedures that otherwise required the use of separate statistical packages such as BMDP, SPSS, or SAS. Indeed, this philosophy of incorporating all the newest computational, statistical, and ease of use strategies into the EQS program continues to this day.

Amos (Arbuckle, 2009)

The Amos program, following closely on the heels of the first Windows version of EQS (Bentler & Wu, 2002), formally entered the world of SEM computing as Amos 3.5 (Arbuckle, 1995). Although there had been published articles reporting on the development of this program (see Arbuckle, 1989, 1994), there was no actual program available for purchase prior to version 3.5, which operated solely within a graphical interface. In 1999, Amos 4 provided for two alternative model specification environments—one structured within a graphical interface (Amos Graphics), and the other based on equation statements (Amos Basic). Using Amos Graphics, the researcher worked directly from a path diagram; using Amos Basic, he or she worked directly from equation statements. Whereas model specification and testing in EQS tended to be weighted heavily toward the equation approach, in Amos, it was weighted toward the path diagram approach.

The ease with which users could build and submit models to analyses in Amos appealed greatly to SEM neophytes and, as a result, most users of the program worked within the framework of Amos Graphics. Indeed, based on my own experience from interaction with students, colleagues, and others, I found that most users were completely unaware of the availability of the alternate Amos Basic approach to model specification. As a consequence, I became increasingly uneasy about the rapidly expanding perception that Amos Graphics was the easy way to learn SEM, as it required no work with either equations or matrices. Concern that these users, although keen to create structural equation models and apply the methodology to their data, lacked sufficient understanding of the underlying theory and, as a consequence, were unable to appropriately and adequately interpret the program output, motivated me to write the first edition of my Amos book (Byrne, 2001). Accordingly, this undertaking gave me the opportunity to weave together aspects of SEM theory with interpretation of the Amos output pertinent to diverse model applications.

Amos has undergone almost yearly revisions since 2003, at which time Version 5 introduced the capability to do specification searches and automated multiple-group analyses. A few of the major additions to the program since that time have been the introduction of (1) Bayesian estimation (Amos 6); (2) analysis of ordered categorical and censored data (Amos 7); (3) mixture modeling (Amos 16); (4) latent growth curve modeling (Amos 17); and (5) estimation through bootstrapping of any user-defined function of model parameters (Amos 19). At the time of writing this chapter, Amos 19 operates as a beta version.

Mplus (Muthén & Muthén, 1998–2010)

Given Mplus's relatively recent emergence in 1998, it might be perceived as the proverbial "new kid on the block." However, this perception definitely is not the case, as its seminal roots were originally established during the development of an earlier program, LISCOMP (Muthén, 1987). An interesting aspect of the LISCOMP program was its close similarity, in terms of both structure and syntax, to LISREL. Indeed, Muthén acknowledged this fact in his statement that "the LISREL modeling framework and program has obviously been one strong source of inspiration for LISCOMP (Muthén, 1988, Preface). Although Mplus operates within the Windows framework, whereas LISCOMP did not, these former structure and syntax features remain evident in Mplus today.

In her review of the LISCOMP program, Hutchinson (1995) noted three characteristics that distinguished it from other SEM programs of its period: (1) It had an exceptionally expansive and analytically strong capability of dealing with categorical, censored, and truncated data; (2) it made available several estimators that could be used in the analysis of non-normal continuous, as well as categorical, data; and (3) it was clearly designed for use by advanced researchers having a strong background in statistical theory. In my view, each of these program attributes similarly characterizes the Mplus program today, with the exception that its strengths in addressing categorical and non-normal data have expanded substantially. Perhaps the most striking difference between LISREL and Mplus can be found in the way it addressed Hutchinson's disparagement of its capability to make the program more accessible for use by a wider band of practical rather than only statistical researchers—and this it has done in spades via an exceptionally efficient customer support facility and superb website, with both facilities providing a wealth of information to its users.

During the time spanning its inaugural version in 1998 (Mplus 1.0) and its most recent version in 2010 (Mplus 6.12), Mplus has made innumerable improvements and expansions of existing models that make possible the estimation of many different structural equation models involving a host of diverse data conditions. Due to space restrictions, and consistent with my review of the three previous programs, I cite only a few of these highlights here. Selected key example modifications include the following: (1) in the interest of extra convenience, addition of a language generator, output data-saving capabilities, and expanded output options (Mplus 2.0); (2) introduction of multilevel modeling applicable to both cross-sectional and longitudinal research designs (Mplus 2.1); (3) classification of the program into a base program and three optional add-on modules that feature specific modeling frameworks (Mplus 3.0); (4) introduction of data transformation features and expansion of parameter constraint commands that both simplify and make more flexible family genetic modeling (Mplus 4.0); (5) expanded exploratory factor analytic (EFA) capabilities related to complex survey data, exploratory factor mixture analysis with class-specific rotations, and two-level exploratory factor analysis of both continuous and categorical data (Mplus 5.0), and (6) Bayesian analysis using Markov Chain Monte Carlo (MCMC) algorithms. A more ex-

tensive review of Mplus developments can be found on the program website (*http://www.statmodel.com*).

CURRENT PERSPECTIVES

I now present a general description of each program based on the current version as this handbook goes to press; features considered to be unique to a particular program are noted.

LISREL (Version 8.8)

LISREL is packaged as a suite of programs that includes its initial companion program, PRELIS.[2] Both programs are compatible with Windows 7. The LISREL program, as noted earlier, is structured around the "LISREL" model and is the workhorse for all SEM analyses.

PRELIS was designed specifically to serve as a preprocessor for LISREL, hence the acronym PRElis. Nonetheless, because it can be used effectively to manipulate and save data files, as well as to provide an initial descriptive overview of data, it can also function as a stand-alone program. In addition to providing descriptive statistics and graphical displays of the data, PRELIS can prepare the correct matrix to be read by LISREL when the data (1) are continuous, ordinal, censored, or any combination thereof, (2) are severely non-normally distributed, and/or (3) have missing values. In addition, PRELIS can be used for a variety of data management functions such as recoding and transformation of variables, case selection, computation of new variables, and creation and merger of raw data files. Finally, PRELIS can be used to generate bootstrapped samples and estimates, as well as to conduct simulation studies with variables specified to have particular distributional characteristics.

Model specification in LISREL can take one of three distinctive forms, each of which is conducted interactively. *First*, and most complex, is via the original LISREL commands, the syntax of which requires an understanding of matrix algebra in general, and matrices pertinent to specification of confirmatory factor analysis (CFA) and full SEM path analytic models in particular. In LISREL, these matrices are denoted by uppercase Greek letters, while their elements, which represent the model parameters, are denoted by lowercase Greek letters. Unlike earlier versions of LISREL, however, the Windows interface enables an interactive approach whereby the user is prompted for model and data information; once this information is entered, the related command syntax is completed automatically. The *second* and less complex form of model specification is through use of SIMPLIS, a command language introduced in the initial version of LISREL 8 (Jöreskog & Sörbom, 1993b). This approach requires only that the user name the observed and latent (if any) variables, together with the estimated regression paths. Indeed, Jöreskog & Sörbom (1993a), in their introduction of this new command language, stated, "It is not necessary to be familiar with the LISREL model or any of its submodels. No Greek or matrix notations are required" (p. i). The *third* and most intuitive approach to model specification in LISREL is via the graphical interface. In this instance, the user simply constructs the path diagram on the screen and then identifies the regression paths to be estimated.

Of the three approaches to model specification, it would appear (at least from a review of reported SEM analyses), that the SIMPLIS command language is the most popular; use of the original LISREL command language seems limited to researchers who are familiar with its earlier versions and/or have a strong statistical background.

Only raw data in ASCII (.dat) format can be read directly by LISREL. Other data forms such as SPSS (.sav) and Excel (.xls) must first be imported to PRELIS, whereupon the file is then converted to covariance matrix format. Estimation methods include unweighted least squares (ULS), generalized least squares (GLS), maximum likelihood (ML), robust ML, weighted least squares (WLS), and diagonally weighted least squares (DWLS). Finally, LISREL enables tests applicable to a broad range of structural equation models that include CFA, full SEM path, structured means, multiple-group, multilevel, latent growth curve, and mixture models.

In my view, two features in particular distinguish LISREL from the other three programs reviewed in this chapter: (1) its continued use of the original LISREL command language, and (2) its companion preprocessor program PRELIS. With respect to the original LISREL matrix-linked syntax, I consider this feature to be highly constructive in the sense that it compels users to think through their model specification within the framework of its related parameter matrices. As such, this approach can be extremely instructive in assisting those new to SEM to develop a solid understanding of the SEM methodology. With respect to my second point, I consider the need for a separate preprocessor program to be somewhat limiting when compared, for example, with the EQS program, which is capable of performing these same tasks, in addition to many more, without the need of an additionally supporting program.

Contact information: Scientific Software International

(general): *http://www.ssicentral.com/lisrel*

(technical support): *lisrel@ssicentral.com*

EQS (Version 6.1)

To the best of my knowledge, EQS is the only SEM program capable of performing comprehensive data management tasks, preanalytic data screening, and exploratory non-SEM analyses, over and above its full range of SEM capabilities, thereby eliminating the need of other statistical packages for these purposes. As EQS is a Windows-based program, all procedures are selected from drop-down menus, with subsequent operations being completed interactively. A few of the many management tasks include conditional case selection, variable labeling and transformation, group formation, data merging, and coding of missing data. Examples of data screening capabilities include graphical presentation via charts or plots such as histograms, pie charts, scatterplots, boxplots, and error bar plots, with color coding preferences available for each. Finally, exploratory analyses available to users include descriptive statistics (although this information is always provided in all SEM output), frequencies, *t*-tests, analysis of variance (ANOVA), cross-tabulations, factor analyses, nonparametric tests, multiple regression (standard, stepwise, and hierarchical), and intraclass correlations. One additional set of exploratory analyses pertinent to the detection of missing data are worthy of separate mention. In this instance, the user is provided with options related to (1) display of missing data (e.g., exclusion of cases having a specified percentage of missing data); (2) search for evidence of missing values and, if detected, a thorough diagnosis and reporting of these findings; and (3) imputation of missing values based on means, group means, regression, or unstructured expectation maximization (EM).

Model specification in EQS is based on the Bentler–Weeks (1980) representation system. As such, all variables in a model, regardless of whether measured (i.e., observed) or unmeasured (i.e., latent), can be categorized as either dependent or independent variables. Any variable having a single-headed arrow pointing at it represents a dependent variable; if no arrow is present, it represents an independent variable. This simple representation system therefore makes it very easy to conceptualize and specify any structural equation model. Likewise, the EQS notation is equally straightforward. All *measured* variables are designated as *V* and constitute the actual data of a study. All other (unmeasured) variables are hypothetical and represent the structural network of the phenomenon under investigation. There are three such variables: (1) the latent construct, regarded generally as a factor in EQS and designated as *F*; (2) a residual (i.e., error term) associated with any measured variable, designated as *E*; and (3) a residual associated with the prediction of each factor, designated as *D* (disturbance term).

Model specification in EQS can be conducted in one of three ways—manually, interactively, or graphically. The *manual* approach requires users to type a one-page input file. Though simple and straightforward, it is nonetheless the most time-consuming. This reality notwithstanding, the manual approach can be invaluable in helping users make the link between a schematic portrayal of the model under study and the equivalent equation statements expressed in EQS language. The *interactive* approach to EQS model specification is implemented through use of a feature called "Build_ EQS." Accordingly, the user is presented with a series of dialog boxes, each of which relates to a particular section of the input file. Completion of each dialog box results in a line-by-line automatic building of the input file. Finally, the EQS *graphical* approach to model specification is enabled through use of the "Diagrammer" facility. For a comprehensive review of the EQS notation and input file, together with a step-by-step walk-through in building an EQS file based on each of the three approaches noted earlier, readers are referred to Byrne (2006).

EQS can read ASCII (.dat), covariance matrix, and SPSS (.sav) data; imported data are automatically converted to EQS format (.ess). This transition, however, is a boon rather than a hindrance, as all information related to the data file (e.g., labels, scaling, sample size) is retained by the program, thereby facilitating any subsequent structuring of files and/or graphical displays. Estimation methods include ULS; GLS; ML; robust ML, including residual-based chi-square and *F*-tests;

and asymptotic distribution-free (ADF), including corrected ADF tests, as well as their counterparts for correlation structure models.[3] Finally, EQS tests a full range of structural equation models for both continuous and categorical data that include latent regression, CFA, full SEM path, structured means, multiple-group, latent growth curve, and multilevel models, with the latter capable of being based on three different analytic estimation approaches: (1) ML, (2) Muthén's (1994) approximate estimator (MUML), and (3) hierarchical linear-like modeling (HLM). In addition, EQS provides for the conduct of easy-to-use bootstrapping procedures and simulation analyses with summaries.

Particular strengths of the EQS program are numerous, but restriction of space allows only a succinct summary here. First, the ease with which a user can build an input file, manage and explore data, and graphically construct models of publication-acceptable quality is incomparable among its program contemporaries. Second, the large number of different statistical methods available in the analysis of diverse types of non-normal data is again unrivaled. Third, EQS provides for a wide and varied range of graphical and analytic procedures in the detection, diagnosis, and estimation of missing data. Fourth, EQS has established statistical methods for testing samples that may be of less than optimal size. Fifth, unlike other SEM programs that calculate only an alpha coefficient of reliability, EQS, in addition, reports maximal, model-based, and greatest lower-bound reliability coefficients. Finally, the EQS support facility is efficient and operates within a very fast turnaround time frame.

Contact information: Multivariate Software Inc.

(general): *http://www.mvsoft.com*

(technical support): *support@mvsoft.com*

Amos (Version 18.0)

As noted earlier, most people tend to equate Amos with only a graphical approach to SEM. Indeed, this perception seemingly remains as strong today as it was 20 years ago and likely derives from the ease, speed, and wide array of modeling tools with which the program enables the building and testing of models. Thus, it is not surprising that, by and large, the majority of users base their analyses on the Amos Graphics interface. In this regard, Amos provides users with all the tools they will ever need in creating and working with SEM path diagrams. Each tool is represented by an icon (or button) and performs one particular function; there are 42 from which to choose. Whereas some icons represent drawing functions, others represent specific aspects of the modeling process itself. A few examples of the latter are as follows: Data icon (selects and reads data files); Calculate Estimates icon (calculates default and/ or requested estimates; Analysis Properties icon (allows for additional calculations; e.g., modification indices, squared multiple correlations); Multiple Groups icon (enables analyses of multiple groups); and Bayesian icon (enables particular analyses based on Bayesian statistics). Immediately upon opening the program, this toolbox of icons appears to the left of a blank workspace. For a step-by-step guide to using these icons in building and testing a wide variety of structural equation models, readers are referred to Byrne (2009).

Despite the popularity of its Graphics module, Amos does provide for an alternative approach to SEM that operates within a programming interface, complete with a built-in editor. Accordingly, the user specifies a model via equation-like statements. Initially, this programming mode was termed "Amos Basic." However, with the introduction of Version 6.0 in 2005, Amos Basic was subsequently replaced by the VB.net (Visual Basic) and C# languages. (For a review of model input files based on Amos Basic, see Byrne, 2001.[4])

Regardless of which approach to structuring model input is preferred, all options related to the analyses are available from drop-down menus, and all parameters can be presented in text format. In addition, Amos Graphics allows for the estimates to be displayed graphically in a path diagram. Thus, the choice between these two Amos approaches to building and testing structural equation models ultimately boils down to one's comfort level in working within a graphical versus a mathematically oriented framework.

In contrast to the other three programs considered here, Amos does not accept data in ASCII (.dat) format; rather, only data formats that include Excel (.xls), SPSS (.sav), and text delimited files (.txt) are supported. Estimation methods include ULS, GLS, ML, ADF,[5] and scale-free least squares (SLS). In addition to providing for the testing of CFA, full SEM path, structured means, multiple-group, and latent growth curve models, Amos can now (as of Version 16) facilitate the analysis of mixture models. A second, recent addition to the Amos program is the capability to handle categorical data. Of import, however, is that analyses based on categorical data in general, and analysis of mixture models in particular, are enabled only through use of the Amos Bayesian statistics facility. (For a step-by-step illustration of the Bayesian approach to analyses based on categorical data, readers are referred to Byrne, 2009.)

Although the Amos Graphics interface is most typically used in the analysis of structural equation models, it also has extensive capabilities for the conduct of exploratory analyses based on a Specification Search function. In using this facility, the researcher allocates certain paths in the model diagram to be optional. The program then fits the model to the data using every possible subset of paths. The models are subsequently sorted according to their fit to the data based on particular fit statistics. Most appropriately, however, the final best-fitting model must be substantiated by theory and other empirical research. Finally, Amos has a broad array of bootstrapping capabilities, in that it is able to (1) generate bootstrapped standard errors and confidence intervals for all parameter and effect estimates, as well as for sample means, variances, covariances, and correlations; (2) implement percentile intervals and bias-corrected percentile estimates (Stine, 1989); and (3) perform the bootstrap approach to model testing proposed by Bollen and Stine (1992).

Although Amos distinguishes itself from the other programs considered here with respect to its unique Specification Search function, this capability may generally not be perceived as a particular strength of the program. In my view, Amos's primary strength unquestionably lies with the Graphics interface in terms of its model building, model specification, and model execution capabilities. In addition, however, the ease with which one can access and use an extensive selection of bootstrapping capabilities has long been popular with researchers who may or may not have a solid understanding of SEM methodology. On the other hand, one notable weakness of the Amos program, in my experience, has been its lack of a viable and efficient technical support facility.

Contact information: SPSS an IBM Company

(general): *http://www-01.ibm.com*

(technical support): *http://www-947.ibm.com/support*

Mplus (Version 6.12)

Mplus provides for the specification and testing of a broad array of models based on a wide choice of estimators and algorithms for analyses of data that are continuous, ordered categorical (ordinal), unordered categorical (nominal), censored, and binary and any combination thereof. The program is divided into a basic program and three optional add-on modules. The basic unit (Mplus Base) provides for the estimation of regression, CFA, EFA, SEM, and latent growth models, as well as discrete- and continuous-time survival models. Module 1 and Module 2 support the estimation of a wide variety of mixture and multilevel models, respectively. Module 3 contains all features of the first two modules and, in addition, enables the estimation of several advanced models that combine the features of both. Consistent with the other three programs, Mplus is Windows-based with drop-down menus allowing the full range of usual editing procedures, as well as model execution. In addition, Mplus provides for specification of graphical displays of observed data and analysis results based on a postprocessing graphics model. Unlike the other three programs, however, Mplus does not have a graphical interface and works solely within the framework of a programming interface. As a result, the building of its input files is equation-based.

Model specification in Mplus is relatively straightforward and entails a maximum of 10 command statements. As might be expected, however, each of these commands provides for several options that can further refine model specification and desired outcome information. Given that, typically, only a small subset of these 10 commands and their options is needed, even specification of very complex models requires only minimal input. This minimization of input structure has been made possible largely as a consequence of numerous programmed defaults chosen on the basis of models that are the most commonly tested in practice.

To assist with the building of input files, Mplus provides for the optional use of its Language Generator, an interactive facility that leads users through a series of screens that prompt for information pertinent to their data and analyses. One limitation of this feature, however, is that its functioning terminates at the point where details related to the model under test must be specified. As such, this information must be added manually to the input file. Additionally, commands related to the transformations of variables (DEFINE), postanalysis graphical displays (PLOT), simulation analyses (MONTECARLO), and any features added to the program following Version 2.0 must be manually inserted. New users of Mplus, in particular, will find this language-generating resource to be extremely

helpful because it not only reduces the time involved in structuring the file, but it also ensures the correct formulation of commands and their options. (For a step-by-step illustration of the Mplus Language Generator as applied to the model and data addressed later in this chapter, see Byrne, 2011.)

Mplus reads data in ASCII (.dat) format only. Thus, to use data saved in another format (e.g., SPSS .sav), conversion to ASCII format is essential. Furthermore, any variable labels appearing on the first line must be deleted. Primary estimation methods in Mplus include ULS, GLS, WLS, and ML. In addition, however, robust variants of the ML estimator (mean-adjusted ML [MLM], mean- and variance-adjusted ML [MLMV], ML with standard errors computed using a sandwich estimate [MLR]), and weight variants of both the ULS (mean- and variance-adjusted ULS [ULSMV]) and WLS (mean-adjusted WLS [WLSM], mean- and variance-adjusted WLS [WLSMV]) estimators, provide users with a wide variety from which to choose. Importantly, selection of the most appropriate estimator is further conditioned by both the type of model under test and the type of *outcome* variables being analyzed (i.e., all continuous; at least one binary or ordered categorical variable; at least one censored, unordered categorical, or count variable). Furthermore, certain conditions (e.g., missing data) can apply.

Models capable of being tested in Mplus are many and can be classified according to whether they include continuous latent variables (e.g., CFA, full SEM, and latent growth models), categorical latent variables (e.g., path analysis mixture, loglinear, and multiple-group models), or a combination of both (e.g., factor mixture, SEM mixture, and latent growth mixture models). In addition, Mplus provides for two approaches to the analysis of complex survey data. Whereas the first approach takes into account stratification, non-independence of observations resulting from cluster sampling, and/or unequal probability of selection, the second approach (commonly known as "multilevel modeling") allows for the modeling of nonindependence of observations (due to clustering) at each level of the data. Beyond these modeling capabilities, Mplus has wide-ranging Monte Carlo simulation capabilities for both data generation and data analysis and, in addition, allows for both standard and Bollen–Stine (Bollen & Stine, 1992) residual bootstrapping facilities.

Although Mplus has many superior model-specific capabilities, limitations of space permit only reflections on the program in general. In my view, the most outstanding aspect of Mplus is its capacity to estimate an absolutely amazing number of different models based on an equally expansive variety of data types. In this regard, it is unquestionably in a class all its own. Of course, a second outstanding strength of Mplus is its long-standing capabilities in dealing with categorical data. Finally, although not specific to the program itself, the Mplus website serves as an exceptionally rich and invaluable source of information in the form of articles, training materials, group discussions, and program updates, all of which bear on various aspects of both SEM and particular program applications. This resource, together with regular e-mail notifications and almost instantaneous technical support assistance, in my view, is unique to Mplus and certainly one of its most valuable assets.

Contact information: Muthén and Muthén

(general): *http://www.statmodel.com*

(technical support): *support@statmodel.com*

COMPARATIVE APPROACHES TO ANALYSIS OF NON-NORMAL DATA

By default, all SEM programs are based on ML estimation. However, a critically important assumption in these analyses is that the data have a multivariate normal distribution in the population. Violation of this assumption can seriously invalidate statistical hypothesis-testing with the result that the normal theory test statistic (χ^2) may not reflect an adequate evaluation of the model under study (Hu, Bentler, & Kano, 1992), thereby leading to results that may be seriously misleading. We turn now to the manner in which each of the four computer programs addresses this issue of data non-normality.

LISREL (Version 8.8)

One approach to working with data that are non-normally distributed is use of asymptotic (large sample) distribution-free (ADF) estimators for which normality assumptions are not required. The early work of Browne (1984) was instrumental in the development of this methodology. This ADF approach is the one embraced by the LISREL program in dealing with this non-normality issue. Implementation of this strategy, however, involves a two-step process. Whereas Step

1 involves use of the PRELIS companion package in recasting the data into asymptotic matrix form, Step 2 focuses on analysis of this matrix based on the use of LISREL with WLS estimation.

One major limitation associated with this approach in addressing non-normality has been its excessively demanding sample-size requirement. It is now well known that unless sample sizes are extremely large (1,000 to 5,000 cases; West, Finch, & Curran, 1995), the ADF estimator performs very poorly and can yield severely distorted estimated values and standard errors (Curran, West, & Finch, 1996; Hu et al., 1992; West et al., 1995). More recently, statistical research has suggested that, at the very least, sample sizes should be greater than 10 times the number of estimated parameters; otherwise, the results from the ADF method generally cannot be trusted (Raykov & Marcoulides, 2000).

EQS (Version 6.1)

Although other estimation methods have been developed for use when the normality assumption does not hold (e.g., ADF; elliptical; heterogeneous kurtotic), Chou, Bentler, and Satorra (1991) and Hu and colleagues (1992) have argued that it may be more appropriate to correct the test statistic rather than use a different method of estimation. Satorra and Bentler (1988) developed such a statistic that incorporates a scaling correction for the χ^2 statistic when distributional assumptions are violated; its computation takes into account the model, the estimation method, and the sample kurtosis values. The resulting (corrected) chi-square value (S-Bχ^2) and standard errors are said to be "robust," meaning that their computed values are valid despite violation of the normality assumption underlying the estimation method. The S-Bχ^2 has been shown to be the most reliable test statistic for evaluating mean and covariance structure models under various distributions and sample sizes (Curran et al., 1996; Hu et al., 1992). In addition, EQS computes robust versions of the comparative fit index (CFI), root mean square error of approximation (RMSEA), and 90% confidence interval (CI) for the latter.

In addition to its usual application with continuous data, the S-Bχ^2 can be used with non-normal categorical data. Although it basically treats the ordered data as if they were continuous, DiStefano (2002) has reported this scaled approach to be beneficial in yielding standard errors that are more precise than ML estimates for non-normally distributed data having as few as three ordered categories.

In SEM, data are often incomplete, as well as non-normally distributed. When this condition holds, correction based on the S-Bχ^2 is not appropriate. Rather, analyses should be based on the Yuan–Bentler (Yuan & Bentler, 2000) scaled statistic (Y-Bχ^2), which corrects both the test statistics and standard errors when the input file specifies the use of robust statistics and indicates the presence of missing data.

In addition to these scaled statistics, EQS has three distribution-free statistics based on the distribution of residuals; robust versions of these test statistics are automatically computed when this option is specified. The first of these, the residual-based statistic, is of a type developed by Browne (1984). As noted earlier, however, use of this statistic is curtailed by the fact that its interpretation is meaningful only when sample size is very large. In contrast, the Yuan–Bentler residual-based statistic (Yuan & Bentler, 1998) represents an extension of Browne's (1984) residual-based test such that it can be used with smaller samples. Of particular note, however, is that in addition to performing better in small samples than the original residual-based statistic, it does so without any loss of its large-sample properties (Bentler, 2005). Finally, the Yuan–Bentler residual-based F-statistic (Yuan & Bentler, 1998), designed to take sample size into account more adequately, represents a more extensive modification of Browne's (1984) statistic and is considered by Bentler (2005) to be the best available residual-based test at this time.

Amos (Version 18.0)

One approach to the analysis of non-normal data in Amos is to base analyses on ADF estimation (Browne 1984), which can be selected from the estimators offered on the *Estimation* tab of the *Analysis Properties* icon or drop-down *View* menu of Amos Graphics. However, given the restrictions of sample size noted earlier, this option is typically of little use to most practical researchers.

Although the robust test statistics described earlier with respect to EQS are not available in the Amos program, there remains at least one other viable approach to analyses of non-normal data based on a procedure known as "the bootstrap" (Efron, 1979; West et al., 1995; Yung & Bentler, 1996; Zhu, 1997). This approach is the one most commonly taken by Amos users in addressing the issue of non-normality. The bootstrapping

technique enables the researcher to compare the extent to which the ML estimates deviate across the total number of bootstrapped samples. The Amos output from a bootstrapping analysis yields five columns of results as follows: (1) the bootstrap estimate of the standard error for each selected model parameter (e.g., factor loading), (2) the approximate standard error of the bootstrap standard error itself, (3) the mean parameter estimate computed across the bootstrapped samples, (4) the difference between the bootstrap mean estimate and the original estimate (i.e., bias), and (5) approximate standard error of the bias estimate. In addition, the program reports 90% bias-corrected confidence intervals. (For an example application of this bootstrapping approach, see Byrne, 2009.)

Mplus (Version 6.11)

As with the EQS program, treatment of non-normal data in Mplus is addressed via estimators that can yield corrected test statistics and standard errors. However, these robust estimators vary according to measurement scale of the data, as well as whether the data are complete or incomplete.

For data with outcome variables that are continuous, non-normally distributed, and complete, the MLM estimator is most appropriately used; it provides for correction to the estimates, standard errors, and a mean-adjusted chi-square statistic that is reportedly equivalent to the S-Bχ^2 statistic (Muthén & Muthén, 1998–2010). Likewise, the MLMV estimator, although computationally more intensive than MLM, is similarly robust, with the exception that the chi-square statistic is both mean- and variance-adjusted. In the event that continuous data are both non-normal and incomplete, it is most appropriate to base analyses on the MLR estimator. Muthén and Muthén (1998–2010) posit that the MLR estimator yields a corrected chi-square statistic that is asymptotically equivalent to the Y-Bχ^2.

When data are both categorical and non-normally distributed, Mplus provides for the use of two robust WLS estimators. Although both the WLSM and WLSMV estimators use a diagonal weight matrix with standard errors that use a full weight matrix, the chi-square test statistic for the WLSM estimator is mean-adjusted, whereas this statistic is mean- and variance-adjusted for the WLSMV estimator. Importantly, these estimators are not appropriate for use with data that are incomplete and involve censored, unordered, or count dependent variables.

COMPARATIVE OVERVIEW OF EQS AND Mplus

The intent of this section is to give readers at least a flavor of how programs can differ in terms of (1) specification of the model as documented in the input file, and (2) the reporting of selected results in the output file. Given the popularity of both the EQS and Mplus programs, together with the soundness of their theoretical and methodological underpinnings, their comparison is considered appropriate. Although necessarily limited by space restrictions, this brief overview provides at least a quick glimpse into the extent to which the two programs are similar, as well as dissimilar. Readers interested in more extensive details related to this application based on either EQS or Mplus, are referred to Byrne (2006) and Byrne (2011), respectively.

The application presented here examines a first-order CFA model designed to test the multidimensionality of a theoretical construct. Specifically, it tests the hypothesis that self-concept (SC), for early adolescents (grade 7), is a multidimensional construct composed of four factors—general SC (GSC), academic SC (ASC), English SC (ESC), and mathematics SC (MSC). The theoretical foundation of this hypothesis derives from the hierarchical model of SC proposed by Shavelson, Hubner, and Stanton (1976). The example is taken from a study by Byrne and Worth Gavin (1996) in which four hypotheses related to the Shavelson and colleagues model were tested for three groups of children—preadolescents (grade 3), early adolescents (grade 7), and late adolescents (grade 11). Only tests bearing on the multidimensional structure of SC for children in grade 7 are relevant here. A schematic portrayal of this model within the framework of both EQS and Mplus is presented in Figure 19.1.

Of the two program-specific representations in Figure 19.1, it is evident that the EQS Diagrammer-produced model is much more explicit in the identification of parameters than is the case for the same model as typically presented for Mplus analyses. Although the model shown here is *exactly specified* for each program, the EQS-labeled one informs the reader that the first factor loading in each congeneric set of indicator variables is constrained to a value of 1.00, with asterisks indicating that the remaining loadings are freely estimated, along with the factor covariances and error variances (termed "residuals" in Mplus); although no asterisks are shown here, all factor variances are also freely estimated.[6] Specifically demarcated only in the EQS figure, the regression path leading from each observed variable to its related error term is automatically fixed to 1.00 in all SEM programs, as only the error variance is of interest. Finally, EQS automatically assigns a V-label to all observed variables, as well as a number in accordance with their data entry placement. Analogously, error variances are assigned an E-label that is numerically consistent with its related observed variable.

Let's turn now to Table 19.1, which presents the combined input files for EQS and Mplus. A review of these files again reveals a substantial difference between the two programs in terms of information specified, with the EQS program denoting considerably more detail. The primary factor contributing to this difference is the numerous defaults implemented by Mplus. For example, in specifying the model, whereas EQS requires three paragraphs of input, each of which describes the pattern of factor loadings (**EQUATIONS**), the variances (factors and errors), and covariances (factors), respectively, Mplus needs to know only the variables to be used in the analysis (**USE VARIABLES ARE**) and the variables loading on each factor as defined with a BY statement specified under the **MODEL** command.

A final key component of both input files is notation related to possible model misspecification. Whereas EQS takes a multivariate approach to the detection of misspecified parameters through use of the Lagrange multiplier test (LMTest), Mplus takes a univariate approach based on the modification index (MI; Sörbom, 1989). The EQS input file paragraph labeled **LMTest** addresses this issue, though it limits the search to possible cross-loadings (GVF) and error covariances (PEE), as indicated by the SET= command. The Mplus input file requests computation of modification indices in an **OUTPUT** command; in the present case, sample statistics and standardized estimates are also requested; this information is automatically included in the EQS output.

Table 19.2 presents model goodness-of-fit statistics as reported in the EQS and Mplus output files. As you will readily note, the information reported, in terms of both estimated values and model fit criteria, varies minimally. Worthy of particular note is that the EQS fit statistics reported here represent the complete list when **FIT=ALL** is specified in the **PRINT** paragraph of the input file (see Table 19.1); in the absence of this command, results include only a few key fit statistics. Also worthy of note (although not applicable in the present case) is when the researcher wishes to base analyses on robust statistics. In EQS, this command results in two sets of fit statistics being reported: (1) those based on

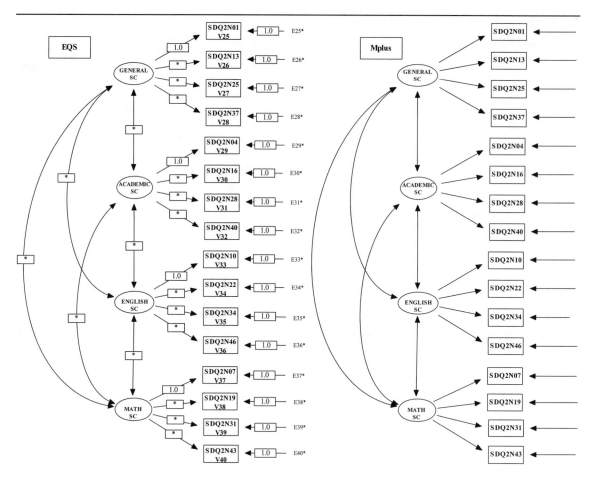

FIGURE 19.1. Hypothesized model of self-concept structure within the frameworks of the EQS (Bentler, 2005) and Mplus (Muthén & Muthén, 1998–2010) programs.

the ML estimator, and (2) those based on the robust ML estimator. In contrast, Mplus reports only the robust statistics requested. For readers who may be unfamiliar with both the EQS and Mplus programs, I assure you that although the numbers are not exactly the same (due likely to computational rounding errors), the information conveyed is definitely consistent in revealing exceptionally good model fit to the sample data. To assist you in your comparison of the two sets of results, I have assigned matching parenthesized numerals to each of the four key model fit statistics typically reported in the SEM literature.

For a final comparison of EQS and Mplus, we turn to Table 19.3, which reports results for tests of possible model misspecification. Although results for a greater number of parameters are reported in the EQS output, the primary parameters considered to be misspecified are essentially the same for both programs despite their different approaches to the analyses.[7] In EQS, one looks for the point at which there is a substantial drop in the univariate chi-square Increment values, which in this case is after the second value reported (16.986). In Mplus, the program separates the BY from the WITH statements. As we see here, the two largest values

TABLE 19.1. Input Files for Hypothesized CFA Model

EQS

/TITLE
CFA OF ASC Structure - GRADE 7 "ASC7F4I"
/SPECIFICATIONS
CASE=265; VAR=46; ME=ML; MA=RAW; FO='(40F1.0,X,6F2.0)';
DATA='C:\EQS61\Files\Data\ASC7INDM.DAT';
/LABELS
V1=SPPCN08; V2=SPPCN18; V3=SPPCN28; V4=SPPCN38; V5=SPPCN48; V6=SPPCN58; V7=SPPCN01; V8=SPPCN11;
V9=SPPCN21; V10=SPPCN31; V11=SPPCN41; V12=SPPCN51; V13=SPPCN06; V14=SPPCN16; V15=SPPCN26;
V16=SPPCN36; V17=SPPCN46; V18=SPPCN56; V19=SPPCN03; V20=SPPCN13; V21=SPPCN23; V22=SPPCN33;
V23=SPPCN43; V24=SPPCN53; V25=SDQ2N01; V26=SDQ2N13; V27=SDQ2N25; V28=SDQ2N37; V29=SDQ2N04;
V30=SDQ2N16; V31=SDQ2N28; V32=SDQ2N40; V33=SDQ2N10; V34=SDQ2N22; V35=SDQ2N34; V36=SDQ2N46;
V37=SDQ2N07; V38=SDQ2N19; V39=SDQ2N31; V40=SDQ2N43; V41=MASTENG1; V42=MASTMAT1; V43=TENG1;
V44=TMAT1; V45=SENG1; V46=SMAT1;
/EQUATIONS
V25= F1+E25;
V26= *F1+E26;
V27= *F1+E27;
V28= *F1+E28;
  V29= F2+E29;
  V30= *F2+E30;
  V31= *F2+E31;
  V32= *F2+E32;
    V33= F3+E33;
    V34= *F3+E34;
    V35= *F3+E35;
    V36= *F3+E36;
      V37= F4+E37;
      V38= *F4+E38;
      V39= *F4+E39;
      V40= *F4+E40;
/VARIANCES
F1 TO F4= *;
E25 TO E40= *;
/COVARIANCES
F1 TO F4= *;
/PRINT
FIT=ALL;
/LMTEST
SET=GVF, PEE;
/END

Mplus

TITLE: CFA of Academic SC Structure for Grade 7 Adolescents
DATA:
FILE IS "C:\Mplus\Files\ASC7INDM.DAT";
FORMAT IS 40F1.0,X,6F2.0;
VARIABLE:
NAMES ARE SPPCN08 SPPCN18 SPPCN28 SPPCN38 SPPCN48 SPPCN58 SPPCN01 SPPCN11 SPPCN21 SPPCN31
SPPCN41 SPPCN51 SPPCN06 SPPCN16 SPPCN26 SPPCN36 SPPCN46 SPPCN56 SPPCN03 SPPCN13 SPPCN23
SPPCN33 SPPCN43 SPPCN53 SDQ2N01 SDQ2N13 SDQ2N25 SDQ2N37 SDQ2N04 SDQ2N16 SDQ2N28 SDQ2N40
SDQ2N10 SDQ2N22 SDQ2N34 SDQ2N46 SDQ2N07 SDQ2N19 SDQ2N31 SDQ2N43 MASTENG1 MASTMAT1 TENG1
TMAT1 SENG1 SMAT1;
USEVARIABLES ARE SDQ2N01- SDQ2N43;
MODEL:
F1 by SDQ2N01-SDQ2N37;
F2 by SDQ2N04-SDQ2N40;
F3 by SDQ2N10-SDQ2N46;
F4 by SDQ2N07-SDQ2N43;
OUTPUT:
SAMPSTAT MODINDICES STANDARDIZED;

TABLE 19.2. Output Files: Goodness-of-Fit Statistics

EQS

GOODNESS OF FIT SUMMARY FOR METHOD = ML

INDEPENDENCE MODEL CHI-SQUARE = 1696.728 ON 120 DEGREES OF FREEDOM

INDEPENDENCE AIC = 1456.72826 INDEPENDENCE CAIC = 907.16068
    MODEL AIC = -37.48818   MODEL CAIC = -486.30170

(1) CHI-SQUARE = 158.512 BASED ON 98 DEGREES OF FREEDOM
    PROBABILITY VALUE FOR THE CHI-SQUARE STATISTIC IS .00011

THE NORMAL THEORY RLS CHI-SQUARE FOR THIS ML SOLUTION IS 152.727.

FIT INDICES

    BENTLER-BONETT NORMED FIT INDEX = .907
    BENTLER-BONETT NON-NORMED FIT INDEX = .953
(2) COMPARATIVE FIT INDEX (CFI) = .962
    BOLLEN (IFI) FIT INDEX = .962
    MCDONALD (MFI) FIT INDEX = .892
    LISREL GFI FIT INDEX = .933
    LISREL AGFI FIT INDEX = .906
    ROOT MEAN-SQUARE RESIDUAL (RMR) = .104
(3) STANDARDIZED RMR = .048
(4) ROOT MEAN-SQUARE ERROR OF APPROXIMATION (RMSEA) = .048
    90% CONFIDENCE INTERVAL OF RMSEA (.034, .062)

Mplus

(1) Chi-Square Test of Model Fit

Value	159.112
Degrees of Freedom	98
P-Value	0.0001

Chi-Square Test of Model Fit for the Baseline Model

Value	1703.155
Degrees of Freedom	120
P-Value	0.0000

CFI/TLI

(2)	CFI	0.961
	TLI	0.953

Information Criteria

Number of Free Parameters	54
Akaike (AIC)	13233.356
Bayesian (BIC)	13426.661
Sample-Size Adjusted BIC	13255.453
$(n^* = (n + 2) / 24)$	

(4) RMSEA (Root Mean Square Error Of Approximation)

Estimate	0.049
90 Percent C.I.	0.034 0.062
Probability RMSEA <= .05	0.556

(3) SRMR (Standardized Root Mean Square Residual)

Value	0.045

TABLE 19.3. Output Files: Modification Indices

EQS

| | | CUMULATIVE MULTIVARIATE STATISTICS | | | | UNIVARIATE INCREMENT | | | |
| | | | | | | | | HANCOCK'S SEQUENTIAL | |
STEP	PARAMETER	CHI-SQUARE	D.F.	PROB.	CHI-SQUARE	PROB.	D.F.	PROB.
1	**E39,E38**	**17.753**	**1**	**.000**	**17.753**	**.000**	**98**	**1.000**
2	**E27,E25**	**34.739**	**2**	**.000**	**16.986**	**.000**	**97**	**1.000**
3	E32,E29	44.003	3	.000	9.264	.002	96	1.000
4	V35,F4	51.317	4	.000	7.313	.007	95	1.000
5	E40,E32	58.310	5	.000	6.993	.008	94	1.000
6	E29,E26	63.870	6	.000	5.560	.018	93	1.000
7	E33,E29	68.972	7	.000	5.102	.024	92	1.000
8	E40,E36	73.905	8	.000	4.933	.026	91	1.000
9	E32,E28	78.590	9	.000	4.685	.030	90	1.000
10	V39,F1	82.726	10	.000	4.136	.042	89	1.000
11	E39,E37	87.433	11	.000	4.707	.030	88	1.000

Mplus

NOTE: Modification indices for direct effects of observed dependent variables regressed on covariates may not be included. To include these, request MODINDICES (ALL).

Minimum M.I. value for printing the modification index   10.000

	M.I.	E.P.C.	Std E.P.C.	StdYX E.P.C.

BY Statements

F2	BY SDQ2N07	11.251	-0.563	-0.422	-0.237

WITH Statements

SDQ2N25	**WITH SDQ2N01**	**17.054**	**0.359**	**0.359**	**0.319**
SDQ2N31	WITH SDQ2N07	10.696	0.305	0.305	0.546
SDQ2N31	**WITH SDQ2N19**	**17.819**	**-0.331**	**-0.331**	**-0.495**

replicate the results of the EQS program. Thus, both programs suggest that if the error variances between items SDQ2N31 and SDQ2N19, as well as between SDQ2N25 and SDQ2N01, were allowed to covary, the chi-square value would drop by approximately 35.00 (see the first χ^2 value of 34.739 reported at step 2 of the EQS output).[8] Of course, from a macro perspective, this differential is trivial, and there is no logical reason, either statistically or substantively, to incorporate these parameters into the model, as the originally hypothesized model already yields an excellent fit to the data.

SELECTING THE BEST PROGRAM FOR YOU

Having reviewed several different aspects of the LISREL, EQS, Amos, and Mplus programs, the likely question now is which program is best for you? The answer to this question, I believe, depends on at least three factors: (1) how familiar you are with the basic concepts and applications of SEM, (2) the types of models you are likely to be testing, and (3) whether you prefer to work within a graphical versus a textual framework via an input file. For readers who may be fairly new to

SEM, I believe you will likely find the EQS program the most informative and easiest; if you tend to prefer working graphically rather than textually, then you may prefer to work with the Amos program. On the other hand, users who are familiar with the use and application of SEM and/or are interested in and need to work with more advanced models, may prefer to work with the LISREL, EQS, and/or Mplus programs. In general, however, many researchers and practitioners will likely work with at least two or a combination of SEM programs, thereby capitalizing on the unique aspects and strengths of each. For a comprehensive, yet nonmathematical, introduction to the basic concepts of SEM, in addition to a detailed walk-through of several different single- and multiple-group model applications based on LISREL, EQS, Amos, or Mplus, readers are referred to books by Byrne (1998, 2006, 2009, 2011, respectively).

NOTES

1. The only other major SEM computer program at that time (LISREL) was available only on the mainframe.
2. An additional five programs address non-SEM statistical analyses of (a) hierarchical linear and nonlinear modeling (MULTILEV); (b) generalized linear modeling (SURVEYGLIM); and (c) formative inference-based recursive modeling for categorical response variables (CATFIRM), formative inference-based recursive modeling for continuous response variables (CONFIRM), and generalized linear modeling for multilevel data (MAPGLIM).
3. Termed arbitrary generalized least squares (AGLS) in EQS (Brown, 2006).
4. Given apparent user preference for Amos Graphics over the equations format, no example files based on VB.net or C# are included in the second edition of Byrne (2009).
5. Brown (2006) notes that the ADF estimator in Amos is actually the WLS estimator.
6. In Mplus, the first factor loading in each congeneric set is automatically fixed to 1.00 by default. Likewise, the factor variances and covariances pertinent to independent factors in a model such as the CFA model discussed here are estimated by default. Importantly, however, all defaults in Mplus can be overridden.
7. Although it may appear that EQS considers substantially more parameters to be misspecified than Mplus, this is not so. Rather, this discrepancy derives from the Mplus default in reporting no MI values less than 10.00 (see Table 19.3). Alternatively, EQS input could likewise be tailored to limit potentially misspecified parameters to those having values equal to or greater than 10.00.
8. The difficulty in matching these parameters across the two

programs is a function of (a) program notation, and (b) automated labeling in EQS. *First*, error parameters in EQS are labeled as E's, with E representing an error variance and EE representing an error covariance. *Second*, EQS automatically assigns a numbered label to each variable in accordance with its location in the data file; V39, for example, occupies Column 39. A review of the EQS **LABELS** paragraph in Table 19.1 will identify this variable as SDQ2N31. In combination, then, E39, E38 represents a covariance between the error terms associated with the observed variables SDQ2N31 (V39) and SDQ2N19 (V38).

REFERENCES

Arbuckle, J. L. (1989). Amos: Analysis of moment structures. *American Statistician, 43*, 66–67.

Arbuckle, J. L. (1994). Amos: Analysis of moment structures. *Psychometrika, 59*, 135–137.

Arbuckle, J. L. (1995). *Amos for Windows: Analysis of moment structures (Version 3.5)*. Chicago: SmallWaters.

Arbuckle, J. L. (2009). *Amos18 User's Guide*. Chicago: SPSS.

Bentler, P. M. (1985). *Theory and implementation of EQS, a structural equations modeling program*. Los Angeles: BMDP Statistical Software.

Bentler, P. M. (1986). Structural modeling and *Psychometrika*: An historical perspective on growth and achievements. *Psychometrika, 51*, 35–51.

Bentler, P. M. (1990). Comparative fit indexes in structural models. *Psychological Bulletin, 107*, 238–246.

Bentler, P. M. (2005). *EQS 6 structural equations program manual*. Encino, CA: Multivariate Software.

Bentler, P. M., & Bonett, D. G. (1980). Significance tests and goodness of fit in the analysis of covariance structures. *Psychological Bulletin, 88*, 588–606.

Bentler, P. M., & Weeks, D. G. (1980). Linear structural equations with latent variables. *Psychometrika, 45*, 289–308.

Bentler, P. M., & Wu, E. J. C. (2002). *EQS for Windows user's guide*. Encino, CA: Multivariate Software.

Bollen, K. A., & Stine, R. A. (1992). Bootstrapping goodness-of-fit measures in structural equation models. *Sociological Methods and Research, 21*, 205–229.

Brown, T. A. (2006). *Confirmatory factor analysis for applied research*. New York: Guilford Press.

Browne, M. W. (1984). Asymptotically distribution-free methods for the analysis of covariance structures. *British Journal of Mathematical and Statistical Psychology, 37*, 62–83.

Byrne, B. M. (1994). *Structural equation modeling with EQS and EQS/Windows: Basic concepts, applications, and programming*. Thousand Oaks, CA: Sage.

Byrne, B. M. (1998). *Structural equation modeling with LISREL, PRELIS, and SIMPLIS: Basic concepts, applications, and programming*. Mahwah, NJ: Erlbaum.

Byrne, B. M. (2001). *Structural equation modeling with Amos: Basic concepts, applications, and programming.* Mahwah, NJ: Erlbaum.

Byrne, B. M. (2006). *Structural equation modeling with EQS: Basic concepts, applications, and programming* (2nd ed.). Mahwah, NJ: Erlbaum.

Byrne, B. M. (2009). *Structural equation modeling with Amos: Basic concepts, applications, and programming* (2nd ed.). New York: Taylor & Francis/Routledge.

Byrne, B. M. (2011). *Structural equation modeling with Mplus: Basic concepts, applications and programming.* New York: Taylor & Francis/Routledge.

Byrne, B. M., & Worth Gavin, D. A. (1996). The Shavelson model revisited: Testing for the structure of academic self-concept across pre-, early, and late adolescents. *Journal of Educational Psychology, 88,* 215–228.

Chou, C.-P., Bentler, P. M., & Satorra, A. (1991). Scaled test statistics and robust standard errors for nonnormal data in covariance structure analysis. *British Journal of Mathematical and Statistical Psychology, 44,* 347–357.

Curran, P. J., West, S. G., & Finch, J. F. (1996). The robustness of test statistics to nonnormality and specification error in confirmatory factor analysis. *Psychological Methods, 1,* 16–29.

DiStefano, C. (2002). The impact of categorization with confirmatory factor analysis. *Structural Equation Modeling, 9,* 327–346.

Duncan, O. D. (1975). *Introduction to structural equation models.* New York: Academic Press.

Efron, B. (1979). Bootstrap methods: Another look at the jackknife. *Annals of Statistics, 7,* 1–26.

Goldberger, A. S., & Duncan, O. D. (1973). *Structural equation models in the social sciences.* New York: Seminar Press.

Hu, L.-T., Bentler, P. M., & Kano, Y. (1992). Can test statistics in covariance structure analysis be trusted? *Psychological Bulletin, 112,* 351–362.

Hutchinson, S. R. (1995). Software review [Review of LISCOMP 1.1 distributed by Scientific Software International]. *Structural Equation Modeling, 2,* 383–386.

Jöreskog, K. G. (1969). A general approach to confirmatory maximum likelihood factor analysis. *Psychometrika, 34,* 183–202.

Jöreskog, K. G. (1970). A general method for analysis of covariance structures. *Biometrika, 57,* 239–251.

Jöreskog, K. G. (1971). Simultaneous factor analysis in several populations. *Psychometrika, 36,* 409–426.

Jöreskog, K. G., & Sörbom, D. (1981). *LISREL V: Analysis of linear structural relationships by the method of maximum likelihood.* Chicago: National Educational Resources (later renamed Scientific Software International).

Jöreskog, K. G., & Sörbom, D. (1984). *LISREL VI user's guide.* Mooresville, IN: Scientific Software International.

Jöreskog, K. G., & Sörbom, D. (1988). *LISREL 7: A guide to the program and applications.* Chicago: SSPS, Inc.

Jöreskog, K. G., & Sörbom, D. (1993a). *LISREL 8: Structural equation modeling with the SIMPLIS command language.* Chicago: Scientific Software International.

Jöreskog, K. G., & Sörbom, D. (1993b). *New features in LISREL 8.* Chicago: Scientific Software International.

Jöreskog, K. G., & Sörbom, D. (1996). *PRELIS 2.* Chicago: Scientific Software International.

Jöreskog, K. G., & Sörbom, D. (1999). *LISREL 8.30 and PRELIS 2.30.* Chicago: Scientific Software International.

Jöreskog, K. G., & Sörbom, D. (2006). *LISREL 8.8 for Windows.* Lincolnwood, IL: Scientific Software International.

Jöreskog, K. G., & van Thillo, M. (1972). *A general computer program for estimating a linear structural equation system involving multiple indicators of unmeasured variables* (Research Bulletin No. RB-72-56). Princeton, NJ: Educational Testing Service.

Muthén, B. (1987). *LISCOMP: Analysis of linear structural equations with a comprehensive measurement model: Theoretical integration and user's guide.* Mooresville, IN: Scientific Software.

Muthén, B. (1988). *LISCOMP: Analysis of linear structural equations with a comprehensive measurement model* (2nd ed.). Mooresville, IN: Scientific Software.

Muthén, B. O. (1994). Multilevel covariance structure analysis. *Sociological Methods and Research, 22,* 376–398.

Muthén, L. K., & Muthén, B. O. (1998–2010). *Mplus user's guide* (6th ed.). Los Angeles: Authors.

Neale, M. C., Boker, S. M., Xie, G., & Maes, H. H. (2003). *Mx: Statistical modeling* (6th ed.). Richmond, VA: Virginia Commonwealth University, Virginia Institute for Psychiatric and Behavioral Genetics.

Raykov, T., & Marcoulides, G. A. (2000). *A first course in structural equation modeling.* Mahwah, NJ: Erlbaum.

SAS Institute Inc. (2009). *SAS/STAT(r) user's guide* (2nd ed.). Cary, NC: Author.

Satorra, A., & Bentler, P. M. (1988). Scaling corrections for chi square statistics in covariance structure analysis. In *American Statistical Association 1988 Proceedings of the Business and Economic Sections* (pp. 308–313). Alexandria, VA: American Statistical Association.

Shavelson, R. J., Hubner, J. J., & Stanton, G. C. (1976). Self-concept: Validation of construct interpretations. *Review of Educational Research, 46,* 407–441.

Sörbom, D. (1989). Model modification. *Psychometrika, 54,* 371–384.

Sörbom, D. (2001). Karl Jöreskog and LISREL: A personal story. In R. Cudeck, S. du Toit, & D. Sörbom (Eds.), *Structural equation modeling: Present and future: A festschrift in honor of Karl Jöreskog.* Lincolnwood, IL: Scientific Software International, Inc.

StatSoft Inc. (2009). *STATISTICA 9* [Computer software]. Tulsa, OK: Author.

Stine, R. A. (1989). An introduction to bootstrap methods: Examples and ideas. *Sociological Methods and Research, 18,* 243–291.

Systat Software Inc. (2009). *SYSTAT (Version 13)* [Computer software]. Chicago: Author.

West, S. G., Finch, J. F., & Curran, P. J. (1995). Structural equation models with nonnormal variables: Problems and remedies. In R. H. Hoyle (Ed.), *Structural equation modeling: Concepts, issues, and applications* (pp. 56–75). Thousand Oaks, CA: Sage.

Wolfle, L. M. (2003). The introduction of path analysis to the social sciences, and some emergent themes: An annotated bibliography. *Structural Equation Modeling, 10,* 1–34.

Yuan, K.-H., & Bentler, P. M. (1998). Normal theory based test statistics in structural equation modeling. *British Journal of Mathematical and Statistical Psychology, 51,* 289–309.

Yuan, K.-H., & Bentler, P. M. (2000). Three likelihood-based methods for mean and covariance structure analysis with nonnormal missing data. In M. P. Becker (Ed.), *Sociological methodology 2000* (pp. 165–200). New York: Wiley-Blackwell.

Yung, Y.-F., & Bentler, P. M. (1996). Bootstrapping techniques in analysis of mean and covariance structures. In G. A. Marcoulides & R. E. Schumacker (Eds.), *Advanced structural equation modeling: Issues and techniques* (pp. 195–226). Mahwah, NJ: Erlbaum.

Zhu, W. (1997). Making bootstrap statistical inferences: A tutorial. *Research Quarterly for Exercise and Sport, 68,* 44–55.

CHAPTER 20

Structural Equation Modeling in R with the sem and OpenMx Packages

John Fox
Jarrett E. Byrnes
Steven Boker
Michael C. Neale

The purpose of this chapter is to introduce and illustrate the use of the sem (structural equation modeling) and OpenMx packages in R for fitting structural equation models. R, an open-source implementation of the S statistical programming language and computing environment, is now standard software in statistics, having eclipsed its commercial cousin S-PLUS, and is becoming increasingly popular in other disciplines, including the social and behavioral sciences.

The sem package has been around for several years (see Fox, 2006); it provides basic structural equation modeling (SEM) facilities and is capable of fitting observed-variable and latent-variable structural equation models by full-information maximum likelihood assuming multivariate-normal data. Employing polychoric and polyserial correlations computed with the polycor package, and with statistical inference based on the bootstrap, the sem package may also be used for ordinal observed variables. In this chapter, we describe a new version of the sem package, currently under development, which augments its capabilities in several directions (e.g., more convenient model specification, the computation of robust standard errors and statisti-

cal tests, provision for alternative "fit" functions, and—we anticipate in the near future—multigroup models).

The OpenMx package (Boker et al., 2011), in contrast, is new. It provides advanced SEM facilities in R. Based on the stand-alone freeware Mx (Neale, Boker, Xie, & Maes, 2003), the R-language package OpenMx encompasses the same functionality as the stand-alone program in a user-extensible environment. In addition to standard fit functions, users are at liberty to specify their own likelihood functions for maximization. Multiple data sets, mixture distributions, latent-variable moderation, and other advanced methods are relatively straightforward to implement in OpenMx.

Because the chapter is brief, we will not be able to describe in detail either the sem package or, especially, the OpenMx package. Rather, we intend to demonstrate how these packages can be used to fit a representative set of structural equation models to data, and to mention the capabilities of the packages that are not demonstrated in the example.

The chapter begins with a very brief introduction to R, which we hope will be sufficient to orient the reader who has not previously encountered R. We then present a representative latent-variable structural equation model to provide an example, and proceed to show how the model can be fit using the sem and OpenMx packages. Finally, we briefly mention other SEM facilities in R.

INTRODUCING R

Descended from S (e.g., Becker, Chambers, & Wilks, 1988; Chambers & Hastie, 1992) and originally developed by Robert Gentleman and Ross Ihaka at the University of Auckland (Ihaka & Gentleman, 1996), R (R Development Core Team, 2010) is a statistical computing environment, incorporating a programming language tuned to the development of statistical applications. R is available for all major computing platforms, including Windows, Mac OS X, and Linux and Unix systems. R comes with a set of manuals, including an introductory manual, and many books describe its various capabilities (see, e.g., Fox & Weisberg, 2011; Venables & Ripley, 2002).

Although the basic R system is highly capable out of the box, one of the great strengths of R is its package system, which allows users to develop and contribute extensions to R. At the time of this writing, more than 2,800 such extension packages are freely available on the Comprehensive R Archive Network ("CRAN," at *cran.r-project.org*), which also hosts the base R software, and several hundred more packages are available from the closely associated Bioconductor Project (*www. bioconductor.org*), which develops software for bioinformatics. R packages incorporate programs (called *functions* or *operators*), data, and documentation. To be included in the CRAN or Bioconductor archives, packages must meet certain quality-control standards. Many packages come with extensive manuals called *vignettes*, accessible through the vignette command in R.

The user interacts directly with the R interpreter, entering commands in the R language, which are then interpreted and executed. R includes a complete set of standard mathematical operators and functions:

```
> 1 + 2 # addition

[1] 3

> 2 - 3*4 # subtraction and multiplication

[1] -10
```

```
> (2 - 3)/4 # parentheses and division

[1] -0.25

> log(10) # a function call

[1] 2.3026

> log(10, base=10) # an optional function argument

[1] 1
```

In this dialog with the interpreter, the greater-than sign (>) is the R *command prompt*, and is issued by the interpreter. The text to the right of the prompt is a command typed by the user. A command is executed when the user presses the Enter key. The pound sign (#) is a comment character; everything to the right of # in a line is ignored by the interpreter. In this chapter, R input is represented in a *slanted typewriter font*, while R output is shown in an upright typewriter font. These simple examples illustrate several general characteristics of R commands: The mathematical operators for addition (+), subtraction (−), multiplication (*), division (/), and exponentiation (^ or **) obey the usual precedence conventions, which may be modified through the use of parentheses; blanks may be used around operators to clarify an expression but are not required. The *arguments* to R functions are enclosed in parentheses and separated by commas; again, blanks are optional. Arguments may be specified by position or by name. Some arguments, such as the base argument to the log function, have default values, which are assumed if the argument is not specified; for example, the default for base is the mathematical constant $e \approx 2.718$, and thus by default log computes natural logarithms. To find information about a function, including its arguments and defaults, use the help function or operator: help(log) or ?log.

If a command is syntactically incomplete (e.g., if there is an unclosed parenthesis), then it is continued on a subsequent line, with the command prompt changing to a plus sign (+):

```
> log(100,
+     base=10)

[1] 2
```

In serious work with R—either data analysis or programming—it is advisable to use a programming editor that can communicate with the R interpreter, rather than entering commands directly at the command prompt. Both the Windows and Mac OS X versions of R come with simple programming editors, and many other editors (e.g., Emacs, WinEdt, Eclipse) have been adapted to work with R.

R supports a variety of data structures, including vectors, matrices, higher-dimensional arrays, lists (which are heterogeneous collections of other objects), and data frames (rectangular case-by-variable data sets). There are two standard object-oriented programming systems in R, which support the definition and manipulation of user-defined objects, and a third standard object system is in the process of implementation.

The basic R distribution also includes literally hundreds of functions for defining and manipulating objects of various sorts. For example, the following R commands use the assignment operator (<-, composed of the less-than sign and hyphen, with no intervening blanks) to create a variable named x, containing 100 values sampled from the standard-normal distribution and produced by the `rnorm` function; display some of the entries in x by indexing the vector using square brackets ([ ]); compute the mean and standard deviation of this variable with the `mean` and `sd` functions; and compute a numeric summary for the variable, including the mean and several quantiles, using the `summary` function—a *generic function* that adapts its behavior to the class of its argument (in this case a numeric vector):

```
> x <- rnorm(100)
> x[1:10]

 [1] -1.20707  0.27743  1.08444 -2.34570  0.42912
 [6]  0.50606 -0.57474 -0.54663 -0.56445 -0.89004

> x[abs(x) > 2]

 [1] -2.3457  2.4158 -2.1800  2.5490  2.0703
 [6]  2.1211

> mean(x)

 [1] -0.15676

> sd(x)

 [1] 1.0044

> summary(x)

   Min. 1st Qu.  Median   Mean 3rd Qu.    Max.
 -2.350  -0.895  -0.385  -0.157   0.471   2.550
```

An R command in which the left-most operation is an assignment, such as x <- rnorm(100), prints nothing. Standard names for R variables and other objects consist of an arbitrary number of characters including lower- and uppercase letters, numerals, periods, and underscores, and must begin either with a letter or a period. R is case-sensitive, and so, for example, the objects mean, Mean, and MEAN are all distinct. The expression 1:10 creates an integer vector with the numbers 1 through 10, and thus x[1:10] returns the first 10 entries of x. In contrast, the relational greater-than operator in the expression abs(x) > 2 returns a logical vector each of whose entries is either TRUE or FALSE, depending upon whether the absolute value of the corresponding entry of x exceeds 2; x[abs(x) > 2] selects the entries of x for which abs(x) > 2 is TRUE. If the elements of x were named, then they could also be indexed by names (with the names specified as character values, enclosed in single or double quotes). The various forms of indexing extend to more complex data structures.

Users can also define their own functions and operators, which are syntactically indistinguishable from those supplied with the R system. For example, we define a function to compute the standard deviation of a numeric vector:

```
> SD <- function(var){
+     n <- length(var)
+     m <- sum(var)/n
+     sqrt(sum((var - m)^2)/(n - 1))
+ }
> SD(x)

[1] 1.0044
```

The argument var to function is the *formal argument* to the function SD that is returned by function; formal arguments have arbitrary names; are matched with *real arguments* (in this case the vector x) when the function is called; and are *local* to the function, in that they exist only while the function executes and do not interfere with global variables of the same names. Variables defined within a function, such as n and m in our example, are also local to the function. The commands comprising the function are enclosed in curly braces, and the last command executed, here the computation of the standard deviation, is the value returned by the function. We named our function SD so that it doesn't *mask* (i.e., hide) the standard R function sd.

The basic R system comes with a variety of functions for statistical modeling, including the `lm` function for least squares linear regression and the `glm` function for fitting generalized linear models. R also has exceptional facilities for creating statistical graphs. We can barely scratch the surface here, but to demonstrate, the following commands create panel (a) of Figure 20.1, showing Anscombe's famous "quartet" of data sets with identical least squares regression lines (Anscombe, 1973):

```
> par(mfrow=c(2, 2)) # 2-by-2 plot array
> plot(y1 ~ x1, pch=16, cex=1.5,
+    xlim=c(3, 20), ylim=c(3, 13),
+    xlab=expression(x[1]), ylab=expression(y[1]),
+    cex.lab=1.25, main="(a)", las=1,
```

```
+    data=anscombe)
> abline(lm(y1 ~ x1, data=anscombe), lwd=2)
```

Although we do not have the space to explain these commands in detail, we used the `par` command, for setting graphical parameters, to divide the plotting device into a two-by-two array of graphs. Each scatterplot is drawn by the `plot` command. A basic command such as `plot(y1 ~ x1, data=anscombe)` would create quite a nice graph, but we have specified a variety of additional arguments to customize the plot—for example, to ensure that all of the panels have the same axes and to typeset subscripts in the axis labels. We use the `lm` function to compute the least squares line, which is plotted by the `abline` function, illustrating

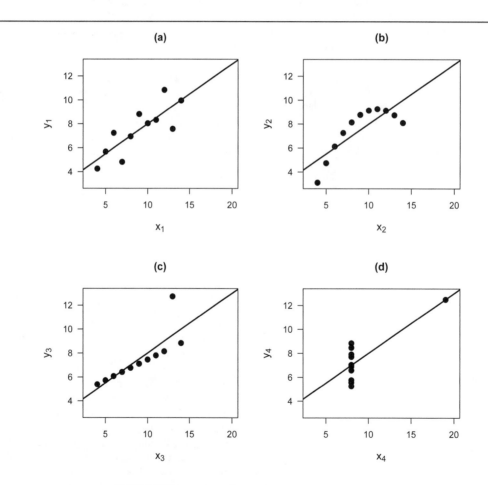

FIGURE 20.1. Anscombe's "quartet" of regression data sets.

how the result returned by one function can supply an argument to another. The commands to draw panels (b) through (d) in Figure 20.1 are similar.

AN ILLUSTRATIVE PROBLEM: CONFIRMATORY FACTOR ANALYSIS

To illustrate fitting structural equation models with the sem and OpenMx packages, we will use a staple of the factor-analysis and SEM literatures, Holzinger and Swineford's data on psychological tests conducted on schoolchildren in two Chicago-area schools (Holzinger & Swineford, 1939; see, e.g., Harman, 1976). The complete data set, available in the MBESS package (Kelley & Lai, 2010), contains 32 variables for 301 children:

```
> library(MBESS)
> data(HS.data)
> dim(HS.data)

[1] 301  32
```

The `library` command loads the MBESS package (in R, *packages* reside in a *library*); the `data` command reads the `HS.data` data frame into memory; and the `dim` command returns the size of the data frame. Twenty-four variables in the data set are scores on various psychological tests, with two additional tests recorded for students in the second school. We use 15 variables in the models fit in this chapter, with three variables meant to tap each of five factors, as recorded in Table 20.1, using the variable names in the `HS.data` data set. To open a spreadsheet-like data viewer to examine the data set, the user can issue the command `View(HS.data)`.

We intend to fit various confirmatory factor-analysis models to the Holzinger and Swineford (1939) data by multinormal maximum likelihood (ML); thus, it might help to ensure that the data are as close to multivariate-normal as possible. Transforming the data *toward*

multinormality does not, of course, guarantee that the transformed data are multinormal, and we therefore will still be interested in statistics such as robust coefficient standard errors. Transformation will make the distributions of the variables more symmetric, will make it more likely that the variables are linearity related, and should improve the efficiency of the ML estimator.

We start by selecting the subset of variables that we intend to normalize, which is not a necessary step but is convenient:

```
> HS <- HS.data[, c(7:9, 12:13, 15:16, 18:25)]
```

We will use power transformations to try to normalize the multivariate distribution of the data, but the variables in the data set have very different ranges; some variables have minimum values of 0, ruling out transformations such as log, which require positive data; and other variables have a very small ratio of their maximum to minimum values, making a power transformation unpromising. We proceed to rescale the data so that all variables run from 1 to 100:

```
> HS.s <- 1 + 99*scale(HS,
+    center=sapply(HS, min),
+    scale=sapply(HS, function(x)
+      diff(range(x))))
```

The `scale` command subtracts the argument `center`, here the minimum of each variable, and divides by `scale`, the range of the variable. The `sapply` function takes the data frame HS as its first argument, and applies the function given as its second argument (e.g., `min`, to compute the minimum) to each column, returning a vector of values. In the second call to `sapply`, we define an *anonymous function* (i.e., defined "on the fly" and never given a name) to compute the difference between the maximum and minimum value of each variable, which are returned by `range`. We then use the `powerTransform` function in the car pack-

TABLE 20.1. Five Factors and 15 Variables from the `HS.data` Data Set

Spatial	Verbal	Speed	Recognition	Memory
visual	paragrap	addition	wordr	object
cubes	sentence	counting	numberr	numberf
paper	wordm	straight	figurer	figurew

age (Fox & Weisberg, 2011) to estimate the required transformations by an unconditional adaptation of the traditional Box–Cox method (Box & Cox, 1964):

```
> library(car)
. . .
> trans <- powerTransform(HS.s ~ 1)
> summary(trans)

bcPower Transformations to Multinormality

        Est.Power Std.Err. Wald Lower Bound
visual      1.300   0.1355            1.035
cubes       0.756   0.0986            0.563
. . .
figurew     1.334   0.1197            1.099
          Wald Upper Bound
visual             1.566
cubes              0.950
. . .
figurew            1.569

Likelihood ratio tests
  about transformation parameters
. . .
                                      pval
LR test, lambda = (0 0 0 0 0 0 0 0 0
                    0 0 0 0 0)  0.000
LR test, lambda = (1 1 1 1 1 1 1 1 1 1
                    1 1 1 1)  0.000
LR test, lambda = (1.3 0.76 1 0.79 1 0.
    5 0.5 0.5 0.8 2 1 2 0.5 0.71 1.33)  0.832
```

In the interest of saving space, we have edited the output and elided some of the lines (represented by the three widely spaced dots, . . .); the output shows the p-values for likelihood-ratio tests of the hypotheses that log transformations of all variables are appropriate (all $\lambda = 0$); that no transformations are necessary (all $\lambda = 1$); and that transformations rounded to "nice" values are sufficient, when a nice value is inside the marginal confidence interval for the transformation parameter. Neither all logs nor no transformations are acceptable, but the rounded powers are. We proceed to apply these powers to the data set, restoring the original names of the variables (which would otherwise have names like "cubes^0.76"), and finally standardizing the variables, which don't have meaningful units, to 0 means and unit standard deviations (the default behavior of the scale function):

```
> HS.t <- bcPower(HS.s,
+   lambda=coef(trans, round=TRUE))
> colnames(HS.t) <- names(HS)
> HS.t <- data.frame(scale(HS.t))
```

We will use the standardized data frame HS.t to fit three confirmatory factor-analysis models (see the path diagrams in Figure 20.2):

■ The first model [Figure 20.2(a)] is closest to the original source, positing that each observed variable is directly affected by one of the five factors and by a general factor, all of which are uncorrelated. The general factor induces correlations among variables loading on distinct factors.

■ The second model [Figure 2(b)] eliminates the general factor but allows the five factors to be correlated, with the factor correlations treated as free parameters to be estimated from the data.

■ The third model [Figure 2(c)] is similar to the second but treats the five factors as endogenous latent variables, each directly affected by an exogenous general factor.

The path diagrams in Figure 20.2 are given in "RAM" (rectricular action model) format (McArdle, 1980; McArdle & McDonald, 1984), with double-headed self-directed arrows representing variances of exogenous variables and error variances of endogenous variables.

THE sem PACKAGE

The sem package contains two functions for fitting structural equation models:

1. The tsls function fits individual observed-variable structural equations by two-stage least squares regression; tsls uses a standard R formula interface (similar, e.g., to lm and glm) to specify structural equations and instrumental variables.

2. The sem function fits observed- and latent-variable models by full-information maximum likelihood or another method, and employs a path-centric interface for model specification.

We illustrate the use of the sem function in this section. For an illustrative application of tsls, see the help page for the function (accessible via ?tsls) or enter the command example(tsls).

Using sem to fit a structural equation model is a two-step process. In the first step, we use the specify-

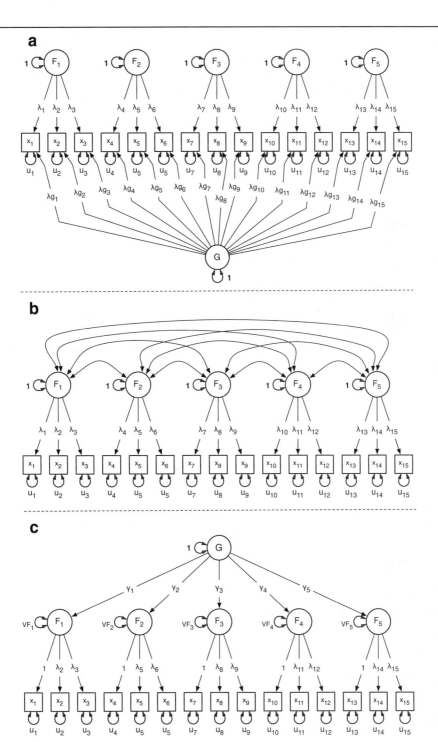

FIGURE 20.2. Three example factor models for 15 variables (represented as $x_1, \ldots, x_{15}$) from the Holzinger and Swineford data; $F_1, \ldots, F_5$ represent the factors Spatial, Verbal, Speed, Recognition, and Memory, respectively.

Model function, as illustrated below, to describe the model, producing a model-specification object. In the second step, we pass this object as an argument to sem, along with a data source—which may be a data frame containing the observed variables in the model, or a moment matrix containing covariances, correlations, or raw sums of squares and products among the observed variables. The readMoments function facilitates entering moment matrices directly (obtained, e.g., from a published source), while the cov, cor, and rawMoments functions—the first two of which are in the standard R system and the third in the sem package—compute covariances, correlations, and raw moments, consecutively. Similarly, the hetcor function in the polycor package can compute a matrix of Pearson, polychoric, and polyserial correlations among a potentially "heterogeneous" set of numeric and ordinal variables.

By default, specifyModel reads path specifications from the standard input stream. Each input line contains up to three elements, separated by commas, the first of which is required:

1. The path, in the form of a single-headed arrow (-> or <-) or double-headed arrow (<->) connecting two variables. For example, in the context of the model in Figure 20.2(a), spatial -> visual represents the path from the spatial factor to the visual test. Similarly, spatial <-> spatial represents the variance of the spatial factor, and visual <-> visual the error variance associated with the visual test (although, as we will see, it is not necessary to specify error variances for endogenous variables explicitly).

2. A name for the parameter associated with the path; if the name is absent or given as NA (the missing-data indicator in R), then the "parameter" is considered to be a fixed value rather than a free parameter to be estimated from the data. If two parameters are given the same name, then they are assumed to be equal.

3. A number giving the start value for the path, if the path is associated with a free parameter, or the value of the parameter, if it is fixed. If the start value is absent or NA, then one will be computed by the sem program.

Here is the complete specification of the model in Figures 20.2(a), allowing specifyModel to supply

error-variance parameters for the endogenous variables, which it does by default when the paths specifying the error variances are not given explicitly:

```
> holzinger.mod.a <- specifyModel ()

1:      spatial -> visual, lam1
2:      spatial -> cubes, lam2
3:      spatial -> paper, lam3
4:      verbal -> paragrap, lam4
5:      verbal -> sentence, lam5
6:      verbal -> wordm, lam6
7:      speed -> addition, lam7
8:      speed -> counting, lam8
9:      speed -> straight, lam9
10:     recogn -> wordr, lam10
11:     recogn -> numberr, lam11
12:     recogn -> figurer, lam12
13:     memory -> object, lam13
14:     memory -> numberf, lam14
15:     memory -> figurew, lam15
16:     G -> visual, lamg1
17:     G -> cubes, lamg2
18:     G -> paper, lamg3
19:     G -> paragrap, lamg4
20:     G -> sentence, lamg5
21:     G -> wordm, lamg6
22:     G -> addition, lamg7
23:     G -> counting, lamg8
24:     G -> straight, lamg9
25:     G -> wordr, lamg10
26:     G -> numberr, lamg11
27:     G -> figurer, lamg12
28:     G -> object, lamg13
29:     G -> numberf, lamg14
30:     G -> figurew, lamg15
31:     spatial <-> spatial, NA, 1
32:     verbal <-> verbal, NA, 1
33:     speed <-> speed, NA, 1
34:     recogn <-> recogn, NA, 1
35:     memory <-> memory, NA, 1
36:     G <-> G, NA, 1
37:

Read 36 records
NOTE: adding 15 variances to the model
```

The number at the beginning of each line is supplied by specifyModel, and input terminates with a blank line. The last six input lines fix the variances of the factors to 1, while the error variances for the 15 tests are added to the model as free parameters.

We then call the sem function to estimate the model (specifying the optional argument par.size="startvalues" to obtain convergence):

```
> holzinger.sem.a <- sem(holzinger.mod.a,
+    data=HS.t, par.size="startvalues")
```

The first argument to `sem` is the model specification object returned by `specifyModel`, and the `data` argument gives the data frame containing the data. If, alternatively, we had supplied a covariance matrix as input, we would have used the `S` (covariance matrix) and `N` (sample size) arguments in place of data.

The `sem` function returns a fitted structural equation model object, on which we can perform further computations. For example, the `summary` function produces a printed report:

```
> summary(holzinger.sem.a)

Model Chisquare =  172    Df =  75
  Pr(>Chisq) = 1.33e-09
Chisquare (null model) =  1367    Df =  105
Goodness-of-fit index =  0.929
Adjusted goodness-of-fit index =  0.886
RMSEA index =  0.0657    90% CI: (0.0528, 0.0787)
Bentler-Bonnett NFI =  0.874
Tucker-Lewis NNFI =  0.892
Bentler CFI =  0.923
SRMR =  0.0637
AIC =  262
AICc =  188
BIC =  429
CAIC =  -331


Normalized Residuals
  Min. 1st Qu.  Median   Mean 3rd Qu.   Max.
 -2.42   -0.60    0.00   0.01    0.51   3.97

R-square for Endogenous Variables
 visual     cubes    paper paragrap sentence
  0.524     0.188    0.305    0.700    0.809
 wordm   addition counting straight    wordr
  0.700     0.392    0.700    0.389    0.437
numberr   figurer   object numberf  figurew
  0.352     0.448    0.213    0.738    0.236


Parameter Estimates
         Estimate Std Error z value Pr(>|z|)
lam1       0.385    0.1094    3.521 4.30e-04
lam2       0.317    0.1025    3.090 2.00e-03
lam3       0.451    0.1281    3.524 4.26e-04
lam4       0.676    0.0521   12.985 1.48e-38
lam5       0.805    0.0511   15.765 5.39e-56
lam6       0.677    0.0521   12.989 1.41e-38
lam7       0.564    0.0804    7.011 2.36e-12
lam8       0.761    0.0913    8.342 7.28e-17
lam9       0.379    0.0663    5.718 1.08e-08
lam10      0.537    0.1050    5.113 3.17e-07
lam11      0.513    0.1043    4.916 8.85e-07
lam12      0.328    0.0774    4.239 2.25e-05
lam13      0.281    0.1457    1.932 5.34e-02
```

```
lam14         0.742    0.3408    2.176 2.95e-02
lam15         0.190    0.1076    1.769 7.69e-02
lamg1         0.613    0.0640    9.578 9.93e-22
lamg2         0.296    0.0700    4.223 2.41e-05
lamg3         0.318    0.0697    4.561 5.09e-06
lamg4         0.493    0.0653    7.553 4.25e-14
lamg5         0.401    0.0670    5.988 2.13e-09
lamg6         0.491    0.0653    7.523 5.37e-14
lamg7         0.272    0.0685    3.969 7.21e-05
lamg8         0.346    0.0676    5.125 2.97e-07
lamg9         0.495    0.0650    7.617 2.59e-14
lamg10        0.386    0.0683    5.656 1.55e-08
lamg11        0.298    0.0695    4.286 1.82e-05
lamg12        0.583    0.0643    9.069 1.20e-19
lamg13        0.365    0.0680    5.373 7.75e-08
lamg14        0.433    0.0669    6.481 9.13e-11
lamg15        0.447    0.0666    6.710 1.95e-11
V[visual]     0.476    0.0830    5.739 9.51e-09
V[cubes]      0.812    0.0814    9.980 1.86e-23
V[paper]      0.695    0.1138    6.106 1.02e-09
V[paragrap]   0.300    0.0345    8.680 3.97e-18
V[sentence]   0.191    0.0384    4.976 6.48e-07
V[wordm]      0.301    0.0346    8.690 3.61e-18
V[addition]   0.608    0.0808    7.528 5.16e-14
V[counting]   0.300    0.1193    2.519 1.18e-02
V[straight]   0.611    0.0611   10.003 1.48e-23
V[wordr]      0.563    0.1018    5.526 3.28e-08
V[numberr]    0.648    0.1000    6.481 9.09e-11
V[figurer]    0.552    0.0615    8.975 2.83e-19
V[object]     0.787    0.0946    8.319 8.88e-17
V[numberf]    0.262    0.5004    0.523 6.01e-01
V[figurew]    0.764    0.0729   10.478 1.09e-25

Iterations =  220
```

Satorra–Bentler-corrected fit statistics and standard errors (Bentler & Dudgeon, 1996; Satorra & Bentler, 1988) are available only if, as earlier, the data argument is given in the call to `sem`, and are obtained by setting the argument `robust=TRUE` in the call to `summary` (with output abbreviated):

```
> summary(holzinger.sem.a, robust=TRUE)

Satorra-Bentler Corrected Fit Statistics
  and Standard Errors:

Adjusted Model Chisquare =  175    Df =  75
  Pr(>Chisq) = 6.15e-10
Chisquare (null model) =  1388    Df =  105
Goodness-of-fit index =  0.929
Adjusted goodness-of-fit index =  0.886
RMSEA index =  0.0657    90% CI: (0.0538, 0.0795)
Bentler-Bonnett NFI =  0.874
Tucker-Lewis NNFI =  0.891
Bentler CFI =  0.922
SRMR =  0.0637
AIC =  262
AICc =  188
```

```
BIC =   429
CAIC =  -331

Normalized Residuals
   Min. 1st Qu.  Median   Mean 3rd Qu.    Max.
  -2.42   -0.60    0.00   0.01   0.51    3.97

R-square for Endogenous Variables
 visual    cubes   paper paragrap sentence
  0.524    0.188   0.305    0.700    0.809
 wordm  addition counting straight    wordr
  0.700    0.392   0.700    0.389    0.437
numberr  figurer  object numberf  figurew
  0.352    0.448   0.213    0.738    0.236

Parameter Estimates
          Estimate Cor. SE z value Pr(>|z|)
lam1       0.385    0.0989   3.894 9.85e-05
lam2       0.317    0.0967   3.276 1.05e-03
lam3       0.451    0.1269   3.558 3.73e-04
. . .
V[object]  0.787    0.0975   8.076 6.68e-16
V[numberf] 0.262    0.4404   0.594 5.52e-01
V[figurew] 0.764    0.0619  12.347 5.08e-35


Iterations =  220
```

In this instance, the corrected standard errors are quite similar to the uncorrected ones, possibly reflecting the success of our data transformations.

The second model [Figure 20.2(b)] eliminates the general factor (G) but permits correlations among the other five common factors. A relatively compact way to specify this model is as follows, using the covs argument to specifyModel to generate the covariances among the factors while, as before, setting the variance of each factor explicitly to 1 (we have suppressed much of the input and output in the interest of brevity):

```
> holzinger.mod.b <- specifyModel(
+   covs=
+     "spatial, verbal, speed, recogn, memory")
1:  spatial -> visual, lam1
2:  spatial -> cubes, lam2
. . .
15: memory -> figurew, lam15
16: spatial <-> spatial, NA, 1
17: verbal <-> verbal, NA, 1
18: speed <-> speed, NA, 1
19: recogn <-> recogn, NA, 1
20: memory <-> memory, NA, 1
21:

> holzinger.sem.b <- sem(holzinger.mod.b,
  data=HS.t, par.size="startvalues")
> summary(holzinger.sem.b)

 Model Chisquare = 176.15   Df = 80
  Pr(>Chisq) = 3.445e-09
```

```
Chisquare (null model) =  1366.9   Df =  105
Goodness-of-fit index =  0.92475
Adjusted goodness-of-fit index =  0.88712
RMSEA index =  0.063293
  90% CI: (0.050651, 0.075955)
Bentler-Bonnett NFI =  0.87114
Tucker-Lewis NNFI =  0.9
Bentler CFI =  0.92381
SRMR =  0.061634
AIC =  256.15
AICc =  188.76
BIC =  404.43
CAIC =  -360.42

. . .
```

Finally, we fit the model in Figure 20.2(c), in which the five common factors are endogenous, each directly affected by a higher-order general factor. We could (as it turns out, more compactly) specify this model from scratch, but we instead illustrate how the generic update function can be used to modify a previously specified model:

```
> holzinger.mod.c <- update(holzinger.mod.b)
1:    delete, spatial <-> spatial
. . .
5:    delete, memory <-> memory
6:    delete, spatial <-> verbal
. . .
15:   delete, recogn <-> memory
16:   delete, spatial -> visual
. . .
20:   delete,  memory -> object
21:   add, G -> spatial, gam1
. . .
25:   add, G -> memory, gam5
26:   add, G <-> G, NA, 1
27:   add, spatial <-> spatial, theta1
. . .
31:   add, memory <-> memory, theta5
32:   add, spatial -> visual, NA, 1
. . .
36:   add, memory -> object, NA, 1
37:

Read 36 records
```

We removed the variances and covariances among the five first-order factors; specified the first-order-factor error variances as free parameters (named theta1, ..., theta5); deleted one factor loading for each first-order factor, subsequently fixing the path to 1 to establish a reference indicator for the factor; and introduced loadings (named gam1, ..., gam5) of the first-order factors on the higher-order factor G.

We proceed to fit this model to the data:

```
> holzinger.sem.c <- sem(holzinger.mod.c, data=HS.t,
+    par.size="startvalues")
> summary(holzinger.sem.c)

 Model Chisquare =  211.84   Df =  85
   Pr(>Chisq) = 8.195e-13
 Chisquare (null model) =  1366.9   Df =  105
 Goodness-of-fit index =  0.9106
 Adjusted goodness-of-fit index =  0.8738
 RMSEA index =  0.070527
   90% CI: (0.058685, 0.082497)
 Bentler-Bonnett NFI =  0.84502
 Tucker-Lewis NNFI =  0.87584
 Bentler CFI =  0.89949
 SRMR =  0.072576
 AIC =  281.84
 AICc =  221.35
 BIC =  411.59
 CAIC =  -358.27

. . .
```

Because the third model, which constrains the correlations among the first-order factors, is a special case of the second model, we can compare the two by a likelihood ratio test, using the generic `anova` function:

```
> anova(holzinger.sem.b, holzinger.sem.c)

LR Test for Difference Between Models

                 Model Df Model Chisq Df LR Chisq
holzinger.sem.b        80      176.15
holzinger.sem.c        85      211.84  5   35.692
```

```
                       Pr(>Chisq)
holzinger.sem.b    1.095e-06 ***
holzinger.sem.c
---
Signif. codes:  0 '***' 0.001
   '**' 0.01 '*' 0.05 '.' 0.1 ' ' 1
```

The test is statistically significant, rejecting the constraints placed on the second-order model; the Bayesian information criterion (BIC) also prefers the more complex model.

The principal facilities of the sem package are summarized in Table 20.2, including methods for standard R generic functions, such as `anova`. Some functions, such as `print` and `summary` methods, are not shown.

THE OpenMx PACKAGE

The OpenMx software provides flexible and powerful methods for specifying and fitting extended structural equation models (XSEMs). XSEMs include not only normal structural equation models but also classes such as multivariate multilevel models, mixture distribution models, hidden Markov models, multivariate ordinal models with thresholds, latent class and latent transition models, and many others. Mechanisms for fitting standard SEM and many XSEM models with maximum likelihood and full-information maximum likelihood are built in. In addition, OpenMx provides methods for

TABLE 20.2. Some of the Functions in the sem Package

anova	Likelihood-ratio test comparing two models
bootSem	Bootstrap a model fit by sem
fscores	Factor scores for latent variables
modIndices	"Modification indices"' (score tests)
rawMoments	Raw sums of squares and products
readMoments	Input correlations, covariances, or raw moments
residuals	Residual moments
sem	Estimation of observed- and latent-variable models
specifyModel	Define structural equation model for sem
standardizedCoefficients	Standardized parameter estimates
tsls	2SLS estimation of observed-variable equation
update	Modify a structural equation model

users to specify their own objective functions so that new model types can be quickly implemented.

The basic philosophy behind the OpenMx interface is "What you say is what it does." This means that OpenMx functions encourage users to be very specific about their models. That is to say, the OpenMx scripting interface does not hide what it will do behind a layer of defaults that try to guess what you want. Similarly, the user does not have to guess what these defaults might be. Instead, we believe that it is better for users to think carefully about what they want and then write it explicitly in the script.

In this section, we will reproduce the three models that were fit in the previous section using sem. We will only reproduce output for the first model because the estimates agree with those from sem presented earlier. As we proceed, we will focus on the two main ways that an OpenMx model can be specified. These are (1) path-based, which is similar to the sem method; and (2) matrix-based, which greatly extends the types of statistical models that can be fit. We start with the same transformed data frame as was used in the previous section, and use the path-based approach. This description is followed by brief consideration of the matrix-based model specification.

Prior to specifying the model, it is useful to define a few character vectors that can be used to label multiple paths at once. The factor names are specified explicitly. Next, the indicator variable names are extracted from the data frame. Finally, three character vectors (lams, lamgs, and uniqs) are constructed by pasting numbers onto the end of a selected string:

```
> library(OpenMx)
> latentsA <- c("Spatial", "Verbal", "Speed",
+    "Recognition", "Memory", "G")
> indicators <- names(HS.t)
> lams <- paste("lam",
+    1:length(indicators), sep="")
> lamgs <- paste("lamg",
+    1:length(indicators), sep="")
> uniqs <- paste("uniq",
+    1:length(indicators), sep="")
```

We next define the model object, an R object of class "MxModel" named ModelA. Inside the MxModel object, OpenMx maintains its own namespace so that the latent variables, manifest variables, and parameters can refer to each other. Because the first argument to mxModel is a character string, "ModelA", a new Mx-Model object, is created. The argument type="RAM" says that this will be a model defined by mxPath state-

ments. Next the latent variables and manifest variables in the model are specified from the character vectors defined in the code section earlier. The mxPath statements define single- and double-headed arrows from the diagram in Figure 20.2(a). Finally, the data are attached to the model using the mxData statement. In OpenMx, if the data are a covariance matrix, then a type="RAM" model will perform an analysis similar to that performed in the previous section. If one were to use a dataframe (type="raw"), the likelihood for each row of data would be calculated, requiring a model for both the expected means and the expected covariances:

```
> ModelA <- mxModel(model="ModelA", type="RAM",
+    latentVars=latentsA, manifestVars=indicators,
+    mxPath(from="Spatial", to=indicators[1:3],
+      arrows=1, free=TRUE, values=0.1,
+      labels=lams[1:3]),
+    mxPath(from="Verbal", to=indicators[4:6],
+      arrows=1, free=TRUE, values=0.1,
+      labels=lams[4:6]),
+    mxPath(from="Speed", to=indicators[7:9],
+      arrows=1, free=TRUE, values=0.1,
+      labels=lams[7:9]),
+    mxPath(from="Recognition",
+      to=indicators[10:12],
+      arrows=1, free=TRUE, values=0.1,
+      labels=lams[10:12]),
+    mxPath(from="Memory",
+      to=indicators[13:15],
+      arrows=1, free=TRUE, values=0.1,
+      labels=lams[13:15]),
+    mxPath(from="G", to=indicators,
+      arrows=1, free=TRUE, values=0.1,
+      labels=lamgs),
+    mxPath(from=indicators,
+      arrows=2, free=TRUE, values=0.8,
+      labels=uniqs),
+    mxPath(from=latentsA,
+      arrows=2, free=FALSE, values=1.0),
+    mxData(observed=cov(HS.t), type="cov",
+      numObs=301)
+ )
```

Finally, we fit the model and print a summary. The result of the mxRun function is itself an object of class "MxModel", so results of one fitted model can be used to define another model. These results are the same, within rounding error, as those produced by the sem function in the sem package (p. 333):

```
> ModelAFit <- mxRun(ModelA)
> summary(ModelAFit)

. . .
```

```
free parameters:
   name matrix     row      col Estimate Std.Error
1  lam1      A   visual  Spatial   0.385   0.1208
2  lam2      A    cubes  Spatial   0.317   0.1065
3  lam3      A    paper  Spatial   0.451   0.1288
4  lam4      A paragrap   Verbal   0.676   0.0529
5  lam5      A sentence   Verbal   0.805   0.0518
6  lam6      A    wordm   Verbal   0.677   0.0529
7  lam7      A addition    Speed   0.564   0.0833
8  lam8      A counting    Speed   0.761   0.0928
9  lam9      A straight    Speed   0.379   0.0667
10 lam10     A    wordr Recognition 0.537  0.1110
11 lam11     A  numberr Recognition 0.513  0.1065
12 lam12     A  figurer Recognition 0.328  0.0843
13 lam13     A   object   Memory   0.281   0.1618
14 lam14     A  numberf   Memory   0.742   0.3517
15 lam15     A  figurew   Memory   0.190   0.1179
16 lamg1     A   visual        G   0.613   0.0740
17 lamg2     A    cubes        G   0.296   0.0750
18 lamg3     A    paper        G   0.318   0.0742
19 lamg4     A paragrap        G   0.493   0.0666
20 lamg5     A sentence        G   0.401   0.0690
21 lamg6     A    wordm        G   0.491   0.0666
22 lamg7     A addition        G   0.272   0.0728
23 lamg8     A counting        G   0.346   0.0684
24 lamg9     A straight        G   0.495   0.0679
25 lamg10    A    wordr        G   0.386   0.0796
26 lamg11    A  numberr        G   0.298   0.0761
27 lamg12    A  figurer        G   0.583   0.0660
28 lamg13    A   object        G   0.365   0.0815
29 lamg14    A  numberf        G   0.433   0.0711
30 lamg15    A  figurew        G   0.447   0.0703
31 uniq1     S   visual   visual   0.476   0.0834
32 uniq2     S    cubes    cubes   0.812   0.0814
33 uniq3     S    paper    paper   0.695   0.1142
34 uniq4     S paragrap paragrap   0.300   0.0345
35 uniq5     S sentence sentence   0.191   0.0385
36 uniq6     S    wordm    wordm   0.301   0.0346
37 uniq7     S addition addition   0.608   0.0816
38 uniq8     S counting counting   0.300   0.1213
39 uniq9     S straight straight   0.611   0.0632
40 uniq10    S    wordr    wordr   0.563   0.1024
41 uniq11    S  numberr  numberr   0.648   0.1009
42 uniq12    S  figurer  figurer   0.552   0.0620
43 uniq13    S   object   object   0.787   0.0948
44 uniq14    S  numberf  numberf   0.262   0.5216
45 uniq15    S  figurew  figurew   0.764   0.0732
. . .
observed statistics:  120
estimated parameters:  45
degrees of freedom:  75
-2 log likelihood:  3305
saturated -2 log likelihood:  3133
number of observations:  301
chi-square:  172
p:  1.33e-09
Information Criteria:
      df Penalty Parameters Penalty Sample-Size Adjusted
AIC   22.1                262                          NA
BIC  -255.9               429                         286
CFI: 0.923
```

```
TLI: 0.892
RMSEA:  0.0656
timestamp: 2012-02-01 14:56:12
frontend time: 0.244 secs
backend time: 0.269 secs
independent submodels time: 0 secs
wall clock time: 0.513 secs
cpu time: 0.513 secs
openmx version number: 1.1.2-1818
```

Note that the summary output includes the free parameter estimates and their standard errors as estimated by the inverse Hessian. A number of fit statistics are presented that are likely to be familiar to structural equation modelers, all based on some penalized scaling of the difference between the saturated –2 log likelihood and the model's –2 log likelihood. In a covariance model such as the one we present here, the saturated –2 log likelihood is automatically calculated. In a full information maximum likelihood model (i.e., fitting a model to raw data), we do not automatically calculate the saturated model likelihood since this can be a lengthy calculation when the data set is large. Instead, we recommend that the saturated model be fit in a separate step and then compared to each constrained model using the function mxCompare, discussed later in this section.

Also presented are some timing statistics. The front-end time is the time spent in R, while the back-end time is the time spent by the optimizer. The timing statistics include a listing for "independent submodels." This points out a major difference between OpenMx and other SEM software in that OpenMx has been written from the ground up to be able to take advantage of parallel computational resources. A hierarchy of models can be defined by the user, along with information about these models' dependence on one another. Independent branches of the model hierarchy can then be estimated in parallel across many central processing unit (CPU) cores or even across distributed computational clusters. One does not need to use this feature for small models such as the ones we are presenting here, but for large data problems or for bootstrapping problems, this facility can reduce computation time by orders of magnitude.

Once the R object ModelA has been defined, it can be used to define other models. In defining ModelB0, the first argument to mxModel is model=ModelA. Because ModelA is an R object of class "MxModel", we make a copy of ModelA and modify it by removing the latent variable "G" and all of the paths associated with it. Next, we create `ModelB` by making a copy of `ModelB0` and modifying it to add covariances between all combinations of latent variables (`all=TRUE`) and fix the variances of the latent variables to be equal to 1.0:

```
> latentsB <- c("Spatial", "Verbal", "Speed",
+    "Recognition", "Memory")
> latBvs <- paste("Var", latentsB, sep="")
> ModelB0 <- mxModel(model=ModelA,
+    name="ModelB0", latentVars="G", remove=TRUE)
> ModelB <- mxModel(model=ModelB0, name="ModelB",
+    mxPath(from=latentsB, to=latentsB, all=TRUE,
+       arrows=2, free=TRUE, values=0.8),
+    mxPath(from=latentsB, arrows=2,
+       free=FALSE, values=1.0, labels=latBvs)
+ )
> ModelBFit <- mxRun(ModelB)
> summary(ModelBFit) # output not shown
```

To create `ModelC`, we start with `ModelA`, remove the paths from "G" to the indicators, and instead add them to predict the first-level factors. We also need to free the variances of the first-level factors and fix one loading for each first-level factor to be 1.0 so that the factors take their scale from one of their respective indicators:

```
> gams <- paste("gam", 1:length(latentsB),
+    sep="")
> thetas <- paste("theta", 1:length(latentsB),
+    sep="")
> ModelC <- mxModel(model=ModelA, name="ModelC",
+    mxPath(from="G", to=indicators,
+       arrows=1, free=FALSE, values=0.0),
+    mxPath(from="G", to=latentsB,
+       arrows=1, free=TRUE, values=0.1,
+       labels=gams),
+    mxPath(from="G",
+       arrows=2, free=FALSE, values=1,
+       labels="VarG"),
+    mxPath(from=latentsB, to=latentsB, all=TRUE,
+       arrows=2, free=FALSE, values=0.0),
+    mxPath(from=latentsB,
+       to=indicators[c(1,4,7,10,13)],
+       arrows=1, free=FALSE, values=1.0),
+    mxPath(from=latentsB,
+       arrows=2, free=TRUE, values=0.8,
+       labels=thetas)
+ )
> ModelCFit <- mxRun(ModelC)
Running ModelC
> summary(ModelCFit) # output not shown
```

Finally, we compare `ModelC` and `ModelB` to test whether the second-order factor model fits significantly

worse than the full latent-covariance model. The difference of 35.7 in −2 log-likelihood values is significantly larger than we would expect for a difference of 5 degrees of freedom (cf. the sem `anova` output on p. 335):

```
> mxCompare(ModelBFit, ModelCFit)
```

	base	comparison	ep	minus2LL	df	AIC	diffLL
1	ModelB	<NA>	40	3309	80	16.1	NA
2	ModelB	ModelC	35	3345	85	41.8	35.7
	diffdf	p					
1	NA	NA					
2	5	1.09e-06					

In order to illustrate how OpenMx differs from other SEM software, we include a short example that fits a two-group model (Females and Males) starting with `ModelC`. First we will constrain all parameters to be equal across the two groups, then allow only the second-order factor loadings to differ across the two groups.

We start by defining two selection vectors, `isFemale` and `isMale`. We define two models, `ModelCFemale` and `ModelCMale`, by copying `ModelC` and subsetting the data prior to calculating the covariances. Then we add each of these single-group models into a "container model" that sums their respective objective functions and uses that sum as its objective function. One might think of the container model as a "parent model" that has two "child models." This defined hierarchical structure of models is, to our knowledge, unique in SEM software, and has proven to be an extremely powerful paradigm for constructing ensembles of models. Also notice that because all the estimated parameters have the same names in both groups, the parameters are constrained be equal across the groups.

```
> isFemale <- HS.data$Gender=="Female"
> isMale <- HS.data$Gender=="Male"
> ModelCFemale <- mxModel(model=ModelC,
+    name="ModelCFemale",
+    mxData(observed=cov(HS.t[isFemale,]),
+       type="cov", numObs=sum(isFemale))
+ )
> ModelCMale <- mxModel(model=ModelC,
+    name="ModelCMale",
+    mxData(observed=cov(HS.t[isMale,]),
+       type="cov", numObs=sum(isMale))
+ )
> ModelCInvar <- mxModel(model="ModelCInvar",
+    ModelCFemale, ModelCMale,
+    mxAlgebra(ModelCFemale.objective +
+       ModelCMale.objective, name="sumLL"),
```

```
+   mxAlgebraObjective("sumLL")
+ )
> ModelCInvarFit <- mxRun(ModelCInvar)
> summary(ModelCInvarFit) # output not shown
```

We next free the constraints on the second-order factor loadings by giving the males' parameters unique names. We then add the two single-group models into a container model as before. Now the females' second-order factor loadings are no longer constrained to be equal to the males' second-order factor loadings.

```
> gamsMale <- paste("gamMale",
+   1:length(latentsB), sep="")
> ModelCMaleFree <- mxModel(model=ModelCMale,
+   name="ModelCMaleFree",
+   mxPath(from="G", to=latentsB, arrows=1,
+     free=TRUE, values=0.1, labels=gamsMale)
+ )
> ModelCFree <- mxModel(model="ModelCFree",
+   ModelCFemale, ModelCMaleFree,
+   mxAlgebra(ModelCFemale.objective +
+     ModelCMaleFree.objective, name="sumLL"),
+   mxAlgebraObjective("sumLL")
+ )
> ModelCFreeFit <- mxRun(ModelCFree)
> summary(ModelCFreeFit) # output not shown
```

Finally, we compare the two models. The model with between-group constraints does not fit significantly worse than the model with the free second-order factor loadings:

```
> mxCompare(ModelCFreeFit, ModelCInvarFit)
```

```
        base  comparison ep minus2LL  df AIC
1 ModelCFree       <NA> 40     3277 200  NA
2 ModelCFree ModelCInvar 35     3286 205  NA
    diffLL diffdf      p
1      NA     NA     NA
2    9.42      5 0.0935
```

OTHER SEM PACKAGES IN R

Several other R packages are capable of fitting various kinds of structural equation models:

■ Currently in a beta version, but available on CRAN, the lavaan package (Rosseel, 2010), whose name is an acronym for "latent variable analysis," fits a wide variety of latent variable models, using an equation-like syntax for model specification.

■ The systemfit package (Henningsen & Hamann,

2007) fits observed-variables structural equation models by ordinary least squares, weighted least squares, two-stage least squares (unweighted or weighted), and three-stage least squares.

■ The semPLS package (Monecke, 2010) fits observed and latent variable structural equation models by partial least squares.

■ The ivreg function in the AER package (Kleiber & Zeileis, 2008) fits regression equations by unweighted or weighted two-stage least squares.

■ The Zelig package (Imai, King, & Lau, 2010) can perform two-stage and three-stage estimation for observed-variables models.

REFERENCES

Anscombe, F. J. (1973). Graphics in statistical analysis. *American Statistician, 27,* 17–22.

Becker, R. A., Chambers, J. M., & Wilks, A. R. (1988). *The new S language: A programming environment for data analysis and graphics.* Pacific Grove, CA: Wadsworth.

Bentler, P. M., & Dudgeon, P. (1996). Covariance structure analysis: Statistical practice, theory, and directions. *Annual Review of Psychology, 47,* 563–592.

Boker, S. M., Neale, M., Maes, H., Wilde, M., Spiegel, M., Brick, T., et al. (2011). OpenMx: An open source extended structural equation modeling framework. *Psychometrika, 76,* 306–317.

Box, G. E. P., & Cox, D. R. (1964). An analysis of transformations. *Journal of the Royal Statistical Society B, 26,* 211–252.

Chambers, J. M., & Hastie, T. J. (Eds.). (1992). *Statistical models in S.* Pacific Grove, CA: Wadsworth.

Fox, J. (2006). Structural equation modeling with the sem package in R. *Structural Equation Modeling, 13,* 465–486.

Fox, J., & Weisberg, S. (2011). *An R companion to applied regression* (2nd ed.). Thousand Oaks, CA: Sage.

Harman, H. H. (1976). *Modern factor analysis* (3rd rev. ed.). Chicago: University of Chicago Press.

Henningsen, A., & Hamann, J. D. (2007). systemfit: A package for estimating systems of simultaneous equations in r. *Journal of Statistical Software, 23*(4), 1–40. Available from *http://www.jstatsoft.org/v23/i04/.*

Holzinger, K. J., & Swineford, F. (1939). *A study in factor analysis: The stability of a bi-factor solution* [Monograph]. Chicago: University of Chicago Press.

Ihaka, R., & Gentleman, R. (1996). R: A language for data analysis and graphics. *Journal of Computational and Graphical Statistics, 5,* 299–314.

Imai, K., King, G., & Lau, O. (2010). *Zelig: Everyone's*

statistical software [Computer software manual]. Available from *http://CRAN.R-project.org/package=Zelig* (R package version 3.4-8).

Kelley, K., & Lai, K. (2010). *Mbess* [Computer software manual]. Available from *http://CRAN.R -project.org/package=MBESS* (R package version 3.0.1).

Kleiber, C., & Zeileis, A. (2008). *Applied econometrics with R*. New York: Springer-Verlag. Available from *http://CRAN.R-project.org/package=AER* (ISBN 978-0-387-77316-2).

McArdle, J. J. (1980). Causal modeling applied to psychonomic systems simulation. *Behavior Research Methods and Instrumentation, 12*, 193–209.

McArdle, J. J., & McDonald, R. P. (1984). Some algebraic properties of the reticular action model. *British Journal of Mathematical and Statistical Psychology, 37*, 234–251.

Monecke, A. (2010). *sempls: Structural equation modeling using partial least squares* [Computer software manual] (R package version 0.8-1).

Neale, M. C., Boker, S. M., Xie, G., & Maes, H. H. (2003). *Mx: Statistical modeling* (6th ed.). Available from Department of Psychiatry, VCU Box 900126, Richmond, VA 23298.

R Development Core Team. (2010). *R: A language and environment for statistical computing* [Computer software manual]. Vienna: R Foundation for Statistical Computing. Available from *http://www.R-project.org* (ISBN 3-900051-07-0).

Rosseel, Y. (2010). *lavaan: Latent variable analysis* [Computer software manual]. Available from *http://CRAN.R-project.org/package=lavaan* (R package version 0.3-1).

Satorra, A., & Bentler, P. M. (1988). Scaling corrections for chi-square statistics in covariance structure analysis. In *Proceedings of the Business and Economics Statistics Section* (pp. 308–313). Alexandria, VA: American Statistical Association.

Venables, W. N., & Ripley, B. D. (2002). *Modern applied statistics with S* (4th ed.). New York: Springer.

CHAPTER 21

The Structural Equation Modeling Research Report

Anne Boomsma
Rick H. Hoyle
A. T. Panter

As applications of structural equation modeling (SEM) increasingly incorporate state-of-the-art developments, including the diverse areas covered in the latter half of this handbook, students, researchers, reviewers, and editors continue to seek guidance about the necessary content and appropriate format for reporting results in their publications and presentations. Several existing publications have provided useful guidance about reporting norms for the more basic SEM cases, as well as a few of the newer modeling approaches (e.g., American Psychological Association, 2010; Boomsma, 2000; Gefen, Rigdon, & Straub, 2011; Hoyle & Panter, 1995; McDonald & Ho, 2002; Schreiber, Nora, Stage, Barlow, & King, 2006). These publications also have served as a needed supplement to enhance the limited quantitative training opportunities available in many social and behavioral science graduate programs (Aiken, West, & Millsap, 2008) by offering researchers a way to keep pace with some of the continually evolving SEM developments.

Although these publications have provided good coverage of the reporting essentials that apply broadly to applications of SEM, they offer little advice for specific applications, particularly newer and more technically challenging applications. Our goal in this chapter is to complement earlier publications on reporting SEM results by offering guidance on five specific model types. We begin with item factor analysis, the modeling of latent variables with noncontinuous indicators. Coverage of this model type provides a basis for some general comments about reporting SEM results and sets the stage for coverage of measurement invariance. To these two model types, we add latent variable interaction, latent growth curve analysis, and Monte Carlo simulations, as applied to SEM. For each of these model types there have been significant improvements in our ability to model data generated by sophisticated research designs and measurement strategies that align closely with complex research questions. Analysis of these model types generates more results and, in some cases, results that are not generated by analyses of more basic models. As such, the production of a satisfactory research report poses unique challenges.

For each model type, we begin with a brief description of the prototypic form of the model, including citations to general treatments of such models. We then discuss the analytic issues associated with the model type, offering practical suggestions for describing these issues and how they are addressed in research reports. Although our focus is not analysis strategy, we nonetheless point out important considerations and occasionally offer recommendations about analyses associated with the different model types. Next, we discuss the presentation of results, focusing specifically on information beyond what might typically be presented in an SEM research report. We conclude each section with a brief presentation of published examples that illustrate good reporting practice for the model type in question.

REPORTING ITEM FACTOR ANALYSIS

Our understanding of how to factor analyze indicators that are "other than" continuously measured has increased substantially in the past few decades, especially with developments in the generalized linear model (Rindskopf, in press). These developments, combined with an emphasis on data properties and improvements in computer programs for handling factor analysis of dichotomous and ordered categorical data (e.g., Jöreskog, 1990; Muthén & Muthén, 2010), have created exciting new modeling opportunities for applied researchers. With an emphasis on these new opportunities, our focus in this section of the chapter is item factor analysis of a set of items or the use of item-level indicators to model latent variables that will be incorporated into a larger structural equation model.

Researchers who use these item factor models acknowledge that in their specific research situation—whether in an experiment in a laboratory setting, in narratives coded by independent judges, in a set of items on a survey, or observed on a playground—the main study indicators are "less than" continuous. These indicators may be some combination of responses types, including dichotomies/binary data (*no–yes*; *incorrect–correct*; *behavior absent–behavior present*), ordered categories (*not at all like me* to *very much like me*; *rarely or none of the time [less than 1 day]* to *most or all of the time [5–7 days]*), count data (number of cigarettes smoked in a week; number of bullying episodes), and other data types that reflect noncontinuously measured variables (e.g., Tobit, censored, zero-inflated Poisson).

Because establishing the latent structure of a set of observed indicators continues to be a basic use of SEM, as in the classic psychometric tradition (Cudeck & MacCallum, 2007; Thurstone, 1947), item-level data, often from surveys, attitude and personality scales, or knowledge measures, are frequently of research interest. Recent reviews of item-level factor analysis, including its relation to item response theory, can be found in publications by Edwards, Wirth, Houts, and Xi (Chapter 12, this volume), Bovaird and Koziol (Chapter 29, this volume), Stucky, Gottfredson, and Panter (in press), and Wirth and Edwards (2007).

Analysis Decisions to Document

The question often arises whether it is more advantageous to retain the individual items as the modeling unit (typically not continuously measured) or to aggregate these smaller units into larger, more reliable composites or parcels, based on some criterion such as content (e.g., Bandalos, 2002; Nesselroade & Cattell, 1988). There is some debate about this issue. In confirmatory factor analysis the conditions are most optimal for item-level analysis when they include relatively large samples, not too many items, and not too many proposed factors (Edwards et al., Chapter 12, this volume). It is generally preferred to factor-analyze the individual items rather than use allocations of individual items to larger parcels as a "corrective measure" simply to improve model fit. Indeed, to the extent that model fit varies from item-level to parcel-level models, the allocation of items to parcels instead of using individual items does improve model fit by creating more continuously measured units, parcels (Sterba, 2011; Sterba & MacCallum, 2010). Due to the critical role of the specific indicators for item factor analysis, researchers need to clearly document the number of items, their measurement level, and their response formats.

There are several estimation options (Bovaird & Koziol, Chapter 29, this volume; Lei, 2006; Lei & Wu, Chapter 10, this volume), including "limited information" types such as mean variance weighted least squares in Mplus (Muthén & Muthén, 2010) and "full-information types" such as full-information maximum likelihood approaches in LISREL (Jöreskog & Moustaki, 2006; Jöreskog & Sörbom, 2006) and EQS (Bentler & Wu, 2002). Because it is useful for readers to see and interpret the magnitude of a factor loading relative to its standard error, we also recommend that researchers use and report estimation methods that allow for computation of standard errors; thus, analyzing only latent correlations, thereby bypassing specialized software programs, is not recommended. Currently, estimation method and choice of computer program are strongly linked in item factor analysis (i.e., certain approaches are associated with certain programs). It is thus important to note and justify the choice of estimation method and computer program (with version).

As is typical of data gathered from human participants, there is likely to be some degree of missing data. Thus, we also need to account for these incomplete data using modern missing data approaches (Acock, in press; Graham & Coffman, Chapter 17, this volume), while also handling noncontinuously measured items. Not all of the more popular SEM programs allow for categorical indicators and missing data to be handled simultaneously, thus limiting researchers' analysis choices.

Clustering may also be an aspect of the research design and cannot be ignored in the analysis and write-up (Rabe-Hesketh, Skrondal, & Zheng, Chapter 30, this volume). Multilevel designs are of great interest to applied researchers because they allow for modeling effects within and between various natural groupings or dependencies, such as data collection sites, twins, romantic couples, peer groups, families, educational institutions, establishments, and companies. Optimally, there are many of these groupings, and their size may vary from small to large. Rabe-Hesketh and colleagues provide an excellent description of several of these models and how they are estimated. Grilli and Rampichini (2007) and Goldstein and Browne (2005) address multilevel modeling in SEM using ordered categorical variables. Gottfredson, Panter, Daye, Allen, and Wightman (2009) provide an example of a longitudinal multilevel model with ordered categories based on a national sample of law students nested within 64 law schools. Because not all SEM programs have options that allow users to simultaneously handle noncontinuously measured indicators in addition to multilevel structures, researchers need to be able to address in their report how they chose to analyze the nestedness in their design, as well as the ordered-categorical indicators.

Finally, there are several ways that item-level indicators may be conceptualized and modeled. Model comparison continues to be a critical aspect of how a research community understands underlying data structure, so the researcher is encouraged to identify meaningful nested comparisons for consideration (e.g., four-factor orthogonal, four-factor oblique, bifactor model, one-factor second-order model). For example, a researcher may be interested in conducting (1) an exploratory factor analysis; (2) a confirmatory factor analysis in which a measurement model for a specific construct or scale is evaluated (see Brown & Moore, Chapter 22, this volume); (3) a hierarchical structure in which a set of higher-order factors gives rise to a set of first-order factors, which in turn gives rise to the observed categorical indicators; (4) a bifactor model (Gibbons et al., 2007) in which items load on a general factor, for example, but certain item subsets form additional factors; and (5) an analysis in which these indicators are part of a larger SEM with various latent predictors and outcomes. In all cases the researcher should be clear which set of hypothesized structures of the item-to-latent variable relations will be evaluated and compared. All models can be estimated in conventional SEM software, as well as specialized software intended for analyses in the item response theory tradition (e.g., IRTPRO; Cai, du Toit, & Thissen, 2011; BIFACTOR; Gibbons & Hedeker, 2007). Cai, Yang, and Hansen (2011) provide a comprehensive review of these models, as special cases of their two-tiered estimation approach.

Tables and Figures

Similar to reporting of factor-analytic models with continuously measured indicators (American Psychological Association, 2010), item factor analyses can be summarized in tables or figures, in addition to the details provided in text. The first table typically lists the different item-level factor-analytic solutions being compared. A second table compares the main model fit information across researcher-selected nested models. A figure is concise and vivid yet limited in that it is usually selected to include estimates from the "final" model, not the set of alternative models.

In tables showing factor solutions for item factor analysis, it is standard for the items to appear in the first column (often paraphrased for brevity or due to copyright issues). Factor loadings and their standard errors for specific solutions are shown in subsequent columns, with column heads differentiating the alternative solutions. It generally helps readers if the items are sorted in some way in the table, such as by factor content and then factor loading magnitude. Also, as is typical, the correlations between factors are provided right below the factor solution.

Because item-level factor analyses involve the estimation of $k - 1$ thresholds per item (where k is the number of points on the item response scale), a 20-item depression scale with a 4-point response format would require reporting of 60 thresholds. In typical SEM reporting, a reader should be able to recreate parameter counts of estimated models from the tables and figures alone. Yet in the item factor analysis case a researcher may not be able to report results associated with each threshold in the tabled results or in the figure. A table note or a figure caption can fill some of that gap by indicating that threshold information is not shown. A full accounting of the degrees of freedom for the model is recommended so the reader can follow which model parameters are free, fixed, or constrained to a value for identification or for another purpose.

The table note can include the *N*, the item response format, the estimation approach, the SEM program, any constrained model parameters constraints, interpretations of the estimates to standard errors, an interpretation of the loading based on whether a full-information or limited-information estimation method was used, an accounting of the estimated model parameters, the rotation (if exploratory factor analyses are reported), and full model statistics (the estimator used for the analysis) for each model shown. If thresholds are not reported in the table, then this should be documented in the note.

The model comparison table provides each specific model labels, preferably with labels that link to the conceptual models being evaluated, along with separate columns for the estimation-specific χ^2 used in the analysis, *df* (or number of estimated parameters), and the researcher's personal selection of fit indices such as root mean square error of approximation (RMSEA), comparative fit index (CFI), and Tucker–Lewis index (TLI). Not all estimators produce a full array of fit statistics, especially in the presence of missing data, so the researcher needs to be creative about how to express model fit information (see, e.g., Gottfredson et al., 2009, Footnote 1). Change statistics can also be provided. A good table would point the reader to a clear conclusion about the preferred models from the larger set. The table note should include the *N*, the estimation method and computer program, specific parameterization if relevant (see Note 10 in Bovaird & Koziol, Chapter 29, this volume), correlated errors in the initial model, and explanations of abbreviations.

When the item factor analysis involves data generated by a multilevel design, additional information should be reported in tables and/or figures. One of the first tables presented can describe key study variables at each major level of the analysis. In Gottfredson and colleagues (2009) this basic descriptive table comprised student-level information (e.g., age, gender, household income, standardized test scores, political orientation, race/ethnicity), as well as institution/law school–related data (e.g., racial diversity of the law school, private–public status, selectivity of the school, enrollment). As part of that table, the number of units, the number of clusters, the mean number of units/clusters, and range of units/clusters should be reported.

A table of parameter estimates might also be presented for the final model, in which the first column is the different model parameters sorted by construct

and type of relation, and the second and third columns are parameter estimates and standard errors, and an optional standardized parameter. The table note should restate the *N* for the analysis (for the individual units and clustering variables), the full model statistic, estimator-specific χ^2, degrees of freedom, and goodness-of-fit indices.

The figure in the multilevel SEM has a different look than the standard SEM figure and warrants a more detailed description in the figure caption. Generally, the within model is shown in a large box or boxes, with between-unit, cluster-level variables shown outside the box, influencing the within system in various ways. Rabe-Hesketh and colleagues (Chapter 30, this volume) show several alternative versions of these models in their figures, including an example of three-level SEM with *t* times nested within *j* units nested within *k* clusters. Several details are important to convey in the figure caption, including which model is actually shown (assuming that multiple competing models were tested), and which paths are shown and not shown (e.g., correlations among certain indicators may not be shown for clarity).

Examples

Hays, Liu, Spritzer, and Cella (2007) investigated the latent structure and item response characteristics of 15 items with three discrete response options related to physical functioning of individuals with chronic health conditions. They found support for a single-factor model that provides good discrimination at lower levels of physical functioning but relatively poor discrimination at higher levels of functioning. Their description of analytic strategy is thorough and complete. They make excellent use of tables and figures to present a large amount of information, including item characteristic curves for every item. Their discussion is a model of thorough interpretation and application of findings from an item factor analysis.

Bowles, Grimm, and McArdle (2005) used item factor analysis to examine the latent structure of vocabulary knowledge, then evaluated the relation between the resultant latent variables and age. Responses to the 10 knowledge items were binary; each response, chosen from among five options, was either correct or incorrect. Bowles and colleagues used a nonlinear method available in the Mplus computer program for the item factor analysis, then output factor scores for use in a dual exponential growth analysis of age differences.

Theirs is an unusually sophisticated use of item factor analysis, but the description of the analytic strategy and presentation of the results is comprehensible without sacrificing important detail. Because their principal focus is the relation between knowledge and age, they understandably devote less attention in the report to the item factor analysis than to the analysis of the knowledge–age relation. Their presentation of the latter, particularly their use of figures, is a fine model for other researchers.

REPORTING MEASUREMENT INVARIANCE WITH ITEM-LEVEL DATA

An essential research question when evaluating the psychometric validity of new and existing instruments is: Does this measure behave similarly across different groups? Typically, these groups are assumed to be independent (e.g., culture; treatment conditions; demographic grouping variables; various other natural, nonoverlapping clusters of individuals). Building on this initial question, a researcher may be interested in an even broader set of questions concerning whether an entire structural equation system of relations—with covariates, predictors, and outcomes at one point in time or over time—behaves similarly across groups. These *measurement invariance*, or *measurement equivalence*, questions presume a very stringent criterion for evidence of similarity. These criteria are as follows: Does every single aspect of the set of relations between indicators and latent variables behave similarly across groups? Does every single relation implied by a predictive model involving several types of latent variables behave similarly across groups?

Two outstanding sources for SEM researchers navigating these types of invariance questions, particularly for determining feasible orderings for testing and evaluating these nested comparisons, are Cheung and Rensvold (2002, especially Table 1) and Vandenberg and Lance (2000, especially the Figure 2 flowchart). Millsap and Olivera-Aguilar (Chapter 23, this volume) also describe the specific steps required to show invariance across different model types. However, with the exception of the review in Bovaird and Koziol (Chapter 29, this volume), discussions of measurement invariance approaches have been limited to a fairly specific, basic case: invariance testing in models (usually measurement models) for continuously measured indicators with an assumed first-order factor structure.

In this section we address SEM reporting for item-level data across any of a number of hypothesized structures (only first-level factors, second-level factors, bifactor models). We can also assume that a design may include some level of incomplete data and possibly multilevel structure or cluster sampling. Different pedagogical articles in the literature addressed various pieces of this puzzle. Chen, Sousa, and West (2005) discussed the series of nested comparisons needed for evaluating invariance in second-order factor structures with continuously measured variables, as did Byrne and Stewart (2006). Millsap and Tein (2004) examined the sequence of tests required for evaluating invariance in basic first-order measurement models with ordered categorical data, with specific emphasis on estimation options, constraints, and analytic results across LISREL and Mplus. Bovaird and Koziol (Chapter 29, this volume) provide an example of measurement invariance with ordered categorical data using three estimation approaches in Mplus: the linear measurement model (ignoring the ordinal nature of the data), the weighted least squares mean- and variance-adjusted (WLSMV) method, and the full-information maximum likelihood (FIML) method.

Analysis Decisions to Document

As with item factor analysis, readers needs clarity about which specific indicators are included in the baseline model and how the researcher chose to treat these indicators. Thus, the items, their response formats, and their assumed measurement level should be noted in the research report. If composites or subscales are modeled (using appropriate caution about the use of item parcels for the purpose of improving model fit), reliability and validity information of those larger units should be reported, as well as their substantive justification.

A major aspect of invariance testing involves identifying a specific order of the tests, starting with an initial structure that would be reasonable to compare across groups. The initial structure is a very important starting point because model fit progressively degrades with each additional set of invariance constraints. We do not recommend that researchers identify baseline structure by pooling data across the groups (i.e., ignoring group membership) and examining the hypothesized structure.

The ordered categorical metric of some item sets introduces a few differences in how invariance is tested.

As noted, the $k - 1$ item thresholds are analyzed; item intercepts are considered to be 0. In addition, residual variances are not freely estimated; they are usually constrained to 1 in the first group and free in other groups. Following the sequence of Bovaird and Koziol (Chapter 29, this volume), the invariance testing for item-level data can proceed as follows: (1) configural invariance (i.e., unconstrained models by group); (2) constrained lower-order factor loadings and intercepts/thresholds; (3) constrained higher-order factor loadings; (4) constrained lower-order factor intercepts; (5) constrained lower-order residual variances; (6) constrained lower-order factor disturbances; and (7) constrained higher-order factor variances.

Presenting Results

Measurement invariance testing requires many decisions that need to be documented clearly in text. For example, readers need to understand how the baseline model was derived and the planned ordering of tests to be conducted. Also, specific constraints are needed to identify these multiple-group invariance models when dealing with ordered categorical data (Millsap & Tein, 2004; Bovaird & Koziol, Chapter 29, this volume) and testing of higher-order factor solutions (Chen et al., 2005). Each of these constraints needs to be specified in a way that would allow the reader to count the number of freely estimated parameters and replicate findings in another set of analyses.

In addition to the documentation provided in text about the sequence of invariance tests, there are two major ways that invariance testing results with ordered categorical indicators are typically displayed. The first is a model comparison summary table that has as its rows each major model and as its columns model statistics (an estimator-specific χ^2, df, a selection of goodness-of-fit indices, difference from the prior better fitting model, and sometimes significance level and difference in such levels). Some authors have chosen to describe these tests using only Greek symbols. We recommend that the researcher use conceptual language in the first column of the table expressing the content of the evaluated models, such as "Social Support Model 1: Fully Unconstrained Model," "Social Support Model 2: Equal Item Loadings and Item Thresholds." Matrix or double-label notation may be added to these descriptions if desired.

If the WLSMV estimator is selected in Mplus, results across models cannot be compared directly and need to be evaluated using the DIFFTEST. Sometimes this test can lead to confusion among reviewers and journal editors because the degrees of freedom do not seem to "add up" as they typically do in nested invariance testing. The researcher may choose to report the number of free parameters of each model to help make transparent for readers what happens when different sets of constraints are added for each model.

A table note is particularly critical for these nested comparisons because it is used to provide further clarity about the performed tests. The table note should include N, the estimation method and computer program used, the overall baseline model statistics, further explanatory detail about the first main column, and how difference tests were conducted, which is especially important for ordered categorical data. The general goal is the following: A reader who finds just the table from an invariance manuscript should be able to understand the context of the analysis, the order of the tests, and where, if at all, invariance breaks down.

A second table typically presents the parameter estimates for the most constrained model. This table takes the form of a typical parameter estimate, but recall that the presence of thresholds for a large model with more than a few response options could make it particularly large and cumbersome.

For continuously measured indicators, figures showing invariance results typically can capture in one place estimates across groups, per parameter, in a transparent way. With categorical indicators, figures need to reflect thresholds as well. If a figure is shown, the caption might report that thresholds were not shown.

Examples

Motl and colleagues (2000) examined the measurement invariance of four measures commonly used in research on the determinants of physical activity. Specifically, they asked whether the latent structure of these measures was invariant prior to and after the transition to high school. These authors describe well their approach to invariance analysis, explaining and justifying their choice of estimator, approach to missing data, and model fit criteria. Atypical for reports of SEM analyses, they provide in table format extensive information regarding the multivariate distribution of indicators for all measures at both time points. They also make good use of tables for presenting model fit information for successive tests of invariance. The Motl and colleagues report is a fine example of providing essential information for a large number of SEM analyses in a single research report.

Morin, Moullee, Maïano, Layet, Just, and Ninot (in press) examined the measurement invariance of a French version of a widely used self-report measure of depression. Their report is a useful model of invariance testing of models for ordered categorical responses. They offer a persuasive argument for why four response options are not sufficient for standard maximum likelihood estimation, an argument reinforced by diagnostic information showing strong evidence of non-normality (as is typical of measures of psychopathology in nonclinical populations). In an appendix that many readers may find useful for understanding the general activity of invariance testing, they provide detailed information about the sequence they followed in evaluating invariance. They also provide an instructive argument for their specification of the measurement equations given the ordered categorical data and weighted least squares estimation. The report by Morin and colleagues is one of a small number showcasing the use of SEM to address important questions about measurement equivalence with appropriate concern for the validity of standard estimation methods for response formats that offer relatively few options.

REPORTING LATENT VARIABLE INTERACTIONS

In contrast to the routine practice of modeling constructs as latent variables to overcome the attenuating effect of unreliability on estimates of the relations between constructs, the constructs involved in statistical interaction tests are rarely modeled as latent variables. Instead, if interaction effects are considered at all, they are modeled using products of observed variables, or one construct is treated as an observed grouping variable in a multigroup model, and invariance is evaluated. This is unfortunate because unreliability is compounded when the indicators are multiplied to produce manifest interaction terms (Busemeyer & Jones, 1983), further reducing the likelihood of detecting elusive interaction effects (McClelland & Judd, 1993). The reluctance of SEM users to model latent interaction effects stems in part from known challenges of specifying latent interaction variables. In the seminal paper on specifying and estimating latent interaction effects using SEM, Kenny and Judd (1984) made clear that although latent interaction effects could be modeled, a full specification would result in a potentially large

number of indicators of the latent interaction variable and a need for nonlinear constraints on many of the parameters associated with those indicators. These specification challenges were sufficiently difficult to overcome that substantive researchers either modeled interaction effects using manifest variables or did not model them at all.

A series of important methodological developments related primarily to specification have now brought the modeling of latent interaction variables within reach of the typical SEM user. These range from strategies for dramatically reducing the number of indicators of the latent interaction variable (Jöreskog & Yang, 1996), to strategies for simplifying the imposition of nonlinear constraints (Ping, 1995), or eliminating them altogether (Marsh, Wen, Nagengast, & Hau, Chapter 26, this volume). Because most published reports describing these strategies are methodological in focus, relatively few examples are available for substantive researchers to consult when considering how to report research using SEM to study latent interaction effects. We therefore offer recommendations and highlight two instructive, published examples.

Analysis Decisions to Document

Because of the widely varied options for specifying latent interaction variables, it is important that full information be given and relevant justifications provided for the chosen specification strategy and estimator. We review four approaches to modeling latent interaction variables, pointing out for each the information and justifications that should be included in a research report.

The most straightforward specification strategy involves selecting one indicator from each latent variable involved in the interaction, producing a single product indicator of the latent interaction variable. Jöreskog and Yang (1996) showed that a latent interaction variable modeled in this way is more likely to result in convergence and produce consistent estimates across estimators than a model that includes all product indicators produced from two latent variables with multiple indicators. The appeal of this simplified specification strategy is evident, but its validity rests on several assumptions that should be documented in reports of findings it produced. Foremost of these is that the indicators of each latent variable are congeneric; that is, their uniquenesses are uncorrelated. Yang Jonsson (1998) described and illustrated a means of testing this and other assumptions that must be met if the Jöreskog–Yang approach to modeling latent interaction variables is used (see Saris, Batista-Foguet, & Coenders, 2007, for an alternative strategy). The results of these tests should be reported in any manuscript based on findings from analyses modeling latent interaction variables using a single product of indicators. Jöreskog and Yang (1996) also argued that intercepts of the measurement equations must be modeled to properly estimate the structural equation including the latent interaction effect. As such, models specified using this strategy include mean structure, a feature that should be clear in the description of the specification and reflected in tables presenting the matrix that was analyzed.

Once evidence has been provided to show that assumptions have been satisfied within the limits of robustness, the next concern is how to justify the selection of a particular indicator from each constituent latent variable to produce the product indicator. Saris and colleagues (2007) recommended choosing the most reliable indicator from each latent variable, a strategy that will yield the most reliable product indicator and the most powerful test of the latent interaction effect. Assuming no specificity, indicator reliability is indexed by the square of the standardized loading. The pair of most-reliable indicators would be determined by a preliminary analysis of the measurement model absent a latent interaction variable. Whether this optimal strategy is chosen to select indicators to include in forming the product indicator, or whether some other strategy is selected, the rationale and identification of the chosen indicators should be provided in the research report.

When the constituent latent variables have a small number of indicators and the researcher is skilled in the use of SEM software to impose nonlinear constraints on specific parameters, the full product indicator specification detailed by Kenny and Judd (1984) is an option. Because all possible products are included, no justification is required regarding the indicators of the latent interaction variable. The correct specification of nonlinear constraints is critical to the specification. Relevant syntax should be provided in an appendix or on a website to show readers how such constraints were implemented, allowing for replication and extension.

A critical concern both for the full- and single-product indicator specification is the choice of estimation method. For this reason, reports of findings from models that include one of these specifications must provide justification for the choice of estimation method, including specific information relevant to its performance. Maximum likelihood (ML), the default

estimation method in most SEM computer programs, assumes the joint distribution of the observed variables is multivariate normal, a condition not met when product indicators are included. Jöreskog and Yang (1996) suggest that ML may be robust to the departure from multivariate normality expected with a single-product indicator, but such robustness should not be assumed. Rather, the comparison of ML fit statistics against those that account for non-normality (e.g., Satorra & Bentler's, 1994, robust estimation and scaled statistics) should be reported as a means of supporting or rejecting the validity of uncorrected ML estimates. Although an estimation method that explicitly incorporates higher-order moments such as WLS might seem appropriate, Jöreskog and Yang (1996) point out that other unmet assumptions argue against WLS. Generalized least squares, by incorporating additional information, is not subject to this assumption (see Neale, 1998, for an example). Klein and Moosbrugger's (2000) latent moderated structural equations approach is also an option, though it becomes prohibitively computationally intensive with more than a few indicators. The choice of estimation method should always be justified in reports of SEM results, but in light of the distributional characteristics of product indicators, even when other observed variables are normally distributed, extra attention should be devoted to choice of estimation method in reports of latent interaction effects when product indicators and nonlinear constraints on parameters are used.

Alternative approaches to specifying latent interaction variables involve circumventing the need for nonlinear constraints on parameters. The approach most similar to Kenny and Judd's (1984) product indicator specification and Jöreskog and Yang's (1996) simplification of it is that of Ping (1995), who proposed that the need for nonlinear constraints could be avoided if the parameters of the latent interaction variable were fixed rather than estimated. This is accomplished by estimating a model that includes only the constituent latent variables, then using the resulting parameter estimates to calculate the values for the parameters associated with the latent interaction variable. If each constituent latent variable has a small number of indicators, producing a relatively small number of indicators of the latent interaction variable, then this implementation of the Kenny–Judd approach is feasible. When it is used, full information about the computation of the fixed parameters associated with the latent interaction variable should be provided. Assuming the observed data are otherwise multivariate normal, ML estimation of free parameters using this setup produced unbiased parameter estimates. Nonetheless, as suggested earlier, standard ML statistics should be compared with statistics from robust ML estimation and reported with reference to the choice of estimation method.

A final alternative for specifying latent interaction variables involves strategically creating the product indicators so as to eliminate any biasing effect of ignoring the nonlinearity of parameters in the latent interaction variable. Little, Bovaird, and Widaman (2006) propose orthogonalizing indicators prior to creating product indicators. Orthogonalizing, or residual centering, follows the logic of mean centering prior to creating observed product terms for moderated multiple regression analysis (Aiken & West, 1991). Little and colleagues (2006) showed that models in which all possible product indicators were used following orthogonalization of indicators produced little bias in estimates when nonlinear constraints were not imposed. Marsh, Wen, and Hau (2004) proposed an alternative strategy in which the indicators are simply mean-centered prior to creation of the product indicators. Moreover, rather than including all product indicators, their mean-centering approach requires including only the number of product indicators necessary to ensure that each indicator is included in one (and only one) product. A key difference in these two approaches is that the mean-centering approach requires the inclusion of a mean structure, whereas the orthogonalizing approach does not (see Marsh, Wen, Hau, Little, Bovaird, & Widaman, 2007, for a direct comparison between the two approaches). As such, an additional set of parameters would need to be accounted for and perhaps reported when the mean-centering approach is used.

Regardless of the specification strategy chosen, the choice of estimator should be deliberate and justified. As noted earlier, even when all indicators of the two latent variables involved in the interaction are normally distributed, the product indicators will not be. Evidence to date suggests that ML is robust to the violation of the normality assumption typical of product indicators, but this robustness should be demonstrated for each investigation (Jöreskog & Yang, 1996). The simplest strategy for accomplishing this is to compare model fit statistics from estimates using ML and those using robust ML estimation. If the difference is nontrivial (e.g., ratio of the former to the latter > 1.5), findings from the robust and scaled solution should be presented in the research report.

Summarizing Results

Once specified, a latent interaction variable is comparable to other latent variables in a structural model. As such, the presentation of parameters from that portion of the model should be no different than the presentation of other parameters and tests. The lone exception is with the Ping (1995) specification, in which the parameters associated with the latent interaction variable are fixed and therefore not estimated. This property of those parameter values should be made clear in any presentation of them.

The relatively few published examples of latent interaction effects suggest little consensus regarding their representation in path diagrams. A review of those examples suggests two common strategies:

1. Show paths from the latent variable(s) involved in the interaction to the outcome variables. Show a path from the latent variable presumed to be the moderator to *paths* from the other latent variable, whose magnitude it is assumed to qualify.

2. Show the latent interaction variable, appropriately labeled, and its presumed effects in the same way the latent variables involved in the interaction are shown.

The first approach is both unconventional in its depiction of paths pointing to other paths and inaccurate in its failure to show the full array of variables in the model. For those reasons, we recommend the second approach.

Because much of the published research on latent interaction effects is methodological in focus, little attention has been devoted to interpretation. A variety of patterns (e.g., crossover, increasing or decreasing strength of effect) with very different implications for interpretation might underlie a signification interaction effect; thus, it is essential that such effects are probed and the underlying pattern is presented in the report. Typically, interactions involving two continuous variables are probed using simple slopes analysis (Aiken & West, 1991), which involves using the estimated parameters to find the slopes for one variable at different points (typically one standard deviation above and below the mean) on the other variable. We are unaware of published examples of simple slopes analysis following estimation of a latent interaction effect, though one of the examples we present includes an informal probing of a significant latent interaction effect.

Examples

Perhaps because of the specification challenges associated with latent interaction variables, there are few published examples. We highlight two that are instructive regarding the reporting of results of SEM tests of latent interaction effects. Wei, Mallinckrodt, Russell, and Abraham (2004) examined the degree to which the effects of stress in the form of attachment anxiety on depressive mood are moderated by a tendency toward perfectionism. Indicators of attachment anxiety were three parcels, and indicators of perfectionism were three subscale scores from standard measures. They used Jöreskog and Yang's (1996) single product indicator strategy, choosing the highest loading indicator of each latent variable to create the product term. They estimated the model using ML but did not examine the potential ill effects of non-normality in the product indicator on the estimates and tests. They depicted the interaction effect using both of the strategies described earlier, illustrating the concept using the path-affecting-path approach, then presenting the parameter estimates on a path diagram with the latent interaction variable shown alongside the two constituent latent variables. To probe the effect, they used factor scores for the latent moderator variable to create low, moderate, and high groups, then plotted the attachment anxiety effect at each level. All in all, aspects of the report by Wei and colleagues (2004) relevant to latent interaction effects are reported thoroughly, making it a good example, particularly for applications that use the Jöreskog–Yang specification strategy.

A second informative example is found in an article by Steinmetz, Davidov, and Schmidt (2011), illustrating the use of the orthogonalizing and mean-centering approaches to specifying latent interaction variables. Substantively, the focus of their analysis was the interaction between perceived behavioral control and behavioral intention on the behavior of using public transportation. Like Wei and colleagues (2004), they showed the interaction effect using both the path-affecting-path and latent interaction variable approaches. They provide a thorough though succinct explanation of the creation of orthogonalized product indicators that is a useful model for researchers reporting studies in which they used that strategy. They highlighted the non-normal distributions of the product indicators as justification for using robust ML estimation. Although they detect the interaction effect of interest using both methods, they

find multicollinearity to be a problem with the mean-centering approach, likely due to their inclusion of all possible product indicators rather than just enough that each individual indicator is represented only once, as required in the Marsh and colleagues (2004) implementation. Although they do not probe the significant interaction effect, their application is a useful model for researchers reporting the outcome of SEM analyses of latent interaction using the orthogonalizing or mean-centering approach.

REPORTING LATENT GROWTH CURVE MODELS

Although the preponderance of SEM involves modeling covariance structure, researchers are increasingly discovering the advantages of SEM for modeling mean structure as well (see Green & Thompson, Chapter 24, this volume, for a review). We have noted the secondary focus on mean structure in some analyses of measurement invariance and specifications of latent variable interaction. In models of latent growth, mean structure is the central focus. Given the focus on patterns of means and variability in the parameters that characterize those patterns, reports of findings from the analysis of latent growth vary somewhat from the norm for SEM analyses.

Latent growth curve models, sometimes referred to as "latent trajectory models" or simply "latent curve models," generally are of two types: unconditional and conditional (see Bollen & Curran, 2006; McArdle, Chapter 32, this volume, for a review). Unconditional models are concerned with characterizing the average trajectory for a population and documenting the degree of variability in specific parameters, termed "growth parameters," associated with the characteristic trajectory (e.g., intercept, slope; Willett & Sayer, 1994). Conditional models build on unconditional models by including additional variables, potentially other variable trajectories, in order to account for variability in growth parameters. In this regard, many analyses of latent growth follow the logic of the two-step approach to estimating models of covariance structure: First establish the adequacy of the measurement model, then evaluate relations in the structural model (Anderson & Gerbing, 1988). In full implementations of latent growth curve analysis, only after the unconditional, or characteristic, trajectory is established are additional variables brought into the model for conditional analyses.

In some instances, relevant variables are not available to account for variability around the characteristic curve. Moreover, variability in the patterns may be more profound with, for example, some individuals evidencing a linear and others a curvilinear trajectory. In such cases, growth mixture modeling is a means of identifying a latent class variable that accounts for the heterogeneity of trajectories (Muthén & Asparouhov, 2006). Although our focus here is latent growth curve analysis, we touch briefly on reporting issues specific to growth mixture modeling at relevant points in the presentation.

Analysis Decisions to Document

Because latent growth curve analysis focuses on means, it is important that the research report provides information about the scale of the variable for which trajectories are to be estimated; this includes the theoretical range, the observed range, and interpretive context for scores. If the scores for which trajectories are to be estimated are composite scores, then reliability information should be supplied. Although unreliability is not accounted for in typical applications of latent growth curve analysis, it should be acknowledged and accounted for in the interpretation of the results.

In the unconditional case, two specification decisions should be stated and justified. The first concerns the origin of the trajectories—the intercept. Because the value of zero has no inherent meaning for most time periods (e.g., age, grade, assessment wave), it can be assigned with a consideration for interpretability. For some studies, this will be the first assessment, meaning the intercept estimate will be the group mean at the first time point. For other studies, it might be the midpoint, or even the endpoint. The midpoint is useful when curvilinear trajectories are modeled and the goal is orthogonal shape coefficients. In any case, the choice of origin should be clearly stated and justified.

A second specification decision for unconditional models concerns the choice of coefficients to reflect the trajectory shape. In the simplest case, the space between assessments is equal, and therefore the space between coefficients for linear trajectories is equal. If the spacing of assessments is not equal, then any adjustment to these coefficients to accurately reflect the spacing should be made explicit and justified. Once the coefficients for the linear trajectory have been chosen, coefficients for any higher-order curves should be selected and made explicit in the report. Because of the relatively small number of paths involved, path diagrams are useful for illustrating these models, including presentation of the trajectory coefficients.

Conditional models incorporate other variables of various types. These include latent or observed variables that are not time varying, time-varying covariates, and other latent growth variables (Curran & Hussong, 2003). Each variable type involves particular specification considerations; these should be outlined and related to the hypotheses guiding the research. As with unconditional models, path diagrams are a useful means of presenting model specification for conditional latent growth curve models. If, as described earlier, a diagram might be provided for the conditional model, then a second diagram is provided for the unconditional model, excluding the paths from the observed variables for which trajectories are being estimated to the latent growth variables.

When growth mixture models are to be estimated, the initial specification considerations are not unlike those for unconditional models, with the exception that given the somewhat exploratory nature of this analytic approach, curvilinear terms might be included as a means of discovering latent classes. Growth mixture modeling requires the somewhat subjective comparison of solutions for different numbers of classes in order to arrive at a final solution. The criteria for making this decision should be specified a priori based on the best simulation work on decision criteria for this purpose. Once the number of classes has been determined, then growth mixture analyses typically proceed like conditional growth models, with other variables influencing the class variable. Given the exploratory nature of these analyses, the basis for choosing predictors and the criteria used to retain those evaluated should be articulated clearly.

The estimation concerns for latent growth curve models do not differ from those for standard models analyzed using SEM. Sample size and variable distributions should be taken into account when choosing an estimator. That choice should be made explicit and justified.

Presenting Results

There is no substitute for visualization when it comes to trajectories. As such, well-constructed figures are a key feature of the presentation of results from latent growth curve analyses. Depending on the sample size, it might be informative to present a diagram in which individual curves are overlaid (the equivalent of a scatterplot in zero-order correlation). These could be observed or fitted; however, given that the statistical outcomes concern fitted trajectories, fitted individual trajectories are most relevant to the analysis. In a separate figure, or potentially an overlay of the plot of individual trajectories, the mean trajectory (or trajectories if higher-order curves are included) should be presented. In the case of growth mixture modeling, it often is most informative to overlay fitted trajectories for the different classes, though in certain cases it might be more appropriate to overlay each trajectory and the individual curves for individuals in that class.

The key parameters in latent growth curve analysis are the means and variances of the latent growth variables. As noted earlier, the mean for the intercept variable corresponds to the group mean at the point of origin. This value may or may not have substantive relevance for the research question but should nonetheless be presented. Likely of greater interest is the variance of this variable, which reflects the degree to which individuals in the data set vary in their scores on the variable for which a trajectory is being estimated at the point of origin. If this variance is near zero, then individuals are at about the same standing on that variable at the time of origin. To the extent its value departs from zero, there the individuals vary, presenting the possibility of predicting variance in intercept in conditional models. Many latent growth curve models include only a linear slope variable, and the mean of this variable is the average increase in the focal variable per unit change in time (typically from one assessment period to the next). Variance in this variable reflects variability in the linear slope; if this variance is near zero, then the slope might be interpreted as characteristic of or normative for the population represented by the sample. In the more likely case of nonzero variance, conditional analyses provide a means of potentially accounting for that variance.

When conditional models are estimated, parameter estimates and tests should be provided in the form typical for presentations of SEM results (Boomsma, 2000; Hoyle & Panter, 1995). For growth mixture models, statistical criteria that are used to determine the number of classes should be presented for all numbers of classes considered; a single table with a row for each number of classes and a column for each criterion is an efficient means of presenting these results. Additional information to be reported for growth mixture analysis includes the number of individuals per class and the results of any analyses comparing classes for the purpose of shedding light on the nature of the latent class variable.

Examples

Because latent growth curve analysis is useful for addressing many interesting research questions and is relatively straightforward in terms of specification and estimation, its use has increased substantially since it was first introduced to social and behavioral scientists (e.g., Willett & Sayer, 1994). Thus, published examples are relatively easy to find and provide concrete examples of the various ways in which results from latent growth curve analyses might be presented. Here we highlight three publications that we view as especially good models for applied researchers reporting results of latent growth curve analyses.

Hussong, Curran, Moffitt, Caspi, and Carrig (2004) examined trajectories of antisocial behavior from ages 18 to 26, focusing specifically on the role of substance use in shaping those trajectories. Their published report is particularly strong in the use of graphs and path diagrams to illustrate their hypotheses and show how they tested them using SEM. An application of latent growth curve analysis by Paxton, Hughes, and Painter (2010) is interesting for its use of country-level data. They modeled patterns of change from 1970 to 2000 in women's political representation in 110 countries. They illustrate the use of matrix notation to describe latent growth models, and the specification and interpretation of a conditional model with time-varying covariates. Simons-Mortin, Chen, Abroms, and Haynie (2004) examine trajectories of change in smoking by adolescents from grades 6–9. They simultaneously estimated trajectories of change in affiliation with friends who smoke and parental involvement. The intervals between their four assessments were unequal, providing an example of reporting the selection of trajectory coefficients in this situation. Ultimately, their model conditions latent trajectories of smoking on time-invariant predictors and latent growth variables associated with trajectories of affiliation with friends who smoke and parental monitoring. Together these published reports model the reporting of findings from a wide array of latent growth curve models.

REPORTING MONTE CARLO STUDIES

Since the 1970s Monte Carlo studies have played an increasing role in examining properties of estimators and procedures in SEM. In about one-third of the articles that appeared in the journal *Structural Equation Modeling* from its inception in 1994 to 2011, the sole focus was reporting findings from a Monte Carlo study (Boomsma, in press). It is clear that Monte Carlo simulations play an important role in SEM research. The mechanics of Monte Carlo experiments, with an emphasis on their use in research on SEM, are provided by Paxton, Curran, Bollen, Kirby and Chen (2001) and Skrondal (2000).

It is important to note that "a Monte Carlo study uses an *experiment*, and the principles of scientific experimentation should be observed" (Gentle, 2003, p. viii, original emphasis). The classification of Monte Carlo studies as experiments has repercussions for their reporting: "It is essential that enough details are given for the experiments to be repeated and the results checked" (Ripley, 1987, p. 4). Boomsma (2000) considered replication of analysis as a key element of any scientific reporting. That rationale may serve as primary motivation in reporting about Monte Carlo experimentation in SEM.

In principle, the research question in a Monte Carlo study is guided by solid theory. Queries to be covered in a theoretical account are as follows: Why is the question to be answered of substantive importance? What answers are to be expected given the nomological network of the theory, which includes empirical evidence by definition, and hence results from earlier simulation studies as well? And why is it necessary to conduct Monte Carlo simulations to answer the question posed? A proper outline of the research question, including substantive theoretical support, is a critical aspect of the research report.

Analysis Decisions to Document

Population Models

A major Monte Carlo design feature is the choice of one or more population models M_j with covariance structure $\Sigma(\theta_j)$, where θ_j is the vector of population model parameter values. This decision is one of the determinative factors for the external validity of the results, that is, the extent to which the findings of the Monte Carlo experiment can be generalized to a set of commonly applied structural equation models. Paxton and colleagues (2001) discussed a variety of considerations in this matter that could be reflected in reporting. In selecting a population model, the choice of the path diagram representing M_j is the first step, that of specific values for θ_j, the second. Together they define the covariance structure $\Sigma(\theta_j)$ of the multivariate population distribution $f[\mathbf{z}; \mu, \Sigma(\theta_j)]$ from which R pseudorandom samples $\mathbf{Z}$ ($N \times k$) will be drawn; N denotes the number of observations, k is the number of (observed) random variables, and μ is a vector of means. Often samples will be taken from a multivariate normal distribution, but not necessarily: Discrete, ordinal variables, or nonsymmetric continuous random variables have been studied as well. This should all be reported adequately, that is, exact specification of (1) the population model and models to be estimated if misspecification is a design factor, and (2) the associated population distributions from which R pseudorandom samples will be drawn.

Experimental Factors and Response Variables

Monte Carlo experiments are the means by which the specific research problem is investigated. Examples include the relationships between the performance of some model estimators (e.g., model fit estimators), modeling procedures (e.g., effectiveness of model selection routines), or estimation characteristics (e.g., occurrence of improper solutions), and a number of experimental factors. This general objective sets a framework for further reporting (see also, Skrondal, 2000).

Basic SEM Statistics. The set of statistics of interest regarding a model, as dictated by the research question, will be denoted by the vector $\hat{\vartheta}$. Its elements can, for example, be estimators of model parameters, estimators of confidence intervals for population parameters, or estimators of model fit. These basic statistics should be clearly defined.

Response Variables $\mathbf{y}$ *and Criteria for Acceptable Performance.* The behavior of the basic statistics needs to be evaluated according to well-defined performance criteria. To that purpose a number of performance statistics $\mathbf{y} = g(\hat{\vartheta})$ have to be chosen first; they are a function of basic SEM statistics and will also be referred to as the response variables. Investigators might, for example, be interested in the bias of parameter estimators, in coverage rates of confidence interval estimators, and in differences between empirical and nominal Type I error rates of model fit statistics.

For descriptive and inferential evaluation of the simulation results, researchers next have to make decisions about and report cutoff criteria or ranges of values for acceptable performance of these response variables **y**. Which statistical behavior is considered to be acceptable and which not? For performance evaluation of parameter and standard error estimators, Hoogland (1999), for example, looked at their absolute and relative bias, and decided that it would be acceptable if it were less than .05 and .10, respectively.

Of special interest is how to define acceptable departures from nominal Type I error rates, α. Robey and Barcikowski (1992) proposed refined performance criteria for them, which were used by Hancock, Lawrence, and Nevitt (2000), for example. Similar choices should be clarified for each element of the response vector **y**.

Explanatory Variables **x**. Investigators are interested in the effects of a number of explanatory variables **x**, the experimental factors or design conditions, on the response or performance variables **y**. The experimental conditions usually have a number of levels, or categories. The research question could for instance be what the effect is of the explanatory variable sample size, with say three levels ($N = 200, 400, 800$), on the relative bias of model parameter estimators as the response variable. Even without misspecification, population models can be implicit explanatory factors as well. The choice of performance variables $\mathbf{y} = g(\hat{\vartheta})$ and explanatory variables **x** will foremost be determined by the research question, and should be properly specified and justified. Jaccard and Wan (1995), for example, extracted their choice of two sample size levels from a study of journals published by the American Psychological Association.

By defining the response variables **y** and the experimental conditions **x**, the framework for a full factorial design is set, and the contents of each cell in that design are, in principle, R replications of the vector **y**. Authors should refer to the size of the design, and indicate whether the design is unbalanced, incomplete, or fractional, if applicable.

Relationships between **x** *and* **y**. The presentation and evaluation of the relationships between **x** and **y** can be handled in a descriptive or a more inferential way, or both. Most often descriptive means are used only,

commonly in the form of cross-tables of (elements of) **x** and **y**, but inferential statistical procedures are also feasible. Skrondal (2000) encouraged researchers to examine the relationships under study by using statistical models, so-called metamodels in Monte Carlo research, following Kleijnen (1974–1975). That could, for example, be analysis of variance (univariate or multivariate) models with main and interaction effects of experimental conditions.

Significance testing is usually not a sensible objective in metamodeling due to the excessive power of such tests given the frequently large number of replications. Therefore, the performance criterion is often one of practical significance (effect size), rather than statistical significance (p-values). Bandalos (2002), for example, used partial η^2 measures of effect size, focusing on effects of large practical significance only. We recommend that researchers make explicit their interpretational criteria, including specific effect sizes that will be considered as important.

The number of replications, R, sampled for each of the cells of the experimental design should be reported and justified in this context. Kleijnen (1975, Part 2, p. 698f.) and Serlin (2000) introduced methods for calculating the size of R required to detect robustness according a particular criterion for desired Type I and Type II error rates.

Expectations

Given the theoretical framework and the experimental design of the Monte Carlo study, we strongly recommend that researchers formulate expectations or hypotheses regarding the relationships between **x** and **y**; for example, by reporting expected trends of associations when results will be presented descriptively. In cases of metamodeling, researchers might state the expected sign and size of unknown primary parameters (regression coefficients, say) of such models, or at least the expected relative effect sizes (e.g., partial η^2's). Anderson (1996), for example, gives a systematic overview of hypothesized outcomes.

Computer Programs

The reasons for choosing a specific computer program are usually not discussed. Researchers, however, should state and justify their choice. Often, but not necessarily, different programs are used for data generation, for model estimation, and for the descriptive and inferential analysis of the crucial simulation results. In each case, name and version of the programs should be reported. We advise including nonobvious SEM program syntax used for model specification and data generation in an appendix or on the Web (see, e.g., Cheung, 2009).

Executing the Simulations

Given population model M_j under study, R pseudorandom samples **Z** are drawn from a specific multivariate distribution f [**z**; **μ**, **Σ**(**θ**$_j$)]. Any of the starting values used for this sample data generation should be reported. Similarly, because most estimation methods in SEM are iterative procedures, the choice of starting values for such routines should be addressed: Are population values **θ**$_j$ used as starting values or not? Authors also should be clear about whether standardized or unstandardized parameter estimates are produced and analyzed subsequently.

Model estimation problems may occur for any of the R random samples for which data are generated. Some of those samples may not lead to a converged solution within a preassigned number of iterations. Others may produce improper solutions due to Heywood cases and boundary or redundancy problems. Authors should be clear about their decision to include or exclude improper solutions, always report the number of occurrences of each type of estimation problem, and indicate whether or not R is fixed for all cells of the design.

Paxton and colleagues (2001) mention a number of options to check whether the Monte Carlo simulations have been executed correctly. The results of any such checks might be summarized briefly in the report. LaGrange and Cole (2008), for example, used more than one SEM program to check whether their results were affected by software-specific characteristics.

Presenting Results

The presentation of results from Monte Carlo SEM research is challenging given the large amount of available output that needs efficient reduction. The researchers' target in the results section is to (1) focus on answering the main research questions; (2) link the interpretation of results to theoretical expectations throughout the analysis; (3) present the essential results in a concise and elucidative format; and (4) formulate unambiguous conclusions and consequences thereof.

Results of Monte Carlo simulation studies are usually presented in tables and graphs or figures. It often is

the case that graphs convey information that might not be noticed otherwise. Even if not reported, they should routinely be generated and examined by researchers. In Monte Carlo studies the empirical (simulated) sampling distribution of statistics of interest can often be compared with a theoretical distribution. Graphs, like quantile–quantile (Q–Q) plots, can be very informative for visualizing such comparisons. These Q-Q plots, along with box plots, can effectively display deviating tails and outliers in empirical sampling distributions. Researchers should clearly state any concerns about possible effects of outlying responses and other distributional irregularities. Gold and Bentler (2000), for example, analyzed generated data with and without outliers.

The choice of graphics and tables has to be determined primarily by the research question and the main results of the study. Always, the most salient and unexpected findings should be presented clearly. Particularly in Monte Carlo studies, the number of figures and tables should not be excessive. Optionally, reference can be made to more elaborate results that have been made available on the Web, or that can be obtained from the author (see, e.g., Williams & MacKinnon, 2008).

CONCLUSIONS

For this chapter we have selected model types typically studied using SEM for which clear reporting norms have not yet been established. For each type, we highlighted specific considerations regarding the use of SEM and offered recommendations for describing the analysis and findings in research reports. In the course of our presentation, we also have offered suggestions regarding analytic strategy, including liberal reference to didactic publications about the modeling types. Although our aim was to highlight distinctive aspects of each model type, a number of cross-cutting considerations are evident. The model specification should be clearly articulated and, when feasible, shown in a path diagram. When multiple specification options are available for addressing a single research question, justification for the one chosen should be provided. Information about the variables is important both for a full understanding of the performance of the measurement strategy and as part of the justification for the selected estimation method. Some model types, when estimated, result in a large amount of information. Although not all of that information warrants inclusion in a research report, the readership of some publications will expect ample details. Well-constructed tables and graphs are indispensable for presenting such information in research reports. We briefly have described informative examples of published research reports for each model type. As the use of these promising models grows, the number of published examples will increase, eventually giving rise to norms for reporting them. In the meantime, we hope the considerations we have highlighted and the recommendations we have offered will prove useful to applied researchers who have made appropriate use of one of the model types we covered and are ready to share their findings.

REFERENCES

Acock, A. (in press). What to do about missing values? In H. Cooper, P. Camic, D. Long, A. T. Panter, D. Rindskopf, & K. Sher (Eds.), *APA handbook of research methodology in psychology*. Washington, DC: APA Books.

Aiken, L. S., & West, S. G. (1991). *Multiple regression: Testing and interpreting interactions*. Newbury Park, CA: Sage.

Aiken, L. S., West, S. G., & Millsap, R. E. (2008). Doctoral training in statistics, measurement, and methodology in psychology: Replication and extension of Aiken, West, Sechrest and Reno's (1990) survey of PhD programs in North America. *American Psychologist, 63*, 32–50.

American Psychological Association. (2010). *Publication manual of the American Psychological Association* (6th ed.). Washington, DC: Author.

Anderson, J. C., & Gerbing, D. W. (1988). Structural equation modeling in practice: A review and recommended two-step approach. *Psychological Bulletin, 103*, 411–423.

Anderson, R. D. (1996). An evaluation of the Satorra–Bentler distributional misspecification correction applied to the McDonald Fit Index. *Structural Equation Modeling, 3*, 203–227.

Bandalos, D. L. (2002). The effects of item parceling on goodness-of-fit and parameter estimate bias in structural equation modeling. *Structural Equation Modeling, 9*, 78–102.

Bentler, P. M., & Wu, E. J. C. (2002). *EQS for Windows: User's guide*. Encino, CA: Multivariate Software.

Bollen, K. A., & Curran, P. J. (2006). *Latent curve models: A structural equation perspective*. Hoboken, NJ: Wiley-Interscience.

Boomsma, A. (2000). Reporting analyses of covariance structures. *Structural Equation Modeling, 7*, 461–483.

Boomsma, A. (in press). Reporting Monte Carlo studies in structural equation modeling. *Structural Equation Modeling*.

Bowles, R. P., Grimm, K. J., & McArdle, J. J. (2005). A struc-

tural factor analysis of vocabulary knowledge and relations to age. *Journals of Gerontology B: Psychological Sciences, 60*, 234–241.

Busemeyer, J. R., & Jones, L. D. (1983). Analysis of multiplicative combination rules when the causal variables are measured with error. *Psychological Bulletin, 93*, 549–562.

Byrne, B. M., & Stewart, S. M. (2006). The MACS approach to testing for multigroup invariance of a second-order factor structure: A walk through the process. *Structural Equation Modeling, 13*, 287–321.

Cai, L., du Toit, S. H. C., & Thissen, D. (2011). *IRTPRO: Flexible, multidimensional, multiple categorical IRT modeling* [Computer software]. Chicago: Scientific Software International.

Cai, L., Yang, J. S., & Hansen, M. (2011). Generalized full-information item bifactor analysis. *Psychological Methods, 16*, 221–248.

Chen, F. F., Sousa, K. H., & West, S. G. (2005). Testing measurement invariance of second-order factor models. *Structural Equation Modeling, 12*, 471–492.

Cheung, G. W., & Rensvold, R. B. (2002). Evaluating goodness-of-fit indexes for testing measurement invariance. *Structural Equation Modeling, 9*, 233–255.

Cheung, M. W.-L. (2009). Constructing approximate confidence intervals for parameters with structural equation models. *Structural Equation Modeling, 16*, 267–294.

Cudeck, R., & MacCallum, R. C. (Eds.). (2007). *Factor analysis at 100: Historical developments and future directions*. Mahwah, NJ: Erlbaum.

Curran, P. J., & Hussong, A. M. (2003). The use of latent trajectory models in psychopathology research. *Journal of Abnormal Psychology, 112*, 526–544.

Gefen, D., Rigdon, E. E., & Straub, D. (2011). An update and extension to SEM guidelines for administrative and social science research. *Management Information Systems Quarterly, 35*, A1–A7.

Gentle, J. E. (2003). *Random number generation and Monte Carlo methods* (2nd ed.). New York: Springer.

Gibbons, R. D., & Hedeker, D. (2007). BIFACTOR [Computer software]. Chicago: Center for Health Statistics, University of Illinois at Chicago.

Gold, M. S., & Bentler, P. M. (2000). Treatments of missing data: A Monte Carlo comparison of RBHDI, iterative stochastic regression imputation, and expectation-maximization. *Structural Equation Modeling, 7*, 319–355.

Goldstein, H., & Browne, W. J. (2005). Multilevel factor analysis models for continuous and discrete data. In A. Maydeu-Olivares & J. J. McArdle (Eds.), *Contemporary psychometrics: A Festschrift for Roderick P. McDonald* (pp. 453–475). Mahwah, NJ: Erlbaum.

Gottfredson, N., Panter, A. T., Daye, C. E., Allen, W. R., & Wightman, L. F. (2009). The effects of educational diversity in a national sample of law students: Fitting multilevel latent variable models in national data with categorical indicators. *Multivariate Behavioral Research, 44*, 305–331.

Grilli, L., & Rampichini, C. (2007). Multilevel factor models for ordinal variables. *Structural Equation Modeling, 14*, 1–25.

Hancock, G. R., Lawrence, F. R., & Nevitt, J. (2000). Type I error and power of latent mean methods and MANOVA in factorially invariant and noninvariant latent variable systems. *Structural Equation Modeling, 7*, 534–556.

Hays, R. D., Liu, H., Spritzer, K., & Cella, D. (2007). Item response theory analyses of physical functioning outcomes in the Medical Outcomes Study. *Medical Care, 45*(Suppl. 1), S32–S38.

Hoogland, J. J. (1999). *The robustness of estimation methods for covariance structure analysis*. Doctoral dissertation, University of Groningen, Groningen, The Netherlands.

Hoyle, R. H., & Panter, A. T. (1995). Writing about structural equation models. In R. H. Hoyle (Ed.), *Structural equation modeling: Concepts, issues, and applications* (pp. 158–176). Thousand Oaks, CA: Sage.

Hussong, A. M., Curran, P. J., Moffitt, T. E., Caspi, A., & Carrig, M. M. (2004). Substance abuse hinders desistance in young adults' antisocial behavior. *Development and Psychopathology, 16*, 1029–1046.

Jaccard, J., & Wan, C. K. (1995). Measurement error in the analysis of interaction effects between continuous predictors using multiple regression: Multiple indicator and structural equation approaches. *Psychological Bulletin, 117*, 348–357.

Jöreskog, K. G. (1990). New developments in LISREL: Analysis of ordinal variables using polychoric correlations and weighted least squares. *Quality and Quantity, 24*, 387–404.

Jöreskog, K. G., & Moustaki, I. (2006). *Factor analysis of ordinal variables with full information maximum likelihood estimation* [Research report]. Chicago: Scientific Software International.

Jöreskog, K. G., & Sörbom, D. (2006). *LISREL 8.8 for Windows* [Computer software]. Lincolnwood, IL: Scientific Software International.

Jöreskog, K. G., & Yang, F. (1996). Nonlinear structural equation models: The Kenny–Judd model with interaction effects. In G. A. Marcoulides & R. E. Schumacker (Eds.), *Advanced structural equation modeling* (pp. 57–88). Mahwah, NJ: Erlbaum.

Kenny, D. A., & Judd, C. M. (1984). Estimating the nonlinear and interactive effects of latent variables. *Psychological Bulletin, 96*, 201–210.

Kleijnen, J. P. C. (1974–1975). *Statistical techniques in simulation* (Parts 1 and 2). New York: Marcel Dekker.

Klein, A. G., & Moosbrugger, H. (2000). Maximum likelihood estimation of latent interaction effects with the LMS method. *Psychometrika, 65*, 457–474.

LaGrange, B., & Cole, D. A. (2008). An expansion of the trait–state–occasion model: Accounting for shared method variance. *Structural Equation Modeling, 15*, 241–271.

Lei, P. W. (2006). Evaluating estimation methods for ordinal data in structural equation modeling. *Quality & Quantity, 43*, 495–507.

Little, T. D., Bovaird, J. A., & Widaman, K. F. (2006). On the merits of orthogonalizing powered and product terms: Implications for modeling interactions among latent variables. *Structural Equation Modeling, 13*, 497–519.

Marsh, H. W., Wen, Z., & Hau, K.-T. (2004). Structural equation models of latent interactions: Evaluation of alternative estimation strategies and indicator construction. *Psychological Methods, 9*, 275–300.

Marsh, H. W., Wen, Z., Hau, K.-T., Little, T. D., Bovaird, J. A., & Widaman, K. F. (2007). Unconstrained structural equation models of latent interactions: Contrasting residual- and mean-centered approaches. *Structural Equation Modeling, 14*, 570–580.

McClelland, G. H., & Judd, C. M. (1993). Statistical difficulties of detecting interactions and moderator effects. *Psychological Bulletin, 114*, 376–390.

McDonald, R. P., & Ho, M. R. (2002). Principles and practice in reporting structural equation analyses. *Psychological Methods, 7*, 64–82.

Millsap, R. E., & Tein, J. (2004). Assessing factorial invariance in ordered-categorical measures. *Multivariate Behavioral Research, 39*, 479–515.

Morin, A. J. S., Moullee, G., Maïano, C., Layet, L., Just, J.-L., & Ninot, G. (in press). Psychometric properties of the Center for Epidemiological Studies Depression Scale (CES-D) in French clinical and nonclinical adults. *Epidemiology and Public Health*.

Motl, R. W., Dishman, R. K., Trost, S. G., Saunders, R. P., Dowda, M., Felton, G., et al. (2000). Factorial validity and invariance of questionnaires measuring social-cognitive determinants of physical activity among adolescent girls. *Preventive Medicine, 31*, 584–594.

Muthén, B., & Asparouhov, T. (2006). Growth mixture analysis: Models with non-Gaussian random effects. In G. Fitzmaurice, M. Davidian, G. Verbeke, & G. Molenberghs (Eds.), *Advances in longitudinal data analysis* (pp. 143–165). Boca Raton, FL: Chapman & Hall/CRC Press.

Muthén, L. K., & Muthén, B. O. (2010). *Mplus user's guide* (6th ed.). Los Angeles: Authors.

Neale, M. C. (1998). Modeling interaction and nonlinear effects with Mx: A general approach. In R. E. Schumacker & G. A. Marcoulides (Eds.), *Interactions and nonlinear effects in structural equation modeling* (pp. 43–61). Mahwah, NJ: Erlbaum.

Nesselroade, J. R., & Cattell, R. B. (1988). *Handbook of multivariate experimental psychology* (2nd ed.). New York: Plenum.

Paxton, P., Curran, P. J., Bollen, K. A., Kirby, J., & Chen, F. (2001). Monte Carlo experiments: Design and implementation. *Structural Equation Modeling, 8*, 287–312.

Paxton, P., Hughes, M. M., & Painter, M. A. (2010). Growth in women's political representation: A longitudinal exploration of democracy, electoral system and gender quotas. *European Journal of Political Research, 49*, 25–52.

Ping, R. A., Jr. (1995). A parsimonious estimating technique for interaction and quadratic latent variables. *Journal of Marketing Research, 32*, 336–347.

Rindskopf, D. (in press). Generalized linear models. In H. Cooper, P. Camic, D. Long, A. T. Panter, D. Rindskopf, & K. Sher (Eds.), *APA handbook of research methodology in psychology*. Washington, DC: APA Books.

Ripley, B. D. (1987). *Stochastic simulation*. New York: Wiley.

Robey, R. R., & Barcikowski, R. S. (1992). Type I error and the number of iterations in Monte Carlo studies of robustness. *British Journal of Mathematical and Statistical Psychology, 45*, 283–288.

Saris, W. E., Batista-Foguet, J. M., & Coenders, G. (2007). Selection of indicators for the interaction term in structural equation models with interaction. *Quality & Quantity, 41*, 55–72.

Satorra, A., & Bentler, P. M. (1994). Corrections to test statistics and standard errors in covariance structure analysis. In A. von Eye & C. C. Clogg (Eds.), *Latent variables analysis: Applications for developmental research* (pp. 399–419). Thousand Oaks, CA: Sage.

Schreiber, J. B., Nora, A., Stage, F. K., Barlow, E. A., & King, J. (2006). Reporting structural equation modeling and confirmatory factor analysis results: A review. *Journal of Educational Research, 99*, 323–337.

Serlin, R. C. (2000). Testing for robustness in Monte Carlo studies. *Psychological Methods, 5*, 230–240.

Simons-Morton, B., Chen, R., Abroms, L., & Haynie, D. L. (2004). Latent growth curve analyses of peer and parent influences on smoking progression among early adults. *Health Psychology, 23*, 612–621.

Skrondal, A. (2000). Design and analysis of Monte Carlo experiments: Attacking the conventional wisdom. *Multivariate Behavioral Research, 35*, 137–167.

Steinmetz, H., Davidov, E., & Schmidt, P. (2011). Three approaches to estimate latent interaction effects: Intention and perceived behavioral control in the theory of planned behavior. *Methodological Innovations Online, 6*, 95–110.

Sterba, S. K. (2011). Implications of parcel-allocation variability for comparing fit of item-solutions and parcel-solutions. *Structural Equation Modeling, 18*, 554–577.

Sterba, S. K., & MacCallum, R. C. (2010). Variability in parameter estimates and model fit across random allocations of items to parcels. *Multivariate Behavioral Research, 45*, 322–358.

Stucky, B., Gottfredson, N. C., & Panter, A. T. (in press). Item factor analysis. In H. Cooper, P. Camic, D. Long, A. T. Panter, D. Rindskopf, & K. Sher (Eds.), *APA handbook of research methodology in psychology*. Washington, DC: APA Books.

Thurstone, L. L. (1947). *Multiple factor analysis*. Chicago: University of Chicago Press.

Vandenberg, R. J., & Lance, C. E. (2000). A review and synthesis of the measurement invariance literature: Suggestions, practices, and recommendations for organizational research. *Organizational Research Methods, 3*, 4–69.

Wei, M., Mallinckrodt, B., Russell, D. W., & Abraham, W. T. (2004). Maladaptive perfectionism as a mediator and moderator between adult attachment and depressive mood. *Journal of Counseling Psychology, 51*, 201–212.

Willett, J. B., & Sayer, A. G. (1994). Using covariance structure analysis to detect correlates and predictors of individual change over time. *Psychological Bulletin, 116*, 363–381.

Williams, J., & MacKinnon, D. P. (2008). Resampling and distribution of the product methods for testing indirect effects in complex models. *Structural Equation Modeling, 15*, 23–51.

Wirth, R. J., & Edwards, M. C. (2007). Item factor analysis: Current approaches and future directions. *Psychological Methods, 12*, 58–79.

Yang Jonsson, F. (1998). Modeling interaction and nonlinear effects in structural equation modeling: A step-by-step LISREL example. In R. E. Schumacker & G. A. Marcoulides (Eds.), *Interactions and nonlinear effects in structural equation modeling* (pp. 17–42). Mahwah, NJ: Erlbaum.

PART IV

BASIC APPLICATIONS

CHAPTER 22

Confirmatory Factor Analysis

Timothy A. Brown
Michael T. Moore

"Confirmatory factor analysis" (CFA) is a type of structural equation modeling that deals specifically with measurement models, that is, the relationships between observed measures or "indicators" (e.g., test items, test scores, behavioral observation ratings) and latent variables or "factors." The goal of latent variable measurement models (i.e., factor analysis) is to establish the number and nature of factors that account for the variation and covariation among a set of indicators. A factor is an unobserved variable that influences more than one observed measure and accounts for the correlations among these observed measures. In other words, the observed measures are intercorrelated because they share a common cause (i.e., they are influenced by the same underlying construct); if the latent construct were partialed out, the intercorrelations among the observed measures would be zero. Thus, a measurement model such as CFA provides a more parsimonious understanding of the covariation among a set of indicators because the number of factors is less than the number of measured variables.[1]

These concepts originate from the "common-factor model" (Thurstone, 1947), which states that each indicator in a set of observed measures is a linear function of one or more common factors and one unique factor. Factor analysis partitions the variance of each indica-

tor (derived from the sample correlation or covariance matrix) into two parts: (1) "common variance," or the variance accounted for by the latent variable(s), which is estimated on the basis of variance shared with other indicators in the analysis; and (2) "unique variance," which is a combination of reliable variance specific to the indicator (i.e., systematic latent variables that influence only one indicator) and random error variance (i.e., measurement error or unreliability in the indicator). There are two main types of analyses based on the common-factor model: exploratory factor analysis (EFA) and CFA (Jöreskog, 1969, 1971). EFA and CFA both aim to reproduce the observed relationships among a group of indicators with a smaller set of latent variables. However, EFA and CFA differ fundamentally by the number and nature of a priori specifications and restrictions made on the latent variable measurement model. EFA is a data-driven approach such that no specifications are made in regard to the number of common factors (initially) or the pattern of relationships between the common factors and the indicators (i.e., the factor loadings). Rather, the researcher employs EFA as an exploratory or descriptive data technique to determine the appropriate number of common factors, and to ascertain which measured variables are reasonable indicators of the various latent dimensions (e.g., by the size and differential magnitude of the factor loadings). In CFA, the researcher specifies the number of factors and the pattern of indicator–factor loadings in advance, as well as other parameters, such as those bearing on the independence or covariance of the factors and indicator unique variances. The prespecified factor solution is evaluated in terms of how well it reproduces the sample covariance matrix of the measured variables. Unlike EFA, CFA requires a strong empirical or conceptual foundation to guide the specification and evaluation of the factor model. Accordingly, EFA is often used early in the process of scale development and construct validation, whereas CFA is used in the later phases, when the underlying structure has been established on prior empirical and theoretical grounds. Other differences between EFA and CFA are discussed throughout this chapter (for a more detailed discussion, see Brown, 2006).

PURPOSES OF CFA

CFA can be used for a variety of purposes, such as psychometric evaluation, the detection of method effects, construct validation, and the evaluation of measurement invariance. Nowadays, CFA is almost always used in the process of scale development to examine the latent structure of a test instrument. CFA verifies the number of underlying dimensions of the instrument (factors) and the pattern of item–factor relationships (factor loadings). CFA also assists in the determination of how a test should be scored. For instance, when the latent structure is multifactorial (i.e., two or more factors), the pattern of factor loadings supported by CFA will designate how a test might be scored using subscales; that is, the number of factors is indicative of the number of subscales, and the pattern of item–factor relationships (which items load on which factors) indicates how the subscales should be scored. CFA is an important analytic tool for other aspects of psychometric evaluation, such as the estimation of scale reliability (e.g., Raykov, 2001).

Unlike EFA, the nature of relationships among the indicator unique variances can be modeled in CFA. Because of the nature of the identification restrictions in EFA, factor models must be specified under the assumption that measurement error is random. In contrast, correlated measurement error can be modeled in a CFA solution provided that this specification is substantively justified and that other identification requirements are met. When measurement error is specified to be random (i.e., the indicator unique variances are uncorrelated), the assumption is that the observed relationship between any two indicators loading on the same factor is due entirely to the shared influence of the latent variable; that is, if the factor were partialed out, the correlation of the indicators would be zero. The specification of correlated indicator uniquenesses assumes that whereas indicators are related in part because of the shared influence of the latent variable, some of their covariation is due to sources other than the common factor. In CFA, the specification of correlated errors may be justified on the basis of *method effects* that reflect additional indicator covariation that results from common assessment methods (e.g., observer ratings, questionnaires); reversed or similarly worded test items; or differential susceptibility to other influences, such as response set, demand characteristics, acquiescence, reading difficulty, or social desirability. The inability to specify correlated errors is a significant limitation of EFA because the source of covariation among indicators that is not due to the substantive latent variables may be manifested in the EFA solution as additional factors (e.g., "methods" factors stemming from the assessment of a unidimensional trait with a questionnaire comprising both positively and negatively worded items; cf. Brown, 2003; Marsh, 1996).

CFA is an indispensable analytic tool for construct validation. The results of CFA can provide compelling evidence of the convergent and discriminant validity of theoretical constructs. "Convergent validity" is indicated by evidence that different indicators of theoretically similar or overlapping constructs are strongly interrelated (e.g., symptoms purported to be manifestations of a single mental disorder load on the same factor). "Discriminant validity" is indicated by results showing that indicators of theoretically distinct constructs are not highly intercorrelated (e.g., psychiatric symptoms thought to be features of different types of disorders load on separate factors, and the factors are not so highly correlated as to indicate that a broader construct has been erroneously separated into two or more factors). One of the most elegant uses of CFA in construct validation is the analysis of multitrait–multimethod matrices (cf. Campbell & Fiske, 1959; Kenny & Kashy, 1992) aided by the fact that indicator error variances can be estimated in CFA to model method effects. A fundamental strength of CFA approaches to construct validation is that the resulting estimates of convergent and discriminant validity are adjusted for measurement error and an error theory. Thus, CFA is superior to traditional analytic methods that do not account for measurement error (e.g., ordinary least squares approaches such as correlation/multiple regression assume that variables in the analysis are free of measurement error).

In addition, CFA offers a very strong analytic framework for evaluating the equivalence of measurement models across distinct groups (e.g., demographic groups such as sexes, races, or cultures). This is accomplished by either multiple-group solutions (i.e., simultaneous CFAs in two or more groups) or multiple-indicator, multiple-cause (MIMIC) models (i.e., the factors and indicators are regressed onto observed covariates representing group membership). These capabilities permit a variety of important analytic opportunities in applied research, such as the evaluation of whether a scale's measurement properties are invariant across population subgroups (e.g., are the factors, factor loadings, item intercepts, etc., that define the latent structure of a questionnaire equivalent in males and females?). Indeed, "measurement invariance" is an important aspect of scale development, as this endeavor determines whether a testing instrument is appropriate for use in various groups (e.g., does the score issued by the test instrument reflect the same level of the underlying characteristic or ability in males and females?). Another chapter in this handbook is devoted to this topic (Millsap & Olivera-Aguilar, Chapter 23).

CFA should be employed as a precursor to structural equation models that specify structural relationships (e.g., regressions) among the latent variables. Structural equation models consist of two major components: (1) the "measurement model," which specifies the number of factors, how the various indicators are related to the factors, and the relationships among indicator errors (i.e., a CFA model); and (2) the "structural model," which specifies how the various factors are related to one another (e.g., direct or indirect effects, no relationship). When poor model fit is encountered in SEM studies, it is more likely that this is due to misspecifications in the measurement portion of the model than in the structural component. This is because there are usually more things that can go wrong in the measurement model than in the structural model (e.g., problems in the selection of observed measures, misspecified factor loadings, additional sources of covariation among observed measures that cannot be accounted for by the specified factors). Thus, although CFA is not the central analysis in SEM studies, an acceptable mea-

surement model should be established before estimating and interpreting the structural relationships among latent variables.

CFA MODEL PARAMETERS

All CFA models contain the parameters of factor loadings, unique variances, and factor variances. "Factor loadings" are the regression slopes for predicting the indicators from the factor. "Unique variance" is variance in the indicator that is not accounted for by the factors. Unique variance is typically presumed to be measurement error and is thus usually referred to as such (synonymous terms include "error variance" and "indicator unreliability"). A "factor variance" expresses the sample variability or dispersion of the factor, that is, the extent to which sample participants' relative standings on the latent dimension are similar or different. If substantively justified, a CFA can include "error covariances" (also referred to as "correlated uniquenesses," "correlated residuals," or "correlated errors"), which designate that two indicators covary for reasons other than the shared influence of the latent factor (e.g., method effects). When the CFA solution has two or more factors, a factor covariance is almost always specified to estimate the relationship between the latent dimensions.

The latent variables may be either exogenous or endogenous. An "exogenous variable" is a variable that is not caused by other variables in the model. Conversely, an "endogenous variable" is caused by one or more variables in the model (i.e., other variables in the model exert direct effects on the variable). Thus, exogenous variables can be viewed as synonymous with X, independent, or predictor (causal) variables. Similarly, endogenous variables are equivalent to Y, dependent, or criterion (outcome) variables. CFAs are typically considered to be exogenous (latent X) variable models because the latent variables are specified to be freely intercorrelated without directional relationships among them. However, when the CFA analysis includes covariates (i.e., predictors of the factors or indicators, as in MIMIC models; see Brown, 2006) or higher-order factors (e.g., superordinate dimensions specified to account for the correlations among the CFA factors), the factors are endogenous (latent Y).

A data-based example is now introduced to illustrate some of these concepts. In this example, a 10-item questionnaire of the symptoms of obsessive–compulsive disorder (OCD) has been administered to a sample of 400 outpatients with anxiety and mood disorders. Participants responded to each item on a 0- to 8-point scale. A two-factor model is anticipated; that is, the first five items ($X1$–$X5$) are conceptualized as indicators of the latent construct of Obsessions, and the remaining five items ($X6$–$X10$) are conjectured to be features of the underlying dimension of Compulsions. A method effect (i.e., error covariance) was anticipated for items $X9$ and $X10$ because these items were reverse-worded (i.e., unlike the other eight items, these items were phrased in the nonsymptomatic direction). The posited CFA measurement model is presented in Figure 22.1. Per conventional path diagram notation, the latent variables are depicted by circles, and indicators by squares or rectangles. Figure 22.1 also provides the LISREL notation (Greek symbols) used to indicate the various parameters in this CFA model (Jöreskog & Sörbom, 1996). Factor loadings are symbolized by lambdas (λ), which are subscripted by two numbers to denote the order of the factors and indicators, respectively (e.g.,

$\lambda_{2,1}$ = the second indicator, $X2$, loads on the first factor, Obsessions). The unidirectional arrows ($\rightarrow$) from the factors to the indicators depict direct effects (regressions) of the latent dimensions onto the observed measures; the specific regression coefficients are the λ's. Thetas (Θ) represent matrices of indicator error variances and covariances: Θ_δ in the case of indicators of latent X variables, and Θ_ε for indicators of latent Y variables. For notational ease, the symbols δ and ε are often used in place of θ_δ and θ_ε, respectively, in reference to elements of Θ_δ and Θ_ε (as in Figure 22.1). Although unidirectional arrows connect the thetas to the observed measures, these arrows are not regressive paths (i.e., Θ_δ and Θ_ε are symmetric variance–covariance matrices consisting of error variances on the diagonal, and error covariances, if any, in the off-diagonal). In fact, some notational systems do not use directional arrows in the depiction of error variances to avoid this potential source of confusion (one notational variation is to symbolize error variances with ovals because, like

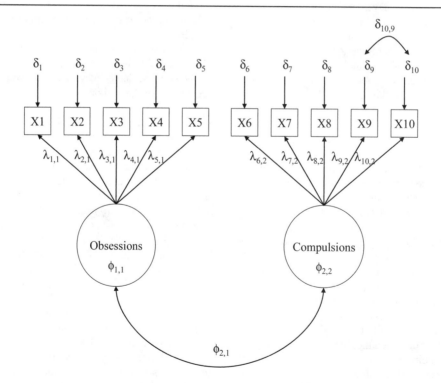

FIGURE 22.1. Two-factor measurement model of obsessions and compulsions.

latent variables, measurement errors are not observed). Factor variances and covariances are notated by phi (ϕ) and psi (ψ) in latent X and latent Y models, respectively. Curved, bidirectional arrows are used to symbolize covariances (correlations) among factors (e.g., $\phi_{2,1}$ reflects the covariance between Obsessions and Compulsions).

In practice, CFA is often confined to the analysis of variance–covariance structures. In this case, the aforementioned parameters (factor loadings, error variances and covariances, factor variances and covariances) are estimated to reproduce the input variance–covariance matrix. The analysis of covariance structures is based on the assumption that indicators are measured as deviations from their means (i.e., all indicator means equal zero). However, the CFA model can be expanded to include the analysis of mean structures, in which case the solution also strives to reproduce the observed sample means of the indicators (which are included along with the sample variances and covariances as input data). The analysis of mean structures is the topic of Chapter 24 by Green and Thompson, this volume.

CFA MODEL SPECIFICATION

Types of Parameters

There are three types of parameters that can be specified in a CFA model: free, fixed, or constrained. A "free parameter" is unknown, and the researcher allows the analysis to find its optimal value that, in tandem with other model estimates, minimizes the differences between the observed and predicted variance–covariance matrices. A "fixed parameter" is prespecified by the researcher to be a specific value, most commonly either 1.0 (e.g., in the case of marker indicators or factor variances to define the metric of a latent variable; see next section) or 0 (e.g., the absence of indicator cross-loadings or error covariances). A third type of estimate is a "constrained parameter," which, like a free parameter, is unknown. However, the parameter is not free to be any value; rather, the specification places restrictions on the values it may assume. The most common type of constrained parameter is an "equality constraint," in which some of the parameters in the CFA solutions are restricted to be equal in value. For instance, equality constraints are used in the evaluation of measurement invariance to determine whether the measurement parameters of the CFA model (e.g., factor loadings) are equivalent in subgroups of the sample (see Millsap & Olivera-Aguilar, Chapter 23, this volume).

The output of CFA can render parameter estimates in three different metrics: completely standardized, unstandardized, and partially standardized. In the case of a "completely standardized" estimate, both the latent variable and the indicator are in standardized metrics (i.e., $M = 0$, $SD = 1$). For instance, if an indicator is specified to load on only one factor (as is true for each item in the Figure 22.1 measurement model), the completely standardized factor loading can be interpreted as the correlation between the indicator and the factor (although, strictly speaking, this estimate is a standardized regressive path reflecting the degree of standardized score change in the indicator given a standardized unit increase in the factor). In many popular software programs (e.g., SPSS), EFA is exclusively a completely standardized analysis (i.e., a correlation matrix is used as input and all results are provided in the completely standardized metric). However, unlike EFA, the results of CFA also include an "unstandardized solution" (parameter estimates expressed in the original metrics of the latent variables and indicators), and possibly a "partially standardized solution" (relationships where either the indicator or the latent variable is standardized and the other is unstandardized). Although completely standardized and unstandardized estimates are usually the primary focus in applied CFA research, partially standardized estimates can also be informative in some contexts. For example, when a latent variable is regressed onto a "dummy code" (e.g., a binary variable indicating whether the participant is male or female), the resulting partially standardized path is more substantively meaningful than a completely standardized estimate (e.g., when the latent variable is standardized and the dummy code is unstandardized, the partially standardized path estimate reflects the extent to which males and females differ on the latent variable in SD units; cf. Cohen's d index of effect size; Cohen, 1988).

Model Identification

To estimate a CFA solution, the measurement model must be "identified." A model is identified if, on the basis of known information (i.e., the variances and covariances in the sample input matrix), a unique set of estimates for each parameter in the model can be obtained (factor loadings, factor covariances, etc.). The two necessary (but not sufficient) aspects of CFA model identification are scaling the latent variables and statistical identification. Additional rules for model identification in SEM are discussed by Kenny and

Milan (Chapter 9, this volume; see also Brown, 2006, for identification rules specific to CFA).

Latent variables have no inherent metrics; thus, their units of measurement must be defined by the researcher. In CFA, this is accomplished in one of two ways. The most widely used method is the "marker indicator" approach, whereby the unstandardized factor loading of one observed measure per factor is fixed to a value of 1.0. As will be illustrated shortly, this specification serves the function of passing the metric of the marker indicator along to the latent variable. In the second method, the variance of the latent variable is fixed to a value of 1.0. Although most CFA results are identical to the marker indicator approach when the factor variance is fixed to 1.0, this method does not produce an unstandardized solution. The absence of an unstandardized solution often contraindicates the use of this approach (e.g., when the researcher is interested in evaluating the measurement invariance of a test instrument; see Millsap & Olivera-Aguilar, Chapter 23, this volume).

"Statistical identification" refers to the concept that a CFA solution can be estimated only if the number of freely estimated parameters (e.g., factor loadings, uniquenesses, factor correlations) does not exceed the number of pieces of information in the input matrix (e.g., number of sample variances and covariances). A model is "overidentified" when the number of knowns (i.e., individual elements of the input matrix) exceeds the number of unknowns (i.e., the freely estimated parameters of the CFA solution). The difference in the number of knowns and the number of unknowns constitutes the model's degrees of freedom (df). Overidentified solutions have positive df. For overidentified models, goodness-of-fit evaluation can be implemented to determine how well the CFA solution was able to reproduce the relationships among indicators observed in the sample data. If the number of knowns equals the number of unknowns, the model has zero df and is said to be "just-identified." Although just-identified models can be estimated, goodness-of-fit evaluation does not apply because these solutions perfectly reproduce the input variance–covariance matrix. When the number of freely estimated parameters exceeds the number of pieces of information in the input matrix (e.g., when too many factors are specified for the number of indicators in the sample data), df is negative and the model is "underidentified." Underidentified models cannot be estimated because the solution cannot arrive at a unique set of parameter estimates.

In some cases, the researcher may encounter an "empirically underidentified" solution. In these solutions the measurement model is statistically just- or overidentified, but there are aspects of the input data or the model specification that prevent the analysis from arriving at a valid set of parameter estimates (i.e., the estimation will not reach a final solution, or the final solution will include one or more parameter estimates that have out-of-range values, such as a negative indicator error variance). Although the various causes and remedies for empirically underidentified solutions are beyond the scope of this chapter (for further discussion, see Brown, 2006; Wothke, 1993), a basic example would be the situation where the observed measure selected to be the marker indicator is in fact uncorrelated with all other indicators of the latent variable (thus, the metric of the latent variable would be unidentified).

Example

The sample data for the measurement model of the OCD questionnaire are provided in Table 22.1, which specifically presents the sample standard deviations (SD) and correlations (r) for the 10 questionnaire items. These data are read into the latent variable software program and converted into variances and covariances, which are used by the analysis as the input matrix (e.g., $VAR_{X1} = SD_{X1}^2$; $COV_{X1,X2} = r_{X1,X2}SD_{X1}SD_{X2}$). Generally, it is preferable to use a raw data file as input for CFA (e.g., to avoid rounding error and to adjust for missing or non-normal data, if needed). In this example, however, the sample SD's and r's are presented to foster the illustration of concepts covered later in this chapter. Also, the data in Table 22.1 can be readily used as input if the reader is interested in replicating the analyses presented in this chapter.

The measurement model in Figure 22.1 is overidentified with df = 33. The model df indicates that there are 33 more elements in the input matrix than there are freely estimated parameters in the two-factor CFA model. Specifically, there are 55 variances and covariances in the input matrix (cf. Table 22.1) and 22 freely estimated parameters in the CFA model; that is, eight factor loadings (the factor loadings of X1 and X6 are not included in the tally because they are fixed to 1.0 to serve as marker indicators), two factor variances, one factor covariance, 10 error variances, and one error covariance (see Figure 22.1). With the exception of X9 and X10, all error covariances are fixed to zero (no curved, double-headed arrows connecting the unique variances

TABLE 22.1. Sample Correlations and Standard Deviations (*SD*) for the Ten-Item Questionnaire of Obsessive and Compulsive Symptoms (*N* = 400)

	X1	X2	X3	X4	X5	X6	X7	X8	X9	X10
X1	1.000									
X2	0.516	1.000								
X3	0.563	0.465	1.000							
X4	0.453	0.462	0.395	1.000						
X5	0.457	0.479	0.480	0.436	1.000					
X6	0.331	0.133	0.210	0.214	0.147	1.000				
X7	0.286	0.170	0.211	0.187	0.148	0.633	1.000			
X8	0.287	0.177	0.253	0.200	0.196	0.639	0.550	1.000		
X9	0.247	0.094	0.130	0.166	0.114	0.519	0.500	0.467	1.000	
X10	0.243	0.128	0.112	0.118	0.156	0.463	0.430	0.419	0.621	1.000
SD:	2.078	1.346	1.958	1.247	1.588	1.820	2.460	2.368	2.666	1.745

of items *X*1 through *X*8), which assumes measurement error in these indicators is random.

A noteworthy aspect of the model specification depicted in Figure 22.1 is that each indicator loads on only one factor—this parameterization does not include "cross-loadings," where an indicator is predicted by more than one factor (i.e., all cross-loadings are fixed to zero). This is another key difference between EFA and CFA. In traditional EFA, all possible relationships (factor loadings) between the indicators and factors are freely estimated in the factor loading matrix. Thus, for EFA models with two or more factors, a mathematical transformation referred to as "rotation" is conducted to foster the interpretability of the solution by maximizing (primary) factor loadings close to 1.0 and minimizing cross-loadings close to 0.0. Rotation does not apply to CFA because most or all indicator cross-loadings are typically fixed to zero. Consequently, CFA models are usually more parsimonious than EFA solutions because, while primary loadings and factor correlations are freely estimated, no other relationships are specified between the indicators and factors.[2]

CFA MODEL ESTIMATION

The objective of CFA is to obtain estimates for each parameter of the measurement model (i.e., factor loadings, factor variances and covariances, indicator error variances and possibly error covariances) that produce a predicted variance–covariance matrix (also referred to as the "model-implied variance–covariance matrix") that resembles the sample variance–covariance matrix as closely as possible. For instance, in overidentified

models (e.g., the model in Figure 22.1), perfect fit is rarely achieved. Thus, the goal of the analysis is to find a set of parameter estimates (e.g., factor loadings, factor correlations) that yield a predicted variance–covariance matrix that best reproduces the input variance–covariance matrix.

In the example shown in Figure 22.1, the following three equations provide the model-implied covariances of the 10 indicators in this measurement model. Given the absence of additional restrictions in this model (e.g., equality constraints on the factor loadings), the variances of the indicators are just-identified (i.e., guaranteed to be perfectly reproduced by the CFA solution; see "CFA Model Evaluation"). For two indicators that load on the same factor (and do not load on any other factors), the model-implied covariance is the product of their factor loadings and the factor variance. For instance, the predicted covariance of *X*2 and *X*3 is

$$COV(X2, X3) = \lambda_{2,1}\phi_{1,1}\lambda_{3,1} \qquad \textbf{(22.1)}$$

If the two indicators load on different factors (but do not cross-load on other factors), the model-implied covariance is the product of their factor loadings and the factor covariance; for example, for *X*2 and *X*7:

$$COV(X2, X7) = \lambda_{2,1}\phi_{2,1}\lambda_{7,2} \qquad \textbf{(22.2)}$$

It is worth mentioning here that for a given indicator set and factor model (e.g., a two-factor solution), factor correlation estimates are usually larger in CFA than in EFA with oblique rotation (unlike orthogonal rotations, oblique rotations in EFA allow the factors to be intercorrelated). This stems from how the factor loading matrix is parameterized in CFA and EFA. Unlike EFA where the factor loading matrix is saturated, in CFA most if not all cross-loadings are fixed to zero. Thus, the model-implied correlation of indicators loading on separate factors in CFA is reproduced solely by the primary loadings and the factor correlation (see Equation 22.2). Compared to oblique EFA (where the model-implied correlation of indicators with primary loadings on separate factors can be estimated in part by the indicator cross-loadings), in CFA there is more burden on the factor correlation to reproduce the correlation between indicators specified to load on different factors because there are no cross-loadings to assist in this model-implied estimate (i.e., in the mathematical process to arrive at CFA parameter estimates that best reproduce the sample matrix, the magnitude of the factor correlation estimate may be increased somewhat to better account for the relationships of indicators that load on separate factors).

Finally, if the model specification includes an indicator error covariance, this estimate must be added to Equation 22.1 or 22.2 to yield the model-implied covariance for the indicators. For the X9 and X10 indicators in Figure 22.1, the equation would be:

$$COV(X9, X10) = \lambda_{9,2}\phi_{2,2}\lambda_{10,2} + \delta_{10,9} \qquad (22.3)$$

The equations are illustrated in subsequent sections of this chapter using the parameter estimates from the OCD questionnaire example.

The estimation process in CFA (and SEM, in general) entails a "fitting function," a mathematical operation to minimize the difference between the sample- and model-implied variance–covariance matrices. By far, the fitting function most widely used in applied CFA and SEM research is "maximum likelihood" (ML), the default statistical estimator in most latent variable software programs. The underlying principle of ML estimation is to find the model parameter estimates that would maximize the probability of observing the available data if the data were collected from the same population again. In other words, ML aims to find the parameter values that make the observed data most likely (or conversely, maximize the likelihood of the parameters given the data). Finding the parameter estimates for an overidentified CFA model is an "iterative" procedure. That is, the computer program (e.g., Mplus, LISREL, EQS, or Amos) begins with an initial set of parameter estimates (referred to as "starting values" or "initial estimates," which can be automatically

generated by the software or specified by the user), and repeatedly refines these estimates in effort to minimize the difference between the sample- and model-implied variance–covariance matrices. Each refinement of the parameter estimates is an "iteration." The program conducts internal checks to evaluate its progress in obtaining the best set of parameter estimates. "Convergence" is reached when the program arrives at a set of parameter estimates that cannot be improved upon to further reduce the difference between the input and predicted matrices.

It is important to note that ML is only one of several methods that can be used to estimate CFA models. ML has several requirements that render it an unsuitable estimator in some circumstances. Some key assumptions of ML are that (1) the sample size is large (asymptotic); (2) the indicators of the factors have been measured on continuous scales (i.e., approximate interval-level data); and (3) the distribution of the indicators is multivariate normal. Although the actual parameter estimates (e.g., factor loadings) may not be affected, non-normality in ML analysis can result in biased standard errors (hence, faulty significance tests) and goodness-of-fit statistics. If non-normality is extreme (e.g., marked floor effects, as would occur if the majority of the sample responded to items using the lowest response choice—0 on the 0- to 8-point scale of the OCD questionnaire if the symptoms were infrequently endorsed by participants), then ML will produce incorrect parameter estimates (i.e., the assumption of a linear model is invalid). Thus, in the case of non-normal, continuous indicators, it is better to use a different estimator, such as ML with robust standard errors and χ^2 (e.g., Satorra & Bentler, 1994). These robust estimators provide the same parameter estimates as ML, but both the goodness-of-fit statistics (e.g., χ^2) and standard errors of the parameter estimates are corrected for non-normality in large samples. If one or more of the factor indicators is categorical (or non-normality is extreme), normal theory ML should not be used. In this instance, estimators such as mean- and variance-adjusted weighted least squares (e.g., WLSMV; Muthén, du Toit, & Spisic, 1997) and unweighted least squares (ULS) are more appropriate. WLS estimators can also be used for non-normal, continuous data, although robust ML is often preferred given its ability to outperform WLS in small and medium-size samples (Curran, West, & Finch, 1996; Hu, Bentler, & Kano, 1992). For more details, the reader is referred to Lei and Wu (Chapter 10, this volume).

CFA MODEL EVALUATION

Using the information in Table 22.1 as input, the two-factor model presented in Figure 22.1was fit to the data using the Mplus software program (version 6.0; Muthén & Muthén, 1998–2010). The Mplus syntax and selected output are presented in Table 22.2. As shown in the Mplus syntax, both the indicator correlation matrix and standard deviations (TYPE = STD CORRELATION;) were input because this CFA analyzed a variance–covariance matrix. The CFA model specification occurs under the "MODEL:" portion of the Mplus syntax. For instance, the line "OBS BY X1-X5" specifies that a latent variable to be named "OBS" (Obsessions) is measured by indicators $X1$ through $X5$. The Mplus programming language contains several defaults that are commonly implemented aspects of model specification (but nonetheless can be easily overridden by additional programming). For instance, Mplus automatically sets the first indicator after the "BY" keyword as the marker indicator (e.g., $X1$) and freely estimates the factor loadings for the remaining indicators in the list ($X2$ through $X5$). By default, all error variances (uniquenesses) are freely estimated, and all error covariances and indicator cross-loadings are fixed to zero; the factor variances and covariances are also freely estimated by default. These and other convenience features in Mplus are very appealing to the experienced CFA researcher. However, novice users should become fully aware of these system defaults to ensure their models are specified as intended. In addition to specifying that $X5$ through $X10$ are indicators of the second factor (COM; Compulsions), the Mplus "MODEL": syntax includes the line "$X9$ WITH $X10$." In Mplus, "WITH" is the keyword for "correlated with"; in this case, this allows the X9 and X10 uniquenesses to covary (based on the expectation that a method effect exists between these items because only these two items of the OCD questionnaire are reverse-worded). Thus, this statement overrides the Mplus default of fixing error covariances to zero.

Three major aspects of the results should be examined to evaluate the acceptability of the CFA model: (1) overall goodness of fit; (2) the presence or absence of localized areas of strain in the solution (i.e., specific points of ill fit); and (3) the interpretability, size, and statistical significance of the model's parameter estimates. As discussed earlier, goodness of fit pertains to how well the parameter estimates of the CFA solution (i.e., factor loadings, factor correlations, error covariances) are able to reproduce the relationships that were observed in the sample data. For example, as seen in Table 22.2 (under the heading, "STDYX Standardization"), the completely standardized factor loadings for $X1$ and $X2$ are .760 and .688, respectively. Using Equation 22.1, the model-implied correlation of these indicators is the product of their factor loading estimates; that is, .760(1) (.688) = .523 (the factor variance = 1 in the completely standardized solution). Goodness of fit addresses the extent to which these model-implied relationships are equivalent to the relationships seen in the sample data (e.g., as shown in Table 22.1, the sample correlation of $X1$ and $X2$ was .516, so the model-implied estimate differed by only .007 standardized units).

There are a variety of goodness-of-fit statistics that provide a global descriptive summary of the ability of the model to reproduce the input covariance matrix. The classic goodness-of-fit index is χ^2. In this example, the model $\chi^2 = 46.16$, $df = 33$, $p = .06$. The critical value of the χ^2 distribution ($\alpha = .05$, $df = 33$) is 47.40. Because the model χ^2 (46.16) does not exceed this critical value (computer programs provide the exact probability value, e.g., $p = .06$), the null hypothesis that the sample- and model-implied variance–covariance matrices do not differ is retained. On the other hand, a statistically significant χ^2 would lead to rejection of the null hypothesis, meaning that the model estimates do not sufficiently reproduce the sample variances and covariances (i.e., the model does not fit the data well).

Although χ^2 is steeped in the traditions of ML and SEM, it is rarely used in applied research as a sole index of model fit. There are salient drawbacks of this statistic, including the fact that it is highly sensitive to sample size (i.e., solutions involving large samples would be routinely rejected on the basis of χ^2 even when differences between the sample and model-implied matrices are negligible). Nevertheless, χ^2 is used for other purposes, such as nested model comparisons (discussed later in this chapter) and the calculation of other goodness-of-fit indices. While χ^2 is routinely reported in CFA research, other fit indices are usually relied on more heavily in the evaluation of model fit.

Indeed, in addition to χ^2, the most widely accepted global goodness-of-fit indices are the standardized root mean square residual (SRMR; Bentler, 1995), root mean square error of approximation (RMSEA; Browne & Cudeck, 1993; Steiger & Lind, 1980), the Tucker–Lewis index (TLI; Tucker & Lewis, 1973), and the comparative fit index (CFI; Bentler, 1990). In practice, it is suggested that each of these fit indices be reported and considered because they provide different information

TABLE 22.2. Mplus Syntax and Selected Output for CFA Model of Obsessions and Compulsions

```
TITLE: TWO-FACTOR CFA OF OBSESSIONS AND COMPULSIONS
DATA:
  FILE IS CFA.DAT;
  NOBSERVATIONS = 400;
  TYPE = STD CORRELATION;
VARIABLE:
  NAMES ARE X1-X10;
ANALYSIS:
  ESTIMATOR IS ML;
MODEL:
  OBS BY X1-X5;
  COM BY X6-X10;
  X9 WITH X10;
OUTPUT: STANDARDIZED MODINDICES(4) RES;
```

MODEL RESULTS

		Estimate	S.E.	Est./S.E.	Two-Tailed P-Value
OBS	BY				
X1		1.000	0.000	999.000	999.000
X2		0.586	0.047	12.479	0.000
X3		0.874	0.068	12.764	0.000
X4		0.488	0.043	11.277	0.000
X5		0.658	0.055	11.922	0.000
COM	BY				
X6		1.000	0.000	999.000	999.000
X7		1.215	0.079	15.355	0.000
X8		1.168	0.076	15.324	0.000
X9		1.100	0.088	12.526	0.000
X10		0.639	0.059	10.912	0.000
COM	WITH				
OBS		0.948	0.159	5.954	0.000
X9	WITH				
X10		1.249	0.184	6.781	0.000
Variances					
OBS		2.490	0.305	8.162	0.000
COM		2.322	0.244	9.529	0.000
Residual Variances					
X1		1.817	0.183	9.956	0.000
X2		0.953	0.083	11.412	0.000
X3		1.924	0.173	11.127	0.000
X4		0.958	0.078	12.274	0.000
X5		1.437	0.121	11.866	0.000
X6		0.983	0.120	8.181	0.000
X7		2.607	0.242	10.785	0.000
X8		2.428	0.224	10.818	0.000
X9		4.280	0.343	12.484	0.000
X10		2.088	0.161	12.963	0.000

(cont.)

TABLE 22.2. *(cont.)*

STANDARDIZED MODEL RESULTS

STDYX Standardization

		Estimate	S.E.	Est./S.E.	Two-Tailed P-Value
OBS	BY				
X1		0.760	0.029	26.282	0.000
X2		0.688	0.033	20.838	0.000
X3		0.705	0.032	22.029	0.000
X4		0.618	0.037	16.747	0.000
X5		0.655	0.035	18.783	0.000
COM	BY				
X6		0.838	0.023	36.280	0.000
X7		0.754	0.028	27.322	0.000
X8		0.752	0.028	27.185	0.000
X9		0.630	0.035	17.906	0.000
X10		0.559	0.039	14.236	0.000
COM	WITH				
OBS		0.394	0.052	7.563	0.000
X9	WITH				
X10		0.418	0.045	9.343	0.000
Variances					
OBS		1.000	0.000	999.000	999.000
COM		1.000	0.000	999.000	999.000
Residual Variances					
X1		0.422	0.044	9.592	0.000
X2		0.527	0.045	11.620	0.000
X3		0.503	0.045	11.147	0.000
X4		0.618	0.046	13.533	0.000
X5		0.571	0.046	12.510	0.000
X6		0.297	0.039	7.677	0.000
X7		0.432	0.042	10.381	0.000
X8		0.434	0.042	10.423	0.000
X9		0.604	0.044	13.633	0.000
X10		0.688	0.044	15.664	0.000

R-SQUARE

Observed Variable	Estimate	S.E.	Est./S.E.	Two-Tailed P-Value
X1	0.578	0.044	13.141	0.000
X2	0.473	0.045	10.419	0.000
X3	0.497	0.045	11.015	0.000
X4	0.382	0.046	8.374	0.000
X5	0.429	0.046	9.392	0.000
X6	0.703	0.039	18.140	0.000
X7	0.568	0.042	13.661	0.000
X8	0.566	0.042	13.592	0.000
X9	0.396	0.044	8.953	0.000
X10	0.312	0.044	7.118	0.000

about model fit (i.e., absolute fit, fit adjusting for model parsimony, fit relative to a null model; see Brown, 2006, for further details). Considered together, these indices provide a more conservative and reliable evaluation of the fit of the model. In one of the more comprehensive and widely cited evaluations of cutoff criteria, the findings of simulation studies by Hu and Bentler (1999) suggest the following guidelines for acceptable model fit: (1) SRMR values close to .08 or below; (2) RMSEA values close to .06 or below; and (3) CFI and TLI values close to .95 or greater. For the two-factor solution in this example, each of these guidelines was consistent with acceptable overall fit; SRMR = .035, RMSEA = 0.032, TLI = 0.99, CFI = .99 (provided by Mplus but not shown in Table 22.2). However, it should be noted that this topic is debated by methodologists. For instance, some researchers assert that these guidelines are far too conservative for many types of models (e.g., measurement models that comprise many indicators and several factors in which the majority of cross-loadings and error covariances are fixed to zero; see Marsh, Hau, & Wen, 2004). Additional information on the evaluation of model goodness of fit can be found in West, Taylor, and Wu (Chapter 13, this volume).

The second aspect of model evaluation is to determine whether there are specific areas of ill fit in the solution. A limitation of goodness-of-fit statistics (e.g., SRMR, RMSEA, CFI) is that they provide a *global*, descriptive indication of the ability of the model to reproduce the observed relationships among the indicators in the input matrix. However, in some instances, overall goodness-of-fit indices suggest acceptable fit despite the fact that some relationships among indicators in the sample data have not been reproduced adequately (or alternatively, some model-implied relationships may markedly exceed the associations seen in the data). This outcome is more apt to occur in complex models (e.g., models that entail an input matrix that comprises a large set of indicators) where the sample matrix is reproduced reasonably well on the whole, and the presence of a few poorly reproduced relationships has less impact on the global summary of model fit. On the other hand, overall goodness-of-fit indices may indicate that a model poorly reproduced the sample matrix. However, these indices do not provide information on the reasons why the model fit the data poorly (e.g., misspecification of indicator–factor relationships, failure to model salient error covariances).

Two statistics that are frequently used to identify specific areas of misfit in a CFA solution are *standard-*

ized residuals and *modification indices*. A residual reflects the difference between the observed sample value and model-implied estimate for each indicator variance and covariance (e.g., the deviation between the sample covariance and the model-implied covariance of indicators $X1$ and $X2$). When standardized, these residuals are analogous to standard scores in a sampling distribution and can be interpreted like z-scores. Stated another way, these values can be considered conceptually as the number of standard deviations by which the residuals differ from the zero-value residuals associated with a perfectly fitting model. For instance, a standardized residual at a value of 1.96 or higher would indicate significant additional covariance between a pair of indicators that was not reproduced by the model's parameter estimates. Modification indices can be computed for each fixed parameter (e.g., parameters that are fixed to zero, such as indicator cross-loadings and error covariances) and each constrained parameter in the model (e.g., parameter estimates that are constrained to be the same value). The modification index reflects an approximation of how much the overall model χ^2 will decrease if the fixed or constrained parameter is freely estimated. Because the modification index can be conceptualized as a χ^2 statistic with 1 df, indices of 3.84 or greater (i.e., the critical value of χ^2 at $p < .05$, $df = 1$) suggest that the overall fit of the model could be significantly improved if the fixed or constrained parameter were freely estimated. For instance, when the two-factor model is specified without the $X9$–$X10$ error covariance, the model $\chi^2(34) = 109.50$, $p < .001$, and the modification index for this parameter is 65.20 (not shown in Table 22.2). This suggests that the model χ^2 is expected to decrease by roughly 65.20 units if the error covariance of these two indicators is freely estimated. As can be seen, this is an approximation because the model χ^2 actually decreased 63.34 units (109.50 – 46.16) when this error covariance is included. Because modification indices are also sensitive to sample size, software programs provide expected parameter change (EPC) values for each modification index. As the name implies, EPC values are an estimate of how much the parameter would be expected to change in a positive or negative direction if it were freely estimated in a subsequent analysis. In the current example, the completely standardized EPC for the $X9$–$X10$ correlated error was .480. Like the modification index, this is an approximation (as seen in Table 22.2, the estimate for the correlated error of $X9$ and $X10$ was .420). Although standardized residuals and modification indices provide specific information for how the fit of the model can be improved, such revisions should only be pursued if they can be justified on empirical or conceptual grounds (e.g., MacCallum, Roznowski, & Necowitz, 1992). Atheoretical specification searches (i.e., revising the model solely on the basis of large standardized residuals or modification indices) will often result in further model misspecification and overfitting (e.g., inclusion of unnecessary parameter estimates due to chance associations in the sample data).

The final major aspect of CFA model evaluation pertains to the interpretability, strength, and statistical significance of the parameter estimates. The parameter estimates (e.g., factor loadings and factor correlations) should only be interpreted in the context of a good-fitting solution. If the model does not provide a good fit to the data, the parameter estimates are likely biased (incorrect). For example, without the error covariance in the model, the factor loading estimates for $X9$ and $X10$ are considerably larger than the factor loadings shown in Table 22.2 because the solution must strive to reproduce the observed relationship between these indicators solely through the factor loadings. In context of a good-fitting model, the parameter estimates should first be evaluated to ensure that they make statistical and substantive sense. The parameter estimates should not take on out-of-range values (often referred to as "Heywood cases") such as a negative indicator error variance. These results may be indicative of model specification error or problems with the sample- or model-implied matrices (e.g., a non-positive definite matrix, small N). Thus, the model and sample data must be viewed with caution to rule out more serious causes of these outcomes (again, for further discussion, see Brown, 2006; Wothke, 1993). From a substantive standpoint, the parameters should be of a magnitude and direction that is in accord with conceptual or empirical reasoning (e.g., each indicator should be strongly and significantly related to its respective factor, and the size and direction of the factor correlations should be consistent with expectations). Small or statistically nonsignificant estimates may be indicative of unnecessary parameters (e.g., a nonsalient error covariance or indicator cross-loading). In addition, such estimates may highlight indicators that are not good measures of the factors (i.e., a small and nonsignificant primary loading may suggest that the indicator should be removed from the measurement model). On the other hand, extremely large parameter estimates may be substantively problematic. For example, if the factor correlations approach 1.0 in a multifactorial solution, there is strong evidence to question whether the latent variables represent distinct constructs (i.e., they have poor discriminant validity). If two factors are highly overlapping, the model could be respecified by collapsing the dimensions into a single factor. If the fit of the respecified model is acceptable, it is usually favored because of its better parsimony.

Selected results for the two-factor solution are presented in Table 22.2. The unstandardized and completely standardized estimates can be found under the headings "MODEL RESULTS" and "STANDARDIZED MODEL RESULTS," respectively (partially standardized estimates have been deleted from the Mplus output). Starting with the completely standardized solution, the factor loadings can be interpreted along the lines of standardized regression coefficients in multiple regression. For instance, the factor loading estimate for $X1$ is .760, which would be interpreted to indicate that a standardized unit increase in the Obsessions factor is associated with a .76 standardized score increase in $X1$. However, because $X1$ loads on only one factor, this estimate can also be interpreted as the correlation between $X1$ and the Obsessions latent variable. Accordingly, squaring the factor loading provides the proportion of variance in the indicator that is explained by the factor; for example, 58% of the variance in $X1$ is accounted for by Obsessions ($.76^2 = .58$). In the factor analysis literature, these estimates are referred to as "communalities" (also provided in the Mplus output in Table 22.2 under the "R-SQUARE" heading).

The completely standardized estimates under the "Residual Variances" heading (see Table 22.2) represent the proportion of variance in the indicators that has not been explained by the latent variables (i.e., unique variance). For example, these results indicate that 42% of the variance in $X1$ was not accounted for by the Obsessions factor. Note that the analyst could readily hand-calculate these estimates by subtracting the indicator communality from one (e.g., $\delta_1 = 1 - \lambda_{1,1}^2 = 1 - .76^2 = .42$). Recall that we previously stated that the indicator variances in this model are just-identified (not a potential source of poor fit in this solution). Accordingly, it can be seen that the sum of the indicator communality (λ^2) and the residual variance (δ) will always be 1.0 (e.g., $X1$: $.578 + .422$). Finally, the completely standardized results also provide the correlation of the Obsessions and Compulsions factors ($\phi_{2,1} = .394$) and the correlated error of the $X9$ and $X10$ indicators ($\delta_{10,9} = .418$). Using these estimates, the model-implied correlations for the 10 indicators can be computed using Equations 22.1 through 22.3. For instance, using

Equation 22.1, the model-implied correlation for the $X2$ and $X3$ indicators is $.688(1).705 = .485$. Inserting the completely standardized estimates into Equation 22.2 yields the following model-implied correlation between $X2$ and $X7$: $.688(.394).754 = .204$. Per Equation 22.3, the correlation of $X9$ and $X10$ that is predicted by the model's parameter estimates is $[.630(.559)] + .268 = .620$.[3] Comparison of the sample correlations in Table 22.1 indicates that these relationships were well approximated by the solution's parameter estimates. This is further reflected by satisfactory global goodness-of-fit statistics, as well as standardized residuals and modification indices indicating no salient areas of strain in the solution.

The first portion of the Mplus results shown in Table 22.2 is the unstandardized factor solution (under the heading "MODEL RESULTS"). In addition to each unstandardized estimate (under the "Estimate" column), Mplus provides the standard error of the estimate ("S.E."), the test ratio which can be interpreted as a z-statistic ("Est./S.E."; i.e., values greater than 1.96 are significant at $\alpha = .05$, two-tailed), and the exact two-sided probability value. In more recent versions of this software program, Mplus also provides standard errors and test statistics for completely (and partially) standardized estimates (also shown in Table 22.2). The standard errors and significance tests for the unstandardized factor loadings for $X1$ and $X6$ are unavailable because these variables were used as marker indicators for the Obsessions and Compulsions factors, respectively (i.e., their unstandardized loadings were fixed to 1.0). The variances for the Obsessions and Compulsions latent variables are 2.49 and 2.32, respectively. These estimates can be calculated using the sample variances of the marker indicators multiplied by their respective communalities. As noted earlier, the communality for $X1$ was .578, indicating that 57.8% of the variance in this indicator was explained by the Obsessions factor. Thus, 57.8% of the sample variance of $X1$ ($SD^2 = 2.078^2 = 4.318$; cf. Table 22.1) is passed along as variance of the Obsessions latent variable; that is, $4.318(.578) = 2.49$. As in the completely standardized solution, the factor loadings are regression coefficients expressing the direct effects of the latent variables on the indicators, but in the unstandardized metric (e.g., a unit increase in Obsessions is associated with a .586 increase in $X2$). The "COM WITH OBS" estimate (0.948) is the factor covariance of Obsessions and Compulsions, and the "X9 WITH X10" estimate (1.249) is the error cova-

riance of these indicators. The residual variances are the indicator uniquenesses or errors (i.e., variance in the indicators that was not explained by the Obsessions and Compulsions latent variables); for example, $\delta_1 = 4.318(.422) = 1.82$ (again, .422 is the proportion of variance in $X1$ not explained by Obsessions; see completely standardized residual variances in Table 22.2).

CFA MODEL RESPECIFICATION

In applied research, a CFA model often will have to be revised. The most common reason for respecification is to improve the fit of the model because at least one of the three aforementioned criteria for model acceptability has not been satisfied (i.e., inadequate global goodness of fit, large standardized residuals or modification indices denoting salient localized areas of ill fit, or not uniformly interpretable parameter estimates). On occasion, respecification is conducted to improve the parsimony and interpretability of the model. In this scenario, respecification does not improve the fit of the solution; in fact, it may worsen fit to some degree. For example, the parameter estimates in an initial CFA may indicate the factors have poor discriminant validity; that is, two factors are correlated so highly that the notion they represent distinct constructs must be rejected. The model might be respecified by collapsing the redundant factors (i.e., the indicators that loaded on separate, overlapping factors are respecified to load on one factor). Although this respecification might foster the parsimony and interpretability of the measurement model, it will lead to some decrement in model fit (e.g., χ^2) relative to the more complex initial solution.

The next sections of this chapter review the three primary ways a CFA model may be misspecified: (1) the selection of indicators and patterning of indicator–factor relationships, (2) the measurement error theory (e.g., uncorrelated vs. correlated measurement errors); and (3) the number of factors (too few or too many). A more general discussion of model respecification in SEM can be found in Chou and Huh (Chapter 14, this volume). As we discuss further in the ensuing sections, modification indices and standardized residuals are often useful for determining the particular sources of strain in the solution when the model contains minor misspecifications. However, it cannot be overemphasized that revisions to the model should only be made if they can be strongly justified by empirical evidence or theory. This underscores the importance of having sound knowledge of the sample data and the measurement model before proceeding with a CFA.

In many situations, the success of a model modification can be verified by the χ^2 difference test (χ^2_{diff}). This test can be used when the original and respecified models are nested. A "nested model" contains a subset of the free parameters of another model (the parent model). Consider the two-factor model of Obsessions and Compulsions, where the model was evaluated with and without the error covariance for the $X9$ and $X10$ indicators. The latter model is nested under the former model because it contains one less freely estimated parameter (i.e., the error covariance is fixed to zero instead of being freely estimated). A nested model will have more df's than the parent model; in this example the df difference was 1, reflecting the presence–absence of one freely estimated error covariance. If a model is nested under a parent model, the simple difference in the model χ^2's produced by the solutions is distributed as χ^2 in many circumstances (e.g., adjustments must be made if a fitting function other than ML is used to estimate the model; see Brown, 2006). The χ^2_{diff} test in this example would be calculated as follows:

	df	χ^2
Model without error covariance	34	109.50
Model with error covariance	33	46.16
χ^2 difference (χ^2_{diff})	1	63.34

Because the models differ by a single degree of freedom, the critical value for the χ^2_{diff} test is 3.84 (α = .05, df = 1). Because the χ^2_{diff} test value exceeds 3.84 (63.34), we can conclude that the two-factor model with the error covariance provides a significantly better fit to the data than the two-factor model without the error covariance. It is important to note that this two-factor model fits the data well. Use of the χ^2_{diff} test to compare models is not justified when neither solution provides an acceptable fit to the data.

Moreover, the χ^2_{diff} test should not be used if the models are not nested. For instance, two models cannot be compared to each other with the χ^2_{diff} test if the input matrix is changed (e.g., an indicator has been dropped from the revised model) or the model has been structurally revised (e.g., two factors have been collapsed into a single latent variable). If the competing models are not nested, in many cases they can be compared using infor-

mation criterion fit indices such as the Akaike information criterion (AIC) and the expected cross-validation index (ECVI). Both indices take into account model fit (as reflected by χ^2) and model complexity/parsimony (as reflected by the number of freely estimated parameters). The ECVI also incorporates sample size—specifically, a more severe penalty function for fitting a nonparsimonious model in a smaller sample. Generally, models that produce the smallest AIC and ECVI values are favored over alternative specifications.

Selection of Indicators and Specification of Factor Loadings

A common source of CFA model misspecification is the incorrect designation of the relationships between indicators and the factors. This can occur in the following manner (assuming that the correct number of factors was specified): (1) The indicator was specified to load on a factor but actually has no salient relationship to any factor; (2) the indicator was specified to load on one factor but actually has salient loadings on two or more factors; or (3) the indicator was specified to load on the wrong factor. Depending on the problem, the remedy is either to respecify the pattern of relationships between the indicator and the factors or eliminate the indicator from the model.

If an indicator does not load on any factor, this misspecification will be readily detected by results showing the indicator has a nonsignificant or nonsalient loading on the conjectured factor, as well as modification indices suggesting that the fit of the model could not be improved by allowing the indicator to load on a different factor. This conclusion would be further supported by inspection of standardized residuals and sample correlations, which points to the fact that the indicator is weakly related or unrelated to other indicators in the model. Although the proper remedial action is to eliminate the problematic indicator, the overall fit of the model will usually not improve appreciably (because the initial solution does not have difficulty reproducing covariance associated with the problematic indicator).

The other two types of indicator misspecifications (failure to specify the correct primary loading or salient cross-loadings) will usually be diagnosed by large modification indices, suggesting that the model will be significantly improved if the correct loading is freely estimated (moreover, if the indicator was specified to load on the wrong factor, the factor loading estimate may be small or statistically nonsignificant). However, it is important to emphasize that specification searches based on modification indices are most likely to be successful when the model contains only minor misspecifications. If the initial model is grossly misspecified (e.g., incorrect number of factors, many misspecified factor loadings), specification searches are unlikely to lead the researcher to the correct measurement model (Mac-Callum, 1986). In addition, even if only one indicator–factor relationship has been misspecified, this can have a serious deleterious impact on overall model fit and fit diagnostic statistics (standardized residuals, modification indices) in small measurement models or when a given factor has been measured by only a few indicators. Although an acceptable model might be obtained using the original set of indicators (after correct specification of the indicator–factor relationships), it is often the case that a better solution will be attained by dropping bad indicators from the model. For example, an indicator may be associated with several large modification indices and standardized residuals, reflecting that it is rather nonspecific (i.e., evidences similar relationships to all latent variables in the model). Dropping this indicator will eliminate multiple strains in the solution.

Measurement Error Theory

Another common source of CFA model misspecification pertains to the relationships among the indicator residual variances. When no error covariances are specified, the researcher is asserting that all of the covariation among indicators is due to the latent variables (i.e., all measurement error is random). Indicator error covariances are specified on the basis that some of the covariance of the indicators not explained by the latent variables is due to an exogenous common cause. For instance, in measurement models involving multiple-item questionnaires, salient error covariances may arise from items that are very similarly worded, reverse-worded, or differentially prone to social desirability (e.g., see Figure 22.1). In construct validation studies of multitrait–multimethod (MTMM) matrices, an error theory must be specified to account for method covariance arising from disparate assessment modalities (e.g., self-report, behavioral observation, interview rating; compare the correlated uniqueness approach to MTMM; Brown, 2006).

Unnecessary error covariances can be readily detected by results indicating their statistical or clinical nonsignificance. The next step would be to refit the model with the error covariance fixed to zero, and verify that the respecification does not result in a significant decrease in model fit. The χ^2_{diff} test can be used in this situation. The more common difficulty is the failure to include salient error covariances in the model. The omission of these parameters is typically manifested by large standardized residuals, modification indices, and EPC values.

Because of the large sample sizes typically involved in CFA, researchers often encounter "borderline" modification indices (e.g., larger than 3.84 but not of particularly strong magnitude) that suggest the fit of the model could be improved if error covariances were added. As with all parameter specifications in CFA, error covariances must be supported by a substantive rationale and should not be freely estimated simply to improve model fit. The magnitude of EPC values should also contribute to the decision about whether to free these parameters. The researcher should resist the temptation to use borderline modification indices to overfit the model. These trivial additional estimates usually have minimal impact on the key parameters of the CFA solution (e.g., factor loadings) and are apt to be highly unstable (i.e., reflect sampling error rather than an important relationship). In addition, it is important to be consistent in the decision rules used to specify correlated errors; that is, if there is a plausible reason for correlating the errors of two indicators, then all pairs of indicators for which this reasoning applies should also be specified with correlated errors (e.g., if it is believed that method effects exist for questionnaire items that are reverse-worded, error covariances should be freely estimated for all such indicators, not just a subset of them).

Number of Factors

This final source of misspecification should be the least frequently encountered by applied CFA researchers. If the incorrect number of latent variables has been specified, it is likely that the researcher has moved into the CFA framework prematurely. CFA hinges on a strong conceptual and empirical basis. Thus, in addition to strong conceptual justification, the CFA model is usually supported by prior exploratory analyses (i.e., EFA) that have established the appropriate number of factors and the correct pattern of indicator–factor relationships. Accordingly, gross misspecifications of this nature should be unlikely if the proper groundwork for CFA has been established.

As we discussed earlier, overfactoring is often reflected by excessively high factor correlations. The remedial action would to be collapse factors or perhaps eliminate a redundant factor altogether (e.g., if an objective is to make a test instrument as brief as possible). An underfactored CFA solution will fail to adequately reproduce the observed relationships among the indicators. Generally speaking, if indicators are incorrectly specified to load on the same factor (but belong on separate factors), standardized residuals will reveal that the solution's parameter estimates markedly underestimated the observed relationships among these indicators. It is noteworthy that if a one-factor model has been specified (but the "true" model consists of two factors), modification indices will only appear in sections of the results that pertain to indicator measurement errors (i.e., modification indices will not appear as possible cross-loadings because a single factor has been specified). The fact that modification indices appear in this fashion might lead the novice CFA researcher to conclude that indicator error covariances are required. However, modification indices can point to problems with the model that are not the real source of ill fit (e.g., a salient modification index may suggest a revision that makes no conceptual sense). This again underscores the importance of having a clear substantive basis (both conceptual and empirical) to guide the model specification.

SUMMARY

This chapter has provided an overview of the purposes and methods of applied CFA. CFA is in fact the foundation of SEM because all latent variable analyses rely on a sound measurement model. The fundamental principles and procedures discussed in this chapter are indispensable to a variety of common research applications, such as psychometric evaluation, construct validation, data reduction, and identification of bias in measurement. More advanced applications of CFA offer a host of other modeling opportunities, such as the analysis of categorical outcomes (as a complement or alternative to item response theory [IRT]), measurement invariance (across time or across population subgroups), higher-order factor analysis (e.g., second-order factor analysis, bifactor analysis), and the analysis of mean structures

(see Brown, 2006, for detailed discussion of these applications). Moreover, recent developments in statistical software packages have fostered the integration of CFA with other analytic traditions such as latent class modeling (e.g., factor mixture models; Lubke & Muthén, 2005) and hierarchical linear modeling (e.g., multilevel factor analysis; Muthén & Asparouhov, 2010). Based on its pertinence to a wide range of empirical endeavors, CFA will continue to be one of the most frequently used statistical methods in the applied social and behavioral sciences.

NOTES

1. This chapter focuses exclusively on models with *reflective indicators*, where the direction of causality is from the latent construct to the observed measure (i.e., the paths relating the indicator to the factor emanate from the latent variable to the indicator). Although rarely used in applied research, it is also possible to specify measurement models with formative indicators, whereby the direction of causality is from the observed measures to the construct (cf. Edwards & Bagozzi, 2000; MacCallum & Browne, 1993). A detailed discussion of formative indicator models can be found in Brown (2006).

2. An exception to the distinctions between EFA and CFA discussed in this chapter is a new method called "exploratory structural equation modeling" (ESEM; Asparouhov & Muthén, 2009), available only in the Mplus software program (beginning with version 5.21). ESEM integrates EFA and CFA measurement models within the same solution. That is, within a given measurement model, some factors can be specified per the conventions of CFA (i.e., zero cross-loadings), whereas other factors can be specified as an EFA (i.e., rotation of a full factor loading matrix). Unlike traditional EFA, the EFA measurement model in ESEM provides the same information as CFA, such as multiple indices of goodness of fit, standard errors for all rotated parameters, and modification indices (i.e., highlighting possible correlated residuals among indicators). Moreover, most of the modeling possibilities of CFA are available in ESEM, including correlated residuals, regressions of factors on covariates, regression among factors (among different EFA factor blocks or between EFA and CFA factors), multiple-group solutions, mean structure analysis, and measurement invariance examination across groups or across time. A technical description of ESEM can be found in Asparouhov and Muthén (2009); see Marsh and colleagues (2009, 2010) and Rosellini and Brown (2011) for initial applied studies.

3. In recent releases, Mplus began to compute standardized error covariances differently than other leading software programs (e.g., LISREL). The following formula converts a covariance into a correlation: $CORR_{1,2} = COV_{1,2} / SQRT(VAR_1 * VAR_2)$.

While the unstandardized error covariances ($COV_{1,2}$) are the same across software programs, Mplus computes the error correlation using the indicator residual variances (VAR_1, VAR_2) rather than the sample variances of the indicators. Consequently, the standardized error covariances reported by Mplus are larger than those derived from the same unstandardized factor solution in another software program. To obtain the correct model-implied correlation (e.g., between $X9$ and $X10$) the more traditional computational method should be used; for example, error correlation of $X9$ and $X10$ = 1.249/ (2.666 * 1.745) = .268 (cf. error correlation = .418 in Mplus output, Table 22.2).

REFERENCES

Asparouhov, T., & Muthén, B. (2009). Exploratory structural equation modeling. *Structural Equation Modeling, 16,* 397–438.

Bentler, P. M. (1990). Comparative fit indices in structural models. *Psychological Bulletin, 107,* 238–246.

Bentler, P. M. (1995). *EQS structural equations program manual.* Encino, CA: Multivariate Software, Inc.

Brown, T. A. (2003). Confirmatory factor analysis of the Penn State Worry Questionnaire: Multiple factors or method effects? *Behaviour Research and Therapy, 41,* 1411–1426.

Brown, T. A. (2006). *Confirmatory factor analysis for applied research.* New York: Guilford Press.

Browne, M. W., & Cudeck, R. (1993). Alternate ways of assessing model fit. In K. A. Bollen & J. S. Long (Eds.), *Testing structural equation models* (pp. 136–162). Newbury Park, CA: Sage.

Campbell, D. T., & Fiske, D. W. (1959). Convergent and discriminant validation by the multitrait–multimethod matrix. *Psychological Bulletin, 56,* 81–105.

Cohen, J. (1988). *Statistical power analysis for the behavioral sciences.* Hillsdale, NJ: Erlbaum.

Curran, P. J., West, S. G., & Finch, J. F. (1996). The robustness of test statistics to nonnormality and specification error in confirmatory factor analysis. *Psychological Methods, 1,* 16–29.

Edwards, J. R., & Bagozzi, R. P. (2000). On the nature and direction of relationships between constructs and measures. *Psychological Methods, 5,* 155–174.

Hu, L., & Bentler, P. M. (1999). Cutoff criteria for fit indexes in covariance structure analysis: Conventional criteria versus new alternatives. *Structural Equation Modeling, 6,* 1–55.

Hu, L., Bentler, P. M., & Kano, Y. (1992). Can test statistics in covariance structure analysis be trusted? *Psychological Bulletin, 112,* 351–362.

Jöreskog, K. G. (1969). A general approach to confirmatory maximum likelihood factor analysis. *Psychometrika, 34,* 183–202.

Jöreskog, K. G. (1971). Statistical analysis of sets of congeneric tests. *Psychometrika, 36,* 109–133.

Jöreskog, K. G., & Sörbom, D. (1996). *LISREL 8: User's reference guide.* Chicago: Scientific Software International.

Kenny, D. A., & Kashy, D. A. (1992). Analysis of the multitrait–multimethod matrix by confirmatory factor analysis. *Psychological Bulletin, 112,* 165–172.

Lubke, G. H., & Muthén, B. O. (2005). Investigating population heterogeneity with factor mixture models. *Psychological Methods, 10,* 21–39.

MacCallum, R. C. (1986). Specification searches in covariance structure modeling. *Psychological Bulletin, 100,* 107–120.

MacCallum, R. C., & Browne, M. W. (1993). The use of causal indicators in covariance structure models: Some practical issues. *Psychological Bulletin, 114,* 533–541.

MacCallum, R. C., Roznowski, M., & Necowitz, L. B. (1992). Model modifications in covariance structure analysis: The problem of capitalization on chance. *Psychological Bulletin, 111,* 490–504.

Marsh, H. W. (1996). Positive and negative global self-esteem: A substantively meaningful distinction or artifactors? *Journal of Personality and Social Psychology, 70,* 810–819.

Marsh, H. W., Hau, K. T., & Wen, Z. (2004). In search of golden rules: Comment on hypothesis testing approaches to setting cutoff values for fit indexes and dangers in overgeneralizing Hu and Bentler's (1999) findings. *Structural Equation Modeling, 11,* 320–341.

Marsh, H. W., Lüdtke, O., Muthén, B., Asparouhov, T., Morin, A. J. S., Trautwein, U., et al. (2010). A new look at the Big Five factor structure through exploratory structural equation modeling. *Psychological Assessment, 22,* 471–491.

Marsh, H. W., Muthén, B., Asparouhov, T., Lüdtke, O., Robitzsch, A., Morin, A. J. S., et al. (2009). Exploratory structural equation modeling, integrating CFA and EFA: Application to students' evaluations of university teaching. *Structural Equation Modeling, 16,* 439–447.

Muthén, B., & Asparouhov, T. (2010). Beyond multilevel regression modeling: Multilevel analysis in a general latent variable framework. In J. Hox & J. K. Roberts (Eds.), *Handbook of advanced multilevel analysis* (pp. 15–40). New York: Taylor & Francis.

Muthén, B., du Toit, S. H. C., & Spisic, D. (1997). *Robust inference using weighted least squares and quadratic estimating equations in latent variable modeling with categorical and continuous outcomes.* Unpublished technical report, University of California, Los Angeles.

Muthén, L. K., & Muthén, B. O. (1998–2010). *Mplus user's guide* (6th ed.). Los Angeles: Author.

Raykov, T. (2001). Estimation of congeneric scale reliability using covariance structure analysis with nonlinear constraints. *British Journal of Mathematical and Statistical Psychology, 54,* 315–323.

Rosellini, A. J., & Brown, T. A. (2011). The NEO Five Factor Inventory: Latent structure and relationships with dimensions of anxiety and depressive disorders in a large clinical sample. *Assessment, 18*, 27–38.

Satorra, A., & Bentler, P. M. (1994). Corrections to test statistics and standard errors in covariance structure analysis. In A. von Eye & C. C. Clogg (Eds.), *Latent variable analysis: Applications for developmental research* (pp. 399–419). Thousand Oaks, CA: Sage.

Steiger, J. H., & Lind, J. M. (1980, June). *Statistically based tests for the number of common factors.* Paper presented at the annual meeting of the Psychometric Society, Iowa City, IA.

Thurstone, L. L. (1947). *Multiple-factor analysis.* Chicago: University of Chicago Press.

Tucker, L. R., & Lewis, C. (1973). A reliability coefficient for maximum likelihood factor analysis. *Psychometrika, 38*, 1–10.

Wothke, W. A. (1993). Nonpositive definite matrices in structural modeling. In K. A. Bollen & J. S. Long (Eds.), *Testing structural equation models* (pp. 256–293). Newbury Park, CA: Sage.

CHAPTER 23

Investigating Measurement Invariance Using Confirmatory Factor Analysis

Roger E. Millsap
Margarita Olivera-Aguilar

Measurement invariance is a concept with roots in early work on factorial invariance (Ahmavaara, 1954; Meredith, 1964; Thomson & Lederman, 1939; Thurstone, 1947). It is based on the idea that a measured variable, X, such as a test score, is intended as a measure of one or more latent variables, W, with X having a relationship to W that can be expressed via probability. For example, we might be interested in the probability that an individual with latent variable score $W = 2.0$ achieves a score of $X = 15$ on a test. We can express this as a conditional probability, written as $P(X = 15 | W = 2.0)$. Now we might ask: To what extent does this probability depend on other characteristics of the individual, such as gender? Is this probability the same for males and females, given that all of these males and females have $W = 2.0$? Formally, we want to know if the following is true:

$$P(X = 15 | W = 2.0, male) \qquad (23.1)$$
$$= P(X = 15 | W = 2.0, female)$$

If this is true for all values of X and W, we say that X has *measurement invariance* in relation to W and gender (Mellenbergh, 1989; Meredith & Millsap, 1992). In

that case, gender influences X only through W, the intended latent variable that is targeted by the test. If the statement in Equation 23.1 is false, we say that X shows *measurement bias* in relation to W and gender. In that case, there are gender differences on X that cannot be explained by differences on W. We suspect in this case that X is measuring something other than W alone.

Many special cases of measurement invariance can be considered by assuming particular latent variable models for the relationship between X and W. When a common-factor model is assumed to hold, with W representing the common factors, we discuss invariance in terms of *factorial invariance*. The general idea is as follows. Let $\mathbf{X}$ be a $p \times 1$ vector of observed measures, such as a set of test scores across p tests in a battery of tests. Let $\mathbf{W}$ be an $r \times 1$ vector of common factor scores, with $r < p$. In the applications to be considered here, $(\mathbf{X}, \mathbf{W})$ will be measured for individuals who can be divided into groups based on some grouping variable V, such as gender, ethnicity, age, or language. Our interest lies in knowing whether the factor structure of $\mathbf{X}$ is the same across these groups. Factorial invariance holds for $\mathbf{X}$ in relation to these groups if this factor structure is the same across groups. The original purpose for studying factorial invariance was to establish a basis for comparing groups on the measured variables as a way of studying group differences on the latent variables. Violations of invariance would mean that systematic group differences on the measured variables could be due to influences apart from the targeted latent variables. In that case, group comparisons on the measured variables would have uncertain interpretations.

The chapter is organized as follows. The next section describes the common-factor model that underlies most applications of confirmatory factor analysis (CFA) in studying factorial invariance. The model to be described is for measured variables that are continuous in scale. The discrete case is briefly discussed at the end of the chapter. Following this, different models representing various levels of invariance as traditionally conceived are described. The next section presents some descriptions of possible measures of "effect size" for violations of invariance in factor analysis. We then present an example using real data. In the final section we discuss some general issues in conducting investigations of factorial invariance, along with limitations and strategies.

THE COMMON-FACTOR MODEL FOR MULTIPLE POPULATIONS

We can express the factor model for X_{ijk}, the score for the ith individual in the kth group on the jth measured variable, as

$$X_{ijk} = \tau_{jk} + \lambda'_{jk} \mathbf{W}_{ij} + u_{ijk} \qquad (23.2)$$

Here τ_{jk} is a measurement intercept parameter, λ_{jk} is an $r \times 1$ vector of factor loading parameters, $\mathbf{W}_{ik}$ is the $r \times 1$ vector of common factor scores for the ith person in the kth group, and u_{ijk} is the unique factor score for the ith person on the jth unique factor in the kth group. We assume that the unique factor scores $(u_{i1k}, u_{i2k}, \ldots, u_{ipk})$ are all mutually uncorrelated, and that the unique factor scores are uncorrelated with the common factor scores $\mathbf{W}_{ik}$. We also define

$$E(\mathbf{W}_{ik}) = \kappa_{k'} \quad E(u_{ijk}) = 0 \quad \text{cov}(\mathbf{W}_{ik}) = \Phi_k \quad (23.3)$$

We define the covariance matrix for the unique factor scores $\mathbf{U}_{ik} = (u_{i1k}, u_{i2k}, \ldots, u_{ipk})$ to be the diagonal matrix

$$\text{cov}(\mathbf{U}_{ik}) = \Theta_k \qquad (23.4)$$

The diagonal matrix reflects the fact that the unique factors are mutually uncorrelated. Putting these assumptions together, the covariance matrix for the measured variables $\mathbf{X}_{ik}$ will have the factor structure

$$\text{cov}(\mathbf{X}_{ik}) = \Sigma_k = \Lambda_k \Phi_k \Lambda'_k + \Theta_k \qquad (23.5)$$

Here Λ_k is a $p \times r$ matrix whose rows are the vectors λ_{jk}. Similarly, the mean vector for $\mathbf{X}_{ik}$ is

$$E(\mathbf{X}_{ik}) = \mu_k = \tau_k + \Lambda_k \kappa_k \qquad (23.6)$$

Here $\tau'_k = (\tau_{1k}, \tau_{2k}, \ldots, \tau_{pk})$, the vector of measurement intercepts. With these definitions in place, we can define "strict factorial invariance" (Meredith, 1993) as holding for $\mathbf{X}$ in relation to the groups defined by V if the parameters $(\tau_k, \Lambda_k, \Theta_k)$ do not vary across groups, or if for all k,

$$\tau_k = \tau, \quad \Lambda_k = \Lambda, \quad \Theta_k = \Theta \qquad (23.7)$$

If strict factorial invariance holds, we can express the mean μ_k and covariance matrix Σ_k as

$$\mu_k = \tau + \Lambda \kappa_k, \quad \Sigma_k = \Lambda \Phi_k \Lambda' + \Theta \qquad (23.8)$$

In Equation 23.8, note that the mean vector and covariance matrix still have subscripts, indicating that these parameters will vary across groups: The measured variables will still have different means, variances, and correlations for different groups under strict factorial invariance. Strict factorial invariance implies that these group differences are due to the group differences in common factor means, variances, and correlations. If strict factorial invariance fails to hold, we can conclude that some of the group differences in means, variances, and/or correlations among the measured variables are due to influences that operate apart from the common factors. We are trying to measure the common factors, so these influences that operate apart from the common factors are unwanted. It may or may not be possible to identify these alternative influences once strict factorial invariance is rejected. Researchers typically evaluate factorial invariance using a sequence of model fit evaluations, beginning with the less restrictive models. In the next section we describe the traditional sequence of models.

MODELS FOR FACTORIAL INVARIANCE

The Baseline Model

The evaluation of factorial invariance usually begins with a baseline model that stipulates a fixed number of common factors in each group, along with some within-group restrictions on the factor loadings and/or the factor covariance structure. The typical within-group restrictions will force each measured variable to load on a single common factor, with variables grouped into factors based on theory or prior empirical work. This structure is an independent cluster structure, which for a $p = 6$, $r = 2$ example might appear as

$$\Lambda_k = \begin{bmatrix} \lambda_{11k} & 0 \\ \lambda_{21k} & 0 \\ \lambda_{31k} & 0 \\ 0 & \lambda_{42k} \\ 0 & \lambda_{52k} \\ 0 & \lambda_{62k} \end{bmatrix} \qquad (23.9)$$

The scale for each factor could be fixed by either fixing one loading per factor to 1, or by fixing the variances for each factor to 1. Covariances between factors are unconstrained. This baseline model has been said to represent *configural invariance* (Thurstone, 1947). The model says that the same number of factors holds for each group, and the same variables define each factor across groups.

The configural invariance model also requires some constraints on the measurement intercepts or factor means for identification purposes (Sörbom, 1974). These constraints serve as identification constraints only, and do not yet restrict the means of the measured variables across groups. Two choices are typical. Either a subset of the measurement intercepts can be fixed to 0, or the factor means can be fixed to 0. If the former choice is adopted, the variables chosen are usually the variables whose loadings were fixed to 1 when the loadings were identified. These constraints on either the measurement intercepts or the factor means are adopted within each group, with the same intercepts being constrained in each group if this option is chosen.

The baseline model is evaluated for fit using all of the standard fit assessment methods for structural equation modeling in general. A good fit should be achieved if further models are to be evaluated. Lack of fit in the baseline model could have a number of explanations, each of which could be investigated. For example, the choice for the number of factors may be correct, but the independent cluster structure shown in Equation 23.9 may be wrong in one or more groups. If no concrete hypotheses are available that would define a new factor structure, it may well be premature to pursue further invariance hypotheses. In this case, not enough is known about the basic factor structure in the groups being studied to warrant further model evaluations. One could adopt an alternative baseline model that would impose minimal constraints on the factor loading structure (Mulaik & Millsap, 2000), while keeping the number of factors fixed across groups. This option is not pursued here.

Metric Invariance

If the baseline model fits adequately in each group, the next model will be one that restricts the factor loadings to invariance across groups. This model is said to represent *metric invariance* (Horn & McArdle, 1992: Thurstone, 1947), *weak factorial invariance* (Widaman & Reise, 1997), or *pattern invariance* (Millsap, 2011). The measurement intercepts and unique factor variances are not restricted beyond what was done in the baseline model. The metric invariance model may require some alterations to the loading or factor variance constraints used in the baseline model. Suppose, for example, that the factor variances were fixed to one in each group in the baseline model. Under metric invariance, one could remove the factor variance restrictions in all groups, except for one chosen group (denoted the reference group here). The factor variances are fixed to one in the reference group. These restrictions, combined with the invariant loadings, will fully identify loadings.

If metric invariance holds across all groups, any population differences in the covariances between the measured variables are due to the common factors. Population differences in means on the measured variables, or in correlations between those variables, are still ambiguous under metric invariance. These differences could be due either to group differences on the common factors or to unknown influences beyond the common factors. If metric invariance fails to hold for all groups, a common practice is to attempt to locate the violation of invariance in one or more measured variables. This type of respecification of the model is addressed below.

Scalar Invariance

Assuming that metric invariance is found to hold, the next step in model evaluation is to place invariance constraints on the measurement intercepts. The combination of metric invariance and invariance in the measurement intercepts is known as *scalar invariance* (Steenkamp & Baumgartner, 1998) or *strong factorial invariance* (Meredith, 1993). Metric invariance is generally required before scalar invariance is evaluated because differences in factor loadings imply that the regressions of the measured variables on the factor scores are not parallel across groups. If these regressions are varying, group differences in the measurement intercepts are also likely because two regression lines with different slopes (i.e., factor loadings) will ordinarily also have different intercepts.

Tests of invariance for the measurement intercepts are a recent development historically in comparison to tests for metric invariance, which has been of interest since the earliest days of factor analysis (Thomson & Lederman, 1939; Thurstone, 1947). Scalar invariance is a highly useful property because it implies that population differences in the means of the measured variables must be due to the influence of the common factors. Hence scalar invariance eliminates a major source of ambiguity in the explanation of group differences in means. Given that group differences in means on the measured variables are typically of interest in multigroup studies, scalar invariance is also of interest.

Once invariance constraints are imposed on all measurement intercepts, the entire mean structure for the factor model across groups can be identified by fixing the factor means to zero in one group, freeing the factor means in all other groups, and eliminating any fixed intercept values. These identification constraints are sufficient to identify the measurement intercepts under scalar invariance. As we discuss later, this particular pattern of identification constraints has some advantages as well in eliminating the need to locate a specific measurement intercept that will be fixed for identification.

Strict Factorial Invariance

Assuming that scalar invariance holds, the final model to be tested adds invariance constraints on the unique factor variances, resulting in *strict factorial invariance* (Meredith, 1993). Under strict factorial invariance, only the factor means and factor covariance matrices

are permitted to vary across groups. As a result, population differences in means or covariance structures for the measured variables are attributable to the common factors rather than other, unknown influences. Given that the measured variables are viewed as measures of those common factors, strict factorial invariance is a desired condition. Group comparisons on the measured variables can be performed without being systematically confounded by unwanted influences on the measured variables. In practice, investigators sometimes omit this final set of constraints on the unique factor variances, arguing that these constraints are not really needed to be able to compare the groups on the means of the measured variables. Other investigators have argued that strict factorial invariance should be the goal even if mean comparisons are of primary interest (DeShon, 2004; Lubke & Dolan, 2003). For example, DeShon (2004) argues that group differences in the unique but reliable sources of variance will complicate the interpretation of mean differences across groups. Strict factorial invariance eliminates this problem.

Partial Invariance

Any of the previous models following the baseline configural model may be rejected as being inconsistent with the data. Once the metric invariance model is rejected, for example, we may wish to locate which loadings vary across groups. We may want to define an intermediate model in which some, but not all, of the loadings are invariant. This type of model, in which a subset of the model parameters is invariant, is denoted as a *partial invariance* model (Byrne, Shavelson, & Muthén, 1989). Partial metric invariance represents a condition in which some loadings are invariant and the rest are not. Partial scalar invariance would represent a model in which some measurement intercepts are invariant and others are not. Going forth with a model of partial invariance requires that we determine which subset of the parameters is invariant. This determination may be difficult and prone to error, particularly when no prior experience or theory is available to light the way. We return to this topic below.

Once a partially invariant model is decided upon, we can ask whether the configuration of invariant parameters is sufficient to support use of the measured variables "as if" strict invariance actually holds. Suppose that one out of 10 measured variables is found to have varying loadings across groups, with the other nine variables meeting strict invariance. If we plan to use the sum of the 10 measures as a scale, can we ignore the loading difference in the single measure? Should we drop the measure and use the other nine? Questions such as these arise often in practical applications, but little guidance is available in the literature (Millsap & Kwok, 2004). Part of the difficulty is that these questions may have different answers depending on the intended purpose of the scale. If the measures are to be used to make decisions about individuals, as in selection for employment or educational purposes, it may be possible to evaluate the impact of ignoring violations of invariance on decision accuracy (see Millsap & Kwok, 2004, for one approach). On the other hand, in the absence of any clear immediate use for the measures, the impact of partial invariance may be correspondingly unclear. In such cases, it is difficult to rigorously justify any simple rules of thumb for how many violators of invariance are tolerable.

VIOLATIONS OF INVARIANCE: EFFECT SIZE

If group differences in factor model parameters are found and invariance is violated at some level, it is useful to have some way of describing the size of the differences that goes beyond simply reporting parameter estimates. It is hard to judge the importance of group differences in factor loadings, for example. In creating an "effect size" measure for a violation of invariance, one must decide whether to consider the effect size at the level of an individual measured variable, or at the level of a scale that might be formed from the set of measured variables. An effect size that is large at the individual-variable level may be washed out at the scale level if enough variables are included in the scale, with few other violators (Stark, Chernyshenko, & Dragsow, 2004). We focus mainly on the individual-variable level here, and confine discussion to the case of two groups throughout.

In describing the impact of violations of invariance, it is useful to consider the following equation, which expresses the difference in means for the jth measured variable across Groups 1 and 2 as a function of factor model parameters:

$$\mu_{j1} - \mu_{j2} = (\tau_{j1} - \tau_{j2}) + (\lambda'_{j1}\kappa_1 - \lambda'_{j2}\kappa_2) \quad \textbf{(23.10)}$$

Here λ_{jk} is an $r \times 1$ vector of loadings for the jth measured variable on the r common factors. There are three

sources for the group mean difference in Equation 23.10: the group difference in measurement intercepts, the group difference in factor loadings, and the group difference in common factor means. Ideally, only the group difference in common-factor means is present, but violations of the metric and/or scalar invariance would lead to one or both other sources.

Intercept Differences

Suppose that metric invariance holds but scalar invariance does not. Then Equation 23.10 simplifies as

$$\mu_{j1} - \mu_{j2} = (\tau_{j1} - \tau_{j2}) + \lambda'_j(\kappa_1 - \kappa_2) \quad \textbf{(23.11)}$$

Equation 23.11 reveals a clear partitioning of the mean difference into (1) a portion due to intercept differences, and (2) a portion due to the common factors. In this case, one way of measuring the effect size for the violation of scalar invariance is through the ratio

$$\frac{\tau_{j1} - \tau_{j2}}{\mu_{j1} - \mu_{j2}} \quad \textbf{(23.12)}$$

This ratio is the proportion of the group difference in means on the measured variables that is due to the measurement intercept difference. We assume here that the ratio is positive in sign, with both differences having the same sign. If a relatively small proportion (e.g., < 20%) of the group difference in means is due to the intercept difference, we may decide to ignore the intercept difference. The threshold for what should be considered a meaningful proportion will vary by context.

In some cases, one may not need to calculate the ratio in Equation 23.12 because the scale of the measured variable is familiar and meaningful. Given that the intercept difference is expressed in the same units as the scale for the measured variable, it is possible in this case to evaluate the intercept difference directly. This approach may be the best option in those cases in which the intercept difference and factor mean difference in Equation 23.11 have opposite signs. The ratio in Equation 23.12 will not be meaningful in that case.

Factor Loading Differences

For the case in which metric invariance is violated, the clean partitioning leading to the ratio in Equation 23.11 is no longer present, and we must go back to Equation 23.10. Furthermore, violations of metric invariance will affect the covariance structures within each group. Differences in factor loadings represent interactions: The relationship between the common factor and the measured variable is different across groups. Under the factor model, this relationship is a linear regression of the measured variable on the factor scores. This regression is expressed

$$E(X_{ijk} | \mathbf{W}_{ik}) = \tau_{jk} + \lambda'_{jk}\mathbf{W}_{ik} \tag{23.13}$$

At any given factor score, we can express the distance between the regression surfaces for the two groups as

$$E(X_{j1} - X_{j2} | \mathbf{W}) = (\tau_{j1} - \tau_{j2}) + (\lambda_{j1} - \lambda_{j2})'\mathbf{W} \tag{23.14}$$
$$= \tau_d + \lambda_d'\mathbf{W}$$

Here we have dropped the person subscript for convenience. Equation 23.14 itself represents a linear regression of the group difference in raw scores for two hypothetical persons having identical factor scores, with intercept τ_d and regression coefficients λ_d. We can estimate τ_d and λ_d using the estimates available for $(\tau_{j1}, \tau_{j2}, \lambda_{j1}, \lambda_{j2})$. We can then ask: What difference on the measured variable scale is meaningful? Suppose that we decide that a difference of $X_d = |X_{j1} - X_{j2}|$ is meaningful. We can then ask if, under the regression in Equation 23.14, what values of $\mathbf{W}_k$ would produce

$$|E(X_{j1} - X_{j2} | \mathbf{W})| > X_d \tag{23.15}$$

The answer will be calculable as a range of values $\mathbf{W} < \mathbf{W}_1$ and $\mathbf{W} > \mathbf{W}_u$ for calculated bounds $(\mathbf{W}_1, \mathbf{W}_u)$ These bounds are most easily calculated in the single-factor case but can also be developed for multiple factors. The final step would be to consider whether enough individuals are likely to be in the region identified through this process. In other words, is anyone really in the region $\mathbf{W} < \mathbf{W}_1$ or $> \mathbf{W}_u$? Consideration of the means and variances of $\mathbf{W}$ as estimated from the data in each group should help answer the question.

The preceding procedure for evaluating the impact of violations of metric invariance requires the investigator to specify what difference on the measured variable scale would be considered meaningful. If a meaningful difference cannot be specified, the procedure cannot be used. We would argue, however, that it will be difficult in this case to evaluate the results of any invariance study of the measure. A better course of action may be to acquire more experience with the measure itself before beginning any invariance studies.

Differences in Unique Variances

Violations of strict factorial invariance that result from group differences only in unique factor variances can also be studied via effect size measures. These violations contribute to group differences in the variances of the measured variables. In this situation, we can express the variance of the jth measured variable in the kth group as

$$\sigma^2_{jk} = \lambda'_j\Phi_k\lambda_j + \theta_{jk} \tag{23.16}$$

Differences in variances are not easily interpreted, but we can evaluate what proportion of the group difference in variance is due to the difference in unique factor variances:

$$\frac{\theta_{j1} - \theta_{j2}}{\sigma^2_{j1} - \sigma^2_{j2}} \tag{23.17}$$

We assume here that the signs of the numerator and denominator are consistent, and consistent with the difference:

$$\lambda'_j(\Phi_1 - \Phi_2)\lambda_j \tag{23.18}$$

In the single-factor case, Equation 23.18 simplifies to

$$\lambda^2_j(\phi_1 - \phi_2) \tag{23.19}$$

Here one need only consider the sign of $(\phi_1 - \phi_2)$. If the signs of the differences in Equations 23.17 and 23.18 are inconsistent, interpretation is complicated and the ratio in Equation 23.17 is less useful.

AN EXAMPLE

The example presented here uses data from a large field trial of an intervention designed to enhance school retention and performance among Hispanic middle school and high school students. Dillman-Carpentier and colleagues (2008) describes the origin and recruitment of this sample. The groups to be compared are defined by the primary language spoken in the home: English or Spanish. The measured variables are five items from a 10-item scale that measures parent–child conflict. The subset of five items was selected based on previous analyses with the data that had supported a single-factor model for the five items. Each item asks about the frequency with which conflicts occur, or behaviors associated with these conflicts. The response scale is a 1- to 5-point scale, with 1 being *almost never or never* and 5 being *almost always or always.* All items were scored so that higher scores are associated with more conflict or conflict behaviors. The Spanish-speaking respondents received a Spanish version of the items, and the English speakers received an English version. The respondents were 450 female caregivers (usually the mother), with 193 English speakers and 257 Spanish speakers. All data were collected via interviews with the caregivers. Given the discrete response scale, the use of the continuous factor model, as illustrated below, should be regarded as an approximation. All of the CFAs reported here were conducted using the Mplus (Muthén & Muthén, 1998–2006) software program, Version 5.21. Maximum likelihood estimation was used in all analyses, and no missing data were present.

Table 23.1 gives the sample means, standard deviations, and correlations for the English and Spanish groups. The means show that conflict events and behaviors occur at a greater frequency in the English-speaking group, and the correlations between the items tend to be higher as well among the English speakers.

TABLE 23.1. Descriptive Statistics for the English and Spanish Samples

	FC1	FC4	FC5	FC6	FC9
Correlations for the English-speaking group ($n = 193$)					
FC1	1				
FC4	0.381	1			
FC5	0.599	0.393	1		
FC6	0.416	0.445	0.476	1	
FC9	0.601	0.404	0.661	0.519	1
Means	2.280	1.518	2.052	1.689	1.684
SD	0.887	0.925	0.972	1.014	0.901
Correlations for the Spanish-speaking group ($n = 257$)					
FC1	1				
FC4	0.227	1			
FC5	0.400	0.322	1		
FC6	0.324	0.330	0.354	1	
FC9	0.473	0.370	0.486	0.540	1
Means	2.113	1.175	1.708	1.366	1.319
SD	1.034	0.597	0.836	0.785	0.701

TABLE 23.2. Fit Statistics for the Invariance Models

Model	Chi-square	df	p-value	RMSEA (90% interval)	SRMR
Congeneric	15.304	10	.1214	.049 (0, .094)	.026
Metric	21.181	14	.0971	.048 (0, .087)	.044
Scalar	30.392	18	.0338	.055 (.015, .088)	.045
Partial scalar	25.490	17	.0843	.047 (0, .083)	.043
Partial strict	96.641	22	< .001	.123 (.098, .148)	.152
Partial strict (release 1,4,6)	29.940	19	.0539	.050 (0, .083)	.043

With the exception of Item 1, the variability in the item scores is also higher in the English group. The higher level of conflict in the English group is consistent with the fact that this group has been in the United States longer, is more acculturated, and shows a higher rate of problem behaviors generally than does the Spanish group.

A series of two-group factor models was fit to the data, beginning with a configural invariance baseline model that specified a single factor for the items in each group. Table 23.2 gives the fit results for this model and all other subsequent models. The configural model fit well, with the global chi-square statistic not reaching statistical significance at $\alpha = .05$. The next model of interest specified metric invariance, with all factor loadings invariant. This model fits slightly less well than the configural model, but the difference in the chi-square statistics ($\chi^2_{\text{diff}} = 5.817$, $df_{\text{diff}} = 4$) does not reach significance at $\alpha = .05$. We therefore retain the invariance on the loadings and move to the next model, which specifies scalar invariance. All measurement intercepts are invariant under this third model. The model fits less well than the metric invariance model, and the change in chi-square is close to significance ($\chi^2_{\text{diff}} = 9.211$, $df_{\text{diff}} = 4$). Scrutiny of the residuals for the sample means showed that Items 1 and 4 seem to have the largest contribution to misfit in the mean structure. We created a partially invariant scalar model by permitting the intercept for Item 4 to vary across groups. This model fit well, as shown in Table 23.2. The change in chi-square from the metric invariance model to this was not significant ($\chi^2_{\text{diff}} = 4.309$, $df_{\text{diff}} = 3$). We retain the scalar invariance constraints on all items except Item 4. Next, we add invariance constraints on all of the unique factor variances, resulting in a partially strict invariance model. This model does not fit well, as shown in Table 23.2. Scrutiny of the residuals and modification indices suggests releasing constraints on the unique variances for Items 1, 4, and 6. A new model was created that retained invariance constraints for the unique factor variances only for Items 5 and 9. This model fit adequately, and was not significantly different in fit from the partial scalar model ($\chi^2_{\text{diff}} = 4.400$, $df_{\text{diff}} = 2$).

Table 23.3 presents the parameter estimates for the final partially strict model. For identification purposes, the mean and variance of the factor scores in the English-speaking group were set to 0 and 1, respectively. The factor mean in the Spanish-speaking group is negative, consistent with the lower item means in that sample. The intercept difference in Item 4 shows a larger intercept for the English group. The ratio in Equation 23.12 for this intercept difference is calcu-

TABLE 23.3. Parameter Estimates from the Final Partially Strict Model

Parameter	English	Spanish
λ_1		.656
λ_4		.424
λ_5		.740
λ_6		.660
λ_9		.766
κ	0[a]	−.446
ϕ	1[a]	.539
τ_1		2.330
τ_4	1.518	1.364
τ_5		2.044
τ_6		1.669
τ_9		1.671
θ_1	.378	.759
θ_4	.633	.269
θ_5		.400
θ_6	.628	.366
θ_9		.197

[a]Fixed for identification.

lated as .45, or 45%. A substantial portion of the item mean difference on this item is due to the intercept difference in this case. If the item variances for Item 4 are pooled between groups, the mean difference on the item is close to one-half of a pooled standard deviation. The intercept difference accounts for about half of that mean difference. This difference would probably not reach the level of practical significance in most applications. A plausible explanation for the intercept difference may lie in the content of the item. Item 4 states, "You and (the child) gave each other the silent treatment (purposely did not talk to each other)." The Spanish-speaking group in this sample is less acculturated than the English-speaking group, and is more traditional in its parenting practices. In this group, it is likely to be more unusual for the child to give the parent the "silent treatment" (Gonzales, Deardorff, Formoso, Barr, & Berrera, 2006), even if conflict exists. Hence, fewer Spanish-speaking caregivers may endorse this item even when conflict is present, leading to a lower measurement intercept for the Spanish-speaking group.

The group differences in unique factor variances are substantial. The differences in unique factor variances for Item 1 go in a direction that is opposite to the difference in sample item variances; hence, the ratio in Equation 23.17 is not useful for that item. For Items 4 and 6, the differences are consistent with the English-speaking group having larger variances. The ratio in Equation 23.17 is equal to .73 for Item 4 and .64 for Item 6. These ratios are substantial, indicating that most of the differences in variances on the items are due to unique factor variance differences rather than to differences on the common factor. In practice, one would ask whether the differences in variance are important for the role that the scale or item will play.

ISSUES IN INVARIANCE MODELING

Many of the technical problems associated with evaluating factorial invariance have been resolved, and efficient software for studying invariance now exists. A number of widely available software programs can conduct CFA in multiple groups (LISREL: Jöreskog & Sörbom, 2003; Mplus: Muthén & Muthén, 1998–2006; EQS: Bentler, 1995). If investigations of factorial invariance could be successfully resolved through computational algorithms alone, the invariance problem would now be solved. The reality is that while good software is indispensable, effective use of these methods relies heavily on the skill and experience of the investigator. In the process of investigating invariance, choices must often be made that can have unforeseen consequences. In this final section, we describe some of the larger issues that should be considered when conducting an investigation of factorial invariance.

The Baseline Model

As described earlier, the starting point for any invariance investigation is a factor model that specifies a fixed number of factors in each group, a certain pattern for the factor loadings, and the placement of identification constraints. This model should incorporate the investigator's best hypothesis about the factor structure of the measured variables, apart from questions of invariance. Ideally, prior research and experience will inform this hypothesis and lead to a baseline model with excellent fit. In some cases, however, the measured variables may be relatively new, with the factor structure being uncertain. For example, a new scale may have been developed, and the invariance study may be intended to establish that the scale can be used in multiple populations. Initial attempts to establish a baseline model may fail. The measures created to determine a common latent dimension may turn out to be related to multiple latent variables.

A virtue of the factor-analytic approach to invariance is that multiple latent variables can be specified without difficulty. The problem here is that mistakes in specification at this level can have important consequences. Camilli (1992) illustrates the point that in omitting factors from a baseline model, one may subsequently reject invariance erroneously due to simple group differences on the omitted factors. On the surface, this result seems to suggest that we should strive to include as many factors as needed in the baseline model to achieve a good fit to the data. On the other hand, one of the most common explanations for lack of invariance is that unwanted "nuisance" factors are operating in the measures, beyond the factor(s) that are the intended target of the measures (Ackerman, 1992; Kok, 1988; Shealy & Stout, 1993). For example, a math test may include a mixture of multiple-choice items and problem-solving items, with the latter being story problems. The problem-solving items might form a separate factor as a function of their verbal content, and this additional factor could be responsible for violations of invariance in some groups (e.g., foreign language speakers). In this example, there are multiple factors, but it

is unclear whether they should all be included in the baseline model. What is the proper baseline model in such cases?

This example illustrates an important principle: that the factors to be specified in the baseline model should represent the latent variables that we intend to measure. In the math test, we do not intend to measure verbal skill, so it is not useful to add such factors to the baseline model. More generally, it is not helpful to expand the number of factors in the baseline model simply to achieve a good fit to the data, if the added factors have no interpretation as intended foci of measurement. If the set of measured variables is intended to form a single factor, the baseline model should specify a single factor. If some secondary factors have clear interpretations, then these must be included as well. For example, some additional factors may reflect known method effects (e.g., common wording effects) that are neutral with regard to group differences. A poor fit for the baseline model will preclude further investigations of models that incorporate invariance constraints, but the poor fit also tells us that the intended set of factors simply does not work for all groups simultaneously. This finding is itself a violation of invariance at a fundamental level.

The Search for Violators

Another issue that arises with questions of partial invariance concerns how we should identify measured variables that are violators, or whose loadings, intercepts, and/or unique variances have values that differ across groups. For example, suppose that metric invariance has been tested and rejected for a set of measured variables. The next step might be to specify a model representing partial metric invariance, but which factor loadings are invariant? To answer this question, a series of respecified models may be fit to the data in the hope of locating the proper configuration of invariant loadings. When the number of measured variables is large, this process can be complex and time-consuming. The best strategy for conducting a search of this type is not obvious.

A number of studies have examined this question directly, most employing simulations to explore how various data and model conditions may affect search accuracy (Oort, 1998; Meade & Bauer, 2007; Meade & Lautenschlager, 2004; Yoon & Millsap, 2007). The problem of model respecification is a general one in structural equation modeling (Kaplan, 1988; Mac-

Callum, 1986; MacCallum, Roznowski, & Necowitz, 1992). We know from this general theory that when the starting model is very different from the data-generating model, it is often difficult to arrive at the latter through a series of data-based modifications of the starting model. Applied to invariance modeling, we might predict that it will be difficult to find the correct partial invariance model when many of the measured variables are violators. Simulation evidence supports this prediction (Meade & Lautenschlager, 2004; Yoon & Millsap, 2007). In the ideal case, theory or prior research would suggest which measured variables might be violators, but in actual practice we must often rely on sample statistical information. Local fit indices such as residuals and modification indices are typically used. Expected parameter change statistics are useful in large samples (Kaplan, 1989). Many data and model conditions may affect these indices, however. Sample size, the size of the parameter difference, the direction of the difference, the number of measured variables, the communalities of the measured variables, and the proportion of the measured variables that are violators all are important.

A related issue that affects the success of the specification search is the presence of some parameter constraints needed for identification purposes. These constraints are typically introduced in an identical fashion across groups. The identification of the factor loadings, for example, is often accomplished by requiring at least one measured variable per factor (denoted here as a "reference variable") to load strictly on that factor, with no nonzero loadings on other factors. Also, each of the reference variables is given a fixed unit value for its nonzero loading. This identification pattern is adopted in each group, with the same reference variables being chosen in each group. As a result, some invariance constraints are adopted for identification purposes. Suppose, however, that one of the chosen reference variables is a violator: Its loading actually varies across groups. It can be shown that if this situation goes undetected and the identification constraints are kept in place, distortions in the specification search can result (Johnson, Meade, & DuVernet, 2009; Yoon & Millsap, 2007).

This problem can be avoided by making sure that no violators are selected as reference variables for identification purposes, but this is not always possible. One helpful practice is to include measures that have been shown to be invariant in previous research, if such measures are available. Assuming they are not available, other approaches must be taken. Woods (2009) proposed some exploratory procedures to identify measures that are invariant, prior to choosing placement of identification constraints. Rensvold and Cheung (2001) proposed an approach to the problem that systematically varies placement of the identification constraints in the hope of revealing patterns that suggest which measures to choose as reference variables. Another approach is to adopt identification constraints that lessen the problem. In the conflict example given earlier, no fixed loadings or measurement intercepts were needed in the final model. As shown in Table 23.3, under metric invariance, one need only fix the factor variances in one group to identify the factor scale. Under scalar invariance, one need only fix the factor means in one group. In either case, local fit information can be used to evaluate which invariance constraints might be related. Yoon and Millsap (2007) found this approach to be useful, within limits. Finally, Little, Slegars, and Card (2006) proposed a new set of identification constraints that might be useful in addressing the problem.

Alternative Models

Most CFA studies of invariance use simple factor structures that stipulate an independent cluster loading pattern: Each measured variable loads on only a single factor. More complex structures may be useful in some research areas, however. The bifactor loading pattern is a good example of such a structure (Gibbons & Hedeker, 1992; Holzinger & Swineford, 1937; Reise, Morizot, & Hays, 2007). In the bifactor model, each measured variable loads on two factors: one general factor on which all measures load, and one "group factor" that influences only a subset of the measured variables. All of the factors are specified as mutually uncorrelated (i.e., Φ is a diagonal matrix). This model has proven to be useful in clinical or personality measurement (Patrick, Hicks, Nichol, & Krueger, 2007; Reise et al., 2007), even though its original development was in cognitive applications. The bifactor model is best suited for measures that are believed to be primarily unidimensional but may be influenced by additional "small" factors whose role is understood. These group factors may account for less variance than the general factor, but they are too influential to permit a good fit for a model that specifies only a general factor. Invariance applications that involve primarily unidimensional measures may benefit from the bifactor representation if some additional limited factors are needed. Bifactor models are also closely related to second-order factor models (Yung, Thissen, & McLeod, 1999), and can be used to evaluate invariance in either set of models.

When the measured variables are test or questionnaire items with few response categories, the traditional continuous factor model may provide a poor approximation (Carroll, 1945, 1983; McDonald & Ahlawat, 1974). One strategy in this case is to adopt a factor model that explicitly recognizes the discrete nature of the measures: the factor model for ordered categorical data (Bartholomew, 1983, 1984, 1987; Bock & Aitkin, 1981; Browne & Arminger, 1995; Christoffersson, 1975; Jöreskog, 1993; Maydeu-Olivares, 2005; Mislevy, 1986; Muthén, 1978, 1984; Wirth & Edwards, 2007). Invariance applications involving this model have been relatively rare until recently. Millsap and Yun-Tein (2004) describe the use and specification of the model for invariance applications. At least two structural equation modeling software programs offer this capability (LISREL: Jöreskog & Sörbom, 2003; Mplus: Muthén & Muthén, 1998–2006). Studies of the power and Type I error performance of these models in invariance applications are needed.

Outside of the factor-analytic framework, discrete measures in invariance studies can be modeled using item response theory (IRT) (De Ayala, 2009; Embretson & Reise, 2000; Fischer & Molenaar, 1995; Lord, 1980; van der Linden & Hambleton, 1997). The factor model for ordered categorical measures can be shown to be equivalent to certain models in IRT (Kamata & Bauer, 2008; Lord & Novick, 1968; Takane & de Leeuw, 1987), but IRT offers other models that have no factor-analytic counterparts. IRT has been used extensively in the study of measurement invariance (for a summary, see Millsap, 2011).

CONCLUSION

In this chapter, we have described how measurement invariance is defined within the common-factor model, and how CFA is used to detect violations of factorial invariance. We have also described some of the tactical issues that often arise in these investigations, such as the creation of effect size measures and the search for violators once invariance has been rejected. Throughout the chapter, we have emphasized the need for some knowledge about the intended latent structure of the measures under study as a requirement for effective

use of the methods described here. We close by reiterating this point. The confirmatory methods described here proceed by evaluating departures from hypothesized factor models. These model evaluations must start from an initial or baseline model that represents our understanding of the intended factor structure of the measures. If we do not know enough to specify the intended factor structure (e.g., know how many factors should underlie the measures), we do not know enough to investigate factorial invariance using CFA. In this case, even if we are able to evaluate a series of models representing varying degrees of invariance, as illustrated earlier, we will not be able to interpret the results. For example, it would not be very useful to know that there are group differences in loadings on a factor whose nature we do not understand. In this sense, the use of CFA in studying invariance must proceed from an understanding of psychological attributes that were the intended targets of the measures.

REFERENCES

Ackerman, T. A. (1992). A didactic explanation of item bias, item impact, and item validity from a multidimensional perspective. *Journal of Educational Measurement, 29,* 67–91.

Ahmavaara, Y. (1954). The mathematical theory of factorial invariance under selection. *Psychometrika, 19,* 27–38.

Bartholomew, D. J. (1983). Latent variable models for ordered categorical data. *Journal of Econometrics, 22,* 229–243.

Bartholomew, D. J. (1984). Scaling binary data using a factor model. *Journal of the Royal Statistical Society B, 46,* 120–123.

Bartholomew, D. J. (1987). *Latent variable models and factor analysis.* London: Griffin.

Bentler, P. M. (1995). *EQS Structural Equations Program manual.* Encino, CA: Multivariate Software, Inc.

Bock, R. D., & Aitkin, M. (1981). Marginal maximum likelihood estimation of item parameters: An application of the EM algorithm. *Psychometrika, 46,* 443–449.

Browne, M. W., & Arminger, G. (1995). Specification and estimation of mean and covariance structure models. In G. Arminger, C. C. Clogg, & M. E. Sobel (Eds.), *Handbook of statistical modeling for the social and behavioral sciences* (pp. 185–249). New York: Plenum Press.

Byrne, B. M., Shavelson, R. J., & Muthén, B. (1989). Testing for equivalence of factor covariance and mean structures: The issue of partial measurement invariance. *Psychological Bulletin, 105,* 456–466.

Camilli, G. (1992). A conceptual analysis of differential item functioning in terms of a multidimensional item response model. *Applied Psychological Measurement, 16,* 129–147.

Carroll, J. B. (1945). The effect of difficulty and chance success on correlations between items and between tests. *Psychometrika, 26,* 347–372.

Carroll, J. B. (1983). The difficulty of a test and its factor composition revisited. In H. Wainer & S. Messick (Eds.), *Principles of modern psychological measurement* (pp. 257–283). Hillsdale, NJ: Erlbaum.

Christoffersson, A. (1975). Factor analysis of dichotomized variables. *Psychometrika, 40,* 5–32.

De Ayala, R. J. (2009). *The theory and practice of item response theory.* New York: Guilford Press.

DeShon, R. P. (2004). Measures are not invariant across groups without error variance homogeneity. *Psychology Science, 46,* 137–149.

Dillman-Carpentier, F. R., Mauricio, A. M., Gonzales, N. A., Millsap, R. E., Meza, C. M., Dumka, L. E., et al. (2008). Engaging Mexican origin families in a school-based preventive intervention. *Journal of Primary Prevention, 28,* 521–546.

Embretson, S. E., & Reise, S. P. (2000). *Item response theory for psychologists.* Mahwah, NJ: Erlbaum.

Fischer, G. H., & Molenaar, I. W. (Eds.). (1995). *Rasch models: Foundations, recent developments, and applications.* New York: Springer-Verlag.

Gibbons, R. D., & Hedeker, D. (1992). Full-information item bifactor analysis. *Psychometrika, 57,* 423–436.

Gonzales, N. A., Deardorff, J., Formoso, D., Barr, A., & Berrera, M. (2006). Family mediators of the relation between acculturation and adolescent mental health. *Family Relations, 55,* 318–330.

Holzinger, K. J. & Swineford, F. (1937). The bifactor method. *Psychometrika, 2,* 41–54.

Horn, J. L., & McArdle, J. J. (1992). A practical guide to measurement invariance in research on aging. *Experimental Aging Research, 18,* 117–144.

Johnson, E. C., Meade, A. W., & DuVernet, A. M. (2009). The role of referent indicators in tests of measurement invariance. *Structural Equation Modeling, 16,* 642–657.

Jöreskog, K. G. (1993). Latent variable modeling with ordinal variables. In K. Haagen, D. J. Bartholomew, & M. Deistler (Eds.), *Statistical modeling and latent variables* (pp. 163–171). Amsterdam: North Holland.

Jöreskog, K. G., & Sörbom, D. (2003). *LISREL 8.54 for Windows.* Lincolnwood, IL: Scientific Software.

Kamata, A., & Bauer, D. J. (2008). A note on the relation between factor analytic and item response theory models. *Structural Equation Modeling, 15,* 136–153.

Kaplan, D. (1988). The impact of specification error on the estimation, testing, and improvement of structural equation models. *Multivariate Behavioral Research, 23,* 69–86.

Kaplan, D. (1989). Model modification in covariance structure analysis: Application of the expected parameter

change statistic. *Multivariate Behavioral Research, 24,* 285–305.

Kok, F. (1988). Item bias and test multidimensionality. In R. Langeheine & J. Rost (Eds.), *Latent trait and latent class models* (pp. 263–275). New York: Plenum Press.

Little, T. D., Slegars, D. W., & Card, N. A. (2006). A non-arbitrary method of identifying and scaling latent variables in SEM and MACS models. *Structural Equation Modeling, 13,* 59–72.

Lord, F. M. (1980). *Applications of item response theory to practical testing problems.* Hillsdale, NJ: Erlbaum.

Lord, F. M., & Novick, M. E. (1968). *Statistical theories of mental test scores.* Reading, MA: Addison-Wesley.

Lubke, G. H., & Dolan, C. V. (2003). Can unequal residual variances across groups mask differences in residual means in the common factor model? *Structural Equation Modeling, 10,* 175–192.

MacCallum, R. C. (1986). Specification searches in covariance structure modeling. *Psychological Bulletin, 100,* 107–120.

MacCallum, R. C., Roznowski, M., & Necowitz, L. B. (1992). Model modifications in covariance structure analysis: The problem of capitalization on chance. *Psychological Bulletin, 111,* 490–504.

Maydeu-Olivares, A. (2005). Linear item response theory, nonlinear item response theory, and factor analysis: A unified framework. In A. Maydeu-Olivares & J. J. McArdle (Eds.), *Contemporary psychometrics* (pp. 73–100). Mahwah, NJ: Erlbaum.

McDonald, R. P., & Ahlawat, K. S. (1974). Difficulty factors in binary data. *British Journal of Mathematical and Statistical Psychology, 27,* 82–99.

Meade, A. W., & Bauer, D. J. (2007). Power and precision in confirmatory factor analytic tests of measurement invariance. *Structural Equation Modeling, 14,* 611–635.

Meade, A. W., & Lautenschlager, G. J. (2004). A Monte-Carlo study of confirmatory factor analytic tests of measurement invariance. *Structural Equation Modeling, 11,* 60–72.

Mellenbergh, G. J. (1989). Item bias and item response theory. *International Journal of Educational Research, 13,* 127–143.

Meredith, W. (1964). Notes on factorial invariance. *Psychometrika, 29,* 177–185.

Meredith, W. (1993). Measurement invariance, factor analysis, and factorial invariance. *Psychometrika, 58,* 525–543.

Meredith, W., & Millsap, R. E. (1992). On the misuse of manifest variables in the detection of measurement bias. *Psychometrika, 57,* 289–311.

Millsap, R. E. (2011). *Statistical approaches to measurement invariance.* New York: Routledge.

Millsap, R. E., & Kwok, O.-M. (2004). Evaluating the impact of partial factorial invariance on selection in two populations. *Psychological Methods, 9,* 93–115.

Millsap, R. E., & Yun-Tein, J. (2004). Assessing factorial

invariance in ordered-categorical measures. *Multivariate Behavioral Research, 39*, 479–515.

Mislevy, R. J. (1986). Recent developments in the factor analysis of categorical variables. *Journal of Educational Statistics, 11*, 3–31.

Mulaik, S. A., & Millsap, R. E. (2000). Doing the four-step right. *Structural Equation Modeling, 7*, 36–73.

Muthén, B. O. (1978). Contributions to factor analysis of dichotomized variables. *Psychometrika, 43*, 551–560.

Muthén, B. O. (1984). A general structural equation model with dichotomous, ordered categorical and continuous latent variable indicators. *Psychometrika, 49*, 115–132.

Muthén, L., & Muthén, B. O. (1998–2006). *Mplus user's guide* (4th ed.). Los Angeles: Authors.

Oort, F. J. (1998). Simulation study of item bias detection with restricted factor analysis. *Structural Equation Modeling, 5*, 107–124.

Patrick, C. J., Hicks, B. M., Nichol, P. E., & Krueger, R. F. (2007). A bifactor approach to modeling the structure of the Psychopathy Checklist—Revised. *Journal of Personality Disorders, 21*, 118–141.

Reise, S. P., Morizot, J., & Hays, R. D. (2007). The role of the bifactor model in resolving dimensionality issues in health outcomes measures. *Quality of Life Research, 16*, 19–31.

Rensvold, R. B., & Cheung, G. W. (2001). Testing for metric invariance using structural equation models: Solving the standardization problem. In C. A. Schriesheim & L. L. Neider (Eds.), *Research in management* (pp. 25–50). Greenwich, CT: Information Age.

Shealy, R., & Stout, W. (1993). An item response theory model for test bias and differential test functioning. In P. Holland & H. Wainer (Eds.), *Differential item functioning* (pp. 197–240). Hillsdale, NJ: Erlbaum.

Sörbom, D. (1974). A general method for studying differences in factor means and factor structure between groups. *British Journal of Mathematical and Statistical Psychology, 27*, 229–239.

Stark, S., Chernyshenko, O. S., & Drasgow, F. (2004). Examining the effects of differential item (functioning and differential) test functioning on selection decisions: When are statistically significant effects practically important? *Journal of Applied Psychology, 89*, 497–508.

Steenkamp, J. E. M., & Baumgartner, H. (1998). Assessing measurement invariance in cross-national consumer research. *Journal of Consumer Research, 25*, 78–90.

Takane, Y., & de Leeuw, J. (1987). On the relationship between item response theory and factor analysis of discretized variables. *Psychometrika, 52*, 393–408.

Thomson, G. H., & Lederman, W. (1939). The influence of multivariate selection on the factorial analysis of ability. *British Journal of Psychology, 29*, 288–305.

Thurstone, L. L. (1947). *Multiple factor analysis.* Chicago: University of Chicago Press.

van der Linden, W. J., & Hambleton, R. K. (Eds.). (1997). *Handbook of modern item response theory.* New York: Springer.

Widaman, K. F., & Reise, S. P. (1997). Exploring the measurement invariance of psychological instruments: Applications in the substance abuse domain. In K. J. Bryant (Ed.), *Alcohol and substance use research* (pp. 281–324). Washington, DC: American Psychological Association.

Wirth, R. J., & Edwards, M. C. (2007). Item factor analysis: Current approaches and future directions. *Psychological Methods, 12*, 58–79.

Woods, C. M. (2009). Empirical selection of anchors for tests of differential item functioning. *Applied Psychological Measurement, 33*, 42–57.

Yoon, M., & Millsap, R. E. (2007). Detecting violations of factorial invariance using data-based specification searches: A Monte Carlo study. *Structural Equation Modeling, 14*, 435–463.

Yung, Y., Thissen, D., & McLeod, L. D. (1999). On the relationship between the higher-order factor model and the hierarchical factor model. *Psychometrika, 64*, 113–128.

CHAPTER 24

A Flexible Structural Equation Modeling Approach for Analyzing Means

Samuel B. Green
Marilyn S. Thompson

Social scientists frequently conduct tests to assess differences in means (Aiken, West, & Millsap, 2008; Keselman, Algina, Lix, Wilcox, & Deering, 2008). These tests are performed to evaluate hypotheses for one-way and higher-way analysis of variance (ANOVA) and multivariate analysis of variance (MANOVA) designs, with and without covariates. All too often these tests are applied in a cookbook fashion without critically evaluating whether the hypotheses tested are maximally consistent with the researcher's hypotheses, or considering whether the assumptions underlying the statistical tests are met. These potential problems could, to a large extent, be avoided by approaching these tests of differences in means using structural equation modeling (SEM). An important advantage of evaluating hypotheses within an SEM framework, such as those regarding differences in means, may be the adoption of a general approach to modeling that stresses the specification of a series of alternative models carefully matched to the substantive theory and methods employed in a study (e.g., Fan & Hancock, 2012; Green & Thompson, 2006; Hancock, 2010; Rodgers, 2010). Estimation of these alternative models is accompanied by the careful assessment of model fit with the observed data to provide evidence for reaching conclusions. Additionally, as a general modeling framework, SEM offers the benefit of being extremely flexible, allowing for testing of means on latent, as well as observed, dependent variables for a wide range of designs. A critical advantage of SEM's flexibility is that by making informed choices regarding model specification and estimation methods, most of the assumptions required by standard ordinary least squares (OLS) regression methods can be obviated. Missing data can even be accommodated, assuming patterns of missingness meet certain criteria.

MODELING MEANS IN SEM

Our chapter incorporates several modeling perspectives advocated previously in the literature. First, we utilize a model comparison approach for evaluating alternative models (e.g., Judd & McClelland, 1989; Maxwell & Delaney, 2004; Namboodiri, Carter, & Blalock, 1975; Thompson & Green, 2006). In addition, we join others in employing SEM as a framework for modeling means (e.g., Bagozzi, 1977; Bollen, 1989; Green & Thompson, 2003, 2006; Hancock, 1997, 2004, 2010; Kano, 2001; Thompson & Green, 2006). Hancock (2010) outlined a general approach for rethinking ANOVA/MANOVA analyses using an SEM likelihood-based framework in which information criteria are used for comparisons of models. Our approach shares Hancock's argument that applied constraints should be based on researchers' hypotheses and on the characteristics of the data rather than a set of restrictive assumptions required for applying traditional ANOVA techniques. In addition, we generally endorse Rodgers's (2010) perspective that SEM offers a critical contribution to what he describes as the "modeling revolution," which involves theory-based evaluations of competing models. We are non-radical participants in this modeling revolution in that we include hypothesis testing as part of the statistical decision-making process.

The advantage of SEM over traditional ANOVA techniques in accommodating a variety of distributional properties should not be minimized. There exists a popular belief that tests performed with the traditional ANOVA methods are generally robust to violations of the assumptions of normality of scores in the populations and, to a lesser extent, homogeneity of population variances. As discussed in several reviews of the robustness literature, this perspective is rooted in early studies that focused on Type I error rates under violation of the normality or homogeneity-of-variance assumption but rarely considered power or simultaneous violations of both of these assumptions (Erceg-Hurn & Mirosevich, 2008; Glass, Peckham, & Sanders, 1972; Lix, Keselman, & Keselman, 1996; Wilcox, 1995, 2005). For example, although ANOVA may be regarded as relatively robust to violation of the normality assumption, it is possible that non-normality, and particularly leptokurtosis, will result in larger standard errors of sample mean and produce adverse effects on power for tests of mean differences (Glass et al., 1972; Wilcox, 1995, 2005). Also, simultaneous violations of the normality and homogeneous variances assumptions can lead to inaccurate Type I error rates, even if sample sizes are equal (Zimmerman, 2004). Although recommended alternative test procedures are geared toward addressing particular violations of standard OLS assumptions, none of these methods performs uniformly best, particularly when population distributions are both non-normal and display heterogeneous variances (e.g., Fan & Hancock, 2012; Lix et al., 1996). SEM offers promise as a viable alternative in that it can allow for the joint occurrence of heterogeneous population variances and non-normality.

The flexibility of SEM supports analyses of mean differences on observed or latent dependent variables. Researchers are more likely to make deliberate choices regarding whether analyses should be conducted on observed or latent dependent variables if the modeling method offers the capacity to handle either type. For example, we might have six scales assessing positive and negative emotions as outcome measures in a design to compare the effectiveness of three methods to cope with the death of a spouse. The three coping methods are (1) contacting two or more intimate friends or relatives who agree to listen and talk about the loss at least once per week for 15 weeks; (2) participating in an online grief support group at least once per week for 15 weeks; and (3) creating an individualized program that involves steps to ensure emotional support for 15 weeks, as well as define a new life routine. Within this research context, we argue that researchers would be more likely to actively engage in choices among statistical methods if they approach the analyses from an SEM framework. Alternative strategies might include analyzing differences in means on (1) each of the six emotion scales; (2) a single negative emotion index that is a sum of the negative emotion scales minus a sum of the positive emotion scales (after standardization); (3) a negative emotion index, which is a sum of the negative emotion scales, and a positive emotion index, which is a sum of the positive emotion scales; or (4) two latent variables representing negative and positive emotions, or perhaps an alternative latent variable structure if the a priori unidimensional hypothesis is not supported empirically. A number of difficulties are likely to be encountered if analyses of individual scales are conducted using strategy 1. For example, it would be unclear how to interpret results if one positive and two negative emotion scales were strongly related to the coping factor, but the other three scales were not. Strategies 2 and 3 are problematic if the created indices are not representative of the dimensions underlying the six scales for the population of interest. Strategies 1, 2, and 3 also are problematic in that they do not directly take into account the unreliability of the dependent variable(s). Strategy 4, involving latent variables, is preferable to the other three options in that it permits the researcher to assess empirically the choice of dependent variables in the context of the research study, as well as to take into account the unreliability of the scales. As we discuss later, researchers may still face analytic problems when they assess mean differences on latent variables. They must be able to support a latent variable structure that has meaning statistically and conceptually across groups before testing differences in latent variable means.

A FRAMEWORK FOR UNDERSTANDING ANALYSES OF DIFFERENCES IN MEANS WITH SEM

In this chapter we take a building-blocks approach to the analyses of means using SEM. We initially consider tests of differences in means on observed measures. We demonstrate how to conduct analyses on measures for a one-way ANOVA design and then for more complex designs. For each design, we discuss approaches using OLS regression analysis prior to presenting tests of the same hypotheses using SEM with maximum likelihood (ML) estimation. The presentation of OLS methods is helpful in understanding SEM methods from a number of perspectives: (1) The constraints on means used with the OLS model are comparable to those imposed with structural equation models; (2) it is reassuring to know that OLS and SEM parameter estimates are comparable; (3) it allows for recognition and discussion of differences in *p*-values obtained with OLS regression methods and SEM methods; and (4) it fosters a discussion of the restrictiveness of the OLS regression methods in terms of underlying assumptions and, in contrast, the flexibility of SEM methods. With respect to this latter point, we demonstrate why it is unnecessary to make restrictive parametric assumptions using SEM methods (e.g., Fan & Hancock, 2012; Green & Thompson, 2006).

We spend considerable time developing methods for assessing mean differences on observed variables because they generalize to those for evaluating mean differences on latent variables. The same constraints are imposed on models for analyses involving observed and latent dependent variables in one-way and multiway designs, with and without covariates; however, the direct effects of the grouping variable are on latent rather than observed variables. In discussing methods for analyzing mean differences on latent variables, we focus primarily on one-way designs because the methods discussed for multiway designs with observed variables generalize to more complex designs with latent variables. We emphasize the flexibility of latent variable methods and discuss the potential problems researchers may encounter, in some sense, as a function of this flexibility. Although considerable space is devoted to mean differences on observed variables because we take a building-blocks approach, we believe SEM methods for assessing latent mean differences are underutilized in practice and, through this chapter, would like to encourage greater use of these methods by researchers in substantive areas.

UNIVARIATE TESTS OF DIFFERENCES IN MEANS ON OBSERVED MEASURES

Before considering methods for assessing mean differences on observed measures, three comments are worth noting. First, we restrict the word *factor* to mean an independent variable in an ANOVA/MANOVA design and use terms like *latent variables* and *dimensions* to represent constructs underlying a set of measures. Second, we use a very simple notational system that we think best allows for understanding the similarities and the differences among the OLS and SEM methods to assess mean differences. *X*'s and *Y*'s represent independent and dependent observed variables, respectively. *F*'s are latent variables, and *E*'s and *D*'s are residual variables for *Y*'s and *F*'s, respectively. Also, using the *a*–*b*–*c* system introduced by Hancock and Mueller (2006), we denote structural equation model parameters as follows: *a* is an intercept; *b* is an effect of one variable on another variable, and *c* is a variance or covariance. Third, the SAS and Mplus syntax and output for all analyses described in this chapter are available on the handbook's website (*handbookofsem.com*).

There are two well-known, general approaches for testing differences in means on observed measures: regression models, which include coded predictors (e.g., indicator variables) for factors, as well as an intercept (Cohen, Cohen, West, & Aiken, 2008; Pedhazur, 1997), and the overparameterized general linear model (e.g., Green, Marquis, Hershberger, Thompson, & Mc-Collam, 1999; Searle, 1971). An alternative to these approaches is the cell means model (e.g., Kirk, 1995; Searle, 1987). Although the cell means model is not as well known, the constraints required to conduct tests with this model are more transparent than those for the other two approaches, and they are easier to apply and understand. In addition, as we will see, the cell means model generalizes easily to SEM methods for testing means.

With the cell means model, an indicator variable is created for each cell, which is a combination of the levels of the between-subjects factors. For any one indicator variable, a 1 is assigned to all individuals within a cell and a 0 to all other individuals. The cell means model includes all of the indicator variables but no intercept.

With this model, the OLS coefficients for the indicator variables are the cell means. To assess hypotheses, a second model is estimated in which the coefficients of the indicator variables (i.e., cell means) are constrained to be consistent with the hypothesis of interest. The fit of the first model (i.e., the less constrained [LC] model) is compared to the fit of the second model (i.e., the more constrained [MC] model), taking into account the degrees of freedom of the two models, to evaluate the hypothesis of interest.

We illustrate univariate tests of means on measured variables using a cell means regression model approach and demonstrate its generalization to SEM analyses. In Table 24.1, we present data from a fictitious study. In the context of an ongoing longitudinal study, a researcher administered a relationship survey and identified 12 men and 12 women who had experienced termination of committed relationships within the previous 2 months because their partners had met other individuals whom they wanted to date. None of the respondents knew each other. On this same survey, the respondents indicated the approach they were using most frequently to cope with this stressor: no strategy, discussion with significant others, and exercise. Study participants also were administered a life satisfaction measure both 6 months before and 6 months after completing the relationship survey. The purpose of the study was to assess the relationship between choice of coping method and life satisfaction.

One-Way ANOVA

We initially conduct analyses for a one-way ANOVA design, with coping method as the factor and the post-satisfaction measure as the dependent variable. For these analyses, we are ignoring the gender of the research participants and the presatisfaction measure. If we were reporting these analyses in a Results section, they would likely be presented as preliminary analyses. In this section, we describe the cell means model using OLS regression and ML SEM. Partial results from these analyses are presented in Table 24.2.

OLS Regression Method

For the less constrained model, we created three indicator variables (X_1, X_2, and X_3), one for each of the three cells (i.e., no strategy, discussion, or exercise). The three indicator variables are predictors in a regression equation, and the postsatisfaction measure, Y, is the outcome variable:

$$Y = b_{YX1}X_1 + b_{YX2}X_2 + b_{YX3}X_3 + E_{LC} \qquad \textbf{(24.1)}$$

TABLE 24.1. Life Satisfaction before and after Using an Approach for Coping with the Stressor of Termination of a Serious Relationship

| Gender | Coping approach | | | | | |
| | No strategy | | Discuss with significant others | | Exercise | |
	Before stressor	After stressor	Before stressor	After stressor	Before stressor	After stressor
Men	21	22	23	30	27	24
	19	22	23	26	25	30
	22	24	21	22	24	26
	21	25				
	24	27				
	23	30				
Women	21	22	19	25	25	26
	24	23	22	26	23	27
	23	24	21	27	22	28
					23	29
					28	40
					26	42

TABLE 24.2. Results for the One-Way ANOVA Example: Comparison of LC and MC Models to Assess Population Constraints That $\mu_{YG1} = \mu_{YG2} = \mu_{YG3}$

Models	Parameter estimates (means)		Pooled error variance = SS_E/df_E		Test to compare fit of LC and MC models	
	OLS regression	SEM multiple group	OLS regression	SEM multiple group	OLS regression	SEM multiple group
Less constrained	$\begin{bmatrix} b_{YX1} \\ b_{YX2} \\ b_{YX3} \end{bmatrix} = \begin{bmatrix} 24.33 \\ 26.00 \\ 31.33 \end{bmatrix}$	$\begin{bmatrix} a_{YG1} \\ a_{YG2} \\ a_{YG3} \end{bmatrix} = \begin{bmatrix} 24.33 \\ 26.00 \\ 31.33 \end{bmatrix}$	$18.19 = \\ 382.00/21$	$15.92 = \\ 382.00/24$	$F(2,21) = \dfrac{\left(\dfrac{617.62-382}{23-21}\right)}{382/21}$ $= 6.48, \quad p = .006$	$\chi^2(4-2) = 19.52 - 7.99$ $= 11.53, p = .003$
More constrained	$\begin{bmatrix} b_{YX} \\ b_{YX} \\ b_{YX} \end{bmatrix} = \begin{bmatrix} 27.38 \\ 27.38 \\ 27.38 \end{bmatrix}$	$\begin{bmatrix} a_Y \\ a_Y \\ a_Y \end{bmatrix} = \begin{bmatrix} 27.38 \\ 27.38 \\ 27.38 \end{bmatrix}$	$26.85 = \\ 617.62/23$	$25.73 = \\ 617.62/24$		

Note. The results for the SEM multiple indicator variable (MIV) method were comparable with those for the multiple group (MG) method. However, the means are represented by different parameters for the MIV model. In addition, although the values for the chi-square difference test were the same for the MIV and MG models, the chi-square value for the LC MIV model was equal to 0, and the chi-square for the MC MIV model was equal to 11.53.

where b_{YX1}, b_{YX2}, and b_{YX3} are the coefficients for the three indicator variables, and E_{LC} represents the errors in prediction for the less constrained model. It should be noted that in contrast to the typical regression equation, we have not included an intercept.

As shown in Table 24.2, the coefficients that minimize the sum of squared errors (SSE) are the cell means of 24.33, 26.00, and 31.33. Thus, the predicted scores for an individual in any one cell is the cell mean in that an individual has a score of 1 on the indicator variable associated with that cell and a score of 0 on all other indicator variables in the model. Given the predicted scores are cell means, the SSE around these cell means (SSE_{LC}) is 382, and the mean squared error (MSE_{LC}) is 18.19.

Next, we specify a more constrained model, in which the three parameters are constrained to be equal to a common coefficient, b_{YX}:

$$Y = b_{YX}X_1 + b_{YX}X_2 + b_{YX}X_3 + E_{MC}$$

The more constrained model can also be expressed as

$$Y = b_{YX}(X_1 + X_2 + X_3) + E_{MC} = b_{YX}(1) + E_{MC} \quad \textbf{(24.2)}$$

The coefficient b_{YX} for this model is the grand mean, 27.375. For the more constrained model, SSE_{MC} is 617.62, and MSE_{MC} is 26.85.

When we compare the less and more constrained models, we are evaluating whether the cell means are equal because the only difference between the LC and MC models is the imposition of the equality constraint. The test of equality of population cell means is conducted by comparing the errors of the less and more constrained models:

$$F(2,21) = \frac{\left(SSE_{MC} - SSE_{LC}\right) \big/ \left(DFE_{MC} - DFE_{LC}\right)}{SSE_{LC} \big/ DFE_{LC}}$$

$$= \frac{\left(617.625 - 382\right) \big/ \left(23 - 21\right)}{382 \big/ 21} = 6.48 \quad \textbf{(24.3)}$$

Based on this test, the null hypothesis that the population means are equal was rejected at the .05 level, $p = .006$.

Within a general data analytic perspective, we can reach one of two conclusions based on hypothesis testing: (1) If the null hypothesis is rejected, we conclude the factor is related to some extent to the dependent variable in the population; or (2) if the null hypothesis is not rejected, we withhold judgment about the population relationship between the factor and the dependent variable. Regardless of the conclusion we reach based on the hypothesis test, we should provide additional information by computing an R^2 as an estimate of how strong the relationship is between the factor and the dependent variable in the sample. One interpretation of R^2 is the proportion reduction in the SSE with the LC model relative to the MC model:

$$R^2 = \frac{\text{SSE}_{MC} - \text{SSE}_{LC}}{\text{SSE}_{MC}} \qquad \textbf{(24.4)}$$
$$= \frac{617.625 - 382}{617.625} = .38$$

The test of equality of population cell means, as well as the coefficients and fit indices for the LC model, can be computed with PROC REG in SAS[c]:

```
PROC REG;
MODEL Y=X1 X2 X3/NOINT;
TEST X1 – X2=0, X2 – X3=0;
```

The coefficients and fit indices for the more constrained model can be calculated with SAS by replacing the TEST statement with a RESTRICT statement.

SEM Multiple-Group Method

We conducted comparable analyses using multiple-group SEM. For these analyses, each of the three levels of the coping factor is a different group. The LC, multiple-group model is shown in the top panel of Figure 24.1. For any one group g, the postsatisfaction measure (Y) is a function of a unit predictor, which has the value of 1 for all individuals:

$$Y = a_{Yg}(1) + E_{LC} \qquad \textbf{(24.5)}$$

In Figure 24.1, the unit predictor is represented by the triangle containing a 1. The coefficient for the unit predictor is an intercept a_{Yg}, and, as indicated by its subscript, it is allowed to vary among the three groups (and as shown in Figure 24.1 as a_{YG1}, a_{YG2}, and a_{YG3} for the three coping groups). Because Y is affected only by a unit predictor, the ML estimates of these intercepts are means, more specifically, the Y means for the three coping groups (i.e., $\hat{\mu}_{YG1}$, $\hat{\mu}_{YG2}$, and $\hat{\mu}_{YG3}$). To be consistent with the assumption of homogeneity of error variances for our OLS model, we constrain the error variances to be equal across groups. We represent error variances

as double-headed curved arrows in the path diagrams, but do not include c's to denote these variances to minimize clutter. The chi-square for the less constrained model is significant at the .05 level: $\chi^2(2) = 7.99$, $p = .018$. The lack of fit is due to heterogeneity among the three error variances. As we discuss later, we do not have to assume homogeneity of error variances using the SEM approach and can allow these variances to be freely estimated.

The more constrained model is identical to the less constrained model except the intercepts are constrained to be equal to a common value a_Y:

$$Y = a_Y(1) + E_{MC} \qquad \textbf{(24.6)}$$

where a_Y is the grand mean of Y, which is 27.38. The chi-square for this model is $\chi^2(4) = 19.52$, $p < .001$. By comparing the MC and LC models, we are assessing whether the population means for the three coping methods are equal, $\chi^2(2) = 19.52 - 7.99 = 11.53$, $p = .003$.

The model equations are equivalent for the SEM multiple-group and the OLS regression approaches (i.e., Equations 24.5 and 24.6 relative to Equations 24.1 and 24.2), and the coefficients for these equations are identical. On the other hand, the error variances for the two models differ. ML estimates of variances do not take into account degrees of freedom. More specifically, the error variances are computed by dividing the sums of squared errors by the total sample size (N) for ML estimates rather than N minus the number of nonredundant estimated means for least squares estimates (in our example, $N - 3$ for the LC model and $N - 1$ for the MC model). For SEM estimates, the error variances were 15.92 (= 382/24) for M_{LC} and 25.73 (= 617.62/24) for M_{MC}. Because the SSEs are easily computed from the SEM results, the R^2 also can be calculated using Equation 24.4.

The major difference in results between OLS and ML is with respect to the significance tests. The p-value for the chi-square difference test between M_{LC} and M_{MC} was .003 in comparison with .006 for the test with OLS. From our perspective, it was surprising that the p-values were as similar as they were, given that the test statistic for the SEM analyses is only approximately distributed as a chi-square in large samples. We discuss later the robustness of SEM tests of means with small to moderate sample sizes. Additional methods could be used to assess fit and to make choices between models, such as information statistics (Hancock, 2010).

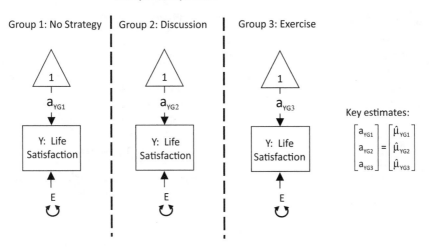

Multiple-Group Model

Group 1: No Strategy | Group 2: Discussion | Group 3: Exercise

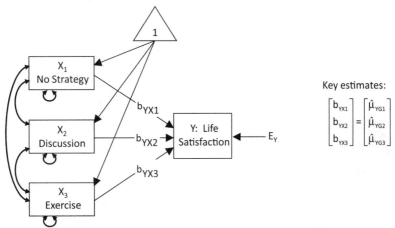

Multiple Indicator Variable Model

FIGURE 24.1. Less constrained models for the one-way ANOVA data. For the more constrained multiple-group model, the *a* intercepts are restricted to be equal to each other. For the more constrained multiple-indicator model, the *b* coefficients are restricted to be equal to each other. The error variances for both the LC and MC multiple-group models are constrained to be equal across groups to demonstrate similarity of results with those based on OLS regression methods.

SEM Multiple Indicator Variable Method

With SEM, we can also assess differences in means by developing models with multiple indicators. We refer to these models as SEM multiple indicator variable (MIV) models. Their form is equivalent to the ones for the OLS regression models (Equations 24.1 and 24.2). The less constrained MIV model includes three indicator variables, but no intercept term to predict the post-satisfaction measure:

$$Y = b_{YX1}X_1 + b_{YX2}X_2 + b_{YX3}X_3 + E_{LC}$$

The model is displayed in the path diagram at the bottom of Figure 24.1. As shown in the diagram, we allow for variances (i.e., double-headed curved arrows to the X's) and covariances (i.e., double-headed curved arrows between X's) among the three indicator variables, as well as for a nonzero mean (i.e., arrows from the 1's triangle to the X's).

For the more constrained model, the coefficients for the three indicator variables are constrained to be equal to a common coefficient b_{YX}:

$$Y = b_{YX}X_1 + b_{YX}X_2 + b_{YX}X_3 + E_{MC}$$

A mathematically equivalent model includes only an intercept term for the predicted score (see Equation 24.2). However, we chose to impose equality constraints on the coefficients for the more constrained MIV model in our analyses with Mplus.

For both the LC and MC models, the estimated coefficients for the MIV models are equivalent to the estimated intercepts for the multiple-group models. In addition, the results of the significance tests are identical across the two SEM methods. It should be noted that the LC MIV model is just-identified (i.e., model has 0 df and must fit perfectly); therefore, the test on the more constrained MIV model is equivalent to the test comparing the MC and LC MIV models and evaluates the null hypotheses that the population means are equal between groups. As we discuss later, the only disadvantage with the MIV model relative to the multiple-group approach is that it is less flexible. For example, the MIV model does not allow for unequal variances between groups.

MIV models, as we have described them, cannot be estimated with all SEM software packages. Because indicator variables are included in the models for all cells, the covariance matrix among predictors is singular, and no results are presented for some packages.

However, Mplus provides appropriate results (if Type = RANDOM is included in the ANALYSIS section), with one exception. Mplus adds one df to the MIV models to account for the perceived redundancy in the covariance matrix among the indicator variables. Accordingly, the df for both the LC and MC models can be corrected by subtracting one from the reported df. The ANOVA null hypothesis can then be evaluated based on the chi-square and the corrected df for the MC model. Alternatively, the hypothesis can be evaluated by computing a chi-square difference test between the MC and LC models (with the uncorrected df) in that the chi-squares reported for both models have one too many df. The same df-correction methods can be applied for all univariate MIV models. We discuss correction methods for multivariate MIV models later.

One-Way ANCOVA

The methods for conducting a one-way ANOVA can be easily extended to analyze data using a one-way analysis of covariance (ANCOVA). We briefly illustrate how to conduct a one-way ANCOVA using our example data (see Table 24.1). The covariate for our example is the life satisfaction measure obtained prior to the stressor (presatisfaction measure), whereas the dependent variable is the postsatisfaction measure. The gender factor was ignored for the one-way ANCOVA analyses. Partial results for one-way ANCOVA based on the various methods are presented in Table 24.3.

OLS Regression Method

For this method, we included in the LC and MC models not only the three indicator variables (X_1, X_2, and X_3), representing the three coping approaches, but also the covariate, the presatisfaction measure (X_4), which was grand mean–centered (i.e., subtracting the grand mean of the presatisfaction measure from all scores on that measure):

$$Y = b_{YX1}X_1 + b_{YX2}X_2 + b_{YX3}X_3 + b_{YX4}X_4 + E_{LC} \quad \textbf{(24.7)}$$

For the LC model, the estimated coefficients for the indicator variables are the estimated means on the dependent variable for individuals who have a score of zero on the covariate, as given in Table 24.3. Because the covariate was grand mean–centered, these coefficients are the estimated means on the postsatisfaction measure for subjects who are at the mean on the presatisfaction

TABLE 24.3. Results for the One-Way ANCOVA Example: Comparison of LC and MC Models to Assess Population Constraints That $\mu_{YG1 \bullet X4} = \mu_{YG2 \bullet X4} = \mu_{YG3 \bullet X4}$

Models	Parameter estimates (means)		Pooled error variance = SS_E/df_E		Test to compare fit of LC and MC models	
	OLS regression	SEM multiple group	OLS regression	SEM multiple group	OLS regression	SEM multiple group
Less constrained	$\begin{bmatrix} b_{YX1} \\ b_{YX2} \\ b_{YX3} \end{bmatrix} = \begin{bmatrix} 24.33 \\ 26.00 \\ 31.33 \end{bmatrix}$	$\begin{bmatrix} a_{YG1} \\ a_{YG2} \\ a_{YG3} \end{bmatrix} = \begin{bmatrix} 24.33 \\ 26.00 \\ 31.33 \end{bmatrix}$	$11.46 =$ $229.31/20$	$9.56 =$ $229.31/24$	$F(2,21) = \dfrac{\left(\dfrac{617.62 - 382}{23 - 21}\right)}{382/21}$ $= 6.48, \ p = .006$	$\chi^2(6-4) = 10.87 - 7.60$ $= 3.27, p = .195$
More constrained	$\begin{bmatrix} b_{YX} \\ b_{YX} \\ b_{YX} \end{bmatrix} = \begin{bmatrix} 27.38 \\ 27.38 \\ 27.38 \end{bmatrix}$	$\begin{bmatrix} a_Y \\ a_Y \\ a_Y \end{bmatrix} = \begin{bmatrix} 27.38 \\ 27.38 \\ 27.38 \end{bmatrix}$	$11.94 =$ $262.74/22$	$10.95 =$ $262.74/24$		

Note. The covariate was grand mean–centered for all analyses. The coefficients associated with the covariate were 1.53 for the LC model and 1.75 for the MC model. In addition, the results for the SEM multiple indicator variable (MIV) method were comparable with those for the multiple-group (MG) method. However, the means are represented by different parameters for the MIV model. In addition, although the values for the chi-square difference test were the same for the MIV and MG models, the chi-square value for the LC MIV model was equal to 0, and the chi-square for the MC MIV model was equal to 3.27.

measure. Using the jargon of ANCOVA, the coefficients are the adjusted means on the dependent variable. To assess whether these adjusted means are equal in the population, the coefficients associated with the indicator variables are constrained to be equal to a common coefficient b_{YX} in the more constrained model:

$$Y = b_{YX}X_1 + b_{YX}X_2 + b_{YX}X_3 + b_{YX4}X_4 + E_{MC} \quad \textbf{(24.8)}$$
$$= b_{YX}(1) + b_{YX4}X_4 + E_{MC}$$

The constrained coefficient, b_{YX}, is the mean on the postsatisfaction measure at the mean of the presatisfaction measure (ignoring groups).

An F-test can then be computed based on the errors in prediction for the LC and MC models, as shown in Table 24.3. The resulting F-test was nonsignificant at the .05 level ($p = .256$). We also can compute a partial R^2, the proportion of variance of postsatisfaction measure accounted for by coping approach, controlling for the presatisfaction measure (i.e., $R^2_{YX1X2X3 \bullet X4}$). In terms of the LC and MC models, this partial R^2 is the proportion reduction in the SSEs with the LC model relative to the MC model:

$$R^2_{YX1X2X3 \bullet X4} = \frac{SSE_{MC} - SSE_{LC}}{SSE_{MC}}$$
$$= \frac{262.74 - 229.31}{262.74} = .127 \quad \textbf{(24.9)}$$

SEM Multiple-Group Method

Models similar to the OLS regression models were specified when applying the SEM multiple-group method. For each group, the grand mean–centered covariate was included as a predictor in the LC models in addition to a constant (i.e., the intercept):

$$Y = a_{Yg}(1) + b_{YX4}X_4 + E_{LC} \quad \textbf{(24.10)}$$

The coefficients for the covariate were constrained to be equal across groups to be consistent with the standard assumption of homogeneity of slopes; consequently, we did not include a subscript for group for the covariate coefficient. In addition, we constrained the error variance to be equal across groups. The estimated intercepts for the LC SEM model are identical to those for OLS coefficients for the indicator variables; that is, they are the adjusted means on the postsatisfaction measure.

To assess the ANCOVA hypothesis, the intercepts for the three groups were constrained to be equal:

$$Y = a_Y(1) + b_{YX4}X_4 + E_{MC} \quad \textbf{(24.11)}$$

The chi-square for the MC model was compared to the chi-square for the LC model. The SEM ANCOVA was not significant at the .05 level ($p = .195$). It should be noted that if the residual variances for the two models are multiplied by N (i.e., 24), the sums of squares for the MC and LC models are obtained, and then the equation for computing the partial R^2 can now be applied using Equation 24.9.

SEM MIV Approach

Identical results can be obtained with a MIV model approach as were found with the SEM multiple-group approach. The equations for the LC and MC models are essentially comparable to those used for OLS regression analyses (Equations 24.7 and 24.8). The parameter estimates for both the LC and MC MIV models were equivalent to those for the multiple-group analyses. In addition, the significance tests for the MIV and multiple-group approaches were the same once the degrees of freedom were corrected (subtract 1 from the df given by Mplus) for the MIV models.

Two-Way ANOVA

In this section, we demonstrate analyses for conducting a two-way ANOVA. The methods discussed in this section and the previous section on one-way ANCOVA easily generalize to higher-way ANOVA and ANCOVA designs. We demonstrate how to conduct a two-way ANOVA using our example data (see Table 24.1).

We include gender as well as coping as factors and the postsatisfaction measure as the dependent variable. The gender and coping factors are correlated for our example (Cramer's $V = .29$). Men were more likely to use no strategy to deal with a breakup, whereas women were more likely to use exercise.

Before considering the different methods for conducting a two-way ANOVA, we briefly discuss choices we need to make when factors are correlated in defining marginal means and thus the main effects that evaluate these marginal means (see Maxwell & Delaney, 2004, for a more complete discussion of this topic). As illustrated in Table 24.4 with our example data, we consider two standard ways for defining marginal means: unweighted and weighted means.

With unweighted means, the row (or column) marginal means are computed by adding all cell means in a row (or column) and dividing by the number of cells. Differences in unweighted means are assessed using a generalized linear model (GLM) approach by evaluating the effects of one factor on the dependent variable, partialing out the effects of the other factor and the interaction between factors (i.e., Type III sums of squares). For example, the test of unweighted means for the coping main effect evaluates differences in population means for satisfaction among coping strategies, given that each strategy was utilized equally by men and women.

TABLE 24.4. Cell and Marginal Means on the Postsatisfaction Measure for the Two-Way ANOVA

Gender		Coping approach			Unweighted row means ($_u\hat{\mu}_{j\bullet}$)	Weighted row means ($_w\hat{\mu}_{j\bullet}$)
		No strategy	Discuss with others	Exercise		
Men	$\hat{\mu}_{jk}$	25	26	30	$\frac{24+26+30}{3}=27.00$	$\frac{(6)25+(3)26+(3)30}{12}=26.50$
	n_{jk}	6	3	3		
Women	$\hat{\mu}_{jk}$	23	26	32	$\frac{23+26+32}{3}=27.00$	$\frac{(3)23+(3)26+(6)32}{12}=28.25$
	n_{jk}	3	3	6		
Unweighted column means ($_u\hat{\mu}_{\bullet k}$)		$\frac{25+23}{2}=24.00$	$\frac{26+26}{2}=26.00$	$\frac{30+32}{2}=31.00$		
Weighted column means ($_w\hat{\mu}_{\bullet k}$)		$\frac{(6)25+(3)23}{9}=24.33$	$\frac{(3)26+(3)26}{6}=26.00$	$\frac{(3)30+(6)32}{9}=31.33$		

With weighted means, the row (or column) marginal means are computed by weighting the cell means by their cell frequencies in a row (or column) and dividing by the sum of the cell frequencies in a row (or column). Differences in weighted means are evaluated with a GLM approach by assessing the effects of one factor on the dependent variable, disregarding the effects of the other factor and the interaction between factors (i.e., Type I sums of squares with the focal factor entered first into the model). For our example, the test of weighted means for the coping main effect evaluates differences in population means for satisfaction among coping strategies, *given that each strategy was utilized with the proportions for men and women found in the sample.* To the extent that the sample proportions are not representative of the population proportions, this approach is inappropriate.

It is important to note that the choice between weighted and unweighted means is dictated by the researcher's questions. For simplicity, we present in Table 24.5 the OLS regression and ML SEM results only for the coping main effect based on weighted means.

OLS Regression Method

The cell means model is particularly helpful in formulating hypotheses concerning two-way ANOVA designs. With these designs, indicator variables do not represent distinctions among levels of a factor, but rather distinctions among combinations of levels of between-subjects factors, that is, the cells of a design. For our example, the LC model includes the six indicator variables for the six cells of the 2 × 3 ANOVA (but no intercept):

$$Y = b_{YX1}X_1 + b_{YX2}X_2 + b_{YX3}X_3 + b_{YX4}X_4 \quad \textbf{(24.12)}$$
$$+ b_{YX5}X_5 + b_{YX6}X_6 + E_{LC}$$

X_1 through X_3 are the indicator variables for the three coping strategies for men, and X_4 through X_6 are the indicator variables for the three coping levels for women.

TABLE 24.5. Results for Coping Main Effect with Weighted Means for Two-Way ANOVA Example: Comparison of LC and MC Models to Assess Population Constraint That $(2/3)\mu_{YG1} + (1/3)\mu_{YG4} = (1/2)\mu_{YG2} + (1/2)\mu_{YG5} = (1/3)\mu_{YG3} + (2/3)\mu_{YG6}$

Models	Parameter estimates (cell means)		Pooled error variance = SS_E/df_E		Test to compare fit of LC and MC models	
	OLS regression	SEM multiple group	OLS regression	SEM multiple group	OLS regression	SEM multiple group
Less constrained	$\begin{bmatrix} b_{YX1} \\ b_{YX2} \\ b_{YX3} \\ b_{YX4} \\ b_{YX5} \\ b_{YX6} \end{bmatrix} = \begin{bmatrix} 25.00 \\ 26.00 \\ 30.00 \\ 23.00 \\ 26.00 \\ 32.00 \end{bmatrix}$	$\begin{bmatrix} a_{YX1} \\ a_{YX2} \\ a_{YX3} \\ a_{YX4} \\ a_{YX5} \\ a_{YX6} \end{bmatrix} = \begin{bmatrix} 25.00 \\ 26.00 \\ 30.00 \\ 23.00 \\ 26.00 \\ 32.00 \end{bmatrix}$	$20.33 = 366.00/18$	$15.25 = 366.00/24$		
More constrained[a]	$\begin{bmatrix} \tilde{b}_{YX1} \\ \tilde{b}_{YX2} \\ \tilde{b}_{YX3} \\ \tilde{b}_{YX4} \\ \tilde{b}_{YX5} \\ \tilde{b}_{YX6} \end{bmatrix} = \begin{bmatrix} 28.04 \\ 27.38 \\ 26.04 \\ 26.04 \\ 27.38 \\ 28.04 \end{bmatrix}$	$\begin{bmatrix} \tilde{a}_{YX1} \\ \tilde{a}_{YX2} \\ \tilde{a}_{YX3} \\ \tilde{a}_{YX4} \\ \tilde{a}_{YX5} \\ \tilde{a}_{YX6} \end{bmatrix} = \begin{bmatrix} 28.04 \\ 27.38 \\ 26.04 \\ 26.04 \\ 27.38 \\ 28.04 \end{bmatrix}$	$30.08 = 601.62/20$	$25.07 = 601.62/24$	$F_{(2,18)} = \dfrac{\left(\dfrac{601.62-366}{20-18}\right)}{366/18}$ $= 5.79, \quad p = .011$	$\chi^2(7-5) = 30.69 - 18.76$ $= 11.93, p = .003$

Note. The results for the SEM multiple indicator variable (MIV) method were comparable with those for the multiple-group (MG) method. However, the means were represented by different parameters for the MIV model. In addition, although the values for the chi-square difference test were the same for the MIV and MG models, the chi-square value for the LC MIV model was equal to 0, and the chi-square for the MC MIV model was equal to 11.93.
[a] The tildes above the coefficients indicate equality constraints were imposed on these parameters that are consistent with the coping main effect hypothesis for weighted means.

The coefficients for the predictors in this model are freely estimated and yield the cell means.

Main and interaction hypotheses, as well as others, can be evaluated by imposing constraints on the parameters of the indicator variables that are consistent with the null hypothesis of interest. For example, using weights that reflect the proportions of men and women using each of the coping strategies in our example, the null hypothesis for the coping main effect based on weighted means is

$$(2/3)\mu_{YG1} + (1/3)\mu_{YG4} = (1/2)\mu_{YG2} + (1/2)\mu_{YG5}$$
$$= (1/3)\mu_{YG3} + (2/3)\mu_{YG6}$$

Given that the coefficients for the LC model represent cell means, the following equality constraints were consistent with this hypothesis and were imposed on the regression coefficients:

$$(2/3)b_{YX1} + (1/3)b_{YX4} = (1/2)b_{YX2} + (1/2)b_{YX5}$$
$$(1/2)b_{YX2} + (1/2)b_{YX5} = (1/3)b_{YX3} + (2/3)b_{YX6}$$

In Table 24.5, we give the estimated coefficients for the MC model. The resulting coefficients can be viewed as the best estimates of the cell means given the imposed constraints. We then compared the errors in prediction for the LC and MC models to test the coping main effect for weighted means (shown in Table 24.5), as well as to compute the partial R^2 (not shown).

The same procedure was applied to assess the main effects for coping based on the unweighted means, the main effects for gender based on the unweighted and weighted means, and the interaction. For example, we assessed the interaction hypothesis by comparing the errors in prediction for the LC model (Equation 24.12) with those for the MC model with the following equality constraint:

$$b_{YX1} - b_{YX4} = b_{YX2} - b_{YX5}$$
$$b_{YX2} - b_{YX5} = b_{YX3} - b_{YX6}$$

These additional analyses are available on this handbook's website (*www.handbookofsem.com*).

SEM Multiple-Group Method

The multiple groups for this method represent the cells in the higher-way design. Thus, in our example, the groups are the six cells created by our 2×3 ANOVA.

The LC model is essentially identical to the model for a one-way ANOVA, except with six groups (i.e., $Y = a_{Yg}(1) + E_{LC}$). Accordingly, the intercepts, a_{Yg}, estimate the cell means. For the more constrained model we impose constraints to assess the hypothesis of interest. The imposed constraints are comparable to those for the OLS regression analysis, except they are imposed on the intercepts rather than the coefficients of the indicator variables. For both the LC and MC structural equation models, we required the variances for the six groups to be equal to each other to obtain results equivalent to those for OLS regression. As with ANOVA and ANCOVA designs, the SEM multiple-group analyses yielded comparable results to those based on OLS regression, except with respect to the p-values for the hypothesis tests. As illustrated in Table 24.5 with the test of the coping main effects for weighted means, the p-values for chi-square tests with the SEM multiple-group analyses were smaller than the p-values based on the OLS regression analyses.

SEM MIV Approach

The MIV models are comparable to the OLS regression models. For the LC model, the coefficients for the six indicator variables associated with the six cells are the cell means. Constraints are imposed on these parameters to assess the hypotheses of interest. The constraints are equivalent to those discussed with the OLS regression and SEM multiple-group approaches.

One-Way MANOVA

The procedures for conducting ANOVA and ANCOVA designs easily generalize to multivariate analysis of variance (MANOVA) and multivariate analysis of covariance (MANCOVA) designs. However, due to space limitations, we will consider analyses for only a one-way MANOVA. To illustrate a one-way MANOVA (as well as analyses of differences in factor means), we created a new data set. In this fictitious study, 200 women who exercise on a regular basis wrote an essay about how they cope with stressors involving relationships with close friends and dating partners. Based on the essay, the participants were classified as using no well-defined coping strategy ($n_1 = 60$), a strategy involving discussion about stressors with significant others ($n_2 = 60$), or a strategy of exercise to promote a positive emotional mood state ($n_3 = 80$). All 200 women also completed four satisfaction measures: satisfaction with emotional status, satisfaction with romantic relationships, satisfaction with friendships, and satisfaction with self-achievements. The data set is available on this handbook's website (*www.handbookofsem.com*). Results for the one-way MANOVA using OLS regression and SEM approaches are shown in Table 24.6.

Faced with our example data, many researchers would conduct a one-way MANOVA, as we do next. However, they could also evaluate differences in means on a latent variable underlying the four dependent measures. When faced with designs with multiple dependent variables, it is important for researchers to consider whether it would be preferable to assess differences in means on observed or latent variables. These issues are discussed later in the chapter.

OLS Multivariate Regression Method

For this method, the LC model includes three indicator variables predicting each of the dependent variables. The model can be represented as follows for our data:

$$
\begin{aligned}
Y_1 &= b_{Y1X1}X_1 + b_{Y1X2}X_2 + b_{Y1X3}X_3 + E_{Y1LC} \\
Y_2 &= b_{Y2X1}X_1 + b_{Y2X2}X_2 + b_{Y2X3}X_3 + E_{Y2LC} \\
Y_3 &= b_{Y3X1}X_1 + b_{Y3X2}X_2 + b_{Y3X3}X_3 + E_{Y3LC} \\
Y_4 &= b_{Y4X1}X_1 + b_{Y4X2}X_2 + b_{Y4X3}X_3 + E_{Y4LC}
\end{aligned}
\quad \textbf{(24.13)}
$$

The MANOVA model assumes that the population covariance matrices among errors are the same across the three levels of the factor. The MC model is similarly specified but restricts the coefficients associated with the three indicator variables to be equal to each other for each dependent variable, which simplifies to the following model:

$$
\begin{aligned}
Y_1 &= b_{Y1X}(1) + E_{Y1MC} \\
Y_2 &= b_{Y2X}(1) + E_{Y2MC} \\
Y_3 &= b_{Y3X}(1) + E_{Y3MC} \\
Y_4 &= b_{Y4X}(1) + E_{Y4MC}
\end{aligned}
\quad \textbf{(24.14)}
$$

As shown in Table 24.6, the parameter estimates for the indicator variables associated with each dependent variable are the group means for the LC model and the grand means for the MC model. Based on these models, error sums of squares and cross-products (SSCP) matrices are computed. Wilks's lambda (Λ) is a function of the determinants of these two matrices. An effect size statistic can be computed from Wilks's lambda (e.g., $1 - \Lambda$), as well as an F-test to assess the hypothesis that the population means for all dependent variables are equal across groups. For our example, $\Lambda = .887$; therefore, the proportion of generalized variance accounted for was .113. The null hypothesis of equal population means

TABLE 24.6. Results for the One-Way MANOVA Example: Comparison of LC and MC Models to Assess Population Constraints That $\mu_{Y1G1} = \mu_{Y1G2} = \mu_{Y1G3}, \mu_{Y2G1} = \mu_{Y2G2} = \mu_{Y2G3}, \mu_{Y3G1} = \mu_{Y3G2} = \mu_{Y3G3},$ **and** $\mu_{Y4G1} = \mu_{Y4G2} = \mu_{Y4G3}$

Models	Means for the three groups and four dependent variables	Error sums of squares and cross-products matrix	Test to compare fit of LC and MC models	
			OLS regression	SEM multiple group
Less constrained	$\begin{bmatrix} 24.62 & 52.57 & 40.58 & 33.48 \\ 24.60 & 54.45 & 41.48 & 42.08 \\ 26.22 & 55.10 & 33.68 & 35.28 \end{bmatrix}$	$\begin{bmatrix} 2650.53 & 1403.08 & 1358.67 & 1675.57 \\ 1403.08 & 2726.78 & 1228.52 & 1362.92 \\ 1358.67 & 1228.52 & 2633.12 & 1278.62 \\ 1675.57 & 1362.92 & 1278.62 & 3387.92 \end{bmatrix}$	$\Lambda = \dfrac{\lvert E_{LC} \rvert}{\lvert E_{MC} \rvert} = .89$	
			$F_{(8,388)} = \dfrac{(1 - .89^{\frac{1}{2}})/8}{(.89^{\frac{1}{2}})/388}$ $= 3.00, \ p = .003$	$\chi^2(28 - 20) = 40.40$ $- 16.40$ $= 24.00,$ $p = .002$
More constrained	$\begin{bmatrix} 25.26 & 54.14 & 41.45 & 34.26 \\ 25.26 & 54.14 & 41.45 & 34.26 \\ 25.26 & 54.14 & 41.45 & 34.26 \end{bmatrix}$	$\begin{bmatrix} 2776.00 & 1525.60 & 1439.05 & 1806.74 \\ 1525.60 & 2954.80 & 1358.95 & 1503.46 \\ 1439.05 & 1358.95 & 2709.50 & 1368.60 \\ 1806.74 & 1503.46 & 1368.60 & 3526.48 \end{bmatrix}$		

Note. The means are represented by comparable parameters for the OLS regression and the SEM multiple indicator variable (MIV) method, but by different parameters for the multiple-group (MG) method. The parameter estimates representing these means yielded identical results across methods. Also, although the values for the chi-square difference test are the same for the MIV and MG models, the chi-square value for the LC MIV model was equal to 0, and the chi-square for the MC MIV model was equal to 24.00.

across the three coping groups for all four dependent variables was rejected at the .05 level, $p = .003$.

SEM Multiple-Group Method

The multiple groups for this method represent the levels of a factor. For our example, there are three levels of the coping factor, as shown in the path model in the top panel of Figure 24.2. The less constrained model allows the intercepts (means) on the dependent variables to differ across groups:

$$
\begin{aligned}
Y_1 &= a_{Y1g} + E_{Y1LC} \\
Y_2 &= a_{Y2g} + E_{Y2LC} \\
Y_3 &= a_{Y3g} + E_{Y3LC} \\
Y_4 &= a_{Y4g} + E_{Y4LC}
\end{aligned}
\tag{24.15}
$$

The more constrained model restricts these means to be equal across groups. To maintain comparability with the OLS multivariate regression model, we constrained the variances and covariances among dependent variables to be the same across the three groups for both the LC and MC models.

Comparable results were obtained with the SEM multiple-group model and the OLS multivariate regression approaches, except those associated with the hypothesis tests. As with previous analyses, the p-value for the SEM chi-square test was less than the p-value for the F-test. The values in the error SSCP matrices were perfectly reproduced by multiplying the variances and covariances in the SEM output by the total sample size.

SEM MIV Model Approach

The models for this method are specified in an identical fashion to those for the OLS regression approach. The LC MIV model for MANOVA involves predicting each of the dependent variables from the three indicator variables with freely estimated coefficients, as shown in the bottom panel of Figure 24.2, whereas the coefficients for the indicator variables are constrained to be equal across groups for each dependent variable for the MC model. The results for the SEM MIV model method are identical to those for the SEM multiple-group approach.

It should be noted that the correction to the df for the MIV model differs slightly with the MANOVA analyses. For ANOVA/ANCOVA analyses, Mplus adds

1 to the df for the MIV models to account for the perceived redundancy in the covariance matrix among the indicator variables to predict a dependent variable. For MANOVA/MANCOVA analyses, there are multiple dependent variables and, accordingly, Mplus adds 1 df to correct for perceived predictor redundancy for each dependent variable. Thus, for MANOVA analyses, the df for the MIV models must be corrected by subtracting the number of dependent variables from the df reported by Mplus. The MANOVA null hypothesis can be evaluated based on the chi-square and the corrected df for the MC model. Alternatively, the hypothesis can be evaluated by computing a chi-square difference test between the MC and LC models (with the uncorrected df) in that the chi-squares reported for both models are incorrect by the same number of df.

TESTS OF DIFFERENCES IN MEANS ON OBSERVED MEASURES DISREGARDING OLS ASSUMPTIONS

At this point, we have demonstrated that OLS regression and SEM approaches for ANOVA/MANOVA designs are specified similarly, and, despite differences in estimation methods, yield comparable results, with the exception that the p-values of the tests differ across approaches. Although we hope this presentation was interesting, we have not yet made arguments that would sway readers to use SEM methods in place of OLS regression approaches. In fact, the OLS methods appear superior in that the F-test is exact if its underlying assumptions are met, whereas the chi-square test is approximate and generally too frequently rejects the null hypothesis for small sample sizes (Boomsma, 1983). We argue in this section that, in practice, the bias of the p-values for SEM tests may not be as severe as one might perceive. In addition, SEM methods are more flexible than OLS methods in that they do not require distributional assumptions. To the extent that these arguments are valid, OLS ANOVA/MANOVA should be abandoned for SEM methods or other approaches that offer similar advantages, such as bootstrap methods (Keselman, Wilcox, & Lix, 2003; Keselman et al., 2008).

We begin by considering the accuracy of Type I error rates for ANOVA/MANOVA hypotheses using SEM. We could find no Monte Carlo studies that investigated the robustness of these tests under very small sample sizes; therefore, we conducted a limited study to ex-

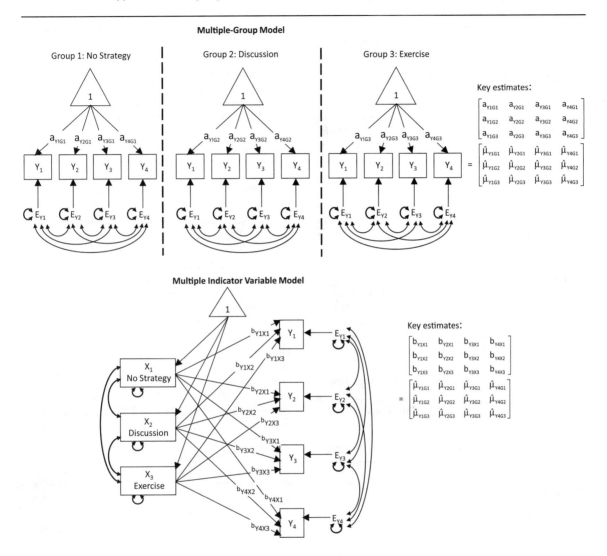

FIGURE 24.2. LC models for the one-way MANOVA data. For the MC multiple-group model, the *a* intercepts are restricted to be equal to each other for each dependent variable. For the MC multiple-indicator model, the *b* coefficients are restricted to be equal to each other for each dependent variable. The error variances for both the LC and MC multiple-group models are constrained to be equal across groups to demonstrate similarity of results with those based on OLS regression methods.

plore this issue using Mplus. All data were generated to meet the assumptions of ANOVA/MANOVA and to be consistent with the null hypotheses for these tests. In addition, we restricted our investigation to analyses with three groups and either one dependent variable (ANOVA) or four dependent variables (MANOVA). The population correlations among all dependent variables within groups were .30. We varied the total number of subjects from 24 to 384 for ANOVA and from 48 to 384 for MANOVA. Under all conditions, the number of subjects was evenly split among the three groups. All data were analyzed using a multiple-group approach, and the chi-square difference tests were evaluated at the .05 level. Empirical Type I error rates for these tests were computed based on 10,000 replications and are presented in Table 24.7.

Consistent with previous research (Anderson & Gerbing, 1984; Boomsma, 1983), the results suggest that the null hypothesis is too frequently rejected when sample size is small. Nevertheless, we had expected the chi-square test for the SEM multiple-group analysis to perform even more poorly. Empirical Type I error rates that fall between .025 and .075 meet Bradley's liberal criterion (Bradley, 1978) when the nominal alpha is .05. The empirical Type I error rates met Bradley's liberal criterion even for sample sizes as low as 24 (i.e., eight subjects per group). In contrast, larger sample sizes

were needed for the more complex MANOVA models. Empirical Type I error rates based on a sample size of 96 or greater met Bradley's liberal criterion. Based on our limited results, it would appear that the true Type I error rate for a chi-square test is likely to be relatively close to the nominal alpha for most studies that are designed with adequate power. Additional conditions need to be explored with more than three levels of a factor, more than four dependent variables, unequal sample sizes, and alternative correlational structures among dependent variables.

An attractive feature of the SEM methods is that the distributional assumptions required by ANOVA and MANOVA can be avoided (Fan & Hancock, 2012; Green & Thompson, 2006). For all SEM analyses we have conducted to this point, we met the distributional assumptions of ANOVA/MANOVA. However, the normality assumption can be obviated using SEM multiple-group and MIV model approaches. In addition, the homogeneity-of-variance/covariance assumption can be circumvented with the SEM multiple-group approach. In fact, Fan and Hancock (2012) conducted a Monte Carlo study and showed that in terms of Type I error rates and power, SEM multiple-group analyses yielded results that compared favorably to other robust methods to assess ANOVA hypotheses. Accordingly, although standard ANOVA/MANOVA methods have some advantage over SEM methods for small sample sizes when distributional assumptions are met, this advantage quickly disappears when these assumptions are violated—an omnipresent condition in the analysis of real data. However, neither method is likely to perform well with small sample sizes. We strongly advocate the use of larger sample sizes to increase precision of parameter estimates and obtain satisfactory statistical power.

To illustrate the advantage of the SEM multiple-group approach, let's reconsider our analysis of the MANOVA data. We specify our MC and LC models in exactly the same manner, except now we do not constrain the variances and covariances of the dependent variable to be equivalent across groups. Once the equality constraints are removed, the LC model is just-identified and only the MC model needs to be evaluated. In addition to changing the specification of the models, we could use robust maximum likelihood methods (MLM in Mplus; Satorra & Bentler, 1994) to correct the chi-square test for non-normality. When the variances and covariances among errors are allowed to differ across groups, the LC model is just-identified and

TABLE 24.7. Empirical Type I Error Rates for One-Way ANOVA with Three Groups and One-Way MANOVA with Three Groups and Four Dependent Variables Using Structural Equation Modeling and a Nominal Alpha of .05

Total sample size (N)	Type of analysis	
	One-way ANOVA	One-way MANOVA[a]
24	.071	—
36	.064	.092
48	.058	.077
96	.057	.066
192	.052	.056
384	.050	.052

Note. For all conditions, there were equal numbers of subjects in the three groups. Empirical Type I error rates were computed based on 10,000 replications.
[a]Data for the one-way MANOVA were generated such that within groups the variances for four dependent variables were 1.00 and the covariances between any two variables were .30.

the MC model directly assesses the MANOVA hypothesis, $\chi^2_{\text{Robust}}(8) = 23.33$, $p = .003$.

It could be argued that prior to conducting this chi-square test, it would be advantageous to determine whether the variance–covariance constraints and normality assumption are inappropriate. Thus, one could compare the fit of a model with unconstrained variances and covariances across groups to the fit of a model with constrained variances and covariances. To avoid unnecessary constraints and assumptions, no constraints need to be imposed on the means across groups for either of the two models, and robust ML can be used. With our example data, the test of homogeneity of covariance matrices was not rejected, $\chi^2(20) = 16.68$, $p = .674$, suggesting that the sample variances and covariances did not differ dramatically across groups. To assess the normality assumption, we could assess residual plots and compute skewness and kurtosis on residual scores within groups. It is informative to conduct these analyses, and the results may have substantive meaning in the context of a study. However, it is unclear whether these data analyses have utility in determining how to proceed with tests of differences in means. Until studies are conducted to address this issue, we suggest that researchers are likely to obtain as good or better results by conducting tests of means with unconstrained variances and covariances, and with methods that do not require normality. This recommendation is analogous to using the Welch–Satterthwaite approach to test differences between two independent means without first assessing the homogeneity-of-variance assumption.

TESTS OF DIFFERENCES IN MEANS ON LATENT VARIABLES

Knowing the large investment of resources involved in conducting scholarly research, investigators typically select a diversified portfolio of dependent measures to include in their studies. Prior to conducting a study, they develop conceptual maps to help them determine what dependent constructs are most relevant, taking into account the purpose and design of the study. Within practical limitations, they then try to include multiple measures of each construct, realizing that different measures of the same construct have varying methodological and conceptual boundaries. In the context of our example, the focus is on the effect of coping strategies on life satisfaction. Assuming the interest is in life satisfaction in general, four scales might

be included in the design to assess this single dependent construct in different contexts: emotional status, romantic relationships, relationships with friends, and self-achievements. If measures are selected to represent constructs (i.e., latent variables), it is preferable to assess differences among groups on the latent variables using SEM rather than to conduct a MANOVA on a set of measured variables, for a number of reasons. In contrast to SEM analyses, MANOVA does not directly address differences on latent variables, but rather on measured variables or linear combinations of measured variables (Huberty & Olejnik, 2006). Even if follow-up ANOVAs and discriminant analyses are conducted to evaluate differences in linear combinations of measures that are believed to represent underlying constructs, these analyses evaluate differences on scores measured with error and do not allow for an assessment of fit of the construct system. Also, as shown by Hancock, Lawrence, and Nevitt (2000), it is more powerful to conduct tests of differences on latent variables using SEM than to conduct tests on measured variables using MANOVA.

A reasonable question is "When should one use MANOVA-type analyses, regardless of whether one chooses OLS multivariate regression or ML SEM methods to conduct these analyses?" We suggest a few possible MANOVA applications. If researchers select measures to represent underlying dependent constructs, but are unable to find empirical support for their hypothesized model or an alternative conceptually meaningful latent variable model using SEM, they might choose MANOVA to assess differences on the set of measures. Similarly, if researchers choose a potpourri of dependent measures without conceptualizing an underlying structure, they may be unable to specify a model underlying their measures and, by default, have to analyze their data using MANOVA. Finally, if researchers believe measures combine together to create composite variables (in contrast to measures that are a function of latent variables), then MANOVA might be preferred. However, methodologists have described a number of statistical and conceptual difficulties associated with formative factors (e.g., Franke, Preacher, & Rigdon, 2008; Howell, Brevik, & Wilcox, 2007; MacCallum & Browne, 1993). In summary, we believe MANOVA is overutilized in practice and, often, SEM analysis of latent mean differences is more consistent with hypotheses that are framed at the construct level.

To illustrate SEM analyses to assess differences in latent variables, we use the same data employed to illustrate MANOVA. We consider initially models in which a single latent variable underlies a set of measures and assume all three coping groups are invariant with respect to latent variable loadings and intercepts of dependent measures. We consider later more complex analyses. The path diagrams for the initial SEM multiple-group and MIV analyses are shown in Figure 24.3, and the results for these analyses are presented in Table 24.8.

SEM Multiple-Group Method

In conducting a multiple-group analysis, we specify one or more latent variables underlying the dependent measures in each of the groups. The structure underlying the dependent measures must be similar across groups to assess group differences in latent means. Ideally, measures are chosen that reflect strongly the constructs of interest and demonstrate comparable statistical properties across groups. As we discuss later, the measurement model underlying the measures must, at a minimum, be partially invariant between populations. In addition, we must also impose constraints on the latent means because the values of the means are arbitrary. We typically specify the means of the latent variables to be zero in one group to have an identified model.

For our coping example, we initially specify an LC model to test group differences on latent variables. The measures were specified to be a function of a single factor model:

$$Y_1 = a_{Y1} + b_{Y1F1}F_1 + E_{Y1LC}$$
$$Y_2 = a_{Y2} + b_{Y2F1}F_1 + E_{Y2LC}$$
$$Y_3 = a_{Y3} + b_{Y3F1}F_1 + E_{Y3LC}$$
$$Y_4 = a_{Y4} + b_{Y4F1}F_1 + E_{Y4LC}$$

(24.16)

For simplicity, we required strict invariance across groups for the measurement parameters; that is, the observed variable intercepts and coefficients for F_1 were constrained to be equal across groups (as indicated in Equation 24.16 by excluding subscripts to indicate a coping group), as well as the error variances and covariances. In addition, we specified the latent variable, F_1, to be a function of an intercept plus a residual source, D_1:

$$F_1 = a_{F1g} + D_{1LC}$$

(24.17)

The latent variable intercepts for the groups are the group means on the latent variable. In that the means on latent variables are arbitrary, we fixed the intercept (i.e., mean) for the first group to be equal to zero but allowed the intercepts for the remaining groups to be freely estimated. Although unnecessary, we constrained the variances for the disturbances to be equal across groups. The less constrained model is shown in the top panel of Figure 24.3. The MC and LC models are specified identically, except the intercepts (i.e., means) on the latent variables are restricted to zero for all groups in the MC model; thus, the means on latent variables are constrained to be equal across groups.

Partial results comparing the MC and LC models are shown in the first row of Table 24.8. The LC model fit adequately, that is, $\chi^2(28) = 28.72$, $p = .428$, comparative fit index (CFI) = .997, Tucker–Lewis index (TLI) = .998, root mean square error of approximation (RMSEA) = .020, 90% confidence interval (CI) [.000, .097], indicating that the single latent variable model is consistent with the data. In other words, we have no empirical reason for rejecting our single latent variable model. In contrast, the MC model with equated latent variable means fit less well: $\chi^2(30) = 41.82$, $p = .074$, CFI = .947, TLI = .968, RMSEA = .077, 90% CI [.000, .128]. Based on the comparison of the less and more constrained models, we reject the hypothesis that the population means on satisfaction (the latent variable) are equivalent across the three groups: $\chi^2(2) = 13.11$, $p = .001$. See West, Taylor, and Wu (Chapter 13, this volume) for discussion of model fit and model selection.

We can compute a standardized effect size statistic to assess the differences in latent means between any two groups by dividing the difference between the latent means by the square root of the variance of the latent variable within groups (Hancock, 2001). Thus, the effect size for the comparison between the no-strategy and discussion groups is $(.664 - 0)/\sqrt{8.135} = .23$, whereas the difference between the no-strategy and exercise groups is $(1.945 - 0)/\sqrt{8.135} = .68$. This effect size statistic is comparable to the d statistic discussed by Cohen (1988), who suggested that values of 0.2, 0.5, and 0.8 may be regarded as small, medium, and large, respectively. Because a latent variable is error free, we would expect the magnitudes of the d statistic would be larger than those found with measured variables. Accordingly, we might judge the first effect size as small and the second as moderate in value.

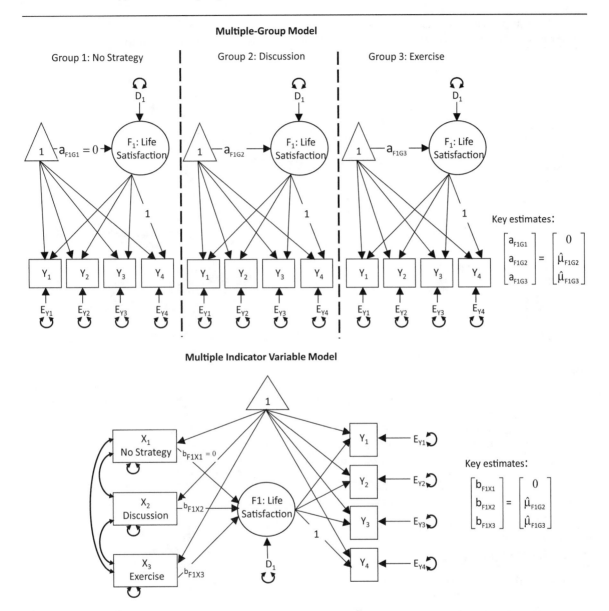

FIGURE 24.3. The LC latent variable models with homogeneous error variances. For the MC multiple-group model, the *a* intercepts are restricted to be equal to zero and thus to each other. For the MC multiple indicator variable model, the *b* coefficients are restricted to be equal to zero and thus to each other. To allow for comparison with the MANOVA results, the error variances for both the LC and MC multiple-group models are restricted to be equal across groups.

TABLE 24.8. Results for Example of a One-Way ANOVA with a Latent Variable as the Dependent Variable: Comparison of LC and MC Models to Assess Population Constraint That $\mu_{F1G1} = \mu_{F1G2} = \mu_{F1G3}$

Measures of latent variable with invariant parameters	Latent variable means for three groups	Error variance of latent variable: pooled or separate by group	Test to compare fit of LC and MC models	Results for measure with invariant parameters		
				Means of measure for each group	Variances of measure for each group	Residual variances of measure for each group
All measures	$\begin{bmatrix} 0 \\ 0.66 \\ 1.94 \end{bmatrix}$	$\begin{bmatrix} 8.14 \end{bmatrix}$	$\chi^2(30-28) = 41.82 - 28.72$ $= 13.11, p = .001$	—	—	—
One measure—Y_1	$\begin{bmatrix} 0 \\ -0.02 \\ 1.61 \end{bmatrix}$	$\begin{bmatrix} 8.20 \\ 6.70 \\ 10.08 \end{bmatrix}$	$\chi^2(8-6) = 13.11 - 4.28$ $= 8.83, p = .012$	$\begin{bmatrix} 24.62 \\ 24.60 \\ 26.22 \end{bmatrix}$	$\begin{bmatrix} 11.74 \\ 12.57 \\ 14.90 \end{bmatrix}$	$\begin{bmatrix} 3.53 \\ 5.87 \\ 4.82 \end{bmatrix}$
One measure—Y_2	$\begin{bmatrix} 0 \\ 1.88 \\ 2.53 \end{bmatrix}$	$\begin{bmatrix} 7.36 \\ 4.41 \\ 6.19 \end{bmatrix}$	$\chi^2(8-6) = 19.51 - 4.28$ $= 15.23, p < .001$	$\begin{bmatrix} 52.57 \\ 54.45 \\ 55.10 \end{bmatrix}$	$\begin{bmatrix} 14.41 \\ 13.55 \\ 13.12 \end{bmatrix}$	$\begin{bmatrix} 7.05 \\ 9.13 \\ 6.92 \end{bmatrix}$

If analyses include more than two groups and the hypothesis that the means on a latent variable are equal across all groups is rejected, then follow-up analyses are conducted to assess pairwise differences among groups. For example, to assess the hypothesis that the population means on satisfaction are equal for the no-strategy and discussion groups, we would compare the LC model, as previously discussed, with an MC model in which the coefficient for the indicator variable representing the discussion coping method was fixed to zero. We may control for Type I errors across the three pairwise comparisons by using methods such as the modified Shaffer method (Shaffer, 1986).

SEM MIV Model Method

For the LC MIV model, and as shown in the bottom panel of Figure 24.3, we included three indicator variables to represent the three coping groups. As with other SEM MIV models discussed in this chapter, the indicator variables have a direct effect on the dependent variable(s), and their coefficients are the means on the dependent variable(s) for the different groups. With latent variable models, the indicator variables are hypothesized to affect the latent variable(s) underlying the measured variables; for our example,

$$F_1 = b_{F1X1}X_1 + b_{F1X2}X_2 + b_{F1X3}X_3 + D_{1LC} \quad \text{(24.18)}$$

Because the mean of the latent variable is arbitrary, we define the mean for the first group to be zero by restricting the coefficient for the first indicator variable (i.e., b_{F1X1}) to be zero. The remaining coefficients represent the means on the latent variable for the second and third groups. Alternatively, because the F_1 mean is zero, these coefficients are the differences in means on F_1 between the first and second groups and between the second and third groups. For the LC model, the measurement model for F_1 was specified in a manner similar to the measurement model for the multiple-group analyses:

$$\begin{aligned} Y_1 &= a_{Y1} + b_{Y1F1}F_1 + E_{Y1LC} \\ Y_2 &= a_{Y2} + b_{Y2F1}F_1 + E_{Y2LC} \\ Y_3 &= a_{Y3} + b_{Y3F1}F_1 + E_{Y3LC} \\ Y_4 &= a_{Y4} + (1)\,F_1 + E_{Y4LC} \end{aligned} \quad \text{(24.19)}$$

The MC model is specified similarly to the LC model except that the coefficients for the second and third indicator variables (i.e., b_{F1X2} and b_{F1X3}) are restricted to zero, implying no differences in means among groups on the latent variable. The results for the MIV model comparisons are presented in Table 24.8 and are identical to those for the multiple-group method. It should be noted that we do not encounter *df* problems for these MIV analyses in that we have constrained the coefficient associated with one of the indicator variables to be equal to zero, thereby eliminating redundancy in the indicator variables. As with the multiple-group analyses, we would conduct follow-up tests if a test of an omnibus hypothesis involving more than two groups were rejected.

More Complex Models

Our example is simple in that the model includes only a single factor and a latent variable. Using a building-block approach, it is straightforward to add more factors, covariates, or latent variables to an analysis.

We have previously discussed two-way and higher-way designs with observed dependent variables. We can apply the same SEM methods but substitute latent dependent variable(s) (with their indicators) for observed dependent variables. For example, with the multiple-group approach, a group would be defined for each cell in a design. Comparable measurement models would be specified across groups. Constraints, like those previously discussed for analyses of observed dependent variables, would then be imposed on the means of the latent variables to test main and interaction effects. Covariates could be included in designs, as we have demonstrated with a one-way ANCOVA.

We could also incorporate more complexity into the dependent variable side of the equation. In our example, we specified a single latent variable model underlying the four satisfaction measures. In many applications, more complex measurement models will need to be specified to have adequate fit to the data, such as models with multiple correlated latent variables or with a hierarchical structure. For example, the bifactor model has received a lot of attention (e.g., Chen, West, & Sousa, 2006; Reise, Waller, & Comrey, 2000; Rindskopf & Rose, 1988) and could yield provocative results in conjunction with analyses involving differences in latent variable means. For simple bifactor models, two types of latent variables are specified to underlie a set of measures: a general latent variable, which affects all measures, and group latent variables, which affect only a subset of the measures. The covariances among general and group latent variables are constrained to zero. With this model, a researcher conducting a experiment would be in a position to conclude that a treatment produced an effect in general on the targeted construct (e.g., depression) and, above and beyond this general effect, on a specific component of this complex construct (e.g., somatic depression).

MORE FLEXIBLE TESTS OF DIFFERENCES IN MEANS ON LATENT VARIABLES

We have demonstrated through our example that the MIV model and the multiple-group approaches yield identical results if they are specified equivalently. In addition, we could introduce with either model more flexibility with respect to the assumption of normality by using robust methods to assess individual parameters, as well as the overall model. However, the advantage of the multiple-group approach is that it is highly flexible in terms of specifying model parameters and, in that sense, it is preferable. In most applications, we would expect the variances and covariances among factors, as well as the error variances, to differ among groups. We could conduct SEM analyses to assess differences in these parameters and, based on the results, decide whether to constrain parameters. However, we argue that it is preferable just to allow for differences on these parameters in our multiple-group analysis, therefore avoiding biased estimates due to misspecification.

Although it is ideal if all measures for each latent variable have equivalent loadings and intercepts across groups, this is not always tenable in practice. The multiple-group approach allows for testing of differences in latent means when the measurement model is only partially invariant. Partial invariance was discussed in detail by Millsap and Olivera-Aguilar (Chapter 23, this volume) as well as in other sources (Byrne, Shavelson, & Muthén, 1989; Thompson & Green, 2006). We summarize below the minimal requirements for partial invariance to assess latent mean differences.

■ The same form of the model must be specified for all groups. For our example, we specified a single latent variable (i.e., satisfaction) to underlie the four measures (Y_1 through Y_4), as shown in the top panel of Figure 24.3. We could not assess differences in latent variable means if we specified, for example, a unidimensional model for one group and multidimensional models for other groups.

■ At least one latent variable loading (arrows between the latent variable and the measures) must be constrained to be equal between any two groups. For our example, we constrained all loadings to be equivalent among the three groups (not shown in Figure 24.3).

■ At least one intercept for a measured variable (arrows between the triangle and the measures) must be constrained to be equal between any two groups. In general, if a latent variable loading for a measure is allowed to vary, the intercept for the same measure is also allowed to vary. For our example, we constrained all intercepts to be equivalent among the three groups (not shown in Figure 24.3).

As previously indicated, partial invariance does not require variances and covariances of latent variables or error variances of measured variables to be equivalent across groups.

As discussed previously (Millsap & Olivera-Aguilar, Chapter 23, this volume), given these minimal requirements, a number of researchers have explored various methodologies to determine how to choose which latent variable loadings and intercepts to constrain to be equal across groups. Based on this literature, one can feel either despondent (Hancock, Stapleton, & Arnold-Berkovits, 2009) or guardedly optimistic (e.g., Yoon & Millsap, 2007) about making these decisions.

It is preferable not to take advantage of the minimal requirement of partial invariance to test latent variable means. Researchers are more likely to reach valid conclusions to the extent that they carefully choose measures that have the same meaning in all groups or, expressed in SEM language, that have the same parameter values across groups. Measures with invariant parameters across groups are called "referent variables" or "indicators." If all measures associated with a latent variable are referent indicators, then the means and variances of this latent variable are a function of the means and variances of all measures. On the other extreme, if a latent variable has only a single referent variable, the means and variances of the latent variables are a function of only the means and variances of this variable.

To illustrate this point, we reanalyzed our multivariate data set and constrained as few parameters as possible to be equal across groups. For the first set of analyses, we imposed between-group equality constraints on the latent variable loadings and intercepts for only the first measured variable. For the second set of analyses, we imposed comparable constraints for only the second measured variable. The results of these analyses are presented in Table 24.8. First, it should be noted that the differences between these latent means for an analysis were exactly the same as the differences in means as assessed on the referent variable. Also, the variances on the latent variable were equal to the referent variable's

variance minus the referent variable's error variance. These results are very disconcerting. The conclusions we reach based on the latent variable are essentially a function of the single referent variable.

Potentially there may be measures that could be used as single referent variables; that is, they are "gold standards" for the assessment of constructs that function well and equivalently across populations. However, it would be the responsibility of researchers who use single referent variables to make this difficult argument. Recognizing the fallibility of individual measures, we prefer to base conclusions on multiple referent variables, preferably using different measurement methods to minimize particular types of bias for any one population. The differences in means on the latent variables would then reflect these multiple measures. Nevertheless, ultimately the ability to reach conclusions about means in the latent world is tied to the quality of our measures to assess different populations in the real world.

SUMMARY

When evaluating mean differences between groups, researchers typically use standard ANOVA/MANOVA OLS methods. Use of these methods may result in missed insights that can be obtained with SEM. Perhaps the biggest benefit in using SEM is the ability to evaluate mean differences in latent variables. Assuming studies are designed to assess mean differences within a construct system, researchers can use SEM analyses to (1) support their measurement theory linking constructs to indicators or make revisions to it, (2) evaluate differences on dimensions that should be measurement-error free, and (3) reach unified conclusions about constructs rather than piecemeal statements from results based on a series of ANOVAs that are supportive with respect to some but not all measures of a construct. If the focus is not on constructs, researchers can still use SEM methods and, within a single framework, assess hypotheses about not only means but also variances and covariances. In addition, the SEM analyses of observed or latent dependent variables can be conducted with one-way or higher-way designs, with or without covariates, and do not require a normality assumption. We have also argued that we think that in most situations, hypothesis tests using SEM should yield relatively accurate p-values if the sample sizes are sufficiently large to have adequate power, although this issue needs further research. In summary, we believe that SEM offers major advantages over OLS regression analysis as a general model for investigating mean differences.

REFERENCES

Aiken, L. S., West, S. G., & Millsap, R. E. (2008). Doctoral training in statistics, measurement, and methodology in psychology: Replication and extension of the Aiken, West, Sechrest, and Reno (1990) survey of PhD programs in North America. *American Psychologist, 63*, 32–50.

Anderson, J. C., & Gerbing, D. W. (1984). The effect of sampling error on convergence, improper solutions, and goodness-of-fit indices for maximum likelihood confirmatory factor analysis. *Psychometrika, 49*, 155–173.

Bagozzi, R. P. (1977). Structural equation models in experimental research. *Journal of Marketing Research, 14*, 209–226.

Bollen, K. A. (1989). *Structural equations with latent variables*. New York: Wiley.

Boomsma, A. (1983). *On the robustness of LISREL (maximum likelihood estimation against small sample size and nonnormality)*. Amsterdam: Sociometric Research Foundation.

Bradley, J. V. (1978). Robustness? *British Journal of Mathematical and Statistical Psychology, 34*, 144–152.

Byrne, B. M., Shavelson, R. J., & Muthén, B. (1989). Testing for the equivalence of factor covariance and means structures: The issue of partial measurement invariance. *Psychological Bulletin, 105*, 456–466.

Chen, F., West, S. G., & Sousa, K. H. (2006). A comparison of bifactor and second-order models of quality of life. *Multivariate Behavioral Research, 41*, 189–225.

Cohen, J. (1988). *Statistical power analysis for the behavioral sciences* (2nd ed.). Hillsdale, NJ: Erlbaum.

Cohen, J., Cohen, P., West, S. G., Aiken, L. S. (2003). *Applied multiple regression/correlation analysis for the behavior sciences* (3rd ed.). Mahwah, NJ: Erlbaum.

Erceg-Hurn, D. M., & Mirosevich, V. M. (2008). Modern robust statistical methods: An easy way to maximize the accuracy and power of your research. *American Psychologist, 63*, 591–601.

Fan, W., & Hancock, G. R. (2012). Robust means modeling: An alternative to hypothesis testing of independent means under variance heterogeneity and nonnormality. *Journal of Educational and Behavioral Statistics, 37*, 137–156.

Franke, G. R., Preacher, K. J., & Rigdon, E. E. (2008). Proportional structural effects of formative indicators. *Journal of Business Research, 61*, 1229–1237.

Glass, G. V., Peckham, P. D., & Sanders, J. R. (1972). Con-

sequences of failure to meet assumptions underlying the analysis of variance and covariance. *Review of Educational Research, 42*, 237–288.

Green, S. B., Marquis, J. G., Hershberger, S. L., Thompson, M., & McCollam, K. (1999). The overparameterized analysis-of-variance model. *Psychological Methods, 4*, 214–233.

Green, S. B., & Thompson, M. S. (2003). Structural equation modeling in clinical research. In M. C. Roberts & S. S. Illardi (Eds.), *Methods of research in clinical psychology: A handbook* (pp. 138–175). London: Blackwell.

Green, S. B., & Thompson, M. S. (2006). Structural equation modeling for conducting tests of differences in multiple means. *Journal of Psychosomatic Medicine, 68*, 706–717.

Hancock, G. R. (1997). Structural equation modeling methods of hypothesis testing of latent variable means. *Measurement and Evaluation in Counseling and Development, 20*, 91–105.

Hancock, G. R. (2001). Effect size, power, and sample size determination for structured means modeling and MIMIC approaches to between-groups hypothesis testing of means on a single latent construct. *Psychometrika, 66*, 373–388.

Hancock, G. R. (2004). Experimental, quasi-experimental, and nonexperimental design and analysis with latent variables. In D. Kaplan (Ed.), *The Sage handbook of quantitative methodology for the social sciences* (pp. 317–334). Thousand Oaks, CA: Sage.

Hancock, G. R. (2010, May). *Life after ANOVA: Reframing and extending analysis of variance using a likelihood/ information paradigm.* Paper presented in the Structural Equation Modeling Special Interest Group of the American Educational Research Association, Denver, CO.

Hancock, G. R., Lawrence, F. R., & Nevitt, J. (2000). Type I error and power of latent mean methods and MANOVA in factorially invariant and noninvariant latent variable systems. *Structural Equation Modeling, 7*, 534–556.

Hancock, G. R., & Mueller, R. O. (Eds.). (2006). *Structural equation modeling: A second course*. Greenwich, CT: Information Age.

Hancock, G. R., Stapleton, L. M., & Arnold-Berkovits, I. (2009). The tenuousness of invariance tests within multisample covariance and mean structure models. In T. Teo & M. S. Khine (Eds.), *Structural equation modeling: Concepts and applications in educational research* (pp. 137–174). Rotterdam, Netherlands: Sense Publishers.

Howell, R. D., Brevik, E., & Wilcox, J. B. (2007). Reconsidering formative measurement. *Psychological Methods, 12*, 205–218.

Huberty, C. J., & Olejnik, S. (2006). *Applied MANOVA and discriminant analysis*. Hoboken, NJ: Wiley.

Judd, C. M., & McClelland, G. H. (1989). *Data analysis: A model comparison approach*. San Diego, CA: Harcourt Brace Jovanovich.

Kano, Y. (2001). Structural equation modeling for experimental data. In R. Cudeck, S. du Toit, & D. Sörbom (Eds.), *Structural equation modeling: Present and future—Festschrift in honor of Karl Jöreskog* (pp. 381–402). Lincolnwood, IL: Scientific Software International.

Keselman, H. J., Algina, J., Lix, L. M., Wilcox, R. R., & Deering, K. (2008). A generally robust approach for testing hypotheses and setting confidence intervals for effect sizes. *Psychological Methods, 13*, 110–129.

Keselman, H. J., Huberty, C. J., Lix, L. M., Olejnik, S., Cribbie, R., Donahue, B., et al. (1998). Statistical practices of educational researchers: An analysis of their ANOVA, MANOVA, and ANCOVA analyses. *Review of Educational Research, 68*, 350–386.

Keselman, H. J., Wilcox, R. R., & Lix, L. M. (2003). A generally robust approach to hypothesis testing in independent and correlated groups designs. *Psychophysiology, 40*, 586–596.

Kirk, R. E. (1995). *Experimental design: Procedures for the behavioral sciences* (3rd ed.). Pacific Grove, CA: Brooks/Cole.

Lix, L. M., Keselman, J. C., & Keselman, H. J. (1996). Consequences of assumption violations revisted: A quantitative review of alternatives to the one-way analysis of variance *F* test. *Review of Educational Research, 66*, 579–619.

MacCallum, R. C., & Browne, M. W. (1993). The use of causal indicators in covariance structure models: Some practical issues. *Psychological Bulletin, 114*, 533–541.

Maxwell, S. E., & Delaney, H. D. (2004). *Designing experiments and analyzing data: A model comparison perspective* (2nd ed.). Mahwah, NJ: Erlbaum.

Namboodiri, N. K., Carter, L. F., & Blalock, H. M. (1975). *Applied multivariate analysis and experimental designs.* New York: McGraw-Hill.

Pedhazur, E. J. (1997). *Multiple regression in behavioral research* (3rd ed.). Orlando, FL: Harcourt Brace.

Reise, S. P., Waller, N. G., & Comrey, A. L. (2000). Factor analysis and scale revision. *Psychological Assessment, 12*, 287–297.

Rindskopf, D., & Rose, T. (1988). Some theory and applications of confirmatory second-order factor analysis. *Multivariate Behavioral Research, 23*, 51–67.

Rodgers, J. L. (2010). The epistemology of mathematical and statistical modeling: A quiet methodological revolution. *American Psychologist, 65*, 1–12.

Satorra, A., & Bentler, P. M. (1994), Corrections to test statistic and standard errors in covariance structure analysis. In A. Von Eye & C. C. Clogg (Eds.), *Analysis of latent variables in developmental research* (pp. 399–419). Newbury Park, CA: Sage.

Searle, S. R. (1971). *Linear models.* New York: Wiley.

Searle, S. R. (1987). *Linear models for unbalanced data.* New York: Wiley.

Shaffer, J. P. (1986). Modified sequentially rejective multiple test procedures. *Journal of the American Statistical Association, 81*, 826–831.

Thompson, M. S., & Green, S. B. (2006). Evaluating between-group differences in latent variable means. In G. R. Hancock & R. O. Mueller (Eds.), *A second course in structural equation modeling* (pp. 119–169). Greenwich, CT: Information Age.

Wilcox, R. R. (1995). ANOVA: A paradigm for low power and misleading measures of effect size? *Review of Educational Research, 65*, 51–77.

Wilcox, R. R. (2005). *Introduction to robust estimation and hypothesis testing* (2nd ed.). San Diego, CA: Academic Press.

Yoon, M., & Millsap, R. E. (2007). Detecting violations of factorial invariance using data-based specification searches: A Monte-Carlo study. *Structural Equation Modeling: A Multidisciplinary Journal, 14*, 435–463.

Zimmerman, D. W. (2004). Inflation of Type I error rates by unequal variances associated with parametric, nonparametric, and rank-transformation tests. *Psicologica, 25*, 103–133.

CHAPTER 25

Mediation/Indirect Effects
in Structural Equation Modeling

JeeWon Cheong
David P. MacKinnon

Thus, the correlation between two variables is equal to the sum of the products
of chains of path coefficients along all of the paths by which they are connected.
—WRIGHT (1921, p. 568)

HISTORY

Modern approaches to quantifying indirect effects or mediation began with Sewall Wright's work on the path analysis (Wolfle, 1999; Wright, 1920, 1921). Investigating the relative influences of heredity and environment on the breeding of guinea pigs, he used a system of equations and a path diagram to display the causal relations among the variables. He showed that the contribution of the intermediate variables connecting the two variables in a complex system of causally related variables was the product of the path coefficients in the chain of paths connecting the two variables (Wright, 1923). He further argued that path analysis is not a method to infer causation but a method to quantify the supposed causal relations. Causal sequences of the variables are already assumed, based on available information including theory, prior correlations, and results of prior experiments; path analysis is used to gauge the strength of the causal relations. The specification of causal relations among the variables continues to be one of the main issues in the use of structural equation modeling (SEM), and we discuss this issue in relation to indirect or mediation effects later in the chapter.

Early substantive conceptualization of mediation can be traced back to Woodworth's (1928) stimulus–organism–response (S-O-R) model, which postulates that a stimulus acts upon the organism or individual, thus eliciting a response. In this formulation, the organism, more specifically the mechanisms or processes within the organism, is the mediator that translates the stimulus into the response. For example, when shopping, a pleasant store environment (S) may enhance the shoppers' positive emotional states (O), which in turn may increase their purchasing (R; Donovan & Rossiter, 1982). In such cases, the individuals' emotional states, such as pleasure and arousal, are mediators. Although the S-O-R model provided the framework for the modern mediation analysis, it conceptualized the intervening variables as abstract, unobservable variables. The issue of measuring them only emerged later. MacCorquodale and Meehl (1948) and Ginsberg (1954) differentiated theoretical mediating variables and intervening variables to distinguish hypothetical constructs representing mediating variables and specific variables used to measure them.

One major treatment of mediating variables was the elaboration model by Kendall and Lazarsfeld (1950;

Lazarsfeld, 1955), who systematically differentiated third-variable effects based on how the relation between two variables changed after introducing a third variable. A third variable is considered as a mediating or intervening variable when the previously observed bivariate relation becomes zero or is significantly reduced after introducing the third variable in the model. The third variable should occur between the two variables to be interpreted as a mediator as opposed to a confounding variable, which has a similar effect on the bivariate relations but is antecedent to both of the original variables. The elaboration model has been extended beyond what Kendall and Lazarsfeld (1950) formalized. For example, Rosenberg (1968) described the notion of a distorter, which is a third variable that might make a relation become stronger or reverse the sign of the original bivariate relation. The elaboration model provided a framework for one of the main approaches to testing mediation in social science research.

Since path analysis as developed by Wright was rediscovered and introduced to sociologists by Duncan (1966), investigation of mediating processes and the quantification of mediation effects have become a central focus in social science research. Because in path analysis the causal relations among the variables can be explicitly specified, path analysis has become a major tool for investigating direct and indirect effects of causal variables to explain the detailed underlying processes of sociological phenomena (Sobel, 1982). With the development of covariance structure modeling during the 1970s (Jöreskog, 1970, 1973; Wiley, 1973) and 1980s (Bentler, 1980), the multiple-equation tradition in path analysis was combined with the psychometric tradition in its focus on measurement; thus, measurement and structural models were incorporated in the quantification and modeling of indirect effects. General methods to decompose the association between the antecedent and the dependent variables into direct and indirect effects were developed (Alwin & Hauser, 1975; Graff & Schmidt, 1982) for covariance structure models, and Sobel (1982) derived the standard error of these direct and indirect effects. These standard errors based on the multivariate delta method (Sobel, 1982) have been implemented in most of the SEM programs to compute confidence intervals and conduct formal significance tests for indirect effects. More recently, methods to accommodate the non-normal distribution of indirect effects were introduced (MacKinnon, Lockwood, & Williams, 2004) and are now part of several SEM programs.

DEFINITIONS

A "mediator," or "mediating variable," is defined as a third variable that intervenes in the relation between an independent variable and a dependent variable, transmitting the effect of the independent variable on the dependent variable. Mediators are often called "intervening" or "intermediate" variables, reflecting that these variables come between an independent and a dependent variable. Baron and Kenny (1986) defined mediation as "the generative mechanism through which the focal independent variable is able to influence the dependent variable of interest" (p. 1173). Last (1988) and Sobel (1982) also emphasized that a mediator is a variable that occurs in a causal pathway, by which the independent variable causes the dependent variable. Statistically, a third variable is considered a significant mediator when the relation between the independent and the dependent variables is completely or partially accounted for by the third-variable intermediate in the causal chain.

A mediator is differentiated from other third variables in that it is an intermediate variable in the causal sequence from the independent variable to the mediator to the dependent variable. For example, a confounder may explain the effect of the independent variable and the dependent variable because it is related to both variables. However, a mediator explicates the effect as an intermediate variable in the causal sequence, whereas a confounder causes both the independent and the dependent variables. In many situations, it may be difficult to determine whether the third variable is a mediator or other type of third variable, such as a confounder. Researchers may need to rely on theory for making such decisions. In this chapter we assume that the third variable is a mediator, and that the model specifying the causal sequence of the independent variables, the mediators, and the dependent variables is correct. Other differentiations that researchers often make are the names of variables involved in the causal sequence in a mediation model. Kenny, Kashy, and Bolger (1998) used initial variable, mediator, and outcome. James and Brett (1984) incorporated the time sequence of the variables by referring to them as the antecedent, mediating, and consequent variables. Although certain names for the variables in the mediation model fit specific modeling situations better, the names we use in this chapter are *independent variable, mediator*, and *dependent variable*.

MATRIX REPRESENTATION OF MEDIATION MODELS

Our focus is indirect or mediation effects estimated in the SEM framework. These models typically have more than one independent variable, mediating variable, or dependent variable, and all or part of the variables are modeled as latent variables. Figure 25.1 presents a single-mediator model with observed variables. The coefficients relating the exogenous variable to the endogenous variables are indicated as γ's and the coefficients relating the endogenous variables to other endogenous variables are indicated as β's. Figure 25.1 also contains actual path coefficients, obtained by analyzing a real data set from 1,208 high school football players (Goldberg et al., 2000). The football players were randomly assigned to either treatment or control group. The treatment program (ξ) was expected to increase peer influence on healthy diet (η_1), which then was expected to improve the athletes' nutrition behaviors (η_2). The relations between the independent variable, the mediator, and the dependent variables are specified in the structural relations as follows:

$$\eta = B\eta + \Gamma\xi + \zeta \qquad (25.1)$$

where η is a 2×1 vector representing the mediator and the dependent variable in Figure 25.1, ζ is a 2×1 vector of their residuals, and ξ is a vector representing an independent variable. The Γ matrix is a 2×1 vector representing the relations of the independent variable to the mediator and the dependent variable, and the B matrix is a 2×2 matrix representing the relation between the mediator and the dependent variable. Specifically, the relations between the variables in Equation 25.1 can be laid out as follows:

$$\begin{bmatrix} \eta_1 \\ \eta_2 \end{bmatrix} = \begin{bmatrix} 0 & 0 \\ \beta_{21} & 0 \end{bmatrix}\begin{bmatrix} \eta_1 \\ \eta_2 \end{bmatrix} + \begin{bmatrix} \gamma_{11} \\ \gamma_{21} \end{bmatrix}[\xi] + \begin{bmatrix} \zeta_1 \\ \zeta_2 \end{bmatrix} \qquad (25.2)$$

The unstandardized estimates of the elements in B and Γ are:

$$\hat{B} = \begin{bmatrix} 0 & 0 \\ 0.171 & 0 \end{bmatrix} \qquad \hat{\Gamma} = \begin{bmatrix} 0.993 \\ 0.177 \end{bmatrix}$$

In models with manifest variables, it is assumed that each variable is measured without error (i.e., with perfect reliability). In the presence of measurement error, the relations between the variables can be attenuated as a function of the reliability of the predictor variable and, consequently, the reliability of the mediator variable can lead to reduced mediation effects (Hoyle & Kenny, 1999). Introducing latent variables can improve estimation of mediation effects by specifying a measurement model for each construct and separating measurement error from the true score. Including measurement models for the constructs requires additional matrices specifying the relations between each indicator and the relevant latent construct, and matrices representing the remaining unexplained variability of each indicator.

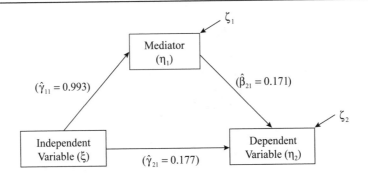

FIGURE 25.1. A single-mediator model with three manifest variables.

Figure 25.2 depicts a two-mediator model with all latent variables, each with three indicators. For illustration, we used the data from 818 high school football players (Goldberg et al., 2000). It was hypothesized that athletic competence (ξ_1) would affect body image (η_1) and self-esteem (η_2), which then would affect athletes' attitudes toward anabolic steroids (η_3). In addition, body image (η_1) was hypothesized to affect self-esteem (η_2). All the parameters are presented in Greek letters in Figure 25.2, with actual estimates of the relations between the latent variables. The measurement models in Figure 25.2 are specified as Equations 25.3 and 25.4, and the structural model is specified as Equations 25.5 and 25.6:

$$y = \Lambda_y \eta + \varepsilon; \quad \begin{bmatrix} y_1 \\ y_2 \\ y_3 \\ y_4 \\ y_5 \\ y_6 \\ y_7 \\ y_8 \\ y_9 \end{bmatrix} = \begin{bmatrix} 1 & 0 & 0 \\ \lambda_{y21} & 0 & 0 \\ \lambda_{y31} & 0 & 0 \\ 0 & 1 & 0 \\ 0 & \lambda_{y52} & 0 \\ 0 & \lambda_{y62} & 0 \\ 0 & 0 & 1 \\ 0 & 0 & \lambda_{y83} \\ 0 & 0 & \lambda_{y93} \end{bmatrix} \begin{bmatrix} \eta_1 \\ \eta_2 \\ \eta_3 \end{bmatrix} + \begin{bmatrix} \varepsilon_1 \\ \varepsilon_2 \\ \varepsilon_3 \\ \varepsilon_4 \\ \varepsilon_5 \\ \varepsilon_6 \\ \varepsilon_7 \\ \varepsilon_8 \\ \varepsilon_9 \end{bmatrix} \quad \textbf{(25.4)}$$

$$\eta = B\eta + \Gamma\xi + \zeta \quad \textbf{(25.5)}$$

$$x = \Lambda_x \xi + \delta; \quad \begin{bmatrix} x_1 \\ x_2 \\ x_3 \end{bmatrix} = \begin{bmatrix} 1 \\ \lambda_{x21} \\ \lambda_{x31} \end{bmatrix} [\xi_1] + \begin{bmatrix} \delta_1 \\ \delta_2 \\ \delta_3 \end{bmatrix} \quad \textbf{(25.3)}$$

$$\begin{bmatrix} \eta_1 \\ \eta_2 \\ \eta_3 \end{bmatrix} = \begin{bmatrix} 0 & 0 & 0 \\ \beta_{21} & 0 & 0 \\ \beta_{31} & \beta_{32} & 0 \end{bmatrix} \begin{bmatrix} \eta_1 \\ \eta_2 \\ \eta_3 \end{bmatrix} + \begin{bmatrix} \gamma_{11} \\ \gamma_{21} \\ \gamma_{31} \end{bmatrix} [\xi_1] + \begin{bmatrix} \zeta_1 \\ \zeta_2 \\ \zeta_3 \end{bmatrix} \quad \textbf{(25.6)}$$

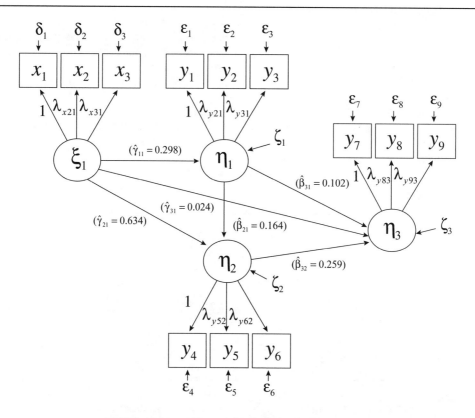

FIGURE 25.2. A two-mediator model with latent variables.

The relations of the independent variable to each of the mediators and the dependent variable are specified in the Γ matrix, and the relations between the mediators and the dependent variable are specified in the $\mathbf{B}$ matrix.

The unstandardized estimates of the elements in $\mathbf{B}$ and Γ are:

$$\hat{\mathbf{B}} = \begin{bmatrix} 0 & 0 & 0 \\ 0.164 & 0 & 0 \\ 0.102 & 0.259 & 0 \end{bmatrix} \quad \hat{\Gamma} = \begin{bmatrix} 0.298 \\ 0.634 \\ 0.024 \end{bmatrix}$$

DECOMPOSITION OF EFFECTS

Decomposition of the effects of causal variables involves differentiation of the effects in terms of the mediated, or indirect effects, and the direct effect (Alwin & Hauser, 1975; Duncan, Featherman, & Duncan, 1972; Graff & Schmidt, 1982). The direct effect is the influence of the causal variables on the other variables involving "a chain of length one" (Sobel, 1987) in the sequence of causal relations. The matrices specifying the relations between two variables in the previous equations provide the direct effects in a model. The Γ matrix contains the direct effects of the exogenous independent variables (ξ's) on the mediators and the dependent variables (η's), and the $\mathbf{B}$ matrix contains the direct effects of the mediators on the dependent variables. The indirect effect is the effect of one variable on another variable that is intervened by at least one additional variable in the "chains of length r ($r \geq 2$)" (Sobel, 1987) causal relations. The total indirect effect is the sum of the specific indirect effects in a model, and the total effect is the sum of the total indirect effect and the direct effect (Bollen, 1987; Fox, 1980).

To illustrate how the total effects, total indirect effects, and direct effects are obtained using matrix form, let $\mathbf{T}_{\eta\eta}$ denote the matrix for the total effects of endogenous variables on endogenous variables and let $\mathbf{T}_{\eta\xi}$ denote the matrix for the total effects of exogenous variables on endogenous variables. In recursive models where $\mathbf{B}$ is strictly triangular, $\mathbf{T}_{\eta\eta}$ is defined as follows (Brown, 1997; Fox, 1980):

$$\mathbf{T}_{\eta\eta} = \sum_{k=1}^{\infty} \mathbf{B}^k \quad (25.7)$$

where k is equal to powers of the direct effects between the endogenous variables in the model. For the recursive

model with q endogenous variables, it is not possible for an endogenous variable to affect another endogenous variable through a chain of length q or higher. Thus, $\mathbf{B}^q$ or higher powered matrix is 0, resulting in Equation 25.8:

$$\mathbf{T}_{\eta\eta} = \mathbf{B} + \mathbf{B}^2 + \mathbf{B}^3 + \ldots + \mathbf{B}^{q-1} \quad (25.8)$$

For example, in Figure 25.2 ($q = 3$), the total effects of the endogenous variables on the other endogenous variables can be obtained as Equation 25.9:

$$\mathbf{T}_{\eta\eta} = \mathbf{B} + \mathbf{B}^2 = \begin{bmatrix} 0 & 0 & 0 \\ \beta_{21} & 0 & 0 \\ \beta_{31} & \beta_{32} & 0 \end{bmatrix} + \begin{bmatrix} 0 & 0 & 0 \\ 0 & 0 & 0 \\ \beta_{21}\beta_{32} & 0 & 0 \end{bmatrix}$$

$$= \begin{bmatrix} 0 & 0 & 0 \\ \beta_{21} & 0 & 0 \\ \beta_{31} + \beta_{21}\beta_{32} & \beta_{32} & 0 \end{bmatrix} \quad (25.9)$$

Using the actual estimates in Figure 25.2, Equation 25.9 can be written as follows:

$$\hat{\mathbf{T}}_{\eta\eta} = \hat{\mathbf{B}} + \hat{\mathbf{B}}^2 = \begin{bmatrix} 0 & 0 & 0 \\ \hat{\beta}_{21} & 0 & 0 \\ \hat{\beta}_{31} + \hat{\beta}_{21}\hat{\beta}_{32} & \hat{\beta}_{32} & 0 \end{bmatrix}$$

$$= \begin{bmatrix} 0 & 0 & 0 \\ 0.164 & 0 & 0 \\ 0.102 + 0.164 \times 0.259 & 0.259 & 0 \end{bmatrix} \quad (25.10)$$

$$= \begin{bmatrix} 0 & 0 & 0 \\ 0.164 & 0 & 0 \\ 0.144 & 0.259 & 0 \end{bmatrix}$$

The total effect of η_1 on η_2 equals $\hat{\beta}_{21} = 0.164$, and the total effect of η_1 on η_3 equals $\beta_{31} + \beta_{21}\beta_{32} = 0.144$.

To obtain the total effects of the exogenous variables on the endogenous variables, the Γ matrix can be incorporated as follows:

$$\mathbf{T}_{\eta\xi} = \Gamma + \mathbf{B}\Gamma + \mathbf{B}^2\Gamma + \mathbf{B}^3\Gamma + \ldots + \mathbf{B}^{q-1}\Gamma \quad (25.11)$$
$$= (\mathbf{I} + \mathbf{B} + \mathbf{B}^2 + \mathbf{B}^3 + \ldots \mathbf{B}^{q-1})\Gamma$$

where $\mathbf{I}$ is an identity matrix. For the model in Figure 25.2, the total effects of the exogenous variable on the endogenous variables can be obtained as Equation 25.12:

$$\mathbf{T}_{\eta\xi} = (\mathbf{I} + \mathbf{B} + \mathbf{B}^2)\Gamma$$

$$= \left[\begin{bmatrix} 1 & 0 & 0 \\ 0 & 1 & 0 \\ 0 & 0 & 1 \end{bmatrix} + \begin{bmatrix} 0 & 0 & 0 \\ \beta_{21} & 0 & 0 \\ \beta_{31} & \beta_{32} & 0 \end{bmatrix} + \begin{bmatrix} 0 & 0 & 0 \\ 0 & 0 & 0 \\ \beta_{21}\beta_{32} & 0 & 0 \end{bmatrix}\right]\begin{bmatrix} \gamma_{11} \\ \gamma_{21} \\ \gamma_{31} \end{bmatrix}$$

$$= \begin{bmatrix} \gamma_{11} \\ \gamma_{11}\beta_{21} + \gamma_{21} \\ \gamma_{11}\beta_{31} + \gamma_{11}\beta_{21}\beta_{32} + \gamma_{21}\beta_{32} + \gamma_{31} \end{bmatrix}$$

$$(25.12)$$

Using the path coefficients between the latent variables in Figure 25.2, we can obtain the total effects of the exogenous variable on the endogenous variables as follows:

$$\hat{\mathbf{T}}_{\eta\xi} = (\mathbf{I} + \hat{\mathbf{B}} + \hat{\mathbf{B}}^2)\hat{\Gamma} = \begin{bmatrix} \hat{\gamma}_{11} \\ \hat{\gamma}_{11}\hat{\beta}_{21} + \hat{\gamma}_{21} \\ \hat{\gamma}_{11}\hat{\beta}_{31} + \hat{\gamma}_{11}\hat{\beta}_{21}\hat{\beta}_{32} + \hat{\gamma}_{21}\hat{\beta}_{32} + \hat{\gamma}_{31} \end{bmatrix}$$

$$= \begin{bmatrix} 0.298 \\ 0.298 \times 0.164 + 0.634 \\ 0.298 \times 0.102 + 0.298 \times 0.164 \times 0.259 + 0.634 \times 0.259 + 0.024 \end{bmatrix}$$

$$= \begin{bmatrix} 0.298 \\ 0.683 \\ 0.231 \end{bmatrix}$$

$$(25.13)$$

The total effects in Equations 25.8 and 25.11 can be simplified as follows (Bollen, 1987):

$$\mathbf{T}_{\eta\eta} = (\mathbf{I} - \mathbf{B})^{-1} - \mathbf{I} \qquad (25.14)$$

$$\mathbf{T}_{\eta\xi} = (\mathbf{I} - \mathbf{B})^{-1}\Gamma \qquad (25.15)$$

Because the total indirect effects in the recursive models are obtained by subtracting the direct effects from the total effects, the total indirect effects of the endogenous variables on the endogenous variables may be calculated as follows:

$$\mathbf{I}_{\eta\eta} = \mathbf{T}_{\eta\eta} - \mathbf{B} = (\mathbf{I} - \mathbf{B})^{-1} - \mathbf{I} - \mathbf{B} \qquad (25.16)$$

Applying Equation 25.16 to Figure 25.2, the total indirect effects of the endogenous variables are

$$\hat{\mathbf{I}}_{\eta\eta} = \hat{\mathbf{T}}_{\eta\eta} - \hat{\mathbf{B}}$$

$$= \begin{bmatrix} 0 & 0 & 0 \\ \hat{\beta}_{21} & 0 & 0 \\ \hat{\beta}_{31} + \hat{\beta}_{21}\hat{\beta}_{32} & \hat{\beta}_{32} & 0 \end{bmatrix} - \begin{bmatrix} 0 & 0 & 0 \\ \hat{\beta}_{21} & 0 & 0 \\ \hat{\beta}_{31} & \hat{\beta}_{32} & 0 \end{bmatrix} \qquad (25.17)$$

$$= \begin{bmatrix} 0 & 0 & 0 \\ 0 & 0 & 0 \\ \hat{\beta}_{21}\hat{\beta}_{32} & 0 & 0 \end{bmatrix} = \begin{bmatrix} 0 & 0 & 0 \\ 0 & 0 & 0 \\ 0.042 & 0 & 0 \end{bmatrix}$$

Similarly, the total indirect effects of the exogenous variables on the endogenous variables can be obtained as follows:

$$\mathbf{I}_{\eta\xi} = \mathbf{T}_{\eta\xi} - \Gamma = (\mathbf{I} - \mathbf{B})^{-1}\Gamma - \Gamma \qquad (25.18)$$

Applying Equation 25.18 to Figure 25.2, the total indirect effects of the exogenous variable are:

$$\hat{\mathbf{I}}_{\eta\xi} = \hat{\mathbf{T}}_{\eta\xi} - \hat{\Gamma}$$

$$= \begin{bmatrix} \hat{\gamma}_{11} \\ \hat{\gamma}_{11}\hat{\beta}_{21} + \hat{\gamma}_{21} \\ \hat{\gamma}_{11}\hat{\beta}_{31} + \hat{\gamma}_{11}\hat{\beta}_{21}\hat{\beta}_{32} + \hat{\gamma}_{21}\hat{\beta}_{32} + \hat{\gamma}_{31} \end{bmatrix} - \begin{bmatrix} \hat{\gamma}_{11} \\ \hat{\gamma}_{21} \\ \hat{\gamma}_{31} \end{bmatrix} \qquad (25.19)$$

$$= \begin{bmatrix} 0 \\ \hat{\gamma}_{11}\hat{\beta}_{21} \\ \hat{\gamma}_{11}\hat{\beta}_{31} + \hat{\gamma}_{11}\hat{\beta}_{21}\hat{\beta}_{32} + \hat{\gamma}_{21}\hat{\beta}_{32} \end{bmatrix} = \begin{bmatrix} 0 \\ 0.049 \\ 0.207 \end{bmatrix}$$

For example, the total indirect effect of ξ_1 on η_3 is $\hat{\gamma}_{11}\hat{\beta}_{31} + \hat{\gamma}_{11}\hat{\beta}_{21}\hat{\beta}_{32} + \hat{\gamma}_{21}\hat{\beta}_{32} = 0.207$. The total indirect effect of ξ_1 on η_3 is further decomposed into three specific indirect effects, each of which is obtained by the product of path coefficients that are involved in the mediational pathways: (1) the indirect effect via η_1 only (i.e., $\hat{\gamma}_{11}\hat{\beta}_{31} = 0.030$), (2) the indirect effect via η_1 and η_2 (i.e., $\hat{\gamma}_{11}\hat{\beta}_{21}\hat{\beta}_{32} = 0.013$), and (3) the indirect effect via η_2 only (i.e., $\hat{\gamma}_{21}\hat{\beta}_{32} = 0.164$).

STANDARD ERRORS OF INDIRECT EFFECTS

In order to conduct significance tests or to construct confidence intervals for the indirect effects, standard errors of the indirect effects are helpful. One of the most widely used methods for estimating standard errors of indirect effects is the method Sobel (1982, 1986) derived, based on first derivatives using the multivariate delta method (Bishop, Fienberg, & Holland, 1975; Folmer, 1981). According to the multivariate delta method, the asymptotic variance of a function of random variables, such as the product of path coefficients, can be obtained by pre- and postmultiplying the covariance matrix of the random variables by a vector of first partial derivatives of the random variable function. For example, let $\theta = [\theta_1, \theta_2, \ldots, \theta_u]'$, a vector of direct effects, $f(\theta)$ be a function of direct effects, $\Sigma(\theta)$ be the asymptotic covariance matrix of the direct effects, and $f^1(\theta)$ be the first derivative of $f(\theta)$ with respect to θ, that is, $[\partial f/\partial \theta_1, \partial f/\partial \theta_2, \ldots, \partial f/\partial \theta_u]'$. Then, the variance of the function of random variables is as follows (Sobel, 1982, 1987):

$$\mathrm{Var}(f(\theta)) = [f^1(\theta)]'\Sigma(\theta)f^1(\theta) \qquad \textbf{(25.20)}$$

Provided $f(\theta)$ is continuously differentiable and $\Sigma(\theta)$ is a continuous function of θ, the quantity in Equation 25.20 can be estimated using the sample estimates as follows:

$$\mathrm{Var}(f(\hat\theta)) = [f^1(\hat\theta)]'S(\hat\theta)f^1(\hat\theta) \qquad \textbf{(25.21)}$$

where $S(\hat\theta)$ is the sample estimate of $\Sigma(\theta)$. Then, the square root of the term in Equation 25.21 can be used to test the significance of $f(\hat\theta)$ and to construct its confidence interval.

Applying the delta method described above to the specific indirect effect of ξ_1 on η_3 via η_2 ($\xi_1 \to \eta_2 \to \eta_3$) in Figure 25.2, $f(\hat\theta) = \hat\gamma_{21}\hat\beta_{32}$, where $\hat\gamma_{21}$ and $\hat\beta_{32}$ are sample estimates of the two path coefficients, and $[f^1(\hat\theta)]' = [\partial f/\partial\hat\gamma_{21}\ \ \partial f/\partial\hat\beta_{32}] = [\hat\beta_{32}\ \ \hat\gamma_{21}]$. With the sample estimates of $S(\hat\theta)$, the estimated variance of $\hat\gamma_{11}\hat\beta_{31}$ the indirect effect is obtained as follows:

$$\mathrm{Var}(\hat\gamma_{21}\hat\beta_{32}) = [\hat\beta_{32}\ \ \hat\gamma_{21}]\begin{bmatrix} s^2_{\gamma_{21}} & s_{\gamma_{21}\beta_{32}} \\ s_{\beta_{32}\gamma_{21}} & s^2_{\beta_{32}} \end{bmatrix}\begin{bmatrix} \hat\beta_{32} \\ \hat\gamma_{21} \end{bmatrix} \qquad \textbf{(25.22)}$$
$$= \hat\gamma^2_{21}s^2_{\beta_{32}} + \hat\beta^2_{32}s^2_{\gamma_{21}} + 2\hat\gamma_{21}\hat\beta_{32}s_{\gamma_{21}\beta_{32}}$$

where $s^2_{\beta_{32}}$, $s^2_{\gamma_{21}}$, and $s_{\gamma_{21}\beta_{32}}$ are the maximum likelihood estimates of the variances and covariance of the relevant path coefficients. Using the estimates in Figure 25.2, the variance in Equation 25.22 can be calculated as follows:

$$\mathrm{Var}(\hat\gamma_{21}\hat\beta_{32}) = [\hat\beta_{32}\ \ \hat\gamma_{21}]\begin{bmatrix} s^2_{\gamma_{21}} & s_{\gamma_{21}\beta_{32}} \\ s_{\beta_{32}\gamma_{21}} & s^2_{\beta_{32}} \end{bmatrix}\begin{bmatrix} \hat\beta_{32} \\ \hat\gamma_{21} \end{bmatrix}$$
$$= [0.259\ \ 0.634]\begin{bmatrix} 0.002 & 0 \\ 0 & 0.002 \end{bmatrix}\begin{bmatrix} 0.259 \\ 0.634 \end{bmatrix}$$
$$= 0.634^2 \times 0.002 + 0.259^2 \times 0.002 + 2 \times 0.634 \times 0 = 0.001$$
$$\textbf{(25.23)}$$

In the single-mediator model, the covariance between coefficients is equal to zero, resulting in the simplified formula, $\mathrm{Var}(\hat\gamma_{21}\hat\beta_{32}) = \hat\gamma^2_{21}s^2_{\beta_{32}} + \hat\beta^2_{32}s^2_{\gamma_{21}}$. In many models, however, the covariances between path coefficients may be nonzero, and more accurate standard errors can be obtained by including the covariance terms.

Other researchers have suggested different methods to estimate the standard error of indirect effects (MacKinnon & Dwyer, 1993). For example, Allison (1995) used a reduced form parameterization for indirect effect models with no latent variables estimated with ordinary least squares estimation, and derived the same standard error formula as Sobel (1982, 1986). The formula derived with second-order Taylor series and exact variance (Goodman, 1960; Mood, Graybill, & Boes, 1974) includes the product of the variances of the path coefficients, instead of the covariance between the path coefficients, resulting in $\mathrm{Var}(\hat\gamma_{21}\hat\beta_{32}) = \hat\gamma^2_{21}s^2_{\beta_{32}} + \hat\beta^2_{32}s^2_{\gamma_{21}} + s^2_{\beta_{32}}s^2_{\gamma_{21}}$. In the formula for the unbiased variance estimator shown by Goodman (1960), the product of the variances of the path coefficients is subtracted rather than added: $\mathrm{Var}(\hat\gamma_{21}\hat\beta_{32}) = \hat\gamma^2_{21}s^2_{\beta_{32}} + \hat\beta^2_{32}s^2_{\gamma_{21}} - s^2_{\beta_{32}}s^2_{\gamma_{21}}$. Despite the differences in the formulas, the estimates of the standard error of the indirect effect are very close to each other. However, simulation studies show that the estimator based on the first-order multivariate delta method (Sobel, 1982) produces the least biased estimates (MacKinnon & Dwyer, 1993; MacKinnon, Lockwood, Hoffman, West, & Sheets, 2002; MacKinnon, Warsi, & Dwyer, 1995). The first-order multivariate delta method estimator is implemented in most SEM software programs, including EQS (Bentler, 1997), LISREL (Jöreskog & Sörbom, 2006), Amos (Arbuckle & Wothke, 1999), and Mplus (Muthén & Muthén, 2010). More detailed information about different estimators of the standard error of the indirect effect can be found in MacKinnon and colleagues (2002).

The rules just described can be extended to cases in which there are multiple indirect effects to be examined. In such cases, the indirect effects in $\hat{I}_{\eta\eta}$ and $\hat{I}_{\eta\xi}$ can be stacked in one long vector of $F(\hat{\theta})$. As shown in Sobel (1982, 1986), the large sample variance covariance matrix of the vector of indirect effects, $F(\hat{\theta})$, can then be approximated as follows:

$$[(\partial F/\partial\hat{\theta})'S(\hat{\theta})(\partial F/\partial\hat{\theta})] \qquad (25.24)$$

where $S(\hat{\theta})$ is the estimated covariance matrix of the parameters, and $(\partial F/\partial\hat{\theta})$ is the matrix of partial derivatives of the vector of indirect effects $F(\hat{\theta})$ with respect to $\hat{\theta}$. For the total indirect effects of the endogenous variables (Equation 25.16), the partial derivatives in $(\partial F/\partial\hat{\theta})$ are given in Equation 25.25:

$$\partial \text{vec}I_{\eta\eta}/\partial\theta = V_B'[(\mathbf{I}-\mathbf{B})^{-1}\otimes((\mathbf{I}-\mathbf{B})^{-1})' - I_q \otimes I_q] (25.25)$$

where $\otimes$ denotes the Kronecker product, q is the number of endogenous variables, and

$$V_B = [\text{vec}(\partial B/\partial\theta_1),...,\text{vec}(\partial B/\partial\theta_u)]$$

$$= \begin{bmatrix} \partial\beta_{11}/\partial\theta_1 & \cdots & \partial\beta_{11}/\partial\theta_u \\ \partial\beta_{21}/\partial\theta_1 & \cdots & \partial\beta_{21}/\partial\theta_u \\ \vdots & \cdots & \vdots \\ \partial\beta_{qq}/\partial\theta_1 & \cdots & \partial\beta_{qq}/\partial\theta_u \end{bmatrix}$$

Similarly, the partial derivatives in $(\partial F/\partial\hat{\theta})$ for the total indirect effects of the exogenous variables are:

$$\partial \text{vec}I_{\eta\xi}/\partial\theta = V_B'[(\mathbf{I}-\mathbf{B})^{-1}\mathbf{\Gamma}\otimes((\mathbf{I}-\mathbf{B})^{-1})'] \\ + V_\Gamma'[I_p \otimes ((\mathbf{I}-\mathbf{B})^{-1}-\mathbf{I})'] \qquad (25.26)$$

where p is the number of exogenous variables in the model and

$$V_\Gamma = [\text{vec}(\partial\Gamma/\partial\theta_1),...,\text{vec}(\partial\Gamma/\partial\theta_u)]$$

$$= \begin{bmatrix} \partial\gamma_{11}/\partial\theta_1 & \cdots & \partial\gamma_{11}/\partial\theta_u \\ \partial\gamma_{21}/\partial\theta_1 & \cdots & \partial\gamma_{21}/\partial\theta_u \\ \vdots & \cdots & \vdots \\ \partial\gamma_{qp}/\partial\theta_1 & \cdots & \partial\gamma_{qp}/\partial\theta_u \end{bmatrix}$$

To illustrate the procedures, we use the model in Figure 25.2 as an example. From Equation 25.5, V_B is constructed as a 9×6 matrix and V_Γ is a 3×6 matrix, with $\hat{\gamma}_{11} = \hat{\theta}_1$, $\hat{\gamma}_{21} = \hat{\theta}_2$, $\hat{\gamma}_{31} = \hat{\theta}_3$, $\hat{\beta}_{21} = \hat{\theta}_4$, $\hat{\beta}_{31} = \hat{\theta}_5$, and $\hat{\beta}_{32} = \hat{\theta}_6$. Most of the elements of V_B are zero, except

three elements, $\partial\hat{\beta}_{21}/\hat{\theta}_4 = 1$, $\partial\hat{\beta}_{31}/\hat{\theta}_5 = 1$, and $\partial\hat{\beta}_{32}/\hat{\theta}_6 = 1$. Similarly, there are only three nonzero elements of V_Γ: $\partial\hat{\gamma}_{11}/\hat{\theta}_1 = 1$, $\partial\hat{\gamma}_{21}/\hat{\theta}_2 = 1$, and $\partial\hat{\gamma}_{31}/\hat{\theta}_3 = 1$. Thus, the following V_Γ and V_B are replaced into Equations 25.25 and 25.26 and the solutions and the estimated covariance matrix of parameter estimates $S(\hat{\theta})$ are substituted into Equation 25.24 to produce the large-sample variance–covariance matrix of the total indirect effects $\hat{I}_{\eta\eta}$ and $\hat{I}_{\eta\xi}$.

$$V_B = \begin{bmatrix} 0 & 0 & 0 & 0 & 0 & 0 \\ 0 & 0 & 0 & 1 & 0 & 0 \\ 0 & 0 & 0 & 0 & 1 & 0 \\ 0 & 0 & 0 & 0 & 0 & 0 \\ 0 & 0 & 0 & 0 & 0 & 0 \\ 0 & 0 & 0 & 0 & 0 & 1 \\ 0 & 0 & 0 & 0 & 0 & 0 \\ 0 & 0 & 0 & 0 & 0 & 0 \\ 0 & 0 & 0 & 0 & 0 & 0 \end{bmatrix}$$

$$V_\Gamma = \begin{bmatrix} 1 & 0 & 0 & 0 & 0 & 0 \\ 0 & 1 & 0 & 0 & 0 & 0 \\ 0 & 0 & 1 & 0 & 0 & 0 \end{bmatrix}$$

$$S(\hat{\theta}) = \begin{bmatrix} s^2_{\gamma_{11}} & s_{\gamma_{11}\gamma_{21}} & s_{\gamma_{11}\gamma_{31}} & s_{\gamma_{11}\beta_{21}} & s_{\gamma_{11}\beta_{31}} & s_{\gamma_{11}\beta_{32}} \\ s_{\gamma_{21}\gamma_{11}} & s^2_{\gamma_{21}} & s_{\gamma_{21}\gamma_{31}} & s_{\gamma_{21}\beta_{21}} & s_{\gamma_{21}\beta_{31}} & s_{\gamma_{21}\beta_{32}} \\ s_{\gamma_{31}\gamma_{11}} & s_{\gamma_{31}\gamma_{21}} & s^2_{\gamma_{31}} & s_{\gamma_{31}\beta_{21}} & s_{\gamma_{31}\beta_{31}} & s_{\gamma_{31}\beta_{32}} \\ s_{\beta_{21}\gamma_{11}} & s_{\beta_{21}\gamma_{21}} & s_{\beta_{21}\gamma_{31}} & s^2_{\beta_{21}} & s_{\beta_{21}\beta_{31}} & s_{\beta_{21}\beta_{32}} \\ s_{\beta_{31}\gamma_{11}} & s_{\beta_{31}\gamma_{21}} & s_{\beta_{31}\gamma_{31}} & s_{\beta_{31}\beta_{21}} & s^2_{\beta_{31}} & s_{\beta_{31}\beta_{32}} \\ s_{\beta_{32}\gamma_{11}} & s_{\beta_{32}\gamma_{21}} & s_{\beta_{32}\gamma_{31}} & s_{\beta_{32}\beta_{21}} & s_{\beta_{32}\beta_{31}} & s^2_{\beta_{32}} \end{bmatrix}$$

CONFIDENCE INTERVALS OF INDIRECT EFFECTS

The application of the first-order multivariate delta method described earlier requires three conditions: (1) the parameters in $\hat{\theta}$ are consistent and normally distributed estimators of θ in large samples, (2) the indirect effect, $f(\hat{\theta})$, is continuously differentiable with respect to θ, and (3) $S(\hat{\theta})$ is a continuous function of $\hat{\theta}$. Under these conditions, the ratio of the indirect effect to its standard error is approximately normally distributed in large samples with mean of 0 and variance of 1. Thus, using the standard normal distribution, the confidence limits for the indirect effect $f(\hat{\theta})$ is obtained as follows:

$$f(\hat{\theta}) \pm z_{\text{Type I error}} \sqrt{[f'(\hat{\theta})]' S(\hat{\theta}) f'(\hat{\theta})} \quad \text{(25.27)}$$

Applying this rationale to the specific indirect effect ξ_1 on η_3 via η_2 ($\xi_1 \rightarrow \eta_2 \rightarrow \eta_3$) in Figure 25.2, the indirect effect $\hat{\gamma}_{21}\hat{\beta}_{32}$ is normally distributed with the variance of $\hat{\gamma}_{21}^2 s_{\hat{\beta}_{32}}^2 + \hat{\beta}_{32}^2 s_{\hat{\gamma}_{21}}^2 + 2\hat{\gamma}_{21}\hat{\beta}_{32} s_{\gamma_{21}\beta_{32}}$. The 95% confidence intervals for $\hat{\gamma}_{21}\hat{\beta}_{32}$ are then calculated as follows:

$$\hat{\gamma}_{21}\hat{\beta}_{32} \pm 1.965 \sqrt{\hat{\gamma}_{21}^2 s_{\hat{\beta}_{32}}^2 + \hat{\beta}_{32}^2 s_{\hat{\gamma}_{21}}^2 + 2\hat{\gamma}_{21}\hat{\beta}_{32} s_{\gamma_{21}\beta_{32}}} \quad \text{(25.28)}$$

$$= 0.164 \pm 1.965 \sqrt{0.001}$$

The resulting lower confidence limit is 0.102 and the upper confidence limit is 0.226. Because the sample interval does not include 0, the indirect effect is considered statistically significant.

Because the standard error of the indirect effect just described is based on the normal theory of the product of path coefficients, the confidence intervals obtained in the preceding equations are assumed to be symmetrical, with the upper and the lower limits at an equal distance from the estimated indirect effect. In addition, with the Type I error rate of .05, 2.5% of the confidence intervals are expected to be on the left side of the true value of the indirect effect, and another 2.5% of the confidence intervals on the right side of the true value. Simulation studies, however, demonstrate that the distributions of indirect effects based on the product of coefficients are often non-normal. Confidence intervals based on Equation 25.28 tend to fall to the left of the true value of indirect effect more often than to the right (MacKinnon et al., 1995, 2004; Stone & Sobel, 1990), although, with increased sample sizes, the proportions of times that confidence intervals fall on either side of the true value become similar. The imbalance of confidence intervals of the indirect effect and the non-normality of the distributions of indirect effects have been also observed when bootstrapping methods are used (Bollen & Stine, 1990; MacKinnon et al., 2004). One of the practical issues of non-normal distributions and imbalanced confidence intervals of indirect effects is low statistical power. Because the distributions of the indirect effects can be skewed with varying kurtosis, assuming the standard normal distribution of the ratio of the indirect effect to its standard error may be incorrect, and applying the critical values from the standard

normal distribution may lead to an incorrect conclusion about the significance of the indirect effect.

Alternative methods have been developed to take into account the non-normality of distributions of indirect effects. One of these methods relies on the distributions of the product of the normally distributed random variables (Craig, 1936; Meeker, Cornwell, & Aroian, 1981; Springer & Thompson, 1966). Given that the indirect effect is obtained as the product of the path coefficients between two variables in the causal chain and the coefficients are assumed to be normally distributed asymptotically (Hanushek & Jackson, 1977), confidence intervals based on the product of normally distributed random variables can be more accurate. The product of normally distributed random variables is not always normally distributed. For the two random variables with means of zero, the distribution of the product is symmetrical with kurtosis of 6 for any sample size (Craig, 1936). When the two random variables have nonzero means, the distribution of their product is skewed with excess kurtosis and becomes normal as the absolute size of the means of the variables increases (Aroian, Taneja, & Cornwell, 1978). Using the frequency distributions of the product of the two random variables (Meeker et al., 1981), upper and lower critical values can be obtained for certain values of path coefficients, and confidence intervals for the indirect effect can be calculated (MacKinnon et al., 2002, 2004; MacKinnon, Fritz, Williams, & Lockwood, 2007). These confidence intervals are usually asymmetrical, unlike those calculated using Equation 25.28. A software program, PRODCLIN (MacKinnon et al., 2007), is available for computing the asymmetric confidence intervals of indirect effects involving one mediator.

Another group of alternative methods for obtaining the confidence intervals of indirect effects uses resampling methods such as bootstrap (Efron & Tibshirani, 1993), permutation (Edgington, 1995), randomization (Edgington, 1995), and jackknife (Mosteller & Tukey, 1977). In these methods, a large number of resamples are taken from the original observed sample, and the statistic in question is computed in each of the resamples. For example, in the bootstrap method for indirect effects, random sampling with replacement is carried out a large number of times from the original observed sample. Typically, the size of the resample is the same as the original sample. In each of these samples, the indirect effect is calculated, and based on the indirect effects computed across the resamples, the empirical distribution of the indirect effects is created. The mean and the standard deviation of this distribution are the bootstrap estimates of the indirect effect and standard error of the indirect effect, respectively. Upper and lower confidence limits are then obtained from the empirical distribution of these indirect effects.

Bootstrap methods have been used more frequently than other resampling methods to construct confidence intervals of indirect effects. Bollen and Stine (1990) showed that the confidence limits obtained by the bootstrap method are asymmetric except in moderately large samples. MacKinnon and colleagues (2004) also found that confidence intervals of indirect effects obtained with resampling methods are asymmetric, and certain bootstrap methods, such as percentile and bias-corrected bootstrap methods, produced more accurate confidence limits than the single-sample methods that assume a normal distribution. Shrout and Bolger (2002) recommended bootstrap methods rather than single-sample methods because the distributions of indirect effects are usually unknown. Bootstrap procedures are now available in SEM programs such as Amos, Mplus, and EQS, and can be readily utilized for testing the significance of indirect effects. SPSS and SAS codes for using the bootstrap method for simpler models are also available (Preacher & Hayes, 2004, 2008).

SIGNIFICANCE TESTING

The null hypothesis for the estimated indirect effect states that the indirect effect is equal to zero. The method based on the multivariate delta method tests the significance of the point estimate of the indirect effect by dividing the estimated indirect effect by its standard error. Then, the ratio of the indirect effect to its standard error is compared to the standard normal distribution. For example, if the ratio for a positive indirect effect is greater than 1.965, the indirect effect is considered significantly different from 0 at the .05 Type I error rate. For the interval test, the upper and lower confidence limits are estimated. If the confidence interval does not include the value of 0, the estimated indirect effect is considered significant. The upper and lower confidence limits can be computed in several ways depending on the method of choice. For multivariate delta method, the confidence limits can be estimated using Equation 25.27. For the method based on the distribution of the product of normal random variables, the asymmetric confidence intervals can be constructed. Alternatively,

one can use resampling methods to obtain the confidence intervals based on the empirical distribution of the indirect effect. Again, if the confidence intervals do not include the value of 0, it is concluded that the estimated indirect effect is statistically significant.

CAUSAL INFERENCE

One way to view the use of SEM is that it provides a way to consider all variables relevant to a phenomenon under study. This is in contrast to examining bivariate relations separately, which has been criticized for not including the omitted variables that would be relevant for the bivariate relation. From this perspective, SEM was developed to provide a solution to the omitted variables problem for causal inference by including as many relevant variables as possible for a phenomenon under study. Nevertheless, causal inference in SEM, including estimation of indirect effects, has been a controversial topic since it was first introduced. Wright's path analysis method (1920, 1921) introduced the definition of a model in terms of mathematical equations and the display of the model in a diagram to clarify the causal relations between variables, with arrows to indicate the direction of the relations. Wright specified that the path coefficient for a mediating process was the product of all the path coefficients in a causal chain.

Soon after Wright's original papers, the method was criticized on causal grounds by Niles (1922, 1923). One of Niles's strongest criticisms was that it was impossible to specify a correct system of the action of causes, so the path analysis was wrong unless somehow the researcher was able to specify the actual model for causes. Wright's response was that the model combined knowledge of correlations with knowledge of causal relations, and noted that prior knowledge of the causal relations is assumed as a prerequisite for the modeling. Regarding a criticism specific to mediation, Wright agreed with Niles's criticism that the chain of causation (i.e., mediation) must be cut off at some point in order to study some part of the mediation process. Wright argued that this was true of all scientific research. This discussion of the chain of mediation was later described as the difference between molar and micromediation, whereby a researcher must decide what part of the chain of mediation to examine and also at what level the mediation should be explored (e.g., neuronal, individual, school, country; MacKinnon, 2008). Overall, Wright argued that path analysis is not a method to infer causation;

it is a method to quantify already assumed causal relations, including chains of mediation.

Many of Niles's criticisms and responses have been repeated in modern criticisms of SEM, which includes path analysis as a special case (Cliff, 1983; Ling, 1982; MacCallum, Wegener, Uchino, & Fabrigar, 1993). These criticisms focus on the additional information that is necessary to generate causal claims about mediation, rather than inferring relations based on correlations or associations (Berk, 1991; Blalock, 1991; Freedman, 1991; Meehl & Waller, 2002). During the 1970s and 1980s, many criticisms of causality in SEM led to avoidance of the term *causal* across many fields (Heise, 1975; Kenny, 1979; James, Mulaik, & Brett, 1982). An important aspect of this literature was a focus on conditions for causal inference. Generally, these conditions included (1) association: if variable A causes B, a researcher should find that A and B have an association; (2) direction: if variable A causes B, then A should precede B; and (3) isolation: if variables A and B are isolated from other influences, then change in variable A will cause change in variable B. These conditions provided a way to formulate ideas about causality. This tradition has further clarified causal effects with more precise mathematical definition of causal relations, including criteria based on actual and counterfactual data (Pearl, 2009; Rubin, 1974, 2004; VanderWeele & Robins, 2008). Considering "counterfactual conditions," conditions in which research participants had not served, as well as the condition in which they had served, enabled a mathematical formulation of causal inference.

Much work on causal inference has focused on the relation between two variables, X and Y, demonstrating the importance of randomization for causal inference of X to Y, as well as other assumptions (Holland, 1988a, 1988b; Robins, 1999; Rubin, 1974). Causal inference for the mediation model is a natural next step for the development of causal inference approaches because it is a more complex model than the bivariate case, and the task of inferring true causal relations from measures of three variables has several new challenges, including the estimation of both direct and indirect effects. In addition, there are several different ways that a third variable may affect the relation between the two variables; for example, as a mediator, confounder, moderator, or covariate. As a result, mediation is an active area for development of new ideas about causal inference. Several new and important approaches that have been developed are useful for the case of mediation, including principal stratification (Frangakis & Rubin, 2002), marginal structural models (Robins, 1999), and instrumental variable methods (Angrist, Imbens, & Rubin, 1996). An important benefit of all these detailed causal approaches is the careful consideration of the limitations and strengths of different types of evidence for causal mediation. In particular, more recent work in this area has focused on alternative methods to test and evaluate results for sensitivity of assumptions (Lynch, Cary, Gallop, & ten Have, 2008; ten Have et al., 2007; VanderWeele, 2008, 2009, 2010; VanderWeele & Vansteelandt, 2009).

One important causal inference approach in SEM in general and indirect effects focuses on causal mathematics and the meaning of parameters in SEM (Pearl, Chapter 5, this volume). In this framework, there are clearly specified inputs and outputs. The first set of the inputs consists of assumptions that the investigator will defend for a model. A second input is a series of research questions that focus on specific aspects of the model, including whether the independent variable affects the dependent variable through a mediator. Only research questions that can be answered by the model are admissible. The third set of inputs comprises data generated by the processes defined by the assumptions and model described earlier. The first output includes a set of statements that are implications of qualitative assumptions that are not based on data. A second output is a set of claims about the research questions in the input, and a third output would be the list of testable statistical implications of the qualitative assumptions that are input. A critical aspect of this approach is that all the causal claims for the results of a structural equation model are given following the qualitative assumptions of the model. Compared to current practice, the extensive specification of inputs, especially qualitative assumptions, is a critical step in the process. The focus on model input addresses critics of SEM who press for clearer specifications of assumptions. This includes additional detective work related to the variables in the model (Berk, 2003; Freedman, 1987) and the clear specification of models to avoid plausible alternative models (Lee & Hershberger, 1990; MacCallum et al., 1993; Spirtes, Glymour, & Scheines, 1993).

Based on this theory, Pearl (2001, 2009; Chapter 5, this volume) derived a nonparametric mediation formula that applies for linear, as well as nonlinear, models and requires no additional assumptions beyond those used in traditional linear analysis. An important aspect of the mediation formula is the notion of controlled and natural direct effects. Controlled direct effects are changes in the dependent variable Y induced by a unit change in X, while holding M constant at a specified value, m. The natural direct effect refers to the same changes in Y, but holding M at whatever value it would have attained in each individual prior to change in X. A similar definition applies to natural indirect effects, which have no controlled version. In the analysis of linear models, the natural and controlled direct effects are equivalent, and reduce to the usual formulas obtained from path coefficients and matrix formulations. They differ however, in nonlinear systems involving continuous or discrete variables with arbitrary distributions and arbitrary interactions (often encoded in logistic regression models). In this case, the natural direct and indirect effects do not add up to the total effect but estimate, respectively, the fraction of individuals who do not owe their response to mediation (through M) and the fraction whose response can be explained by mediation alone.

ADVANCES IN MEDIATION ANALYSIS

Due to recent advancements in technology and research in mediation analysis, more complex models have been proposed and utilized to investigate mediation. In this section, we present recent developments in methods for testing multilevel and longitudinal mediation.

Multilevel Mediation

Often research studies involve clustered data, such as individuals nested within families and students nested within schools. In such cases, the responses of the individuals in the same higher-level units (e.g., students in the same schools) tend to be more similar to each other than to those of individuals in other higher-level units. Ignoring the dependence of observations in clustered data would lead to inflated Type I error rates due to downward biases in the standard error of estimate (Krull & MacKinnon, 1999, 2001). Furthermore, when the data are clustered, the independent variables, the mediators, and the dependent variables can be assessed at different levels. For example, the independent variable can be a school characteristic that is hypothesized to affect individual student motivation, which is expected to improve students' academic performance. This case is called a 2-1-1 design, indicating that inde-

pendent variable, mediator, and dependent variable are measured at Level 2 (cluster-level), Level 1 (individual-level), and Level 1, respectively. The advantage of multilevel modeling of indirect effects is that it allows us to appropriately specify the relations between the variables as level specific effects, while adjusting for the biases in standard errors and Type I error rates that result from the dependence of observations (Kenny, Bolger, & Korchmaros, 2003; Krull & MacKinnon, 2001). Another advantage of multilevel modeling of indirect effects is that the effects can be modeled as fixed or random. At least one of the effects in the mediational pathways may be treated as either constant or varying across upper-level units, and indirect effects may be tested for both lower- and upper-level units (Bauer, Preacher, & Gil 2006; Kenny et al., 1998).

In recent years, multilevel modeling of indirect effects has been actively studied and is increasingly applied to answering research questions on indirect effects. Various studies have outlined multilevel indirect effect models, although mainly in the hierarchical linear modeling (HLM) framework (Krull & MacKinnon, 1999, 2001; MacKinnon, 2008; Raudenbush & Sampson, 1999), and simulation studies have been conducted to evaluate the statistical performance of multilevel modeling of indirect effects (Kenny et al., 2003; Krull & MacKinnon, 1999, 2001; Pituch, Stapleton, & Kang, 2006). Furthermore, researchers have described comprehensive approaches of multilevel indirect models in the SEM framework (Preacher, Zyphur, & Zhang, 2010).

When multilevel modeling of indirect effects is carried out in the SEM framework, namely, multilevel structural equation modeling (MSEM), the variances of variables and effects can be partitioned into uncorrelated between-cluster and within-cluster components (Muthén & Asparouhov, 2011). If there is no between-cluster variability, it is not necessary to estimate indirect effects in MSEM, and the single-level analysis can be carried out applying the methods described in the previous sections. On the other hand, if there is statistically significant between-cluster variability, indirect effects can be estimated more in detail in the MSEM framework. In addition to testing whether the potential mediator significantly intervenes in the relation between the independent and the dependent variables, one can investigate to what extent the indirect effect is due to the cluster-level variability in the mediator or to what extent the cluster-level variability in the dependent variable is mediated by the cluster-level variability in the mediator. For example, in a 2-1-1 design, the independent variable is a cluster-level variable; thus, it can predict only between-cluster variability in the mediator and the dependent variable. In such cases, one can assess the extent to which the between-cluster variability in the mediator mediates the effect of the independent variable on the between-cluster variability in the dependent variable. In a 1-1-1 design, where all the variables are measured at the lower level (e.g., individual level), one may wish to model the relations between the variables as random effects and investigate the cluster-level variables that may affect the relations between the variables (Bauer et al., 2006; Kenny et al., 2003).

In this section, we focus on multilevel modeling of indirect effects specified in the structural model, although the measurement model can be specified in MSEM as well. Detailed information on the multilevel specification for the fuller model can be found elsewhere (Kaplan, Kim, & Kim, 2009; Muthén & Asparouhov, 2011). The single-level specification of indirect effects (Equation 25.5) can be extended to the multilevel specification as follows:

$$\eta_{ij} = \alpha_j + B_j\eta_{ij} + \Gamma_j\xi_{ij} + \zeta_{ij} \qquad (25.29)$$

where subscript j denotes cluster and having the subscript j in both the variables and the parameters indicates that the elements in these matrices can vary across clusters. In Equation 25.29, η_{ij} is a p-dimensional vector of endogenous variables for individual i in cluster j and ξ_{ij} is a q-dimensional vector of within-cluster exogenous variables. The matrices α_j, B_j, and Γ_j are parameter matrices whose elements can vary across clusters. Specifically, α_j is a vector of random intercepts, and B_j and Γ_j are matrices for structural relations. The last term in Equation 25.29, ζ_{ij}, is a p-dimensional vector of within-cluster disturbances. Random effects in α_j, B_j, and Γ_j are then specified at the between-cluster level as functions of between-cluster level variables as in Equations 25.30, 25.31, and 25.32, where the between-cluster level endogenous variable Z_j and exogenous variable W_j can be introduced as predictors of the random effects:

$$\alpha_j = \alpha_{00} + \alpha_{01}Z_j + \alpha_{02}W_j + \varepsilon_j \qquad (25.30)$$

$$B_j = B_{00} + B_{01}Z_j + B_{02}W_j + \upsilon_j \qquad (25.31)$$

$$\Gamma_j = \Gamma_{00} + \Gamma_{01}Z_j + \Gamma_{02}W_j + \delta_j \qquad (25.32)$$

Equation 25.30 specifies the random intercepts as a function of Z_j and W_j. Equations 25.31 and 25.32 specify random slopes as functions of Z_j and W_j. Random slopes denoting the relations between endogenous variables are modeled in B_j, while random slopes relating exogenous variables to endogenous variables are modeled in Γ_j.

For a specific example, let us assume we have a 2-1-1-1 design in which the independent variable is a school-level measure of antidrug attitudes that may affect individual students' attitudes toward drug users and intention to use drugs, and eventually affect an individual student's drug use. This model is similar to that in Figure 25.2, except that the independent variable is measured at the cluster level. Figure 25.3 follows the presentation scheme used by Muthén and Asparouhov (2011). The filled circles indicate random intercepts or mean of the latent variables that vary across schools,

Within-cluster level

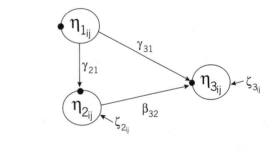

Between-cluster level

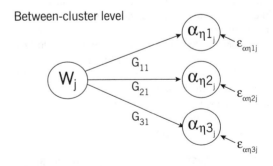

FIGURE 25.3. A multilevel mediation model for a 2-1-1-1 design.

which are presented as latent variables, $\alpha_{\eta_{1j}}$, $\alpha_{\eta_{2j}}$, and $\alpha_{\eta_{3j}}$. The relations between the three endogenous latent variables are specified at the within-school level, whereas the relations between the school-level exogenous variable and the latent mean and intercepts of the within-school level variables are specified at the between-cluster level. The indirect effect of W_j (school-level antidrug attitude) on η_{3ij} (individual student drug use) via η_{1ij} (students' attitudes toward drug users) and η_{2ij} (students' intention to use drugs) is estimated by the product of coefficients, $G_{11}\gamma_{21}\beta_{32}$. In this example, random slopes are not modeled; thus, the elements in the parameter matrices of $\mathbf{B}_j$ and Γ_j are not specified. When the relations between the within-school latent variables are modeled as random slopes, school-level covariates can be introduced to predict these random slopes. In such cases, the relations between the within-school latent variables are represented as cross-level interactions between school-level covariates and the within-school latent variables, and the indirect effects can be further probed as moderated by school-level characteristics.

Longitudinal Mediation

When the same variables are measured repeatedly on the same individuals, researchers can investigate more complex questions regarding mediation mechanisms. With longitudinal data, the time sequence of independent variables, mediators, and dependent variables can be specified in the model, rendering more confident temporal statements regarding indirect effects. In addition, indirect effects can be modeled in terms of individual changes, such that the independent variable affects changes in the mediator over time, which, in turn, affects changes in the dependent variable over time. Despite the rich opportunities for investigating longitudinal mediation, however, it is not easy to identify the optimal timing of measurements that allows accurate assessment of when longitudinal effects occur. Researchers also need to be careful about potential model misspecification problems, since there are more measurement time points and more relations than can be included in hypothesizing correct mediation pathways (Cheong, MacKinnon, & Khoo, 2003; Cole & Maxwell, 2003; Collins & Graham, 2002; MacKinnon, 2008). With the advancements in modeling techniques for longitudinal data analysis, various ways of modeling longitudinal indirect effects have been proposed and utilized in empirical studies. One such method is

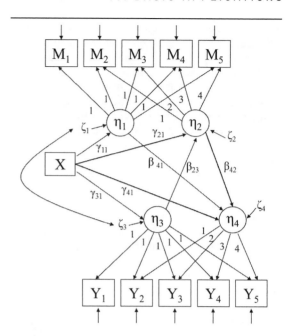

FIGURE 25.4. A parallel process latent growth curve model for mediation.

the latent growth curve modeling (LGCM) approach to testing mediation (Cheong, 2011; Cheong et al., 2003).

When LGCM is used for testing mediation, the mediation process is typically modeled using parallel process models, where the growth trajectories of the independent variable, the mediator, and the dependent variable are modeled as distinctive growth trajectories, and the mediation is hypothesized in the relations among the growth factors. Figure 25.4 shows an example of a parallel-process LGCM model for mediation. Using the repeated measures across five time points spaced equally, the trajectories of the mediator and the dependent variable are modeled as two distinctive processes. The independent variable is specified as affecting the trajectory of the dependent variable directly and also indirectly, through its influence on the trajectory of the mediator. In other cases, the repeated measures of the independent variable may also be modeled as another growth process. Indirect effects are specified in the relations among the growth factors.

In the model depicted in Figure 25.4, mediational pathways can be hypothesized in several ways. One possibility is the independent variable X affecting the growth rate of the dependent variable process η_4 via the growth rate of the mediator process η_2 (i.e., $\gamma_{21}\beta_{42}$). Another potential mediation process is the independent variable affecting the growth rate of the dependent variable process η_4 via the initial level of the dependent variable process η_3 and the growth rate of the mediator process η_2 (i.e., $\gamma_{31}\beta_{23}\beta_{42}$). It is also possible to investigate mediation process from the independent variable to the initial level of the mediator η_1 to the growth rate of the dependent variable process η_4 (i.e., $\gamma_{11}\beta_{41}$). The unique aspect of the LGCM approach to testing mediation is that the mediation is modeled in terms of individual changes in the mediator and the dependent variable, rather than the levels of individuals on the variables. Significant mediation is supported when the greater (or smaller) growth rate in the mediator is associated with the greater (or smaller) growth rate in the dependent variable.

When indirect effects are investigated in the parallel-process LGCM approach, within-individual changes in the mediator and the dependent variable are estimated as overall, as opposed to time-specific, changes based on the multiple waves of measurements. To examine more detailed time-specific indirect effects, researchers may apply other longitudinal data analysis techniques. For example, if researchers are interested in examining whether the effect of the independent variable on the mediator and the effect of the mediator on the dependent variable vary across time, or if they are interested in assessing when the mediated effect ceases to occur in longitudinal studies, autoregressive cross-lagged modeling can be applied for testing mediation (Cole & Maxwell, 2003). If researchers are interested in estimating indirect effects that are based on the change scores between two measurement occasions, rather than the overall changes across several measurement occasions, latent difference score models can be applied (Ferrer & McArdle, 2003; McArdle, 2001). In addition to the approaches described in this section, there are other longitudinal modeling approaches, including models combining autoregressive and LGCM models (Bollen & Curran, 2004), models with a person-centered approach to identify individuals whose response patterns are consistent with the mediation hypothesis (Collins, Graham, & Flaherty, 1998), and models specifying parameters in time metric to reflect different time intervals between measurements (Boker & Nesselroade, 2002; Fritz, 2007).

SUMMARY AND CONCLUSIONS

Mediation analysis is beneficial in that it provides information on the underlying mechanisms by which the independent variable affects the dependent variable. Especially in experimental studies such as randomized clinical trials, mediation analysis informs researchers whether the experimental manipulation has worked as hypothesized and whether the intermediate variable is a good mediator as specified in the theory (MacKinnon & Dwyer, 1993). Such detailed information can be further utilized to improve intervention/prevention programs for the future studies. In recent years, extensive research has been conducted on the statistical approaches to testing indirect effects. Methods for estimating indirect effects and their standard errors have been developed, and numerous simulation studies have been conducted to evaluate statistical performance of these methods. Research in causal inference for mediation effect and the structural equation models is currently an active field of study. With recent development in causal inference for mediation, our understanding of the limitations and strengths of contemporary mediation analysis methods has been accelerated. Due to advances in computing techniques and developments in complex modeling techniques, evaluation of indirect effects has been expanded to include more complicated data structures, such as multilevel and longitudinal data. Although the utilities of these complex modeling techniques have been demonstrated, we have relatively little knowledge about the statistical performance of such complex techniques. Further studies are warranted to evaluate the methodological properties and the potential of those techniques.

REFERENCES

Allison, P. D. (1995). Exact variance of indirect effects in recursive linear models. *Sociological Methodology, 25*, 253–266.

Alwin, D. F., & Hauser, R. M. (1975). The decomposition of effects in path analysis. *American Sociological Review, 40*, 37–47.

Angrist, J. D., Imbens, G. W., & Rubin, D. B. (1996). Identification of causal effects using instrumental variables. *Journal of the American Statistical Association, 91*, 444–472.

Arbuckle, J. L., & Wothke, W. (1999). *Amos users' guide (Version 4.0)*. Chicago: Smallwaters Corporation.

Aroian, L. A., Taneja, V. S., & Cornwell, L. W. (1978). Mathematical forms of the distribution of the product of two normal variables. *Communications in Statistics: Theory and Methods, A7*, 165–172.

Baron, R. M., & Kenny, D. A. (1986). The moderator–mediator variable distinction in social psychological research: Conceptual, strategic, and statistical considerations. *Journal of Personality and Social Psychology, 51*, 1173–1182.

Bauer, D. J., Preacher, K. J., & Gil, K. M. (2006). Conceptualizing and testing random indirect effects and moderated mediation in multilevel models: New procedures and recommendations. *Psychological Methods, 11*, 142–163.

Bentler, P. M. (1980). Multivariate analysis with latent variables: Causal modeling. *Annual Review of Psychology, 31*, 419–456.

Bentler, P. M. (1997). *EQS for Windows (Version 5.6)*. Encino, CA: Multivariate Software, Inc.

Berk, R. A. (1991). Toward a methodology for mere mortals. *Sociological Methodology, 21*, 315–324.

Berk, R. A. (2003). *Regression analysis: A constructive critique*. Thousand Oaks, CA: Sage.

Bishop, Y. M. M., Fienberg, S. E., & Holland, P. W. (1975). *Discrete multivariate analysis: Theory and practice*. Cambridge, MA: MIT Press.

Blalock, H. M. (1991). Are there really any constructive alternatives to causal modeling? *Sociological Methodology, 21*, 325–335.

Boker, S. M., & Nesselroade, J. R. (2002). A method for modeling the intrinsic dynamics of intraindividual variability: Recovering the parameters of simulated oscillators in multi-wave panel data. *Multivariate Behavioral Research, 37*, 127–160.

Bollen, K. A. (1987). Total, direct, and indirect effects in structural equation models. *Sociological Methodology, 17*, 37–69.

Bollen, K. A., & Curran, P. J. (2004). Autoregressive latent trajectory (ALT) models: A synthesis of two traditions. *Sociological Methods and Research, 32*, 336–383.

Bollen, K. A., & Stine, R. A. (1990). Direct and indirect effects: Classical and bootstrap estimates of variability. *Sociological Methodology, 20*, 115–140.

Brown, R. L. (1997). Assessing specific mediational effects in complex theoretical models. *Structural Equation Modeling, 4*, 142–156.

Cheong, J. (2011). Accuracy of estimates and statistical power for testing mediation in latent growth modeling. *Structural Equation Modeling, 18*, 195–211.

Cheong, J., MacKinnon, D. P., & Khoo, S. (2003). Investigation of mediational processes using parallel process latent growth curve modeling. *Structural Equation Modeling, 10*, 238–262.

Cliff, N. (1983). Some cautions concerning the application of causal modeling methods. *Multivariate Behavioral Research, 18*, 115–126.

Cole, D. A., & Maxwell, S. E. (2003). Testing mediational models with longitudinal data: Questions and tips in the use of structural equation modeling. *Journal of Abnormal Psychology, 112*, 558–577.

Collins, L. M., & Graham, J. W. (2002). The effect of the timing and spacing of observations in longitudinal studies of tobacco and other drug use: Temporal design considerations. *Drug and Alcohol Dependence, 68*, S85–S96.

Collins, L. M., Graham, J. W., & Flaherty, B. P. (1998). An alternative framework for defining mediation. *Multivariate Behavioral Research, 33*, 295–312.

Craig, C. C. (1936). On the frequency function of xy. *Annals of Mathematical Statistics, 7*, 1–15.

Donovan, R. J., & Rossiter, J. R. (1982). Store atmosphere: An environmental psychology approach. *Journal of Retailing, 58*, 34–57.

Duncan, O. D. (1966). Path analysis: Sociological examples. *American Journal of Sociology, 72*, 1–16.

Duncan, O. D., Featherman, D. L., & Duncan, B. (1972). *Socioeconomic background and achievement*. New York: Seminar Press.

Edgington, E. S. (1995). *Randomization tests* (3rd ed.). New York: Marcel Dekker.

Efron, B., & Tibshirani, R. J. (1993). *An introduction to the bootstrap*. New York: Chapman & Hall.

Ferrer, E., & McArdle, J. J. (2003). Alternative structural models for multivariate longitudinal data analysis. *Structural Equation Modeling, 10*, 493–524.

Folmer, H. (1981). Measurement of the effects of regional policy instruments by means of linear structural equation models and panel data. *Environment and Planning A, 13*, 1435–1448.

Fox, J. (1980). Effect analysis in structural equation models: Extensions and simplified methods of computation. *Sociological Methods and Research, 9*, 3–28.

Frangakis, C. E., & Rubin, D. B. (2002). Principal stratification in causal inference. *Biometrics, 58*, 21–29.

Freedman, D. A. (1987). As others see us: A case study in path analysis (with discussion). *Journal of Educational Statistics, 12*, 101–223.

Freedman, D. A. (1991). Statistical models and shoe leather. *Sociological Methodology, 21*, 291–313.

Fritz, M. S. (2007). *An exponential decay model for mediation*. Unpublished doctoral dissertation, Arizona State University, Tempe.

Ginsberg, A. (1954). Hypothetical constructs and intervening variables. *Psychological Review, 61*, 119–131.

Goldberg, L., MacKinnon, D. P., Elliot, D., Moe, E., Clarke, G., & Cheong, J. (2000). Adolescents Training and Learning to Avoid Steroids program: Preventing drug use and promoting health behaviors among adolescent athletes: Results of the program. *Archives of Pediatric and Adolescent Medicine, 154*, 332–338.

Goodman, L. A. (1960). On the exact variance of products.

Journal of the American Statistical Association, 55, 708–713.

Graff, J., & Schmidt, P. (1982). A general model for decomposition of effects. In K. G. Jöreskog & H. Wold (Eds.), *Systems under indirect observation: Causality, structure, prediction* (pp. 131–148). Amsterdam: North-Holland.

Hanushek, E. A., & Jackson, J. E. (1977). *Statistical methods for social scientists.* New York: Academic Press.

Heise, D. (1975). *Causal analysis.* Oxford, UK: Wiley.

Holland, P. W. (1988a). Causal inference, path analysis, and recursive structural equation models. *Sociological Methodology, 18*, 449–484.

Holland, P. W. (1988b). Comment: Causal mechanism or causal effect: Which is best for statistical science? *Statistical Science, 3*, 186–188.

Hoyle, R. H., & Kenny, D. A. (1999). Sample size, reliability, and tests of statistical mediation. In R. H. Hoyle (Ed.), *Statistical strategies for small sample research* (pp. 195–222). Thousand Oaks, CA: Sage.

James, L. R., & Brett, J. M. (1984). Mediators, moderators, and tests for mediation. *Journal of Applied Psychology, 69*, 307–321.

James, L. R., Mulaik, S. A., & Brett, J. M. (1982). *Causal analysis: Assumptions, models, and data.* Beverly Hills, CA: Sage.

Jöreskog, K. G. (1970). A general method for analysis of covariance structures. *Biometrika, 57*, 239–251.

Jöreskog, K. G. (1973). A general method for estimating a linear structural equation system. In A. S. Golberger & O. D. Duncan (Eds.), *Structural equation models in the social sciences* (pp. 85–112). New York: Seminar Press.

Jöreskog, K. G., & Sörbom, D. (2006). *LISREL.* Chicago: Scientific Software International.

Kaplan, D., Kim, J.-S., & Kim, S.-Y. (2009). Multilevel latent variable modeling: Current research and recent developments. In R. E. Millsap & A. Maydeu-Olivares (Eds.), *Sage handbook of quantitative methods in psychology* (pp. 592–612). Thousand Oaks, CA: Sage.

Kendall, P. L., & Lazarsfeld, P. F. (1950). Problems of survey analysis. In R. K. Merton & P. F. Lazarsfeld (Eds.), *Continuities in social research: Studies in the scope and method of "The American Soldier"* (pp. 133–196). Glencoe, IL: Free Press.

Kenny, D. A. (1979). *Correlation and causality.* New York: Wiley.

Kenny, D. A., Bolger, N., & Korchmaros, J. D. (2003). Lower level mediation in multilevel models. *Psychological Methods, 8*, 115–128.

Kenny, D. A., Kashy, D. A., & Bolger, N. (1998). Data analysis in social psychology. In D. T. Gilbert, S. T. Fiske, & G. Lindzey (Eds.), *The handbook of social psychology* (4th ed., pp. 233–265). Boston: McGraw-Hill.

Krull, J. L., & MacKinnon, D. P. (1999). Multilevel mediation modeling in group-based intervention studies. *Evaluation Review, 23*, 418–444.

Krull, J. L., & MacKinnon, D. P. (2001). Multilevel modeling of individual and group level mediated effects. *Multivariate Behavioral Research, 36*, 249–277.

Last, J. M. (1988). *A dictionary of epidemiology* (2nd ed.). New York: Oxford University Press.

Lazarsfeld, P. F. (1955). Interpretation of statistical relations as a research operation. In P. F. Lazarsfeld & M. Rosenberg (Eds.), *The language of social research: A reader in the methodology of social research* (pp. 115–125). Glencoe, IL: Free Press.

Lee, S., & Hershberger, S. (1990). A simple rule for generating equivalent models in covariance structure modeling. *Multivariate Behavioral Research, 25*, 313–334.

Ling, R. (1982). Review of the book: *Correlation and causation,* by D. A. Kenny. *Journal of the American Statistical Association, 77*, 489–491.

Lynch, K. G., Cary, M., Gallop, R., & ten Have, T. R. (2008). Causal mediation analyses for randomized trials. *Health Services and Outcome Methodology, 8*, 57–76.

MacCallum, R. C., Wegener, D. T., Uchino, B. N., & Fabrigar, L. R. (1993). The problem of equivalent models in applications of covariance structure analysis. *Psychological Bulletin, 114*, 185–199.

MacCorquodale, K., & Meehl, P. E. (1948). On a distinction between hypothetical constructs and intervening variables. *Psychological Review, 55*, 95–107.

MacKinnon, D. P. (2008). *Introduction to statistical mediation analysis.* New York: Erlbaum.

MacKinnon, D. P., & Dwyer, J. H. (1993). Estimating mediated effects in prevention studies. *Evaluation Review, 17*, 144–158.

MacKinnon, D. P., Fritz, M. S., Williams, J., & Lockwood, C. M. (2007). Distribution of the product confidence limits for the indirect effect: Program PRODCLIN. *Behavior Research Methods, 39*, 384–389.

MacKinnon, D. P., Lockwood, C. M., Hoffman, J. M., West, S. G., & Sheets, V. (2002). A comparison of methods to test mediation and other intervening variable effects. *Psychological Methods, 7*, 83–104.

MacKinnon, D. P., Lockwood, C. M., & Williams, J. (2004). Confidence limits for the indirect effect: Distribution of the product and resampling methods. *Multivariate Behavioral Research, 39*, 99–128.

MacKinnon, D. P., Warsi, G., & Dwyer, J. H. (1995). A simulation study of mediated effect measures. *Multivariate Behavioral Research, 30*, 41–62.

McArdle, J. J. (2001). A latent difference score approach to longitudinal dynamic structural analysis. In R. Cudeck, S. du Toit, & D. Sörbom (Eds.), *Structural equation modeling: Present and future: A festschrift in honor of Karl Jöreskog* (pp. 341–380). Lincolnwood, IL: Scientific Software International.

Meehl, P. E., & Waller, N. G. (2002). The path analysis controversy: A new statistical approach to strong appraisal of verisimilitude. *Psychological Methods, 7*(3), 283–300.

Meeker, W. Q., Jr., Cornwell, L. W., & Aroian, L. A. (1981). The product of two normally distributed random variables. In W. J. Kennedy & R. E. Odeh (Eds.), *Selected tables in mathematical statistics, Vol. VII* (pp. 1–256). Providence, RI: American Mathematical Society.

Mood, A. M., Graybill, F. A., & Boes, D. C. (1974). *Introduction to the theory of statistics* (3rd ed.). New York: McGraw-Hill.

Mosteller, F., & Tukey, J. W. (1977). *Data analysis and regression: A second course in statistics.* Reading, MA: Addison-Wesley.

Muthén, B. O., & Asparouhov, T. (2011). Beyond multilevel regression modeling: Multilevel analysis in a general latent variable framework. In J. Hox & J. K. Roberts (Eds.), *Handbook of advanced multilevel analysis.* New York: Taylor & Francis.

Muthén, L. K., & Muthén, B. O. (2010). *Mplus user's guide.* Los Angeles: Authors.

Niles, H. E. (1922). Correlation, causation, and Wright's theory of "path coefficients." *Genetics, 7,* 258–273.

Niles, H. E. (1923). The method of path coefficients: An answer to Wright. *Genetics, 8,* 256–260.

Pearl, J. (2001). Direct and indirect effects. In *Proceedings of the 17th Conference on Uncertainty in Artificial Intelligence* (pp. 411–420). San Francisco: Morgan Kaufmann.

Pearl, J. (2009). *Causality* (2nd ed.). New York: Cambridge University Press.

Pituch, K. A., Stapleton, L. M., & Kang, J.-Y. (2006). A comparison of single sample and bootstrap methods to assess mediation in cluster randomized trials. *Multivariate Behavioral Research, 41,* 367–400.

Preacher, K. J., & Hayes, A. F. (2004). SPSS and SAS procedures for estimating indirect effects in simple mediation models. *Behavior Research Methods, Instruments, and Computers, 36,* 717–731.

Preacher, K. J., & Hayes, A. F. (2008). Asymptotic and resampling strategies for assessing and comparing indirect effects in multiple mediator models. *Behavior Research Methods, 40,* 879–891.

Preacher, K. J., Zyphur, M. J., & Zhang, Z. (2010). A general multilevel SEM framework for assessing multilevel mediation. *Psychological Methods, 15,* 209–233.

Raudenbush, S. W., & Sampson, R. (1999). Assessing direct and indirect effects in multilevel designs with latent variables. *Sociological Methods and Research, 28,* 123–153.

Robins, J. M. (1999). Marginal structural models versus structural nested models as tools for causal inference. In M. E. Halloran & D. Berry (Eds.), *Statistical models in epidemiology, the environment, and clinical trials* (pp. 95–134). New York: Springer-Verlag.

Robins, J. M., & Greenland, S. (1992). Identifiability and exchangeability for direct and indirect effects. *Epidemiology, 3,* 143–155.

Rosenberg, M. (1968). *The logic of survey analysis.* New York: Basic Books.

Rubin, D. B. (1974). Estimating causal effects of treatments in randomized and nonrandomized studies. *Journal of Educational Psychology, 66,* 688–701.

Rubin, D. B. (2004). Direct and indirect causal effects via potential outcomes. *Scandinavian Journal of Statistics, 31,* 161–170.

Shrout, P. E., & Bolger, N. (2002). Mediation in experimental and nonexperimental studies: New procedures and recommendations. *Psychological Methods, 7,* 422–445.

Sobel, M. E. (1982). Asymptotic confidence intervals for indirect effects in structural equation models. *Sociological Methodology, 13,* 290–312.

Sobel, M. E. (1986). Some new results on indirect effects and their standard errors in covariance structure models. *Sociological Methodology, 16,* 159–186.

Sobel, M. E. (1987). Direct and indirect effects in linear structural equation models. *Sociological Methods and Research, 16,* 155–176.

Spirtes, P., Glymour, C., & Scheines, R. (1993). *Causation, prediction, and search.* New York: Springer-Verlag.

Springer, M. D., & Thompson, W. E. (1966). The distribution of products of independent random variables. *SIAM Journal on Applied Mathematics, 14,* 511–526.

Stone, C. A., & Sobel, M. E. (1990). The robustness of estimates of total indirect effects in covariance structure models estimated by maximum likelihood. *Psychometrika, 55,* 337–352.

ten Have, T. R., Joffe, M. M., Lynch, K. G., Brown, G. K., Maisto, S. A., & Beck, A. T. (2007). Causal mediation analyses with rank preserving models. *Biometrics, 63,* 926–934.

VanderWeele, T. J. (2008). Simple relations between principal stratification and direct and indirect effects. *Statistics and Probability Letters, 78,* 2957–2962.

VanderWeele, T. J. (2009). Marginal structural models for the estimation of direct and indirect effects. *Epidemiology, 20,* 18–26.

VanderWeele, T. J. (2010). Bias formulas for sensitivity analysis for direct and indirect effects. *Epidemiology, 21,* 540–551.

VanderWeele, T. J., & Robins, J. M. (2008). Empirical and counterfactual conditions for sufficient cause interactions. *Biometrika, 95,* 49–61.

VanderWeele, T. J., & Vansteelandt, S. (2009). Conceptual issues concerning mediation, interventions and composition. *Statistics and Its Interface, 2,* 457–468.

Wiley, D. E. (1973). The identification problem for structural equation models with unmeasured variables. In A. S. Goldberger & O. D. Duncan (Eds.), *Structural equa-*

tion models in the social sciences (pp. 69–83). New York: Seminar Press.

Wolfle, L. M. (1999). Sewall Wright on the method of path coefficients: An annotated bibliography. Structural Equation Modeling, 6, 280–291.

Woodworth, R. S. (1928). Dynamic psychology. In C. Murchison (Ed.), Psychologies of 1925 (pp. 111–126) Worcester, MA: Clark University Press.

Wright, S. (1920). The relative importance of heredity and environment in determining the piebald pattern of guinea-pigs. Proceedings of the National Academy of Sciences, 6, 320–332.

Wright, S. (1921). Correlation and causation. Journal of Agricultural Research, 20, 557–585.

Wright, S. (1923). The theory of path coefficients: A reply to Niles's criticism. Genetics, 8, 239–255.

CHAPTER 26

Structural Equation Models of Latent Interaction

Herbert W. Marsh
Zhonglin Wen
Benjamin Nagengast
Kit-Tai Hau

In their classic presentation of moderation, Baron and Kenny (1986, p. 1174) defined a moderator variable to be a "variable that affects the direction and/or strength of the relationship between an independent or predictor variable and a dependent or criterion variable." An interaction effect occurs when the effect of at least one predictor variable on an outcome variable is moderated by one other predictor (i.e., depends upon or varies as a function of this variable). Moderation studies address questions like "when (under what conditions/situations)" or "for whom" does X have a stronger–weaker (positive–negative) relation with or effect on Y.

Moderation and interactions between variables—we use both terms interchangeably in the remainder of the chapter—are important concerns in psychology and the social sciences more generally. In educational psychology, for example, it is often hypothesized that the effect of an instructional technique on achievement outcomes will depend on characteristics of individual students, an aptitude–treatment interaction (Cronbach & Snow, 1977). For example, a special remediation program developed for slow learners may not be an effective instructional strategy for bright students

(i.e., the effect of the special remediation "treatment" is moderated by the ability "aptitude" of the student). Developmental psychologists are frequently interested in how the effects of a given variable are moderated by age in longitudinal or cross-sectional studies. Social psychologists are concerned with how the effects of individual characteristics are moderated by groups in which people interact with others. Organizational psychologists study how the effects of individual employee characteristics interact with workplace characteristics. Fundamental to the rationale of differential psychology is the assumption that people differ fundamentally in the way they respond to all sorts of external stimuli. The opposite of interaction or moderation is generalization. For example, if the effect of an intervention is the same for males and females, the effect is said to generalize across gender. However, if the effect of the intervention differs for men and women, it is said to be moderated by gender.

Moderators can be categorical variables (e.g., gender, race, school type) or continuous variables (e.g., age, years of education, self-concept, test scores, reaction time). They can be a manifest observed variable (e.g., gender, race) or a latent variable measured with multiple indictors (e.g., self-concept, test scores). Different analytic methods of testing interactions are associated with the types of moderators. This chapter mostly focuses on techniques to analyze interaction effects when at least one of the predictors is a latent variable with multiple indicators. However, for didactical reasons, we begin by briefly discussing multiple moderated regression (Cohen, Cohen, West, & Aiken, 2003) as the dominant technique for analyzing interactions between observed variables. We believe it is important that the applied researcher has basic knowledge in understanding issues in testing manifest interactions before proceeding to more sophisticated latent variable models for interactions.

The presentation of the latent variable models is structured as follows. We first deal with interactions between a categorical manifest variable (e.g., gender or immigrant status) and a latent variable. Multigroup structural equation models are appropriate for analyzing this type of interaction effect, if the manifest variable is truly categorical. The main focus of our chapter is on structural equation models for interactions between two latent variables that are each measured with multiple indicators. We introduce three families of approaches to the analyses of these models: (1) Product indicator approaches that identify a latent product variable with products of the indicators of the original latent variables, (2) distribution analytic approaches that estimate the latent interaction directly, and (3) Bayesian approaches using prior information. We give a brief historical overview of the development of the product indicator approaches culminating in the flexible and easy-to-implement unconstrained approach (Marsh, Wen, & Hau, 2004). We then discuss in more detail some of the issues relating to specifying latent interaction models with the unconstrained approach. In particular, we will discuss issues relating to building the product indicators, transforming the indicator variables for easy model specification and obtaining a standardized solution with appropriate standard errors. Next, we introduce distribution analytic approaches and discuss their merits relative to each other and to the product indicator approaches. Finally, we briefly illustrate the Bayesian approach to latent interactions. Our chapter concludes with further directions for research on latent variable interactions, particularly the assessment of model fit, the consequences and estimation of quadratic effects, and interactions in multilevel structural equation models.

MULTIPLE REGRESSION MODEL FOR ANALYZING INTERACTION EFFECTS BETWEEN OBSERVED VARIABLES

Historically, interaction effects have been analyzed with methods that only allowed the constructs and variables to be represented by a single indicator. When the predictor variables X_1 and X_2 are both categorical variables that can take on a relatively small number of levels, and the dependent variable is a continuous variable, interaction effects can be easily estimated with traditional analysis of variance (ANOVA) procedures (for more general discussions of ANOVA see classic textbooks; e.g., Kirk, 1982; see also Jaccard, 1998). In the simplest factorial design, both X_1 and X_2 have two levels (i.e., a 2×2 design). In addition to the first-order effects (i.e., main effects) of X_1 and X_2, ANOVA provides a test of the statistical significance of the interaction between X_1 and X_2.

More generally, interaction effects based on manifest variables can be evaluated with the moderated multiple regression approach in which the predictor variables X_1 and X_2 can be continuous, categorical, or a mixture of the two. The ANOVA model is a special case of the more general multiple regression approach.

Consider the effect of observed variables X_1 and X_2 on an outcome Y. When the independent variables X_1 and X_2 are reasonably continuous variables, the following multiple regression with a product term is widely used to estimate both first-order and interaction effects (e.g., Aiken & West, 1991; Cohen & Cohen, 1983; Cohen et al., 2003; Friedrich, 1982; Jaccard, Turrisi, & Wan, 1990):

$$Y = \beta_0 + \beta_1 X_1 + \beta_2 X_2 + \beta_3 X_1 X_2 + e \qquad (26.1)$$

where β_1 and β_2 represent the first-order effects, β_3 represents the interaction effect, and e is a random disturbance term with zero mean that is uncorrelated with X_1 and X_2. In order to test whether the interaction effect is statistically significant, the test statistic is

$$t = \frac{\hat{\beta}_3}{\text{SE}(\hat{\beta}_3)}$$

where $\text{SE}(\hat{\beta}_3)$ is the standard error of the estimate.

Alternatively, the significance of the interaction effect could be tested by evaluating whether the model including the interaction effect predicts significantly more variance than the model without the interaction effects using an F-test. For a single interaction term (based on a single degree of freedom), the t-test and F-test are equivalent. When the interaction effect is significant, the R^2 increment of the model with the interaction effect compared to the model without the interaction effect represents the effect size of the interaction.

Whenever a statistically significant interaction effect is found, it is useful to graph the relations between the predictors and the outcome variable at several values of the predictors. However, the graph should only be the starting point of the evaluation of the nature of the interaction. It should be supplemented by post hoc strategies, such as testing the statistical significance of simple slopes (i.e., whether the effect of one predictor variable is statistically significant at a certain value of the other predictor variable), regions of significance (i.e., the range of the moderator values for which the relation between X_1 and Y is statistically significant), and, when one predictor is categorical and the interaction is disordinal, the crossing point of the two regression lines (see, e.g., Preacher, Curran, & Bauer, 2006).

Interaction effects are central to theory and practice in the social sciences. Nevertheless, particularly in applied research, even interactions hypothesized on the basis of strong theory and good intuition are typically small, nonsignificant, or not easily replicated. One of the potential reasons for this failure is the existence of measurement error in observed variables: While measurement error biases parameter estimates in general if not appropriately controlled, it is particularly damaging for tests of interaction effects. The reliability of a product variable used to model the interaction effect will always be smaller than the reliability of the original variables (Busemeyer & Jones, 1983; Dimitruk, Schermelleh-Engel, Kelava, & Moosbrugger, 2007). This leads to an underestimation of the regression coefficients—the estimated coefficients will be biased toward zero—and hence to reduced power of detecting interaction effects. This is particularly worrisome as the power to detect interaction effects with moderated regression models is usually quite low, even in the absence of measurement error. Latent variable models of interaction effects that control for measurement error substantially reduce measurement error and increase power, as well as having more general strategic advantages. Hence we now turn to an overview of these approaches, which is the main focus of this chapter.

LATENT VARIABLE APPROACHES TO TESTS OF INTERACTION EFFECTS

Particularly when there are multiple indicators of constructs (e.g., multiple items in rating scales or achievement tests), latent variable approaches provide a much stronger basis for evaluating the underlying factor structure, relating multiple indicators to their factors, controlling for measurement error, reducing bias in the estimation of the effects, and, ultimately, providing more defensible interpretations of the interaction effects.

Models of latent interactions fall into two broad categories. In the first and generally simpler situation, at least one of the variables involved in the interaction is a categorical variable with only a few categories (e.g., gender: male and female). In this situation, a multiple-group SEM is appropriate in which the different categories are treated as separate groups. In the second situation, both independent variables involved in the interaction are latent and continuous. Here there are various approaches to estimating interaction effects— "best practice" is still evolving. We first briefly discuss the use of multiple-group structural equation modeling (SEM) of interaction effects between categorical manifest and latent continuous variables, before turning to a discussion of models for interactions between latent continuous variables.

Multiple-Group SEM

Consider an interaction between a latent variable (ξ_1) and an observed variable (X_2) on a latent variable (η), and assume that X_2 is a categorical variable with a few naturally existing categories. We can use a multiple-group SEM approach (see, e.g., Bagozzi & Yi, 1989; Byrne, 1998; Rigdon, Schumacker, & Wothke, 1998; Vandenberg & Lance, 2000) with the categorical variable (X_2) as the grouping variable. Once the sample is divided into a small number of groups, we conduct multiple-group SEM and compare the model with and without restraining the effect of ξ_1 on the dependent variable η to be equal across groups. Let χ_1^2 (with df_1) and χ_2^2 (with df_2) be chi-square test statistics, respectively, with and without restraining the effect of ξ_1 on η to be equal in all groups. If there is substantial decline in the goodness of fit with the invariance constraint (e.g., significant increase in χ^2 with the difference in df between the two models; i.e., $\chi_1^2 - \chi_2^2$ with $df_1 - df_2$ is significant and substantial deterioration in selected goodness-of-fit indices), then the effects in the different groups are not identical and the interaction is said to be significant. Of course, the invariance of the corresponding loadings and factor variances must have been examined earlier (for details, see, e.g., Marsh, Muthén, et al., 2009; Marsh et al., 2010; Vandenberg & Lance, 2000).

If one of the independent variables is an observed categorical variable that can be used to divide the sample naturally into a small number of groups, then multiple-group SEM is a simple, direct, yet effective approach (Bagozzi & Yi, 1989; Rigdon, Schumacker, & Wothke, 1998) that can be easily implemented in most common commercial SEM software. This approach is particularly useful if there are differences in the error variances at different levels of the moderator.

However, the multiple-group approach is generally not appropriate when two or a small number of groups are formed from a reasonably continuous predictor variable, in that it ignores measurement error in the variable used to divide the sample into multiple groups and actually increases the unreliability in the grouping variable relative to the original continuous variable. In addition, it is well known that categorizing continuous variables is fraught with other problems, such as loss of information, reduced power, increased Type I error, and sample-dependent cutoff values (see, e.g., Butts & Ng, 2008; MacCallum, Zhang, Preacher, & Rucker, 2002), and is in general not recommended. Hence, the multiple-group approach should only be used if one of the interacting variables is a true categorical variable with a small number of categories. Interactions between two continuous latent variables require other, more advanced techniques that we introduce next.

Structural Equation Models for Analyzing Interaction Effects between Latent Variables

There are many methods to test the interactions between two latent variables that are both inferred from multiple indicators (see Schumacker & Marcoulides, 1998). Generally, structural equation models provide many advantages over the use of analyses based on observed variables but are more complicated to conduct. Here we focus on the fully latent variable approaches in which all of the dependent and independent variables are modeled as latent constructs. We first introduce the family of product–indicator approaches to latent

interactions and discuss issues related to their implementation. We then focus on more recent distribution–analytic and Bayesian approaches to the analysis of latent interactions that do not rely on the specification of product–indicators. For other partially latent variable approaches (e.g., factor scores and two-stage least squares approaches) to the problem of latent interaction effects, the reader is referred to the overview by Marsh and colleagues (2006).

PRODUCT INDICATOR APPROACHES

Although there are many approaches to estimating interaction effects between two latent variables, historically product indicator approaches have been the most influential class of models. These approaches were initially proposed in an ingenious paper by Kenny and Judd (1984), who estimated a structural equation model with a latent product term and used products of indicators to identify the latent product variable. Their work was heuristic, stimulating many published studies of alternative approaches to the use of products of indicators to estimate latent interactions (e.g., Algina & Moulder, 2001; Coenders, Batista-Foguet, & Saris, 2008; Hayduk, 1987; Jaccard & Wan, 1995; Jöreskog & Yang, 1996; Marsh et al., 2004; Wall & Amemiya, 2001). However, due in part to the limitations of software available at the time, their original approach was unduly cumbersome and overly restrictive in terms of the assumptions upon which it was based (see, e.g., Marsh et al., 2004), leading to the development of new approaches discussed here. For convenience, we summarize all models that use products of indicators under the heading "product indicator approaches."

For the sake of simplicity, suppose that endogenous latent variable η has three indicators: y_1, y_2, y_3; exogenous latent variables ξ_1 and ξ_2 also have three indicators, respectively: x_1, x_2, x_3 and x_4, x_5, x_6. In order to analyze the interaction effect of ξ_1 and ξ_2 on η, following the interaction model for the continuous manifest variables (Cohen et al., 2003), we use the structural model with product term as below:

$$\eta = \gamma_1\xi_1 + \gamma_2\xi_2 + \gamma_3\xi_1\xi_2 + \zeta \qquad \textbf{(26.2)}$$

where γ_1 and γ_2 represent the first order effects, and γ_3 represents the interaction effect. The intercept term in Equation 26.2 is set to zero for identification of the latent outcome variable η (see Jöreskog & Yang, 1996; Yang, 1998).

When treating the product term $\xi_1\xi_2$ as the third latent variable after ξ_1 and ξ_2, Marsh and colleagues (2004) suggested matching of three indicators of ξ_1 and three indicators of ξ_2 to form three pairs of product indicators (x_1x_4, x_2x_5, x_3x_6) as the indicators of $\xi_1\xi_2$. The corresponding path diagram of such a latent interaction model is illustrated in Figure 26.1. The usual supposition is that ξ_1, ξ_2, ζ, and all δ and ε terms are multivariate normal with mean of zero, and each is uncorrelated with the other (except that ξ_1 and ξ_2 are allowed to be correlated).

Main Issues Related to Latent Interaction Modeling with Product Indicator Approaches

At the first sight, the model is very similar to a conventional structural equation model. However, there are many issues involved in the model that need to be addressed. The four main issues are as follows:

1. There are many different ways in which the indicators of ξ_1 and ξ_2 can be combined to form the product indicators of $\xi_1\xi_2$. How many product indicators should be used? How do we form the best set of product indicators to be used?

2. Kenny and Judd (1984) introduced a large number of constraints on parameters in terms of the relationship between the product indicators and ξ_1, ξ_2 and $\xi_1\xi_2$. This *constrained approach* was applied by many researchers (see, e.g., Algina & Moulder, 2001; Jaccard & Wan, 1995; Jöreskog & Yang, 1996), making the latent interaction modeling very tedious and difficult. Are those constraints absolutely necessary?

3. Even if both ξ_1 and ξ_2 have a mean of zero, the mean of the product term $\xi_1\xi_2$ is not zero. Hence the mean structure has to be included as a necessary part of a usual latent interaction model. The mean structure typically makes the implementation of the latent interaction model more

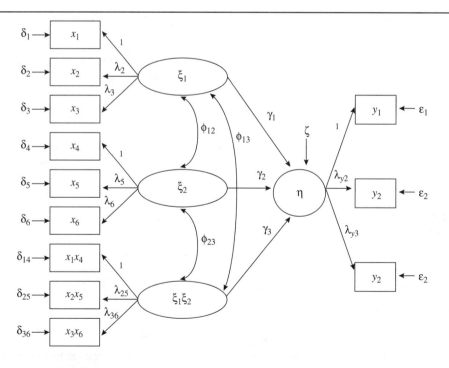

FIGURE 26.1. The path diagram of the latent interaction model using product indicators to identify the latent product variable.

complex and thus encumbers its applications in the empirical studies. Is the mean structure really necessary?

4. Even in conventional linear structural equation models, many commercially available software programs do not provide appropriate standard errors for standardized effects (Champoux & Peters, 1987; McDonald & Ho, 2002). For structural equation models with latent interaction terms, the situation is more serious because the standardized parameter estimate for the interaction effect is typically inappropriate when estimated with a product indicator approach. How does one obtain an appropriate standardized solution and standard errors for the latent interaction effect?

These issues have been a focus of recent research into the application of latent interaction models.

STRATEGIES FOR CREATING PRODUCT INDICATORS

Types of Product Indicators

In a series of simulation studies, Marsh and colleagues. (2004) compared three types of product indicators formed from the three indicators of ξ_1 and the three indicators of ξ_2: (1) all possible products (nine products in this example): $x_1x_4, x_1x_5, x_1x_6, x_2x_4, x_2x_5, x_2x_6, x_3x_4, x_3x_5, x_3x_6$; (2) matched pair products (three matched pairs in this example): x_1x_4, x_2x_5, x_3x_6; and (3) one pair: x_1x_4. Different combinations of matched pairs and one pair were also compared. Their results showed that the precision of estimation for matched pairs was systematically better than other types of products. Based on their results, they posited two guidelines in the selection of the most appropriate strategies for the estimation of latent interactions:

1. *Use all of the information.* All of the multiple indicators should be used in the formation of the indicators of the latent variable interaction factor.

2. *Do NOT reuse any of the information.* Each of the multiple indicators should only be used once in the formation of the multiple indicators of the latent variable interaction factor, to avoid creating artificially correlated residuals when the same variable is used in the construction of more

than one product term. Importantly, when the indicators are not reused, the variance–covariance matrix of errors will become diagonal. This subsequently decreases the number of constraints in constrained-type analyses. Batista-Foguet, Coenders, and Saris (2004) obtained the same result, and also suggested use of the matched pairs as the product indicators. The matched pairs strategy satisfies both guidelines given by Marsh and colleagues (2004), whereas using one pair violates the first guideline, and using all possible products violates the second guideline.

Strategies for Matching Indicators

Matched pairs can be produced by different combination of cross-products; for example, x_1x_4, x_2x_5, x_3x_6 is a set of matched pairs of product indicators; so is x_1x_5, x_2x_4, x_3x_6. A problem is how to form the product indicators. In some situations there is a natural matching that should be used to form product indicators (e.g., if the items used to infer ξ_1 and ξ_2 have parallel wording). More generally, when the two first-order effect factors ξ_1 and ξ_2 have the same number of indicators, Marsh and colleagues (2004; see also Saris et al., 2007) suggested that it would be better to match indicators in order of the reliabilities of the indicators; that is, the items with the highest reliability from one predictor will be matched to the item with the highest reliability in measuring the other latent predictor, and so on. This will lead to more reliable indicators of the latent interaction term. Subsequent research by Coenders, Batista-Foguet, and Saris (2008) confirmed these results.

However, if the number of indicators differs for the two first-order effect factors, then the previous simple matching strategy does not work. Assume, for example, that there were five indicators for the first factor and 10 for the second. In this situation we recommend that the product indicators for the latent interaction variable are created using parcels of indicators of the second factor. One approach would be to use the 10 items from the second factor to form five (item pair) parcels by taking the average of the first two items to form the first item parcel, the average of the second two items to form the second parcel, and so on. In this way, the first factor would be defined in terms of five (single-indicator) indicators, the second factor would be defined by 10 (single-indicator) indicators, and the latent interaction factor would be defined in terms of five matched product indicators based on single indicators from the first factor and item parcels from the second factor. This strategy has the advantage of satisfying both of the previous principles: "use all" and "do not reuse." Strategic application of this strategy can be adapted to accommodate any number of indicators of the ξ_1 and ξ_2 factors. Because our interest is in modeling relations among the latent constructs, item parceling can be efficacious (Little, Cunningham, Shahar, & Widaman, 2002). However, the sets of indicators being parceled should be strictly unidimensional; otherwise, use of parceling can result in high levels of bias in estimates of structural parameters, as well as high Type II error rates (Bandalos, 2008).

CONSTRAINED AND UNCONSTRAINED APPROACHES

In the following section, we review different historical approaches to the specification of product indicator approaches. These models required a large number of parameter constraints to deal with dependencies between the indicators of the original indicators and the product indicators, as well as between the original latent variables and the latent product variable. These constraints made the implementation of the models very cumbersome. However, as we discuss below, the constraints can be removed.

Constrained Approach

Although there are many approaches to estimating interaction effects between two latent variables, the historical starting point has been to constrain the loadings and variances of the product term. Kenny and Judd (1984) initially proposed this method. In their demonstration, there were two indicators for each latent factor (x_1 and x_2 of ξ_1, and x_3 and x_4 of ξ_2) such that

$$x_1 = \xi_1 + \delta_1, \, x_2 = \lambda_2\xi_1 + \delta_2 \quad \text{(26.3)}$$
$$x_3 = \xi_2 + \delta_3, \, x_4 = \lambda_4\xi_2 + \delta_4$$

where λ_1 and λ_3 were fixed to 1 for purposes of identification (and thus are excluded from Equation 26.3). They used product variables x_1x_3, x_1x_4, x_2x_3, and x_2x_4 as indicators of $\xi_1\xi_2$. Each product indicator has a measurement equation, for example,

$$x_2x_4 = \lambda_{24}\xi_1\xi_2 + \delta_{24} \quad \text{(26.4)}$$

where λ_{24} is the loading of x_2x_4 on $\xi_1\xi_2$, and δ_{24} is the measurement error. From Equation 26.3 we have

$$x_2x_4 = (\lambda_2\xi_1 + \delta_2)(\lambda_4\xi_2 + \delta_4)$$
$$= \lambda_2\lambda_4\xi_1\xi_2 + \lambda_2\xi_1\delta_4 + \lambda_4\xi_2\delta_2 + \delta_2\delta_4 \quad \text{(26.5)}$$

Then nonlinear constraints can be derived from comparing Equations 26.4 and 26.5:

(i) $\lambda_{24} = \lambda_2\lambda_4$

(ii) $\text{var}(\delta_{24}) = \lambda_2^2\text{var}(\xi_1)\,\text{var}(\delta_4) + \lambda_4^2\text{var}(\xi_2)\,\text{var}(\delta_2)$
$\qquad\qquad + \text{var}(\delta_2)\,\text{var}(\delta_4)$

Generally, two constraints were required whenever one product indicator was added, one constraint for the loading of the product indicator and the other for the variance of measurement error. However, the constraints were not so straightforward until Jaccard and Wan's (1995) work.

Jöreskog and Yang (1996) provided a general model and thorough treatment of this approach. When observed variables are not mean-centered, they used measurement equations with intercept terms

$$x_1 = \tau_1 + \xi_1 + \delta_1, \, x_2 = \tau_2 + \lambda_2\xi_1 + \delta_2 \quad \text{(26.6)}$$
$$x_3 = \tau_3 + \xi_2 + \delta_3, \, x_4 = \tau_4 + \lambda_4\xi_2 + \delta_4$$

However, the additional intercept terms of indicators (i.e., τ terms) not only require the specification of the mean structure of the model, but also produce many additional nonlinear constraints. Generally, five constraints were required whenever one product indicator was added.

Algina and Moulder (2001) revised the Jöreskog and Yang (1996) model so that observed variables are mean-centered. Although their model is the same as Jöreskog and Yang's model except for mean centering, they found that their model was more likely to converge. Even in cases when both models converged, their simulation results still favored their model. When Moulder and Algina (2002) compared six models for estimating and testing an interaction under a wide range of conditions, the result showed that Algina and Moulder's (2001) model was the most effective one for evaluating interactions, in terms of less bias, better control of Type I error rate, and higher power. For this reason, we recommend Algina and Moulder's model among the variety of constrained approaches, and refer to it simply as the *constrained approach*.

Unconstrained Approach

Marsh and colleagues (2004) evaluated an unconstrained approach in which the product of observed variables is used to form indicators of the latent interaction term, as in the constrained approach. Their approach, however, was fundamentally different in that they did not impose any nonlinear constraints to define relations between product indicators and the latent interaction factor. They demonstrated that the unconstrained model is identified when there are at least two product indicators.

In the unconstrained approach, the structural model is the same as that in the constrained approach (when ξ_1 and ξ_2 are normally distributed) except that constraints are not imposed. (For details of modeling with the unconstrained approach, see the example presented later.) Since the unconstrained approach does not constrain parameters based on assumptions of normality of ξ_1 and ξ_2, both of these approaches provide less biased estimates of the latent interaction effects than the constrained approach under widely varying conditions of non-normality. Importantly, however, the unconstrained approach is much easier for applied researchers to implement, eliminating the need for the imposition of complicated, nonlinear constraints required by the traditional constrained approaches. However, when the sample size is small and normality assumptions are met, the precision of the unconstrained approach is somewhat lower than for the constrained approach.

Robustness to Violations of Normality Assumptions in Product Indicator Approaches

There are three fundamentally different problems associated with violating the assumption of multivariate normality that must be considered in the evaluation of the product indicator approaches. First, the maximum likelihood (ML) estimation typically used with each of these approaches is based on the assumption of the multivariate normality of all indicators. This problem is common to all confirmatory factor analysis (CFA) and SEM research based on ML estimation, and is not specific to the latent interaction effects. Second, even when the indicators of ξ_1 and ξ_2 are normally distributed, the distributions resulting from the products of these indicators are known to be non-normal (Jöreskog & Yang, 1996). The distribution analytic approaches discussed later model this non-normality explicitly and are not affected by it. However, both the constrained and the unconstrained product indicator approaches are negatively affected when ML estimation is used. Fortunately, ML estimation tends to be robust to violations of normality such as these in terms of parameter estimates (e.g., Boomsma, 1983; Hau & Marsh, 2004). However, previous research suggests that the likelihood ratio test is biased, and that ML standard errors are too small under some conditions of non-normality (Hu, Bentler, & Kano, 1992; West, Finch, & Curran, 1995). Although there are alternative estimators that do not assume multivariate normality (e.g., asymptotically distribution-free or weighted least squares estimators; Bollen, 1989), simulation studies of latent interaction effects suggest that ML estimation outperforms these alternative estimation procedures under most conditions (Jaccard & Wan, 1995; Wall & Amemiya, 2001; see also Marsh et al., 2004). Nevertheless, it may be appropriate to impose adjustments on the standard errors and χ^2-statistics to correct for this bias (Marsh et al., 2004; Yang-Wallentin & Jöreskog, 2001). Alternatively, a bootstrap approach can be used to estimate standard errors that are not based on assumptions of normality.

The third problem associated with violations of the assumptions of normality is specific to the constrained approach but does not apply to the unconstrained approach. As emphasized by Wall and Amemiya (2001) and Marsh and colleagues (2004), the nature of the constraints imposed in the constrained approach depends fundamentally on the assumption that ξ_1 and ξ_2 are normally distributed. Importantly, estimates of the interaction effect based on these constraints are not robust in relation to violations of this assumption of normality; neither the size nor even the direction of this bias is predictable a priori, and the size of the bias does not decrease systematically with increasing N. However, the unconstrained approach provides relatively unbiased estimates of the latent interaction effects under the widely varying conditions of non-normality considered by Marsh and colleagues (2004).

CENTERING OF INDICATORS AND THE MEAN STRUCTURE OF THE LATENT INTERACTION MODELS

Historically, transformations of indicators such as centering and standardization have been important in the development of latent interaction models using the product indicator approach. In this section, we describe how different centering strategies affect the model setting and parameter specification in the unconstrained approach. For the following presentation, we use a small example: The endogenous latent variable η has three indicators: y_1, y_2, y_3, and the exogenous latent variables ξ_1 and ξ_2 have two indicators, respectively: $x_1, x_2; x_3, x_4$. The indicators of the product term $\xi_1\xi_2$ are the matched pairs: x_1x_3, x_2x_4.

Raw Indicators

When raw indicators are used, intercept terms are needed in the measurement equations, as shown in Equation 26.6. In this case, the measurement equations of the product indicators are very complicated because they consist of two first-order terms in addition to the intercept term, product term, and error term. For example,

$$x_2x_4 = (\tau_2 + \lambda_2\xi_1 + \delta_2)(\tau_4 + \lambda_4\xi_2 + \delta_4)$$
$$= \tau_2\tau_4 + \tau_4\lambda_2\xi_1 + \tau_2\lambda_4\xi_2 + \lambda_2\lambda_4\xi_1\xi_2 + \delta_{24}$$

where $\delta_{24} = \tau_4\delta_2 + \lambda_4\xi_2\delta_2 + \tau_2\delta_4 + \lambda_2\xi_1\delta_4 + \delta_2\delta_4$ denotes the error term of x_2x_4. The loadings of x_2x_4 on ξ_1 and ξ_2 are generally not zero.

More importantly, Jöreskog and Yang (1996) noted that even if ξ_1, ξ_2, and ζ are centered so as to have means of zero, $\kappa_3 = E(\xi_1\xi_2) = \text{cov}(\xi_1,\xi_2)$ will typically not be zero. Hence, it is always necessary to specify a mean structure for the structural and the measurement model when raw indicators are used.

Mean-Centered Indicators

As seen earlier, specification of the latent interaction model with product indicators is complicated when raw x-indicators are used. Hence, as in multiple regression analysis with manifest variables, mean-centering the indicators of the latent predictor variables became a routine step for latent interaction models (Aiken & West, 1991; Algina & Moulder, 2001; Marsh et al., 2004). Centering these indicators simplifies the model considerably. Denote x^C as the mean-centered variable of x, that is, $x^C = x - E(x)$. The measurement models given in Equation 26.6 become

$$x_1^C = \xi_1 + \delta_1, x_2^C = \lambda_2\xi_1 + \delta_2$$
$$x_3^C = \xi_2 + \delta_3, x_4^C = \lambda_4\xi_2 + \delta_2 \quad \textbf{(26.7)}$$

The matched product indicators are $x_1^C x_3^C, x_2^C x_4^C$. After the indicators of the latent predictors have been centered, the intercept terms of the measurement equations of the original and the product indicators are no longer necessary. The intercept terms of the measurement equations of indicators of the latent outcome variable, however, are still necessary even if they have been centered (see Algina & Moulder, 2001; Marsh et al., 2004). Furthermore, even if ξ_1 and ξ_2 are centered so as to have means of zero, $E(\xi_1\xi_2) = \text{cov}(\xi_1,\xi_2)$ will typically not be zero. Hence, the latent mean of $\xi_1\xi_2$ must be included in the model (see Algina & Moulder, 2001; Marsh et al., 2004).

Therefore, although the latent interaction model is simpler after indicators are centered, the mean structure of the model is still necessary. More precisely, intercepts of indicators of the latent outcome variable and the mean of $\xi_1\xi_2$ have to be included in the model. While the specification of the mean structure is straightforward in many modern SEM software packages, further simplifications are possible that make the application of these models easier.

Orthogonalized Product Indicators

An alternative to mean-centering is to orthogonalize the interaction term by regressing the product term $\xi_1\xi_2$ on both ξ_1 and ξ_2 (Little, Bovaird, & Widaman, 2006; Marsh et al., 2007). In latent interaction models with product indicators, this is achieved by forming the product indicators (x_1x_3 and x_2x_4 in our example) based on the raw indicators. The product indicators are then regressed separately on the full set of indicators (x_1, x_2, x_3, and x_4, in our example). The residuals of this regression (denoted as $O\_x_1x_3$, $O\_x_2x_4$, respectively) are then used as indicators for the latent residualized product variable

$$O\_\xi_1\xi_2 = \xi_1\xi_2 - (\beta_0 + \beta_1\xi_1 + \beta_2\xi_2)$$

Marsh and colleagues (2007) showed that the corresponding latent interaction model did not require any mean structure.

Orthogonalizing the latent product variable does not change the estimate of the latent interaction effect. However, the corresponding first-order effects may differ substantially from estimates obtained with mean-centering the predictors (Marsh et al., 2007). While the orthogonalizing strategy makes model specification somewhat simpler, as a mean structure is no longer required, it involves a cumbersome two-step procedure: In the first step, the product term is regressed onto all of the first-order indicators, and the orthogonalized product indicators are produced; in the second step, a latent interaction model is analyzed as usual. Furthermore, Lin, Wen, Marsh, and Lin (2010) illustrated that there exists a problem with consistency of the orthogonalizing strategy unless the third-order moments of latent predictor variables are zero. This problem, when it occurs, results in a nonrandom bias for each indicator of the interaction construct. In general, the third-order moments of (ξ_1, ξ_2) are not zero when the distribution of (ξ_1, ξ_2) is not bivariate normal and non-normal data are very common (Micceri, 1989; Pyzdek, 1995).

Double-Mean-Centered Indicators

Lin and colleagues (2010) proposed a double-mean-centering strategy, an extension of the conventional mean-centering approach. As in Equation 26.7, the indicators of the latent variables are mean-centered and used to identify the original latent variables and to calculate the initial matched product indicators. Then the matched product indicators $x_1^C x_3^C, x_2^C x_4^C$ are mean-centered again (i.e., double-mean-centering), and are denoted as $(x_1^C x_3^C)^C, (x_2^C x_4^C)^C$. From Equation 26.7 we have

$$
\begin{aligned}
(x_2^C x_4^C)^C &= x_2^C x_4^C - E\left(x_2^C x_4^C\right) \\
&= (\lambda_2 \lambda_4 \xi_1 \xi_2 + \lambda_2 \xi_1 \delta_4 + \lambda_4 \xi_2 \delta_2 + \delta_2 \delta_4) \\
&\quad - \lambda_2 \lambda_4 E(\xi_1 \xi_2) \\
&= \lambda_{24}[\xi_1 \xi_2 - E(\xi_1 \xi_2)] + \delta_{24}
\end{aligned}
\tag{26.8}
$$

where

$$
\delta_{24} = \lambda_2 \xi_1 \delta_4 + \lambda_4 \xi_2 \delta_2 + \delta_2 \delta_4
$$

has a zero mean. Obviously (see Equation 26.8)

$$
\xi_1 \xi_2 - E(\xi_1 \xi_2)
$$

is the latent interaction variable and has a zero mean. Therefore, when we use

$$
x_1^C, x_2^C; x_3^C, x_4^C; (x_1^C x_3^C)^C, (x_2^C x_4^C)^C
$$

as the indicators to model a latent interaction framework, we actually analyze the following structural model

$$
\eta = \gamma_1 \xi_1 + \gamma_2 \xi_2 + \gamma_3 [\xi_1 \xi_2 - E(\xi_1 \xi_2)] + \zeta
\tag{26.9}
$$

This implies that the specification of a mean structure is not necessary when all indicators are mean centered and the product indicators are doubly mean centered. However, the parameter estimates of first-order and interaction effects are the same as those with the single-mean-centering strategy in theory. In practice, the product indicators $x_1^C x_3^C, x_2^C x_4^C$ do not need really to be recentered if no mean structure is specified (the default in some packages but not others). When the model does not include a mean structure, the estimated first-order and interaction effects are identical with and without recentering the product indicators. Noting this point, Wu, Wen, and Lin (2009) suggested that researchers can directly use single-mean-centered data to analyze a latent interaction model without any mean structure. They ran a simulation study to compare the estimated parameters and goodness-of-fit indices of the two latent interaction models with and without the mean structure by using matched-pair product indicators and the unconstrained approach. The simulation results were consistent with the theoretical predictions. However, when only a single sample was considered, the estimation results obtained from the models with and without mean structure were not exactly the same, though the differences were negligible, because the fit functions of the two models were not exactly identical.

More importantly, both the first-order effects and the interaction effect will not change after double-mean-centering, whereas the first-order effects will change after orthogonalizing. That is, the explanation of the first-order effects and the interaction effect with the double-mean-centering strategy is the same as that with the single-mean-centering strategy.

In short, the latent interaction model with $\xi_1 \xi_2 - E(\xi_1 \xi_2)$ as the interaction term does not require any mean structure by using single-mean-centering strategy: First, mean-center all indicators; second, create product indicators for the latent product variable; finally, fit a latent model (for which a mean structure is not required).

AN APPROPRIATE STANDARDIZED SOLUTION AND ITS SCALE-FREE PROPERTIES

In typical regression analyses based on manifest variables, standardized parameter estimates are commonly used to facilitate the comparison of the effects of different predictor variables. By transforming the model parameters to reflect a situation where all variables have a mean of 0 and a variance of 1 (i.e., z-scores), standardization allows the comparison of effects of variables originally measured on different scales.

In analyses of structural equation models, it is also common to present results in terms of standardized parameter estimates. Because the scale of the latent variables can be set arbitrarily by different identification constraints (e.g., fixing either factor variances or one loading per factor to 1.0), published SEM results typically include completely standardized parameter estimates. However, the appropriate standardized solution for an interaction model estimated with the product indicator approaches is not directly provided by the SEM packages and is discussed in this section. Hereafter, we use the term "solution" associated with a model to refer to a set of parameter estimates based on that model, and the term "usual standardized solution" to refer to a set of standardized parameter estimates produced by statistical packages.

Appropriate Standardized Solution for Nonlatent Interaction

For didactical reasons, we start by defining the appropriate standardized solution in the context of a manifest interaction. In this case, the interaction model formulated in Equation 26.1 is rewritten here for convenience:

$$Y = \beta_0 + \beta_1 X_1 + \beta_2 X_2 + \beta_3 X_1 X_2 + e$$

In the conventional standardized solution from the following equation, where Z_{X_1}, Z_{X_2}, and $Z_{X_1 X_2}$ are the standardized versions of X_1, X_2, and $X_1 X_2$,

$$Z_Y = b_1 Z_{X_1} + b_2 Z_{X_2} + b_3 Z_{X_1 X_2} + \varepsilon \qquad (26.10)$$

is not appropriate because $Z_{X_1 X_2}$ does not represent the product term of Z_{X_1} and Z_{X_2}. Rather, Friedrich (1982) suggested a straightforward way that standardizes the interaction model. One first standardizes Y, X_1, X_2 to Z_Y, Z_{X_1}, Z_{X_2}, then forms the product term $Z_{X_1} Z_{X_2}$. The unstandardized coefficients of the equation

$$Z_Y = c_0 + c_1 Z_{X_1} + c_2 Z_{X_2} + c_3 Z_{X_1} Z_{X_2} + \varepsilon \qquad (26.11)$$

are the appropriate standardized coefficients of the interaction Model 1. Hereafter, we use the term "appropriate standardized" rather than "standardized" to

distinguish the standardized coefficients obtained from Equation 26.11 from the conventional standardization procedure that is inappropriate for models with an interaction term. In contrast to Equation 26.10, the intercept term c_0 in Equation 26.11 is necessary and generally not equal to 0 because the product term $Z_{X_1 X_2}$ usually does not have a mean of 0. In fact, $E(Z_{X_1} Z_{X_2}) = \text{cov}(Z_{X_1}, Z_{X_2})$, which is not 0 unless X_1 and X_2 are uncorrelated.

Appropriate Standardized Solution for Latent Interaction Models

Wen, Marsh, and Hau (2010; see also Wen, Hau, & Marsh, 2008) derived an appropriate standardized solution for latent interaction. They proved that these appropriate standardized versions of the main and interaction effects are scale-free, and the standard error and z-values of the appropriate standardized estimates of the main and interaction effects are also scale-free (Wen et al., 2010). When a parameter estimate is scale-free, it is invariant whatever units (e.g., height in centimeters, feet, or inches) of indicators are used.

Suppose that γ_1, γ_2 represent the first-order effects and that γ_3 represents the interaction effect. Their conventional standardized coefficients are denoted as γ_1', γ_2', and γ_3' respectively; their appropriate standardized coefficients are denoted as γ_1'', γ_2'', and γ_3'' respectively. We can obtain the appropriate standardized coefficients (γ_1'', γ_2'', and γ_3'') from the usual standardized coefficients (γ_1', γ_2', and γ_3') as provided by many SEM software packages as follows:

$$\gamma_1'' = \gamma_1', \ \gamma_2'' = \gamma', \ \gamma_3'' = \gamma_3' \frac{\sqrt{\phi_{11}\phi_{22}}}{\sqrt{\phi_{33}}} \qquad (26.12)$$

where $\phi_{11} = \text{var}(\xi_1)$, $\phi_{22} = \text{var}(\xi_2)$, and $\phi_{33} = \text{var}(\xi_1 \xi_2)$, are from the unstandardized solution (Wen et al., 2010). That is, for the main (first order) effects, the usual standardized coefficients (γ_1', γ_2') are also the appropriate standardized coefficients (γ_1'' and γ_1''). But the appropriate standardized coefficient of the interaction should be calculated from the formula involving information from both the original parameter estimates (e.g., ϕ_{11}) and the usual standardized parameter estimates (γ_3').

Hence, once we get the unstandardized estimates of ϕ_{11}, ϕ_{22}, and ϕ_{33}, and the usual standardized estimate of the interaction effect γ_3', we can calculate the appropriate standardized interaction effect γ_3'' by Equation 26.12.

For example, suppose we get the following original estimates from the LISREL output: $\gamma_1 = 0.425$, $\gamma_2 = 0.331$, $\gamma_3 = 0.197$; $\phi_{11} = 0.501$, $\phi_{22} = 0.529$, $\phi_{33} = 0.308$; and the completely standardized estimates: $\gamma_1' = 0.423$, $\gamma_2' = 0.338$ and $\gamma_3' = 0.153$. From Equation 26.12, the appropriate standardized estimates of the main (first-order) effects are identical to the above standardized estimates: $\gamma_1'' = 0.423$, $\gamma_2'' = 0.338$. The appropriate standardized estimate of the interaction effect is

$$\gamma_3'' = \gamma_3' \frac{\sqrt{\phi_{11}\phi_{22}}}{\sqrt{\phi_{33}}} = 0.153 \times \frac{\sqrt{0.501 \times 0.529}}{\sqrt{0.308}} = 0.142$$

The Scale-Free Properties of the Standardized Solution

When an estimate is scale-free, it is invariant whatever scales are used in the indicators (Cudeck, 1989). Indeed, as shown by Cudeck, the usual standardized solution of a structural equation model is generally invariant with respect to the scales used in the indicators, thus popularizing the report of the usual standardized solutions in the comparison of effect sizes associated with different independent variables. In SEM applications, the typical standardized solution refers to the completely standardized solution obtained from the model in which both the latent variables and their respective indicators are standardized. However, as indicated earlier, this typical standardized solution is not appropriate for a latent interaction model estimated with the product indicator approach. Rather, the appropriate standardized estimates of the first-order effects and interaction effect need to be computed by Equation 26.12. Wen and colleagues (2010) proved that these appropriate standardized estimations have the scale-free properties:

1. The appropriate standardized estimates of the main and interaction effects are scale-free.

2. All the appropriate standardized estimates of loadings are scale-free.

When a parameter estimate is scale-free, the corresponding standard error and z-value is also scale-free. Wen and colleagues (2010; see also Wen et al., 2008) illustrated these scale-free properties of the appropriate standardized estimation by simulated data.

Calculation of Standard Errors of Appropriate Standardized Coefficients through Bootstrap Samples

Cudeck (1989) noted that when a parameter estimate and its standard error estimate are both rescaled by the same scaling factor, the corresponding z-statistic for evaluating the significance of the parameter will not change because of the simultaneous canceling in the rescaling process. Hence, in SEM models without an interaction effect, the significance of the standardized parameter estimates is determined by examining the z-values of the original parameter estimates.

For interaction models, is it reasonable to follow this tradition? More specifically, are the z-values of the appropriate standardized estimates the same as those of the original estimates? Wen and colleagues (2010) dealt with the issues by using the bootstrap method, where they treated the original data set as a population and sampled from it with replacement so as to obtain bootstrap samples with the same sample size as the original data set. They found that there are minor differences between the z-values associated with the original estimates and those with the appropriate standardized estimates (from the bootstrap method)—as is to be expected when bootstrap estimates are used. These differences, however, are often ignorable unless the z-values are close to the cutoff point for testing, in which case the bootstrap estimates should be used.

AN EXAMPLE OF THE LATENT INTERACTION MODEL AND ITS APPROPRIATE STANDARDIZED SOLUTION

We use simulated data to illustrate the estimation of the effect of the interaction between ξ_1 and ξ_2 on η with the unconstrained approach. In our simulated data, the structural model with the interaction term is

$$\eta = \gamma_1\xi_1 + \gamma_2\xi_2 + \gamma_3[\xi_1\xi_2 - E(\xi_1\xi_2)] + \zeta$$

where the endogenous latent variable η has 3 indicators: y_1, y_2, y_3; the exogenous latent variables ξ_1 and ξ_2 also have three indicators, respectively: x_1, x_2, x_3 and x_4, x_5, x_6. For present purposes, we considered only one sample generated from the population (described in Study 1 of Marsh et al., 2004). In order to provide a context for this example, assume that η is mathematics achievement, ξ_1 is prior mathematics ability, ξ_2 is mathematics motivation, and $\xi_1\xi_2$ is the interaction of prior mathematics ability and mathematics motivation; ξ_1 and ξ_2 are correlated. The population values used for data generation were $\gamma_1 = \gamma_2 = 0.4$, $\gamma_3 = 0.2$. The covariance between ξ_1 and ξ_2 was set to 0.3.

In our generated data set, all indicators, y_1, y_2, y_3, x_1, x_2, x_3, and x_4, x_5, x_6, were standardized to z-scores (mean = 0, SD = 1). Then the product indicators x_1x_4, x_2x_5, x_3x_6 were created, but not restandardized. [*Note.* The covariance matrix of the nine indicators and the three (matched pair) product indicators are available on this handbook's accompanying website (*www. handbookofsem.com*), where you will also find the model example and model syntax to specify the unconstrained approach without mean structure in LISREL and Mplus.]

The completely standardized solution is shown in Figure 26.2. Note that the estimate of the latent interaction effect is not correctly standardized by the LISREL program. From the LISREL output we obtain: $\gamma_1 = 0.425$, $\gamma_2 = 0.331$, $\gamma_3 = 0.197$; $\phi_{11} = 0.501$, $\phi_{22} = 0.529$,

$\phi_{33} = 0.308$; and the completely standardized estimates: $\gamma_1' = 0.423$, $\gamma_2' = 0.338$, $\gamma_3' = 0.153$, and $\phi_{21}' = 0.391$. By using Equation 26.12, $\gamma_1'' = 0.423$, $\gamma_2'' = 0.338$, and $\gamma_3'' = 0.142$; of course $\phi_{21}'' = 0.391$ remains the same.

To calculate the standard errors and the z-values of the appropriate standardized estimates, the nonparametric bootstrap is applied to the original sample with size 500; a total of 800 bootstrap samples was generated by PRELIS 2.72. The PRELIS syntax for creating bootstrap samples is available from this handbook's accompanying website (*www.handbookofsem.com*).

For each resample, the original solution and usual standardized solution were obtained; one set of appropriate standardized estimates of main and interaction effects is calculated by using Equation 26.12. The standard deviations of the 800 appropriate standardized estimates of the latent interaction effect are the standard errors estimated by the bootstrap method from which the z-values (denoted as z_bs) are calculated. The results are shown in Table 26.1. We note that there are minor differences between the z-values associated

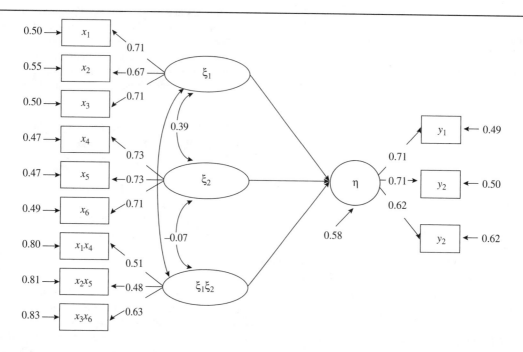

FIGURE 26.2. Path diagram and appropriate standardized parameter estimates of the interaction model by the unconstrained approach.

TABLE 26.1. Comparison of z-Values Obtained from LISREL Output and the Bootstrap Method

	γ_1	γ_1''	γ_2	γ_2''	γ_3	γ_3''
Estimation	0.425	0.423	0.331	0.338	0.197	0.142
z-value	6.197		5.230		2.358	
z_bs		7.295		5.460		2.395

Note. The z-value is obtained from LISREL output, corresponding to the original estimation. z_bs is calculated by bootstrap method for the appropriate standardized estimation.

with the original estimates (from the LISREL output) and those with the appropriate standardized estimates (from the bootstrap method) that is due to sampling fluctuations in the bootstrap procedure.

Both first-order effects and the interaction effect are statistically significant ($p < .05$). Hence, mathematics achievement is higher when prior mathematics ability is higher ($\gamma_1'' = 0.423$), when mathematics motivation is higher ($\gamma_2'' = 0.338$), and when the $\xi_1\xi_2$ term is higher ($\gamma_3'' = 0.142$). Whereas both prior ability and motivation contribute substantially to subsequent achievement, the positive effect of mathematics ability (i.e., 0.423 + 0.142 × motivation) is more substantial for highly motivated students. Equivalently, the positive effect of mathematics motivation (i.e., 0.338 + 0.142 × ability) is more substantial for students with higher levels of prior ability. Because simulated data were used, it is not surprising that the model fit the data very well: $\chi^2(48) = 37.35$ ($p = .87$), root mean square error of approximation (RMSEA) = 0.000, standardized root mean square residual (SRMR) = 0.026, non-normed fit index (NNFI) = 1.008, and comparative fit index (CFI) = 1.000.

DISTRIBUTION-ANALYTIC APPROACHES

While the approaches to the estimation of latent interactions discussed so far are based on cross-products of the indicator of the latent predictor variables and rely on conventional SEM techniques, the so-called distribution analytic approaches (Klein & Moosbrugger, 2000; Klein & Muthén, 2007) are specialized alternatives for the estimation of nonlinear structural equation models. These approaches explicitly model the non-normal distribution of the manifest indicator variables that is im-

plied by the presence of latent interaction effects. Two methods are currently available: The latent moderated structural equations (LMS) approach (Klein & Moosbrugger, 2000) that is implemented in Mplus (Muthén & Muthén, 1997–2010) and the quasi-maximum likelihood (QML) approach (Klein & Muthén, 2007) that has not been implemented in a readily available software package but is available on request as a standalone program from its author, Andreas Klein. An alternative procedure based on marginal ML estimation is described by Cudeck, Harring, and du Toit (2009).

Both QML and LMS can be used to directly estimate the latent structural model with a latent interaction, as presented in Equation 26.2, without the need to identify the latent product variable with the corresponding product indicators. In addition, they also allow the inclusion of latent quadratic effects in the structural model. LMS and QML differ in the distributional assumptions made about the latent dependent variable η and its indicators, and in the specialized estimation method used to obtain the parameter estimates. Here we summarize and discuss the particulars of each method briefly. A more thorough technical, yet accessible, overview is given by Kelava and colleagues (2011).

LMS

The LMS approach (Klein & Moosbrugger, 2000) models the non-normal distribution of the latent outcome variable η and its indicators with a finite mixture of normal distributions. LMS assumes that the indicators x of the latent predictor variables ξ, the structural disturbance term ζ, and all residuals in the measurement model are normally distributed. The indicators y of the latent outcome variable, which will have an unconditionally non-normal distribution in the presence of nonlinear effects, are assumed to be normally distributed conditionally on the latent outcome variable η and the latent predictor variables ξ. Based on these assumptions, the coefficients for the first-order and interaction effects in the structural model are obtained with the expectation maximization algorithm (Dempster, Laird, & Rubin, 1977). For this purpose, a numerical integration technique is used to estimate the finite mixture distribution of the latent outcome variable and its indicators. Compared to conventional SEM estimation, this procedure is computationally demanding and becomes unfeasible in applications with a large number of nonlinear effects.

QML

The QML approach (Klein & Muthén, 2007) also estimates the latent nonlinear structural equation model in Equation 26.2 but is based on a different, less restrictive set of distributional assumptions compared to the LMS procedure. Whereas LMS assumes that the distribution of the latent outcome variable η and its indicators can be approximated by a finite—and potentially large—number of normal mixture components, QML reduces the number of components used to represent the distribution of the indicators to two; the distribution of the indicators is approximated only by the product of a normal and a conditionally normal density function. Parameter estimates are obtained by the maximization of a quasi-log-likelihood function using the Newton–Raphson algorithm. Compared to LMS, the QML method is theoretically more robust against violations of the normal distribution of the indicator variables and residuals, but also slightly less efficient if the distributional assumptions of LMS are fulfilled (Kelava et al., 2011). Computationally, QML is more efficient and can be used to fit models with a larger number of nonlinear effects and interactions.

Comparison to Product Indicator Approaches

There are two main differences between the product indicator approaches discussed earlier in this chapter and the distribution analytic approaches we just introduced:

1. In the unconstrained approach, as in all other product indicator approaches, products of the indicator variables have to be formed to identify the latent interaction variable. In the distribution analytic approaches, it is not necessary to construct products of indicators, as the product of the latent predictor variables ξ and the non-normal distribution of the latent outcome variable η and its indicators y are modeled directly.

2. As discussed earlier, the product indicator approaches optimize conventional SEM fitting functions to obtain parameter estimates and standard errors that usually assume normality of the latent variables and indicators. In general, both assumptions are violated in models with latent interactions. The distribution analytic approaches, on the other hand, maximize special fitting functions that take into account the non-normality of the indicators and the dependent latent variable that

is due to the presence of interaction effects explicitly. However, they still assume that the latent predictor variable and its indicators are normally distributed and rely on assumptions about the latent outcome variable and its indicators that are based on mixtures or conditionally normal distributions.

Simulation studies that compared QML to the unconstrained approach for models with a latent interaction effect showed that when QML's distributional assumptions are fulfilled (i.e., when the indicator variables of the latent predictors and the residuals are normally distributed), the parameter estimates for the interaction effect are unbiased and are estimated more precisely than with the unconstrained approach (Klein & Muthén, 2007; Marsh et al., 2004). When the distributional assumptions are violated, the current implementation of the QML program and the unconstrained approach still yield unbiased estimates of the interaction effect. Again, the QML estimates were slightly more efficient, and the power to detect interaction effects with a likelihood ratio test was higher than with other methods. The standard error of the interaction seems to be slightly overestimated by QML, whereas it is slightly underestimated by the unconstrained approach (Klein & Muthén, 2007). Similar results have been obtained in simulation studies that included both latent interaction and latent quadratic effects (Kelava & Brandt, 2009). Comparisons of LMS and QML (Kelava et al., 2011; Klein & Muthén, 2007) indicate that LMS is slightly more efficient when its distributional assumptions are fulfilled, but QML is comparatively more robust to violations of normality.

The theoretical advantages of the distribution analytic approaches are in the appropriate modeling of quadratic forms of latent variables, without the need to specify an involved measurement model with product indicators, constraints on the mean structure, and standardizing of variables. At least the QML method appears to be sufficiently robust against violations of its distributional assumptions. However, these advantages are offset by the need to use specialized software to estimate these models and the sometimes prohibitive computational demands. So far, LMS is only available in Mplus (Muthén & Muthén, 1997–2010). QML has not been incorporated in any of the conventional SEM packages, but it is available on request from its author, Andreas Klein. The unconstrained approach, on the other hand, can be implemented in most SEM packages, including the freely available R packages (Fox, 2006; Kelava & Brandt,

2009) and OpenMx (Boker et al., 2010). Due to the lack of a properly defined null model, there are no general fit statistics for the distribution analytic approaches yet. However, nested models can be compared using the chi-square difference tests, and non-nested models can be compared using information criteria such as the Akaike information criterion (AIC) and the Bayesian information criterion (BIC). The QML program provides a fully standardized solution that assumes all manifest and latent variables are standardized, but no standard errors for the standardized effects. These estimates are equal to the parameters of the appropriately standardized solution defined in Equation 26.12.

Example

An analysis of the example data set analyzed here with the QML program (Version 2.63, Klein, 2009) and Mplus 5.2 (Muthén & Muthén, 1997–2010) yielded the following results (only the structural coefficients are reported for comparison purposes):

In the QML analysis (Version 2.63) the raw parameter estimates of the structural first-order effects were estimated as $\gamma_1 = 0.438$ ($SE = 0.075$) and $\gamma_2 = 0.320$ ($SE = 0.058$). The unstandardized latent interaction effect was estimated as $\gamma_3 = 0.174$ ($SE = 0.057$). The variances of the latent predictor variables were $\phi_{11} = 0.496$ and $\phi_{22} = 0.528$. The fully standardized estimates for the structural parameters obtained from QML were $\gamma_1'' = 0.434$, $\gamma_2'' = 0.327$, and $\gamma_3'' = 0.125$; standard errors for the standardized parameter effects are not provided. The likelihood ratio test for the latent interaction effect was significant ($\chi^2(1) = 6.317$, $p = .012$). As expected, these results closely match the results obtained with the unconstrained approach in LISREL.

The LMS analysis with Mplus 5.2 (Muthén & Muthén, 1997–2010) yielded the following unstandardized parameter estimates for the latent first-order effects: $\gamma_1 = 0.437$ ($SE = 0.075$) and $\gamma_2 = 0.318$ ($SE = 0.058$), and for the latent interaction effect $\gamma_3 = 0.172$ ($SE = 0.057$). The variances of the latent variables were estimated as $\phi_{11} = 0.501$ and $\phi_{22} = 0.526$, respectively. Parameter estimates for the appropriate standardized solution were $\gamma_1'' = 0.436$, $\gamma_2'' = 0.325$, and $\gamma_3'' = 0.124$.

BAYESIAN APPROACH

Bayesian approaches to SEM are becoming increasingly more popular (Asparouhov & Muthén, 2010;

Lee, 2008) due to their flexibility and easy-to-use implementation in popular software packages such as WinBugs (Spiegelhalter, Thomas, Best, & Lunn, 2004) and Mplus (Muthén & Muthén, 1997–2010). Lee, Song, and Tang (2007) developed a Bayesian approach for the analysis of structural equation models with latent interactions that is fundamentally different from the likelihood-based approaches discussed so far. The particulars of the general Bayesian approach to structural equation models and its implementation are described by Kaplan and Depaoli (Chapter 38, this volume) and in more detail by Lee (2008).

In contrast to conventional frequentist approaches, Bayesian modeling techniques assume that all parameters are random variables and model their distribution conditionally on prior information and the data (Gelman, Carlin, Stern, & Rubin, 2004). This approach explicitly allows incorporating prior knowledge about parameter values into the model, although the specification of noninformative priors is possible. The prior information is combined with the information contained in the data and summarized in posterior distributions of all model parameters. The larger the sample size, the more the final results are influenced by the data as compared to the prior distributions. In smaller samples, the choice of the prior distribution will have a stronger influence on the posterior parameter estimation. When noninformative priors are specified, the final parameter estimates are only a function of the data, and Bayesian approaches converge with conventional frequentist ML estimation methods. The posterior distributions of the parameters are often analytically intractable, so that parameter estimates and their distributions cannot be obtained with conventional estimation methods. A prominent alternative for Bayesian models in general, and for Bayesian structural equation models in particular, is the Markov Chain Monte Carlo (MCMC) methods (e.g., Geman & Geman, 1984; Hastings, 1970). These procedures are simulation-based and used to approximate the posterior distributions of the parameters with large numbers of random draws from the corresponding conditional distributions. Inferences about parameters are then based on measures of central tendency (e.g., as the median or the mean) and dispersion (e.g., the standard deviation) of these simulated distributions. For a thorough discussion of Bayesian SEM, the reader is referred to Lee (2008).

Similar to the distribution analytic approaches discussed earlier, Bayesian structural equation models with latent interactions do not require the calculation of product indicators for the latent product variable. Instead, they draw simulated values of the latent variables at each step of the MCMC method from their posterior distribution and calculate their cross-product based on these simulated values. Thus, they automatically account for the nonlinear distribution of the latent outcome variable and its indicators.

Simulation studies (e.g., Lee et al., 2007) have generally hinted at good performance of the Bayesian approach to nonlinear structural equation models, especially in small samples. However, due to the great flexibility of the Bayesian approach and its implementations, model specification requires sound statistical knowledge and careful thinking about the distributions of all model parameters and their priors. Although the simulation results of Lee and colleagues (2007) suggest that the choice of the different priors did not unduly affect the parameter estimates even in relatively small samples, care should be taken and sensitivity analyses with different priors are called for—especially for small samples. Due to the flexibility of implementation, the Bayesian approach to latent interactions can be easily extended to include quadratic and other polynomial effects of latent variables, as well as higher-order interactions between more than two latent variables. The corresponding nonlinear functions can simply be implemented as part of the structural model. While this flexibility adds much to the appeal of the Bayesian approach, it also makes implementation of the model to be estimated quite cumbersome: Sound statistical knowledge for the specification of models and priors is currently necessary. Currently, the free WinBugs software (Spiegelhalter et al., 2004) is the only widely available program that allows the implementation of

the Bayesian approach. The user-friendly implementation of Bayesian structural equation models in Mplus (Muthén & Muthén, 1997–2010) currently allows only the specification of linear structural models.

We analyzed the example data set using WinBugs 1.4 (Spiegelhalter et al., 2004) with noninformative conjugate priors, in line with the recommendations by Lee (2008), using three MCMC chains with 10,000 replications each and discarding the first 4,000 replications of each chain for burn-in. The unstandardized parameter estimates of the structural model were $\gamma_1 = 0.451$ ($SD = 0.073$) and $\gamma_2 = 0.329$ ($SD = 0.065$) for the latent first-order effects and $\gamma_3 = 0.186$ ($SD = 0.077$) for the latent interaction effect; the estimates for the variances of the predictor variables were $\phi_{11} = 0.487$ and $\phi_{22} = 0.511$, respectively. The standardized parameters are $\gamma_1'' = 0.432$ ($SD = 0.059$), $\gamma_2'' = 0.323$ ($SD = 0.060$), and $\gamma_3'' = 0.126$ ($SD = 0.050$). See Table 26.2.

SUMMARY

Nonlatent variable tests of interaction effects traditionally underestimate interaction effects if there is measurement error in the predictors that becomes exacerbated when product variables are formed. In this chapter we have described new and evolving approaches to testing latent interaction effects. When one of the predictor variables is a manifest grouping variable with a small number of categories (e.g., male–female) the traditional approach to multigroup SEM can be applied. This approach is well established, easily implemented, and facilitates a detailed evaluation of invariance assumptions (e.g., invariance of factor load-

TABLE 26.2. Comparison of Latent Interaction Effects Obtained with the Unconstrained Approach in LISREL, QML, LMS, and the Bayesian Approach in WinBugs

	Unconstrained		QML		LMS		Bayesian	
	Raw	Standardized	Raw	Standardized	Raw	Standardized	Raw	Standardized
γ_1	0.425	0.423	0.438	0.434	0.437	0.436	0.451	0.432
γ_2	0.331	0.338	0.320	0.327	0.318	0.325	0.329	0.323
γ_3	0.197	0.142	0.174	0.125	0.172	0.124	0.186	0.126
ϕ_{11}	0.501		0.496		0.501		0.487	
ϕ_{22}	0.529		0.528		0.526		0.511	
ϕ_{33}	0.308							

ings over groups) that is largely ignored in other approaches. However, the multigroup approach is generally not recommended when all the predictor variables are continuous or based on multiple indicators. Historically, the product indicator approaches have dominated latent interaction research. Although this approach is still evolving, there is good evidence in support of the unconstrained approach in terms of robustness and ease of implementation in terms of all commercial SEM packages. More recently, distribution analytic approaches (LMS and QML) hold considerable promise and apparently have strategic advantages over the product indicator approach. While LMS is available in Mplus, the QML approach is not available in any major SEM package (but is available from its author, Andreas Klein, upon request).

LIMITATIONS AND DIRECTIONS FOR FURTHER RESEARCH

We now turn to a set of issues that is beyond the scope of this chapter and represents areas of ongoing research. In particular, we discuss recent developments in detecting latent interaction effects and testing model fit for models with latent interaction effects, quadratic and other nonlinear latent variable effects, and latent interactions in multilevel structural equation models.

Detecting Latent Interaction Effects and Assessing Model Fit

One of the most important issues in structural equation models is assessing whether the model fits the data. There are two complications with assessing model fit for structural equation models with latent interactions using these strategies: (1) The conventional likelihood ratio test (and fit indices based on the likelihood function more generally) is not sensitive to latent interaction effects; and (2) the appropriate saturated and null models for structural equation models with latent interactions are not well-defined when making the use of conventional (absolute) model tests, and fit indices are suspect when product indicators are used or impossible when distribution analytic approaches are employed. We discuss each issue briefly and summarize some of the initial solutions that have been proposed.

Mooijaart and Satorra (2009) proved that the conventional likelihood ratio test of a linear SEM based on the covariance structure is insensitive to a missing interaction effect and cannot be used to detect this misspecification. Their findings are derived under very general conditions that include a saturated linear structural model, the most common setting in which latent interaction effects have been considered. To address this problem, Mooijaart and Bentler (2010) introduced a new estimator for latent interaction effects that models selected third-order moments and trivariate measures of skew, in addition to the mean and covariance structure. Including the third-order moment structure allows for testing whether the linear structural model is misspecified and inclusion of an interaction effect is necessary. Their method proved to be unbiased in small simulation studies but had larger standard errors (i.e., was less efficient) than the LMS method. Although some of the technical details of this new estimator are yet to be resolved and its finite sample properties need to be studied in more extensive simulation studies, it seems to be a promising and principled alternative to the product indicator and distribution analytic approaches discussed earlier. In particular, it offers well-defined tests of model fit and standard errors that can be easily extended to robust alternatives (see Mooijart & Bentler, 2010). This includes the potential to develop relative indices of model fit. The pending implementation in the commercial software package EQS (Bentler, 2004) should make it an attractive alternative for applied researchers.

Klein and Schermelleh-Engel (2010) used a different approach to assess misspecification of the linear structural models, such as a missing latent interaction effect that can be implemented with conventional SEM software. They reasoned that a missing latent interaction effect would show up as heteroscedasticity of the residuals of the latent outcome variable: If an interaction were incorrectly left out of the model, the variance of the residuals would be different at different values of the predictors. Violations of the equal residual variance assumptions in a linear structural model can be assessed with a likelihood ratio test statistic. Klein and Schermelleh-Engel derived this test statistic and its distribution, and demonstrated how it can be calculated, based on predicted and actual factor scores of the latent outcome variable. Using simulated data sets, they showed that it was sensitive to missing interaction and quadratic effects in the structural model. Their easy-to-implement approach seems very promising for specification problems for structural equation models, but further research into its sensitivity and specificity is necessary.

Nonlinear Effects: Confounding Quadratic Effects and Interaction Effects

Theories that hypothesize quadratic effects of a predictor variable are common. For example, nonlinear effects may be hypothesized between strength of interventions (or dosage level) and outcome variables such that benefits increase up to an optimal level, then level off or even decrease beyond this optimal point. At low levels of anxiety, for example, increases in anxiety may facilitate performance, but at higher levels of anxiety, further increases in anxiety may undermine performance. However, the existence of quadratic effects (and other higher-order polynomials) can complicate the analysis and interpretation of interaction effects.

In the context of manifest interaction models, it is well known that the presence of unmodeled quadratic effects may give the appearance of a significant interaction effect that is spurious (Ganzach, 1997; Kromrey & Foster-Johnson, 1999; Lubinski & Humphreys, 1990; MacCallum & Mar, 1995). This is particularly relevant when the predictor variables are strongly correlated and measured with error. Thus, without the inclusion of quadratic effects in the regression model, the investigator might easily misinterpret, overlook, or mistake a quadratic effect as an interaction effect. Testing quadratic effects is relatively straightforward in manifest approaches (the squared predictors have to be entered into the regression equation), but when latent variable models in which the latent predictor variables are based on multiple indicators, the simultaneous inclusion of latent interaction and latent quadratic terms is more complicated.

Quadratic effects can be easily specified and estimated within the distribution analytic approaches: Both LMS and QML have provisions for estimating interaction effects and quadratic effects simultaneously (Klein & Moosbrugger, 2000; Klein & Muthén, 2007). Recent work on extensions of the unconstrained approach to latent interactions (Kelava & Brandt, 2009; Kelava et al., 2011; Moosbrugger, Schermelleh-Engel, Kelava, & Klein, 2009) has demonstrated how product indicator approaches can be extended to account for quadratic effects of latent variables. Initial, limited simulation studies (Kelava et al., 2011; Moosbrugger et al., 2009) suggest that all three approaches result in unbiased estimators for quadratic and interaction effects when normality assumptions for the indicators of the latent predictor variables and their indicators are

fulfilled. In general, the recommendation of routinely including quadratic terms when estimating interaction effects, given in the context of manifest variable models (Ganzach, 1997). can now also be followed with latent interaction models. This might be even more important in these models because violations of the assumption of multivariate normality (that are not made in manifest regression models) have been shown to bias interaction effects when quadratic effects were not controlled for at the same time (Klein, Schermelleh-Engel, Moosbrugger, & Kelava, 2009).

The specification of higher-order polynomials (e.g., cubic effects) or higher-order interactions that involve more than two latent variables becomes increasingly more difficult with product indicator approaches or not possible with current implementations of distribution analytic approaches. Within these approaches, little progress has been made on deriving latent variable models for these—more complex—relations between latent variables. Note, however, that including higher-order polynomials and higher-order interactions is straightforward within the Bayesian framework. As measurement error associated with the separate predictor variables combines multiplicatively, it will affect higher-order polynomials and interactions even more adversely than simple products of latent variables. Although the simple two-way interaction effects are not biased by higher-order polynomials if there is a linear relation between the two predictor variables (Klein et al., 2009), further research into expanding nonlinear latent variable models to include higher-order polynomials and higher-order latent variable interactions is needed.

Semiparametric approaches (e.g., Bauer, 2005; Bauer & Curran, 2004; Pek, Sterba, Kok, & Bauer, 2009) offer an attractive alternative for modeling complex nonlinear relations between latent variables. Bauer (2005) showed how a latent variable mixture model could be used to approximate the nonlinear relation between two latent variables. In contrast to direct applications of the latent variable mixture model (Dolan & van der Maas, 1998), the mixture components are not given a substantive interpretation, but they are used as a computational tool to flexibly approximate the nonlinear regression function with linear within-group regressions (see Bauer, 2005, for details). Pek and colleagues (2009) provided an easy-to-use and freely available R package that can be used to summarize and visualize the findings obtained with this method. So far, the semiparametric approaches have only been used to study the nonlinear relations between two latent variables and have not been extended to cover interactions between two latent variables in the prediction of a latent outcome variable. Extensions of the semiparametric approach could be a welcome addition to the toolbox for latent interaction analysis and would be a straightforward way of handling latent interactions and other nonlinear effects at the same time.

Multilevel Designs and Clustered Samples

In many real-world applications, data are collected in multilevel systems in which units (e.g., students, employees) are nested in clusters (e.g., schools, organizations). This nesting introduces dependencies between the units in the same clusters that have to be handled with the appropriate modeling strategies. Historically, multilevel systems researchers have tended to work with manifest variables that ignore measurement error, while SEM researchers have tended to work with latent variable models that ignore multilevel structures in their data. However, these two dominant analytic approaches are increasingly being integrated within more comprehensive, multilevel structural equation models (e.g., Lüdtke et al., 2008; Marsh, Lüdtke, et al. 2009; Mehta & Neale, 2005).

While the initial implementations of multilevel structural equation models only allowed random intercepts (e.g., see Rabe-Hesketh, Skrondal, & Zheng, Chapter 30, this volume) of indicators and latent variables, recent developments have become much more flexible by allowing the relations between latent variables at the individual level to vary with the higher-level units. For example, parental influence on students' achievement can depend on the school the student attends. The search for group-level variables that can explain variance in the effect of individual variables between schools is a key question in many multilevel studies. The advent of flexible, multilevel structural equation models now allows applied researchers to address this question based not only on manifest variables but also with respect to latent variables. Initial demonstrations of models including latent interactions within and across levels (e.g., Marsh, Lüdtke, et al., 2009) underscore their great potential. Although more work on their applicability and robustness is warranted before their promise will be fully realized, multilevel structural equation modeling with latent interactions is an important emerging area in quantitative analysis.

REFERENCES

Aiken, L. S., & West, S. G. (1991). *Multiple regression: Testing and interpreting interactions.* Newbury Park, CA: Sage.

Algina, J., & Moulder, B. C. (2001). A note on estimating the Jöreskog–Yang model for latent variable interaction using LISREL 8.3. *Structural Equation Modeling, 8*, 40–52.

Asparouhov, T., & Muthén, B. (2010). Bayesian analysis of latent variable models using Mplus (Technical Report, Version 4). Unpublished report. Available at *www.statmodel.com.*

Bagozzi, R. P., & Yi, Y. (1989). On the use of structural equation models in experimental designs. *Journal of Marketing Research, 26*, 271–284.

Bandalos, D. L. (2008). Is parceling really necessary?: A comparison of results from item parceling and categorical variable methodology. *Structural Equation Modeling, 15*, 211–240.

Baron, R. M., & Kenny, D. A. (1986). The moderator–mediator variable distinction in social psychological research: Conceptual, strategic, and statistical considerations. *Journal of Personality and Social Psychology, 51*, 1173–1182.

Batista-Foguet, J. M., Coenders, G., & Saris, W. E. (2004). A parsimonious approach to interaction effects in structural equation models: an application to consumer behavior. *Working Papers d'ESADE, 183*, 1–28.

Bauer, D. J. (2005). A semiparametric approach to modeling nonlinear relations among latent variables. *Structural Equation Modeling, 12*, 513–535.

Bauer, D. J., & Curran, P. J. (2004). The integration of continuous and discrete latent variable models: Potential problems and promising opportunities. *Psychological Methods, 9*, 3–29.

Bentler, P. M. (2004). *EQS 6 structural equations program manual.* Encino, CA: Multivariate Software, Inc.

Boker, S., Neale, M., Maes, H., Wilde, M., Spiegel, M., Brick, T., et al. (2010). *OpenMx: The OpenMx statistical modeling package* (R package version 0.3.0-1217). Available at *http://openmx.psyc.virginia.edu* .

Bollen, K. A. (1989). *Structural equations with latent variables.* New York: Wiley.

Boomsma, A. (1983). *On the robustness of LISREL against small sample size and non-normality.* Doctoral dissertation, University of Groningen, Groningen, the Netherlands.

Busemeyer, J. R., & Jones, L. E. (1983). Analysis of multiplicative combination rules when the causal variables are measured with error. *Psychological Bulletin, 93*, 549–562.

Butts, M. M., & Ng, T. W. H. (2008). Chopped liver? OK. Chopped data? Not OK. In C. E. Lance & R. J. Vandenberg (Eds.), *Statistical and methodological myths and urban legends: Received doctrine, verity, and fable in the organizational and social sciences* (pp. 563–585). New York: Routledge.

Byrne, B. M. (1998). *Structural equation modeling with LIS-REL, PRELIS, and SIMPLIS: Basic concepts, applications and programming*. Mahwah, NJ: Erlbaum.

Champoux, J. E., & Peters, W. S. (1987). Form, effect size, and power in moderated regression analysis. *Journal of Occupational Psychology, 60*, 243–255.

Coenders, G., Batista-Foguet, J. M., & Saris, W. E. (2008). Simple, efficient and distribution-free approach to interaction effects in complex structural equation models. *Quality and Quantity, 42*(3), 369–396.

Cohen, J., & Cohen, P. (1983). *Applied multiple regression/correlational analysis for the behavioral sciences*. Hillsdale, NJ: Erlbaum.

Cohen, J., Cohen, P., West, S. G., & Aiken, L. S. (2003). *Applied multiple regression/correlation analysis for the behavior sciences* (3rd ed.). Mahwah, NJ: Erlbaum.

Cronbach, L. J., & Snow, R. E. (1977). *Aptitudes and instructional methods: A handbook for research on interactions*. Oxford, UK: Irvington.

Cudeck, R. (1989). Analysis of correlation matrices using covariance structure models. *Psychological Bulletin, 105*, 317–327.

Cudeck, R., Harring, J. R., & du Toit, S. H. C. (2009). Marginal maximum likelihood estimation of a latent variable model with interaction. *Journal of Educational and Behavioral Statistics, 34*, 131–144.

Dempster, A. P., Laird, N. M., & Rubin, D. B. (1977). Maximum likelihood from incomplete data via the EM algorithm. *Journal of the Royal Statistical Society B, 39*, 1–38.

Dimitruk, P., Schermelleh-Engel, K., Kelava, A., & Moosbrugger, H. (2007). Challenges in nonlinear structural equation modeling. *Methodology, 3*, 100–114.

Dolan, C. V., & van der Maas, H. (1998). Fitting multivariage normal finite mixtures subject to structural equation modeling. *Psychometrika, 63*, 227–253.

Fox, J. (2006). Structural equation modeling with the SEM package in R. *Structural Equation Modeling, 13*, 465–486.

Friedrich, R. J. (1982). In defense of multiplicative terms in multiple regression equations. *American Journal of Political Science, 26*, 797–833.

Ganzach, Y. (1997). Misleading interaction and curvilinear terms. *Psychological Methods, 2*, 235–247.

Gelman, A., Carlin, J. B., Stern, H. S., & Rubin, D. B. (2004). *Bayesian data analysis* (2nd ed.). London: Chapman & Hall.

Geman, S., & Geman, D. (1984). Stochastic relaxation, Gibbs distribution, and the Bayesian restoration of images. *IEEE Transactions on Pattern Analysis and Machine Intelligence, 6*, 721–741.

Hastings, W. K. (1970). Monte Carlo sampling methods using Markov chains and their application. *Biometrika, 57*, 97–109.

Hau, K. T., & Marsh, H. W. (2004). The use of item parcels in structural equation modeling: Non-normal data and small sample sizes. *British Journal of Mathematical Statistical Psychology, 57*, 327–351.

Hayduk, L. A. (1987). *Structural equation modeling with LISREL: Essentials and advances*. Baltimore: Johns Hopkins University Press.

Hu, L., Bentler, P. M., & Kano, Y. (1992). Can test statistics in covariance structure analysis be trusted? *Psychological Bulletin, 112*, 351–362.

Jaccard, J. (1998). *Interaction effects in factorial analysis of variance*. Thousand Oaks, CA: Sage.

Jaccard, J., Turrisi, R., & Wan, C. K. (1990). *Interaction effects in multiple regression*. Newbury Park, CA: Sage.

Jaccard, J., & Wan, C. K. (1995). Measurement error in the analysis of interaction effects between continuous predictors using multiple regression: Multiple indicator and structural equation approaches. *Psychological Bulletin, 117*, 348–357.

Jöreskog, K. G., & Yang, F. (1996). Nonlinear structural equation models: The Kenny–Judd model with interaction effects. In G. A. Marcoulides & R. E. Schumacker (Eds.), *Advanced structural equation modeling: Issues and techniques* (pp. 57–88). Mahwah, NJ: Erlbaum.

Kelava, A., & Brandt, H. (2009). Estimation of nonlinear latent structural equation models using the extended unconstrained approach. *Review of Psychology, 16*, 123–131.

Kelava, A., Werner, C. S., Schermelleh-Engel, K., Moosbrugger, H., Zapf, D., Ma, Y., et al. (2011). Advanced nonlinear latent variable modeling: Distribution analytic LMS and QML estimators of interaction and quadratic effects. *Structural Equation Modeling, 18*, 465–491.

Kenny, D. A., & Judd, C. M. (1984). Estimating the nonlinear and interactive effects of latent variables. *Psychological Bulletin, 96*, 201–210.

Kirk, R. (1982). *Experimental design: Procedures for the Behavioral Sciences*. Belmont, CA: Brooks/Cole.

Klein, A. G. (2009). *QuasiML 2.63: Quick reference manual*. Unpublished manuscript, University of Western Ontario, London, Ontario, Canada.

Klein, A. G., & Moosbrugger, H. (2000). Maximum likelihood estimation of latent interaction effects with the LMS method. *Psychometrika, 65*, 457–474.

Klein, A. G., & Muthén, B. O. (2007). Quasi-maximum likelihood estimation of structural equation models with multiple interaction and quadratic effects. *Multivariate Behavioral Research, 42*, 647–663.

Klein, A. G., & Schermelleh-Engel, K. (2010). Introduction of a new measure for detecting poor fit due to omitted nonlinear terms in SEM. *Advances in Statistical Analysis, 94*, 157–166.

Klein, A. G., Schermelleh-Engel, K., Moosbrugger, H., &

Kelava, A. (2009). Assessing spurious interaction effects. In T. Teo & M. S. Khine (Eds.), *Structural equation modeling in educational research: Concepts and applications* (pp. 13–28). Rotterdam, the Netherlands: Sense Publishers.

Kromrey, J. D., & Foster-Johnson, L. (1999). Statistically differentiating between interaction and nonlinearity in multiple regression analysis: A Monte Carlo investigation of a recommended strategy. *Educational and Psychological Measurement, 59*, 392–413.

Lee, S. Y. (2008). *Structural equation modelling. A Bayesian approach.* London: Wiley.

Lee, S. Y., Song, X. Y., & Tang, N. S. (2007). Bayesian methods for analyzing structural equation models with covariates, interaction, and latent quadratic variables. *Structural Equation Modeling, 14*, 404–434.

Lin, G. C., Wen, Z., Marsh, H. W., & Lin, H. S. (2010). Structural equation models of latent interactions: Clarification of orthogonalizing and double-mean-centering strategies. *Structural Equation Modeling, 17*, 374–391.

Little, T. D., Bovaird, J. A., & Widaman, K. F. (2006). On the merits of orthogonalizing powered and product term: Implications for modeling interactions among latent variables. *Structural Equation Modeling, 13*(4), 497–519.

Little, T. D., Cunningham, W. A., Shahar, G., & Widaman, K. F. (2002). To parcel or not to parcel: Exploring the question, weighing the merits. *Structural Equation Modeling, 9*, 151–173.

Lubinski, D., & Humphreys, L. G. (1990). Assessing spurious "moderator effects": Illustrated substantively with the hypothesized ("synergistic") relation between spatial and mathematical ability. *Psychological Bulletin, 107*, 385–393.

Lüdtke, O., Marsh, H. W., Robitzsch, A., Trautwein, U., Asparouhov, T., & Muthén, B. (2008). The multilevel latent covariate model: A new, more reliable approach to group-level effects in contextual studies. *Psychological Methods, 13*, 203–229.

MacCallum, R. C., & Mar, C. M. (1995). Distinguishing between moderator and quadratic effects in multiple regression. *Psychological Bulletin, 118*, 405–421.

MacCallum, R. C., Zhang, S., Preacher, K. J., & Rucker, D. D. (2002). On the practice of dichotomization of quantitative variables. *Psychological Methods, 7*, 19–40.

Marsh, H. W., Lüdtke, O., Muthén, B., Asparouhov, T., Morin, A. J. S., Trautwein, U., et al. (2010). A new look at the Big-Five factor structure through exploratory structural equation modeling. *Psychological Assessment, 22*, 471–491.

Marsh, H. W., Lüdtke, O., Robitzsch, A., Trautwein, U., Asparouhov, T., Muthén, B., et al. (2009). Doubly-latent models of school contextual effects: Integrating multilevel and structural equation approaches to control measurement and sampling error. *Multivariate Behavioral Research, 44*, 764–802.

Marsh, H. W., Muthén, B., Asparouhov, T., Lüdtke, O., Robitzsch, A., Morin, A. J. S., et al. (2009). Exploratory structural equation modeling, integrating CFA and EFA: Application to students' evaluations of university teaching. *Structural Equation Modeling, 16*, 439–476.

Marsh, H. W., Wen, Z., & Hau, K. T. (2004). Structural equation models of latent interactions: Evaluation of alternative estimation strategies and indicator construction. *Psychological Methods, 9*(3), 275–300.

Marsh, H. W., Wen, Z., & Hau, K. T. (2006). Structural equation models of latent interaction and quadratic effects. In G. R. Hancock & R. O. Mueller (Eds.), *Structural equation modeling: A second course* (pp. 225–265). Greenwich, CT: Information Age.

Marsh, H. W., Wen, Z. L., Hau, K. T., Little, T. D., Bovaird, J. A., & Widaman, K. F. (2007). Unconstrained structural equation models of latent interactions: Contrasting residual- and mean-centered approaches. *Structural Equation Modeling, 14*(4), 570–580.

McDonald, R. P., & Ho, M. R. (2002). Principles and practice in reporting structural equation analyses. *Psychological Methods, 7*, 64–82.

Mehta, P. D., & Neale, M. C. (2005). People are variables too: Multilevel structural equation modeling. *Psychological Methods, 10*, 259–284.

Micceri, T. (1989). The unicorn, the normal curve, and other improbable creatures. *Psychological Bulletin, 105*, 156–166.

Mooijaart, A., & Bentler, P. M. (2010). An alternative approach for nonlinear latent variable models. *Structural Equation Modeling, 17*, 357–373.

Mooijaart, A., & Satorra, A. (2009). On insensitivity of the chi-square model test to nonlinear misspecification in structural equation models. *Psychometrika, 74*, 443–455.

Moosbrugger, H., Schermelleh-Engel, K., Kelava, A., & Klein, A. G. (2009). Testing multiple nonlinear effects in structural equation modeling: A comparison of alternative estimation approaches. In T. Teo & M. Khine (Eds.), *Structural equation modeling in educational research: Concepts and applications* (pp. 103–136). Rotterdam, the Netherlands: Sense Publishers.

Moulder, B. C., & Algina, J. (2002). Comparison of methods for estimating and testing latent variable interactions. *Structural Equation Modeling, 9*, 1–19.

Muthén, L. K., & Muthén, B. O. (1997–2010). *Mplus user's guide.* Los Angeles: Authors.

Pek, J., Sterba, S. K., Kok, B. E., & Bauer, D. J. (2009). Estimating and visualizing nonlinear relations among latent variables: A semiparametric approach. *Multivariate Behavioral Research, 44*, 407–436.

Preacher, K. J., Curran, P. J., & Bauer, D. J. (2006). Computational tools for probing interactions in multiple linear regression, multilevel modelling and latent curve analysis. *Journal of Educational and Behavioral Statistics, 31,* 437–448.

Pyzdek, T. (1995). Why normal distributions aren't [all that normal]. *Quality Engineering, 7,* 769–777.

Rigdon, E. E., Schumacker, R. E., & Wothke, W. (1998). A comparative review of interaction and nonlinear modeling. In R. E. Schumacker & G. A. Marcoulides (Eds.), *Interaction and nonlinear effects in structural equation modeling* (pp. 1–16). Mahwah, NJ: Erlbaum.

Saris, W. E., Batista-Foguet, J. M., & Coenders, G. (2007). Selection of indicators for the interaction term in structural equation models with interaction. *Quality and Quantity, 41*(1), 55–72.

Schumacker, R. E., & Marcoulides, G. A. (Eds.). (1998). *Interaction and nonlinear effects in structural equation modeling.* Mahwah, NJ: Erlbaum.

Spiegelhalter, D. J., Thomas, A., Best, N. G., & Lunn, D. (2004). *WinBugs user manual (Version 1.4).* Cambridge, UK: MRC Biostatistics Unit.

Vandenberg, R. J., & Lance, C. E. (2000). A review and synthesis of the measurement invariance literature: Suggestions, practices, and recommendations for organizational research. *Organizational Research Methods, 3,* 4–69.

Wall, M. M., & Amemiya, Y. (2001). Generalized appended product indicator procedure for nonlinear structural equation analysis. *Journal of Educational and Behavioral Statistics, 26,* 1–29.

Wen, Z., Hau, K. T., & Marsh, H. W. (2008). Appropriate standardized estimates for moderating effects in structural equation models. *Acta Psychologica Sinica, 40*(6), 729–736.

Wen, Z., Marsh, H. W., & Hau, K. T. (2010). Structural equation models of latent interactions: An appropriate standardized solution and its scale-free properties. *Structural Equation Modeling, 17,* 1–22.

West, S. G., Finch, J. F., & Curran, P. J. (1995). Structural equation models with nonnormal variables: Problems and remedies. In R. H. Hoyle (Ed.), *Structural equation modeling: Concepts, issues and applications* (pp. 56–75). Newbury Park, CA: Sage.

Wu, Y., Wen, Z., & Lin, G. C. (2009). Structural equation modeling of latent interactions without using the mean structure. *Acta Psychologica Sinica, 41*(12), 1252–1259.

Yang, F. (1998). Modeling interaction and nonlinear effects: A step-by-step LISREL example. In R. E. Schumacker & G. A. Marcoulides (Eds.), *Interaction and nonlinear effects in structural equation modeling* (pp. 17–42). Mahwah, NJ: Erlbaum.

Yang-Wallentin, F., & Jöreskog, K. G. (2001). Robust standard errors and chi-squares for interaction models. In G. A. Marcoulides & R. E. Schumacker (Eds.), *New developments and techniques in structural equation modeling* (pp. 159–171). Mahwah, NJ: Erlbaum.

CHAPTER 27

Autoregressive Longitudinal Models

Jeremy C. Biesanz

The analysis of longitudinal data has a long and rich history (see Bollen & Curran, 2006, for a brief review). The development of specialized statistical software, new and sophisticated analytical models, and technological innovations to collect data over time continues with a seemingly accelerating pace. This combination of readily available statistical software, rich statistical models, and novel technologies for collecting longitudinal data has substantially reduced the barriers to collecting and analyzing longitudinal data. Given a longitudinal data set and rich analytical options, how should one proceed? Collins (2006) recently argued for the ideal of integrating the three elements of (1) a well-articulated theoretical model of change based on (2) a temporal design that allows assessment of this theoretical model through (3) a statistical model that captures the theoretical model. This ideal situation that one should strive toward will often run aground on the rocks of reality. Theoretical models may not be sufficiently detailed to articulate the precise analytical model required. Even given strong a theoretical framework that specifies the analytical model, the observed data may not conform to the initial theory and analytical model. For these reasons it is important to understand the different analytical options for longitudinal data and their strengths and weaknesses. A comprehensive review of longitudinal data analysis is beyond the scope the present chapter.

In the current handbook, Shiyko, Ram, and Grimm (Chapter 31), McArdle (Chapter 32), Wood (Chapter 33), Cole (Chapter 34), and Ferrer and Song (Chapter 35) present in detail different models for longitudinal data (see also Collins & Horn, 1991; Collins & Sayer, 2001). This chapter focuses on one of the historically dominant analytical approaches to examining longitudinal data—the autoregressive (AR) model.

The chapter is organized as follows. First I briefly present an overview of the history of AR models. Next I present a basic AR structural equation model and provide interpretation of the model parameters and implications of the model. I then discuss technical and practical issues, followed by an empirical example, extensions to cross-lagged AR models, and discussion of continuous versus discrete time. Finally I contrast, compare, examine, and discuss different analytical models that include the AR structure either explicitly or implicitly within the model.

A BRIEF HISTORY OF THE AR MODEL AND TERMINOLOGY

The AR model has a rich history across different disciplines and is routinely used in econometrics, forecasting, psychology, and sociology, among other disciplines. The AR model posits that the observed value for a given point in time, t, is a function of p earlier assessments where p is specified. This is known as an AR model of order p, or AR(p). The AR model may be used to analyze as few as one unit across a moderate to large number of time points to data sets where many units are assessed on several variables for a few time points. For a single observed variable, Y, assessed across m different points in time ($t = 2, 3, \ldots, m$) on a single unit, this relationship is expressed as follows:

$$Y_t = \beta_0 + \sum_{j=1}^{p} \beta_p Y_{t-j} + \varepsilon_t \qquad (27.1)$$

When $p = 1$, a specific pattern emerges for the covariance matrix of the assessed variables across units which Guttman (1950) termed *simplex* in the context of factor analysis across different variables. Following this work a number of researchers including Harris (1963), Jones (1959, 1960) and Jöreskog (1970) extended the modeling framework where this covariance pattern is observed across different temporal assessments, as expressed in Equation 27.1. The simplex model now generally refers to a first-order autoregressive model, or AR(1). In general, there may be multiple units assessed ($i = 1, 2, 3, \ldots, n$) on q variables at each assessment. A classic time series design represents m assessments, where m is a large number for as few as one unit on just one variable. However, this chapter focuses on designs where there are multiple units measured on q variables at each of m assessments and n is generally much larger than m, and appropriately modeling the latent construct of interest that is assessed at each time point is of concern.

A Basic Quasi-Simplex AR Model

As discussed in Hoyle (Chapter 8, this volume), relationships among observed variables can be seriously biased if there is measurement error present in each assessed variable that is not accounted for in the model. Jöreskog (1970, 1979) first extended autoregressive models to latent variables. To illustrate, the basic simplex AR model, AR(1), models the latent value for each assessment as a function of the immediately preceding latent value plus a residual as follows,

$$\eta_t = \beta_{t,t-1} \eta_{t-1} + \zeta_t \qquad (27.2)$$

where $t = 2, 3, \ldots, m$. At each assessment the latent variable differs from the previous assessment by the latent disturbance $\zeta_t \sim N(0, \Psi)$. Note that all latent and manifest variables are assumed to be centered without loss of generality. Graphically this is represented in Figure 27.1, where the measurement equation is

$$y_t = 1.0\eta_t + \varepsilon_t \qquad (27.3)$$

If observed measures y_t are not fallible (i.e., $\Theta_{\varepsilon_t} = 0$ for all t), this is the standard *simplex* model as in Equation 27.1. In this case the latent variables are indeed not actually latent but instead directly observed (i.e., see Bollen & Hoyle, Chapter 4, this volume). Standard regression programs can estimate this model for small numbers of assessments; for large numbers of assessments time series programs may prove more useful. If the observed measures have at least some degree of measurement error (i.e., $\Theta_{\varepsilon_t} > 0$), this model is referred to as the *quasi-simplex*.

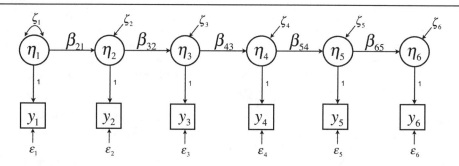

FIGURE 27.1. First-order autoregressive model (simplex) for six assessments of the same observed measure.

To understand the quasi-simplex model, an observed assessment, y_t, is a function of the previous assessment's latent value, η_{t-1}, a latent disturbance, and measurement error. This is seen by combining Equations 27.2 and 27.3, $y_t = 1.0(\beta_{t,t-1}\eta_{t-1} + \zeta_t) + \varepsilon_t$, as follows:

$$y_t = 1.0\eta_t + \varepsilon_t = 1.0(\beta_{t,t-1}\eta_{t-1} + \zeta_t) + \varepsilon_t \quad \textbf{(27.4)}$$
$$= \beta_{t,t-1}\eta_{t-1} + \zeta_t + \varepsilon_t$$

The relationship between the latent factors, $\beta_{t,t-1}$, describes the stability of individual differences across two adjacent assessments. High values indicate strong stability in the rank ordering of individuals on the latent variable. The latent disturbances, ζ_t, are often referred to as "random shocks." These are unexplained changes to each individual's latent value at a specific assessment. The uniqueness ε_t is simple measurement error. Although in Equation 27.4 ζ_t and ε_t appear as "error" terms, what distinguishes these are the structural relationships they have across time. As presented in Figure 27.1, the uniquenesses (ε's) have no relationship to future assessments. In contrast, the latent disturbance for a given point in time t will influence future assessments. To illustrate, consider the fourth assessment, $y_4 = \eta_4 + \varepsilon_4$. The latent value η_4 is a function of the previous latent value, $\eta_4 = \beta_{43}\eta_3 + \zeta_4$, which in turn is a function of the second latent value, $\eta_4 = \beta_{43}(\beta_{32}\eta_2 + \zeta_3) + \zeta_4$, and so on. Thus, the fourth assessment can be written as $y_4 = \beta_{43}(\beta_{32}(\beta_{21}\eta_1 + \zeta_2) + \zeta_3) + \zeta_4 + \varepsilon_4$. The effect of the latent disturbances promulgate across time, whereas the uniqueness has no temporal effect.

At first glance, estimating the model in Figure 27.1 appears relatively simple. Six assessments result in a covariance matrix with 21 unique variances and covariances. The model has 17 parameters: 12 variances (six variances in Ψ, and six variances in Θ_ε) and five structural coefficients (β's), resulting in $21 - 17 = 4$ df. However, this model is not identified without two further constraints. To understand the identification problem in Figure 27.1, consider the first latent assessment, η_1. The model shown in Figure 27.1 attempts to estimate both the latent variance of η_1 as well as the uniqueness Θ_{ε_1} based on a single fallible indicator. The latent variable η_1 is consequently not identified (see Kenny & Milan, Chapter 9, this volume). The last latent assessment is not identified either and constraints must be placed in order to identify this latent variable and allow the model to be estimated. Interestingly, the middle assessments are empirically identified as they

borrow strength from previous and subsequent assessments when $\hat{\beta} \neq 0$. If the assessments are not related to each other (e.g., $\hat{\beta} \approx 0$), then none of the latent variables is identified. One solution to the identification problem is to simply constrain Θ_{ε_1} and Θ_{ε_6} to 0. This will identify the model but presumes that the second through fifth assessments are fallible, whereas the first and last are not. Alternatively, the uniqueness variances for the first and last assessments can be constrained to be equal to their adjoining assessments (i.e., $\Theta_{\varepsilon_1} = \Theta_{\varepsilon_2}$ and $\Theta_{\varepsilon_6} = \Theta_{\varepsilon_5}$), resulting in a model with 6 df as there are now only 15 parameters to be estimated.

Additional constraints beyond those required for identification can be placed on the model. For instance, with equally temporally spaced assessments, all of the AR regression coefficients can be constrained to be equal ($\beta_{21} = \beta_{32} = \beta_{43} = \beta_{54} = \beta_{65} = \beta$), which may or may not be a realistic assumption. When assessments are not spaced equally across time, the autoregressive parameters are not constant even if the autoregressive relationship is constant across time. I address this issue later under the topic of discrete versus continuous time modeling in AR models. As well, a single common uniqueness variance and a single latent disturbance for assessments $t > 1$ can be estimated. These sets of constraints reduce the number of parameters estimated to a parsimoniously small four, resulting in a model with 17 df. Model 2A is presented in Figure 27.2. An empirical example of this model is examined next, along with models that are equivalent in that they produce the exact same model-implied covariance matrix.

EMPIRICAL EXAMPLE

As part of a larger longitudinal study, 140 University of British Columbia undergraduates completed online assessments of their personality (104 females, 31 males, 5 unknown; mean age $= 19.6$, $SD = 2.36$) approximately every month for 6 months. The present example focuses on measuring Subjective Well-Being (SWB; also known as the Satisfaction with Life Scale; Diener, Emmons, Larsen, & Griffen, 1985), a 5-item scale measured on a 1 (*disagree strongly*) to 7 (*agree strongly*) rating scale.[1] As is common in longitudinal research, there was attrition, with participants either withdrawing from the study or missing one or more assessments. All presented models were estimated in LISREL 8.71 (Jöreskog & Sörbom, 1996) using full information maximum likelihood and all available data (see Graham & Coffman,

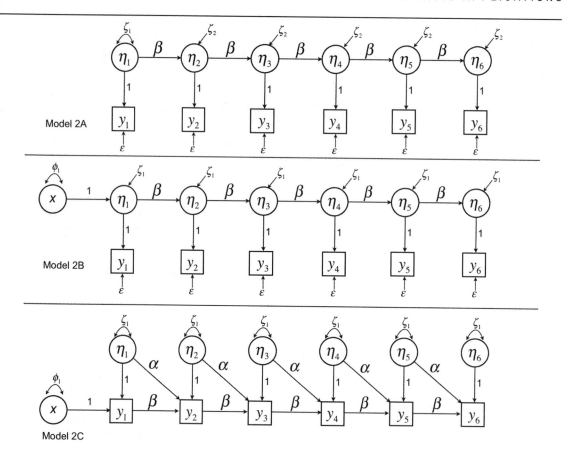

FIGURE 27.2. Equivalent autoregressive models.

Chapter 17, this volume, for more discussion of missing data in structural equation modeling [SEM]). I first examine and interpret AR models based on the SWB scale mean score data, presented in Table 27.1, before considering models that assess SWB as a latent factor defined by the individual items at each assessment.

Across the 6 monthly assessments of SWB the basic quasi-simplex AR model 2A presented in Figure 27.2 results in a fairly poor fit to the observed data, $\chi^2(17)$ = 49.00, root mean square error of approximation (RMSEA) = .12, $CI_{.90}$ = [.079, .155]. In the present case it is useful for didactic purposes to examine and interpret this model and related equivalent models before attempting to understand the source of misfit and relax constraints. Parameter estimates and standard errors

are presented in Table 27.2. Of note, the unstandardized autoregressive parameter (β) is very close to 1, indicating a very high degree of stability in the rank ordering of individuals' SWB. Indeed, the variance for the latent disturbances, $\hat{\Psi}_2 = 0.03$, is very small. Together these results suggest that there is very little change in SWB across the monthly assessments and that most of the observed change in actual assessments is simply due to measurement error that is unrelated to actual (latent) SWB. In other words, this interpretation appears quite consistent with a single latent SWB factor that does not change over the observed 6 months. This interpretation is misleading, as I illustrate shortly.

Model 2A presented in Figure 27.2 estimates the variance for the first latent "disturbance" separately from

TABLE 27.1. Relationship of Subjective Well-Being across Time

Month	Month					
Month	1	2	3	4	5	6
1	1.00					
2	0.84	1.00				
3	0.80	0.83	1.00			
4	0.88	0.86	0.89	1.00		
5	0.86	0.88	0.92	0.93	1.00	
6	0.79	0.86	0.86	0.89	0.90	1.00
Mean	4.84	4.84	4.94	4.82	4.93	4.82
SD	1.37	1.48	1.47	1.42	1.34	1.49
N	138	124	99	88	76	67

Note. Correlations represent pairwise relationships given available data.

the rest of the latent disturbances. This first assessment is treated as an exogenous latent variable that provides the initial value on SWB. Future assessments are then a function of the preceding assessments and latent disturbances. In reality, there were previous values of SWB that simply were not assessed—individuals' levels of SWB before the study commenced are simply missing data. These can be incorporated into the model through a phantom latent variable X that captures the unassessed stable part of SWB. Phantom latent variables have no corresponding manifest variables but nonetheless can be estimated given sufficient constraints. In the present

TABLE 27.2. Autoregressive Parameter Estimates (Standard Errors) from Models 2A–C

Parameter	Model estimate		
	2A	2B	2C
β	0.99 (0.01)	0.99 (0.01)	0.99 (0.01)
α	—	—	−0.69 (0.09)
Φ_1	—	1.59 (0.21)	1.51 (0.22)
Ψ_1	1.62 (0.22)	0.03 (0.02)	0.36 (0.03)
Ψ_2	0.03 (0.02)	—	—
Θ_ε	0.26 (0.03)	0.26 (0.03)	—
$\chi^2(17)$	49.00	49.00	49.00
RMSEA	0.116	0.116	0.116

case, by defining $\Psi_1 = \Psi_2$, and thus equating all of the variances of the latent disturbances across assessments, and fixing the unstandardized relationship between X and η_1 to be 1.0, X is identified and its variance can be estimated. Model 2B is illustrated in Figure 27.2 and is exactly equivalent to model 2A. All of the parameter estimates for this model are identical to those of model 2A. The variance for η_1 is now decomposed into the sum of the variances for Φ_1 and Ψ_1 (i.e., 1.62 = 1.59 + 0.03).

In Figure 27.2, since models 2A and 2B are equivalent models with common parameters whose interpretation is the same for both models, it does not matter which model is estimated. However, model 2B has several benefits over model 2A. First, the variance of X can be constrained to achieve stationarity. A model is stationary if the model-implied covariance matrix is independent of the exact timing of the assessments. In other words, if everyone were assessed an arbitrary number of days earlier or later, thus shifting t by some arbitrary constant, then the expected value of all parameter estimates, the expected value for each assessment, and the population covariance matrix of the assessments, $\Sigma(\theta)$, all remain the same. This implies that if a model is stationary, then the model-implied variance for each assessment is identical. Even though the AR parameter estimates are the same and the latent disturbances and uniquenessess are all the same, in the present case the model is close to but not fully stationary. Examining the fitted covariance matrix $\hat{\Sigma}(\theta)$ shows that the model implied variance is 1.877 for y_1 and 1.874 for y_6. Although very close in value, these are not exactly identical. A quasi-simplex AR(1) model is stationary if $\Phi_1 = \beta^2\Psi_1/(1 - \beta^2)$ in the population (see Browne & Zhang, 2007, p. 31). Imposing that constraint during estimation ensures that the resulting model-implied covariance matrix is stationary if so desired.

The second benefit that model 2B in Figure 27.2 provides is conceptual and aesthetic. The timing of the first assessment is often arbitrary in longitudinal research and theoretically no different than the second, third, and subsequent assessments. In other words, the latent disturbance influencing SWB at the first assessment is present there, just as it is for subsequent assessments. Specifying the model such that there is a latent disturbance at the first assessment provides a cleaner match to the theoretical process, even though the remaining parameter estimates are isomorphic between models 2A and 2B in Figure 27.2.

Both models 2A and 2B are fully equivalent to an alternative formulation known as the AR moving average (ARMA) model illustrated in Figure 27.2C. Here each observed assessment is a function of the previous observed assessment, a disturbance, and the previous assessment's disturbance.

$$y_t = \beta y_{t-1} + \zeta_t + \alpha \zeta_{t-1} \qquad (27.5)$$

The ARMA model has the equivalent AR parameter to that in models 2A and 2B in Figure 27.2 but no longer separates latent disturbances from measurement error at each assessment. The importance of considering the ARMA model in Figure 27.2C lies in the observation that the nature of the autoregressive relationship on the manifest variables is not the same as that on the latent variables, as in models 2A and 2B in Figure 27.2. In other words, conducting a time series analysis on the observed assessments will not provide the model that exists at the latent structure after explicitly modeling measurement error at each assessment. Thus, in Figure 27.2, model 2C, although fully equivalent to models 2A and 2B in its fit to the observed data and yielding the same model-implied covariance matrix $\hat{\Sigma}(\theta)$, has a substantively different interpretation of the nature of the AR relationship and how change on SWB occurs over time. Model 2C presumes no measurement error in the assessment of SWB; thus, the disturbance is *any* change from the previous assessment that then promulgates across time. In other words, there is no longer the traditional latent variable of which the observed *y*'s are imperfect assessments. The latent variables in the ARMA model represent disturbances that impact the current and future assessment(s) and each assessment in model 2C in Figure 27.2 is considered to be without measurement error.

Returning to Models 2A and 2B in Figure 27.2, the fit of these models is rather modest and warrants reconsidering the set of parameter constraints across time. Relaxing the constraints that either the uniqueness variances or latent disturbances are homogenous improves the model fit to more acceptable levels. For instance, allowing the latent disturbances Ψ to vary across the six assessments results in a much better fitting model, $\chi^2(13) = 24.98$, RMSEA = .081, CI$_{.90}$ = [.029, .13], and provides a reasonable fit to the observed data. West, Taylor, and Wu (Chapter 13, this volume) provide a detailed and nuanced perspective on evaluating model fit. Of substantive import, note that the interpretation of the overall model remains unchanged as the AR parameter is the same β = .99. In other words, the broad interpretation of the overall AR model remains unchanged after relaxing these constraints.

A Quasi-Simplex AR Model with an Explicit Measurement Model

The results of models 2A and 2B in Figure 27.2 suggest that there is an extraordinarily high degree of stability in SWB across monthly assessments. Any change in an individual's actual latent SWB is minimal. At first glance this seems reasonable given the relatively short interval between assessments. However, alternative explanations should be explored. The observed assessments that are modeled represent scale scores by simply averaging the five SWB items. Although analyzing summary scale scores across time is a common longitudinal data analytical practice for cross-lagged panel analyses and growth curve models, it is a practice born out of convenience. Model 2B in Figure 27.2 presumes that the only relationship across time on SWB occurs at the latent trait level. If the model is correctly specified, then parameter estimates are unbiased. However, misspecification of the model can bias parameter estimates and lead to erroneous conclusions. One possible misspecification is that there is a temporal relationship among the uniquenesses that, by definition, is not related to the latent variable. For instance, responses to the first SWB item, "In most ways my life is close to my ideal," may be consistent across time due to temporal stability in the uniqueness for this specific item that is independent of the latent variable defined by all five items in the scale. In this example, the net result of not modeling temporal relationships among uniquenesses in models 2A and 2B would be the potential inflation of the AR parameter estimate as the temporal relationship among the uniquenesses could only manifest itself through the relationship among the latent variables.

With multiple indicators of the same underlying construct assessed at each of the time points, the AR structure among the latent variables defined by commonality among those five indicators can be assessed. The additional complexity of the analysis carries several benefits. First, the assumption of measurement invariance across time can be examined explicitly. When examining change on a construct across time it is assumed that the measurement relationship between the indicator variables and the latent variable does not change as well (see Millsap & Olivera-Aguilar, Chapter 23, this volume, for a more complete discussion of measurement invariance). To illustrate, the frequency of biting may be a good marker of aggression in a 3-year old but a poor one for a 30-year-old. The relationship between the measured variable (biting) and the latent construct (aggression) changes across time, and the scale of the latent variable needs to be calibrated to be constant across time in order to interpret any change across time as reflecting change on the latent variable as opposed to change on the scale of the latent variable. In other words, observing that biting frequency declines from age 3 to age 30 is not necessarily indicative of a change in level of aggression if the relationship between that variable and the latent construct of aggression changes over time as well.

The second benefit for modeling the latent variables through the individual items, and indeed the *raison d'être* for it in this example, is to identify the latent variables in a manner that is independent of the structural relationships across time. The latent SWB variable is identified at each point in time and no longer relies on either constraints to identify the first and last assessments or the structural relationships across time. Although it is tempting to jump to the final model and present and interpret the results, this example follows the linear progression of what I did, as this is more useful didactically.

Assessing Measurement Structure

The five SWB items intercorrelate strongly (*r*'s range from .54 to .85). Yet examining the measurement model at the first assessment indicates that a single latent SWB factor has poor fit to the observed data: $\chi^2(5, N = 140) = 16.35$, $p = .006$, RMSEA = 0.128. Items 4 and 5 have lower correlations with the other items; however, removing Item 5 did not substantially improve fit: $\chi^2(2, N = 140) = 5.96$, $p = .05$, RMSEA = 0.119. Traditional exploratory factor-analytic techniques for determining the number of factors (dimensions) may provide results that do not hold well when examined through the lens of confirmatory factor analysis. The current data set presents one such example; the traditional scree test and more diagnostically useful parallel test strongly suggest that a single factor underlies the five items, and that the second factor is not reliable. Yet the one-factor model is clearly rejected in the present case.

Revisiting the measurement structure through writing and assessing new items is not feasible in this example. What then are the options for examining the overall model? One possibility is to simply ignore the lack of fit

at the measurement level. This may be justifiable in circumstances where there are sufficient data in the literature to believe that the single dimension is warranted, and that the current sample is representative of previously assessed populations. However, the final model will have potential misfit arising from three difference sources: (1) measurement misfit at each assessment, (2) measurement variance across assessments, and (3) misfit at the structural model (i.e., the specified AR(1) model is incorrect). Understanding the overall fit of the model becomes more difficult when it is known a priori that the measurement model is not fully satisfactory.

With more than five items, bundling items into parcels of equal numbers of items often has the empirical benefit of minimizing the impact of minor but statistically significant deviations from unidimensionality when the goal is to assess the broader higher-order construct across all of the items (e.g., in the context of well-being, see Gallagher, Lopez, & Preacher, 2009). For instance, with a 12-item scale, four bundles of three items each could be created and then the four bundles could be treated as the assessed items in the overall model of the broad construct of interest. With five items this approach is not feasible.

The approach taken in this example is to simply remove measurement misfit from the overall model and model SWB as a function of just the first three items across time. Use of three items identifies a latent factor exactly but does not provide a test of dimensionality. Adopting this approach simply circumvents the strict lack of a single dimension underlying SWB in the present data and defines SWB based solely on the first three items. At the same time, since there is no misfit in the measurement of the latent SWB factors, any misfit observed in the overall quasi-simplex model can be interpreted as stemming from either measurement variance over time and/or structural misspecification.

Assessing Measurement Invariance

If measurement invariance holds across time, then factor loadings, uniqueness variances, and intercepts for each item (if assessed) remain constant across time and do not vary. Assessing measurement invariance can be done by constraining these parameter estimates to be equal across assessments and evaluating the change in the overall model fit when the constraint is relaxed. As presented in Figure 27.3, the quasi-simplex model of SWB with both loadings and uniquenesses for common items constrained to be equal across time had a mod-

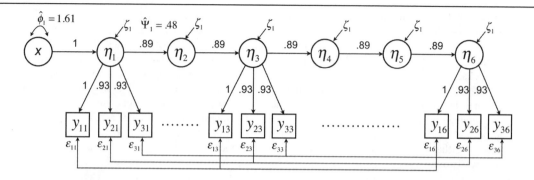

FIGURE 27.3. Quasi-simplex autoregressive model with an explicit measurement model.

est fit to the observed data: $\chi^2(110) = 259.47$, RMSEA $= .099$, $CI_{.90} = [.083, .11]$. Allowing loadings to vary across time did not change the model fit in a substantively important manner: $\Delta\chi^2(10; N = 140) = 18.33$, $p < .05$. Allowing uniquenesses to vary across time did significantly improve model fit: $\Delta\chi^2(15; N = 140) = 53.10$, $p < .0001$, RMSEA $= .092$, $CI_{.90} = [.074, .11]$. Model parameter estimates were consistent between these two specifications. Model 3, where loadings are constrained to be equal across time but uniquenesses may vary, is presented in Figure 27.3. In sum, the relationship between SWB and individual items is constant across assessments; however, the amount of noise present in the assessment did change over time.

Comparing Model 3 with 2B

What is striking in the present example are the similarities and differences in the substantive conclusions reached about the nature of SWB across time. Modeling SWB through specific items shows a high degree of stability with the AR parameter estimate $\hat{\beta} = .89$, $z = 37.09$, $p < .00001$. Although the AR parameter estimate is large in both models, it is decidedly smaller in model 3. This can be seen as well in the variance of the latent disturbances: $\hat{\Psi} = .48$, $z = 10.43$, $p < .0001$. Whereas in model 2B latent disturbances were not statistically distinguishable from 0, here we see in model 3 that there are substantial disturbances in latent SWB. In other words, there were changes in the rank ordering in SWB across individuals over the monthly assessments. Indeed, the model-implied correlation for model 3 between adjacent monthly assessments of SWB is $r = .88$,

which represents a strong level of temporal stability. However, as the interval between assessments grows, this relationship diminishes; the model-implied correlation between assessments 6 months apart is $r = .54$.

Why does model 3 presented in Figure 27.3 yield a different substantive conclusion? One explanation, alluded to earlier, is that model 2B in Figure 27.2 misspecifies the nature of the latent variable. Examining the uniquenesses for the same item across time in model 3 generally indicates substantially reliable covariances, as 36 of the 45 uniqueness covariances were significantly positive. Model 2B essentially constrains those covariances to be 0, which forced that relationship to manifest itself through the association of latent SWB and in a higher estimate of β. Model 3, by allowing uniquenesses to correlate across time, presents a more defensible estimate of the stability of latent SWB. Although the estimate of the autoregressive parameter β is lower in model 3 compared to model 2B, it still represents a substantial level of stability across time.

Cross-Lagged Panel Designs

At times simply assessing how a construct changes over time is solely of interest. At other times this may be a prelude to examining how a construct changes and covaries across time with other constructs. One such common application of AR models is the cross-lagged panel design. Originally developed by Lazarsfeld and Fiske (1938), a "panel design" involves assessing the same cohort of individuals across time and is distinguished from the cross-sectional design in which a different sample is assessed at each point in time. Cross-lagged

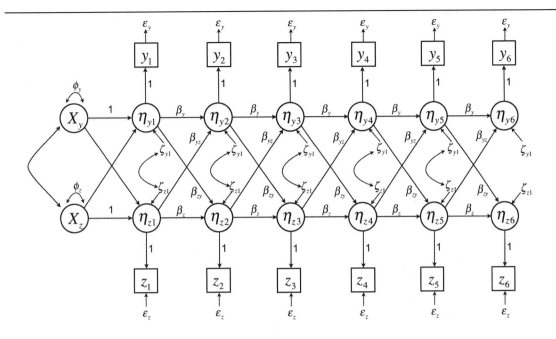

FIGURE 27.4. Cross-lagged panel design with six assessments.

panel designs involve examining two or more variables across time, where (1) each variable is modeled with an AR structure, (2) simultaneously assessed disturbances may correlate, and (3) each latent variable is also a function of previous values of the other latent variables (see also Kessler & Greenberg, 1981). A general model of a cross-lagged panel design for two constructs with a single manifest variable defining the latent structure is presented in Figure 27.4. Here are two variables, y_t and z_t, with corresponding latent values η_{y_t} and η_{z_t}, respectively. The AR structure is carried by β_y and β_z, and each construct may have a different AR structure.

The substantive benefit of the cross-lagged design lies in the relationships between the two variables. These cross-lagged temporal relationships, β_{yz} and β_{zy}, are often the substantive impetus for the model and the research. The former indicates the predictive relationship that has $\eta_{z_{t-1}}$ with η_{y_t}, controlling for $\eta_{z_{t-1}}$. In other words, does z predict changes in y? Similarly, β_{zy} indicates the predictive relationship that $\eta_{y_{t-1}}$ has with η_{z_t}, controlling for $\eta_{z_{t-1}}$. At the same point in time, the covariance between the two disturbances may be assessed by Ψ_{yz}. This captures the extent to which changes on

one variable are associated with changes on the other variable at the exact same point in time.

Simply observing a covariance between two variables y and z at a single point in time is insufficient without additional information to draw causal inferences (i.e., the well-known refrain "correlation does not imply causation"). Longitudinal data and models such as those in Figure 27.4 offer the ability to estimate and determine temporal precedence, a necessary condition for making stronger causal inferences. The cross-lagged relationships help identify the directionality of potential causal relationships between the two variables. For further discussion of causality in longitudinal designs see Finkel (1995) and Williams and Podsakoff (1989) for the panel design and West, Biesanz, and Kwok (2004) more generally.

Empirical Example

Participants in the previous empirical example provided responses to two items reflecting their levels of extraversion at each assessment. Specifically participants assessed the extent to which they were *talkative*

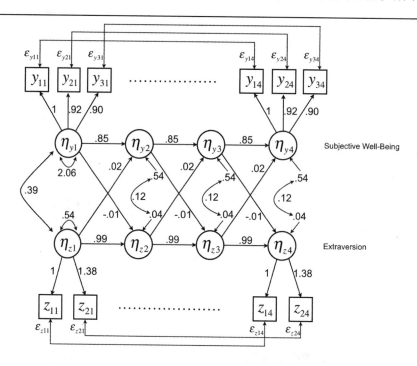

FIGURE 27.5. Cross-lagged panel design with four assessments between Subjective Well-Being and Extraversion. Note that SWB Items 1–3 correspond with the first three items listed in Note 1, and z_1 is *talkative* and z_2 is *energetic*.

and *energetic* using the same rating scale as SWB. The relationship between SWB and extraversion has long been well documented and is robust. This observed correlation has been suggested as a causal relationship, in that extraversion leads to SWB (e.g., see Harris, & Lightsey, 2005; Lee, Dean, & Jung, 2008; Lucas, Le, & Dyrenforth, 2008). The cross-lagged design allows this contemporaneous relationship to be examined prospectively. To simplify the presentation of the model only the first four assessments were modeled, as presented in Figure 27.5.

Overall model fit was acceptable: $\chi^2(147) = 226.44$, RMSEA = .062, $CI_{.90}$ = [.046, .078]. The AR nature of SWB is consistent with the previous models, where SWB was considered in isolation. In contrast, latent extraversion, defined by the two indicator variables, was remarkably stable across assessments with an AR parameter of $\hat{\beta}$ = .99, z = 25.39, p < .00001. This is consistent with a general trait of extraversion that did not change appreciably across monthly assessments; concordant with this interpretation, the latent disturbance

for extraversion had a variance that was marginally reliably different from 0, $\hat{\Psi}$ = .04, z = 1.94, p = .052. Of note, the correlation between latent SWB and extraversion was r = .37 at the first assessment, replicating previous research. In addition, the latent disturbances at each assessment significantly covaried: $\hat{\Psi}_{SWB,EX}$ = .12, z = 4.35, p < .0001.

Of substantive import, neither SWB nor extraversion was significantly temporally related to the other construct, z's < .4, nonsignificant. SWB did not meaningfully predict change in extraversion and neither did extraversion predict change in SWB. The only associations between these constructs in the present data set were contemporaneous temporal relationships—disturbances at the same point in time reliably covaried, but neither construct was associated with the other after accounting for the AR relationship. Interpretation of these results must be made cautiously, as they are predicated on the spacing of the assessments. A temporal design where assessments were much more closely spaced may have yielded different results. For more discussion of temporal spacing and causal models in the context of mediation see Shrout and Bolger (2002).

Discrete versus Continuous Time

In the traditional single construct autoregressive as well as cross-lagged panel models, as presented in Figures 27.1–27.5, time is an inherent feature of the model in that observations are ordered temporally. However, time is discrete in the sense that the timing between assessments is not part of the overall model. In other words, there is nothing present in the model to indicate or account for the spacing of assessments. Although they are spaced 1 month apart, they could just as well be 12 months or 10 years. Essentially time is treated as an ordered category. Why is this important? Even with equally spaced assessments, as in the current examples, the AR parameter is itself a function of the temporal spacing. In Figure 27.5 we observe a high AR parameter estimate for extraversion. This value would be much smaller if the assessments were substantially further apart. The scaling between assessments is inherently part of the AR parameter. Importantly, the impact of the timing between assessments on the AR parameter is not transparent.

This scaling issue becomes critical either when assessments are not equally spaced or when one wishes to compare results to other studies that used different spacing between assessments. If assessments are not equally spaced, then even with a stationary process the AR parameter would not be constant and *should not* be constrained to be equal across time, as in Figures 27.2–27.5. As well, comparing results of studies that used different spacing between assessments is equivalent to trying to determine the relative heights of two individuals reflected in different funhouse mirrors—even if they are the same height, the observed data will differ.

The solution to these problems is to reexpress the AR relationships in a manner that is independent of the scaling of time. To illustrate, consider the regression coefficient from Equation 27.2 expanded to include the intercept term as follows: $\eta_t = \beta_{0t} + \beta_{t,t-1}\eta_{t-1} + \zeta_t$. This expresses the relationship between a given assessment at point in time t as it is related to the previous assessment, $t - 1$. That the assessment in the empirical example is 1 month is irrelevant, as we could have scaled time as 30 days, a point considered in more detail shortly. Equation 27.2 can be rewritten as

$$\eta_t = f(c_0) + e^{c_1\Delta t}\eta_{t-1} + \zeta_t \qquad (27.6)$$

where e is the natural logarithm, Δt is the time between assessments (1 month in the present examples), and c_1 is the derivative of η_t with respect to t (i.e., $d\eta_t/dt = c_0 + c_1\eta_{t-1}$). Importantly, the coefficient c_1 can be determined from Equation 27.2 as $c_1 = \ln(\beta_{t,t-1})/\Delta t$. Note that $c_0 = \beta_{0t}\ln(\beta_{t,t-1})/(\Delta t(\ \beta_{t,t-1} - 1))$ when the mean structure is estimated in Equation 27.2 (see Finkel, 1995). Equation 27.6 provides the ability to determine the AR parameter for different spacings. Note that if $\Delta t = 1$, then $e^{c_1\Delta t} = \beta_{t,t-1}$. For different values of Δt the model-implied AR relationship can easily be determined. This allows one to compare models where the AR relationship is determined from different temporal spacings (e.g., monthly vs. yearly). As well, if the temporal spacing between assessments varies within the same study, nonlinear constraints between the AR parameter estimated can be placed to ensure that c_1 is constant for all parts of the model. The scale of time here is considered to be held constant (months, days, weeks, years, etc.). In the present example, the estimate of what the AR relationship for extraversion would be if assessments were made on an annual basis (12 months) is calculated as follows. The coefficient $c_1 = \ln(.99)/1 = -.01005$. The estimated AR parameter for 12 months is then $e^{-.01005\times12} = .886$. For more details and examples of constraints to ensure continuous time metric, as well as extensions to cross-lagged relationships and specific equations for the intercept coefficient, see Oud (2007) and Finkel (1995, pp. 16–19).

Analytical Models with AR Components

Very similar statistical models are often developed in different disciplines to serve slightly different functions. Consequently, different terminology and notation will often refer to the same essential concepts and parameters. More troublesome is the tendency for particular analytical techniques to become entwined with specific research questions and designs carrying inferential limitations that are not inherent in the analytical technique. Panel analysis and cross-lagged panel designs in general are frequently employed when the motivating question is one of causal direction among a set of constructs. The focus is on understanding relationships among variables. This approach is eschewed when the motivating question relates to understanding and modeling growth and change within individuals. This latter question is often associated with techniques such as latent curve analysis (McArdle, Chapter 32, this volume), also known as latent growth curves. The AR model is aesthetically unpleasing from a developmental perspective, as it does not provide a succinct summary or model of an individual's change over time. It is inherently stochastic in asserting that unknown— and, more importantly, unmodeled—random disturbances or shocks alter the latent construct's score for each individual. However, these are not incompatible perspectives or models. Change and growth over time can be lawful, systematic, and modeled. At the same time, there can be random disturbances that change the latent constructs. An integration of an autoregressive model with the latent curve modeling framework is provided in the aptly named autoregressive latent trajectory (ALT) model (Bollen & Curran, 2004, 2006; Curran & Bollen, 2001). This modeling framework allows for individual differences in a functional basis form of growth over time that is coupled with an AR component on the observed measures, as opposed to the latent constructs. As a consequence, this modeling assumption, which can be modified, does allow measurement uniquenesses to promulgate across time.

Kenny and Zautra (1995) proposed an extension of the AR modeling framework where the AR effect occurs at the latent level in a state variable—the trait–state error model. At the same time, a general trait latent factor provides stable individual difference across time. Further extensions of this modeling framework are found in the trait–state occasion model (e.g., Ciesla, Cole, & Steiger, 2007; Cole, Martin, & Steiger, 2005). More extensive discussion of these frameworks is provided in Cole (Chapter 34, this volume).

An alternative formulation of the AR model is provided within the general latent change score (LCS) modeling framework (see McArdle, 2001). Here the change on a construct across sequential assessments is modeled as a latent variable. This modeling framework more closely aligns with the developmental perspective and desire for assessing change within individuals. At the same time, cross-lagged panel designs can easily be accommodated within this model. For a brief and accessible introduction to this framework, see Ferrer and McArdle (2010).

SUMMARY AND CONCLUSION

The present chapter has reviewed the AR longitudinal model and focused on empirical examples examining

the relatively simple case of a single lag, that is, AR(1). Extensions to the basic AR model include more lags (e.g., AR(p) models), as well as models where there are trait factors and or growth factors. In addition, the choice of where to model the AR effect carries implications for the interpretation of the basic nature of the construct of interest. AR effects can be modeled as functions of the observed manifest variables, the latent trait construct at a given point in time, or state components. The choice of these different models carries substantive implications and thus requires well-articulated theoretical models of change in order to properly assess the appropriate model for a given construct and longitudinal design.

ACKNOWLEDGMENTS

This research was supported by Social Sciences and Humanities Research Council of Canada Grant Nos. SSHRC 410-2005-2287 and 410-2008-2643 to Jeremy C. Biesanz.

NOTE

1. The five items are (1) "In most ways my life is close to my ideal," (2) "The conditions of my life are excellent," (3) "I am satisfied with my life," (4) "So far I have gotten the important things I want in life," and (5) "If I could live my life over, I would change almost nothing."

REFERENCES

Bollen, K. A., & Curran, P. J. (2004). Autoregressive latent trajectory (ALT) models: A synthesis of two traditions. *Sociological Methods and Research, 32*, 336–383.

Bollen, K. A., & Curran, P. J. (2006). *Latent curve models: A structural equation approach* (Wiley Series on Probability and Mathematical Statistics). Hoboken, NJ: Wiley.

Browne, M. W., & Zhang, G. (2007). Repeated time series models for learning data. In S. M. Boker & M. J. Wenger (Eds.), *Data analytic techniques for dynamical systems in the social and behavioral sciences* (pp. 25–46). Mahwah, NJ: Erlbaum.

Ciesla, J. A., Cole, D. A., & Steiger, J. H. (2007). Extending the trait-state-occasion model: How important is within-wave measurement equivalence? *Structural Equation Modeling, 14*, 77–97.

Cole, D. A., Martin, N. C., & Steiger, J. H. (2005). Empirical and conceptual problems with longitudinal trait-state models: Support for a trait-state-occasion model. *Psychological Methods, 10*, 3–20.

Collins, L. M. (2006). Analysis of longitudinal data: The integration of theoretical model, temporal design and statistical model. *Annual Review of Psychology, 57*, 505–528.

Collins, L. M., & Horn, J. L. (1991). *Best methods for the analysis of change*. Washington, DC: American Psychological Association.

Collins, L. M., & Sayer, A. G. (2001). *New methods for the analysis of change*. Washington, DC: American Psychological Association.

Curran, P. J., & Bollen, K. A. (2001). The best of both worlds: Combining autoregressive and latent curve models. In L. Collins & A. Sayer (Eds.), *New methods for the analysis of change* (pp. 107–135). Washington, DC: American Psychological Association.

Diener, E., Emmons, R. A., Larsen, R. J., & Griffen, S. (1985). The Subjective Well-Being scale. *Journal of Personality Assessment, 49*, 71–75.

Ferrer, E., & McArdle, J. J. (2010). Longitudinal modeling of developmental changes in psychological research. *Current Directions in Psychological Science, 19*, 149–154.

Finkel, S. E. (1995). *Causal analysis with panel data* (QASS #105). Thousand Oaks, CA: Sage.

Gallagher, M. W., Lopez, S. J., & Preacher, K. J. (2009). The hierarchical structure of well-being. *Journal of Personality, 77*, 1025–1049.

Guttman, L. (1950). The basis for scalogram analysis. In S. A. Stouffer, L. Guttman, E. A. Suchman, P. Lazarsfeld, S. A. Star, & J. A. Clausen (Eds.), *Measurement and prediction* (pp. 60–90). Princeton, NJ: Princeton University Press.

Harris, C. W. (1963). Canonical factor models for the description of change. In *Problems in measuring change* (pp. 138–155). Madison: University of Wisconsin Press.

Harris, P. R., & Lightsey, O. R., Jr. (2005). Constructive thinking as a mediator of the relationship between extraversion, neuroticism, and subjective well-being. *European Journal of Personality, 19*, 409–426.

Hershberger, S. L., Molenaar, P. C. M., & Corneal, S. E. (1996). A hierarchy of univariate and multivariate structural time series models. In G. A. Marcoulides & R. E. Schumacker (Eds.), *Advanced structural equation modeling: Issues and techniques* (pp. 159–194). Mahwah, NJ: Erlbaum.

Jones, M. B. (1959). *Simplex theory* (Monograph No. 3). Pensacola, FL: U.S. Naval Aviation Medicine.

Jones, M. B. (1960). *Molar correctional analysis* (Monograph No. 4). Pensacola, FL: U.S. Naval Aviation Medicine.

Jöreskog, K. G. (1970). Estimation and testing of simplex models. *British Journal of Mathematical and Statistical Psychology, 23*, 121–145.

Jöreskog, K. G. (1979). Statistical models and methods for analysis of longitudinal data. In J. Magidson (Ed.), *Advances in factor analysis and structural equation models* (pp. 129–169). Cambridge, MA: Abt Books.

Jöreskog, K. G., & Sörbom, D. (1996). *LISREL 8: User's reference guide*. Chicago: Scientific Software International.

Kenny, D. A., & Zautra, A. (1995). The trait-state-error model for multiwave data. *Journal of Consulting and Clinical Psychology, 63*, 52–59.

Kessler, R. C., & Greenberg, D. F. (1981). *Linear panel analysis*. New York: Academic Press.

Lazarsfeld, P. F., & Fiske, M. (1938). The panel as a new tool for measuring opinion. *Public Opinion Quarterly, 2*, 596–612.

Lee, R. M., Dean, B. L., & Jung, K.-R. (2008). Social connectedness, extraversion, and subjective well-being: Testing a mediation model. *Personality and Individual Differences, 45*, 414–419.

Lucas, R. E., Le, K., & Dyrenforth, P. S. (2008). Explaining the extraversion/positive affect relation: Sociability cannot account for extraverts' greater happiness. *Journal of Personality, 76*, 385–414.

Marsh, H. W. (1993). Stability of individual differences in multiwave panel studies: Comparison of simplex models and one-factor models. *Journal of Educational Measurement, 30*, 157–183.

McArdle, J. J. (2001). A latent difference score approach to longitudinal dynamic structural analysis. In R. Cudeck, S. du Toit, & D. Sörbom (Eds.), *Structural equation modeling: Present and future* (pp. 342–380). Lincolnwood, IL: Scientific Software International.

Oud, J. H. L. (2007). Continuous time modeling of reciprocal relationships in the cross-lagged panel design. In S. M. Boker & M. J. Wenger (Eds.), *Data analytic techniques for dynamical systems in the social and behavioral sciences* (pp. 87–129). Mahwah, NJ: Erlbaum.

Shrout, P. E., & Bolger, N. (2002). Mediation in experimental and nonexperimental studies: New procedures and recommendations. *Psychological Methods, 7*, 422–445.

Sivo, S. A., & Willson, V. L. (2000). Modeling causal error structures in longitudinal panel data: A Monte Carlo study. *Structural Equation Modeling, 7*, 174–205.

West, S. G., Biesanz, J. C., & Kwok, O.-M. (2004). Within-subject and longitudinal experiments: Design and analysis issues. In C. Sansone, C. C. Morf, & A. T. Panter (Eds.), *The SAGE handbook of methods in social psychology* (pp. 287–312). Thousand Oaks, CA: Sage.

Williams, L. J., & Podsakoff, P. M. (1989). Longitudinal field methods for studying reciprocal relationships in organizational behavior research: Toward improved causal analysis. In B. M. Staw & L. L. Cummings (Eds.), *Research in organizational behavior* (Vol. 11, pp. 247–292). Greenwich, CT: JAI Press.

CHAPTER 28

Scale Construction and Development Using Structural Equation Modeling

Tenko Raykov

Researchers in the social, behavioral, educational, and biomedical sciences are frequently concerned with construction and development of multiple-component measuring instruments. Over the past several decades, such instruments have become highly popular in these and cognate disciplines. A major feature responsible for their widespread use is the fact that they provide multiple converging pieces of information about studied latent constructs of main interest, such as abilities, attitudes, traits, or attributes. For these and related reasons, scales, tests, inventories, self-reports, subscales, testlets, questionnaires, test batteries, and so forth, are currently very often utilized behavioral measurement instruments for collecting data on examined phenomena. (In the remainder of this chapter I employ synonymously the terms "scale" and "multiple-component measuring instrument," or "instrument" for short.)

A particular characteristic of many investigations in the social and behavioral disciplines is their concern with latent variables and their relationships (cf. Raykov & Marcoulides, 2011). Theories in these sciences are oftentimes developed in terms of unobservable dimensions that can be only indirectly evaluated, referred to as "constructs" in this chapter. While the constructs cannot be directly measured, their manifestations in overt behavior can be evaluated using various measuring instruments that consist of multiple components, such as the aforementioned scales. Being only proxies of the constructs of substantive interest, their evaluated manifestations—often referred to as "indicators"—typically contain sizable measurement error. The latter may be considered to consist of random error of measurement entangled with possible discrepancies between the targeted latent construct and what is actually evaluated with the pertinent indicator. Reducing as much as possible this complex measurement error is of critical relevance for the development of high-quality instruments, which are essential for construct validation, theory development, knowledge accumulation, and progress in the social and behavioral sciences.

A methodology that is especially suited for addressing many of these and related concerns is structural equation modeling (SEM). This comprehensive modeling approach provides also a means for examining psychometric properties of multiple-component measuring instruments, and contributes in this way substantially to the enhancement of their quality. One special feature of the SEM methodology, which is of particular relevance in this endeavor, is the fact that models developed within it explicitly account for measurement error by including such terms and, specifically, their variances among the model parameters. These models allow evaluation of important aspects of measurement quality of considered scales, and can indicate possible courses of instrument improvement.

This chapter deals with the potential that SEM offers to behavioral and social researchers involved in scale construction and development, an activity in which they frequently engage in their quest for high-quality measuring instruments. The plan of the chapter is as follows. It begins with a discussion of a modeling approach that permits point and interval estimation of important indices characterizing an original set of items considered for inclusion in a scale of interest, attending also to issues pertaining to the study of their latent structure. Revision of resulting tentative instrument versions is discussed next, including reliability and criterion validity evaluation, as well as discussion of their change due to removal or addition of scale components. The discussion is subsequently extended to the concepts of maximal reliability and validity. Applications of the general modeling approach with missing data are finally attended to, as is the two-level setup where studied subjects are nested within higher-order units. Throughout the chapter, repeated reference is made to the application of this SEM approach in empirical research. Source codes for the popular software Mplus (Muthén & Muthén, 2010) and R (Venables, Smith, and the R Core Development Team, 2007), which accomplish the underlying parameter estimation, model testing, and instrument development analyses, are provided at the book's website (*www.handbookofsem.com*).

SELECTION FROM AN INITIAL ITEM SET

Scale construction and development is usually a multistage process. At its beginning one may view the initial selection from a relatively large set of items, which are deemed on substantive grounds to be indicative of a latent construct of research interest, as an important activity. In the rest of the chapter it is assumed that these items are (1) prespecified—that is, given or fixed, rather than sampled from potentially a very large pool to which inferences are to be made; and (2) administered to a large sample from a subject population of concern—the population for which the measuring instrument is being constructed. The initial item set is usually created beforehand based on expertise and thorough substantive and validity considerations, as well as accumulated knowledge in the pertinent subject-matter domain; the specifics of its development go beyond the confines of this discussion and are not dealt with here (see, e.g., Downing & Haladyna, 2006).

Once the initial set of items becomes available, SEM can be used for evaluation of their interrelationships—an activity often referred to as "classical item analysis"—as well as for examination of their latent structure (Raykov & Marcoulides, 2011). In classical item analysis, interest frequently centers on item-difficulty-related parameters, where applicable, and interitem as well as item–total score correlations (possibly adjusted for corresponding item). As is well known (e.g., McDonald, 1999), in this context a given item's "difficulty parameter" is defined as the probability of correct response in a studied population, and evaluated in a sample by the proportion of "correct" answers, or "yes," "endorse," "present" responses. (For simplicity, in the rest of the chapter, such a response is referred to as "correct," the pertinent item as "binary scored," and this parameter as "classical item difficulty," abbreviated CID.) With Likert-type items, CID is not readily defined but examination of their distributions (empirical response frequencies) can be quite useful. The CID parameter can be especially informative when constructing measuring instruments that target particular parts of a population distribution on a studied construct (e.g., low-, or alternatively, high-achieving students), as well as in general ability range evaluation. The interitem and (adjusted) item–total correlations may indicate items with weak relations to the bulk of the item set or intended overall score that may then be deemed undesirable to retain in an initial version of the scale, based on substantive considerations (e.g., Crocker & Algina, 1986). The value of these analyses is enhanced substantially when carried out in conjunction with possibly repeated examination of the latent structure of the initial and related item sets, a topic addressed shortly, since interitem and item–total correlations may be hard to interpret—if not uninformative or even misleading—for composites of items with unknown underlying structure.

Evaluation of Classical Item Analysis Indices

Point estimation of CID for binary scored items and especially interitem and item–total correlations for discrete (categorical, ordinal) items has been possible using SEM since the 1970s, and a large body of pertinent literature has accumulated over the past 30 years or so (see, e.g., Muthén, 1984, for an underlying three-step estimation procedure, eventually employing the weighted least squares method). While their point estimation is relatively direct, SEM can also be used as outlined next to obtain standard errors and confidence intervals for these parameters, as well for the purpose of latent structure examination of a considered item set, instrument, or versions of it that are of interest (cf. Raykov & Marcoulides, 2011).

Evaluation of Classical Item Difficulty

Suppose one were concerned with estimation of classical item analysis parameters for a given set $\wp$ of p binary scored items, denoted $X_1, X_2, \ldots, X_p$ ($p \geq 1$). Designate by π_i the population CID parameter of X_i, that is, the probability of correct response on it ($1 \leq i \leq p$; $0 < \pi_i < 1$ is assumed in this chapter, to avoid triviality considerations). In a sample, as is well known, π_i can be estimated by the relative frequency of correct response, designated $\hat{\pi}_i$, whose variance is (e.g., Agresti & Finlay, 2009)

$$\mathrm{Var}(\hat{\pi}_i) = \frac{\pi_i(1-\pi_i)}{n} \tag{28.1}$$

where n is sample size, caret symbolizes estimator of the parameter underneath, and Var(.) denotes variance ($i = 1, \ldots, p$). The variance (Equation 28.1) can itself be estimated in empirical research by, say,

$$\mathrm{V\hat{a}r}(\hat{\pi}_i) = \frac{\hat{\pi}_i(1-\hat{\pi}_i)}{n} = v_i^2 \tag{28.2}$$

(with a positive square root taken to obtain v_i; $i = 1, \ldots, p$). Since π_i as a probability is bounded by 0 and 1, a confidence interval (CI) for π_i must entirely reside within the interval (0, 1) in order for it not to contain meaningless values (e.g., Browne, 1982). This can be ensured by first constructing a CI for a suitable monotone increasing transformation of π_i, such as the logit:

$$\kappa_i = \ln(\pi_i/(1-\pi_i)) \tag{28.3}$$

where ln(.) denotes natural logarithm, which leads to the transformed CID estimator

$$\hat{\kappa}_i = \ln(\hat{\pi}_i/(1-\hat{\pi}_i)) \tag{28.4}$$

($i = 1, \ldots, p$). Its standard error can be rendered with the popular delta-method as

$$SE(\hat{\kappa}_i) = v_i/[\hat{\pi}_i(1-\hat{\pi}_i)] \tag{28.5}$$

where $SE(.)$ denotes standard error ($i = 1, \ldots, p$; for a discussion of the delta-method, see, e.g., Raykov & Marcoulides, 2004; cf. Browne, 1982). Since $\hat{\kappa}_i$ is a maximum likelihood (ML) estimator, being a function of such, $\hat{\kappa}_i$ is asymptotically normal; thus, a large-sample $100(1-\delta)\%$-CI ($0 < \delta < 1$) for κ_i is

$$(\hat{\kappa}_i - z_{\delta/2}SE(\hat{\kappa}_i), \hat{\kappa}_i + z_{\delta/2}SE(\hat{\kappa}_i)) \tag{28.6}$$

where $z_{\delta/2}$ denotes the $(1 - \delta/2)$th quantile of the standard normal distribution ($i = 1, \ldots, p$). Then a large-sample $100(1-\delta)\%$-CI for the CID parameter π_i of actual interest is furnished via the inverse of the logit function, namely, the logistic function:

$$(1/(1+e^{-\kappa_{i,lo}}), 1/(1+e^{-\kappa_{i,up}})) \tag{28.7}$$

where $\kappa_{i,lo}$ and $\kappa_{i,up}$ are the lower and upper endpoints of the CI (28.6), respectively ($i = 1, \ldots, p$).

The estimate of the CID, $\hat{\pi}_i$, and the limits of its CI (28.7) can be readily calculated for a given item using the popular SEM program Mplus (Muthén & Muthén, 2010) in two estimation steps. In the first, one carries out basic analyses for the set of items under consideration in order to obtain $\hat{\pi}_i$. (This step can also provide a test of the unidimensionality hypothesis for the initial, or subsequently considered, item set; see below.) In the second step, the estimate $\hat{\pi}_i$ is used via Equations 28.5, 28.6, and 28.7 to obtain the CI limits for a prespecified confidence level. The source codes for both analytic steps are provided in Appendix 1 on the handbook webpage (*www.handbookofsem.com*) for this chapter.[1] As an alternative to the second step, one can use the popular software R with a specifically defined function (see the R function 'ci.cid' in Appendix 1; in the rest of the chapter, reference will be made to numbered appendices available on that webpage). The CID estimates and corresponding CIs provide important insights into the items' psychometric properties, which, in addition to substantive and validity related considerations, allow a researcher to make a more informed decision at this stage as to which items from the original set $\wp$ could be further considered in the scale construction endeavor. In particular, as indicated earlier, items with CIs for their CID that are close to 0 could be considered for retention in an instrument aimed at screening high achievers (high-ability subjects); conversely, items with CID CIs close to 1 could be suitable for measures helping to identify persons at the low end of the underlying latent dimension; and items with CID CIs in the middle range would likely be useful in general ability range measurement (e.g., Crocker & Algina, 1986).

Estimation of Interitem and Item–Total Interrelationship Indices

Interitem and (adjusted) item–total correlations have been traditionally of interest in classical item analysis and especially in early phases of scale construction, since they contain information about the extent to which items in a given set relate to one another, as well as to the overall sum score. In particular one may expect that if an item set evaluates a common underlying attribute, the interrelationships among its members will be pronounced, as will be the relationships of each item with the total score (possibly adjusted for the item by not including it in the overall sum). The methodological literature over the past several decades indicates that when one is interested in interitem relationships, it is generally more appropriate to be concerned with their polychoric correlations (e.g., McDonald, 1999). If one considers in addition an (approximately) continuous variable, such as the sum score of certain items, it would be generally more suitable to be concerned with the pertinent polyserial correlations when evaluating the relationships between individual items and that score.

The polychoric and polyserial correlation coefficients have been developed based on the assumption of an underlying normal variable (UNV) behind each categorical item or component (e.g., Muthén, 1984; Skrondal & Rabe-Hesketh, 2004; cf. Raykov & Mels, 2009; in the remainder of the chapter, I use the terms "item" and "component" interchangeably, indicating their nature—i.e., continuous or discrete—where necessary). In the rest of this section, the items in a given set (e.g., $X_1, X_2, \ldots, X_p$) are not necessarily assumed to be binary or evaluated using a binary format, but can be categorical (e.g., Likert-type or ordinal measures; $p > 1$). To facilitate the developments that follow, denote by $X_1^*, X_2^*, \ldots, X_p^*$ these items' corresponding UNVs. (If any of the variables $X_1, X_2, \ldots, X_p$ are continuous, or it is decided that they be treated as such, then one can set $X_i^* = X_i$ in the following discussion; $1 \leq i \leq p$.) As mentioned earlier, the degree to which $X_1, X_2, \ldots, X_p$ are interrelated is reflected in their associated polychoric (polyserial) correlations, for the purposes of this section (i.e., in the elements of the correlation matrix of the underlying variables $X_1^*, X_2^*, \ldots, X_p^*$). Similarly, the extent to which each item is related to the total score is reflected in the polyserial correlations, which are the correlations between each of $X_1^*, X_2^*, \ldots, X_p^*$ and the total sum score $X = X_1 + X_2 + \ldots + X_p$ (possibly adjusted for an item by subtracting its score from X; e.g., Jöreskog & Sörbom, 1996).

Point estimation of polychoric and polyserial correlations can be readily accomplished using SEM, as discussed in detail in the literature over the past 30 years or so (e.g., Muthén, 1984; Muthén & Muthén, 2010). Their interval estimation is similarly possible using the same modeling framework, as described in Raykov and Marcoulides (2011; see also Raykov & Mels, 2009). Specifically, if one denotes generically by ρ a polychoric or polyserial correlation of concern, a large-sample $100(1 - \delta)\%$-CI ($0 < \delta < 1$) for the Fisher-transform $z(\rho)$ of ρ, defined as $z(\rho) = .5\ln[(1 + \rho)/(1 - \rho)]$, is

$$(z(\hat{\rho}) - z_{\delta/2}SE(\hat{\rho}) / (1-\hat{\rho}^2), z(\hat{\rho}) + z_{\delta/2}SE(\hat{\rho}) / (1-\hat{\rho}^2)) \quad \textbf{(28.8)}$$

where $SE(\hat{\rho})$ is the standard error of the polychoric/polyserial correlation estimator (cf. Browne, 1982). Then the large-sample $100(1 - \delta)\%$-CI ($0 < \delta < 1$) for the correlation ρ of concern is furnished via the inverse of Fisher's z-transform:

$$((\exp(2z_{\rho,lo}) - 1)/(\exp(2z_{\rho,lo}) + 1), \quad \textbf{(28.9)}$$
$$(\exp(2z_{\rho,up}) - 1)/(\exp(2z_{\rho,up}) + 1))$$

with $\exp(.)$ indicating the exponential function and $z_{\rho,lo}$, $z_{\rho,up}$ denoting the lower and upper limits, respectively, of the interval (28.8).

The interitem (polychoric) correlation estimates and standard errors can be easily obtained with the software Mplus using the basic analysis procedure discussed in the preceding section on CID evaluation (Step 1), and CIs for these correlations are furnished as outlined below in this paragraph. To render item–total (polyserial) correlation estimates, one includes in that analysis the total score X. (If interested in an adjusted item–total correlation, this score is defined as the sum of all items but the one in question.) This activity is readily accomplished with the corresponding Mplus command file in Appendix 1 of the handbook website (*www.handbookofsem.com*) (Step 3). Once having obtained the interitem and/or (adjusted) item–total correlation estimates and their standard errors, use of the

R function 'ci.pc' in Appendix 1 can be made to furnish CIs for these parameters. (Application of Mplus is also possible for this purpose, though it is at present somewhat more tedious; e.g., Raykov & Marcoulides, 2011). The point and interval estimates of interitem and in particular item–total correlations are best viewed as preliminary guides for selection from an initial item set. They become more helpful, as mentioned earlier, when used in conjunction with substantive and validity considerations, as well as with results from examination of the latent structure of the original and related item sets (see next section).

In conclusion of this section, another avenue for interval estimation of classical item analysis indices is provided by the bootstrap methodology (e.g., Efron & Tibshirani, 1993). Such an application, in addition to being generally quite computer intensive at present, would initially need evidence that with increasing sample size and number of resamples, the pertinent bootstrap distribution (i.e., of the CID and above polychoric/polyserial correlation estimates) indeed approaches the sampling distribution of the corresponding index estimator (see, e.g., Bollen & Stein, 1993, for counterexamples in a more general setting and related references). It is left to future studies to pursue such evidence and examine more thoroughly the properties of resulting bootstrap CIs, as well as to make possible recommendations with regard to choice of method for interval estimation of classical item analysis indices (under corresponding conditions, if applicable).

LATENT STRUCTURE EXAMINATION OF AN ITEM SET

The point and interval estimates of interitem and item–total interrelationship indices obtained with the procedure outlined in the last section, in addition to substantive and validity considerations, can substantially aid the process of selecting from a potentially large original item set $\wp$ a subset that is of interest for the purpose of measuring a latent construct of concern. Denote the items in a set under consideration by $Y_1, Y_2, \ldots, Y_q$, and let $\underline{Y} = (Y_1, Y_2, \ldots, Y_q)'$ be their vector (underlining denotes vector and priming transposition in this chapter; in this section, $2 < q \leq p$ is assumed).[2] As indicated earlier, a main step in the scale construction process consists of examination of the latent structure of the item set $\underline{Y}$. To this end, exploratory factor analysis (EFA) can be carried out for $\underline{Y}$ on a random half of the available sample of studied subjects. EFA is a statistical method covered in detail in other sources (e.g., Cudeck & MacCallum, 2007, and references therein), and its discussion will not be part of the present chapter. The particular value of an EFA application on the set $\underline{Y}$ consists in the possibility of generating hypotheses about its latent structure that can be tested on the remaining half of the original sample. The hypothesis of unidimensionality (homogeneity) of $\underline{Y}$ is then of special interest, since most behavioral measuring instruments are constructed so as to allow evaluation of a single latent construct. In the rest of this section, it is assumed that this is the aim of a scale construction effort, and the alternative of general structure scales is addressed subsequently.

When EFA suggests a single substantively interpretable construct underlying the item set $\underline{Y}$, it is important to test the unidimensionality hypothesis for $\underline{Y}$ using the second random half of the original sample. To this end, SEM can be employed as outlined in the next paragraph. If, however, EFA indicates two or more meaningful constructs as latent sources of variability in the elements of $\underline{Y}$, the appropriate of two avenues may be pursued. Along the first, the possibility of constructing correspondingly two or more (sub)scales from the item set $\underline{Y}$ can be examined, using pertinent subject-matter considerations. In that case, SEM can be utilized subsequently on each hypothetical (sub)scale, for the purpose of testing its own unidimensionality (see below). Alternatively, one may consider dropping items from the set $\underline{Y}$ that are associated with relatively small/weak loadings (and possibly large unique factor/residual variances) on a latent construct of substantive interest that is suggested by the remaining items in $\underline{Y}$. Denote by $\underline{Z}$ the vector of components (scale) focused on in the former case, or remaining in $\underline{Y}$ if one decides to remove such "weak" items after additional subject-matter and validity related considerations. (If no such items are found in $\underline{Y}$, set $\underline{Z} = \underline{Y}$ in the remaining discussion in this section; see also Note 2.) For the purposes of this chapter, the set of components $\underline{Z}$ may be considered a prototype of a scale of interest, which will be subjected to the modeling efforts that follow.

As a next step in the process of instrument development, the unidimensionality hypothesis for the item set $\underline{Z}$—or subsets of it corresponding to subscales of interest—is examined. (In this paragraph, the notation $\underline{Z}$ is used generically to denote a set of items under consideration.) To this end, SEM can be used by employing the analytic framework of confirmatory factor analysis

(CFA; e.g., Jöreskog & Sörbom, 1996; Muthén, 1984; Muthén & Muthén, 2010). Within this framework, an empirical test of homogeneity for $\underline{Z}$ (or appropriate subset) amounts to testing the following congeneric model (Jöreskog, 1971):

$$\underline{Z} = \underline{a} + \underline{b}\,T + \underline{E} \qquad (28.10)$$

where T denotes the assumed common latent construct evaluated by the items in question, $\underline{a}$ is a correspondingly sized vector of intercepts (see below), $\underline{b}$ the vector of observed measure loadings on T, and $\underline{E}$ is the vector of error terms with zero means and assumed positive variances, and uncorrelated with T. When examining the hypothesis of unidimensionality in an empirical setting where some of the components involved are discrete, the corresponding model of relevance is

$$\underline{Z}^* = \underline{\tau} + \underline{b}f + \underline{e} \qquad (28.11)$$

where $\underline{Z}^*$ is the vector consisting of the UNVs for the discrete components augmented by the remaining continuous components (if any), $\underline{\tau}$ is a vector with pertinent thresholds, and f is the common factor underlying $\underline{Z}^*$.

Fitting the models in Equations 28.10 and 28.11 to the second half of the original sample of subjects is accomplished using a parameter estimation method that corresponds to the observed variable distribution. Specifically, ML can be used then with multinormality, robust maximum likelihood (MLR) with mild deviations from normality (other than those resulting from piling of cases at extreme ends of a measure, clustering effect, or highly discrete items), or weighted least squares with more serious deviations from normality (and fairly large samples; Muthén & Muthén, 2010). Source codes for conducting these analyses using Mplus are provided in Appendix 2 of this handbook's website (*www.handbookofsem.com*). Lack of fit of the model in Equations 28.10 and 28.11 may be the result of the presence in $\underline{Z}$ of items that are still weak if not poor indicators of a latent construct evaluated by the remaining elements of $\underline{Z}$. These indicators will be typically associated with relatively small (perhaps even nonsignificant) loadings and/or large residual error variances relative to the majority of the items in $\underline{Z}$. Dropping these items subsequently from $\underline{Z}$ following substantive and validity related considerations, which would lead to an item subset denoted $\underline{U}$ with the property that unidimensionality is found plausible for it, can be expected to provide a considerably better tentative measuring instrument

for the latent construct(s) of interest. (If no items are removed thereby from $\underline{Z}$, set $\underline{U} = \underline{Z}$ in the remainder of the chapter; as indicated earlier, in case homogeneity is not plausible for $\underline{U}$, it may be possible to develop more than one scale from it with the methods in this chapter.) Evaluation and improvement of the psychometric qualities of this tentative scale(s) are of concern in the next steps of the instrument development process.

REVISION OF TENTATIVE SCALE VERSIONS

At the end of the activities outlined in the last section, one may consider the resulting item subset $\underline{U}$ as representing a tentative scale for measuring a latent construct of interest. The questions next concern the psychometric features of this scale, and whether particular revisions of it may be undertaken, if need be, to enhance its quality. To this end, denote first by U the sum of the items in the set $\underline{U}$, that is,

$$U = U_1 + U_2 + \ldots + U_r \qquad (28.12)$$

where r ($r \geq 1$) denotes their number. (For simplicity of reference, I often refer to U as a "scale" in the rest of this discussion.) In the remainder of the chapter, the overall sum score of scales under consideration (i.e., unit-weighted scales like U) will be of primary interest, since this is the case having drawn so far the most attention in empirical social and behavioral research. I also address in a later section the case of weighted linear combinations W of the items U_j ($j = 1, \ldots, r$), which are defined as

$$W = w_1 U_1 + w_2 U_2 + \ldots + w_r U_r \qquad (28.13)$$

where $w_1, w_2, \ldots, w_r$ are corresponding weights with certain optimality properties and need not be known beforehand ($r > 1$).

Main indices of psychometric quality of behavioral measuring instruments are reliability and validity, which have received a great deal of discussion in the literature (e.g., Crocker & Algina, 1986; McDonald, 1999; and references therein). According to the fundamental classical test theory (CTT) decomposition, $U = T_U + E_U$ holds, with T_U and E_U being the true and error score of U (e.g., Zimmerman, 1975). In this chapter, I use the traditional and widely adopted definition of "reliability" as the ratio of true variance to observed variance in the studied subject population:

$$\rho_U = \text{Var}(T_U)/\text{Var}(U) \qquad \textbf{(28.14)}$$

where ρ_U denotes the reliability coefficient of the scale U (assuming $\text{Var}(U) > 0$, which can be considered fulfilled for most current research in the social and behavioral disciplines; for convenience and simplicity, in the remainder of the chapter I nearly always refer to the ρ_U as "reliability").

Unlike reliability, the concept of validity—which can be seen as the bottom line of measurement (e.g., Shadish, Cook, & Campbell, 2002)—cannot be quantified in a single index. The reason is that validity is a multifaceted and very comprehensive notion, with diverse interrelated aspects of relevance in various empirical settings in behavioral and social research (e.g., Messick, 1995). A particular form of validity, "criterion validity," is often evaluated by the correlation between a criterion variable, denoted C, say, and a scale score under consideration. Accordingly,

$$v_U = \text{Corr}(U, C) \qquad \textbf{(28.15)}$$

is the criterion validity coefficient for the scale U, where $\text{Corr}(.,.)$ designates correlation (assuming $\text{Var}(C) > 0$). Similarly evaluated as appropriate correlation coefficients are the discriminant and convergent validity coefficients, specifically as (linear) interrelationship indices between a scale score in question and other observed measures that on substantive grounds would be expected to be closely or, alternatively, weakly related to that score (e.g., Campbell & Fiske, 1959; Raykov, 2011b).

From the definition of reliability in Equation 28.14, ρ_U represents the percentage of true individual differences in observed individual differences. That is, "reliability" is the degree to which there are true individual differences in an observed score, such as those generated by the scale U. Since reliability is also equal to the squared correlation between true and observed score (when both have positive variances, as assumed in the remainder), ρ_U is thus the R^2 index of (1) the regression of true score upon observed score, and (2) the regression of observed score upon true score. Hence, reliability gives the proportion of observed scale variance that is explained by the true scale score and, conversely, the proportion of true scale variance that is explained by observed scale variability. No less important, recalling the classical correction for attenuation and related formulas (e.g., Crocker & Algina, 1986; Raykov & Marcoulides, 2011), the reliability coefficients of two

fallible measures—as are most measures in social and behavioral research—"connect" true and observed correlations. With this important property, reliability coefficients allow evaluation of true correlations of actual interest based on available observed correlations among studied construct measures. Further, low reliability implies substantial error of measurement and/or limited true individual differences, and hence limited capability of differentiation between the subjects' true scale scores of real concern using observed scale scores. Conversely, high reliability implies substantial true individual differences and/or limited error variance, that is, enhanced capability of differentiation among subjects' true scores using their observed scale scores. By virtue of all these features, reliability is an essential concept that permits social and behavioral scholars to obtain insights into the true relationships among examined aspects of observed phenomena and the individual differences on studied latent dimensions.

Similarly, "validity"—being the bottom line of measurement—is a critical concept that reflects the degree to which an instrument indeed evaluates the construct it purports to measure. Low validity implies that inferences based on the observed scores are likely not to be veridical and are potentially seriously misleading. For these reasons, high validity and high reliability are essential psychometric quality indices of measuring instruments. When constructing and developing social and behavioral scales, therefore, it is of special relevance to ensure that these indices are sufficiently high for measuring instruments recommended for further use. The process of comprehensive validity assessment consists of multiple activities that are characterized also by thorough and multifaceted substantive considerations specific to the pertinent subject-matter domain. In the remainder of this chapter I will be concerned only with "criterion validity," the available validity coefficient as mentioned, which quantifies particular aspects of validity pertaining to the relationship between a scale score in question and a prespecified criterion measure. (The following discussion applies also to concurrent and predictive validity coefficients that may be considered forms of criterion validity; e.g., Messick, 1995.) In particular, in the rest of this section I discuss applications of SEM for the purpose of scale development and revision aimed at enhancing reliability and criterion validity of tentative scales. Before I embark on this activity, however, it is fitting to determine which specific coefficient informing the scales' reliability will have to be the focus of the subsequent developments, and what type of analytic approach will be used in them.

Reliability Coefficient of Relevance in Scale Construction and Development

When addressing questions about reliability, I find it essential to adhere to the following fundamental principle of logic and science: When a question about concept *A* is to be answered, one should be concerned (as much as possible) with providing an answer that is phrased only in terms of the very notion asked about, namely, *A*. In particular, one should not aim at responding to this question in terms of another concept *B* that only under certain conditions—possibly very restrictive—equals *A*. In the context of reliability evaluation, this principle demands that when questions are asked about the reliability coefficient, answers to them ought to be sought that are phrased entirely in terms of the reliability coefficient itself, rather than in terms of another quantity that only in very special cases equals this coefficient, even if data from an entire studied population were to be available.

This fundamental principle has been violated repeatedly in scale construction and development activities in the social and behavioral sciences for more than half a century. This has occurred at times when the popular coefficient alpha (α; e.g., Cronbach, 1951) has been used with no compelling reasons (see below) for scale reliability evaluation purposes, and in particular when the aim has been to find items/components whose removal from a tentative instrument would increase its reliability. As is well known from the literature, α is defined in the population as the (approximate) interitem covariance per unit of scale score variance:

$$\alpha = \frac{r}{r-1}\left[1 - \frac{\sum_{i=1}^{r} \mathrm{Var}(U_i)}{\mathrm{Var}(U)}\right] = \frac{r}{r-1}\cdot\frac{\sum_{i\neq j}\mathrm{Cov}(U_i, U_j)}{\mathrm{Var}(U)} \quad \textbf{(28.16)}$$

(for the preceding scale *U*), and bears a distinct relationship to earlier work by Guttman (1945; cf. McDonald, 1999). Part of the reason why α is currently popular across the social and behavioral disciplines is the fact that if $U_1, U_2, \ldots, U_r$ are (a) true-score equivalent—that is, evaluate the same underlying latent construct with the same units of measurement—or even parallel, and (b) are associated with uncorrelated error scores E_{U_i} (i

$= 1, \ldots, r$), then $\alpha = \rho_U$ in the population; otherwise $\alpha < \rho_U$ (as long as the component errors are uncorrelated; e.g., Novick & Lewis, 1967; see next section).

Correct and Incorrect Uses of Coefficient Alpha in Scale Construction and Development

The last mentioned relationship between population α and the population scale reliability coefficient has been frequently overinterpreted in empirical and related research as being indicative of a "lower-bound property of α" which researchers have often incorrectly referred to and relied on. (The rest of this section on scale revision, like its preceding part, is developed at the population level unless otherwise explicitly stated.) In actual fact, this lower bound property holds for α only when the component errors are uncorrelated. In the general case, however, the relationship of α to scale reliability is more complex. In particular, when some of the component error terms are correlated, α can overestimate, underestimate, or equal reliability, depending on underlying parameter relationships.[3] This population discrepancy between reliability and α can be quite sizable both when error terms are correlated and in cases when they are not (e.g., Maxwell, 1968; Raykov, 1997, 1998a, 2001a, 2001b). Hence, reliance on α can be seriously misleading.

Conversely, when the set $\underline{U}$ of components is (1) unidimensional (i.e., congeneric) (2) with uncorrelated errors and (3) has uniformly high loadings on the underlying true score (say, in excess of .6 on a 0–1 metric), then α is not underestimating by much composite reliability. In those cases, α can be fairly close to scale reliability. Their discrepancy has been quantified, as well as tabulated, for a number of empirically relevant cases in Raykov (1997) for the case of unidimensional scale components with uncorrelated errors. However, uniformly high loadings are typical primarily for advanced stages of the process of instrument construction and development, and do not seem likely in its early phases. In those early stages, as well as in other settings when the triple conditions (1) through (3) are not all fulfilled, I would like to reiterate that α can markedly under- or overestimate composite reliability (e.g., Raykov, 1997, 1998b, 2001a, 2001b). Furthermore, interval estimates (standard errors and confidence intervals) for α that are obtained with existing methods for α cannot generally be trusted either. The reason is that they are of a parameter, namely, α, that is possibly quite distinct from the one of actual concern, which is reliability itself. Specifically, when conditions (1) through (3) are not fulfilled, confidence intervals for α cannot be expected to have the required (nominal) coverage with respect to the reliability coefficient of real relevance, and can in fact be seriously misleading (see also below).

This discussion makes it appropriate to emphasize the following cautionary points in relation to the many past and recent applications of α in social and behavioral research (various aspects of some of these points have been highlighted in Bentler, 2007, 2009; Crocker & Algina, 1986; Green & Yang, 2009a, 2009b; McDonald, 1981, 1999; Raykov, 1997, 1998b, 2001a, 2001b; Revelle & Zinbarg, 2009; Sijtsma, 2009a, 2009b; cf. Raykov & Marcoulides, 2011).

1. The relationship of α to composite reliability is further complicated by the fact that typically an empirical scientist has access only to sample data, and thus can only estimate the parameters of interest as opposed to determining their population values. Hence, in a particular sample, α can actually overestimate (or, alternatively, underestimate or even equal) population reliability, but one has no way of knowing it has happened because that reliability is unknown. (If the population reliability of an instrument were known, there would be no need to even look at α or an estimate of reliability.)

2. Alpha is the mean of all possible split-half coefficients calculated via Rulon's method (cf. Crocker & Algina, 1986). There is, however, at best limited value in most split-half reliability estimates, since they do not yield a unique estimate of reliability for any single, given set of observed data; for this reason, the value of a split-half reliability estimate is at least unclear in general (cf. McDonald, 1999). Thus, I do not consider this relationship of α to split-half reliability coefficients as adding much if anything to the utility of α in the scale development and revision process.

3. Alpha is not an index of unidimensionality, contrary to what may still be the view among some applied researchers (see Green, Lissitz, & Mulaik, 1977, for an insightful discussion and counterexamples; also see McDonald, 1981). Alpha is only an approximate measure of interitem covariance per unit sum score variance (see Equation 28.16), and a reasonably good index of reliability only under certain restrictive conditions, namely, (1) through (3) in the last paragraph on page 479. If one is indeed interested in unidimensionality, there is no need to use or refer to α, since it does not index unidimensionality and thus can be misleading (even if known in

an entire studied population). Instead, what is required then is direct examination of the homogeneity hypothesis itself. For this aim, use of EFA and especially CFA (on independent samples) is recommended (discussed earlier). With the latter approach, one tests statistically the unidimensionality hypothesis and evaluates the extent to which it may be viewed as "supported" in (i.e., consistent with) a given data set.[4]

4. The fact demonstrated next—that α is in general *not* a consistent estimator of scale reliability—does not seem to have received the attention it deserves in the literature. This inconsistency of α contradicts a widely held view that consistency, at a minimum, should be required from a parameter estimator. Specifically, as is well known, the routinely used estimator of the population α is defined as

$$\hat{\alpha} = \frac{r}{r-1}\left[1 - \frac{\sum\limits_{i=1}^{r}\hat{Var}(U_i)}{\hat{Var}(U)}\right] \qquad (28.17)$$

where $\hat{Var}(U_i)$ and $\hat{Var}(U)$ denote the conventional variance estimators for the individual items and overall scale score, respectively ($i = 1, \ldots, r$; I will often refer to Equation 28.17 as "sample α" or "empirical α" in the rest of this chapter). However, these variance estimators are continuous functions of empirical moments; hence, $\hat{\alpha}$ itself is a continuous function of those moments. In addition, the empirical moments converge in probability to (i.e., are consistent estimators of) the corresponding theoretical moments (e.g., Casella & Berger, 2002). Therefore, $\hat{\alpha}$ converges in probability to α (i.e., $\hat{\alpha}$ is a consistent estimator for the population α). Yet, as indicated earlier, population α is in general not equal to population reliability. Hence, the widely used α estimator in Equation 28.17 in general converges in probability to a quantity (namely, population α) that is not equal to population reliability—the very coefficient that the estimator in Equation 28.17 is supposed to inform about. That is, the popular sample α is in general *not* a consistent estimator of reliability. In particular, for unidimensional scales with uncorrelated errors, the sample α is *not* a consistent estimator of the reliability coefficient that it purports to evaluate. (For the amount of inconsistency, that is, bias that does not vanish with sample size, see Raykov, 1997.) Also with correlated scale component errors, the empirical α in

Equation 28.17 in general is *not* a consistent estimator of reliability (e.g., Raykov, 1998a, 2001a; see also discussion earlier in this chapter). Owing to this inconsistency of α (whether component errors correlate or not), the popular α estimator in Equation 28.17 converges in distribution to a cumulative distribution function that has a jump of 1 at a point that is generally distinct from the population scale reliability coefficient (since convergence in distribution follows from that in probability—here, to a constant distinct from the population reliability; e.g., Casella & Berger, 2002). Hence, CIs for α in general have other than nominal coverage if used as CIs for reliability. (In fact, from the preceding discussion it follows that empirical settings and sample sizes exist where CIs for α can be expected to have coverage smaller than any given, arbitrarily close to 0 positive number.)

Model-Free Evaluation of Reliability

In recent years, the possibility of a so-called "model-free evaluation" of scale reliability has received considerable interest in the measurement related literature. (I find that this approach may be interpreted as another way of suggesting more general use of α as an estimator of reliability.) The model-free approach is based in part on the argument that it is not contingent on tenability of the unidimensionality hypothesis with regard to the components of a scale under consideration, and allows violation of this hypothesis in a given empirical setting (data set). In my view, model-free scale reliability evaluation can be associated with multiple problems. Some of them stem from the previously discussed limitations of α as an index informing about reliability. No less important is another potential problem that consists in the fact that this model-free approach may be seen as (1) implying that there is no need to examine the latent structure of a given set of items/components, while in particular (2) recommending estimation of model-independent indexes of reliability (e.g., of α). However, with lacking knowledge of the latent structure of a scale under consideration, there may be any number of sources of latent variance underlying it (limited from above only by the number of its components). Not having examined, then, the instrument's underlying structure, a researcher runs the danger of using a pertinent sum score—whether weighted or unweighted—that is in fact evaluating an unknown mixture (of an unknown number) of latent sources of variance contributing to variability on the observed components. With this

property of their sum score, even if it is acknowledged or borne in mind that the scale may not be unidimensional, one has in general no possibility of making a convincing statement of what this instrument is actually measuring. For this reason, there cannot be a strong argument, then, in favor of validity of the scale, if any of relevance, yet validity is the bottom line of measurement in the social and behavioral sciences. Therefore, giving up the need for basing reliability evaluation on a model for the relationships between latent source(s) of variance and a scale's components entails in general serious, if not worse, difficulties for a scholar trying to reason in favor of validity of the instrument in question. Moreover, if a (sub)scale is of interest—on validity grounds, say—that is not unidimensional, then it is possible to point- and interval-estimate its reliability using the SEM approach in this chapter (see below). In particular, as elaborated in a later section, there is no need to utilize a model-free procedure for these aims. Thereby, an essential element of this SEM approach application is that it properly accounts for latent structure of the instrument under consideration that need not be unidimensional in general.

Scale Development Enhancing Reliability

After the previous discussion on the importance of model-based evaluation of scale reliability and its traditional definition (Equation 28.14), the next questions of interest are (1) how to point- and interval-estimate the reliability of a tentative scale version, with scale score U (see Equation 28.12); and (2) in case its reliability is deemed unsatisfactory, how to identify components in this scale that, if deleted, would entail increase in its reliability. This subsection outlines an SEM method applicable for answering these questions. In addition, with the procedure described next one can also respond to the query of how to identify components from the more general sets $\underline{Y}$ or even $\wp$ discussed earlier, which are not included in the scale (score) U but if added to the latter would increase its reliability. In the following developments, I assume that the scale consisting of the items in the set $\underline{U}$ is homogeneous (i.e., the items are congeneric). When addressing the question of how to find components not in U that would enhance its reliability if included, it is also assumed that the more general set containing these components and the ones in $\underline{U}$ is unidimensional. I extend the discussion subsequently to the case of a general structure measuring instrument.

Point and Interval Estimation of Scale Reliability

According to the homogeneity assumption, the item set in question—namely, U in case one is interested in component deletion, or Y or $\wp$ if one is concerned with component addition—is congeneric (e.g., Jöreskog, 1971). Then the CTT decomposition into true and error scores for these items is

$$U_j = a_j + b_j T + E_j$$

where for notational simplicity T denotes their common true score and E_j the pertinent error scores ($j = 1, \ldots, r$; $r > 1$; see Note 2). The scale score is then $U = U_1 + \ldots + U_r = (a_1 + \ldots + a_r) + (b_1 + \ldots + b_r) T + E_1 + \ldots + E_p$, with $(a_1 + \ldots + a_r) + (b_1 + \ldots + b_p) T$ being its true score and $E_1 + \ldots + E_p$ its error score. From Equation 28.14 defining the reliability coefficient, it follows that (e.g., Bollen, 1989; cf. McDonald, 1999; Raykov & Marcoulides, 2011)

$$\rho_U = \frac{\text{Var}[(a_1 + \ldots + a_p) + (b_1 + \ldots + b_p)T]}{\text{Var}[(a_1 + \ldots + a_p) + (b_1 + \ldots + b_p)T + E_1 + \ldots + E_p]}$$
$$= \frac{(b_1 + \ldots + b_p)^2 \text{Var}(T)}{(b_1 + \ldots + b_p)^2 \text{Var}(T) + \text{Var}(E_1 + \ldots + E_p)}$$
$$= \frac{(b_1 + \ldots + b_p)^2 \text{Var}(T)}{(b_1 + \ldots + b_p)^2 \text{Var}(T) + \theta_1 + \ldots + \theta_p}$$

where $\theta_j = \text{Var}(E_j)$ denote the error variances ($j = 1, \ldots, p$), in case of uncorrelated errors. For model identification, assume $\text{Var}(T) = 1$, which leads to

$$\rho_U = \frac{(b_1 + \ldots + b_p)^2}{(b_1 + \ldots + b_p)^2 + \theta_1 + \ldots + \theta_p} \tag{28.18}$$

In case of correlated scale component errors, the denominator in Equation 28.18 is extended as follows (assuming the overall model is identified, when of interest to fit it to a given data set; e.g., Bollen, 1989):

$$\rho_U = \frac{(b_1 + \ldots + b_p)^2}{(b_1 + \ldots + b_p)^2 + \theta_1 + \ldots + \theta_p + 2\sum_{j<k} \text{Cov}(E_j, E_k)}$$

where the added sum includes the nonzero error covariances. With maximum likelihood (ML) estimation in

case of multinormality of the scale components, the ML estimator of scale reliability results from Equation 28.18 as

$$\hat{\rho}_U = \frac{(\hat{b}_1 + \ldots + \hat{b}_p)^2}{(\hat{b}_1 + \ldots + \hat{b}_p)^2 + \hat{\theta}_1 + \ldots + \hat{\theta}_p} \tag{28.19}$$

and correspondingly its denominator is extended by twice the sum of estimated error covariances, with correlated errors (and identified overall model). I note in passing that due to Equation 28.19 being an ML estimator, it is a consistent estimator of scale reliability (e.g., Casella & Berger, 2002; this consistency holds also in case of correlated errors, when the denominator of Equation 28.18 is correspondingly extended; discussed earlier in this section).

In an empirical setting where the congeneric model in Equation 28.10 is plausible, an estimate of the reliability for the scale score U is directly obtained following Equation 28.19. (As follows from the preceding discussion in this section, it is only logical (1) to use the reliability estimator in Equation 28.19 when the underlying unidimensionality hypothesis is plausible in a given data set, and (2) not to use Equation 28.19 if that hypothesis is not plausible; in the latter case, see the later section on reliability evaluation for general structure scales.) To this end, one can readily use the software Mplus, which can also provide upon request a delta-method-based approximate (large-sample) standard error for scale reliability (see Appendix 3 in this handbook's webpage [www.handbookofsem.com] for source code). With this standard error, one can furnish a $100(1 - \delta)\%$-CI for reliability of the scale score U via the logit transformation, as in the earlier section on CID estimation ($0 < \delta < 1$). Specifically, this CI is easily rendered by calling the R function 'ci.rel' provided in Appendix 3 in this handbook's webpage (www.handbookofsem.com), with arguments being the scale reliability estimate in Equation 28.19 and its associated standard error obtained from the mentioned software application (see Raykov & Marcoulides, 2011, for further details and illustrations).

The outlined reliability evaluation method is also applicable with non-normal, approximately continuous components that do not exhibit piling of cases (e.g., ceiling or floor effects) or a pronounced clustering effect. The only change needed in the described procedure is the application of the robust maximum likelihood method (MLR; see Appendix 3 and its note in this handbook's webpage [*www.handbookofsem.com*]). This procedure may also be applicable in a trustworthy way with items having at least five to seven possible values (cf. Raykov & Marcoulides, 2011, and references therein). Alternatively, a CI for reliability can be obtained using the bootstrap methodology, as indicated earlier (e.g., Raykov, 1998b). Future research should examine its large-sample properties, with the aim of providing possible guidelines for choosing between an application of the method outlined in this section and the bootstrap-based CIs, depending on empirical setting characteristics.

When the items in the set $\underline{U}$ are binary or binary scored (i.e., scored ultimately 0 and 1, say, depending on response), the CTT framework remains applicable for the purpose of reliability evaluation (e.g., Dimitrov, 2003; see also Raykov & Marcoulides, 2011, for several misconceptions about CTT in this context). Point and interval estimation of reliability of the sum score U can still be conducted using SEM, as outlined in Raykov, Dimitrov, and Asparouhov (2010; the issue of point and interval estimation of reliability following revision is also covered in that work, for binary scored items). If at least one of the items involved contains more than two possible values/options (no higher than, say, five to seven), one may utilize an approximate method based on item parceling that employs the preceding estimation procedure for (approximately) continuous components with respect to the resulting parcel scores (Raykov & Marcoulides, 2011). That method will be trustworthy when resulting reliability estimates and confidence intervals do not vary considerably across possible parceling choices.

Scale Revision for Improving Reliability

Oftentimes in behavioral and social research, tentative instrument versions do not possess what may be considered satisfactory reliability (e.g., .80 or higher, with this number being largely arbitrary, while meeting some consensus among empirical researchers). Enhancing their reliability then may be achieved by (1) removing some components that possibly contribute to lower reliability or, alternatively, (2) adding components that are congeneric with the ones already in the scale version under consideration and entail increase in its reliability. The rest of this subsection deals with a SEM-based procedure that is equally applicable for the purposes (1) and (2).

Over the past several decades, a widely used procedure in empirical research for achieving aims pertaining to activity (1) has been the repeated evaluation in a given sample of α for a tentative scale and revised versions of it that result when each of its components is removed (one at a time). This procedure is widely available in popular statistical software, such as SPSS and SAS, and currently the pertinent statistic nearly routinely employed for this purpose is referred to as "Alpha if item deleted." Based on the discussion in a previous section, however, it is readily seen that this statistic is potentially misleading, since, as I mentioned, α is in general unequal to reliability even if the individual scores on all components $U_1, \ldots, U_r$ under consideration were to be available from an entire population (cf. Raykov & Marcoulides, 2011). Unfortunately, while α's limitations have received a substantial amount of attention, in the past this index "Alpha if item deleted" has not. Raykov (2007; see also 1997, 2001b) showed that "Alpha if item deleted" can suggest and lead to component deletions that enhance α considerably in a studied population yet at the same time entail marked loss in reliability there. Subsequently, Raykov (2008) demonstrated that the same can happen with respect to validity. Specifically, deleting a component so as to enhance α may in fact cause considerable loss in a scale's criterion validity in the population. These unsettling findings of possible loss in reliability and/or validity as a result of adopting a revision that increases α, are explained by the fact mentioned earlier that in certain circumstances α can greatly underestimate reliability (at the population level; e.g., Raykov, 1997, 2001b). Then removing an appropriately chosen component may in fact cause α to increase toward the population reliability coefficient that is however decreased through that component's deletion from the scale version in question.

Instead of examining the potentially misleading index "Alpha if item deleted" that is in addition reported only in the form of a point estimate from a given sample by widely circulated software, such as SPSS or SAS—while one is obviously interested in making conclusions about revision effect in the population for which the instrument is being constructed—a researcher can utilize the SEM approach of this chapter and especially the method discussed in the last section dealing with reliability estimation. Specifically, a candidate component(s) for deletion from a scale under consideration can be that associated with a relatively small loading(s) on the latent dimension evaluated by the pre-revised composite, and/or large residual variance(s) (cf. McDonald, 1999). This component(s) can be found based on a preceding confirmatory factor analysis aimed at testing unidimensionality of the instrument version in question, for example while evaluating its reliability (see, e.g., this handbook's webpage [*www.handbookofsem.com*], Appendices 2 and 3), or from pertinent exploratory factor analysis (e.g., this handbook's webpage [*www.handbookofsem.com*], Appendix 2). Using, then, the SEM procedure described in the previous section, one can point- and interval-estimate scale reliability before and after that component(s) deletion, denoted correspondingly by $\rho_{U,B}$ and $\rho_{U,A}$ in the population of concern. Then the revision effect upon reliability is

$$D = \rho_{U,A} - \rho_{U,B}$$

whereby it is worthwhile emphasizing (1) that D can be positive, 0, or negative in the population; and (2) that in an empirical setting both reliability coefficients involved in D are related to one another, since their estimates are based on the same sample of subjects.

The reliability estimation procedure described in the previous section can be readily modified to provide also a point and interval estimate of the reliability change D of interest, via application of the widely used delta-method, which, as mentioned, is implemented in Mplus and invoked upon request (Muthén & Muthén, 2010). By comparing the resulting reliability estimates and associated CIs, before and after revision, and the associated effect D, and based on substantive and validity related considerations, one can make a more informed conclusion whether a scale revision under consideration is worthwhile to carry out (e.g., Raykov, 2008). The Mplus command file in this handbook's website (*wwwhandbookofsem.com*, Appendix 4; see also Appendix 3) accomplishes point and interval estimation of reliability of a scale after deleting a component, as well as the associated change D in reliability. (This source code is readily modified for the case when more components are deleted from the scale.) As mentioned earlier, in the same way, a researcher can point- and interval-estimate reliability before and after addition of one or more components to an initial instrument that are congeneric with those already in it (Raykov, 2007, 2008).

I stress that the described SEM method for point and interval estimation of revision effect upon reli-

ability is completely unrelated to the currently widely used index "Alpha if item deleted." Instead, the present method is concerned exclusively with reliability itself, since the question pursued is about reliability to begin with; hence, logically, it is the reliability coefficient rather than another quantity (e.g., α), that is to be evaluated for this aim. Furthermore, the focus in this procedure is on the two involved population scale reliabilities and their difference. The reason is that the method (1) furnishes CIs for these coefficients at large and (2) is not exclusively concerned with their sample estimates—as would be the case, with regard to α, if the traditionally used index "Alpha if item deleted" were consulted instead. Furthermore, the outlined procedure is also applicable in a trustworthy way with up to mild deviations from normality, namely, via use of the robust ML estimation method indicated earlier (see also Appendix 4 and its note in this handbook's website; *www.handbookofsem.com*). A binary item version of this procedure is provided in Raykov and colleagues (2010), and a corresponding variant for highly discrete items with more than two possible values could be used via parceling (see also earlier discussion in this chapter).

In concluding this subsection, I mention several limitations of the discussed SEM method. It requires analyzing the same data set more than once (and possibly more than twice, if the first revision is deemed not to have yielded satisfactory reliability), while conclusions and decisions about population parameters involved at each stage may lead to capitalization on chance (e.g., MacCallum, 1986). In particular, *p*-values and CIs obtained for the revised scales in question need to be interpreted with caution. (One may then consider use of CIs obtained at confidence levels corresponding to a Bonferroni-protected significance level; e.g., Johnson & Wichern, 2002). For this reason, one can rely on suggestion(s) for scale improvement, as indicated by analyses with this SEM procedure, only if its results are replicated in a subsequent study with the same components on an independent sample from the studied population. Moreover, I stress that the described method is concerned merely with one feature of a "good" scale, namely, reliability. As discussed in a later section, there is another, highly important aspect of measuring instrument quality that also needs to be assessed for each considered scale version during a revision process: validity. Therefore, an informed decision regarding component removal from or addition to tentative scales can only be made after validity and related substantive considerations.

Reliability and Revision Effect Evaluation for Scales with General Structure

Unidimensionality is a very useful and desirable property of a behavioral measuring instrument, mostly due to the fact that it contributes substantially to unambiguous interpretation of the resulting scores in a given subject-matter domain. In some empirical situations, however, there may be important substantive and, in particular, validity reasons that lead a scientist to consider a scale with a more general structure than that of unidimensionality (i.e., an instrument associated with two or more sources of latent variability) (e.g., McDonald, 1970, 1978, 1981, 1985, 1999; Raykov & Shrout, 2002; Zinbarg, Revelle, Yovel, & Li, 2005). As indicated earlier in this chapter, α does not represent in general a dependable index of reliability for multidimensional scales, irrespective of whether their component errors are correlated. Specifically, depending on parameter relationships, α can overestimate or underestimate reliability in a studied population for a general structure scale (e.g., Novick & Lewis, 1967; Raykov, 1998a; see also Note 3).

The SEM methodology provides also a generally applicable approach to evaluation of reliability and revision effects for multidimensional measuring instruments. To this end, consider the set of items U_1, U_2, ..., U_r comprising a general structure scale under consideration. Denote by E_1, E_2, ..., E_r their corresponding error scores, and by T_1, T_2, ..., T_r their true scores, which are also random variables (cf. McDonald, 1999; Raykov & Marcoulides, 2011; Raykov & Shrout, 2002). Given the scale's general structure, there are at least two sources of interindividual variability behind T_1, T_2, ..., T_r. Accordingly, assume the validity of the corresponding model

$$\underline{T} = \underline{d} + A\underline{f} + \underline{u} \tag{28.20}$$

where $\underline{T}$ is the $r \times 1$ vector of true scores, $\underline{f}$ is that of their t $(t < r)$ underlying factors, A is the associated $r \times t$ loading matrix relating the true scores to these factors, d is an $r \times 1$ vector of intercepts, and $\underline{u}$ is the pertinent $r \times 1$ vector of residual terms with zero means and positive variances, and uncorrelated with $\underline{f}$. Then for the overall scale score $U = \mathbf{1} \bullet (\underline{T} + \underline{E})$ holds, where

$\mathbf{1}$ denotes the $r \times 1$ vector consisting of 1's only, and from Equation 28.14 its reliability follows with some algebra as

$$r_U = \frac{(\mathbf{1}' \bullet A\Phi A \bullet \mathbf{1} + \mathbf{1}' \bullet \Omega \bullet \mathbf{1})}{(\mathbf{1}' \bullet A\Phi A \bullet \mathbf{1} + \mathbf{1}' \bullet \Omega \bullet \mathbf{1} + \mathbf{1}' \bullet \Theta \bullet \mathbf{1})} \tag{28.21}$$

where Φ is the covariance matrix of the common factors $\underline{f}$, Ω is that of the unique factors $\underline{u}$, Θ is the covariance matrix of the error score vector $\underline{E}$, and $\bullet$ denotes corresponding vector multiplication. (There is no need to assume Θ diagonal given overall model identification; see Equation 28.19 and discussion following it.) The coefficient in Equation 28.21 bears close resemblance to the so-called "omega" coefficient (McDonald, 1999; see also Revelle & Zinbarg, 2009). The right-hand side of Equation 28.21 represents a nonlinear function of model parameters, like that in Equation 28.18. Hence, in case of tenability of the model in Equation 28.20, one can point- and interval-estimate scale reliability using the general SEM approach outlined earlier, with only a minor corresponding modification (see Appendix 5 in this handbook's website [*www.handbookofsem.com*] for Mplus source code and specific details of that approach's application in a two-dimensional scale case; I stress that the model in Equation 28.20, and hence the present method for reliability evaluation, does not incorporate the unidimensionality hypothesis).

This SEM method is also readily applicable with a particular form of lack of unidimensionality often found in so-called "hierarchical scales" (e.g., McDonald, 1999; Zinbarg et al., 2005; cf. Raykov & Marcoulides, in press). In these instruments, several interrelated sources of latent variability account for the interrelationships among a set of observed components, with these sources drawing part of their variability from a second-order factor, frequently referred to as a "general (hierarchical) factor." The degree to which this factor accounts for variability in the overall sum score can provide important information about instrument score interpretation (e.g., Uliaszek et al., 2009; Zinbarg et al., 2005, 2006). SEM procedures for point and interval estimation of the proportion of general factor variance in a hierarchical scale are outlined in Raykov and Zinbarg (2011), and for evaluation of reliability and criterion validity of such scales in Raykov and Marcoulides (in press; the cited papers contain the Mplus source codes accomplishing these goals).

The outlined SEM procedure of reliability evaluation for scales with general structure is directly applicable in the process of instrument revision and development. This is achieved by point and interval estimation of reliability before and after revision, as well as of the reliability change due to revision, by complete analogy to the SEM method described earlier in this section for unidimensional scales (see also Appendices 4 and 5 on this handbook's website [*www.handbookofsem. com*]).

Scale Development Enhancing Validity

While high reliability is a very desirable feature of a multicomponent instrument, it is validity that is the bottom line of social and behavioral measurement. Validity is a complex and comprehensive concept, as discussed at length in the literature (e.g., Messick, 1995, and references therein), and may be viewed as the degree to which a scale under consideration is indeed evaluating the construct it purports to measure. Examples of measuring instruments that possess high reliability but low validity can be readily given. In this sense, high reliability can be seen as a necessary but not sufficient condition for high validity, in particular for high construct validity, which has been argued to encompass most other types of validity (e.g., Crocker & Algina, 1986). Unlike reliability, as mentioned earlier, validity cannot be quantified in a single index. However, criterion validity, a form of validity that is relevant when predictions with regard to a criterion variable are to be made using the score from a scale under consideration, can be evaluated by their correlation coefficient (assuming positive variance on both measures, which are also presumed to be approximately continuous in this section; see also Raykov & Marcoulides, in press; the following discussion is similarly applicable for evaluation of concurrent and predictive validity). Other forms of validity, such as convergent and discriminant validity coefficients, can be point- and interval-estimated using SEM in a multitrait–multimethod context, as discussed in detail in alternative sources (e.g., Marsh, 1989; Marsh & Hocevar, 1983; Raykov, 2011b).

Denoting as before by U the scale score in question and by C that on a criterion variable, point and interval estimation of the criterion validity of this scale, $\mathrm{Corr}(U, C)$, is readily furnished using standard methods for estimation of a correlation coefficient and obtaining a confidence interval for it (e.g., Agresti & Finlay, 2009). When criterion validity is not deemed

sufficiently high in an empirical setting, the question naturally arises as to which revisions of a unidimensional instrument under development could enhance its validity. As in the preceding section on estimation of revision effect upon reliability, these revisions are considered to consist here either in deletion of certain components of a unidimensional scale or addition of components congeneric with those already in it. The concern, then, is to evaluate the change in criterion validity that this revision entails.

SEM provides a readily applicable method for accomplishing this aim. To outline it, denote by U_B the scale's score before the revision, by U_A its score after the revision, and by Δ the difference in criterion validity coefficients of the two scale versions with regard to a prespecified criterion C, that is,

$$\Delta = \mathrm{Corr}(C, U_A) - \mathrm{Corr}(C, U_B)$$

(It is assumed that the variances of all three measures involved are positive.) Similarly to change in scale reliability following revision, I stress that (1) Δ can be positive, 0, or negative in the population of concern; and (2) the two criterion validity coefficients in Δ are dependent rather than independent, since they are based on variables observed on the same subjects.

To furnish a point estimate and, in particular, interval estimate (CI) for the change in criterion validity due to revision, we can use the following modeling approach within the SEM methodology (see Raykov & Marcoulides, in press). Consider three dummy latent variables f_1 through f_3 that equal the three scores of concern (i.e., $f_1 = U_B$, $f_2 = U_A$ and $f_3 = C$), as well as the saturated CFA model

$$\underline{v} = \Lambda \underline{f} + \underline{e} \qquad (28.22)$$

where Λ is the 3×3 identity matrix, $\underline{f} = (f_1, f_2, f_3)'$, $\underline{v} = (U_B, U_A, C)'$, and $\underline{e} = \underline{0}$ is a 3×1 vector consisting of zeros only (e.g., Jöreskog & Sörbom, 1996; Raykov, 2001c). From Equation 28.22, then, it follows that the correlation matrix of $\underline{f}$ equals that of $\underline{v}$. Thus, the previous definition of the revision effect on criterion validity, Δ, entails

$$\Delta = \mathrm{Corr}(f_3, f_2) - \mathrm{Corr}(f_3, f_1) \qquad (28.23)$$

That is, the loss or gain in criterion validity due to revision is a function of parameters of the model in Equation 28.22. Therefore, in an empirical setting, after fitting this saturated model to data, an estimate of the change in criterion validity is obtained by substituting the resulting estimates of the two correlations involved in Equation 28.23. As was the case with reliability change due to revision, an interval estimate of loss or gain in criterion validity thereby is obtained by applying the widely used delta-method (Muthén & Muthén, 2010). Appendix 6 in this handbook's website (*www.handbookofsem.com*) contains the needed source code for point and interval estimation of change in criterion validity following revision. This procedure is also directly applicable in case of a multidimensional scale, since it critically depends on the sum scores U_B and U_A on the scale before and after revision, whose criterion correlations are not affected by the structure of the instrument.

Reliability and Validity of Weighted Linear Combinations

The discussion so far in the chapter has been concerned with unweighted scales, also referred to as unit-weighted scales. The resulting overall sum scores have the convenient feature that the same weights, namely, all equal to 1, are attached to the individual components before taking their sum anytime the scale is considered or used. A natural question that arises in this context is whether one could find weights (constants) for each of the instrument components, such that their linear combination with the former would have higher reliability than that of their simple overall sum. This query has received considerable attention in the methodological literature over the past several decades and has led to the concept of maximal reliability (MR; e.g., Li, 1997; Li, Rosenthal, & Rubin, 1996; see also Bentler, 2007, and references therein). For a given homogeneous scale consisting of the items $U_1, U_2, \ldots, U_r$, for which the congeneric model

$$U_j = a_j + b_j T + e_j \ (j = 1, \ldots, r) \qquad \textbf{(28.24)}$$

holds (with uncorrelated errors), MR is achieved with their linear combination

$$W = w_1 U_1 + w_2 U_2 + \ldots + w_r U_r \qquad \textbf{(28.25)}$$

where

$$w_j = b_j / \theta_j \qquad \textbf{(28.26)}$$

(assuming as before that $\theta_j > 0$, $j = 1, \ldots, r$; e.g., $r >$

1; Bartholomew, 1996). Due to this feature of yielding the maximal possible reliability (for a linear combination of the scale components), the ratios (28.26) are referred to as optimal weights and the associated linear combination in Equation 28.25 as the optimal linear combination (OLC). I stress that the optimal weights are population parameters, and thus are typically unknown in empirical research; once a sample becomes available from a studied population, the weights can be estimated (on the condition of tenability of the congeneric model [Equation 28.24] and positive error variances). Hence, the OLC in an empirical study depends on the data and in general will differ from the OLC in another sample (as will the associated MR estimate). Likely as a result of this sample dependency, the concepts of OLC and MR have so far received relatively limited interest among substantive social and behavioral scholars.

For the congeneric model (Equation 28.24), the MR, denoted $\rho_{U,m}$, can be straightforwardly shown to equal (assuming true score variance is set at 1, as earlier, for model identification; e.g., Bartholomew, 1996):

$$\rho_{U,m} = \frac{\sum_{j=1}^{r} b_j^2 / \theta_j}{1 + \sum_{j=1}^{r} b_j^2 / \theta_j} \qquad \textbf{(28.27)}$$

Several interesting features of MR—in case the model in Equation 28.24 is tenable—are worth mentioning at this point. First, the MR $\rho_{U,m}$ is always defined, since its denominator is positive. Second, like the "conventional" reliability coefficient ρ_U in Equation 28.14, MR is never negative and does not exceed 1. Third, unlike the reliability coefficient ρ_U, MR has the properties that it (1) never decreases with the addition of a component (adhering to the model in Equation 28.24), and (2) never increases as a result of deletion of a component (e.g., Raykov & Hancock, 2005). Fourth, if two components are being considered for addition to measures that are congeneric among themselves and with the two in question, then MR will be increased by a greater amount if one adds the measure (say, the qth) for which the ratio b_q^2/θ_q is higher ($1 \leq q \leq r$).[5] Fifth, the OLC W in Equation 28.25 is associated also with maximal criterion validity for a given criterion variable (e.g., Penev & Raykov, 2006).

From Equation 28.27 it is readily seen that if one wishes to construct a linear combination of components chosen optimally from a given set of r measures satisfying the model in Equation 28.24, one should proceed in the following manner: (1) Start by selecting the component with the highest ratio b_q^2/θ_q among all r measures $(1 \leq q \leq r)$; (2) add to that component the measure with the highest ratio of squared loading to error variance among the remaining $r - 1$ components, and so on, until a desired, prespecified level of MR is achieved (e.g., say, .90; this number is given only for the sake of example rather than to suggest any rule of thumb). This scale construction approach achieves the highest MR with the smallest possible number of components, and bears a close relationship to the item response theory concept of information (see McDonald, 1999, for a discussion of an item selection procedure that is not based explicitly on the MR concept while using the concept of information; see also Raykov & Hancock, 2005).

In an empirical setting with (approximately) continuous components, MR is estimated by substituting estimates of the observed measure loadings and error term variances into the right-hand side of Equation 28.26, which are obtained using the SEM approach in this chapter. Since MR is by definition the reliability coefficient of the OLC, a confidence interval for MR is readily furnished simultaneously—as a by-product of this activity—via the logit transformation, as discussed in the earlier section on interval estimation of reliability. The necessary Mplus and R source codes are provided in Appendix 7 in this handbook's website (*www. handbookofsem.com*).

EXTENSIONS OF THE MODELING APPROACH

The discussed SEM approach for scale construction and development has been presented thus far in a setting (1) with complete data on all scale components and (2) where subjects were not nested in higher-order units. The approach can also be extended, however, to cover the cases of missing values and two-level data. Missing data pervade social and behavioral research, and in many current empirical settings there is realistically little, if anything, one can do to prevent their occurrence. In those cases where a scholar has to work with an incomplete data set for the purpose of instrument construction and development, it is important to keep in mind that the goals of his or her analysis should be the same as if he or she had to deal with a complete data set: fitting models to all available data, estimating parameters with standard errors, evaluating model fit, and test-

ing of parameter restrictions, if of interest (e.g., Little & Rubin, 2002). When the missing at random (MAR) assumption can be considered plausible, full-information maximum likelihood (FIML; Arbuckle, 1996) can be readily used with the SEM approach outlined in this chapter (in particular, all Mplus and R source codes provided in Appendices 1–7 at *www.handbookofsem. com* are applicable then, and resulting outputs are interpretable, as in the case of complete data, after ensuring that all missing values are indicated with uniform symbols throughout the raw data and the MISSING subcommand is added to the VARIABLE section of the Mplus input files; Muthén & Muthén, 2010). When the MAR assumption is considered violated, the inclusion of auxiliary variables "predictive" of the missing values can enhance substantially its plausibility, and is thus recommended (Graham, 2003; Little & Rubin, 2002; see also Raykov, 2011a). This is achieved by adding the AUXILIARY (M) subcommand in the pertinent Mplus source code (Muthén & Muthén, 2010). With a large number of available additional variables, application of multiple imputation may well be recommendable, especially when an appropriate imputation model is available (Schafer, 1997). Due to space limitations, these and related issues that arise with incomplete data cannot be discussed further here (see Graham & Coffman, Chapter 17, this volume).

Social and behavioral scientists often collect data that are hierarchical in nature (patients nested within treatment centers, employees nested within firms, respondents nested within cities, students nested within schools, etc.). When this clustering effect is not negligible, ignoring it and proceeding with conventional single-level methods of analysis may be misleading by yielding spuriously small standard errors and thus too short confidence intervals, as well as incorrect statistical test results (in particular, spurious findings of significance). The general SEM approach outlined in this chapter is still applicable for scale construction and development purposes in two-level settings, after appropriate and relatively minor modifications. Raykov and du Toit (2005) provide an SEM method for point and interval estimation of scale reliability in a two-level setup, which is also readily utilized for instrument revision goals. Similarly, Raykov (2011c) describes an SEM procedure for point and interval estimation of criterion validity in a hierarchical setting, which can also be employed for scale development. (The last two cited papers also provide source codes to accomplish these estimation and related goals.)

CONCLUSION

This chapter has outlined a generally applicable SEM approach for scale construction and development, an activity in which social and behavioral scientists frequently engage in their measurement-related research. A utilization of the approach may commence with point and interval estimation of classical item analysis indices—such as item difficulty, interitem correlations, and (adjusted) item–total score correlations—and examination of the latent structure for an item set of concern in the early phases of an instrument development process. These steps aim to inform initial efforts to select, based also on substantive and validity related considerations, a subset of items from a large original set that may be considered to be tapping into a latent construct of research interest. Examination of the latent structure of the relevant item set is also facilitated by EFA and CFA, conducted on independent subsamples from an original sample of studied subjects, potentially leading to tentative instrument versions. Their revision and development can be carried out then with corresponding procedures developed within the outlined SEM approach, in addition to substantive and validity considerations that are also applicable, with minor modifications in cases of general structure scales. These procedures are concerned with point and interval estimation of scale reliability and validity, as well as their change due to removal or addition of components. An extension of this approach to a two-level setup can be employed with hierarchical data. The described estimation procedures can also be utilized in empirical settings with missing data under the MAR assumption, or with inclusion of auxiliary variables "predictive" of the missing values when it is deemed violated, which enhance its plausibility.

An important requirement of the outlined general SEM approach is the availability of large samples of subjects. While at present no specific guidelines can be provided with regard to determining necessary sample size, as it generally depends on number of scale components and underlying sources of latent variability, psychometric features of the former, possible amount of missing values, and model complexity (to name a few of the factors potentially affecting sample size), one may conjecture that the need for a large sample may be less pronounced when the robust maximum likelihood method is applicable and used for model fitting and parameter estimation purposes. Since some of the discussed procedures of the SEM approach in this chapter involve repeated inferences carried out on the same sample, more trust in its findings can be placed only after a replication study is carried out on an independent sample from the studied subject population. Last, but not least, the benefit of this SEM approach can only be realized when it is employed in conjunction with well-informed, substantive considerations based on all accumulated knowledge in the pertinent substantive area.

ACKNOWLEDGMENTS

This research was supported in part by The College Entrance and Examination Board. I am grateful to R. Hoyle, an anonymous referee, and A. Traynor for valuable comments and criticism on an earlier version of the chapter, which have contributed considerably to its improvement. I am indebted to T. Asparouhov, D. M. Dimitrov, G. A. Marcoulides, S. Penev, P. E. Shrout, and R. E. Zinbarg for valuable discussions related to behavioral measurement and reliability estimation.

NOTES

1. An alternative, symmetric CI of the CID for a given item may be obtained by invoking the normality approximation with large samples, adding to and subtracting from its estimate 1.96 times its standard error rendered via the delta method in the software used (for a 95% CI; Muthén & Muthén, 2010). This symmetric CI is not likely to have good coverage properties in general, however, since it can obviously produce CIs that extend below 0 and/or beyond 1. This can occur in particular for sufficiently small or, alternatively, large population difficulty parameters (or sufficiently small samples and/or large confidence levels), which are not infrequent in empirical research on scale construction and development, especially in its early phases. Even if one were then to truncate the symmetric CI at 0 or 1, the resulting interval could still contain generally implausible values, in particular those very close to 0 or 1. The same argument is also applicable to symmetric CIs of other bounded parameters (e.g., reliability; see later section).

2. The developments in this section are also relevant in case of $q = 2$ components, after appropriate constraints are imposed to ensure identifiability of fitted models (e.g., equality of observed measure loadings on common true scores, or of associated error variance equality). Similarly, the following discussion in this section is also applicable when $q = p$.

3. For simplicity of reference, I also use the verbs *overestimate* and *underestimate* at times in population-related discussions, to indicate that the population value of a particular parameter (e.g., coefficient alpha) is correspondingly larger or lower than the population value of another parameter (e.g., scale

reliability; cf. Raykov, 1997, for a more detailed discussion of the population discrepancy/slippage of coefficient alpha in the unidimensional case with uncorrelated errors; for the correlated error case, see also Raykov, 1998a, 2001a).

4. In this context, I find that much of the reliability-related literature—particularly in empirical applications dealing with scale construction and development, and some theoretical discussions—makes frequently unnecessary and potentially misleading references to the concepts of "internal consistency" and "internal consistency reliability." These references can also be counterproductive, since they contribute to confusion among social and behavioral researchers. The concept of internal consistency has not been defined rigorously and in a unique form, at least not in a way that would show its possible contribution to the literature over and above (a) the notion of reliability as defined in Equation 28.14, and (b) coefficient alpha (Equation 28.16). In my view, all too frequently, internal consistency is utilized as just another reference to α (cf. McDonald, 1981), and as such is a largely unneeded separate notion. Its use in the literature can well mislead scholars into employing subsequently α as an index purportedly informing about reliability also in cases when it seriously misestimates the latter (even at the population level; see Note 3). Further, it can be just as misleading to speak of "internal consistency reliability," since doing so creates the impression that this is another (third) important type of reliability. With the view that internal consistency is effectively α, there is no need for yet another "type" of reliability (beyond the earlier widely accepted definition in Equation 28.14 and α, in the instances when it is close to population scale reliability). Instead, I submit (a) that we should strive to use (as often as possible) only one definition of reliability rather than two or more, which should be employed and referred to routinely in the literature and in theoretical as well as empirical research; and (b) that for many current settings in the social and behavioral disciplines, it is unlikely that there would be a real reason for or benefit in using a definition of reliability other than the traditional one in Equation 28.14.

5. This fact obviously is a corollary from the following proposition that is readily demonstrated: If

$$b_j^2/\theta_j > b_q^2/\theta_q \ (1 \leq j, q \leq r)$$

then

$$\frac{A + b_j^2/\theta_j}{1 + A + b_j^2/\theta_j} > \frac{A + b_q^2/\theta_q}{1 + A + b_q^2/\theta_q}$$

for any $A \geq 0$ (assuming positive error variances, as done in this section of the main text).

REFERENCES

Agresti, A., & Finlay, B. (2009). *Statistical methods for the social sciences* (4th ed.). Upper Saddle River, NJ: Prentice-Hall.

Arbuckle, J. L. (1996). Full information estimation in the presence of incomplete data. In G. A. Marcoulides & R. E. Schumacker (Eds.), *Advanced structural equation modeling* (pp. 243–277). Mahwah, NJ: Erlbaum.

Bartholomew, D. J. (1996). *The statistical approach to social measurement*. London: Arnold.

Bentler, P. M. (2007). Covariance structure models for maximal reliability of unit-weighted composites. In S.-Y. Lee (Ed.), *Handbook of latent variable and related models* (pp. 1–19). New York: Elsevier.

Bentler, P. M. (2009). Alpha, dimension-free, and model-based internal consistency reliability. *Psychometrika, 74,* 137–144.

Bollen, K. A. (1989). *Structural equations with latent variables*. New York: Wiley.

Bollen, K. A., & Stein, R. A. (1993). Bootstrapping goodness of fit measures in structural equation models. In K. A. Bollen & J. S. Long (Eds.), *Testing structural equation models*. Thousand Oaks, CA: Sage.

Browne, M. W. (1982). Covariance structures. In D. M. Hawkins (Ed.), *Topics in applied multivariate analysis* (pp. 72–141). Cambridge, UK: Cambridge University Press.

Campbell, D. T., & Fiske, D. W. (1959). Convergent and discriminant validity by the multitrait–multimethod matrix. *Psychological Bulletin, 56,* 81–105.

Casella, G., & Berger, R. L. (2002). *Statistical inference.* Monterey, CA: Wadsworth.

Crocker, L., & Algina, J. (1986). *Introduction to classical and modern test theory.* Fort Worth, TX: Harcourt College Publishers.

Cronbach, L. J. (1951). Coefficient alpha and the internal structure of tests. *Psychometrika, 16,* 297–334.

Cudeck, R., & MacCallum, R. C. (Eds.). (2007). *Factor analysis at 100.* Mahwah, NJ: Erlbaum.

Dimitrov, D. M. (2003). Marginal true-score measures and reliability for binary items as a function of their IRT parameters. *Applied Psychological Measurement, 27,* 440–458.

Downing, S. M., & Haladyna, T. M. (Eds.). (2006). *Handbook of test development.* Mahwah, NJ: Erlbaum.

Efron, B., & Tibshirani, R. J. (1993). *An introduction to the bootstrap.* London: Chapman & Hall/CRC.

Graham, J. W. (2003). Adding missing-data relevant variables to FIML-based structural equation models. *Structural Equation Modeling, 10,* 80–100.

Green, S. B., Lissitz, R. W., & Mulaik, S. A. (1977). Limitations of coefficient alpha as an index of test unidimensionality. *Educational and Psychological Measurement, 37,* 827–838.

Green, S. B., & Yang, Y. (2009a). Commentary on coefficient alpha: A cautionary tale. *Psychometrika, 74,* 121–136.

Green, S. B., & Yang, Y. (2009b). Reliability of summed item scores using structural equation modeling: An alternative to coefficient alpha. *Psychometrika, 74,* 155–167.

Guttman, L. (1945). A basis for analyzing test–test reliability. *Psychometrika, 10,* 255–282.

Johnson, R. A., & Wichern, D. W. (2002). *Applied multivariate statistical analysis.* Upper Saddle River, NJ: Prentice-Hall.

Jöreskog, K. G. (1971). Statistical analysis of sets of congeneric tests. *Psychometrika, 36,* 109–133.

Jöreskog, K. G., & Sörbom, D. (1996). *LISREL8 user's guide.* Chicago: Scientific Software International.

Li, H. (1997). A unifying expression for the maximal reliability of a linear composite. *Psychometrika, 62,* 245–249.

Li, H., Rosenthal, R., & Rubin, D. B. (1996). Reliability of measurement in psychology: From Spearman-Brown to maximal reliability. *Psychological Methods, 1,* 97–108.

Little, R. J., & Rubin, D. B. (2002). *Statistical analysis with missing data.* New York: Wiley.

MacCallum, R. C. (1986). Specification searches in covariance structure modeling. *Psychological Bulletin, 100,* 107–120.

Marsh, H. W. (1989). Confirmatory factor analyses of multitrait–multimethod data: Many problems and a few solutions. *Applied Psychological Measurement, 13,* 335–361.

Marsh, H. W., & Hocevar, D. (1983). Confirmatory factor analysis of multitrait–multimethod matrices. *Journal of Educational Measurement, 20,* 231–248.

Maxwell, A. E. (1968). The effect of correlated errors on estimates of reliability coefficients. *Educational and Psychological Measurement, 28,* 803–811.

McDonald, R. P. (1970). The theoretical foundations of principal factor analysis, canonical factor analysis, and alpha factor analysis. *British Journal of Mathematical and Statistical Psychology, 23,* 1–21.

McDonald, R. P. (1978). Generalizability in factorable domains: Domain validity and reliability. *Educational and Psychological Measurement, 38,* 75–79.

McDonald, R. P. (1981). The dimensionality of tests and items. *British Journal of Mathematical and Statistical Psychology, 34,* 100–117.

McDonald, R. P. (1985). *Factor analysis and related methods.* Hillsdale, NJ: Erlbaum.

McDonald, R. P. (1999). *Test theory. A unified treatment.* Mahwah, NJ: Erlbaum.

Messick, S. (1995). Validation of inferences from persons' responses and performances as scientific inquiry into score meaning. *American Psychologist, 50,* 741–749.

Muthén, B. (1984). A general structural equation model with dichotomous, ordered categorical, and continuous latent variables indicators. *Psychometrika, 49,* 115–132.

Muthén, L. K., & Muthén, B. (2010). *Mplus user's guide.* Los Angeles: Authors.

Novick, M. R., & Lewis, C. (1967). Coefficient alpha and the reliability of composite measurement. *Psychometrika, 32,* 1–13.

Penev, S., & Raykov, T. (2006). On the relationship between maximal reliability and maximal validity for linear composites. *Multivariate Behavioral Research, 41,* 105–126.

Raykov, T. (1997). Scale reliability, Cronbach's coefficient alpha, and violations of essential tau-equivalence for fixed congeneric components. *Multivariate Behavioral Research, 32,* 329–354.

Raykov, T. (1998a). Cronbach's alpha and reliability of composite with interrelated nonhomogenous items. *Applied Psychological Measurement, 22,* 375–385.

Raykov, T. (1998b). A method for obtaining standard errors and confidence intervals of composite reliability for congeneric items. *Applied Psychological Measurement, 22,* 369–374.

Raykov, T. (2001a). Bias of coefficient alpha for congeneric measures with correlated errors. *Applied Psychological Measurement, 25,* 69–76.

Raykov, T. (2001b). Estimation of congeneric scale reliability via covariance structure models with nonlinear constraints. *British Journal of Mathematical and Statistical Psychology, 54,* 315–323.

Raykov, T. (2001c). Testing multivariable covariance structure and means hypotheses via structural equation modeling. *Structural Equation Modeling, 8,* 224–257.

Raykov, T. (2007). Reliability if deleted, not "alpha if deleted": Evaluation of scale reliability following component deletion. *British Journal of Mathematical and Statistical Psychology, 60,* 201–216.

Raykov, T. (2008). "Alpha if item deleted": A note on loss of criterion validity in scale development if maximising coefficient alpha. *British Journal of Mathematical and Statistical Psychology, 61,* 275–285.

Raykov, T. (2011a). Estimation of latent construct correlations in the presence of missing data: A note on a latent variable modeling approach. *British Journal of Mathematical and Statistical Psychology.*

Raykov, T. (2011b). Evaluation of convergent and discriminant validity with multitrait–multimethod correlations. *British Journal of Mathematical and Statistical Psychology, 64,* 38–52.

Raykov, T. (2011c). Scale validity evaluation with congeneric measures in hierarchical designs. *British Journal of Mathematical and Statistical Psychology.*

Raykov, T., Dimitrov, D. M., & Asparouhov, T. (2010). Evaluation of scale reliability with binary measures. *Structural Equation Modeling, 17,* 122–132.

Raykov, T., & du Toit, S. H. C. (2005). Evaluation of reliability for multiple-component measuring instruments in hierarchical designs. *Structural Equation Modeling, 12,* 536–550.

Raykov, T., & Hancock, G. R. (2005). Examining change in maximal reliability for multiple-component measuring instruments. *British Journal of Mathematical and Statistical Psychology, 58,* 65–82.

Raykov, T., & Marcoulides, G. A. (2004). Using the delta

method for approximate interval estimation of parametric functions in covariance structure models. *Structural Equation Modeling, 11*, 659–675.

Raykov, T., & Marcoulides, G. A. (2011). *Introduction to psychometric theory.* New York: Routledge.

Raykov, T., & Marcoulides, G. A. (in press). Evaluation of validity and reliability for hierarchical scales using latent variable modeling. *Structural Equation Modeling.*

Raykov, T., & Mels, G. (2009). Interval estimation of inter-item and item–total correlations for ordinal items of multiple-component measuring instruments. *Structural Equation Modeling, 16*, 99–108.

Raykov, T., & Shrout, P. E. (2002). Reliability of scales with general structure: Point and interval estimation using a structural equation modeling approach. *Structural Equation Modeling, 9*, 195–202.

Raykov, T., & Zinbarg, R. E. (2011). Proportion of general factor variance in a hierarchical multiple-component measuring instrument: A note on a confidence interval estimation procedure. *British Journal of Mathematical and Statistical Psychology, 64*(pt. 2), 193–207.

Revelle, W., & Zinbarg, R. E. (2009). Coefficients alpha, beta, omega, and the GLB: Comments on Sijtsma. *Psychometrika, 74*, 145–154.

Schafer, J. L. (1997). *Analysis of incomplete multivariate data.* London: Chapman & Hall.

Shadish, W. R., Cook, T. D., & Campbell, D. T. (2002). *Experimental and quasi-experimental designs for generalized causal inference.* Boston: Houghton Mifflin.

Sijtsma, K. (2009a). On the use, the misuse, and the very limited usefulness of Cronbach's alpha. *Psychometrika, 74*, 107–120.

Sijtsma, K. (2009b). Reliability beyond theory and into practice. *Psychometrika, 74*, 169–174.

Skrondal, A., & Rabe-Hesketh, S. (2004). *Generalized latent variable modeling: Multilevel, longitudinal and structural equation models.* Boca Raton, FL: Chapman & Hall/CRC.

Uliaszek, A. A., Hauner, K. K., Zinbarg, R. E., Craske, M. G., Mineka, S., Griffith, J. W., et al. (2009). An examination of content overlap and disorder-specific predictions in the associations of neuroticism with anxiety and depression. *Journal of Research in Personality, 43*, 785–794.

Venables, W. N., Smith, D. M., & the R Development Core Team. (2007). *An introduction to R.* Bristol, UK: Network Theory Limited.

Zimmerman, D. W. (1975). Probability spaces, Hilbert spaces, and the axioms of test theory. *Psychometrika, 40*, 395–412.

Zinbarg, R. E., Revelle, W., Yovel, I., & Li, W. (2005). Cronbach's α, Revelle's β, McDonald's ω_H, their relations with each other, and two alternative conceptualizations of reliability. *Psychometrika, 70*, 123–134.

Zinbarg, R. E., Yovel, I., Revelle, W., & McDonald, R. P. (2006). Estimating generalizability to a latent variable common to all of a scale's indicators: A comparison for estimates of ω_H. *Applied Psychological Measurement, 30*, 121–144.

PART V

ADVANCED APPLICATIONS

CHAPTER 29

Measurement Models for Ordered-Categorical Indicators

James A. Bovaird
Natalie A. Koziol

Latent constructs are inherent to many areas of social, behavioral, and educational inquiry. Consequently, confirmatory factor analysis (CFA) and, more generally, structural equation modeling (SEM) have become critical analytic frameworks because of their capacity to model such latent constructs. While traditional CFA and SEM assume constructs are measured at least at the interval level of measurement, only discrete measurement at the ordinal level is frequently achieved in practice. With the intent of surveying the principles and practices of establishing measurement models for latent variables with ordered-categorical (i.e., ordinal) indicators, this chapter integrates and expands upon ideas presented in three of the previous chapters included in this volume—categorical data (Edwards, Wirth, Houts, & Xi, Chapter 12), confirmatory factor analysis (Brown & Moore, Chapter 22), and measurement invariance (Millsap & Olivera-Aguilar, Chapter 23).

We begin this chapter by discussing the fundamental assumptions of measurement and relating them to traditional CFA for continuous indicators. We then discuss the empirical literature surrounding two indirect approaches to modeling or otherwise overcoming some of the complications brought on by ordinal items in a measurement context, including (1) reliance on the "robustness" of traditional maximum likelihood (ML)

estimation procedures, and (2) data reduction/normalization through aggregation. Subsequently, we discuss modeling ordinal data explicitly with either a full- or limited-information estimation method. We conclude the chapter with a practical example of latent variable measurement with ordinal indicators in the context of evaluating invariance of a construct across genders.

FUNDAMENTALS OF MEASUREMENT

A basic concept in statistics is the classification of four scales of measurement: nominal, ordinal, interval, and ratio (Stevens, 1960). Measurement at the *nominal* level is the process of classifying like-observations into groups. Importantly, there is no inherent ordering among the groups, only qualitative distinctions. Measurement at the *ordinal* level is the process of rank-ordering distinct observations according to some attribute. In an ordinal scale, observations can be logically ordered on the basis of the attribute, but the degree to which one individual has more or less of the attribute than another individual cannot be quantified. Measurement at the *interval* level is like measurement at the ordinal level, but it permits meaningful quantitative comparisons between observations. Importantly, it does *not* permit inferences about the absolute magnitude of the entity being measured. Finally, measurement at the *ratio* level is comparable to, and often treated as equivalent in practice, to measurement at the interval level; however, with the presence of a true zero point, the ratio level permits further inferences about the absolute magnitude of the entity being measured.

Understanding the classification of measurement scales is important because it defines the validity of inferences made about relationships in the data. Each measurement scale permits increasingly stronger inferences. Table 29.1 provides the measurement rules corresponding to each measurement scale (Hays, 1994, pp. 73–75).

Different families of models require different levels of measurement. The well-known family of *general* linear models, of which traditional SEM is a multivariate extension, assumes that endogenous variables are measured on an interval or ratio scale (West, Finch, & Curran, 1995). In contrast, the family of *generalized* linear models (a family that subsumes general linear models) can additionally model data that are measured on a nominal or ordinal scale (e.g., Skrondal & Rabe-Hesketh, 2004). Regardless of measurement level, all general and generalized models include three components: (1) a random component, (2) a systematic component, and (3) a link function (Agresti, 2002). The random component is the probability distribution of the outcome variable, *y*. In CFA it is the probability distribution of all responses on a particular item. Conversely, the systematic component is a set of variables (e.g., X_1, X_2, . . . , X_k) that linearly combine to predict the outcome variable, *y*. Finally, the link function determines the relationship between the random and systematic components, where $\mu = E(y)$, $g(\mu) = \alpha + \beta_1 X_1 + . . . \beta_k X_k$, $g(.)$ is the link function, and $gA''(.)$ is its inverse. While all models have these components, the assumed distribution of the random component and particular link function used depend on the measurement level of the data. In the following sections we first review traditional CFA with continuous indicators, then transition to CFA with ordinal indicators.

CFA WITH CONTINUOUS INDICATORS

Because latent variables, or latent constructs, are not directly observable, their presence is generally inferred by measuring a profile of two or more related behaviors and assuming that the relationship between the observed behaviors is due to the hypothesized latent construct as the antecedent event. In other words, we infer that because the construct exists, we should be able to observe its manifestation given the availability of appropriate indicators or measures. Most often, this is accomplished through the use of multi-item instruments, giving rise to the need for a model to evaluate how well the items measure the construct of interest.

In the general SEM context, we typically test a hypothesis that the observed variance–covariance matrix among the measured variables, Σ_{xx}, is equal to the model-implied variance–covariance matrix, $\Sigma_{xx}(\theta)$, where θ is a vector of model parameters. In the specific context of a measurement model tested in the CFA framework, where CFA is a special case of the broader SEM framework, the observed variance–covariance matrix represents the variances and covariances among measured indicators of the presumed construct(s). The variance–covariance matrix implied by $\Sigma(\theta)$ is a function of factor loadings relating the indicators to the latent construct(s), Λ_x; variances and covariances among one or more latent variables, $\Psi_{\xi\xi}$; and indicator residual variances, or measurement errors, $\Theta_{\delta\delta}$:

$$\Sigma_{xx}(\theta) = \Lambda_x \Psi_{\xi\xi} \Lambda_x' + \Theta_{\delta\delta} \qquad (29.1)$$

Traditional CFA using continuous observed variables makes three key assumptions. First, the sample variance–covariance matrix representing the linear associations among variables is based on only normally distributed continuous endogenous variables. This sample variance–covariance matrix accompanied by a

TABLE 29.1. Measurement Rules for the Scales of Measurement

Measurement scale	Measurement rule
Nominal	$m(o_i) \neq m(o_j)$ implies that $t(o_i) \neq t(o_j)$
Ordinal	$m(o_i) > m(o_j)$ implies that $t(o_i) > t(o_j)$
Interval	$t(o_i) = x$ if and only if $m(o_i) = ax + b$, where $a \neq 0$
Ratio	$t(o_i) = x$ if and only if $m(o_i) = ax$, where $a > 0$

Note. o, object; *m(o)*, numerical measurement of object; *t(o)*, true value of object.

vector of the variables' means then provides the sufficient statistics necessary for ML estimation (see Little, 1997). The other two assumptions are typically made for all modeling applications: The model is correctly specified, and residuals are independent from (i.e., uncorrelated with) all other residuals and latent factors. Given these conditions and assuming an adequately large sample size, ML estimation results in (1) parameter estimates that are consistent, efficient, and unbiased, and (2) accurate standard errors. An omnibus test of model fit that can be evaluated using a standard chi-square distribution is also available.

The validity of conclusions based on test statistics and fit indices depends on the degree of congruence between the measurement model and estimation method used to obtain parameter estimates and the actual measurement characteristics of the data (level of measurement and approximation of normality); failure to obtain a sufficient degree of congruity weakens statistical conclusion validity (Shadish, Cook, & Campbell, 2002). As one might expect, available data do not always match the traditional assumptions of standard mean and covariance structure modeling. Although latent construct(s) are typically considered to be of a continuous nature, the individual observed measures of the construct (i.e., the items) are often discrete, with a small number of measurement categories, such that the requirements for interval-level measurement are not generally met. When this is the case, traditional CFA assuming continuous indicators is no longer appropriate.

CFA WITH ORDINAL INDICATORS

A number of approaches exist for modeling the measurement of latent variables with ordinal indicators. We first discuss two indirect (and potentially less preferred) methods, including (1) ignoring the ordinality and relying on the "robustness" of traditional ML estimation procedures, and (2) using data reduction or normalizing techniques through aggregation. We then describe two alternative frameworks—a full-information approach and a limited-information approach—that more explicitly address the indicators' ordinal nature. Estimation using a full-information approach parallels the item response theory (IRT) tradition, whereas estimation using a limited-information approach expands on traditional CFA for continuous indicators through a series of modifications.

Ignoring Ordinality

Estimation of SEM through ML estimation with normally distributed continuous variables is well understood, and behavior of the chi-square test statistic under ideal and less than ideal conditions has also been widely studied. Unfortunately, in a CFA measurement context with observed items of the Likert-type, the necessary ML assumptions are not met because the data are discrete and ordinal rather than continuous and of at least an interval level of measurement. This leads to estimation problems (Muthén & Kaplan, 1985), especially when there are four or fewer response options in the Likert-type scale.

Numerous studies have examined the robustness of normal theory test statistics and fit indices to the presence of ordinality. When ordinal data are based on at least five response options and approximate a normal distribution, normal theory ML chi-square Type I error rates are relatively unaffected (Babakus, Ferguson, & Jöreskog, 1987; Muthén & Kaplan, 1985, 1992; Olsson, 1979). On the other hand, increasingly skewed and kurtotic ordinal distributions produce inflated Type I error rates (Babakus et al., 1987; Muthén & Kaplan, 1985), especially when the pattern of skewness varies across items (Olsson, 1979) and the data follow a leptokurtic distribution (Muthén & Kaplan, 1992). Lubke and Muthén (2004) also found that normal theory ML chi-square Type I error rates were more inflated when factor loadings were strong and thresholds varied across items.

One way to address these issues is through the use of alternative "corrected" normal theory estimation methods that are appropriate when data are assumed to be continuous and normally distributed in the population, but demonstrate skewness and/or kurtosis in a particular sample. These methods are frequently used by practitioners who argue that discrete ordinal variables with a sufficient number of response alternatives may be considered "essentially continuous." The term "corrected" refers to the fact that although the data are modeled using normal theory ML, the chi-square test of overall model fit and/or estimated standard errors is adjusted for the presence of non-normality (i.e., additional information about the third and fourth moments of the distribution is included in the calculation of the statistics; Kline, 2011). Corrections range from implementing mean- and variance-adjusted, or just mean-adjusted, chi-square test statistics (also known as the Satorra–Bentler chi-square statistic) with robust standard errors to calculating only adjusted or robust standard errors using a Huber–White "sandwich" estimator (Huber, 1967; White, 1982) or first-order derivatives. The practical example at the end of this chapter contrasts such a "robust" approach with two direct approaches for modeling ordered categorical indicators.

Data Normalizing through Parceling

"Parceling" is an approach to modeling ordinal data in which multiple items are aggregated into one or more composite scores, or *parcels*, that are intended to better approximate measurement at the interval level, so that traditional CFA methods can be applied. The most common approach to parceling is to use a sum or mean of a set of items instead of the individual items themselves (Cattell, 1956). Bandalos and Finney (2001) outline a number of arguments for and against parceling. In support of parceling, parcels tend to have increased reliability, communality, and common-to-unique factor variance ratios. Parcels also have an increased likelihood of meeting distributional assumptions such as normality and an interval level of measurement. Due to the smaller number of parameters involved when modeling parcels rather than the full battery of individual items, parcels also may be used to accommodate a smaller sample size, reduce influence of abnormal items, simplify overall model interpretation, and improve model fit.

In opposition to parceling, others argue that parcels may mask dimensionality and model misspecification concerns such as true multidimensionality or cross-loadings, thus increasing the Type II error rate (failing to reject a model that should indeed be rejected). While there are fewer parameters to interpret when using parcels versus individual items, the interpretation of model parameters can become less clear as well. Additional concerns include loss of information, change of original relations from nonlinear to linear (Coenders, Satorra, & Saris, 1997), potential limited range that may bias variances and covariances, and underestimation of structural parameters if scale reliability is low. See Bandalos (2002), Bandalos and Finney (2001), Little, Cunningham, and Shahar (2002), or Yang, Nay, and Hoyle (2010) for excellent reviews and additional detail on parceling.

The approaches just discussed do not model ordinal data directly. Rather, they attempt to modify (or simply ignore) the data so that measurement models

and estimation techniques for continuous data can be employed. We now discuss more explicit methods for modeling the measurement of latent variables with ordinal indicators.

Full-Information Estimation Using Sample Response Patterns

Edwards and colleagues (Chapter 12, this volume) describe ML estimation directly accounting for the discrete nature of ordinal data as a *full-information* approach due to the requirement of estimating from the raw empirical data rather than summary statistics. That is, instead of obtaining model parameter estimates by means of covariance structure modeling, as done in traditional CFA, full-information parameter estimates are those values that maximize the likelihood of the sample response patterns (see, e.g., de Ayala, 2009). Like traditional CFA, the parameters to be estimated are defined by the measurement model.

Perhaps the most relevant model for measurement involving ordinal data is the two-parameter logistic (2PL) model for dichotomous data from the IRT tradition:

$$P\left(y_{ij}=1\mid\theta_i,a_j,b_j\right)=\frac{1}{1+e^{-Da_j\left(\theta_i-b_j\right)}} \qquad (29.2)$$

According to the 2PL model, the probability that the dichotomous response, y_{ij}, to a given item j is observed to be an endorsement (i.e., a "1" vs. "0") is a function of individual i's standing on the latent construct, θ; a discrimination or slope parameter, a_j, reflecting the strength of association between the latent factor and indicator; a difficulty parameter, b_j, indicating the extent to which the individual must possess the latent trait in order to endorse the indicator at a chance level (i.e., 50% for dichotomous items); and a scaling factor, D, which is essentially a historical artifact.[1]

Outside of the IRT tradition, SEM software packages generally estimate factor loadings in place of discrimination parameters, and thresholds (identical to intercepts but with the opposite sign) in place of difficulty parameters. For estimation involving a logit link, and assuming the distribution for the random component is the Bernoulli distribution for binary data, the 2PL model for dichotomous data specified in terms of factor loadings and thresholds is

$$P\left(y_{ij}=1\mid f_i,\lambda_j,\tau_j\right)=\frac{1}{1+e^{\left(\tau_j-\lambda_jf_i\right)}} \qquad (29.3)$$

where f_i is individual i's factor score (equivalent to θ_i given earlier), τ_j is the threshold for item j, and λ_j is the factor loading for item j. For estimation involving a probit link, the same model is formulated as

$$P\left(y_{ij} = 1 \mid f_i, \lambda_j, \tau_j\right) = \Phi\left(-\tau_j + \lambda_j f_i\right) \qquad (29.4)$$

where Φ is the standard cumulative normal distribution.

A dichotomous variable can be conceptualized as an ordinal variable with only two levels. Samejima (1969) proposed an extension of the 2PL model for polytomous data called the "graded response model" (GRM), which is then appropriate for ordinal data with more than two discrete measurement categories:

$$P\left(y_{ij} = c \mid \theta_i, a_j, b_{j,c}\right) = \frac{1}{1 + e^{-Da_j\left(\theta_i - b_{j,c}\right)}} - \frac{1}{1 + e^{-Da_j\left(\theta_i - b_{j,c+1}\right)}}$$

$$= P(y_{ij} \geq c) - P(y_{ij} \geq c+1) \qquad (29.5)$$

Parameter definitions in the GRM are generally the same as in the 2PL model. The notable exception is the presence of $c - 1$ difficulty parameters, which are now referred to as "thresholds" indicating the level of the latent trait after which the respondent transitions from a lower category to the next higher category. In the 2PL model for dichotomous data, this was the transition between a "0" and a "1." For polytomous data, there are multiple difficulty parameters because there are multiple transitions between categories. For estimation involving a logit link, the corresponding model for polytomous data specified in terms of factor loadings and thresholds is

$$P\left(y_{ij} = c \mid f_i, \lambda_j \tau_{j,c}\right) = \frac{1}{1 + e^{\left(\tau_{j,c} - \lambda_j f_i\right)}} - \frac{1}{1 + e^{\left(\tau_{j,c+1} - \lambda_j f_i\right)}}$$

$$= P(y_{ij} \geq c) - P(y_{ij} \geq c+1) \qquad (29.6)$$

For estimation involving a probit link, the corresponding expression of the GRM is

$$P(y_{ij} = c \mid f_i, \lambda_j, \tau_{j,c}) = \phi(-\tau_{j,c} + \lambda_j f_i) - \Phi(-\tau_{j,c+1} + \lambda_j f_i) \qquad (29.7)$$

$$= P(y_{ij} \geq c) - P(y_{ij} \geq c+1)$$

These models formulate the probability of a particular individual endorsing a particular response on a particular item. While full-information approaches to estimating these model parameters do not require intermediate steps such as calculating sufficient summary statistics, these direct modeling approaches do require sophisticated computational methods based on numerical integration and result in little model fit information. In contrast, direct modeling of the latent construct(s) based on estimation through the use of sufficient statistics obtained from the empirical data derived from a set of assumptions is classified as a *limited-information* approach by Edwards and colleagues (Chapter 12, this volume). According to Edwards and colleagues, these approaches are simpler to implement in practice, but they also sacrifice some information.

Limited-Information Estimation Using Polychoric Correlations

Limited-information approaches utilize covariance modeling as done in traditional CFA but incorporate a series of conceptual and statistical modifications/extensions to account for the ordinal nature of the data. Muthén (1983, 1984) defined a "latent response distribution" (LRD) as an unobserved continuous distribution that leads to an ordinal observed distribution. For categorical ordinal data characterized by a small number of discretely measured categories, an observed variable, y, is related to its corresponding latent response variable by means of

$$y = c, \quad if \quad \tau_c < y^* < \tau_{c+1} \qquad (29.8)$$

That is, when the true latent value changes on the latent response variable, y^*, such that a discrete threshold, τ, is crossed, the observed discrete categorical value of y changes as well. When the latent response variable is continuous and the observed data are also continuous, then parameter estimation using a product–moment-based variance–covariance matrix with ML estimation holds. However, when the observed data are not continuous (what we consider to be the norm), the traditional covariance structure assumptions hold only for the latent response variable (Bollen, 1989).

The need for the LRD to formalize the relationship between a discrete observed variable and the corresponding latent response variable is a central component in the *categorical* confirmatory factor analysis (CCFA) model. Modeling in the CCFA context follows the same general structure as when testing a CFA with continuous indicators:

$$\Sigma^*_{xx}(\theta) = \Lambda^*_x \Phi^*_{\xi\xi} \Lambda^{*'}_x + \Theta^*_{\delta\delta} \qquad \textbf{(29.9)}$$

However, the estimation process becomes more demanding because of the presence of latent variables in the variance–covariance matrix, Σ^*_{xx}, due to modeling the associations between latent response variables rather than observed variables. As in the common CFA model, the variance–covariance matrix implied by $\Sigma^*_{xx}(\theta)$ is a function of a factor loading matrix, Λ^*_x; latent variances and covariances among one or more latent variables, $\Phi^*_{\xi\xi}$ (similar to an individual i's standing on the latent construct(s), θ, from the 2PL IRT model in Equation 29.2); and a diagonal matrix of unique variances, $\Theta^*_{\delta\delta}$.

As previously established, while individual Likert-type items are intended to measure a continuous latent construct, the observed rating scale responses are actually discrete and are most appropriately considered to be at the ordinal level of measurement rather than at the interval level. A logical alternative, then, is to model the measurement association between such ordinal indicators through polychoric and/or polyserial correlations rather than the traditional product–moment coefficients. In a tradition that dates back to Pearson (1901), a polychoric correlation models a linear association between two continuous latent response variables given ordinal (more than two ordered categories) observed data, while a polyserial correlation coefficient models the linear association between two continuous latent response variables given that one is ordinal and the other is measured at the interval or ratio level.[2] The actual calculation of polychoric correlations is not central to this chapter, but the interested reader is referred to Olsson (1979). While it might follow that a correlation matrix based on polychoric associations could be used with ML estimation procedures (instead of product–moment covariances), significant problems have been reported, including incorrect test statistics and standard errors (Babakus et al., 1987; Dolan, 1994; Rigdon & Ferguson, 1991).

An alternative to using ML estimation with a polychoric correlation matrix—which is perhaps best grouped with the indirect corrected normal theory approach—is to specify a "distribution-free" estimator from the weighted least squares (WLS) family. These estimators incorporate calculations of kurtosis into the estimation process rather than assuming its absence (Kline, 2011). When data are specified as continuous and the correct asymptotic covariance matrix is used, the WLS estimator is also referred to as the asymp-

totic distribution-free (ADF) estimator (Browne, 1982, 1984). Muthén (1983, 1984) proposed a continuous/categorical variable methodology (CVM) to generalize Browne's work with WLS beyond non-normal continuous data to categorical data such as dichotomous or ordinal observed variables. This enabled the use of either continuous or categorical endogenous variables, or a combination of both.

While full WLS appeared to present a suitable solution to the ordinal indicator problem by addressing the non-normality (but not the categorical nature of the data), the dimensions of the necessary weight matrix, **W**, increase as model complexity increases, and **W** becomes unstable (Bentler, 1995; West et al., 1995). In addition, stable estimation of the weight matrix and asymptotic covariance matrix under WLS requires a large sample size, which is often a concern and prohibitive in practice (Muthén & Kaplan, 1992). Further limitations of WLS are presented when endogenous variables are categorical because the sample variance–covariance matrix will not sufficiently consider the variables' categorical nature (Hipp & Bollen, 2003); hence, there is a need to replace the normal product–moment matrix with the polychoric correlation matrix. As pointed out by Flora and Curran (2004), although estimation of the polychoric correlations themselves are known to be robust to violations of bivariate normality for continuous latent response variables with ordinal observed data, there is limited research on whether such robustness extends to issues of model fit, parameter estimation (i.e., factor loadings), or standard errors when using WLS and a correct covariance matrix in the CFA modeling context. In fact, Dolan (1994) has shown that chi-square test statistics are frequently inflated and standard errors are negatively biased when estimating models based on polychoric correlation matrices with WLS estimation, and the problem increases as a function of increased model complexity and decreased sample size. Difficulty inverting the weight matrix, **W**, is also reported (Muthén & Kaplan, 1992).

As a counter to the problems encountered when using full WLS with small samples and/or complex models, a robust WLS approach is recommended that substitutes a diagonal matrix of asymptotic variances of the original weight matrix diagonal elements (e.g., Christoffersson, 1975; Muthén, du Toit, & Spisic, 1997). In the robust WLS approach, the weight matrix, **W**, does not need to be inverted, thus avoiding the computational difficulties encountered in full WLS. Muthén and colleagues (1997) also provide a mean- and variance-adjusted chi-square test statistic with empirical degrees of freedom based on the Satterthwaite (1941) method. Hipp and Bollen (2003) point out, though, that the use of Satterthwaite-inspired degrees of freedom makes the testing of nested models unclear. Research is promising, however, as the mean- and variance-adjusted WLS estimator has proven robust to various categorical indicators with large samples (Muthén & Kaplan, 1985, 1992).

The full- and limited-information approaches described earlier provide two alternative methods for estimating measurement model parameters in the context of ordinal data. We now provide an example to demonstrate and compare these approaches in the context of evaluating measurement invariance. We further contrast these explicit approaches with the "method" of simply ignoring ordinality. We illustrate a number of the strengths and limitations of each of these approaches.

AN EMPIRICAL EXAMPLE

Measurement models play different roles depending on the focus of one's research questions; measurement models may be of interest in their own right (e.g., one might use CFA to support the factor structure of a recently developed psychological scale), or they may be used to provide necessary evidence of measurement invariance prior to evaluating construct-level relationships of interest. We use a single running example in the remainder of the chapter to illustrate a real-world application of measurement models for ordered-categorical indicators *within* the context of evaluating measurement invariance. The goal of this example is to provide the reader with a framework for analyzing and evaluating measurement models with ordered-categorical data, both when interest lies solely in the measurement model and when the measurement model simply serves as a foundation for structural-level comparisons. While measurement invariance is more thoroughly addressed by Millsap and Olivera-Aguilar (Chapter 23, this volume), there are additional complexities specific to ordered-categorical measurement models that need to be addressed.

The data used in this example come from 992 undergraduate students (50.4% males) enrolled in a large Midwestern university who completed a newly developed Sense of Duty (SOD) scale (in addition to numerous other measures) in exchange for course credit

(see Bovaird & Gallant, 2002, for more details). The SOD scale is composed of 20 Likert scale items, each of which is based on six response options (1 = *Strongly disagree*, 2 = *Disagree*, 3 = *Slightly disagree*, 4 = *Slightly agree*, 5 = *Agree*, 6 = *Strongly agree*). Example items include, "If responsibilities pile up, I start to ignore them" and "If I promise to do something, I do it no matter what." Upon reverse-coding 11 of the items, higher scores are assumed to represent higher levels of dutifulness.

Bovaird and Gallant (2002) used these data to evaluate the factor structure, with the intent of providing validity evidence for the SOD scale through both exploratory factor analysis and CFA. In performing the CFA—and due in part to a lack of accessible software for CFA with ordered-categorical indicators at the time—Bovaird and Gallant specified a measurement model for continuous indicators and used ML estimation with the Satorra–Bentler scaled chi-square test statistic to account for the presence of multivariate nonnormality. Based on their results, the authors proposed the existence of a higher-order construct representing *dutifulness*, as well as three lower-order constructs representing *responsibility*, *diligence*, and *commitment*. See Figure 29.1 for a simplified path diagram representing the relationship among SOD items and factors.

Because of the ordinal and nonsymmetrical nature of the SOD scale data, Bovaird and Gallant (2002) could alternatively have specified a measurement model for ordered-categorical indicators. This example utilizes the GRM to reanalyze the data used in Bovaird and Gallant, and further, evaluates the degree to which the model demonstrates measurement invariance across males and females.

Although a number of software environments exist for analyzing SEMs (see Byrne, Chapter 19, and Fox, Byrnes, Boker, & Neale, Chapter 20, this volume), this example utilizes Mplus (Muthén & Muthén, 1998–2010) due to the flexibility by which it permits categorical data modeling. In Mplus, measurement models for ordinal data are generally estimated using either a limited-information estimator, WLSMV (the mean- and variance-adjusted WLS estimator), or a full-information estimator, as in ML with numerical integration.[3] As previously discussed, these estimators have different advantages and limitations, and may even lead researchers to slightly different statistical conclusions (Wirth & Edwards, 2007). Thus, results from both estimators are discussed below. In addition, results are presented for a model that is comparable[4] to Bovaird

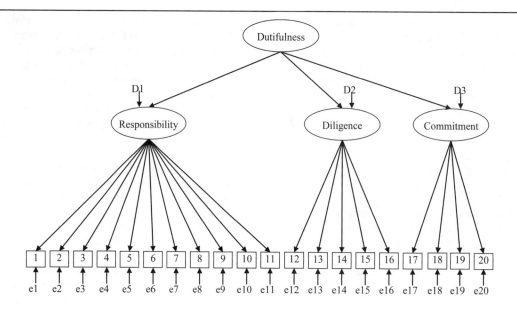

FIGURE 29.1. A simplified path diagram representing the factor structure of the SOD scale.

and Gallant's (2002) model in order to illustrate the similarities and differences among measurement models for continuous indicators and measurement models for ordered-categorical indicators. For clarity of presentation, we refer to the model estimated through the limited-information approach as WLSMV, the full-information approach as FIML, and the Bovaird and Gallant approach assuming non-normal continuous indicators as MLR.

The primary differences between continuous and ordered-categorical measurement models need to be addressed/revisited before discussing the invariance results, as these differences affect the interpretation of parameter estimates and comparability of model results. Three differences are of note. First, in Mplus the WLSMV- and FIML-estimated categorical model factor loadings are based on a probit and logit scale, respectively,[5] whereas the MLR continuous model loadings are based on an identity scale. Second, the ordered-categorical measurement models include item thresholds (item intercepts are constrained at zero), whereas the continuous measurement model includes item intercepts. The number of estimated thresholds for ordered-categorical models equals the number of response options minus one, so $6 - 1 = 5$ thresholds

are estimated per item for this example (a total of 100 thresholds is estimated for the 20 items). The number of estimated intercepts for continuous models equals the number of items, so a total of 20 intercepts is estimated for the 20 items in this example. The third primary difference is that residual variances are not freely estimated parameters in the categorical measurement models. Using WLSMV estimation with the Mplus option of theta parameterization, residual variances of the latent response variables (y^*'s) are included in the model ($\Theta^*_{\delta\delta}$ from the CCFA model presented in Equation 29.9) but are constrained at one for identification purposes (although, because this is a multiple-groups analysis, they will be freely estimated for the female group once additional constraints are placed on the model; see Muthén & Muthén, 1998–2010, for further explanation). Residual variances are not tangible parameters for the FIML estimated model.

Besides the primary differences just described, a few logistical differences among models and estimators should be noted. In terms of syntax, the Mplus GROUP-ING option is used to evaluate multiple-group measurement invariance of continuous models or ordered-categorical models with WLSMV estimation, whereas the KNOWNCLASS option is required for evaluating invariance of ordered-categorical models with FIML estimation. Unique to WLSMV, the Mplus DIFFTEST option is required for calculating nested model chi-square difference tests. For continuous measurement models with Yuan–Bentler corrected ML estimation (denoted MLR in Mplus), the chi-square difference test requires the calculation of a correction factor. For categorical measurement models with FIML estimation, nested model comparisons are based on -2^*log-likelihood ($-2LL$) deviance difference test statistics.

A final notable difference among models and estimators is that FIML estimation with numerical integration may not be computationally feasible if there are too many dimensions of integration (Wirth & Edwards, 2007). The present example requires three dimensions of integration (corresponding to the three lower-order factors with ordered-categorical indicators). Although FIML was computationally feasible in this example, the analyses took much longer (approximately 30 minutes per analysis on a dual-core processor) than the analyses based on the other estimators (3 and 2 seconds per analysis for WLSMV and MLR,[6] respectively). Speed of processing can be increased by reducing the number of integration points or utilizing Monte Carlo integration instead of the default adaptive numerical integration in Mplus, but both of these options may result in less precise log-likelihood values. In general, the overall chi-square test for categorical outcome variables should not be interpreted, so suppressing its calculation through the NOCHISQUARE option will also increase processing speed. Despite the time associated with numerical integration, Wirth and Edwards suggest that FIML is preferred over limited-information estimators (e.g., WLSMV) for evaluating models with categorical indicators when FIML is in fact computationally feasible.

Further differences among measurement models and estimators will be highlighted within the discussion of the invariance results. As explained by Millsap and Olivera-Aguilar (Chapter 23, this volume), evaluating measurement invariance involves a number of steps. In the case of higher-order factor models, such as the one used in this example, additional steps are required. Based on the recommendations of Chen, Sousa, and West (2005) and Widaman and Reise (1997), the example in this chapter evaluates the following tests of measurement invariance (in this order): configural invariance; lower-order item factor loading and threshold invariance; higher-order factor loading invariance; lower-order factor intercept invariance; lower-order residual variance invariance; and lower-order factor

disturbance invariance. In addition, tests of structural invariance—invariance of the higher-order factor variance and factor mean—are evaluated. Had the higher-order factor been omitted, only the first two measurement invariance tests (configural invariance and item factor loading and threshold invariance) would have been necessary. All syntax used in this example can be obtained from this handbook's website (*www.handbookofsem.com*).

Configural Invariance

Configural invariance was evaluated by estimating the unconstrained measurement model separately for males and females. Based on initial modification indices, the residual variances of items 15 and 16 were allowed to covary in the WLSMV estimated categorical measurement model and the MLR continuous measurement model (there were no residual variances in the FIML estimated categorical measurement model). For all three measurement models, lower-order latent factors were identified by fixing the first factor loading (i.e., loadings of items 1, 12, and 17) at 1 and the latent factor intercepts at 0. The higher-order latent factor was identified by fixing its variance and mean at 1 and 0, respectively. In addition, it was necessary to fix all residual variances at 1 in the measurement model with WLSMV estimation. The total number of freely estimated parameters varied across measurement models. A total of 128 parameters were estimated for the MLR measurement model: 17 lower-order factor loadings per group, three higher-order factor loadings per group, 20 item intercepts per group, 20 residual variances per group, one residual variance covariance per group, and three factor disturbances per group. A total of 248 parameters were freely estimated for the WLSMV ordered-categorical measurement model: 17 lower-order factor loadings per group, three higher-order factor loadings per group, 100 thresholds per group, one residual variance covariance per group, and three factor disturbances per group. With the exception of the residual variance–covariance, the same parameters were estimated for the FIML-ordered categorical measurement model (i.e., a total of 246 parameters were estimated).

See Table 29.2 for the overall model fit indices for the test of configural invariance. Because FIML with numerical integration does not allow for meaningful interpretation of the chi-square test statistic, overall model fit can only be evaluated for the MLR continu-

TABLE 29.2. Model Fit Indices for Evaluating Measurement Invariance of a Higher-Order Factor Model for the SOD Scale

	Linear measurement model (MLR[a])				Graded response model (WLSMV)				Graded response model (FIML)	
	χ^2 (df)	p	CFI	RMSEA	χ^2 (df)	p	CFI	RMSEA	LL ($\hat{\theta}$)	p
M1	689.98 (332)	< .001	.930	.047	1125.662 (332)	< .001	.962	.069	−24606.73 (246)	. . .
	$\Delta\chi^2$ (Δdf)	p	ΔCFI	ΔRMSEA	$\Delta\chi^2$ (Δdf)[b]	p	ΔCFI	ΔRMSEA	Δ-2LL ($\Delta\hat{\theta}$)	p
M2	127.71 (34)	< .001	.017	−.002	172.597 (94)	< .001	−.005	.012	225.54 (114)	< .001
M3	1.49 (2)	.474	.000	.000	6.159 (2)	.046	.000	.000	1.42 (2)	.491
M4	21.22 (3)	< .001	.003	−.001	16.982 (3)	< .001	−.002	.002	23.10 (3)	< .001
M5	34.18 (20)	.025	.002	.001	68.876 (20)	< .001	−.001	.002	. . .	. . .
M6	1.50 (3)	.681	−.001	.000	1.71 (3)	.634	−.001	.001	.81 (3)	.848
M7	.69 (1)	.406	.000	.000	.295 (1)	.587	−.009	.009	.07 (1)	.786

Note. $\hat{\theta}$, number of freely estimated parameters; M1, no constraints; M2, lower-order factor loadings and intercepts/thresholds constrained; M3, higher-order factor loadings constrained; M4, lower-order factor intercepts constrained; M5, lower-order residual variances constrained; M6, lower-order factor disturbances constrained; M7, higher-order factor variance constrained; ΔCFI = CFI$_{Previous}$ − CFI$_{Nested}$ (positive values indicate decrease in model fit); ΔRMSEA = RMSEA$_{Previous}$ − RMSEA$_{Nested}$ (negative values indicate decrease in model fit).
[a]Yuan–Bentler adjusted test statistics.
[b]Calulations based on DIFFTEST command.

ous measurement model and categorical measurement model with WLSMV estimation. The chi-square test statistic was significant for both models, suggesting a lack of *exact* model fit across gender groups (the chi-square contribution from males and females was approximately equal). However, the chi-square test statistic is often criticized for being too sensitive to small discrepancies in fit (e.g., Meade, Johnson, & Braddy, 2008), so alternative criteria of approximate fit have been developed. Using Hu and Bentler's (1999) suggested criteria of comparative fit index (CFI) < .95 and root mean square error of approximation (RMSEA) > .06[7] as an indication of *inadequate* model fit, the MLR continuous measurement model demonstrated acceptable fit based on its RMSEA but not the CFI. The opposite pattern held for the categorical measurement model with WLSMV estimation. Such an inconsistency of results makes it difficult to say with any confidence that the same SOD factor structure holds for males and females. However, because this is a demonstration, configural invariance is assumed.

Lower-Order Loading and Intercept/Threshold Invariance

Assuming evidence of configural invariance, it is meaningful to evaluate invariance of the lower-order factor loadings and item intercepts/thresholds. While loadings and intercepts of continuous measurement models are typically constrained in a sequential manner, loadings and thresholds of categorical measurement models are often constrained simultaneously. The rationale of this latter approach is that both item parameters (the loading and thresholds) influence the item probability function, so both parameters must be invariant in order to make meaningful structural-level comparisons across groups.

Upon constraining the loadings and intercepts/thresholds to be equal across genders, the lower-order factor intercepts for the female group were allowed to be freely estimated (identification is maintained through the constrained thresholds). In addition, the residual variances for the female group were allowed to be freely estimated for the categorical measurement model with WLSMV estimation (as recommended by Muthén & Muthén, 1998–2010). The chi-square/likelihood ratio difference test[8] for each measurement model was significant, as shown in Table 29.2. This suggests that the lower-order factor loadings and intercepts/thresholds of the SOD scale are noninvariant across genders in this particular sample. However, like the overall chi-square test statistic, the chi-square difference test statistic is often criticized for being too sensitive to large sample sizes and small discrepancies in fit (e.g., Meade et al., 2008). It has been suggested that alternative criteria, |ΔCFI| ≥ .01 (Cheung & Rensvold, 2002) and |ΔRMSEA| ≥ .01 (Chen, 2007), be used to indicate a meaningful decrease in model fit, but these criteria need more independent validation. Furthermore, these criteria were developed for models with continuous indicators, so it is unclear whether they are appropriate for ordered-categorical indicators. Nevertheless, using these criteria, the MLR continuous measurement model still demonstrated a decrease in fit based on ΔCFI, but not based on ΔRMSEA. The categorical measurement model with WLSMV estimation did not show a decrease in fit according to either of the criteria. At this point, the decision to move forward depends on the criterion used. For illustration purposes, the next level of invariance is evaluated. In practice, a closer inspection of the loadings and intercepts/thresholds would be warranted.

Higher-Order Loading Invariance

The next step was to constrain the higher-order factor loadings to be equal across genders, which allowed the higher-order factor variance to be freely estimated in the female group (identification is maintained through the constrained loadings). Table 29.2 shows complete agreement among all three criteria and all three measurement models (with the exception of the significant chi-square difference test, *p* = .046, for the WLSMV estimated model), providing evidence that the higher-order factor loadings are indeed invariant across genders. That is, the proportion of true score variance in dutifulness is equivalent across genders.

Because the higher-order factor loadings demonstrated invariance, the lower-order factor intercepts were constrained to be equal across genders (the factor intercepts in the female group were constrained back at zero). Similar to the test of lower-order loadings and intercepts/thresholds, the chi-square/likelihood ratio difference test was significant for all three measurement models. In contrast, ΔCFI and ΔRMSEA suggested no decrease in model fit. Again, because this is just an example, invariance of the lower-order factor intercepts is assumed, and we proceed to the next test of invariance.

Residual and Disturbance Invariance

Residual variance invariance was evaluated by constraining the residual variances to be equal across gen-

ders (the residual variances in the female group were previously fixed for identification in the WLSMV estimated model back at the configural invariance stage). This test of invariance was not evaluated for the categorical measurement model with FIML estimation, as residual variances are not testable parameters. As before, the chi-square difference tests were significant, but ΔCFI and ΔRMSEA did not indicate a decrease in model fit. Regardless of criterion, residual variance invariance is not usually seen as a requirement for evaluating structural-level relationships (Chen et al., 2005). Thus, the next level of invariance was evaluated.

Constraining the lower-order factor disturbances to be equal across genders did not decrease the fit of any of the measurement models (see Table 29.2). This suggests that the variance in responsibility, diligence, and commitment that is not accounted for by the dutifulness factor is the same across genders. Like the test of residual variances, invariance of the lower-order factor disturbances is not required for evaluating structural-level relationships (Chen et al., 2005).

Structural Invariance

Measurement invariance of the SOD scale has been fully evaluated at this point. Assuming there is sufficient evidence of measurement invariance (such an assumption is certainly debatable and is only made here for illustration purposes), it is meaningful to compare the higher-order dutifulness factor variance and factor mean across genders. To assess factor variance invariance, the factor variance in the female group was constrained back at one (i.e., it was constrained equal to the factor variance in the male group). As evidenced by the nonsignificant chi-square/likelihood ratio difference tests and satisfactory ΔCFI and ΔRMSEA values provided in Table 29.2, the dutifulness factor variance was invariant across genders. As such, the factor mean in the female group was subsequently freed to determine whether males and females have different average levels of dutifulness. Table 29.3 shows the estimated mean differences. On average, females had significantly higher levels of dutifulness than males, and this estimated difference was slightly greater for the WLSMV categorical measurement model ($\kappa_{Dutiful,Women} - \kappa_{Dutiful,Men} = .21$) than for the MLR continuous measurement model and FIML categorical measurement model ($\kappa_{Dutiful,Women} - \kappa_{Dutiful,Men} = .15$).

In terms of the omnibus tests of measurement and structural invariance, the continuous and categorical

TABLE 29.3. Selected Parameter Estimates from the Fully Constrained Sense of Duty Factor Model

	Linear measurement model (MLR)[a]			Graded response model (WLSMV)[b]			Graded response model (FIML)[c]		
	$\hat{\theta}$	SE	StdYX($\hat{\theta}$)	$\hat{\theta}$	SE	StdYX($\hat{\theta}$)	$\hat{\theta}$	SE	StdYX($\hat{\theta}$)
$\lambda_{11,Resp}$	.87	.06	.60	1.11	.07	.64	1.11	.09	.65
$\lambda_{16,Dilig}$	.81	.07	.60	.75	.06	.65	.86	.08	.65
$\lambda_{20,Commit}$	1.16	.07	.60	1.29	.09	.63	1.22	.10	.66
$E_{11,Resp}$	.71	.07	.64	1.00	...	.59	...	...	...
$E_{16,Dilig}$	.89	.08	.64	1.00	...	.58	...	...	...
$E_{20,Commit}$	.63	.06	.64	1.00	...	.60	...	...	...
ν_{11}	5.07	.04	3.58	...	...	...	...	...	...
$\tau_{11,1}$	...	...	...	−3.53	.22	−2.31	−6.65	.53	−2.34
$\tau_{11,2}$	...	...	...	−2.71	.12	−1.32	−4.89	.26	−1.29
$\tau_{11,3}$	...	...	...	−1.84	.08	−.41	−3.29	.17	−.45
$\tau_{11,4}$	...	...	...	−1.03	.07	.35	−1.85	.13	.28
$\tau_{11,5}$	...	...	...	.38	.06	1.39	.62	.11	1.37
ν_{16}	4.15	.04	4.20	...	...	...	...	...	...
$\tau_{16,1}$	...	...	...	−2.77	.15	−2.39	−5.47	.37	−2.47
$\tau_{16,2}$	...	...	...	−1.97	.09	−1.65	−3.74	.19	−1.64
$\tau_{16,3}$	...	...	...	−.74	.06	−.92	−1.39	.11	−.89
$\tau_{16,4}$	...	...	...	.42	.05	−.02	.67	.10	−.04
$\tau_{16,5}$	...	...	...	1.62	.07	1.04	2.96	.15	.99
ν_{20}	4.26	.04	4.52	...	...	...	...	...	...
$\tau_{20,1}$	...	...	...	−3.36	.18	−2.42	−6.21	.41	−2.54
$\tau_{20,2}$	...	...	...	−2.36	.11	−1.80	−4.19	.21	−1.80
$\tau_{20,3}$	...	...	...	−1.06	.08	−1.13	−1.96	.14	−1.10
$\tau_{20,4}$	...	...	...	.28	.07	−.23	.35	.12	−.23
$\tau_{20,5}$	...	...	...	1.77	.09	.91	3.12	.17	.87
$\lambda_{Resp,Dutiful}$	.55	.03	.82	.70	.04	.84	1.32	.09	.85
$\lambda_{Dilig,Dutiful}$	.60	.04	.95	.80	.05	.95	1.46	.10	.95
$\lambda_{Commit,Dutiful}$	.58	.03	.94	.77	.04	.94	1.50	.10	.95
D_{Resp}	.15	.02	.33	.21	.02	.30	.66	.09	.28
D_{Dilig}	.04	.02	.09	.07	.02	.10	.23	.07	.10
D_{Commit}	.04	.02	.11	.07	.02	.11	.27	.08	.11
$\kappa_{Dutiful,Women} - \kappa_{Dutiful,Men}$	.15	.07	.15	.21	.07	.21	.15	.07	.15

Note. $\hat{\theta}$, estimated parameter; λ, factor loading; E, item residual variance; ν, item intercept; τ, item threshold; D, factor disturbance; κ, higher-order factor mean.
[a]Lower-order factor loadings on a linear scale.
[b]Lower-order factor loadings on a probit scale.
[c]Lower-order factor loadings on a logit scale.

measurement models were very similar. The chi-square/likelihood ratio difference tests generally provided the same statistical conclusions, and ΔCFI and ΔRMSEA showed good agreement across the continuous measurement model and categorical measurement model with WLSMV estimation. Nevertheless, it is important to keep in mind that different parameters are estimated under each of the three measurement models. Thus, the meaning or practical implication of each statistical conclusion depends on the measurement model.

Model Interpretations

To illustrate the interpretational differences among models, the estimated loading and intercept/thresholds for Item 11 are interpreted. See Table 29.3 for the parameter estimates for Item 11 (as well as for Items 16 and 20). These estimates are based on the final model evaluated earlier, so all parameters are constrained to be equal across genders with the exception of the dutifulness factor mean. Under the measurement model for continuous indicators and MLR estimation, individuals with average levels of responsibility are expected to have a response of 5.07 on Item 11, and this response is expected to be .87 units greater for each additional unit of responsibility they possess. Figure 29.2 illustrates the linear relationship implied by these coefficients. There are two related problems with the continuous model estimates. First, a response of 5.07 is not an option on the integer-based SOD scale. Second, individuals who have responsibility scores 2 units above average are expected to have a response on Item 11 of 5.07 + (.87*2) =

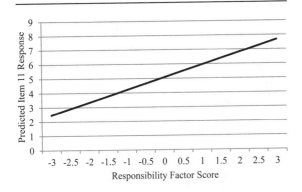

FIGURE 29.2. Predicted response for Item 11 based on the continuous measurement model with MLR estimation.

6.81. This response is outside the 1- to 6-point response option boundary of the SOD scale.

These problems are avoided by the categorical measurement models. Under the WLSMV estimated model, the *probit* of individuals' response to Item 11 is expected to be 1.11 units greater for each additional unit of responsibility they possess. Likewise, under the FIML estimated model, the *logit* of individuals' response to Item 11 is expected to be 1.11 units greater for each additional unit of responsibility they possess. In contrast to the interpretation of factor loadings, the interpretation of thresholds is the same across the WLSMV- and FIML-estimated ordered-categorical models (i.e., there are no differences in metric). Table 29.2 shows that the WLSMV- and FIML-estimated thresholds for Item 11 are quite different. Because this example is based on real data as opposed to simulated data, we do not know which estimates are better approximations of truth.[9] Under the WLSMV estimated model, a responsibility score of –3.53 is needed to endorse response Option 2 or higher with 50% probability; a score of –2.71 is needed to endorse response Option 3 or higher with 50% probability; a score of –1.84 is needed to endorse response Option 4 or higher with 50% probability; a score of –1.03 is needed to endorse response Option 5 or higher with 50% probability; and a score of .38 is needed to endorse response Option 6 with 50% probability. Under the FIML-estimated model, very little responsibility (a factor score of –6.65) is needed to endorse response Option 2 or higher with 50% probability. In fact, the amount of responsibility needed (–3.29) to endorse response Option 4 with 50% probability under FIML is approximately the same amount that is needed to endorse response Option 2 with 50% probability under WLSMV.

Rather than discussing probits/logits and thresholds, it is perhaps more meaningful to interpret Item 11 in terms of probabilities. Figure 29.3 illustrates the category response curve (CRC) for Item 11 as estimated by both models. For WLSMV, each of the six response options has the highest probability of endorsement at some point within the range from –3 to 3 on the responsibility continuum. In contrast, only response Options 4, 5, and 6 have the highest probability of endorsement at some point within the same range from –3 to 3 on the responsibility continuum for the FIML estimated model. According to the FIML estimates, then, the lowest three response options will generally be unused by 99.7% of the population (assuming the responsibility factor is normally distributed).

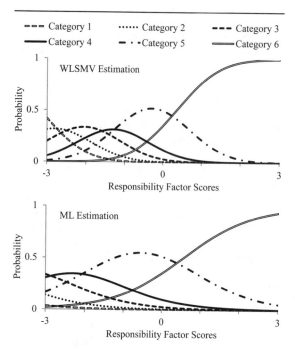

FIGURE 29.3. Category response curve for Item 11 as a function of the Responsibility factor.

$$P(y=1)=P(y\geq1)-P(y\geq2)=1-.999=.001$$
$$P(y=2)=P(y\geq2)-P(y\geq3)=.999-.997=.002$$
$$P(y=3)=P(y\geq3)-P(y\geq4)=.997-.968=.029$$
$$P(y=4)=P(y\geq4)-P(y\geq5)=.968-.853=.115$$
$$P(y=5)=P(y\geq5)-P(y\geq6)=.853-.326=.527$$
$$P(y=6)=P(y\geq6)-0=.326-0=.326$$

(29.11)

Thus, an individual with average responsibility is most likely to endorse response Option 5 on Item 11 as estimated by the WLSMV model (which is evidenced by the corresponding CRC).

Under FIML estimation, the probability of an individual with average responsibility endorsing each response option or higher is:

$$P(y\geq1)=1$$
$$P(y\geq2)=\frac{1}{1+e^{(-6.65-1.11*0)}}=.999$$
$$P(y\geq3)=\frac{1}{1+e^{(-4.89-1.11*0)}}=.993$$
$$P(y\geq4)=\frac{1}{1+e^{(-3.29-1.11*0)}}=.964$$
$$P(y\geq5)=\frac{1}{1+e^{(-1.85-1.11*0)}}=.864$$
$$P(y\geq6)=\frac{1}{1+e^{(.62-1.11*0)}}=.350$$

(29.12)

Given an individual's level of responsibility and the Item 11 parameters, the probability of a particular response option being endorsed for Item 11 can be calculated directly using parameter estimates reported in Table 29.3. Under WLSMV, the probability of an individual with average responsibility endorsing each response option or higher can be determined using Equation 29.4[10]:

$$P(y\geq1)=1$$
$$P(y\geq2)=\Phi\big((-1)(-3.53)+1.11*0\big)=\Phi(3.53)=.999$$
$$P(y\geq3)=\Phi\big((-1)(-2.71)+1.11*0\big)=\Phi(2.71)=.997$$
$$P(y\geq4)=\Phi\big((-1)(-1.84)+1.11*0\big)=\Phi(1.84)=.968$$
$$P(y\geq5)=\Phi\big((-1)(-1.03)+1.11*0\big)=\Phi(1.03)=.853$$
$$P(y\geq6)=\Phi\big((-1)(.38)+1.11*0\big)=\Phi(-.38)=.326$$

(29.10)

Then, the probability of an individual with average responsibility endorsing a *particular* response option can be determined using Equation 29.7:

Then, based on Equation 29.7 as before, the probability of an individual with average responsibility endorsing a *particular* response option under ML estimation is $P(y=1)=.001$, $P(y=2)=.006$, $P(y=3)=.029$, $P(y=4)=.100$, $P(y=5)=.514$, $P(y=6)=.350$. Therefore, an individual with average responsibility is most likely to endorse response Option 5 on Item 11 as estimated by the ML model (which again matches the corresponding CRC). These calculations show that the WLSMV and ML estimated models predict the same response option for individuals with average levels of responsibility; however, these models would predict different response options for individuals with particularly low levels of responsibility (WLSMV would predict response Option 1 or 2, whereas FIML would predict response Option 4).

CONCLUSIONS

This chapter surveys the principles and practices of establishing measurement models for latent variables with ordered-categorical indicators. Through a practical example, we have illustrated several similarities and differences between a corrected normal theory approach for developing measurement models for continuous indicators that indirectly addressed issues raised by categorical indicators, and two estimation approaches designed for modeling the categorical nature of ordinal indicators directly. Further differences between estimating measurement models for categorical indicators using a limited information approach, WLSMV, and a full information approach, FIML, were highlighted. Omnibus tests of model fit and change in model fit generally led to similar conclusions of measurement invariance regardless of measurement model; however, there were important differences in the interpretations of individual parameters across models. Importantly, the categorical measurement models were shown to avoid the problems faced by a measurement model assuming continuous indicators in which predicted values were outside plausible bounds. In addition, choice of estimator for the categorical measurement models influenced the predicted response of individuals at the lowest end of the continuum, with WLSMV-estimated thresholds tending to be less extreme than FIML-estimated thresholds. Overall, this chapter demonstrates that applicable methods exist for proper modeling of ordered-categorical indicators. With the continued advancement of increasingly efficient computing resources, researchers are encouraged to consider direct methods for modeling ordinal indicators that utilize all of the information available to them.

NOTES

1. The scaling factor, D, actually serves to place results from the original normal ogive model expressed on a probit scale on the same scale with the newer formulation presented in Equation 29.2 which uses a logistic approximation.
2. This mismatch between observed indicators and latent constructs gave rise to the latent response distribution (Muthén, 1983, 1984) as the distribution of the latent variable given certain assumptions about the observed indicators.
3. Mplus Version 6.0 additionally offers Bayesian estimation, an alternative type of estimation that is becoming increasingly popular (see Kaplan & Depaoli, Chapter 38, this volume).
4. The continuous measurement model used in this example

differs from the one used in Bovaird and Gallant's (2002) study because of its inclusion of a single residual variance–covariance (instead of multiple residual covariances) and its use of the Yuan–Bentler corrected ML estimator (which does not require listwise deletion in Mplus) instead of the Satorra–Bentler scaled ML estimator.
5. The logit link function is the default in Mplus for FIML, but the probit link function can also be specified. Only the probit link function is available for WLSMV in Mplus (Muthén & Muthén, 1998–2010).
6. All ML-based estimators require numerical integration in the context of evaluating models with categorical indicators. Thus, MLR would have been equally slow had it been paired with a categorical model.
7. These criteria were developed for continuous indicators; more research is needed to determine their acceptability for ordered categorical indicators.
8. While an overall test of model fit is not available when using FIML estimation with numerical integration, differences between nested models can be evaluated through the likelihood ratio difference test.
9. Although we do know that FIML is generally preferred over WLSMV when it is computationally feasible (Wirth & Edwards, 2007).
10. The interested reader is referred to the Mplus IRT webnote available at *http://www.statmodel.com/download/MplusIRT2.pdf*. This document describes how formulas for the IRT 2PL and GRM models vary depending on the delta versus theta parameterization, and how the factor is identified.

REFERENCES

Agresti, A. (2002). *Categorical data analysis* (2nd ed.). Hoboken, NJ: Wiley.

Babakus, E., Ferguson, C. E., Jr., & Jöreskog, K. G. (1987). The sensitivity of confirmatory maximum likelihood factor analysis to violations of measurement scale and distributional assumptions. *Journal of Marketing Research, 24*, 222–228.

Bandalos, D. L. (1997). Assessing sources of error in structural equation models: The effects of sample size, reliability, and model misspecifications. *Structural Equation Modeling, 4*, 177–192.

Bandalos, D. L. (2002). The effects of item parceling on goodness-of-fit and parameter estimate bias in structural equation modeling. *Structural Equation Modeling, 9*, 78–102.

Bandalos, D. L., & Finney, S. J. (2001). Item parceling issues in structural equation modeling. In G. A. Marcoulides & R. E. Schumacker (Eds.), *New developments and techniques in structural equation modeling* (pp. 269–275). Mahwah, NJ: Erlbaum.

Bentler, P. M. (1995). *EQS structural equations program manual*. Encino, CA: Multivariate Software, Inc.

Bollen, K. A. (1989). *Structural equations with latent variables* (Wiley Series in Probability and Mathematical Statistics). New York: Wiley.

Bovaird, J. A., & Gallant, S. J. (2002, August). *The SOD scale: An initial study of reliability and validity.* Paper presented at the annual meeting of the American Psychological Association, Chicago.

Browne, M. W. (1982). Covariance structures. In D. M. Hawkins (Ed.), *Topics in applied multivariate analysis* (pp. 72–141). Cambridge, UK: Cambridge University Press.

Browne, M. W. (1984). Asymptotically distribution-free methods for the analysis of covariance structures. *British Journal of Mathematical and Statistical Psychology, 37,* 62–83.

Cattell, R. J. (1956). Validation and intensification of the sixteen personality factor questionnaire. *Journal of Clinical Psychology, 12,* 205–214.

Chen, F. F. (2007). Sensitivity of goodness of fit indexes to lack of measurement invariance. *Structural Equation Modeling, 14,* 464–504.

Chen, F. F., Sousa, K. H., & West, S. G. (2005). Testing measurement invariance of second-order factor models. *Structural Equation Modeling, 12,* 471–492.

Cheung, G. W., & Rensvold, R. B. (2002). Evaluating goodness-of-fit indexes for testing measurement invariance. *Structural Equation Modeling, 9,* 233–255.

Christoffersson, A. (1975). Factor analysis of dichotomized variables. *Psychometrika, 40,* 5–32.

Coenders, G., Satorra, A., & Saris, W. E. (1997). Alternative approaches to structural equation modeling of ordinal data: A Monte Carlo study. *Structural Equation Modeling, 4,* 261–282.

de Ayala, R. J. (2009). *The theory and practice of item response theory.* New York: Guilford Press.

Dolan, C. V. (1994). Factor analysis of variables with 2, 3, 5, and 7 response categories: A comparison of categorical variable estimators using simulated data. *British Journal of Mathematical and Statistical Psychology, 47,* 309–326.

Flora, D. B., & Curran, P. J. (2004). An empirical evaluation of alternative methods of estimation for confirmatory factor analysis with ordinal data. *Psychological Methods, 9,* 466–491.

Hays, W. L. (1994). *Statistics* (5th ed.). Belmont, CA: Wadsworth.

Hipp, J. R., & Bollen, K. A. (2003). Model fit in structural equation models with censored, ordinal, and dichotomous variables: Testing vanishing tetrads. *Sociological Methodology, 33,* 267–305.

Hu, L., & Bentler, P. M. (1999). Cutoff criteria for fit indexes in covariance structure analysis: Conventional criteria versus new alternatives. *Structural Equation Modeling, 6,* 1–55.

Huber, P. J. (1967). The behavior of maximum likelihood estimates under non-standard conditions. In *Proceedings of the Fifth Berkeley Symposium on Mathematical Statistics and Probability* (pp. 221–233). Berkeley: University of California Press.

Jöreskog, K. G., Sörbom, D., du Toit, S., & du Toit, M. (1999). *LISREL 8: New statistical features.* Chicago: Scientific Software.

Kline, R. B. (2011). *Principles and practice of structural equation modeling* (3rd ed.). New York: Guilford Press.

Little, T. D. (1997). Mean and covariance structures (MACS) analyses of cross-cultural data: Practical and theoretical issues. *Multivariate Behavioral Research, 32,* 53–76.

Little, T. D., Cunningham, W. A., & Shahar, G. (2002). To parcel or not to parcel: Exploring the question, weighing the merits. *Structural Equation Modeling, 9,* 151–173.

Lubke, G. H., & Muthén, B. O. (2004). Applying multigroup confirmatory factor models for continuous outcomes to Likert scale data complicates meaningful group comparisons. *Structural Equation Modeling, 11,* 514–534.

Meade, A. W., Johnson, E. C., & Braddy, P. W. (2008). Power and sensitivity of alternative fit indices in tests of measurement invariance. *Journal of Applied Psychology, 93,* 568–592.

Muthén, B., & Kaplan, D. (1985). A comparison of some methodologies for the factor analysis of non-normal Likert variables. *British Journal of Mathematical and Statistical Psychology, 38,* 171–189.

Muthén, B. O. (1983). Latent variable structural equation modeling with categorical data. *Journal of Econometrics, 22,* 48–65.

Muthén, B. O. (1984). A general structural equation model with dichotomous, ordered categorical, and continuous latent variable indicators. *Psychometrika, 49,* 115–132.

Muthén, B. O. (1993). Goodness of fit with categorical and other nonnormal variables. In K. A. Bollen & J. S. Long (Eds.), *Testing structural equation models* (pp. 205–234). Newbury Park, CA: Sage.

Muthén, B. O., du Toit, S. H. C., & Spisic, D. (1997). Robust inference using weighted least squares and quadratic estimating equations in latent variable modeling with categorical and continuous outcomes (Mplus webnote). Available at *pages.gseis.ucla.edu/faculty/muthen/articles/Article-075.pdf.*

Muthén, B. O., & Kaplan, D. (1992). A comparison of some methodologies for the factor analysis of non-normal Likert variables: A note on the size of the model. *British Journal of Mathematical and Statistical Psychology, 45,* 19–30.

Muthén, L. K., & Muthén, B. O. (1998–2010). *Mplus user's guide* (6th ed.). Los Angeles: Authors.

Olsson, U. (1979). Maximum likelihood estimation of the polychoric correlation coefficient. *Psychometrika, 44,* 443–460.

Pearson, K. (1901). Mathematical contribution to the theory of evolution, VII: On the correlation of characters not quantitatively measureable. *Philosophical Transactions of the Royal Society of London A, 195,* 1–47.

Rigdon, E. E., & Ferguson, C. E. (1991). The performance of the polychoric correlation coefficient and selected fitting functions in confirmatory factor analysis with ordinal data. *Journal of Marketing Research, 28,* 491–497.

Samejima, F. (1969). *Estimation of latent trait ability using a response pattern of graded scores* (Psychometric Monograph No. 17). Bowling Green, OH: Psychometric Society.

Satorra, A., & Bentler, P. M. (1988). Scaling corrections for chi square statistics in covariance structure analysis. In *1988 Proceedings of the Business and Economic Statistics Section of the American Statistical Association* (pp. 308–313). Alexandria, VA: American Statistical Association.

Satterthwaite, F. E. (1941). Synthesis of variance. *Psychometrika, 6,* 309–316.

Shadish, W. R., Cook, T. D., & Campbell, D. T. (2002). *Experimental and quasi-experimental designs for generalized causal inference.* Boston: Houghton Mifflin.

Skrondal, A., & Rabe-Hesketh, S. (2004). *Generalized latent variable modeling: Multilevel, longitudinal, and structural equation models.* Boca Raton, FL: Chapman & Hall/CRC.

Stevens, S. S. (1960). On the theory of scales of measurement. In A. Danto & S. Morgenbesser (Eds.), *Philosophy of science* (pp. 141–149). New York: Meridian.

West, S. G., Finch, J. F., & Curran, P. J. (1995). Structural equation models with non-normal variables: Problems and remedies. In R. Hoyle (Ed.), *Structural equation modeling: Concepts, issues, and applications* (pp. 56–75). Thousand Oaks, CA: Sage.

White, H. (1982). Maximum likelihood estimation of misspecified models. *Econometrica, 50,* 1–25.

Widaman, K. F., & Reise, S. P. (1997). Exploring the measurement invariance of psychological instruments: Applications in the substance use domain. In K. J. Bryant, M. Windle, & S. G. West (Eds.), *The science of prevention: Methodological advances from alcohol and substance abuse research* (pp. 281–324). Washington, DC: American Psychological Association.

Wirth, R. J., & Edwards, M. C. (2007). Item factor analysis: Current approaches and future directions. *Psychological Methods, 12,* 58–79.

Yang, C., Nay, S., & Hoyle, R. H. (2010). Three approaches to using lengthy ordinal scales in structural equation models: Parceling, latent scoring, and shortening scales. *Applied Psychological Measurement, 34,* 122–142.

CHAPTER 30

Multilevel Structural Equation Modeling

Sophia Rabe-Hesketh
Anders Skrondal
Xiaohui Zheng

Multilevel structural equation models represent a synthesis of multilevel regression models and structural equation models.

The motivation for multilevel regression models is to handle hierarchical data where elementary units are nested in clusters, such as students in schools, which in turn may be nested in higher-level clusters (e.g., school districts or states). The latent variables, often called "random effects" in this context, can be interpreted as the effects of unobserved covariates at different levels that induce dependence among lower-level units. In contrast, the motivation for structural equation models is to handle variables that cannot be measured directly, and are hence latent, and to model their relationships with each other and with observed or manifest variables. The latent variables, often called "common factors" in this context, are measured by manifest variables and induce dependence among them.

As would be expected, the early development of multilevel structural equation modeling (SEM) was confined solely to continuous responses or measures. Early, rather ad hoc attempts at multilevel factor analysis, separately analyzing the within-cluster and between-cluster covariance matrices, include the unpublished manuscript by Cronbach (1976) and the paper by Härnquist (1978). However, remarkable earlier work in the unpublished PhD dissertation by Schmidt (1969) put multilevel factor analysis on a firm statistical footing by considering the theory and implementation of maximum likelihood estimation of a general multilevel covariance structure model (see also Schmidt & Wisenbaker, 1986).

The idea of jointly modeling within-cluster and between-cluster covariance matrices was later pursued in a series of papers by Muthén. In contrast to the work by Cronbach and Härnquist, the "varying factor means model" of Muthén and Satorra (1989) implied equal within- and between-factor loading matrices, but this was relaxed in later work (e.g., Muthén, 1994). These contributions (see in particular Muthén, 1989) were of vital practical importance, showing how multilevel SEM for continuous responses could simply be implemented in standard software for SEM. From a more theoretical perspective, a milestone in the earlier literature was the unifying work by McDonald and Goldstein (1989) and Goldstein and McDonald (1988), who proposed a general model framework for multilevel SEM of continuous responses.

Reflecting general trends in statistics, the research frontier in multilevel SEM recently moved to approaches accommodating unbalanced data and noncontinuous responses, such as dichotomous, ordinal, and nominal responses; durations and counts; as well as cross-level effects among latent variables. These developments toward "generalized multilevel SEM" were instigated by Rabe-Hesketh, Skrondal, and Pickles (2004a) in their *Psychometrika* paper with the same title that was submitted in 2001. This work unified a wide range of latent variable models, including multilevel structural equation models, within their "generalized linear latent and mixed models" (GLLAMM) framework.

More importantly from a practical point of view, Rabe-Hesketh, Skrondal, and Pickles also made available their accompanying gllamm software (e.g., Rabe-Hesketh, Skrondal, & Pickles, 2004b; Rabe-Hesketh & Skrondal, 2012) for maximum likelihood estimation of GLLAMM and empirical Bayes prediction using adaptive quadrature (Rabe-Hesketh, Skrondal, & Pickles, 2005). Alternative software handling different kinds of multilevel structural equation models include Mplus (Muthén & Muthén, 2010) and the R software developed by Fox (2010). The Latent GOLD software (Vermunt & Magidson, 2008) that was originally developed for latent class models can increasingly handle models with continuous latent variables and several levels of nesting.

The plan of the chapter is as follows: In the "Measurement Models" section, we describe single-level and multilevel measurement models. In the "Multilevel Structural Equation Models" section, we give an overview of different kinds of multilevel structural equation models, and we apply one of these models to data from a large-scale educational assessment study in the "Application" section. We use mostly path diagrams to represent the models, but in the "Modeling Frameworks" section we describe two modeling frameworks for defining models and compare them by using both frameworks to express the model used in the "Application" section. In the "Estimation" section we briefly review estimation methods before concluding with a "Discussion" section.

We adopt the following conventions regarding notation and terminology. Measures of latent variables are indexed by i, persons by j, and clusters (e.g., schools) by k. When measures are continuous they are often called "indicators" in the literature on factor analysis and SEM. Categorical (dichotomous, ordinal, or nominal) measures are typically called "items" in the literature on item response theory (IRT). We use these terms interchangeably and often use the generic term "unit" j (instead of person j) and "cluster" k, but most hypothetical and real examples refer to students j nested in schools k.

MEASUREMENT MODELS

We start by describing conventional single-level measurement models such as factor models, item response models, and generalized latent variable models before extending such models to the multilevel setting where persons are nested in clusters.

Factor Models, IRT, and Generalized Latent Variable Models

A one-dimensional factor model for continuous indicators can be written as

$$y_{ij} = \beta_i + \lambda_i \eta_j + \varepsilon_{ij}, \quad \eta_j \sim N(0, \psi), \quad \varepsilon_{ij} \sim N(0, \theta_i^{(\varepsilon)}),$$
$$\text{Cov}(\eta_j, \varepsilon_{ij}) = 0$$

Here, η_j is the common factor for person j with zero expectation and variance ψ, and λ_i represents the factor loading for indicator i. ε_{ij} is the unique factor for indicator i and person j with expectation zero and variance $\theta_i^{(\varepsilon)}$. Finally, β_i is an intercept for indicator i (often omitted when responses have been mean-centered).

IRT was developed for binary indicators in the context of ability testing (e.g., Lord, 1952; Lord & Novick, 1968). In the simplest IRT model, the one-parameter logistic (1-PL) model, the conditional response probability for item i, given ability θ_j, is specified as

$$\Pr(y_{ij} = 1 \mid \theta_j) = \frac{\exp(\theta_j - b_i)}{1 + \exp(\theta_j - b_i)}, \quad \theta_j \sim N(0, \psi)$$

This model is called a one-parameter model because there is one parameter, the item difficulty b_i, for each item. It is also known as the Rasch model (Rasch, 1960), although Rasch treated θ_j as a fixed unknown parameter instead of a latent random variable. Using conventions from generalized linear models, the model can be expressed using a logit link as

$$\text{logit} [\Pr(y_{ij} = 1 \mid \theta_j)] = \theta_j - b_i$$

We see that this model is similar to the one-dimensional factor model where the ability θ_j corresponds to the common factor η_j, and the difficulty b_i corresponds to minus the intercept, $-\beta_i$. The two differences are (1) it is a logistic regression instead of a linear regression, and (2) all factor loadings are set to 1.

The two-parameter logistic (2-PL) model has a second parameter a_i for each item i, known as a "discrimination parameter," that corresponds to a factor loading λ_i. This model can be written as

$$\text{logit}[\Pr(y_{ij} = 1 \mid \theta_j)] = a_i(\theta_j - b_i) = a_i\theta_j - a_ib_i$$

where the difficulty parameter b_i now corresponds to the ratio $-\beta_i/\lambda_i$.

Replacing the logit link by a probit link gives one-parameter and two-parameter normal ogive IRT models. These models are equivalent to the factor models for dichotomous items proposed by Bock and Lieberman (1970) and extended to the multidimensional case by Christoffersson (1975). These authors specified a traditional common-factor model for an underlying (latent) continuous response y^* (called the "response strength" by Bock and Lieberman). In the unidimensional case, the model is typically written as

$$y_{ij}^* = \beta_i + \lambda_i\eta_j + \varepsilon_{ij},$$
$$\eta_j \sim N(0, \psi), \ \varepsilon_{ij} \sim N(0, 1), \ \text{Cov}(\eta_j, \varepsilon_{ij}) = 0 \quad (30.1)$$

where

$$y_{ij} = \begin{cases} 1 & \text{if } y_{ij}^* > 0 \\ 0 & \text{otherwise} \end{cases}$$

Bartholomew (1987) and Takane and de Leeuw (1987) demonstrated that this model is equivalent to the two-parameter normal ogive IRT model. To see this, consider the probability that y_{ij} equals 1, given the common factor,

$$\Pr(y_{ij} = 1 \mid \eta_j) = \Phi(\beta_i + \lambda_i\eta_j) \equiv \Phi(a_i(\theta_i - b_i))$$

where $\Phi(\bullet)$ is the standard normal cumulative density function, or the inverse probit link function. When a standard logistic distribution is specified for ε_{ij} in Equation 30.1, the 2-PL IRT model is obtained.

It has been recognized by Bartholomew (1980), Mellenbergh (1994), and others that, conditional on the latent variables, the response model of many latent variable models is a generalized linear model (McCullagh & Nelder, 1989). We write this general model as

$$g(\mu_{ij}) = \nu_{ij} = \beta_i + \lambda_i\eta_j \qquad \textbf{(30.2)}$$

where $g(\bullet)$ is the link function, μ_{ij} is the conditional expectation of y_{ij} given the common factor η_j, ν_{ij} is the linear predictor, and the model specification is completed by choosing a distribution for $y_{ij}\mid\mu_{ij}$ from the family of exponential distributions. Bartholomew and Knott (1999) refer to the multidimensional version of this model with uncorrelated common factors as the "generalized latent variable model" (GLVM).

For nominal or unordered polytomous measures, such as the responses to multiple-choice items, the nominal response model (Bock, 1972) is typically used. Measurement models for ordered polytomous responses include the graded response model (Samejima, 1969), the partial credit model (Masters, 1982) and closely related rating scale model (Andrich, 1978), and the sequential or continuation ratio model (Hemker, van der Ark, & Sijtsma, 2001; Mellenbergh, 1995; Tutz, 1990). Given the latent variables, the response distribution for a graded response model is a cumulative logit or probit model; for partial credit and rating scale models, the response model is an adjacent-category logit model, and for the continuation ratio model it is typically a continuation ratio logit model. We describe the graded response or cumulative logit model in more detail in the "Application" section.

Although the relationship between a unidimensional factor model and a normal ogive two-parameter IRT model was already pointed out by Lord and Novick (1968) and has been emphasized by several authors in different contexts, the literature on IRT has remained largely separate from the literature on factor analysis and SEM. However, in this chapter, we ignore the largely artificial distinction between these types of models. We focus on the kinds of models that can be specified for the linear predictors of the indicators, given on the right-hand side of Equation 30.2.

When all factor loadings λ_i are known (typically set to 1), as in the 1-PL IRT model, the model in Equation 30.2 can be thought of as a generalized linear mixed model or multilevel generalized linear model. Seeing this connection requires us to view the indicators not as different variables in a multivariate setting but rather as different observations or realizations of a single variable. In other words, think of i as units at level 1, nested in persons j at level 2, and sharing a "random intercept" η_j (or random coefficient of a variable containing the factor loadings).

The similarity of latent variable models and multilevel models has been recognized for a long time, mostly in the context of growth curve modeling (McArdle, 1988; Mehta & Neale, 2005; Meredith & Tisak, 1990; Rao, 1958) and more recently in factor analysis

(Raudenbush, Rowan, & Kang, 1991; Raudenbush & Sampson, 1999) and IRT (Adams, Wilson, & Wu, 1997; De Boeck & Wilson, 2004; Kamata, 2001; Rijmen, Tuerlinckx, De Boeck, & Kuppens, 2003) and is discussed in Rabe-Hesketh and colleagues (2004a) and Skrondal and Rabe-Hesketh (2004). In this chapter, we consider measures to be at level 1 and persons at level 2. Hence, the conventional measurement models discussed in this section are two-level models, and multilevel measurement models have more than two hierarchical levels.

Multilevel Measurement Models

When persons are nested in clusters, for instance, students in schools, employees in firms, or patients in hospitals, it may be necessary to introduce cluster-level latent variables representing variability between clusters. For instance, it is well known that student achievement, a student-level latent variable, tends to vary between schools. The simplest way of modeling such variability is using a variance components factor model (Rabe-Hesketh et al., 2004a), depicted in Figure 30.1(a). Here, three observed indicators (rectangles) are regressed on a latent variable $\eta_1^{(2)}$ (circle) as shown by the arrows pointing from the latent variable to the indicators. The short arrows pointing to the indicators represent the unique factors. This measurement model lies inside a frame labeled "unit j," implying that all the variables involved vary between units, typically persons. It also

lies inside a frame labeled "cluster k," so all these variables also vary between clusters. To make this clear, we use the subscripts jk for these variables, for instance, the first and only common factor is denoted $\eta_{1jk}^{(2)}$, where the superscript (2) denotes the level at which the latent variable varies. For continuous indicators i, the measurement model can be written as

$$y_{ijk} = \beta_i + \lambda_i \eta_{1jk}^{(2)} + \varepsilon_{ijk}$$

The latent variable $\eta_{1k}^{(3)}$ varies between clusters, since it is inside the frame for clusters, but does not vary between units, since it is not inside the frame for units. The unit-level latent variable is regressed on the cluster-level latent variable with disturbance $\zeta_{1jk}^{(2)}$. As mentioned earlier, we consider indicators to be at level 1, so that units are at level 2 and clusters at level 3. In this model, $\eta_{1k}^{(3)}$ can be thought of as a school-level random intercept in a linear model for student ability,

$$\eta_{1jk}^{(2)} = \eta_{1k}^{(3)} + \zeta_{1jk}^{(2)}$$

The random intercept $\eta_{1k}^{(3)}$ induces a correlation between the abilities $\eta_{1jk}^{(2)}$ and $\eta_{1j'k}^{(2)}$ of any two students jk and $j'k$ in the same school k. We do not generally enclose random intercepts (or slopes) in circles because this helps to distinguish such random effects from latent variables measured by multiple indicators.

Fox and Glas (2001) considered such a model for binary indicators and called it a one-way random effects IRT model. If the factor loadings are set to known constants, as in one-parameter IRT models for binary data, the model becomes an ordinary multilevel random intercept model (e.g., Kamata, 2001; Maier, 2001; Raudenbush et al., 1991; Raudenbush & Sampson, 1999). Sometimes the cluster-level latent variable $\eta_{1k}^{(3)}$ is not merely viewed as a random intercept, but as a higher-level "ecological" construct (e.g., Raudenbush & Sampson, 1999).

A more complicated multilevel measurement model is given in Figure 30.1(b). Here, a cluster-level common factor $\eta_{1k}^{(3)}$ affects each indicator directly. In addition, there are cluster-level unique factors $\eta_{i+1,k}^{(3)}$ for the items. The corresponding measurement model for a continuous indicator i can be written as

$$y_{ijk} = \beta_i + \lambda_i^{(2)} \eta_{1jk}^{(2)} + \lambda_i^{(3)} \eta_{1k}^{(3)} + \eta_{i+1,k}^{(3)} + \varepsilon_{ijk}$$

where $\lambda_i^{(2)}$ and $\lambda_i^{(3)}$ are factor loadings for the unit-level and cluster-level common factors, respectively.

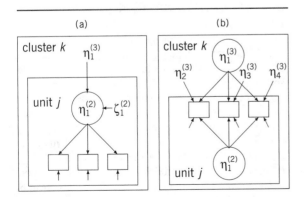

FIGURE 30.1. (a) A variance components factor model and (b) a general two-level factor model. From Rabe-Hesketh, Skrondal, and Pickles (2004a). Copyright 2004 by the Psychometric Society. Reprinted by permission.

In Longford and Muthén's (1992) application of such a model to test scores in eight areas of mathematics for students j nested in classes k, the cluster-level unique factors were interpreted as representing variability in emphases between classrooms, partly due to tracking. In IRT models, such cluster-level unique factors, or random cluster by item interactions, can be viewed as random cluster-level differential item functioning (De Jong & Steenkamp, 2007; Zheng, 2009).

By relaxing the constraint implicit in the variance components factor model that the loadings at levels 2 and 3 are the same and by including specific factors at the cluster level, the model can be thought of as comprising two separate factor models, one for each level,

$$y_{ijk} = \mu_{ik} + \beta_i + \lambda_i^{(2)}\eta_{1jk}^{(2)} + \varepsilon_{ijk}$$
$$\mu_{ik} = \lambda_i^{(3)}\eta_{1k}^{(3)} + \eta_{i+1,k}^{(3)}$$

Taking this idea further, multidimensional factor models can be specified at each level, possibly with different numbers of dimensions at the two levels (e.g., Linda, Lee, & Poon 1993; Longford, 1993; Longford & Muthén, 1992; Poon & Lee, 1992). This more general approach is commonly used in factor analysis for continuous indicators, whereas the highly structured variance components approach is more common in IRT for binary and ordinal items (e.g., Fox & Glas, 2001; Kamata, 2001; Maier, 2001). Exceptions include Steele and Goldstein (2006) and Grilli and Rampichini (2007), who consider a multidimensional multilevel measurements model for ordinal indicators.

MULTILEVEL STRUCTURAL EQUATION MODELS

In multilevel measurement models, the common factors at a given level are typically allowed to be correlated, corresponding to symmetric relationships among pairs of latent variables. In contrast, multilevel structural equation models specify regressions among latent variables, where relationships are no longer symmetric, but some latent variables serve as response variables and others as explanatory variables (sometimes referred to as "endogenous" and "exogenous" variables, although we do not like this use of the terms because they have more rigorous definitions in econometrics). In addition, there can be cross-level regressions of lower-level latent or observed variables on higher-level latent or observed variables.

We focus on the different kinds of multilevel structural equation models considered by Rabe-Hesketh and colleagues (2004a), relating them to the more recent literature whenever we are aware of connections. We also mention some kinds of multilevel structural equation models not considered by Rabe-Hesketh and colleagues (2004a). For simplicity, the measurement models considered here are unidimensional; see Goldstein, Bonnet, and Rocher (2007) for a structural equation model with multidimensional measurement models.

We start with multilevel structural equation models in which latent explanatory variables can vary at different levels. For example, predictors of student achievement may include a classroom-level latent variable, such as teachers' knowledge, and a school-level latent covariate, such as school climate. The corresponding indicators typically vary at the same level as the latent variable (e.g., tests given to teachers, or questionnaires given to principals). Figure 30.2, from Rabe-Hesketh and colleagues (2004a), shows different multilevel structures for a latent covariate, assuming that the latent response variable varies at the unit level. Variables pertaining to the latent covariate have a C subscript, whereas those pertaining the latent response variable have an R subscript. In the model shown in the top-left panel, the latent covariate varies at the cluster level and is measured by cluster-level indicators, such as school climate measured by answers to a questionnaire by the principal. In the top-right panel, the latent covariate and its indicators vary at the unit level, such as students' self-efficacy measured by a self-completion questionnaire. The latent covariate has a cluster-level random intercept $\eta_{Ck}^{(3)}$.

In the bottom-left panel, the latent covariate also varies between units, but now the school-level random intercept also affects the student outcome. The corresponding regression coefficient b_{14} can be thought of as the contextual effect of the student-level variable, for example, the effect of the school mean self-efficacy after controlling for the student's own efficacy. Marsh and colleagues. (2009) refer to this kind of model as a "doubly latent contextual model." This terminology is most easily understood by first considering a doubly manifest contextual model as used, for instance, by Raudenbush and Bryk (2002). Here, the student-level covariate is manifest instead of latent, such as socioeconomic status (SES) represented by an index x_{jk} and treated as observed without error. The contextual effect is then estimated by including the school mean SES,

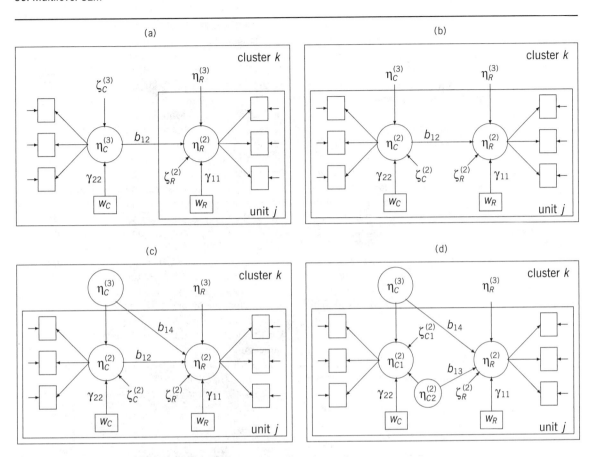

FIGURE 30.2. Path diagrams for structural equation models with latent covariates at different levels. From Rabe-Hesketh, Skrondal, and Pickles (2004a). Copyright 2004 by the Psychometric Society. Reprinted by permission.

$$\frac{1}{n_k}\sum_{j=1}^{n_k}x_{jk}$$

in the model, together with the student-level SES. Hence, the school-level aggregate is also manifest. In the terminology of Marsh and colleagues, a manifest latent contextual model is obtained by introducing a school-level random intercept for student-level SES and letting this random intercept affect the response variable. The corresponding path diagram would be the same as that in Figure 30.2(c) but with $\eta_C^{(2)}$ replaced by a manifest variable (and with the indicators of $\eta_C^{(2)}$ removed). This model would account for the sampling error due to sampling students from schools. The doubly latent

contextual model accounts for not only the sampling error but also the measurement error for the student-level latent construct. Note that the idea of using doubly latent models for contexts or ecological settings was already proposed by Raudenbush and Sampson (1999), who used multiple indicators at the housing-block level to measure neighborhood-level latent constructs such as physical and social disorder. However, their models treated factor loadings as known.

Another possibility is to consider the effect of deviations of students' latent self-efficacy from the school means. In the model in the bottom-right panel of Figure 30.2, $\zeta_{C1jk}^{(2)}$ represents such a centered latent variable since it is the error term of the regression of students' efficacy on their schools' mean efficacy. In the GLLAMM framework discussed in the "Modeling Frameworks" section, the disturbance $\zeta_{C1jk}^{(2)}$ cannot be a predictor. We therefore replace it by the latent variable $\eta_{C2jk}^{(2)}$ by setting the variance of $\zeta_{C1jk}^{(2)}$ to zero. The notion of such centered effects is common in sociological research, for instance, when studying relative deprivation. Cluster mean centering is also often used in multilevel modeling, in the doubly manifest contextual model.

The path diagrams in Figure 30.3 show random coefficient models. Specifically, the coefficient of z_{bjk} varies between clusters, as indicated by the arrow pointing from $\eta_{b2k}^{(3)}$ to the corresponding path. The latent variable $\eta_{b2k}^{(3)}$ is a cluster-level random slope of z_{bjk}. An application of such a model would be to allow the effect of student SES z_{bjk} on achievement to vary between schools. In Figure 30.3(a), there is also a latent covariate in the model, such as intelligence. Fox and Glas (2003) and Segawa, Emery, and Curry (2008) extend this idea by also allowing the slopes of latent covariates to be random.

In Figure 30.3(b), the response variable is latent. Such a model would be applicable, for instance, if achievement is latent and measured by multiple items. This kind of model, possibly with several random coefficients, is a natural extension of a multiple-indicator,

multiple-cause (MIMIC) model (e.g., Jöreskog & Goldberger, 1975) or IRT model with a latent regression (e.g., Mislevy, 1987) to a multilevel setting (Fox & Glas, 2001; Li, Oranje, & Jiang, 2009). To relax measurement invariance, or allow differential item functioning, models can include direct effects of covariates on indicators (e.g., Muthén & Lehman, 1985; Thissen & Steinberg, 1988). Chaimongkol, Huffer, and Kamata (2006) specify a random slope for such a direct effect to allow differential item functioning, say between males and females, to vary randomly between schools.

Figure 30.4 shows a random coefficient model or growth curve model for longitudinal data. In the left panel, the innermost frame on the right represents occasions or time points and contains a regression of the response variable on a time-varying variable (e.g., time itself) z_{btjk}. From the left, the unit-level random intercept $\eta_{Rjk}^{(2)}$ affects the response directly, whereas the unit-level random slope $\eta_{bjk}^{(2)}$ affects the slope of y_{tjk} on z_{btij}. The random intercept and slope are regressed on a cluster-level latent covariate $\eta_{Ck}^{(3)}$ measured by three cluster-level indicators. The figure on the right represents the same model for the case where there are three occasions with identical values of ($z_{b1jk} = 0$, $z_{b2jk} = z_{b2}$, $z_{b3jk} = z_{b3}$) for all jk. The coefficient for the path from $\eta_{bjk}^{(2)}$ to y_{2jk} is z_{b2}, and the coefficient for the path from $\eta_{bjk}^{(2)}$ to y_{3jk} is z_{b3}.

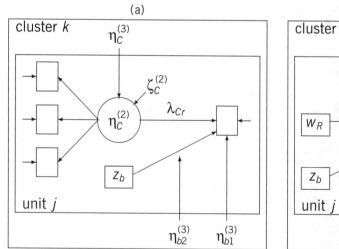
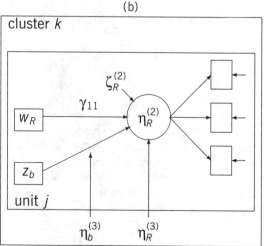

FIGURE 30.3. Random coefficient models with latent covariate (a) and latent response (b). From Rabe-Hesketh, Skrondal, and Pickles (2004a). Copyright by the Psychometric Society. Reprinted by permission.

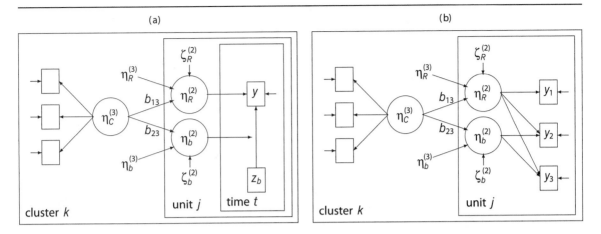

FIGURE 30.4. Level 2 random intercept and slope regressed on level 3 latent covariate. (a) General representation; (b) representation for balanced covariate. Correlations between the random effects $\eta_R^{(3)}$ and $\eta_b^{(3)}$ or between $\zeta_R^{(2)}$ and $\zeta_b^{(2)}$ would be indicated by curved double-headed arrows. From Rabe-Hesketh, Skrondal, and Pickles (2004a). Copyright 2004 by the Psychometric Society. Reprinted by permission.

Clearly, the models discussed so far do not exhaust the possibilities, but they are intended to give an idea of the kinds of models that might be useful for multilevel data.

Also important are multilevel path models with direct effects of explanatory variables on response variables, as well as indirect effects via intervening variables. Such models have attracted increasing attention in psychology, where mediation effects are of great interest. Bauer, Preacher, and Gil (2006) consider multilevel path models without latent variables and distinguish three kinds of mediation effects, each corresponding to a different kind of model. In upper-level mediation, a level 2 variable x affects a level 2 mediator M, which affects a level 1 response variable y. For example, teacher professional development may improve teacher content knowledge, which in turn improves student achievement. x may also have a direct effect on y, not mediated by the intervening variable. Bauer and colleagues (2006) represent the models as path diagrams using the conventions of Rabe-Hesketh and colleagues (2004a), with two nested frames representing variability at levels 1 and 2. In addition, they also use the short-form representation $2 \rightarrow 2 \rightarrow 1$ for upper-level mediation. Lower-level mediation of an upper-level effect is represented by $2 \rightarrow 1 \rightarrow 1$, meaning that a level 2 variable x affects a level 1 mediator M, which affects y. For example, a new curriculum may improve student engagement, which subsequently improves student achieve-

ment. Finally, lower-level mediation of a lower-level effect only involves level 1 variables and is represented by $1 \rightarrow 1 \rightarrow 1$. Any path from 1 to 1 may correspond to a coefficient that varies randomly between level 2 units. Raudenbush and Sampson (1999) consider multilevel models with mediation of the kind $2 \rightarrow 2 \rightarrow 2$, where the mediator and response variables are latent variables and factor loadings are treated as known.

APPLICATION

Here we consider an application to Progress in International Reading Literacy Study (PIRLS) data from Zheng (2009). A similar model was applied to Program for International Student Assessment (PISA) data by Rabe-Hesketh, Skrondal, and Zheng (2007).

PIRLS Data

PIRLS is a series of international comparative assessments of reading literacy of fourth-grade students. PIRLS is coordinated by the International Association for the Evaluation of Educational Achievement (IEA). In 2006, 45 countries and subnational education systems took part.

PIRLS examines three aspects of reading literacy, purposes for reading, processes of comprehension, and reading behaviors and attitudes (Mullis, Kennedy, Martin, & Sainsbury, 2006). The purposes include reading for literacy experience and reading to acquire and use information. For each of these purposes, four types of comprehension processes are assessed, and we consider one of these, making straightforward inferences. In addition to the reading assessment, participating students and schools were asked to complete background questionnaires to provide information about reading behaviors and attitudes.

Here we analyze the American sample of the PIRLS 2006 assessment data that comprise 5,190 fourth-grade students j from 183 U.S. schools k. Six items i about making inferences were chosen from a reading passage (Flowers); three multiple-choice questions and three constructed response questions (where the student writes down the answer). All items were scored as 1 (correct) or 0 (incorrect).

Four observed covariates from the student questionnaire are included in the analyses: student gender ([girl]; 1: girl, 0: boy), language spoken at home ([English]; 1: speak English at home, 0: no English at home), time spent reading ([reading]; 1: some time spent reading every day, 0: otherwise), and number of books at home ([books]; 1: more than 25 books, 0: otherwise).

At the school level, we focus on school climate measured by six survey questions in the school questionnaire completed by school principals. The six questions concern teachers' job satisfaction, teachers' expectations for student achievement, parental support for student achievement, students' regard for school property, students' desire to do well in school, and students' regard for each other's welfare. The ordinal responses to the six questions originally had five categories that were collapsed into three categories due to sparseness.

School climate is reflected in the practice of teachers and school administrators, as well as aspects of the school environment that affect the attitudes, behavior, and achievement of students. Studies have suggested that school climate is associated with academic success (Ma, Ma, & Bradley, 2008; Raudenbush & Willms, 1995). The main research question motivating our analysis is whether there is a relationship between the school-level latent variable "school climate" and the student-level latent variable "reading ability."

Model

We number the six student assessment items as $i = 1$, ..., 6 and the six school-level items as $i = 7, \ldots, 12$.

The student-level measurement model for reading item i for student j from school k is a 2-PL IRT model,

$$
\begin{aligned}
\mathrm{logit}[\Pr(y_{ijk} = 1 \mid \eta_{1jk}^{(2)})] &= \beta_i + \lambda_i^{(2)}\eta_{1jk}^{(2)} \\
&= \lambda_i^{(2)}[\eta_{1jk}^{(2)} - (-\beta_i/\lambda_i^{(2)})], \quad i = 1, \ldots, 6
\end{aligned}
$$

with discrimination parameter $\lambda_i^{(2)}$, difficulty parameter $-\beta_i/\lambda_i^{(2)}$, and student-level latent variable, reading ability $\eta_{1jk}^{(2)}$. The first discrimination parameter, $\lambda_1^{(2)}$, is set to 1 for identification (the residual ability variance is a free parameter, see below).

The measurement model for school climate is a 2-PL graded response model. In terms of a latent response y_{ik}^* for item i and school k, the model can be written as

$$
y_{ik}^* = \lambda_i^{(3)}\eta_{1k}^{(3)} + \varepsilon_{ik}, \quad i = 7, \ldots, 12
$$

where $\eta_{1k}^{(3)}$ is the school-level latent variable, school climate, and $\lambda_i^{(3)}$ are discrimination parameters (with $\lambda_1^{(3)} = 1$ for identification). The error term ε_{ik} has a standard logistic distribution. The observed ordinal responses to the survey items are generated from the threshold model

$$
y_{ik} = \begin{cases}
1 & \text{if} \quad -\infty \le y_{ik}^* < \alpha_1 + \tau_{i1} \\
2 & \text{if} \quad \alpha_1 + \tau_{i1} \le y_{ik}^* < \alpha_2 + \tau_{i2} \quad \tau_{71} = \tau_{72} = 0 \\
3 & \text{if} \quad \alpha_2 + \tau_{i2} \le y_{ik}^* < \infty
\end{cases}
$$

In the threshold model α_s ($s = 1, 2$) represents the sth threshold for item 7 and τ_{is} ($i = 8, \ldots, 12$) the difference in the sth threshold between item i and item 7. Thus, $\alpha_s + \tau_{is}$ becomes the threshold parameter for the sth threshold of item i. When there are no latent variables, this kind of model is called a "cumulative ordinal logit model" or a "proportional odds model." The cumulative probabilities are given by

$$
\begin{aligned}
\mathrm{logit}\,[\Pr(y_{ik} > s \mid \eta_k^{(3)})] &= \lambda_i^{(3)}\eta_{1k}^{(3)} - (\alpha_s + \tau_{is}) \\
&= \lambda_i^{(3)}[\eta_{1k}^{(3)} - (\alpha_s + \tau_{is})/\lambda_i^{(3)}], \quad s = 1, 2
\end{aligned}
$$

so that $(\alpha_s + \tau_{is})/\lambda_i^{(3)}$ can be interpreted as the difficulty of rating item i above s.

The structural models are

$$
\begin{aligned}
\eta_{1k}^{(2)} &= b_{12}\zeta_{1k}^{(3)} + \gamma_1 w_{1jk} + \gamma_2 w_{2jk} + \gamma_3 w_{3jk} + \gamma_4 w_{4jk} + \zeta_{2k}^{(3)} + \zeta_{1jk}^{(2)} \\
\eta_{1k}^{(3)} &= \zeta_{1k}^{(3)}
\end{aligned}
$$

where b_{12} is the cross-level effect of school climate on student reading proficiency, w_{1jk} to w_{4jk} are the student-level covariates, and γ_1 to γ_4 are the associated regression coefficients. The disturbances are independently identically distributed as $\zeta_{2k}^{(3)} \sim N(0, \psi_2^{(3)})$, $\zeta_{1jk}^{(2)} \sim N(0, \psi_1^{(2)})$, and $\zeta_{1k}^{(3)} \sim N(0, \psi_1^{(3)})$.

A path diagram for the model, for simplicity showing only three items at the student and school levels and only one student-level covariate, is given in Figure 30.5. Note that the model is very similar to the model in Figure 30.2(a) but does not include a school-level predictor for school climate, such as the crime rate in the school's neighborhood.

Results and Interpretation

Maximum likelihood estimates for the model are given in Table 30.1. All estimates were obtained using gllamm (Rabe-Hesketh et al., 2004b; Rabe-Hesketh & Skrondal, 2012), which uses adaptive quadrature (Rabe-Hesketh, Skrondal, & Pickles, 2002, 2005) and runs in Stata (StataCorp, 2011).

Confirming our main hypothesis, the estimated effect of school climate on student reading ability is positive and significant at the 5% level ($p = .01$) after controlling for student-level covariates. Student gender, time spent reading, and number of books at home also have statistically significant effects on student reading performance. After controlling for the other variables, girls on average perform better than boys; students who report spending some time reading every day perform better than those who do not and having more than 25 books at home is positively associated with reading achievement. Although students whose home lan-

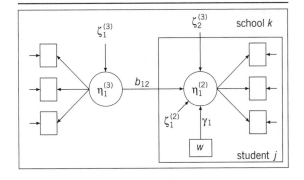

FIGURE 30.5. Multilevel structural equation model for PIRLS data.

TABLE 30.1. Maximum Likelihood Estimates for Reading Achievement Study

Parameter		Est.	(SE)	Difficulty
Reading ability				
Measurement model				$-\beta_i/\lambda_i^{(2)}$
β_1	(Item 1)	0.78	(0.31)	−0.78
β_2	(Item 2)	1.05	(0.52)	−0.60
β_3	(Item 3)	−0.36	(0.50)	0.21
β_4	(Item 4)	−0.18	(0.42)	0.13
β_5	(Item 5)	−0.06	(0.51)	0.04
β_6	(Item 6)	2.50	(0.66)	−1.13
$\lambda_1^{(2)}$	(Item 1)	1	—	
$\lambda_2^{(2)}$	(Item 2)	1.75	(0.39)	
$\lambda_3^{(2)}$	(Item 3)	1.71	(0.38)	
$\lambda_4^{(2)}$	(Item 4)	1.40	(0.31)	
$\lambda_5^{(2)}$	(Item 5)	1.75	(0.38)	
$\lambda_6^{(2)}$	(Item 6)	2.22	(0.56)	
Structural model				
b_{12}	(School climate)	0.10	(0.04)	
γ_1	(Girl)	0.16	(0.08)	
γ_2	(Reading)	0.16	(0.06)	
γ_3	(English)	0.16	(0.09)	
γ_4	(Books)	0.38	(0.28)	
$\psi_2^{(3)}$	(Rand. intercept. var.)	0.14	(0.11)	
$\psi_1^{(2)}$	(Residual var.)	0.76	(0.13)	
School climate				
Measurement model				$(\alpha_s + \tau_{is})/\lambda_i^{(3)}$
α_1	(T's satisfaction)	−2.43	(0.29)	−2.43
$\tau_{8,1}$	(T's expectations)	−0.64	(0.45)	−2.53
$\tau_{9,1}$	(Parental support)	2.39	(0.35)	−0.02
$\tau_{10,1}$	(S's regard for property)	0.27	(0.43)	−1.11
$\tau_{11,1}$	(S's ambition)	0.14	(0.53)	−0.83
$\tau_{12,1}$	(S's regard for each other)	0.84	(0.44)	−0.65
α_2	(T's satisfaction)	1.22	(0.22)	1.22
$\tau_{8,2}$	(T's expectations)	−0.79	(0.27)	0.35
$\tau_{9,2}$	(Parental support)	1.51	(0.44)	1.44
$\tau_{10,2}$	(S's regard for property)	1.26	(0.41)	1.27
$\tau_{11,2}$	(S's ambition)	2.93	(0.75)	1.49
$\tau_{12,2}$	(S's regard for each other)	2.96	(0.71)	1.71
$\lambda_7^{(3)}$	(Item 7)	1	—	
$\lambda_8^{(3)}$	(Item 8)	1.22	(0.27)	
$\lambda_9^{(3)}$	(Item 9)	1.90	(0.43)	
$\lambda_{10}^{(3)}$	(Item 10)	1.95	(0.44)	
$\lambda_{11}^{(3)}$	(Item 11)	2.78	(0.72)	
$\lambda_{12}^{(3)}$	(Item 12)	2.45	(0.60)	
Structural model				
$\psi_1^{(3)}$	(School climate var.)	1.37	(0.24)	

guage was English score higher than students with a home language other than English, controlling for the other variables, the difference is not significant at the 5% level.

We can interpret the exponentiated regression coefficients as adjusted student-specific odds ratios for getting the first item right, as this item has a discrimination parameter of 1. The estimated odds ratios are 1.17 for girl, reading, and English, implying a 17% increase in the odds associated with these dummy variables, and 1.46 for books, implying a 46% increase in the odds of getting the first item right for those who read occasionally compared with those who do not, controlling for the other variables. For item 6 the corresponding odds ratios are 1.42 (= exp(2.22 × 0.16)) for girl, reading, and English and 2.32 (= exp(2.22 × 0.38)) for books. Regarding the effect of school climate, we consider a 0.69 increase in school climate, as this corresponds to doubling the odds that the principal will rate question 7 (with discrimination parameter 1) above a given category (above 1 or above 2), since exp(0.69) = 2. Such an increase in school climate is associated with a 7% (= 100%[exp(0.69 × 0.10) − 1]) increase in the odds of getting the first item right and a 17% (= 100%[exp(0.69 × 0.10 × 2.22) − 1]) increase in the odds of getting the last item right, so the estimated effect size is rather small.

The school-level random intercept for reading proficiency has an estimated variance of 0.14, and the student-level residual variance is estimated as 0.76. Therefore, an estimated 16% of the residual variance in reading proficiency is between schools.

In the student-level measurement model for the binary reading items, we see that the estimated discrimination parameters range from 1.00 to 2.22 and the estimated difficulties, given in the last column, range from −1.13 to 0.21. In the school-level measurement model, the estimated discrimination parameters range from 1.00 to 2.76. The estimated difficulties of rating questions above 1 (given in the last column) range from −2.51 to −0.02. We see that teachers' expectations for student achievement (item 8) is the easiest item and parental support for student achievement (item 9) is the hardest item for ratings above 1. Regarding ratings above 2 (i.e., in the top category), the estimated difficulties range from 0.35 to 1.71. Teacher's expectations is again the easiest, whereas students' regard for each other's welfare (item 12) now is the hardest, followed by students' desire to do well in school (item 11). The variance of school climate is estimated as 1.37.

MODELING FRAMEWORKS

We consider two modeling frameworks, GLLAMM, and the within–between framework. For each framework there is a software package, gllamm and Mplus, respectively, with a syntax that allows models to be specified within the corresponding frameworks.

GLLAMM Framework

The generalized linear latent and mixed (GLLAMM) framework, introduced by Rabe-Hesketh, Skrondal, and Pickles (2004a) and described by Skrondal and Rabe-Hesketh (2004), treats the different response variables, such as indicators or item responses, as level 1 units i that can be viewed as nested in units (e.g., subjects) j at level 2, which in turn may be nested in clusters k at level 3, and so forth, up to level L. Given the latent and observed explanatory variables, the responses are conditionally independent and follow generalized linear models with link functions $g_{ijk\ldots}(\bullet)$, linear predictors $v_{ijk\ldots}$ and distributions from the exponential family.

The linear predictor has the following form (omitting subscripts):

$$v = \mathbf{x}'\boldsymbol{\beta} + \sum_{l=2}^{L}\sum_{m=1}^{M_l} \eta_m^{(l)} \mathbf{z}_m^{(l)'} \boldsymbol{\lambda}_m^{(l)}$$

where $\eta_m^{(l)}$ is the mth latent variable at level l, $m = 1, \ldots, M_l$, $\mathbf{x}$, and $\mathbf{z}_m^{(l)}$ are vectors of covariates and known constants, and $\boldsymbol{\beta}$ and $\boldsymbol{\lambda}_m^{(l)}$ are parameter vectors. This part of the model is the GLLAMM response model.

The two-level ($L = 2$) version of the GLLAMM response model can generate a wide range of standard multilevel and measurement models. It is convenient to write these two-level models using the following vector notation:

$$\mathbf{v}_j = \mathbf{X}_j \boldsymbol{\beta} + \sum_{m=1}^{M_2} \eta_{mj}^{(2)} \mathbf{Z}_{mj}^{(2)} \boldsymbol{\lambda}_m^{(2)}$$

where $\mathbf{v}_j$ is the vector of linear predictors for unit j, $\mathbf{X}_j$ is a matrix with rows $\mathbf{x}'_{ij}$, and $\mathbf{Z}_{mj}^{(2)}$ are matrices with rows $\mathbf{z}_{mij}^{(2)'}$. Then a unidimensional generalized measurement model can then be expressed as

$$
\underbrace{\begin{bmatrix} v_{1j} \\ v_{2j} \\ v_{3j} \end{bmatrix}}_{\mathbf{v}_j} = \underbrace{\begin{bmatrix} 1 & 0 & 0 \\ 0 & 1 & 0 \\ 0 & 0 & 1 \end{bmatrix}}_{\mathbf{X}_j} \underbrace{\begin{bmatrix} \beta_1 \\ \beta_2 \\ \beta_3 \end{bmatrix}}_{\boldsymbol{\beta}} + \eta_{1j}^{(2)} \underbrace{\begin{bmatrix} 1 & 0 & 0 \\ 0 & 1 & 0 \\ 0 & 0 & 1 \end{bmatrix}}_{\mathbf{Z}_{1j}^{(2)}} \underbrace{\begin{bmatrix} \lambda_{11}^{(2)} \\ \lambda_{12}^{(2)} \\ \lambda_{13}^{(2)} \end{bmatrix}}_{\boldsymbol{\lambda}_1^{(2)}}
$$

$$= \begin{bmatrix} \beta_1 + \eta_{1j}^{(2)}\lambda_{11}^{(2)} \\ \beta_2 + \eta_{1j}^{(2)}\lambda_{12}^{(2)} \\ \beta_3 + \eta_{1j}^{(2)}\lambda_{13}^{(2)} \end{bmatrix}$$

and a two-level regression model as

$$\underbrace{\begin{bmatrix} v_{1j} \\ v_{2j} \\ v_{3j} \end{bmatrix}}_{\mathbf{v}_j} = \underbrace{\begin{bmatrix} 1 & t_{1j} \\ 1 & t_{2j} \\ 1 & t_{3j} \end{bmatrix}}_{\mathbf{X}_j} \underbrace{\begin{bmatrix} \beta_1 \\ \beta_2 \end{bmatrix}}_{\boldsymbol{\beta}} + \eta_{1j}^{(2)} \underbrace{\begin{bmatrix} 1 \\ 1 \\ 1 \end{bmatrix}}_{\mathbf{Z}_{1j}^{(2)}} + \eta_{2j}^{(2)} \underbrace{\begin{bmatrix} t_{1j} \\ t_{2j} \\ t_{3j} \end{bmatrix}}_{\mathbf{Z}_{2j}^{(2)}}$$

$$= \begin{bmatrix} \beta_1 + \eta_{1j}^{(2)} + (\beta_2 + \eta_{2j}^{(2)})t_{1j} \\ \beta_1 + \eta_{1j}^{(2)} + (\beta_2 + \eta_{2j}^{(2)})t_{2j} \\ \beta_1 + \eta_{1j}^{(2)} + (\beta_2 + \eta_{2j}^{(2)})t_{3j} \end{bmatrix}$$

In the GLLAMM structural model, the latent variables can be regressed on same and higher-level latent variables and on observed covariates via the following system of equations:

$$\boldsymbol{\eta} = \mathbf{B}\boldsymbol{\eta} + \boldsymbol{\Gamma}\mathbf{w} + \boldsymbol{\zeta}$$

where $\boldsymbol{\eta}$ is the vector of all latent variables, arranged from lowest level to highest level, with corresponding vector of disturbances $\boldsymbol{\zeta}$,

$$\boldsymbol{\eta}' = (\overbrace{\eta_1^{(2)},\eta_2^{(2)},...,\eta_{M_2}^{(2)}}^{\text{Level 2}},...,\overbrace{\eta_1^{(l)},...,\eta_{M_l}^{(l)}}^{\text{Level }l},...,\overbrace{\eta_1^{(L)},...,\eta_{M_L}^{(L)}}^{\text{Level }L})$$

$$\boldsymbol{\zeta}' = (\zeta_1^{(2)},\zeta_2^{(2)},...,\zeta_{M_2}^{(2)},...,\zeta_1^{(l)},...,\zeta_{M_l}^{(l)},...,\zeta_1^{(L)},...,\zeta_{M_L}^{(L)})$$

To disallow regressions of higher-level latent variables on lower-level latent variables and avoid loops or feedback relationships, $\mathbf{B}$ is a strictly upper triangular matrix of regression coefficients (the diagonal and all elements below the diagonal are zero). $\mathbf{w}$ is a vector of observed covariates, and $\boldsymbol{\Gamma}$ is a matrix of regression coefficients. The disturbances $\boldsymbol{\zeta}$ are specified as multivariate normal with correlations among disturbances at the same level, but not among disturbances at different levels.

Within–Between Framework

The within–between framework (e.g., Asparouhov & Muthén, 2007; Longford & Muthén, 1992; Muthén, 1989, 1994) for continuous responses and data with only one clustering level (e.g., students nested in schools)

defines the models in terms of two standard structural equation models.

The within-cluster model specifies how responses vary around the cluster means, whereas the between-cluster model specifies how the cluster means vary. Stacking the responses for different items in a vector $\mathbf{y}_{jk}$ for unit j in cluster k and assuming multivariate normality, the decomposition into within and between models can be written as

$$\mathbf{y}_{jk} \sim N(\boldsymbol{\mu}_k, \boldsymbol{\Sigma}_W)$$
$$\boldsymbol{\mu}_k \sim N(\boldsymbol{\mu}, \boldsymbol{\Sigma}_B)$$

where $\boldsymbol{\mu}_k$ are the cluster means for cluster k, $\boldsymbol{\Sigma}_W$ is the within-cluster covariance matrix, $\boldsymbol{\mu}$ are the grand means, and $\boldsymbol{\Sigma}_B$ is the between-cluster covariance matrix. Ansari and Jedidi (2000) use the same formulation for binary data with y_{jk} replaced by the corresponding latent responses y_{jk}^*, giving a probit model. Asparouhov and Muthén (2007) use this formulation for mixtures of continuous, binary, and censored responses.

Leaving $\boldsymbol{\mu}_k$ unspecified, the within-cluster model is a structural equation model of the form

$$\mathbf{y}_{jk} = \boldsymbol{\mu}_k + \boldsymbol{\Lambda}^{(2)}\boldsymbol{\eta}_{jk}^{(2)} + \boldsymbol{\varepsilon}_{jk}^{(2)}$$
$$\boldsymbol{\eta}_{jk}^{(2)} = \mathbf{B}^{(2)}\boldsymbol{\eta}_{jk}^{(2)} + \boldsymbol{\zeta}_{jk}^{(2)}$$

In the measurement model, $\boldsymbol{\eta}_{jk}^{(2)}$ is the vector of unit-level latent variables with factor-loading matrix $\boldsymbol{\Lambda}^{(2)}$, and $\boldsymbol{\varepsilon}_{jk}^{(2)}$ is a vector of unit-level unique factors. (We use the (2) superscript to denote unit-level variables for consistency with the GLLAMM framework.) In the structural model, $\mathbf{B}^{(2)}$ is a matrix of regression coefficients for relationships among unit-level latent variables, and $\boldsymbol{\varepsilon}_{jk}^{(2)}$ is a vector of unit-level disturbances.

The between-cluster model is a structural equation model of the form

$$\boldsymbol{\mu}_k = \boldsymbol{\mu} + \boldsymbol{\Lambda}^{(3)}\boldsymbol{\eta}_k^{(3)} + \boldsymbol{\varepsilon}_k^{(3)}$$
$$\boldsymbol{\eta}_k^{(3)} = \mathbf{B}^{(3)}\boldsymbol{\eta}_k^{(3)} + \boldsymbol{\zeta}_k^{(3)}$$

where $\boldsymbol{\eta}_k^{(3)}$, $\boldsymbol{\varepsilon}_k^{(3)}$, and $\boldsymbol{\zeta}_k^{(3)}$ are the cluster-level counterparts of $\boldsymbol{\eta}_{jk}^{(2)}$, $\boldsymbol{\varepsilon}_{jk}^{(2)}$, and $\boldsymbol{\zeta}_{jk}^{(2)}$. Covariates can be included via phantom variables (i.e., by treating the covariate as the only indicator of a phantom latent variable and setting the unique factor variance to zero) so that the phantom variable equals the covariate. In the within–between framework, this corresponds to partitioning the covariate into a latent variable at each level. Asparouhov and Muthén (2007) use the notation $\mathbf{x} = \mathbf{x}_b + \mathbf{x}_w$ and add terms $\mathbf{\Gamma}_w \mathbf{x}_w$ and $\mathbf{\Gamma}_b \mathbf{x}_b$ to the within and between structural models, respectively.

Path diagrams for these models consist of separate diagrams for the within and between models. Using the conventions of Muthén and Muthén (2010), the unidimensional factor model in Figure 30.1(b) is represented in Figure 30.6. In the within model, the filled circles represent the cluster means $\mathbf{\mu}_k = (\mu_{1k}, \mu_{2k}, \mu_{3k})'$ that are referred to as y_1, y_2, and y_3 in the between model. In the between model, the cluster means are shown as circles because they are continuous latent variables at the cluster level. The between model looks the same as the within model, apart from the circles replacing the rectangles for the response variables. (Note that Mplus can also handle noncontinuous responses and has several options for handling covariates at the different levels.)

Example

To compare the frameworks, we now express the model in Figure 30.5 using each framework. Although the application had more than three indicators at the student and school levels, we write the models for the case of three continuous indicators at each level. We also omit the covariates for simplicity.

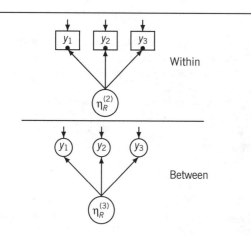

FIGURE 30.6. Two-level unidimensional factor model using within–between formulation.

In GLLAMM

For compactness, we write the GLLAMM response model for a vector containing the three indicators for a student jk and the three indicators for the school k to which the student belongs, separating rows that pertain to the student-level indicators from rows that pertain to the school-level indicators with a horizontal line:

$$
\underbrace{\begin{bmatrix} v_{1jk} \\ v_{2jk} \\ v_{3jk} \\ \hline v_{4jk} \\ v_{5jk} \\ v_{6jk} \end{bmatrix}}_{\mathbf{v}_{jk}} = \underbrace{\mathbf{I}\mathbf{\beta}}_{\mathbf{X}_k \mathbf{\beta}} + \eta_{Rjk}^{(2)} \underbrace{\begin{bmatrix} 1 & 0 & 0 \\ 0 & 1 & 0 \\ 0 & 0 & 1 \\ 0 & 0 & 0 \\ 0 & 0 & 0 \\ 0 & 0 & 0 \end{bmatrix}}_{\mathbf{Z}_{1k}^{(2)}} \underbrace{\begin{bmatrix} \lambda_1 \\ \lambda_2 \\ \lambda_3 \end{bmatrix}}_{\mathbf{\lambda}_1^{(2)}}
$$

$$
+ \eta_{Rk}^{(3)} \underbrace{\begin{bmatrix} 0 & 0 & 0 \\ 0 & 0 & 0 \\ 0 & 0 & 0 \\ 1 & 0 & 0 \\ 0 & 1 & 0 \\ 0 & 0 & 1 \end{bmatrix}}_{\mathbf{Z}_{1k}^{(3)}} \underbrace{\begin{bmatrix} \lambda_4 \\ \lambda_5 \\ \lambda_6 \end{bmatrix}}_{\mathbf{\lambda}_1^{(3)}} + \eta_{Ck}^{(3)} \underbrace{\begin{bmatrix} 0 \\ 0 \\ 0 \\ 0 \\ 0 \\ 0 \end{bmatrix}}_{\mathbf{Z}_{2k}^{(3)}} \underbrace{\begin{matrix} 1 \\ \lambda_2^{(3)} \end{matrix}}_{}
$$

For simplicity, we have used the notation λ_i ($i = 1$, 2, 3) for the elements of $\mathbf{\lambda}_1^{(2)}$, and λ_i ($i = 4, 5, 6$) for the elements of $\mathbf{\lambda}_1^{(3)}$. For continuous indicators, the model above for the linear predictors $\mathbf{v}_{jk}$ would be combined with an identity link and a normal distribution for the responses given the linear predictors.

The structural model can be written as

$$
\underbrace{\begin{bmatrix} \eta_{Rjk}^{(2)} \\ \eta_{Rk}^{(3)} \\ \eta_{Ck}^{(3)} \end{bmatrix}}_{\mathbf{\eta}} = \underbrace{\begin{bmatrix} 0 & b & 1 \\ 0 & 0 & 0 \\ 0 & 0 & 0 \end{bmatrix}}_{\mathbf{B}} \underbrace{\begin{bmatrix} \eta_{Rjk}^{(2)} \\ \eta_{Rk}^{(3)} \\ \eta_{Ck}^{(3)} \end{bmatrix}}_{\mathbf{\eta}} + \underbrace{\begin{bmatrix} \zeta_{Rjk}^{(2)} \\ \zeta_{Rk}^{(3)} \\ \zeta_{Ck}^{(3)} \end{bmatrix}}_{\mathbf{\zeta}}
$$

In Within–Between Formulation

As for the GLLAMM formulation, we consider the three indicators for a student and for the school to which the student belongs. The within model can then be written as

$$
\begin{bmatrix} y_{1jk} \\ y_{2jk} \\ y_{3jk} \\ y_{4jk} \\ y_{5jk} \\ y_{6jk} \end{bmatrix} = \begin{bmatrix} \mu_{1k} \\ \mu_{2k} \\ \mu_{3k} \\ \mu_{4k} \\ \mu_{5k} \\ \mu_{6k} \end{bmatrix} + \begin{bmatrix} \lambda_1 \\ \lambda_2 \\ \lambda_3 \\ 0 \\ 0 \\ 0 \end{bmatrix} \begin{bmatrix} \left(\eta_{Rjk}^{(2)} \right) \\ \zeta_{Rjk}^{(2)} \end{bmatrix} + \begin{bmatrix} \varepsilon_{1jk}^{(2)} \\ \varepsilon_{2jk}^{(3)} \\ \varepsilon_{3jk}^{(3)} \\ 0 \\ 0 \\ 0 \end{bmatrix}
$$

Note that it is necessary to set the unique factors, or their variances, and the factor loadings to zero for the school-level indicators, since these indicators do not vary within clusters.

The between model can be written as

$$
\begin{bmatrix} \mu_{1k} \\ \mu_{2k} \\ \mu_{3k} \\ \mu_{4k} \\ \mu_{5k} \\ \mu_{6k} \end{bmatrix} = \begin{bmatrix} \lambda_1 & 0 \\ \lambda_2 & 0 \\ \lambda_3 & 0 \\ 0 & \lambda_4 \\ 0 & \lambda_5 \\ 0 & \lambda_6 \end{bmatrix} \begin{bmatrix} \eta_{Rk}^{(3)} \\ \eta_{Ck}^{(3)} \end{bmatrix} + \begin{bmatrix} 0 \\ 0 \\ 0 \\ \varepsilon_{4k}^{(3)} \\ \varepsilon_{5k}^{(3)} \\ \varepsilon_{6k}^{(3)} \end{bmatrix},
$$

$$
\begin{bmatrix} \eta_{Rk}^{(3)} \\ \eta_{Ck}^{(3)} \end{bmatrix} = \begin{bmatrix} 0 & b \\ 0 & 0 \end{bmatrix} \begin{bmatrix} \eta_{Rk}^{(3)} \\ \eta_{Ck}^{(3)} \end{bmatrix} + \begin{bmatrix} \zeta_{Rk}^{(3)} \\ \zeta_{Ck}^{(3)} \end{bmatrix}.
$$

For the student-level indicators, the factor loadings in the between model are constrained to be equal to those in the within model, and the unique factor variances are set to zero because this is a variance components factor model (no arrows pointing from the cluster frame directly to the student-level indicators in Figure 30.5). In the structural part of the between model, the between component $\eta_{Rk}^{(3)}$ of the student-level latent variable is regressed on the school-level latent variable.

We can see that we obtain the correct model by first writing the structural part of the between-model for $\eta_{Rk}^{(3)}$ as $\eta_{Rk}^{(3)} = b\eta_{Ck}^{(3)} + \zeta_{Rk}^{(3)}$ and substituting this into the measurement part of the between model. To make this more transparent, we write separate between models for items 1 to 3 and 4 to 6:

$$
\begin{bmatrix} \mu_{1k} \\ \mu_{2k} \\ \mu_{3k} \end{bmatrix} = \begin{bmatrix} \lambda_1 \\ \lambda_2 \\ \lambda_3 \end{bmatrix} (b\eta_{Ck}^{(3)} + \zeta_{Rk}^{(3)})
$$

$$
\begin{bmatrix} \mu_{4k} \\ \mu_{5k} \\ \mu_{6k} \end{bmatrix} = \begin{bmatrix} \lambda_4 \\ \lambda_5 \\ \lambda_6 \end{bmatrix} \eta_{Ck}^{(3)} + \begin{bmatrix} \varepsilon_{4k}^{(3)} \\ \varepsilon_{5k}^{(3)} \\ \varepsilon_{6k}^{(3)} \end{bmatrix}
$$

Substituting these equations into the within model equations gives

$$
\begin{bmatrix} y_{1jk} \\ y_{2jk} \\ y_{3jk} \end{bmatrix} = \begin{bmatrix} \lambda_1 \\ \lambda_2 \\ \lambda_3 \end{bmatrix} \underbrace{(\zeta_{Rjk}^{(2)} + b\eta_{Ck}^{(3)} + \zeta_{Rk}^{(3)})}_{\eta_{Rjk}^{(2)}} + \begin{bmatrix} \varepsilon_{1jk}^{(2)} \\ \varepsilon_{2jk}^{(2)} \\ \varepsilon_{3jk}^{(2)} \end{bmatrix}
$$

$$
\begin{bmatrix} y_{4jk} \\ y_{5jk} \\ y_{6jk} \end{bmatrix} = \begin{bmatrix} \lambda_4 \\ \lambda_5 \\ \lambda_6 \end{bmatrix} \eta_{Ck}^{(3)} + \begin{bmatrix} \varepsilon_{4jk}^{(3)} \\ \varepsilon_{5jk}^{(3)} \\ \varepsilon_{6jk}^{(3)} \end{bmatrix}
$$

as required.

The path diagram for the within and between formulation is given in Figure 30.7. Note that Mplus allows variables to be declared as between or within variables. Declaring y_4, y_5, and y_6 as between variables means that these variables will disappear from the within model in Figure 30.7 and the corresponding circles in the between model will be replaced by rectangles, as shown in Figure 30.8.

We see that the cross-level effect is obtained by regressing the between component of the unit-level latent response variable on the cluster-level latent covariate. This specification is equivalent to a direct regression of the unit-level response variable on the cluster-level covariate only if the factor loadings in the within and between measurement models of the unit-level latent variable are constrained to be equal. Unfortunately, it is not apparent from the diagram that the model includes a cross-level effect.

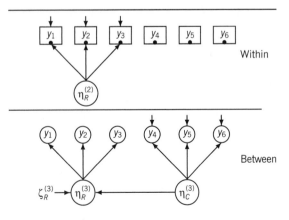

FIGURE 30.7. Path diagram for within–between formulation of multilevel SEM.

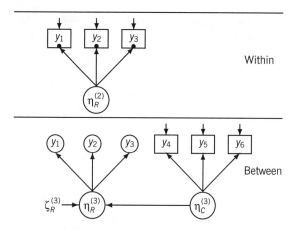

FIGURE 30.8. Path diagram for within–between formulation of multilevel SEM where y_4, y_5, and y_6 have been declared as between variables.

ESTIMATION

Continuous Responses

For continuous responses, Goldstein and McDonald (1988), McDonald and Goldstein (1989), and Lee (1990) derived theory and succinct expressions for the likelihood, allowing two-level structural equation models to be estimated. For unbalanced multilevel designs with missing items, Longford and Muthén (1992) proposed a Fisher scoring algorithm whereas Raudenbush (1995) and Poon and Lee (1998) suggested expectation maximization (EM) algorithms.

Because maximum likelihood approaches in general require specialized software, several ad hoc methods have been proposed. Muthén (1989) suggests an approach that corresponds to maximum likelihood in the usually unrealistic case where all clusters have the same size n, but not otherwise. In this balanced case, the empirical covariance matrix $\mathbf{S}_W$ of the cluster–mean-centered responses is a consistent and unbiased estimator for $\boldsymbol{\Sigma}_W$,

$$E(\boldsymbol{\Sigma}_W) = \boldsymbol{\Sigma}_W$$

In contrast, the expectation of the empirical covariance matrix $\mathbf{S}_B$ of the cluster means is

$$E(\mathbf{S}_B) = \boldsymbol{\Sigma}_B + \frac{1}{n}\boldsymbol{\Sigma}_W$$

Within and between structural equation models are specified for $\boldsymbol{\Sigma}_W$ and $\boldsymbol{\Sigma}_B$. Since $\boldsymbol{\Sigma}_W$ contributes to both $E(\mathbf{S}_B)$ and $E(\mathbf{S}_W)$, both models must be fitted jointly to the empirical covariance matrices $\mathbf{S}_B$ and $\mathbf{S}_W$. This can be accomplished by treating the two matrices as if they corresponded to different groups of subjects, and performing two-group analysis with the required constraints. If there are only a relatively small number of different cluster sizes, a multiple-group approach (with more than two groups) can be used to obtain maximum likelihood estimates. This approach, as well as an ad hoc solution for the completely unbalanced case, are described in detail in Hox (2010) and Muthén (1994).

Various two-stage approaches have also been proposed. Goldstein (1987, 2003) suggests using multivariate multilevel modeling to estimate $\boldsymbol{\Sigma}_W$ and $\boldsymbol{\Sigma}_B$ consistently by either maximum likelihood or restricted maximum likelihood. Structural equation models can then be fitted separately to each estimated matrix. Advantages of this approach are that unbalanced data and missing values are automatically accommodated, and that it is straightforward to extend to more hierarchical levels and to models where levels are crossed instead of nested.

An alternative two-stage approach, similar in spirit to the work by Korn and Whittemore (1979), was proposed by Chou, Bentler, and Pentz (2000). Here, a factor or structural equation model is estimated separately for each cluster. The estimates are subsequently treated as responses in a between model, typically a regression model with between-cluster covariates and an unstructured multivariate residual covariance matrix. This approach allows, and indeed requires, all parameters to vary between clusters, including factor loadings.

A common feature of these two-stage procedures is that standard errors provided from the second stage are incorrect, since they treat the output from the first stage as data or as empirical covariance matrices.

Noncontinuous Responses

For models with noncontinuous responses, maximum likelihood estimation or Bayesian methods are typically used. Although computationally demanding, these methods automatically handle lack of balance and missing data, and are straightforward to extend in order to include, for instance, mixed responses and nonlinear relations among latent variables.

The major challenge in maximum likelihood estimation of multilevel latent variable models for noncontinuous responses is to integrate out the latent variables, since closed-form results typically do not exist. Thus, integration usually proceeds by using either Monte Carlo simulation or numerical methods.

Lee and Shi (2001) and Lee and Song (2004) use Monte Carlo EM (MCEM) algorithms, employing Gibbs sampling to evaluate the integrals in the E-step. Rabe-Hesketh and colleagues (2004a) suggest using the Newton–Raphson algorithm where the latent variables are integrated out using adaptive quadrature; see also Rabe-Hesketh and colleagues (2005). Maximum likelihood estimation using adaptive quadrature is also implemented in Mplus, but as far as we know, there is no publication describing the Mplus implementation or assessing its performance.

The ad hoc approaches of Goldstein (1987, 2003) and Chou and colleagues (2000) discussed earlier for continuous responses can also be used for noncontinuous responses. In a similar spirit, the unpublished work by Asparouhov and Muthén (2007) describes limited-information weighted least squares estimation for mixtures of categorical, censored, and continuous responses.

As in other areas of statistics, Bayesian estimation via Markov Chain Monte Carlo (MCMC) methods has recently attracted considerable interest in multilevel SEM. This is probably due to the general purpose program WinBUGS (Spiegelhalter, Thomas, Best, & Gilks, 1996) that makes estimation of complex models relatively easy. Diffuse or vague priors are almost invariably specified in practice. The mean of the posterior distribution is in this case often quite close to the mode of the likelihood. MCMC can thus be viewed as a convenient way of implementing maximum likelihood estimation for complex models. MCMC methods have been used by Ansari and Jedidi (2000), Fox and Glas (2001), and Goldstein and Browne (2005) for binary responses, and by Lee and Song (2004) for continuous and ordinal responses. See also the books by Fox (2010) and Lee (2007).

DISCUSSION

We have provided a survey of models that combine features from two general modeling frameworks, multilevel regression models and structural equation models. We first reviewed different types of multilevel structural equation models and illustrated one of them using large-scale educational assessment data. We then introduced two frameworks for multilevel SEM: GLLAMM and the within–between framework. Unlike GLLAMM, the within–between framework is not a natural framework for including effects of higher-level variables on lower-level variables, as was demonstrated by expressing such a model using both frameworks and presenting the associated path diagrams. Another limitation of the within–between framework is that it cannot be easily extended to more levels.

In multilevel SEM, all latent variables are continuous, whereas latent class models include discrete latent variables only. Features of both model types can be combined to specify multilevel structural equation models with discrete latent variables. One approach is to have latent classifications at the lowest level and either continuous or discrete latent variables at higher levels. Vermunt (2003) specifies multilevel latent class models where units belong to latent classes and the probability of latent class membership depends on random effects that vary between clusters. Vermunt (2008) also specifies models where the probability of latent class membership for units depends on the latent class membership of the clusters. Cognitive diagnosis models for item response data include several binary latent variables, interpretable as latent indicators for mastery of several skills involved in solving the items. de la Torre and Douglas (2004) specify an item response model for the latent skill mastery indicators, whereas von Davier (2010) specifies a latent class model for students, where students' class membership can depend on a clustering variable, such as schools.

Another approach is to have continuous latent variables at the lowest level and categorical latent variables at higher levels. Muthén and Asparouhov (2009) model the random effects of a standard two-level model using a finite mixture of normal densities, where membership in a mixture component or latent class is modeled as a multinomial logit model with random cluster effects, as in Vermunt (2003). Cho and Cohen (2010) define mixture IRT models with latent classifications of students and schools, where latent class membership can depend on covariates at both levels. De Jong and Steenkamp (2010) allow the item parameters in a multidimensional graded response model to vary randomly between countries according to a finite mixture distribution.

Other model features that could extend multilevel structural equation models include nonlinear relations and interactions among latent variables (e.g., Klein & Moosbrugger, 2000); models with non-nested clusters, such as schools and neighborhoods (e.g., Browne,

Goldstein, & Rasbash, 2001; Jeon & Rabe-Hesketh, in press); models with random variances (e.g., Segawa et al., 2008); spatial or longitudinal models with complex dependence structures, such as Gaussian Markov random fields (Rue & Held, 2005); and more. See Skrondal and Rabe-Hesketh (2007) for a survey of latent variable models.

Complex models can be important for understanding complex processes. However, as models become increasingly large and convoluted, several important problems can arise. A model may not be well identified or it may be equivalent to an alternative model with a very different interpretation, and such problems may be difficult to discover as models become more complex. Estimation can become time-consuming and challenging, with risks of finding local instead of global maxima, in particular for complex models involving finite mixtures (e.g., Hipp & Bauer, 2006; Hoeksma & Kelderman, 2006). Furthermore, explaining the model and interpreting the estimates become increasingly difficult, and this is not helped by the tendency of authors not to report all parameter estimates, so that the reader may be left guessing about aspects of model specification.

Another challenge with ever more complex models is to keep them within a modeling framework that comes with a notation for writing the models down and corresponding software, syntax, and intuitive path diagrams. The LISREL framework (e.g., Jöreskog, 1973) and software (e.g., Jöreskog & Sörbom, 1989) was a great accomplishment in this regard. The GLLAMM framework is an attempt to extend the range of models, while retaining a coherent framework. Such coherent frameworks are important for communication among researchers, and between researchers and software, both in terms of specifying the model correctly and interpreting the output correctly.

There has been an increasing number of applications of multilevel structural equation models, mostly in psychology and education. In statistics, latent variable modeling has gradually become more accepted and popular. We expect these trends to continue as computers become more powerful and ever more sophisticated algorithms and software are developed.

ACKNOWLEDGMENTS

We would like to thank Taehun Lee and Rick Hoyle for their helpful comments and suggestions.

REFERENCES

Adams, R. J., Wilson, M., & Wu, M. L. (1997). Multilevel item response models: An approach to errors in variables regression. *Journal of Educational and Behavioural Statistics, 22,* 46–75.

Andrich, D. (1978). A rating formulation for ordered response categories. *Psychometrika, 43,* 561–573.

Ansari, A., & Jedidi, K. (2000). Bayesian factor analysis for multilevel binary observations. *Psychometrika, 65,* 475–496.

Asparouhov, T., & Muthén, B. O. (2007). Computationally efficient estimation of multilevel high-dimensional latent variable models. In *Proceedings of the American Statistical Association* (pp. 2531–2535). Alexandria, VA: American Statistical Association.

Bartholomew, D. J. (1980). Factor analysis for categorical data (with discussion). *Journal of the Royal Statistical Society B, 42,* 293–321.

Bartholomew, D. J. (1987). *Latent variable models and factor analysis.* London: Griffin.

Bartholomew, D. J., & Knott, M. (1999). *Latent variable models and factor analysis.* London: Arnold.

Bauer, D. J., Preacher, K. J., & Gil, K. M. (2006). Conceptualizing and testing random indirect effects and moderated mediation in multilevel models: New procedures and recommendations. *Psychological Methods, 11,* 142–163.

Bock, R. D. (1972). Estimating item parameters and latent ability when responses are scored in two or more nominal categories. *Psychometrika, 37,* 29–51.

Bock, R. D., & Lieberman, M. (1970). Fitting a response model for n dichotomously scored items. *Psychometrika, 33,* 179–197.

Browne, W. J., Goldstein, H., & Rasbash, J. (2001). Multiple membership multiple classification (MMMC) models. *Statistical Modelling, 1, 103–124.*

Chaimongkol, S., Huffer, F. W., & Kamata, A. (2006). A Bayesian approach for fitting a random effect differential item functioning across group units. *Thailand Statistician, 4,* 27–41.

Cho, S. J., & Cohen, A. S. (2010). A multilevel mixture IRT model with an application to DIF. *Journal of Educational and Behavioral Statistics, 35,* 336–370.

Chou, C.-P., Bentler, P. M., & Pentz, M. A. (2000). Two-stage approach to multilevel structural equation models: Application to longitudinal data. In T. D. Little, K. U. Schnabel, & J. Baumert (Eds.), *Modeling longitudinal and multilevel data: Practical issues, applied approaches, and specific examples* (pp. 33–49). Mahwah, NJ: Erlbaum.

Christoffersson, A. (1975). Factor analysis of dichotomized variables. *Psychometrika, 40,* 5–32.

Cronbach, L. J. (1976). *Research on classrooms and schools: Formulation of questions, design, and analysis* (Technical Report Stanford Evaluation Consortium). Palo Alto, CA: School of Education, Stanford University.

De Boeck, P., & Wilson, M. (Eds.). (2004). *Explanatory item response models: A generalized linear and nonlinear approach.* New York: Springer.

De Jong, M. G., & Steenkamp, J. B. E. M. (2007). Relaxing measurement invariance in cross-national consumer research using a hierarchical IRT model. *Journal of Consumer Research, 34,* 260–278.

De Jong, M. G., & Steenkamp, J. B. E. M. (2010). Finite mixture multilevel multidimensional ordinal IRT models for large-scale cross-cultural research. *Psychometrika, 75,* 3–32.

de la Torre, J., & Douglas, J. (2004). Higher-order latent trait models for cognitive diagnosis. *Psychometrika, 69,* 333–353.

Fox, J. P. (2010). *Bayesian item response modeling: Theory and applications.* New York: Springer.

Fox, J. P., & Glas, C. A. W. (2001). Bayesian estimation of a multilevel IRT model using Gibbs sampling. *Psychometrika, 66,* 271–288.

Fox, J. P., & Glas, C. A. W. (2003). Bayesian modeling of measurement error in predictor variables using item response theory. *Psychometrika, 68,* 169–191.

Goldstein, H. (1987). Multilevel covariance component models. *Biometrika, 74,* 430–431.

Goldstein, H. (2003). *Multilevel statistical models* (3rd ed.). London: Arnold.

Goldstein, H., Bonnet, G., & Rocher, T. (2007). Multilevel structural equation models for the analysis of comparative data on educational performance. *Journal of Educational and Behavioral Statistics, 32,* 252–286.

Goldstein, H., & Browne, W. J. (2005). Multilevel factor analysis models for continuous and discrete data. In A. Maydeu-Olivares & J. J. McArdle (Eds.), *Contemporary psychometrics: A Festschrift for Roderick P. McDonald* (pp. 453–475). Mahwah, NJ: Erlbaum.

Goldstein, H., & McDonald, R. P. (1988). A general model for the analysis of multilevel data. *Psychometrika, 53,* 455–467.

Grilli, L., & Rampichini, C. (2007). Multilevel factor models for ordinal variables. *Structural Equation Modeling, 14,* 1–25.

Härnquist, K. (1978). Primary mental abilities of collective and individual levels. *Journal of Educational Psychology, 70,* 706–716.

Hemker, B. T., van der Ark, L., & Sijtsma, K. (2001). On measurement properties of continuation ratio models. *Psychometrika, 66,* 487–506.

Hipp, H. J., & Bauer, D. J. (2006). Local solutions in the estimation of growth mixture models. *Psychological Methods, 11,* 36–53.

Hoeksma, J. B., & Kelderman, H. (2006). On growth curves and mixture models. *Infant and Child Development, 15,* 627–634.

Hox, J. (2010). *Multilevel analysis: Techniques and applications* (2nd ed.). New York: Routledge.

Jeon, M., & Rabe-Hesketh, S. (in press). Profile-likelihood approach for estimating generalized linear mixed models with factor structures. *Journal of Educational and Behavioral Statistics.*

Jöreskog, K. G. (1973). A general method for estimating a linear structural equation system. In A. S. Goldberger & O. D. Duncan (Eds.), *Structural equation models in the social sciences* (pp. 85–112). New York: Seminar.

Jöreskog, K. G., & Goldberger, A. S. (1975). Estimation of a model with multiple indicators and multiple causes of a single latent variable. *Journal of the American Statistical Association, 70,* 631–639.

Jöreskog, K. G., & Sörbom, D. (1989). *LISREL 7: A guide to the program and applications.* Chicago: SPSS.

Kamata, A. (2001). Item analysis by hierarchical generalized linear model. *Journal of Educational Measurement, 38,* 79–93.

Klein, A., & Moosbrugger, H. (2000). Maximum likelihood estimation of latent interaction effects with the LMS method. *Psychometrika, 65,* 457–474.

Korn, E. L., & Whittemore, A. S. (1979). Methods for analyzing panel studies of acute health effects of air pollution. *Biometrics, 35,* 795–804.

Lee, S.-Y. (1990). Multilevel analysis of structural equation models. *Biometrika, 77,* 763–772.

Lee, S.-Y. (2007). *Structural equation modelling: A Bayesian approach.* New York: Wiley.

Lee, S.-Y., & Poon, W.-Y. (1998). Analysis of two-level structural equation models via EM-type algorithm. *Statistica Sinica, 8,* 749–766.

Lee, S.-Y., & Shi, J.-Q. (2001). Maximum likelihood estimation of two-level latent variable models with mixed continuous and polytomous data. *Biometrics, 57,* 787–794.

Lee, S.-Y., & Song, X.-Y. (2004). Maximum likelihood analysis of a general latent variable model with hierarchically mixed data. *Biometrics, 60,* 624–636.

Li, D., Oranje, A., & Jiang, Y. (2009). On the estimation of hierarchical latent regression models for large-scale assessments. *Journal of Educational and Behavioral Statistics, 34,* 433–463.

Linda, N. Y., Lee, S.-Y., & Poon, W.-Y. (1993). Covariance structure analysis with three level data. *Computational Statistics and Data Analysis, 15,* 159–178.

Longford, N. T. (1993). *Random coefficient models.* Oxford, UK: Oxford University Press.

Longford, N. T., & Muthén, B. O. (1992). Factor analysis for clustered observations. *Psychometrika, 57,* 581–597.

Lord, F. M. (1952). *A theory of test scores* (Psychometric Monograph No. 7). Richmond, VA: Psychometric Corporation.

Lord, F. M., & Novick, M. R. (1968). *Statistical theories of mental test scores.* Reading, MA: Addison-Wesley.

Ma, X., Ma, L., & Bradley, K. D. (2008). Using multilevel modeling to investigate school effects. In A. A. O'Connell

& D. B. McCoach (Eds.), *Multilevel modelling of educational data* (pp. 59–110). Charlotte, NC: Information Age.

Maier, K. S. (2001). A Rasch hierarchical measurement model. *Journal of Educational and Behavioral Statistics, 26,* 307–330.

Marsh, H. W., Lüdtke, O., Robitzsch, A., Trautwein, U., Asparouhov, T., Muthén, B., et al. (2009). Doubly-latent models of school contextual effects: Integrating multilevel and structural equation approaches to control measurement and sampling error. *Multivariate Behavioral Research, 44,* 764–802.

Masters, G. N. (1982). A Rasch model for partial credit scoring. *Psychometrika, 47,* 149–174.

McArdle, J. J. (1988). Dynamic but structural equation modeling with repeated measures data. In J. R. Nesselroade & R. B. Cattell (Eds.), *Handbook of multivariate experimental psychology* (Vol. II, pp. 561–614). New York: Plenum Press.

McCullagh, P., & Nelder, J. A. (1989). *Generalized linear models* (2nd ed). London: Chapman & Hall.

McDonald, R. P., & Goldstein, H. (1989). Balanced and unbalanced designs for linear structural relations in two-level data. *British Journal of Mathematical and Statistical Psychology, 42,* 215–232.

Mehta, P. D., & Neale, M. C. (2005). People are variables too: Multilevel structural equations modeling. *Psychological Methods, 10,* 259–284.

Mellenbergh, G. J. (1994). Generalized linear item response theory. *Psychological Bulletin, 115,* 300–307.

Mellenbergh, G. J. (1995). Conceptual notes on models for discrete polytomous item responses. *Applied Psychological Measurement, 19,* 91–100.

Meredith, W., & Tisak, J. (1990). Latent curve analysis. *Psychometrika, 55,* 107–122.

Mislevy, R. J. (1987). Exploiting auxiliary information about examinees in the estimation of item parameters. *Applied Psychological Measurement, 11,* 81–91.

Mullis, I., Kennedy, A. M., Martin, M. O., & Sainsbury, M. (2006). *PIRLS 2006 Assessment Framework and Specifications* (2nd ed.). Chestnut Hill, MA: Boston College.

Muthén, B. O. (1989). Latent variable modeling in heterogeneous populations. *Psychometrika, 54,* 557–585.

Muthén, B. O. (1994). Multilevel covariance structure analysis. *Sociological Methods and Research, 22,* 376–398.

Muthén, B. O., & Asparouhov, T. (2009). Multilevel regression mixture analysis. *Journal of the Royal Statistical Society A, 172,* 639–657.

Muthén, B. O., & Lehman, J. (1985). A method for studying the homogeneity of test items with respect to other relevant variables. *Journal of Educational Statistics, 10,* 121–132.

Muthén, B. O., & Satorra, A. (1989). Multilevel aspects of varying parameters in structural models. In R. D. Bock (Ed.), *Multilevel analysis of educational data* (pp. 87–99). San Diego, CA: Academic Press.

Muthén, L. K., & Muthén, B. O. (2010). *Mplus user's guide* (6th ed.). Los Angeles: Authors.

Poon, W.-Y., & Lee, S.-Y. (1992). Maximum likelihood and generalized least squares analyses of two-level structural equation models. *Statistics and Probability Letters, 14,* 25–30.

Rabe-Hesketh, S., & Skrondal, A. (2012). *Multilevel and longitudinal modeling using Stata: Volume II. Categorical responses, counts, and survival* (3rd ed.). College Station, TX: Stata Press.

Rabe-Hesketh, S., Skrondal, A., & Pickles, A. (2002). Reliable estimation of generalized linear mixed models using adaptive quadrature. *Stata Journal, 2,* 1–21.

Rabe-Hesketh, S., Skrondal, A., & Pickles, A. (2004a). Generalized multilevel structural equation modeling. *Psychometrika, 69,* 167–190.

Rabe-Hesketh, S., Skrondal, A., & Pickles, A. (2004b). *GLLAMM Manual* (2nd ed.). UC Berkeley Division of Biostatistics Working Paper Series—Working Paper 160). Berkeley: University of California.

Rabe-Hesketh, S., Skrondal, A., & Pickles, A. (2005). Maximum likelihood estimation of limited and discrete dependent variable models with nested random effects. *Journal of Econometrics, 128,* 301–323.

Rabe-Hesketh, S., Skrondal, A., & Zheng, X. (2007). Multilevel structural equation modeling. In S. Y. Lee (Ed.), *Handbook of latent variable and related models* (pp. 209–227). Amsterdam: Elsevier.

Rao, C. R. (1958). Some statistical methods for comparison of growth curves. *Biometrics, 14,* 1–17.

Rasch, G. (1960). *Probabilistic models for some intelligence and attainment tests.* Copenhagen: Danmarks Pædagogiske Institut.

Raudenbush, S. W. (1995). Maximum likelihood estimation for unbalanced multilevel covariance structure models via the EM algorithm. *British Journal of Mathematical and Statistical Psychology, 48,* 359–370.

Raudenbush, S. W., & Bryk, A. S. (2002). *Hierarchical linear models.* Thousand Oaks, CA: Sage.

Raudenbush, S. W., & Sampson, R. (1999). Assessing direct and indirect effects in multilevel designs with latent variables. *Sociological Methods and Research, 28,* 123–153.

Raudenbush, S. W., Rowan, B., & Kang, S. J. (1991). A multilevel, multivariate model for studying school climate with estimation via the EM algorithm and application to U.S. high-school data. *Journal of Educational Statistics, 16,* 295–330.

Raudenbush, S. W., & Willms, J. D. (1995). Estimation of school effects. *Journal of Educational and Behavioral Statistics, 20,* 307–335.

Rijmen, F., Tuerlinckx, F., De Boeck, P., & Kuppens, P. (2003). A nonlinear mixed model framework for item response theory. *Psychological Methods, 8,* 185–205.

Rue, H., & Held, L. (2005). *Gaussian Markov random fields.* Boca Raton, FL: Chapman & Hall/CRC.

Samejima, F. (1969). *Estimation of latent ability using a response pattern of graded scores* (Psychometric Monograph No. 17). Richmond, VA: Psychometric Society.

Schmidt, W. H. (1969). *Covariance structure analysis of the multivariate random effects model.* PhD thesis, University of Chicago, Chicago, IL.

Schmidt, W. H., & Wisenbaker, J. (1986). *Hierarchical data analysis: An approach based on structural equations* (Technical Report 4). Ann Arbor: Department of Counseling Educational Psychology and Special Education, University of Michigan.

Segawa, E., Emery, S., & Curry, S. J. (2008). Extended generalized linear latent and mixed models. *Journal of Educational and Behavioral Statistics, 33*, 464–484.

Skrondal, A., & Rabe-Hesketh, S. (2004). *Generalized latent variable modeling: Multilevel, longitudinal, and structural equation models.* Boca Raton, FL: Chapman & Hall/CRC.

Skrondal, A., & Rabe-Hesketh, S. (2007). Latent variable modelling: A survey. *Scandinavian Journal of Statistics, 34*, 712–745.

Spiegelhalter, D. J., Thomas, A., Best, N. G., & Gilks, W. R. (1996). *BUGS 0.5 Bayesian analysis using Gibbs sampling: Manual (version ii).* Cambridge, UK: MRC-Biostatistics Unit. Downloadable from *http://www.mrcbsu.cam.ac.uk/bugs/documentation/contents.shtml.*

StataCorp. (2009). *Stata statistical software: Release 11.0.* College Station, TXL Stata Press.

Steele, F., & Goldstein, H. (2006). A multilevel factor model for mixed binary and ordinal indicators of women's status. *Sociological Methods and Research, 35*, 137–153.

Takane, Y., & de Leeuw, J. (1987). On the relationship between item response theory and factor analysis of discretized variables. *Psychometrika, 52*, 393–408.

Thissen, D., & Steinberg, L. (1988). Data analysis using item response theory. *Psychological Bulletin, 104*, 385–395.

Tutz, G. (1990). Sequential item response models with an ordered response. *British Journal of Mathematical and Statistical Psychology, 43*, 39–55.

Vermunt, J. K. (2003). Multilevel latent class models. In R. M. Stolzenberg (Ed.), *Sociological methodology 2003* (Vol. 33, pp. 213–239). Oxford: Blackwell.

Vermunt, J. K. (2008). Latent class and finite mixture models for multilevel data sets. *Statistical Methods in Medical Research, 17*, 33–51.

Vermunt, J. K., & Magidson, J. (2008). *Latent GOLD 4.5 user's guide.* Belmont, MA: Statistical Innovations.

von Davier, M. (2010). Hierarchical mixtures of diagnostic models. *Psychological Test and Assessment Modeling, 52*, 8–28.

Zheng, X. (2009). *Multilevel item response modeling: Applications to large-scale assessment of academic achievement.* PhD thesis, University of California, Berkeley.

CHAPTER 31

An Overview of Growth Mixture Modeling
A Simple Nonlinear Application in OpenMx

Mariya P. Shiyko
Nilam Ram
Kevin J. Grimm

Among the central tasks in the study of behavioral processes is describing how individuals change over time and how those changes differ across persons (Baltes & Nesselroade, 1979; Collins & Horn, 1991; Nesselroade, 1991). In the last few decades, growth curve models (GCMs), and the analytical conceptualizations underlying their use, have become the prime choice for such descriptions (Laird & Ware, 1982; McArdle & Epstein, 1987; Meredith & Tisak, 1990; Raudenbush & Bryk, 2002; Rogosa & Willett, 1985; Singer & Willett, 2003). The models provide a set of parameters that describe observed means, variances, and covariances in terms of average longitudinal trajectories and between-person differences in those trajectories. Typically, though, the classic GCMs impose a homogeneity assumption, requiring that all individuals in the sample (and by inference the population) follow qualitatively similar trajectories. When true, the collection of individuals being studied can be described adequately by a single set of parameters (i.e., means, variances, and covariances). However, there are many situations where the samples are heterogeneous (e.g., include men and women) and the homogeneity assumption is not tenable. Heterogeneous samples introduce another layer of complexity. GCMs must be expanded to both acknowledge and adequately model the trajectories of each subgroup of individuals.

When individual group membership is known a priori, specification and examination of change and differences therein proceed in a straightforward manner. The classic "single-group" GCM is expanded into a multiple-group GCM (McArdle, 1989; McArdle & Bell, 2000; McArdle & Epstein, 1987; Rovine & Molenaar, 2000). Multiple sets of parameters are used, each of which describes the average longitudinal trajectory and between-person variance around that trajectory for each specific subgroup of individuals (e.g., males and females). Between-group differences in average trajectories, patterns of change, and extent of between-person differences in change can be tested formally via likelihood ratio tests. When individual group membership is *not* known a priori, the description and examination of group differences is less straightforward. Unable to assign individuals to groups based on observed characteristics, researchers must infer their membership from patterns within the available data. Luckily a number of models that have emerged allow for description and examination of heterogeneity in longitudinal change, even when group membership is unobserved.

The idea of describing heterogeneity of developmental patterns for individuals with no observable grouping indicators was raised half a century ago in works of Rao (1958) and Tucker (1958, 1966). Among these proposals, Tucker (1966) forwarded a principal component analysis (PCA) approach in which the person-by-occasion matrix of scores was decomposed into two sets of scores: component loadings that represent distinct developmental profiles observed in a sample of data, and component scores, representing the extent to which an individual exhibits a particular developmental profile. The method was applied, for example, to analysis of trajectories of IQ development in children (e.g., McCall, Appelbaum, & Hogarty, 1973) to uncover distinct developmental patterns and eventually morphed into growth curve modeling and related techniques.

Similar to these classic approaches for describing qualitatively distinct developmental shapes, growth mixture modeling (GMM; Muthén & Shedden, 1999; Nagin, 1999) uses a *latent* categorical variable to place the heterogeneity in observed developmental trajectories into likely subgroups/classes. The substantive objective is to identify the latent classes and to describe the trajectories within each of those classes and the differences in trajectories between those classes. Examples of phenomena that have been studied with GMM include trajectories of antisocial and aggressive behaviors (Bradshaw, Schaeffer, Petras, & Ialongo, 2010; Park, Lee, Sun, Vazsonyi, & Bolland, 2010), substance use (Jacob, Koenig, Howell, Wood, & Randolphaber, 2009; Martino, Ellickson, & Mc-Caffrey, 2009), depression (Chen & Simons-Morton, 2009; Lincoln & Takeuchi, 2010; Romens, Abramson, & Alloy, 2009), anxiety (Crocetti, Klimstra, Keijsers, Hale, & Meeus, 2009), academic achievement (Espy, Fang, Charak, Minich, & Taylor, 2009; Pianta, Belsky, Vandergrift, Houts, & Morrison, 2008), and differential treatment response (Stulz, Thase, Klein, Manber, & Crits-Christoph, 2010), among others. In the absence of observed grouping distinctions, the objective in these inquiries has been to identify groups of individuals that follow distinct trajectories of change (e.g., healthy and pathological development), to describe those trajectories, and potentially to better understand the determinants of interindividual differences in development.

Our goal in this chapter is to describe and illustrate the use of GMMs for identifying and describing qualitative between-person differences in longitudinal trajectories. After briefly reviewing basic elements of the classic GCM and its multiple-group counterpart model, we introduce GMM as a straightforward extension. Subsequently, we describe our step-by-step approach to conducting GMM analysis in application to an empirical example of stress response patterns in a sample of adults. Finally, we demonstrate how GMMs can be implemented using the OpenMx statistical analysis framework (Boker et al., 2009).

GROWTH CURVE MODELING

The objective of growth curve modeling (an inclusive term for various similar and often identical approaches for modeling change, including multilevel models of change, latent trajectory analysis, latent curve modeling, and mixed effects or random effects models of change) is to describe and test hypotheses about between-person differences in within-person change. Comprehensive introductions may be found in this handbook (Chapter 32 on latent curve modeling by McArdle), as well as in works by Bollen and Curran (2006), Burchinal, Nelson, and Poe (2006), Duncan, Duncan, Stryker, Li, and Alpert (2006), Preacher, Wichman, MacCallum, and Briggs (2008), and Singer and Willett (2003), among others. A brief overview of the model is provided below as a foundation for our presentation of GMM.

Consider the hypothetical data inspired by the body of literature on substance abuse and behavioral pathways leading to nicotine dependence in adolescence and early adulthood (e.g., Brook et al., 2008; Maggi, Hertzman, & Vaillancourt, 2007; Orlando, Tucker, Ellickson, & Klein, 2004, 2005), in Panel A of Figure 31.1. Observed trajectories for 30 individuals' smoking behavior (the outcome is measured on the 0- to 4-point scale, capturing frequency of daily smoking; Brook et al., 2008) across six waves of assessment are depicted by the thin gray lines. The objective of growth curve modeling is to provide a parsimonious representation of those trajectories: specifically, to describe the average trajectory of change (denoted by the solid black line) and the extent of between-person differences in change (the shaded gray area around the line).

Mathematically, a GCM can be specified as a structural equation model. For an individual i measured at time t (where $t = 0, \ldots, T - 1$), a univariate longitudinal outcome y_{ti} is expressed as a combination of a *measurement* model

$$y_{ti} = \lambda \eta_i + \varepsilon_{ti} \qquad \textbf{(31.1a)}$$

and a *structural* model

$$\eta_i = \alpha + \zeta_i \qquad \textbf{(31.1b)}$$

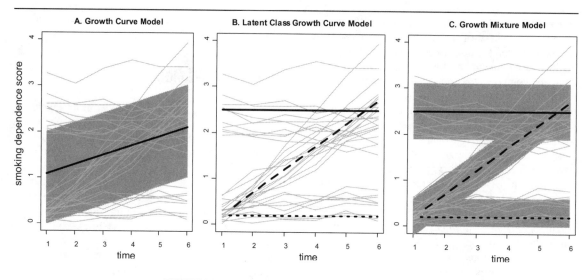

FIGURE 31.1. Simulated smoking trajectories ($N = 30$).

Summarizing across multiple individuals, the model provides a set of mean and variance–covariance expectations that can be fitted to the data. Specifically, the mean expectations describe the average trajectory, and the variance–covariance expectations describe the extent of between-person differences. The expected vector of means for the GCM is

$$\mu = \Lambda \alpha \qquad (31.2a)$$

where μ is the $T \times 1$ longitudinal vector of the expected means, α is a $p \times 1$ vector of latent variable means (e.g., average starting point = intercept, and average amount of linear change = slope), and Λ is a $T \times p$ design matrix, specifying the characteristics that define specific components of change. Depending on a shape of developmental curves and the modeling approach, the dimension and content of the columns of Λ, and the corresponding elements of α, allow for a wide variety of change patterns (linear, polynomial, sigmoid, etc., see Grimm & Ram, 2009, 2012; Ram & Grimm, 2007). For example, a linear pattern of change can be articulated by constraining the elements of the design matrix Λ to be

$$\Lambda = \begin{bmatrix} 1, & 1, & 1, & 1, & 1, & 1, & 1 \\ 0, & .167, & .33, & .5, & .668, & .835, & 1 \end{bmatrix}'$$

where the first column (row in the transpose) isolates the level of y at a baseline occasion ($t = 0$), and the second isolates a linear progression over time. The associated means (i.e., elements of α) describe the average linear trajectory for the sample (e.g., the solid black line in Panel A of Figure 31.1).

Portending our empirical example in the later section (data plotted in Figure 31.3), the GCM can be easily adapted for modeling of nonlinear trajectories, including trajectories that are described using higher-order polynomials (quadratic, cubic, etc.), exponential, sigmoid, and many other mathematical functions (Burchinal & Appelbaum, 1991; Grimm & Ram, 2009; Grimm, Ram, & Hamagami, 2011; Ram & Grimm, 2007). Given that the GCM is in fact a constrained common-factor model, further flexibility can be incorporated by simply estimating the elements of Λ (with minimal identification constraints) directly from the data—the latent-basis GCM (McArdle & Epstein, 1987; Meredith & Tisak, 1990). For example, the elements of the design matrix Λ can be specified as

$$\Lambda' = \begin{bmatrix} 1, & 1, & 1, & 1, & 1, & 1, & 1 \\ 0, & \lambda_1, & \lambda_2, & \lambda_3, & \lambda_4, & \lambda_5, & 1 \end{bmatrix}$$

where only the first and the last elements of the second column are constrained, to 0 and 1, respectively.

This assures model identification, while allowing for representation of a wide variety of patterns of change. Later, we make use of this flexibility in our empirical example.

Complementary to the description of average change (mean expectations), the GCM also provides a description of the extent of between-person differences in change. The covariance expectations for the GCM are

$$\Sigma = \Lambda \Psi \Lambda' + \Theta \qquad \text{(31.2b)}$$

where Σ, the expected $T \times T$ covariance matrix, is a function of Λ, a $T \times p$ design matrix; Ψ is the $p \times p$ symmetrical variance–covariance matrix of between-person differences in the change components, ζ_i (see Equation 31.1b); and Θ is a $T \times T$ covariance matrix of residuals, ε_{ti} (see Equation 31.1a), that is often specified to be diagonal. The elements of Ψ describe the extent of between-person differences in the change components describing individuals' trajectories (e.g., the shaded gray area in Panel A of Figure 31.1) and the associations among them.

MULTIPLE-GROUP GCMs

When an average trajectory does not fit the data well and interindividual variability is captured largely by either variances of latent variables or the residual terms, the model can be extended to incorporate grouping information that is explicitly observed (males and females, low and high socioeconomic status, etc.). Multiple-group GCMs explicitly examine developmental differences among prespecified groups of people on all aspects of the growth process (McArdle, 1989; McArdle & Bell, 2000; McArdle & Epstein, 1987). To specify the model, a categorical grouping variable, c, is introduced:

$$\mu_c = \Lambda_c \alpha_c$$
$$\Sigma_c = \Lambda_c \Psi_c \Lambda_c' + \Theta_c \qquad \text{(31.3)}$$

For multiple-group GCMs, data are split into two or more nonoverlapping, mutually exclusive subsets (based on the grouping variable c) and estimations are made for each subgroup. In principle, group-based growth models can be specified to be unique for each subgroup of individuals in all parameters, and the equivalence or differences in all or a portion of those parameters

tested explicitly. In multiple-group GCMs, different developmental shapes for each group allow for interpretation of qualitative differences in group trajectories (e.g., linear for males and quadratic for females).

GMMs AND LATENT-CLASS GGMs

For most developmental trends, a single grouping indicator (e.g., gender) rarely defines intrinsically different etiologies that drive temporal changes (e.g., increasing use of tobacco and stable nonuse). Instead, one needs to rely on observed data patterns that cluster together and follow similar developmental shapes to distinguish between qualitatively different trajectories. A subjective categorization of trajectories based on visual examination is one approach for creating developmental taxonomies (e.g., typology of antisocial behavior; Haapasalo & Tremblay, 1994; Moffitt, 1993). However, this often leads to conflicting findings and over- or underfitting of developmental profiles. Instead, GMM and latent-class GCMs (Muthén & Shedden, 1999; Nagin, 1999, 2005) present an analytical opportunity to distinguish between distinct developmental shapes in the absence of a priori group specification. These models build on the foundations of finite mixture modeling (e.g., McLachlan & Peel, 2000) to relax the homogeneity assumption of GCMs.

Two main approaches have been developed to address the issue of unobserved heterogeneity. They primarily differ in how the mixture is conceptualized, specified, and estimated. The latent-class growth curve modeling approach (LCGCM; Nagin, 1999, 2005) takes a semiparametric approach to approximate a continuous distribution (Everitt & Hand, 1981; McLachland & Peel, 2000; Nagin, 1999; Titterington, Smith, & Makov, 1985). Panel B in Figure 31.2 demonstrates how a hypothetical continuous non-normal distribution of slopes can be approximated with four "points of support" (Nagin, 2005, p. 47). These pillars, then, correspond to latent classes of individuals with different values of slope parameters. In contrast, GMM (Everitt & Hand, 1981; McLachlan & Peel, 2000; Muthén & Shedden, 1999) is a parametric approach that aims to uncover different normally distributed populations with means and variances within a mixture, often represented by non-normally distributed data. Rather than approximating a nonstandard shape, the philosophical foundation of GMM is that different distributions are driven by fundamentally different developmental pro-

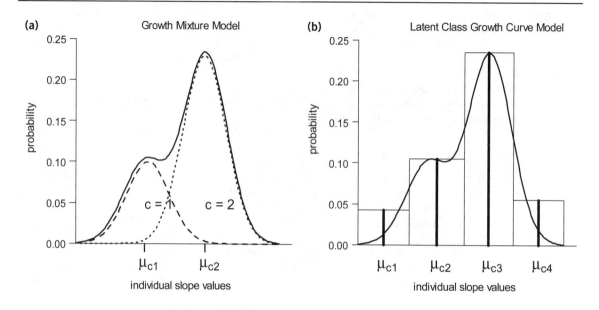

(a) Growth Mixture Model

(b) Latent Class Growth Curve Model

FIGURE 31.2. Conceptual differences between GMM and latent LCGCM.

cesses (e.g., Muthén, 2002). Then, the mixture arises due to the fact that the underlying driving processes of change have no observable or measurable grouping indicator. Figure 31.2, Panel A, demonstrates how the same observed non-normal distribution can be split into two normal components.

We further provide a mathematical representation of both approaches. Formulae for GMM expectations resemble those of multiple-group GCM, extending them to *latent* developmental classes and introducing a probabilistic classification (similar to logistic regression):

$$\mu = \sum_{c=1}^{C} \pi_c [\Lambda_c \alpha_c]$$

$$\Sigma = \sum_{c=1}^{C} \pi_c [\Lambda_c \Psi_c \Lambda_c' + \Theta_c] \qquad \textbf{(31.4)}$$

where $0 \le \pi_{nc} \le 1$ and $\sum_{c=1}^{C} \pi_{nc} = 1$. Equation 31.4 is a general form of the model, where both mean and variance parameters are estimated separately for each latent class, c. In practice, however, researchers tend to constrain some or all Λ, Ψ, and Θ, and set matrices as invariant across latent classes, and, instead, focus on the mean differences in latent variables, α_c.

The interpretation of parameters (mean initial level, change pattern, and variability around the means) is similar to that in multiple-group GCM, and it is done on a class-by-class basis. The elements of Λ_c are specific to each latent class, reflecting the unique developmental pattern of that subgroup. An individual's class membership is probabilistic, with each individual having an estimated probability of being in one or more classes.

With GMM, the hypothetical trajectories in Figure 31.1, Panel C are well described by three qualitatively different patterns and emergent typology of (1) consistent low nicotine users, (2) consistent high nicotine users, and (3) increasing nicotine users. Distinctively, the gray shaded areas around the average latent class trajectories reflect within-class heterogeneity.

Mathematically, LCGCM is a simplified version of GMM that focuses on latent variable means, α_c, that characterize specific aspects of temporal change for each latent class, while constraining between-person differences around the class-specific means to zero. Thus, the model in Equation 31.4 reduces to

$$\mu = \sum_{c=1}^{C} \pi_c [\Lambda_c \alpha_c]$$

$$\Sigma = \sum_{c=1}^{C} \pi_c [\Theta_c] \qquad \textbf{(31.5)}$$

with all the elements of Ψ_c constrained to zero, and the trajectories in each latent class described by mean growth parameters, α_c. Panel B in Figure 31.1 provides an example of mean developmental trajectories that are fitted to the hypothetical data, where absence of shaded gray rectangles around averages signifies a constant per-group development.

To be clear, LCGCM and GMM are similar in their aims to describe unobserved heterogeneity; however, the two approaches differ in how the heterogeneity is defined and estimated. Conceptually, LCGCM finds clusters of individuals with similar and homogenous developmental profiles, uncovering *between-class* heterogeneity. In contrast, GMM sets apart different developmental classes (*between-class* heterogeneity) and allows for interindividual differences within classes (*within-class* heterogeneity). In fitting GMM models, it may be noted that the added complexity often leads to estimation and identification problems (see Nagin, 2005, p. 55). Further difficulties arise in the interpretation of results. For example, non-normality of the outcome distribution may inadvertently be perceived as a mixture in cases when the underlying data were drawn from a single non-Gaussian distribution (Bauer & Curran, 2003a, 2004). Often, a mixture distribution is indistinguishable from a non-Gaussian distribution, and, if the deviation from normality is substantial, model fit indices almost always incorrectly point toward a multiple-class solution because the mixture model is simply attempting to account for the observed (non-Gaussian) data. Normality checks in forms of graphical summaries, skewness and kurtosis statistics, data transformations, and a number of Bayesian approaches (Rindskopf, 2003) are ways to explore distributional properties. In addition, theoretical justification for a mixture can serve as a major deciding factor. Latent-class covariates and distal outcomes can also serve as validating indicators of model utility (Muthén, 2003).

In comparison, LCGCM makes no assumption of conditional normality, as it approximates a non-normal distribution in a nonparametric manner. For that reason, the model is often criticized for making an unrealistic theoretical assumption about within-class homogeneity (Muthén, 2002). It also generally requires more classes to describe the underlying complexity of trajectories. Finally, since groups are an approximation to a non-normal distribution, questions arise about generalizability of classes to population (Bauer & Curran, 2003b). Thus, replication is crucial when using these approaches.

When making a decision about using LCGCM or GMM, it is worth considering the theoretical and practical implications of each approach. Depending on the analytical implications (e.g., Does overextraction or underextraction pose a problem?), research questions (e.g., Are mean latent trajectories of primary interest?), and data characteristics (e.g., Does the sample size preclude fitting of complex models?), a choice between the modeling approaches can be made. In addition, a theoretical foundation for model building is necessary for model validation purposes, as the decision to pursue the exploration of distinct latent developmental classes should be sound and justifiable. In the following section, we present more details on the model selection and model fitting issues, and demonstrate how the method can be applied to a set of empirical data.

Model Fitting

Fitting of GMMs to data follows an iterative process that can be roughly subdivided into phases of hypothesis formulation, model enumeration and specification, and model estimation and interpretation. A number of demonstrations of the GMM fitting procedures can be found in Connell and Frye (2006), Jung and Wickrama (2008), Li, Duncan, Duncan, and Acock (2001), Muthén (2004), Ram and Grimm (2009), and Wang and Bodner (2007). In this section, we primarily focus on important aspects of model building, demonstrate each step in application to an empirical example, and share syntax details for the free and open-source statistical software OpenMx (Boker et al., 2009), developed for use with R (R Development Core Team, 2010). This software can fit a variety of multivariate models including GMM. Chapter 20, introducing OpenMx, can be found in the current volume. Our previous work (Ram & Grimm, 2009) demonstrated how the same model can be fit in Mplus (Muthén & Muthén, 2009), yielding identical solutions.

Empirical Example

As an empirical example, we analyze data collected as part of the MacArthur Successful Aging Studies to investigate interindividual differences in stress responses (Seeman, Berkman, et al., 1995; Seeman, Singer, & Charpentier, 1995). To assess hypothalamic–pituitary–adrenocortical axis activity, saliva cortisol samples (mmol/l) were taken from 34 adults on nine successive occasions: two baseline measures ($t = 0$ and 1), followed by three assessments during a stress-invoking challenge task ($t = 2$–4) and four during a poststress recovery period ($t = 5$–8). This example has no missing data, but the model can accommodate data that do have some missingness.

A graphical summary of trajectories in Figure 31.3, as well as our previous analyses (Ram & Grimm, 2007, 2009), demonstrate a nonlinear developmental pattern in cortisol production over the observational period. The overall trend appears to follow an initial increase in cortisol production associated with the stress exposure, followed by dissipation during the stress withdrawal period. There are also clear interindividual differences in responses. Some individuals appear to have a quick poststress recovery, exhibiting a rapid reduction in cortisol level; others exhibit a lingering stress response, maintaining high levels of cortisol long after the stress exposure. The outcome distribution was nonskewed ($-.049$, $SE = .14$) but kurtotic (2.063, $SE = .28$), pointing toward the possible presence of mixture components. Thus, the main research question of the current analysis is to assess whether one or more stress response patterns are present in the data. While no intention is made to provide a complete taxonomy of stress patterns in this small sample of individuals, previous literature suggests differential stress regulatory patterns associated with healthy and heightened cortisol trajectories (Heim, Elhert, & Hellhammer, 2000; Miller, Chen, & Zhou, 2007). In the following sections,

we apply LCGCM and GMM to distinguish between unobserved groups that can be distinguished by their cortisol response trajectories.

Hypotheses Formulation

In GMM, the central research question is that of determining the number of latent classes. This is carried out by sequentially fitting models with different numbers of classes and comparing model fit. Relying purely on data for determining the best-fitting model, however, is unadvisable, and setting hypotheses about the number of classes and developmental shapes within each class is of primary importance. In fact, theory should be the driving force when the outcome distribution is not normal and could consist of a mixture (Bauer & Curran, 2003a; Muthén, 2003; Rindskopf, 2003). Thus, the method can be thought of as a guided and constrained exploration of the data, as decisions made prior to analyses heavily affect the obtained results. Generally speaking, more complex models (with more latent classes and free variances) tend to fit data better; however, a statistical improvement in model fit does not always elicit valid model interpretation. Thus, consideration of a priori hypotheses protects against a mindless search for a best-fitting model.

A philosophical conceptualization of latent classes can also aid in selecting a particular analytical approach. Thinking of classes as homogeneous groups,

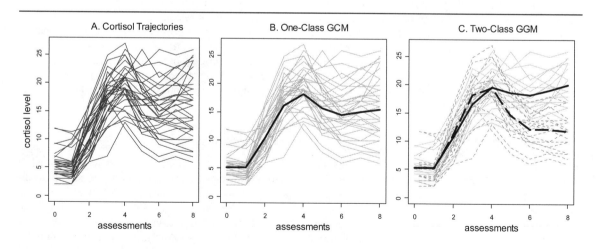

FIGURE 31.3. Results of empirical data analysis for cortisol data.

with a primary focus on mean developmental trajectories, calls for the LCGCM approach. In contrast, when groups are defined as distinct subpopulations, with corresponding mean and variance parameters, a more complex model may be suitable. Often, a particular analytical approach is chosen to accompany and illustrate a narrative the researchers have chosen to relate (see Ram, Grimm, Gatzke-Kopp, & Molenaar, 2012). Thus, it is important that an analyst has some general hypotheses and expectations about what might emerge during the process of model fitting.

Model Enumeration and Specification

Once the hypotheses are established, two important aspects of the analytical process are model enumeration and model specification. "Model enumeration" refers to the process of selecting the correct number of latent classes, which is essential for understanding distinctions in developmental trajectories. "Model specification" refers to defining model parameters and may entail constraining or freeing mean and variance parameters across latent classes, determining developmental shapes within classes, and specifying variances of growth parameters. Both procedures are iterative and codependent, as the model specification may influence the number of latent classes needed to describe data complexity. The simpler the model is (i.e., with mean trajectories describing latent groups), the more likely it is to require more latent classes. Thus, model enumeration and model specification should be viewed as part of the model-fitting continuum and be considered together.

The model-fitting sequence for GMM largely resembles the process of model fitting in multiple-group GCM. Depending on the conceptualized between-class differences, GMM can range from fully unconstrained, where all model parameters are specific to each latent class, to mostly constrained, with the majority of parameters being equal across classes. To aid model estimation and identification, it is common to set some constraints on the class-specific parameters even when the most flexible model is envisioned.

The starting analytical point is to estimate a single-group GCM, which assumes a homogeneous developmental pattern for all individuals in the study. Such a model becomes a reference point (baseline model) for describing a general developmental shape of data and assessing the degree of interindividual differences with variance components of growth parameters and

residuals. Subsequently, the homogeneity assumption is relaxed when the model is extended to more than one class. A simple way to describe heterogeneity is to model means of growth parameters, α_c, separately for each latent class and assess the number of latent classes needed to describe all present developmental profiles. When mean differences in developmental trajectories are not sufficient to describe data complexity, the model can be extended to accommodate different factor loadings, Λ_c, and nonzero variances, Ψ_c, which can be either constrained to remain equal across classes or estimated separately for each latent class. A full class-varying model would have all class-specific parameters (see Ram & Grimm, 2009).

Because of the multitude of possible models, it is practical to view the process of model selection in two dimensions. First, models with a different number of latent classes (e.g., one-class vs. two-class models) can be compared. Unlike multiple-group structural equation modeling (SEM), such models are not nested, and the likelihood ratio tests cannot be used for model selection. Instead, relative fit *information criteria* such as the Bayesian information criterion (BIC; Schwarz, 1978) and Akaike information criterion (AIC; Akaike, 1974) are used for relative model comparisons. Lower values on the information criteria indicate better-fitting models (Nylund, Asparouhov, & Muthén, 2007; Tofighi & Enders, 2008; Tolvanen, 2007). The general principle is to select models with the value on the information criteria, in terms of the absolute value, and models that do not fit better than the baseline model can be dismissed.

In addition to statistical indicators of model fit, researchers should carefully examine the estimation output. Given that solutions obtained during model estimation may not be accurate or useful (see Hipp & Bauer, 2006), it is important to check that the model makes sense mathematically. For example, the issue of out-of-bounds parameter values (e.g., negative variances) can be avoided by setting constraints on the parameter space. Further, model interpretation plays a crucial role in model selection. For instance, when parameter estimates for two or more groups indicate practically identical change patterns, such solutions should be questioned and perhaps set aside while models with fewer classes are examined more closely. In all cases, knowledge of the substantive area regarding the distinctiveness of the obtained trajectories should inform model selection. Inadmissible or inappropriate models should be dismissed.

A number of additional ways to assess the model fit include classification tables (Boscardin, Muthén, Francis, & Baker, 2008; Wang & Bodner, 2007) and graphical summaries (Boscardin et al., 2008; Muthén & Asparouhov, 2008). Classification tables are summaries of average posterior probabilities for each class membership for individuals who are the likeliest members of a specific class. High values on a diagonal correspond to high classification certainty. Graphical summaries include comparisons of observed and estimated mean curves as well as estimated mean curves and actual developmental trajectories. Generally, we recommend that researchers pay attention to all of the available fit indices, numerical and graphical summaries, and the relevant theory when selecting the GMM that provides the best representation of the data.

Model Estimation

During the process of model fitting, model estimation can be carried out in one of a number of available software packages. Previously, we have described the use of Mplus for fitting GMMs (Ram & Grimm, 2009). Here, we describe use of the OpenMx software, which maximizes the likelihood of the data given the model parameters (maximum likelihood [ML]). Missing data on the outcome variable can be accommodated using full-information ML under missing at random assumptions (Little & Rubin, 1987).

MODEL FITTING IN OpenMx: ILLUSTRATION WITH CORTISOL DATA

In this section we present details of model fitting in the OpenMx software. First, the latent-basis GCM is fit to cortisol data to establish a baseline model and to introduce main syntax components. We further proceed to LCGCM and GMM, and compare fits across one-, two-, three-, and four-class models. A complete script of the OpenMx syntax is provided at the handbook website (*www.handbookofsem.com*). We focus on the OpenMx statements, assuming that readers are familiar with the object-oriented R environment. For didactic purposes, we focus only on two types of models: LCGCM and GMM with freely estimated variance parameters of growth terms. Our previous work (Ram & Grimm, 2009) provides a more thorough overview of the model selection process. However, components of

the presented models can be easily reconfigured to fit a wide variety of alternative models (Ram et al., 2012).

GCM in OpenMx

The OpenMx software can be downloaded free of charge from *http://openmx.psyc.virginia.edu/*. A general introduction and a list of commands can be found in the User Guide and Reference Manual on the same website. As with other statistical R packages, the **library (OpenMx)** command loads the software. The model is specified in the matrix format and all the building components are explicitly defined. For GCM, Equations 31.2a and 31.2b, indicating mean and variance expectations, need to be supplied as part of the OpenMx syntax. Any model modifications are carried out by modifying corresponding matrices. All OpenMx commands have the prefix **mx**, followed by either **Data** when a data object is created, **Matrix** when a matrix is specified, **Algebra** when a mathematical expression is provided, **Model** when a model is defined, or **Run** when the program is called to execute the model estimation procedure.

Based on Equations 31.2a and 31.2b, Λ, α, Ψ, and Θ matrices define the GCM. Taking a stepwise approach, we first create all necessary matrices and later supply these objects in the **mxModel** statement for model estimation. While matrices are stored as R objects, they are also named, and any further manipulation requires calling matrices by assigned names. Several default types of matrices are available in OpenMx, including **Full** (a rectangular matrix with specified dimensions), **Symm** (a symmetrical matrix for off-diagonal elements), **Diag** (a diagonal matrix with off-diagonal elements set to 0), and **Unit** (a matrix with all elements set to 1). Other types are also available but are not used in the current model.

Referring to OpenMx syntax for GCM (*www.handbookofsem.com*) first, the raw data object **cortdataMX** is created and names of variables are stored in **names**. Second, the **mxMatrix** command is used to create a 2×1 vector of growth parameter means, α, both elements of which are freely estimated by stating **free = TRUE** and providing initial starting values with **values = c (15, 1)**. Elements of the vector are labeled as **int** and **sl**, and the overall matrix name is **alpha**. Furthermore, a 2×2 variance–covariance matrix of intercept and slope parameters, Ψ (**"psy"**), is specified to be freely estimated. The residual variance matrix is diagonal with variances constrained to be equal across all time points by supplying a single label **"residual"** for all 9 elements. Label names can be used as part of the syntax to set constraints on model parameters either within a single-class model or across groups in a multiclass model.

The GCM with free factor loadings was fit to data. Thus, to create the factor loading matrix, Λ, the vector of intercept loadings (ones) was created in the **Unit** matrix, and the vector of slope loadings was estimated from data with an exception of the first and fifth loadings, fixed to 0 and 1 and specified as **free = FALSE**. These constraints were given due to time centering at the first time point ($t = 0$) and scaling of total change by setting the fifth loading ($t = 4$) to 1 at the point where peak levels of cortisol are observed (end of stress challenge). The loadings **lambdaInt** and **lambdaSl** were combined into a single matrix **lambda** with the **mxAlgebra** statement.

Model expectations, **mean** and **cov** matrices, were created by supplying necessary parts of the formulae (Equations 31.2a and 31.2b) and referring to previously created matrices by assigned names. In the final step, the **mxModel** statement was used to collect all relevant model components and specify parts of the model (**cov**, **mean**) that need to be maximized with full-information ML (**mxFIMLObjective**). The model is run with the **mxRun** statement, and the results are stored in the **results** R objects, which can be examined.

Extending GCM to LCGCM in OpenMx

LCGCM is a straightforward extension of the GCM. It can be conceptualized as a multiple-group GCM where the class membership is unknown. Most of the same model elements are created (see full code on the handbook website at *www.handbookofsem.com*). However, growth factor means, factor loadings, and expectations are created on a class-by-class basis and are, in this example, specified twice with distinct class labels (e.g., **factorMean1**, **factorMeans2**). In this two-class GCM, factor means, α_c, are freely estimated. By supplying different names (i.e., **int1**, **sl1**, and **int2**, **sl2**), parameters are allowed to differ across latent classes. Since the variance component of the model consists only of the residual matrix Θ (Equation 31. 5), variances of the factor means, Ψ_c, are set to zero and omitted. A single residual variance matrix Θ represents a common variance of residuals for both latent classes. Factor loadings, Λ_c (**lambda1** and **lambda2**), are class-specific,

with developmental shapes estimated for each latent class. Mean and variance expectations for each latent class are constructed from corresponding class-specific elements.

Further, two class-specific **mxModel**s are defined, including the **mxFIMLObjective** functions. These interim models break the estimation process into several steps by, first, optimizing class-specific means and variance and, then, combining obtained estimates in the overarching model. This stepwise approach speeds the estimation process for complex models.

Since class membership is unobserved, a 2×1 vector of class probabilities (**pclass1** and **pclass2**) is created, with the first of the elements being estimated and the second equated to **1 – pclass1**. Based on Equation 31.5, individual model expectations are weighted by class probabilities, and the **mxAlgebra** object **algObj** specifies the likelihood function of the overall model, which is maximized through **mxAlgebraObjective** statement. The overall **mixedModel** combines interim models (**model1**, **model2**), data, class probabilities, and objective functions in the overall model estimation.

Extending Latent-Class GCM to GMM in OpenMx

The only part of the script that distinguished GMM from LCGCM is the specification of the variance–covariance growth factor matrices, where elements of **psy1** and **psy2** are freely estimated. When specifying model covariance expectations (Equation 31.4) these factor–covariance matrices are incorporated in the formulae. The rest of the estimation process resembles that of the latent LCGCM.

It is straightforward to extend the models to three or four latent-class scenarios by specifying additional components of the expectation matrices for additional classes. Similarly, models that deviate from latent LCGCM and GMM with freely estimated covariance matrices can be created by modifying parts of the provided syntax.

Results

In the current section we present results of the model-fitting procedure for cortisol data. A latent basis GCM served as a baseline model, with a single growth line capturing changes in cortisol over nine assessment points. Results of the model are summarized in Table

31.1 and the graphical summary is presented in Figure 31.3, Panel B. The intercept mean, μ_0, represents the initial level of cortisol production at baseline ($t = 0$), and the significant intercept variance, σ_0^2, points to a substantial amount of variability in baseline cortisol production across individuals. The parameter values of the basis vector Λ_1 were estimated to be [=0, 0, .40, .84, =1, .81, .72, .76, .79] across $t = 0$ to 8. In combination with the mean slope parameter, μ_1, slope loadings represent the proportion of the maximum change that occurred up to a specific point in time. For example, a loading of 0 corresponds to no change from baseline cortisol production, and a loading of .4 corresponds to a 13*.4 = 5.2-point increase in cortisol since baseline (40% of the maximum amount of expected change). From the model representation in Figure 31.3, Panel B, it is clear that a significant increase in cortisol level took place during stress exposure, slightly reducing after stress withdrawal. The significant value of the slope variance parameter, σ_1^2, represents a large amount of interindividual variability in developmental trajectories.

To describe interindividual differences in cortisol trajectories beyond the covariance parameters of the latent basis model, we fit two-, three-, and four-class LCGCM and two- and three-class GMM. Values of the AIC and BIC indices and class sizes for the tested models are summarized in Table 31.2. For LCGCM, no improvement in AIC and BIC over the baseline model was found. While the AIC was smaller for the four-class solution, the model was deemed nonuseful due to instability of parameter estimates and was dropped from consideration. For GMM, there was a clear improvement in model fit beyond the single-class model. The two-class solution had the smallest AIC and BIC values. Thus, in conjunction with theoretical considerations, the two-class GMM was considered the best-fitting model.

Figure 31.3, Panel C, and Table 31.1 summarize results of the final two-class GMM. Values of mean intercept and slope parameters for two classes, μ_1 and μ_2, appear to be similar. Both groups exhibited a comparable increase in cortisol production in response to stress

TABLE 31.1. Parameter Estimates for the Single-Class Latent-Basis GCM and Two-Class GMM

		Two-class GMM	
	Latent-basis GCM	Class 1	Class 2
Group size	34	16.62	17.38
Latent variable means			
Intercept mean, μ_0	5.19 (.51)	5.11 (.66)	5.28 (.60)
Slope mean, μ_1	13.00 (.88)	14.04 (1.14)	14.38 (.92)
Slope loadings, Λ_1			
Time 0	=0 (fixed)	=0 (fixed)	=0 (fixed)
Time 1	−.01 (.04)	−.01 (.04)	−.02 (.04)
Time 2	.40 (.04)	.43 (.04)	.38 (.03)
Time 3	.84 (.04)	.91 (.04)	.79 (.04)
Time 4	=1 (fixed)	=1 (fixed)	=1 (fixed)
Time 5	.81 (.04)	.66 (.04)	.93 (.04)
Time 6	.72 (.04)	.49 (.04)	.89 (.04)
Time 7	.76 (.04)	.49 (.04)	.96 (.04)
Time 8	.79 (.04)	.46 (.04)	1.03 (.04)
Latent variable covariances			
Intercept variance, σ_0^2	2.89 (1.37)	4.50 (1.94)	3.54 (1.61)
Slope variance, σ_1^2	13.87 (4.86)	16.28 (6.78)	9.03 (3.78)
Intercept–slope covariance, σ_{01}	−0.27 (1.95)	−1.81 (2.71)	−1.93 (1.92)
Residual variance, σ_e^2	6.35 (.58)	2.83 (.26)	2.83 (.26)

TABLE 31.2. Model Fit of LCGCM and GMM

Model type	Parameters	AIC	BIC	Class sizes
GCM				
1-Class	13	956	254	34
LCGCM				
2-Class	20	988	276	18.2, 15.8
3-Class	30	968	274	15.6, 15.3, 3.1
4-Class[a]	40	923	258	
GMM				
2-Class	**26**	**822**	**197**	**17.4, 16.6**
3-Class[b]	37	847	218	

Note. AIC, Akaike information criteria; BIC, Bayes information criteria.
[a]The model did not estimate properly: one of the classes had no members in it.
[b]Slope variance in Class 1 was estimated as negative. When fixing the slope to 0, one of the classes had no members in it.

exposure. The between-class differences emerge in the poststress period of cortisol production, with "healthy" responders showing a clear downward trajectory [Λ_1 = .66, .49, .49, .46 for t = 5–8] and "heightened" responders demonstrating high cortisol levels even after stress withdrawal [Λ_2 = .93, .89, .96, 1.03 for t = 5–8]. Significant variability around the mean growth parameters captures interindividual differences within each response pattern even after the etiological differences in stress-response patterns were taken into account.

DISCUSSION

In the current chapter, we have reviewed how interindividual developmental differences can be described beyond covariance parameters of GCM and the multigroup analysis of change. With increased computational capabilities, methods such as LCGCM and GMM are increasingly used to answer a realm of complex questions about human development. Specifically, these methods recover and/or identify unique developmental processes with qualitatively distinct patterns of change from observed trajectories with no measurable grouping indicators. Our empirical example demonstrates how an average developmental trajectory (Figure 31.3, Panel B) masks important practical differences in stress response patterns that are uncovered with GMM analysis (Figure 31.3, Panel C).

There are theoretical debates about the types of approaches suitable for recovering latent patterns and the conceptualization of latent classes (Bauer & Curran, 2003a, 2003b, 2004; Muthén, 2003; Rindskopf, 2003). While we acknowledge the existing controversy, it should not preclude method applications. Instead, we encourage researchers to invest heavily in the preparatory steps of model fitting, setting up the theoretical stage, clarifying research hypotheses, and exploring data with theory-based expectations. GMM can be used for a number of practical implications. For example, identifying subgroups of at-risk individuals with suboptimal behavioral or psychological indicators (Boscardin et al., 2008; Hunter, Muthén, Cook, & Leuchter, 2010; Schaeffer et al., 2006) can directly inform the types of patterns, and a targeted audience for intervention or prevention programs can be determined.

As GMM becomes more widely employed, access to open-source flexible statistical software is invaluable. OpenMx is a program with capabilities to fit a variety of mixture models, including combinations of LCGCM and GMM. An intuitive transition from the SEM model specification to the OpenMx syntax language makes this software manageable to master and navigate. With easily accessible analytical tools, the potential utility of the models for understanding interindividual differences in developmental processes is great and should be exploited further.

ACKNOWLEDGMENTS

We would like to thank Dr. Ryne Estabrook for his assistance with the OpenMx programming. Mariya P. Shiyko's work was supported by the National Institute on Drug Abuse (Grant No. P50 DA010075), Nilam Ram's work was supported by the National Institute on Aging (Grant Nos. RC1-AG035645, R21-AG032379, and R21-AG033109) and the Penn State Social Science Research Institute. Kevin J. Grimm's work was supported by the National Science Foundation (Reece Program Grant No. DRL-0815787). The content of this chapter is solely the responsibility of the authors and does not necessarily represent the official views of the funding agencies.

REFERENCES

Akaike, H. (1974). A new look at the statistical model identification. *IEEE Transactions on Automatic Control, 19*(6), 716–723.
Baltes, P. B., & Nesselroade, J. (1979). History and rationale of longitudinal research. In J. R. Nesselroade & P.B. Baltes

(Eds.), *Longitudinal research in the study of behavior and development* (pp. 1–40). New York: Academic Press.

Bauer, D. J., & Curran, P. (2003a). Distributional assumptions of the growth mixture models: Implications for over-extraction of latent trajectory classes. *Psychological Methods, 8,* 338–363.

Bauer, D. J., & Curran, P. (2003b). Overextraction of latent trajectory classes: Much ado about nothing?: Reply to Rindskopf (2003), Muthén (2003), and Cudeck and Henley (2003). *Psychological Methods, 8,* 384–392.

Bauer, D. J., & Curran, P. (2004). The integration of continuous and discrete latent variables models: Potential problems and promising opportunities. *Psychological Methods, 9,* 3–29.

Boker, S., Neale, M., Maes, H., Wilde, M., Spiegel, M., Brick, T., et al. (2009). OpenMx: Multipurpose software for statistical modeling. Available from *http://openmx.psyc.virginia.edu.*

Bollen, K. A., & Curran, P. J. (2006). *Latent curve models: A structural equation perspective.* New York: Wiley.

Boscardin, C. K., Muthén, B., Francis, D. J., & Baker, E. L. (2008). Early identification of reading difficulties using heterogeneous developmental trajectories. *Journal of Educational Psychology, 100*(1), 192–208.

Bradshaw, C. P., Schaeffer, C. M., Petras, H., & Ialongo, N. (2010). Predicting negative life outcomes from early aggressive–disruptive behavior trajectories: Gender differences in maladaptation across life domains. *Journal of Youth and Adolescence, 39,* 953–966.

Brook, D. W., Brook, J. S., Zhang, C., Whiteman, M., Cohen, P., & Finch, S. J. (2008). Developmental trajectories of cigarette smoking from adolescence to the early thirties: Personality and behavioral risk factors. *Nicotine and Tobacco Research, 10*(8), 1283–1291.

Burchinal, M., & Appelbaum, M. (1991). Estimating individual developmental functions: Methods and their assumptions. *Child Development, 62,* 23–43.

Burchinal, M., Nelson, L., & Poe, M. (2006). Growth curve analysis: An introduction to various methods for analyzing longitudinal data. *Monographs of the Society for Research in Child Development, 71,* 65–87.

Chen, R., & Simons-Morton, B. (2009). Concurrent changes in conduct problems and depressive symptoms in early adolescents: A developmental person-centered approach. *Development and Psychopathology, 21*(1), 285–307.

Collins, L., & Horn, J. L. (1991). *Best methods for the analysis of change.* Washington, DC: American Psychological Association.

Connell, A. M., & Frye, A. A. (2006). Growth mixture modeling in developmental psychology: Overview and demonstration of heterogeneity in developmental trajectories of adolescent antisocial behaviour. *Infant and Child Development, 15,* 609–621.

Crocetti, E., Klimstra, T., Keijsers, L., Hale, W. W., III, & Meeus, W. (2009). Anxiety trajectories and identity de-

velopment in adolescence: A five-wave longitudinal study. *Journal of Youth and Adolescence, 38*(6), 839–849.

Duncan, T., Duncan, S., Stryker, L., Li, F., & Alpert, A. (2006). *An introduction to latent variable growth curve modeling.* Mahwah, NJ: Erlbaum.

Espy, K. A., Fang, H., Charak, D., Minich, N., & Taylor, H. G. (2009). Growth mixture modeling of academic achievement in children of varying birth weight risk. *Neuropsychology, 23* (4), 460–474.

Everitt, B. S., & Hand, D. J. (1981). *Finite mixture distributions.* London: Chapman & Hall.

Grimm, K. J., & Ram, N. (2009). Non-linear growth models in M*plus* and SAS. *Structural Equation Modeling, 16,* 676–701.

Grimm, K. J., & Ram, N. (2012). Growth curve modeling from a structural equation modeling perspective. In B. Laursen, T. D. Little, & N. A. Card (Eds.), *Handbook of developmental research methods* (pp. 411–431). New York: Guilford Press.

Grimm, K. J., Ram, N., & Hamagami, F. (2011). Nonlinear growth curves in developmental research. *Child Development, 85,* 1357–1371.

Haapasalo, J., & Tremblay, R. (1994). Physically aggressive boys from ages 6 to 12: Family background, parenting behavior, and prediction of delinquency. *Journal of Consulting and Clinical Psychology, 62,* 1044–1052.

Heim, C., Elhert, U., & Hellhammer, D. (2000). The potential role of hypocortisolism in the pathophysiology of stress-related bodily disorders. *Psychoneuroendocrinology, 25,* 1–35.

Hipp, J. R., & Bauer, D. J. (2006). Local solutions in the estimation of growth mixture models. *Psychological Methods, 11,* 36–53.

Hunter, A. M., Muthén, B. O., Cook, I. A., & Leuchter, A. F. (2010). Antidepressant response trajectories and quantitative electroencephalography (QEEG) biomarkers in major depressive disorder. *Journal of Psychiatric Research, 44,* 90–98.

Jacob, T., Koenig, L. B., Howell, D. N., Wood, P. K., & Randolphaber, J. (2009). Drinking trajectories from adolescence to the fifties among alcohol-dependent men. *Journal of Studies on Alcohol and Drugs, 70*(6), 859–869.

Jung, T., & Wickrama, K. A. S. (2008). An introduction to latent class growth analysis and growth mixture modeling. *Social and Personality Psychology Compass, 2,* 302–317.

Laird, N. M., & Ware, J. H. (1982). Random-effects models for longitudinal data. *Biometrics, 38,* 963–974.

Li, F., Duncan, T. E., Duncan, S. C., & Acock, A. (2001). Latent growth modeling of longitudinal data: A finite growth mixture modeling approach. *Structural Equation Modeling, 8,* 493–530.

Lincoln, K. D., & Takeuchi, D. (2010). Variation in the trajectories of depressive symptoms: Results from the Americans' changing lives study. *Biodemography and Social Biology, 56,* 24–41.

Little, R. J. A., & Rubin, D. B. (1987) *Statistical analysis with missing data*. New York: Wiley.

Maggi, S., Hertzman, C., & Vaillancourt, T. (2007). Changes in smoking behaviors from late childhood to adolescence: Insights from the Canadian National Longitudinal Survey of Children and Youth. *Health Psychology, 26*(2), 232–340.

Martino, S. C., Ellickson, P. L., & McCaffrey, D. F. (2009). Multiple trajectories of peer and parental influence and their association with the development of adolescent heavy drinking. *Addictive Behaviors, 34*(8), 693–700.

McArdle, J. J. (1989). Structural modeling experiments using multiple growth functions. In P. Ackerman, R. Kanfer, & R. Cudeck (Eds.), *Learning and individual differences: Abilities, motivation and methodology* (pp. 71–117). Hillsdale, NJ: Erlbaum.

McArdle, J. J., & Bell, R. Q. (2000). An introduction to latent growth models for developmental data analysis. In T. D. Little, K. U. Schnabel, & J. Baumert (Eds.), *Modeling longitudinal and multilevel data: Practical issues, applied approaches, and specific examples* (pp. 69–107, 269–281). Mahwah, NJ: Erlbaum.

McArdle, J. J., & Epstein, D. B. (1987). Latent growth curves within developmental structural equation models. *Child Development, 58*(1), 110–133.

McCall, R. B., Appelbaum, M. I., & Hogarty, P. S. (1973). Developmental changes in mental performance. *Monographs of the Society for Research in Child Development, 38*(3), 1–85.

McLachlan, G., & Peel, D. (2000). *Finite mixture models*. New York: Wiley.

Meredith, W., & Tisak, J. (1990). Latent curve analysis. *Psychometrica, 55*, 107–122.

Miller, G. E., Chen, E., & Zhou, E. S. (2007). If it goes up, must it come down?: Chronic stress and the hypothalamic–pituitary–adrenocortical axis in humans. *Psychological Bulletin, 133*, 25–45.

Moffitt, T. E. (1993). Adolescence-limited and life-course persistent antisocial behavior: A developmental taxonomy. *Psychological Review, 100*, 674–701.

Muthén, B. (2002). Beyond SEM: General latent variable modeling. *Behaviormetrika, 29*(1), 81–117.

Muthén, B. (2003). Statistical and substantive checking in growth mixture modeling: Comment on Bauer and Curran (2003). *Psychological Methods, 8*(3), 369–377.

Muthén, B. (2004). Latent variable analysis: Growth mixture modeling and related techniques for longitudinal data. In D. Kaplan (Ed.), *The Sage handbook of quantitative methodology for the social sciences* (pp. 345–368). Thousand Oaks, CA: Sage.

Muthén, B., & Asparouhov, T. (2008). Growth mixture modeling: Analysis with non-Gaussian random effects. In G. Fitzmaurice, M. Davidian, G. Verbeke, & G. Molenberghs (Eds.), *Longitudinal data analysis* (pp. 143–165). Boca Raton, FL: Chapman & Hall/CRC Press.

Muthén, B. O., & Shedden, K. (1999). Finite mixture modeling with mixture outcomes using the EMA algorithm. *Biometrics, 55*, 463–469.

Muthén, L. K., & Muthén, B. (2009). *Mplus user's guide* (5th ed.). Los Angeles: Authors.

Nagin, D. S. (1999). Analyzing developmental trajectories: A semiparametric, group-based approach. *Psychological Methods, 4*, 139–157.

Nagin, D. S. (2005). *Group-based modeling of development*. Cambridge, MA: Harvard University Press.

Nesselroade, J. R. (1991). Interindividual differences in intraindividual change. In L. Collins & J. L. Horn (Eds.), *Best methods for analysis of change* (pp. 92–105). Washington, DC: American Psychological Association.

Nylund, K. L., Asparouhov, T., & Muthén, B. O. (2007). Deciding on the number of classes in latent class analysis and growth mixture modeling: A Monte Carlo simulation study. *Structural Equation Modeling, 14*(4), 535–569.

Orlando, M., Tucker, J. S., Ellickson, P. L., & Klein, D. J. (2004). Developmental trajectories of cigarette smoking and their correlates from early adolescence to young adulthood. *Journal of Consulting and Clinical Psychology, 72*(3), 400–410.

Orlando, M., Tucker, J. S., Ellickson, P. L., & Klein, D. J. (2005). Concurrent use of alcohol and cigarettes from adolescence to young adulthood: An examination of developmental trajectories and outcomes. *Substance Use and Misuse, 40*, 1051–1069.

Park, N. S., Lee, B. S., Sun, F., Vazsonyi, A. T., & Bolland, J. M. (2010). Pathways and predictors of antisocial behaviors in African American adolescents from poor neighborhoods. *Children and Youth Services Review, 32*(3), 409–415.

Pianta, R. C., Belsky, J., Vandergrift, N., Houts, R., & Morrison, F. J. (2008). Classroom effects on children's achievement trajectories in elementary school. *American Educational Research Journal, 45*(2), 365–397.

Preacher, K. J., Wichman, A. L., MacCallum, R. C., & Briggs, N. E. (2008). *Latent growth curve modeling*. Thousand Oaks, CA: Sage.

Ram, N., & Grimm, K. J. (2007). Using simple and complex growth models to articulate developmental change: Matching theory to method. *International Journal of Behavioral Development, 31*, 303–316.

Ram, N., & Grimm, K. J. (2009). Growth mixture modeling: A method for identifying differences in longitudinal change among unobserved groups. *International Journal of Behavioral Development, 33*(6), 565–576.

Ram, N., Grimm, K. J., Gatzke-Kopp, L. M., & Molenaar, P. C. M. (2012). Longitudinal mixture models and the identification of archetypes. In B. Laursen, T. D. Little, & N. A. Card (Eds.), *Handbook of developmental methods*. (pp. 481–500). New York: Guilford Press.

Rao, C. R. (1958). Some statistical methods for comparison of growth curves. *Biometrics, 14*, 1–17.

Raudenbush, S. W., & Bryk, A. S. (2002). *Hierarchical linear models: Applications and data analysis methods* (2nd ed.). Thousand Oaks, CA: Sage.

R Development Core Team. (2010). *R: A language and environment for statistical computing.* Vienna: R Foundation for Statistical Computing. Available from *http://www.r-project.org.*

Rindskopf, D. (2003). Mixture or homogeneous?: Comment on Bauer and Curran (2003). *Psychological Methods, 8*(3), 364–368.

Rogosa, D. R., & Willett, J. B. (1995). Understanding correlates of change by modeling individual differences in growth. *Psychometrika, 50,* 203–228.

Romens, S. E., Abramson, L. Y., & Alloy, L. B. (2009). High and low cognitive risk for depression: Stability from late adolescence to early adulthood. *Cognitive Therapy and Research, 33*(5), 480–498.

Rovine, M. J., & Molenaar, P. C. M. (2000). A structural modeling approach to a multilevel random coefficients model. *Multivariate Behavioral Research, 35*(1), 51–88.

Schaeffer, C. M., Petras, H., Ialongo, N., Masyn, K. E., Hubbard, S., Poduska, J., et al. (2006). A comparison of girl's and boy's aggressive-disruptive behavior trajectories across elementary school: Prediction to young adult antisocial outcomes. *Journal of Consulting and Clinical Psychology, 74,* 500–510.

Schwarz, G. (1978). Estimating the dimension of a model. *Annals of Statistics, 6*(2), 461–464.

Seeman, T. E., Berkman, L. F., Gulanski, B., Robbins, R., Greenspan, S., Charpentier, P., et al. (1995). Self-esteem and neuroendocrine response to challenge: MacArthur Successful Aging Studies. *Psychosomatic Research, 39,* 69–84.

Seeman, T. E., Singer, B., & Charpentier, P. (1995). Gender differences in pattern of HPA axis response to challenge: MacArthur Studies of Successful Aging. *Psychoneuroendicrinology, 20,* 711–725.

Singer, J. D., & Willett, J. B. (2003). *Applied longitudinal data analysis: Modeling change and event occurrence.* New York: Oxford University Press.

Stulz, N., Thase, M. E., Klein, D. N., Manber, R., & Crits-Christoph, P. (2010). Differential effects of treatments for chronic depression: A latent growth model reanalysis. *Journal of Consulting and Clinical Psychology, 78*(3), 409–419.

Titterington, D. M., Smith, A. F. M., & Makov, U. E. (1985). *Statistical analysis of finite mixture distributions.* New York: Wiley.

Tofighi, D., & Enders, C. (2008). Identifying the correct number of classes in growth mixture models. In G. R. Hancock & K. M. Samuelsen (Eds.), *Advances in latent variable mixture models* (pp. 317–341). Charlotte, NC: Information Age.

Tolvanen, A. (2007). *Latent growth mixture modeling: A simulation study.* Unpublished doctoral dissertation, University of Jyvaskyla, Finland.

Tucker, L. R. (1958). Determination of parameters of a functional relation by factor analysis. *Psychometrika, 23,* 19–23.

Tucker, L. R. (1966). Learning theory and multivariate experiment: Illustration by determination of generalized learning curves. In R. B. Cattell (Ed.), *Handbook of multivariate experimental psychology* (pp. 476–501). Chicago: Rand McNally.

Wang, M., & Bodner, T. E. (2007). Growth mixture modeling: Identifying and predicting unobserved subpopulations with longitudinal data. *Organizational Research Methods, 10,* 635–656.

CHAPTER 32

Latent Curve Modeling of Longitudinal Growth Data

John J. McArdle

Longitudinal growth curve data have unique features: (1) The same entities are repeatedly observed; (2) the same procedures of measurement and scaling of observations are used; and (3) the timing of the observations is known. These features lead to unusual opportunities for developmental data analysis, and researchers have created many methods for this purpose. For example, many behavioral scientists have relied on advanced versions of the linear growth models formalized in terms of *analysis of variance* (ANOVA) techniques (e.g., Bock, 1975; Pothoff & Roy, 1964). These classical methods provide powerful and accurate tests of "group trends."

But the newest analyses of longitudinal data are often based on the concept of a "trajectory over time" with parameters that are "maximum likelihood estimates" (MLEs). Many new presentations seem to promote the available techniques as entirely new methodology (e.g., Miyazaki & Raudenbush, 2000; cf. McArdle & Bell, 2000). Formal models for the analysis of complex longitudinal data have been developed in many different substantive domains. Early work on these problems led to the polynomial growth models by Wishart (1938), where an individual regression coefficient was used to describe a growth characteristic of the person (see Rogosa & Willett, 1983, 1985; Vandenberg & Falkner, 1965). The contemporary basis of latent growth curve analyses can also be found in the recent developments of *multilevel models* (Bryk & Raudenbush, 1992; Goldstein, 1995) or *mixed-effects models* (Laird & Ware, 1982; Littell, Miliken, Stoup, & Wolfinger, 1996), or *latent curve analysis* (McArdle, 1988; Meredith & Tisak, 1990). In further work by Browne and du Toit (1991), classical nonlinear models were added to this same framework (Cudeck & du Toit, 2001; McArdle & Hamagami, 1996; Pinherio & Bates, 2000).

This general concept of integrating cross-sectional and longitudinal data has come up often, and this was explored by Horn and McArdle (1980), McArdle and Anderson (1990), McArdle and Hamagami (1992), and McArdle and Bell (2000), and in related work by Miyazaki and Raudenbush (2000). All of these models can be based on fitting observed raw-score longitudinal growth data to a theoretical model using likelihood-based techniques (as in Little & Rubin, 1987; McArdle, 1994). These latent curve models have since been expanded upon and described by many others (McArdle & Woodcock, 1997; Metha & West, 2000; Muthén & Curran, 1997). When these options are added to standard latent-variable path analysis structural equation modeling (SEM; e.g., McArdle & Prescott, 1992) some limitations of previous research can be overcome (McArdle, 2007, 2009).

This chapter does not review the classical growth curve data collections or provide the historical perspective of different kinds of mathematical and statistical models for the analyses of these data (but see Baltes & Nesselroade, 1979; McArdle & Nesselroade, 2003; Zeger & Harlow, 1987). This is a very big story, and too lengthy for presentation in this chapter. Instead, I mainly emphasize the use of an SEM approach, including the use of existing software (e.g., SAS-MIXED, NLMIXED, Mplus). I discuss technical and substantive features of contemporary model fitting and the inferences that follow. This chapter is not intended to be overly technical, and the general basis of computer software for these analyses is described. The parameters in these kinds of models can be estimated using standard computer programs that allow appropriate. To simplify this presentation, I do not deal with computer program differences but simply restate that the results for the classical SEM for latent curves will produce the same no matter what program is used (for demonstration, see Ferrer, Hamagami, & McArdle, 2004). Input scripts from recent programs are presented on the handbook's website (*www.handbookofsem.com*), where parallel versions of SAS PROC MIXED and Mplus are included.

To illustrate five key issues about latent curve structural equation models, contemporary techniques are used here to fit the longitudinal data on physical growth from the classic study of Bell (1954), presented in Figure 32.1 and discussed below. This application also serves to remind us that a few classical studies actually

set the stage for the majority of contemporary trajectory analyses. The new SEM work is of obvious interest but, as I also claim here, it largely revives old problems and creates new nomenclature for the same solutions. So, while we are fortunate that new SEM computer programs have allowed these classical concepts to be realized, we should recognize that the current SEM work is far less revolutionary than the past work.

PHYSICAL GROWTH DATA FROM BELL (1954)

The data used in this chapter come from the available physical growth data of Bell (1954). The sample initially included a subpopulation of 61 females ages 10–14 who were measured at yearly evaluation at the National Institute of Mental Health (NIMH) laboratory (in Bethesda, Maryland, around 1950) for about 4 years each, with times selected around their birthdays. Figure 32.1 is a plot of the individuals' height in inches plotted against the time at testing to make up a collection of trajectories over time. For various reasons, some of the individuals (10 of 61; 16.3%) did not have complete data on all occasions of measurement. The summary statistics of Table 32.1 include sample sizes, means, standard deviations, minimum and maximum scores, and the "pairwise" correlations (with $n = 61$). It is obvious that the correlations among the physical height measures are very high ($r > .96$), indicating that these people stay on a specific track most of this time. It also indicates that the measurement of height was done using a highly reliable technique. In addition to the height scores, the four specific ages of testing for all occasions are added. Also added is a single variable, age at menarche, which was gathered by the NIMH (using Tanner stage scores) on all individuals at a later time. This additional variable has much lower correlations with height.

In this context, some early conjectures of R. Q. Bell (1953, 1954) were both interesting and provocative. The problems of inferences about changes from cross-sectional differences were already well known, so the longitudinal data collection approach was gaining momentum. As a resolution of these same problems, Bell suggested use of a combination of longitudinal and cross-sectional data, a data collection he termed "accelerated" longitudinal data. In this first paper Bell suggested that this complex data collection design would be a nearly optimal way to understand growth and change processes both within and between individuals. In a second paper Bell (1954) showed that by se-

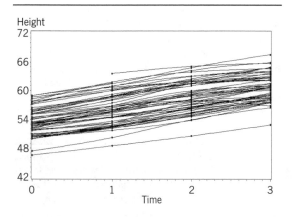

FIGURE 32.1. Bell's (1954) longitudinal physical growth data.

TABLE 32.1. Basic Summary Statistics for Bell's (1954) Physical Growth Data (N = 61)

Univariate statistics	Sample size	Mean	Standard deviation	Minimum	Maximum
Age at Menarche	61	12.98	0.97	10.90	14.75
Age[1]	57	10.49	0.06	10.39	10.61
Age[2]	56	11.49	0.08	11.09	11.61
Age[3]	57	12.48	0.15	11.57	12.93
Age[4]	59	13.48	0.15	12.56	13.66
Inches[1]	57	53.59	2.95	46.53	58.96
Inches[2]	56	56.19	3.43	48.53	63.62
Inches[3]	57	58.74	3.17	50.56	65.10
Inches[4]	59	60.68	2.89	52.86	67.52

Pairwise correlations (n ≤ 54)	Age at menarche	Age[1]	Inches[1]	Inches[2]	Inches[3]
Age at menarche	1.000				
Age[1]	−0.008	1.000			
Inches[1]	−0.402	0.072	1.000		
Inches[2]	−0.478	0.107	0.978	1.000	
Inches[3]	−0.477	0.159	0.945	0.973	1.000
Inches[4]	−0.303	0.157	0.932	0.929	0.960

lecting data from a more time-consuming longitudinal study (i.e., by "masking" of some of the existing data) he could obtain the same results. To ensure uniformity of the outcomes, he suggested a test of "convergence" of the cross-sectional and longitudinal data. He created estimates by joining together the shorter spans of data from people whose scores were most similar at the endpoints, so that he could have complete data to run standard ANOVA. He then demonstrated that the key estimates and inferences were basically the same even though the actual data collection was much shorter. As it turns out, this innovation is now commonly used.

ISSUE 1: MODELING OVER-TIME TRAJECTORIES USING MEANS AND VARIANCE COMPONENTS

We first ask, "How can we do this kind of longitudinal analysis?" Many recent longitudinal curve analyses start by defining longitudinal data as having *repeated measurements* where one can observe the Y variable at multiple occasions ($t = 1$ to T) on the same person ($n = 1$ to N) and symbolize the scores as $Y[t]_n$. In previous

decades, the most common longitudinal approach was based on an autoregressive model (see Jöreskog & Sörbom, 1979; McArdle & Aber, 1990). Due to standard equilibrium assumptions, the means were not the main focus, so we started with deviations around the mean ($Y[t]^* = \mu_y - Y[t]$). A model was written

$$Y[t]^*_n = \beta_0 + Y[t-1]^*_n \beta_1 + e[t]_n \qquad \textbf{(32.1)}$$

where the future deviation at time point t was predicted from deviation at the prior time point ($t - 1$) using a linear regression model with fixed parameters (β_0, β_1) and independent errors ($e[t]$). As usual, the utility of this autoregression approach seems to resonate with some researchers more than others (Molenaar, 1985; cf. McArdle & Epstein, 1987).

During the past decade the most commonly used longitudinal SEM approach is different, and is based on a decomposition of the trajectories over time into mean and variance components (from Meredith & Tisak, 1990; Tisak & Tisak, 1996). This seemingly newer approach, often termed *latent curve modeling* (LCM), starts by writing a classical model in three additive parts:

$$Y[t]_n = f_{0,n} + f_{1,n} B[t] + u[t]_n \qquad \textbf{(32.2)}$$

In this *trajectory* equation the $Y[t]$ is decomposed for each individual as the sum of (1) the f_0, unobserved or *latent scores* representing the individual's *initial latent level*; (2) the f_1, unobserved or latent scores representing the individual's unobserved *change over time* or *latent slope*; and (3) the $u[t]$, unobserved and independent unique features of measurements. In this latent variable longitudinal model the latent slope score (f_1) is assumed to be constant *within* an individual, but it is not assumed to be the same *between* individuals. The latent variables are lowercase letters (f_0, f_1) because they are similar to the predicted scores in a standard regression equation (i.e., we do not use Greek notation here because these scores will not be estimated). However, we usually do estimate several parameters to characterize these scores.

In this model of repeated measures the $B[t]$ are a set of group coefficients or *basis weights* that define the timing or *shape of the trajectory over time* (e.g., $B[t] = t - 1$). To identify all model parameters, the unique terms are assumed to be normally distributed with mean zero and variance (σ_u^2), and are presumably uncorrelated with all other components. It is typical to decompose latent scores into parameters representing *latent means* and *latent variance* terms

$$f_{0n} = \mu_0 + d_{0n}, \text{ and } f_{1n} = \mu_1 + d_{1n} \qquad \textbf{(32.3)}$$

where we have not only the fixed group means for intercept and slopes (μ_0, μ_1) but also implied random variance and covariance terms (σ_0^2, σ_1^2, σ_{01}) describing the distribution of individual deviations (d_{0n}, d_{1n}) around those means. These latent means are the only parameters used to create expectations for the observed means in the model. We typically assume that there is only one unique variance (σ_u^2), but recognize that specific factor influences could be different at each time (Meredith & Horn, 2001). Most importantly, the "trajectory" model (Equations 32.2 and 32.3) is not the same as model in Equation 32.1, so we do not use the "past to predict the future." I return to this point later.

Considering Latent Basis Functions

The previous linear curve model is termed a "latent" variable model because the parameters are calculated under the model-based assumption of "independence of the unique factors and the common factors" (see Equation 32.2). Although a linear scaling of the basis curve (i.e., $B[t] = t - 1$) is very popular (see Singer & Willett, 2003), it is only one of many that could be used. A different alternative to the linear growth model was highlighted by Meredith and Tisak (1990)—the model proposed by Rao (1958) and Tucker (1958, 1966) in the form of summations of "latent curves." Meredith and Tisak (1990) showed how the "Tuckerized curve" models (named in recognition of Tucker's contributions) could be represented and fitted using SEM based on restricted common factors. These important innovative techniques made it possible to represent a wide range of alternative growth and change models by adding the benefits of the SEM techniques (McArdle, 1986, 1997, 2009; McArdle & Aber, 1990; McArdle & Anderson, 1990; McArdle & Hamagami, 1992).

Use of this latent curve concept here is relatively simple. The curve basis is allowed to take on a form based on the empirical data, and one simply writes a model where

$$\begin{aligned}
Y[1]_n &= f_{0,n} + f_{1,n} \bullet 0 + u[1]_n \\
Y[2]_n &= f_{0,n} + f_{1,n} \bullet 1 + u[2]_n \\
Y[3]_n &= f_{0,n} + f_{1,n} \bullet \beta[3] + u[3]_n, \text{ and} \\
Y[4]_n &= f_{0,n} + f_{1,n} \bullet \beta[4] + u[4]_n
\end{aligned} \qquad \textbf{(32.4)}$$

implying that the last two basis coefficients $\beta[3]$ and $\beta[4]$ are *free to be estimated*. The actual time of the measurement is known, but the basis parameters are allowed to be freely estimated so than one ends up with different latent distances between time points (i.e., an optimal shape for the whole curve). In this model the $B[t]$ is estimated just like a common-factor loading and has the same mathematical and statistical identification problems (see McArdle, 1989, 2007). In the typical case at least two entries of the $B[t]$ need to be fixed (e.g., $\alpha[1] = 0$ and $\alpha[2] = 1$) as done here to provide a reference point for the changes in the other model parameters. There are many alternative ways to estimate these parameters but, in general, the number of free parameters in the two-component growth model is $p = 6 + T - 1$. The use of an estimated basis has been termed a "meta-meter" or "latent time" scale that can be plotted against the actual age curve for visual interpretation (McArdle & Epstein, 1987; Rao, 1958; Tucker, 1958, 1966).

Growth Models as SEM Path Diagrams

The path diagram of Figure 32.2 provides an exact translation of the necessary matrix formulation of these models (see McArdle, 1986, 1988). Path diagrams are also practically useful because they can be used to represent the input and output of any of the computer programs (see Appendix 32.1 at *www.handbookofsem. com*). In this path diagram the observed variables are drawn as squares, the unobserved variables are drawn as circles, and the required constant is included as a triangle. Model parameters representing "fixed" or "group" coefficients are drawn as one-headed arrows, while "random" or "individual" features are drawn as two-headed arrows. In this model the initial level and slopes are assumed to be latent variables with "fixed" means (μ_0, μ_1) but "random" variances (σ_0^2, σ_1^2) and correlations (ρ_{01}). The standard deviations (σ_j) are drawn as arrows to permit the interpretation of the scaled correlations (see McArdle, 1996; McArdle & Hamagami, 1992).

These path diagrams can be conceptually useful devices for understanding the basic modeling concepts. For example, the path diagram presented here can also be interpreted as a two-common-factor model with means. The first latent factor score is an intercept or level score (f_0), and the second latent factor score is a slope or change score (f_1). The relationships between the latent levels f_0 and all observed scores $Y[t]$ are fixed at a value of 1. In contrast, the relationships between the latent slopes f_1 and all observed scores $Y[t]$ are assigned a value based on the time parameter $B[t]$, which may be fixed or estimated from the data. The unique components ($u[t]$) have mean of zero and constant deviation (σ_u), and are uncorrelated with other components. Variations of this model may be acceptable, but such variations may not be needed.

One note of caution—the path diagrams do not fully substitute for the algebraic interpretations, and they often can be misleading. For example, while path diagrams were originally used with autoregression models (e.g., Equation 32.1), these models seemed to reflect actions or predictions over time, even though they did not. Subsequent work showed how these diagrams can be used in the context of growth and change as latent variables (e.g., McArdle, 1986, 1991; McArdle & Epstein, 1987; McArdle & Woodcock, 1997). Clearly, the promotion of this path diagram was my main contribution to this area of research.

Numerical Results from Fitting Latent Curve Models

The results of a series of models fitted to these longitudinal data are presented in Table 32.2. These latent curve models were fitted to Bell's data using both SAS MIXED and Mplus, and the computer codes used here are on the handbook's website (*www.handbookofsem. com*).

In a typical sequence we start with utterly simple models, most of which we typically hope do not fit the data. Then we add extra parameters representing substantive issues, and we try to stop model fitting when the models seem to create unwarranted overfitting— that is, nothing is added to the fit by adding parameters. Using this classical strategy here, we first consider a *no-growth* model (column a in Table 32.2) fitted with only three parameters: an initial level mean ($\mu_0 = 57.24$), an initial level variance ($\sigma_0^2 < 6.63$), and a unique variance ($\sigma_u^2 = 10.09$). The values of the basis function are all set to zero ($\beta[t] = 0$) by design. We list the *t*-values associated with the estimated parameters are in parentheses, and these are all significantly different from

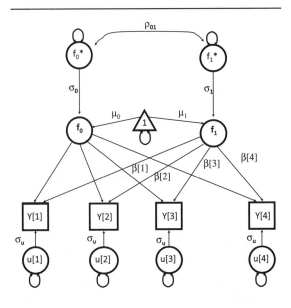

FIGURE 32.2. Latent growth as a path diagram with multiple components.

TABLE 32.2. Initial Results for Complete and Incomplete Longitudinal Physical Growth Curve Data

Latent curve parameters	Level (intercepts) only	Level + linear time	Level+ latent time
Fixed effects			
$\beta[1]$	=0	=0	=0
$\beta[2]$	=0	=1	=1
$\beta[3]$	=0	=2	2.09 (25)
$\beta[4]$	=0	=3	2.92 (25)
Intercept $1 \rightarrow f_0 \ (\mu_0)$	57.24 (147)	53.82 (131)	53.75 (131)
Slope $1 \rightarrow f_1 \ (\mu_1)$	=0	2.39 (45)	2.43 (21)
Random Effects			
Intercept (σ_0^2)	6.63 (3.9)	9.92 (5.3)	8.69 (4.9)
Slope (σ_1^2)	=0	0.08 (2.4)	0.07 (2.3)
Correlation (ρ_{01})	=0	-0.26 (1.4)	-0.19 (1.0)
Unique (σ_u^2)	10.09 (9.2)	0.38 (7.3)	0.35 (7.1)
Goodness-of-fit			
Likelihood/ parameters	1260/3	746/6	733/8
Change ΔL^2/degrees of freedom	0/0	514/3	13/2

zero at conventional test levels ($\alpha = .05$, $t > 1.96$). This model yields a constant mean, a constant variance, and a constant correlation over time (i.e., calculated as $\eta^2 = [6.63/(6.63 + 10.09)] = 0.397$). This model is useful because it makes an explicit prediction about every individual observed score $Y[t]$. We can form "individual misfits" as residuals (McArdle, 1997), and the sum of all these misfits yields a model likelihood ($L^2 = 1,260$). Of course, next we hope to improve the fit.

The first substantive model is a *linear growth* (column b in Table 32.2) with fixed-basis-coefficient form $B[t] = [0, 1, 2, 3]$. In the physical growth example, we can use a fixed $B[t] = [1, 2, 3, 4]$, so that it permits a practical interpretation of the slope parameters in terms of the physical growth data as *per-year change*. (If we fit $B[t] = [0, 1, 2, 3]$, then we would still have 1 year of

change but the intercept would then be set at the first occasion.) This linear growth model can be estimated by adding a few more free parameters: a slope mean ($\mu_1 = 53.82$) representing height in inches at the first time, and a slope mean ($\mu_1 = 2.39$) representing changes in height per year. In addition, this model also gives estimated latent variances—for the latent intercept ($\sigma_0^2 = 9.92$), the latent slope ($\sigma_1^2 = 0.08$), the correlation between them ($\rho_{01} = -0.26$), and for the latent unique variance ($\sigma_u^2 = 0.38$). If this model were correct, then the variance of the intercept would largely account for the variance of the initial time score—the estimate of the intraclass reliability ($\eta^2 = [9.92/(9.92 + 0.38)] = 0.963$).

This linear model yields a new likelihood ($L^2 = 746$), and the basis of this likelihood is discussed in the next section. For now, it is easiest to state that under the assumption that all other impacts are random noise, the difference between likelihoods is distributed as a chi-square variate, which in this case does not seem random ($\chi^2 = 1,260 - 746 = 514$ on $df = 3$). Thus, the latent concept of linear change in height over time seems like a reasonable idea (see Figure 32.1). In this model, all persons are assumed to have linear slopes, but they do not add up to zero (μ_1), and the size of the slope is assumed to vary (based on both σ_1^2 and σ_{01}; see Equation 32.3). In this last concept, this latent curve model is different than repeated-measures ANOVA (O'Brien & Kaiser, 1985).

The results of the more complete latent-basis alternative (column c in Table 32.2) was fitted and the free basis functions are estimated at $\beta[3] = 2.09$ and $\beta[4] = 2.92$, with a small but potentially useful improvement in fit ($\chi^2 = 13$ on $df = 2$). Of course, the estimated values of the basis are very close to the fixed linear slope values—$\beta[3] = 2.09$ instead of 2, and $\beta[4] = 2.92$ instead of 3. So, although the fit is slightly better, the result is only very small changes from a simple linear slope for each person, and this should not be viewed as a considerable improvement on that linear slope.

ISSUE 2: DEALING WITH INCOMPLETE DATA USING INDIVIDUAL LIKELIHOODS

Dealing with the incomplete longitudinal data can be complicated, but it is typically necessary in any real longitudinal study because some persons who start do not come back at all occasions. There is an extremely simple way to view this problem in this case, as illustrated in Figure 32.3. Here we separate the plot of trajectories for those individuals with complete data (Figure 32.3a; $n = 51$) and those without complete data (Figure 32.3b; $n = 10$). In the analyses to follow I show how these kinds of problems can be dealt with using contemporary latent curve modeling. The main question is: "Does the pattern of change appear to be the same over groups?"

For all analyses, standard SAS programs were used here, including PROC MIXED and PROC NLMIXED, but SEM programs can be used as well (Mplus, Open-Mx, etc.) because the results are identical. In addition, most of these programs can deal with incomplete data patterns using a likelihood-based approach (McArdle, 1994; McArdle & Hamagami, 1996; McArdle, Prescott, Hamagami, & Horn, 1998). In some cases, the SEM programming does not seem as convenient as the mixed-effects program input, and some "bracketing" or "bucketing" of time is needed, but SEM is far more flexible when one considers a range of alternative models.

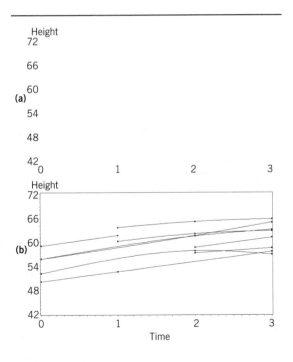

FIGURE 32.3. Time plots of (a) complete and (b) incomplete data.

Numerical Calculations in Fitting Standard Latent Curve Models

One essential idea is that the data have a likelihood ($L^2[0]$, termed "fully saturated"), the specific model has a different likelihood ($L^2[1]$, based on "some restrictions"), and the distance between these can be indexed by a difference in the likelihoods ($L^2[0 - 1]=L^2[0] - L^2[1]$), which, due to the simplifying device of the logarithm, is termed a likelihood ratio (*LR*). Under additional regularity assumptions of normality of the residuals, this *LR* may follow a chi-square distribution with specific degrees of freedom (*df* = parameters[0] – parameters[1]).

Numerical estimates of such parameters can come from calculations based on the concepts from the optimization of a likelihood. Details of this important calculation were initially provided by Anderson (1958), Lawley and Maxwell (1963), and Rao (1965); used by Jöreskog and Sörbom (1979); and repeated by others (e.g., Bollen, 1989). In most cases, these derivations start with (1) an assumption of multivariate normality of the scores (*v*) taken over all observations (*N*), (2) calculation of the joint density of all such observations via a product of all scores for a given sample—a likelihood function, followed by (3) calculation of the log of the likelihood function (–2*LL*, to turn multiplication into addition but retain the same functional form). In simplified terms, the log-likelihood function (L^2) for one group can be written as

$$L^2 = K1 + K2 + K3 \qquad (32.5)$$

where

$$K1 = (-N*v)/2, \ K2 = (-N/2) \ln(\Sigma),$$
$$\text{and } K3 = (\mu - Y) \ \Sigma^{-1} \ (\mu - Y)'$$

In this organization of the likelihood function, $K1$ is a constant based on the size of the data, $K2$ is based on the expected covariances (Σ), and $K3$ is based on the observed data (Y), the expected means (μ), and the expected covariances (Σ). We note that $K3$ is equivalent to Hotelling's classical formulation of the T^2 or Mahalanobis's classical formulation of the Euclidean distance Δ^2, and is possibly useful for identifying multivariate outliers (e.g., Rocke & Woodruff, 1997). The calculation of the scalar likelihood indicates some distance from the data, so smaller numbers imply closer fit, and larger numbers imply poorer fit.

The way to carry out the calculations when the data are less than complete is to assign each individual in the analysis (N) to one and only one group (g = 1 to G) based on the common pattern of available data ($Y^{[g]}$). In simplified terms, the joint likelihood function for several can be decomposed into a likelihood for each group written as

$$L^{2[g]} = K1^{[g]} + K2^{[g]} + K3^{[g]} \qquad (32.6)$$

where

$$K1^{[g]} = (-n^{[g]}*v^{[g]})/2, \; K2^{[g]} = (-n^{[g]}/2) \ln(\Sigma^{[g]}),$$
$$\text{and } K3 = (\mu^{[g]} - Y^{[g]}) \; \Sigma^{[g]-1} \; (\mu^{[g]} - Y^{[g]})'$$

In this organization of the likelihood function, each group $K1^{[g]}$ is a constant based on the size of the data in that group, $K2^{[g]}$ is based on the expected covariances ($\Sigma^{[g]}$) within the group, and $K3^{[g]}$ is based on the observed data ($Y^{[g]}$), the expected means ($\mu^{[g]}$), and the expected covariances ($\Sigma^{[g]}$) within the group. The overall likelihood for the model given the G patterns of independent and available data is calculated as the weighted sum of the group likelihoods, so it is written as

$$L^2 = \Sigma(g = 1 \text{ to } G) \; w^{[g]} * L^{2[g]} \qquad (32.7)$$

where the weight is $w^{[g]} = n^{[g]}/N$, or the ratio of the sample size in each group compared to the total size. Because we can easily create models or data collections where each individual has a unique pattern of data collected, this approach is generally termed "raw score maximum likelihood," or full-information maximum likelihood, or individual likelihood.

It follows that when carrying out an analysis with incomplete data one is not only using the observed data but also is dealing with incomplete data as *unobserved but important scores* that can alter estimates of any parameter. This becomes much more of an issue when one considers the longitudinal data at every age, including considerations of the loss of participants due to selective attrition (see McArdle, Small, Backman, & Fratiglioni, 2005). Estimates based on incomplete data statistics are an essential part of all models used here. A relatively complex expression is required when one wishes to include a great deal of incomplete data patterns (e.g., McArdle, 1994).

The Individual Likelihood Model Applied to the Physical Growth Data

Most current SEM computer programs that offer this raw data approach (Amos, LISREL, Mplus, semR, OpenMx, etc.) and built-in options allow us to estimate parameters using all the available data (e.g., SAS-MIXED, Mplus) in this way.

Using this likelihood logic, we can examine the impact of attrition of the previous estimates. Table 32.3 (column a) repeats the previous results for the linear time-based curve model of individuals with any data (N = 61). Next are results (column b) for the same model fitted to those people with complete data (n = 51). The estimated model parameters are very similar to the pre-

TABLE 32.3. More In-Depth Results for Complete and Incomplete Longitudinal Physical Growth Curve Data

Latent curve parameters	Level + linear time	Only complete cases	Only incomplete cases
Sample Sizes			
Persons (*N*)	61	51	10
Data points (*D*)	230	204	26
Fixed Effects			
Intercept $1 \rightarrow f_0 \; (\mu_0)$	53.82 (131)	53.44 (128)	55.99 (49)
Slope $1 \rightarrow f_1 \; (\mu_1)$	2.39 (46)	2.42 (47)	2.12 (9.4)
Random Effects			
Intercept (σ_0^2)	9.92 (5.3)	8.69 (4.9)	9.92 (5.4)
Slope (σ_1^2)	0.08 (2.4)	0.07 (2.3)	0.09 (2.7)
Correlation (ρ_{01})	−0.26 (1.4)	−0.19 (1.0)	−0.24 (1.3)
Unique (σ_u^2)	0.38 (7.3)	0.35 (7.1)	0.34 (7.3)
Goodness-of-Fit			
Likelihood/ parameters	746/6	632/6	104/6
Change ΔL^2/degrees of freedom	514/3	458/3	20/3

vious model (column a), and the new likelihood (L^2 = 632) is a large distance from a no-growth model (χ^2 = 453 on df = 3) for the same data. In the next model (column c in Table 32.3) we give results for the same time-based curve model based only on individuals with incomplete data (n = 10). The estimated model parameters are fairly similar to the previous linear model (column b), and the new likelihood (L^2 = 104) is only a short distance from a no-growth model (χ^2 = 20, df = 3).

Most importantly here, since the two sets of persons (Figure 32.3a and 32.3b) are independent of one another, we can add the two likelihoods together as if they were all fit as one model with separate parameters—this is most simply done by creating a simple sum of these likelihoods (L^2 = [632 + 104] = 736), and we find that this combined model is only a small distance away from the initial model (column b in Table 32.2, χ^2 = [746 − 736] = 10), where essentially all parameters were forced to be the same. This is clearly a test of parameter invariance, and this small relative difference (χ^2 = 10 on df = 6) suggests that not much is gained by treating these two samples of individuals as different groups, each requiring its own parameters. This likelihood difference is the formal statistical test often termed *missing completely at random* (MCAR; from Little & Rubin, 1987). This small difference found here suggests that the complete and incomplete data are not presenting a different story about trajectories, so we will combine them in all analyses to follow.

Initial results from this first SEM model can also be seen in a test of the "incomplete data" estimate of the sample means, variances, and correlations based on some kind of MLE–MAR (missing at random) algorithm (Cnaan, Laird, & Slasor, 1997; Little, 1995; Little & Rubin, 1987; McArdle, 1994). This approach allows us to examine these basic summary statistics "as if all persons were measured on all variables." As stated earlier, these estimated statistics are fairly close to the pairwise estimates, so they are not presented here. But it is important to note that this typically indicates these data meet the minimal conditions of MAR (Little & Rubin, 1987), where the observed scores are not different between groups after some important measured covariates have been considered. Most importantly, these estimated statistics do not suffer from some common statistical problems (local linear dependency); also, we can routinely use whatever information is available from every person (McArdle, 2004).

ISSUE 3: FLEXIBILITY IN THE DEFINITION OF A LATENT BASIS

One concept that was made clear in the early work of Bell and others is that the assignment of a set of basis functions ($B[t]$) is not a fixed feature of the statistical model. Instead, the basis is a potentially important aspect of the substantive question. Of course, the basis function represents the axis of interest to the investigator and, as such, needs to be defined in a unique way, or using the latent basis suggested by Meredith and Tisak (1990). But, in this context, what Bell (1953, 1954) suggested was more revolutionary that this. He suggested that (1) we typically did not need all the longitudinal data we collected, so we could *accelerate* the data collection, then that (2) we could test the adequacy of this acceleration through *convergence* analysis. This approach seems a bit easier to understand given that one can deal with incomplete data vectors (as earlier), but I illustrate these points in several ways.

Introducing Individualized Alternative Bases

One way to deal with this general problem of model fitting is to have $\beta[t]$ take on known values based on the data collection for each person. For example, we can easily set $\beta[t]$ = Age$[t]_n$ so that we can fit a model based on the age of the person at a particular time (t). To illustrate the basic concepts involved here, Figure 32.4a shows the same raw data on height as in Figure 32.1 now plotted as a function of the "age at which the persons were tested." In a typical study no persons were measured at exactly the same ages, so this can be seen as an alternative form of the convergence design. The differentiation of complete and incomplete data becomes a bit muddled here because we are making an inference about all ages even though no person has been measured at every age. Whether or not an age-based model allows a clearer representation of the data is strictly a substantive issue and is viewed here as an empirical question.

This age-based approach is not novel, and it is implied by the work of Bell (1953, 1954), but it was initially revived and used by McArdle and Anderson (1990). This approach has been refined in more recent statistical (Mizayaki & Raudenbush, 2000) and theoretical treatments (e.g., Metha & West, 2000). Longitudinal data collection often includes different num-

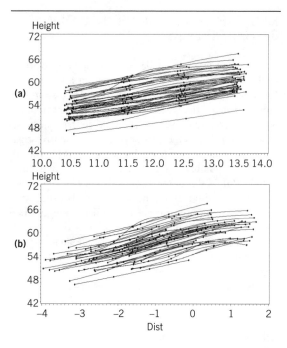

FIGURE 32.4. (a) Age- and (b) puberty-based plots of the longitudinal data.

bers of data points for different people and different variables, and there are several good ways to deal with these kinds of statistical problems (e.g., Cnaan et al., 1997; Little, 1995). Thus, it may be wise to view this simply as an issue of dealing directly with incomplete data. So, in the approach used here, we fit structural models to the *raw score information for each person on each variable at each time* (Hamagami & McArdle, 2001; McArdle & Bell, 2000). The currently available computer programs (SAS-MIXED, SAS-NLMIXED, Mplus) now make this an incredibly easy task (see McArdle, 1997; McArdle & Bell, 2000; programs on this handbook's website at *www.handbookofsem. com*).

Once again, the fundamental reason to consider these alternatives is to recognize that the basis is not a fixed element of the model. Once we open up the possibilities for altering the basis and dealing with incompleteness, we need to recognize that many other options are possible. That is, since we can deal with incomplete data

so easily, possibly we should evaluate different ways to create incomplete data (after McArdle, 1994; McArdle & Hamagami, 1992).

In one substantively reasonable alternative, Figure 32.4b presents the same observed height data using a slightly different *X*-axis—as a function of the "individual's distance to puberty when tested." In Figure 32.4b it is clear that the zero point (i.e., age at menarche) was often observed after the data collection began. However, if the growth of individual height is in fact regulated by individual characteristics, and some of these are captured by this measured variable (age at menarche), then this could be an improved axis upon which to pattern the growth (i.e., biological age). Of course, we do not really know until we fit these model to the data.

Numerical Results for Flexible Basis

The time-based model (column a in Table 32.4) is repeated from the initial analysis. Here the loadings of $B[t] = [0, 1, 2, 3]$ are made clear. For the purposes of the second analysis, the age basis at each time point was initially centered at 12. Thus, the results for this age-based model (column b in Table 32.4) are used to estimate the average height at age 12 ($\alpha_0 = 57.47$) with individual differences at age 12 ($\sigma_0^2 = 9.49$). In addition, the average linear slope for every year is similar ($\mu_0 = 2.41$) with individual differences ($\sigma_1^2 = 0.10$). The estimate of the unique variance is a bit larger than before ($\sigma_u^2 = 0.44$), but this could be a correct estimate. This model has the same numbers of parameters as the time based model, but the fit is not as good as the time-based model ($L^2 = 773$; $\Delta L^2 = -27$). These models are not strictly nested, so a formal statistical test is difficult to create.

In the third analysis, the pubertal basis at each time point was the age at testing the person minus the distance from the age at menarche ($B[t] = Age[t] - $ Menarche). This means the results for this puberty-based model (column c in Table 32.4) are used to estimate the average height at menarche ($\alpha_0 = 59.90$) with individual differences at menarche ($\sigma_0^2 = 9.00$). In addition, the average linear slope for every year is similar ($\mu_0 = 2.41$) with individual differences ($\sigma_1^2 = 0.10$). The estimate of the unique variance is a bit larger than before ($\sigma_u^2 = 0.44$), and this could be an improved estimate. The goodness of fit is larger than before ($L^2 = 765$; $\Delta L^2 = -21$), but this may still be a reasonable approach.

TABLE 32.4. Fitting Flexible Linear Bases for Latent Curve Models of Longitudinal Physical Growth Data

Latent curve parameters	Linear time basis	Linear age basis	Linear puberty basis
Fixed effects			
Linear basis $B[t]$	$=0$	$=Age[1]_n-12$	$=\Delta Mena[1]_n-13$
	$=1$	$=Age[2]_n-12$	$=\Delta Mena[2]_n-13$
	$=2$	$=Age[3]_n-12$	$=\Delta Mena[3]_n-13$
	$=3$	$=Age[4]_n-12$	$=\Delta Mena[4]_n-13$
Intercept	53.82	57.47	59.90
$1 \rightarrow f_0$ (μ_0)	(131)	(145)	(154)
Linear Slope	2.39	2.41	2.41
$1 \rightarrow f_1$ (μ_1)	(46)	(42)	(42)
Random effects			
Intercept (σ_0^2)	9.92	9.49	9.00
	(5.3)	(5.4)	(5.4)
Linear Slope (σ_1^2)	0.08	0.10	0.10
	(2.4)	(2.2)	(2.3)
Correlation (ρ_{01})	−0.26	−0.04	0.32
	(1.4)	(0.2)	(1.9)
Unique (σ_u^2)	0.38	0.44	0.44
	(7.3)	(7.0)	(7.1)
Goodness of fit			
Likelihood/parameters	746/6	773/6	765/6
Change ΔL^2/degrees of freedom	514/3	527/3	535/3

Convergence with Accelerated Longitudinal Data

In order to examine this issue further, I now recreate the "accelerated" design of Bell (1954) by "masking" or not using some of the available data—in other words, randomly restricting the analysis to data from only two consecutive occasions of measurement (for selection, see Appendix 32.1 on this handbook's website at *www.handbookofsem.com*), and the resulting "unmasked" data are presented in Figure 32.5.

For example Figure 32.5a shows a time plot of the resulting data as if we only had information from two time points on the individuals here, but notice we have plotted the data as if different people were chosen for four different occasions. Since this data collection only requires two occasions of measurement it would only take 1 year to collect these data. Figure 32.5b is more illustrative because it uses the same data with an age basis, and now it looks as if we simply started differ-

ent people at different ages, but measured everyone for about 1 year. This is not at all an unusual feature of real longitudinal lifespan data, and we should consider this very carefully. Figure 32.5c shows a plot of the same data versus the distance to menarche. It is interesting that puberty is a variable that could not be known in advance of the early data collection. In addition to chronological age, this kind of biological age may be very important when dealing with biologically relevant outcomes (i.e., height).

The resulting statistics that come from dropping almost all but two occasions of measurement are similar to those in Table 32.1, but it is clear that this statistical information is impoverished at best. While variation in these summary statistics appears to create the hopeless situation of not having enough longitudinal data to estimate the longitudinal model parameters uniquely (e.g., Rogosa, 1978), it is possible to estimate the previous models based only on two-occasion time-lagged data

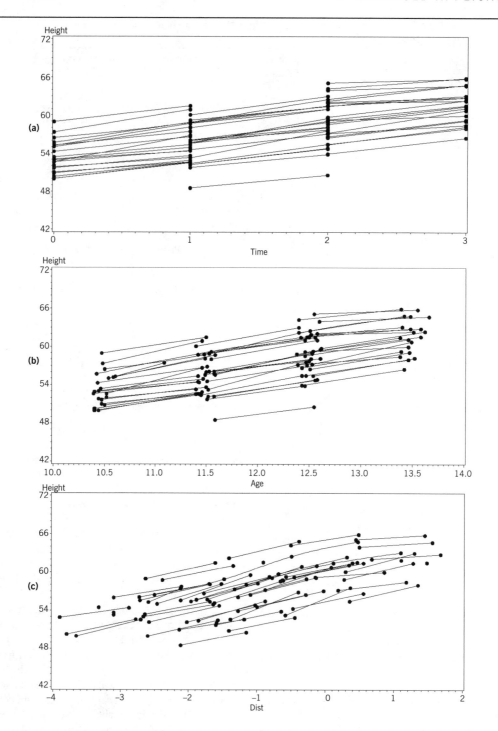

FIGURE 32.5. (a) Time-, (b) age-, and (c) puberty-based plots of the accelerated data.

(i.e., McArdle, Ferrer-Caja, Hamagami, & Woodcock, 2002).

Some modeling results appear in Table 32.5. The first model fitted (column a) uses a linear time basis (see Figure 32.5a) and the estimates of fixed effects (group trajectory) are remarkably similar to those using all the four occasion data (compare to column b). The variance of the intercepts and the uniqueness are also similar, but the slope variance and the correlation of the level and slope are unreasonable. It is clear that we lose some precision to deal with individual differences in changes when we lose the data representing changes. The overall change in fit for this model is slightly less ($\chi^2 = 620$ on $df = 3$) but there are less data points fitted ($d = 119$ rather than $D = 230$).

The next model (column b in Table 32.5) uses the age basis (Figure 32.5a) and has similar recovery of the fixed and random effects, and a loss of individual differences in slope. The subsequent model (column c in Table 32.5) uses distance from menarche as the basis (Figure 32.5b), and the results for all parameters, including the individual difference in slopes, are re-

markably similar to the full data model (see column c in Table 32.4). Even though it seems that there are not enough data measured to estimate all model parameters, the key fixed results, including the level of significance, are nearly identical. Not surprisingly, the big loss is that most of the random components cannot be estimated with accuracy.

ISSUE 4: DEFINING NONLINEAR LATENT TRAJECTORIES VIA LATENT CHANGES

Including Nonlinearity in Growth

It is possible to add a lot of nonlinear complexity to the simple growth curve models for the study of within-person changes. In one popular approach, Wishart (1938) introduced a useful way to examine a nonlinear shape—the use of power polynomials to better fit the curvature apparent in growth data. The individual growth curve (consisting of $t = 1, T$ occasions) is summarized into a small set of linear orthogonal polynomial coefficients based on a fixed-power time series ($B[t]$, $1/2 B[t]^2$, $1/3 B[t]^3$, ... $1/p B[t]^p$) describing the general nonlinear shape of the growth curve. A second-order (quadratic) polynomial growth model can be written as

$$Y[t]_n = f_{0n} + f_{1n} \bullet B[t] + 1/2\ B[t]^2 + u[t]_n \quad (32.8)$$

where the loadings of the second component are fixed to be a function of the first component (and so the derivative is linear with this time). A new set of component scores (e.g., f_p) can be introduced to represent another level of change with a set of powered coefficients ($1/p\ B[t]^p$).

A quadratic form of this basic model is depicted as a path diagram in Figure 32.6. This model leads to an implied change that is proportionally linear with time (i.e., acceleration). Of course, a model of growth data might require this form of a second-order (quadratic), third-order (cubic), or even higher-order polynomial model fitted to the data. In all cases, additional variance and covariance terms are added to account for individual differences in latent scores. This polynomial growth curve approach remains popular (e.g., Bryk & Raudenbush, 1992). Others have pointed out how the quadratic model can be reparameterized in terms of key inflection points and maximum scores (Cudeck & du Toit, 2001; Stimson, Carmines, & Zeller, 1978).

TABLE 32.5. Fully "Accelerated and Converged" Longitudinal Latent Curve/Mixed Effects Results for Bell's (1954) Physical Growth Data ($N = 61$, but $D = 119$)

Latent curve parameters	Linear time	Linear age	Linear Puberty
Basis $B[t]$	Time 0–3	Age[t]–12	ΔMena–13
Intercept $1 \rightarrow f_0\ (\mu_0)$	53.55 (134)	57.28 (153)	59.67 (156)
Linear slope $1 \rightarrow f_1\ (\mu_1)$	2.47 (26)	2.48 (25)	2.27 (24)
Intercept (σ_0^2)	8.08 (4.5)	8.11 (5.3)	7.82 (5.2)
Slope (σ_1^2)	0.0001 (0.7)	>0.00 (=0)	0.05 (0.4)
Correlation (ρ_{01})	<1.00 (=0)	=0 (=0)	=0 (=0)
Unique (σ_u^2)	0.36 (5.5)	0.38 (55)	0.35 (2.8)
Likelihood/ parameters	442/6	445/6	444/6
Change ΔL^2/degrees of freedom	620/3	623/3	624/3

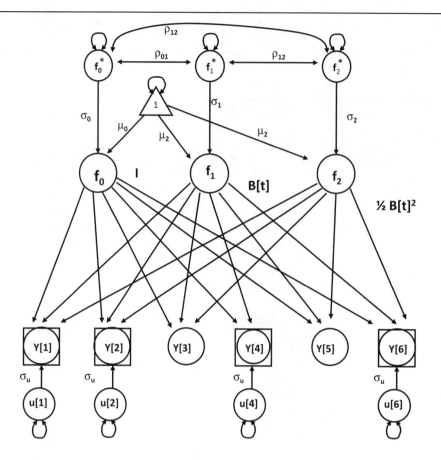

FIGURE 32.6. Representing a "quadratic polynomial" as a latent growth curve.

A different alternative to the linear growth model was proposed by Rao (1958) and Tucker (1958, 1966) in a form of simple summations of additional ($k > 1$) latent-basis curves:

$$Y[t]_n = f_{0,n} + \Sigma(k = 1 \text{ to } K)\{f_{k,n} B_k[t]\} + u[t]_n \quad \textbf{(32.9)}$$

Of course, these latent curve models can be combined with the polynomial models, with critical cutoff ages (C_n) estimated as well, or with a nonlinear function (e.g., logistic, exponential) using structured latent basis curves. These can be very useful models when they match substantive concerns, but I do not deal with these issues here (Browne & du Toit, 1991; Cudeck & du Toit, 2001; Cudeck & Harring, 2007; McArdle

& Hamagami, 2001; McArdle & Nesselroade, 2003; McArdle & Wang, 2008; Nesselroade & Boker, 1994; Preece & Baines, 1978).

Results for Quadratic Models

Table 32.6 is a list of results for three quadratic models fitted to these data. The first model (column a) uses time as the basis of the quadratic model, and the results show a distinct improvement in fit over the comparable linear time model (vs. column a in Table 32.5: $\chi^2 = 48$ on $df = 4$). Also, the estimate of the unique variance is much smaller than before ($\sigma_u^2 = 0.15$), so this is probably an improved model for these data. The second model (column b in Table 32.6) uses age as the basis of

TABLE 32.6. Fitting Alternative Quadratic ($B2[t]$ = $1/2B[t]^2$) Latent Bases for Latent Curve Models with Longitudinal Physical Growth Data

Latent curve parameters	Quadratic time basis	Quadratic age basis	Quadratic puberty basis
Linear basis $B[t]$	Time$[t] - 1$	Age$[t] - 12$	ΔMena–13
Intercept 1 → f_0 (μ_1)	53.69 (140)	57.64 (134)	60.18 (153)
Linear slope 1 → f_1 (μ_1)	2.79 (20)	2.41 (44)	2.48 (35)
Quadratic slope 1 → f_2 (μ_1)	–0.13 (2.6)	–0.15 (2.8)	–0.10 (2.7)
Intercept (σ_0^2)	8.82 (5.4)	11.11 (5.5)	9.26 (5.3)
Linear slope (σ_1^2)	0.83 (3.6)	0.14 (3.8)	0.13 (2.5)
Quadratic (σ_2^2)	0.11 (3.8)	0.13 (3.5)	0.07 (0.5)
Correlation (ρ_{01})	0.45 (3.1)	–0.04 (0.2)	0.10 (0.5)
Correlation (ρ_{02})	–0.48 (3.8)	–0.64 (6.4)	–0.08 (0.5)
Correlation (ρ_{12})	–0.94 (42)	0.10 (0.6)	=1.00 (0.0)
Unique (σ_u^2)	0.15 (5.1)	0.18 (5.0)	0.22 (6.9)
Likelihood/parameters	698/10	729/10	711/10
Change ΔL^2/degrees of freedom	48/4	44/4	54/4

the quadratic model, and the results show an improvement in fit over the comparable linear age model (vs. column b in Table 32.4: $\chi^2 = 44$ on $df = 4$). Also, the estimate of the unique variance is much smaller than before ($\sigma_u^2 = 0.18$), so this last model is probably an improved understanding of these data.

The first two models are fairly similar. In the age-based model, for example, the quadratic parameters show an intercept for the average height at age 12 ($\alpha_0 = 57.64$) with individual differences at age 12 ($\sigma_0^2 = 11.11$). In addition, the average linear slope for every year is similar ($\beta_0 = 2.41$) with individual differences

($\sigma_1^2 = 0.14$). The quadratic slope is small but significant and negative ($\gamma_0 = -0.15$), with some variance ($\sigma_2^2 = 0.13$). The mean expectations indicate a parabolic form to the age-based curve. From standard quadratic formulas, we can calculate the peak height at about age 20 (max = $-\beta_0/2\gamma_0$ = [–2.41/–0.30] = [+8.0 + 12] = 20)—of course, this age is well over the ages actually measured here, so it has a large standard error of estimate. These parameters are correlated, and an estimate of the unique contribution due to each variance component is possible, but this will not be carried out here (see McArdle, 2004).

The third model (column c in Table 32.6) uses the individual distance from puberty as the basis of the quadratic model, with a basis centered at what would be approximately 13 years of age. The results again show an improvement in fit over the comparable linear model (vs. column c in Table 32.4: $\chi^2 = 54$ on $df = 4$). Also, the estimate of the unique variance is much smaller than before ($\sigma_u^2 = 0.22$), so this is probably an improved model for these data. The quadratic parameters show an intercept for the average height at pubertal age ($\alpha_0 = 60.18$) with individual differences at this age ($\sigma_0^2 = 9.26$). The average linear slope for every year is similar ($\beta_0 = 2.48$) with individual differences ($\sigma_1^2 = 0.13$). The quadratic slope is small but significant and negative ($\gamma_0 = -0.10$), with some variance ($\sigma_2^2 = 0.13$). The mean expectations indicate a parabolic form to the puberty-based curve. From standard quadratic formulas, we can calculate the peak height at about age 20 (max = $-\beta_0/2\gamma_0$ = [–2.48/–0.20] = 12.4)—of course, this age is directly in the middle of the ages actually measured here, so it has a small standard error of estimate. Although some of the correlations have reached a boundary condition and are unreasonable in size (e.g., $\rho_{12} \sim 1$), this seems to be the best fitting model to these physical growth data. This kind of an estimation problem can imply the data are weak, or the model is wrong, or both. This seems to be a common problem in using real data.

ISSUE 5: ADDING GROUP COMPARISONS AND TREATMENT EFFECTS

The previous latent curve representations lead to an increasingly popular way to add external variables. We can write a *mixed* or *multilevel* model where the X variable has a direct effect on the parameters of the growth curve as

$$Y[t]_n = f_{0n} + f_{1n} \bullet B[t] + u[t]_n \text{ with}$$
$$f_{0n} = \gamma_{00} + \gamma_{01} X_n + d_{0n}, \text{ and} \qquad (32.10)$$
$$f_{1n} = \gamma_{10} + \gamma_{11} X_n + d_{1n,}$$

where the intercepts (γ_{0j}) and the regression slopes (γ_{1j}) for the effects of grouping variables in set X on the two latent components of $Y[t]$. It may be useful to write this as a reduced form SEM so it is now clear that the three unobserved residual terms are not simply separable by standard linear regression or covariance equation (see McArdle & Hamagami, 1996).

This path diagram of Figure 32.7 is the same as the diagram of Figure 32.3 except that it includes the variable (or set of variables) labeled X as a predictor of the levels and slope components. This is termed a "multilevel model" because the *first-level* model is based on levels and slopes, while the *second-level* model adds predictors X for the intercepts and the slopes (e.g., Bryk & Raudenbush, 1992). Researchers in early SEM considered these models using the factor-analytic terminology *latent growth models with extension variables* (e.g., McArdle & Epstein, 1987). In either terminology, these models can be generically represented by the parameters in the path diagram of Figure 32.7, and this is

a common way to understand the between-group differences in within-group changes. Once considered in this way, no additional SEM fitting techniques or procedures are required.

These models combine static information from groups (X) with dynamic information from people within groups (Y_n), and this can be useful for many specific purposes. For example, if the treatment were assigned on a random basis (McArdle & Prindle, 2008), the comparison of the group trajectories would be considered a "causal" effect (i.e., Muthén & Curran, 1997; Rubin, 2006; Steyer, Partchev, & Shanahan, 2000). Variations on these kinds of causal models can represent a fruitful way to use and examine longitudinal data.

This approach allows us to consider another potential problem: There are potentially important individual differences at each occasion. Obviously it would be impractical to require everyone to be measured on exactly the same date (i.e., his or her birthday), so some variation in age is always apparent. One popular way to deal with this variation is to use "age as a covariate" in a multilevel account (Equation 32.10). This is an easy concept to introduce into modern computer programs, but this is not the only way to deal with group differences (see next section).

Results for Second-Level Effects

Although random assignment was not possible here, other modeling possibilities are explored in the results of Table 32.7. The first model (column a) gives the numerical results for a model where the age at time 1 (Age[1]) is used as a second-level predictor. Here the impacts of age on the initial level are small ($\beta_0 = -1.2$, $t = 1.7$), but the effects of age on the slope are negative and significant ($\beta_1 = -0.13$ per year, $t = 3.1$). This second effect means that the linear slopes of height over time are slightly lower for the older persons, or slightly higher for the younger persons. The inclusion of these age effects does degrade the model fit ($\Delta L^2 = 12$ on $df = 2$), indicating the need to consider other possibilities for age, but it only accounts for a small portion of the slope variance (from 0.08 to 0.07, or $R^2 = 13\%$).

The previous estimates can also be compared to the second model (column b in Table 32.7) where the age at menarche (Mena-13) is included as a second-level predictor. In this accounting, both the predictions of latent scores are significant: The initial level ($\beta_0 = -1.6$, $t = 4.1$) indicates lower initial height for persons with higher age of menarche, and the latent slope ($\beta_1 = +0.13$

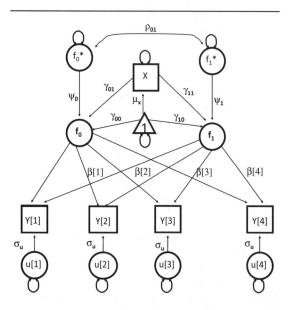

FIGURE 32.7. Latent growth as a path diagram with mixed-effects or multilevel predictor model.

TABLE 32.7. Results from Adding Second-Level Covariates into All Longitudinal Physical Growth Data

Latent curve parameters	Testing + age[1] − 12 at level 2	Menarche + age − 13 at level 2	Testing age + age at menarche at level 2
Fixed effects			
Intercept $1 \to f_0 \, (\gamma_0)0)$	51.91 (45)	53.80 (149)	51.88 (46)
Slope $1 \to f_1 \, (\gamma_1)0)$	3.75 (5.3)	2.40 (48)	3.76 (5.3)
Age[1]−12→$f_0 \, (\gamma_0)1)$	−1.19 (1.7)	=0	−1.19 (1.7)
Age[1]−12→$f_1 \, (\gamma_1)1)$	−0.13 (3.1)	=0	0.12 (3.1)
Mena−13→$f_0 \, (\gamma_2)0)$	=0	−1.55 (4.1)	−1.55 (4.1)
Mena−13→$f_1 \, (\gamma_2)1)$	=0	0.13 (2.4)	0.12 (2.6)
Random effects			
Intercept (σ_0^2)	9.56 (5.4)	7.65 (5.4)	7.71 (5.3)
Slope (σ_1^2)	0.07 (2.4)	0.07 (2.2)	0.06 (2.2)
Correlation (ρ_{01})	−0.29 (1.6)	−0.07 (0.4)	−0.09 (0.5)
Unique (σ_u^2)	0.35 (7.3)	0.38 (7.3)	0.35 (7.4)
Goodness of fit			
Likelihood/parameters	734/8	729/8	716/10
Change ΔL^2/degrees of freedom	12/2	17/2	30/4

per year, $t = 2.4$), indicates positive changes for those with higher age of menarche. The inclusion of these age effects also degrades the model fit ($\Delta L^2 = 17$ on $df = 2$), possibly indicating the need to consider other possibilities for age at menarche, and this accounts for a larger portion of the level variance (from 9.9 to 7.7, or $R^2 = 22\%$).

The third model (column c in Table 32.7) includes both of the measured variables, age at testing and age of menarche, as second-level predictors, and the joint results are much the same as the separate results (columns a and b). This may not be surprising because these variables are largely uncorrelated in this sample (see Table 32.1). In any case, there is some relationship between these measured ages and the height variables that may require further exploration.

A final model was fitted in an attempt to add a predictor variable to the quadratic components of height. This actual age at menarche (Mena-13) was used here as a predictor, and the results show small but significant predictions of both the initial level ($\gamma_{20} = 0.83$) and the acceleration ($\gamma_{21} = 0.16$), but not for the linear slope. The fact that people who start growing earlier for their age both reach a higher peak and do so at a faster pace seems to be a relatively well-known phenomenon in classic research on physical height (see Tanner, 1987). However, the main problem with this analysis is similar to that in the previous model: It was extremely difficult to estimate all seven variance components required by the full quadratic model. In this case, all three correlations and the quadratic variance were fixed to zero in order to resolve these uncertainties. This is not justified by statistical theory, since these components are obviously identifiable with enough data and the correct model, but these kinds of restrictions are often used in practice, mainly to allow numerical convergence. Although many other nonlinear models may be carried out using these data (e.g., McArdle, 2009), these examples illustrate the issues and problems.

DISCUSSION

The main goal of this work was to point out that there are many new elegant models for dealing directly with unbalanced, incomplete, or missing data. Recent work on linear and nonlinear mixed and multilevel models has surfaced, making it possible to estimate growth curves and test hypotheses by collecting only small segments of data on each individual (Bryk & Raudenbush, 1992; Pinherio & Bates, 2000; Raz et al., 2005). These statistical models are being used in many longitudinal studies to deal with self-selection and subject attrition, multivariate changes in dynamic patterns of development (e.g., McArdle et al., 2002, 2005). This leads us to consider the trade-offs between statistical power and costs of person and variable sampling. When considered in terms of R. Q. Bell's (1954) classic call for "accelerated longitudinal designs," the statistical power questions of the future may not be "How *many* occasions do we need?" but "How *few* occasions are adequate?" and "Which persons should we measure at which occasions?" (McArdle & Bell, 2000; McArdle & Woodcock, 1997).

Statistical researchers such as Rao (1958) and Tucker (1958, 1966) clearly understood that with multiple growth curves a simple structure rotation was not appropriate, and they sought out other simplifying rules (also see Arbuckle & Friendly, 1977). Thus, the term "latent growth models" seems appropriate for any technique that describes the underlying growth in terms of latent changes using the classical assumptions (e.g., independence of errors). One of the reasons we use the contemporary modeling approach is to overcome classical statistical problems. I find it convenient to *describe* the data using the observed change scores but make *inferences* about the underlying growth processes by estimating parameters of the latent change scores.

Modern statistical procedures have been developed to avoid some of these problems by fitting the model of an *implied trajectory over time* directly to the observed scores. Various kinds of mathematical forms of growth can be considered using various statistical restrictions (e.g., independence of the residual error terms). But these new latent variable techniques also lead to a set of new challenges that must be met before these techniques can be fully realized.

Challenging Assumptions about Latent Curves

In order to uniquely identify and estimate the model, all parameters are *forced to be invariant over all groups* (for details, see McArdle, 1994; McArdle & Anderson, 1990; McArdle & Hamagami, 1992). In some cases groups are not necessarily measured at the same ages, or the same number of times, so the data from any one age group may not overlap very much with those of another group. Thus, a model of "longitudinal convergence" (after Bell, 1954; McArdle & Bell, 2000) is a reasonable goal in many studies, but it is not necessarily a hypothesis that can be tested adequately with incomplete patterns (McArdle & Anderson, 1990; Willett & Sayer, 1994).

One common assumption in our use of these MLE-based techniques is that the incomplete data are MAR (Little & Rubin, 1987). This assumption does not require the data to be MCAR, but MAR does assume there is some observed information that allows us to completely account for the pattern of incomplete data we know about (e.g., McArdle, 1994; McArdle & Hamagami, 1992). This MAR assumption is a convenient starting point that allows us to use all the available information in one analysis, but it could be incorrect for a number of reasons (e.g., Cnaan et al., 1997; Little, 1995; McArdle, 1994), so these key assumptions should be examined. Thus, instead of simply stating MAR is a reasonable assumption, we should investigate methods for evaluating the failure of these assumptions. In future research we should make more efforts to evaluate the adequacy of this helpful MAR assumption, and to find out where we went wrong (see Hedeker & Gibbons, 1997).

These kind of convergence analyses described here raise the important question, "Exactly what data are needed?" This is obviously related to the question,

"Exactly what model estimates are most critical?" (McArdle, 2010). If we only need the fixed effects, or if a good separation of the intercept and unique variances is desired, then very little longitudinal data are actually required. McArdle and Anderson (1990) showed how multiple-basis functions could be estimated using standard SEM programs as long as the bases were not collinear. Thus, in this case, we could fit both distance from birth (age) and distance from menarche (puberty) together, but here I do not deal with this kind of complexity further. However, if we want good estimates of the latent slopes, we need more longitudinal repetitions. Until we formalize the parameters for the model, we should not expect a formal solution to the primary question of the requirements of data collections. Of course, this illustrates what Bell (1953, 1954) seemed to know fairly well.

The choice between using a latent basis or a polynomial, or other nonlinear model, can be substantively important. The initial idea from Wishart (1938) was that the basic shape of each individual curve could be captured with a small number of fixed parameters and random variance components. In some cases a fixed-basis polynomial model is more parsimonious than a free-basis model. However, the polynomial model also (1) has a relatively fixed curvature and (2) requires an additional estimation of covariances among the new latent scores. (*Note.* This is true even if orthogonal polynomial coefficients are used.) Thus, the polynomial model may add more complexity (via parameters to be estimated) than is actually needed, and the latent basis model may prove to be more efficient and interpretable. Although many recent textbooks overlook the latent basis model (e.g., Duncan, Duncan, & Stryker, 2006; Singer & Willett, 2003), my colleagues and I typically treat this as an empirical choice (McArdle & Bell, 2000; McArdle & Nesselroade, 2003).

It is very clear that the interpretation of change in any model comes from the theoretical definition of the derivative or change score ($\Delta y[t]_n = y[t]_n - y[t - 1]_n$). For example, in the quadratic model, the latent change from one time to another is a linear function of the slope, the rate of change score, and the time. Indeed, the introduction of individual differences in change analyses has led to a great deal of statistical controversy in model fitting. For example, in many published data analyses the *observed difference scores* or *rate-of-change scores* are used as outcomes in data analyses (e.g., Allison, 1990; Nesselroade & Bartsch, 1977). These kinds of

difference score calculations are relatively simple and theoretically meaningful. The confounds due to the accumulation of random errors have been a key concern in previous studies using observed change scores or rate-of-change scores (e.g., Burr & Nesselroade, 1990; McArdle & Nesselroade, 1994; Rogosa & Willett, 1983, 1985; Willett, 1990).

One way to combine recent ideas about dynamics and retain the statistical and practical benefits of SEM is to use a model directly based on *latent change scores* (Hamagami & McArdle, 2000; McArdle, 2001; McArdle & Hamagami, 2001; Nesselroade & Boker, 1994; Oud & Jansen, 2000). Although not emphasized here, the recent approaches allow us to write a model in terms of the first- or second- or higher-order latent differences, and have the SEM program create the required nonlinear expectations. In other cases we are interested in the representation of a *group difference dynamic change score* model. These dynamic models can be fitted and used in the same way as any multiple-group structural equation models (e.g., Ferrer & McArdle, 2010; McArdle & Hamagami, 1996, 2006). Most importantly, these kinds of models permit a practical way to (1) represent the dynamics of change and (2) study group dynamics. Variations on these models can be used to examine many different combinations of concepts.

Practical problems in the fitting of any statistical model with longitudinal data begin with scaling and metrics. The basic requirements of meaningful and age-equivalent measurement models remain a key problem in the behavioral sciences, and future research is needed to address these fundamental concerns (see Fischer & Molenaar, 1995). These ideas can be examined at the item level by forming a scoring system for any construct we used from item response theory (IRT). The resulting item–trait score parameters for all items can be displayed as a set of "common rulers" or "translation tables" (see McArdle, Grimm, Hamagami, Bowles, & Meredith, 2009). These IRT techniques generalize to a wide range of batteries and measurement systems.

Additional scaling issues deal with the exact timing of observations. A variety of transformations of these original data could be examined (e.g., Boker & McArdle, 1995) and, as usual, these transformations can change the statistical patterns. Also, all models require a well-defined time axis where, say, the youngest age ($B[0] = 10$) is considered the initial time score ($t = 0$), and the gap between assessments is set at a fixed interval (e.g., $\Delta t = 1$ year). This means the intercept parameters will reflect age = 10, and all one-unit changes will represent 1 year. While we hope these measurement decisions have no impact on our results, this hope is not necessarily valid. In all measurement problems, it is necessary to gather new information to see whether different scaling lead to different inferences about growth and change.

The SEM analyses presented here make specific assumptions about latent changes in individuals and groups. Certainly these are one step beyond the more typical ANOVA or analysis of covariance (ANCOVA) used so frequently in the behavioral sciences (see McArdle & Prescott, 2010). But it is now also clear that growth curve models of arbitrary complexity can be fitted to the observed trajectory over time (i.e., the integral), and the unknown parameters can be estimated to minimize some statistical function (e.g., weighted least squares, maximum likelihood) using, for example, nonlinear programming. Several different computer programs were used for the analyses discussed here.

SEM has an advantage over other forms of mixed-effect modeling because we can examine different shapes for different groups. This highlights the classical problem of discriminating models of multiple curves for the same people from models of *multiple groups with different curves*. Whether we know it or not, we could have three or more subgroups or clusters of people, each with a distinct growth curves, but when we summarize over all the people we end up with multiple factors and mixed curves. These problems set the stage for models that test hypotheses about *growth curves between latent groups*.

The recent techniques termed *growth mixture models* have been developed for this purpose (Hipp & Bauer, 2006; Li, Duncan, Duncan, & Acock, 2001; Muthén, 2004, 2006). In these kinds of analyses the distribution of the latent parameters is assumed to come from a "mixture" of two or more overlapping distributions (McLachlan & Peel, 2000). Current techniques in mixture models have largely been developed under the assumption of a small number of discrete or probabilistic "classes of persons" based on mixtures of multivariate normals. The resulting MLEs yield a likelihood that can be compared to the results from a model with one less class, so the exploratory mixture model distribution might be treated as a hypothesis to be investigated. As in standard discriminant analysis, we can also estimate the probability of assignment of individuals to each class in the mixture. A variety of new computer programs have been developed for this purpose (e.g., Mplus; Muthén & Muthén, 2002), and experiments into the stability and replicability of statistical and substantive results are still needed (Hamagami & McArdle, 2000; McArdle & Nesselroade, 2003).

Final Comments

These illustrations are intended to show how it is now possible to fit all kinds of "accelerated" longitudinal data, and that the model results are meaningful if the summary statistics meet the condition of "convergence." These were ideas originally created by R. Q. Bell (1953, 1954), and these basic concepts have been used by many others since. For example, although it is not widely recognized, this mixture of longitudinal and cross-sectional information clearly predated but is consistent with K. W. Schaie's (1965) elaboration of the "cohort sequential design" and R. B. Cattell's (1969) subsequent call for the separation of ecogenic and epogenic curves. Novel statistical techniques for calculating the misfit due to convergence have been a focus of many recent analyses of lifespan data (McArdle, 1994; McArdle & Anderson, 1990; McArdle et al., 2002), but these are simply contemporary versions of the basic ideas in Figure 32.1. These ideas have formed the basis of much of our recent research (e.g., Albert, Blacker, Moss, Tanzi, & McArdle, 2007; Ferrer, Salthouse, McArdle, Stewart, & Schwartz, 2005; Ferrer et al., 2007; Ghisletta & McArdle, 2001; Ghisletta, McArdle, & Lindenberger, 2007; Grimm & McArdle, 2007; Grimm, McArdle, & Hamagami, 2007; McArdle, Fisher, & Kadlec, 2007; McArdle et al., 2004). We recognize that all this work is a direct descendant of Bell's prior ideas.

In broader terms, the representation of change processes can be accomplished using the variety of methods we have been referring to as latent growth curve, mixed effect, multilevel, or multiple-group growth curve modeling. These developments represent an important but limited class of longitudinal data analyses. So we also need to recognize that some of the most difficult problems for future work on latent growth curves will not involve the statistical analysis or computer programming, but will be based on the rather elusive meaning of the values of the growth model parameters themselves, and the minimal set of data needed for powerful tests of hypotheses about development. These are the key challenges for future longitudinal research.

ACKNOWLEDGMENTS

This work was supported by the National Institute on Aging (Grant No. AG-7137-21). I thank my colleagues John R. Nesselroade (University of Virginia), Kevin Grimm (University of California at Davis), John Prindle (University of Southern California), and Rick Hoyle (Duke University) for their useful contributions to earlier versions of this work.

REFERENCES

Albert, M., Blacker, D., Moss, M. B., Tanzi, R., & McArdle, J. J. (2007). Longitudinal change in cognitive performance among individuals with mild cognitive impairment. *Neuropsychology, 21*(2), 158–169.

Allison, P. D. (1990). Change scores as dependent variables in regression analysis. In C. C. Clogg (Ed.), *Sociological methodology 1990* (pp. 93–114). San Francisco: Jossey-Bass.

Anderson, T. W. (1958). *An introduction to multivariate statistics.* New York: Wiley.

Arbuckle, J. L., & Friendly, M. (1977). On rotation to smooth functions. *Psychometrika, 42, 127–140.*

Baltes, P. B., & Nesselroade, J. R. (1979). History and rationale of longitudinal research. In J. R. Nesselroade & P. B. Baltes (Eds.), *Longitudinal research in the study of behavior and development.* New York: Academic Press.

Bell, R. Q. (1953). Convergence: an accelerated longitudinal approach. *Child Development, 24,* 145–152.

Bell, R. Q. (1954). An experimental test of the accelerated longitudinal approach. *Child Development, 25,* 281–286.

Bock, R. D. (1975). *Multivariate statistical methods in behavioral research.* New York: McGraw-Hill.

Boker, S. M., & McArdle, J. J. (1995). Statistical vector field analysis applied to mixed cross- sectional and longitudinal data. *Experimental Aging Research, 21,* 77–93.

Bollen, K. A. (1989). *Structural equation models.* New York: Wiley.

Browne, M., & du Toit, S. H. C. (1991). Models for learning data. In L. Collins & J. L. Horn (Eds.), *Best methods for the analysis of change* (pp. 47–68). Washington, DC: APA Press.

Bryk, A. S., & Raudenbush, S. W. (1992). *Hierarchical linear models: Applications and data analysis methods.* Newbury Park, CA: Sage.

Burr, J. A., & Nesselroade, J. R. (1990). Change measurement. In A. von Eye (Ed.), *New statistical methods in developmental research* (pp. 3–34). New York: Academic Press.

Cattell, R. B. (1970). Separating endogenous, exogenous, ecogenic and epogenic component curves in developmental data. *Developmental Psychology, 3*(2), 151–162.

Cnaan, A., Laird, N. M., & Slasor, P. (1997). Using the general linear mixed model to analyse unbalanced repeated measures and longitudinal data. *Statistics in Medicine, 16,* 2349–2380.

Cudeck, R., & du Toit, S. H. C. (2001). Mixed-effects models in the study of individual differences with repeated measures data. *Multivariate Behavioral Research, 31,* 371–403.

Cudeck, R., & Harring, J. R. (2007). The analysis of nonlinear patterns of change with random coefficient models. *Annual Review of Psychology, 58,* 615–637.

Duncan, T. E., Duncan, S. C., & Stryker, L. A. (2006). *An introduction to latent growth curve modeling* (2nd ed.) Mahwah, NJ: Erlbaum.

Ferrer, E., Hamagami, F., & McArdle, J. J. (2004). Modeling latent growth curves with incomplete data using different types of structural equation modeling and multilevel software. *Structural Equation Modeling, 11*(3), 452–483.

Ferrer, E., & McArdle, J. J. (2010). Longitudinal modeling of developmental changes in psychological research. *Current Directions in Psychological Science, 19*(3), 149–154.

Ferrer, E., McArdle, J. J., Shaywitz, B. A., Holahan, J. M., Marchione, K., & Shaywitz, S. E. (2007). Longitudinal models of developmental dynamics between reading and cognition from childhood to adolescence. *Developmental Psychology, 43,* 1460–1473.

Ferrer, E., Salthouse, T. A., McArdle, J. J., Stewart, W. F., & Schwartz, B. (2005). Multivariate modeling of age and retest effects in longitudinal studies of cognitive abilities. *Psychology and Aging, 20*(3), 412–442.

Fischer, G. H., & Molenaar, I. (Eds.). (1995). *Rasch models—foundations, recent developments, and applications.* New York: Springer.

Ghisletta, P., & McArdle, J. J. (2001). Latent growth curve analyses of the development of height. *Structural Equation Modeling, 8*(4), 531–555.

Ghisletta, P., McArdle, J. J., & Lindenberger, U. (2006). Longitudinal cognition–survival relations in old and very old age: 13-year data from the Berlin Aging Study. *European Psychologist, 11*(3), 204–223.

Goldstein, H. (1995). *Multilevel statistical models, second edition.* New York: Oxford University Press.

Grimm, K. J., & McArdle, J. J. (2007). A dynamic structural analysis of the potential impacts of major context shifts on lifespan cognitive development. In T. D. Little, J. A. Bovaird, & N. A. Card (Eds.), *Modeling contextual effects in longitudinal studies* (pp. 363–386). Mahwah, NJ: Erlbaum.

Grimm, K. J., McArdle, J. J., & Hamagami, F. (2007). Nonlinear growth mixture models in research on cognitive aging. In K. van Montfort, H. Oud, & A. Satorra (Eds.), *Longitudinal models in the behavioral and related sciences* (pp. 267–294). Mahwah, NJ: Erlbaum.

Hamagami, F., & McArdle, J. J. (2000). Advanced studies of individual differences linear dynamic models for longitudinal data analysis. In G. Marcoulides & R. Schumacker

(Eds.), *Advanced structural equation modeling: Issues and technique* (pp. 203–246). Mahwah, NJ: Erlbaum.

Hedeker, D., & Gibbons, R. (1997). Application of random-effects pattern-mixture models for missing data in longitudinal studies. *Psychological Methods, 2*, 64–78.

Hipp, J. R., & Bauer, D. J. (2006). Local solutions in the estimation of growth mixture models. *Psychological Methods, 11*, 36.

Horn, J. L., & McArdle, J. J. (1980). Perspectives on mathematical and statistical model building (MASMOB) in research on aging. In L. Poon (Ed.), *Aging in the 1980's: Psychological issues* (pp. 503–541). Washington, DC: American Psychological Association.

Jöreskog, K. G., & Sörbom, D. (1979). *Advances in factor analysis and structural equation models*. Cambridge, MA: Abt Books.

Laird, N. M., & Ware, J. H. (1982). Random effects models for longitudinal data. *Biometrics, 38*, 963–974.

Lawley, D. N., & Maxwell, A. E. (1963). *Factor analysis as a statistical method*. London: Butterworths.

Li, F., Duncan, T. E., Duncan, S. C., & Acock, A. (2001). Latent growth modeling of longitudinal data: A finite growth mixture modeling approach. *Structural Equation Modeling, 8*, 493–530.

Littell, R. C., Miliken, G. A., Stoup, W. W., & Wolfinger, R. D. (1996). *SAS system for mixed models*. Cary, NC: SAS Institute.

Little, R. J. A. (1995). Modeling the dropout mechanism in repeated-measures studies. *Journal of the American Statistical Association, 90*, 1112–1121.

Little, R. J. A., & Rubin, D. J. (1987). *Statistical analysis with missing data*. New York: Wiley.

McArdle, J. J. (1986). Latent variable growth within behavior genetic models. *Behavior Genetics, 16*(1), 163–200.

McArdle, J. J. (1988). Dynamic but structural equation modeling of repeated measures data. In J. R. Nesselroade & R. B. Cattell (Eds.), *The handbook of multivariate experimental psychology* (Vol. 2, pp. 561–614). New York: Plenum Press.

McArdle, J. J. (1989). Structural modeling experiments using multiple growth functions. In P. Ackerman, R. Kanfer, & R. Cudeck (Eds.), *Learning and individual differences: Abilities, motivation, and methodology* (pp. 71–117). Hillsdale, NJ: Erlbaum.

McArdle, J. J. (1991). Structural models of developmental theory in psychology. In P. Van Geert & L. P. Mos (Eds.), *Annals of theoretical psychology, Volume VII* (pp. 139–160). New York: Springer.

McArdle, J. J. (1994). Structural factor analysis experiments with incomplete data. *Multivariate Behavioral Research, 29*(4), 409–454.

McArdle, J. J. (1996). Current directions in structural factor analysis. *Current Directions in Psychological Science, 5*(1), 11–18.

McArdle, J. J. (1997). Modeling longitudinal data by latent growth curve methods. In G. Marcoulides (Ed.), *Modern methods for business research* (pp. 359–406). Mahwah, NJ: Erlbaum.

McArdle, J. J. (2001). A latent difference score approach to longitudinal dynamic structural analyses. In R. Cudeck, S. du Toit, & D. Sörbom (Eds.), *Structural equation modeling: Present and future* (pp. 342–380). Lincolnwood, IL: Scientific Software International.

McArdle, J. J. (2004). Latent growth curve analysis using structural equation modeling techniques. In D. M. Teti (Ed.), *The handbook of research methods in developmental psychology* (pp. 340–466). New York: Blackwell.

McArdle, J. J. (2007). Five steps in the structural factor analysis of longitudinal data. In R. Cudeck & R. MacCallum (Eds.), *Factor analysis at 100 years* (pp. 99–130). Mahwah, NJ: Erlbaum.

McArdle, J. J. (2009). Latent variable modeling of longitudinal data. *Annual Review of Psychology, 60*, 577–605.

McArdle, J. J. (2010). Contemporary challenges of longitudinal measurement using HRS data. In G. Walford, E. Tucker, & M. Viswanathan (Eds.), *The SAGE handbook of measurement* (pp. 509–536). London: Sage.

McArdle, J. J., & Aber, M. S. (1990). Patterns of change within latent variable structural equation modeling. In A. von Eye (Ed.), *New statistical methods in developmental research* (pp. 151–224). New York: Academic Press.

McArdle, J. J., & Anderson, E. (1990). Latent variable growth models for research on aging. In J. E. Birren & K. W. Schaie (Eds.), *The handbook of the psychology of aging* (pp. 21–43). New York: Plenum Press.

McArdle, J. J., & Bell, R. Q. (2000). An introduction to latent growth curve models for developmental data analysis. In T. D. Little, K. U. Schnabel, & J. Baumert (Eds.), *Modeling longitudinal and multiple-group data: Practical issues, applied approaches, and scientific examples* (pp. 69–107). Mahwah, NJ: Erlbaum.

McArdle, J. J., & Epstein, D. B. (1987). Latent growth curves within developmental structural equation models. *Child Development, 58*(1), 110–133.

McArdle, J. J., Ferrer-Caja, E., Hamagami, F., & Woodcock, R. W. (2002). Comparative longitudinal multilevel structural analyses of the growth and decline of multiple intellectual abilities over the life-span. *Developmental Psychology, 38*(1), 115–142.

McArdle, J. J., Fisher, G. G., & Kadlec, K. M. (2007). Latent variable analysis of age trends in tests of cognitive ability in the health and retirement survey, 1992–2004. *Psychology and Aging, 22*(3), 525–545.

McArdle, J. J., Grimm, K., Hamagami, F., Bowles, R., & Meredith, W. (2009). Modeling life-span growth curves of cognition using longitudinal data with multiple samples and changing scales of measurement. *Psychological Methods, 14*(2), 126–149.

McArdle, J. J., & Hamagami, F. (1992). Modeling incomplete longitudinal and crosssectional data using latent growth structural models. *Experimental Aging Research*, *18*(3), 145–166.

McArdle, J. J., & Hamagami, F. (1996). Multilevel models from a multiple group structural equation perspective. In G. Marcoulides & R. Schumacker (Eds.), *Advanced structural equation modeling techniques* (pp. 89–124). Hillsdale, NJ: Erlbaum.

McArdle, J. J., & Hamagami, F. (2001). Linear dynamic analyses of incomplete longitudinal data. In L. Collins & A. Sayer (Eds.), *Methods for the analysis of change* (pp. 137–176). Washington, DC: APA Press.

McArdle, J. J., Hamagami, F., Jones, K., Jolesz, F., Kikinis, R., Spiro, A., et al. (2004). Structural modeling of dynamic changes in memory and brain structure using longitudinal data from the normative aging study. *Journals of Gerontology B*, *59*(6), P294–P304.

McArdle, J. J., & Nesselroade, J. R. (1994). Using multivariate data to structure developmental change. In S. H. Cohen & H. W. Reese (Eds.), *Lifespan developmental psychology: Methodological innovations* (pp. 223–267). Hillsdale, NJ: Erlbaum

McArdle, J. J., & Nesselroade, J. R. (2003). Growth curve analyses in contemporary psychological research. In J. Schinka & W. Velicer (Eds.), *Comprehensive handbook of psychology: Vol. 2. Research methods in psychology* (pp. 447–480). New York: Pergamon Press.

McArdle, J. J., & Prescott, C. A. (1992). Agebased construct validation using structural equation modeling. *Experimental Aging Research*, *18*(3), 87–115.

McArdle, J. J., & Prescott, C. A. (2010). Contemporary modeling of Gene-by-Environment effects in randomized multivariate longitudinal studies. *Perspectives on Psychological Science*, *5*, 606–621.

McArdle, J. J., Prescott, C. A., Hamagami, F., & Horn, J. L. (1998). A contemporary method for developmentalgenetic analyses of age changes in intellectual abilities. *Developmental Neuropsychology*, *14*(1), 69–114.

McArdle, J. J., & Prindle, J. J. (2008). A latent change score analysis of a randomized clinical trial in reasoning training. *Psychology and Aging*, *23*(4), 702–719.

McArdle, J. J., Small, B. J., Backman, L., & Fratiglioni, L. (2005). Longitudinal models of growth and survival applied to the early detection of Alzheimer's disease. *Journal of Geriatric Psychiatry and Neurology*, *18*(4), 234–241.

McArdle, J. J., & Wang, L. (2007). Modeling age-based turning points in longitudinal life-Span growth curves of cognition. In P. Cohen (Ed.), *Turning points research* (pp. 105–127). Mahwah, NJ: Erlbaum.

McArdle, J. J., & Woodcock, J. R. (1997). Expanding test–retest designs to include developmental timelag components. *Psychological Methods*, *2*(4), 403–435.

McLachlan, G. J., & Peel, D. (2000). *Finite mixture models*. New York: Wiley.

Meredith, W., & Horn, J. L. (2001). The role of factorial invariance in measuring growth and change In L. Collins & A. Sayer (Eds.), *New methods for the analysis of change* (pp. 201–240). Washington, DC: APA Press.

Meredith, W., & Tisak, J. (1990). Latent curve analysis. *Psychometrika*, *55*, 107–122.

Metha, P. D., & West, S. G. (2000). Putting the individual back into individual growth curves. *Psychological Methods*, *5*(1), 23–43.

Miyazaki, Y., & Raudenbush, S. W. (2000). Tests for linkage of multiple cohorts in an accelerated longitudinal design. *Psychological Methods*, *5*, 24–63.

Molenaar, P. C. M. (1985). A dynamic factor model for the analysis of multivariate time series. *Psychometrika*, *50*, 181–202.

Muthén, B. (2004). Latent variable analysis: Growth mixture modeling and related techniques for longitudinal data. In D. Kaplan (Ed.), *Handbook of quantitative methodology for the social sciences* (pp. 345–368). Newbury Park, CA: Sage.

Muthén, B. (2006). The potential of growth mixture modeling. *Infant and Child Development*, *15*, 623–625.

Muthén, B. O., & Curran, P. (1997). General longitudinal modeling of individual differences in experimental designs: A latent variable framework for analysis and power estimation. *Psychological Methods*, *2*, 371–402.

Muthén, L. K., & Muthén, B. O. (2002). *Mplus, the comprehensive modeling program for applied researchers user's guide*. Los Angeles: Authors.

Nesselroade, J. R., & Bartsch, T. W. (1977). Multivariate perspectives on the construct validity of the trait–state distinction. In R. B. Cattell & R. M. Dreger (Eds.), *Handbook of modern personality theory* (pp. 221–238). Washington, DC: Hemisphere.

Nesselroade, J. R., & Boker, S. M. (1994). Assessing constancy and change. In T. F. Heatherton & J. L. Weinberger (Eds.), *Can personality change?* Washington, DC: American Psychological Association.

O'Brien, R. G., & Kaiser, M. K. (1985). MANOVA method for analyzing repeated measures designs: An extensive primer. *Psychological Bulletin*, *97*(2), 316–333.

Oud, J. H. L., & Jansen, R. A. R. G. (2000). Continuous time state space modeling of panel data by means of SEM. *Psychometrika*, *65*, 199–215.

Pinherio, J. C., & Bates, D. M. (2000). *Mixed-effects models in S and S-PLUS*. New York: Springer.

Pothoff, R. F., & Roy, S. N. (1964). A generalized multivariate analysis model useful especially for growth curve problems. *Biometrics*, *51*, 313–326.

Preece, M. A., & Baines, M. J. (1978). A new family of mathematical models describing the human growth curve. *Annals of Human Biology*, *5*(1), 1–24.

Rao, C. R. (1958). Some statistical methods for the comparison of growth curves. *Biometrics*, *14*, 1–17.

Rao, C. R. (1965). *Linear statistical inference and its applications*. New York: Wiley.

Raz, N., Lindenberger, U., Rodrigue, K. M., Kennedy, K. M., Head, D., Williamson, A., et al. (2005). Regional brain changes in aging healthy adults: General trends, individual differences and modifiers. *Cerebral Cortex, 15*(11), 1676–1689.

Rocke, D. M., & Woodruff, D. L. (1997). Robust estimation of multivariate location and shape. *Journal of Statistical Planning and Inference, 57,* 245–255.

Rogosa, D. (1978). Causal models in longitudinal research: Rationale, formulation, and interpretation. In J. R. Nesselroade & P. B. Baltes (Eds.), *Longitudinal research in the study of behavior and development.* New York: Academic Press.

Rogosa, D., & Willett, J. B. (1983). Demonstrating the reliability of the difference score in the measurement of change. *Journal of Educational Measurement, 20*(4), 335–343.

Rogosa, D., & Willett, J. B. (1985). Understanding correlates of change by modeling individual differences in growth. *Psychometrika, 50*(2), 203–228.

Rubin, D. B. (2006). *Matched sampling for causal effects.* New York: Cambridge University Press.

Schaie, K. W. (1965). A general model for the study of developmental problems. *Psychological Bulletin, 64*(2), 92–107.

Shadish, W., Cook, T. D., & Campbell, D. T. (2002). *Experimental and quasi-experimental design for generalized causal inference.* Boston: Houghton Mifflin.

Singer, J. D., & Willett, J. (2003). *Applied longitudinal data analysis.* New York: Oxford University Press.

Steyer, R., Partchev, I., & Shanahan, M. (2000). Modeling true individual change in structural equation models: The case of poverty and children's psychosocial adjustment. In T. D. Little, K. U. Schnabel, & J. Baumert (Eds.), *Modeling longitudinal and multiple-group data: Practi-cal issues, applied approaches, and scientific examples* (pp. 109–126). Mahwah, NJ: Erlbaum.

Stimson, J. A., Carmines, E. G., & Zeller, R. A. (1978). Interpreting polynomial regression. *Sociological Methods and Research, 6*(4), 515–524.

Tanner, J. M. (1987). Growth as the mirror of the condition of society: Secular trends and class distinctions. *Pediatrics International, 29*(1), 93–103.

Tisak, J., & Tisak, M. S. (1996). Longitudinal models of reliability and validity: A latent curve approach. *Applied Psychological Measurement, 20*(3), 275–288.

Tucker, L. R. (1958). Determination of parameters of a functional relation by factor analysis. *Psychometrika, 23,* 19–23.

Tucker, L. R. (1966). Learning theory and multivariate experiment: Illustration by determination of generalized learning curves. In R. B. Cattell (Ed.), *Handbook of multivariate experimental psychology.* Chicago: Rand McNally.

Vandenberg, S. G., & Falkner, F. (1965). Heredity factors in human growth. *Human Biology, 37,* 357–365.

Willett, J. B. (1990). Measuring change: The difference score and beyond. In H. J. Walberg & G. D. Haertel (Eds.), *The international encyclopedia of education evaluation* (pp. 632–637). Oxford, UK: Pergamon.

Willett, J. B., & Sayer, A. G. (1994). Using covariance structure analysis to detect correlates and predictors of individual change over time. *Psychological Bulletin, 116,* 363–381.

Wishart, J. (1938). Growth rate determinations in nutrition studies with the bacon pig, and their analyses. *Biometrika, 30,* 16–28.

Zeger, S. L., & Harlow, S. D. (1987). Mathematical models from laws of growth to tools for biologic analysis: Fifty years of growth. *Growth, 51,* 1–21.

CHAPTER 33

Dynamic Factor Models for Longitudinally Intensive Data

Description and Estimation via Parallel Factor Models of Cholesky Decomposition

Phillip Wood

Advances in computing technology and communication make it increasingly practical for researchers to gather longitudinally intensive data in a variety of contexts. For example, the existence of compact and portable electronic equipment makes it feasible to conduct nearly instantaneous ambulatory assessments of individuals' physiological responses across multiple days (e.g., Buckley, Holohan, Greif, Bedard, & Suvak, 2004; Ebner-Priemer & Kubiak, 2010). Electronic diaries, which can be assessed using Palm Pilots or other electronic planners, permit longitudinally intensive assessment of self-reports of constructs such as positive or negative affect or interpersonal conflict, as well as consumption patterns or craving associated with food, alcohol, or tobacco (e.g., Finan et al., 2010; Piasecki, Slutske, Wood, & Hunt-Carter, 2010). Individuals' frequent contact with social networking sites such as Facebook (Lewis, Kaufman, Gonzalez, Wimmer, & Christakis, 2008) or commercial sites such as eBay (e.g., Jank & Shmueli, 2008) means that their records of electronic interactions over daily or even hourly time periods can be investigated. Finally, the connectivity afforded by the Internet makes it feasible for participants to continue to contribute data to a longitudinal study even when geographically removed from the original study (e.g., Littlefield, Sher, & Wood, 2010).

A major upshot of these technological advances is that researchers are now able to consider longitudinally intensive models to better understand how change occurs over time. Although dynamic factor models present researchers with types of factor models that incorporate time-bound effects, it is not the case that all multivariate longitudinally intensive models are well modeled as dynamic factors. In order to provide the reader a context for selecting the appropriate type of dynamic factor model (or, alternatively, using another, more appropriate analytic approach) I first discuss types of data commonly encountered in longitudinally intensive assessment.

In brief, the term "dynamic factor models" is used to describe a class of stochastic latent variable models that, in addition to modeling contemporaneous patterns of covariation between manifest variables, also explains patterns of covariation in manifest variables over time. As such, dynamic factor models include traditional "P-technique" factor models (traditional factor analysis of a given individual's data over time) as a special case. Dynamic factor models have been extended to a variety of research designs, and several approaches to the statistical estimation of dynamic factor models have also been proposed (see, e.g., Brown & Nesselroade, 2005; Zhang, Hamaker, & Nesselroade, 2008). A formal exposition of all these applications and technical developments is beyond the scope of this chapter; however, the applied researcher may benefit from some general guidance about the nature of these models and the location of appropriate literature on the topic. As such, the first goal in this chapter is to outline, in simple terms, some of the time series terms used in describing dynamic factor models and characteristics of data appropriate for dynamic factor models, and to reference appropriate literature that interested readers may explore according to their needs. In the second section, the use of Cholesky decomposition and parallel factor analysis is described as a (relatively) quick means for assessing the dimensionality and lagged structure of such time series data, without the need to enumerate and estimate all possible dynamic factor models.

EXAMPLES OF TIME-BOUND BEHAVIOR

To begin, consider Figure 33.1A, which shows the trajectory of a series which could represent one of multiple manifest variables appropriate for analysis under the P-technique approach mentioned earlier (i.e., a factor model containing no time-bound effects). This series appears to demonstrate no discernible trend over time (i.e., performance does not appear to systematically increase or decrease over time), and these data appear to demonstrate no local time-bound relationships (e.g., a score above the mean at one measurement occasion is just as likely to be followed by another observation above the mean as to be followed by an observation below the mean). These data also appear to represent a "stochastic" process, meaning that the data represent a sequence of random variability over time, and that the observed variables over time are distributed identically. Informally, one way to visualize the stochastic nature of the series is to observe that essentially the same pattern of data is observed regardless of whether data reflected on the Y axis have roughly the same characteristics as the original series.

By contrast, time-bound relationships that may be present in a given series are illustrated in Figure 33.1B, in which values at one measurement occasion that occur above (or below) the mean tend remain above (or below) the mean on subsequent measurement oc-

casions. Similar to the unlagged series in Figure 33.1A, these data appear to be stochastic and to represent a series of "random shocks" over the course of time, with no systematic increase or decrease in scores. In dynamic factor models, the observed lagged relationships in such series are thought to be the result of previous values of one or more latent variables. Although lagged relationships that are positive over time are fairly common in time series data, they are not the only possibility. Figure 33.1C, for example, shows data from a lagged series in which negative lagged effects are present. Although these data appear visually similar to data in Figure 33.1A, they represent a series with negative lag (i.e., observations at one time of measurement are negatively correlated with subsequent observations). Such a series could result, for example, if the variable under consideration is subject to random stochastic shocks but is accompanied by a refractory effect subsequent to an elevated response (or a "recharging effect" anticipatory to an elevated response). Even if a set of manifest variables appears to demonstrate a pattern of time-bound stochastic shocks, however, the time-lagged dynamic factor model presented here may not be the most tractable dynamic factor model for the data. In contexts where the measurement of time is finely resolved (e.g., as occurs, in functional magnetic resonance imaging or electroencephalographic data), a dynamic factor model based on a spectral decomposition is more appropriate for the data (see Molenaar, 1987, for a presentation of the model and exemplar analysis).

ALTERNATIVES TO STATIONARY STOCHASTIC MODELS

A particular study involving longitudinally intensive data, however, does not imply that it necessarily is appropriately modeled using a dynamic factor model approach. Consider, for example, the series in Figure 33.1D, which, in addition to demonstrating a series of stochastic variation over time, also appears to show a significant linear trend over time. Molenaar, Sinclair, Rovine, Ram, and Corneal's (2009) analysis of the dynamics and decreases in anger and anxiety in children over the course of meetings with a stepfather is one example of a stochastic process that systematically changes in overall level over time. Dynamic models with trends vary in terms of the nature and underlying process by which such trends occur. For example, linear trends in observed variables may be conceptualized as being

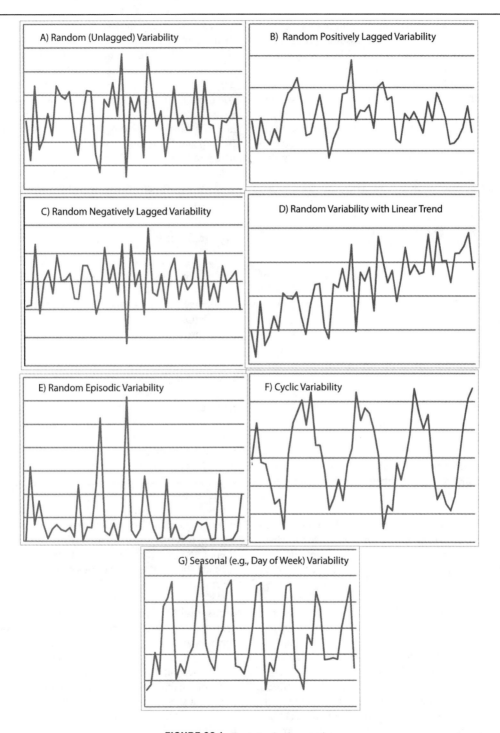

FIGURE 33.1. Prototypic time series.

due to changes in level associated with the latent variables of the model, or they may be assumed to be due to systematic changes in the level of individual manifest variables. Although these trends appear in the data, the researcher must basically make an analytic choice. If, conceptually, the researcher is interested in proposing a statistical model that explains the differential rates of growth present in the data, as well as (possibly time-lagged) patterns of variability and covariation between variables, he or she uses dynamic factor models that include linear or similar large-scale trends (see, e.g., Molenaar, de Gooijer, & Schmitz [1992] or Zuur, Fryer, Jolliffe, Dekker, & Beukema [2003] for descriptions of maximum likelihood [ML] or expectation maximization [EM] estimation of such models, and Molenaar et al. [2009] for an example of such a model applied to children's affect over time). If, however, the researcher is only interested in better understanding patterns of contemporaneous and lagged relationships between the manifest variables of the study, it is necessary to make some adjustment of the data to remove these large-scale trends prior to analysis. If no adjustment is made, observed contemporaneous or time-bound associations are open to the third-variable explanation that such associations are due to both variables sharing the same general trend over time. Although a variety of techniques exist for adjusting time series for the effects of a long-term trend, one rather straightforward method to adjust each series for the effects of a general trend is to calculate a simple regression for each manifest variable that models the general trend of interest (e.g., a linear trend as a function of time), then use the residuals from this analysis as the variables of interest for a dynamic factor model.

Other series, although longitudinally intensive, do not appear to represent continuously measured stochastic series. The data in Figure 33.1E represent one such example in which the elevations that appear to occur due to random shocks seem to be accompanied by a relatively rapid return to a baseline. Such data may occur, for example, in studies of affective instability or aggression. As with models involving general trends, the researcher is again faced with a choice. Analyses based on a dynamic factor model that assume continuous and stochastic response are prone to the criticism that the estimated parameters of the model are artifacts of the failure of the data to meet model assumptions. If modeling of the spikes in performance is the primary attribute of interest, the researcher may more appropriately consider use of a generalized mixed modeling approach such as that described by Jahng, Wood, and Trull (2008), in which a gamma link function is used to model the phenomenon of instability. If, however, the evident spikes in the continuously measured variable are assumed to be artifacts of the measurement process, some scaling transformation of the data prior to analysis is appropriate, such as rank normalization or use of any of a variety of scaling techniques. Alternatively, if the repeated-measures variable is not a continuously measured variable and consists of a fixed number of categories, the data may be more appropriately modeled as an ordinal dynamic factor model (Zhang & Browne, 2010).

Cyclic Trends

Other longitudinally intensive data, rather than showing stochastic variability over time, also appear to show regular periodicities over time. These periodicities may be relatively smooth cycles, as shown in Figure 33.1F, in which a smooth cycle, such as that of a sine or cosine, appears in addition to random variability over time. Such data may occur, for example, in studies of variables that show a strong diurnal effect over time. In other data sets, however, these periodicities are not so smoothly cyclical, as shown in Figure 33.1G. In this data set, a regular "period" or "seasonality" of seven measurement occasions regularly occurs in the series. Such periodic effects in the data may occur when the phenomenon of interest is closely associated with characteristics associated with time of day, week, or month. For example, if an individual's affect is systematically higher or lower on weekends versus weekdays, the data series will demonstrate a pattern similar to that seen in Figure 33.1G. Note that this series differs from the cyclical pattern shown in Figure 33.1F, in that the duration of elevated response (during the 2 weekend days) is much shorter than the periods of depressed response (during the 5-day workweek).

As with the other series, the researcher must make a decision as to whether this systematic variation represents part of the phenomenon to be modeled or represents a source that must be removed from the data prior to analysis. If, on the other hand, these periodic effects are of substantive interest, then they should be components of the dynamic model, for example, either by employing a spectral approach, as described by Molenaar (1987), or by appropriately coding for these cyclicities by, for example, effect or dummy coding the weekday versus weekend effects.

SPECIFICATION OF THE STATIONARY DFA MODEL

In its stationary form, a column vector of m manifest variables representing individuals' scores assessed at time t can be explained under the dynamic factor model as

$$y_t = \sum_{i=0}^{s} \Lambda_i B_i f_t + u_t \qquad (33.1)$$

where f_t is a row vector of l latent variables associated with the individual at time t, u_t is a row vector of errors of measurement associated with each of their respective manifest variables at time t, the Λ_i are $m \times 1$ matrices of factor loadings associated with the ith prior measurement occasion, and B is the backshift operator such that $B f_t = f_{t-i}$. It is usually assumed that the error component vectors u_t are mutually uncorrelated with mean 0 and diagonal covariance θ_k at lag k ($k = 0, \pm 1, \pm 2, \ldots$). This implies that apart from serial autocorrelation of the error vectors, all variation and covariation between manifest variables is due to variation in the factor series weighted by the factor loading matrices Λ_i. In the stationary dynamic factor model, it is assumed that the means of the unobserved latent series are zero, and that the expectations of each manifest variable over time are stationary and separately estimated or, equivalently, that the manifest variables are centered prior to factor analysis. The stationary dynamic factor model assumes that the "random shocks" to variables wear themselves out over time, and imply that factor loadings associated with longer lagged effects will be smaller in magnitude than lagged effects of shorter duration or contemporaneous effects.

DYNAMIC FACTOR MODELS OF TOEPLITZ MATRICES

Estimation of dynamic factor analysis (DFA) proceeds via confirmatory factor models in which contemporaneous patterns of covariation are modeled across blocks of replicates of the variables. The first method of estimation proposed by Molenaar (1985) involved estimation based on a Toeplitz-transformed matrix. Under this approach, it is assumed that the researcher is able to specify a priori a "window size," w, which represents the maximum lag length of effects +1 present in the data. This windows size is used to calculate the rectangular

matrices of lagged covariances of the manifest variables. These rectangular blocks of covariances are then used along with the triangular matrix of contemporaneous variances and covariances between variables to create a block diagonal Toeplitz matrix, which is used as the variance–covariance matrix for analysis. The block diagonal nature of the Toeplitz matrix is shown in Figure 33.2. The diagonal triangular blocks represent variances and covariances within variables within a block. Thus, in this example, the manifest variables of the study are replicated three times and the structural equation modeling software used must specify wm rather than m manifest variables. The rectangular blocks shown in Figure 33.2 represent the covariances between blocks of a given lag length. For example, the two rectangular blocks labeled Lag 1 Covariances represent covariances of lag length 1 of the m manifest variables with their m Lag 1 counterparts. Note that the block of Lag 1 Covariances, unlike the triangular matrix of contemporaneous variances and covariances, need not be symmetric; that is, the covariance of variable 1 with the lag of variable 2 need not equal the covariance of variable 2 with the lag of variable 1. In similar fashion, the block in the lower left-hand corner represents covariances of lag length 2.

It can be noted that the block diagonal nature of the Toeplitz matrix produces the best available summary of covariance patterns between a given measurement occasion, the immediately preceding measurement occasions associated up to the maximum lag length considered. Specifically, the triangular matrix of the usual variance–covariance matrix between variables represents patterns of covariation of variables at time t, but also represents covariation of variables at time $t - 1$ with other variables at time $t - 1$, as well as covariation of variables at time $t - 2$ with other variables at time $t - 2$. Because of this, in dynamic factor models with l latent variable, it is necessary to specify the l*w latent factors in the confirmatory model in which the Λ_0 loadings are fixed to equality across their respective blocks. In addition, lagged effects across factors must also be specified to be equal across the blocks of the Toeplitz matrix. Figure 33.3 illustrates the equality constraints for an example of four manifest variables for which the maximum lag length considered is 2, in which a single dynamic factor model of lag length 1 is considered. In this diagram, the Λ_0 factor loadings [$\lambda_1 \lambda_2 \lambda_3 \lambda_4$] occur across the three blocks of the Toeplitz matrix and are denoted as $l1$ through $l4$, respectively. Similarly, lagged latent variable relationships of length 1 (the matrix of

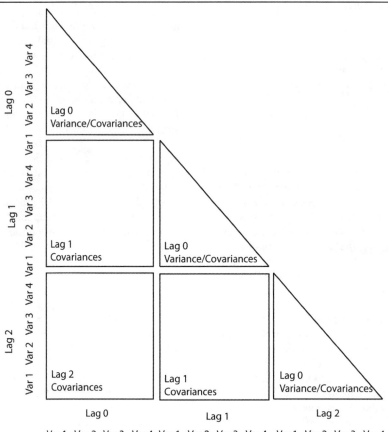

FIGURE 33.2. The Toeplitz transform.

Λ_1 loadings associated with the B_1 backshift operator) occur twice in this diagram and are labeled lag1L1 through lag1L4, respectively. Although not indicated in Figure 33.3, it would be possible to also include an additional matrix of $L2$ loadings which would represent lag length 2 effects from the $f3$ latent variable to the variables X1 through X4. The "striped diagonal" matrix of error variances and covariances, Θ_k, is represented by the freely estimated error variances, e1 through e4, which are, like the Λ_0, constrained to equality across the three respective blocks. Lag length 1 serial autocorrelations of the manifest variables are modeled via the error covariances c1 through c4 in the diagram and appear twice: once between the manifest variables and their lag 1 counterparts, and once between the lag 1

variables and their lag 2 counterparts. Finally, lag 2 autocorrelations are modeled by the covariances labeled $l2c$1 through $l2c$4 between the manifest variables and their lag 2 counterparts.

As Molenaar (1985) notes, the fit indices usually reported from SEM software are incorrect and must be calculated from the fit function used, due to the fact that the Toeplitz matrix input to the software contains redundant replications of the contemporaneous and lagged covariance blocks. As a result, the number of unique values in the Toeplitz matrix is $m^2{*}s + (m + 1){*}m/2$ rather than the $m{*}s{*}(m{*}s + 1)/2$ elements assumed by the software, which assumed that the input matrix was a simple variance–covariance matrix of $m{*}s$ distinct variables.

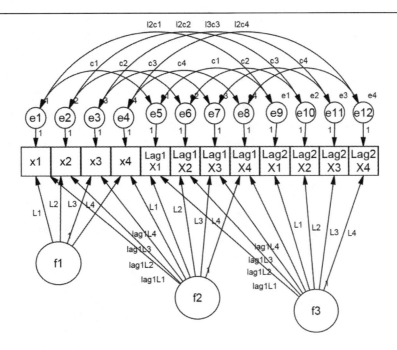

FIGURE 33.3. DFA model.

Several approaches to the estimation of dynamic factor models exist. These include use of EM or asymptotically distribution-free (ADF) estimation approaches (Molenaar & Nesselroade, 1998), or the use of Bayesian models and software (see Ferrer & Song, Chapter 35, this volume). Although these methods have conceptual and often computational advantages over the confirmatory factor model based on the Toeplitz matrix outlined earlier, they also share a common obstacle in that the researcher must enumerate and explore the dimensionality and lag length of various latent variable models. The computational burden on the researcher in exploring these enumerated models is often quite great in practice. Although use of the numerous equality constraints necessary to fit such models is burdensome, some statistical software automatically generates the required Toeplitz matrices and program files (Wood & Brown, 1992; Zhang, 2006). Even using such programs, however, it is sometimes unclear whether the researcher has adequately explored the dimensionality and lag length of the series. There is some reason to believe, for example, that rates of improper solutions and nonconvergence in fitted DFA models depend on the window size used in the models. Wood and Brown (1992) note that larger window sizes are associated with a lower rate of nonconvergence and improper solutions. Even if researchers examine a set of dynamic models that explore the dimensionality and lag length of a series, the question often remains as to whether additional factors or lags could have been considered.

Thus, although the fitting of dynamic factor models via confirmatory models seems appropriate based on conceptual grounds, with the ability to reexpress such structural models in terms of state-space expressions, it seems useful to explore the dimensionality of such time series using techniques that permit a full rank factorization of the series as a way to explore the dimensionality length of time-lagged components of the model. To this end, a Cholesky factorization of the Toeplitz matrix is proposed. In order to use this factorization to make decisions regarding the appropriate number of factors and lag lengths to retain, the method of parallel factor analysis is used (Horn, 1965). Because researchers using dynamic factor models must make decisions regarding both the number of factors to extract and the appropriate lag length associated with such factors, use of the parallel factor model involves an initial decision regarding the dimensionality of the solution and a subsequent examination of the lag length appropriate for such factors. These decisions can then be used to either extract the dynamic factor model in its orthogonal form or reexpress the dynamic factor model in a rotated form.

CHOLESKY FACTORIZATION

Cholesky decomposition is used as a triangular factorization of symmetric, positive definite matrices such that the original matrix C is expressed as LL'. The triangular nature of the factorization entails that factor loadings are estimated across all manifest variables for the first factor, all but the first for the second factor, and so on. Although the Cholesky decomposition is sometimes expressed using eigenvectors $L*$ (whose squared sum across rows is equal to unity) and positive diagonal matrix D, such that $C = L*DL*'$, the relationship of Cholesky decomposition to factor models can be seen by substituting $\sqrt{D^2}$ for D and expressing L as $L*\sqrt{D}$. One may also consider the LL' Cholesky factorization as a latent variable model by noting that any identity matrix representing orthogonal latent variables with unit variance may be inserted between L and L'. When time-lagged data are considered in a block Toeplitz matrix such as that described above, the sum of squared loadings within a block can be considered an eigenvalue associated with the latent variable represented in the row.

SIMULATED EXAMPLE

To see how Cholesky factorizations and parallel factor analysis can be used to make decisions about the dimensionality, structure, and length of lagged relationships in dynamic factor models, a simulated series composed of four manifest variables with 300 times of measurement was created. A two-factor model was used to generate the data. The first two manifest variables were based on a latent variable with no lagged effects, but the second two manifest variables were based on another latent variable with lagged effects. If the subscript t from Equation 33.1 is dropped, the matrix form of the dynamic factor model can be expressed as follows:

$$[y_1\ y_2\ y_3\ y_4] = \begin{bmatrix} 0.71 & 0.71 & 0 & 0 \\ 0 & 0 & 0.71 & 0.71 \end{bmatrix} \begin{bmatrix} F_1 \\ F_2 \end{bmatrix}$$
$$+ \begin{bmatrix} 0 & 0 & 0 & 0 \\ 0 & 0 & 0.4 & 4 \end{bmatrix} \begin{bmatrix} \text{lag}_1 F_1 \\ \text{lag}_2 F_2 \end{bmatrix} + [e_1\ e_2\ e_3\ e_4]$$

The variance–covariance matrix of the latent F variables was an identity matrix, the diagonal of the variance–covariance matrix of the error variables was selected to produce manifest variables with unit variance and were chosen to be [0.71 0.71 0.59 0.59], with zeros in the off-diagonal and no serial autocorrelation among error terms. The top panel of Figure 33.4 shows the generated series for these data for the first 100 observations. A Toeplitz matrix of lag length 5 was considered for the data and was constructed by first constructing the lagged variables and then using PROC CORR to generate the appropriate covariance matrices. These matrices were then used as input to PROC IML, the desired Cholesky decomposition of the Toeplitz matrix calculated using the statement cb5=root(Toeplitz(l0|||1|||2|||3|||4|||5)). The first four rows of the resulting Cholesky factorization are shown in the first two columns of Table 33.1. The triangular nature of the decomposition can be seen in the lag 0 loadings in the upper-left-hand corner of the table; factor loadings for all four variables are extracted for the first factor, factor loadings for all but the first variable are extracted in the second factor, factor loadings for all but first two variables are extracted in the third factor, and only a single factor loading associated with the last variable is extracted in the final row. Informal examination of the loadings associated with the lag 0 variances and covariances reveals that the first two variables appear to load primarily on this factor, with minor loadings on the third and fourth variables. As mentioned earlier, the sum of the squared factor loadings within this block are eigenvalues associated with these dimensions. Within a time block, the sum of the squared loadings represents a partial eigenvalue associated with the particular time unit of interest. For example, loadings associated with contemporaneous factor loadings are shown in the column labeled "Lag 0 eigenvalues" in Table 33.1, and contain information about the dimensionality associated with lag 0 effects. It should be kept in mind that in contrast to traditional parallel factor analysis, eigenvalues associated with successive factors need not uniformly decrease over time because eigenvalues reflect the successive factor patterns under the triangular

100 Simulated Observations taken: 2 factor Example

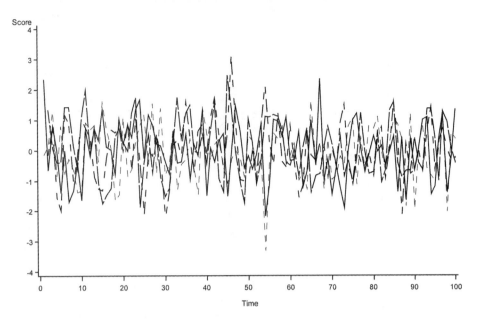

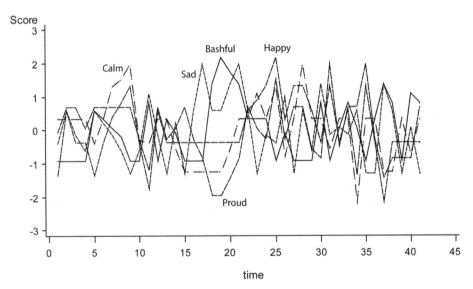

FIGURE 33.4. Simulated four-variate series and affect time series.

TABLE 33.1. Cholesky Decomposition of 300 Simulated Observations

Factor/ variable	Cholesky decomposition								Parallel eigenvalues			
	v1	v2	v3	v4	v1	v2	v3	v4	Eigenvalue	Parallel eigenvalue	Eigenvalue	Parallel eigenvalue
	Lag 0				Lag 1				Lag 0		Lag 1	
1	0.940	0.444	0.006	−0.099	−0.042	0.013	−0.012	0.016	*1.090*	0.893	0.002	*0.005*
2	0.000	0.877	−0.055	0.013	−0.026	0.003	0.044	−0.068	0.773	*0.976*	0.007	*0.022*
3	0.000	0.000	0.967	0.647	−0.032	−0.045	0.228	0.286	*1.353*	0.944	*0.137*	0.015
4	0.000	0.000	0.000	0.786	0.014	−0.044	0.105	0.164	0.619	*1.021*	*0.040*	0.010
	Lag 2				Lag 3				Lag 2		Lag 3	
1	0.078	0.063	0.003	0.038	−0.010	−0.078	0.060	0.013	0.012	0.008	0.010	0.006
2	0.068	−0.022	−0.111	−0.082	−0.018	−0.075	−0.103	−0.074	0.024	0.020	0.022	0.018
3	−0.016	−0.043	−0.110	−0.083	−0.037	0.005	−0.020	−0.124	*0.021*	0.007	*0.017*	0.006
4	0.051	−0.002	−0.039	−0.044	−0.069	−0.001	−0.102	−0.044	0.006	0.005	0.017	0.007
	Lag 4				Lag 5				Lag 4		Lag 5	
1	−0.022	0.019	0.017	−0.036	−0.043	−0.122	0.055	0.050	0.002	0.014	0.022	0.010
2	0.068	0.015	0.084	0.037	0.032	0.101	0.032	0.017	0.013	0.008	0.013	0.008
3	−0.050	0.023	−0.063	−0.069	0.018	0.005	−0.066	−0.054	0.012	0.011	0.008	0.012
4	−0.019	−0.083	0.026	−0.034	−0.026	0.025	0.048	0.063	0.009	0.011	0.008	0.015

Note. $v1$ and $v2 = .7F1 + .7e1$; $v3$ and $v4 = .7F1 + .4Lag_1F1$; error and factor variances = 1.

decomposition. For these data, for example, eigenvalues are markedly higher for the first and third factors relative to the remaining two.

PARALLEL FACTOR ANALYSIS

Informal comparison of these eigenvalues, however, can be misleading, due to possible capitalization on chance associated with more as opposed to fewer factor loadings, the influence of measurement scale, and (for real-world data) failure of the data to meet normality assumptions. Horn's (1965) method of parallel factor analysis has been proposed as a way to determine the dimensionality of a factor space. In parallel factor analysis, each column of the data matrix is randomized separately and the resulting column-randomized data set is then factored. Within the context of dynamic factor analysis, the parallel factor analysis proceeds by column-randomizing the data, then calculating lagged coefficients based on this data set. Although traditional column-randomized data only serve to remove

dependencies between manifest variables, when lagged variables are calculated from such column-randomized data, the result removes covariation between successive measurement occasions as well. The results for one such column-randomized data set are shown in Table 33.1 in the column labeled "Parallel eigenvalues." Whenever the eigenvalue from the data exceeds that obtained for the column-randomized data set, this is taken as evidence for the existence of the factor in the data. As can be seen, the eigenvalues for the first and third factors exceed those based on the column-randomized data and therefore argue for the existence of these two factors in the data. In practice, factorizations from several column-randomized data sets are usually considered in order to get a better idea of the degree of variability associated with the column-randomized extractions. For these data, when 100 replications of such column-randomized data are calculated, the variability in lag 0 eigenvalues is relatively proscribed, with the first and 99th percentiles of the eigenvalues falling between .81 and .96. As a result, it seems reasonable to believe that the data are well-modeled by a two-factor model in which the first factor loads predominantly on the first two variables, and the second factor loadings on the remaining two variables.

LAGGED RELATIONSHIPS

Once it has been determined which latent variables are present in the model, these factors can then be examined for their lagged effects using the same parallel factor analysis approach. In the column in Table 33.1 labeled as the "Lag 1" Cholesky decomposition, estimates of the lagged effects can be seen for all variables. In contrast to the triangular decomposition of lag 0 contemporaneous variances and covariances, these lagged estimates of lagged effects for all four latent variables are estimable. When these loadings are squared and summed, they are a form of partial eigenvalue estimate of lagged effects. Because the dynamic factor model assumes that the effect of latent variables "wear themselves out over time," only those latent variables found to exist in the lag 0 factor analysis may be examined for the presence of lagged effects. Of the factors identified in the lag 0 parallel analysis, the first factor is correctly identified as not having a lagged effect because the obtained partial eigenvalue of 0.002 is less then the eigenvalues observed for the column-randomized value of 0.005 and a significant lagged effect is found for the third factor, as shown by the partial eigenvalue of 0.137, which is larger than the value of 0.015 for the column-randomized data shown in the column labeled "Parallel eigenvalue." Although it might initially seem reasonable to conclude that additional lagged effects exist for these data, based on the partial eigenvalues associated with the lag 2, lag 3, and lag 4 partial eigenvalues, examination of the percentiles associated with repeated replications of the data reveal that these differences reflect chance variation. The observed partial eigenvalue of 0.021 of the lag 2 effect for the third factor approximately represents the 75th percentile of values observed over 100 replications of the column-randomized factorizations.

REAL-WORLD EXAMPLE: LONGITUDINAL AFFECT

From these analyses, it can be seen that the Cholesky factorization method correctly recovers both the dimensionality and the lag length associated with the randomly generated data. This was, to some extent, to be expected given that the data contained no serial autocorrelations and were generated using normal variates of both latent and error variables. It is helpful, therefore, to examine whether the same clear patterns emerge using a real-world data set. An ecological momentary assessment of a patient with borderline personality disorder is taken as such an illustration. In this data set, an individual who as diagnosed with borderline personality disorder was asked to complete ratings of being happy, calm, sad, proud, and bashful by entering ratings on a 5-point Likert scale each half-hour for approximately 6 hours across 4 days. The resulting time series contains 44 measurement occasions for analysis and constitutes a relatively short series for the purposes of dynamic factor analysis. Possible nonstationarity across days as a function of time of day were explored by calculating multiple regressions in which each of the mood variables was predicted from day and hour information. No systematic variation was found in the data as a function of these larger trends. In addition, analyses based on raw data were also compared in which the manifest variables were rank normalized over time. Results from these two analyses were the same regarding decisions about the dimensionality and lagged effects in the data and so it was decided to report the rank normalized results here because the magnitude of effects across variables were in largely the same metric. The number of manifest variables (5) and the relatively short series observed make it impossible to consider lag lengths greater than 2 for these data because the Toeplitz matrix composed of more three or more lags is rank deficient.

As can be seen from the lag 0 partial eigenvalues in Table 33.2, a single factor seems to be present in the data, and the magnitude of the eigenvalue associated with the first factor appears to be larger than those associated with the column-randomized data. When 100 column-randomized replications are considered, the 99th percentile of the eigenvalues associated with the first factor is 1.09, indicating that the first factor partial eigenvalue of 1.7392 should be retained. The remaining factors, however, all were less than partial eigenvalues observed for column-randomized data, thereby indicating that no additional factors beyond the first factor need be retained. All observed partial eigenvalues ranged between the first and 10th percentile rank of their column-randomized counterparts. Conceptually, the first factor extracted appears to indicate a general arousal or surgency factor, with positive loadings on the variables Happy, Proud, and Calm, and negative loadings on the

TABLE 33.2. Cholesky Decomposition of Affect Ratings

Factor	Cholesky decomposition					Parallel eigenvalues	
	Happy	Proud	Sad	Calm	Bashful	Eigenvalue	Parallel eigenvalue
				Lag 0 effects			
1	0.9310	0.5317	−0.3638	0.5591	−0.3803	*1.7392*	0.9089
2	0	0.7866	−0.2831	0.1120	−0.4135	0.8823	*1.0268*
3	0	0	0.8320	−0.1757	0.1478	0.7448	*0.8716*
4	0	0	0	0.7216	0.0205	0.5211	*0.7969*
5	0	0	0	0	0.7049	0.4969	*0.7802*
				Lag 1 effects			
1	0.1886	0.0765	0.1700	0.1690	0.0695	*0.1037*	0.0589
2	−0.1524	0.3061	−0.0572	0.1040	−0.0214	0.1315	*0.3858*
3	−0.1448	−0.2532	0.0838	−0.0574	0.1237	*0.1107*	0.0796
4	0.1820	0.1954	−0.1844	0.2803	−0.1103	*0.1960*	0.1286
5	−0.1671	−0.3010	0.1389	−0.1054	0.4468	*0.3486*	0.2131
				Lag 2 effects			
1	0.1997	0.0282	0.0920	0.0836	0.1706	0.0852	0.0782
2	−0.0425	0.1863	−0.3250	0.3035	−0.1386	*0.2534*	0.1022
3	0.2518	−0.0342	−0.1290	−0.0212	−0.0417	0.0834	*0.1934*
4	−0.1059	0.0398	0.2317	0.0876	0.1358	0.0926	0.0992
5	−0.0622	−0.1690	0.2232	−0.1280	0.1426	0.1190	0.1102

variables Sad and Bashful. Analysis then proceeds to a consideration of possible lagged effects of this factor on subsequent measurement occasions, where it is found that a significant lagged effect exists for the factor, as evidenced by the observed partial eigenvalue for the Lag 1 effects of 0.1037, which is larger than the value of 0.0589 for the column-randomized data. Although inference based on this single column-randomized data set would seem to indicate that a lagged effect is present for this factor, when the data from 100 replications of column-randomized data are considered, the observed value of 0.10 is at approximately the 50th percentile of the distribution. As a result, it does not seem reasonable to assume that a lagged effect is present in the data.

Based on these considerations, a dynamic factor model that was then specified postulated a single factor model with no lagged factor effects but which allowed for error covariances to be lagged in time. EM estimates of these factor loadings were

$$
\begin{bmatrix}
\text{Happy} & 0.80 \\
\text{Proud} & 0.73 \\
\text{Sad} & -0.58 \\
\text{Calm} & 0.56 \\
\text{Bashful} & -0.55
\end{bmatrix}
$$

and all statistically significant, estimated error variances were

$$
\begin{bmatrix}
\text{Happy} & 0.67 \\
\text{Proud} & 0.37 \\
\text{Sad} & 0.54 \\
\text{Calm} & 0.53 \\
\text{Bashful} & 0.47
\end{bmatrix}
$$

Lag length 1 error autocovariances were

$$
\begin{bmatrix}
\text{Happy} & 0.09 \\
\text{Proud} & 0.13* \\
\text{Sad} & -0.05 \\
\text{Calm} & 0.12 \\
\text{Bashful} & 0.16*
\end{bmatrix}
$$

with * indicating significance at the $p < .05$ level. Similarly Lag length 2 error autocovariances were

$$
\begin{bmatrix}
\text{Happy} & 0.61** \\
\text{Proud} & -0.07 \\
\text{Sad} & -0.06 \\
\text{Calm} & 0.15 \\
\text{Bashful} & 0.01
\end{bmatrix}
$$

These values appear reasonable, with the possible exception of the lag length 2 autocovariance for Happy, which was larger in magnitude than its lag 1 counterpart, suggesting that some cyclicity may be present in the data for this variable.

DISCUSSION

In this chapter I have discussed the use of dynamic factor models for stochastic data and provided a brief review of appropriate dynamic factor models (and alternatives) for such data. It is important to describe both contexts in which dynamic factor models may be appropriate and those contexts which, even though longitudinally intensive, fail to meet the assumptions of regularly spaced assessments in time, stationarity, or stochastic behavior over time. If, for example, some of the phenomena of interest (e.g., randomly spaced spikes in performance) are not well described by the continuously measured random shock model implicit in dynamic factor models, then other statistical models or prior adjustments to the data should be explored.

Although various programs help to automate the rapid specification of dynamic factor models, exploration of candidate models by enumeration of all possible models is burdensome, and it is often unclear whether estimation difficulties are due to rank conditions or misspecification of the universe of possible lags or factors in the model. To this end, use of the Cholesky decomposition of the Toeplitz variance–covariance matrix and a parallel factor analysis analogue permits the researcher to examine and evaluate dimensionality and

lagged effects relatively quickly. The computational burden associated with generating and evaluating replicates of column-randomized data is quite minimal and may be conducted using commonly available software for which the Toeplitz transform and Cholesky decomposition are available. So long as the Toeplitz matrix itself is of full rank, researchers need not be concerned about dependencies in estimation as a function of window size, as the factorizations extracted are identical under Toeplitz matrices of varying lag lengths.

Although the proposed technique may serve as a useful first step, the question of how researchers may best explore whether the data appear to reasonably meet the assumptions of the dynamic factor model is underresearched. As described in the earlier substantive example, researchers should, at a minimum, explore whether the data show signs of nonstationarity or seasonality and, if present, should either employ statistical models that incorporate such effects or make adjustments to the data in order to determine whether such possible violations affect the model selected and the magnitude of effects. Additional explorations that may be appropriate include influence diagnostics and/or examination of the estimated distributions of error variances in the data. Given that most appropriate diagnostic tests for structural equation models assume independence of successive observations, there is clearly much additional work to be done in the development of diagnostics that help researchers judge whether model assumptions have been met for the data and the degree to which a proposed model is robust relative to these assumptions.

Although the real-world example considered here appeared to indicate that affect measures over time were described by a single, unlagged factor structure, it may well be that lagged effects in the data were obstructed by the presence of either short-term cyclical effects due to time-of-day assessment or to "secular" differential lagged structures due to the day of the week. Although the series under consideration was probably adequately powered for tests of simple covariation over time, the series is underpowered to detect and estimate parameters associated with such differential effects. The existence of such plausible differential cyclical or secular trends over time is somewhat typical of day-to-day mood and behavior assessments.

In summary, I hope that this discussion of dynamic factor models helps researchers clarify some of the broad classes of psychological phenomena that appear in time-intensive data. I also hope that the described parallel Toeplitz factorization approach helps researchers to not only assess more quickly the dimensional-ity and nature of time-bound relationships at the latent variable level, but also to consider more readily a universe of possible models than are frequently entertained in the interests of keeping analyses tractable.

REFERENCES

Browne, M. W., & Nesselroade, J. R. (2005). Representing psychological processes with dynamic factor models: Some promising uses and extensions of ARMA time series models. In A. Maydeu-Olivares & J. J. McArdle (Eds.), *Advances in psychometrics: A Festschrift for Roderick P. McDonald* (pp. 415–452). Mahwah, NJ: Erlbaum.

Buckley, T. C., Holohan, D., Greif, J. L., Bedard, M., & Suvak, M. (2004). Twenty-four-hour ambulatory assessment of heart rate and blood pressure in chronic PTSD and non-PTSD veterans. *Journal of Trauma Stress, 17,* 163–171.

Ebner-Priemer, U., & Kubiak, T. (2010). The decade of behavior revisited: Future prospects for ambulatory assessment. *European Journal of Psychological Assessment, 26,* 151–153.

Finan, P. H., Zautra, A. J., Davis, M. C., Lemery-Chalfant, K., Covault, J., & Tennen, H. (2010). Genetic influences on the dynamics of pain and affect in fibromyalgia. *Health Psychology, 29,* 134–142.

Horn, J. L. (1965). A rationale and test for the number of factors in factor analysis. *Psychometrika, 32,* 179–185.

Jahng, S., Wood, P. K., & Trull, T. J. (2008). Analysis of affective instability in EMA: Indices using successive difference and group comparison via multilevel modeling. *Psychological Methods, 13,* 345–375.

Jank, W., & Shmueli, G. (2008). *Statistical methods in eCommerce research.* Hoboken, NJ: Wiley.

Lewis, K., Kaufman, J., Gonzalez, M., Wimmer, A., & Christakis, N. A. (2008). Tastes, ties, and time: A new (cultural, multiplex, and longitudinal) social network dataset using *facebook.com. Social Networks, 30,* 330–342.

Littlefield, A. K., Sher, K. J., & Wood, P. K. (2010). Do changes in drinking motives mediate the relation between personality change and "maturing out" of problem drinking? *Journal of Abnormal Psychology, 119,* 93–105.

Molenaar, P. (1987). Dynamic factor analysis in the frequency domain: Causal modeling of multivariate psycho physi-

ological time series. *Multivariate Behavioral Research, 22*(3), 329–353.

Molenaar, P. C. M. (1985). A dynamic factor analysis model for the analysis of multivariate time series. *Psychometrika, 50,* 181–202.

Molenaar, P. C. M., de Gooijer, J. G., & Schmitz, B. (1992). Dynamic factor analysis of non-stationary multivariate time series. *Psychometrika, 57,* 333–349.

Molenaar, P. C. M., & Nesselroade, J. R. (1998). A comparison of pseudo-maximum likelihood and asymptotically distribution-free dynamic factor analysis parameter estimation in fitting covariance-structure models to block-Toeplitz matrices representing single subject multivariate time series. *Multivariate Behavioral Research, 33,* 313–342.

Molenaar, P. C. M., & Nesselroade, J. R. (2009). The recoverability of P-technique factor analysis. *Multivariate Behavioral Research, 44,* 130–141.

Molenaar, P. C. M., Sinclair, K. O., Rovine, M. J., Ram, N., & Corneal, S. E. (2009). Analyzing developmental processes on an individual level using nonstationary time series modeling. *Developmental Psychology, 45,* 260–271.

Piasecki, T. M., Slutske, W. S., Wood, P. K., & Hunt-Carter, E. E. (2010). Frequency and correlates of diary-measured hangoverlike experiences in a college sample. *Psychology of Addictive Behaviors, 24,* 163–169.

Wang, S., Jank, W., & Shmueli, G. (2008). Functional data analysis in electronic commerce research. *Journal of Business and Economic Statistics, 26,* 144–160.

Wood, P. K., & Brown, D. (1984). The study of intraindividual differences by means of dynamic factor models: Rationale, implementation, and interpretation. *Psychological Bulletin, 116,* 166–186.

Zhang, G., & Browne, M. (2010). Dynamic factor analysis with ordinal manifest variables. In *Statistical methods for modeling human dynamics: An interdisciplinary dialogue* (pp. 241–263). New York: Routledge.

Zhang, Z. (2006). Codes for DyFA using least square method to estimate dynamic factor models. Retrieved September 1, 2010, from *http://www.psychstat.org/us/article. php/70.htm.*

Zhang, Z., Hamaker, E. L., & Nesselroade, J. R. (2008). Comparisons of four methods for estimating a dynamic factor model. *Structural Equation Modeling, 15,* 377–402.

Zuur, A. F., Fryer, A. F., Jolliffe, I. T., Dekker, I. T., & Beukema, J. J. (2003). Estimating common trends in multivariate time series using dynamic factor analysis. *Environmetrics, 14,* 665–685.

CHAPTER 34

Latent Trait–State Models

David A. Cole

Historically, researchers tended to conceive of measures as tapping either trait-like or state-like characteristics (Spielberger, 1966). Following John Nesselroade's seminal works (e.g., Herzog & Nesselroade, 1987; Nesselroade, 1988), researchers began to conceptualize measures as being sensitive (in varying degrees) to both trait and state components of the underlying construct. This insight highlighted the importance of understanding not just the cross-sectional structure but also the longitudinal structure of the measures used in psychological research. The goal of this chapter is to present several structural equation approaches to modeling the longitudinal structure of one or more measures of a particular construct. In particular, the chapter focuses on what have been referred to as trait–state models. Not every longitudinal data set will be amenable to analysis by these models. Some of the data set characteristics necessary for these analyses are discussed. Further, strengths and limitations of each of these models are also presented. Finally, I present an example data set to which several of these structural equation methods may be applied.

Before we begin, however, I need to discuss terminology. Most of these models have been presented in previous work using the words *trait* and *state*—often meaning very different things in different publications (e.g., Herzog & Nesselroade, 1987; Kenny & Zautra,

1995; Steyer & Schmitt, 1990). Furthermore, the words *trait* and *state* have been tied to numerous social, personality, developmental, and clinical theories (e.g., Allen & Potkay, 1981; Allport, 1966; Epstein, 1979; Jones, 1979; Mischel, 1968; Spielberger, 1966; Zuckerman, 1983). Most structural equation trait–state models incorporate relatively few of these theoretical nuances. To avoid inadvertently suggesting that structural equation trait–state models represent or test more than they do, I begin this chapter by suggesting a different terminology.

Inherent in all of the models I discuss is the idea that a particular psychological construct assessed at a given point in time can be partitioned into two parts. One part is completely stable over time and has often been called the *trait* component of the construct. The other part fluctuates from time to time and has been referred to as either the *state* component or the *occasion-specific* component. Here I use a different terminology to describe all trait–state models, irrespective of the language the original authors used in their presentation of these models.

First, I refer to the completely stable part of a construct as the *time-invariant* component (not, as many other authors have called it, the "trait component"). This chapter symbolizes the time-invariant factor as *I*. In every model, individual differences in the time-invariant component or factor are perfectly stable over time. This definition implies that the correlation of individual differences in the time-invariant factor from one time point to the next is 1.0, irrespective of the amount of time that has elapsed (within the constraints of a particular study). Note that this definition does not imply that the entire psychological construct of interest is perfectly stable over time. Perfect stability refers only to individual difference in that part of the psychological construct under investigation.

Second, I refer to the fluctuating part of a construct as the *time-varying* component (in contrast to terms such as the "state component" or "occasion factor"). This chapter symbolizes the time-varying factor as *V*. Individual differences in the time-varying component are not perfectly stable over time. That is, the over-time correlation of individual differences in this component is less than 1.0. In fact, the over-time correlation will diminish as the time lag increases in duration.

Theoretically, these models are an appropriate way of understanding the longitudinal structure of a psychological construct when the variance of that construct can be partitioned into exactly these two components. The percent of variance attributable to one component or the other, theoretically, can vary from 0% to 100% (depending on the construct, the population, and the time frame under investigation), as long as the two components sum to 100%. For example, in certain populations, the variance of a relatively mercurial construct such as anger might be 10% time-invariant and 90% time-varying, whereas a more stable construct such as introversion might be 90% time-invariant and only 10% time-varying. These percentages (or proportions) are two of the parameters that can be estimated using trait–state models.

Interestingly, several meta-analyses of longitudinal studies suggest that a wide variety of constructs may lend themselves to trait–state models. For example, Tram and Cole (2006) examined the test–retest reliabilities of various measures of children's dysphoric mood. From study to study, the test–retest time intervals ranged from 1 week to 84 weeks. Plotting the magnitudes of these correlations against their respective retest time intervals revealed the pattern depicted by the dots (and the solid line) in the upper panel of Figure 34.1. As the retest interval increases from 1 week to about 24 weeks, the over-time correlations drop from a high of around .92 to approximately .50. As the time interval grows even longer, the correlations drop at a slower and slower rate; however, they do not drop to

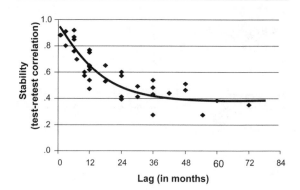

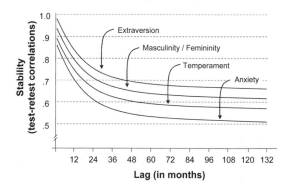

FIGURE 34.1. Test–retest correlations as a function of lag time: for depression measures (upper panel) and for personality/temperament (lower panel).

zero even over extremely long intervals (Conley, 1984). Rather, they asymptote at a value of approximately .38 (Tram & Cole, 2006).

Interestingly, this pattern pertains not just to dysphoric mood but to a wide range of psychological/temperament variables (Roberts & DelVecchio, 2000; Schuerger, Tait, & Tavernelli, 1982). As shown in the lower panel of Figure 34.1, the trends are strikingly similar across constructs.

These data are compatible with the coexistence of the two temporal processes that characterize most trait–state models: one, a time-invariant process; the other, a time-varying process. The initial drop in correlations could reflect the effects of a time-varying process. If we let *V* symbolize the time-varying component of the target variable *Y*, the process could be represented by an autoregressive function in which *V* at time *t* is par-

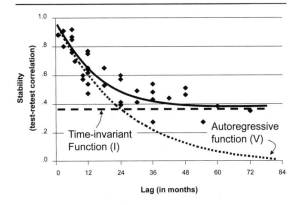

FIGURE 34.2. Observed test–retest correlations (symbolized by black diamonds) for depression measures plotted with a time-invariant (I) function and a time-varying (V) autoregressive function.

tially predicted by *V* at time *t* – 1. One such instantiation of this function is represented by the dotted line in Figure 34.2 as part of an overlay to the Figure 34.1 data. We see that the function anticipates the initial drop in correlations rather nicely; however, the function dramatically deviates from the data when the retest intervals become longer. A second process is needed to explain the nonzero asymptote of the correlations: a time-invariant part of *Y* symbolized simply as *I*, an intraindividual constant. One possible manifestation of *I*

is depicted in Figure 34.2 as the horizontal dashed line. This line anticipates the latter correlations quite nicely; however, it dramatically misses the correlations for the briefer time lags. The trait–state models discussed in the remainder of this chapter incorporate both of these processes in ways that appear to be compatible with longitudinal data on a wide variety of psychological variables.

UNIVARIATE MODEL

The first model we discuss is Kenny and Zautra's (1995, 2001) trait–state–error model. It has a considerable advantage over other models in that it only requires that the researcher have one measure of the construct at each of four waves. Its disadvantage, however, is that it is finicky, often failing to converge or generating out-of-range parameter estimates. Nevertheless, the model is elegant in its simplicity and is relatively intuitive. Therefore, it provides an excellent starting place for this chapter.

The univariate model is represented by the path diagram in Figure 34.3, in which, the rectangles represent a time series of *J* repeated measures on a single manifest variable, represented as Y_t for time point *t*. The circles represent latent variables or factors. At each time point, the manifest variable is a function of three latent variables: a time-invariant factor (*I*), a time-varying factor (V_t), and random measurement error (δ_t):

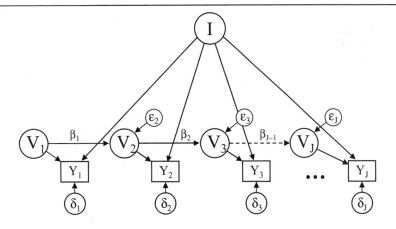

FIGURE 34.3. Univariate trait–state model (Kenny & Zautra, 1995).

$$Y_t = I + V_t + \delta_t, \, t = 1, 2, 3, \ldots, J$$

The time-varying variables are connected by single-headed arrows, reflecting an autoregressive function:

$$V_t = \beta_{t-1} V_{t-1} + \varepsilon_t$$

(for $t = 2, 3, \ldots, J$), where $\beta_1 = \beta_2 \ldots \beta_{J-1} = \beta$, and where ε_t represents the autoregressive residuals. To be sure that the model was mathematically identified, Kenny and Zautra (1995) required that the variances of the time-varying factor, the error terms, and the residuals (respectively) were equivalent over time. Consequently, this model requires the estimation of only five parameters: σ_I^2, σ_V^2, σ_ε^2, σ_δ^2, and β. To be structurally overidentified, the model must have at least four time points.

As mentioned earlier, one strength of the Kenny–Zautra model is that it requires only a single measure of the underlying construct at each of four (or more) time points. These relatively few requirements are characteristic of many longitudinal studies. A second strength is that the covariance of Y with itself over time will diminish as the time lag increases (as long as $\beta \neq 1$). This feature is characteristic of many psychological constructs, as is evident in Roberts and DelVecchio's (2000) literature review. A third strength is that as long as there is nonzero variance for the time-invariant factor, the covariance of Y with itself over time will not approach zero, reflecting another of the key features I described earlier as being characteristic of many psychological constructs (Conley, 1984; Roberts & DelVecchio, 2000; Tram & Cole, 2005). Applying the Kenny–Zautra model to a popular measure of children's depressive symptoms, Cole and Martin (2005) reported qualitatively different longitudinal structures depending on whether the measure was completed by children about themselves or by parents about their children. When parents were the informants, 61–72% of the variance was due to a time-invariant factor, and only 17–18% of the variance was due to a time-varying factor. When children were the informants, however, only 29–55% of the variance was due to a time-invariant factor, whereas 28–58% of the variance was due to a time-varying factor.

As elegant as it is, the Kenny–Zautra model can be a bit cantankerous. Cole, Martin, and Steiger's (2005) Monte Carlo analyses revealed a variety of circumstances that can cause this model to generate out-of-range and potentially biased parameter estimates. One set of such circumstances pertains to the stability of the time-varying factors, V_t. When the stability of the time-varying factor is either relatively low ($\beta < .20$) or relatively high ($\beta > .80$), the likelihood of out-of-range parameter estimates increases substantially, as does the magnitude of bias in some of the parameter estimates. When stability is ~.50, these problems are relatively rare. We suspect that such problems emerge because (1) at low stability, distinguishing between the time-varying factors and measurement error becomes difficult, and (2) at high stability, distinguishing the time-varying factors from the time-invariant factor becomes difficult.

A second problem pertains to sample size. Almost all structural equation models require a lot of subjects. The Kenny–Zautra model appears to need even more. Again, based on their Monte Carlo work, Cole and colleagues (2005) recommended having at least 500 cases in order to avoid problems with out-of-range values and to reduce bias in the parameter estimates.

A third problem pertains to the number of waves. Although the Kenny–Zautra model is technically identified with four waves, Monte Carlo analyses revealed that having so few waves gives rise again to unacceptably high rates of out-of-range estimates and large bias in the estimation of some parameters (Cole et al., 2005).

Taken together, these problems can make the interpretation of such models difficult, if not impossible. We speculate that problems such as these have emerged in other laboratories and may be one reason why we see relatively few published studies using this method (Kenny & Zautra, 2001). That said, this model is elegant in its simplicity, provides a very helpful heuristic through which to understand more complex models (described below), and certainly can be used successfully on certain data sets.

BASIC MULTIVARIATE MODEL

The univariate model is obviously a trait–state model applied to a time series of fallible, manifest variables. Often, investigators are more interested in the longitudinal structure of the factor that underlies such measures, not the measures themselves. Toward this end, a variety of latent variable trait–state models have been proposed (Cole et al., 2005; Courvoisier, Nussbeck, Eid, Geiser, & Cole, 2008; Eid, 2002; Nussbeck, Eid, Geiser, Courvoisier, & Cole, 2012; Steyer, Ferring, & Schmitt, 1992; Steyer & Schmitt, 1990, 1994; Steyer, Schmitt, & Eid, 1999). Of these, the Cole and colleagues (2005) trait–state–occasion (TSO) model is the clearest multivariate extension of the Kenny–Zautra model and is the focus of this section. (*Note.* We have since discovered that Ormel and Schaufeli [1991] embedded a TSO-like model in a larger model designed to assess the relation of self-esteem and external locus of control to a completely stable component of psychological distress.)

The basic TSO model is depicted in the upper panel of Figure 34.4. At every wave, the TSO model requires multiple (two or more) measures of the same underlying variable. At each wave, a latent variable (L_t) is extracted from this set of manifest variables (Y_{ti}), such that $Y_{ti} = L_t + \delta_{ti}$. At each wave, this latent variable is conceptualized as a function of both a time-invariant

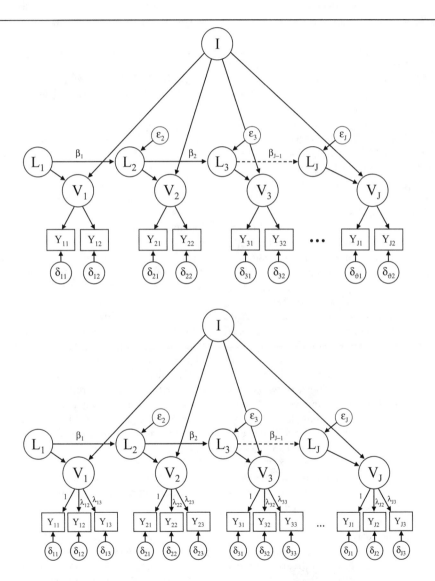

FIGURE 34.4. Upper panel: Basic multivariate trait–state model (Cole et al., 2005). Lower panel: Multivariate model with nonequivalent measures (Cole et al., 2007).

factor (I) and a time-varying factor (V_t): $L_t + I + V_t$. In a manner analogous to that in the Kenny–Zautra model, the time-varying factors are part of an autoregression process: $V_t = \beta_{t-1} V_{t-1} + \varepsilon_t$. An important advantage of this model over the univariate model, however, is that the variance of the target variable (L_t) is partitioned into only two sources, whereas the variance of Y_t in the univariate model is partitioned into three sources. This difference is due to the fact that the measurement error in the latent variable model is part of manifest variables (Y_{ti}), not the variable of interest (L_t).

Other advantages accrue to the TSO model. First, like the univariate model, the over-time covariance of the target variable with itself diminishes (but not to zero) as the time lag increases (as long as $0 < \beta_t < 1$ and $\sigma^2 > 0$) in a manner consistent with empirical observations (e.g., Roberts & DelVecchio, 2000). Second, the basic multivariate TSO model affords the opportunity to test many of its simplifying assumptions, including homogeneity of regression ($\beta_1 = \beta_2 = \ldots \beta_{J-1} = \beta$),), and the homoscedasticity of σ_V^2, σ_ε^2, and σ_δ^2 over time. Third, the TSO model is identified with three waves as long as these simplifying assumptions pertain.

Monte Carlo trials have revealed a number of desirable characteristics of the basic TSO model (Cole et al., 2005). First, virtually no improper solutions emerged when the stability of V_t was low. Second, the multivariate model was more manageable than the univariate model when the stability of V_t was moderately high. With only four waves of data and an N of only 200, models with V_t stability as high as .7 generated out-of-range parameter estimates at most only 12% of the time. When the stability of V_t was greater than .7, however, out-of-range parameter estimates were problematic unless either the sample size or the number of waves was increased. Third, the likelihood of improper solutions was appreciably smaller when the sample sizes were larger. Fourth, the likelihood of improper solutions and the magnitude of bias in parameter estimates were substantially reduced in designs with five or six waves, or N's of 500. The only change from the univariate model to the multivariate model was the use of multiple measures to represent the latent variable at each wave. This change enables the distinction between measurement error and V_t in a manner that is not dependent upon the stability of V_t.

Two shortcomings of the basic multivariate model are noteworthy. First, in this model the manifest variables at a particular time are equivalent measures of L_t. This feature would be unusual for most longitu-dinal designs; more commonly, the measures of L_t would have different factor loadings. Second, the basic multivariate model does not allow for shared method variance over time. Because most longitudinal studies utilize the same measures at each wave, the measurement error associated with a given measure at one wave may well be related to the measurement error associated with the same measure administered at other waves. Fortunately, extensions of the basic multivariate model have been developed to account for these situations.

MULTIVARIATE TSO MODEL WITH NONEQUIVALENT MEASURES

In their original presentation of the TSO model, Cole and colleagues (2005) made two important simplify-ing assumptions. One assumption was that the factor loadings and error variances (respectively) were equal within and across waves. This assumption facilitated the initial presentation of this model; however, it un-necessarily restricts its applicability. Most multivariate longitudinal studies involve measures that are conge-neric within wave, but not necessarily tau-equivalent. Classical test theory states that measures are "conge-neric" if their true score components are perfectly cor-related. Tests are tau-equivalent if they have equal true score variances but possibly different error variances (Steyer, 2001). Utilization of tau-equivalent measures within wave is rare in longitudinal research, except when investigators use alternate forms or split halves of the same instrument. Such equivalence comes at a noteworthy price, insofar as the latent variable that is extracted will typically reflect not just the construct of interest but also the method of measurement. For exam-ple, if a researcher obtained a set of tau-equivalent self-report measures of depression, the latent variable that is extracted is better conceptualized as "self-reported depression" than as "depression" per se. According to Cook's (1985) concept of critical multiplism, a stronger measurement design would involve multiple measures of the same construct that utilize maximally dissimilar methods.

The second restriction in Cole and colleagues' (2005) model was its limitation to two indicators per wave. Gerbing and Anderson's (1987) research suggests that having only two (nonequivalent) indicators per la-tent variable will increase various parameter estimation problems (e.g., biased factor loadings, large standard errors, and out-of-range parameter estimates), probably as a result of empirical underidentification.

Ciesla, Cole, and Steiger (2007) examined the feasibility of expanding the basic TSO model in ways that relax these simplifying restrictions. They used Monte Carlo simulations to test the effects of (1) dropping the tau-equivalence assumption and (2) increasing the number of indicators per wave from two to three. They tested these effects under a variety of conditions, varying sample size, the stability of the time-varying factors, and the ratio of $\sigma_I^2 : \sigma_V^2$. These changes create a model like the one depicted in the lower panel of Figure 34.4, where one factor loading per wave for L_t is fixed at 1.0, but the other two factor loadings (symbolized as λ_{ti}) are unconstrained within wave. (Factor loadings and measurement error variances were constrained to be equal to their counterparts across waves.)

Results were encouraging. The TSO model with nonequivalent measures was viable under a wide variety of conditions. One such condition involved having three, not just two, indicators per wave. Adding a third indicator at each wave slightly reduced the likelihood of nonconvergence and substantially reduced the probability of out-of-range parameter estimates. These findings reflect Anderson and Gerbing's (1984) research on simpler models, showing that out-of-range variance estimates were more likely when only two indicators per factor are utilized. In Ciesla and colleagues (2007), adding a third indicator was especially helpful when other conditions were especially troublesome. That is, even when the stability of V_t and the variance of I were low, the likelihood of out-of-range estimates dropped from 27% in two-indicator models to only 8% in three-indicator models. They speculated that problems with the two-indicator models were the result of empirical underidentification (Dillon, Kumar, & Mulani, 1987; Kenny, 1979; Rindskopf, 1984).

A second condition pertained to the magnitude of the factor loadings. In general, fewer problems with nonconvergence and out-of-range parameter estimates emerged when measurement factor loadings were relatively large. These effects were not trivial. Under some conditions, a drop in the standardized factor loadings from .91 to .55 increased the probability of out-of-range parameter estimates from .10 to .30. Ciesla and colleagues (2007) further noted that the benefit associated with adding a third indicator diminishes with the quality of the added variable. Adding a weak third measure did little to reduce the likelihood of problematic solutions.

MULTIVARIATE TSO MODEL ALLOWING FOR SHARED METHOD VARIANCE

A limitation of the models presented in both Cole and colleagues (2005) and Ciesla and colleagues (2007) is their assumption that all longitudinal covariance is entirely due to the time-varying and time-invariant factors of interest. In many longitudinal studies (and certainly in those for which the TSO model is appropriate), the repeated administration of the same set of measures wave after wave opens the door for "shared method variance," which can be defined as the covariance between two or more variables that is not explained by the constructs of interest but instead derives from the method inherent to the specific set of measures. In longitudinal research, this definition implies that the relation of measure to itself over time may reflect not only the stability of the targeted construct but also the method used to measure that construct. When the researcher is primarily interested in characteristics of the targeted construct, the effects of shared method variance must be controlled. Failure to control for such effects in longitudinal research typically results in the overestimation of longitudinal stabilities (Marsh, 1993). In TSO models, such overestimation would likely generate upwardly biased estimates of both the variance of the time-invariant factor and the stability of the time-varying factors.

Recognizing similarities between such multivariate longitudinal designs and cross-sectional multitrait–multimethod (MTMM) designs, LaGrange and Cole (2008) examined several MTMM approaches for handling shared method variance in TSO designs. Results of their Monte Carlo simulations suggested that one approach was particularly versatile and generated relatively few problems. As shown in Figure 34.5, this model is an elaboration of the model in the lower panel of Figure 34.4, in which selected measurement error terms are allowed to covary. More specifically, error terms associated with repeated administrations of the same measure are allowed to covary from wave to wave of the longitudinal design. Figure 34.5 explicitly shows the six over-time correlations for the error terms associated with Y_{t1}. Analogous correlations are allowed for the error terms associated with the other two variables, Y_{t2} and Y_{t3}, but are not depicted so as to avoid visual clutter. Adapting this approach from previous MTMM designs (Kenny & Kashy, 1992; Marsh, 1989), LaGrange and Cole (2008) referred to this TSO design as the correlated uniqueness (or CU) approach.

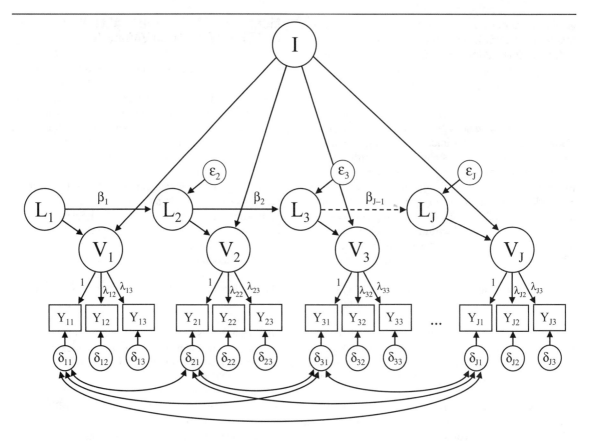

FIGURE 34.5. Multivariate model allowing for shared method variance (LaGrange & Cole, 2008). (*Note.* Comparable correlated disturbances among d_{t2} and among d_{t3} exist but are not depicted so as to avoid visual clutter.)

LaGrange and Cole's (2008) Monte Carlo results revealed that the CU model fit a wide variety of data sets quite well. Furthermore, implementation of the CU model generated few if any out-of-range parameter estimates. Similar findings have resulted from the comparison of methods for handling shared method variance in MTMM designs (e.g., Becker & Cote, 1994; Byrne & Goffin, 1993; Conway, 1996; Marsh & Bailey, 1991). Although the CU method for handling shared method variance is indeed highly versatile, this flexibility comes at a price. The model may not readily *fail* to fit data sets with which it is *incompatible*. In general, the ability to fit a misspecified model can lead to serious misinterpretations, as described by Lance, Woehr, and Meade (2007). Whether or not the implementation

of a CU approach to TSO data is subject to such problems has not yet been thoroughly investigated.

ADDING LATENT VARIABLE MEANS TO THE TSO MODEL

One last addition to the TSO model is that of latent variable means. In many applications of SEM, researchers focus only on the examination of covariance structure (i.e., means are not part of the analysis). The most common exception is latent growth curve (LGC) analysis, in which one must anticipate (and model) a specific pattern of mean-level change or growth over time. In some cases, however, the researcher may anticipate a kind of mean structure that does not neatly correspond to the concept of growth. In the trait–state conceptualization, one might expect an individual's scores to reflect an overall level (due to the time-invariant factor) plus some time-to-time deviation from this level (due to the effects of the time-varying factor). The expected value of the time-invariant factor, $E(I_g)$, would represent the level or amount of this factor in a specific group, g. The expected value of the time-varying factor, $E(V_{tg})$, would represent the average deviation of scores around $E(I_g)$ at a specific time in a given group. Although an individual's scores may vary considerably from time to time, the absence of circumstances that systematically affect all members of a group would suggest that $E(V_{tg})$ should be zero. With the addition of latent variable means to the TSO

model, we can estimate $E(I_g)$, test for group differences in $E(I_g)$, estimate $E(V_{tg})$, and test the hypothesis that $E(V_{tg}) = 0$. We refer to the TSO model with structured means as the enhanced TSO model. In this section, I describe this model and apply it to a two-group example data set to test group differences in measurement, covariance structure, and latent means.

Figure 34.6 depicts an example of the enhanced TSO model. The figure is virtually identical to the model in Figure 34.5 except that it makes explicit the addition of latent variable means (or intercepts). In most covariance models where means are not examined, the expected values of all variables (latent and manifest) are zero. In models like the one shown in Figure 34.6, however, the manifest variable means are a function of their underlying latent variables: $E(Y_{tig}) = \tau_{tig} + \lambda_{tig}E(L_{tg})$,

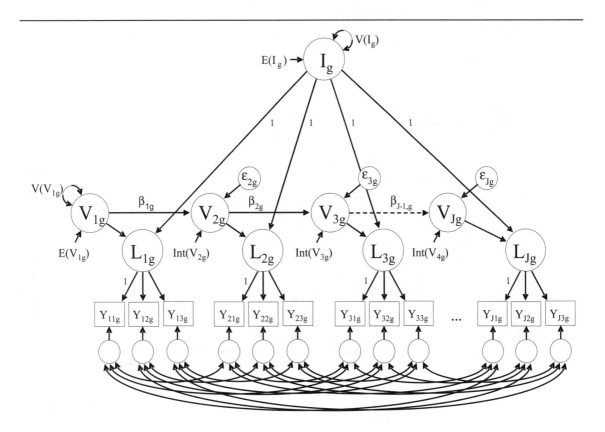

FIGURE 34.6. Enhanced multivariate TSO model with structured means.

where τ_{tig} s the intercept in the regression of Y_{tig} onto L_{tg}. In turn, the means of these latent variables can be expressed as a function of the time-invariant and time-varying factors: $E(L_{tg}) = E(I_g) + E(V_{tg})$.

Although this model can be tested in a single group, the examination of latent means often becomes more interesting when cross-group comparisons are also tested. In making both within- and cross-group comparisons, one should give serious consideration to the testing of a series of hypotheses via the comparison of various hierarchically nested models. In making such comparisons regarding the TSO model, one should consider the following key questions.

1. Is there within-group measurement equivalence across waves? Without such longitudinal equivalence, the interpretation of means can become difficult and potentially misleading. This question is addressed by examining whether or not the unstandardized factor loadings λ_{tig} at one wave are equal to their counterparts at other waves within each group.

2. Are the within-group measurement intercepts equivalent across waves? Changes in intercept for a given measure across time would suggest the intrusion of an additive measurement bias at one or more waves, which could be misinterpreted as true change in the construct of interest. This question can be addressed by testing whether or not the manifest variable intercepts τ_{tig} at one wave are equal to their counterparts at other waves within each group.

3. Does the stability of the time-varying factor change from wave to wave within group? This substantive question can provide evidence of temporal windows when the latent variable, V_t, is less stable (and possibly more amenable to instigated change).

4. Is there cross-group measurement equivalence? That is, are the factor loadings for the measures in one group equal to their counterparts in the other groups?

5. Are the intercepts of the manifest variables in one group equal to their counterparts in the other groups?

6. Is the stability β_g of the time-varying factor equal across groups? This question addresses the issue of whether or not individual differ-

ences in V_t are more stable in one group than the others.

7. Is the amount of variance attributable to the time-invariant factor equal across groups? This substantive hypothesis addresses the question of whether or not the latent variable of interest L_g is as time-invariant in one group as the others.

8. Likewise, is the amount of variance attributable to the time-varying factor equal across groups? Support for question 7 does not necessarily imply support for this question, as the total variance of L may differ from group to group.

9. If the examination of question 4 reveals systematic change in V over time in any group, one can ask further whether the pattern or magnitudes of these deflections differ from one group to another.

10. Are there mean differences in the time-invariant factor across groups? In other words, do the groups differ with regard to their overall level on the time-invariant factor?

Note. Estimation of $E(I_g)$ and $E(V_{tg})$ is not possible without the imposition of certain model-identifying constraints. A variety of such constraints can be implemented, but the meaning of $E(I_g)$ and $E(V_{tg})$ will vary depending on this choice. One particular constraint is especially commensurate with the current conceptualization of I and V_t: that is, $E(V_1) + E(V_2) + E(V_3) + \ldots + E(V_t) = 0$ (Maxwell, personal communication, October 2010). Using this constraint causes $E(V_{tg})$ to represent the average deviation of V_g at time t around a grand mean, $E(I_g)$. Thus, $E(I_g)$ represents the over-time average level of the latent variable in a given group, and $E(V_{tg})$ represents the fluctuation of the latent variable around $E(I_g)$ at a specific time. This is very different from latent growth models, which typically add constraints designed to test linear (or other) mean trends across time.

To facilitate the understanding and testing of these hypotheses, the enhanced TSO model is applied to an example data set. We used LISREL version 8.71 (Jöreskog & Sörbom, 2004) to test some of the hypotheses listed earlier. The example data set contains two groups, with 400 observations each. Both groups have three congeneric measures administered at each of four waves. Population parameters included the following: $\lambda_{t1g} = .80$, $\lambda_{t2g} = .70$, $\lambda_{t3g} = .60$, $\beta_{tg} = .40$, $V(I_{g=1}) = .70$,

$V(I_{g=2}) = .30$, $V(V_{t,g=1}) = .30$, $V(V_{t,g=2}) = .70$, $E(I_{g=1}) = 2.35$, $E(I_{g=2}) = 2.00$, and $E(V_{tg}) = 0$ for all t and both g, unless otherwise specified. (Also, the measurement intercepts were arbitrarily set at $\tau_{t1g} = 0$, $\tau_{t2g} = 4.0$, and $\tau_{t3g} = 8.0$, and modest correlations (0 to .18) were set between the measurement residuals in a manner commensurate with the pattern depicted in Figure 34.6.) Thus, population differences existed only in $V(I)$, $V(V_t)$, and $E(I)$. We used SEPath (STATISTICA; StatSoft, 2003) to obtain multivariate random deviates around these parameters. The resulting sample correlation matrices, standard deviations, and means for the two groups are embedded in the LISREL program for the base model (Model 1), presented in Appendix 34.1 and available at the handbook's website (*www.handbookofsem.com*). (*Note.* In this model the identifying constraints, $E(V_{1g}) + E(V_{2g}) + E(V_{3g}) + E(V_{4g}) = 0$ for groups 1 and 2, were achieved via the lines 55 and 73, respectively, in the LISREL program.) This base model provided a good fit to the data (see Table 34.1).

Model 2 was tested next and is identical to Model 1 except that it contained a number of within- and cross-group constraints, corresponding to earlier questions 1–6. Each of these constraints could be tested separately in a series of hierarchically nested models. Here they are tested together to save space and to expedite progress toward questions 7–10.

■ *Question 1.* Are the unstandardized factor loadings λ_{tig} at one wave are equal to their counterparts at other waves within each group? One can address this question by adding the following lines to the base model LISREL program:

```
21a)   EQ LY(2,4) LY(5,5) LY(8,6) LY(11,7)
21b)   EQ LY(3,4) LY(6,5) LY(9,6) LY(12,7)
72a)   EQ LY(2,2,4) LY(2,5,5) LY(2,8,6) LY(2,11,7)
72b)   EQ LY(2,3,4) LY(2,6,5) LY(2,9,6) LY(2,12,7)
```

■ *Question 2.* Are the manifest variable intercepts τ_{tig} at one wave are equal to their counterparts at other waves within each group? This question is addressed by adding the lines:

```
50a)   EQ TY(2) TY(5) TY(8) TY(11)
50b)   EQ TY(3) TY(6) TY(9) TY(12)
72c)   EQ TY(2,2) TY(2,5) TY(2,8) TY(2,11)
72d)   EQ TY(2,3) TY(2,6) TY(2,9) TY(2,12)
```

TABLE 34.1. Goodness-of-Fit Statistics for the Enhanced TSO Model, Applied to an Artificial Data Set

Model	df	χ^2	Δdf	$\Delta\chi^2$	NFI	CFI	RFI	RMSEA (90% CI)
Model 1. Base model with no cross-wave or cross-group measurement or stability equality constraints	64	59.99	—	—	.993	1.00	.985	.000 (0–.026)
Model 2. Same as Model 1 plus cross-wave and cross-group measurement and stability equality constraints: see LISREL program in Appendix 34.1	97	114.32	33[a]	54.33	.986	.998	.981	.022 (0–.036)
Model 3. Same as Model 2 plus constraints requiring that $V(I)$ is equal across groups: EQ PH(1,1,1) PH(2,1,1) after line 97	98	**140.86***	1[b]	26.54**	.983	.995	.977	.034 (.021–.045)
Model 4. Same as Model 2 plus constraints requiring that $V(V_t)$ are equal across groups.	101	**174.59****	4[b]	60.27**	.979	.991	.973	.043 (.032–.054)
Model 5. Same as Model 2 plus constraints requiring that $E(V_t)$ are equal across groups: AL=IN in line 91	100	115.15	3[b]	0.83	.986	.998	.982	.021 (0–.035)
Model 6. Same as Model 2 plus constraints requiring that $E(I)$ is equal across groups: EQ KA(1,1) KA(2,1) after line 97	98	**141.49***	1[b]	27.17**	.983	.995	.997	.034 (.020–.045)

Note. df, degrees of freedom; Δ, change in; NFI, normed fit index; CFI, comparative fit index; RFI, relative fit index; RMSEA, root mean square error of approximation; CI, confidence interval.
[a] Compared to Model 1.
[b] Compared to Model 2.
*$p < .01$; ** $p < .001$.

◼ *Question 3.* Does the within-group stability of V_t change over time? This question is addressed by adding the lines:

```
27a)   EQ GA(1,2) BE(2,1) BE(3,2)
72e)   EQ GA(2,1,2) BE(2,2,1) BE(2,3,2)
```

◼ *Question 4.* Are the factor loadings for the measures in group 1 equal to their counterparts in group 2? This question can be addressed by dropping lines 94a and 94b and then changing the LY specification in line 90 to read:

```
68)    MO … LY=IN
```

◼ *Question 5.* Are the intercepts of the manifest variables in group 1 equal to their counterparts in group 2?

This question can be addressed by dropping lines 94c and 94d and then changing the TY specification in line 90 to read:

```
MO … TY=IN
```

◼ *Question 6.* Is the stability of the time-varying factor V_t in group 1 the same as in group 2? This question can be addressed by dropping line 94e and adding a line:

```
72d)   EQ GA(2,1,2) BE(2,2,1) BE(2,3,2)
```

With these within- and cross-group constraints in place, Model 2 also fits the data well (see Table 34.1). For both groups, the parameter estimates and their standard errors from this model are presented in Table 34.2. All

TABLE 34.2. Key Parameter Estimates, Standard Errors, and Selected Cross-group Tests from the Application of the Enhanced TSO Model 2 to an Artificial Two-Group Data Set

Parameter (population value)	Group 1		Group 2		Selected group differences tested by specific model comparisons
	Est.	SE	Est.	SE	
λ_{11} (.8, fixed loading for $y11$)	.80	—	.80	—	
λ_{12} (.7, loading for $y12$)[a]	.71	.02	.71	.02	
λ_{13} (.6, loading for $y13$)[a]	.60	.02	.60	.02	
τ_{11} (0, fixed intercept for $y11$)[a]	0	—	0	—	
τ_{12} (4.0, intercept for $y12$)[a]	3.96	.06	3.96	.06	
τ_{13} (8.0, intercept for $y13$)[a]	7.98	.05	7.98	.05	
$\gamma_{12} = \beta_{21} = \beta_{32}$ (.4, stability of V_t)[a]	.41	.07	.41	.07	
$V(V_1)$ (.3, for $g = 1$; .7 for $g = 2$)	.27	.07	.75	.11	$\chi^2_{(4)} = 60.27$ ($p < .01$); compare models 3 vs. 2
$V(V_2)$ (.3, for $g = 1$; .7 for $g = 2$)	.37	—[b]	.74	—[b]	
$V(V_3)$ (.3, for $g = 1$; .7 for $g = 2$)	.34	—[b]	.68	—[b]	
$V(V_4)$ (.3, for $g = 1$; .7 for $g = 2$)	.29	—[b]	.74	—[b]	
$V(I)$ (.7 for $g = 1$; .3 for $g = 2$)	.76	.08	.27	.08	$\chi^2_{(1)} = 26.54$ ($p < .01$); compare models 4 vs. 2
$E(V_1)$ (0, mean of V at $t = 1$)	−.02	.03	−.07	.04	$\chi^2_{(3)} = 0.83$ (ns); compare models 5 vs. 2
$E(V_2)$ (0, mean of V at $t = 2$)	.05	.03	.07	.04	
$E(V_3)$ (0, mean of V at $t = 3$)	.00	.03	.00	.04	
$E(V_4)$ (0, mean of V at $t = 4$)	−.03	.03	.00	.04	
$E(I)$ (2.35 for $g = 1$; 2.00 for $g = 2$)	2.36	.05	2.01	.04	$\chi^2_{(1)} = 27.17$ ($p < .01$); compare models 6 vs. 2

[a]Constrained to be equal across groups in Model 2.
[b]Computed based on other parameter estimates, so *SE*s are not directly available via the Model 2 LISREL program.

estimates are close to the population parameter values that were used to generate the sample data. Of special interest are the apparent group differences (or lack thereof) in $V(I)$, $V(V_t)$, $E(V_t)$, and $E(I)$. These are the focus of the next series of questions and models.

■ *Question 7.* Is the amount of variance in L_{tg} that is attributable to the time-invariant factor I_g equal across groups? One can address this question by adding the following line to the Model 2 program:

73a)   EQ PH(1,1,1) PH(2,1,1)

With this one modification, Model 2 became Model 3. Model 3 did not fit the data well, as shown in Table 34.1 by the large and significant chi-square. Further, Model 3 provided a significantly worse fit to the data than did Model 2 ($\Delta\chi^2_{(1)} = 26.54$, $p < .001$). Examination of the parameter estimates clearly shows that $V(I_{g=1}) > V(I_{g=2})$. In the trait–state parlance, the latent variable L contains more "trait" variance in group 1 than in group 2.

■ *Question 8.* Is the amount of variance attributable to the time-varying factor equal across groups? Given the already-established cross-group equivalence of the V_t stability coefficients, one can address this question by modifying line 90 of the Model 2 program to read

68)   MO … PS=IN

and adding the following line to the program:

73a)   EQ GA(2,1,2) BE(2,2,1) BE(2,3,2)

With these changes, Model 2 becomes Model 4. As shown in Table 34.1, Model 4 also provided a poor fit to the data. Further, the change in chi-square relative to Model 2 was large and statistically significant ($\Delta\chi^2_{(4)} = 60.27$, $p < .001$). Examination of the variance estimates consistently reveals that $V(V_{tg=1}) < V(V_{tg=2})$. In the trait–state terminology, the latent variable L contains more "state" variance in group 1 than in group 2.

■ *Question 9.* Are there group differences in the means of the time-varying variable; that is, does $E(V_{tg=1}) = E(V_{tg=2})$? Given the constraint, $E(V_{1g}) + E(V_{2g}) + E(V_{3g}) + (V_{4g}) = 0$ that is already in place for both groups (see lines 66 and 95), this question becomes a 3 degrees of freedom test, accomplished by modifying line 90 of the Model 2 program to read

68)   MO … AL=IN

This modification created Model 5, which provided a good absolute fit to the data, as shown by the small and nonsignificant chi-square (see Table 34.1). Further, the change in chi-square compared to Model 2 was negligible ($\Delta\chi^2_{(3)} = 0.83$, $p > .50$). Examination of the unconstrained parameter estimates in Table 34.2 reveals that the estimates of $E(V_{tg})$ were all very close to zero.

■ *Question 10.* Are there mean differences in the time-invariant factor across groups; that is, does $E(I_{g=1}) = E(I_{g=2})$? This question is addressed by adding a line to the Model 2 program:

73a)   EQ KA(1,1) KA(2,1)

thus creating Model 6. As shown in Table 34.1, Model 6 provided a poor absolute fit to the data. Further, it provided a significantly worse fit to the data than did Model 2 ($\Delta\chi^2_{(1)} = 27.17$, $p < .001$). Examination of the parameter estimates in Table 34.2 clearly shows that $E(I_{g=1}) > E(I_{g=2})$.

At least three interesting results emerge from these analyses. First, the latent variable of interest has a stronger time-invariant component in group 1 than in group 2. Such a result would imply that individual differences in the latent variable are far more stable in group 1 than in group 2, perhaps reflecting the greater influence of stable biological and/or environmental factors in group 1. Attempts to instigate change in the latent variable in group 1 might not be successful unless such an intervention successfully targets these stability-maintaining factors. Second, the latent variable has a stronger time-varying component in group 2 than in group 1. Such a result would suggest greater lability of the latent variable in group 2 and potentially greater responsivity to intervention. Third, group 1 has a higher mean level of the time-invariant factor than does group 2; that is, the long-term average level of the latent variable (controlling for time-specific fluctuations) is higher in group 1 than in group 2. If the latent variable is a positive characteristic (e.g., problem solving), one might expect better long-term outcomes for members of group 1. Conversely, if the latent variable is a risk factor, members of group 1 would be more likely to experience a problematic outcome compared to members of group 2.

CONCLUSIONS

This chapter reviews a series of increasingly complex (and increasingly applicable) "trait–state" models, all designed to examine the latent longitudinal structure of one or more variables selected to measure the same underlying construct over time. All of the models reviewed here allow for the extraction of two kinds of latent variables, a time-invariant (aka "trait") factor and a set of time-varying (aka "state" or "occasion") factors.

The first of these models was a univariate model, sometimes called the trait–state–error model (Kenny & Zautra, 1995). Elegant in its conception and minimalistic in its design requirements, the model has empirical difficulties, often failing to converge or resulting in out-of-range parameter estimates (Cole et al., 2005). Some of these problems resolve with very large sample sizes but, unfortunately, others do not.

The second model can be conceptualized as a multivariate upgrade of the univariate model and has been called the trait–state–occasion (TSO) model (Cole et al., 2005). Although this basic multivariate model is better behaved than its univariate predecessor, it is limited in several very practical ways. First, it assumed that the multiple variables at each wave were tau-equivalent. In practice, relatively few such data sets exist. Second, it assumed that all cross-wave covariance was due to the latent variables of interest—that is, a time-invariant factor and a time series of time-varying factors. In reality, the repeated administration of the same measures over multiple waves typically requires the modeling of other longitudinal processes, such as the effects of the repeated method. Failing to account for the longitudinal effects of shared method variance constitutes a model specification error that can result in either a poor fit to the data, biased parameter estimation, or both (Marsh, 1993).

Third, the basic multivariate model was subsequently upgraded to accommodate (1) measures that are congeneric but not necessarily tau-equivalent, and (2) the shared method variance that likely results from the repeated administration of the same measures over time (Ciesla et al., 2007; LaGrange & Cole, 2008). Like the basic multivariate model, these upgrades are relatively well-behaved when applied to a wide variety of data sets. Problems do emerge, however, in data sets where the time-varying factor is highly stable ($\beta \geq .70$) or the sample size is relatively small ($N < 200$). .

Finally, the enhanced TSO model is introduced. It contains all the features of the previously discussed upgraded multivariate model plus the capacity to model latent variable means. With the constraint that the time-varying factor means sum to zero, two things happen. First, the mean of the time-invariant factor represents the longitudinal grand mean of the latent variable over time. Second, the means of the time-varying factors represent the time-specific deviations of the latent variable around the grand mean. This parameterization is quite commensurate with the conceptualization of both kinds of factors. That is, the mean of the time-invariant factor becomes the long-term average of the latent variable, and the means of the time-varying factor represent the up and down average deflections from the grand mean. The end of the chapter describes the application of this model to an example data set, demonstrating how group differences can be detected in both the amount of variance and the mean levels of the time-invariant and time-varying components of a longitudinal latent variable.

The models described in this chapter are only a few of those on which vibrant new research continues. For example, Steyer, Nussbeck, Eid, and Geiser continue to elaborate very sophisticated multitrait–multimethod models, some of which have been adapted to longitudinal applications (Courvoisier et al., 2008; Eid, 2002; Nussbeck et al., 2012; Steyer et al., 1999; Steyer & Schmitt, 1990, 1994). Also, Kenny has continued to elaborate his STARTS model (Kenny & Zautra, 2001). A recent multivariate version of this model (Donnellan, Kenny, Trzesniewski, Lucas, & Conger, 2010) is remarkable for three reasons. First, like the 2001 model, it successfully partitions the variance of the latent variable into three sources: a time-invariant factor, a set of time-varying factors, and a set of completely time-specific factors. Second, it relaxes the stationarity assumption, thus allowing the variance of the latent variable to change over time (either for substantive or methodological reasons). Third, it links the stability coefficient to age, making it a rate of change parameter, and allows it to vary from wave to wave—again either for methodological or substantive reasons. Both of these classes of models have been successfully applied to real data. Unclear, however, is the degree to which naturally occurring features of such data sets may cause convergence or boundary problems for such models, clearly suggesting topics for future research.

ACKNOWLEDGMENT

This research was supported by funding from Patricia and Rodes Hart.

REFERENCES

Allen, B. P., & Potkay, C. R. (1981). On the arbitrary distinction between states and traits. *Journal of Personality and Social Psychology, 41*, 916–928.

Allport, G. W. (1966). Traits revisited. *American Psychologist, 21*, 1–10.

Anderson, J. C., & Gerbing, D. W. (1984). The effect of sampling error on convergence, improper solutions, and goodness-of-fit indices for maximum likelihood confirmatory factor analysis. *Psychometrika, 49*(2), 155–173.

Becker, T. E., & Cote, J. A. (1994). Additive and multiplicative effects in applied psychological research: An empirical assessment of three models. *Journal of Management, 20*, 625–641.

Byrne, B. M., & Goffin, R. D. (1993). Modeling MTMM data from additive and multiplicative covariance structures: An audit of construct validity concordance. *Multivariate Behavioral Research, 28*, 67–96.

Ciesla, J. A., Cole, D. A., & Steiger, J. H. (2007). Extending the Trait–State–Occasion Model: How important is within-wave measurement equivalence? *Structural Equation Modeling, 14*, 77–97.

Cole, D. A., Ciesla, J., & Steiger, J. H. (2007). The insidious effects of completely justifiable correlated residuals in latent variable covariance structure analysis. *Psychological Methods, 12*, 381–398.

Cole, D. A., & Martin, N. C. (2005). The longitudinal structure of the children's depression inventory: Testing a latent trait–state model. *Psychological Assessment, 17*(2), 144–155.

Cole, D. A., Martin, N. C., & Steiger, J. H. (2005). Empirical and conceptual problems with longitudinal trait–state models: Introducing a trait–state–occasion model. *Psychological Methods, 10*, 3–20.

Conley, J. J. (1984). Longitudinal consistency of adult personality: Self-reported psychological characteristics across 45 years. *Journal of Personality and Social Psychology, 47*, 1325–1333.

Conway, J. M. (1996). Analysis and design of multitrait–multirater performance appraisal studies. *Journal of Management, 22*, 139–162.

Cook, T. D. (1985). Postpositivist critical multiplism. In R. L. Shotland & M. M. Mark (Eds.), *Social science and social policy* (pp. 21–62). Beverly Hills, CA: Sage.

Courvoisier, D. S., Nussbeck, F. W., Eid, M., Geiser, C., & Cole, D. A. (2008). Analyzing the convergent and discriminant validity of states and traits: Development and applications of multimethod latent state–trait models. *Psychological Assessment, 20*, 270–280.

Dillon, W. R., Kumar, A., & Mulani, N. (1987). Offending estimates in covariance structure analysis: Comments on the causes and solutions to Heywood cases. *Psychological Bulletin, 101*, 126–135.

Donnellan, M. B., Kenny, D. A., Trzesniewski, K. H., Lucas, R. E., & Conger, R. D. (2010). *Using trait–state models to evaluate the longitudinal consistency of global self-esteem from adolescence to adulthood.* Unpublished manuscript.

Eid, M. (2002). A closer look at the measurement of change: Integrating latent state–trait models into the general framework of latent mixed Markov modeling [Special issue]. *Methods of Psychological Research, 7*, 33–52.

Epstein, S. (1979). The stability of behavior: I. On predicting most of the people most of the time. *Journal of Personality and Social Psychology, 37*, 1097–1126.

Gerbing, D. W., & Anderson, J. C. (1987). Improper solutions in the analysis of covariance structures: Their interpretability and a comparison of alternative respecifications. *Psychometrika, 52*, 99–111.

Herzog, C., & Nesselroade, J. R. (1987). Beyond autoregressive models: Some implication of the trait–state distinction for the structural modeling of developmental change. *Child Development, 58*, 93–109.

Kenny, D. A. (1979). *Correlation and causality.* New York: Wiley.

Kenny, D. A., & Kashy, D. A. (1992). Analysis of the multitrait–multimethod matrix by confirmatory factor analysis. *Psychological Bulletin, 112*, 165–172.

Kenny, D. A., & Zautra, A. (1995). The trait–state–error model for multiwave data. *Journal of Consulting and Clinical Psychology, 63*, 52–59.

Kenny, D. A., & Zautra, A. (2001). Trait–state models for longitudinal data. In L. M. Collins & A. G. Sayer (Eds.), *New methods for the analysis of change* (pp. 243–263). Washington, DC: American Psychological Association.

LaGrange, B., & Cole, D. A. (2008). An expansion of the trait–state–occasion model: Accounting for shared method variance. *Structural Equation Modeling, 15*(2), 241–271.

Lance, C. E., Woehr, D. J., & Meade, A. W. (2007). Case study: A Monte Carlo investigation of assessment center construct validity models. *Organizational Research Methods, 10*, 430–448.

Jones, E. E. (1979). The rocky road from acts to dispositions. *American Psychologist, 34*, 107–117.

Jöreskog, K., & Sörbom, D. (2004). *Linear structural relations* (version 8.71). Lincolnwood, IL: Scientific Software International.

Marsh, H. W. (1989). Confirmatory factor analysis of multitrait–multimethod data: Many problems and a few solutions. *Applied Psychological Measurement, 13*, 335–361.

Marsh, H. W. (1993). Stability of individual differences in multiwave panel studies: Comparison of simplex models and one-factor models. *Journal of Educational Measurement, 30*, 157–183.

Marsh, H. W., & Bailey, M. (1991). Confirmatory factor analyses of multitrait–multimethod data: A comparison of alternative models. *Applied Psychological Measurement, 15*, 47–70.

Mischel, W. (1968). *Personality and assessment.* New York: Wiley.

Nesselroade, J. R. (1988). Some implications of the trait–state distinction for the study of development over the life span: The case of personality. In P. B. Baltes, D. L. Featherman, & R. M. Lerner (Eds.), *Life-span development and behavior* (Vol. 8, pp. 163–189). Hillsdale, NJ: Erlbaum.

Nussbeck, F. W., Eid, M., Geiser, C., Courvoisier, D. S., & Cole, D. A. (2012). Konvergente und diskriminante Validität über die Zeit: Integration von Multitrait–Multimethod-Modellen und der Latent-State–Trait-Theorie. In H. Moosbrugger & A. Kelava (Eds.), *Testtheorie und Fragebogenkonstruktion.* Berlin: Springer.

Ormel, J., & Schaufeli, W. B. (1991). Stability and change in psychological distress and their relationship with self-esteem and locus of control: A dynamic equilibrium model. *Journal of Personality and Social Psychology, 60*(2), 288–299.

Rindskopf, D. (1984). Structural equation models: Empirical identification, Heywood cases, and related problems. *Sociological Methods and Research, 12*, 109–110.

Roberts, B. W., & DelVecchio, W. F. (2000). The rank-order consistency of personality traits from childhood to old age: A quantitative review of longitudinal studies. *Psychological Bulletin, 126*, 3–25.

Schuerger, J. M., Tait, E., & Tavernelli, M. (1982). Temporal stability of personality by questionnaire. *Journal of Personality and Social Psychology, 43*, 176–182.

Spielberger, C. D. (1966). Theory and research on anxiety. In C. D. Spielberger (Ed.), *Anxiety and behavior* (pp. 3–20). New York: Academic Press.

StatSoft. (2003). *STATISTICA (version 6)* [Computer software]. Tulsa, OK: Author.

Steyer, R. (2001). Classic test theory. In C. Ragin & T. Cook (Eds.), *International encyclopedia of the social and behavioral sciences: Logic of inquiry and research design* (pp. 1955–1962). Oxford, UK: Pergamon.

Steyer, R., Ferring, D., & Schmitt, M. J. (1992). States and traits in psychological assessment. *European Journal of Psychological Assessment, 8*, 79–98.

Steyer, R., & Schmitt, M. J. (1990). The effects of aggregation across and within occasions on consistency, specificity and reliability. *Methodika, 4*, 58–94.

Steyer, R., Schmitt, M. J., & Eid, M. (1999). Latent state–trait theory and research in personality and individual differences. *European Journal of Personality, 13*, 389–408.

Steyer, R., & Schmitt, T. (1994). The theory of confounding and its application in causal modeling with latent variables. In A. von Eye & C. C. Clogg (Eds.), *Latent variables analysis: Applications for developmental research* (pp. 36–67). Thousand Oaks, CA: Sage.

Tram, J., & Cole, D. A. (2006). A multimethod examination of the stability of depressive symptoms in childhood and adolescence. *Journal of Abnormal Psychology, 115*, 674–686.

Zuckerman, M. (1983). The distinction between trait and state scales is not arbitrary: Comment on Allen and Potkay's "On the arbitrary distinction between traits and states." *Journal of Personality and Social Psychology, 44*, 1083–1086.

CHAPTER 35

Longitudinal Structural Models for Assessing Dynamics in Dyadic Interactions

Emilio Ferrer
Hairong Song

Aprimary goal in research involving dyads is to identify patterns of interrelations between the two members of the dyad (e.g., parent–child, teacher–student, husband–wife). When the interactions between both dyad members develop over time, the goal is to capture such interrelations, as they unfold over time. To detect and quantify dyadic interactions accurately, longitudinal techniques are needed that can model the time course of the interactions, taking into consideration the interdependent nature of the members in the dyad. Dynamic factor analysis (DFA; Browne & Nesselroade, 2005; Molenaar, 1985) is an analytic technique that can accomplish these goals. In spite of its potential, DFA has been underused in the social and behavioral sciences. DFA models are traditionally applied to time series data collected from a single unit of study, such as a single individual or dyad (Ferrer & Nesselroade, 2003), or have been implemented to various units separately, from which a summary of results across units is then extracted (e.g., Ferrer & Widaman, 2008; Hamaker, Dolan, & Molenaar, 2005). In this chapter we first describe DFA as a technique to examine the dynamics of dyadic interactions over time. We then apply this model to time series data on affect from multiple dyads and examine variability in the affect dynamics across dyads.

DYNAMIC FACTOR ANALYSIS

DFA is a statistical technique developed to model lagged structure in covariance matrices. DFA emerged as a way to solve one of the main limitations of Cattell's P-technique factor analysis (Cattell, 1963; Cattell, Cattell, & Rhymer, 1947), namely, the lack of specification of lagged relations. Such lagged relations are meant to account for time-related dependencies among manifest and latent variables. P-technique consists of factor analysis of multivariate time series data collected from a single individual across multiple occasions. The number of factors from P-technique is indicative of the number of potential drives that bring about within-individual variation, and the pattern of factor loadings indicates the structure of such variation (Jones & Nesselroade, 1990).

To overcome the limitations of the P-technique, Anderson (1963) suggested that time series analyses should be carried out on the common factors, so that the dynamics of the implied psychological processes could be appropriately identified. Several types of DFA models were then proposed in various disciplines. These models differ mainly in the specification of lagged relations between manifest and latent variables (Engle &

Watson, 1981; Molenaar, 1985; for reviews see Browne & Nesselroade, 2005; Ferrer & Zhang, 2009; Nesselroade, McArdle, Aggen, & Meyer, 2002; Wood & Brown, 1994). One such specification is the so-called process factor analysis (PFA) model formulated by Browne and colleagues (Browne & Nesselroade, 2005; Browne & Zhang, 2007). In this specification, the latent variables represent unobserved constructs through which the lagged relations are structured. In its more general form, the PFA can be expressed as a function of two equations. The first equation is written as

$$y_t = \Lambda f_t + u_t \tag{35.1}$$

where y_t is a vector of j manifest variables measured at time t, Λ is a matrix of factor loadings that is assumed to be invariant over time, f_t is a vector of common factors at time t, and u_t is a vector of unique factors at time t assuming $u_t \sim (0, \sigma_j^2 I)$. The second equation of the model can be written as

$$f_t = \sum_{l=1}^{L} \Phi_l f_{t-l} + \sum_{p=1}^{P} B_p z_{t-p} + z_t \tag{35.2}$$

where Φ_l are the autoregressive (AR) weight matrices at lag l, f_{t-l} is a vector of common factors at time $t-1$, the B_p are moving average weight matrices, and $z_t \sim (0, \Psi)$ is a random shock vector.

Equation 35.1 represents a standard factor-analytic representation of a set of manifest variables in y_t as linear functions of a set of common latent variables in f_t and uncorrelated unique factors in u_t. In Equation 35.2, the set of latent variables at a given time, in f_t, are represented as a function of three components: (1) AR or cross-lagged relations from latent variables at prior times, where regression weights associated with latent variables at prior times are contained in the Φ_l matrix; (2) moving average relations from random shocks at prior times, with associated regression weights in the B_p matrix; and (3) random shocks at time t, represented as z_t. If the latent variables only follow AR processes, namely, that the middle term on the right side of Equation 35.2 is omitted, then the PFA model has its reduced form of PFA(Q, L), where Q is the number of factors, and L is the number of lagged relationships.

Figure 35.1 shows a path diagram of a PFA (2,2) model (i.e., two factors and two lags in this notation). Here, circles represent latent variables and squares represent observed variables. The depicted model includes two latent variables, labeled as $f1$ and $f2$, at each time

of measurement, and these two latent variables are measured by six manifest variables $M_1, M_2, \ldots, M_6$ at each time. The lag 2 status of the model in Figure 35.1 is embodied in the direct AR paths to a given latent variable, such as $f1_t$, from itself at the prior two times of measurement, $f1_{t-1}$ and $f1_{t-2}$. Cross-lagged paths of lag 1 are also shown in Figure 35.1, from one latent variable at a given time of measurement to the other latent variable at the next time of measurement, such as from $f1_{t-2}$ to $f2_{t-1}$ and from $f2_{t-1}$ to $f1_t$. Although not shown in Figure 35.1, lag 2 cross-lagged paths, such as from $f2_{t-2}$ to $f1_t$, are also included in this model. All of these AR and cross-lagged path coefficients are contained in the Φ_t matrix in Equation 35.2. In addition, the variable z_t, labeled z_1 and z_2 at each time of measurement, represents unobserved exogenous forces that produce random shocks on the system. Also noticeable in Figure 35.1 are the latent variables at times $t-3$ and $t-4$ depicted without manifest variables. These variables are meant to represent that, on any given occasion, the process shows influences of the same order (i.e., lag 2) and is stationary across the observed measurement occasions.[1]

One important feature of the model displayed in Figure 35.1 is the latent variables, labeled as $f1$ and $f2$. If the data were from a single individual and $f1$ and $f2$ represented, say, positive and negative affect, respectively, any cross-lagged paths between $f1$ and $f2$ across time could be interpreted as intraindividual dynamics. But, if the various latent variables correspond to each of the individuals in a dyad, then cross-lagged paths from one member in the dyad to the other represent interindividual dynamic processes within the dyad (see Ferrer & Widaman, 2008).

Although initially developed to analyze data from a single individual, DFA is a general framework that is well suited to examine interactions within dyads over time (Ferrer, 2006; Ferrer & Nesselroade, 2003). In these interactions, data are measured across multiple points in time from two individuals who form an interdependent system. Several important questions about dyadic interactions can be examined with DFA models. The first set of questions has to do with the structure of the data. For example, which variables are most strongly indicative of which factors? Are the factors representing one member in the dyad the same as those representing the other member? Another set of questions about dyadic interactions concerns the dynamics of the latent variables over time. One could ask, for

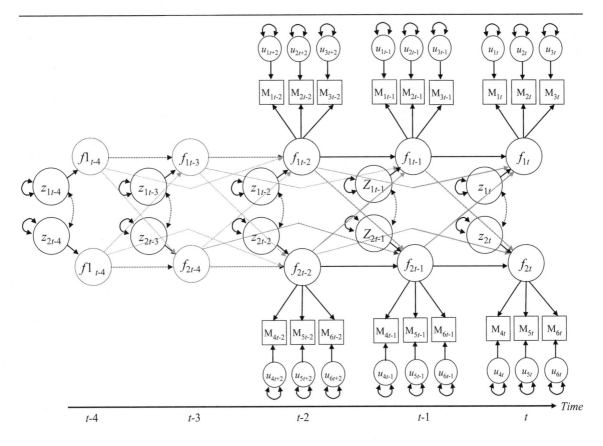

FIGURE 35.1. Path diagram of a lag 2 PFA (2,2) model.

example, what is the optimal number of lags required to represent relations among latent variables? Are the identified dynamic processes stable across time and/or measurement occasions? Does one member of the dyad have lagged influences of larger magnitude on the other member of the dyad? (see Ferrer & Nesselroade, 2003).

A third set of questions is related to possible differences in the dynamics across dyads. As typically implemented, DFA models apply to time series data collected from a single unit (e.g., individual, dyad). This single-unit-based approach, however, is limited when data from multiple dyads are available and the goal is to study variation of the dyadic dynamics in the population. We discuss this issue in the next section.

DYNAMIC FACTOR ANALYSIS WITH MULTIPLE UNITS

Most of the applications of DFA on psychological research consist of univariate or multivariate time series from a single individual. This approach, focused exclusively on a person, is important to identify patterns of intraindividual variability (Molenaar, 2004; Nesselroade & Ford, 1985). However, it is limited in its applicability to the population. That is, it cannot provide any information regarding differences in the intraindividual variability across individuals (or dyads). Several methods have been used over the years to solve this issue.

Perhaps the first effort to handle multivariate time series from multiple individuals was put forward by

Cattell in what he called the "chained P-technique" (Cattell, 1966; see also Russell, Bryant, & Estrada, 1996), which consists of pooling several multivariate time series from different individuals into a single, longer multivariate time series. The resulting pooled series is then submitted to a P-technique factor analysis, as if it came from a single individual, yielding an overall factor structure for all the time series. The chained P-technique can be practical when the available time series from the different individuals are short. However, it presents a number of limitations, not the least important being the integration of the various time series without considering possible—or likely—differences in the underlying processes across individuals. In other words, by combining the data from all the individuals into a single time series, one assumes that all individuals' data have the same factorial structure and follow the same pattern of dynamics over time. This important assumption, however, is untested in the chained P-technique.

One method for testing the "poolability" of time series from different individuals was developed by Nesselroade and Molenaar (1999). This method consisted of identifying a group of individuals whose time series meet certain conditions of homogeneity, then pooling the lagged covariance matrices across those individuals to obtain an estimate of a single-population lagged covariance matrix. The test that Nesselroade and Molenaar proposed was based on the differences between each individual lagged-covariance function and the pooled, expected population lagged covariance function. These differences are then evaluated based on a chi-square distribution. The procedure would start with the data from all the individuals in the sample and apply the test to the resulting pooled lagged covariance matrix. If the test leads to rejection of the complete pooling, the next step is to remove those individual lagged covariance matrices that depart most significantly from the pooled matrix and reapply the test. This sequence is implemented with the goal of identifying groups of individuals with homogeneous (i.e., poolable) pooled covariance matrix (for applications of this approach, see Chow, Nesselroade, Shifren, & McArdle, 2004; Nesselroade & Molenaar, 1999).

In several recent applications, researchers have applied DFA models to data from multiple individuals using invariance analyses (Hamaker et al., 2005; Hamaker, Nesselroade, & Molenaar, 2007; Shifren, Wood, Hooker, & Nesselroade, 1997). The goal in this approach is to use invariance tests to identify subgroups of individuals with the same factorial structure. In situations where factorial invariance holds, data from the different individuals can be combined for the subsequent analyses. If, however, factorial invariance does not hold, a DFA model is fitted to each individual (or dyad) separately. To illustrate, Hamaker and colleagues (2007) applied this method to time series from 22 individuals and identified five different groups whose individuals showed factorial invariance, although the largest group consisted of three individuals only. To make comparisons across groups of individuals, the authors suggested a visual inspection.

An example of a similar individual-based DFA approach to multiple dyads with comparisons of results across dyads was performed by Ferrer and Widaman (2008). They applied a DFA model to time series from multiple dyads. They first fitted the same model to the time series data from each dyad separately and then obtained empirical distributions (e.g., sample means and variances) of the parameter estimates across all dyads in the sample. They found that although the number of factors can be reasonably considered to be the same across all dyads, the dynamics between the two members of the dyad over time show substantial variation across the dyads. Although this method is practical for examining similarities and differences in specific parameter estimates across subjects (or dyads), the distribution of the parameters in the population cannot be formally assessed, and there is not a single set of standard errors that reflect the uncertainty in the variability within units (individual time series) and across units (sample) (see Song & Ferrer, 2012). One method proposed to formally examine variation in dynamic parameters across multiple subjects is mixed models. This idea is well validated and widely used in many disciplines using clustered cross-sectional data or repeated-measures data from multiple subjects. This approach, however, is not standard practice in the case of multivariate time series data from multiple individuals. One available application of this method consists of univariate time series from multiple subjects (Rovine & Walls, 2006). The researchers used mixed models to examine within-individual variability and between-individual differences in such variability simultaneously. This application was successful and informative but required a number of restrictive assumptions. For example, all observed time series were assumed to follow the same stationary process (a first-order AR model) and the univariate time series data were measured without error. In most situations, however, time series data, either univariate or multivariate, collected from multiple individuals (or dyads), have proved to show substantial heterogeneity (Ferrer & Widaman, 2008; Hamaker et al., 2005, 2007).

In this chapter we present analyses trying to overcome some of the limitations described previously. For this, we apply a DFA model to multivariate time series of daily affect from multiple dyads. The goals of these analyses are (1) to examine patterns of variability in affect for each individual in the dyad, (2) to identify dynamics of affect between both members of the dyad; and (3) to examine variability in such dynamics across all dyads in the study. The DFA model that we apply is a PFA model, as described in previous sections. We estimate the parameters of this PFA model using a Bayesian procedure (for a general introduction to Bayesian estimation, see Franić, Dolan, Borsboom, & Boomsma, Chapter 36, this volume; see also Song & Ferrer, 2012, for technical details about fitting PFA models with multiple units using Bayesian estimation).

METHOD

Participants

The data for the analyses in this chapter are from romantic couples in a project dealing with dyadic interactions (see, e.g., Ferrer & Widaman, 2008). As part of the overall project, all participants were asked to complete a daily questionnaire about their affect. In this chapter we present data from 171 couples who had at least 56 daily observation days of complete data (M = 70 days, SD = 17 days). The ages of the participants ranged from 18 to 74 years (M = 33; SD = 13). The time that they had been involved in the relationship ranged from 0.8 to 35.1 years (M = 9.80; SD = 9.31); 2.29% of the couples reported that they were dating casually, 81.7% reported that they were living together, 3% were engaged, and 13% reported that they were married.

Measures of Relationship-Specific Affect

As part of the daily questionnaire, participants responded to 18 adjectives reflective of positive (e.g., "emotionally intimate," "trusted") and negative (e.g., "trapped," "lonely") emotional experiences specific to their relationship. Participants were asked to complete these items by responding to the instruction "Indicate to what extent you have felt this way about your relationship today." Thus, these items were intended to tap into participants' positive and negative affect specific to their relationship. Figure 35.2 displays plots of composites created from the positive and negative items, for four separate dyads. These plots display differences in the emotional experiences among the dyads. Such differences are apparent with regard to the levels of affect (i.e., high vs. low), fluctuation, and stability.

For all items, participants were asked to respond using a 5-point Likert-type scale ranging from 1 (*very slightly or not at all*) to 5 (*extremely*). The alpha coefficients of reliability (computed using the data from all individuals at the first measurement occasion) for the positive and negative affect scales were .93 and .92, respectively. Moreover, we also computed the reliability of change within person using generalizability analysis (Cranford et al., 2006). This reliability index represents the precision with which systematic change of persons across days is being measured. The resulting reliability coefficients for positive and negative affect were .83 and .86 respectively (see Steele & Ferrer, 2011).

RESULTS

Descriptive Analyses, Data Preparation, and Diagnostics

Means, standard deviations, and skewness of all the items are shown in Table 35.1, with statistics based on the first time of measurement t_1, and all times of measurement T. The means on positive items are of higher magnitude than those on negative items. As expected from a standard sample (i.e., as opposed to, say, a clinical sample of depressed individuals), participants reported much higher levels of positive affect relative to their levels of negative affect. The skewness values indicate that most positive items have distributions close to normal, whereas the negative items show positive skewness (i.e., most scores cluster around low values).

To confirm that two dimensions underlie the current data (e.g., Ferrer & Widaman, 2008), we fitted a P-technique factor analysis to the pooled data from all 342 individuals. This analysis produced a two-factor structure (see Table 35.2). All items for positive affect loaded on the same factor, and so did all the items for negative affect, with no cross-loadings between the two factors. Positive and negative affect were correlated at

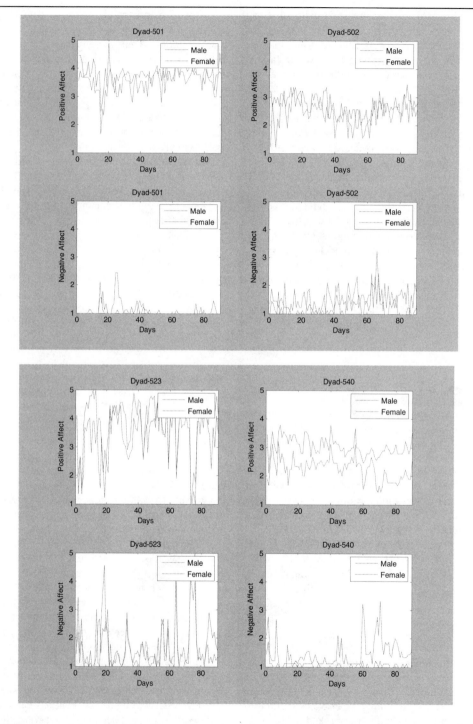

FIGURE 35.2. Observed time series data for positive and negative affect for the two individuals in four different dyads.

TABLE 35.1. Means, Standard Deviations, and Skewness of Items

Items	t_1 Mean	SD	Skewness	T Mean	SD	Skewness
Positive affect						
Emotionally intimate	3.36	1.10	−.36	3.24	1.21	−.22
Physically intimate	3.09	1.33	.04	2.70	1.39	.27
Trusted	3.95	.94	−.92	3.86	1.11	−.90
Committed	4.18	.95	−1.31	3.95	1.09	−1.09
Free	3.09	1.15	−.35	3.07	1.03	−.26
Loved	4.03	.95	−.92	3.88	1.05	−.80
Happy	3.86	1.04	−.68	3.76	1.12	−.71
Loving	3.84	1.04	−.80	3.80	1.08	−.68
Socially supported	3.35	1.16	−.44	3.16	1.27	−.28
Negative affect						
Sad	1.60	1.00	2.09	1.54	.89	2.11
Blue	1.59	.91	1.84	1.48	.88	2.38
Trapped	1.31	.74	3.21	1.39	.81	2.58
Argumentative	1.92	1.12	1.28	1.55	.93	1.98
Discouraged	1.62	.96	1.77	1.45	.84	2.29
Doubtful	1.51	.87	2.16	1.41	.81	2.59
Lonely	1.55	.93	2.13	1.58	.98	2.06
Angry	1.54	.94	2.10	1.39	.82	2.66
Deceived	1.19	.61	4.36	1.23	.65	3.86

Note. t_1, data from the first measurement occasion only; T, data from all measurement occasions.

−.48. Four items representative of positive affect, including *emotionally intimate* (E), *trust* (T), *loved* (L), and *happy* (H), were selected and used for subsequent analyses. This selection was done to reduce the number of items for the analyses and facilitate parameter estimation. The selected items were expected to define well the latent construct of positive affect due to their large loadings.

Within-Person Dynamics of Affect

In the first set of analyses, we carried out a PFA analysis of the detrended time series of all the individuals simultaneously. In other words, we did not consider the fact that these data came from interdependent dyads. For this, we used a PFA model with one factor, four manifest indicators, and AR components of one and two lags [i.e., PFA(1,1) and PFA(1,2)]. These lag orders

seem reasonable when using time series consisting of self-report data, especially regarding affect and emotion (Ferrer & Widaman, 2008; Hamaker et al., 2005). The PFA(1,1) model that we used can be written in matrix form as

$$\begin{pmatrix} y_E \\ y_T \\ y_L \\ y_H \end{pmatrix}_{it} = \begin{pmatrix} \lambda_1 \\ \lambda_2 \\ \lambda_3 \\ \lambda_4 \end{pmatrix} f_{it} + \begin{pmatrix} u_1 \\ u_2 \\ u_3 \\ u_4 \end{pmatrix}_{it}$$

$$f_{it} = \phi_i \cdot f_{i,t-1} + z_{it}$$

$$\phi_i \sim N(\mu_\phi, \sigma_\phi^2) \qquad \text{(35.3)}$$

New in Equation 35.3 is ϕ_i, which includes a subscript i indicating that the AR coefficients can vary

TABLE 35.2. Factor Loading Estimates for the Items

Items	Positive affect	Negative affect
Emotionally intimate	.77	.08
Physically intimate	.57	.06
Trusted	.79	−.01
Committed	.77	−.00
Free	.53	−.00
Loved	.82	−.06
Happy	.77	−.16
Loving	.83	−.02
Socially supported	.62	−.01
Sad	.01	.77
Blue	.01	.77
Trapped	−.06	.58
Argumentative	.06	.66
Discouraged	−.04	.77
Doubtful	−.06	.73
Lonely	−.06	.56
Angry	.02	.77
Deceived	.02	.65

across individuals. Furthermore, the vector of such autoregressive coefficients is assumed to approximate a normal distribution with mean μ_φ and variance σ^2_φ. To identify this model, we constrained the first factor loading λ_1 to unity. Fitting this PFA(1,1) model to the data produced estimates for a set of nine parameters $\theta = (\lambda_2, \lambda_3, \lambda_4, \sigma^2_1, \sigma^2_2, \sigma^2_3, \sigma^2_4, \mu_\phi, \sigma^2_\phi)$. The PFA model was fitted to the data using the program WinBUGS (Windows version of Bayesian inference using Gibbs sampling; Spiegelhalter, Thomas, Best, Gilks, & Lunn, 2003).[2]

A semi-informative prior was specified for the factor loading parameters, $\lambda_2, \lambda_3, \lambda_4 \sim N(.8, 10,000)$, because the results from the factor analysis showed that .8 was a reasonable value (see also Ferrer & Widaman, 2008). For the precision of the uniqueness (i.e., $1/\sigma^2_i$, $i = 1,\ldots,$ 4), a noninformative gamma distribution was specified as the priors, $1/\sigma^2_i \sim$ Gamma(0.1,0.001), which is the most common prior for variance terms in Bayesian analyses. The priors for μ_φ and $1/\sigma^2_\varphi$ were set up as $\sim N(0, 1,000)$ and Gamma (.01, .01), respectively.[3]

A total of 10,000 iterations were run for each of three sequences generated with different starting values. The sequences for all parameters converged very rapidly, and the parallel chains mixed well together (see Figure 35.3). Based on this information, the first 1,000 iterations were discarded as burn-in. We then thinned the converged sequence by collecting every 10th random draw to reduce the possible independence among the draws. This yielded a total of 2,700 (i.e., 3 sequences × (10,000 − 1,000)/10) random draws from which to obtain the Bayesian estimates for each parameter. In addition, to test the convergence for each parameter statistically we used the Gelman–Rubin test $\hat{R}$ (using the R package "coda"). After convergence, we computed the deviance information criterion (DIC) index (Spiegelhalter et al., 2003), which considers the trade-off between model fit and complexity, and is useful to compare among competing models.

Results from these analyses are presented in the upper panel of Table 35.3. Included are point estimates, standard errors, and 2.5 and the 97.5 percentiles of the point estimates (i.e., certainty intervals). All the Gelman–Rubin indices $\hat{R}$ were around 1, indicating that the sequences generated from the Markov Chain Monte Carlo (MCMC) mixed very well. Examples of $\hat{R}$ over iterations for parameters are given in Figure 35.4, showing that $\hat{R}$ gets close to 1 as iterations increase. The estimates for the factor loadings were $\lambda_2 = .839$, $\lambda_3 = 1.031$, and $\lambda_4 = 1.041$ (the first loading was fixed to one for identification). The estimates for the uniqueness were $\sigma^2_1 = .490$, $\sigma^2_2 = .295$, $\sigma^2_3 = .177$, and $\sigma^2_4 = .218$. The mean of the AR(1) coefficient was estimated at .266 ($SE = .013$), representing the average influence of positive affect on itself from one day to the next. The variance of this AR(1) coefficient was .035 ($SE = .004$). Hence, the AR coefficients range from −.101 to .633 in the population, with a probability of .95. This variability indicates that the degree with which positive affect influences itself from one day to the next varies significantly across individuals.

In the next analysis, we fitted a 2-lag model PFA (1,2) following the same procedure as in the previous analyses. Results from these analyses are presented in the lower panel of Table 35.3. As shown, adding a second order to the lag component of the factor series did not affect the magnitude of the factor loading estimates ($\lambda_2 = .839$, $\lambda_3 = 1.031$, and $\lambda_4 = 1.040$) or the uniqueness estimates ($\sigma^2_1 = .490$, $\sigma^2_2 =. 294$, $\sigma^2_3 = .177$, and $\sigma^2_4 = .217$). The estimate of the lag 1 coefficient AR(1) decreased slightly, from .266 to .261 ($SE = .013$), with variance also decreasing from .035 to .032 ($SE = .004$). Importantly, the mean of the lag 2 coefficient AR(2) ($\mu_{\varphi 2} = .012$, $SE = .010$) was unlikely to be different

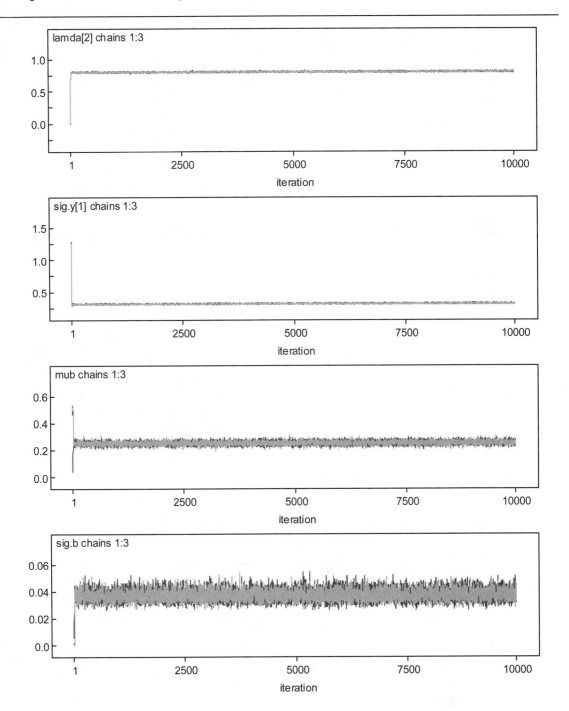

FIGURE 35.3. Trace plots of the parameters from fitting a PFA(1) to data from $N = 342$. Lambda, factor loadings; sig.y, uniqueness; mub, mean of the AR coefficients; sig.b, variance of the AR coefficients.

TABLE 35.3. Parameter Estimates from PFA(1,1) and PFA(1,2) Fitted to Individual Data

	$\hat{R}$	Est.	SE	2.5	97.5
PFA (1,1)					
λ_2	1.00	.839	.007	.826	.852
λ_3	1.00	1.031	.007	1.017	1.045
λ_4	1.00	1.041	.007	1.027	1.056
σ_1^2	1.00	.490	.005	.480	.500
σ_2^2	1.00	.295	.003	.289	.301
σ_3^2	1.00	.177	.003	.172	.182
σ_4^2	1.00	.218	.003	.211	.223
μ_φ	1.00	.266	.013	.240	.291
σ_φ^2	1.01	.035	.004	.029	.043
PFA (1,2)					
λ_2	1.00	.839	.007	.825	.853
λ_3	1.00	1.031	.007	1.017	1.045
λ_4	1.00	1.040	.007	1.026	1.055
σ_1^2	1.00	.490	.005	.491	.491
σ_2^2	1.00	.294	.003	.289	.295
σ_3^2	1.00	.177	.003	.172	.177
σ_4^2	1.00	.217	.003	.211	.212
$\mu_{\varphi 1}$	1.00	.261	.013	.235	.286
$\sigma_{\varphi 1}^2$	1.00	.032	.004	.025	.040
$\mu_{\varphi 2}$	1.01	.012	.010	−.008	.031
$\sigma_{\varphi 2}^2$	1.01	.007	.002	.004	.010

Note. λ_1 was fixed to 1. $N = 342$ individuals. $T \geq 56$ days.

from zero, but the variance estimates ($\sigma_{\varphi 2}^2 = .007$, $SE = .002$) indicated that there may be variation around this parameter across individuals (95% interval = −.153, .177). These results indicate that, on average, people's positive affect on a given day was influenced by their positive affect the previous day, although not by that from 2 days earlier. Although these effects were true on average, there were important differences in such influences across all individuals. For example, the lag 1 effect (i.e., influences from one day to the next) was large for some people and weak for others. The lag 2 effect (i.e., influences from one day to 2 days ahead), however, was positive for some individuals and negative for others.

The model comparison index was similar for both models (DIC = 166,608), indicating that both models

were supported statistically by the data. Thus, the decision to retain one model over the other needs to be based on substantive grounds. On the one hand, the PFA(1,1) model is more parsimonious and has been found to be accountable for most of the lagged covariation in these types of affect data (Ferrer & Nesselroade, 2003; Ferrer & Widaman, 2008). On the other hand, the PFA(1,2) provides more information (up to the lag 2 relation) about the dynamics of the affective system and, although the mean of the lag 2 AR parameter was not different from zero, the variance estimate was, indicating enough variation in that parameter across all individuals.

Between-Person Dyadic Dynamics of Affect

In the next set of analyses, we considered the dyadic nature of the data and examined the interrelations of affect over time between the two individuals in the dyad. For this, we fitted a PFA(2,1) model to 158 couples who had observations for at least 56 days. The model that we used can be written in matrix form as

$$
\begin{bmatrix} y_{F\_E} \\ y_{F\_T} \\ y_{F\_L} \\ y_{F\_H} \\ y_{M\_E} \\ y_{M\_T} \\ y_{M\_L} \\ y_{M\_H} \end{bmatrix}_{it} = \begin{bmatrix} \lambda_1 & 0 \\ \lambda_2 & 0 \\ \lambda_3 & 0 \\ \lambda_4 & 0 \\ 0 & \lambda_5 \\ 0 & \lambda_6 \\ 0 & \lambda_7 \\ 0 & \lambda_8 \end{bmatrix} \begin{bmatrix} f_F \\ f_M \end{bmatrix}_{it} + \begin{bmatrix} u_1 \\ u_2 \\ u_3 \\ u_4 \\ u_5 \\ u_6 \\ u_7 \\ u_8 \end{bmatrix}_{it}
$$

$$
\begin{bmatrix} f_F \\ f_M \end{bmatrix}_{it} = \begin{bmatrix} \varphi_{11} & \varphi_{12} \\ \varphi_{21} & \varphi_{22} \end{bmatrix} \begin{bmatrix} f_F \\ f_M \end{bmatrix}_{i,t-1} + \begin{bmatrix} \omega_1 \\ \omega_2 \end{bmatrix}_{it}
$$

$$
\Phi_i = \begin{bmatrix} \varphi_{11} & \varphi_{12} \\ \varphi_{21} & \varphi_{22} \end{bmatrix}_i \sim MN(\mu_\Phi, \Pi)
$$

(35.4)

where the items from the female (F) and the male (M) were assumed to load on their respective factor, the unique variances were assumed to be independent (i.e., σ_{ij}^2 for $i \neq j$), and the two factor disturbances were allowed to correlate with each other. For identification purposes, the first factor loading was constrained to unity for each factor. The resulting parameters estimated from this model were $\theta = (\lambda_2, \lambda_3, \lambda_4, \lambda_6, \lambda_7, \lambda_8, \sigma_1^2, \sigma_2^2, \sigma_3^2, \sigma_4^2, \sigma_5^2, \sigma_6^2, \sigma_7^2, \sigma_8^2, \mu_\Phi, \Pi)$.

All the priors were set up in a similar way as under the one-factor model, whereas the variances of the

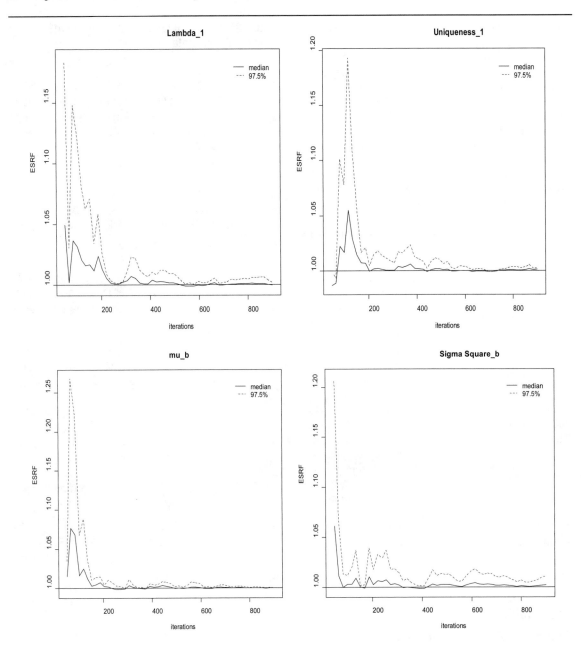

FIGURE 35.4. Gelman–Rubin indices of convergence over iterations from fitting PFA(1) to data from $N = 342$.

factor disturbances and the Φ matrix were given an inverse-Wishart prior distribution (i.e., a multivariate version of inverse-gamma distribution). A total of 10,000 iterations were run for each of three sequences generated with different starting values. The trace plots from the three sequences indicated that the chains mixed well after approximately 2,000 iterations. This was true for all three parameters. To increase accuracy, the first 2,500 iterations were discarded as burn-in and the remaining iterations were used for estimation. As previously, each chain was thinned by collecting every 10th draw. Therefore, the total random draws for each parameter was 2,250 ($3 \times (10,000 - 2,500)/10$).

The estimates from this model, as well as standard errors, and 2.5 and 97.5 certainty intervals of the point estimates, are presented in Table 35.4. The factor loadings and uniqueness estimates were of similar magnitude as those from the one-factor model. Of particular interest here are the estimates representing the means of the AR coefficients μ_{Φ} and their associated variance estimates Π. As shown in Table 35.4, the diagonal elements of the μ_{Φ} matrix were .303 ($SE = .024$) and .245 ($SE = .024$), for μ_{11} and μ_{22}, respectively. These coefficients indicate that, on average, both females and males in this population carry their positive affect from one day to the next. The off-diagonal elements were μ_{21}, small, yet likely different from zero (.043, $SE = .019$), and μ_{12}, unlikely different from zero (.024, $SE = .020$). These estimates imply that, on average, males' positive affect on a given day was influenced by the females' positive affect the day before. Influences from males to females, however, were not perceptible. The estimates of the variances for the AR coefficients were all significant, $\Pi_{11} = .063$, $SE = .009$; $\Pi_{22} = .027$, $SE = .005$; $\Pi_{33} = .029$, $SE = .005$; $\Pi_{44} = .058$, $SE = .009$, indicating significant variability across individuals in each of the lagged AR coefficients, both within- and between-person coefficients.

DISCUSSION

Summary of Results: Intraindividual and Dyadic Processes

In this chapter we applied DFA to multivariate time series data from multiple dyads for examining within-individual and within-dyad variability in affect. In addition, we examined the extent to which such dynamics of affect showed variability across the dyads in the

TABLE 35.4. Parameter Estimates from PFA(2,1) Fitted to Dyadic Data

	$\hat{R}$	Est.	SE	2.5%	97.5%
λ_2	1.00	.958	.013	.933	.984
λ_3	1.00	1.165	.014	1.140	1.194
λ_4	1.00	1.178	.014	1.151	1.207
λ_6	1.00	1.008	.014	.982	1.036
λ_7	1.00	1.207	.016	1.176	1.240
λ_8	1.00	1.202	.016	1.172	1.233
σ_1^2	1.00	.505	.008	.490	.520
σ_2^2	1.00	.293	.005	.284	.302
σ_3^2	1.00	.155	.003	.148	.162
σ_4^2	1.00	.198	.004	.190	.205
σ_5^2	1.00	.489	.007	.475	.504
σ_6^2	1.00	.297	.005	.288	.307
σ_7^2	1.00	.194	.004	.186	.202
σ_8^2	1.00	.229	.004	.220	.237
μ_{11}	1.00	.303	.024	.257	.350
μ_{12}	1.00	.024	.020	−.016	.063
μ_{21}	1.00	.043	.019	.007	.080
μ_{22}	1.00	.245	.024	.197	.292
σ_{11}^2	1.01	.063	.009	.047	.082
σ_{12}	1.01	−.006	.005	−.016	.004
σ_{13}	1.01	.006	.005	−.003	.015
σ_{14}	1.01	.017	.006	.005	.030
σ_{21}	1.01	−.006	.005	−.016	.004
σ_{22}^2	1.01	.027	.005	.019	.038
σ_{23}	1.01	.001	.003	−.006	.007
σ_{24}	1.01	.006	.005	−.003	.016
σ_{31}	1.01	.006	.005	−.003	.015
σ_{32}	1.01	.001	.003	−.006	.007
σ_{33}^2	1.01	.029	.005	.021	.040
σ_{34}	1.01	−.009	.005	−.018	.000
σ_{41}	1.01	.017	.006	.005	.030
σ_{42}	1.01	.006	.005	−.003	.016
σ_{43}	1.01	−.009	.005	−.018	.000
σ_{44}^2	1.01	.058	.009	.043	.077

Note. λ_1 and λ_5 were fixed to 1. $N = 158$ dyads. $T \geq 56$ days.

sample. We implemented a DFA model with random coefficients using a Bayesian estimation procedure. The results of our analyses indicate that (1) positive affect had a reliable time effect, whereby affect on a given day was, on average, related to the previous day, but not to 2 days before; (2) these lagged effects of positive affect showed individual variation, such that 1-day effects were substantial for some people and weak for others, but 2-day influences were positive for some individuals and negative for others; (3) regarding the dyadic dynamics, females appeared to influence their male partners' positive affect the next day, but the reverse pattern was not detectable; (4) such dyadic influences (i.e., both auto- and cross-lagged effects) showed substantial variability across the population; and, (5) in all models, the random effects of the dynamic parameters could be reliably estimated.

These findings are in line with previous research on intraindividual variability and dynamics in affect. With regard to the order of the lagged effects, most studies support either lag 1 relations (Chow et al., 2004; Ferrer & Widaman, 2008) or lag 2 relations (Ferrer & Nesselroade, 2003; Nesselroade et al., 2002). Of particular importance here is the variability in the dynamic parameters across individuals. Previous research has consistently found large heterogeneity in such dynamic parameters. This is the case, for example, regarding the lagged relations within each person (e.g., Chow et al., 2004; Ferrer & Widaman, 2008; Hamaker et al., 2005) and across the two individuals in a dyad, thus showing variability in affective dynamics across couples (Ferrer & Widaman, 2008). This was true in our analyses as well. Although for some dyads there was no prediction of affective dynamics over time, for other dyads such dynamics were strong and systematic. In sum, these results highlight the importance of considering variability across dyads (or individuals) when studying dyadic affective processes over time. Traditional approaches in which the data from various dyads are pooled assume a similar pattern of dynamics across all dyads, and are likely to generate results that do not represent any particular dyad.

The idea of avoiding pooling data from individuals (or dyads) before—or instead of—examining information at the individual level or testing for their homogeneity is part of the old idiographic–nomothetic debate (for reviews see, e.g., Allport, 1937; Lamiell, 1981; Nesselroade, 2002, 2006). How to make inferences that generalize to the population while preserv-

ing information at the individual level is not an easy task. Simply averaging across individuals (or dyads, or whatever unit of study) is misguiding at best, and wrong at worst. Several researchers have demonstrated that aggregating data from individuals to express interindividual changes over time fails to characterize accurately how each person changes over time (Hamaker et al., 2005, Molenaar, 2004; Molenaar & Valsiner, 2005; Nesselroade, 2001, 2002). By incorporating variability in the dynamics across dyads as part of the model, our analyses are consistent with this view. The results further support the idea by revealing that the dynamics of affective processes show large variability across all dyads in our sample.

Methodological Considerations

Our approach for implementing a DFA model with random coefficients is based on a Bayesian estimation procedure. Currently, there are not many available programs for implementing such a model using standard structural equation modeling software (see Zhang, Hamaker, & Nesselroade, 2008; Zhang & Nesselroade, 2007). Although this technical detail will be solved in the near future, the current status of techniques leaves researchers in a difficult position. We opted for Bayesian estimation using the program WinBUGS. Our choice was primarily motivated by the flexibility of this program to specify variance components, as well as the availability of standard errors associated with the parameter estimates. Our analyses show that this is a valid and efficient approach to fit DFA models with random coefficients to data from multiple units (e.g., individuals, dyads). In substantive terms, this approach is an effective way to study both population-average dynamics and interindividual differences in such dynamics. Although the analyses presented in this chapter are based solely on empirical data, simulation studies have demonstrated the effectiveness of this method in a variety of data conditions, even in situations of small sample size ($N = 50$ individuals) and short series ($T = 50$ observations) (Song & Ferrer, 2012).

The specification of all the models that we implemented assumed factorial invariance across all dyads. That is, the factor structure representing the four manifest variables and the latent factor was fixed to be similar across all individuals. Although this is not necessarily an unreasonable assumption in this type of data, it presumes that the way the items represented positive affect relating to the positive affect factor was equivalent across individuals—and across time. One benefit of imposing factorial invariance is the straightforward interpretation of regression coefficients among latent factors. To the extent that this assumption is not tenable, however, our results might have misrepresented the affective structure of the individuals and dyads in the sample. In other analyses with these data (e.g., Ferrer & Widaman, 2008) we did not impose this invariance constraint, thus allowing each individual in the sample to have an idiosyncratic factorial structure. Despite the benefit of representing affect based on information from each individual, such specification did not support equal construct identification across all individuals. In other words, the meaning of the latent factors might have been different across individuals and dyads. Because of this, the interpretation and comparison of the affective dynamics across dyads were less clear.

A recent alternative approach, put forward by Nesselroade (Nesselroade 2002, 2006; Nesselroade, Gerstorf, Hardy, & Ram, 2007), consists of relaxing the traditional invariance restrictions at the level of factor loadings (i.e., relationship of manifest variables to latent factors) but imposing such restrictions at the level of second-order factors, or relationships among factors. Using this method, one would filter out factorial structure features that are unique to each person before estimating relations among the constructs of interest.

Another alternative to address this issue would be to use latent response variable models, such as those involving a probit or logit link function when the variables of interest are categorical. If, for example, the factor loadings from a continuous model are not similar across individuals, it may be because different individuals have different categorical thresholds that map onto the latent continuous response variable. More broadly, the possibility exists that the current model is perhaps not the right model for these data, and other approaches ought to be considered.[4]

CONCLUDING REMARKS

We proposed a DFA model with random components for examining the dynamics of affective processes in dyads. We showed that our indicators of emotional experience have a robust factorial structure over time and show reliable dynamics both within and across individuals in dyads. Finally, we showed that such dynamics

of affective processes vary substantially across dyads, with large effects for some and weak or imperceptible effects for other dyads. We hope that this approach supports the idea of examining dyadic interactions in dynamic terms.

ACKNOWLEDGMENTS

This work was supported in part by grants from the National Science Foundation (Nos. BCS-05-27766 and BCS-08-27021) and the National Institutes of Health–National Institute of Neurological Disorders and Stroke (No. R01 NS057146-01) to Emilio Ferrer, and by a Dissertation Support Award from the Society of Multivariate Experimental Psychology to Hairong Song. We appreciate the help by Kevin Grimm, Keith Widaman, and Robert Shumway, and the members of the DDIP Lab at the University of California, Davis.

NOTES

1. Although not shown in Figure 35.1, an error covariance structure is specified so that the unique variances of specific manifest variables are allowed to covary across measurement occasions.
2. The WinBUGS program and its manual can be freely downloaded from the website *http://www.mrc-bsu.cam.ac.uk/bugs/*.
3. All syntax codes for the analyses are available at the handbook's website (*www.handbookofsem.com*). Also see Song and Ferrer (in press) for some examples of syntax codes.
4. We appreciate an anonymous reviewer for raising these issues.

REFERENCES

Allport, G. W. (1937). *Personality: A psychological interpretation*. New York: Holt, Rinehart & Winston.

Anderson, T. W. (1963). The use of factor analysis in the statistical analysis of time series. *Psychometrika, 28,* 1–25.

Browne, M. W., & Nesselroade, J. R. (2005). Representing psychological processes with dynamic factor models: Some promising uses and extensions of ARMA time series models. In A. Maydeu-Olivares & J. J. McArdle (Eds.), *Advances in psychometrics: A festschrift to Roderick P. McDonald* (pp. 415–451). Mahwah, NJ: Erlbaum.

Browne, M. W., & Zhang, G. (2007). Developments in the factor analysis of individual time series. In R. Cudeck & R. C. MacCallum (Eds.), *Factor analysis at 100: Historical developments and future directions* (pp. 265–291). Mahwah, NJ: Erlbaum.

Cattell, R. B. (1963). The structuring of change by P-technique and incremental R-technique. In C. W. Harris (Ed.), *Problems in measuring change* (pp. 167–198). Madison: University of Wisconsin Press.

Cattell, R. B. (1966). Patterns of change: Measurement in relation to state-dimension, trait change, lability, and process concepts. In R. B. Cattell (Ed.), *Handbook of multivariate experimental psychology* (pp. 355–402). Chicago: Rand McNally.

Cattell, R. B., Cattell, A. K. S., & Rhymer, R. M. (1947). P-technique demonstrated in determining psychophysical source traits in a normal individual. *Psychometrika, 12*, 267–288.

Chow, S.-M., Nesselroade, J. R., Shifren, K., & McArdle, J. J. (2004). Dynamic structure of emotions among individuals with Parkinson's disease. *Structural Equation Modeling, 11*, 560–582.

Cranford, J. A., Shrout, P. E., Iida, M., Rafaeli, E., Yip, T., & Bolger, N. (2006). A procedure for evaluating sensitivity to within-person change: Can mood measures in diary studies detect change reliably? *Personality and Social Psychology Bulletin, 32*, 917–929.

Engle, R., & Watson, M. (1981). A one-factor multivariate time series model of metropolitan wage rates. *Journal of American Statistical Association, 76*, 774–781.

Ferrer, E. (2006). Application of dynamic factor analysis to affective processes in dyads. In A. D. Ong & M. van Dulmen (Eds.), *Handbook of methods in positive psychology* (pp. 41–58). Oxford, UK: Oxford University Press.

Ferrer, E., & Nesselroade, J. R. (2003). Modeling affective processes in dyadic relations via dynamic factor analysis. *Emotion, 3*, 344–360.

Ferrer, E., & Widaman, K. F. (2008). Dynamic factor analysis of dyadic affective processes with inter-group differences. In N. A. Card, J. Selig, & T. Little (Eds.), *Modeling interdependent developmental data* (pp. 107–137). Mahwah, NJ: Erlbaum.

Ferrer, E., & Zhang, G. (2009). Time series models for examining psychological processes: Applications and new developments. In R. E. Millsap & A. Maydeu-Olivares (Eds.), *Handbook of quantitative methods in psychology* (pp. 637–657). London: Sage.

Hamaker, E. L., Dolan, C. V., & Molenaar, P. C. M. (2005). Statistical modeling of the individual: Rationale and application of multivariate stationary time series analysis. *Multivariate Behavioral Research, 40*, 207–233.

Hamaker, E. L., Nesselroade, J. J., & Molenaar, P. C. M. (2007). The integrated trait–state model. *Journal of Research in Personality, 41*, 295–315.

Jones, C. J., & Nesselroade, J. R. (1990). Multivariate, replicated, single-subject, repeated measures designs and P-technique factor analysis: A review of intraindividual change studies. *Experimental Aging Research, 16*, 171–183.

Lamiell, J. T. (1981). Toward an idiothetic psychology of personality. *American Psychologist, 36*, 276–289.

Molenaar, P. C. M. (1985). A dynamic factor model for the analysis of multivariate time series. *Psychometrika, 50*, 181–202.

Molenaar, P. C. M. (2004). A manifesto on psychology as idiographic science: Bringing the person back into scientific psychology—this time forever. *Measurement, 2*, 201–218.

Molenaar, P. C. M., & Valsiner, J. (2005). How generalization works through the single case: A simple idiographic process analysis of an individual psychotherapy. *International Journal of Idiographic Science*, Article 1. Retrieved October 18, 2005, from *http://www.valsiner.com/articles/molenvals.htm.*

Nesselroade, J. R. (2001). Intraindividual variability in development within and between individuals. *European Psychologist, 6*, 187–193.

Nesselroade, J. R. (2002). Elaborating the different in differential psychology. *Multivariate Behavioral Research, 37*, 543–561.

Nesselroade, J. R. (2007). Factoring at the individual level: Some matters for the second century of factor analysis. In R. Cudeck & R. C. MacCallum (Eds.), *Factor analysis at 100: Historical developments and future directions* (pp. 249–264). Mahwah, NJ: Erlbaum.

Nesselroade, J. R., & Ford, D. H. (1985). P-technique comes of age: Multivariate, replicated, single-subject designs for research on older adults. *Research on Aging, 7*, 46–80.

Nesselroade, J. R., Gerstorf, D., Hardy, S. A., & Ram, N. (2007). Idiographic filters for psychological constructs. *Measurement, 5*, 217–235.

Nesselroade, J. R., McArdle, J. J., Aggen, S. H., & Meyer, J. M. (2002). Alternative dynamic factor models for multivariate time-series analyses. In D. M. Moscowitz & S. L. Hershberger (Eds.), *Modeling intraindividual variability with repeated measures data: Advances and techniques* (pp. 235–265). Mahwah, NJ: Erlbaum.

Nesselroade, J. R., & Molenaar, P. C. M. (1999). Pooling lagged covariance structures based on short, multivariate time-series for dynamic factor analysis. In R. H. Hoyle (Ed.), *Statistical strategies for small sample research* (pp. 224–250). Newbury Park, CA: Sage.

Rovine, M. J., & Walls, T. A. (2006). Multilevel autoregressive modeling of interindividual differences in the stability of a process. In T. A. Walls & J. L. Schafer (Eds.), *Models for intensive longitudinal data* (pp. 124–147). New York: Oxford University Press.

Russell, R., Bryant, F., & Estrada, A. (1996). Confirmatory P-technique analysis of therapist discourse: High- versus low-quality child therapy sessions. *Journal of Consulting and Clinical Psychology, 64*, 1366–1376.

Shifren, K., Wood, P., Hooker, K., & Nesselroade, J. R. (1997). Structure and variation of mood in individuals with Parkinson's disease: A dynamic factor analysis. *Psychology and Aging, 12*, 328–339.

Song, H., & Ferrer, E. (2012). Bayesian estimation of random coefficient dynamic factor models. *Multivariate Behavioral Research, 47*, 26–60.

Spiegelhalter, D. J., Thomas, A., Best, N. G., Gilks, W. R., & Lunn, D. (2003). *BUGS: Bayesian inference using Gibbs sampling.* Cambridge, UK: MRC Biostatistics Unit. Available online at *www.mrc-bsu.cam.ac.uk/bugs/.*

Steele, J., & Ferrer, E. (2011). Latent differential equation modeling of self-regulatory and coregulatory affective processes. *Multivariate Behavioral Research, 46*, 956–984.

Wood, P., & Brown, D. (1994). The study of intraindividual differences by means of dynamic factor models: Rationale, implementation, and interpretation. *Psychological Bulletin, 116*, 166–186.

Zhang, Z., Hamaker, E. L., & Nesselroade, J. R. (2008). Comparisons of four methods for estimating dynamic factor models. *Structural Equation Modeling, 15*, 377–402.

Zhang, Z., & Nesselroade J. R. (2007). Bayesian estimation of categorical dynamic factor models. *Multivariate Behavioral Research, 42*, 729–756.

CHAPTER 36

Structural Equation Modeling in Genetics

Sanja Franić
Conor V. Dolan
Denny Borsboom
Dorret I. Boomsma

Our aim in the present chapter is to discuss structural equation modeling (SEM[1]) as applied in human quantitative genetics. Taking the seminal paper by Martin and Eaves (1977) as a starting point, the genetic analysis of covariance structures spans a period of over 30 years (see Hottenga & Boomsma, 2008, for a brief history). Martin and Eaves is the first published account of genetic covariance structure modeling (GCSM) using maximum likelihood (ML) estimation in SEM. Although Martin and Eaves used their own programs to fit multivariate twin models, it was soon realized that the LISREL program (Jöreskog & Sörbom, 2006) could be used to fit genetic models (Boomsma & Molenaar, 1986; Cantor, 1983; Fulker, Baker, & Bock, 1983). The adoption of the LISREL program cemented the view of quantitative genetic modeling as a class of SEM of data observed in family members. In addition, it encouraged the applications of multivariate models developed in SEM (e.g., the common factor, simplex, and growth curve models), and it inspired geneticists to develop their own models. Finally, the incorporation of SEM in genetic modeling resulted in the development of Mx, a SEM program with a flexible matrix syntax, which is well suited to the data structures and modeling requirements of GCSM (Boker et al., 2010; Neale, 2000).

In the present chapter we introduce GCSM, as applied in the classical twin design. We first present the basic method of exploiting familial relationships to infer the effects of unmeasured genetic and environmental factors. We then emphasize that any SEM can be incorporated in GCSM of twin data to study the structures of the genetic and environmental covariances matrices. Next, we discuss several models developed specifically in GCSM, including models that require data collected in twins, pedigrees, or adoption designs for identification. Finally, we briefly discuss the recent incorporation of measured genetic variables in GCSM-based association analyses.

GCSM

A principal aim of GCSM (Boomsma, Martin, & Neale, 1989; Eaves, Last, Young, & Martin, 1978; Martin & Eaves, 1977; Neale & Cardon, 1992) is to estimate the contributions of genetic and environmental variables to individual differences in one or more measured variables (i.e., phenotypes). If the genetic and environmental variables are unobserved (latent), their effects are inferred from resemblance among family members in a SEM. However, measured environmental and (or) genetic variables may also be modeled directly (e.g., Cherny, 2008; van den Oord, 2000).

To infer the contributions of unmeasured genetic and environmental variables to the phenotypic variance, quantitative geneticists employ a number of designs, which include individuals in known genetic and environmental relations (Falconer & Mackay, 1996; Mather & Jinks, 1971). Samples of such individuals are called "genetically informative" because, given various assumptions, genetic and environmental effects are identified in the associated phenotypic covariance structures. The classical twin design, which involves the analysis of phenotypes measured in monozygotic (MZ) and dizygotic (DZ) twins living together, is the best known of such designs (Boomsma, Busjahn, & Peltonen, 2002), but others, such as the adoption design, also achieve identification in GCSM.

In GCSM, different classes of genetic and environmental variables are distinguished. A polygenic factor represents the total effects of multiple, possibly very many, genes. A "gene" refers to a unit of heredity that resides on a stretch of DNA and codes for a protein or for an RNA chain. Genes are situated at a given chromosomal region, referred to as a "locus." If the gene influences a complex (or a quantitative) trait, the location is referred to as a "quantitative trait locus" (QTL). To contribute to phenotypic variation, a gene has to be "polymorphic"; that is, different forms of the gene (i.e., different alleles) must exist. The combination of alleles at a locus determines the effect of the gene (Evans, Gillespie, & Martin, 2002; Slagboom & Meulenbelt, 2002). We distinguish between additive polygenic variable(s) (A), which represent the combined additive effects of alleles within and across loci, and genetic dominance variable(s) (D), which represent intralocus allelic interaction effects. One can also consider interactions between loci (interlocus nonlinear effects, i.e., epistasis), although in practice such effects are hard to resolve in the nonexperimental designs typically used in GCSM. With respect to environmental effects, environmental effects that are shared by family members (shared environment; C) and individual-specific environmental effects (unshared environment; E) are distinguished. In the classical twin design, the latter contribute to the phenotypic differences between the twins, and the former contribute to resemblance between the twins. Note that environmental influences are defined in terms of their *effect*. For instance, twins may be exposed to the shared event of parental divorce,

but the effects of divorce on the individual twin pair members may differ. Thus, a shared event can have a specific (unshared) consequence that will contribute to what is interpreted as specific or unshared environmental effects.

The identification of model parameters in GCSM is achieved by incorporating in the model the information on the degree of genetic and environmental relatedness among different types of relatives (Evans et al., 2002; Falconer & Mackay, 1996; Mather & Jinks, 1971). In the classical twin design, the sample consists of MZ and DZ twin pairs. DZ twins share an average of 50% of their polymorphic (also termed "segregating") genes, and MZ twins share 100% of their genetic material, as they arise from a single fertilized egg. This information is used in model specification as follows: The A factors correlate 1 in MZ twins and .5 in DZ twins, while the D factors correlate 1 in MZ twins and .25 in DZ twins (Falconer & Mackay, 1996). Shared environmental factors (C) correlate unity across twins, regardless of zygosity, and unshared environmental factors (E) correlate zero.[2]

All designs in GCSM include specific assumptions and limitations. For instance, in the classical twin design, a model including effects of A, C, D, and E is not identified. Researchers must therefore limit their comparisons to submodels including three of the four sources of individual differences, i.e., an ACE or ADE model (or submodels thereof). The DE model is biologically implausible (Falconer & Mackay, 1996). The twin design involves many further assumptions, some of which are mentioned below. For an exhaustive treatment we refer the reader to the literature (e.g., Carey, 2009; Plomin, Defries, McClearn, & McGuffin, 2008).

GCSM BASED ON THE TWIN DESIGN

GCSM based on the classical twin design can be used to analyze univariate and multivariate data. In the univariate case, the phenotypic measure is regressed on the genetic and environmental variables. For instance, the univariate ACE model can be expressed as

$$P_{ij} = t + a*A_{ij} + c*C_{ij} + e*E_{ij} \qquad (36.1)$$

where P_{ij} is the continuous phenotypic measure observed in the jth member (j = 1,2) of the ith twin pair. The genetic (A) and environmental variables (C and E) are unobserved, and as such are subject to standard identifying scaling constraints: The variances are fixed to unity, and the means are fixed to zero. The parameter t represents the intercept (i.e., given the scaling constraints, the mean of the phenotype). We assume the phenotypic means of the twin pair members are equal (a testable assumption of the twin model). The parameters a, c, and e represent regression coefficients that express the effects of the A, C, and E factors on the phenotype.

Figure 36.1 depicts two examples of a univariate model for twin data. Assuming the variables have been centered, we can drop the intercept t from the path diagrams. The path diagrams graphically convey some of the assumptions associated with the twin model. For instance, barring the correlations as depicted, the A, C (D), and E variables are uncorrelated within and between twin pair members. The zero correlations between A and D, and between E and C follow from their definitions. However, certain correlations (e.g., between A and E, or A and C) are fixed to zero by assumptions (not by any substantive theory). Any violation of such assumptions will bias estimates in the model (e.g., Purcell, 2002). Note also that absence of any interaction among the latent variables is assumed.[3] Expressing the ACE model for the mean-centered observations in matrix notation we have

$$\mathbf{P}_i = \Lambda\eta_i \tag{36.2}$$

where i represents twin pair, $\mathbf{P}_i^t = [P_{i1} \; P_{i2}]$,

$$\Lambda = \begin{bmatrix} a & c & e & 0 & 0 & 0 \\ 0 & 0 & 0 & a & c & e \end{bmatrix} \tag{36.3}$$

and $\eta_i^t = [A_1 \; C_1 \; E_1 \; A_2 \; C_2 \; E_2]_i$. The expected covariance matrix is $\Sigma = E[\mathbf{P}_i \; \mathbf{P}_i^t] = E[\Lambda\eta_i\eta_i^t\Lambda^t] = \Lambda E[\eta_i\eta_i^t]\Lambda^t = \Lambda\Psi\Lambda^t$, where the correlation matrix of the latent variables is denoted Ψ. The correlation matrix Ψ includes the expected correlations among $\eta_i^t = [A_1 \; C_1 \; E_1 \; A_2 \; C_2 \; E_2]$:

$$\Psi = \begin{bmatrix} 1 & & & & & \\ 0 & 1 & & & & \\ 0 & 0 & 1 & & & \\ \rho_k & 0 & 0 & 1 & & \\ 0 & 1 & 0 & 0 & 1 & \\ 0 & 0 & 0 & 0 & 0 & 1 \end{bmatrix} \tag{36.4}$$

where ρ_k is the correlation between the twins' additive polygenic factors, that is, unity in MZ twins and .5 in DZ twins (the k subscript denotes zygosity). As Ψ differs over zygosity, we require a separate model for MZ and DZ twins (i.e., $\Sigma_{mz} = \Lambda\Psi_{mz}\Lambda^t$ and $\Sigma_{dz} = \Lambda\Psi_{dz}\Lambda^t$). The actual structures of the 2×2 phenotypic covariance matrices are:

$$\Sigma_k = \begin{bmatrix} \sigma_{k11}^2 & \sigma_{k12}^2 \\ \sigma_{k21}^2 & \sigma_{k22}^2 \end{bmatrix} = \begin{bmatrix} a^2 + c^2 + e^2 & \rho_{Ak}a^2 + c^2 \\ \rho_{Ak}a^2 + c^2 & a^2 + c^2 + e^2 \end{bmatrix} \tag{36.5}$$

where k denotes zygosity, and the additive polygenic correlation ρ_{Ak} is 1 in MZ and .5 in DZ twins. The stan-

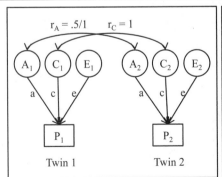
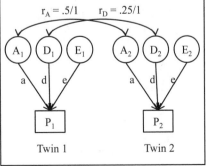

FIGURE 36.1. An ACE (left) and an ADE (right) univariate genetic factor model.

dardized decomposition of variance is a^2/σ^2, c^2/σ^2, and e^2/σ^2, where σ^2 equals the total phenotypic variance (note $\sigma^2 = \sigma^2_{11} = \sigma^2_{22}$). The component a^2/σ^2 is commonly called the "narrow-sense heritability." In the ADE model $(a^2 + d^2)/\sigma^2$, the proportion of total genetic effects, is called the "broad-sense heritability."

Application of the univariate twin model has provided important insights into the structure of individual differences in a variety of psychological phenotypes such as personality, cognitive abilities, and psychopathology. For instance, it is now clear that C plays a minor role in determining individual differences on personality dimensions. Furthermore, the role of C in general intelligence is considerable in young children, but with increasing age, the role of C wanes, while that of A waxes. By young adulthood, the heritability of general intelligence is as high as .7, while shared environmental influences are no longer discernible (e.g., Bartels, Rietveld, van Baal, & Boomsma, 2002; Boomsma et al., 2002).

As demonstrated originally by Martin and Eaves (1977), a powerful feature of GCSM lies in the possibility to analyze multivariate phenotypes. Two examples of a multivariate ACE twin model are depicted in Figure 36.2. First consider the model on the right. While we have dropped the C factors from the model to avoid

clutter in the figure, we include C in the following representation of the model:

$$\mathbf{P}_i = \Lambda \eta_i \tag{36.6}$$

where i represents twin pair, $\mathbf{P}_i^t = [P_{i11}\ P_{i21}\ P_{i31}\ P_{i12}\ P_{i22}\ P_{i32}]_i$,

$$\Lambda = \begin{bmatrix} \Lambda_A & \Lambda_C & \Lambda_E & 0 & 0 & 0 \\ 0 & 0 & 0 & \Lambda_A & \Lambda_C & \Lambda_E \end{bmatrix} \tag{36.7}$$

and

$$\eta_i' = [A_{11}\ A_{21}\ A_{31}\ C_{11}\ C_{21}\ C_{31}\ E_{11}\ E_{21}\ E_{31}\ A_{12}\ A_{22}\ A_{32}\ C_{12}\ C_{22}\ C_{32}\ E_{12}\ E_{22}\ E_{32}] \tag{36.8}$$

Now, the 3×3 matrix Λ_a contains the regression coefficients in the regression of the phenotypes on the additive genetic factors (Λ_C and Λ_E are defined analogously):

$$\Lambda_a = \begin{bmatrix} a_{11} & 0 & 0 \\ a_{21} & a_{22} & 0 \\ a_{31} & a_{32} & a_{33} \end{bmatrix} \tag{36.9}$$

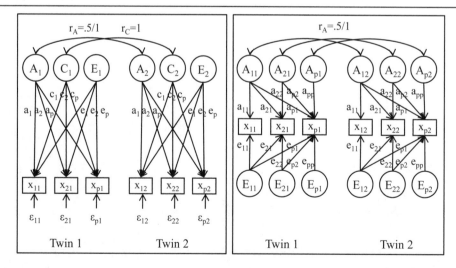

FIGURE 36.2. Multivariate genetic factor models with single (left) and multiple (right) genetic and environmental factors.

The implied phenotypic covariance matrices can be expressed as $\Sigma_{mz} = \Lambda\Psi_{mz}\Lambda^t$ and $\Sigma_{dz} = \Lambda\Psi_{dz}\Lambda^t$, where

$$\Sigma_k = \begin{bmatrix} \Sigma_{k11} & \Sigma_{k12} \\ \Sigma_{k21} & \Sigma_{k22} \end{bmatrix}$$

$$= \begin{bmatrix} \Lambda_A\Lambda_A' + \Lambda_C\Lambda_C' + \Lambda_E\Lambda_E' & \rho_{Ak}\Lambda_A\Lambda_A' + \Lambda_C\Lambda_C' \\ \rho_{Ak}\Lambda_A\Lambda_A' + \Lambda_C\Lambda_C' & \Lambda_A\Lambda_A' + \Lambda_C\Lambda_C' + \Lambda_E\Lambda_E' \end{bmatrix}$$

$$(36.10)$$

and k, as above, denotes zygosity. Given p phenotypes, Σ_{k11} (Σ_{k22}) is the expected $p \times p$ phenotypic covariance matrix of twin 1 (twin 2), and Σ_{k12} is the expected $p \times p$ twin 1 – twin 2 phenotypic cross-covariance matrix.

It is important to note that in the right panel of Figure 36.2, the phenotypic covariance matrix Σ_{11} (Σ_{22}) is decomposed into covariance matrices $\Sigma_A = \Lambda_A\Lambda_A'$, $\Sigma_C = \Lambda_C\Lambda_C'$, and $\Sigma_E = \Lambda_E\Lambda_E'$, where Λ_A (shown in Equation 36.9), Λ_C, and Λ_E are lower triangular matrices. This triangular decomposition has the advantage that the sum of the underlying covariance matrices ($\Sigma_A + \Sigma_C + \Sigma_E$) yields a covariance matrix that is almost certainly positive definite (Neale & Cardon, 1992). Beyond this restriction, the underlying covariance matrices are not modeled. However, the covariance matrices Σ_A, Σ_C, and Σ_E may themselves be subjected to covariance structure modeling. That is, we can specify any model for each of the covariance matrices underlying the phenotypic covariance matrix. For example, see the left panel of Figure 36.2, where we have introduced common A, C, and E factors, and residuals that represent the effects of error and phenotype-specific environment. The model for the unshared environmental effects is now a standard factor model (Lawley & Maxwell, 1971), that is, $\Sigma_E = \Lambda_E\Psi_E\Lambda_E' + \Theta_E$. The path diagram is overly simple (e.g., genetic and shared environmental residuals may be added), but it illustrates the principle of modeling the genetic and environmental covariance matrices.

EXAMPLES OF GCSM BASED ON THE TWIN DESIGN

By multivariate GCSM, we obtain the decomposition of covariances among the phenotypes, and thus insight into the cause of phenotypic covariation. For instance, phenotypic measures of depression and anxiety covary quite considerably (Angold, Costello, & Erkanli, 1999;

Brady & Kendall, 1992). Multivariate GCSM has been used to estimate the contributions of genetic and environmental factors to the phenotypic covariance (e.g., Hettema, Prescott, & Kendler, 2004; Kendler, Heath, Martin, & Eaves, 1987). Interestingly, from these analyses it appears that the distinction between anxiety and depression is not a function of genetic differences, since the additive genetic factors that underlie anxiety and depression are hardly separable; rather, the distinction between these disorders appears to be driven by the unique environmental covariance structure. GCSM has also been used to study the genetic and environmental contributions to the intercorrelations among cognitive ability tests (e.g., subtests of the Wechsler Adult Intelligence Scale [WAIS] or the Wechsler Intelligence Scale for Children [WISC]). For instance, the phenotypic covariance structure of the WAIS can be represented by a hierarchical factor model with three or four first-order factors, and a second-order general factor. Rijsdijk, Vernon, and Boomsma (2002) found that the underlying additive genetic influences resembled the hierarchical phenotypic structure, while the structure of the underlying unshared environmental influences resembled a single-factor model.

Both growth curve and simplex models have been applied to study the roles of genetic and environmental factors in development (Figure 36.3). Applied phenotypically, growth curve models are used to study individual differences in growth curves by regressing repeated measures on the (appropriately coded) time index. Often, a polynomial regression model is used, which may include higher-order components to accommodate nonlinearity (see Neale & McArdle, 2000, for other nonlinear models). A simple linear model may be conveyed as $X_{it} = I_i + t*S_i + \varepsilon_{it}$, where X_{it} is the phenotypic measure of subject i at occasion t ($t = 0, 1, 2, \ldots$), I is the random intercept, and S is the random slope (Figure 36.3). The phenotypic mean at occasion t is $E(X_t) = E(I) + t*E(S)$. In a growth curve model, regression coefficients (S and I) are random over subjects, which allows for individual differences in the form of the growth curve. Therefore, the covariance matrix of interest is

$$\Psi = \begin{bmatrix} \sigma_I^2 & \sigma_{IS} \\ \sigma_{IS} & \sigma_S^2 \end{bmatrix} \qquad (36.11)$$

Using GCSM, this covariance matrix can be decomposed into genetic and environmental components (e.g., $\Psi = \Psi_A + \Psi_C + \Psi_E$), which provides a window on the

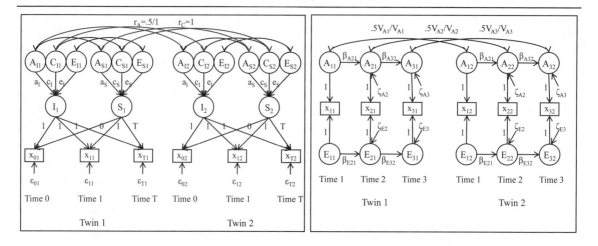

FIGURE 36.3. A linear growth curve (left) and a simplex AE (right) genetic covariance structure model.

role of genetic and environmental factors in growth or decline (e.g., McArdle, 1986). A notable area of application of growth curve modeling is that of age-related changes in cognitive abilities (e.g., McArdle, Prescott, Hamagami, & Horn, 1998; Reynolds, Finkel, Gatz, & Pedersen, 2002; Reynolds et al., 2005), especially with regard to cognitive decline. Multiple studies of aging have demonstrated, for instance, that additive genetic factors account for most of the variance in intercept (or level) in adults age 50 or older, whereas the rate of change (decline) is primarily affected by unshared environmental factors (e.g., Reynolds et al., 2002). The model has also been applied in other areas, such as personality, psychopathology (e.g., Burt, McGue, Carter, & Iacono, 2007; Kendler et al., 2007), and health research (e.g., Hjelmborg et al., 2008).

An alternative approach to the analysis of repeated measures is provided by the simplex model, which is used to assess stability over time, by regressing the data at occasion t ($t = 1, \ldots, T$) on data at the preceding occasion ($t - 1$) (Boomsma & Molenaar, 1987; Eaves, Long, & Heath, 1986; Hewitt, Eaves, Neale, & Meyer, 1988). The simplex model is depicted in Figure 36.3. To ease presentation we limit the model to additive genetic (A) and unshared environmental influences (E). In this model, the phenotypic variable X measured at time point t, X_t, is related to the additive genetic and unshared environmental factors A_t and E_t

($t = 1, \ldots, T$). Simplex models, or first-order autoregressions, are specified to account for the stability and change at the level of the A_t and E_t. For instance, for the unshared environmental part, the autoregression is $E_t = \beta_{Et,t-1} * E_{t-1} + \zeta_{Ei}$, and the implied decomposition of variance is $\beta_{Et,t-1}^2 \sigma_{Ei-1}^2 + \sigma_{\zeta Et}^2$. The simplex model has been applied extensively in GCSM. For a study of repeatedly measured full-scale IQ at ages 5, 7, 10, and 12, see Bartels and colleagues (2002). Hoekstra, Bartels, and Boomsma (2007) applied the model to repeatedly measured verbal and nonverbal IQ tests administered at five occasions from ages 5 to 18 (see also Bishop et al., 2003; Eaves et al., 1986; Petrill, Lipton, Hewitt, & Plomin, 2004; Rietveld, Dolan, van Baal, & Boomsma, 2003). Generally, these studies found that the observed temporal stability in cognitive performance was due to a single common genetic factor, and a common shared environmental factor. The latter declined in effect over the years, such that it was all but absent in early adulthood. In addition, age-specific additive genetic factors emerged at different ages (i.e., $\sigma_{\zeta At}^2 \neq 0$), partly accounting for the lack of complete temporal stability. The genetic simplex model has also been applied in other domains, such as personality (e.g., Gillespie, Evans, Wright, & Martin, 2004; Pedersen & Reynolds, 1998) and psychopathology (e.g., Boomsma, van Beijsterveldt, Bartels, & Hudziak, 2008; Gillespie, Kirk, et al., 2004).

SEM DEVELOPED WITHIN GENETICS

The examples of GCSM we have discussed essentially involve the simultaneous estimation and modeling of the covariance matrices Σ_A, Σ_C (or Σ_D), and Σ_E. The fact that these matrices may be subjected to any identified SEM resulted in the full-scale adoption of SEM in GCSM. However, the twin design itself and its various extensions (e.g., the use of parental ratings of the twins) posed modeling challenges and provided unique modeling possibilities. We now discuss several models that were developed in GCSM of twin data. These models include (1) the common and independent pathway factor models, (2) moderation models, (3) sex interaction models, and (4) direction of causality models.

Factor Models: Common Pathway and Independent Pathway Models

With regard to the relationship between the genetic and environmental factors on the one hand, and the observed phenotypes on the other, two kinds of factor models may be distinguished: the common pathway model (Kendler et al., 1987; McArdle & Goldsmith, 1990) and the independent pathway model. In the common pathway model, depicted in the left panel of Figure 36.4, the influences of A, C (or D), and E on the pheno-

types are mediated by a latent phenotype, represented by the common factors P_1 and P_2 in Figure 36.4. In this model, the factors P_1 and P_2 generally have substantive interpretations (e.g., neuroticism or verbal intelligence). The latent phenotypes mediate the genetic and environmental effects, as the path from the A, C, and E factors to the observed phenotypes runs via the latent phenotype. In the common pathway model, the observed variables may be interpreted as indicators of the latent phenotype (Mellenbergh, 1994).

In the independent pathway model (Kendler et al., 1987), or the biometric factors model (McArdle & Goldsmith, 1990), the common factors A, C, and E influence the phenotypes directly; there is no mediating phenotypic common factor. A simple instance of this model is shown in the right panel of Figure 36.4. We can convey the common pathway model as

$$\Sigma_{k11} = \Sigma_{k22} = \Lambda\Psi\Lambda^t + \Theta_{cp} = \Lambda(\Psi_A + \Psi_C + \Psi_E)\Lambda^t + \Theta_{cp}$$
$$= \Lambda(\Gamma_A\Phi_A\Gamma_A^t + \Gamma_C\Phi_C\Gamma_C^t + \Gamma_E\Phi_E\Gamma_E^t)\,\Lambda^t + \Theta_{cp} \quad \textbf{(36.12)}$$
$$\Sigma_{k21} = \Lambda(\rho_{Ak}\Psi_A + \Psi_C)\,\Lambda^t + \Theta_{cp21}$$
$$= \Lambda(\rho_{Ak}\Gamma_A\Phi_A\Gamma_A^t + \Gamma_C\Phi_C\Gamma_C^t)\,\Lambda^t + \Theta_{cp21}$$

and the independent pathway model as

$$\Sigma_{k11} = \Sigma_{22} = \Lambda_A\Phi_A\Lambda_A^t + \Lambda_C\Phi_C\Lambda_C^t + \Lambda_E\Phi_E\Lambda_E^t + \Theta_{ip} \quad \textbf{(36.13)}$$
$$\Sigma_{k21} = \rho_{Ak}\Lambda_A\Phi_A\Lambda_A^t + \Lambda_C\Phi_C\Lambda_C^t + \Theta_{ip21}$$

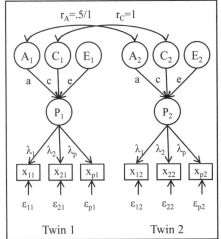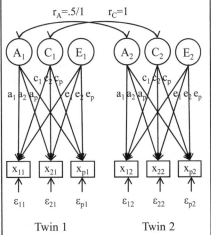

FIGURE 36.4. A common pathway (left) and an independent pathway (right) genetic factor model.

Here, Φ_A, Φ_C, and Φ_E are the covariance matrices of the A, C, and E factors, respectively. In the common pathway model, the covariance matrix of the psychometric factor, Ψ, equals $\Psi_A + \Psi_C + \Psi_E$ (i.e., $\Gamma_A\Phi_A\Gamma_A{}^t + \Gamma_C\Phi_C\Gamma_C{}^t + \Gamma_E\Phi_E\Gamma_E{}^t$), where Γ_A, Γ_C, and Γ_E are the vectors of factor loadings. The Λ (in the common pathway model) and Λ_A, Λ_C, and Λ_E (in the independent pathway model) vectors contain the factor loadings of the indicators on the psychometric factor, and on the biometric (A, C, and E) factors, respectively. Note that in both models the matrices Θ (denoted Θ_{cp} and Θ_{ip}, as they may vary over the models) contain the residuals of the indicators in the model. By considering two phenotypes ($x_{j1}, j = 1, 2$) in the common pathway model

$$
\begin{aligned}
X_1 &= \lambda_1 (aA_1 + cC_1 + eE_1) + \varepsilon_{11} \\
&= \lambda_1 aA_1 + \lambda_1 cC_1 + \lambda_1 eE_1 + \varepsilon_{11} \\
X_{21} &= \lambda_2 (aA_1 + cC_1 + eE_1) + \varepsilon_{21} \\
&= \lambda_2 aA_1 + \lambda_2 cC_1 + \lambda_2 eE_1 + \varepsilon_{21}
\end{aligned}
\tag{36.14}
$$

and the independent pathway model

$$
\begin{aligned}
X_{11} &= a_1 A_1 + c_1 C_1 + e_1 E_1 + \varepsilon_{11} \\
X_{21} &= a_2 A_1 + c_2 C_1 + e_2 E_1 + \varepsilon_{21}
\end{aligned}
\tag{36.15}
$$

we note that the common pathway model is nested under the independent pathway model (i.e., that we may derive the common factor model from the independent pathway model by imposing appropriate proportionality constraints on the factor loadings). Specifically, the introduction of the constraints $a_1/a_2 = c_1/c_2 = e_1/e_2$ renders Equations 36.14 and 36.15 equivalent (see also Yung, Thissen, & McLeod, 1999). Hence, restrictions of the common pathway models can be tested using a likelihood ratio test. Such comparisons are particularly useful in addressing methodological issues pertaining to the conceptual status of latent variables (Franić et al., 2011). Specifically, if the independent pathway fits better than the corresponding common pathway model, we may conclude that the genetic and environmental influences on the indicators in the model are not fully mediated by the phenotypic latent variable (i.e., the psychometric factor). If the measured phenotypes are taken as indicators of the phenotypic latent variable, this calls into question the substantive meaning of the phenotypic latent variable. Ideally, if the common factor obtained in a phenotypic analysis represents a substantive unitary construct, and the phenotypes are indicators of this construct, one would expect the genetic

and environmental influences on the indicators of the construct to be mediated by the construct.

The independent pathway model may also be applied in a purely exploratory manner to determine the (possibly different) dimensionalities of the covariance matrices Σ_A, Σ_C (or Σ_D), and Σ_E. For example, Kendler and colleagues (1987) concluded that the dimensionality of anxiety and depression symptoms differs with respect to genetic and environmental factors; while genetic factors appear to represent a unidimensional structure affecting the overall level of symptoms, environmental influences distinctly affect symptoms of anxiety and symptoms of depression, giving rise to the observed phenotypic clustering of the two disorders.

Genotype–Environment Interaction

The possibility of genotype by environment interaction (G × E) is widely recognized in human genetics and, if present, may have a biasing effect on estimates obtained in the standard twin model. We speak of G × E if an environmental variable moderates the genetic effects in the sense that the magnitude of the genetic variance varies over the levels of the moderator. Similarly, a genetic variable (a given genotype) may moderate environmental effects.

The phenotypic variance in the presence of G × E may be expressed as $\sigma^2_P = \sigma^2_G + \sigma^2_E + \sigma^2_{G\times E}$, where $\sigma^2_{G\times E}$ represents variance due to the interaction. In the twin model, the effect of the interaction depends on the exact nature of the interaction (Purcell, 2002). In the ACE twin model, the variance due to $A \times C$ interaction cannot be distinguished from the A variance. Thus $A \times C$ interaction will result in overestimation of the A variance. On the other hand, variance due to $A \times E$ interaction cannot be distinguished from E variance.

Several methods have been proposed to detect interaction in the twin model. Jinks and Fulker (1970) proposed the regression of MZ twin pair differences on MZ twin pair sums (Eaves, 1984; Jinks & Fulker, 1970). In this method, the MZ pair difference is a measure of environmental variability, and the MZ pair mean is measure of the polygenic effects. In the absence of G × E, the environment variability should not depend on the genotypic level (i.e., the regression coefficient should be zero) (see van der Sluis, Dolan, Neale, Boomsma, & Posthuma, 2006, for a related method).

Modeling G × E is relatively easier if one has measured the variable that moderates the genetic effects. Given a measured moderator, G × E can be modeled by fitting the twin model conditional on the moderator (e.g., in a multigroup model, with groups corresponding to the levels of the moderator). One can then test for homogeneity in *A*, *C*, and *E* variance components over the levels the moderator. For instance, Boomsma, de Geus, van Baal, and Koopmans (1999) found that the heritability of disinhibition (a personality trait related to sensation seeking), as estimated in the twin design, depended on whether the twins had a religious upbringing or not. In the latter case the heritability was about .45 (typical for personality traits; Boomsma et al., 2002), but in the former, it was less than .10.

Purcell (2002) proposed a general method to accommodate a measured moderator in the twin model, where the moderator can be any variable (not necessarily environmental; Kendler & Baker, 2007; Plomin et al., 2008; Vinkhuyzen, van der Sluis, de Geus, Boomsma, & Posthuma, 2010; Vinkhuyzen, van der Sluis, & Posthuma, 2011). This method can also accommodate genetic and environmental effects on the moderator itself, and the possible correlation between the moderator and the trait. For instance, parenting style may moderate the heritability of neuroticism in children, but it is quite possible that the parenting style and neuroticism of the children are correlated, either directly (e.g., common genetic influences), or indirectly (e.g., a highly neurotic child elicits a given parenting style).

Purcell's (2002) approach to modeling G × E is depicted in Figure 36.5. We limit the depiction to an *AE*

model to ease presentation. In this model, *M1* (*M2*) is the moderator measured in twin 1 (twin 2), and *T1* (*T2*) is the phenotype of interest measured in twin 1 (twin 2). The models for the moderator M_i and the trait T_i are

$$M_i = [e_m * E_{ci} + a_m A_{ci}]$$
$$T_i = [(e_c + \beta_{ec} * M_i) * E_{ci} + (a_c + \beta_{ac} * M_i) * A_{ci}] \quad \textbf{(36.16)}$$
$$+ [(e_u + \beta_{eu} * M_i) * E_{ui} + (a_u + \beta_{au} * M_i) * A_{ui}]$$

This model accommodates moderation of the covariance between the moderator and the trait [$(e_c + \beta_{ec} * M_i) * E_{ci} + (a_c + \beta_{ac} * M_i) * A_{ci}$] and moderation of the residual [$(e_u + \beta_{eu} * M_i) * E_{ui} + (a_u + \beta_{au} * M_i) * A_{ui}$], and includes the decomposition of the phenotypic variance of the moderator itself. Tests of moderation can be carried out by means of a likelihood ratio test.

This bivariate moderation model describes the relations between *T* and *M* in such detail that computational problems (e.g., sensitivity to starting values, converging problems) may arise, especially if the covariance between trait *T* and moderator *M* is small. In addition, Rathouz, van Hulle, Rodgers, Waldman, and Lahey (2008) have shown that this model sometimes produces spurious moderation effects. An alternative approach is to regress the trait directly on the moderators, without decomposing the variance of the moderator. The moderation of the regression of the trait on its genetic and environmental factors is retained (van der Sluis, Posthuma, & Dolan, 2012).

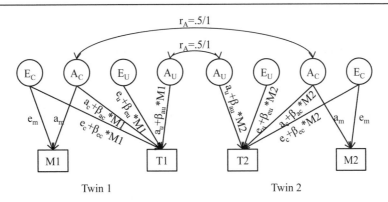

FIGURE 36.5. A G × E model (Purcell, 2002). The model accommodates moderation of the possible covariation between a measured moderator (M) and a phenotype (T), and the moderation of the residual genetic and environmental effects on T. In addition, the model includes the decomposition of the phenotypic variance of moderator itself.

The popularity of the G × E model is evident given its frequent use in twin studies on moderation in the context of, for instance, cognitive abilities (e.g., Bartels, van Beijsterveldt, & Boomsma, 2009), personality (e.g., Brendgen et al., 2009), health (e.g., Johnson & Krueger, 2005), and brain morphology (e.g., Lenroot et al., 2009). This method of handling moderation (i.e., modeling moderation directly on the path parameters of the model) is also used in SEM outside the field of GCSM. Bauer and Hussong (2009) applied it to test whether the parameters in the one-factor model depend on a continuous moderator, or in the present case, a differentiation variable. Molenaar, Dolan, Wicherts, and van der Maas (2010) and Tucker-Drob (2009) used this method to investigate ability differentiation (Spearman, 1927) in the higher-order common-factor model.

Although G × E is frequently discussed in conjunction with genotype–environment correlation (rGE), G × E and rGE represent very different mechanisms. rGE refers to a nonrandom distribution of genotypes over the environments. rGE may arise, for instance, from genetic control of exposure to environmental events (Kendler & Eaves, 1986). Examples of rGE research include, for example, a study by Kendler and Karkowski-Shuman (1997), in which rGE was shown to explain the association between life events and depression. However, not all studies supported this finding (e.g., Middeldorp, Cath, Beem, Willemsen, & Boomsma, 2008).

Sex Interaction in the Twin Model

An important possible moderator of genetic and environmental effects in the twin model is sex. The classical twin design can be broken down by sex; that is, we can distinguish between same-sex pairs (MZ males, DZ males, MZ females, DZ females) and DZ opposite-sex (DZOS) pairs. This extended design, specifically the presence of DZ opposite-sex twins, provides the information to study both qualitative and quantitative sex differences in genetic and environmental effects. Figure 36.6 depicts a partial path diagram of a general sex limitation model (Eaves et al., 1978; Neale & Cardon, 1992), conveying both quantitative and qualitative sex differences. In the former case, the genetic factors are the same, but sex modulates their effects. In the latter case, different genetic factors (different genes) are expressed in men and women. To model quantitative effects, the genetic and environmental correlations (ρ_A and ρ_C) in DZOS twin pairs are constrained to equal those in same-sex DZ twin pairs (.5 and 1, respective-

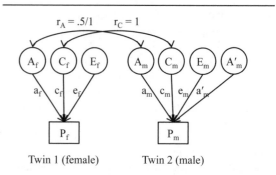

FIGURE 36.6. A general sex-limitation ACE model.

ly), while the genetic and environmental factor loadings (a, c, and e) may differ across the sexes. This covariance structure implies that the A_f (C_f) and A_m (C_m) factors represent sets of genes (environmental influences) common to both sexes, but not necessarily of the same magnitude of effect in males and females. In addition, a sex-specific additive genetic factor (A'_m), uncorrelated with other additive genetic factors in the model, is specified. This factor represents genetic effects unique to the phenotype of one, in this example male, sex. Note that we may also choose to model a sex-specific C factor, but we cannot model both A'_m and C'_m. The model is fitted in a multigroup analysis, in which the parameters pertaining to men are equated across male groups (e.g., MZ males, DZ males, and males from opposite-sex pairs), and the same is done for parameters pertaining to women. As a result, the expectations of variances are equal within, but not necessarily between, the sexes.

Testing for the presence of quantitative and qualitative sex differences may be performed by likelihood ratio tests based on the log-likelihood of the general sex limitation model, and that of its various subset models.

The sex interaction model has been used extensively in various domains of genetics research, such as psychopathology (e.g., Boomsma, van Beijsterveldt, & Hudziak, 2005; Eley & Stevenson, 1999; Rice, Harold, & Thapar, 2002), intelligence (e.g., Bartels et al., 2002), personality (e.g., Eaves, Heath, Neale, Hewitt, & Martin, 1998; Rettew et al., 2006), health and well-being (e.g., Mosing, Pedersen, Martin, & Wright, 2010; Roysamb, Harris, Magnus, Vitterso, & Tambs, 2002; Schousboe et al., 2003), physiological traits (e.g., Weiss, Pan, Abney, & Ober, 2006), and substance abuse research (e.g., Prescott, Aggen, & Kendler, 1999, 2000). These studies generally indicate absence of any substantial sex-related differences. However, there are exceptions. For instance, Eaves and colleagues (1998) found that the relative contribution of nonadditive genetic effects to neuroticism is larger in males. Rettew and colleagues (2006) showed that different genes may produce variation in neuroticism in male and female adolescents.

Direction of Causation Model

So far we have considered models in which the measured phenotypes are dependent variables, and the genetic and environmental variables are independent variables. Twin models in which the measured phenotypes may be related directly (i.e., models in which the phenotypes are not strictly dependent variables) have also been developed. These models include longitudinal models (Eaves et al., 1986), the sibling interaction model (Carey, 1986), and the direction of causality (DOC) model (Heath et al., 1993). The DOC model is interesting from a SEM point of view as this twin model allows one to test hypotheses concerning the direction of causality among two (or more) phenotypes. For instance, a correlation between psychopathology and recall of early childhood environment may be due to a causal influence of the childhood environment on psychopathology ($A \rightarrow B$) or, for instance, to a biasing

effect of current psychopathology on recall of childhood environment ($B \rightarrow A$) (Heath et al., 1993). An instance of a bivariate genetic model with a reciprocal causal relationship between two indicator variables is depicted in Figure 36.7. Note that in this example, the model for trait x is an ADE model, while the model for trait y is a CE model.

The expectations for the cross-relative, cross-trait covariance (CRCTC), that is, the covariance between trait x (y) in relative 1 and trait y (x) in relative 2, derived under this model may be employed to test hypotheses about the direction of causation between the two indicator variables. Specifically, consider the case in which trait x exerts a causal influence on trait y ($x \rightarrow y$). Given that the variances of the latent factors are scaled at 1, the expected covariance structure is

$$\Sigma_{11} = \Sigma_{22} = \begin{matrix} a_x^2 + d_x^2 + e_x^2 & i_{xy}(a_x^2 + d_x^2 + e_x^2) \\ i_{yx}(a_x^2 + d_x^2 + e_x^2) & c_y^2 + e_y^2 + i_y^2(a_x^2 + d_x^2 + e_x^2) \end{matrix}$$

$$\Sigma_{k21} = \Sigma_{k12}{}' = \begin{matrix} r_A a_x^2 + r_D d_x^2 & i_{xy}(r_A a_x^2 + r_D d_x^2) \\ i_{yx}(r_A a_x^2 + r_D d_x^2) & r_C c_y^2 + i_{yx}^2(r_A a_x^2 + r_D d_x^2) \end{matrix}$$

(36.17)

where $i_{yx}(r_A a_x^2 + r_D d_x^2)$ is the expectation for the CRCTC. Conversely, if $y \rightarrow x$, the expected CRCTC can be shown to be $i_{xy} r_C c_y^2$. Given that the CRCTC depends on r_A and r_D if $x \rightarrow y$, and on r_C if $y \rightarrow x$, a comparison of CRCTCs in groups of different degrees

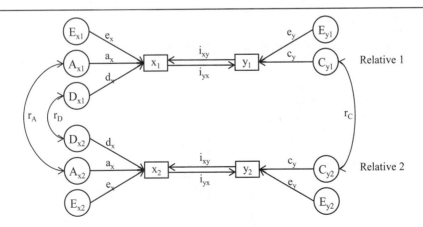

FIGURE 36.7. A bivariate genetic covariance structure model with a reciprocal causal relationship between the two indicator variables (Heath et al., 1993).

of genetic and environmental relatedness is informative about the direction of causality. For instance, if $x \rightarrow y$, CRCTC is positive in biological relatives, but its magnitude will depend on the degree of genetic relatedness. Alternatively, if $y \rightarrow x$, CRCTC will be positive and independent of the degree of genetic relatedness in individuals reared in the same family, and zero in individuals reared in separate families. Family data will, however, only be informative about DOC if the phenotypes have different modes of inheritance (i.e., if the effects of A, C (D), and E differ across the two phenotypes).

In the DOC model depicted in Figure 36.7, the latent genetic and environmental factors affecting each of the two traits are uncorrelated; thus, the *only* mechanism that generates the correlation between traits x and y is the unidirectional causal effect of x on y, or of y on x (or bidirectional causal effects, which may be resolved using models with multiple indicators; Heath et al., 1993). The standard bivariate twin model, in contrast, models the phenotypic correlation between x and y as a function of the underlying genetic and environmental correlations. Given that the DOC model is nested under the general bivariate model (Heath et al., 1993), the fit of both uni- and bidirectional causal models can be compared to that of the general bivariate model by means of a likelihood ratio test.

Thomsen and colleagues (2009) applied this model to data on asthma and severe respiratory syncytial virus (RSV) infection, and found that the high positive association between these phenotypes is not due to RSV causing asthma, but to both phenotypes reflecting a common genetic predisposition. In the area of intelligence research, Luciano and colleagues (2005) showed that the well-established correlation between inspection time (IT; a measure of perceptual discrimination speed) and general cognitive ability is due neither to the efficiency of IT increasing general cognitive ability, nor to general ability affecting IT. Instead, both processes seem to be indicators of common genetic factors. De Moor, Boomsma, Stubbe, Willemsen, and de Geus (2008) used bivariate genetic modeling, analyses of longitudinal data, and intrapair differences in identical twins to show that the association between exercise and symptoms of anxiety and depression is not due to causal effects of (lack of) exercise.

In all models considered here the genetic (or polygenic) factors are featured as latent variables, which represent the action of many polymorphic genes. In the final section of this chapter, we briefly discuss the incorporation of measured genes in genetic association analysis.

ASSOCIATION ANALYSIS

Developments in high-throughput genotyping technologies have enabled geneticists to measure vast amounts of genetic information directly (Slagboom & Meulenbelt, 2002). Consequently, twin and family registries now include measured genotypic material, in the form of genetic markers, alongside phenotypic data. Accordingly, the aim of studies has shifted toward localizing and identifying individual genes that contribute to variation in complex phenotypes (Cherny, 2008; Guo & Adkins, 2008; Vink & Boomsma, 2002). Such genes are generally expected to have a relatively small effect (<1%) and are referred to as quantitative trait loci (QTLs). In this section we outline how information on genetic markers has been incorporated in SEM.

A "genetic marker" is a DNA sequence with a known chromosomal position. This sequence is measurable and is polymorphic; that is, it displays interindividual variation (i.e., there are at least two alleles). The marker may be (part of) a functional gene of interest (i.e., a candidate gene), but that is not necessarily the case. Markers are used in two ways to identify the QTLs that contribute to individual differences in the trait of interest: linkage and association analysis. Both methods hinge on the phenomenon of "cosegregation" (i.e., the fact that DNA variants located closely together on the same chromosome are not inherited independently). This means that a marker can serve as an indicator of functional genes in its chromosomal vicinity. Linkage analysis is carried out in pedigrees, in which long stretches of DNA are shared among family members. Genetic association tests are usually performed in samples of unrelated subjects, either patients (cases) and controls, or subjects who differ phenotypically on a quantitative scale. Although both linkage and association analyses have been incorporated in SEM (e.g., Hottenga & Boomsma, 2008), here we discuss association analysis, as this technique currently dominates gene-hunting enterprises and is characterized by a higher statistical power to identify genes of relatively small effect (see, e.g., Manolio & Collins, 2009).

Distant loci (or loci on different chromosomes) are subject to recombination as a consequence of chromosomal crossing over during meiosis (the formation of gametes). However, when large numbers of markers are genotyped (e.g., typically 0.5 to 1.5 million variants), the chromosomal locations of a QTL and a marker may be so close that configurations of the alleles (i.e., haplotypes) are almost always transmitted from parents to offspring as single units. This means that at the population level a marker allele (say M1 of a marker locus with alleles M1 and M2) almost always forms a haplotype (M1-Q1) with a given allele at a QTL location (say Q1 at a QTL locus with alleles Q1 and Q2). The observed marker allele can therefore serve as an indicator of the QTL allele. The closer the marker is to the QTL on the chromosome (the more tightly they are linked), the more reliable it is as an indicator, as the process of crossing over is less likely. High-resolution microarrays typically assess genetic variants called single nucleotide polymorphisms (SNPs) that have two alleles and whose minor allele frequencies (MAFs) are not extremely low. The reliability of a SNP as an indicator can be expressed in terms of the degree of linkage disequilibrium (i.e., a measure of the extent to which a SNP allele at locus M is predictive of the presence of an allele at locus Q in the population) (Wray & Visscher, 2008).

In the case of a continuous phenotype, association analysis involves the regression of the phenotype on the number of M1 (or M2) alleles observed in each subject (Figure 36.8). If explained variance is statistically significant, the marker itself (say, if it is situated within a candidate gene), or a QTL in the vicinity of the SNP, is associated with the phenotype. Note that this analysis can be carried out in samples of unrelated individuals, if the sample is genotyped across the genome. Given multivariate phenotypes, one can consider a multivariate test. Ferreira and Purcell (2009) considered the power of multivariate analysis of variance (MANOVA) given varying number of phenotypes (5, 10, and 20), a varying number of which were affected by the QTL. They found that the multivariate test was more powerful than univariate tests, with (1) increasing correlations among the phenotypes and (2) increasing number of phenotypes affected (i.e., by the QTL), increasing the power. They noted a sharp loss of power of the multivariate test when all phenotypes were affected by the QTL.

Given multivariate data, one can also consider embedding the test of association in a proper SEM. Medland and Neale (2010) considered single-factor models with three or five indicators in unrelated cases and in sib pairs. They varied the locus of the effect of the QTL in the factor model such that it was part of the

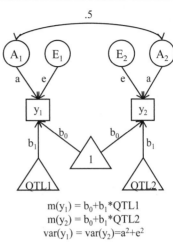

$$m(y_1) = b_0 + b_1 * QTL1$$
$$m(y_2) = b_0 + b_1 * QTL2$$
$$var(y_1) = var(y_2) = a^2 + e^2$$

H-null: $b_1 = 0$

FIGURE 36.8. A genetic association model.

common factor, thus conveying its effect via the factor loadings on all variables, common to all phenotypes, but not conveyed via the factor, or common to some phenotypes but not conveyed via the factor. The main conclusion is that their combined multivariate approach (where the QTL effect is conveyed via the common factor, or the QTL affects the phenotypes directly) was almost universally as powerful as, or, depending on specific circumstances, more powerful than the univariate tests using weighted or unweighted sum scores. Van der Sluis, Verhage, Posthuma, and Dolan (2010) discussed the power to detect the effects of genetic variants in the context of uni- and multidimensional common-factor models, and contrasted the power in these designs to the sum score operationalization when the sum score is not a sufficient statistic (i.e., the sum score entails a loss of information). They showed that the sum score is as powerful as the factor-analytic design only under very specific circumstances. In addition, they discussed how violations of measurement invariance across multiple samples, or with respect to the genetic variant itself, affect the power to detect genetic variants. Violations with respect to the genetic variant itself proved very disadvantageous in both the sum score model and incorrectly specified factor models. Van der Sluis and colleagues considered association tests in factor models fitted to ordinary samples (not genetically informative). Medland and Neale (2010) also considered sib data (e.g., DZ twins), as these allow one to test for "stratification" (i.e., spurious association due to population heterogeneity) (Fulker, Cherney, Sham, & Hewitt, 1999). Minica, Boomsma, van der Sluis, and Dolan (2010) considered the incorporation of the marker information in a variety of SEMs, including the simplex model and the multiple-factor model. They considered both twin samples and ordinary samples. Overall, their results were consistent with those of Medland and Neale (2010) and van der Sluis and colleagues (2010).

Other statistical issues in genetic association studies include the multiple testing problem (e.g., when more than a million SNPs are tested), meta-analyses to combine association tests, and the fact that a statistically significant association is not yet proof of a causal relation between the gene and the phenotype. In addition, rare genetic variants are difficult to hunt down in association tests, and attention has consequently shifted to large sequencing projects.

DISCUSSION

Our aim in this chapter was to discuss SEM as it is applied in human quantitative genetics. We have concentrated on the classical twin design, as this provides a good basis for understanding GCSM. Given its various assumptions, the twin design applied to multivariate phenotypic data provides the information to estimate the genetic and environmental covariance matrices underlying the phenotypic covariance matrix. As we discussed, any SEM that can be fitted to the phenotypic covariance matrix can be fitted to the genetic and environmental covariance matrices. An important fact is that the genetic covariance structure does not necessarily resemble the environmental covariance structure. The phenotypic structure may resemble either or, indeed, neither structure. For instance, Rijsdijk and colleagues (2002), in their analysis of the WAIS, showed that the hierarchical phenotypic structure resembled closely the additive genetic structure, whereas the unshared environmental structure was a single-factor model. One model in which relationships among the genetic, environmental, and phenotypic covariance structures are compared explicitly is the common pathway model (e.g., Franić, et al., under review). This model implies that all three have the same structure (i.e., are isomorphic). This follows from the fact that the phenotypic latent variables mediate the effect of the genetic and environmental factors on the indicators. Interestingly, the isomorphism implied by the common pathway model appears to be the exception rather than the rule. Often, therefore, the phenotypic structure is a function of two qualitatively different underlying structures. The fact that the phenotypic structure is in effect a weighted average of distinct underlying genetic and environmental structures underlines the theoretical importance of GCSM.

In the sections that followed, we reviewed a selection of models developed within genetics and suited specifically to address research questions arising in this particular field (e.g., the possible moderation of genetic and environmental effects on the phenotype, or the DOC between observed variables). The utility of these models is evident given their widespread use in genetics research. However, the classical twin design represents only the most basic design employed in the field, and many extensions to this design are currently in use. These more elaborate designs usually involve adding one or more relatives to the study, which greatly enhances the resolution to detect more subtle effects and increases the assemblage of research questions that may be addressed (for an overview, see, e.g., Boomsma et al., 2002; Truett et al., 1994). For instance, the inclusion of parents of twins allows one to study the effects of social homogamy and cultural transmission (Eaves, Fulker, & Heath, 1989; Rao, Morton, & Yee, 1974) or differential gene expression as a function of age (see, e.g., Snieder, van Doornen, & Boomsma, 1997). Including spouses of twins allows one to study assortative mating (Eaves, 1979; Heath & Eaves, 1985). The inclusion of siblings of twins makes it possible to examine social interactions and special twin effects, such as prenatal hormone transition or shared prenatal environment (see, e.g., Stoel, de Geus, & Boomsma, 2006), and including offspring of MZ twins (who are genetically half-sibs but socially cousins) allows for the study of maternal effects and imprinting (see, e.g., Nance, Kramer, Corey, Winter, & Eaves, 1983). In addition, adding relatives to the twin model results in an increase in power to detect and distinguish between different sources of variation (see also Dolan, Boomsma, & Neale, 1999; Posthuma & Boomsma, 2000).

In this chapter we have focused on continuous outcome measures; however, the possibility to model discrete data using the liability–threshold model (Falconer & Mackay, 1996) has also been developed. The liability-threshold model assumes the discrete phenotype to be a manifestation of an underlying continuous liability distribution, with one or more thresholds imposing a discontinuity on the visible expression. Estimation of thresholds and polychoric correlations allows one to specify models with respect to the underlying liability distributions rather than the observed discrete indicators. This model bears a close resemblance to the ordinal factor model as commonly applied in SEM.

As mentioned, this chapter has addressed only a selection of models employed in GCSM. More recent developments include, for instance, genetics applications of mixture modeling (Muthén, Asparouhov, & Rebollo, 2006) and extensions of GCSM to include linear feedback or recursiveness between multivariate phenotypes (Gianola & Sorensen, 2004). Finally, we note that GCSM may be performed using any standard SEM software, for example, Mx (Neale, 2000), the OpenMx package in R (Boker et al., 2010; R Development Core Team, 2010), MPlus (Muthén & Muthén, 2007), or LISREL (Jöreskog & Sörbom, 2006). Extensive libraries containing Mx specifications of most of the models discussed in this chapter are available at *http://www.psy.vu.nl/mxbib/* (Posthuma & Boomsma, 2005) and *http://www.vcu.edu/mx/examples.html* (Neale, 2007).

NOTES

1. We use this abbreviation to refer to modeling and model(s).
2. Carey (2009) suggested an alternative model in which the *C* and *E* latent variables are replaced by a variable *T* representing total environmental effects, which may correlate among family members to account for shared environmental effects.
3. Modeling genotype–environment correlation and genotype–environment interaction is discussed in subsequent sections.

REFERENCES

Angold, A., Costello, E. J., & Erkanli, A. (1999). Comorbidity. *Journal of Child Psychology and Psychiatry and Allied Disciplines, 40*(1), 57–87.

Bartels, M., Rietveld, M. J. H., van Baal, G. C. M., & Boomsma, D. I. (2002). Genetic and environmental influences on the development of intelligence. *Behavior Genetics, 32*(4), 237–249.

Bartels, M., van Beijsterveldt, C. E. M., & Boomsma, D. I. (2009). Breastfeeding, maternal education and cognitive function: A prospective study in twins. *Behavior Genetics, 39*(6), 616–622.

Bauer, D. J., & Hussong, A. M. (2009). Psychometric approaches for developing commensurate measures across independent studies: Traditional and new models. *Psychological Methods, 14*(2), 101–125.

Bishop, E. G., Cherny, S. S., Corley, R., Plomin, R., DeFries, J. C., & Hewitt, J. K. (2003). Development genetic analysis of general cognitive ability from 1 to 12 years in a sample of adoptees, biological siblings, and twins. *Intelligence, 31*(1), 31–49.

Boker, S., Neale, M., Maes, H., Wilde, M., Spiegel, M., & Brick, T. (2011). OpenMx: An open source extended structural equation modeling framework. *Psychometrika, 76*(2), 306–317.

Boomsma, D. I., Busjahn, A., & Peltonen, L. (2002). Classical twin studies and beyond. *Nature Reviews Genetics, 3*(11), 872–882.

Boomsma, D. I., de Geus, E. J., van Baal, G. C., & Koopmans, J. R. (1999). A religious upbringing reduces the influence of genetic factors on disinhibition: evidence for interaction between genotype and environment on personality. *Twin Research, 2*(2), 115–125.

Boomsma, D. I., Martin, N. G., & Neale, M. C. (1989). Genetic analysis of twin and family data: Structural modeling using LISREL. *Behavior Genetics, 19*(1), 5–7.

Boomsma, D. I., & Molenaar, P. C. M. (1986). Using LISREL to analyze genetic and environmental covariance structure. *Behavior Genetics, 16*(2), 237–250.

Boomsma, D. I., & Molenaar, P. C. M. (1987). The genetic-analysis of repeated measures: I. Simplex models. *Behavior Genetics, 17*(2), 111–123.

Boomsma, D. I., van Beijsterveldt, C. E. M., Bartels, M., & Hudziak, J. J. (2008). Genetic and environmental influences on anxious/depression: A longitudinal study in 3- to 12-year-old children. In J. J. Hudziak (Ed.), *Developmental psychopathology and wellness* (pp. 161–190). Washington DC: American Psychiatric Publishing.

Boomsma, D. I., van Beijsterveldt, C. E. M., & Hudziak, J. J. (2005). Genetic and environmental influences on Anxious/Depression during childhood: a study from the Netherlands Twin Register. *Genes Brain and Behavior, 4*(8), 466–481.

Brady, E. U., & Kendall, P. C. (1992). Comorbidity of anxiety and depression in children and adolescents. *Psychological Bulletin, 111*(2), 244–255.

Brendgen, M., Vitaro, F., Boivin, M., Girard, A., Bukowski, W. M., Dionne, G., et al. (2009). Gene–environment interplay between peer rejection and depressive behavior in children. *Journal of Child Psychology and Psychiatry, 50*(8), 1009–1017.

Burt, S. A., McGue, M., Carter, L. A., & Iacono, W. G. (2007). The different origins of stability and change in antisocial personality disorder symptoms. *Psychological Medicine*, *37*(1), 27–38.

Cantor, R. M. (1983). A multivariate genetic-analysis of ridge count data from the offspring of monozygotic twins. *Acta Geneticae Medicae et Gemellologiae*, *32*(3–4), 161–207.

Carey, G. (1986). Sibling imitation and contrast effects. *Behavior Genetics*, *16*(3), 319–341.

Carey, G. (2009). *The problem with c2*. Paper presented at the annual meeting of the Behavior Genetics Association, Minneapolis, MN. Retrieved from *http://psych.colorado.edu/~carey/Bouchard/docs/Environment%20in%20BG3.pdf*.

Cherny, S. S. (2008). Variance components and related methods for mapping quantitative trait loci. *Sociological Methods Research*, *37*, 227–250.

De Moor, M. H. M., Boomsma, D. I., Stubbe, J. H., Willemsen, G., & de Geus, E. J. C. (2008). Testing causality in the association between regular exercise and symptoms of anxiety and depression. *Archives of General Psychiatry*, *65*(8), 897–905.

Dolan, C. V., Boomsma, D. I., & Neale, M. C. (1999). A note on the power provided by sibships of size 3 and 4 in genetic covariance modeling of a codominant QTL. *Behavior Genetics*, *29*, 163–170.

Eaves, L. (1979). Use of twins in the analysis of assortative mating. *Heredity*, *43*, 399–409.

Eaves, L. J. (1984). The resolution of genotype × environment interaction in segregation analysis of nuclear families. *Genetic Epidemiology*, *1*, 215–228.

Eaves, L. J., Fulker, D. W., & Heath, A. C. (1989). The effects of social homogamy and cultural inheritance on the covariances of twins and their parents—a LISREL model. *Behavior Genetics*, *19*(1), 113–122.

Eaves, L. J., Heath, A. C., Neale, M. C., Hewitt, J. K., & Martin, N. G. (1998). Sex differences and non-additivity in the effects of genes on personality. *Twin Research*, *1*(3), 131–137.

Eaves, L. J., Last, K. A., Young, P. A., & Martin, N. G. (1978). Model-fitting approaches to the analysis of human behavior. *Heredity*, *41*, 249–320.

Eaves, L. J., Long, J., & Heath, A. C. (1986). A theory of developmental change in quantitative phenotypes applied to cognitive development. *Behavior Genetics*, *16*(1), 143–162.

Eley, T. C., & Stevenson, J. (1999). Exploring the covariation between anxiety and depression symptoms: A genetic analysis of the effects of age and sex. *Journal of Child Psychology and Psychiatry and Allied Disciplines*, *40*(8), 1273–1282.

Evans, D. M., Gillespie, N. A., & Martin, N. G. (2002). Biometrical genetics. *Biological Psychology*, *61*(1–2), 33–51.

Falconer, D. S., & Mackay, T. F. C. (1996). *Introduction to quantitative genetics* (4th ed.). Harlow, UK: Pearson.

Ferreira, M. A. R., & Purcell, S. M. (2009). A multivariate test of association. *Bioinformatics*, *25*(1), 132–133.

Franić, S., Dolan, C. V., Borsboom, D., Hudziak, J. J., van Beijsterveldt, C. E. M., & Boomsma, D. I. (2011). *Can genetics help psychometrics?: Improving dimensionality assessment through genetic factor modeling*. Manuscript under review.

Fulker, D. W., Baker, L. A., & Bock, R. D. (1983). Estimating components of covariance using LISREL. *Data Analyst*, *1*, 5–8.

Fulker, D. W., Cherny, S. S., Sham, P. C., & Hewitt, J. K. (1999). Combined linkage and association sib-pair analysis for quantitative traits. *American Journal of Human Genetics*, *64*(1), 259–267.

Gianola, D., & Sorensen, D. (2004). Quantitative genetic models for describing simultaneous and recursive relationships between phenotypes. *Genetics*, *167*(3), 1407–1424.

Gillespie, N. A., Evans, D. E., Wright, M. M., & Martin, N. G. (2004). Genetic simplex modeling of Eysenck's dimensions of personality in a sample of young Australian twins. *Twin Research*, *7*(6), 637–648.

Gillespie, N. A., Kirk, K. M., Evans, D. M., Heath, A. C., Hickie, I. B., & Martin, N. G. (2004). Do the genetic or environmental determinants of anxiety and depression change with age?: A longitudinal study of Australian twins. *Twin Research*, *7*(1), 39–53.

Guo, G., & Adkins, D. E. (2008). How is a statistical link established between a human outcome and a genetic variant? *Sociological Methods and Research*, *37*(2), 201–226.

Heath, A. C., & Eaves, L. J. (1985). Resolving the effects of phenotype and social background on mate selection. *Behavior Genetics*, *15*(1), 15–30.

Heath, A. C., Kessler, R. C., Neale, M. C., Hewitt, J. K., Eaves, L. J., & Kendler, K. S. (1993). Testing hypotheses about direction of causation using cross-sectional family data. *Behavior Genetics*, *23*(1), 29–50.

Hettema, J. M., Prescott, C. A., & Kendler, K. S. (2004). Genetic and environmental sources of covariation between generalized anxiety disorder and neuroticism. *American Journal of Psychiatry*, *161*(9), 1581–1587.

Hewitt, J. K., Eaves, L. J., Neale, M. C., & Meyer, J. M. (1988). Resolving causes of developmental continuity or "tracking": I. Longitudinal twin studies during growth. *Behavior Genetics*, *18*(2), 133–151.

Hjelmborg, J. V. B., Fagnani, C., Silventoinen, K., McGue, M., Korkeila, M., Christensen, K., et al. (2008). Genetic influences on growth traits of BMI: A longitudinal study of adult twins. *Obesity*, *16*(4), 847–852.

Hoekstra, R. A., Bartels, M., & Boomsma, D. I. (2007). Longitudinal genetic study of verbal and nonverbal IQ from early childhood to young adulthood. *Learning and Individual Differences*, *17*(2), 97–114.

Hottenga, J. J., & Boomsma, D. I. (2008). QTL detection in multivariate data from sibling pairs. In B. M. Neale, M. A.

R. Ferreira, S. E. Medland, & D. Posthuma (Eds.), *Statistical genetics: Gene mapping through linkage and association*. New York: Taylor & Francis Group.

Jinks, J. L., & Fulker, D. W. (1970). Comparison of biometrical genetical, MAVA, and classical approaches to analysis of human behavior. *Psychological Bulletin, 73*(5), 311–349.

Johnson, W., & Krueger, R. F. (2005). Genetic effects on physical health: Lower at higher income levels. *Behavior Genetics, 35*(5), 579–590.

Jöreskog, K. G., & Sörbom, D. (2006). *LISREL 8.80 for Windows*. Lincolnwood, IL: Scientific Software International.

Kendler, K. S., & Baker, J. H. (2007). Genetic influences on measures of the environment: A systematic review. *Psychological Medicine, 37*(5), 615–626.

Kendler, K. S., & Eaves, L. J. (1986). Models for the joint effect of genotype and environment on liability to psychiatric illness. *American Journal of Psychiatry, 143*(3), 279–289.

Kendler, K. S., Heath, A. C., Martin, N. G., & Eaves, L. J. (1987). Symptoms of anxiety and symptoms of depression: Same genes, different environments? *Archives of General Psychiatry, 44*, 451–457.

Kendler, K. S., Jacobson, K. C., Gardner, C. O., Gillespie, N., Aggen, S. A., & Prescott, C. A. (2007). Creating a social world—a developmental twin study of peer-group deviance. *Archives of General Psychiatry, 64*(8), 958–965.

Kendler, K. S., & Karkowski-Shuman, L. (1997). Stressful life events and genetic liability to major depression: Genetic control of exposure to the environment. *Psychological Medicine, 27*(3), 539–547.

Lawley, D. N., & Maxwell, A. E. (1971). *Factor analysis as a statistical method* (2nd ed.). London: Butterworths.

Lenroot, R. K., Schmitt, J. E., Ordaz, S. J., Wallace, G. L., Neale, M. C., Lerch, J. P., et al. (2009). Differences in genetic and environmental influences on the human cerebral cortex associated with development during childhood and adolescence. *Human Brain Mapping, 30*(1), 163–174.

Luciano, M., Posthuma, D., Wright, M. J., de Geus, E. J. C., Smith, G. A., Geffen, G. M., et al. (2005). Perceptual speed does not cause intelligence, and intelligence does not cause perceptual speed. *Biological Psychology, 70*(1), 1–8.

Manolio, T. A., & Collins, F. S. (2009). The HapMap and genome-wide association studies in diagnosis and therapy. *Annual Review of Medicine, 60*, 443–156.

Martin, N. G., & Eaves, L. J. (1977). Genetic analysis of covariance structure. *Heredity, 38*, 79–95.

Mather, K., & Jinks, J. L. (1971). *Biometrical genetics* (2nd ed.). New York: Cornell University Press.

McArdle, J. J. (1986). Latent variable growth within behavior genetic models. *Behavior Genetics, 16*(1), 163–200.

McArdle, J. J., & Goldsmith, H. H. (1990). Alternative common factor models for multivariate biometric analyses. *Behavior Genetics, 20*(5), 569–608.

McArdle, J. J., Prescott, C. A., Hamagami, F., & Horn, J. L. (1998). A contemporary method for developmental–genetic analyses of age changes in intellectual abilities. *Developmental Neuropsychology, 14*(1), 69–114.

Medland, S., & Neale, M. C. (2010). An integrated phenomic approach to multivariate allelic association. *European Journal of Human Genetics, 18*(2), 233–239.

Mellenbergh, G. J. (1994). A unidimensional latent trait model for continuous item responses. *Multivariate Behavioral Research, 29*(3), 223–236.

Middeldorp, C. M., Cath, D. C., Beem, A. L., Willemsen, G., & Boomsma, D. I. (2008). Life events, anxious depression and personality: A prospective and genetic study. *Psychological Medicine, 38*(11), 1557–1565.

Minica, C. C., Boomsma, D. I., van der Sluis, S., & Dolan, C. V. (2010). Genetic association in multivariate phenotypic data: Power in five models. *Twin Research and Human Genetics, 13*(6), 525–543.

Molenaar, D., Dolan, C. V., Wicherts, J. M., & van der Maas, H. L. J. (2010). Modeling differentiation of cognitive abilities within the higher-order factor model using moderated factor analysis. *Intelligence, 38*(6), 611–624.

Mosing, M. A., Pedersen, N. L., Martin, N. G., & Wright, M. J. (2010). Sex differences in the genetic architecture of optimism and health and their interrelation: A study of Australian and Swedish twins. *Twin Research and Human Genetics, 13*(4), 322–329.

Muthén, B., Asparouhov, T., & Rebollo, I. (2006). Advances in behavioral genetics modeling using Mplus: Applications of factor mixture modeling to twin data. *Twin Research and Human Genetics, 9*(3), 313–324.

Muthén, L. K., & Muthén, B. O. (2007). *MPlus (Version 5.0)*. Los Angeles: Authors.

Nance, W. E., Kramer, A. A., Corey, L. A., Winter, P. M., & Eaves, L. J. (1983). A causal analysis of birth weight in the offspring of monozygotic twins. *American Journal of Human Genetics, 35*(6), 1211–1223.

Neale, M. C. (2000). MxGui (Version 1.7.03). Richmond: Virginia Commonwealth University.

Neale, M. C. (2007). Mx examples. Retrieved from *http://www.vcu.edu/mx/examples.html*.

Neale, M. C., & Cardon, L. R. (1992). *Methodology for genetic studies of twins and families*. Dordrecht: Kluwer.

Neale, M. C., & McArdle, J. J. (2000). Structured latent growth curves for twin data. *Twin Research, 3*(3), 165–177.

Pedersen, N. L., & Reynolds, C. A. (1998). Stability and change in adult personality: Genetic and environmental components. *European Journal of Personality, 12*(5), 365–386.

Petrill, S. A., Lipton, P. A., Hewitt, J. K., & Plomin, R. (2004). Genetic and environmental contributions to general cognitive ability through the first 16 years of life. *Developmental Psychology*, *40*(5), 805–812.

Plomin, R., Defries, J. C., McClearn, G. E., & McGuffin, P. (2008). *Behavioral genetics* (5th ed.). New York: Freeman.

Posthuma, D., & Boomsma, D. I. (2000). A note on the statistical power in extended twin designs. *Behavior Genetics*, *30*(2), 147–158.

Posthuma, D., & Boomsma, D. I. (2005). Mx scripts library: Structural equation modeling scripts for twin and family data. *Behavior Genetics*, *35*(4), 499–505.

Prescott, C. A., Aggen, S. H., & Kendler, K. S. (1999). Sex differences in the sources of genetic liability to alcohol abuse and dependence in a population-based sample of US twins. *Alcoholism: Clinical and Experimental Research*, *23*(7), 1136–1144.

Prescott, C. A., Aggen, S. H., & Kendler, K. S. (2000). Sex-specific genetic influences on the comorbidity of alcoholism and major depression in a population-based sample of US twins. *Archives of General Psychiatry*, *57*(8), 803–811.

Purcell, S. (2002). Variance components models for gene–environment interaction in twin analysis. *Twin Research*, *5*(6), 554–571.

R Development Core Team. (2010). R: A language and environment for statistical computing. Vienna: R Foundation for Statistical Computing.

Rao, D. C., Morton, N. E., & Yee, S. (1974). Analysis of family resemblance: II. A linear-model for familial correlation. *American Journal of Human Genetics*, *26*(3), 331–359.

Rathouz, P. J., van Hulle, C. A., Rodgers, J. L., Waldman, I. D., & Lahey, B. B. (2008). Specification, testing, and interpretation of gene-by-measured-environment interaction models in the presence of gene–environment correlation. *Behavior Genetics*, *38*(3), 301–315.

Rettew, D. C., Vink, J. M., Willemsen, G., Doyle, A., Hudziak, J. J., & Boomsma, D. I. (2006). The genetic architecture of neuroticism in 3301 Dutch adolescent twins as a function of age and sex: A study from the Dutch Twin Register. *Twin Research and Human Genetics*, *9*(1), 24–29.

Reynolds, C. A., Finkel, D., Gatz, M., & Pedersen, N. L. (2002). Sources of influence on rate of cognitive change over time in Swedish twins: An application of latent growth models. *Experimental Aging Research*, *28*(4), 407–433.

Reynolds, C. A., Finkel, D., McArdle, J. J., Gatz, M., Berg, S., & Pedersen, N. L. (2005). Quantitative genetic analysis of latent growth curve models of cognitive abilities in adulthood. *Developmental Psychology*, *41*(1), 3–16.

Rice, F., Harold, G. T., & Thapar, A. (2002). Assessing the effects of age, sex and shared environment on the genetic aetiology of depression in childhood and adolescence. *Journal of Child Psychology and Psychiatry and Allied Disciplines*, *43*(8), 1039–1051.

Rietveld, M. J. H., Dolan, C. V., van Baal, G. C. M., & Boomsma, D. I. (2003). A twin study of differentiation of cognitive abilities in childhood. *Behavior Genetics*, *33*(4), 367–381.

Rijsdijk, F. V., Vernon, P. A., & Boomsma, D. I. (2002). Application of hierarchical genetic models to Raven and WAIS subtests: A Dutch twin study. *Behavior Genetics*, *32*(3), 199–210.

Roysamb, E., Harris, J. R., Magnus, P., Vitterso, J., & Tambs, K. (2002). Subjective well-being: Sex-specific effects of genetic and environmental factors. *Personality and Individual Differences*, *32*(2), 211–223.

Schousboe, K., Willemsen, G., Kyvik, K. O., Mortensen, J., Boomsma, D. I., Cornes, B. K., et al. (2003). Sex differences in heritability of BMI: A comparative study of results from twin studies in eight countries. *Twin Research*, *6*(5), 409–421.

Slagboom, P. E., & Meulenbelt, I. (2002). Organisation of the human genome and our tools for identifying disease genes. *Biological Psychology*, *61*(1–2), 11–31.

Snieder, H., van Doornen, L. J. P., & Boomsma, D. I. (1997). The age dependency of gene expression for plasma lipids, lipoproteins, and apolipoproteins. *American Journal of Human Genetics*, *60*(3), 638–650.

Spearman, C. (1927). The abilities of man. London: Macmillan.

Stoel, R. D., de Geus, E. J. C., & Boomsma, D. I. (2006). Genetic analysis of sensation seeking with an extended twin design. *Behavior Genetics*, *36*(2), 229–237.

Thomsen, S. F., van der Sluis, S., Stensballe, L. G., Posthuma, D., Skytthe, A., Kyvik, K. O., et al. (2009). Exploring the association between severe respiratory syncytial virus infection and asthma: A registry-based twin study. *American Journal of Respiratory and Critical Care Medicine*, *179*(12), 1091–1097.

Truett, K. R., Eaves, L. J., Walters, E. E., Heath, A. C., Hewitt, J. K., Meyer, J. M., et al. (1994). A model system for analysis of family resemblance in extended kinships of twins. *Behavior Genetics*, *24*(1), 35–49.

Tucker-Drob, E. M. (2009). Differentiation of cognitive abilities across the life span. *Developmental Psychology*, *45*(4), 1097–1118.

van den Oord, E. (2000). Framework for identifying quantitative trait loci in association studies using structural equation modeling. *Genetic Epidemiology*, *18*(4), 341–359.

van der Sluis, S., Dolan, C. V., Neale, M. C., Boomsma, D. I., & Posthuma, D. (2006). Detecting genotype–environment interaction in monozygotic twin data: Comparing the Jinks and Fulker Test and a new test based on marginal maximum likelihood estimation. *Twin Research and Human Genetics*, *9*(3), 377–392.

van der Sluis, S., Posthuma, D., & Dolan, C. (2012). A note on false positives and power in G × E modeling of twin data. *Behavior Genetics, 42*(1), 170–186.

van der Sluis, S., Verhage, M., Posthuma, D., & Dolan, C. V. (2010). Phenotypic complexity, measurement bias, and poor phenotypic resolution contribute to the missing heritability problem in genetic association studies. *PLoS ONE, 5*(11), e13929.

Vink, J. M., & Boomsma, D. I. (2002). Gene finding strategies. *Biological Psychology, 61*(1–2), 53–71.

Vinkhuyzen, A. A. E., van der Sluis, S., de Geus, E. J. C., Boomsma, D. I., & Posthuma, D. (2010). Genetic influences on "environmental" factors. *Genes Brain and Behavior, 9*(3), 276–287.

Vinkhuyzen, A. A. E., van der Sluis, S., & Posthuma, D. (2011). Life events moderate variation in cognitive ability (g) in adults. *Molecular Psychiatry, 16*, 4–6.

Weiss, L. A., Pan, L., Abney, M., & Ober, C. (2006). The sex-specific genetic architecture of quantitative traits in humans. *Nature Genetics, 38*(2), 218–222.

Wray, N. R., & Visscher, P. M. (2008). Population genetics and its relevance to gene mapping. In B. M. Neale, M. A. R. Ferreira, S. E. Medland, & D. Posthuma (Eds.), *Statistical genetics. Gene mapping through linkage and association* (pp. 87–110). New York: Taylor & Francis Group.

Yung, Y., Thissen, D., & McLeod, L. D. (1999). On the relationship between the higher-order factor model and the hierarchical factor model. *Psychometrika, 64*(2), 113–128.

CHAPTER 37

Structural Equation Models of Imaging Data

Anthony R. McIntosh
Andrea B. Protzner

One of the current challenges in neuroscience is to understand how brain operations give rise to mental phenomena ranging from sensation and perception to attention and memory. A dominant assumption is that certain parts of the brain have unique roles in mental function. This idea of one-region/one-function comes from early studies that showed some remarkable cognitive deficits following lesions in specific parts of the brain (Finger, 1994). Most of the available tools have allowed neuroscientists to examine only small parts of the brain at a time; the findings reinforce the notion of discrete functions in specific brain regions.

Modern neuroimaging tools allow us to measure how the *entire* brain reacts as people perform different mental operations. We are finding that many more brain areas "light up" when someone pays attention, thinks, and remembers, than we would have expected based on the results from lesion studies. Emerging neurobiological theories emphasize the combined actions of interacting brain elements as the link between the brain and human mental function (McIntosh, 2000a, 2000b).

If it is the case that brain function results from the action of distributed networks, then analytic approaches tuned to such dynamics would best capture these actions. One method that has proven useful in network analysis is structural equation modeling (SEM). Applications of SEM to neuroimaging data (e.g., 2-deoxyglucose autoradiography [2DG], positron emission tomography [PET], functional magnetic resonance imaging [fMRI], electroencephalography [EEG], and magnetoelectroencephalography [MEG]) make use of the fact that the causal relation between brain regions is essentially a known entity—that being the neuroanatomy (McIntosh & Gonzalez-Lima, 1994). Thus, for neuroimaging data, the main focus of SEM is on whether there are task-dependent changes in the influences regions have on one another—or the effective connections—within the constraints of the same anatomical network. In this chapter, we discuss the theoretical motivation for exploring higher-order statistics in neuroimaging data, which includes mode decomposition methods as well as SEM, then focus on the application of SEM to neuroimaging data, and its strengths and limitations. We also review more recent advances in SEM and related causal modeling methods that take advantage of the temporal information of neuroimaging data and incorporate statistical advances in Bayesian inference.

THEORETICAL BASIS OF NETWORK ANALYSIS

The measurement of neural interactions in neuroimaging has developed under two general approaches. The first emphasizes pairwise interactions, often in terms of correlations or covariances. The second incorporates additional information, such as anatomical connections, and considers an interaction of several neural elements simultaneously to explicitly quantify the effect that one element has on another. These two approaches are known as functional and effective connectivity, respectively. "Functional connectivity" usually refers to the correlations of activity between neural elements in both electrophysiology (Aertsen, Bonhoeffer, & Kruger, 1987) and brain imaging (Friston, Frith, Liddle, & Frackowiak, 1993). To say that two neural elements (neurons or brain regions) have a functional connection is to say that these elements show statistically significant correlated activity, without reference to how that correlation is mediated. "Effective connectivity" is a logical progression from functional connectivity and can be defined as the influence that one neural element has on another (Friston, Frith, & Frackowiak, 1993). The major difference between functional and effective connectivity is best appreciated from the available levels of inference. Because functional connectivity is an estimate of a correlation between neural elements (either pairwise or multivariate), no inferences on the directionality of influences are possible. Effective connectivity estimation requires the specification of a model wherein directional influences are estimated; thus, by definition, inferences on directionality can be made. An illustration may help to clarify: consider two simple networks shown in Figure 37.1. Network 1 has three nodes, where nodes *a* and *b* are connected by a mediating node *c*. Network 2 has a similar configuration save for a direct link between nodes *a* and *b*. Estimation of functional connectivity among the three nodes in either network would not be able to differentiate between the configurations of the two networks because of the focus on zero-order correlations. Effective connectivity, which tries to model directionality, would be able to show that in Network 1, the functional con-

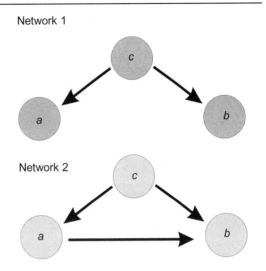

FIGURE 37.1. Example of two networks with different anatomical connection topologies. Functional connectivity estimation between nodes *a*, *b*, and *c* in the two networks would not be able to differentiate the anatomical connectivity between Networks 1 and 2. Effective connectivity, where directionality of effects is modeled, would be able to identify the direct connection between *a* and *b* when the common effect from *c* is accounted for.

nection between *a* and *b* is mediated by node *c*, whereas in Network 2, there is an additional influence from *a* to *b* when the mutual effect from *c* is taken into account. However, additional information must be incorporated into the model to capture such effects. This information, in the case of SEM, comes from the anatomical connectivity between nodes.

TAXONOMY OF TECHNIQUES IN NEUROIMAGING

Given the richness of neuroimaging data, and the potential to reveal critical workings of the human brain, it is no surprise that neuroimaging has attracted scientists from a number of fields. One of the fastest growing components is the development of methods for the estimation of functional and effective connectivity. While the primary focus of our chapter is on use of SEM, it is by no means the only method used for quantifying network dynamics. The sections below briefly characterize the major methods for estimating connectivity and list their advantages and disadvantages. This is not an exhaustive list, but it provides a general orientation for the interested reader.

Functional Connectivity

Regional Correlation

This is perhaps the simplest and most often used method. Pairwise correlations of regions of interest, or "voxels," provide a snapshot of functional connectivity patterns (Horwitz, Duara, & Rapoport, 1984; Horwitz et al., 1991). This method has the advantage of simplicity and uses a minimal number of assumptions beyond linearity. The technique becomes problematic when the number of correlations grows and one must correct for multiple statistical tests (the same problem as with other univariate measures). Moreover, as the number of correlations grows, easily summarizing the patterns becomes difficult. It is at this point that multivariate methods may be helpful (see below).

Psychophysiological Interactions

Linear regression methods sometimes appear to lie in a gray area between functional and effective connectivity. For example, the method to estimate psychophysiological interactions (PPIs) (Friston et al., 1997) in the Statistical Parametric Mapping (SPM) package is used to assess task-dependent changes in the degree that one region (Y) predicts or explains the activity of another (X) (McIntosh & Gonzalez-Lima, 1994). However, the PPI approach provides the same statistical result one would obtain if the roles of X and Y were reversed. Thus, the PPI method is most similar to an estimate of functional connectivity.

Principal Component Analysis

A tried-and-true method, principal component analysis (PCA), has been applied to a number of neuroimaging data sets to summarize complex patterns of interregional correlations (Strother et al., 1995). The PCA solutions are always unique for a given data set (compared with those of independent component analysis [ICA]), and the calculation of the principal components is relatively fast. The main drawbacks include:

- Orthogonality of components, which may impose artifactual groupings within a component. This effect can be alleviated somewhat by orthogonal or oblique rotation.

- The decomposition depends on the rank of matrix. If there are more regions than observations, the matrix will be rank-deficient, which can obscure the "true" grouping of regions.

ICA

ICA is a newer method than PCA and has been applied extensively to fMRI and EEG data. It was originally a denoising method but has since shown to be quite powerful for extracting resting state networks in fMRI data (using a variation of the usual ICA: tensor ICA; Beckmann & Smith, 2005). ICA has the advantage over PCA of assuming not orthogonality but rather maximal independence. In this case, it has the capacity to separate artifactual components from those of interest. This capacity depends, however, on the flavor of ICA used (e.g., single subject vs. group) and the nature of the artifact. The drawbacks of ICA include:

- Nonunique solutions without additional constraints.

- Computationally expensive for large data sets.

Partial Least Squares

The partial least squares (PLS) method has been used in neuroimaging for more than a decade and has been applied to PET, fMRI, EEG, and MEG (McIntosh, Bookstein, Haxby, & Grady, 1996; McIntosh & Lobaugh, 2004). It is related to canonical correlation analysis in that it relates the neuroimaging data to the experimental design (e.g., design contrasts); performance measures; or, for functional connectivity, one or more voxels. In the latter case, it can be considered to be a multivariate extension of PPI. PLS has the flexibility to work on combinations of design, behavior, and voxels, and has been extended to merge multiple imaging data sets (Martinez-Montes, Valdes-Sosa, Miwakeichi, Goldman, & Cohen, 2004). It has the advantage of creating a flexible framework for direct testing of statistical dependency in neuroimaging data. Its main drawbacks are as follows:

◼ Orthogonal extraction of components such as PCA may obscure the true dependencies. To offset this effect, the extraction can be done with ICA (Lin et al., 2003).

◼ Interpretation can be complicated in complex designs.

◼ Statistical assessment through resampling is computationally expensive.

Effective Connectivity

SEM

SEM has been used primarily for PET and fMRI data (Buchel & Friston, 1997; McIntosh & Gonzalez-Lima, 1994), although its use has been extended to EEG data (Astolfi et al., 2004, 2005). Its primary use has been to identify changes in effective connectivity between tasks or groups within a defined anatomical network (Protzner & McIntosh, 2006). It has also been used to identify likely patterns of effective connectivity in a given data set (Bullmore et al., 2000). It has the advantage of allowing fast and robust computations and can be used for rather complicated models (McIntosh, Grady, Haxby, Ungerleider, & Horwitz, 1996); more recently, it was validated for use with neuroimaging data based on large-scale simulations (Kim & Horwitz, 2009; Marrelec, Kim, Doyon, & Horwitz, 2009). It has a long history; thus, several software packages and numerous algorithmic variations are available. For its application to neuroimaging, the main drawbacks are as follows:

◼ Absolute assessment of model fit is very dependent on sample size.

◼ It needs to prespecify connection directions.

◼ It cannot deal with fully reciprocal models.

Granger Causality

Granger causality (GC) is a general methodological approach for analyzing dependencies in time series. Its most common implementation comes in the form of autoregressive modeling (Goebel, Roebroeck, Kim, & Formisano, 2003). There are also variations that operate in the spectral domain (Kaminski, Ding, Truccolo, & Bressler, 2001), although they have not been used in fMRI. Methods that generally fall under this label have the advantage of working directly with the time series, allowing inferences on directionality, without the need to prespecify the direction (cf. SEM and dynamic causal modeling [DCM]). Its main drawbacks are as follows:

◼ Most implementations are pairwise. Multivariate extensions are possible (Deshpande, LaConte, James, Peltier, & Hu, 2009), but with many regions, the solutions may become unstable.

◼ For fMRI, GC requires relatively short repetition time (TR) to get a robust time series.

◼ There has been a recent observation that GC may provide spurious estimates of directional effects in fMRI data (David et al., 2008; but see Roebroeck, Formisano, & Goebel, 2011).

DCM

Unlike SEM and GC, DCM was designed specifically for neuroimaging data and has been applied to fMRI and EEG (Friston, Harrison, & Penny, 2003; Kiebel, Garrido, Moran, Chen, & Friston, 2009). Like SEM, DCM has also received some validation through large-scale simulations (Lee, Friston, & Horwitz, 2006). DCM uses a generative model of the measured signal to infer its neural sources. The effective connectivity estimation then proceeds based on the neural source activity rather than the measured signal (e.g., blood oxygen–dependent [BOLD] or EEG). The model first estimates the intrinsic connections between sources and then the changes in the connections that come about through external perturbation (usually the experimental design). This can be thought of in the general linear model (GLM) framework as estimating the grand mean, and the deviations from the mean for the experimental manipulation. A Bayesian estimation procedure is used to determine the effective connections and their changes, as well as provide evidence for the "best" model. We discuss DCM again later in this chapter.

The advantages of DCM are the tight couplings to biophysical models, which enable an interpretation of the effective connections in terms of neurophysiology. There is a potential for investigating several models for mediation of effective connections using model evidence. Its main drawbacks are as follows:

◼ It is computationally expensive, and in its present form cannot handle more than about six regions.

■ It cannot easily model intrinsic activity, such as resting state networks.

■ Some researchers question the robustness of parameter estimation given the extensive constraints on the generative model (Rowe, 2010; Rowe, Hughes, Barker, & Owen, 2010).

METHODOLOGICAL ISSUES IN SEM FOR NEUROIMAGING

Returning to our focus on SEM and neuroimaging, as we noted earlier, most applications target the statistical inference to task- or group-dependent changes of effective connections (McIntosh & Gonzalez-Lima, 1994). The causal structure, which is derived from the anatomical connections, is considered to be invariant across the samples studied. In that vein, the measures of model fit can be used to assess whether, given the same anatomical foundation, the path coefficients vary significantly between tasks or groups.

An important consideration for SEM in neuroimaging is the determination of the anatomical connections. The anatomical connectivity between selected brain regions is derived from the neuroanatomy literature. This is not a trivial step, and it is at this stage that the theoretical persuasion of the investigator must guide the decision of which connections to include in a model. Any system of equations where there are unknowns to be solved will benefit from constraints to possible solutions. Using the anatomy of the system helps to constrain solutions. However, if all major and minor paths were to be included, most models would contain reciprocal loops between most areas, with some interconnections, both feedforward and feedback, spanning regions. When all possible anatomical connections are included, it is likely that there would be either the same number of known and unknown elements or more unknown elements. In either case, an underdetermined system of equations would result, and unique solutions would not be obtainable. In most cases, some compromise between anatomical accuracy and interpretability is needed. Any compromise would clearly be a simplification of what the reality of the interactions may be, and these compromises need to be made explicit for a complete understanding of the final model. There have been several published accounts where the compromises in model building have been made explicit (Buchel & Friston, 1997; Kohler, McIntosh, Moscovitch, &

Winocur, 1998; McIntosh et al., 1994), although such specificity is often lacking in neurocognitive models that are loosely based on activation patterns. Any modeling effort, whether based on simulations, data fitting, or intuition, is necessarily a simplification of reality, and it is the degree of simplification that determines the utility of the model.

Path coefficients represent the proportion of the activity in one area that is determined by the activity of other areas that project to it. When the coefficients are based on functional activity measured across participants, they reflect what can be thought of as an average functional influence within a given task, and index the reliability and sign of the influence. The final step includes the comparison of path coefficients across tasks to determine if the interactions within the functional network differ. This is done by assuming that path coefficients are the same between tasks, yielding the same implied covariance matrix for each group. This overall measure of fit is compared to a model where the estimated path coefficients are allowed to vary between tasks, yielding a separate implied covariance matrix for each group. If the fit improves significantly when the coefficients are allowed to vary, then there is a significant difference in effective connections between tasks. Using this nested or stacked model approach, one may test for more specific differences involving individual paths (McIntosh, Cabeza, & Lobaugh, 1998).

The approach used by McIntosh and colleagues assumes the causal structure is "true" in the sense that the anatomy defines the structural equations, and the inferential focus is on whether the coefficients (effective connections) in the equation differ between groups or tasks. Bullmore and colleagues (2000) used SEM to test whether a particular causal structure was consistent with the observed interregional covariance, which is the usual application of SEM outside its use for neuroimaging. Their application made use of the long history of neurological models of behaviors (e.g., language networks, attention networks) that purport a causal relationship between brain regions that may or may not be anatomically grounded. The inferential focus is primarily on the overall model fit rather than the specific effects within (see also Zhuang, LaConte, Peltier, Zhang, & Hu, 2005). The approaches of McIntosh and Bullmore are equally valid but have different goals in mind.

Unfortunately, there seems to be a belief that the ability to make inferences about changes in effective connectivity is compromised if the overall model does not fit the data adequately (e.g., Goncalves & Hall, 2003; Goncalves, Hall, Johnsrude, & Haggard, 2001), regardless of the method used to define the causal structure. The absolute model fit may be poor for neuroimaging data given that most models include only a few of the total influences on a region (McIntosh & Gonzalez-Lima, 1994). Within a poorly fitting model, inferences about a given effective connection (path coefficient) may not be meaningful when the goal is to identify the most plausible causal structure (MacCallum, 1995). Neither of these points speaks to the question of whether one can detect a change in effective connections despite having an overall model that fits poorly.

We (Protzner & McIntosh, 2006) sought to address this concern by creating two population networks with different patterns of effective connectivity, extracting three samples sizes ($N = 100, 60, 20$), then assessing whether the ability to detect effective connectivity differences depends on absolute model fit. Four scenarios were assessed: (1) elimination of a region showing no task differences; (2) elimination of connections with no task differences; (3) elimination of connections that carried task differences but could be expressed through alternative indirect routes; and (4) elimination of connections that carried task differences and could not be expressed through indirect routes. We were able to detect task differences in all four cases, despite poor absolute model fit. The main findings of our simulations were as follows:

1. If paths or regions whose effects do not differ across tasks are left out of a model, they have no impact on ability to detect task differences in the rest of the model, regardless of whether the overall model fits the data.

2. If a path that carries a task difference is not part of the model, the difference may manifest in the total effects so long as indirect routes are possible. Importantly, while the magnitude of the direct effects along these indirect routes may change, they themselves do not appear to embody the task-dependent change.

3. If a path carries a task difference that cannot be captured in the total effects, the effect is not represented in the model.

4. Modification indices can be useful to decide whether regions and/or paths are missing from a model.

These conclusions are possible when the focus of SEM is to test for differences in path coefficients within a predefined causal structure. The important point is that the causal structure is independent of the data. In the case where SEM is used to determine causal structure, the interpretation of individual path coefficients is indeed ambiguous in a poorly fitting model. This distinction emphasizes what Bullmore and colleagues (2000) defined as the relativistic versus confirmatory approach. When the purpose of SEM is to evaluate whether the hypothesized causal structure is consistent with the data, one should not interpret path coefficients if the model does not fit (MacCallum, 1995). This is because the coefficients may change when the causal structure is modified. In the case where the causal structure is relatively fixed, the path coefficients are themselves quite interpretable and can be compared between tasks or groups.

Consistent with previous work (McIntosh & Gonzalez-Lima, 1994), Protzner and McIntosh (2006) noted that modification indices are able to indicate possible omissions of connections and regions. However, modification indices alone may not be completely accurate because they only provide clues as to possible omissions. Usually, the regions and direct paths that are included in the model are selected beforehand using either statistical criteria or a theoretical guide. The situation for residual influences is less clear. As noted elsewhere (Hayduk, 1987; McIntosh & Gonzalez-Lima, 1994), model instabilities can be expressed in high PSI estimates and is the most direct way to minimize discrepancy in model fitting. We have previously suggested a rough rule of thumb for constraining PSI values that depend on the anatomical connections for a given region (McIntosh & Gonzalez-Lima, 1994), but a more empirically based means to derive the estimates (Bullmore et al., 2000) would be preferable. When model modification can be made either on the paths between regions or on residual influences, it is preferable to make the modification on the paths (effective connections) first.

APPLICATION OF SEM TO NEUROIMAGING

SEM originally was applied to neuroscience data in a rat auditory learning study by McIntosh and Gonzalez-Lima (1991). They used SEM to assess changes in auditory system 2DG uptake during long- and short-term habituation of the acoustic startle reflex. Habituation consisted of a decrease in the startle reflex with repeated stimulations of an acoustic stimulus. The structural model was based on anatomical connections between central auditory system structures. The analysis revealed that the lemniscal path was dominant during short-term habituation. This was consistent with the function of the lemniscal pathway in basic sensory processing. During long-term habituation, this influence shifted from lemniscal to extralemniscal paths with strong involvement from the superior olivary nuclei and the external nucleus of the inferior colliculus. The extralemniscal pathway has been associated with the learned relevance of auditory stimuli; hence, the movement from the dominant effects in the lemniscal to extralemniscal paths was consistent with the changes in the learned relevance of the auditory stimulus. The change in the relative contribution of the two auditory pathways was substantiated in further studies of auditory classical conditioning (McIntosh & Gonzalez-Lima, 1995).

The first application of SEM to human neuroimaging data examined the effective connections in the cortical visual system (McIntosh et al., 1994). One well-established functional distinction in the brain is between object and spatial visual pathways, which correspond to the dorsal and ventral cortical processing streams, described by Ungerleider and Mishkin (1982). The functional separation was identified in humans with the aid of PET (Haxby, Grady, & Horwitz, 1991). A match-to-sample task for faces was used to explore object vision. For spatial vision, a match-to-sample task for the location of a dot within a square was used. The results from right-hemisphere SEM analysis are presented in Figure 37.2 (left-hemisphere interactions did not differ between tasks). The connections for the model were derived from monkey anatomical tracing studies and defined the dorsal (Brodmann's areas [Bas] 19d, 7) and ventral (BAs 19v, 37 and 21) processing streams. As may be expected, path coefficients along the ventral pathway from cortical BA 19v extending into the frontal lobe were stronger in the face-matching model, whereas interactions along the dorsal pathway from BA 19d to the frontal lobe were relatively stronger in the location-matching model. Among posterior areas, the differences in path coefficients were mainly in magnitude. Occipitotemporal interactions between BAs 19v and 37 were stronger in the face-matching model, whereas the impact of BA 17/18 to BA 19d and the occipitoparietal influences from BA 19d to 7 were stronger in the location-matching model. One important feature of this model was that the anatomical con-

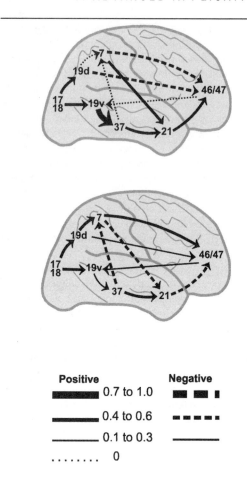

FIGURE 37.2. Graphic depiction of path coefficients between cortical areas in the right hemisphere for object and spatial vision operations. The numbers on the cortical surface refer to Brodmann's areas (d, dorsal; v, ventral). The arrows represent the anatomical connections between areas, and the magnitude of the direct effect from one area to another is proportional to the arrow width for each path.

nections allowed for interactions between the dorsal and ventral pathways, with connections from BAs 37 to 7 and from 7 to 21. The interactions among these areas showed task-dependent differences in magnitude and sign. Thus, the strongest positive interactions in each model may have preferentially been in one pathway, but the parallel pathways were not functioning independently. Strong interactions between parallel pathways have been a consistent finding in all SEM applications to imaging data. Using anatomically guided SEM to explore brain network interactions reinforces the idea that while a certain pathway or area may be critical for a particular function, operations in the intact brain involve interactions among many regions (McIntosh, 2000a; McIntosh & Gonzalez-Lima, 1994).

The interpretation of regional cerebral blood flow (rCBF) decreases can gain an important level of specificity through the use of network analysis. There are at least two different ways that task-dependent rCBF decreases can come about. First, the baseline task may have higher activity in relevant areas than the experimental task. Second, a decrease can represent active suppression. As an example, consider a PET study by Nyberg and colleagues (1996) that used SEM to test the hypothesis that rCBF decreases came about through active inhibition. They measured rCBF in an episodic memory retrieval task relative to a baseline reading task, and identified regions with increased activity (right prefrontal cortex, left anterior cingulate, left occipital cortex, and cerebellum), and regions with decreased activity (bilateral prefrontal, bilateral anterior and posterior temporal, and posterior cingulate cortices). Using SEM, they showed that the influence of activated regions on deactivated regions was more negative during retrieval than during reading, suggesting that regional decreases resulted from active inhibition by regions showing increased activity during retrieval. This application shows the use of SEM to resolve ambiguous interpretations of brain activity changes.

In the first application of SEM to fMRI data, Buchel and Friston (1997) explored effective connectivity patterns related to the posterior visual pathway. Specifically, they examined the effects of attention to visual motion using fMRI. They showed marked attention-related changes in effective connectivity in the pathway from V5 to PP. Furthermore, they showed a modulatory influence from the dorsolateral prefrontal cortex on this pathway by introducing nonlinear interaction terms (Kenny & Judd, 1984).

SEM applied to neuroimaging data has been used to elucidate models of cognitive function. For example, the encoding specificity principle (Tulving & Thomson, 1973) and transfer-appropriate processing concepts (Morris, Bransford, & Franks, 1977) were proposed to account for the typical memory advantage shown when retrieval conditions and processes reinstate those present during encoding. Rugg, Johnson, Park, and

Uncapher (2008) suggested that this reinstatement is also reflected in the neural networks that support encoding and retrieval. Specifically, he argued that hippocampal–neocortical interactions engaged during encoding of information may be reinstated during retrieval. McCormick, Moscovitch, Protzner, Huber, and McAndrews (2010) tested the hypothesis that although the same circuitry of hippocampal–neocortical connections underlies both initial binding of relational information and its subsequent retrieval, these processes can be differentiated by their patterns of effective connectivity. The nodes included in the anatomical model were selected from a functional connectivity analysis using PLS, which indicated functional connectivity between a hippocampal seed voxel and various neocortical areas. The SEM analysis revealed a reversal of directionality between the left hippocampus (LHC) and left inferior parietal cortex (LIPC) at encoding and retrieval. During encoding, activation of the LHC had a positive influence on the LIPC, whereas during retrieval the reverse pattern was found (i.e., the LIPC activation positively influenced LHC activation). This application of SEM shows that examining patterns of connectivity can be important both to elaborate and constrain models of cognitive function.

A handful of studies have applied SEM to EEG data. In these instances, cortical waveforms were estimated from EEG data, and SEM was applied to the source waveforms (Astolfi et al. 2004, 2005). For example, Astolfi and colleagues (2005) applied SEM to simulated data as well as cortical waveforms estimated from high-resolution EEG data collected during a finger-tapping task. In their simulations, they manipulated the signal-to-noise ratio and the length of recordings. They also evaluated the effect of errors made in the a priori model formulation. They found that a signal-to-noise ratio of 3, and 190 seconds of data (equivalent, for instance, to 380 trials of 500 milliseconds each) were satisfactory in order to obtain a good model accuracy. The ability of SEM to perform a good estimate of connectivity patterns in the face of errors made in the a priori model formulation depends on the type of error made. An error consisting of path omission is the worst with respect to the parameter estimate, though it can easily be detected by chi-square statistical testing. In applying SEM to data collected in a human study using high-resolution EEG recordings during finger tapping, they were able to detect changes in effective connectivity between the period preceding and following movement onset in the alpha (8–12 Hz) frequency band. The dominant connections preceeding movement onset were from left parietal to bilateral premotor cortex. Dominant connections following movement onset were from left sensorimotor to left prefrontal and bilateral premotor cortex.

APPLICATION OF SEM TO AGING AND CLINICAL CONDITIONS

Although the majority of studies of network interactions have focused on the young healthy brain, there are tremendous gains to be had in studying these operations in other age groups and patient populations. From a developmental perspective, the fact that brain structure changes across the entire lifespan has obvious implications for network operations. As we see below, even in cases where overt behavior does not show an age-related change there may be quite different sets of regional activity and interactivity between age groups. In clinical populations, the network reorganization may be even more dramatic, depending on the source of pathology. In cases of brain damage, network reorganization will likely be seen in terms of both primary response to damage (degeneration, diaschisis) and secondary responses as the networks reconfigure in an attempt to adapt to the insult (compensatory mechanisms). The interesting implication is that some of the behavioral deficits may reflect the secondary response. It is likely that a similar reorganization also occurs in degenerative disorders, although over a more protracted time scale. Finally, mental disorders will affect the integrity of network operations.

Several studies have examined variations in effective connections related to aging and clinical conditions. In all cases, the target of statistical inference was whether the effective connections differed between groups given the same anatomical network. Consider a study by Della-Maggiore and colleagues (2000) that examined age-related functional reorganization involving the hippocampus while participants performed a visual short-term memory task. Although behavioral performance did not vary with age, the hippocampal network supporting performance did. The hippocampal network engaged by young participants included the prefrontal cortex (BA 10), fusiform gyrus, and posterior cingulate gyrus. The hippocampal network recruited by the elderly comprised more anterior regions, including the dorsolateral prefrontal cortex, middle cingulate gyrus, and caudate nucleus. In this case, SEM analysis showed

that young and older participants recruit distinct neural networks to perform the same cognitive function.

Grady, McIntosh, and Craik (2003) examined the functional connectivity of the hippocampus during encoding in young and old adults, and the way in which this connectivity was related to recognition performance. They found an age-related ventral–dorsal shift in the cognitive resources used from more perceptually based processes to those involved in executive and organizational functions. Older adults showed correlations between hippocampal activity and the dorsolateral prefrontal and parietal regions, and increased activity in these regions was associated with better memory performance. Younger adults showed correlations between hippocampal activity and ventral prefrontal and extrastriate regions, and increased activity in these regions was associated with better recognition. Then they used effective connectivity analysis to address the question of whether inputs to and/or from regions other than the hippocampus were affected by the fact that young and old adults use differential hippocampal networks. They confirmed that functional influences to regions in addition to the hippocampus (e.g., left ventral frontal cortex, right temporal cortex) differed between groups.

Seminowicz and colleagues (2004) developed a structural model for resting-state PET data acquired from depressed patients at multiple labs. They showed that variations in effective connectivity prior to treatment predicted how patients eventually responded to pharmacological and cognitive-behavioral therapy at the group level. This application of SEM would be very useful in clinical decision making if models of effective connectivity could be applied to single subjects. The idea is that if one can create a model for therapeutical success, one can predict which therapies would benefit individual patients the most. A study by James and colleagues (2009) suggests that such an application of SEM is possible. They extended the Seminowicz and colleagues group-level connectivity analysis to individual subjects. First, they modeled baseline resting-state functional connectivity from fMRI scans with 46 treatment-naive depressed patients during baseline resting state. Exploratory SEM was used to derive an optimal group model. Jackknife and split-sample tests confirmed that this model was highly reproducible, and path weights were consistent across the best five group models. Second, they applied the model to data from individual subjects and found that 85% of patients fit the group model. Their results indicate that exploratory SEM is a viable technique for effective connectivity analyses of individual subjects' resting-state fMRI data.

Maguire, Vargha-Khadem, and Mishkin (2001) used SEM to compare effective connectivity during successful retrieval of real-world memories in a patient (Jon) with selective bilateral hippocampal pathology resulting from perinatal hypoxia and in healthy controls. They showed that both Jon and healthy controls activated the same network of brain regions (although Jon activated this network bilaterally). However, the communication between regions in this network differed with respect to hippocampal–cortical connectivity. Controls showed increased connectivity between the parahippocampal cortex and hippocampus during the retrieval of autobiographical events. In contrast, for these events, Jon showed increased connectivity between the hippocampus and the retrosplenial cortex, and retrosplenial and medial frontal cortex. This study suggests that altered patterns of effective connectivity may be an indicator of disordered memory.

APPLICATION OF SEM TO INDIVIDUAL DIFFERENCES

Mechelli, Penny, Price, Gitelman, and Friston (2002) used SEM to examine differences in effective connectivity among subjects. They did this by constructing a multisubject network with m regions of interest for each of the n subjects studied (i.e., resulting in a model with $m \times n$ nodes). Using such a network with regions from different subjects has two advantages. First, it tests directly for differences among subjects by comparing models that do and do not allow a particular connectivity parameter to vary over subjects. Second, it provides additional degrees of freedom to estimate the model's free parameters. Meccelli and colleagues tested whether the effect of word type (single words or pseudowords) on the reading-related coupling differed significantly among subjects. They showed that several of the forward and backward connections in their model were stronger for reading pseudowords than words, and that one connection showed significant intersubject variability.

Glabus and colleagues (2003) used SEM to examine how individual differences in subject performance or strategy are reflected in system-level networks. They used PET data acquired during a working memory (WM) task that allowed the use of different strategies to support successful performance. They assessed how

strategy and performance levels were reflected in the functional networks, both for the group as a whole and in individual subjects. High-performing subjects used a left-hemisphere network involving the inferior parietal lobe and Broca's area, whereas low-performing subjects used a right-hemisphere network involving the inferior parietal lobe and dorsolateral prefrontal cortex. Additionally, self-reported strategy (spatial vs. verbal) was reflected at the cortical level, in that there was a significant positive correlation of increasing spatial strategy and path strength between the left inferior parietal lobe and right parahippocampal gyrus.

DCM

The most recent method for causal modeling in neuroimaging is DCM (Friston et al., 2003). There are two features of DCM that distinguish it from other extant methods: (1) the specific use of a biophysical "inverse solution" to estimate the neural sources of the measured signal, and (2) the bilinear model and Bayesian causal estimation framework. For the first feature, the assumption is that the desire of most investigators is to apply connectivity estimation to the neural sources rather than the measured signal. Because this is not possible, a biophysical model is used to estimate the likely neural signals given the measured signal. It is important to distinguish the use of this model from the source estimation described for EEG/MEG. In EEG/MEG, estimating the electromagnetic sources usually is done independently from the underlying biophysical sources. In DCM, the source estimation comes from both the biophysical model and the underlying causal estimation. As a result, DCM can more properly be considered a generative model, wherein the process of model fitting involves fitting the causal structure that most likely generated the signal. In its first application to fMRI data, the Balloon–Windkessel model, which characterizes the translation between neural activity and regional hemodynamics, was adopted to generate a BOLD fMRI time series from the estimated underlying neural generators.

The bilinear aspect of DCM is implemented by examining what is termed "intrinsic" connectivity, direct inputs, and modulatory effects. This can be related to a standard general linear model:

$$A = bX + cY + dZ \qquad \text{(37.1)}$$

where A is the activity in region A; X is a matrix of areas connected to region A, with their effective connections (regression weights) in the vector b; Y reflects the external/driving input from the experimental design for which c is the parameter estimate; and finally Z is the change in the effects from areas in X that depend on features of the experimental design, with the magnitude estimated in vector d. It should be noted that the actual equations in DCM are more elaborate state equations, and the present expression in Equation 37.1 is meant to convey the concept.

The DCM implementation is meant to specifically estimate the extent of the task-dependent changes in effective connectivity. Intrinsic connectivity, therefore, can be conceived as the grand average effective connectivity across all tasks, and the modulatory effects, as the bilinear term, represent the changes in the intrinsic connections as a result of task demands. The direct inputs represent exogenous influences that are linked to the experimental paradigm. For example, the onset of visual stimuli, regardless of stimulus type, could be a direct input targeting a primary visual cortex. Conversely, the changes in effective connections as a result of stimulus type would represent the modulatory terms.

The same bilinear model is used for EEG and MEG, but the biophysical model is substantially different (Kiebel et al., 2009). Each source is modeled using a neural mass model that emulates the activity of a cortical area using three neuronal subpopulations. Moreover, the biophysical model is applied to cortical source space data rather than EEG or MEG channel data.

Applications of DCM

One of the first applications of DCM was to examine category-specific responses in ventral visual cortex (Mechelli, Price, Noppeney, & Friston, 2003). Category specificity refers to the observation of relatively focal increases in areas such as the anterior fusiform gyrus for faces, or the parahippocampal gyrus for images with complex spatial information. The prevailing hypothesis was that the specificity of the response is generated from a top-down influence from higher-order cortical areas onto the areas showing the category specificity. Using DCM, with both feedforward and feedback connections, the model with the highest Bayesian evidence showed that modulatory effects from the different categories were bottom-up. In other words, the category-specific responses were best explained by a change in the bottom-up rather than top-down effects.

Stephan, Penny, Marshall, Fink, and Friston (2005) used DCM to examine whether hemispheric functional asymmetry was determined by a word stimulus (short words, with one letter colored red) itself or by the task. In one instance, subjects judged whether the word contained the letter A, ignoring the red letter, and in another instance, they made a visuospatial judgment indicating whether the red letter was right or left of center. A direct comparison of the activity (measured with fMRI) revealed strong hemispheric differences. The letter task produced higher activity in the left hemisphere, whereas the visuospatial task produced higher activity in the right hemisphere, despite the identical letter stimulus. Models were constructed to test competing theories of interhemispheric interactions (IHIs). Using a systematic Bayesian model selection procedure, they found that, in the ventral visual stream, which was activated by letter judgments, interhemispheric connections mediated asymmetric information transfer from the right to the specialized left hemisphere. In the dorsal stream, activated by spatial judgments, it did not matter which hemisphere received the stimulus: interhemispheric coupling increased bidirectionally, reflecting recruitment of the left hemisphere. This study provided strong direct neurophysiological evidence for the existence of context-dependent mechanisms of IHI that are implemented by specific visual areas during task-driven lateralization. More generally, this study demonstrates the utility of DCM in testing competing models of network interactions underlying cognitive functions.

FINAL THOUGHTS FOR MODELING OF NEUROIMAGING DATA

The analytic translation of the notion of functional or effective connectivity estimation has benefits for developing theories of brain operation. Brain imaging researchers often discuss the results from regional activation analysis in terms of "functional networks," without specifically referring to how these networks are formed. By requiring that the networks be expressed through either functional or effective connectivity estimation, the researcher's assumptions about the network organization are more obvious.

It is also critical to acknowledge, particularly with effective connectivity, that the results are a model. There are decisions that have to be made in the course of estimation, such as the selection of regions to include in the model and how their interactions are mediated (through specification of anatomical connections). Because it is a model, however, it is an approximation of reality and, by definition, false. To paraphrase the statement from statistician George Box that all models are wrong but some are useful, the utility of any model comes from its capacity to explain neural dynamics and cognitive function, and to suggest further avenues of research to test and develop the model.

Finally, one of the greatest sins in analyzing neuroimaging data is to assume that there is a single correct method. While one can certainly make mistakes in the application of a method, there is little to be gained from "analytic chauvinism." The complexity of the data that are extracted from neuroimaging methods dictates that a single analytic approach is insufficient. We strongly concur with the position advocated by others that a pluralistic approach will provide a much better appreciation of how the brain brings about human mental function (Lange et al., 1999).

REFERENCES

Aertsen, A., Bonhoeffer, T., & Kruger, J. (1987). Coherent activity in neuronal populations: analysis and interpretation. In E. R. Caianiello (Ed.), *Physics of cognitive processes* (pp. 1–34). Singapore: World Scientific Publishing.

Astolfi, L., Cincotti, F., Babiloni, C., Carducci, F., Basilisco, A., Rossini, P. M., et al. (2005). Estimation of the cortical connectivity by high-resolution EEG and structural equation modeling: Simulations and application to finger tapping data. *IEEE Transactions on Biomedical Engineering*, 52(5), 757–768.

Astolfi, L., Cincotti, F., Mattia, D., Salinari, S., Babiloni, C., Basilisco, A., et al. (2004). Estimation of the effective and functional human cortical connectivity with structural equation modeling and directed transfer function applied to high-resolution EEG. *Magnetic Resonance Imaging*, 22(10), 1457–1470.

Beckmann, C. F., & Smith, S. M. (2005). Tensorial extensions of independent component analysis for multisubject FMRI analysis. *NeuroImage*, 25(1), 294–311.

Buchel, C., & Friston, K. (1997). Modulation of connectivity in visual pathways by attention: Cortical interactions evaluated with structural equation modeling and fMRI. *Cerebral Cortex*, 7(8), 768–778.

Bullmore, E., Horwitz, B., Honey, G., Brammer, M., Williams, S., & Sharma, T. (2000). How good is good enough in path analysis of fMRI data? *NeuroImage*, 11(4), 289–301.

David, O., Guillemain, I., Saillet, S., Reyt, S., Deransart, C., Segebarth, C., et al. (2008). Identifying neural drivers with functional MRI: An electrophysiological validation. *PLoS Biology*, 6(12), e315.

Della-Maggiore, V., Sekuler, A. B., Grady, C. L., Bennett, P. J., Sekuler, R., & McIntosh, A. R. (2000). Corticolimbic interactions associated with performance on a short-term memory task are modified by Age. *Journal of Neuroscience*, 20(22), 8410–8416.

Deshpande, G., LaConte, S., James, G. A., Peltier, S., & Hu, X. (2009). Multivariate Granger causality analysis of fMRI data. *Human Brain Mapping*, 30(4), 1361–1373.

Finger, S. (1994). *Origins of neuroscience: A history of explorations into brain function*. New York: Oxford University Press.

Friston, K., Frith, C., & Frackowiak, R. (1993). Time-dependent changes in effective connectivity measured with PET. *Human Brain Mapping*, 1, 69–79.

Friston, K., Frith, C. D., Liddle, P. F., & Frackowiak, R. S. J. (1993). Functional connectivity: The principal-component analysis of large (PET) data sets. *Journal of Cerebral Blood Flow and Metabolism*, 13, 5–14.

Friston, K. J., Buechel, C., Fink, G. R., Morris, J., Rolls, E., & Dolan, R. J. (1997). Psychophysiological and modulatory interactions in neuroimaging. *NeuroImage*, 6, 218–229.

Friston, K. J., Harrison, L., & Penny, W. (2003). Dynamic causal modelling. *NeuroImage*, 19(4), 1273–1302.

Glabus, M. F., Horwitz, B., Holt, J. L., Kohn, P. D., Gerton, B. K., Callicott, J. H., et al. (2003). Interindividual differences in functional interactions among prefrontal, parietal and parahippocampal regions during working memory. *Cerebral Cortex*, 13(12), 1352–1361.

Goebel, R., Roebroeck, A., Kim, D. S., & Formisano, E. (2003). Investigating directed cortical interactions in time-resolved fMRI data using vector autoregressive modeling and Granger causality mapping. *Magnetic Resonance Imaging*, 21(10), 1251–1261.

Goncalves, M. S., & Hall, D. A. (2003). Connectivity analysis with structural equation modelling: An example of the effects of voxel selection. *NeuroImage*, 20(3), 1455–1467.

Goncalves, M. S., Hall, D. A., Johnsrude, I. S., & Haggard, M. P. (2001). Can meaningful effective connectivities be obtained between auditory cortical regions? *NeuroImage*, 14(6), 1353–1360.

Grady, C. L., McIntosh, A. R., & Craik, F. I. (2003). Age-related differences in the functional connectivity of the hippocampus during memory encoding. *Hippocampus*, 13(5), 572–586.

Haxby, J. V., Grady, C. L., & Horwitz, B. (1991). Two visual processing pathways in human extrastriate cortex mapped with positron emission tomography. In N. A. Lassen, D. H. Ingvar, M. E. Raichle, & L. Friberg (Eds.), *Brain work and mental activity (Alfred Benzon Symposium 31)* (pp. 324–333). Copenhagen: Munksgaard.

Hayduk, L. (1987). *Structural equation modeling with LISREL*. Baltimore: Johns Hopkins University Press.

Horwitz, B., Duara, R., & Rapoport, S. I. (1984). Intercorrelations of glucose metabolic rates between brain regions: Application to healthy males in a state of reduced sensory input. *Journal of Cerebral Blood Flow and Metabolism, 4*, 484–499.

Horwitz, B., Grady, C., Haxby, J., Schapiro, M., Carson, R., Herscovitch, P., et al. (1991). Object and spatial visual processing: Intercorrelations of regional cerebral blood flow among posterior brain regions. *Journal of Cerebral Blood Flow and Metabolism, 11*(Suppl. 2), S380.

James, G. A., Kelley, M. E., Craddock, R. C., Holtzheimer, P. E., Dunlop, B. W., Nemeroff, C. B., et al. (2009). Exploratory structural equation modeling of resting-state fMRI: Applicability of group models to individual subjects. *NeuroImage, 45*(3), 778–787.

Kaminski, M., Ding, M., Truccolo, W. A., & Bressler, S. L. (2001). Evaluating causal relations in neural systems: Granger causality, directed transfer function and statistical assessment of significance. *Biological Cybernetics, 85*(2), 145–157.

Kenny, D. A., & Judd, C. M. (1984). Estimating nonlinear and interactive effects of latent variables. *Psychological Bulletin, 96*, 201–210.

Kiebel, S. J., Garrido, M. I., Moran, R., Chen, C. C., & Friston, K. J. (2009). Dynamic causal modeling for EEG and MEG. *Human Brain Mapping, 30*(6), 1866–1876.

Kim, J., & Horwitz, B. (2009). How well does structural equation modeling reveal abnormal brain anatomical connections?: An fMRI simulation study. *NeuroImage, 45*(4), 1190–1198.

Kohler, S., McIntosh, A. R., Moscovitch, M., & Winocur, G. (1998). Functional interactions between the medial temporal lobes and posterior neocortex related to episodic memory retrieval. *Cerebral Cortex, 8*(5), 451–461.

Lange, N., Strother, S. C., Anderson, J. R., Nielsen, F. A., Holmes, A. P., Kolenda, T., et al. (1999). Plurality and resemblance in fMRI data analysis. *NeuroImage, 10*(3, Pt. 1), 282–303.

Lee, L., Friston, K., & Horwitz, B. (2006). Large-scale neural models and dynamic causal modelling. *NeuroImage, 30*(4), 1243–1254.

Lin, F. H., McIntosh, A. R., Agnew, J. A., Eden, G. F., Zeffiro, T. A., & Belliveau, J. W. (2003). Multivariate analysis of neuronal interactions in the generalized partial least squares framework: Simulations and empirical studies. *NeuroImage, 20*(2), 625–642.

MacCallum, R. (1995). Model specification: Procedures, strategies, and related issues. In R. H. Hoyle (Ed.), *Structural equation modeling: Concepts, issues, and applications* (pp. 16–36). Thousand Oak, CA: Sage.

Maguire, E. A., Vargha-Khadem, F., & Mishkin, M. (2001). The effects of bilateral hippocampal damage on fMRI regional activations and interactions during memory retrieval. *Brain, 124*(Pt. 6), 1156–1170.

Marrelec, G., Kim, J., Doyon, J., & Horwitz, B. (2009).

Large-scale neural model validation of partial correlation analysis for effective connectivity investigation in functional MRI. *Human Brain Mapping, 30*(3), 941–950.

Martinez-Montes, E., Valdes-Sosa, P. A., Miwakeichi, F., Goldman, R. I., & Cohen, M. S. (2004). Concurrent EEG/fMRI analysis by multiway partial least squares. *NeuroImage, 22*(3), 1023–1034.

McCormick, C., Moscovitch, M., Protzner, A. B., Huber, C. G., & McAndrews, M. P. (2010). Hippocampal–neocortical networks differ during encoding and retrieval of relational memory: Functional and effective connectivity analyses. *Neuropsychologia, 48*, 3272–3281.

McIntosh, A. R. (2000a). From location to integration: How neural interactions form the basis for human cognition. In E. Tulving (Ed.), *Memory, consciousness, and the brain: The Tallinn Conference* (pp. 346–362). Philadelphia: Psychology Press.

McIntosh, A. R. (2000b). Towards a network theory of cognition. *Neural Networks, 13*, 861–876.

McIntosh, A. R., Bookstein, F. L., Haxby, J. V., & Grady, C. L. (1996). Spatial pattern analysis of functional brain images using partial least squares. *NeuroImage, 3*, 143–157.

McIntosh, A. R., Cabeza, R. E., & Lobaugh, N. J. (1998). Analysis of neural interactions explains the activation of occipital cortex by an auditory stimulus. *Journal of Neurophysiology, 80*, 2790–2796.

McIntosh, A. R., & Gonzalez-Lima, F. (1991). Structural modeling of functional neural pathways mapped with 2-deoxyglucose: Effects of acoustic startle habituation on the auditory system. *Brain Research, 547*, 295–302.

McIntosh, A. R., & Gonzalez-Lima, F. (1994). Structural equation modeling and its application to network analysis in functional brain imaging. *Human Brain Mapping, 2*(1–2), 2–22.

McIntosh, A. R., & Gonzalez-Lima, F. (1995). Functional network interactions between parallel auditory pathways during Pavolvian conditioned inhibition. *Brain Research, 683*, 228–241.

McIntosh, A. R., Grady, C. L., Haxby, J. V., Ungerleider, L. G., & Horwitz, B. (1996). Changes in limbic and prefrontal functional interactions in a working memory task for faces. *Cerebral Cortex, 6*, 571–584.

McIntosh, A. R., Grady, C. L., Ungerleider, L. G., Haxby, J. V., Rapoport, S. I., & Horwitz, B. (1994). Network analysis of cortical visual pathways mapped with PET. *Journal of Neuroscience, 14*, 655–666.

McIntosh, A. R., & Lobaugh, N. J. (2004). Partial least squares analysis of neuroimaging data: Applications and advances. *NeuroImage, 23*(Suppl. 1), S250–S263.

Mechelli, A., Penny, W. D., Price, C. J., Gitelman, D. R., & Friston, K. J. (2002). Effective connectivity and intersubject variability: Using a multisubject network to test differences and commonalities. *NeuroImage, 17*(3), 1459–1469.

Mechelli, A., Price, C. J., Noppeney, U., & Friston, K. J.

(2003). A dynamic causal modeling study on category effects: bottom-up or top-down mediation? *Journal of Cognitive Neuroscience, 15*(7), 925–934.

Morris, C. D., Bransford, J. D., & Franks, J. J. (1977). Levels of processing versus transfer appropriate processing. *Journal of Verbal Learning and Verbal Behavior, 16*, 519–533.

Nyberg, L., McIntosh, A. R., Cabeza, R., Nilsson, L.-G., Houle, S., Habib, R., et al. (1996). Network analysis of positron emission tomography regional cerebral blood flow data: Ensemble inhibition during episodic memory retrieval. *Journal of Neuroscience, 16*, 3753–3759.

Protzner, A. B., & McIntosh, A. R. (2006). Testing effective connectivity changes with structural equation modeling: What does a bad model tell us? *Human Brain Mapping, 27*(12), 935–947.

Roebroeck, A., Formisano, E., & Goebel, R. (2011). The identification of interacting networks in the brain using fMRI: Model selection, causality and deconvolution. *NeuroImage, 58*(2), 296–302.

Rowe, J. B. (2010). Connectivity analysis is essential to understand neurological disorders. *Frontiers in Systems Neuroscience, 4*, 144.

Rowe, J. B., Hughes, L. E., Barker, R. A., & Owen, A. M. (2010). Dynamic causal modelling of effective connectivity from fMRI: Are results reproducible and sensitive to Parkinson's disease and its treatment? *NeuroImage, 52*(3), 1015–1026.

Rugg, M. D., Johnson, J. D., Park, H., & Uncapher, M. R. (2008). Encoding-retrieval overlap in human episodic memory: A functional neuroimaging perspective. *Progresses in Brain Research, 169*, 339–352.

Seminowicz, D. A., Mayberg, H. S., McIntosh, A. R., Goldapple, K., Kennedy, S., Segal, Z., et al. (2004). Limbic–frontal circuitry in major depression: A path modeling metanalysis. *NeuroImage, 22*(1), 409–418.

Stephan, K. E., Penny, W. D., Marshall, J. C., Fink, G. R., & Friston, K. J. (2005). Investigating the functional role of callosal connections with dynamic causal models. *Annals of the New York Academy of Sciences, 1064*, 16–36.

Strother, S. C., Anderson, J. R., Schaper, K. A., Sidtis, J. J., Liow, J.-S., Woods, R. P., et al. (1995). Principal components analysis and the scaled subprofile model compared to intersubject averaged and statistical parametric mapping: I. "Functional connectivity" of the human motor system studied with [15O]water PET. *Journal of Cerebral Blood Flow and Metabolism, 15*, 738–753.

Tulving, E., & Thomson, D. M. (1973). Encoding specificity and retrieval processes in episodic memory. *Psychological Review, 80*, 352–373.

Ungerleider, L. G., & Mishkin, M. (1982). Two cortical visual systems. In D. J. Ingle, M. A. Goodale, & R. J. W. Mansfield (Eds.), *Analysis of visual behavior* (pp. 549–586). Cambridge, MA: MIT Press.

Zhuang, J., LaConte, S., Peltier, S., Zhang, K., & Hu, X. (2005). Connectivity exploration with structural equation modeling: An fMRI study of bimanual motor coordination. *NeuroImage, 25*(2), 462–470.

CHAPTER 38

Bayesian Structural Equation Modeling

David Kaplan
Sarah Depaoli

The history of structural equation modeling (SEM) can be roughly divided into two generations. The *first generation* of structural equation modeling began with the initial merging of confirmatory factor analysis (CFA) and simultaneous equation modeling (see, e.g., Jöreskog, 1973). In addition to these founding concepts, the first generation of SEM witnessed important methodological developments in handling nonstandard conditions of the data. These developments included methods for dealing with non-normal data, missing data, and sample size sensitivity problems (see, e.g., Kaplan, 2009). The *second generation* of SEM could be broadly characterized by another merger; this time, combining models for continuous latent variables developed in the first generation with models for categorical latent variables (see Muthén, 2001). The integration of continuous and categorical latent variables into a general modeling framework was due to the extension of finite mixture modeling to the SEM framework. This extension has provided an elegant theory, resulting in a marked increase in important applications. These applications include, but are not limited to, methods for handling the evaluation of interventions with noncompliance (Jo & Muthén, 2001), discrete-time mixture survival models (Muthén & Masyn, 2005), and models for examining unique trajectories of growth in academic outcomes (Kaplan, 2003). A more comprehensive review of the

history of SEM can be found in Matsueda (Chapter 2, this volume).

A parallel development to first- and second-generation SEM has been the expansion of Bayesian methods for complex statistical models, including structural equation models. Early papers include Lee (1981), Martin and McDonald (1975), and Scheines, Hoijtink, and Boomsma (1999). A recent book by Lee (2007) provides an up-to-date review and extensions of Bayesian SEM. Most recently, B. Muthén and Asparouhov (in press) demonstrate the wide range of modeling flexibility within Bayesian SEM. The increased use of Bayesian tools for statistical modeling has come about primarily as a result of progress in computational algorithms based on Markov chain Monte Carlo (MCMC) sampling. The MCMC algorithm is implemented in software programs such as WinBUGS (Lunn, Thomas, Best, & Spiegelhalter, 2000), various packages within the R archive (R Development Core Team, 2008), and most recently Mplus (Muthén & Muthén, 2010).

The purpose of this chapter is to provide an accessible introduction to Bayesian SEM as an important alternative to conventional frequentist approaches to SEM. However, to fully realize the utility of the Bayesian approach to SEM, it is necessary to demonstrate not only its applicability to first-generation SEM but also how Bayesian methodology can be applied to models characterizing the second generation of SEM. Although examples of Bayesian SEM relevant to first- and second-generation models will be provided, an important goal of this chapter is to develop the argument that MCMC is not just another estimation approach to SEM, but that Bayesian methodology provides a coherent philosophical alternative to conventional SEM practice, regardless of whether models are "first" or "second" generation.

The organization of this chapter is as follows. To begin, the previous chapters in this volume provide a full account of basic and advanced concepts in both first- and second-generation SEM, and we assume that the reader is familiar with these topics. Given that assumption, the next section provides a brief introduction to Bayesian ideas, including Bayes' theorem, the nature of prior distributions, description of the posterior distribution, and Bayesian model building. Following that, we provide a brief overview of MCMC sampling that we use for the empirical examples in this chapter. Next, we introduce the general form of the Bayesian structural equation model. This is followed by three examples that demonstrate the applicability of Bayesian SEM: Bayesian CFA, Bayesian multilevel path analysis, and Bayesian growth mixture modeling. Each example uses the MCMC sampling algorithm in Mplus (Muthén & Muthén, 2010). The chapter closes with a general discussion of how the Bayesian approach to SEM can lead to a pragmatic and evolutionary development of knowledge in the social and behavioral sciences.

BRIEF OVERVIEW OF BAYESIAN STATISTICAL INFERENCE

The goal of this section is to briefly present basic ideas in Bayesian inference to set the framework for Bayesian SEM, and follows closely the recent overview by Kaplan and Depaoli (in press). A good introductory treatment of the subject can be found in Hoff (2009).

To begin, denote by Y a random variable that takes on a realized value y. For example, a person's socioeconomic status could be considered a random variable taking on a very large set of possible values. In the context of SEM, Y could be vector-valued, such as items on an attitude survey. Once the person responds to the survey items, Y becomes realized as y. In a sense, Y is unobserved—it is the probability distribution of Y that we wish to understand from the actual data values y.

Next, denote by θ a parameter that we believe characterizes the probability model of interest. The param-

eter θ can be a scalar, such as the mean or the variance of a distribution, or it can be vector valued, such as the set of all structural model parameters, which later in the chapter we denote using the boldface $\boldsymbol{\theta}$.

We are concerned with determining the probability of observing y given unknown parameters θ, which we write as $p(y|\theta)$. In statistical inference, the goal is to obtain estimates of the unknown parameters given the data. This is expressed as the likelihood of the parameters given the data, denoted as $L(\theta|y)$. Often we work with the log-likelihood, written as $l(\theta|y)$.

The key difference between Bayesian statistical inference and frequentist statistical inference concerns the nature of the unknown parameters θ. In the frequentist tradition, the assumption is that θ is unknown but fixed. In Bayesian statistical inference, θ is random, possessing a probability distribution that reflects our uncertainty about the true value of θ. Because both the observed data y and the parameters θ are assumed random, we can model the joint probability of the parameters and the data as a function of the conditional distribution of the data given the parameters, and the prior distribution of the parameters. More formally,

$$p(\theta, y) = p(y|\theta)p(\theta) \tag{38.1}$$

Because of the symmetry of joint probabilities,

$$p(y|\theta)p(\theta) = p(\theta|y)p(y) \tag{38.2}$$

Therefore,

$$p(\theta \mid y) = \frac{p(\theta, y)}{p(y)} = \frac{p(y \mid \theta)p(\theta)}{p(y)} \tag{38.3}$$

where $p(\theta|y)$ is referred to as the *posterior distribution* of the parameters θ given the observed data y. Thus, from Equation 38.3, the posterior distribution of θ given y is equal to the data distribution $p(y|\theta)$ times the prior distribution of the parameters $p(\theta)$ normalized by $p(y)$ so that the distribution integrates to one. Equation 38.3 is *Bayes' theorem*. For discrete variables

$$p(y) = \sum_{\theta} p(y \mid \theta)p(\theta) \tag{38.4}$$

and for continuous variables

$$p(y) = \int_{\theta} p(y \mid \theta)p(\theta)d\theta \tag{38.5}$$

As earlier, the denominator in Equation 38.3 does not involve model parameters, so we can omit the term and obtain the *unnormalized posterior distribution*

$$p(\theta|y) \propto p(y|\theta)p(\theta) \qquad (38.6)$$

Consider the data distribution $p(y|\theta)$ on the right hand side of Equation 38.6. When expressed in terms of the unknown parameters θ for fixed values of y, this term is the *likelihood* $L(\theta|y)$, which we mentioned earlier. Thus, Equation 38.6 can be rewritten as

$$p(\theta|y) \propto L(\theta|y)p(\theta) \qquad (38.7)$$

Equation 38.6 represents the core of Bayesian statistical inference and is what separates Bayesian statistics from frequentist statistics. Specifically, Equation 38.6 states that our uncertainty regarding the parameters of our model, as expressed by the prior distribution $p(\theta)$, is *weighted* by the actual data $p(y|\theta)$ (or equivalently, $L[\theta|y]$), yielding an updated estimate of the model parameters, as expressed in the posterior distribution $p(\theta|y)$.

Types of Priors

The distinguishing feature of Bayesian inference is the specification of the prior distribution for the model parameters. The difficulty arises in how a researcher goes about choosing prior distributions for the model parameters. We can distinguish between two types of priors, (1) *noninformative* and (2) *informative priors,* based on how much information we believe we have prior to data collection and how accurate we believe that information to be.

Noninformative Priors

In some cases we may not be in possession of enough prior information to aid in drawing posterior inferences. From a Bayesian perspective, this lack of information is still important to consider and incorporate into our statistical specifications. In other words, it is equally as important to quantify our ignorance as it is to quantify our cumulative understanding of a problem at hand.

The standard approach to quantifying our ignorance is to incorporate a noninformative prior into our specification. Noninformative priors are also referred to as "vague" or "diffuse" priors. Arguably, the most common noninformative prior distribution is the uniform distribution over some sensible range of values. Care must be taken in the choice of the range of values over the uniform distribution. Specifically, a uniform $[-\infty, \infty]$ would be an improper prior distribution insofar as it does not integrate to 1.0 as required of probability distributions. Another type of noninformative prior is the so-called "Jeffreys' prior," which handles some of the problems associated with uniform priors. An important treatment of noninformative priors can be found in Press (2003).

Informative Priors

In many practical situations, there may be sufficient prior information on the shape and scale of the distribution of a model parameter that it can be systematically incorporated into the prior distribution. Such priors are referred to as "informative." One type of informative prior is based on the notion of a "conjugate prior" distribution, which is one that, when combined with the likelihood function, yields a posterior distribution that is in the same distributional family as the prior distribution. This is a very important and convenient feature because if a prior is not conjugate, the resulting posterior distribution may have a form that is not analytically simple to solve. Arguably, the existence of numerical simulation methods for Bayesian inference, such as MCMC sampling, may render nonconjugacy less of a problem.

Point Estimates of the Posterior Distribution

Bayes' theorem shows that the posterior distribution is composed of encoded prior information weighted by the data. With the posterior distribution in hand, it is of interest to obtain summaries of the distribution—such as the mean, mode, and variance. In addition, interval summaries of the posterior distribution can be obtained. Summarizing the posterior distribution provides the necessary ingredients for Bayesian hypothesis testing. In the general case, the expressions for the mean and variance of the posterior distribution come from expressions for the mean and variance of conditional distributions generally. Specifically, for the continuous case, the mean of the posterior distribution can be written as

$$E(\theta|y) = \int_{-\infty}^{+\infty} \theta p(\theta|y)d\theta \qquad (38.8)$$

and is referred to as the *expected a posteriori* or EAP estimate. Thus, the conditional expectation of θ is obtained by averaging over the marginal distribution of y. Similarly, the conditional variance of θ can be obtained as (see Gill, 2002)

$$
\begin{aligned}
var(\theta|y) &= E[(\theta - E[(\theta|y])^2|y) \\
&= E(\theta^2|y) - E(\theta|y)^2 \quad \textbf{(38.9)}
\end{aligned}
$$

The conditional expectation and variance of the posterior distribution provide two simple summary values of the distribution. Another summary measure would be the mode of the posterior distribution. Those measures, along with the quantiles of the posterior distribution, provide a complete description of the distribution.

Credibility Intervals

One important consequence of viewing parameters probabilistically concerns the interpretation of "confidence intervals." Recall that the frequentist confidence interval is based on the assumption of a very large number of repeated samples from the population characterized by a fixed and unknown parameter μ. For any given sample, we obtain the sample mean $\bar{x}$ and form, for example, a 95% confidence interval. The correct frequentist interpretation is that 95% of the confidence intervals formed this way capture the true parameter μ under the null hypothesis. Notice that from this perspective, the probability that the parameter is in the interval is either zero or one.

In contrast, the Bayesian perspective forms a "credibility interval" (also known as a "posterior probability interval"). Again, because we assume that a parameter has a probability distribution, when we sample from the posterior distribution of the model parameters, we can obtain its quantiles. From the quantiles, we can directly obtain the probability that a parameter lies within a particular interval. So in this example, a 95% credibility interval means that the probability that the parameter lies in the interval is 0.95. Notice that this is entirely different from the frequentist interpretation, and arguably aligns with common sense.

Formally, a $100(1 - \alpha)\%$ credibility interval for a particular subset of the parameter space θ is defined as

$$
1 - \alpha = \int_C p(\theta \mid x)d\theta \quad \textbf{(38.10)}
$$

Highest Posterior Density

The simplicity of the credibility interval notwithstanding, it is not the only way to provide an interval estimate of a parameter. Following the argument set down by Box and Tiao (1973), when considering the posterior distribution of a parameter θ, there is a substantial part of the region of that distribution where the density is quite small. It may be reasonable, therefore, to construct an interval in which every point inside has a higher probability than any point outside the interval. Such a construction is referred to as the *highest probability density* (HPD) interval. More formally,

Definition 1

Let $p(\theta|y)$ be the posterior probability density function. A region R of the parameter space θ is called the HPD region of the interval $1 - \alpha$ if

1. $P(\theta \in R|y) = 1 - \alpha$
2. *For $\theta_1 \in R$ and $\theta_2 \notin R$, $p(\theta_1|y) \geq p(\theta_2|y)$.*

In words, the first part says that given the data y, the probability is that θ is in a particular region defined as $1 - \alpha$, where α is determined ahead of time. The second part says that for two different values of θ, denoted as θ_1 and θ_2, if θ_1 is in the region defined by $1 - \alpha$, but θ_2 is not, then θ_1 has a higher probability than θ_2 given the data. Note that for unimodal and symmetric distributions, such as the uniform distribution or the normal distribution, the HPD is formed by choosing tails of equal density. The advantage of the HPD arises when densities are not symmetric and/or are not unimodal. In fact, this is an important property of the HPD and sets it apart from standard credibility intervals. Following Box and Tiao (1973), if $p(\theta|y)$ is not uniform over every region in θ, then the HPD region $1 - \alpha$ is unique. Also if $p(\theta_1|y) = p(\theta_2|y)$, then these points are included (or excluded) by a $1 - \alpha$ HPD region. The opposite is true as well, namely, if $p(\theta_1|y) \neq p(\theta_2|y)$, then a $1 - \alpha$ HPD region includes one point but not the other (Box & Tiao, 1973, p. 123).

BAYESIAN MODEL EVALUATION AND COMPARISON

SEM, by its very nature, involves the specification, estimation, and testing of models that purport to represent the underlying structure of data. In this case, SEM is not only a noun describing a broad class of methodologies, but it is also a verb—an activity on the part of a researcher to describe and analyze a phenomenon of interest. The chapters in this handbook have described the nuances of SEM from the frequentist domain—with many authors attending to issues of specification, power, and model modification. In this section, we consider model evaluation and comparison from the Bayesian perspective. We focus on two procedures that are available in Mplus, namely, posterior predictive checking along with posterior predictive p-values as a means of evaluating the quality of the fit of the model (see, e.g., Gelman, Carlin, Stern, & Rubin, 2003), and the deviance information criterion for the purposes of model comparison (Spiegelhalter, Best, Carlin, & van der Linde, 2002). We are quick to note, however, that these procedures are available in WinBUGS as well as various programs within the R environment such as LearnBayes (Albert, 2007) and MCMCpack (Martin, Quinn, & Park, 2010).

Posterior Predictive Checks

The general idea behind posterior predictive checking is that there should be little, if any, discrepancy between data generated by the model, and the actual data itself. In essence, posterior predictive checking is a method for assessing the specification quality of the model from the viewpoint of predictive accuracy. Any deviation between the model-generated data and the actual data suggests possible model misspecification.

Posterior predictive checking utilizes the posterior predictive distribution of replicated data. Following Gelman and colleagues (2003), let y^{rep} be data replicated from our current model. That is,

$$p(y^{rep} \mid y) = \int p(y^{rep} \mid \theta) p(\theta \mid y) d\theta \quad (38.11)$$
$$= \int p(y^{rep} \mid \theta) p(y \mid \theta) p(\theta) d\theta$$

Notice that the second term, $p(\theta|y)$, on the right-hand side of Equation 38.11 is simply the posterior distribution of the model parameters. In words, Equation 38.11 states that the distribution of future observations given the present data, $p(y^{rep}|y)$, is equal to the probability distribution of the future observations given the parameters, $p(y^{rep}|\theta)$, weighted by the posterior distribution of the model parameters. Thus, posterior predictive checking accounts for both the uncertainty in the model parameters and the uncertainty in the data.

As a means of assessing the fit of the model, posterior predictive checking implies that the replicated data should match the observed data quite closely if we are to conclude that the model fits the data. One approach to quantifying model fit in the context of posterior predictive checking incorporates the notion of Bayesian p-values. Denote by $T(y)$ a model test statistic based on the data, and let $T(y^{rep})$ be the same test statistic but defined for the replicated data. Then, the Bayesian p-value is defined to be

$$p\text{-value} = pr(T(y^{rep}) \geq T(y)|y) \quad (38.12)$$

Equation 38.12 measures the proportion of test statistics in the replicated data that exceeds that of the actual data. We will demonstrate posterior predictive checking in our examples.

Bayes Factors

As suggested earlier in this chapter, the Bayesian framework does not adopt the frequentist orientation to null hypothesis significance testing. Instead, as with posterior predictive checking, a key component of Bayesian statistical modeling is a framework for model choice, with the idea that the model will be used for prediction. For this chapter, we will focus on Bayes factors, the Bayesian information criterion, and the deviance information criterion as methods for choosing among a set of competing models. The deviance information criterion will be used in the subsequent empirical examples.

A very simple and intuitive approach to model building and model selection uses so-called "Bayes factors" (Kass & Raftery, 1995). An excellent discussion of Bayes factors and the problem of hypothesis testing from the Bayesian perspective can be found in Raftery (1995). In essence, the Bayes factor provides a way to quantify the odds that the data favor one hypothesis over another. A key benefit of Bayes factors is that models do not have to be nested.

To begin, consider two competing models, denoted as M_1 and M_2, that could be nested within a larger space of alternative models. For example, these could be two regression models with a different number of variables, or two structural equation models specifying very different directions of mediating effects. Further, let θ_1 and θ_2 be two parameter vectors. From Bayes' theorem, the posterior probability that, say, M_1, is the correct model can be written as

$$p(M_1 \mid y) = \frac{p(y \mid M_1)p(M_1)}{p(y \mid M_1)p(M_1) + p(y \mid M_2)p(M_2)} \quad \textbf{(38.13)}$$

Notice that $p(y|M_1)$ does not contain model parameters θ_1. To obtain $p(y|M_1)$ requires integrating over θ_1. That is

$$p(y \mid M_1) = \int p(y \mid \theta_1, M_1)p(\theta_1 \mid M_1)d\theta_1 \quad \textbf{(38.14)}$$

where the terms inside the integral are the likelihood and the prior, respectively. The quantity $p(y|M_1)$ has been referred to as the "integrated likelihood" for model M_1 (Raftery, 1995). Perhaps a more useful term is the "predictive probability of the data" given M_1. A similar expression can be written for M_2.

With these expressions, we can move to the comparison of our two models, M_1 and M_2. The goal is to develop a quantity that expresses the extent to which the data support M_1 over M_2. One quantity could be the posterior odds of M_1 over M_2, expressed as

$$\frac{p(M_1 \mid y)}{p(M_2 \mid y)} = \frac{p(y \mid M_1)}{p(y \mid M_2)} \times \left[\frac{p(M_1)}{p(M_2)} \right] \quad \textbf{(38.15)}$$

Notice that the first term on the right-hand side of Equation 38.15 is the ratio of two integrated likelihoods. This ratio is referred to as the "Bayes factor" for M_1 over M_2, denoted here as B_{12}. In line with Kass and Raftery (1995, p. 776), our prior opinion regarding the odds of M_1 over M_2, given by $p(M_1)/p(M_2)$, is weighted by our consideration of the data, given by $p(y|M_1)/p(y|M_2)$. This weighting gives rise to our updated view of evidence provided by the data for either hypothesis, denoted as $p(M_1|y)/p(M_2|y)$. An inspection of Equation 38.15 also suggests that the Bayes factor is the ratio of the posterior odds to the prior odds.

In practice, there may be no prior preference for one model over the other. In this case, the prior odds are neutral and $p(M_1) = p(M_2) = 1/2$. When the prior odds ratio equals 1, then the posterior odds is equal to the Bayes factor.

The Bayesian Information Criterion

A popular measure for model selection used in both frequentist and Bayesian applications is based on an approximation of the Bayes factor and is referred to as the "Bayesian information criterion" (BIC), also called the "Schwarz criterion" (Schwarz, 1978). A detailed math-

ematical derivation for the BIC can be found in Raftery (1995), who also examines generalizations of the BIC to a broad class of statistical models.

Under conditions where there is little prior information, Raftery (1995) has shown that an approximation of the Bayes factor can be written as

$$\text{BIC} = -2 \log(\hat{\theta}|y) + q \log(n) \quad \textbf{(38.16)}$$

where $-2 \log(\hat{\theta}|y)$ describes model fit, while $q \log(n)$ is a penalty for model complexity, q represents the number of variables in the model, and n is the sample size.

As with Bayes factors, the BIC is often used for model comparisons. Specifically, the difference between two BIC measures comparing, say, M_1 to M_2 can be written as

$$\begin{aligned}\Delta(\text{BIC}_{12}) &= \text{BIC}_{(M_1)} - \text{BIC}_{(M_2)} \\ &= \log(\hat{\theta}_1 \mid y) - \log(\hat{\theta}_2 \mid y) - \frac{1}{2}(q_1 - q_2)\log(n)\end{aligned} \quad \textbf{(38.17)}$$

Rules of thumb have been developed to assess the quality of the evidence favoring one hypothesis over another using Bayes factors and the comparison of BIC values from two competing models. Following Kass and Raftery (1995, p. 777) and using M_1 as the reference model,

BIC difference	Bayes factor	Evidence against M_2
0 to 2	1 to 3	Weak
2 to 6	3 to 20	Positive
6 to 10	20 to 150	Strong
> 10	> 150	Very strong

The Deviance Information Criterion (DIC)

Although the BIC is derived from a fundamentally Bayesian perspective, it is often productively used for model comparison in the frequentist domain. Recently, however, an explicitly Bayesian approach to model comparison was developed by Spiegelhalter and colleagues (2002) based on the notion of *Bayesian deviance*.

Consider a particular probability model for a set of data, defined as $p(y|\theta)$. Then, *Bayesian deviance* can be defined as

$$D(\theta) = -2 \log[p(y|\theta)] + 2 \log[h(y)] \quad \textbf{(38.18)}$$

where, according to Spielgelhalter and colleagues (2002), the term $h(y)$ is a standardizing factor that does not involve model parameters and thus is not involved in model selection. Note that although Equation 38.18 is similar to the BIC, it is not, as currently defined, an explicit Bayesian measure of model fit. To accomplish this, we use Equation 38.18 to obtain a posterior mean over θ by defining

$$\text{DIC} = E_\theta\{-2\log[p(y|\theta)|y] + 2\log[h(y)]\} \quad \textbf{(38.19)}$$

Similar to the BIC, the model with the smallest DIC among a set of competing models is preferred.

BRIEF OVERVIEW OF MCMC ESTIMATION

As stated in the introduction, the key reason for the increased popularity of Bayesian methods in the social and behavioral sciences has been the advent of powerful computational algorithms now available in proprietary and open-source software. The most common algorithm for Bayesian estimation is based on MCMC sampling. A number of very important papers and books have been written about MCMC sampling (see, e.g., Gilks, Richardson, & Spiegelhalter, 1996). Suffice it to say, the general idea of MCMC is that instead of attempting to analytically solve for the moments and quantiles of the posterior distribution, MCMC instead draws specially constructed samples from the posterior distribution $p(\theta|y)$ of the model parameters.

The formal algorithm can be specified as follows. Let θ be a vector of model parameters with elements $\theta = (\theta_1, \ldots, \theta_q)'$. Note that information regarding θ is contained in the prior distribution $p(\theta)$. A number of algorithms and software programs are available to conduct MCMC sampling. For the purposes of this chapter, we use the Gibbs sampler (Geman & Geman, 1984) as implemented in Mplus (Muthén & Muthén, 2010). Following the description given in Hoff (2009), the Gibbs sampler begins with an initial set of starting values for the parameters, denoted as $\theta^{(0)} = (\theta_1^{(0)}, \ldots, \theta_q^{(0)})'$. Given this starting point, the Gibbs sampler generates $\theta^{(s)}$ from $\theta^{(s-1)}$ as follows:

1. sample $\theta_1^{(s)} \sim p(\theta_1 | \theta_2^{(s-1)}, \theta_3^{(s-1)}, \ldots, \theta_q^{(s-1)}, y)$
2. sample $\theta_2^{(s)} \sim p(\theta_2 | \theta_1^{(s)}, \theta_3^{(s-1)}, \ldots, \theta_q^{(s-1)}, y)$
$$\vdots$$
q. sample $\theta_q^{(s)} \sim p(\theta_q | \theta_1^{(s)}, \theta_2^{(s)}, \ldots, \theta_{q-1}^{(s)}, y)$

where $s = 1, 2, \ldots, S$ are the Monte Carlo interations. Then, a sequence of dependent vectors is formed

$$\theta^{(1)} = \left\{\theta_1^{(1)}, \ldots, \theta_q^{(1)}\right\}$$
$$\theta^{(2)} = \left\{\theta_1^{(2)}, \ldots, \theta_q^{(2)}\right\}$$
$$\vdots$$
$$\theta^{(S)} = \left\{\theta_1^{(S)}, \ldots, \theta_q^{(S)}\right\}$$

This sequence exhibits the so-called "Markov property" insofar as $\theta^{(s)}$ is conditionally independent of $\{\theta_1^{(0)}, \ldots \theta_q^{(s-2)}\}$ given $\theta^{(s-1)}$. Under some general conditions, the sampling distribution resulting from this sequence will converge to the target distribution as $S \to \infty$. See Gilks and colleagues (1996) for additional details on the properties of MCMC.

In setting up the Gibbs sampler, a decision must be made regarding the number of Markov chains to be generated, as well as the number of iterations of the sampler. With regard to the number of chains to be generated, it is not uncommon to specify multiple chains. Each chain samples from another location of the posterior distribution based on purposefully disparate starting values. With multiple chains it may be the case that fewer iterations are required, particularly if there is evidence for the chains converging to the same posterior mean for each parameter. Convergence can also be obtained from one chain, though often requiring a considerably larger number of iterations. Once the chain has stabilized, the iterations prior to the stabilization (referred to as the "burn-in" phase) are discarded. Summary statistics, including the posterior mean, mode, standard deviation and credibility intervals, are calculated on the post-burn-in iterations.[1]

Convergence Diagnostics

Assessing the convergence of parameters within MCMC estimation is a difficult task that has received considerable attention in the literature (see, e.g., Sinharay, 2004). The difficulty of assessing convergence stems from the very nature of the MCMC algorithm because it is designed to converge in distribution rather than to a point estimate. Because there is not a single adequate assessment of convergence for this situation, it is common to inspect several different diagnostics that examine varying aspects of convergence conditions.

A variety of these diagnostics are reviewed and demonstrated in Kaplan and Depaoli (in press), including the Geweke (1992) convergence diagnostic, the Heidelberger and Welch (1983) convergence diagnostic, and the Raftery and Lewis (1992) convergence diagnostic. These diagnostics can be used for the single-chain situation.

One of the most common diagnostics in a multiple-chain situation is the Brooks, Gelman, and Rubin diagnostic (see, e.g., Gelman, 1996; Gelman & Rubin, 1992a, 1992b). This diagnostic is based on analysis of variance and is intended to assess convergence among several parallel chains with varying starting values. Specifically, Gelman and Rubin (1992a) proposed a method where an overestimate and an underestimate of the variance of the target distribution are formed. The overestimate of variance is represented by the between-chain variance, and the underestimate is the within-chain variance (Gelman, 1996). The theory is that these two estimates would be approximately equal at the point of convergence. The comparison of between and within variances is referred to as the "potential scale reduction factor" (PSRF), and larger values typically indicate that the chains have not fully explored the target distribution. Specifically, a variance ratio that is computed with values approximately equal to 1.0 indicates convergence. Brooks and Gelman (1998) added an adjustment for sampling variability in the variance estimates and also proposed a multivariate extension (MPSRF), which does not include the sampling variability correction. The changes by Brooks and Gelman reflect the diagnostic as implemented in Mplus (Muthén & Muthén, 2010).

SPECIFICATION OF BAYESIAN SEM

Following general notation, denote the measurement model as

$$y = \alpha + \Lambda\eta + \mathbf{K}x + \varepsilon \qquad (38.20)$$

where y is a vector of manifest variables, α is a vector of measurement intercepts, Λ is a factor loading matrix, η is a vector of latent variables, $\mathbf{K}$ is a matrix of regression coefficients relating the manifest variables y to observed variables x, and ε is a vector of uniquenesses with covariance matrix Ξ, assumed to be diagonal. The structural model relating common factors to each other

and possibly to a vector of manifest variables x is written as

$$\eta = \nu + \mathbf{B}\eta + \Gamma x + \zeta \qquad (38.21)$$

where ν is a vector of structural intercepts, $\mathbf{B}$ and Γ are matrices of structural coefficients, and ζ is a vector of structural disturbances with covariance matrix Ψ, which is assumed to be diagonal.

Conjugate Priors for SEM Parameters

To specify the prior distributions, it is notationally convenient to arrange the model parameters as sets of common conjugate distributions. Parameters with the subscript 'norm' follow a normal distribution, while those with the subscript 'IW' follow an inverse-Wishart distribution. Let $\theta_{norm} = \{\alpha, \nu, \Lambda, \mathbf{B}, \Gamma, \mathbf{K}\}$ be the vector of free model parameters that are assumed to follow a normal distribution, and let $\theta_{IW} = \{\Xi, \Psi\}$ be the vector of free model parameters that are assumed to follow the inverse-Wishart distribution. Formally, we write

$$\theta_{norm} \sim N(\mu, \Omega) \qquad (38.22)$$

where μ and Ω are the mean and variance hyperparameters, respectively, of the normal prior. For blocks of variances and covariances in Ξ and Ψ, we assume that the prior distribution is IW,[2] that is,

$$\theta_{IW} \sim IW(\mathbf{R}, \delta) \qquad (38.23)$$

where $\mathbf{R}$ is a positive definite matrix, and $\delta > q - 1$, where q is the number of observed variables. Different choices for $\mathbf{R}$ and δ will yield different degrees of "informativeness" for the IW distribution.

In addition to the conventional SEM model parameters and their priors, an additional model parameter is required for the growth mixture modeling example given below. Specifically, it is required that we estimate the mixture proportions, which we denote as π. In this specification, the class labels assigning an individual to a particular trajectory class follow a multinomial distribution with parameters n, the sample size, and π is a vector of trajectory class proportions. The conjugate prior for trajectory class proportions is the Dirichlet(τ) distribution with hyperparameters $\tau = (\tau_1, \dots, \tau_T)$, where T is the number of trajectory classes and $\sum_{T=1}^{T} = 1$.

MCMC Sampling for Bayesian SEM

The Bayesian approach begins by considering η as missing data. Then, the observed data y are augmented with η in the posterior analysis. The Gibbs sampler then produces a posterior distribution $[\theta_n, \theta_{IW}, \eta \,|\, y]$ via the following algorithm. At the $(s + 1)$th iteration, using current values of $\eta^{(s)}$, $\theta_{norm}^{(s)}$, and $\theta_{IW}^{(s)}$,

1. sample $\eta^{(s+1)}$ from $p(\eta \,|\, \theta_{norm}^{(s)}, \theta_{IW}^{(s)}, y)$ **(38.24)**

2. sample $\theta_n^{(s+1)}$ from $p(\theta_{norm} \,|\, \theta_{IW}^{(s)}, \eta^{(s+1)}, y)$ **(38.25)**

3. sample $\theta_{IW}^{(s+1)}$ from $p(\theta_{IW} \,|\, \theta_{norm}^{(s+1)}, \eta^{(s+1)}, y)$ **(38.26)**

In words, Equations 38.24–38.26 first require start values for $\theta_{norm}^{(0)}$ and $\theta_{IW}^{(0)}$ to begin the MCMC generation. Then, given these current start values and the data y at iteration s, we generate η at iteration $s + 1$. Given the latent data and observed data, we generate estimates of the measurement model and structural model parameters in Equations 38.20 and 38.21, respectively. The computational details can be found in Asparouhov and Muthén (2010).

THREE EXAMPLES OF BAYESIAN SEM

This section provides three examples of Bayesian SEM. Example 1 presents a simple two-factor Bayesian CFA. This model is compared to an alternative model with only one factor. Example 2 presents an example of a multilevel path analysis with a randomly varying slope. Example 3 presents Bayesian growth mixture modeling.

Bayesian CFA

Data for this example is comprised of an unweighted sample of 665 kindergarten teachers from the fall assessment of the Early Childhood Longitudinal Study—Kindergarten (ECLS-K) class of 1998–1999 (National Center for Education Statistics [NCES], 2001). The teachers were given a questionnaire about different characteristics of the classroom and students. A portion of this questionnaire consisted of a series of Likert-type items regarding the importance of different student characteristics and classroom behavior. Nine of these items were chosen for this example. All items were scored based on a 5-point summative response scale re-

garding the applicability and importance of each item to the teacher.

For this example we presume to have strong prior knowledge of the factor loadings, but no prior knowledge of the factor means, factor variances, and unique variances. For the factor loadings, strong prior knowledge can be determined as a function of both the location and the precision of the prior distribution. In particular, the mean hyperparameter would reflect the prior knowledge of the factor loading value (set at 0.8 in this example), and the precision of the prior distribution would be high (small variances of 0.01 were used here) to reflect the strength of our prior knowledge. As the strength of our knowledge decreases for a parameter, the variance hyperparameter would increase to reflect our lack of precision in the prior.

For the factor means, factor variances, and unique variances, we specified priors that reflected no prior knowledge about those parameters. The factor means were given prior distributions that were normal but contained very little precision. Specifically, the mean hyperparameters were set arbitrarily at 0, and the variance hyperparameters were specified as 10^{10} to indicate no precision in the prior. The factor variances and unique variances also received priors reflecting no prior knowledge about those parameters. These variance parameters all received IW priors that were completely diffuse, as described in Asparouhov and Muthén (2010).

On the basis of preliminary exploratory factor analyses, the CFA model in this example is specified to have two factors. The first factor contains two items related to the importance teachers place on how a student's progress relates to other children. The items specifically address how a student's achievements compare to other students in the classroom and also how they compare to statewide standards. The second factor comprises seven items that relate to individual characteristics of the student. These items include the following topics: improvement over past performance, overall effort, class participation, daily attendance, classroom behavior, cooperation with other students, and the ability to follow directions.

Parameter Convergence

A CFA model was estimated with 10,000 total iterations, 5,000 burn-in and 5,000 post-burn-in. This model converged properly as indicated by the Brooks and Gelman (1998) (PSRF) diagnostic. Specifically, the estimated value for PSRF fell within a specified range surrounding 1.0. This model took less than 1 minute to compute.

Figure 38.1 presents convergence plots, posterior density plots, and autocorrelation plots (for both chains) for the factor loadings for items 2 and 4. Perhaps the most common form of assessing MCMC convergence is to examine the convergence (also called "history")

plots produced for a chain. Typically, a parameter will appear to converge if the sample estimates form a tight horizontal band across this history plot. This method is more likely to be an indicator of nonconvergence. It is typical to use multiple Markov chains, each with different starting values, to assess parameter convergence. For example, if two separate chains for the same parameter are sampling from different areas of the target distribution, there is evidence of nonconvergence. Like-

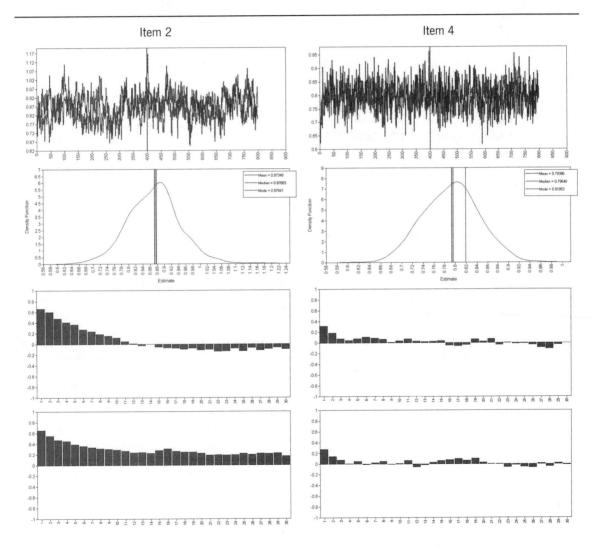

FIGURE 38.1. CFA: Convergence, posterior densities, and autocorrelation plots for select parameters.

wise, if a plot shows substantial fluctuation or jumps in the chain, it is likely the parameter has not reached convergence. The convergence plots in Figure 38.1 exhibit a tight, horizontal band for both of the parameters presented. This tight band indicates the parameters likely converged properly.

Next, Figure 38.1 presents the posterior probability density plots that indicate the posterior densities for these parameters are approximating a normal density. The following two rows present the autocorrelation plots for each of the two chains. Autocorrelation plots illustrate the amount of dependence in the chain. These plots represent the post-burn-in phase of the respective chains. Each of the two chains for these parameters shows relatively low dependence, indicating that the estimates are not being impacted by starting values or by the previous sampling states in the chain.

The other parameters included in this model showed similar results of proper convergence, normal posterior densities, and low autocorrelations for both MCMC chains. Appendix 38.1 contains the Mplus code for this example.

Model Interpretation

Estimates based on the post-burn-in iterations for the final CFA model are presented in Table 38.1. The EAP estimates and standard deviations of the posterior distributions are provided for each parameter. The one-tailed p-value based on the posterior distribution is also included for each parameter. If the parameter estimate is positive, this p-value represents the proportion of the posterior distribution that is below zero. If the parameter estimate is negative, the p-value is the proportion of the posterior distribution that is above zero (B. Muthén, 2010, p. 7). Finally, the 95% credibility interval is provided for each parameter. The first factor consisted of measures comparing the student's progress to others, while the second factor consisted of individual student characteristics. Note that the first item on each factor was fixed to have a loading of 1.00 in order to set the metric of that factor.

The factor comparing the student's progress to state standards has a high loading of 0.87. The factor measuring individual student characteristics also had high factor loadings, ranging from 0.79 to 1.10 (unstandardized). Note that although these are unstandardized loadings, the Bayesian estimation framework can handle any form of standardization as well. Estimates

for factor variances and covariances, factor means, and residual variances are also included in Table 38.1.

The one-sided p-values in Table 38.1 can aid in interpreting the credibility interval produced by the posterior distribution. For example, in the case of the means for factor 1 and factor 2, the lower bound of the 95% credibility interval was negative and the upper bound was positive. The one-sided p-value indicates exactly what proportion of the posterior is negative and what proportion is positive. For the factor 1 mean, the p-value indicated that 13% of the posterior distribution fell below zero. Likewise, results for the factor 2 mean indicated that 45% of the posterior distribution fell below zero. Overall, these p-values, especially for the factor 2 mean, indicated that a large portion of the posterior distribution was negative even though the EAP estimate was positive.

Model Fit and Model Comparison

For this example, we illustrate posterior predictive checking (PPC) for model assessment, and the DIC for model choice. Specifically, PPC was demonstrated for the two-factor CFA model, and the DIC was used to compare the two-factor CFA model to a one-factor CFA model.

In Mplus, PPC uses the likelihood ratio chi-square test as the discrepancy function between the actual data and the data generated by the model. A posterior predictive p-value is then computed based on this discrepancy function. Unlike the classical p-value, the Bayesian p-value takes into account the variability of the model parameters and does not rely on asymptotic theory (Asparouhov & Muthén, 2010, p. 28). As mentioned, the data generated by the model should closely match the observed data if the model fits. Specifically, if the posterior predictive p-value obtained is small, this is an indication of model misfit for the observed data. The PPC test also produces a 95% confidence interval for the difference between the value of the chi-square model test statistic for the observed sample data and that for the replicated data (Muthén, 2010).

Model fit was assessed by PPC for the original two-factor CFA model presented earlier. The model was rejected based on the PPC test with a posterior predictive p-value of .00, indicating that the model does not adequately represent the observed data. The 95% confidence interval for the difference between the observed data test statistic and the replicated data test statistic

TABLE 38.1. MCMC CFA Estimates: ECLS-K Teacher Survey

Parameter	EAP	SD	p-value	95% credibility interval
Loadings: Compared to others				
Compared to other children	1.00			
Compared to state standards	0.87	0.07	0.00	0.73, 1.02
Loadings: Individual characteristics				
Improvement	1.00			
Effort	0.79	0.05	0.00	0.70, 0.89
Class participation	1.09	0.06	0.00	0.97, 1.20
Daily attendance	1.08	0.06	0.00	0.96, 1.20
Class behavior	1.10	0.05	0.00	1.00, 1.20
Cooperation with others	1.10	0.05	0.00	1.00, 1.20
Follow directions	0.82	0.05	0.00	0.72, 0.91
Factor means				
Factor 1 mean	0.30	0.22	0.13	−0.07, 0.65
Factor 2 mean	0.02	0.07	0.45	−0.08, 0.18
Factor variances and covariances				
Factor 1 variance	0.45	0.05	0.00	0.35, 0.55
Factor 2 variance	0.14	0.01	0.00	0.12, 0.17
Factor covariance	0.11	0.01	0.00	0.09, 0.14
Residual variances				
Compared to other children	0.31	0.04	0.00	0.23, 0.39
Compared to state standards	0.60	0.05	0.00	0.52, 0.70
Improvement	0.28	0.02	0.00	0.25, 0.31
Effort	0.21	0.01	0.00	0.18, 0.23
Class participation	0.27	0.02	0.00	0.23, 0.30
Daily attendance	0.29	0.02	0.00	0.26, 0.33
Classroom behavior	0.16	0.01	0.00	0.13, 0.18
Cooperation with others	0.17	0.01	0.00	0.14, 0.19
Follow directions	0.18	0.01	0.00	0.16, 0.20

had a lower bound of 149.67 and an upper bound of 212.81 (see Figure 38.2). Since the confidence interval for the difference in the observed and replicated data is positive, this indicates "that the observed data test statistic is much larger than what would have been generated by the model" (Muthén, 2010, p. 14).

Figure 38.2 illustrates the PPC plot and the corresponding PPC scatterplot for the original two-factor model. The PPC distribution plot shows the distribution of the difference between the observed data test statistic and the replicated data test statistic. In this plot, the observed data test statistic is marked by the *y*-axis line, which corresponds to a value of zero on the *x*-axis. The PPC scatterplot, also presented in Figure 38.2, has a 45 degree line that helps to define the posterior predictive *p*-value. With all of the points below this line, this indicates that the *p*-value (0.00) was quite small and the model can be rejected, indicating model misfit for the observed data. If adequate model fit had been observed, the points would be plotted along the 45 degree line in Figure 38.2, which would indicate a close match between the observed and the replicated data.

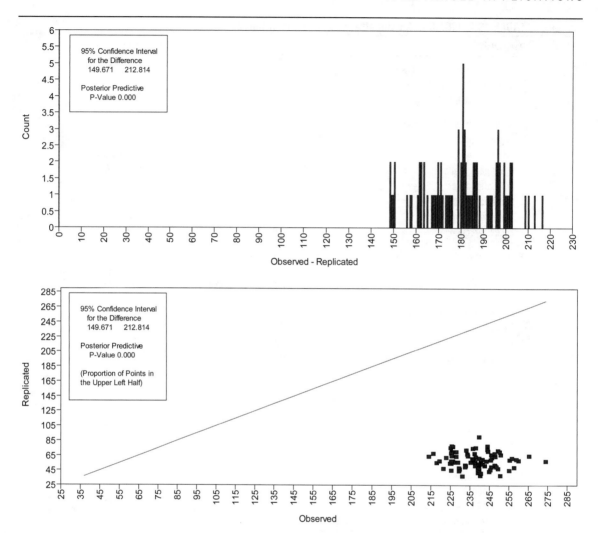

FIGURE 38.2. CFA: PPC 95% confidence interval histogram and PPC scatterplot.

As an illustration of model comparison, the original two-factor model was compared to a one-factor model. The DIC value produced for the original two-factor CFA model was 10,533.37. The DIC value produced for the one-factor CFA model was slightly larger at 10,593.10. This indicates that although the difference in DIC values is relatively small, the two-factor model provides a better representation of the data compared to the one-factor model.

Bayesian Multilevel Path Analysis

This example is based on a reanalysis of a multilevel path analysis described in Kaplan, Kim, and Kim (2009). In their study, a multilevel path analysis was employed to study within- and between-school predictors of mathematics achievement using data from 4,498 students from the Program for International Student Assessment (PISA) 2003 survey (Organization for Economic Co-operation and Development [OECD], 2004). The full multilevel path analysis is depicted in Figure 38.3. The final outcome variable at the student level was a measure of mathematics achievement (MATHSCOR). Mediating predictors of mathematics achievement consisted of whether students enjoyed mathematics (ENJOY) and whether students felt mathematics was important in life (IMPORTNT). Student exogenous background variables included students' perception of teacher qualities (PERTEACH), as well as both parents' educational levels (MOMEDUC and DADEDUC). At the school level, a model was specified to predict the extent to which students are encouraged to achieve their full potential (ENCOURAG). A measure of teachers' enthusiasm for their work (ENTHUSIA) was viewed as an important mediator variable between background variables and encouragement for students to achieve full potential.

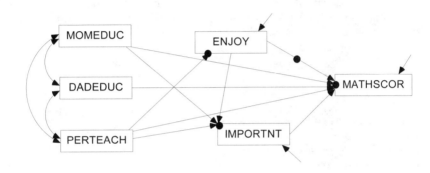

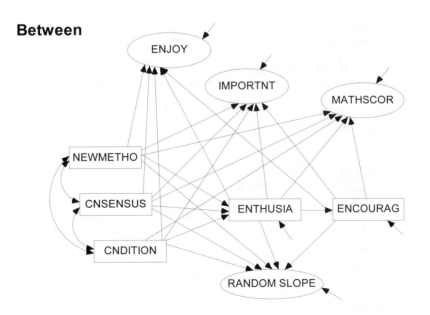

FIGURE 38.3. Multilevel path analysis diagram. Dark circles represent random intercepts and slopes. From Kaplan, Kim, and Kim (2009). Copyright 2009 by SAGE Publications, Inc. Reprinted by permission.

The variables used to predict encouragement via teachers' enthusiasm consisted of math teachers' use of new methodology (NEWMETHO), consensus among math teachers with regard to school expectations and teaching goals as they pertain directly to mathematics instruction (CNSENSUS), and the teaching conditions of the school (CNDITION). The teaching condition variable was computed from the shortage of school's equipment, so higher values on this variable reflect a worse condition.

For this example, we presume to have no prior knowledge of any of the parameters in the model. In this case, all model parameters received normal prior distributions with the mean hyperparameter set at 0 and the variance hyperparameter specified as 10^{10}. The key issue here is the amount of precision in this prior. With this setting, there is very little precision in the prior. As a result, the location of this prior can take on a large number of possible values.

Parameter Convergence

A multilevel path analysis was computed with 5,000 burn-in iterations and 5,000 post-burn-in iterations. The Brooks and Gelman (1998) convergence diagnostic indicated that all parameters properly converged for this model. This model took approximately 1 minute to run.

Figure 38.4 presents convergence plots, posterior density plots, and autocorrelation plots (for both chains) for one of the between-level parameters and one of the within-level parameters. Convergence for these parameters appears to be tight and horizontal, and the posterior probability densities show a close approximation to the normal curve. Finally, the autocorrelation plots are low, indicating that dependence was low for both chains. The additional parameters in this model showed similar results in that convergence plots were tight, density plots were approximately normal, and autocorrelations were low. Appendix 38.2 contains the Mplus code for this example. Note that model fit and model comparison indices are not available for multilevel models and are thus not presented here. This is an area within MCMC estimation that requires further research.

Model Interpretation

Table 38.2 presents selected results for within-level and between-level parameters in the model.[3] For the within-level results, we find that MOMEDUC, DADEDUC, PERTEACH, and IMPORTNT are positive

predictors of MATHSCOR. Likewise, ENJOY is positively predicted by PERTEACH. Finally, MOMEDUC, PERTEACH, and ENJOY are positive predictors of IMPORTNT.

The between-level results presented here are for the random slope in the model that relates ENJOY to MATHSCOR. For example, the results indicate that teacher enthusiasm moderates the relationship between enjoyment of mathematics and math achievement, with higher levels of teacher-reported enthusiasm associated with a stronger positive relationship between enjoyment of math and math achievement. Likewise, the math teachers' use of new methodology also demonstrates a moderating effect on the relationship between enjoyment of math and math achievement, where less usage of new methodology lowers the relationship between enjoyment of mathematics and math achievement. The other random slope relationships in the between level can be interpreted in a similar manner.

Bayesian Growth Mixture Modeling

The ECLS-K math assessment data were used for this example (NCES, 2001). Item response theory (IRT) was used to derive scale scores across four time points (assessments were in the fall and spring of kindergarten and first grade) that were used for the growth mixture model. Estimation of growth rates reflects math skill development over the 18 months of the study. The sample for this analysis comprised 592 children and two latent mixture classes.

For this example, we presume to have a moderate degree of prior knowledge of the growth parameters and the mixture class proportions, but no prior knowledge for the factor variances and unique variances. For the growth parameters, we have specified particular location values, but there is only moderate precision defined in the priors (variances = 10). In this case, we are only displaying moderate confidence in the parameter values, as seen through the larger variances specified. This specification provides a wider range of values in the distribution than would be viable but accounts for our lack of strong knowledge through the increased variance term. Stronger knowledge of these parameter values would decrease the variance hyperparameter term, creating a smaller spread surrounding the location of the prior. However, weaker knowledge of the values would increase the variance term, creating a larger spread surrounding the location of the prior. For the mixture proportions, we presume strong background knowledge

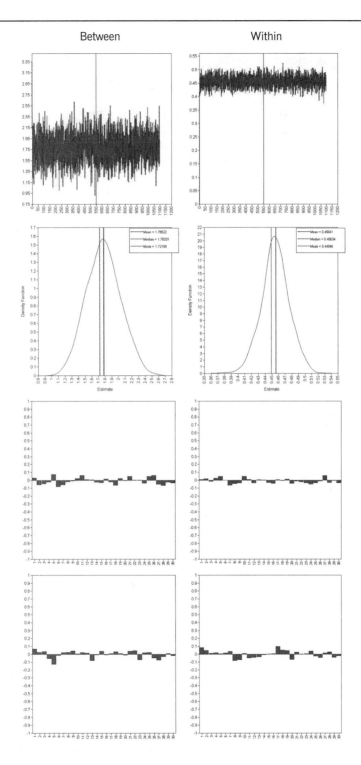

FIGURE 38.4. Multilevel path analysis: Convergence, posterior densities, and autocorrelation plots for select parameters.

TABLE 38.2. Selected MCMC Multilevel Path Analysis Estimates: PISA 2003

Parameter	EAP	SD	p-value	95% credibility interval
Within level				
MATHSCOR ON MOMEDUC	3.93	0.96	0.00	2.15, 5.79
MATHSCOR ON DADEDUC	4.76	0.96	0.00	2.91, 6.68
MATHSCOR ON PERTEACH	6.10	2.31	0.00	1.64, 10.72
MATHSCOR ON IMPORTNT	15.67	1.98	0.00	11.84, 19.72
ENJOY ON PERTEACH	0.45	0.02	0.00	0.41, 0.49
IMPORTNT ON MOMEDUC	0.02	0.00	0.00	0.01, 0.03
IMPORTNT ON PERTEACH	0.24	0.01	0.00	0.21, 0.27
IMPORTNT ON ENJOY	0.53	0.01	0.00	0.51, 0.55
Between level				
SLOPE ON NEWMETHO	−4.26	2.58	0.05	−9.45, 1.02
SLOPE ON ENTHUSIA	8.95	4.81	0.03	−0.76, 18.23
SLOPE ON CNSENSUS	−3.09	3.72	0.20	−10.65, 4.29
SLOPE ON CNDITION	−8.24	2.66	0.00	−13.53, −3.09
SLOPE ON ENCOURAG	−2.06	2.79	0.23	−7.59, 3.58

Note. EAP, expected a posteriori; *SD*, standard deviation.

of the mixture proportions by specifying class sizes through the Dirichlet prior distribution. The factor variances and unique variances received IW priors that reflected no prior knowledge of the parameter values, as specified in Asparouhov and Muthén (2010).

Parameter Convergence

A growth mixture model was computed, with a total of 10,000 iterations with 5,000 burn-in iterations and 5,000 post-burn-in iterations. The model converged properly, signifying that the Brooks and Gelman (1998) convergence diagnostic indicated parameter convergence for this model. This model took less than 1 minute to run.

Figure 38.5 presents convergence plots, posterior density plots, and autocorrelation plots (for both chains) for the mixture class proportions. Convergence for the mixture class parameters appears to be tight and horizontal. The posterior probability densities show a close approximation to the normal curve. Finally, the autocorrelation plots are quite low, indicating relative sample independence for these parameters for both MCMC chains. The additional parameters in this model showed similar results to the mixture class parameters in that convergence plots were tight, density plots were approximately normal, and autocorrelations were low. Appendix 38.3 contains the Mplus code for this example.

Model Interpretation

The growth mixture model estimates can be found in Table 38.3. For this model, the mean math IRT score for the first latent class (mixture) in the fall of kindergarten was 32.11 and the average rate of change between time points was 14.28. The second latent class consisted of an average math score of 18.75 in the fall of kindergarten, and the average rate of change was 10.22 points between time points. This indicates that Class 1 comprised children with stronger math abilities than Class 2 in the fall of kindergarten. Likewise, Class 1 students also have a larger growth rate between assessments. Overall, 14% of the sample was in the first mixture class, and 86% of the sample was in the second mixture class.

Model Fit

Theory suggests that model comparison via the DIC is not appropriate for mixture models (Celeux, Hurn, & Robert, 2000). As a result, only comparisons from the PPC test will be presented for this growth mixture modeling (GMM) example. Figure 38.6 includes the PPC distribution corresponding to the 95% confidence interval for the difference between the observed data test statistic and the replicated data test statistic. The lower bound of this interval was 718.25, and the upper

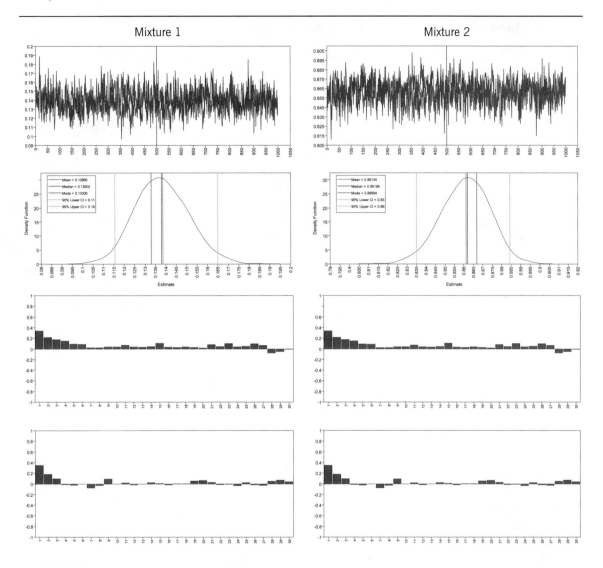

FIGURE 38.5. GMM: Convergence, posterior densities, and autocorrelation plots for mixture class proportions.

bound was 790.56. Similar to the CFA example presented earlier, this positive confidence interval indicates that the observed data test statistic is much larger than what would have been generated by the model. Likewise, Figure 38.6 also includes the PPC scatterplot. All of the points fall below the 45 degree line, which indicates that the model was rejected based on a sufficiently small *p*-value of .00. The results of the PPC test indicate substantial model misfit for this GMM model.

DISCUSSION

This chapter has sought to present an accessible introduction to Bayesian SEM. An overview of Bayesian concepts, as well as a brief introduction to Bayesian computation, was also provided. A general framework of Bayesian computation within the Bayesian SEM framework was also presented, along with three examples covering first- and second-generation SEM.

TABLE 38.3. Mplus MCMC GMM Estimates: ECLS-K Math IRT Scores

Parameter	EAP	SD	p-value	95% credibility interval
Latent class 1				
Class proportion	0.14			
Intercept and slope correlation	−0.06	0.19	0.38	−0.44, 0.32
Growth parameter means				
Intercept	32.11	1.58	0.00	28.84, 35.09
Slope	14.28	0.78	0.00	12.72, 15.77
Variances				
Intercept	98.27	26.51	0.00	54.37, 158.07
Slope	18.34	4.51	0.00	10.60, 27.76
Latent class 2				
Class proportion	0.86			
Intercept and slope correlation	0.94	0.03	0.00	0.87, 0.98
Growth parameter means				
Intercept	18.75	0.36	0.00	17.98, 19.40
Slope	10.22	0.19	0.00	9.86, 10.61
Variances				
Intercept	22.78	3.63	0.00	16.12, 30.56
Slope	7.84	1.15	0.00	5.93, 10.29
Residual variances				
All time points and classes	32.97	1.17	0.00	30.73, 35.34

Note. EAP, expected a posteriori; *SD*, standard deviation.

With the advent of open-source software for Bayesian computation, such as packages found in R (R Development Core Team, 2008) and WinBUGS (Lunn et al., 2000), as well as the newly available MCMC estimator in Mplus (Muthén & Muthén, 2010), researchers can now implement Bayesian methods for a wide range of research problems.

In our examples, we specified different degrees of prior knowledge for the model parameters. However, it was not our intention in this chapter to compare models under different specification of prior distributions, nor to compare results to conventional frequentist estimation methods. Rather, the purpose of these examples was to illustrate the use and interpretation of Bayesian estimation results.

The relative ease of Bayesian computation in the SEM framework raises the important question of why one would choose to use this method—particularly when it can often provide results that are very close to that of frequentist approaches such as maximum like-

lihood. In our judgment, the answer lies in the major distinction between the Bayesian approach and the frequentist approach, that is, in the elicitation, specification, and incorporation of prior distributions on the model parameters.

As pointed out by Skrondal and Rabe-Hesketh (2004, p. 206), there are four reasons why one would adopt the use of prior distributions—one of which they indicate is "truly" Bayesian, while the others represent a more "pragmatic" approach to Bayesian inference. The truly Bayesian approach would specify prior distributions that reflect elicited prior knowledge. For example, in the context of SEM applied to educational problems, one might specify a normal prior distribution on the regression coefficient relating socioeconomic status (SES) to achievement, where the hyperparameter on the mean of the regression coefficient is obtained from previous research. Given that an inspection of the literature suggests roughly the same values for the regression coefficient, a researcher might specify a small value for the

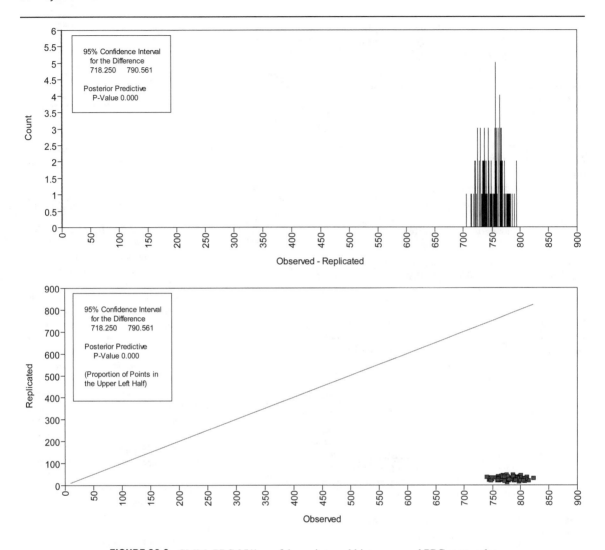

FIGURE 38.6. GMM: PPC 95% confidence interval histogram and PPC scatterplot.

variance of the regression coefficient—reflecting a high degree of precision. Pragmatic approaches, on the other hand, might specify prior distributions for the purposes of achieving model identification, constraining parameters so they do not drift beyond their boundary space (e.g., Heywood cases) or simply because the application of MCMC can sometimes make problems tractable that would otherwise be very difficult in more conventional frequentist settings.

Although we concur with the general point that Skrondal and Rabe-Hesketh (2004) are making, we do not believe that the distinction between "true" Bayesians versus "pragmatic" Bayesians is necessarily the correct distinction to be made. If there is a distinction to be made, we argue that it is between Bayesians and pseudo-Bayesians, where the latter implement MCMC as "just another estimator." Rather, we adopt the pragmatic perspective that the usefulness of a model lies in whether it provides good predictions. The specification of priors based on subjective knowledge can be subjected to quite pragmatic procedures in order to sort out the best predictive model, such as the use of PPC.

What Bayesian theory forces us to recognize is that it is possible to bring in prior information on the distribution of model parameters, but that this requires a deeper understanding of the elicitation problem (see Abbas, Budescu, & Gu, 2010; Abbas, Budescu, Yu, & Haggerty, 2008; O'Hagan et al., 2006). The general idea is that through a careful review of prior research on a problem, and/or the careful elicitation of prior knowledge from experts and/or key stakeholders, relatively precise values for hyperparameters can be obtained and incorporated into a Bayesian specification. Alternative elicitations can be directly compared via Bayesian model selection measures as described earlier. It is through (1) the careful and rigorous elicitation of prior knowledge, (2) the incorporation of that knowledge into our statistical models, and (3) a rigorous approach to the selection among competing models that a pragmatic *and* evolutionary development of knowledge can be realized—and this is precisely the advantage that Bayesian statistics, and Bayesian SEM in particular, has over its frequentist counterparts. Now that the theoretical and computational foundations have been established, the benefits of Bayesian SEM will be realized in terms of how it provides insights into important substantive problems.

ACKNOWLEDGMENTS

The research reported in this chapter was supported by the Institute of Education Sciences, U.S. Department of Education, through Grant No. R305D110001 to the University of Wisconsin–Madison. The opinions expressed are those of the authors and do not represent views of the Institute or the U.S. Department of Education.

We wish to thank Tihomir Asparouhov and Anne Boomsma for valuable comments on an earlier draft of this chapter.

NOTES

1. The *credibility interval* (also referred to as the *posterior probability interval*) is obtained directly from the quantiles of the posterior distribution of the model parameters. From the quantiles, we can directly obtain the probability that a parameter lies within a particular interval. This is in contrast to the frequentist *confidence interval*, where the interpretation is that $100(1 - \alpha)\%$ of the confidence intervals formed a particular way capture the true parameter of interest under the null hypothesis.
2. Note that in the case where there is only one element in the block, the prior distribution is assumed to be inverse-gamma, that is, $\theta_{\mathrm{IW}} \sim \mathrm{IG}(a, b)$.

3. Tables with the full results from this analysis are available upon request.

REFERENCES

Abbas, A. E., Budescu, D. V., & Gu, Y. (2010). Assessing joint distributions with isoprobability countours. *Management Science, 56*, 997–1011.

Abbas, A. E., Budescu, D. V., Yu, H.-T., & Haggerty, R. (2008). A comparison of two probability encoding methods: Fixed probability vs. fixed variable values. *Decision Analysis, 5*, 190–202.

Albert, J. (2007). *Bayesian computation with R*. New York: Springer.

Asparouhov, T., & Muthén, B. (2010). *Bayesian analysis using Mplus: Technical implementation*. Available from *http://www.statmodel.com/download/Bayes3.pdf*.

Box, G., & Tiao, G. (1973). *Bayesian inference in statistical analysis*. New York: Addison-Wesley.

Brooks, S. P., & Gelman, A. (1998). General methods for monitoring convergence of iterative simulations. *Journal of Computational and Graphical Statistics, 7*, 434–455.

Celeux, G., Hurn, M., & Robert, C. P. (2000). Computational and inferential difficulties with mixture posterior distributions. *Journal of the American Statistical Association, 95*, 957–970.

Gelman, A. (1996). Inference and monitoring convergence. In W. R. Gilks, S. Richardson, & D. J. Spiegelhalter (Eds.), *Markov chain Monte Carlo in practice* (pp. 131–143). New York: Chapman & Hall.

Gelman, A., Carlin, J. B., Stern, H. S., & Rubin, D. B. (2003). *Bayesian data analysis, second edition*. London: Chapman & Hall.

Gelman, A., & Rubin, D. B. (1992a). Inference from iterative simulation using multiple sequences. *Statistical Science, 7*, 457–511.

Gelman, A., & Rubin, D. B. (1992b). A single series from the Gibbs sampler provides a false sense of security. In J. M. Bernardo, J. O. Berger, A. P. Dawid, & A. F. M. Smith (Eds.), *Bayesian statistics 4* (pp. 625–631). Oxford, UK: Oxford University Press.

Geman, S., & Geman, D. (1984). Stochastic relaxation, Gibbs distributions and the Bayesian restoration of images. *IEEE Transactions on Pattern Analysis and Machine Intelligence, 6*, 721–741.

Geweke, J. (1992). Evaluating the accuracy of sampling-based approaches to calculating posterior moments. In J. M. Bernardo, J. O. Berger, A. P. Dawid, & A. F. M. Smith (Eds.), *Bayesian statistics 4* (pp. 169–193). Oxford, UK: Oxford University Press.

Gilks, W. R., Richardson, S., & Spiegelhalter, D. J. (Eds.). (1996). *Markov chain Monte Carlo in practice*. London: Chapman & Hall.

Gill, J. (2002). *Bayesian methods*. Boca Raton, FL: CRC Press.

Heidelberger, P., & Welch, P. (1983). Simulation run length control in the presence of an initial transient. *Operations Research, 31*, 1109–1144.

Hoff, P. D. (2009). *A first course in Bayesian statistical methods*. New York: Springer.

Jo, B., & Muthén, B. (2001). Modeling of intervention effects with noncompliance: A latent variable modeling approach for randomized trials. In G. A. Marcoulides & R. E. Schumacker (Eds.), *New developments and techniques in structural equation modeling* (pp. 57–87). Mahwah, NJ: Erlbaum.

Jöreskog, K. G. (1973). A general method for estimating a linear structural equation system. In A. S. Goldberger & O. D. Duncan (Eds.), *Structural equation models in the social sciences* (pp. 85–112). New York: Academic Press.

Kaplan, D. (2003). Methodological advances in the analysis of individual growth with relevance to education policy. *Peabody Journal of Education, 77*, 189–215.

Kaplan, D. (2009). *Structural equation modeling: Foundations and extensions* (2nd ed.). Newbury Park, CA: Sage.

Kaplan, D., & Depaoli, S. (in press). Bayesian statistical methods. In T. D. Little (Ed.), *Oxford handbook of quantitative methods*. Oxford, UK: Oxford University Press.

Kaplan, D., Kim, J.-S., & Kim, S.-Y. (2009). Multilevel latent variable modeling: Current research and recent developments. In R. E. Millsap & A. Maydeu-Olivares (Eds.), *The SAGE handbook of quantitative methods in psychology* (pp. 595–612). Newbury Park, CA: Sage.

Kass, R. E., & Raftery, A. E. (1995). Bayes factors. *Journal of the American Statistical Association, 90*, 773–795.

Lee, S.-Y. (1981). A Bayesian approach to confirmatory factor analysis. *Psychometrika, 46*, 153–160.

Lee, S.-Y. (2007). *Structural equation modeling: A Bayesian approach*. New York: Wiley.

Lunn, D., Thomas, A., Best, N., & Spiegelhalter, D. (2000). Winbugs—a Bayesian modelling framework: concepts, structure, and extensibility. *Statistics and Computing, 10*, 325–337.

Martin, A. D., Quinn, K. M., & Park, J. H. (2010, May 10). *Markov chain Monte Carlo (MCMC) package*. Available online at *http://mcmcpack.wustl.edu*.

Martin, J. K., & McDonald, R. P. (1975). Bayesian estimation in unrestricted factor analysis: A treatment for Heywood cases. *Psychometrika, 40*, 505–517.

Muthén, B. (2001). Second-generation structural equation modeling with a combination of categorical and continuous latent variables: New opportunities for latent class/latent growth modeling. In L. Collins & A. G. Sayer (Eds.), *New methods for the analysis of change* (pp. 289–322). Washington, DC: American Psychological Association.

Muthén, B. (2010). *Bayesian analysis in Mplus: A brief introduction*. Available from *http://www.statmodel.com/download/introbayesversion%203.pdf*.

Muthén, B., & Asparouhov, T. (in press). Bayesian SEM: A more flexible representation of substantive theory. *Psychological Methods*.

Muthén, B., & Masyn, K. (2005). Mixture discrete-time survival analysis. *Journal of Educational and Behavioral Statistics, 30*, 27–58.

Muthén, L. K., & Muthén, B. (2010). *Mplus: Statistical analysis with latent variables*. Los Angeles: Authors.

National Center for Education Statistics (NCES). (2001). *Early childhood longitudinal study: Kindergarten class of 1998–99: Base year public-use data files user's manual* (Tech. Rep. No. NCES 2001-029). Washington, DC: U.S. Government Printing Office.

O'Hagan, A., Buck, C. E., Daneshkhah, A., Eiser, J. R., Garthwaite, P. H., Jenkinson, D. J., et al. (2006). *Uncertain judgements: Eliciting experts' probabilities*. West Sussex, UK: Wiley.

Organization for Economic Cooperation and Development (OECD). (2004). *The PISA 2003 assessment framework: Mathematics, reading, science, and problem solving knowledge and skills*. Paris: Author.

Press, S. J. (2003). *Subjective and objective Bayesian statistics: Principles, models, and applications* (2nd ed.). New York: Wiley.

R Development Core Team. (2008). R: A language and environment for statistical computing [Computer software manual]. Vienna: R Foundation for Statistical Computing. Available from *http://www.R-project.org*.

Raftery, A. E. (1995). Bayesian model selection in social research (with discussion). In P. V. Marsden (Ed.), *Sociological methodology* (Vol. 25, pp. 111–196). New York: Blackwell.

Raftery, A. E., & Lewis, S. M. (1992). How many iterations in the Gibbs sampler? In J. M. Bernardo, J. O. Berger, A. P. Dawid, & A. F. M. Smith (Eds.), *Bayesian statistics 4* (pp. 763–773). Oxford, UK: Oxford University Press.

Scheines, R., Hoijtink, H., & Boomsma, A. (1999). Bayesian estimation and testing of structural equation models. *Psychometrika, 64*, 37–52.

Schwarz, G. E. (1978). Estimating the dimension of a model. *Annals of Statistics, 6*, 461–464.

Sinharay, S. (2004). Experiences with Markov chain Monte Carlo convergence assessment in two psychometric examples. *Journal of Educational and Behavioral Statistics, 29*, 461–488.

Skrondal, A., & Rabe-Hesketh, S. (2004). *Generalized latent variable modeling: Multilevel, longitudinal, and structural equation models*. Boca Raton, FL: Chapman & Hall/CRC.

Spiegelhalter, D. J., Best, N. G., Carlin, B. P., & van der Linde, A. (2002). Bayesian measures of model complexity and fit (with discussion). *Journal of the Royal Statistical Society B, 64*, 583–639.

APPENDIX 38.1. CFA Mplus Code

```
title: MCMC CFA with ECLS-K math data
data: file is cfadata.dat;
variable: names are y1-y9;
analysis:
        estimator = BAYES; !This option uses the MCMC Gibbs sampler as a default
        chains = 2; !Two chains is the default in Mplus Version 6
        distribution = 10,000; !The first half of the iterations is always used as burn-in
        point = mean; !Estimating the median is the default for Mplus
model priors: !This option allows for priors to be changed from default values
        a2 ~ N(.8,.01); !Normal prior on Factor 1 loading: Item 2
        b4 ~ N(.8,.01); !Normal prior on Factor 2 loading: Item 4
        b5 ~ N(.8,.01); !Normal prior on Factor 2 loading: Item 5
        b6 ~ N(.8,.01); !Normal prior on Factor 2 loading: Item 6
        b7 ~ N(.8,.01); !Normal prior on Factor 2 loading: Item 7
        b8 ~ N(.8,.01); !Normal prior on Factor 2 loading: Item 8
        b9 ~ N(.8,.01); !Normal prior on Factor 2 loading: Item 9
model:
        f1 by y1@1 y2*.8(a2); !Normal priors on Factor 1 loadings with arbitrary item identifiers (a2)
        f2 by y3@1 y4-y9*.8(b4-b9); !Priors on Factor 2 loadings with arbitrary item identifiers (b4-b9)
        f1*1;
        f2*1;
        f1 with f2 *.4;
plot:
        type = plot2; !Requesting all MCMC plots: convergence, posterior densities, and autocorrelations
```

APPENDIX 38.2. Multilevel Path Analysis with a Varying-Slope Mplus Code

```
title: Path Analysis
data: File is multi-level.dat;
variable: names are schoolid newmetho enthusia cnsensus
        cndition encourag momeduc dadeduc
        perteach enjoy importnt mathscor;
        Usevariables are newmetho enthusia cnsensus
        cndition encourag momeduc dadeduc
        perteach enjoy importnt mathscor;
        Between = newmetho enthusia cnsensus cndition encourag;
        Cluster is schoolid;
analysis: type = twolevel random;
        estimator = BAYES;
        point=mean;
model:
%Within%
        mathscor ON momeduc dadeduc perteach importnt;
        enjoy ON perteach;
        importnt ON momeduc perteach enjoy;
        momeduc WITH dadeduc perteach;
        dadeduc WITH perteach;
        slope | mathscor ON enjoy;
```

(cont.)

APPENDIX 38.2. *(cont.)*

```
%Between%
        mathscor ON newmetho enthusia cnsensus cndition encourag;
        enjoy ON newmetho enthusia cnsensus cndition encourag; importnt ON
newmetho enthusia cnsensus cndition encourag;
        slope ON newmetho enthusia cnsensus cndition encourag;
        encourag ON enthusia;
        enthusia ON newmetho cnsensus cndition;
plot: type=plot2;
```

APPENDIX 38.3. Growth Mixture Model Mplus Code

```
title: MCMC GMM with ECLS-K math data
data: file is Math GMM.dat;
variable: names are y1-y4;
        classes =c(2);
analysis:
        type = mixture;
        estimator = BAYES; !This option uses the MCMC Gibbs sampler as a default
        chains = 2; !Two chains is the default in Mplus Version 6
        distribution = 10,000; !The first half of the iterations is always used as burn-in
        point = mean; !Estimating the median is the default for Mplus
model priors: !This option allows for priors to be changed from default values
        a ~ N(28,10); !Normal prior on mixture class 1 intercept
        b ~ N(13,10); !Normal prior on mixture class 1 slope
        c ~ N(17,10); !Normal prior on mixture class 2 intercept
        d ~ N(9,10); !Normal prior on mixture class 2 slope
        e ~ D(80,510); !Dirichlet prior on mixture class proportions
model:
%overall%
        y1-y4*.5;
        i s | y1@0 y2@1 y3@2 y4@3;
        i*1; s*.2;
        [c#1*-1](e); !Setting up Dirichlet prior on mixture class proportions with arbitrary identifier (e)
        y1 y2 y3 y4 (1);
%c#1%
        [i*28](a); !Setting up Normal prior on mixture class 1 intercept with arbitrary identifier (a)
        [s*13](b); !Setting up Normal prior on mixture class 1 slope with arbitrary identifier (b)
        i with s;
        i; s;
%c#2%
        [i*17](c); !Setting up Normal prior on mixture class 2 intercept with arbitrary identifier (c)
        [s*9](d); !Setting up Normal prior on mixture class 2 intercept with arbitrary identifier (d)
        i with s;
        i; s;
plot:
        type = plot2; !Requesting all MCMC plots: convergence, posterior densities, and autocorrelations
        output: stand;
        cinterval;
```

CHAPTER 39

Spatial Structural Equation Modeling

Melanie M. Wall

It is becoming more and more common to consider the geographic location of individuals when examining health behaviors and outcomes. Indeed, a recently introduced BioMed Central journal, the *International Journal of Health Geographics*, notes, "Health geographics improves our understanding of the important relationships between people, location (and its characteristics: for example environmental or socioeconomic), time, and health; it therefore assists us in discovering and eliminating disease, in public health tasks like disease prevention and health promotion, and also in better healthcare service planning and delivery" (*www.ij-healthgeographics.com/info/about/*). Place matters for health in the sense that geographic location or "spatial" location often serves as a proxy for a conglomerate of contextual variables including policies, norms, and generally risk and protective factors that may be thought to directly influence health. Moreover, individuals more spatially proximal are likely to be more similar than those farther apart, implying a lack of independence in the data. There is an extensive literature describing statistical methods for modeling different types of spatially referenced data (for recent textbooks with health data examples, see Banerjee, Carlin, & Gelfand, 2004;

Schabenberger & Gotway, 2005; Waller & Gotway, 2004; for economic data examples, see LeSage & Pace, 2009).

A simple yet common spatially referenced data setup is to have summary measures of some outcome (e.g., lung cancer mortality rates) in each of several regions (e.g., counties within a state), and then to also have measures of some potential risk factor summarized at the same region level (e.g., smoking rates by county). A "spatial regression" model can then be fit to these data where county lung cancer rates are regressed on county smoking rates with a model that also accounts for correlation between counties that are nearby one another (i.e., accounts for spatially correlated errors rather than assuming independent identically distributed [IID] errors). This basic spatial regression framework is what is extended with the spatial structural equation model. Spatial structural equation modeling (SSEM[1]) is structural equation modeling (SEM) with data collected at geographic spatial locations and incorporates the proximity of geographic regions into the model. Rather than focusing on just one measured outcome at each spatial location, the SSEM jointly models a multivariate vector of related outcomes that may be reasonably thought of as indicators of some underlying common spatially varying latent variable(s).

As in traditional SEM with latent variables, the SSEM is built from latent factor-analytic models that relate the observed measurements to underlying common latent factors at the different locations. Spatial latent factor models have been developed and recently applied. particularly in disease mapping (for a thorough review see Tzala & Best, 2007). Because many diseases share common risk factors, spatial latent factor models have been used to investigate shared and divergent patterns in risk across regions (Dabney & Wakefield, 2005; Held, Natrio, Fenton, Rue, & Becker, 2005; Hogan & Tchernis, 2004; Knorr-Held & Best, 2001; Wang & Wall, 2003). For example, Wang and Wall (2003) modeled a shared spatial latent factor model underlying cancer-specific mortality across counties in Minnesota. Hogan and Tchernis (2004) proposed a similar spatial factor model where the latent variable summarized area-level material deprivation based on census variables collected in census tracts in Rhode Island. These papers both analyzed multivariate spatial data and described the correlations within and across locations using a single spatially distributed latent factor. A natural extension is then to consider regression-type relationships between multiple underlying spatial factors, hence leading to SSEM (Congdon, 2007, 2010; Hossain & Laditka, 2009; Liu, Wall, & Hodges, 2005; Oud & Folmer, 2008; van Oort, Oud, & Raspe, 2009).

In the SSEM, spatial processes are assumed for the underlying factors and errors, and can generally take into account the proximity of observations to one another across the geographic region. The spatial process can be parameterized so that the strength of the "spatial similarity" across the region can be estimated and tested. That is, a measure or measures quantifying the variability between observations taken more spatially proximal to one another can be obtained. The inclusion of a spatial process model in the SSEM is similar to longitudinal data modeling, where autoregressive structure is commonly assumed in order to properly account for inherent correlation due to measurements taken across time and the strength of the autocorrelation (e.g., a lag 1 autoregressive parameter) can be estimated.

Because geographic location is important for studying many research questions, it is common to find public use data sets that include geographic location indicators (e.g., state, county, zip code, census tract, census block). Due to issues of respondent privacy, there is always a limit to how fine-grained the geographic location can go. In fact, most public use data do not typically provide any finer-grained geographic information than county. Nevertheless, there may be patterns and trends of interest at this geographic level, and even at the broader state level, as will be demonstrated later in this chapter with an example using state-level summary data from the 2009 Behavioral Risk Factor Surveillance Survey (BRFSS).

In the next section I describe the multivariate spatially referenced BRFSS data that will be modeled using a SSEM. In the section on SEM I introduce the specific form of the SSEM, including different types of spatial correlation structure that can be considered. In the section on Bayesian inference I describe estimation and inference for the model within a Bayesian framework using the Markov Chain Monte Carlo (MCMC) method. The next section then applies the SSEM to the BRFSS data to assess the relationship among the latent variables while accounting for and identifying spatial associations. Conclusions and discussion are given in the final section.

MOTIVATING DATA

The 2009 BRFSS, the data source for the illustrative example presented in this chapter, is a national health survey focused on behavioral risk and protective factors (e.g., smoking, heavy drinking, physical activity, and healthful eating). The cross-sectional yearly survey is run by the Centers for Disease Control and Prevention through each of the 50 state health departments and is administered by telephone. In 2009, the BRFSS began conducting surveys by cellular phone in addition to traditional landline telephones.

One question included in the BRFSS asks respondents the single health-related quality-of-life (HRQL) question "Would you say that in general your health is . . ." with response options *Excellent*, *Very good*, *Good*, *Fair*, *Poor*, and *Don't know/Not sure*. This measure has been used to track and identify geographic variation in HRQL (e.g., Jia & Lubetkin, 2009; Jia, Moriarty, & Kanarek, 2009; Jia, Muennig, Lubetkin, & Gold, 2004; Moriarty, Zack, & Kobau, 2003). Age and race are two strong predictors of HRQL, with decreases in positive responses (i.e., *Good* or better) as age increases and for nonwhites compared to whites. In the current chapter I examine quality of general health at the state level, summarized across eight specific subgroups defined by intersecting age (< 65, ≥ 65), race (white, nonwhite), and gender (male, female). Within each of the eight subgroups, and for each state separately, the percentage of people responding that they are in *Good* or better general health is calculated using the state sampling weights provided by the BRFSS. The percentages were additionally regression-adjusted by age separately within the younger and older subgroups to account for differential age distributions across states. Figure 39.1 presents data for the state percentages of good general health. Each map represents a different demographic group, and states with above the median general health in that group are indicated in dark gray and black (black indicating the highest quartile), and those with below the median general health in light gray and white (white indicating the lowest quartile of general health). Considering these eight multivariate measurements of general health at the state level, we notice patterns of correlation both across variables and across states nearby one another. When we look across variables, the Pearson correlations range from .24 (between younger white males and older nonwhite males) to .89 (between older white males and older white females), and there is only a single eigenvalue > 1 explaining 63% of the variability across the eight variables. When we look across states (i.e., location) within variables we can see a general tendency for the Upper Midwest states and the Southern Belt states to have more similar health. Indeed, Moran's I statistic (a test statistic for spatial association; Cressie, 1993) is statistically significant for each of the eight variables, indicating positive spatial association. These correlations are indicative of the potential for a shared common spatial latent factor underlying all eight of the variables. Here, because of the construction of the variables from different demographic subgroups, we name the latent factor "state quality of general health."

It is also of interest to examine potential state-level correlates of the state quality of general health. There is an extensive literature extolling the healthful benefits of eating more fruits and vegetables and engaging in regular physical activity. Both fruit and vegetable intake and physical activity are measured in the BRFSS, and similar subgroup specific summaries of them are constructed at the state level. For fruits and vegetables, we calculate the percentage of people who report eating at least 5 or more fruit and vegetable servings per day, and for physical activity, we calculate the percentage of people who report engaging in the recommended

amount of moderate and/or vigorous physical activity per week (≥ 20 minutes of vigorous activity ≥ 3 days/week, and/or ≥ 30 minutes of moderate activity ≥ 5 days/week). Figures 39.2 and 39.3 show maps of the associated data.

Using SSEM one can examine by state people's overall tendency to follow these healthful behaviors and overall reported health quality. Figure 39.4 presents side-by-side boxplots of the eight different measures of state-level reported health quality. One can see clearly that there are substantial overall differences in reported health quality by race and age. By taking the different demographic groups as separate state-level indicator variables, one also can use an SSEM to pinpoint which if any of the groups deviate from the general relationship trends shared by the latent factors, hence allowing one to pinpoint health disparities in particular states.

THE SSEM

Traditionally, structural equation models (Bentler & Weeks, 1980; Bollen, 1989; Jöreskog, 1979) have been used to model relationships between multiple variables (observed and latent) measured on *independent* individuals. The model is made up of two parts: a measurement and a structural part. The measurement part specifies the relationship between the manifest (observed) variables and the underlying latent factors, while the structural part specifies the relationships among the latent factors. In addition, both parts of the model may also include exogenous covariates that help to describe relationships.

The SSEM follows the same general form as the traditional structural equation model but replaces the common assumption of independence of latent factors and errors across individuals with specific parametric (nonindependent) spatial models linking observations at each location to those at nearby locations. Furthermore, for the type of applications presented herein, the "individuals" or observational units in the SSEM are the spatial regions themselves, typically representing a partition of a larger geographic region (e.g., states within the United States, or counties within a state).

Given a vector of p observed variables $\mathbf{Z}_i$ for the ith spatial region in an area with n regions and a vector of q latent variables $\mathbf{f}_i$ such that $\mathbf{f}_i = (\boldsymbol{\eta}'_i, \boldsymbol{\xi}'_i)'$, where $\boldsymbol{\eta}_i$ are the d endogenous latent variables and $\boldsymbol{\xi}_i$ are the $q - d$ exogenous latent variables, and further given an $(m \times 1)$

FIGURE 39.1. State-by-state percentage of persons reporting good or better general health. Quartiles within each of the eight subpopulations are represented with different shades of gray from white (lowest) to black (highest). "Young" indicates ages 18–65, "Old" indicates ages 65 and older, and "NonWhite" includes all races except non-Hispanic white.

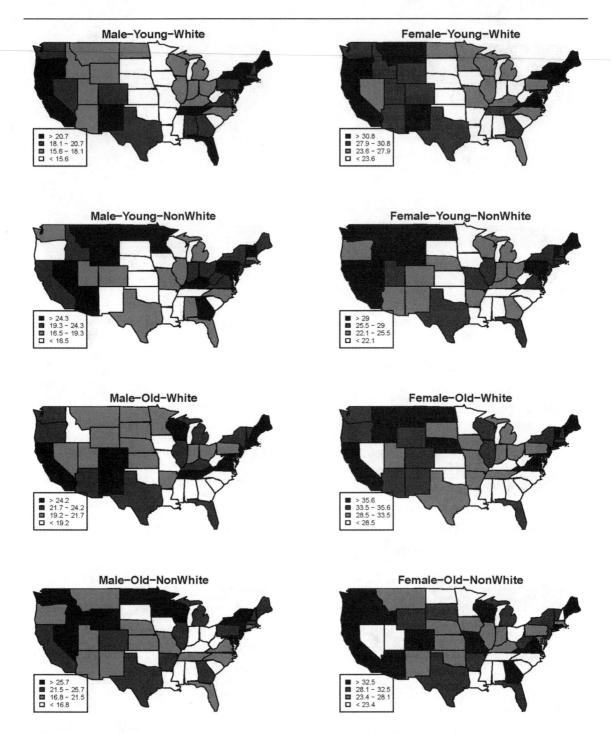

FIGURE 39.2. State-by-state percentage of persons eating five or more fruits and vegetables per day. Quartiles within each of the eight subpopulations are represented with different shades of gray from white (lowest) to black (highest). "Young" indicates ages 18–65, "Old" indicates ages 65 and older, and "NonWhite" includes all races except non-Hispanic white.

FIGURE 39.3. State-by-state percentage of persons meeting recommended amount of moderate and/or vigorous physical activity per week. Quartiles within each of the eight subpopulations are represented with different shades of gray from white (lowest) to black (highest). "Young" indicates ages 18–65, "Old" indicates ages 65 and older, and "NonWhite" includes all races except non-Hispanic white.

vector of observed exogenous covariates $\mathbf{X}_i$ measured for each region, the SSEM is

$$\mathbf{Z}_i = \lambda_0 + \Lambda\mathbf{f}_i + \Lambda_x\mathbf{X}_i + \varepsilon_i \qquad (39.1)$$

$$\eta_i = \gamma_0 + \Gamma\xi_i + \Gamma_x\mathbf{X}_i + \delta_i \qquad (39.2)$$

$$\xi_i = \mathbf{A}\mathbf{w}_i \qquad (39.3)$$

$$\varepsilon_i, \delta_i, \mathbf{w}_i \sim \text{zero-mean, spatial processes} \qquad (39.4)$$

where in the measurement model (Equation 39.1), the matrices λ_0 ($p \times 1$), Λ ($p \times q$), and Λ_x ($p \times m$) contain fixed or unknown scalars describing the linear relation between the observations $\mathbf{Z}_i$ and the common latent factors $\mathbf{f}_i$ and covariates, and ε_i represents the ($p \times 1$) vector of random measurement errors; and in the structural model (Equation 39.2) the matrices γ_0 ($d \times 1$), Γ ($d \times (q - d)$), and Γ_x ($d \times m$) contain fixed or unknown scalars describing the relationship among latent variables and covariates, and δ_i ($d \times 1$) are the random equation errors.

In the traditional independent observations structural equation model, the specification of the random errors (ε_i, δ_i) and exogenous latent factors ξ_i would be completed by stating that they are assumed to be IID Instead in Equations 39.3 and 39.4 for the spatial structural equation model, these random variables are specified to come from spatial processes.

Multivariate Spatial Process Specification

The spatial processes assumed for the p elements of the ε_i vector are assumed to be independent, as are the $q - d$ elements of the δ_i vector. This independence mimics the usual assumption in latent variable models, which is that the correlation between the variables is explained solely by the latent variable itself (i.e., no correlated measurement errors between variables). Indeed, this assumption could be weakened by forming a multivariate spatial distribution for ε_i and δ_i in the same way that it is done for ξ_i. Nevertheless, the addition of potential spatial correlation for the errors provides information about the similarity across nearby locations of the unexplained part of the variables.

The spatial process model for the exogenous latent ξ_i should allow for correlation between elements both

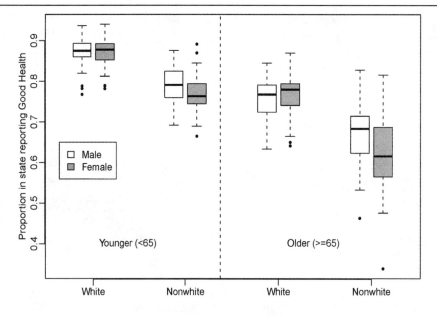

FIGURE 39.4. Each boxplot represents 51 proportions (50 states + Washington, DC) of persons reporting good or better general health. Each box indicates interquartile range with median drawn as a horizontal line. Extending lines go out to value within 1.5 × (interquartile range). Values outside this range are shown with dots. White race includes only non-Hispanic white race.

within and across location, and hence requires a multivariate spatial process. There are many well-developed univariate spatial process models (Banerjee et al., 2005; Cressie, 1993) that specify how observations are correlated with one another across spatial locations. In particular let us consider two general classes of univariate spatial processes in the next subsection. The basic idea of Equations 39.3 and 39.4 is to specify a *multivariate spatial process* for ξ by taking linear combinations of *independent, univariate* spatial processes, $\mathbf{w}$. For a multivariate spatial process, we want to model not only the correlation between variables within locations but also the correlation between the same and different variables across locations.

Using linear combinations of independent spatial processes for modeling multivariate spatial data is called the "linear model of coregionalization" (LMC) (Banerjee et al., 2005; Wackernagel, 2003). LMC was originally developed to transform a multivariate spatial process into linear combinations of components of different spatial scales by using principal component analysis on the variance–covariance matrix. Here it is used to generate a rich and flexible class of variance–covariance structures to model the multivariate spatial process of the latent factors in the SSEM.

The exogenous latent factors ξ_i are defined as

$$\xi_i = \mathbf{A}\mathbf{w}_i$$

where $\mathbf{A}$ is a $(q - d) \times (q - d)$ full-rank matrix and the components of $\mathbf{w}_i$, w_{ij} ($j = 1, \ldots (q - d)$) are univariate spatial processes defined across the entire region $i = 1, \ldots, n$ and assumed to be independent across j. Let $\mathbf{C}(\alpha_j)$ be the $n \times n$ covariance matrix for the jth spatial process $(w_{1j}, w_{2j}, \ldots, w_{nj})$, where α_j represents the parameters in the spatial covariance matrix. Let $\xi = (\xi_1', \xi_2', \ldots, \xi_n')'$ be the $((q - d) * n) \times 1$ vector which stacks the $(q - d)$ exogenous latent variables at each of the n locations into one long vector. Then the $((q - d) * n) \times ((q - d) * n)$ covariance matrix for ξ is

$$\Sigma = \sum_{j=1}^{q-d} \mathbf{C}(\alpha_j) \otimes \mathbf{T}_j$$

where $\mathbf{T}_j = \mathbf{A}_j \mathbf{A}_j'$ and $\mathbf{A}_j$ is the jth column of $\mathbf{A}$. In practice, $\mathbf{A}$ is commonly assumed to be lower or upper triangular without loss of generality, since for any positive definite matrix $\mathbf{T}$, there is a unique lower or upper triangular matrix $\mathbf{A}$ such that $\mathbf{T} = \mathbf{A}\mathbf{A}'$.

We note some important special cases of this multivariate spatial process specification. If the spatial co-variance matrix $\mathbf{C}(\alpha_j)$ is the same across all j, then $\Sigma = \mathbf{C}(\alpha) \otimes \mathbf{T}$, where $\mathbf{C}(\alpha)$ is the common spatial covariance matrix for each of the j spatial processes in $\mathbf{w}$ and $\mathbf{T} = \mathbf{A}\mathbf{A}'$. Hence, $\mathbf{T}$ is interpreted as the within-location covariance matrix between variables, and $\mathbf{C}(\alpha)$ is interpreted as the across-site covariance matrix. This special case is equivalent to a "separable" covariance specification, as in Mardia and Goodall (1993). Another special case is if the matrix $\mathbf{A}$ is diagonal (i.e., elements are fixed to zero on the off diagonal). In this case, the $(q - d)$ latent factors in ξ_i are uncorrelated with one another within spatial location but still exhibit spatial correlation across sites, due to the $\mathbf{C}(\alpha_j)$. Finally, in the special case where the spatial covariance matrices $\mathbf{C}(\alpha_j)$ are in fact diagonal, this implies no relationships between observations at different locations (i.e., independence). This can be tested by examining the appropriate spatial parameters in $\mathbf{C}(\alpha_j)$.

Specific Spatial Process Models

To complete the specification of the SSEM, it is necessary to describe the specific spatial models used for ε, δ, and $\mathbf{w}$. We denote $\mathbf{C}(\alpha_\varepsilon)$, $\mathbf{C}(\alpha_\delta)$, and $\mathbf{C}(\alpha_\mathbf{w})$ to be the $n \times n$ model spatial covariance matrix for an arbitrary element of ε, δ, or $\mathbf{w}$. In general the spatial functional form $\mathbf{C}()$ could be different across different processes, but we will take the general parametric form to be the same and allow the parameters α to potentially differ.

Two common types of models for the spatial structure can be considered. One is "geostatistical" models, in which spatial locations where observations are made are assumed to be continuously indexed across the spatial region, and the spatial correlation depends on the distance between two locations. Models of the "geostatistical" type can take into account direction as well as distance, or make an assumption that the process is "isotropic," meaning that direction does not matter. "Geostatistical" spatial processes are often modeled through the variogram function, which describes the variability of the difference between two locations as a function of the distance between those locations. Models of this type are appropriate for data with a continuous spatial support (i.e., that can be collected at any point throughout the region of interest).

The other type of model for spatial structure is called a lattice or areal data model, in which the process is discretely indexed over a partitioned area, and the spatial correlations depend on the neighborhood structure. Regional summary data of the type considered in this chapter are an example of areal data where the states make up a partition of the United States, and the observations (state summaries) can only be made at the discrete "locations" indexed by the states. Furthermore, the states are related to one another by their "neighborhood structure," which is taken to mean whether they share a border or not. There are several areal spatial models, but a common one used particularly in public health is the conditional autoregressive (CAR) model (Besag, 1974; Cressie, 1993). The CAR model, considered for use here in the SSEM, is a Gaussian spatial process model completely defined by its covariance matrix. The associated $n \times n$ covariance matrix for the CAR is

$$\mathbf{C}(\alpha) = \frac{1}{\tau}\mathbf{D}(\mathbf{I}_n - \rho\mathbf{H})^{-1} \qquad (39.5)$$

where $\alpha = (\tau, \rho)$ and ρ is referred to as the spatial association parameter, τ is a parameter that is proportional to the conditional precision of the random variable at a particular location i given all the neighboring random variables, $\mathbf{I}_n$ is an $n \times n$ identity matrix, and $\mathbf{D}$ is a diagonal matrix with elements equal to $1/d_i$, where d_i is the count of the number of neighbors for location i. The neighbor adjacency matrix $\mathbf{H} = (h_{ij})$ is an $n \times n$ matrix containing the row-normalized neighboring information, where $h_{ij} = 1/d_i$ implies that region i is adjacent to region j and otherwise $h_{ij} = 0$, including $h_{ii} = 0$. Note that $\mathbf{D}$ and $\mathbf{H}$ will not differ across the different spatial processes modeled (i.e., elements of ε, δ, $\mathbf{w}$), implying that the neighborhood structure is the same for all spatial processes, but the strength of the association ρ and the variability $1/\tau$ will be allowed to vary. The row normalization leads to an upper boundary value of $\rho = 1$. Notice that if $\rho = 0$, then $\mathbf{C}(\alpha)$ is a diagonal matrix and the associated spatial process is simply independent random variables. We denote $y \sim CAR(\rho, \tau)$, if y has a CAR covariance structure (Equation 39.5), with parameters ρ and τ.

BAYESIAN INFERENCE FOR THE SSEM

Some statistical software packages useful for SEM allow for nonindependence due to multilevel clustering (e.g., Mplus, GLLAMM), but as of yet, they are not flexible enough to allow for more general forms of nonindependence, including spatial dependence. To overcome this limitation, we use the WinBUGS soft-

ware, which allows for very general specifications of models and in particular includes canned syntax for the spatial CAR model employed herein. The WinBUGS software is freely available (*www.mrc-bsu.cam.ac.uk/bugs/*) and utilizes a Bayesian approach to modeling that relies on specification of not only the likelihood but also priors for all model parameters. Posterior distributions of all the model parameters are simulated in WinBUGS using MCMC methods. An advantageous by-product of MCMC sampling is that it produces empirical estimates of the entire posterior distribution (not just the most likely parameter value—or posterior mode) and hence provides credible intervals directly for all model parameters. Further, because in the Bayesian framework there is no distinction between fixed and random parameters, this means that posterior estimates and credible intervals are available for all the latent variables as well. The disadvantage of MCMC sampling can be a practical one; that is, it can take a long time for the computational method to converge to stationarity.

Identifiability

The model presented in Equations 39.1 to 39.4 with CAR models specified for ε, δ, and $\mathbf{w}$ is very general, and all the parameters are not likely to be completely identified without some constraints (simplifications). The first simplifying assumption we make is that Λ exhibits simple structure, implying that each observed variable $\mathbf{Z}$ is an indicator of one and only one latent factor. This assumption avoids any identifiability issues related to rotation of the latent factors. Furthermore, it is often the most natural assumption for Λ, since often there is a priori specification of which variables measure which factors.

Further, it is necessary to fix the scale of the latent factors. This is accomplished for the exogenous latent factors ξ by fixing the τ parameters in the spatial processes $\mathbf{w}$ to 1, as well as fixing the diagonal elements of $\mathbf{A}$ to 1. Because the endogenous factor η is a convolution (linear combination) of spatial processes from $\mathbf{w}$ and δ, its variance is fixed by additionally fixing the τ parameter governing the δ spatial process to be 1. It is also necessary, since we include unrestricted intercepts λ_0 in the measurement model of the SSEM (Equation 39.1), to fix the mean of the exogenous latent factors to zero, and also to fix the intercept for the structural model $\gamma_0 = 0$, so that the endogenous factor also has mean zero.

Priors

To do the Bayesian inference for the model (Equations 39.1 to 39.4) where the CAR model (Equation 39.5) is assumed for each spatial process in (Equation 39.4), we need to assign prior distributions to all the parameters. The general rule we follow is to put noninformative priors on the parameters, with the goal of minimizing the influence of the prior on the final posterior estimates. The unknown regression-type coefficients in the measurement and structural models (i.e., λ_0, Λ, Λ_x, γ_0, Γ, and Γ_x) are all assigned normal priors, $N(\mu_0, \sigma_0^2)$, where μ_0 is taken to be 0, and σ_0^2 is chosen to be a large number to make the prior vague (e.g., we use $\sigma_0^2 = 10^4$ in the latter example). Note that we assign the same vague normal prior to these parameters for convenience, but this is not necessary. Recall that the diagonal elements of A are fixed to 1 for identifiability purposes; similar vague normal priors are assigned to the off-diagonal elements. The spatial association parameters (ρ) that govern the different CAR spatial processes are taken to be uniformly distributed from (−0.1,1.0). Note that we assume a priori that the spatial association will tend toward being positive, but we allow zero to be a possibility in order to allow for complete independence. Further, we point out that the lower end of the possible range for the spatial association parameter is not −1, as might be expected, but a function of the eigenvalues of the neighbor matrix **H**.

Let Φ be the vector that contains all the unknown parameters in the model; then the joint priors can be expressed as $P(\Phi)$, which is the product of the priors of all the parameters specified earlier.

Posterior Inference

The main target of Bayesian inference is the posterior distribution of the parameters given the observed data $\mathbf{Z} = (Z_1, \ldots, Z_n)$ and $\mathbf{X} = (X_1, \ldots, X_n)$. The posterior is obtained by Bayes' rule. It is possible to focus specifically on the posterior for just the "fixed" parameters Φ, but it is also straightforward to derive the posterior jointly for the latent factors $\mathbf{f} = (\eta, \xi)$ as well. The spatial structural equation model (Equations 39.1–39.5) with CAR spatial processes leads to the following joint posterior distribution of all the unknown parameters and latent factors:

$$P(\Phi, \eta, \xi | \mathbf{Z}, \mathbf{X}) \propto P(\mathbf{Z}|\mathbf{X}, \eta, \xi, \lambda_0, \Lambda, \Lambda_x, \alpha_\varepsilon)$$
$$\times P(\eta|\xi, \gamma_0, \Gamma, \Gamma_x, \alpha_\delta)\, P(\xi|\mathbf{A}, \alpha_w)\, P(\Phi)$$

When describing the Bayesian method, it is common to point out that the posterior distribution updates prior knowledge about parameters using information in the observed data found through the likelihood. The posterior is proportional to the likelihood times the prior. What is required for Bayesian inference is to know what the posterior distribution looks like (e.g., where it is centered and how variable it is). The basic idea of MCMC is to sample from a distribution (e.g., the joint posterior distribution) by constructing a Markov chain that has the desired distribution as its equilibrium distribution. Rather than sampling directly from the joint posterior distribution, MCMC methods sample the conditional posteriors of the individual parameters conditional on the last sampled value of all the other parameters and the data. These full conditional distributions often have forms from which one can simulate straightforwardly. Samples are then drawn iteratively from the chain, and after a sufficiently large number of iterations (say, B), when the chain has converged to its equilibrium distribution (in this case the joint posterior), the continued draws from the chain represent simulated observations of the parameters from the posterior. Then, by continuing to take a large number of additional samples from the chain after it has converged (at iteration B), a simulated (empirical) sample of the posterior distribution is produced and can be used to perform any desired inference. Typically the expected mean of the posterior is computed by taking the empirical mean of the MCMC samples and is treated as the Bayesian estimate of the parameter. Similarly, the standard deviation of the posterior samples is the standard error, and quantiles can be calculated that correspond to some desired credible intervals. B draws from the chain needed to allow the Markov chain to reach its equilibrium at the joint posterior are discarded and are often referred to as the burn-in samples. Before convergence, the draws do not represent samples from the joint posterior and thus are not useful to keep. There are recommendations for monitoring the convergence of the chain in order to know how big B should be (Gelman, 1996), but there is no single best solution. A common technique is to generate multiple chains with different starting values and decide that convergence has occurred when the chains (which all started at different places) are mixed well together, indicating they have reached the same equilibrium distribution.

The SSEM can be implemented using the WinBUGS software, and specific code is made available from the author.

Model Comparison

Commonly used criteria for model comparison in hierarchical Bayesian models are the deviance information criteria (DIC; Spiegelhalter, Best, Carlin, & Van Der Linde, 2002). The DIC is useful for comparing complex hierarchical models in which the number of parameters is not clearly defined. Latent variable models such as the spatial structural equation model fall into this category, since it is not immediately obvious how to count the latent variables to obtain the so-called "effective number of parameters." DIC is given as

$$\text{DIC} = \overline{D(\Theta)} + p_D$$

where $\overline{D(\Theta)}$ is the average of $D(\Theta)$ for all MCMC samples of Θ, and $D(\Theta)$, which is called Bayesian deviance, can be defined as $D(\Theta) = -2 \log(f(Z|\Theta))$, where $f(Z|\Theta)$ is the likelihood function of the observed data given the parameter Θ. The quantity p_D is called the effective number of parameters and is defined as $p_D = \overline{D(\Theta)} - D(\overline{\Theta})$, where $\overline{\Theta}$ is the average of MCMC samples of Θ. The DIC, similar to the Akaike information criterion (AIC) and the Bayesian information criterion (BIC), has no well-defined meaning, so when it is used in model selection, the difference of DIC across models is considered and "smaller" implies better fit.

APPLICATION OF SSEM TO STATE-LEVEL BRFSS DATA

We return to the state-level BRFSS data presented earlier summarizing different subgroups' responses to the questions about general quality of health, fruit and vegetable intake, and physical activity. It is of interest to examine how a latent factor underlying the eight general health measurements across the country are predicted by latent factors representing state-level fruit and vegetable intake, as well as physical activity. An SSEM is used, and the basic measurement and structural model relationships are shown in Figure 39.5 using the conventional SEM graphical notation. What is unique to

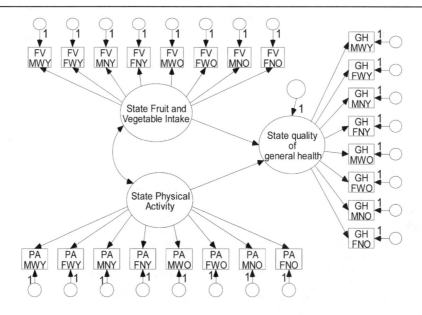

FIGURE 39.5. SSEM: Rectangles indicate observed variables; ovals and circles indicate latent factors and errors, respectively. FV, PA, GH indicate fruit and vegetable, physical activity, and general health (respectively) measures. Three-letter code indicates sex, race, and age subgroups forming the observed variables: MWY is male, white, young (< 65) and FNO is female, nonwhite, old (≥ 65). Spatial measurement errors, ε, are indicated by circles with arrows going to observed variables; spatial equation error, δ, is indicated by a circle with an arrow going to latent state quality of general health.

the SSEM and not explicitly shown in Figure 39.5 is the spatial correlation structure assumed for the latent factors and errors (i.e., correlation across locations). We consider and compare the fit of three models:

- $\varepsilon_i \sim \text{CAR}(\alpha_\varepsilon, \tau_\varepsilon)$ and $\delta_i \sim \text{CAR}(\alpha_\delta, \tau_\delta)$ (spatial measurement and equation error)
- $\varepsilon_i \sim \text{IID}$ and $\delta_i \sim \text{CAR}(\alpha_\delta, \tau_\delta)$ (spatial equation error only)
- $\varepsilon_i \sim \text{IID}$ and $\delta_i \sim \text{IID}$ (traditional IID model)

For simplicity of the presentation, only the 48 contiguous U.S. states are used, with Alaska and Hawaii deleted. These two states could be included in the analysis and would be treated as "islands" in the spatial model, which would mean that they are assumed to be independent of the other states. For the CAR spatial structure, the neighbor adjacency matrix **H** used (shown in Appendix 39.1) took as neighbors any two states that shared any part of their border with one another. The ρ parameter governing the spatial similarity is allowed to be different for the each of the different error terms.

Comparing the DIC of the three different models, the spatial equation error-only model has the smallest DIC and hence the fit best: spatial measurement and equation error, DIC = −3,333; spatial equation error only, DIC = −4,112; traditional IID model, DIC = −4,037.

These results indicate that while there is improvement over the traditional IID model by adding spatial association to the residual equation error term in the structural model, no additional benefit comes from including spatial association for the measurement errors. In other words, there is residual spatial correlation in the latent factor representing state general quality of health that is not explained by state fruit and vegetable intake and/or physical activity.

The resulting posterior mean estimates and 95% credible intervals for the structural regression parameters Γ from the spatial equation error-only model are 0.33 (−0.02, 0.76) for the state fruit and vegetable factor and 0.62 (0.22, 1.18) for the state physical activity factor. Hence, for a 1 standard deviation increase in the state physical activity factor, there is a significant 0.62 standard deviation increase in the general health factor controlling for fruit and vegetable intake, and while the fruit and vegetable intake factor is trending toward a similar, albeit smaller, positive association, there is still a nontrivial probability that its association is null. A map of the posterior mean value for the latent spatial factor for general quality of health is shown in Figure 39.6. The spatial equation error, which makes up part of this endogenous latent spatial factor, had an estimated spatial association parameter that was clearly positive, indicating spatial similarity that can be seen clearly in the map. Recall that the prior for the spatial parameter

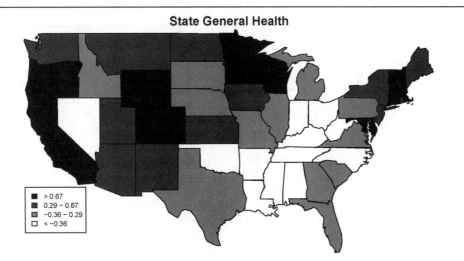

State General Health

> 0.67
0.29 – 0.67
−0.36 – 0.29
< −0.36

FIGURE 39.6. Posterior estimates from the SSEM of the spatial latent factor for state quality of general health.

ρ was uniform (–0.01,1). Its posterior distribution is skewed to the left, with the interquartile of its distribution ranging from (0.51,0.90) and posterior mean 0.60. Indeed, its 95% credible interval also does not contain zero (i.e., 0.01,0.96).

Finally, Figure 39.7 shows the "measurement" relationship between the eight different observed general health variables and how they relate to the latent factor representing state general health. The intercept and slopes of the linear relationships in these plots represent the "factor loadings" and intercepts (i.e., the associated elements of Λ and λ_0). It is of interest to note particular state-by-variable combinations that do not follow the general linear relationships in Figure 39.7. This summary is descriptive and does not follow from any specific hypotheses that are formally tested. For example, Tennessee (TN) in the MNY plot, and both Tennessee and West Virginia (WV) in the MNO plots, appear to be higher in their percentage of people reporting good general health than that predicted based on the overall state latent factor. Thus, although TN is low overall in terms of general state health and WV is, indeed, lowest, older nonwhite males in those states are not faring as poorly. On the flip side, California (CA) is a state that falls in the top quartile in terms of the overall state general health factor, but nonwhites in that state tend to fall on the lower end when reporting good health.

DISCUSSION

The SSEM is a natural extension of traditional IID structural equation models. The SSEM builds in spatial structure through spatially distributed latent factors and errors. While the example presented on state-level BRFSS incorporated spatial structure using the CAR model, the general formulation of the SSEM is flexible enough to incorporate other spatial models. Despite the ambiguity involved when one single-parameter ρ represents the overall spatial association (Wall, 2004), the reasons for preferring the CAR model here are its simplicity for testing whether a positive spatial association exists and, practically, because it is readily available in software.

One straightforward extension of the SSEM from what is presented here is to replace the linear measurement model (Equation 39.1) with a generalized linear measurement model structure. Indeed, that is the structure presented in Liu, Wall, and Hodges (2005), which allows for binomial or Poisson count data at each loca-

tion to be directly modeled. Furthermore, this extension is easily accommodated in Winbugs. Another extension of the SSEM would be to allow for nesting of observations within spatial location while still accounting for spatial similarity. That is, spatial correlation could be incorporated into a multilevel SEM framework where the units at level 2 were defined by geography. The usual multilevel SEM assumes independence between the level 2 units and, hence, independence between observations of the level 2 factors. It would be possible to instead assume a spatial process model for the level 2 factors so that these macrolevel factors could be correlated with nearby regions.

Plotting the original observed data and the predicted latent factors is often not a part of standard SEM, which typically is focused more on the relationships among variables than on pinpointing features of any particular observation. In contrast, when data are collected in geographic regions, one immediately wants to plot (map) the data in order to identify spatial patterns across the entire region. A nice advantage of the Bayesian framework is that it is straightforward to obtain the posterior distributions for the underlying latent factors and, hence, have them readily available for plotting.

Finally, no study analyzing aggregated region level data should be finished without at least acknowledging the modifiable area unit problem (MAUP) (Cressie, 1996; Gehlke & Biehl, 1934). This problem is well known in the geography and also the disease mapping literature, and points to the phenomenon that the statistical association between variables measured on geographic regions can change if the partition of the geographic region itself is changed. In the context of our example, the MAUP means that it can be expected that the association between general health and the two predictors, fruit and vegetable intake and physical activity, would change if county-level data instead of state-level were used. Also, if there were some other fabricated way to partition the United States into regions (e.g., square grids), MAUP implies that the association between summary variables on that grid would not be the same as that found at the state level. The point is that the way a region is partitioned matters in terms of the results found. One recommendation for dealing with MAUP is to use "meaningful" regions for the particular variables under study. Certainly an argument can be made that states are natural units for studying health behaviors, since states can and do make policies that may directly impact these particular health behaviors.

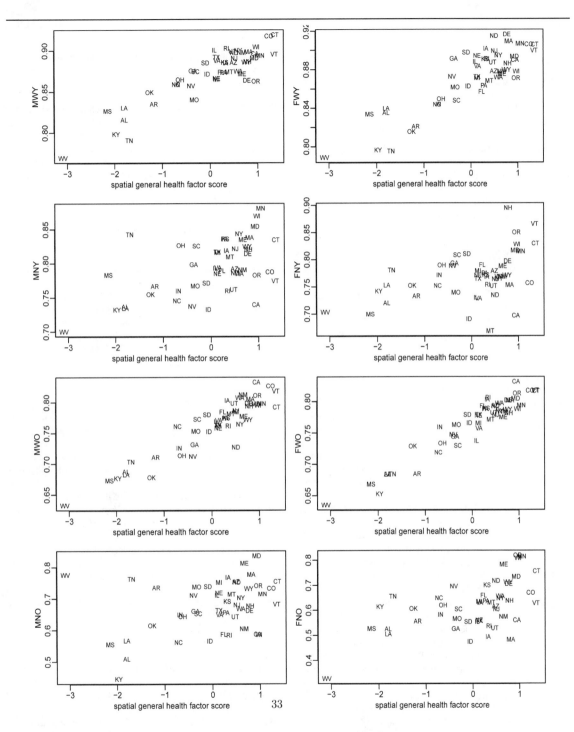

FIGURE 39.7. State-by-state percentage of persons reporting good or better general health (as in Figure 39.1) plotted against the posterior estimates from the SSEM of the spatial latent factor for state quality of general health (as in Figure 39.6). Two-letter labels are state postal abbreviations.

NOTE

1. This abbreviation refers to modeling and model(s).

REFERENCES

Banerjee, S., Carlin, B. P., & Gelfand, A. E. (2004). *Hierarchical modeling and analysis for spatial data.* Boca Raton, FL: Chapman & Hall.

Bentler, P. M., & Weeks, D. G. (1980). Linear structural equations with latent variables. *Psychometrika, 45,* 289–307.

Besag, J. (1974). Spatial interaction and the statistical analysis of lattice systems (with discussion). *Journal of the Royal Statistical Society, Series B, 36,* 192–236.

Bollen, K. (1989). *Structural equations with latent variables.* New York: Wiley.

Congdon, P. (2007). A spatial structural equation modelling framework for health count responses. *Statistics in Medicine, 26,* 5267–5284.

Congdon, P. (2010). A spatial structural equation model with an application to area health needs. *Journal of Statistical Computation and Simulation, 80*(4), 401–412.

Cressie, N. (1993). *Statistics for spatial data.* New York: Wiley.

Cressie, N. (1996). Change of support and the modifiable areal unit problem. *Geographical Systems, 3,* 159–180.

Dabney, A., & Wakefield, J. (2005). Issues in the mapping of two diseases. *Statistical Methods in Medical Research, 14,* 83–112.

Gehlke, C., & Biehl, H. (1934). Certain effects of grouping upon the size of the correlation coefficient in census tract material. *Journal of the American Statistical Association Supplement, 29*(Suppl.), 169–170.

Gelman, A. (1996). Inference and monitoring convergence. In W. R. Gilks, S. Richardson, & D. J. Spiegelhalter (Eds.), *Markov Chain Monto Carlo in practice* (pp. 131–143). Boca Raton, FL: Chapman & Hall/CRC.

Held, L., Natrio, I., Fenton, S., Rue, H., & Becker, N. (2005). Towards joint disease mapping. *Statistical Methods in Medical Research, 14,* 61–82.

Hogan, J., & Tchernis, R. (2004). Bayesian factor analysis for spatially correlated data, with application to summarising area-level material deprivation from census data. *Journal of the American Statistical Association, 99,* 314–324.

Hossain, M., & Laditka, J. (2009). Using hospitalization for ambulatory care sensitive conditions to measure access to primary health care: An application of spatial structural equation modeling. *International Journal of Health Geographics, 8,* 51.

Jia, H., & Lubetkin, E. (2009). Time trends and seasonal patterns of health-related quality of life among US adults. *Public Health Reports, 124*(5), 692–701.

Jia, H., Moriarty, D. G., & Kanarek, N. (2009). County-level social environment determinants of health-related quality of life among US adults: A multilevel analysis. *Journal of Community Health, 34,* 430–439.

Jia, H., Muennig, P., Lubetkin, E. I., & Gold, M. R. (2004). Predicting geographic variations in behavioral risk factors: An analysis of physical and mental healthy days. *Journal of Epidemiology and Community Health, 58*(2), 150–155.

Jöreskog, K. G. (1979). *Advances in factor analysis and structural equation models.* Cambridge, MA: Abt Books.

Knorr-Held, L., & Best, N. (2001). A shared component model for detecting joint and selective clustering of two diseases. *Journal of the Royal Statistical Society A, 164,* 73–85.

LeSage, J., & Pace, R. K. (2009). *Introduction to spatial econometrics.* Boca Raton, FL: CRC Press/Taylor & Francis Group.

Liu, X., Wall, M. M., & Hodges, J. (2005). Generalized spatial structural equation models. *Biostatistics, 6,* 539–557.

Mardia, K. V., & Goodall, R. R. (1993). Spatial temporal analysis of multivariate environmental monitoring data. In G. P. Patil & C. R. Rao (Eds.), *Multivariate environmental statistics* (pp. 347–386). Amsterdam: North-Holland.

Moriarty, D. G., Zack, M. M., & Kobau, R. (2003). The Centers for Disease Control and Preventions healthy days measures population tracking of perceived physical and mental health over time. *Health and Quality of Life Outcomes, 1*(37), 1–8.

Oud, J. H. L., & Folmer, H. (2008). A structural equation approach to models with spatial dependence. *Geographical Analysis, 40,* 152–166.

Schabenberger, O., & Gotway, C. A. (2005). *Statistical methods for spatial data analysis.* Boca Raton, FL: Chapman & Hall/CRC.

Spiegelhalter, D. J., Best, N., Carlin, B. P., & Van Der Linde, A. (2002). Bayesian measures of model complexity and fit (with discussion). *Journal of the Royal Statistical Society B, 64,* 583–639.

Tzala, E., & Best, N. (2007). Bayesian latent variable modeling of multivariate spatio-temporal variation in cancer mortality. *Statistical Methods in Methods Research, 17,* 97–118.

van Oort, F. G., Oud, J. H. L, & Raspe, O. (2009). The urban knowledge economy and employment growth: A spatial structural equation modeling approach. *Annals of Regional Science, 43,* 859–877.

Wackernagel, H. (2003). *Multivariate geostatistics: An introduction with applications* (3rd ed.). New York: Springer.

Wall, M. M. (2004). A close look at the spatial structure implied by the CAR and SAR models. *Journal of Statistical Planning and Inference, 121*(2), 311–324.

Waller, L. A., & Gotway, C. A. (2004). *Applied spatial statistics for public health data.* Hoboken, NJ: Wiley.

Wang, F., & Wall, M. M. (2003). Generalized common spatial factor model. *Biostatistics, 4,* 569–582.

APPENDIX 39.1.

The spatial neighbor matrix **H** contains many zeros. A simple description of the neighbor structure follows, where each row represents one of the 48 contiguous states followed by that state's numerically labeled neighbors. Note that states sharing a common point are also considered neighbors. For example, Arizona (AZ) and Colorado (CO) are considered neighbors.

```
1 AL 8 9 40 22
2 AZ 4 26 42 5 29
3 AR 23 40 22 16 41 34
4 CA 35 26 2
5 CO 48 25 14 34 29 2 42
6 CT 30 19 37
7 DE 28 18 36
8 FL 9 1
9 GA 1 8 38 31 40
10 ID 45 35 26 42 48 24
11 IL4 7 12 15 23 13
12 IN 11 20 33 15
13 IA 2147 11 23 25 39
14 KS 25 23 34 5
15 KY 23 11 12 33 4644 40
16 LA 41 3 22
17 ME 27
18 MD 36 7 44 46
19 MA 43 27 37 6 30
20 MI 12 33 47
21 MN 32 39 13 47
22 MS 16 3 40 1
23 MO 13 11 15 40 3 34 14 25
24 MT 10 48 39 32
25 NE 39 13 23 14 5 48
26 NV 35 10 42 2 4
27 NH 43 19 17
28 NJ 7 30 36
29 NM 2 42 5 34 41
30 NY 43 19 6 28 36
31 NC 44 40 93 8
32 ND 24 39 21
33 OH 20 12 15 46 36
34 OK 14 23 3 41 29 5
35 OR 45 10 26 4
36 PA 30 28 7 18 46 33
37 RI 6 19
38 SC 31 9
39 SD 32 24 48 25 13 21
40 TN 15 44 31 9 1 22 3 23
41 TX 29 34 3 16
42 UT 10 48 5 29 2 26
43 VT 30 19 27
44 VA 46 18 31 40 15
45 WA 35 10
46 WV 33 36 18 44 15
47 WI 20 11 13 21
48 WY 24 39 25 5 42 10
```

CHAPTER 40

Automated Structural Equation Modeling Strategies

George A. Marcoulides
Marsha Ing

There is currently tremendous interest within the statistics and related quantitative methodology communities on developing and applying automated strategies for the analysis of data sets. Some researchers refer to such automated strategies as "discovering structure in data" or "learning from data," while others simply call them "data mining" (Marcoulides, 2010). There is also a generally accepted taxonomy of the different kinds of automated strategies that includes the so-called "supervised," "semisupervised," and "unsupervised" methods (Larose, 2005; Marcoulides, 2005). In statistical terminology, the dividing line between supervised learning and unsupervised learning is the same as that which distinguishes the techniques of discriminant analysis from cluster analysis in multivariate statistics. Supervised learning requires that the target variable be well defined and that a sufficient number of its values be given. In the case of a discriminant analysis, this would imply specifying a priori the number of groups to be considered and focusing on which variables can best be used for the discrimination of the groups. For unsupervised learning, typically, the target variable is unknown, which in the case of cluster analysis corresponds to the number of groupings of observations based upon the selectively considered variables. Semisupervised learning is a combination of both—the algorithms are provided with limited information concerning the must- and/or cannot-link constraints on the model.

Reducing the number of explanatory or predictive variables or selecting a subset of variables from a long list of potential explanatory variables occurs not only in discriminant analysis and cluster analysis but also in structural equation modeling (SEM), where the problem has recently received some attention in the literature (e.g., Marcoulides & Drezner, 2001, 2003; Marcoulides, Drezner, & Schumacker, 1998; Scheines, Spirtes, Glymour, Meek, & Richardson, 1998). SEM has for several decades enjoyed widespread popularity in the behavioral, educational, medical, and social sciences as one of the fastest growing and most dominant multivariate statistical techniques (Hershberger, 2003). A major reason for this popularity is that SEM permits researchers to study complex multivariate relationships among observed and latent variables whereby both direct and indirect effects can be evaluated (see Bollen & Hoyle, Chapter 4, this volume). Another reason for the popularity is the general availability of specialized SEM programs (see Byrne, Chapter 19, this volume). For example, programs such as Amos (Arbuckle & Wothke, 1999), EQS (Bentler, 2004), LISREL (Jöreskog & Sörbom, 2005), Mplus (Muthén & Muthén, 2008), and Mx (Neale, Boker, Xie, & Maes, 1999), to name a few, are all broadly available for the analyses of a wide variety of models. A frequent assumption when using the SEM methodology is that the relationships among observed and/or latent variables are linear (although modeling nonlinear relationships is also increasingly popular in the SEM field, as are specialized programs; see Schumacker & Marcoulides, 1998; Chou & Huh, Chapter 14, this volume).

The basic building block of a structural model is an equation that specifies the hypothesized effects or relationships of certain variables on other variables (regardless of whether they are observed or latent variables). This is essentially a simple statement of the verbal theory that posits the hypothesized relationships among a set of studied variables (Marcoulides, 1989). The relationships are thereby described by parameters that specify their magnitude. A structural equation model is typically represented by a path diagram, which is a mathematical representation of the proposed theoretical model in graphical form (see Ho, Stark, & Chernyshenko, Chapter 3, this volume, for further details).[1]

It might also be helpful to distinguish between using an inference model to specify the relationship between variables, and the statistical procedure that examines and determines the strength of that relationship. One may think of the inference model as specifying the parameters to be estimated or tested, whereas the statistical procedure defines the mathematical procedure used to test the hypothesis about the relationship. So the full power of SEM cannot be attained until the parameters of the model are estimated and tested numerically against empirically obtained data. The process of proposing and testing a theoretical model is commonly referred to as the "confirmatory aspect" of SEM. Although in principle researchers should fully specify and deductively hypothesize a specific model prior to data collection and testing, in practice this is often not possible, because a theory is either poorly formulated or perhaps even nonexistent. Consequently, another aspect of SEM is the exploratory mode, in which theory development can occur. The theory development mode often involves repeated analyses of the same data in order to explore potential relationships among either observed or latent variables of interest (see Chou & Huh, Chapter 14, this volume). A related utilization of SEM where such repeated analyses may occur is to examine the psychometric properties of a given measurement device (see Millsap & Olivera-Aguilar, Chapter 23, and Bovaird & Koziol, Chapter 29, this volume).

To some extent, then, two broad categories of potential applications of automated SEM can be defined: those related to measurement issues, and those to model modification. Measurement issues in essence underlie any variables included in a specified model. If the variables selected do not accurately and consistently represent the construct, this calls into question the inferences based on the model. Attention to measurement issues helps ensure that the variables entered into the model are reflective of the construct of interest. One application of automated SEM to measurement issues includes the development of different forms to measure the same construct (Jöreskog, 1971; Lord, 1957, 1980). This includes situations in which there is a large number of items but it is not practical or feasible to administer all of the items to all of the potential respondents. Shorter versions of the measure are created with the intention of concisely and accurately representing the construct with fewer items. In developing short forms, there is also a need to simultaneously examine any number of prespecified qualities, such as the difficulty, order, content, and type of items (Hambleton, Swaminathan, & Rogers, 1991; Kenny & McCoach, 2003; Lord, 1980; Reise, Widaman, & Pugh, 1993). Any one of these single factors requires an examination of a large number of likely models, and any combination of these factors highlights the need for more efficient procedures to examine properties of the different measures.

Consider two examples of these factors that demonstrate how automated SEM might be useful to address measurement issues. To examine content validity, often items from the different forms are given to a panel of experts that decides whether the items included in each form are equivalent in terms of the content (for review, see Messick, 1989). It would be unfair, for example, to create a mathematics test in which one form of the test focuses on fractions and another focuses on addition. The quality of inferences based on performance on these different forms of the test would be compromised because the tests are measuring different mathematical content. Instead of relying on content experts to determine the content of each form, Ding and Hershberger (2002) constructed parallel forms of a measure using an SEM approach. The researchers examined whether different forms had adequate content coverage, using empirical data from two college-level subject examinations. There were two forms measuring research methods in psychology and another two measuring research in nursing. Within each form were seven subcontent areas for research methods in psychology, including experimental psychology and the scientific method, and three subcontent areas for research in nursing including qualitative research. SEM use helped researchers to compare both the content coverage and balance of the different forms. This approach helps to ensure equivalence between the forms in terms of the overall construct and different subconstructs. Imagine a scenario where there are more than two forms per content area, a greater number of items from which to select, or a greater number of subconstructs. To construct and to compare these different scenarios, particularly when different features about the items are changing simultaneously, require a much more efficient approach, and this is where automated approaches can provide assistance.

Another example pertains to the types of items to include. Some items might be in different response formats, such as fixed response or open-ended response. Both item formats might measure the same construct, but when constructing equivalent forms of the same measures one must consider a host of factors that might influence responses. Even if the item format is similar with different forms, it is still possible that there are different item response options for items measuring the same construct. Ferrando (1999) used an SEM approach to test the equivalence of different item response formats (binary, 5-point Likert, and continuous). More specifically, Ferrando used a nested confirmatory factor analysis model to determine whether the different formats of the same items were equivalent. The five items selected for the study were not redundant in content, and all were worded in the same manner. One limitation cited is that the computational demand makes it "impossible to work with large and moderately large sets of items" (1999, p. 161). An automated structural equation model allows researchers to work with a larger set of items and to test whether forms with different combinations of item response formats provide similar information about respondents.

Fitting a model to empirical data can be difficult, particularly when the number of variables is large. For example, a covariance structure model with 25 variables has 325 variances and covariances that must be modeled correctly. One can envision that many models may not be perfect and might need some minor modification in order to better fit the data (for further details see Chou & Huh, Chapter 14, this volume). Three types of situations can apply to such model fitting and testing (Jöreskog, 1993). The first is the so-called "strictly confirmatory approach," in which the initial proposed

model is tested against data and is either accepted or rejected. The second situation is one in which competing or alternative models are considered. All proposed models are assessed, and selecting the best is based upon which model more appropriately fits the observed data. The third situation is the so-called "model-generating approach," in which an initially proposed model is repeatedly modified until some level of fit is obtained (Jöreskog, 1993). Of course, we strongly believe that the decision with regards to which approach to follow should be based on the initial theory. A researcher who is firmly rooted in his or her theory will elect a different approach than one who is quite tentative about the various relationships being modeled, or one who acknowledges that such information is what actually needs to be determined. Nevertheless, once a researcher agrees that an initially proposed model is to be abandoned, the modeling approach is no longer confirmatory. Indeed, the modeling approach has clearly entered an exploratory mode in which revisions to the model occur. Such modifications can entail simply adding and/or removing parameters in the model (see Chou & Huh, Chapter 14, this volume) or even completely changing the initially proposed model (the topic of this chapter). This process of model exploration is commonly referred to as a "specification search" (Long, 1983; Marcoulides & Drezner, 2001).

For many considered models there may be a finite number of variable combinations possible. For example, a multiple regression prediction model with five potential predictor variables only has $2^5 = 32$ combinations to examine, which can usually be easily evaluated by calculating the value of the objective function (e.g., maximum R^2) for all possible variable combinations. With 26 predictor variables, the number of combinations now increases to 67,108,864, although even these can still be evaluated within a reasonable amount of computer time. However, what happens when the number of possible combinations is prohibitively large? For example, with 100 potential predictor variables the number of possible combinations geometrically increases to the staggering value of $2^{100} = 1,267,650,600,228,229,401,496,703,205,376$ combinations, which even if the evaluation of each combination took one millionth of a second would still take more than 40 thousand trillion years to examine.

In such cases where total enumeration procedures are impractical, various heuristic optimization or automated search algorithms have been developed (Marcoulides et al., 1998). Heuristic search algorithms are specifically designed to determine the best possible solution but do not guarantee that the optimal solution is found—though their performance using empirical testing or worst cases analysis indicates that in many situations they seem to be the only way forward to produce concrete results (Salhi, 1998). So as the models become more complicated, automated procedures can make "chaotic situation(s) somewhat more manageable by narrow(ing) attention to models on a recommendation list" (Marcoulides & Drezner, 2009, p. 266). To date, heuristic procedures have been successfully applied to tackle difficult-to-solve problems in business, economics, and industrial engineering. They have also recently made their way into the general SEM literature. Examples of such numerical heuristic procedures in SEM include ant colony optimization (Leite, Huang, & Marcoulides, 2008; Leite & Marcoulides, 2009; Marcoulides & Drezner, 2003), genetic algorithms (Marcoulides & Drezner, 2002), the ruin and re-create approach (Marcoulides, 2009), simulated annealing (Drezner & Marcoulides, 1999), and Tabu search (Marcoulides et al., 1998; Marcoulides & Drezner, 2004), and over the years a great variety of modifications have been proposed to these heuristic search procedures (e.g., Drezner & Marcoulides, 2003; Marcoulides, 2010). In summary, all of these methods focus on the evaluation of an objective function that is usually based upon some aspect of model fit (e.g., in the case of model modification it could be the Lagrange multiplier; see Chou & Huh, Chapter 14, this volume).

It is important to note that a number of other proposed heuristic search strategies do not specifically require numerical minimization or maximization. For example, the methods based upon the evaluation of tetrads proposed by Glymour, Scheines, Spirtes, and Kelly (1987), Scheines and colleagues (1998), and Spirtes, Scheines, and Glymour (1990) would fall into this category. These search approaches make use of tetrads, which represent the relationships between sets of four covariance elements (h, i, j, k) within any covariance matrix defined as simply $\tau_{hijk} = \sigma_{hi}\,\sigma_{jk} - \sigma_{hj}\,\sigma_{ik}$. When a tetrad is equal to zero, it is called a vanishing tetrad. Glymour and colleagues (1987) also developed the program TETRAD to explore the existence of possible alternative models (now in its version IV; for a recent review of the program, see Landsheer, 2010). They indicated that besides having an advantage over other methods because it does not require numerical minimization, this approach also avoids convergence problems. Unfortunately, because the TETRAD pro-

gram is limited with regard to the number of variables it can handle in a model, its practical value is rather restricted. For this reason, the tetrad approach to automated searches is not discussed further in this chapter (for details, see Landsheer, 2010).

In this chapter, we provide an overview of several numerical, heuristic, automated SEM strategies and elaborate on some conceptual and methodological details related to their application in a variety of settings and situations. The term "automated SEM" used throughout the chapter as a generic notion refers to the application of semisupervised and unsupervised heuristic searches on a wide variety of possible models (e.g., confirmatory factor analysis; multiple regression; path analysis; models for time-dependent data; recursive and nonrecursive models for cross-sectional, longitudinal, and multilevel data; covariance structure analysis; latent class or mixture analysis; and all kinds of variations thereof). For obvious space limitations, we selectively introduce just a few illustrative examples. We also emphasize that because each application of the described heuristic search requires problem- and model-specific construction, programming design, and setup, only the procedural steps or pseudocodes are described throughout the chapter (for more extensive computer and programming details, see Resenda & Sousa, 2003).

The chapter is organized into several sections, each focused on providing an overview of the most current heuristic search procedures that have been applied to SEM methodology. Although a number of criteria can be used to comparatively evaluate the performance of the described heuristic search procedures (e.g., the quality of the solutions provided and the computational effort in terms of central processing time needed to obtain a solution), to date most studies within the SEM field have focused mainly on implementations and empirical tests of the different algorithms to perform various types of model searches. The study by Leite and Marcoulides (2009) appears to be one of the few that has examined performance issues, but it is concentrated solely on the ant colony algorithm. Their results indicated that when faced with specification searches for highly complex SEM models, nonconvergence of solutions occurs quite frequently. However, in a prior study of complex models using ant colony algorithms, Leite et al. (2008) actually found that nonconvergence rarely occurred. Similar good convergence results were also found for the genetic algorithm and Tabu search procedures (see Marcoulides & Drezner, 2002; Marcoulides et al., 1998). As such, at least with SEM applications, it would appear that further research is needed before definitive conclusions can be drawn about preferring one algorithm over another. In contrast, within the operation research/management science areas a number of studies have attempted to compare the different algorithms and appear to recommend the use of genetic algorithms and Tabu search procedures (e.g., Dorigo & Stützle, 2004; Salhi, 1998). For example, Dorigo and Stützle (2004) indicated that ant colony optimization algorithms do not perform as well as genetic algorithms in general optimization problems. Nevertheless, other studies have shown that ant colony optimization algorithms do perform as well as other currently available heuristic search procedures. Some studies have also shown that genetic algorithms and Tabu search procedures often outperform other heuristic procedures in difficult combinatorial problems (e.g., Drezner & Marcoulides, 2003). Given the rather inconclusive evidence with regard to the superiority of one method over another, and for ease of presentation, the heuristic search procedures discussed in this chapter are simply listed in alphabetic order. Throughout the chapter we use a notational system and equations generally considered to be consistent with the so-called Jöreskog–Keesling–Wiley (Jöreskog & Sörbom, 2005) framework, although this choice is to some extent arbitrary, as specialized variants of the equations (e.g., the Bentler–Weeks model; Bentler & Weeks, 1980) can also be readily used.

ANT COLONY OPTIMIZATION ALGORITHMS

Ant colony optimization (ACO) is a class of optimization algorithms based on the foraging behavior of ants (Dorigo & Stützle, 2004). Using a colony of Argentine ants (*Linepithema humile*, formerly *Iridomyrmex humili*) Deneubourg, Pasteels, and Verhaeghe (1983; Deunebourg & Goss, 1989) determined how ants manage to establish a shortest route path back and forth between the colony nest and food sources. Ants are able to find the shortest path between the nest and the food source using a process that starts with the ants randomly trying different paths and leaving feedback on the ground in the form of a chemical substance called pheromone. The pheromone accumulates faster on the shortest path, stimulating other ants to follow the same path, thus ensuring that it is strongly preferred over any other path. Marcoulides and Drezner (2003), Leite and colleagues (2008), and Leite and Marcoulides (2009) demonstrated implementations of an ant colony algo-

rithm to perform various types of model searches in SEM and in the development of short forms of a scale based upon the relationship between the short form and other variables. Selecting a model or a short form of a scale that maintains adequate dimensionality and maximizes the relationship with another variable requires the examination of many different combinations of a potentially large number of models or item subsets. Although any number of heuristic algorithms may be used to deal with such a difficult combinatorial optimization problem (see sections that follow), we begin first with the ACO algorithm (Marcoulides & Drezner, 2003) both for alphabetic reasons and because it has the advantage of being relatively easy to implement.

Marcoulides and Drezner (2003) demonstrated the implementation of ACO to perform model modification in SEM. Their implementation of the ACO algorithm samples parameters in a model to be freely estimated, while the other parameters are fixed at zero. Their ACO algorithm attempts to minimize the non-centrality parameter relative to the specific model considered. If a small noncentrality parameter (NCP) is obtained with a given model configuration, the pheromone levels (i.e., sampling weights) of the parameters freely estimated increase, while the pheromone levels of the parameters fixed at zero stay the same. Consequently, the probability of the same configuration of model parameters being sampled again increases. This process is repeated until parameters that provide the best model fit when freely estimated have very large sampling weights, while the other parameters have small sampling weights. Their ACO converges when a NCP of zero is found or after a preselected fixed number of iterations is completed. In the Marcoulides and Drezner ACO, the actual NCP value is not used directly as the pheromone level. Instead, the function $int[100/(NCP + 1)]$ (where int refers to an integer) is used to provide the pheromone level to be added after each iteration. The use of this function is necessary because the pheromone level should increase as NCP decreases in order to provide the feedback mechanism described previously. For example, consider a simple CFA model with the following known two-factor loading matrix Λ with five observed indicators:

$$\begin{bmatrix} \lambda_{11} & 0 \\ \lambda_{21} & 0 \\ \lambda_{31} & 0 \\ 0 & \lambda_{42} \\ 0 & \lambda_{52} \end{bmatrix} \qquad \textbf{(40.1)}$$

In order to simplify matters for the ACO algorithm, this matrix is binary-coded as the vector **1110000011** (for ease of presentation, we also do not discuss here the correlation between the factors or the error variances normally considered in a factor model). We note that when the value of the factor loading is "set to 0" it implies that the particular element is fixed to 0, whereas "set to 1" implies that the particular element is freely estimated. Let us assume that we did not know the specific structure of this factor loading matrix and wish to use the ACO approach on data to examine an initially proposed misspecified model, which is represented by the vector **1100000111**—in other words, we assume that the first factor is only measured by indicators 1 and 2, whereas the second factor is measured by indicators 3, 4, and 5. To implement the ACO algorithm for the specification search, the following pheromone table can be used (for complete details, see Marcoulides & Drezner, 2003). We note that the initial pheromone level is initially set at a value of 1 for each variable in the model.

Loading to be set = 0 1 1 1 1 1 1 1 1 1 1
Loading to be set = 1 1 1 1 1 1 1 1 1 1 1

Now assuming that the initial misspecified model provides an NCP = 46.47, based on the earlier pheromone level function formula, the obtained NCP yields a value of 2. This obtained pheromone level value, when added to the initial table, leads to the following updated table:

Loading to be set = 0 1 1 3 3 3 3 3 1 1 1
Loading to be set = 1 3 3 1 1 1 1 1 3 3 3

The process of updating the pheromone level based upon the obtained NCP for each randomly generated model continues for a number of iterations until either NCP = 0 or a fixed number of iterations is completed. With respect to the previously considered example model, this occurs after only seven iterations, whereupon the pheromone table displayed next would emerge and one can quickly discern that the model **1110000011** is preferred (i.e., it is dominated in terms of its pheromone levels, which is of course the correct known model given earlier):

Loading to be set = 0 1 1 7 107 104 140 138 102 1 3
Loading to be set = 1 140 140 134 34 37 1 3 39 140 138

The Marcoulides and Drezner (2003) ACO algorithm is aimed at maximizing model fit in terms of converging on the correct model. However, only maximizing fit is not always sufficient for selecting a good short form of a scale. Indeed, as indicated in an earlier section, the ideal short form can depend on a number of additional characteristics. For example, instead of just maximizing a function of model fit, the ACO algorithm can be used to additionally maximize a function of the magnitude of the regression coefficients between the outcome of interest and the latent variables measured (i.e., the so-called γ_j) by the short form.

The selection of a short form should optimally include the evaluation of assorted short forms with different numbers of items, in order to ideally attain an appropriate balance between scale length and validity. For example, if an a priori number of items were set at 22, the number of short-form combinations that need to be considered would be 51,021,117,810 versus, say, a short form with only 15 items, which would lead to just 25,140,840,660 combinations.

Figure 40.1 provides an example multiple-indicator, multiple-cause (MIMIC) model with a variable called *pcsugar*, which is included as a predictor of the five factors measured by the D-39 scale (see Leite et al., 2008). We note that any number of predictors could easily be added for the purposes of conducting an automated search. Because *pcsugar* is in this case dichotomous, the coefficients γ_j are the differences in the j latent variables between individuals with good and poor *pcsugar* (see Figure 40.1). Such a MIMIC model can be easily fit using, say, Mplus and the weighted least squares with adjusted means and variances (WLSMV) estimator (Muthén & Muthén, 2008) and the ACO algorithm programmed using the R statistical package[2] (although other SEM programs could also be used because the ACO algorithm implementation does not compute the parameter estimates and fit statistics but uses the values generated by the SEM program).

It is important to note that Leite and colleagues (2008) also suggested the use of a multiple-ant search strategy with a "best-so-far" pheromone update. This notion of a "best-so-far" pheromone update is similar to that employed in Tabu searches (see complete description in section below), where the best solution is maintained in a list and updated whenever better solutions are encountered. A multiple-ant search strategy consists of evaluating n potential solutions (e.g., short forms) before updating the pheromone level. This process is equivalent to sending a group of ants, instead of a single ant, to look for food at a time, and evaluating

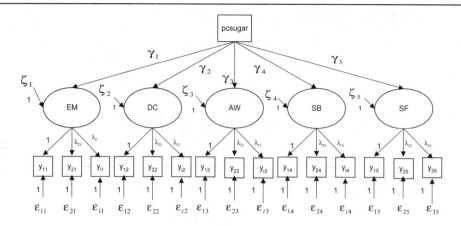

FIGURE 40.1. Example MIMIC model.

the pheromone trails after all the ants from that group return. After the n solutions are evaluated, the best solution from the group is selected. Then, pheromone is added to the search weights if the pheromone level of the current best solution exceeds the largest pheromone level obtained with the previous best solution (i.e., the "best-so-far" pheromone update). We also note that the number of potential solutions examined at a time can be set to any prespecified number (e.g., with $n = 10$ suggesting the use of a group of 10 ants). Although reducing n makes the algorithm converge faster, it can increase the number of nonoptimal solutions found. Additionally, by implementing a process of pheromone evaporation before the pheromone is updated, the pheromone associated with each component of the pheromone table can be reduced (e.g., by 5%). Pheromone evaporation reduces the influence of the solutions obtained at earlier stages of the search, when poor-quality solutions are more likely to be selected (Dorigo & Stützle, 2004).

Finally, we also note that for the sake of simplicity, the example of selecting a short-form presented in this section only took into account model fit and the relationship with a variable. However, a test developer can easily tailor the ACO algorithm to account for any number of prespecified qualities simultaneously, such as content balancing, reliability, test information, and relationship with several variables. To make the ACO algorithm take into account any of these prespecified qualities, it is only necessary to modify the definition of the pheromone level (φ_i) in the ACO according to the

particular needs of the test developer. The implementation of the ACO algorithm to conduct an automated SEM activity is thereby to a great degree problem- and model-specific.

GENETIC ALGORITHMS

A "genetic algorithm" (GA) is a type of adaptive heuristic search procedure carried out on a population of points (i.e., several potential solutions are considered simultaneously). Because of this, GAs are generally considered to be more robust than most other heuristic search methods. A GA performs a sort of multidimensional search by maintaining a population of potential solutions, and encourages information and exchange between solutions. Thus, the population undergoes a simulated evolution in which the relatively good solutions reproduce at each generation, while the relatively bad solutions die or are eliminated. Another characteristic of a GA that makes it somewhat different than other heuristic search procedures is that model parameters are not manipulated; rather, a coding of the parameter set is directly manipulated. Finally, and perhaps most importantly, a GA generates information about a population of candidate solutions over any number of selected iterations.

GAs were first introduced by Holland (1975) as a way to emulate the processes observed in biological evolution to solve game theory and pattern recognition problems. The main idea behind GAs is that a Darwinian survival of the fittest strategy can be modeled for solving optimization problems. Based on this strategy, a population of chromosomes evolves over a number of different generations, with only the best surviving from one generation to the next. Thus, evaluation of an optimization problem takes place on chromosomes (rather than model parameters), and there are chromosomal encoding and decoding processes that relate to the problem under study in a biologically evolutionary process.

In terms of specific optimization processes, the goal of a GA is to find the optimum of a given function F over a given search space S. A point of the search space S is then described by a vector of N bits and F is a function able to compute a real value for each of the vectors

(Drezner & Marcoulides, 2006). In the initialization step, a set of points in the search space or a starting population is selected. Subsequently, a GA iteration occurs in four sequential steps (evaluation, selection, reproduction, and replacement) until a stopping criterion is met. The following four sequential steps are depicted in Figure 40.2 using rabbits for the representation of the population:

1. *Evaluation*—The function F is computed so that a starting population can be ordered from best to worst.

2. *Selection*—Pairs of mates (referred to as parents) are selected (although a mate can appear in any number of pairs).

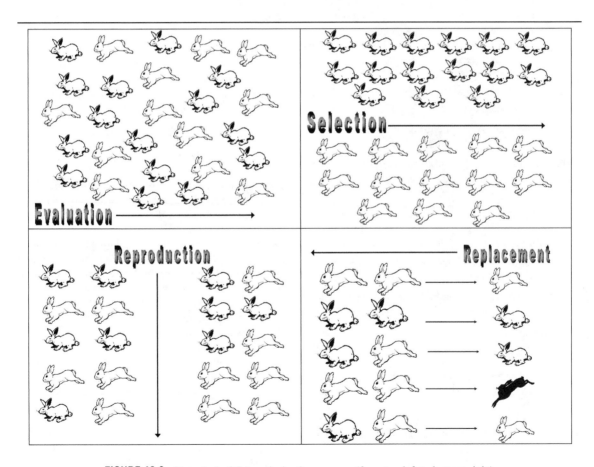

FIGURE 40.2. Steps 1–4 of GA optimization process (from top left to bottom right).

3. *Reproduction*—Offspring are produced by the parents.

4. *Replacement*—A new population is generated through a replacement of some of the old members of the population with new ones.

Because genetic algorithms use a vocabulary borrowed from natural genetics, the following terminology is also useful for understanding how the search process takes place:

1. *Chromosome*: A string of binary codes representing a solution to an objective function. For example, **1110000011** could be used to represent a possible solution to an objective function (somewhat similar to that used with the ACO algorithm). It is important to note that there are a number of possible chromosome coding schemes that can be used to set up a genetic algorithm. Besides the binary code, other popular coding schemes include the decimal, character, and integer number representation.

2. *Genes*: A binary coding representation of a chromosome (i.e., the 0 or 1).

3. *Population*: A set of chromosomes used at each iteration of the algorithm.

4. *Operators*: Manipulations that occur to the chromosomes (these include crossover, mutation, and reproduction).

5. *Crossover*: A manipulation that occurs when two parents exchange parts of their corresponding chromosomes to create a new chromosome.

6. *Mutation*: A manipulation that occurs when the gene is changed to form a new chromosome.

7. *Reproduction*: A manipulation that occurs when two parents join to generate a new chromosome.

8. *Neighbor*: Two chromosomes are considered neighbors if the string of binary codes representing each chromosome differs by one gene (e.g., the two chromosomes 111111 and 111110 are considered neighbors).

To illustrate the basic features of a genetic algorithm, consider the optimization of the following simple function:

$$f = x_1^2 + x_2^2 + x_3^2 + x_4^2 + x_5^2 - x_1 x_2 - x_2 x_3 - x_3 x_4 - x_4 x_5 \quad \textbf{(40.2)}$$

The function is defined with the value of x being equal to either 0 or 1. The values of the objective function vary from $f = 0$ to $f = 3$, so for simplicity let us just consider the maximization of the function f.

To construct a genetic algorithm, the following must be defined.

An Initial Population

Using a binary vector as a chromosome to represent values of the variables x_i, an initial population size of 4 is selected (this initial population may even be randomly generated). Let us assume that the following four chromosomes were generated to provide the solutions below:

1.	01001	$f = 2$	2.	11011	$f = 2$
3.	01100	$f = 1$	4.	11111	$f = 1$

We note that the binary vector defined as a chromosome changes according to the type of problem examined. More complicated problems will require large chromosome strings. For example, Marcoulides and Drezner (2001)[3] illustrated that the binary vector

$$\Lambda \quad \Phi \quad \Theta$$
1110000011 | 1 | 11111

would need to be used to represent the matrices Λ, Φ, and Θ for the confirmatory factor analysis (CFA) model considered in Equation 40.1 (the model with five observed variables and two correlated common factors). This chromosome has 16 genes, with each ordered according to the proposed structure for the first column in the factor loading matrix Λ, the second column in Λ (see Equation 40.1), the covariance between the two factors in Φ, and the five error terms in Θ. A value of 0 is used in the chromosome to denote that the particular element is fixed, and a 1 means that it is free. Of course, more complicated models would lead to longer chromosome coding vectors. We also emphasize again that model parameters are never directly manipulated in a GA; only the chromosomal coding is manipulated.

Genetic Operators

During the search operations of the GA, several genetic operators are used. As mentioned previously, genetic operators (crossover, mutation, and reproduction) are manipulations that occur to the chromosomes. To illustrate the crossover operator for chromosomes 1 and 2 listed earlier in the initial population table, assume that the crossover point was to occur after the third gene:

$$010|01$$
$$110|11$$

The resulting offspring are

$$010|11$$
$$110|01$$

These offspring both evaluate to $f = 2$. Since the resulting offspring are better than chromosomes 3 and 4 in the initially utilized population, the old chromosomes are replaced in the population with the new ones.

To illustrate mutation (i.e., the altering of one or more genes in a chromosome), assume that the second gene of chromosome 2 was selected for mutation. Since the second gene in this chromosome is a 1, it would be flipped to a 0. So the chromosome after this mutation would become equal to 10011. This particular mutation leads to $f = 2$, and so it is also replaced in the population. The whole process of crossover and mutation continues for several cycles until finally the following best chromosome is generated 10101, which, of course, corresponds to the (in this case, known) optimal value of $f = 3$.

A Summary of GA Steps

A GA consists of the following sequential steps and can be readily modified to accommodate any type of automated structural equation model search:

1. An initial (starting) population is generated (based on a proposed model).

2. A pair of parents is randomly selected.

3. The parents are merged to produce offspring.

4. The offspring are improved by a steepest-descent algorithm (or by a Tabu search; see section below).

5. If the offspring's objective function is better than (or equal to) the worst population member, the worst population member is replaced by the offspring as long as it is not identical to an existing population member.

6. A mutation that is not related to the process of generating an offspring is executed. This means that a population member is randomly selected and one of its genes is randomly selected and changed. If the mutation results in a better population member, it is accepted as long as it is not identical to an existing population member. If not, the mutation is ignored. The algorithm returns to Step 2 for another iteration.

TABU SEARCH

Tabu search is a memory-based search strategy to guide the function being optimized away from parts of the solution space that have already been explored. This is usually achieved by forbidding solutions already visited and stored in the Tabu list. Tabu search procedures are closely tied to the field of artificial intelligence, in which intelligent uses of memory help to exploit useful historical information concerning interrelationships within data (for a complete discussion, see Salhi, 1998). Tabu search procedures are basically local search strategies that proceed by examining a neighborhood of the current solution. Unlike most common procedures (e.g., steepest descent) where the search terminates when there is no further improvement with respect to the function examined, Tabu allows the search to exploit inferior solutions. This flexibility helps the search get out of local optimality when taking uphill moves, and to avoid cycling, Tabu search imposes a sort of off-limits status (i.e., a "tabu status") to those attributes recently involved in the choice of the new solution.

In order to implement a Tabu search procedure in SEM, several definitions and parameters must be considered (Drezner, Marcoulides, & Salhi, 1999).[4] These include (1) the criterion for the selection of a model; (2) the definition of the neighborhood; (3) a starting model; (4) a definition of the Tabu list, Tabu size (the length of the Tabu list), and admissible models; (5) the search parameters; and, finally, (6) a stopping criterion. Each of these is described next, followed by a listing of the Tabu search procedure steps for implementation with any type of structural equation model.

Criterion for the Selection of a Model

Numerous criteria have been proposed in the SEM literature to evaluate the goodness of fit of a specified model (Marsh, Balla, Hau, 1996; West, Taylor, & Wu,

Chapter 13, this volume). Most criteria define goodness of fit in terms of the discrepancy between the observed and the model-implied covariance matrices. Given the plethora of fit indices available in the SEM literature and because there is no "best" index, one can essentially choose to rely on any one (or more) fit index as the criterion for the selection of a model when using a Tabu search.

Definition of the Neighborhood

A variety of neighborhood definitions can be utilized. For example, two CFA models can be considered neighbors if the set of free terms in the Λ matrix differs by the definition of just one term. This implies that the neighborhood of a model K is a model for which either one fixed parameter is freed, or one free parameter is fixed to zero (or any other value).

A Starting Model

A variety of models can be utilized as the starting model, for example, a user-specified theoretical model, a randomly generated initial model, or even a model where all parameters are constrained to zero (or all parameters are set free—a null model).

The Tabu List, Tabu Size, Admissible Models, and Search Parameters

The Tabu list contains a list of all Tabu moves. When a move is performed (e.g., a constrained term in the model is freed), reversing this action is added to the Tabu list. The Tabu list contains the names of the terms whose status has been changed. A prespecified maximum length of the Tabu list is termed the "Tabu size." When the Tabu size is exceeded, the last member in the Tabu list is discarded in a "first in, first out" manner. A model in the neighborhood is termed "admissible" if the term changed in the current model (i.e., one that is freed or fixed) is not in the Tabu list. The Tabu size used in the search procedure can be set to any number (e.g., 5 times the number of observed variables). When a new best model is found, the Tabu list is emptied as if it were a new starting solution.

Stopping Criterion

The stopping criterion for a Tabu search can be set to any number according to the complexity of the model examined (e.g., when 100 consecutive iterations do not produce a new best solution).

A Summary of Tabu Search Procedure Steps

1. An initial model K is specified.
2. The best current model K_{best} is set to K.
3. The iteration counter is set to iter = 0 (current iteration).
4. The neighborhood $N(K)$ of the model K is created.
5. The objective function $F(K')$ for all K' in $N(K)$ are evaluated.
6. If $F(K') < F(K_{best})$ for any K' in $N(K)$, set $K_{best} = K'$ (if there are several K' that fulfill this condition, select the best one). Go to Step 8.
7. If for all K' in $N(K)$: $F(K') \geq F(K_{best})$, choose the best admissible model K' in $N(K)$.
8. Set $K = K'$ and iter = iter + 1.
9. The Tabu list is updated. Go to Step 4, unless the stopping criterion is met.

RUIN AND RE-CREATE

The ruin and re-create (R & R) approach was originally formulated by Scrimpf, Schneider, Stamm-Wilbrandt, and Dueck (2000), and a modified version was implemented within the SEM framework by Marcoulides (2009).[5] The modified version utilizes an iterative process and local neighborhood search of the considered solutions in a manner somewhat similar to that used in Tabu search (see previous section). The basic element of the R & R principle is to try and obtain better optimization results by a reconstruction (ruin) of a large fraction of an obtained or existing modeling solution and a subsequent improvement (re-create) procedure, which seeks to obtain a new result that is better in terms of model fit (or any other criteria considered) than the previous one.

Suppose we begin with an initial or current solution to our modeling problem. We now "ruin" a significant part of the solution. When ruining the solution, think of a complete disintegration of the model fit. For example, in a CFA model, mathematically speaking, we would completely remove some of the observed and latent variables from the model and then connect the remaining (or surviving) variables. This process can be either completely random or based upon some minimum specified connections between variables. For example, in the case of a regression model on latent variables, this might include imposing constraints that certain indicators can only load on particular latent variables. In the next step, a partial solution is re-created after its ruin to a full model solution. So in a sense there is an attempt to restore the solution as best as possible, with the hope that the new solution is better than the previous one. This disintegration of a large part of the model from a previous solution approach offers the advantage of providing increased freedom to create a new, improved admissible solution. There are quite a few different ways to recreate and improve obtained solutions, so some researchers think of this approach as a metaheuristic, not a pure heuristic.

The R & R approach is similar in structure to all of the algorithms discussed in this chapter (particularly the Tabu search and simulated annealing; see discussion below) and functions much like an iterative improvement algorithm. It starts with an initial configuration of a model and proceeds by small changes in the current solution to get a tentative new solution. The tentative new solution is evaluated based on the specified objective function evaluation approach (the magnitude of the NCP, etc.) and an automated algorithmic decision rule is applied. If it fulfills the specified criteria, it is kept as the current solution and the search proceeds. A typical R & R approach is outlined by the following pseudo code:

procedure ruin and recreate ( )
    a starting solution S is provided (the initial model specified)
    $S' = recreate\ S$ (create new improved models)
    $S* = S'$
    repeat
    $S* =$ next model for ruin
    $S'' = ruin\ S*$
    $S' = recreate\ S''$
    until
    stopping criterion is met
end

As can be seen from this pseudocode, all that is needed to implement an R & R algorithm for any specific problem are four components. First, an initial solution should be provided (this is usually the first step

of any type of SEM implementation). Second, a solution improvement method must be determined—in this case, a Tabu search (see description in previous section). Third, a solution reconstruction (a mutation) procedure must be developed (see GA section). Finally, a decision rule is need.

SIMULATED ANNEALING

"Simulated annealing" (SA) is a heuristic search procedure that simulates the annealing of metals by starting with a high temperature and cooling the metal off (Drezner & Marcoulides, 1999; Kirkpatrick, Gelat, & Vecchi, 1983). SA is also quite similar in structure to other algorithms discussed here because it too functions much like an iterative improvement algorithm. It starts with an initial configuration of a model and proceeds by small changes in the current solution to get a tentative new solution. The tentative new solution is evaluated based on some objective function evaluation, and an automated decision rule is used. If the tentative new solution fulfills the criteria, it is kept as the current solution and the search proceeds. The process of SA is ideally suited for solving all types of large-scale optimization problems and has been successfully used for the solution of variable selection in multiple regression analysis and related variable selection problems (Drezner & Marcoulides, 1999[6]; see also Salhi, 1998, for a review and detailed description of the method).

The general SA approach can best be described using the following pseudocode:

1. A starting solution to the problem being examined is selected.

2. A starting temperature T_0 is selected (T_i is the temperature at iteration i).

3. The following iterations are repeated N times.

4. At iteration i:

    a. A perturbation of the current selected set is randomly generated.

    b. The difference between the values of the objective function of the current set and the perturbed set, Δf, is calculated.

    c. If the perturbation results in a better objective function, it is accepted and the set of selected variables updated.

    d. If the perturbation results in a worse objective function, the quantity $\delta = \Delta f / T_i$ is calculated.

e. The perturbed set is accepted with a probability of $e^{-\delta}$. Otherwise, the selected set remains unchanged and the perturbation is ignored.

f. The temperature T_i is changed to T_{i+1}.

It is important to note that the success of a SA procedure depends on the selection of the starting temperature T_0, the way the temperature is lowered, and the number of iterations. Drezner and Marcoulides (1999) suggested that the temperature should be kept constant for blocks of 100 iterations each. When a block of 100 iterations is completed, the temperature is multiplied by the value 0.95 (i.e., the temperature is lowered by the product). One hundred blocks of 100 iterations each are executed for a total of 10,000 iterations.

For example, to conduct a best possible subset selection in multiple regression analysis, the following process would be followed:

1. The empty set is selected as a starting solution (i.e., where no independent variables are used in the model).

2. The starting temperature is set to $T_0 = 1$

3. A perturbation of the current selected set is created by randomly selecting an independent variable. If the variable is in the current set, it is moved out, and if it is not in the current set it is put in.

4. The number of iterations is set to $N = 10,000$.

5. Using the significance level as the objective function, replace the change in the objective function Δf with the relative change in the objective function df/f, where f is the value of the objective function of the current set.

6. The last selected set is chosen as the solution. One may keep the best solution encountered throughout the iterations as the solution.

SUMMARY AND CONCLUSIONS

This chapter provided an overview of algorithms that can be used to perform a variety of automated SEM activities. There is no doubt that such model searches within SEM are extremely difficult, especially whenever the number of possible variables and potential models might be high. Indeed, there is without doubt

a definite usefulness to any automated procedure that can make such a potentially chaotic situation somewhat more manageable. As discussed throughout the chapter, all of the algorithms introduced have the potential to be quite helpful for examining models, particularly those that are not fundamentally misspecified but are incorrect only to the extent that they have some missing paths or parameters involved in unnecessarily restrictive constraints. Nevertheless, despite the fact that such automated searches can find the best models according to a given fit criterion, all final generated models must be cross-validated with new data before any real validity to the determined models can be claimed. For example, when equivalent models are encountered, such automated searches only lead one to a list of feasible models, but it is the responsibility of the researcher to decide which model to accept as the best model. To date, no automated search can make such a decision for the researcher. Therefore, as long as researchers keep in mind that the best use of automatic search procedures is to narrow attention to models on a recommendation list (a sort of top-10 list), the algorithms will not be abused in empirical applications.

NOTES

1. In addition to facilitating the conceptualization and communication of a model, path diagrams also substantially contribute to the creation of the appropriate input file for the computer program that is necessary to test and fit the model to the collected data (see Byrne, Chapter 19, this volume).

2. The R program that implements the ACO algorithm alongside with Mplus is provided at the handbook's website: *www.handbookofsem.com*.

3. A FORTRAN program that implements the GA algorithm alongside with LISREL is available at *www.handbookofsem.com*.

4. A FORTRAN program that implements the Tabu search algorithm alongside with LISREL is available at *www.handbookofsem.com*.

5. A FORTRAN program that implements the R & R algorithm alongside with LISREL is available at *www.handbookofsem.com*.

6. A FORTRAN program that implements the SA algorithm is available at *www.handbookofsem.com*.

REFERENCES

Arbuckle, J. L., & Wothke, W. (1999). *Amos 4.0 user's guide.* Chicago: SPSS.

Bentler, P. M. (2004). *EQS structural equations program manual.* Encino, CA: Multivariate Software.

Bentler, P. M., & Weeks, D. G. (1980). Linear structural equations with latent variables. *Psychometrika, 45,* 289–308.

Deneubourg, J. L., & Goss, S. (1989). Collective patterns and decision making. *Ethology, Ecology, and Evolution, 1,* 295–311.

Deneubourg, J. L., Pasteels, J. M., & Verhaeghe, J. C. (1983). Probabilistic behaviour in ants: A strategy of errors? *Journal of Theoretical Biology, 105*(2), 259–271.

Ding, C. S., & Hershberger, S. L. (2002). Assessing content validity and content equivalence using structural equation modeling. *Structural Equation Modeling, 9,* 283–297.

Dorigo, M., & Stützle, T. (2004). *Ant colony optimization.* Cambridge, MA: MIT Press.

Drezner, Z., & Marcoulides, G. A. (1999). Using simulated annealing for model selection in multiple regression analysis. *Multiple Linear Regression Viewpoints, 25*(2), 1–4.

Drezner, Z., & Marcoulides, G. A. (2003). A distance-based selection of parents in genetic algorithms. In M. Resenda & J. P Sousa (Eds.), *Metaheuristics: Computer decision-making* (pp. 257–278). Boston: Kluwer Academic.

Drezner, Z., & Marcoulides, G. A. (2006). Mapping the convergence of genetic algorithms. *Journal of Applied Mathematics and Decision Sciences, 15,* 1–16.

Drezner, Z., Marcoulides, G. A., & Salhi, S. (1999). Tabu search model selection in multiple regression analysis. *Communications in Statistics: Computation and Simulation, 28,* 349–367.

Ferrando, P. J. (1999). Likert scaling using continuous, censored, and graded response models: Effects of criterion-related validity. *Applied Psychological Measurement, 23*(2), 161–175.

Glymour, C., Scheines, R., Spirtes, P., & Kelly, K. (1987). *Discovering causal structure: Artificial intelligence, philosophy of science, and statistical modeling.* San Diego: Academic Press.

Hambleton, R. K., Swaminathan, H., & Rogers, J. (1991). *Fundamentals of item response theory.* Newbury Park, CA: Sage.

Hershberger, S. L. (2003). Latent variable models of genotype-environment correlation. *Structural Equation Modeling, 10,* 423–434.

Holland, J. H. (1975). *Adaptation in natural and artificial systems.* Ann Arbor: University Michigan Press.

Jöreskog, K. G. (1971). Statistical analysis of sets of congeneric tests. *Psychometrika, 36,* 109–133.

Jöreskog, K. G. (1993). Testing structural equation models. In K. A. Bollen & J. S. Long (Eds.), *Testing structural equation models* (pp. 294–316). Newbury Park, CA: Sage.

Jöreskog, K. G., & Sörbom, D. (2005). *LISREL 8 user's reference guide.* Chicago: Scientific Software International.

Kenny, D. A., & McCoach, D. B. (2003). Effect of the number of variables on measures of fit in structural equation modeling. *Structural Equation Modeling, 10,* 333–351.

Kirkpatrick, S., Gelat, C. D., & Vecchi, M. P. (1983). Optimization by simulated annealing. *Science, 220,* 671–680.

Landsheer, J. A. (2010). The specification of causal models with TETRAD IV: A review. *Structural Equation Modeling, 17,* 630–640.

Larose, D. T. (2005). *Discovering knowledge in data: An introduction to data mining.* Hoboken, NJ: Wiley.

Leite, W. L., Huang, I. C., & Marcoulides, G. A. (2008). Item selection for the development of short-form of scaling using an ant colony optimization algorithm. *Multivariate Behavioral Research, 43,* 411–431.

Leite, W. L., & Marcoulides, G. A. (2009, April). *Using the ant colony optimization algorithm for specification searches: A comparison of criteria.* Paper presented at the annual meeting of the American Education Research Association, San Diego, CA.

Long, J. S. (1983). *Covariance Structure Models: An Introduction to LISREL.* Beverly Hills, CA: Sage.

Lord, F. M. (1957). A significance test for the hypothesis that two variables measure the same trait except for errors of measurement. *Psychometrika, 22,* 207–220.

Lord, F. M. (1980). *Applications of item response theory to practical testing problems.* Hillsdale, NJ: Erlbaum.

Marcoulides, G. A. (1989). Structural equation modeling for scientific research. *Journal of Business and Society, 2*(2), 130–138.

Marcoulides, G. A. (2005). Review of *Discovering Knowledge in Data: An Introduction to Data Mining. Journal of the American Statistical Association, 100*(472), 1465–1465.

Marcoulides, G. A. (2009, May). *Conducting specification searches in SEM using a ruin and recreate principle.* Paper presented at the annual meeting of the American Psychological Society, San Francisco.

Marcoulides, G. A. (2010, July). *Using heuristic algorithms for specification searches and optimization.* Paper presented at the Albert and Elaine Borchard Foundation International Colloquium, Missillac, France.

Marcoulides, G. A., & Drezner, Z. (2001). Specification searches in structural equation modeling with a genetic algorithm. In G. A. Marcoulides & R. E. Schumacker (Eds.), *New developments and techniques in structural equation modeling* (pp. 247–268). Mahwah, NJ: Erlbaum.

Marcoulides, G. A., & Drezner, Z. (2002). A model selection approach for the identification of quantitative trait loci in experimental crosses: Discussion on the paper by Broman and Speed. *Journal of the Royal Statistical Society B, 64,* 754.

Marcoulides, G. A., & Drezner, Z. (2003). Model specification searchers using ant colony optimization algorithms. *Structural Equation Modeling, 10,* 154–164.

Marcoulides, G. A., & Drezner, Z. (2004). Tabu search variable selection with resource constraints. *Communications in Statistics: Simulation and Computation, 33,* 355–362.

Marcoulides, G. A., & Drezner, Z. (2009). Specification searches in structural equation modeling with a genetic algorithm. In G. A. Marcoulides & R. E. Schumacker (Eds.),

New developments and techniques in structural equation modeling (pp. 247–268). Mahwah, NJ: Erlbaum.

Marcoulides, G. A., Drezner, Z., & Schumacker, R. E. (1998). Model specification searches in structural equation modeling using Tabu search. *Structural Equation Modeling, 5,* 365–376.

Marsh, H. W., Balla, J. R., & Hau, K. (1996). An evaluation of incremental fit indices: A clarification of mathematical and empirical properties. In G. A. Marcoulides & R. E. Schumacker (Eds.), *Advanced structural equation modeling: Issues and techniques* (pp. 315–353). Mahwah, NJ: Erlbaum.

Messick, S. (1989). Validity. In R. L. Linn (Ed.), *Educational measurement* (3rd ed., pp. 13–103). New York: Macmillan.

Muthén, L., & Muthén, B. (2008). *Mplus user's guide* (3rd ed.). Los Angeles: Authors.

Neale, M. C., Boker, S. M., Xie, G., & Maes, H. H. (1999). *Mx: Statistical modeling* (5th ed.). Richmond: Virginia Commonwealth University.

Reise, S. P., Widaman, K. F., & Pugh, R. H. (1993). Confirmatory factor analysis and item response theory: Two approaches for exploring measurement invariance. *Psychological Bulletin, 114,* 552–566.

Resenda, M., & Sousa, J. P. (Eds.). (2003). *Metaheuristics: Computer decision-making.* Boston: Kluwer Academic.

Salhi, S. (1998). Heuristic search methods. In G. A. Marcoulides (Ed.), *Modern methods for business research* (pp. 147–175). Mahwah, NJ: Erlbaum.

Scheines, R., Spirtes, P., Glymour, C., Meek, C., & Richardson, T. (1998). The TETRAD Project: Constraint based aids to causal model specification. *Multivariate Behavioral Research, 33,* 65–117.

Schumacker, R. E., & Marcoulides, G. A. (1998). *Interaction and nonlinear effects in structural equation modeling.* Mahwah, NJ: Erlbaum.

Scrimpf, G., Schneider, K., Stamm-Wilbrandt, H., & Dueck, V. (2000). Record breaking optimization results using the ruin and recreate principle. *Journal of Computational Physics, 159,* 139–171.

Spirtes, P., Scheines, R., & Glymour, C. (1990). Simulation studies of the reliability of computer-aided model specification using the TETRAD II, EQS, and LISREL programs. *Sociological Methods and Research, 19,* 3–66.

Author Index

Subject Index

Page numbers followed by *f* indicate figure; *n*, note; and *t*, table

About the Editor

Rick H. Hoyle, PhD, is Professor of Psychology and Neuroscience at Duke University, where he serves as Associate Director of the Center for Child and Family Policy and Director of the Methodology and Statistics Core in the Transdisciplinary Prevention Research Center. He is a Fellow of the Association for Psychological Science, the American Psychological Association, and the Society of Experimental Social Psychology. He has written extensively on structural equation modeling and other statistical and methodological strategies for the study of complex social and behavioral processes. His other books include *Structural Equation Modeling for Social and Personality Psychology*; *Structural Equation Modeling: Concepts, Issues, and Applications*; *Statistical Strategies for Small Sample Research*; *Research Methods in Social Relations* (with Monica J. Harris and Charles M. Judd); and *Handbook of Individual Differences in Social Behavior* (with Mark R. Leary).

Contributors

Deborah L. Bandalos, PhD, Department of Graduate Psychology, James Madison University, Harrisonburg, Virginia

Jeremy C. Biesanz, PhD, Department of Psychology, University of British Columbia, Vancouver, British Columbia, Canada

Steven Boker, PhD, Department of Psychology, University of Virginia, Charlottesville, Virginia

Kenneth A. Bollen, PhD, Department of Sociology, University of North Carolina at Chapel Hill, Chapel Hill, North Carolina

Anne Boomsma, PhD, Department of Sociology, University of Groningen, Groningen, The Netherlands

Dorret I. Boomsma, PhD, Department of Biological Psychology, Faculty of Psychology and Education, VU University, Amsterdam, The Netherlands

Denny Borsboom, PhD, Department of Psychology, Faculty of Social and Behavioral Sciences, University of Amsterdam, Amsterdam, The Netherlands

James A. Bovaird, PhD, Department of Educational Psychology, University of Nebraska–Lincoln, Lincoln, Nebraska

Timothy A. Brown, PsyD, Center for Anxiety and Related Disorders, Department of Psychology, Boston University, Boston, Massachusetts

Barbara M. Byrne, PhD, School of Psychology, University of Ottawa, Ottawa, Ontario, Canada

Jarrett E. Byrnes, PhD, Santa Barbara Coastal LTER, Marine Science Institute, University of California, Santa Barbara, Santa Barbara, California

Li Cai, PhD, Departments of Education and Psychology, University of California, Los Angeles, Los Angeles, California

JeeWon Cheong, PhD, Department of Psychology, University of Pittsburgh, Pittsburgh, Pennsylvania

Olexander Chernyshenko, PhD, Division of Strategy, Management, and Organization, School of Business, Nanyang Technological University, Singapore

Chih-Ping Chou, PhD, Department of Preventive Medicine, Keck School of Medicine, University of Southern California, Los Angeles, California

Donna L. Coffman, PhD, The Methodology Center, Pennsylvania State University, University Park, Pennsylvania

David A. Cole, PhD, Department of Psychology and Human Development, Peabody College, Vanderbilt University, Nashville, Tennessee

Sarah Depaoli, PhD, Department of Psychological Sciences, University of California, Merced, Merced, California

Conor V. Dolan, PhD, Department of Psychology, Faculty of Social and Behavioral Sciences, University of Amsterdam, Amsterdam, The Netherlands

Michael C. Edwards, PhD, Department of Psychology, Ohio State University, Columbus, Ohio

Emilio Ferrer, PhD, Department of Psychology, University of California, Davis, Davis, California

John Fox, PhD, Department of Sociology, McMaster University, Hamilton, Ontario, Canada

Sanja Franić, MSc, Department of Biological Psychology, Faculty of Psychology and Education, VU University, Amsterdam, The Netherlands

Phillip Gagné, PhD, Institute for Education Sciences, U.S. Department of Education, Washington, DC

John W. Graham, PhD, Department of Biobehavioral Health, Pennsylvania State University, University Park, Pennsylvania

Samuel B. Green, PhD, School of Social and Family Dynamics, Arizona State University, Tempe, Arizona

Kevin J. Grimm, PhD, Department of Psychology, University of California, Davis, Davis, California

Gregory R. Hancock, PhD, Department of Measurement, Statistics, and Evaluation, University of Maryland, College Park, Maryland

Kit-Tai Hau, PhD, Faculty of Education, Chinese University of Hong Kong, Shatin, Hong Kong

Moon-ho Ringo Ho, PhD, Division of Psychology, School of Humanities and Social Sciences, Nanyang Technological University, Singapore

Carrie R. Houts, PhD, Department of Psychology, Ohio State University, Columbus, Ohio

Rick H. Hoyle, PhD, Department of Psychology and Neuroscience, Duke University, Durham, North Carolina

Jimi Huh, PhD, Department of Preventive Medicine, Keck School of Medicine, University of Southern California, Los Angeles, California

Marsha Ing, PhD, Graduate School of Education, University of California, Riverside, Riverside, California

David Kaplan, PhD, Department of Educational Psychology, University of Wisconsin–Madison, Madison, Wisconsin

David A. Kenny, PhD, Department of Psychology, University of Connecticut, Storrs, Connecticut

Rex B. Kline, PhD, Department of Psychology, Concordia University, Montreal, Quebec, Canada

Natalie A. Koziol, MA, Department of Educational Psychology, University of Nebraska–Lincoln, Lincoln, Nebraska

Taehun Lee, PhD, Department of Education, University of California, Los Angeles, Los Angeles, California

Pui-Wa Lei, PhD, Department of Educational Psychology, Counseling, and Special Education, Pennsylvania State University, University Park, Pennsylvania

Min Liu, PhD, Department of Educational Psychology, University of Hawaii, Manoa, Hawaii

Jill B. Lubansky, MA, Department of Psychology, University of South Carolina, Columbia, South Carolina

Robert C. MacCallum, PhD, Department of Psychology, University of North Carolina at Chapel Hill, Chapel Hill, North Carolina

David P. MacKinnon, PhD, Department of Psychology, Arizona State University, Tempe, Arizona

Patrick S. Malone, PhD, Department of Psychology, University of South Carolina, Columbia, South Carolina

George A. Marcoulides, PhD, Graduate School of Education, University of California, Riverside, Riverside, California

Herbert W. Marsh, PhD, Department of Education, University of Oxford, Oxford, United Kingdom; Centre for Positive Psychology in Education, University of Western Sydney, Sydney, Australia; King Saud University, Riyadh, Saudi Arabia

Ross L. Matsueda, PhD, Department of Sociology, University of Washington, Seattle, Washington

John J. McArdle, PhD, Department of Psychology, University of Southern California, Los Angeles, California

Anthony R. McIntosh, PhD, Rotman Research Institute, Baycrest Centre, University of Toronto, Toronto, Ontario, Canada

Stephanie Milan, PhD, Department of Psychology, University of Connecticut, Storrs, Connecticut

Roger E. Millsap, PhD, Department of Psychology, Arizona State University, Tempe, Arizona

Michael T. Moore, PhD, Center for Anxiety and Related Disorders, Department of Psychology, Boston University, Boston, Massachusetts

Benjamin Nagengast, PhD, Center for Educational Science and Psychology, Department of Education, University of Tübingen, Tübingen, Germany; Department of Education, University of Oxford, Oxford, United Kingdom

Michael C. Neale, PhD, Department of Psychiatry and Human Genetics, Virginia Commonwealth University, Richmond, Virginia

Margarita Olivera-Aguilar, MA, Department of Psychology, Arizona State University, Tempe, Arizona

A. T. Panter, PhD, Department of Psychology, University of North Carolina at Chapel Hill, Chapel Hill, North Carolina

Judea Pearl, PhD, Department of Computer Science, University of California, Los Angeles, Los Angeles, California

Andrea B. Protzner, PhD, Department of Psychology, University of Calgary, Calgary, Alberta, Canada

Sophia Rabe-Hesketh, PhD, Graduate School of Education, University of California, Berkeley, Berkeley, California

Nilam Ram, PhD, Department of Human Development and Family Studies, Pennsylvania State University, University Park, Pennsylvania

Tenko Raykov, PhD, Department of Measurement and Quantitative Methods, Michigan State University, East Lansing, Michigan

Mariya P. Shiyko, PhD, Department of Counseling and Applied Psychology, Bouve College of Health Sciences, Northeastern University, Boston, Massachusetts

Anders Skrondal, PhD, Division of Epidemiology, Norwegian Institute of Public Health, Oslo, Norway

Hairong Song, PhD, Department of Psychology, University of Oklahoma, Norman, Oklahoma

Stephen Stark, PhD, Department of Psychology, University of South Florida, Tampa, Florida

Aaron B. Taylor, PhD, Department of Psychology, Texas A & M University, College Station, Texas

Marilyn S. Thompson, PhD, School of Social and Family Dynamics, Arizona State University, Tempe, Arizona

Melanie M. Wall, PhD, Division of Biostatistics, New York State Psychiatric Institute, and Department of Biostatistics, Mailman School of Public Health, Columbia University, New York, New York

Zhonglin Wen, PhD, Department of Psychology, South China Normal University, Guangzhou, China

Stephen G. West, PhD, Department of Psychology, Arizona State University, Tempe Arizona

Larry J. Williams, PhD, Center for the Advancement of Research Methods and Analysis, School of Business Administration, Wayne State University, Detroit, Michigan

R. J. Wirth, PhD, Vector Psychometric Group, LLC, Seattle, Washington

Phillip Wood, PhD, Department of Psychological Sciences, University of Missouri–Columbia, Columbia, Missouri

Qiong Wu, PhD, Center for Population and Development Studies, Harvard University, Cambridge, Massachusetts

Wei Wu, PhD, Department of Psychology, University of Kansas, Lawrence, Kansas

Nuo Xi, PhD, Educational Testing Service, Princeton, New Jersey

Xiaohui Zheng, PhD, Institutional Research, University of California, Office of the President, Oakland, Oakland, California